GUN DIGEST
26th Anniversary Edition

ASSOCIATE EDITOR
Edward Dams

TECHNICAL EDITORS
Bob Bell
John Lachuk
John Maynard
Maj. Geo. C. Nonte, Jr.
A. M. Wynne, Jr.

EUROPEAN EDITORS
Raymond Caranta
Derek Partridge

EDITORIAL ASSISTANT
Lilo Anderson

Edited by
John T. Amber

OUR COVERS

The New Sharps Sporting Rifle graces our front cover, the painting done by James W. Triggs. The back cover pictures the U.S. Grant Commemorative caplock revolver. Both are made by Colt's.

Opening place in this edition goes to "Shooter's Hall of Fame," by Charles Askins. We hope you'll agree with us that this concept is long past due, and that it is workable with your help and support.

For a superb and profusely illustrated article on the "British Volunteer Rifle," don't fail to read the article so-titled in this issue.

"Gun Proof in Italy," the fifth chapter in our new series on proof and proof marks, will be found in this edition.

If you're one of those who believes that England's extremely strict gun controls have been effective, read Colin Greenwood's article on page 212!

MEMBER OF THE
NATIONAL SHOOTING SPORTS FOUNDATION INC.

F **Follett Publishing Company**
Chicago

T-0222

ISBN 0695-80222-4 **Library of Congress Catalog Card Number 44-32588**

IN THE BLACK

Thomas Shelhamer
1890 - 1971

This famed stockmaker, whom I'd known since his long-ago years with the Niedner Rifle Corporation, died at his home in Dowagiac (Michigan) on May 7th, 1971. He is survived by his wife, Elva, and a daughter, Alice.

A most excellent craftsman in wood, we were pleased and proud to show examples of Tom Shelhamer's fine work in various issues of the Gun Digest.

Townsend Whelen Award

Larry S. Sterett is the recipient this year of our annual award for the best contribution to firearms literature. His prize-winning two-part article "The Rifles of James Paris Lee," begins in this 26th edition.

This $500 award, honoring the late Townsend Whelen—whose whole life was devoted to the rifle and marksmanship—is the 6th annual presentation. Mr. Sterett's article, in the judges' opinions, best met our criteria—originality, clarity, readability and lasting value. Our warmest congratulations to Larry Sterett.

Bench Rest Shooting

We regret having to report on the dissension that developed some months ago in the National Bench Rest Shooters Assn., and the subsequent formation by a bloc of essentially Eastern-Midwest shooters into the International Benchrest Shooters. Headquarters of the IBS is in Dolgeville, N.Y. 13329, which is also the address for *Precision Shooting,* official monthly organ of the IBS. Headquarters of the NBRSA is at 607 W. Line St., Minerva, Ohio 44657, and its sponsored monthly publication is *The Rifle* (Box 3030, Prescott, Ariz. 86301), which may be subscribed to separately, without NBRSA membership, as may *Precision Shooting.*

Combined membership/subscription is $8 for both organizations.

W-W Outdoorsman Award

The Winchester-Western Outdoorsman of the Year Award for 1970 was presented in mid-March to John D. Dingell, U.S. Congressman from Michigan.

Dingell, chairman of the House Subcommittee on Fisheries and Wildlife Conservation, received the award from W.E. (Bill) Talley, W-W's vice president for marketing. The award scroll was accompanied by a Winchester Model 101 over-and-under 20-gauge Skeet gun, with interchangeable extra barrels in 410 and 28 gauge.

John D. Dingell was chosen for the award by a poll of more than 5000 outdoor writers and conservationists.

Nash Buckingham 1881-1971

Nash Buckingham, "the grand old man of American conservation," died on March 10, in Knoxville, Tenn., after a long illness. He was 90.

A lifelong sportsman and conservationist, he was an outstanding and prolific writer on outdoor subjects for national magazines, Nash Buckingham was one of the founders of the Outdoor Writers Association of America. In 1928, he helped found the American Wildfowlers, a foundation devoted to the study of waterfowl conditions in this country and Canada, later to become Ducks Unlimited.

Gun Digest NBRSA Trophy

Don Geraci, of New Orleans, La., was the winner in 1970 of our silver-bowl award for the best scores in the Heavy Varmint rifle championship matches. His Grand Aggregate was .3769 MOA (minute of angle), shot on the Midland, Texas, range.

Unfortunately, Geraci didn't get to keep the trophy for the usual year; it had been heavily damaged in shipment. He did, of course, receive our smaller bowl to keep. Our congratulations—and our regrets—to Don Geraci.

Weatherby Trophy

George H. Landreth (center) was awarded the Weatherby Big Game Trophy, at the 15th annual award dinner, by astronaut James A. Lovell, Jr. (right) as donor Roy E. Weatherby looks on. Landreth was selected for the honor from among seven nominees for his hunting achievements round the world, for his contributions to conservation and the betterment of the sport.

Gun Digest IBS Trophy

The International Benchrest Shooters (IBS) held its first International Championship matches—for Varmint and Sporter rifles—at Fassett, Pa. on 23-25 July, 1970. Warren Page, making a nice comeback, won the Gun Digest trophy for Heavy Varmint rifles, his Grand Aggregate .3680 MOA (minute of angle). Mr. Page, president emeritus of the FLS, is now Exec. Vice President of the National Shooting Sports Foundation. Our hearty congratulations—on both counts—and to the NSSF as well.

Doc Garcelon (left) president of the IBS, congratulates Warren Page on winning the HV Class rifle championship and the new GUN DIGEST Trophy.

Page Leaves *F&S*

Warren Page, long-time shooting editor of *Field & Stream,* has left that post to become Executive vice president of the National Shooting Sports Foundation, perhaps better known by its initials—NSSF. Warren Page's excellent stories and articles have graced these pages over the years —his tale on how not to shoot an elephant is in this 26th edition—and they will, I hope, continue to do so.

Our warmest congratulations to the NSSF, and our sympathy to F&S—they'll have a rough time finding someone to fill Lefty's moccasins. They won't, of course, for no man of Page's stature and individualism is fully replaceable, but the best of good wishes, Mr. Calabash, whoever you are.

Book Notes

Loren W. Smith's long out-of-print book on how to repair and rework the Colt Single Action revolver (published in 1955) will be reprinted by Ray Riling some time this year. The title will be *Home Gunsmithing Colt Single Actions,* price not yet set.

Riling will also reissue Clark S. Campbell's excellent work, *The '03 Springfield* by late summer of 1971. Much sought after for its detailed data, the author has completely revised the 2nd edition, adding new information, new drawings, etc. The price will be announced later.

Questions and Answers

Demands on the editors are such that not all letters can be answered, though we try. A stamped, addressed-to-oneself, envelope must be included. However, before writing to us for the location of suppliers, please see our Directory of the Arms pages —you'll probably save a stamp.

New Ruger 45-70 Single Shot Carbine, later to be made in 30-40 Krag, 22 Hornet, other calibers.

CONTENTS

THE SHOOTERS HALL OF FAME

by Col. Charles Askins

There are many institutions honoring the famed players of football, baseball, golf and the like, but there is none, strangely enough, for that most typical of American sports — *shooting!* We urge your support and participation in founding a National Shooter's Hall of Fame.

O. F. Winchester

Ad Topperwein

WE ARE A PEOPLE who look on our ranking athletes as national heroes. We simply wallow in the verbiage that spills forth from our sports writers. We faithfully journey afield to applaud our favorite golfer, tennis whiz, or quarterback while he does his stuff. We do not always confine our worship to the Namaths, the Toomeys and the Palmers, either. We often let our sentiment spill over to include horses, dogs and the like. We cast plaques, put up statues, designate parks and, in a score of ways, do honor to the beast as well as the man.

We are not particularly athletically inclined, really, though we like to think we are. Our participation in the game, more often than not, consists in sitting on the sidelines. We are spectator athletes in great part, but this doesn't seem to dampen the ardor or cool the enthusiasm. Every man who watches the Green Bay Packers imagines himself down there on the field, and while his thrills may be vicarious his interest is no less intense. The most ardent baseball fan of my circle never played a game in his life. Yet he can rattle off the season batting averages of every player in either league.

So compelling is our admiration for our star performers—man and beast—that we seek to enshrine them after their glory has commenced to fade a little. We put them in a hall of fame. Some of these halls are literal but most of them are figurative. We sometimes nominate likely candidates but mostly we content ourselves with permitting the sports writers to do it for us. Record performances are sometimes made a part of a book or scroll, a tablet or memorial. It's even bet-

ter when the record is chiseled into marble or cast in imperishable bronze, so that those exploits are preserved for all future generations to see.

The hall of fame is an established American institution. There must be so many of these hallowed portals, both those that are tangible and those that are transparent, that it would be hard to list them all. Besides those for basketball and football, baseball and golf, tennis and track, hockey and the swimming sports, there are innumerable others. There's a special hall for the ponies, too, those gallant thoroughbreds that gallop at Churchill Downs and the Preakness. There's another for the field trial winners, for retrievers, even one for hounds.

It is a glorious institution, this hall of fame thing. An enriching and ennobling gesture of admiration and good will on the part of man for his fellow. A sort of nomination for knighthood, much as Queen Elizabeth bestows on her liege men. If there are two or three score of such shrines, all rendering unto history the feats of man and beast, then I approve of them all. It gives me a sense of satisfaction to realize that somewhere the prowess of the Jim Thorpes and the Bobby Jones's is set down for all time, for posterity to look upon, to remember.

Strangely enough, among these numerous halls of fame, there is none for that most typical American sport—*shooting*. It seems passing odd that with a great national tradition for guns and the outdoors, with dozens of prominent figures in our history who were outdoorsmen, with an annual sale of some eighteen million hunting licenses—and a slice of our population

counted by the Department of the Interior at fifty millions afield every year—that we have not seen fit to honor our shooters with a special shrine, nor our hunters, if such distinction is needed.

We have not. True, at times in the not too distant past, we've made gestures in that direction. During the mid-30s the National Rifle Association named All-American rifle and pistol teams on an annual basis, the selections based on the shooting of U.S. marksmen throughout the season. The fellow who had the highest average was named No.1 on the All-American Team, which made him a sort of national champion. Jimmy Robinson, who has been Skeet & trap editor for *Sports Afield* for 40-odd years, annually selects his All-America teams. His selections are based on season scores and averages.

In 1956, Roy Weatherby, the prominent West Coast firearms impresario, initiated an annual selection of the outstanding sportsman of the year. This choice was based not on shooting a Weatherby firearm, but on the hunting which the nominee had done over the year before, how widely he had traveled for game, the species he'd shot, his record heads, and his background generally as a big game hunter. This annual award has been continued, with selections now made by a group of 10 committeemen, most of whom have received the Weatherby award at some time in the past.

The Winchester Company annually selects its Sportsman of the Year, then presents him with a fitting tribute to his fame. These selections are broader than those made by Weatherby, and the nominee may have some shooting background. However,

Col. Whelen

A.O. Zischang

that is not essential— he may be nationally prominent, a conservationist or a writer.

These gestures toward the proper recognition of our outstanding sportsmen are wholly commendable, and certainly the majority of those selected, whether by the NRA, the Weatherby committee or Winchester, must surely be eligible for a hall of fame—if we had such an institution!

That romantic figure in the history of this country, the American cowboy, has a hall of fame at Oklahoma City. Housed in a handsome building that was the gift of 17 western states, this edifice does honor to countless trail drivers, ranchers, bronc riders and cowpunchers turned sheriff. There, in the polished marble of those stately halls, these Westerners are enshrined for all time. Along with the likeness and the story of these riders there's also a gathering of memorabilia—the six-shooters, the saddles, spurs and branding irons, the chuckwagons and the other tools of his trade. So while the hall is a memorial to the most glamorous figure of the old West it is a museum, too. It attracts thousands of visitors annually.

There are far more shooters than cowboys. If the cowpuncher can have a hall of fame, and a quite elegant one at that, there isn't any reason why the infinitely more numerous shooting fraternity cannot also have a similar establishment. A fine building where names and scores and trophies and guns could be presented. A place where, preserved for all time, a testimonial would stand to the most traditional American game of them all!

Ideally, a headquarters of this kind would need a custodian, one who did record keeping and the like. As I see it, a committee would be needed to make selections. A shooters hall of fame could not run itself, with nominations offered spontaneously. There would have to be a group whose business it was to ponder likely prospects, to vote on them and, if they appeared worthy, to add their names to the roll of honor.

We have an organization that could do these things. This is the National Rifle Association, our over-a-million-member order, with a fine new headquarters, the necessary record keeping facilities, and faculties within the organization for the consideration of candidates to the hall of fame. Whether the NRA would be agreeable to taking on these new chores is problematical. Certainly it is the logical choice to maintain a shooters hall of fame.*

Who should be named first to the shooters hall of fame? That is an intriguing question. Should the selection committee go back to Daniel Boone, Davy Crockett and Kit Carson, or should there be a cutoff date of, say, 1875? That's almost a hundred years ago, and only those sportsmen and shooters from that time forward might be considered. Is nomination to the hall to be based on target shooting, on hunting, or on

*The editor of the GUN DIGEST has talked with certain NRA officers about this proposal, but their answers were, understandably, noncommittal at this early stage. There would be many problems arising, naturally, as Col. Askins points out—methods of procedure, formulation of rules for qualification, space availability, materials and workers, and so on. However, these things are by no means insurmountable, so we remain hopeful.

both? Shall we include such famous marksmen/gunmakers as Horace Warner, William Billinghurst, Norman Brockway, Milton Farrow, Adolph Niedner and numerous others of like ability? Are we to bring in such prominent men on the American shooting scene in the 19th century as John Chapman, the brothers Edwin and Frank Wesson, Dan Lefever? What about such personages as Sam'l Colt and Eliphalet Remington, both of whom lived before our arbitrary cutoff date? Or should we choose a different date? Neither were especially noteworthy as hunters nor yet marksmen, yet both contributed immeasurably to the shooting tradition. Is our hall to be confined to shooters as such, or can we broaden our scope a bit to include our great designers?

Perhaps an auxiliary to the shooters hall of fame could be set up, making this open to those who, while non-shooters, had made important contributions to the shooting world. James Paris Lee comes to mind; Oliver Winchester, Eli Whitney, Christian Sharps . . .

We owe a great deal to people like John Browning, Peter Paul Mauser and Georg Luger, to the Englishmen Metford, Purdey, Anson and Deeley and Woodward. Is our hall to contain only Americans? If it does, what about our current crop of gun designers? Brilliant people like Bill Ruger, Wayne Leek and Bruce Browning? Are they to be included, even though they may not be shooters and hunters, but because of

their contribution to improved ordnance?

There are firearms writers who should be given consideration. Really great authorities like the late Col. Townsend Whelen and Capt. Ned Crossman. Certainly these two should be on any scroll of fame, but there are many others. Where is the line to be drawn? Must the writer have won a national Skeet championship, hunted in the tops of the Himalayas, or made the Boone & Crockett book before he is eligible? Or can he be included because of

"Buffalo Bill" Cody

the goodness of his literary effort? The committee will have to draw up a set of ground rules, but they'll probably find that frequent exceptions must be made to them.

Would it be wise to attempt to narrowly confine the membership of the hall? Perhaps, say, making a selection at the beginning of only 20 names, and thereafter adding only one name every year, or every five years? Certainly a group as small and as select as this would necessarily represent the very top level shooting men. But can any group make a choice as small as this from a background stretching into the past a full century and not arbitrarily slight those individuals quite equally deserving of a place of honor? I think that no ceiling should be placed on the number who could be nominated, but I don't have any idea what a representative number would be. Certainly it would exceed a score by a very considerable margin.

During the 1880s and '90s, we had a class of shooting men whose type has disappeared from the scene. These were the exhibition marksmen, the trick and fancy shooters. Among these were Doc Carver, Bogardus, Annie Oakley, Doc Ruth and B. A. Bartlett—not forgetting the immortal Ad Toepperwein of a few years later. These people not only put on stage shows before great audiences about the country, but they vied against each other to see who could hit the greatest number of glass balls or wooden blocks tossed into the air. These competitions

Teddy Roosevelt

were rarely staged man to man and shoulder-to-shoulder; the shooter set up an ideal situation where he was surrounded by friends and well-wishers, and then he proceeded to bang away at the flying targets. The results were published in the local news sheets for the other champions to see. Toepperwein, needless to say, finally bested all the records.

These performers of an early day have, most assuredly, earned a niche in our memorial hall. With them too, belongs that nemesis of the stodgy bison, that showman par excellence who galloped about the arena bursting glass balls with his smoothbored 44 Winchester—Buffalo Bill Cody.

Into this century during its formative years, we had other great marksmen. People like Harry Pope, who was not only a ranking Schuetzen rifleman but one of the greatest barrel makers of all time. There was also that dedicated shooter and ballistician, Dr. Franklin Mann, who wrote *The*

Bullet's Flight, a classic which, even today, holds the respect of every shooting man. And there was another, Dr. Walter G. Hudson, a ranking long range rifleman and a stalwart in the shooting wars before there was a Camp Perry.

Now, lest we seem to neglect that great American, that sportsman, statesman, adventurer and conservationist, let us mention his name now, certainly one that will loom large in any shooters hall of fame—Theodore Roosevelt. Rancher, Rough Rider, President of his country, the inimitable Roosevelt found the time to hunt extensively. He spent nine months in Africa, and his wanderings in South America were so strenuous as to have very probably shortened his life.

Chevalier Ira Paine was an early day pistol champion who usually shot on the eastern seaboard. Occasionally, too, he journeyed off to Europe, where he jousted

and generally won against the British and Continental handgunners. A generation later there were other handgunners who were champions in their own right. There were Bracken, Snook, Roper and Himmelwright, to name but a few.

There is a tendency to forget these older handgunners, their names and records retained only in the musty archives of an now all but defunct shooting order— the U.S. Revolver Association. It would take a major excavation project to unearth the scores, the matches and the dates, I suspect, but it is for these very reasons that we need a receptacle somewhere into which the old records may be stowed and preserved for all time.

Two years ago the National Rifle Association published a fine book, *Americans and their Guns,* an attempt to register all the major winnings in national and international competition over the past 40 years. It was a highly commendable job, but there was one grievous omission—Col. Harry Renshaw, USAF, won the 300-meter world rifle championship in 1930, but no record of his momentous victory in international match shooting appears in this book. A well-organized hall of fame might have prevented that oversight.

During the 1920s we twice went to the Olympics and twice carried off the free rifle honors. The winner in each Olympiad was Morris "Bud" Fisher, a Marine Corps gunnery sergeant. Along with him, in one of the Games, Mark Arie annexed the trapshooting diadem. Not until the imperishable Gary Anderson arrived upon the scene, in recent years, have we done as well.

In those same distant days we had a pair of African adventurers, Martin and Osa Johnson, who trekked off to Africa and sometimes remained in the bush for two years or so at a time. They hunted extensively, but they were also still and motion-picture photographers. Financed by Eastman Kodak, the Johnson duo provided us with some of the most thrilling pictures of charging lions, elephants and rhino that have ever been filmed. Generally he made the pictures and his diminutive wife, Osa, did the shooting. While it might be debated whether these two were more picture people than shooters, my vote would be to include them in our gallery. A decade before them was another adventurer who rightly deserves his spot in our archives. This was Paul Rainey, a wealthy Southerner who journeyed off to Kenya and there, in company with a cowboy named Buffalo Jones, rode down and roped lions. Rainey, a thoroughgoing sportsman who had become sated with the run-of-mill shooting safari,

Kit Carson

Samuel F. Colt

determined to enliven the sport a bit. Certainly his name and deeds, however foolhardy, should be retained.

We come down, finally, to those sportsmen who are well remembered for their exploits. Like the younger Roosevelts, sons of the immortal Teddy, who hunted in the tops of the world's most rugged mountains, the Himalayas for that most elusive trophy, the Marco Polo sheep. There's Ben Comfort, who won the Wimbledon in 1925 with a 300 H&H Magnum, thus setting off a spiral which hasn't ended to this day. Comfort's shooting called attention to the superior performances of the big belted cartridge, and his superb rifle work brought this English-designed round to the notice of all Americans.

These sportsmen who are nominated annually for the Weatherby award gain considerable publicity for their game-field shooting. A most interesting pair, never named for the Weatherby honors and yet among our top big game hunters, are Don and Marg Hopkins. They spent nearly 10 years on African safaris, sometimes out in the bush for almost a year at a time. Don Hopkins has long wanted to obtain elephant with 150 pounds of ivory in each tusk, and in that search he's hunted old Tembo more, probably, than any American sportsman. Shunning publicity, denying interviews, never appearing in print, this great Spokane sportsman is highly deserving of remembrance in the hunters hall of fame.

Since the end of World War II the Soviets have been obsessed with a desire to dominate the Olympics. To this end they have made a science of training their athletes, and among them their marksmen. At first their successes were quite ordinary but, with characteristic persistence, they finally achieved shooting teams which were well nigh unbeatable. That is, until our Gary Anderson bowed onto the scene.

This remarkable young shooter is the best in the world today. His forte is the centerfire free-rifle, a firearm that is fired at 300 meters. He has twice been the Olympic champion—in 1964 and '68. He has repeatedly taken the measure of the Russians and of all the other world marksmen. We'd never developed such a rifleman before, and we may never have another. Anderson, barely 30 years old, bids fair to hold and wear the crown of the world champion for a long time. Of all modern shooting men he most deserves a spacious corner in our hall of fame.

Along with Anderson there are others. There is Huelet "Joe" Benner, who has been pistol champion of the United States five times, and there's Harry Reeves, who held the title an equal number of times, Sgt. Bill Blankenship, a six-time champion. There is also Don Hamilton, who offers Bill the toughest sort of competition, and who is currently the No. 1 pistolman in this country. Among the rifle shooters there is the very outstanding Maj. Lones Wigger who, next to Anderson, has more frequently taken the measure of the Soviets.

Match shooting is ordinarily looked upon as a man's game, but there are exceptions. The most extraordinary one is a mere girl, Capt. Margaret Murdock, until this year a member of the U.S. Army rifle team. She was a consistent winner in shoulder-to-shoulder competition, not only among American male gunners but internationally as well. She became the World Champion at Wiesbaden in 1966, shooting in the Women's 3-Position event. Certainly in any summary of our all-time great marksmen this girl rates among the tops —and she rates a prominent place in our shrine for shooters without question.

Certainly the committee considering the stature of our modern shooters would want to consider the qualifications of such sportsmen-writers as Jack O'Connor and Warren Page. Both men, long-time contributors to our largest outdoor magazines, have not only written voluminously and well on guns and shooting but they've also hunted widely. They have trod the length and breadth of North America, and they've shot over much of Africa, Asia and Europe. Each well deserves a place 'mongst our shooting elite.

These names brought to mind are representative of the shooting men, past and present, who richly deserve remembrance. There are others, of course, for hardly two people would come up with a similar listing. If a committee goes to work developing a roster of our most deserving marksmen, hunters and sportsmen, it may decide on an altogether different group. This is not greatly important. The critical need is to commence the selection and, after that's been done, to preserve the names, the dates, the honors and the accomplishments of the individuals in a central repository. In a place—the Shooters Hall of Fame—where it can be cherished as shooting history. Guarded and sequestered for all time, so that a century hence the shooters and hunters of today—and of yesteryear— will not have been forgotten. ●

The Classic Double

A CENTURY OF DEVELOPMENT

by **WALLACE LABISKY**

A survey of the breech-loading side-by-side double gun in its variant forms and action styles.

To THE CASUAL observer, all double barrel shotguns may seem to be of almost identical design. But outward appearances tell only a small part of the story. Excluding the French-made Darne with its sliding breech and perhaps a few others that are neither fish nor fowl, the hammerless side-by-side guns in use today fall within three basic categories. These include the boxlock, the sidelock, and a much less common type known as the trigger-plate action.

Most of such famous American doubles as the A.H. Fox, Parker and Winchester Model 21 are of boxlock design, while such British makers as Boss, Holland & Holland and Purdey lean heavily toward sidelock actions. A large majority of the side-by-side doubles currently being imported to the U.S. for the competitive market from Spain, Italy and Japan are of the boxlock type.

The firm of John Dickson & Son, Edinburgh, Scotland, is (or was) a leading proponent of the trigger-plate type with their "round" action design. Sometimes called the "Blitz" action, this type also has a following among German makers.

The boxlock action can be defined as one in which the various component lock parts (the tumblers or hammers, the sears, and the attendant springs) are contained within the body of the action—in other words, inside the frame.

The sidelock gun differs principally in that the locks are separate from the action body. The lock parts (usually of greater number than for a boxlock action) are mounted on a pair of individual sideplates, being sandwiched between the sideplate and an additional screw-fastened support piece called a "bridle." The sideplates are, in turn, inletted to both the action body and the jaws of the stock.

Each sideplate is generally fastened to the action body by a single short screw, and to each other by a long joining screw running completely through the stock from one sideplate to the other. However, some foreign sidelocks, particularly those of British origin, do not always employ the long joining screw. But regardless of how they are fastened to the action body, these sideplates are readily removable, to one degree or another, for inspection and care of the locks.

It is interesting to note that on Holland & Holland's best-quality sidelock gun (the Royal grade), the sideplates are retained by a single transverse joining screw, the front part of the plate being held by a dove-

tail. This transverse screw is fitted with a small lever which permits it to be turned out by hand; therefore, no screwdriver is needed. Sideplates fastened in this manner are called "hand-detachable." They are also found on some Spanish copies of the Holland & Holland action, perhaps on some Austrian or German doubles.

The Lang is another British sidelock which features hand-detachable locks. In this design, each sideplate has its own retaining screw so that the locks may be removed independently. Moreover, the lever part of the screw is recessed into the plate for a neater appearance.

Hand-detachable locks are confined to a very few makes of sidelock guns and generally are found only in the most expensive grades. In boxlock doubles they are even more rare.

To my knowledge, the only boxlock gun having them is the top-grade Westley Richards. All of the component lock parts, including the cocking levers, are mounted on a pair of plates which are inserted separately, from the bottom, into recesses in the action body. They are covered by a hinged or detachable floorplate secured by a spring fastener. These instantly detachable locks are beautifully fitted and finished, all surfaces being damascened (engine-turned).

Sometimes boxlock guns are fitted with dummy sideplates to give the appearance

> For an explanation of double gun esoterica, much of which is unfamiliar nowadays to the novice, turn to Mr. Labisky's Part II of The Classic Double, immediately following.

of a sidelock action. I doubt that this practice is ever carried out purely with the intention of hoodwinking the prospective buyer. After all, the absence of tumbler, sear and other pins showing through the plate makes it quite apparent—except to the novice, perhaps—that the gun is wearing "falsies." At any rate, dummy sideplates do add to the lines of the boxlock action, and they furnish additional surface for such ornamentation as engraving and inlays.

Just as there are wide differences between boxlock and sidelock doubles, there also is a basic difference between actions of the latter type. In fact sidelocks can be further classified as having either bar-action or back-action locks.

The most commonly encountered sidelock is the bar-action. In this subtype the mainspring (invariably of the V-type) is positioned *ahead* of the tumbler (hammer). It is mounted on the narrow, forward part of the sideplate, which is let into the bar part of the action body. Hence the designation *bar*-action.

In a back-action sidelock the sideplates are generally of the same configuration as for a bar-action gun, but instead of mounting the mainspring forward, it is placed at the upper rear part of the sideplate, *behind* the tumbler.

Another but seldom seen form of the back-action lock employs a differently shaped sideplate which is narrow toward the rear, wide at the front. This type has a small projection (for inletting to the action body) at the front and to accommodate a retaining screw.

From a purely basic standpoint, any hammerless sidelock double could be described as a highly refined version of the old "rabbit-eared" hammer guns of yesteryear. Viewed in this light, the boxlock can be labeled as the more modern of the two, although this action itself dates back deeply into the 19th century.

Early Boxlocks

The first boxlock design of genuine merit was patented in 1875 by Mssrs. Anson and Deeley, both of whom at that time were gunmakers employed by the British firm of Westley Richards. The system stands as a milestone in double gun development, and attesting to its soundness of design is the fact that following the expiration of patent rights it became the most widely copied of all double-gun actions. Many of the boxlock guns being manufactured today show little variation from the original Anson & Deeley pattern, and all follow the same principle.

Boxlock doubles patterned after the Anson & Deeley design have fewer lock parts than the average sidelock. However, in all fairness, it should be pointed out that some well-known American sidelocks (namely, the L.C. Smith, the Syracuse-built Lefever, and the Baker) also featured uncomplicated locks.

In a typical boxlock action the principal lock parts consist of the tumbler, sear, mainspring, sear spring and cocking lever. The tumblers (hammers) and sears—one for each lock—are "pegged" to the action body (frame) by crosspins that extend completely through the frame at a point below

The sideplates on a sidelock double gun (top) provide additional space for ornamentation and offer more pleasing lines than found on boxlock gun with square-sterned frame.

and behind the action face. The mainsprings are always positioned forward of the tumblers in the upper part of the bar of the action body, or just below the water table (action flats). The axle for the cocking levers (one for each lock) is also a transverse pin through the bar of the frame. The ends of the cocking levers protrude from the frame at the knuckle and are accommodated by recesses in the fore-end iron.

Upon pulling the trigger, the integral trigger blade lifts the tail of the sear and disengages the sear nose from the tumbler bent (hammer notch). This allows the tumbler to fall and the firing pin to strike the shotshell primer. In some boxlock guns the firing pins are integral with the hammers; in others, the firing pins are separate.

With the lock in its fired position, the toe or forward part of the tumbler has been lowered into contact with the tail of the cocking lever. As the gun is opened and the fore-end iron revolves around the knuckle, the cocking lever is activated and its tail lifts the toe of the tumbler, causing the latter to rotate on its crosspin until the nose of the sear engages the bent. Simultaneously, the mainspring undergoes compression and thus the lock is again ready for firing.

This explanation of how the Anson & Deeley type lock operates may sound complicated, but the system is extremely simple and reliable. Most sidelock guns, incidentally, cock in much the same manner through the use of cocking levers extending through the bar of the frame.

There are a number of variations of the Anson & Deeley boxlock design, and some gunmakers have further simplified this type of action. An example is the famous old British firm of W. W. Greener (now a part of Webley & Scott, Birmingham). In the Greener "Empire" action, used for the "Blue Book Pigeon" and "Empire" grade boxlocks, long mainsprings of the V-type extend the full length of the bar of the frame and serve a double purpose by also acting as cocking levers. The "Empire" action is certainly the epitome of simplicity, and its reliability has been proven through long use in all corners of the world.

Trigger Plate Actions

The Dickson "round" action, patented in 1880, probably ranks as the most outstanding example of the trigger-plate design. It could be classed as part boxlock and part sidelock, though it more closely approaches the latter than the former. The locks are behind the action body as in a sidelock gun, and the mainsprings are behind the tumblers as in a back-action sidelock.

In this type of action, as the name implies, the locks are fastened to the trigger plate which, of course, is inserted from the bottom of the frame. A center "blade" which is integral with the trigger plate provides the foundation for both locks, the various components being sandwiched between this blade and a pair of screw-fastened bridles. So the lock support parallels that of a sidelock action, except that the single center blade takes the place of a pair of sideplates.

Foremost among the merits of the Dickson action is that the bar of the frame is not slotted to accommodate cocking levers. This function is handled by a flat cocking piece that moves longitudinally just above the trigger plate. The arrangement leaves the frame with exceptional rigidity and strength, exceeding that of even a back-action sidelock gun.

Although this article does not concern itself with ejector systems, I might point out in passing that the Dickson ejector system is contained entirely within the action body, whereas in most boxlock and sidelock actions the ejector mechanism is housed mainly within the fore-end.

An ultra-modern example of the trigger-plate action is found on Perazzi over-under doubles. This Italian firm, founded only a few years ago, furnishes a quickly-detachable trigger group that holds all of the lock work. Coil springs are used, permitting of a compact system, and Perazzi trigger-locks are available—and completely interchangeable—in single trigger, double trigger and "release" trigger construction. The single trigger unit may be had, optionally, to fire the top or the bottom barrel first.

While this Perazzi system is used only on over-under guns at the moment, it is understood that side-by-side doubles with virtually the same trigger-plate action will be offered in the near future.

A few double gun actions are of the "self-opening" type. With these the shooter has only to push the top lever over. Once the bolt(s) is retracted, no further effort is required. The barrels pivot fully down, the tumblers are brought to full cock, and the fired shells are ejected. Actions of this type seem to be the exclusive province of British makers, and all are sidelocks.

Perhaps best known among the self-openers are the best-grade Holland & Holland and the Rosson sidelocks, both makes being bar-action guns. The famous Purdey bar-action sidelock also reduces the opening effort to a large extent, as does the Lan-

caster "Twelve-Twenty" back-action sidelock.

In the Holland & Holland action the self-opening feature consists of a spring-operated slide that is attached to the barrels between the fore-end loop and the forward lug or lump, and the force for opening is applied against a projection at the frame knuckle.

The Rosson action uses a quite different arrangement. Employed here are two V-type springs for each lock, both being positioned on the topside of a uniquely shaped cocking lever that rides in the bar of the frame. When the top lever is pushed over to withdraw the bolt, the forward V-spring forces the cocking lever down to act against the fore-end iron with the result that the barrels are pivoted away from the action flats. Simultaneously, the rear spring (mainspring) acts in conjunction with the cocking lever to rotate the tumbler to full cock.

Obviously, these actions offer effortless opening, but the gain comes at the expense of pronounced stiffness on closing. To my thinking this approach isn't nearly what it is cracked up to be. In the Rosson action, for example, if both barrels have been fired, closing the action means that 6 springs (counting the two ejector springs) must be brought under compression at the same time.

Actions Compared

The weakest point in the action body of any side-by-side double, regardless of the type of lock used, is at the angle of the frame. In other words, it is that part in line with and directly below the action face. Upon firing, the bar of the frame tends to flex downward, and this area immediately below the action face is where the greatest strain occurs.

The rigidity of the bar of the frame governs to a large extent how great this flexing will be, and its rigidity, in turn, depends on the amount of metal that has been removed to make room for the lock

parts and the cocking levers. When judged strictly on this basis, the frame of a conventional Anson & Deeley type boxlock is weaker than that of the bar-action sidelock, and the bar-action comes in second to the back-action sidelock. Strongest of all in this respect is the Dickson or "Blitz" trigger-plate action which has no metal removed from the sides of the action bar, except for a pair of small circular tunnels to take the ejector rods and their coil springs.

Often cited as a major shortcoming of the coventional boxlock is that the transverse hole for the tumbler axle must necessarily be positioned in close proximity to the angle of the action, thus further weakening the frame at this critical point. It is for this reason that the under-bolted boxlock double is often additionally fitted with a barrel top extension in the form of either a cross-bolt or a "doll's head."

In cases where under-bolting is used, the breech or rib extension is not really intended to materially assist in locking the barrels to the action, but rather to alleviate, upon firing, that downward flexing at the angle of the action.

A strong case can be made on paper against the boxlock action in terms of relative frame strength, but metallurgy has come a long way since the 1880s and the argument tends to fall apart in court. When we are dealing with a double gun that is of extremely light weight for the gauge size, such as those feathery 12-bore "game" guns turned out by a bevy of British makers, then the theory has a good deal of merit. In such cases it is wise for the boxlock action to be fitted with a good functional top extension.

However, when a gun is built to a weight that is normal for the gauge, with a proportional increase in action body dimensions and using strong modern steel possessing the right degree of elasticity, I believe the matter becomes largely academic. In my personal battery is a pair of under-bolted boxlock doubles patterned after the Anson

Considerable wood must be removed from stock jaws on sidelock double to accommodate locks and sideplates. Stock joint is weaker than that of a boxlock gun. Cocking lever (arrow) lies in bar of action body. Cylindrical firing pin can be seen protruding above tail of cocking lever. Inletting sideplate to stock jaws and action body calls for precise craftsmanship, boosts price tag on sidelock doubles.

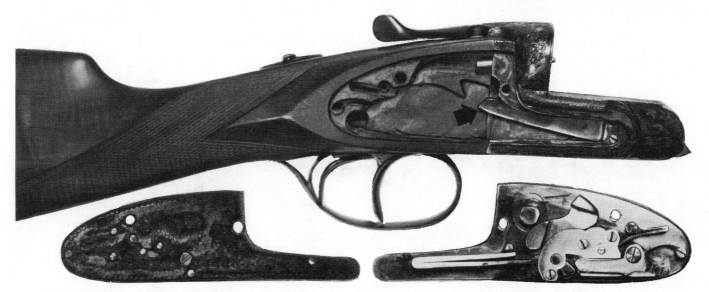

& Deeley system. One is a 12 bore, the other a Magnum 10 bore, and neither has a functional top extension. Both have seen long and continued use with loads producing heavy recoil. Yet they still breech up as tightly as ever, and I am not the least bit worried that the action body of either is suddenly going to give up the ghost.

One undisputable advantage which the boxlock action holds over the sidelock entails the joining of the buttstock to the action body. In the sidelock, much wood has to be removed from the jaws of the stock to make room for the lock parts; so much, in fact, that there is little more than a slender finger of wood contacting the frame at each corner. If the wood-to-metal union is not achieved with absolute precision, recoil will cause longitudinal cracks to develop both beneath and behind the sideplates.

As we have seen, the stock jaw of the boxlock does not have to be inletted to take the lock parts, and the action/stock joint is therefore inherently much stronger. If the fit is reasonably good, cracking from recoil is actually quite rare.

Another advantage held by the boxlock, through one of a minor nature, is that with the locks contained within the frame, the action is slightly more weatherproof than that of a sidelock.

Double Gun Safeties

On the other side of the ledger, an advantage claimed by the sidelock is that the action design lends itself far better to the use of an intercepting safety. Not all sidelocks possess this feature, but it is usually found on guns of British make, as well as on quite a number of sidelocks made on the European continent. Although it is possible to incorporate an intercepting safety in a boxlock, it is rarely found on that action type.

Of the famous American sidelock guns (L. C. Smith, Syracuse-built Lefever and Baker), only the better grades in the Baker line had an intercepting safety. This was in the form of a small block in front of the tumbler which pivoted clear, laterally, when the trigger was pulled.

However, the most widely used type is in the form of an extra sear. The two sears are usually positioned in close proximity, but only one of them actually engages the tumbler. If the engaging sear should happen to be jarred out of its notch, the standby sear catches a shoulder on the tumbler and stops its fall. Hence the term "intercepting safety." Incidentally, the regular safety on a double gun blocks only the trigger blades and cannot prevent discharge due to other causes.

Theoretically, an intercepting safety completely rules out accidental discharge due to jarring off, because tumbler clearance comes about only when this standby sear is functionally negated. This does not occur until the trigger has been pulled. But in actual practice there is always the possibility that a jar that is severe enough to move the engaging sear from its notch may also move the standby sear enough so that the tumbler will clear.

There are other considerations, too, when looking at the so-called advantage of an intercepting safety. In a boxlock action, the location of the sear pin is usually such that better trigger-pull leverage is afforded. Consequently, to combat the possibility of jarring off, the tumbler notch can be cut to provide greater sear engagement without making the actual trigger pull abnormally heavy.

Basically, the "crispness" of a double gun's trigger pull is largely a matter of the angle relationship between the tumbler axle, the tumbler notch, and the sear pin. In this realm, the bar-action sidelock and the trigger-plate actions rate as king of the hill, with the boxlock and back-action sidelock actions finishing second, there actually being little difference between the latter two.

When assessed from a practical point of view, the speed and efficiency of the tumbler fall is really no better in a sidelock than it is in a boxlock action, providing the mainsprings are of the same type. Disre-garding the self-opening guns, both action types pretty much balance out in terms of cocking ease.

Costs and Choice

This brings the comparison around, finally, to the matter of cost. Here we find that the sidelock actions generally carry a much harder-to-swallow price tag than do the boxlock guns.

Assuming that both types are similarly finished in terms of engraving, checkering, et cetera, the higher cost of the sidelock is more a matter of additional hours of hand labor devoted to fitting than anything else. Not only are the locks themselves somewhat more complicated, but the inletting of the side-plates, their lateral spacing and other niceties all require a great deal of painstaking work.

Bargain-priced sidelocks should be avoided like the plague, because in order to trim the price tag the manufacturer has had to skimp on the fitting, and such pieces, as I have sadly learned first-hand, often turn out to be worse than an Excedrin headache.

Dollar for dollar, the boxlock double gun is by far the best investment. Those straight lines at the frame may not be quite as pleasing to the eye, but certainly the action is equally as reliable as a sidelock and probably a good deal more rugged. Other factors being equal, it will pattern and handle just as well. I can't speak for the other fellow, but those points are good enough for me. ●

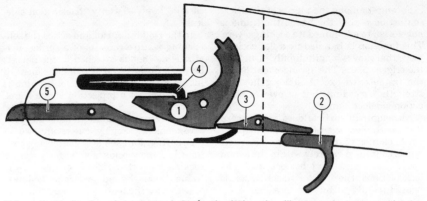

This sectional drawing of an Anson & Deeley boxlock action illustrates the system which has been widely copied by double-gun makers. Here the tumbler (1) or hammer is in the cocked position. When the trigger blade (2) moves the sear (3) nose from the tumbler notch, the force of the compressed mainspring (4) is applied to the tumbler which rotates forward to strike the shotshell primer. Tumbler toe, then in contact with the cocking lever (5), will rotate back to the cocked position when the fore-end iron activates the cocking lever as the gun is opened for loading.

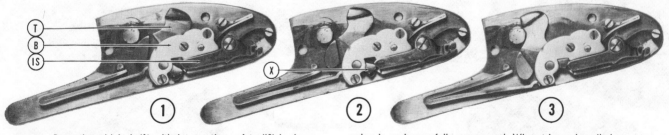

Bar-action sidelock (1) with intercepting safety (IS) is shown with tumbler or hammer (T) in cocked position behind bridle (B). Sear has been jarred out of the tumbler notch (2) and the intercepting safety's nose contacts the tumbler shoulder at point "X," stopping its fall. Note that main-spring is no longer fully compressed. When trigger is pulled (3), intercepting safety pivots on sear axle and provides clearance for the tumbler shoulder. The lock is shown in the fired position, two small springs at the rear of the sideplates tension the sear and intercepting safety.

The Classic Double

A CENTURY OF DEVELOPMENT PART II

A clear explanation of the sometime esoteric and obscure double gun terminology — an Illustrated Glossary.

by WALLACE LABISKY

SURROUNDING THE side-by-side double gun is a vernacularism that often is not clearly understood in the shotgunning world of today. Ever since the early years of this century, pump repeaters and autoloaders have dominated the scene, and in this light it is little wonder that the neophyte shooter or collector goes a little blank when double-gun *aficionados* open up with their special brand of parlance. So, in order that the uninitiated will be better equipped to savvy the lingo, we present the following glossary.

FRAME or ACTION BODY When viewed in profile, the frame of a side-by-side gun can be likened to the letter "L" which has been tipped so that the toe of the letter points upward. Its role is much more than just a simple component for linking the buttstock to the barrels. It is really the nucleus of the gun, serving as a housing or framework for the various action parts—lockworks, cocking levers, bolting system, trigger mechanism and safety. It is sometimes erroneously referred to as the receiver.

ACTION BAR or FRAME BAR This is the long, horizontal section of the frame below the breech end of the barrels. It has a longitudinal cut down its center to accommodate the barrel lumps (which see). Also, it is further "hollowed out" in varying degrees, depending on the type of action (i.e., whether sidelock or boxlock), to accept the cocking levers, mainsprings, under-bolt, et cetera.

STANDING BREECH That part of the frame which is perpendicular (or nearly so) to the bar of the frame. In a boxlock action, this section provides the framework for supporting the hammers and sears. In a sidelock action, it receives the forward end of the lockplate. Regardless of action type, it houses the top-lever spindle which cams the bolt(s) that lock the barrels to the frame. In cases where a top-bolt is adopted, it also houses that component. When the firing pins are not integral with hammers, they, too, are fixed within the standing breech.

TANG or STRAP Integral with the frame, this "finger" of metal extends a few inches rearward from the standing breech and is inletted flush with the top of the stock wood. The tang carries the thumb-slide safety and it also takes the breech pin (large screw) which secures the stock to the frame.

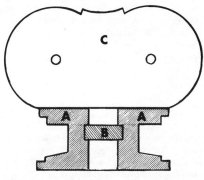

Section of a barlock breech action showing how the bolt holds the lumps. A, is the action bar or frame bar. B, is the action bolt, C is action face.

ACTION FACE The smooth, flat, forward surface of the standing breech through which the firing pin openings are cut, and which is in juxtaposition with the breech end of the barrels when the action is closed.

ACTION VENTS These provide a means for diverting powder gas in the event of a very loose-fitting primer or a primer that has been pierced by the firing pin. As a rule, the vents are in the form of narrow, shallow, line-like channels which circle the firing pin orifice and then lead to the outer edge of the action face. Some double guns have this feature, others do not.

TRIGGER PLATE Serves as a cover, or floor, for the bottom of the frame, and as a platform on which the triggers themselves are pinned. It also furnishes a means of anchoring the front end of the trigger guard. The lower tang is integral with the trigger plate and is the terminus for the stock-retaining breech pin.

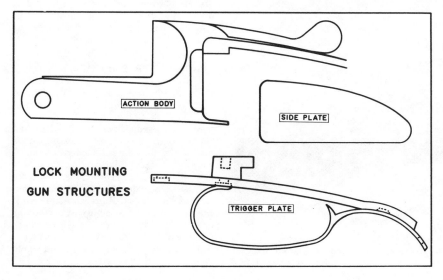

ACTION BODY

SIDE PLATE

LOCK MOUNTING GUN STRUCTURES

TRIGGER PLATE

ACTION FLATS or ACTION TABLE These terms refer to the flat, horizontal surface of the action bar which is in juxtaposition to the bottom of the barrels when the action is closed. This part of the frame also is sometimes called the "water table." The serial number of the gun and certain proof marks are often found stamped on the action flats.

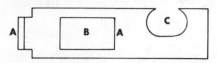

Top view of an action bolt. A, bearing edges; B, slot for rear lump; C, eliptical slot for the cam operated by the top lever.

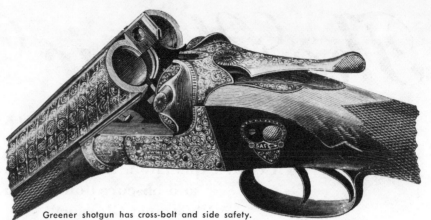

Greener shotgun has cross-bolt and side safety.

BARREL FLATS The flat surface on the bottom of each barrel at its breech end. These flats are in juxtaposition to the action flats when the action is closed. On the barrel flats are usually found such markings as serial number, gauge, chamber length and additional symbols and numerals relating to proof testing.

BOLT LOOP or BARREL LOOP This is the projection found between the two barrels on their bottom side, usually about six or seven inches forward of the breech. Its purpose is to engage the fore-end catch, thereby locking the fore-end to the barrels and, in turn, preventing the barrels from pivoting free of the frame when the action is opened. Both terms listed are correct, but among the more dedicated students the former is usually considered to be more "according to Hoyle."

KNUCKLE The rounded forward end of the action bar which is in juxtaposition to the fore-end iron when the gun is fully assembled and through which the cocking levers protrude.

BARREL LUMPS The rather massive projections that occupy a position between the barrel flats. These are sometimes called *lugs* or *under-lugs*. On an under-bolted action, there are always two lumps, while on an action that is strictly top-bolted there is usually only one.

BITE The slot or opening cut into the rear face of the barrel lump(s). It or they provide a bearing surface(s) for the bolt, which locks the barrels to the frame.

HOOK As the designation implies, this is the circular cut in the front face of the forward barrel lump which hooks the barrels to the action bar.

HINGE Usually described as the hinge pin, this is the heavy cross-pin through the action bar at the knuckle. It forms the axis on which the barrels rotate, via the hook in the forward lump.

UNDER BOLTING A method of locking the barrels to the frame wherein a single bolt (rectangular in cross-section) moves longitudinally (fore-and-aft) within the action bar to engage the barrel lump bites. The bolt (sometimes referred to as the *action bolt*) is actuated by a cam arrangement on the top-lever spindle. This form of bolting originated with the British firm of Purdey and has been extensively copied throughout the world. In some designs, under bolting involves only the rear barrel lump, but the more common practice employs a bolt that engages both barrel lumps and such guns are sometimes described as having "double locking lugs."

RIB EXTENSION or TOP EXTENSION A projecting "limb" at the breech end of the barrels which generally forms a continuation of the top rib. When the action is closed, the rib extension mates with a slot-way in the standing breech.

TOP BOLTING In this method of breech lock-up a bolt engages a bite in the rib extension which, as we have just seen, is flush-fitted into a slot-way in the standing breech. Top bolts vary considerably in de-

sign, as do the bites in the rib extension. A famous example of top bolting is the well-known L.C. Smith's rotary bolt.

CROSS-BOLT Usually a round bolt that moves laterally within the standing breech to engage a matching bite in the rib extension. When retracted, some cross-bolts protrude from the side of the standing breech; others remain concealed when disengaged. A classic example of the cross-bolt in its most efficient form is the W.W. Greener design which has been copied by many gunmakers.

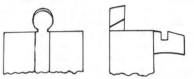

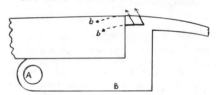

Above—Doll's head extension, top and side views. Below—Cross section view.

DOLL'S HEAD In its most common form this is simply a circular enlargement at the end of the rib extension. As a rule, it is not combined with a top bolt. Its foremost purpose is to transfer some of the stress of firing from the action bar to the standing breech. The doll's head is no longer widely used, but when precisely fitted to the standing breech it is quite effective in preventing the action bar from flexing downward at the moment of discharge.

CONCEALED BREECH EXTENSION This is another form of top bolting, and it also was originated by the firm of Purdey. The extension projects from between the barrels at a point that coincides with the axis of the bores—sometimes a little higher. There is a half-moon recess in the action face to accommodate the extension, and a small bolt moves longitudinally in the standing breech to bear against the upper surface of the extension. A secondary function of the concealed breech extension is that it can be, and usually is, used as an extractor guide. The reason it came to be described as a "concealed" extension is that when the extractors are cammed out it is not at all conspicuous.

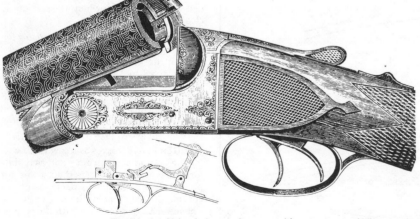

The Westley-Richards hammerless gun with extractors and rib extension for top bolting. Inset shows operation of automatic top tang safety.

MULTIPLE or TRIPLE BOLTING This term is, as a rule, applied to an action that employs double under-bolts in conjunction with one of the various top-bolt designs—the cross-bolt, doll's head or concealed breech extension. The practice is a quite common one.

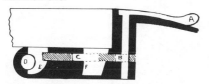

Cross section of Purdey double bolt. A, top lever; B, cam; C, slot for rear lump; D, hinge pin; E, front barrel lump with hook and bite.

FORE-END IRON The metal part of the fore-end that is in juxtaposition to the knuckle of the frame and which actuates the cocking levers when the barrels swing open. On ejector guns of conventional design it serves also as the framework for the ejector lockworks.

FORE-END ESCUTCHEONS The small, various-shaped metal pieces inletted in the bottom surface of the wood for accepting the screws that secure the fore-end iron to the wood. Sometimes the escutcheons are omitted, with shorter screws simply being turned into the wood.

ANSON FORE-END RELEASE The push-rod type of release with a round (usually) stud projecting from the tip of the fore-end. Sometimes called a Purdey-style release.

DEELEY FORE-END RELEASE A release inletted, at a mid-point position, into the belly of the wood. This type is manipulated by lifting a short, hinged finger lever which withdraws the catch from the barrel loop. Sometimes the lever itself is fitted with a self-locking device.

EXTRACTOR GUN In this design the two extractors are made as a single unit (usually) and upon opening the action both shells, whether fired or unfired, are simply withdrawn from the chambers far enough so that they can be easily grasped for manual removal.

EJECTOR GUN The total ejection of fired shells is automatic upon fully opening the action. The ejection is also selective; that is, if only one barrel has been fired that empty is kicked from its chamber, while the unfired shell in the other barrel is lifted in the same manner as for an extractor gun. The partial withdrawal of an unfired shell from the chamber is called primary extraction.

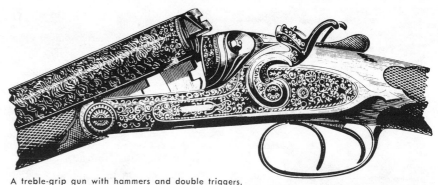

A treble-grip gun with hammers and double triggers.

EXTRACTOR CAM A small component part that contacts the extractor leg(s) to produce primary extraction as the barrels swing away from the action face. On plain extractor guns the camming action is achieved through the use of a small pivoted "limb" fixed at the upper end of the fore-end iron. On an ejector gun, the work is usually done by a stationary "limb" at the center of the frame knuckle, this part performing double duty by also serving as a cocking piece for the ejector hammers.

EXTRACTOR STOP PIN A small screw which passes down through the rear barrel lump, or through the flat area just ahead of the lump, to prevent over-travel of the extractors.

ARTICULATED or HINGED TRIGGER This means that the front trigger on a double-trigger gun is hinged so that it can swing forward under recoil when the rear trigger is pulled. This is a very worthwhile feature, because it eliminates bruising the top of the shooter's trigger finger when firing loads that produce heavy recoil.

MECHANICAL TRIGGER A single trigger which does *not* require recoil to activate the mechanism that readies the second barrel for firing.

INERTIA TRIGGER This type of single trigger does require recoil to accomplish the shift from one barrel to the other. In the case of a misfire or a very weak load on the first pull of the trigger, the second barrel cannot be fired without first manipulating the barrel selector.

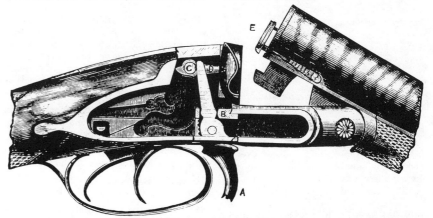

Side view of the Murcott hammerless shotgun—the first successful gun of this type—which used conventional sidelocks.

NON-SELECTIVE TRIGGER A single trigger with a fixed firing order. Invariably the sequence is (except on special order) right barrel/left barrel. If the right barrel only is fired and reloaded, the right barrel will again fire with the first pull of the trigger—not the left barrel.

SELECTIVE TRIGGER A single trigger which can be set to fire either the right barrel first or the left barrel first, and the sequence is automatically reset each time the action is opened, even though only one barrel has been fired.

BARREL SELECTOR A mechanism which regulates the firing sequence of a selective single trigger. There are two common types. One is incorporated with the tang safety, the other is a small cross-bolt affair located in the web of the trigger.

MONOBLOCK BREECH A method of manufacture wherein the breech section of the barrels, including the flats, lumps, top rib section and rib extension (if one is used), is made as a single unit. The front part of the monoblock section is then counter-bored and the tubes (barrels) are inserted. This is an extremely strong system for joining together the two barrels at their breech end.

The Deeley ejector gun was the earliest of the type having separate fore-end ejectors.

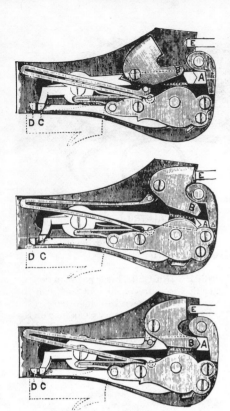

The most popular form of automatic intercepting safety—Scott's design used on most modern shotguns.

AUTOMATIC SAFETY Automatically returns to the "on" or "safe" position immediately the top lever is pushed over to open the action. Most double guns intended primarily for field use have this type of safety. Skeet and trap guns often do not.

MANUAL SAFETY This type is not linked to the top lever and it must be manually returned to the "safe" position. It is usually the preferred type among Skeet and trap shooters, particularly the latter.

INTERCEPTING SAFETY A standby sear which blocks the fall of the hammer in the event the main sear is jarred out of its notch in the hammer. Ordinarily an intercepting safety is found only in a sidelock action and is incorporated with the lockworks.

RIB All side-by-side guns have both a top and bottom rib to fill the "valleys" between the two barrels and thereby enhance the appearance of the gun. The top rib, of course, is the more important of the two inasmuch as it is of tremendous value in aligning the gun on target. Although ventilated top ribs are sometimes employed on a side-by-side, most wear a raised, solid rib. The surface is generally flat (though in some instances slightly concave, often called a "swamped" rib) and is usually checkered or matted to reduce glare.

BOXLOCK ACTION In this type of action the standing breech (which see) supports the hammer, sear, etc. See SIDELOCK.

SIDELOCK or LOCKPLATE The plate to which the various lock parts are attached and which is inletted to both the jaws of the stock and the frame on a sidelock action. A *dummy* lockplate is sometimes fitted on a boxlock gun to improve its appearance or to provide additional space for ornamentation.

LOCKWORKS The hammers, sears, springs, pins and other attendant lock parts.

SEAR and TUMBLER PINS The axles on which the sears and hammers rotate. In a boxlock gun the pins are positioned crosswise through the lower part of the standing breech, one for the two sears and one for the two hammers. In a sidelock action the pins are in the lockplates.

BENT The notch in the hammer which is engaged by the nose of the sear when the lock is brought to full-cock position.

MAINSPRING Usually a V-type spring which provides the power for hammer fall.

TUMBLER A gunmaker's term for the hammer that strikes the firing pin.

SEAR That part of the lock which releases the hammer when actuated by a pull on the trigger.

DOUBLE TRIGGER A simple and highly reliable arrangement in which each lock has its own trigger. The front trigger fires the right barrel, the rear trigger and left barrel, and the shooter has an instant choice of any firing sequence without having to manipulate a barrel selector. A very few foreign two-trigger guns are designed so that one of the triggers will function as a non-selective single trigger.

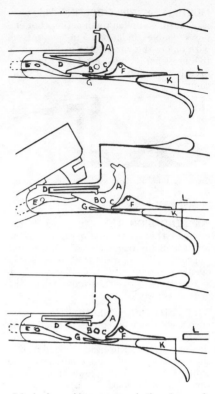

Principal working parts of the Anson & Deeley action. Top—gun is closed and fired, trigger is still depressed. Center—gun is open. Bottom—gun closed and ready to fire.

STOCK JAWS That portion of the buttstock which mates with the frame.

STOCK HAND or WRIST The small of the stock, more commonly referred to as the grip. The various shapes include straight, half-pistol and full-pistol styles.

STOCK THROUGH-BOLT This represents a more modern approach in securing the buttstock to the action. The bolt runs lengthwise in the stock, is accessible through a deep counter-bore in the butt of the stock.

CAST-OFF This refers to the butt of the stock and means that its center is offset slightly to the right of a straight line extending through the sights. Cast-off is preferred by many right-handed shooters (and by those with a full face) as it aids in quickly aligning the eye with the top rib. In custom-built doubles (or other types) cast-off may be greater at heel than at the toe—or vice versa.

CAST-ON Exactly the opposite of cast-off and means that the butt center is offset to the left. Obviously, cast-on is of benefit only to a southpaw shooter.

DOWNPITCH The distance that the barrel muzzle is away from the perpendicular (in inches or degrees) when both toe and heel of the stock are in contact with a flat surface that is square to the perpendicular. Downpitch is governed by the angle on which the stock butt is cut. An easy way to determine the amount of downpitch is to stand the gun on the floor with the top of the standing breech touching the wall. Then measure the distance between the wall and the top rib at the muzzles. ●

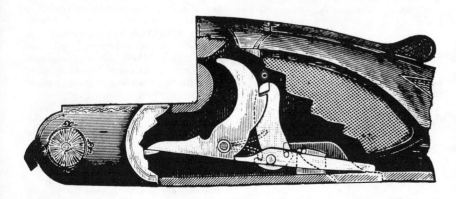

Another type of automatic intercepting safety. This one is by Greener.

HOW CAN YOU MISS AN ELEPHANT?

Well, it ain't easy, but a complete miss isn't the point. The successful elephant hunter must know exactly where to hit, and how to do it. The unsuccessful one seldom talks about it!

by WARREN PAGE

IT HAPPENS all the time. You're gabbing with solid American citizens, perhaps not very savvy about hunting, talking about Africa. Somebody mentions elephants. Immediately up pops the double-barreled question: Why hunt elephants? Who could miss an elephant?

Who indeed? It has been done, I am told. But the hunter seized by a buck ague so colossal as to make him miss a hulk too big for a two-car garage is a rare bird. Such a total miss has naught to do with our case, anyway. The fact is that successful elephant hunting demands that—from moderate to ultra-short range —you be able to hit a 5-gallon can (the heart) nestling in an odd position behind the shoulder; or perhaps a loaf of rye bread (the brain) which is tucked into the stern end of a lumpy, bone-armored head somewhat bulkier than a 50-gallon drum. So the question deals not with missing the elephant entirely, but with knowing his anatomy well enough to punch a bullet precisely into vitals hidden by his very bulk. The penalty for even slight misplacement is quite possibly your own demise. You just don't "miss" elephants, friend, not more than once or twice a lifetime anyway.

Far more interesting, of course, is the question as to why anybody should want to hunt elephant. To the average "civilized" mind, conditioned by all the Disney, Daktari, and Tarzan nonsense—and chiefly familiar with those docile, small-eared Indian elephants common to circuses and zoos—the great grey creatures of Africa must likewise be slow-moving hulks, utterly noncombative. Presumably they, too, divide their time between toting around Hollywood muscle men dressed in loin cloths, and gamboling at the waterhole. This is a false portrait, as are so many on the TV tube. The African elephant is grey, and normally moves slowly, to be sure. Yet in his shambling run he can get up to almost 25 miles an hour, like when he's chasing you. Olympic sprinters do little better. Anger one elephant or a herd and you have turned loose a hurricane. As for toting Tarzan around, well, the grown African elephant has not been successfully domesticated, to any degree, since the days of Hannibal. There is, in the nature of the great beast, very sound reason why every African professional white hunter, off for a busman's holiday, tackles either buffalo or elephant, likely the latter.

That reason is not simple, nor is it easy to convey in words. When, of 12 safaris, I made my first, years back, I felt no urge to hunt elephant. I took out a ticket chiefly because the arms writer of another magazine had made his first safari, the year before, without hunting elephant. A mighty poor reason, perhaps. But after that first hunt, up in the sandy luggas of the Northern Frontier District, I was converted. Now, for my money, the bull elephant of trophy proportions is the Number I hunting challenge in Africa. Not necessarily the nastiest tempered or the

most dangerous—those crowns go either to Cape buffalo or leopard—but the greatest hunting challenge. I say this after 9 elephants taken, and a thousand encountered, in nearly all the safari areas of the Dark Continent.

That first bull wasn't such a muchness. I had set as acceptable ivory weight the modest minimum of 65 pounds per side. Most people agree that 80 is very good; 100 or over—and I've been lucky enough to beat that only once, with 123—rates as most excellent. There are today perhaps only two sections of Africa where you face reasonable odds in trying for a hundred-pounder. But 65 will do to start with, I had told Tony Dyer, back in 1956 on the Merille Lugga. Even that came hard. We scoured around for days tracking elephants, glassing elephants, following up misinformation from the nomadic Sanburu tribesmen who watered their goat herds at shallow wells scraped in the lugga. The elephants we found one day were 40 miles away the next, that being their idea of a casual overnight jaunt in times of scarce water. Every respectable bull seemed to sport a broken tusk or, as is not usually the case, was unapproachable within a mixed herd. Just plain slow going. The forty-pounders began to look good.

But finally long search paid off. We located the right bull in a bunch of five, and from 50 yards I made an acceptable heart shot. Nothing to it, so far.

But Tony hadn't told me about what would happen next. The remaining four bulls, shaken for a moment by the rifle blast, as if by a quarterback's signal wheeled and headed for us. We scrambled up onto a rocky knoll. The elephants charged, screamed, finally stopped and backed off. This was just a demonstration. But I had learned what it could be like to be caught in either a stampede or a deliberate charge. What do you do when 7 tons, or 70, come down on you? Good question.

That first safari was easy to remember when I hunted the Belgian Congo a few seasons later. We were operating on the Rutshuru Plain north of Goma, a panhandle between Albert Park on the Congo side and Queen Elizabeth Park in Uganda. This brushy flat then had, I suspect, the heaviest elephant population in all of Africa. What it is like today, after the bloody revolutions and upheavals that began in the Congo within two

months of our hunt, is hard to say. One windless day we found, my Swiss friend Tommy Aman and I, a group of 30-40 elephant feeding in dense 12-foot bush, by spotting their backs from afar. With no professional hunter along to question our bad judgment we pussyfooted in to look for possible trophy ivory. Sneaking around on hands and knees and looking *up* at a bull elephant is an excellent stimulus for the adrenal glands. When a bull elephant starts tearing up the very bush you are hiding behind, to stuff it into his face, it becomes even better.

When another bunch moved in behind us it was time to go. High time. These were almost entirely cows and calves and the female of the species is vastly more troublesome than the male. Even in open country it is wise to give a bunch of cows a two to three hundred yard berth. No telling what idiocy of maternal fierceness may possess them. In Zambia recently my companion and his professional hunter wandered a shade too close to a nursery group. The cows scented them and turned, immediately protective. The native bearers made the fatal error of running away, focussing the cows' dim eyesight on the two hunters. One cow pressed home a charge that ended only when she died at gun muzzle. No good reason, just female orneriness.

It was much the same on a charge we faced in the Congo. In a 40-acre patch of jungle around a waterhole, Aman and I were trailing up big foot prints that might well mean a big bull, were close enough to hear the purring rumbles that are the sign of full-bellied elephantine contentment. When the rumbles quit we knew the beasts were alerted. Two crashed down past us, small and probably cows. Then a huge-bodied elephant, the tallest I've ever seen but with absolutely no ivory showing, moved out, stopped 15 yards away, unreeled a fire-hose length of trunk to sniff in our direction. Our bearers tried to disappear down a wormhole, Aman and I stood with rifles ready. The critter made up its mind, rolled back its trunk and hiked its ears in the signs preparatory to a real charge, grunted into gear. Two hard-jacketed slugs in its brain halted the elephant seven paces from us. It was a cow, a pregnant one, in whom we had not the slightest interest, save that she go peaceably away. But who can account for the vagaries of a pregnant lady?

The Congo authorities called it *legitime defense*, no count on our licenses. Defense, no doubt about it, and if not legitimate then desperate.

The point I'm making here is that not only can a wounded elephant jam a tusk through your gizzard, or squash you into people-burger, but an unwounded one, especially a female, may come up with the same idea. Its reasons will appear valid only to the pachydermatous mind. Crocodiles kill most native blacks, the buffalo is the runner-up, lion and rhino probably fight for the show spot. Elephants do not rate high in that sweepstakes because they're big enough to be avoided and are generally smart enough to avoid man—but they can indeed put the careless hunter into the obituary column. Still, isn't the

element of personal danger one of the three factors that distinguish those animals that really challenge the hunter?

The two others are difficulty of terrain and the cunning or sensibility of the game. Elephant country holds none of the gut-busting physical difficulty of sheep and goat mountains, of course, though bulls are common in the giant heather regions of Mount Kenya above 11,000 feet. Most of the stories told by safarists who claim to have tracked elephants for endless sole-burning miles are highly exaggerated. But where the elephant of Karamoja Bell's day roamed fearlessly in the open, today's pachyderm hangs more in dense bush, where he's hard to locate. Any elephant, casually wandering from one patch of feed to another, ambles at 5 to 6 miles an hour. That will force a mere human into a puffing trot. There is certainly a degree of physical difficulty.

Far more interesting are the elephant reactions to being hunted, their intelligence, and their abilities to sense the hunter. On the first two scores the animal with the tail on both ends is hard to beat. Tsavo Park got into serious trouble from overgrazing by elephant herds because the pachyderms knew as precisely where the park lines lay, where elephant were and were not protected, as if there had been actual fences. In Zambia, one open-country section of the Luangwa Valley, up near the boundary escarpments, was filthy with elephant when Phil Hankin and I first poked into it. There were a few around the second day. But after the third the word had somehow been passed. The elephant had bugged out for further and thicker places. With a very high IQ, they know, and I think they can communicate.

Game animals come equipped with various levels of sensor, just as do humans. Our powers of scent are downright lousy, our hearing only fair, but our eyesight is excellent, for example. The moose smells and hears well, but has poor eyesight for distance. The sheep has absolutely superb eyes, a good nose, doesn't much give a damn what rock noises he hears. The Cape buffalo is a toughie because all three of his senses work efficiently. And so on.

The elephant—well, those huge flapping ears, effective as hide-cooling fans, will also funnel abnormal noises into remarkably acute ears. His trunk is as sensitive to threatening smell as is radar to an incoming plane—and it can be raised to sniff the upper air currents or swept down along the ground like a vacuum cleaner to snuffle out a footprint. We were, on one occasion, investigating a small waterhole in Kenya, and were driven back from it by the arrival of a dozen elephants. One might turn out to be a good bull, so we stayed close to watch. The leader stepped cautiously into the clearing, paused. Surely he would come to the water. Then that trunk tip swept across where I had stood five minutes before. Silently the leader wheeled and the group oozed off through the bush. Not crashing away in heedless flight, no. Silently. Those 6-inch pads of gristle that elephants use for foot soles squdged down so gently that no twig broke, and no branch cracked as tons of weight swept by it.

The elephant's weakest sense is his eyesight. Stand still and he has a tough time making you out. Move and he can spot you from across a football field. By astute use of the elephant's visual defect and by moving only against a good breeze, a careful man can work up into touching distance, if he has the nerve. The pygmies of the Ituri have done this for centuries. Smeared in elephant dung to kill their human pungency, they sneak in under a bull's belly, stab him in the bladder, and wait for him to die—a method I offer free for those who would prove their courage by killing elephant with bow and arrow or other inadequate weapon. None of these stunts would be possible if elephantine eyes were bird-sharp, and few men would be able to stalk into dead certain range even for a rifle.

For the targets are not large on an elephant. Remember the 5-gallon can and the loaf of bread mentioned early in this piece. The problem is to calculate instantly the angles that will get a bullet surely into an execution area through any intervening flesh or bone. This is a neat trial of judgment.

When we were flying home from Zambia the Alitalia stewardess, a snappy brunette from Rome, asked the inevitable why-do-you-hunt-elephant question. I answered it as best I might. She had somewhere come to know the truth that among Africa's mammals the elephant is doing remarkably well, with the only real threat to it being not hunting but the population explosion, since after all a herd of elephants and a native farmer's banana patch can come together with only one flattened result. Control shooting, for reasons of expanding humanity, kills vastly more elephants each year than trophy hunters ever could. I recall watching John Blower, then Chief Game Warden of Uganda and essentially a man of protectionist views, nonchalantly signing an order for the indiscriminate slaughter of 1500 elephants in one reserve. Such control killings are still common. Finally, in these days of low ivory prices and high taxes, the professional ivory-killer is long since kaput. All this the Roman girl understood. What I found hard to explain to her was the emotional element in the hunt for my Zambian bull.

We had looked at 200 or more, over three weeks and at from 15 to 200 yards, searching for trophy ivory. White hunter Rolf Rohwer had reported a bunch of good tuskers, from which his clients had already taken two, watering at a hidden pond two hours hike back into the *mopane,* but they had gone, driven off by the earlier shooting. Nothing we located seemed good enough. As we stood examining the total wreckage of a baobab, a tree 8 to 10 feet through the trunk, which had been felled and ripped apart by bulls hungry for the damp pulp that passes for baobab wood, we heard a lesser tree crash down in the forest. Only elephant could be responsible.

It was long minutes before we found the bunch, mostly young bulls, noisily feeding by walking down *mopane* trees and then eating the leafy green topping. Nine, but no big ones. To the right we heard other munching sounds. Three bulls. The two finest stood on a small island created by a loop in a deeply eroded creek bed. One carried ivory of excellent weight, curved and bulky tusks so long we could see them either side of a heavy-trunked hardwood. They'd go 75 pounds each tusk, Rolf and I agreed.

The stalk would not have been hard save for that steep-walled creek, its bottom choked with dry leaves. The only quiet way to cross it would be to fly. As we crept over the edge nearest the big bull, he was standing broadside at 15 yards. A heart shot. Just below the top of the crease made by the foreleg would do it. But my foot dislodged a chunk of clay that rattled down into the leaves. The bull whirled to face us.

There wasn't any place to go. The creek gully was too deep to jump back into. Surprised and perhaps even frightened by our sudden arrival, the bull was going to charge. Either my shot would be right or the Zambia newspapers would have front page news. His brain should lie dead behind the center of the trunk base on a line between the two eyes, said my racing mind. The rifle lined up there without further thought. But as he rolled into motion the bull lifted his head. That changed the angle. I must shoot lower by anyway six inches. Right there.

At that moment, to my heightened consciousness, the wrinkles crossing the elephant's trunk seemed as coarsely visible as masonry on a wall. The rifle sight lined automatically and my trigger finger tightened automatically. As the rifle belted me in recoil, the elephant dropped out of sight, instantly dead from only 300 grains of lead and steel that had bitten into a hidden brain located as precisely as if I had used a T-square. For a moment I had lived quite outside myself, had compressed days into seconds.

That was part of what I couldn't explain to the Alitalia girl, plus the supreme satisfaction at having faced the bull in fight as fair as ever conflict between man and beast can be, to slay him with a little projectile thrown as accurately as David slung stone at Goliath. Come to think of it, it is almost impossible to make such things clear, isn't it, save to another hunter? ●

Larry Wilson thought he'd have to shoot this elephant, but he didn't—the big tusker stopped his charge 12 yards away.

Through the years, O. F. Mossberg & Sons has offered scores of gun models. One of the most interesting--because of its historical derivation as well as its low cost and high quality--is this little . . .

MOSSBERG MARTINI

by Harry O. Dean

THE RARE GUN, the unusual gun, the historic gun, the clever gun—each holds a strong fascination for the true firearms enthusiast. I want to discuss one here, a 22 rifle, that possesses all of these attributes and more. It was an early product of O. F. Mossberg & Sons. The older catalogs and folders list it simply as the Model L. First, a bit of background, then let's see what makes it so unusual.

A Visit to the Roundhouse

I was fortunate in being able to visit the old Mossberg factory in New Haven, Conn. prior to their move to new facilities in North Haven. Fortunate, because I was able to see the famed "Roundhouse" factory—a fitting name because the building was formerly a railroad roundhouse! It was quite large and contained several floors but, in general, working conditions were somewhat cramped and much of the metal- and scope work had to be done elsewhere. To make matters worse, the other factory was located several blocks away from the Roundhouse. All these problems were solved when Mossberg moved into their beautiful new factory on Grasso Ave. in North Haven.

I mention this to point up the fact that I was able to see the older manufacturing setup as it was before it became history. Here I met Walter L.

Mossberg Model L, top, was built on a Martini-type falling block action, shown in close-up, upper left. The lever visible at front of action activated the takedown cam. Ithaca Saddlegun, above, in current production, also is made on a Martini style action.

Pierson, then vice president of Mossberg, but since elevated to the presidency. I recall asking him if he remembered the old Model L.

"I certainly do," he replied. "Would you like to see one?" He must have interpreted my surprised stutter as an affirmative answer. The Model L that he handed me from his office gun cabinet looked as if it had just come out of the box. Actually, it had been beautifully refinished. We discussed it for awhile and then turned our attention to the 22 Magnum rifles which were my major point of interest during that tour of the factory.

A couple of years later I wrote Walter in regard to the Model L. He kindly offered to lend me his personal rifle for the photographs you see with this article.

We Examine the Rifle

The Mossberg Model L was a single shot 22-cal. rimfire rifle, built on the time-tested Martini falling block action. Over-all length was 40", weight about 5 lbs. It had a walnut stock with a 13" pull, and a full beavertail fore-end. The tapered barrel measured 3/4" at the breech and was 24" long. The action was a takedown, the barrel being retained in the breech by a rotating cam, which was activated by a small swing lever on the forward left side of the frame. The design of this cam lock allowed for constant take up of wear.

A clever safety feature was incorporated in the operation of the exposed hammer. When the lever was opened, requiring only a two-inch throw, the front end of the breech block dropped and the two-speed ejector automatically expelled the cartridge. This motion also moved the hammer into the half-cock position, which served as a safety. Since the

named Frederich Martini improved the Peabody action by making it hammerless with coil springs within the breechblock.* This version was called the Peabody-Martini. From this evolved the famous Martini-Henry rifle of England.

This was a military model, known for its strength and simplicity. The rear of the action was completely en-

was transmitted, *not* to the bolt upon which it pivoted, but to the rear of the breechblock itself where it contacted the abutment of the frame. This made the action quite strong, even though the thrust was not in a straight line with its final support.

Famed Target Arm

A great number of 22 rimfire target

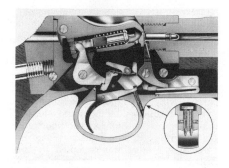

A Peabody-Martini target rifle popular in the 1870s and 1880s for 500-800 yard matches was the No. 1 Mid-Range Creedmoor model, top. It had a pistol grip and half-octagon barrel and used the 40-70-1⅝" Peabody-Martini cartridge with 380-gr. paper patched bullet. Weight about 9½ lbs.

Above, Mossberg's only current lever action rifle, the Palomino model in 22 rimfire.

Left, cutaway view of the BSA Martini-International smallbore target rifle action. This model is a favorite with many shooters. Trigger is adjustable from ½ to 3½ lbs.

shooters still favor the Martini breech for tack-driving accuracy. The modern Martini match rifle is a masterpiece of X-ring machinery. Much of the improved design on current models is a result of the work of Al Freeland. He introduced several group tightening innovations which are incorporated in the imported British bullseye-busters which his company sells.

Mossberg Martini History

You will remember my suggestion to bear in mind the exposed hammer on the original Peabody action. This allows us to note a full circle of evolution from hammer to hammerless and back to the hammer again, for the external hammer also appears on a modern counterpart, the 22-cal. Ithaca Saddlegun. The Martini action concept is again applied here, but with a silhouette styled to emulate the popular Winchester and Marlin lever guns.

The Mossberg Martini was made from 1929 until 1932. Price—$7.65! A Model L-1 variant, listed as a Special Target Rifle, was priced at $17.50. This included a hooded 17-A Lyman front sight with removable inserts and a Lyman 2-A tang sight. Sling and swivels completed the outfit. I recall recommending the revival of this gun in 25 RF caliber in the October, 1945, *American Rifleman*. I favored a solid frame version.

Despite the seemingly low price, the Model L suffered slow sales during the depression years of its manufacture and not many were produced.

Today the Mossberg Martini is quite a rarity and most of these excellent little arms are being snatched up by collectors. ●

hammer had to be manually cocked before each shot, the Model L Mossberg Martini was a fine choice as a training rifle for the beginning shooter. The exposed hammer itself was a good safety feature. Its position always gave visual proof of the rifle's firing status.

Martini Explained

I have used the word "Martini" several times. This bears closer study. The name refers to a famous type of single shot breech action. The original was an American design patented in July, 1862. Named the Peabody, after its inventor, Henry Peabody, it had an *exposed* hammer. Bear this detail in mind. Later, a Swiss designer

closed and the shooter was in no danger if there was an occasional primer leak or burst case head. The top surface of the Martini breechblock had a shallow rounded groove which served as a loading channel. Opening the lever caused the forward end of the breechblock to swing down. A cartridge laid in the groove could be shoved directly into the exposed chamber with a touch of the finger. A simple, smooth procedure.

Upon firing, the breech back-thrust

---

*It is interesting to note that in 1862 Henry Peabody himself designed a hammerless version of his action, having a coiled mainspring located behind the breechblock and a firing pin slanting upward from the rear through that block. A cross-section drawing of this action is shown in *American Breech-Loading Small Arms*, C. B. Norton (New York City, 1872).

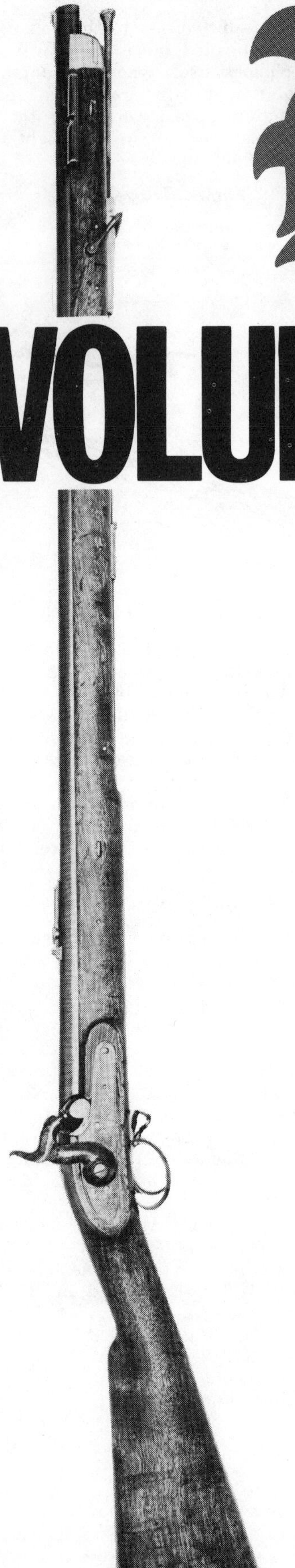

British
VOLUNTEER RIFLES
1850-1870

The Volunteer Movement in mid-19th century England sparked an immense manufacture of volunteer rifles. These admirable firearms, in all their fascinating variety, are here described in smallest detail, their salient points cataloged for the collector's and historian's reliable reference. A scholarly, definitive study.

by DeWitt Bailey II

THE VOLUNTEER Movement in Great Britain during the 1850s received its initial impetus from the unstable composition and erratic actions of the French government after the Revolutions of 1848. To better understand the place of the Volunteer Rifle in arms history and the significance of the socio-political movement which brought about its creation and proliferation, the development of the Volunteer Movement must be examined in some detail. In the United States the Volunteer Rifle has long been associated with the American Civil War, the *Jeff Davis Enfield, Officer's Rifle* and *Checkered Enfield* being terms rather generally applied to it. In point of fact, these names, and the character they imply, are only partially correct and certainly inadequate to describe this class of arms. Hence the necessity for dwelling on the developments behind the rifles as well as on the rifles themselves.

Great Britain lagged sadly behind the

Fig. 1. Pattern 1851 Volunteer Rifle by Deane, Adams & Deane, London. 33" barrel, 577 caliber, 4 grooves, brass mounts. Note key-fastened barrel, ramrod pipes, button-head ramrod, style of sights and curved contours of hammer. Special features include Damascus twist barrel, full length top flat or nocksform, dovetailed front sight, and circular-section bayonet bar.

other European powers in the adoption of effective rifled-bore arms during the 1840s. While few of the rifles adopted by the various European powers during this period would do much justice to a target in comparison with later muzzle-loading rifles, they were still considerably more effective than Britain's Brown Bess smoothbore and the two-groove Brunswick rifle. When the percussion system was accepted by the British military authorities in the mid-1830s, the rifling system used in the flintlock Baker rifle (7 grooves with a ¾-turn in the 30-inch barrel) was abandoned in favor of a more modern system comprised of two deep grooves making one turn in the length of the 30-inch barrel. It was with this arm that the Rifle Brigade and the 60th Rifles were armed until the onset of the Crimean War. The percentage of rifle-equipped troops in the British Army was much lower than that of other powers, notably France—which appeared to upset no one. With the Duke of Wellington as Commander-in-Chief of the British Army, and Louis-Philippe as the peaceful-minded King of the French, matters rested. But not quite—technical developments led by various officers of the French service brought about the introduction, on a limited basis, of various forms of rifled arms during the decade of the 1840s, most of

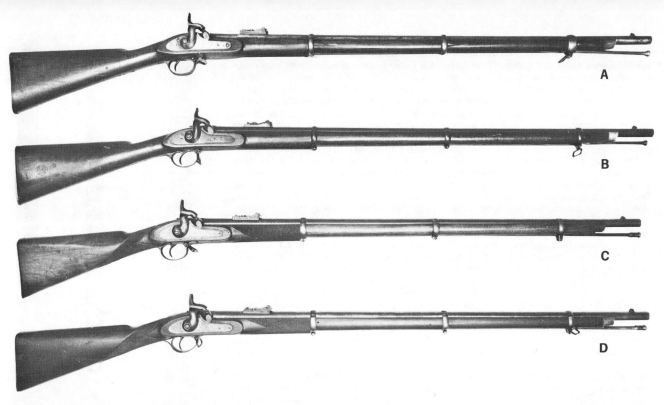

Fig. 2. Volunteer Long Enfield Rifles. (a) Second Model Enfield marked *J. Dickson & Son Edinburgh 1854* on lockplate. Solid bands held by springs, wide front band, button-head ramrod of swell type are typical. Convex flanges of rear sight are holdover from First Model. (b) First Model Enfield marked *Tower 1855* on lockplate. Clamping bands, button-head ramrod and convex-flanged rear sight are typical of this model, as is the rather delicate form of hammer. This is a true Volunteer Long Enfield bearing the Pimlico Arsenal inspection stamp for 1861 and the classification numeral "2." This model and the one above formed the basis for governmental rearming of the Volunteers in 1861-62. (c) A late Volunteer prize rifle with the short butt. Fully engraved lock and iron mounts, with presentation inscription etched into barrel just ahead of rear sight. Won in October, 1862, it is marked *Parker, Field & Son* on the lockplate with *233 Holborn, London* on top of the barrel. (d) London Armoury Company prize rifle, marked L.A. Co. *1861* on lockplate. This is identical with the later pattern issue Long Enfield as made by Enfield and this Company, with the addition of checkering at wrist and forearm. These rifles were much coveted by Volunteer marksmen as they conformed to the definition of "bona fide Government Enfield" specified in most match regulations, but were much superior in accuracy to the patterns generally issued, the rank-and-file rifles of (a) and (b) types.

which cast the performance of the Brunswick rifle quite in the shade. Then came the Revolutions of 1848, shattering stability and order throughout Europe. The result in France was the establishment of a republic with Louis Napoleon Bonaparte, a nephew of the Emperor Napoleon I, "elected" as President. The disorder created by the revolutions unsettled the minds of the government in England, and the almost immediate military activity of the Prince-President of France did nothing to smooth the wrinkled brows of Lord John Russell's cabinet. But they had to contend with the views of the Duke of Wellington, who still preferred to arm the British line soldier with smoothbore muskets. Awareness of the disparity between the weapons of the British soldier and those of other powers had indeed been growing in official circles since the mid-1840s, but beyond small-scale experiments nothing positive had been done. Louis Napoleon's requests for greatly increased naval expenditures, experiments with armor plating, and the success of the trials of the French Captain Minie's bullet, all occurring during 1849 and 1850, created the necessary urgency in the minds of British military authority. By the middle of 1851 even the Duke of Wellington had been induced to arm the infantry with the new "Minie Rifled Musquet." This new rifle still resembled the Brown Bess in external appearance, having a pin-fastened stock and heavy brass mounts, with rammer pipes and button-head ram-

mer of the Brown Bess pattern. They were first issued early in 1852.

It was at this period that the Volunteer Movement got its start, although, as will shortly be seen, it was a false start in some ways. Rifle clubs had long been in existence in England, but the interest had been in sporting arms and target shooting with specialized rifles, patterned on the sporting rifles of the day. With the press beginning to come into its own as a media for public communication outside the very wealthy and literate classes, the imminent danger of French invasion received some attention. In 1852 a book appeared entitled *The Rifle: its Uses and Advantages in War, in the Volunteer Service, and in Sporting Pursuits.** In 1853 John Boucher's *The Volunteer Rifleman and the Rifle* † appeared, a book which went into some detail on the comparative developments of rifled arms in France and England, and on the Minie principle. Public attention had been drawn to the need for public participation in the defense of the country, and for the need to consider the value of military-style shooting. During 1853 the first of the volunteer companies directly concerned in this particular movement were enrolled: The Exeter & South Devon Rifle Volunteer Brigade and the Victoria Rifles. The latter was to become the elite of the Metropolitan—that is, the

---

*By "Long Range" (a pseudonym) London.
†London.

London area—Rifle Corps later in the decade.

Fig. 1 shows a Volunteer Rifle dating from this early "pre-Enfield period," which is typical in that it combines old and new features in one weapon, along with special features requested by the customer, these not necessarily of a military nature. Externally, the rifle closely resembles a scaled-down Pattern 1851 Minie rifle, with a pin-fastened stock and lock, and mounts of the pattern designed by George Lovell when, as Inspector of Small Arms, he improved most of the British military percussion weapons in the early 1840s. The rifling is the typical 4-groove Minie pattern, making one turn in 78 inches, but the caliber is of the new reduced bore, i.e., .577″ rather than the standard .702″ of the Minie. The only other "new" feature of this rifle is the stirrup-fastened mainspring, which is characteristic of the P/53 Enfield rather than the P/51 Minie rifle, which retained the older hook mainspring. The rifle possesses several special features, including a Damascus twist barrel, dovetailed front sight, dovetailed rear sight leaf similar to the Minie's but graduated to 800 yards, and a circular-section bayonet bar mounted in a manner reminiscent of the Baker and Brunswick rifles. In view of the reduced bore of this rifle it probably dates from early 1853.

International developments intervened at this time and created a hiatus in the growth of the Volunteer Movement for about four years. This is not to say that the movement came to a standstill, but it certainly slowed down and it did not receive the attention in the press that had been its chief nutriment during the early years. Rifles are known, during this period from 1854 to 1858, which were obviously made for private purchase and Volunteer use, a typical example being the Long Enfield shown in fig. 2a.

According to the terms of the French Constitution of 1848, Prince-President Louis Napoleon would serve for a term of four years, but was not eligible for re-election. This feature clashed sharply with Napoleon's own ideas on the future and fame of the heir of Bonaparte, and he gradually built up around him a group of adherants and a set of circumstances suited to his ambitions. On the night of December 2, 1851, he executed a *coup d'etat* and proclaimed himself President for 10 years, instituting at the same time a number of basic and dictatorial changes in the form of government. At first these changes were not accomplished or accepted without the shedding of French blood. Although dissent and opposition were largely silenced by the usual violent as well as non-violent methods, they remained beneath the surface, waiting only a significant mistake on the part of the regime to retaliate. In November, 1852, after almost a year of careful planning and preparation, the President of the French Republic became, by popular acclaim, Napoleon III, Emperor of the French.

Historical traditions decreed that a Bonaparte, as a leader of the French nation, must embellish his reign with military glories. Napoleon III's several blunders, involving the shedding of French blood during his progression to the imperial throne, made it a political necessity that military glory wash away civil bloodstains. Fortunately for him and most unfortunately for the rest of Europe, the rising animosity between Russia and Turkey over the rights of Christians within Ottoman territory provided Napoleon with a set of conditions which his clever mind could manipulate to his own ends. The tortuous details of the Anglo-French alliance and the tragic uselessness of the Crimean War do not conern this study except to emphasize certain points:

1. The alliance between France and Great Britain obviated, at least for the moment, the latter's necessity to arm against possible French invasion.

2. The fighting in the Crimea gave further opportunities for French military training in the field, for the perfection of logistic and theoretical developments, and left France at the close of this war in a much improved rather than shattered military condition.

3. The Crimean fighting brought out the incredible backwardness of Britain's military organization both in theory and practice, and the reports published in the press served to acquaint the general public with the utter unpreparedness of the regular British forces to meet any future threats of invasion unless drastic steps were taken to modify existing conditions.

4. So long as the alliance with France remained, a powerful ally would be most useful, but should any rift develop between France and Great Britain, the ability of the latter to defend herself was very questionable in the 1856-58 period.

Following the Peace of Paris in 1856, and the several enquiries from Parliament, which attempted to lay the blame for numerous failures on several heads without conspicuous success, military matters began to settle back into quietude. Reductions in the naval establishment were made, the army reduced as well, while reforms on paper were instituted in various departments. Then, not even a year later, came the outbreak in May, 1857, of the Indian Mutiny, and more troops were hurried off, half-way round the globe. A few months later the Second China War broke out, a much smaller operation, and one in which the French cooperated, but still another drain upon Britain's regular forces and still shaky logistic mechanism. In 1857 the Volunteer Movement began to pick up momentum; articles began appearing in the press, particularly in *The Times* of London, about the defense of the country and the shocking state of the regular establishment, the heavy calls upon its resources. Then, early in 1858, two events occurred which tended largely to bring matters to a head, and which we may justly consider the prime-movers which got the Volunteer Movement properly in motion.

The first of these shocks was the Orsini Plot, in which several Italian revolutionaries attempted (and very nearly succeeded) in assassinating Napoleon III and the Empress Eugenie. While none of the principals was English, it was established that the plot had matured on English soil; the conspirators had lived in England for weeks before converging upon Paris, the bombs had been made in Birmingham, and Orsini had entered France on a British passport. In addition, a Middlesex jury acquitted one of the conspirators who had remained behind. The uproar was tremendous in the French and British press, with speeches of a highly inflammatory nature being made in the legislatures of both countries, and the roots of the earlier alliance were severed. Although the two royal families remained friends to some degree, their subjects did not. A visit to Cherbourg by Queen Victoria and Prince Albert in the early summer of 1856 (where Albert and some of his officers viewed with shock and apprehension the advanced state of French naval armaments, particularly in the ironclad line) set the seal upon an attitude of greatly increased military preparedness on the home front. Thus the stage was set, by mid-1858, for the resurgence and continued growth of the Volunteer Movement.

A Definition

The British Volunteer Rifle, as the term is understood today, varies in several respects from the original and official definition. Today, we tend to include such arms as the 45-caliber "small bore" rifles of Whitworth, Kerr and Alexander Henry, if they are of military style. These were specifically excluded at the time save for particular competitions at long ranges (over

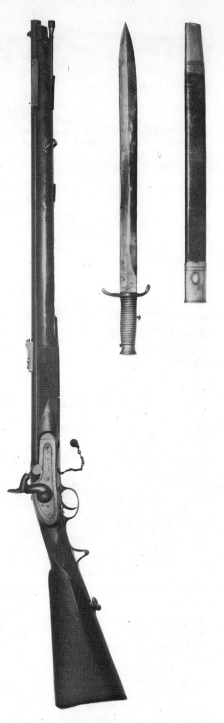

Fig. 3. Brunswick-Enfield Volunteer Rifle. A superb example by W. & C. Scott. Marked with a large crown and *1859* on lockplate, with *W.&C. Scott* or the initials appearing on all major parts. The key-fastened stock carried to the muzzle, the bayonet bar on the right side of the barrel, ramrod pipes, pattern of sights and lock, are typical of this combination of old and new features. Mounts are blued and engraved iron. Special features include Lancaster's oval bore rifling, ringed and knurled bronze ramrod tip, scroll trigger guard, and break-off breech. Bayonet, also marked by Scott, is numbered with the rifle. It was this pattern of rifle, differing so markedly from the issue pattern, which helped greatly to bring about the issuance of the War Office circulars in 1861, ordering the rearming of the Volunteers with the Long Enfield.

600 yards) where the 577 was not considered sufficiently accurate. Only 577-caliber (or 25-gauge) rifles which would accept government ammunition and government musket caps were considered as weapons for Volunteer units. Officer's rifles—more accurately "checkered Enfields"—would have been Volunteer Rifles only if owned and carried by an officer of a Volunteer unit. There was no distinction between the rifle carried by an officer of a regular regiment and one carried by a Volunteer officer. Today these are all included under the broad heading of Volunteer Rifles. Prize

most typical of all. These are the issue Long Enfields received in various centers, refinished and repaired during the early 1860s, then reclassified from 1st to 2nd Class arms. After March, 1860, these arms were held in store specifically for issue to Volunteers and Militia; after 1861 they undoubtedly formed the basis for all issues to newly organized Volunteer regiments or replacements for already existing units. These will be, in appearance, standard Pattern 1853 Long Enfields (in a few cases P/56 Short Rifles as well) which bear a circular stamp on the stock and a large

The Rifles, 1858-1862

The Volunteers were armed with Enfield pattern rifles from the beginning years of the movement until 1871, when pressure was exerted by the British National Rifle Association (NRA) that the breech-loading Snider rifle should be issued to the Volunteer Corps. It was only for the first five years of the development, however, that any great variety of rifles was produced. After 1862, because of the War Office decrees presently to be discussed, and a general levelling off of the

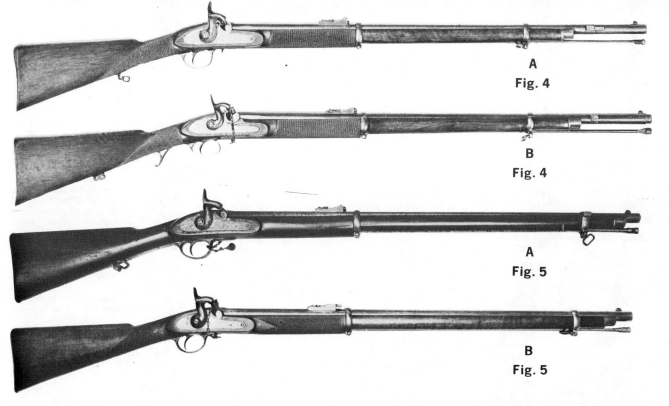

A
Fig. 4

B
Fig. 4

A
Fig. 5

B
Fig. 5

Fig. 4. Pattern 1856 Volunteer Rifles by G.H. Daw, 57 Threadneedle St. London. At top: (a) The "standard" Volunteer Enfield, for which the volunteer recruit paid 5 guineas in 1859-60 (about $25 in 1860 U.S. currency). Note the stock pattern, distance of barrel beyond stock-tip; bayonet bar on right side of barrel, position of barrel bands; also the form of the lock, breech and mounts, and position of butt swivel. 577 caliber (or 25 bore), 3-groove rifling, sighted to 1100 yards. Oval silver escutcheon at top of wrist with crest and initials. The checkering on this and the next rifle is typical of Daw rifles; the pattern is known as "Daw checkering" even when occasionally found on rifles by other retailers. (b) Daw-Jacob Volunteer Rifle. Variations include Jacob's deep 4-groove rifling, patent breech with break-off, semi-scroll trigger guard, and bronze, deeply-cupped ramrod tip made to fit the Jacob percussion shell. Muzzle is

turned round to accept standard sword-bayonet (rest of barrel is egg-shaped in section, having a full length top-flat or nocksform), and has standard bayonet bar on right side. Fig. 5. Pattern 1858 Volunteer Rifles. (a) Standard pattern by Potts & Hunt, London. Note snub-nosed appearance of stock, with bayonet bar on upper barrel band, and pin through band below bayonet bar; also note distance between two bands. Standard weight barrel with 3-groove rifling. (b) Variation marked J. Ashton Hythe on lockplate and Isaac Hollis & Sons, Makers to Her Majesty's War Department on top of barrel. Made by the latter and retailed by the former, who was Armourer to the School of Musketry at Hythe. Checkered and highly finished stock, the heavyweight barrel has 5-groove rifling; the top band lacks a bayonet bar and is not pinned.

rifles—that is, those inscribed as having been presented to a man for winning a shooting contest—can be strictly classified as Volunteer Rifles only if they conform to the caliber specifications. Small-bore rifles, then, are not quite eligible even if awarded to a Volunteer, as they most often were. In fact, it is only as a prize rifle that the small-bore may be said to have any connection with the Volunteers. They were only used in "Any Rifle" competitions and those over 600 yards where Service rifles were not satisfactory. There are, in addition, a very large group of arms which today would not be thought of as Volunteer Rifles, but which are in fact the most correct and

numeral "2" stamped nearby. The majority of those noted were refurbished in 1860, 1861 and 1862 at Pimlico Arsenal in London.

Included in this study, then, will be 577 rifles only, the 45-caliber rifles being in actuality Military Target Rifles and not in the hands of Volunteers except for long range or non-Volunteer competitions. Officer's and sergeant's rifles, offering a wide degree of variation but still adhering to the basic specifications, are included, whether of Regular or Volunteer origins, since they are indistinguishable; and those issue rifles which have been reclassified as 2nd Class arms.

movement, variations found in individual rifles drop off sharply and, in most cases, it would appear that issue rifles came into general use in the ranks of the Volunteers. Only officers and sergeants retained their privately made government pattern rifles.

Two factors governed the design of these early Volunteer Rifles (aside from the government standard bore and nipple size): fashion and individual preference, applied within a military or semi-military frame of reference. The Pattern 1856 Short Rifle, with its blued iron mounts and dashing sword bayonet, being the rifle of the elite Rifle Brigade, was naturally the basis for the overwhelming majority of Volunteer

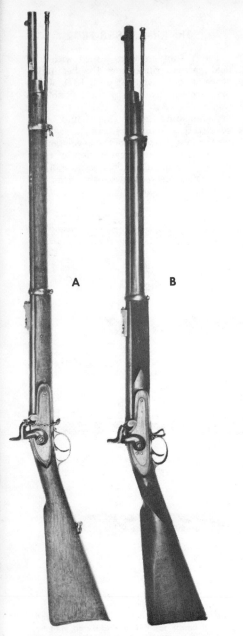

Rifle designs. The choice of both arms and uniform was left to the members of the unit concerned, assuming the concurrence of the commanding officer and of the Lord Lieutenant in the county in which the unit was raised. The usual methods were either for the individual to provide himself with a rifle at whatever cost he chose, or to contribute to a common fund from which a rifle, of a pattern decided upon by the majority, was bought for each man. Officers, of course, supplied their own weapons. The P/56 Short Rifle provided the basic pattern for the great majority of arms ordered by Volunteer regiments, but even a casual glance at the illustrations will indicate the almost infinite variety capable of being achieved within this basic pattern.

Dating Volunteer Rifles is difficult until a large number have been examined and a number of dated examples compared with others of similar types. Presentation plaques offer the most ready means of dating, but this may, in some instances, be as much as six months later than the actual date of manufacture—if not more. A small number of rifles have dated lockplates—almost always 1859 or 1860. The graduations found on rear sights may act as a lead, since the 1250-yard rear sight did not come into official use until the end of 1861, but several rifles of 1860 vintage are known with this graduation of sight, indicating either special order at the time or possible contemporary regraduating of the leaf. Whatever the actual date of manufacture of a given rifle, however, there is no question that the overwhelming majority of Volunteer Rifles were made in 1859 and 1860. During these two years the greatest number of Volunteer companies were formed and equipped; it was not until 1861 that the government began to take a hand in the arming of the Volunteers, with a consequent reduction in the individuality of the rifles.

Grouping the Volunteer Rifles by the military system of model dates is possible, and indeed practicable, but only if a wide degree of latitude is recognized as necessary within the limits of any one dating. Features of one model or another frequently overlap, so that in classifying a given rifle one criterion must be arbitrarily settled upon as the deciding factor. The present study uses rifling and stock form as the major factors wherever possible, and the official dates of corresponding issue Short Rifles—1856, 1858, 1860 and 1861—have been adopted for simplicity and uniformity. There are, of course, some rifles which do not fall into any of these neat brackets, and which must be dealt with separately. These include the sporting/military rifles, half-stocked military rifles, Brunswick/Enfield and P/51 Volunteer Rifles, all of which come under the general heading (because of their barrel length) of Short Rifles. This group also includes Long Enfields and Carbines.

Models and Patterns

Pattern 1851. Fig.1 (noted earlier) illustrates all of the salient characteristics of this pattern: pin- or key-fastened barrel, brass or blued iron mounts of rather more

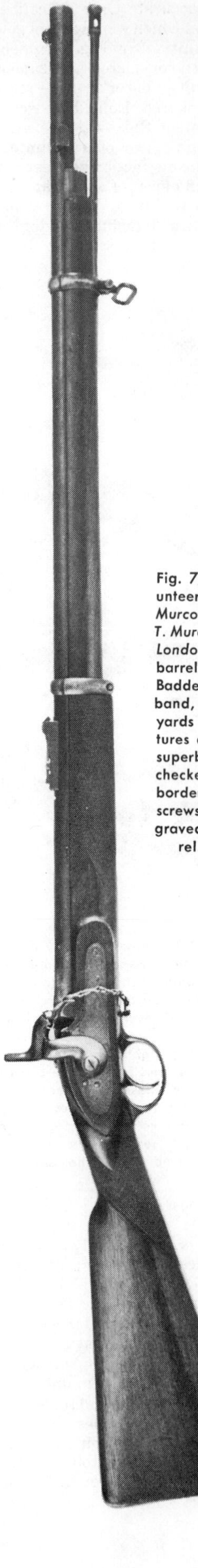

Fig. 6. Pattern 1860 Volunteer Rifles. At left: (a) Marked *Wilkinson, London* on lockplate. This is the quality of rifle which, with that shown in fig. 2a, would have been purchased by the rank and file of Volunteer Corps formed prior to the government's re-arming with long Enfields. Note reversion to shorter stock length at muzzle and bayonet bar on side of barrel, a return to the external appearance of the Pattern 1856. Aside from its superior finish on metal and stock, private retailer's markings and London proofmarks, this very plain rifle conforms exactly to the Government Issue P/60 Short Rifle. (b) Marked *T. Murcott, 68, Haymarket, London, S.W.* on lockplate. A very superior quality rifle in all respects, with fine checkering and metal finish. Butt swivel location follows the Naval Rifle pattern, unusual on Volunteer Short Rifles. All mounts, including the barrel bands have double-border line engraving, and all external screwheads are flower-head engraved. Both of these rifles have 33-inch heavyweight (4 lbs. 1½ ozs.) 5-groove barrels; the rifling twist is 1 in 48 inches, the distinguishing feature of the Pattern 1860 rifle. The Wilkinson is sighted to 1100 yards, while the later Murcott is sighted to 1250 yards—a most unusual variation which makes it differ from the Pattern 1861 only in having standard pattern barrel bands rather than the Baddeley type.

Fig. 7. Pattern 1861 Volunteer Rifle. Marked *T. Murcott* on lockplate and *T. Murcott, 68, Haymarket, London, S.W.* on top of barrel. Fitted with the Baddeley rear type barrel band, and sighted to 1250 yards — the salient features of this rare type. A superb example with fine checkering and all mounts border-line engraved, all screws flower-head engraved. Heavyweight barrel with 5 grooves.

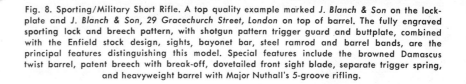

Fig. 8. Sporting/Military Short Rifle. A top quality example marked *J. Blanch & Son* on the lock-plate and *J. Blanch & Son, 29 Gracechurch Street, London* on top of barrel. The fully engraved sporting lock and breech pattern, with shotgun pattern trigger guard and buttplate, combined with the Enfield stock design, sights, bayonet bar, steel ramrod and barrel bands, are the principal features distinguishing this model. Special features include the browned Damascus twist barrel, patent breech with break-off, dovetailed front sight blade, separate trigger spring, and heavyweight barrel with Major Nuthall's 5-groove rifling.

rounded contours than those of the P/53 Enfields, ramrod pipes similar to the Brown Bess and earlier Lovell percussion muskets, and pre-Enfield pattern sights conforming more or less to the P/51 Minie rifle design. These are quite uncommon as Regular Army officers generally carried pistols rather than a long arm at this period, and there were not sufficient Volunteer companies yet in existence in the early 1850s to create much of a demand for the then "service pattern" arm with suitable refinements.

Brunswick-Enfield. This classification of Short Rifle was something of an anachronism even in its own day, and attests to the individuality which could be had while still conforming to standards. Fig.3 shows a typical rifle of this pattern dated 1859. From other examples examined or reported this type does not seem to have survived in popularity past 1859. Markings on this rifle indicate that it was probably one of several made, presumably for a company. The wide combination of features exhibited by this rifle gives some idea of why the War Office finally felt it necessary, by 1861, to take a hand in obtaining something like uniformity of design in the arms of the Volunteer forces.

Pattern 1856. This is the most common style of Volunteer Short Enfield. Fig.4a shows a typical example, which would have cost the purchaser L5/5s. in the late 1850s. This pattern is characterized by a 33-inch barrel with three-groove rifling making one turn in 78 inches, and by a stock which comes to within 5½ inches of the muzzle; this leaves space for the hilt of the sword bayonet to fasten to the bayonet bar mounted on the right side of the barrel about four inches from the muzzle. This type was made from 1856 onwards, and will be found with checkered or plain stocks, usually with blued or case-hardened iron mounts of the pattern shown, but sometimes with brass mounts. In addition, most Lancaster oval-bore rifles and Jacob 4-groove rifles are based on this pat-

tern rather than the later ones, but not invariably. The rear sight, of basic Enfield pattern, is graduated to 1100 yards on the leaf.

Pattern 1858. Easily recognized by the snub-nosed appearance at the muzzle, as the stock is carried forward to within 1¼ inches of the muzzle, the bayonet bar being part of the upper barrel band. This is a scarce Volunteer pattern, and did not last very long even in its issue counterpart; with the introduction of the heavier barrel it was found possible to revert to the P/56 pattern of stock and bayonet bar. This pattern is found with both standard weight (3 lbs. 10½ ozs.) and the later heavyweight barrel of 4 lbs. 1½ ozs., and with three-groove rifling and the later 5-groove rifling. The upper barrel band, which has the bayonet bar on the right side, is generally secured by a thick pin through the band and stock. Fig.5a shows a typical example of this pattern, from which it will be seen that the distinctive features about the muzzle comprise its major identifying marks.

Pattern 1860 Volunteer Short Rifles revert again in external appearance to that of the P/56, with the muzzle extending some 5½ inches forward of the stock tip, and with the bayonet bar brazed onto the right side of the barrel. The P/60 is, however, invariably fitted with the new heavyweight barrel of 4 lbs. 1½ oz., and generally has 5-groove rifling making one turn in 48 inches, which had first been adopted in the Naval Short Rifle in 1858. Some P/60 Volunteer rifles have the heavyweight barrel but the older 3-groove rifling. Both checkered and plain types are known, and this is perhaps the second most common of the various Volunteer Short Rifle patterns. The majority are still fitted with the 1100-yard sight, but some have been observed with the 1250-yard graduations. Fig.6 shows examples (a and b) of these rifles with variations.

Pattern 1861 Volunteer Short Rifles are very rarely seen, largely because at the time when they would have appeared among Volunteer units the government was attempting to arm the Volunteers with issue 2nd Class Long Enfields in the interests of economy and uniformity. Basically, the P/61s are similar to the P/56 and P/60 rifles, but invariably have the heavyweight 5-groove barrel, a 1250-yard rear sight, and are fitted with the new Baddeley patent barrel bands having the clamping screw covered by the metal of the band to avoid catching in clothing. These will be found as rear bands only, since the forward or upper band still carried the upper sling swivel. Fig.7 illustrates a fine example of this very scarce model.

A   B

Fig. 9. Enfield Carbines as issued to Volunteers. At left: (a) Pattern 1853 Artillery Carbine. 24" bbl., brass mounts, sighted to 300 yards. Marked *1861 Tower* on lockplate. This pattern was issued to Volunteer Artillery and to some Mounted Rifle units as well. (b) Pattern 1856 Calvary Carbine. 21" bbl., brass mounts, swivel ramrod. Marked *1858 Tower* on lockplate. Sighted to 300 yards. Issued to Light Horse Volunteers. Both carbines have 3-groove rifling. The Pattern 1861 (not shown) of both models has 5-groove rifling and miniature sliding leaf rear sights sighted to 600 yards. It is highly unlikely that any of these later types were issued to the Volunteers.

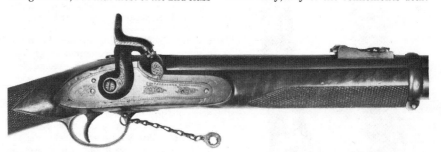

Fig. 10. Pattern 1856 Volunteer Short Rifle by William Greener. Typically Greener is the shape of the well-curved "Belgian" hammer and the markings on lock and breech; otherwise a standard Pattern 1856 rifle. Lockplate marked with large crown over T.V.R.C. (Tynemouth Volunteer Rifle Corps). Nocksform of barrel bears shield with Tynemouth coat of arms, and top of barrel is marked *William Greener Inventor of the Expansive Principle.* The hammer form, and the markings of a particular Volunteer unit on lock and/or barrel, along with Greener's name, are typical of Greener's Volunteer Enfields.

Short Rifle Variants

We pass now from the relatively simple classification by model date to the more difficult definitions made necessary by non-standard combinations of major structural features—primarily mixtures of military and sporting gun parts. Lacking any uniform contemporary reference for guidance, the basic Enfield Short Rifle is accepted as the foundation upon which various degrees of refinement have been made in the form of sporting furniture, locks, breeches, sights, etc. The first of these are the:

Sporting/Military Short Rifles. This combines the short rifle pattern of stock with two barrel bands, Enfield pattern ramrod and stock tip with various degrees of refinement. The rifle shown in fig.8 has a sporting lock complete, patent break-off breech with a musket nipple and, recessed on the left side, a separate trigger spring, sporting pattern buttplate, trigger guard and trigger mechanism, and a Damascus twist barrel made octagonal at the breech. The rear sight is a standard pattern graduated to 1100 yards, but the blade foresight is dovetailed into the base. The rifling is one of Nuthall's 5-groove segmental types. This particular rifle represents, perhaps, the extreme degree of variation to be found within this classification, before one comes to the:

Half-Stocked Enfield. This embodies the same basic principle as the last category but carries it out in a reverse manner. A sporting pattern halfstock is fitted with an Enfield pattern lock and Enfield pattern mounts of brass or steel. The 33-inch round barrel has the usual bayonet bar on its right side, and the normal pattern of Enfield ramrod in most cases. The stock is finished off with a metal or bone tip, and either a rib under the barrel or pipes by themselves hold the ramrod. Sights are of the normal Enfield pattern. Great care must be taken in assessing this classification, as it is possible to find cut-down issue Enfields which have been "sporterized" by modern basement gunsmiths. Small details of finishing on the stock and barrel breech, the style and execution of the checkering, and the style and workmanship with which the single or double barrel-keys have been fitted, both to barrel and stock, are good indicators of the date and origins of the work in this class of rifle.

Volunteer Long Enfields. These may be classified under two headings; those rifles of government-contract origins which were refinished, repaired and reclassified as 2nd Class arms and thereby defined as Volunteer and Militia arms, and those rifles privately made and marked by commercial firms and gunmakers (see fig.2). Prominent among the latter are the checkered Long Enfields made by the London Armoury Company and more generally known in the United States as "Jeff Davis Enfields." These were actually nothing more than issue pattern rifles sometimes stocked with wood of superior quality and checkered at the wrist and foreend, intended for presentation as prizes to Volunteer units. Many of them were in fact so inscribed, but their primary claim to contemporary attention was the fact of their being completely interchangeable in all their parts, as well as with the Long Enfield made at the Royal Small Arms Factory at Enfield. They are the only two Enfields which are completely interchangeable. It may be noted that Volunteer Long Enfields will be found in all of the three major variations of the issue Long Enfield, but that most of the 2nd class arms appear to be second models—with band springs holding the barrel bands in place, and a swelled ramrod. The privately marked Long Enfields are mostly of the latest or third type with clamping bands and a ramrod spring, with a large minority of the second model. Checkered types predominate by only a narrow margin over those privately marked Long Enfields with plain stocks. This is largely accounted for by the checkered London Armoury Company Enfields, which were made in some quantity.

Volunteer Carbines are as rare as issue carbines are among issue Enfields, if not more so. Volunteer artillery units were few in number and small in size, and were armed with the issue Pattern 1853 Artillery Carbine (fig.9a). A few of these are known showing commerical retailer's names, and with checkered stocks, but small arms don't seem to have been of much interest to the Volunteer Artillery units; they concentrated on their heavy gun drills. Volunteer cavalry did not exist as such—the already established Yeoman-ry cavalry largely filling this role. However, there were a few Volunteer Light Horse companies, which were armed, again from government stores, with the issue Pattern 1856 Cavalry Carbine (fig.9b). The Volunteer Mounted Rifles, who were intended to act as dragoons and fight dismounted, were armed with the short rifles but, as with the Light Horse units, there were very few of them to arm.

Variations and Refinements

The basic patterns of Volunteer Rifles have been described, and it remains now to deal with the myriad of small refinements and variations from the standard pattern, which make this class of arm of particular interest to collectors. The most important point to remember in this regard is that there are no variations applicable to one model only; any of the refinements dealt

Fig. 11. Lock and breech of Pattern 1856 rifle by Thomas Fletcher of Gloucester. Note scroll engraved snail and engraved hammer with flattened body. Rifle has Lancaster's oval bore rifling which accounts for rear sight being mounted "reversed" to the normal manner. Side-mounted snap-cap chain is very unusual, as is the checkering pattern on the forearm. Engraving is typical of fine quality on Volunteer rifles.

with here may be found on any of the standard patterns described, and were originally dictated by the preferences and purse of the buyer, and the whims of the maker/retailer (see fig.10).

The most obvious refinements will be in the style and finish of the furniture and sights. While the large bulk of Volunteer Rifle furniture conforms closely to the issue pattern, there are significant minor flourishes which set it above the normal type (figs.7 and 19). The trigger guard bow is sometimes a separate piece from the strap, and an extension or spur guard is sometimes used (figs.3 and 12c). The presence of an eyelet riveted into the forward extension of the guard strap is almost invariable, and was used to anchor the snap-cap chain (figs.6, 11 and 12c). Most furniture is of blued iron, although case-hardened mounts have been noted. Engraving is usually confined to a double border line similar to that found on the border of the lockplate and hammer (fig.13), but scrollwork flourishes are not uncommon (figs.11 and 14). Fully engraved locks and ham-

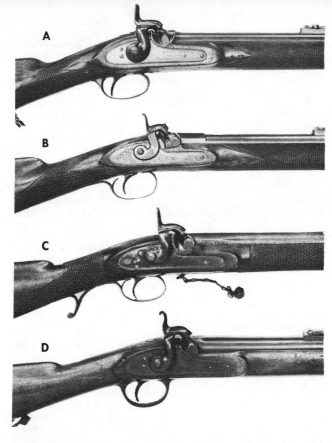
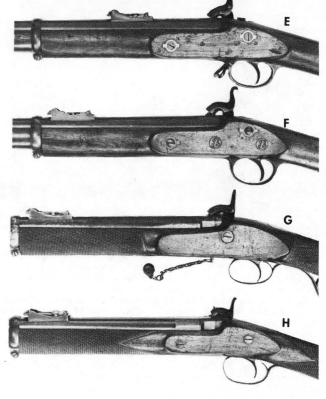

Fig. 12. Volunteer Rifle breeches, front and back. (a) "Hay breech" showing the double-flash fence designed by General Charles Hay, Commandant of the Hythe School of Musketry. Note also the two-piece trigger guard assembly and the thin wrist of this rifle. (b) Sporting/Military Short Rifle breech. Typical sporting design of lock, snail and trigger guard; patent break-off or hook breech, fitted with musket nipple, standing breech fully scroll engraved. (c) Daw's Jacob rifle. Break-off breech, variant form of lock, and scroll guard. Pattern of checkering is so typical of Daw's rifles that it has been called "Daw checkering." (d) Typical William Greener Enfield breech. (e) Issue Enfield, First Model, dated 1855, showing convex sides of rear sight and typical Enfield furniture, including barrel band, lock bolt cups, trigger guard and trigger, also normal lower sling swivel mounting for early Long Enfields with curved type swivel. G. Ewart stamp is name of stocker. (f) Sporting/Military Short Rifle. Has recessed patent break-off breech, octagonal section of barrel, twist barrel, typical Enfield rear sight and barrel band. Compare in proportions and finish with (e). (g) Daw-Jacob breech. Has patent break-off breech, single lock-bolt, and escutcheon inlaid in stock on top of wrist. (h) William Greener Enfield. Monogram stamped in stock is typical of many Greener Enfields. Note standard Birmingham proof marks on breech.

mers of the Enfield pattern are quite rare (fig.15).

Sights, particularly rear sights, are often rounded off in contour where the issue pattern is left square, as on the trailing edge of the sight bed (fig.12). Platinum or gold lines in the center of the V-notches on block, leaf and slide are sometimes found, but it is typical that on some of the most highly finished examples the sights are not so embellished, while on some of the most unassuming examples the lines have been put in. In some instances the full numbers, such as 200, 300, 400 are completed rather than the more normal 2, 3, 4 on the sight bed, and similar treatment is given the numbers on the leaf.

Barrels are subject to considerable variation, both in and out. (See fig.16). The standard government bores of three- and 5-grooves have already been described, and to these should be added the oval bore of Charles Lancaster, which must be considered as a third standard bore-pattern since it was regulation for the Royal Engineer's Short Rifle—and for many Volunteer Engineer units as well. Rifles with this system will invariably be marked with some form of *Lancaster's Patent*. But, as it may occur on top of or beneath the barrel, and be engraved or stamped in large or very minute letters, it may require careful examination to locate the mark. General

Jacob's very deep 4-groove rifling—making about one turn in 40 inches—is also found in some Volunteer rifles, principally those made by London's George H. Daw of 57 Threadneedle Street, and E.M. Reilly & Company of Oxford Street. Other rifling systems, such as Boucher's, Nuthall's, and Rigby's ratchet rifling, are found on small numbers of rifles, constituting rare variations. It is curious that with the exception of Lancaster's, and an occasional exception of Nuthall's, none of the various 577 rifling systems are identified by markings on the rifles. It has already been noted that three-groove government rifling will be found in both standard and heavyweight barrels; this also applies to the 5-groove type, though mostly seen in heavyweight barrels. This has been noted on a number of rifles bearing Scottish names, particularly John Dickson & Son and J. Harkom, both of Edinburgh.

Damascus twist barrels are quite rare and must have increased the cost of a rifle considerably. A full length top flat along the barrel is another rare embellishment (see fig.1). The use of the false, hook, or break-off breech is somewhat more common and is generally accompanied by a more ornamental snail or nipple-lump than the issue pattern, as shown in figs.2 and 12. Octagonal sections at the breech are not common, but an extended top flat

at the breech known as a "nocksform" (from its first general use by the famous gunmaker Henry Nock) is standard even on issue Enfields. This may extend as far forward as the front sight on some examples (fig.17g).

Locks are generally of the standard Enfield pattern, with variations noted only in the amount of engraving on the plate and hammer. Occasionally, a variant form of hammer will be used with the Enfield pattern plate (figs.11 and 15) and, very rarely, an Enfield pattern lock will be found either partially or fully floral and scroll engraved (fig.15).

Sporting locks, such as that used on the Blanch rifle in figs.8 and 14 are rarely found. Detented or "fly-type" tumblers were seldom used, and then with no particular reference to the quality of the remainder of either the lock or the rifle (fig.18). The "double-freed" lock, which has both sides of the tumbler and sear cut away, leaving only circular bearing surfaces immediately around the pivot points, was introduced on the government pattern 1856 Short Rifle. But, surprisingly enough, it is not found on a majority of Volunteer Rifles; its additional cost and perhaps a lack of adequate publicity deprived many very fine rifles of this friction-reducing design.

Stock patterns varied very little from

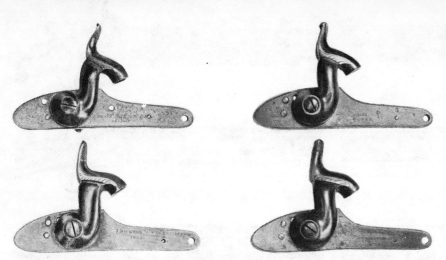

Fig. 13. Typical Volunteer Rifle locks, showing the patterns and style of markings found on the majority of Volunteer Rifles of the 1850-1870 period. Arranged chronologically, beginning at top left with the Pattern 1851 style lock with Deane, Adams & Deane markings. Note slender outline of hammer and curled spur. Bottom left is very early Pattern 1853 Volunteer lock, with Scottish maker's name and dated 1854; very few Enfield pattern locks aside from Tower locks and L.A.C. locks are dated. Top right is issue Tower lock dated 1855, of the sort used on 2nd Class Long Enfields issued to Volunteers. Note slender curved outline of hammer and well-curled spur, features which were "improved" in later types as shown at bottom right. This is the most commonly found form of Volunteer Rifle lock, being of the Enfield pattern adopted in 1857; marks are *Wilkinson, London*. Note the heavier, straighter outline of the hammer and thick straight spur, also the "flame" or "feather" engraving along the side of the nose, standard on almost all Enfield pattern hammers, early or late.

the normal issue types, aside from the finishing of contours around the lock and back-lock, which occasionally create minor differences in over-all appearance (fig.12). Few Volunteer Rifles were made with the post-December, 1859, reduced length butt (13 inches from the trigger to buttplate rather than 14 inches), an example of which is shown in fig.2c. In the design and execution of checkering there exists the widest possible range of style and quality, from the crudest to very nearly the best found on sporting rifles of the period. The average is about midway between the two extremes, with large-diamond patterns of 11 or 12 lines to the inch. Although a superior rifle in almost every other respect, the Blanch rifle (figs.8 and 14) has checkering of only average quality, with 9 lines per inch. Capboxes were virtually never used on Volunteer Enfields.

Presentation plaques vary widely in size, shape and location, and are inscribed with legends from the briefest to the most verbose. Typical examples would be *C.T.G. from O.W.D. 12th S.R.V.C. 1861* or *Presented by the Directors of the London Armoury Comp'y to Francis Bennock, Esqr., in token of his able and Gratuitous Services as Auditor to the Comp'y 16th April 1861.* The plaques may take the form of circles, ovals, shields, octagons or rectangles; they're usually in silver, sometimes of brass (especially on Company prize rifles within a particular Corps), and are most often inlaid into the right side of the butt, and, less frequently, into the left side. In other instances the initial plate or escutcheon is made use of, which may be at the wrist ahead of the checkering or in the underside of the stock to the rear of the trigger guard strap. On still other rifles the inscription is engraved on the buttplate, or on rare occasions etched into the barrel. Most of the inscriptions include the name

of the donor of the rifle, the name and regiment of the winner, with the date and location of the match.

Some rifles, while of a purely military design, such as the Hollis-Aston in fig.5b, lack the full complement of requirements for a truly military rifle; in this case there is not and never has been any provision for a bayonet bar. Other rifles have never been fitted with lower sling swivels (fig.19), while others were fitted originally with sporting nipples rather than the regulation musket nipples. These small but significant variations identify a rather anomalous class of rifles not intended for the drill ground or even for possible use in the field, but purely for military target shooting. In general they are late—that is, post 1861—products which would have been made after the tightening-up, by the War Office, on the individual purchase and ownership of military rifles. It seems reasonable that, while these arms conform in general design to the Volunteer Rifle, they should be considered more in the light of semi-military arms, rather in the same way that 451 military target rifles are regarded.

The Markings Puzzle Who Made What?

If the British military issue firearm presents a problem, with its multiplicity of markings inside and out, the Volunteer Enfield class of rifles adds a few more names and markings to grapple with if its origins are to be discovered. Up to a point it is relatively simple, in the light of recent research, to identify the names—or at least their significance—found on the various components of these rifles. Beyond this point generalities must be resorted to and, in some individual instances, one has to admit defeat!

American practice has long been, in the

case of privately made arms, to identify the name appearing on the barrel as that of the maker of the entire gun, with a name beneath the barrel being either the barrelmaker or possibly, again, the maker of the whole. The name on the lock is taken to be that of the lockmaker only. In the case of British Volunteer Rifles, however, there are marked departures from these practices; this must be thoroughly understood before any further consideration is given to specific material.

The name, and often the address, appearing on the outside of the lock of a British Volunteer Rifle will almost always be that of the retailer who sold the rifle. This individual or firm, on getting the customer's order, subcontracted part or the whole of the necessary operations for the production of the finished arm—depending upon the capabilities, if any, of his own establishment; it may have been no more than a mere salesroom. This applies as well to the name and address which may appear on the top of the barrel instead of, or in addition to, its appearance on the outside of the lock. Names stamped into the stock (usually opposite the lock or behind the trigger guard strap) will be those of the stockmaker or of the setter-up—the person, or sometimes the firm, who put all the components together into a finished piece. The name or most significant set of initials appearing on the inside of the lockplate will be those of the lockmaker; prominent here will be such markings as *R.&W.A.— IB—J. BRAZIER—FINE—J. FRANCIS— DUCE* and *FIELD*, this last being found primarily on rifles by Parker, Field & Son. R&W Aston were large-scale contractors for government Enfield parts, and many Volunteer Rifles will be found with parts bearing their initials. Other and smaller initials will be those of the individual who finished the lock or, perhaps, inspected it upon completion.

On the tops of barrels at the breech will often be found a variety of names and marks, some of which require explanation; in many instances they're self-explanatory. Just at the breech and on the left side will often appear the proof marks of the Gunmaker's Company of London, or those of the Birmingham Proof House. The London marks will be a **GP** and **V**, both surmounted by crowns, along with the number **24** or **25**. These numbers indicate the bore or gauge of the barrel in terms of balls-to-the-pound (as in modern shotgun practice), and represent the bore diameter when proved. Either are roughly equivalent to 577 caliber.

Birmingham proof marks at this period appear as two sets of crossed scepters, both surmounted by crowns; one set also shows the letters **BCP**, the other set a **V** plus the same numbers, **24** or **25**. On the better quality rifles the proof marks are usually found beneath the barrel rather than on top.

Other marks will include the name or the name and address of the retailer of the rifle; in the case of rifles by Hollis & Sheath or their successors Isaac Hollis & Sons, the firm name and *Makers to Her Majesty's War Department* is normally found, and the name of the retailer—often James Aston, Armourer to the School of Musketry at Hythe, Kent—will appear on the lock-plate. Some rifles are found with from two to 5 star-like stamps on the surface of the nocksform; to date no documentary evidence explaining the use of these stars has been found; they may indicate varying degrees of finished bore-size above or below the standard .577-inch size.

Markings on the under side of a Volunteer Rifle barrel can be a nightmare, especially if the barrel went through many hands before reaching its final state. Names such as Henry or John Clive, T. Turner, Deakin, Tranter, E. or W. Millward, Hollis & Sheath, Isaac Hollis & Sons, will be the names of the barrelmaker only except for Hollis & Sheath, Isaac Hollis & Sons and Turner, who also made entire rifles, both for themselves and other firms. A point to be noted here is that Thomas Turner operated under two different styles: *J. T. Turner* was used for barrelmaking only, while *T. Turner* was indicative of rifle manufacture: hence a rifle bearing the initials *JTT*, and the stamp *T. Turner* or *TT* under the barrel, would indicate that the barrel was made by Turner and the rifle set up by a different section of the same firm. Again, this same rifle may bear any other firm's name on the top of the barrel or lockplate as the retailer of the completed rifle, or it may bear Turner's name and address on the lockplate. The variety of initials generally found under the barrel will sometimes be those of barrel filers or finishers, or of firms or inspectors; numerals often indicate inspectors as well. Since parts were not interchangeable, both the rear end of the barrel and the breechplug will often bear identical numbers so that the correct coupling of parts in final assembly could be readily made.

So far as military weapons are concerned, and Volunteer Rifles in particular, hardly any firms made up complete rifles from start to finish. Hollis & Sheath and their successors, Isaac Hollis & Sons, and Thomas Turner are two conspicuous exceptions. There was a much larger number of firms who possessed workshops and other facilities of sufficient size that they could execute large orders to "set-up" rifles; that is, having received an order from another firm or a retailer for a quantity of rifles, they then bought all of the necessary components (locks, hammers, barrels, stocks, furniture, sights—each of these being considered as separate types of purchasable material), and fitted them together to the specifications of the particular order. Such work largely involved stocking, fitting of sights, and finishing of wood and metal. These rifles were then delivered to the purchaser, and may or may not bear more than the initials of the firm which built them. The important point to remember is that the names appearing on the outsides of the locks and barrels of British Volunteer Rifles are those of the shops which sold the arms. Only in a very small percentage of examples will they also be the names of the firms which set-up the rifles.

One other set of markings deserves notice, marks that will be found almost exclusively on the 2nd Class Long Enfields reconditioned and issued to Volunteer Corps from government stores. These markings

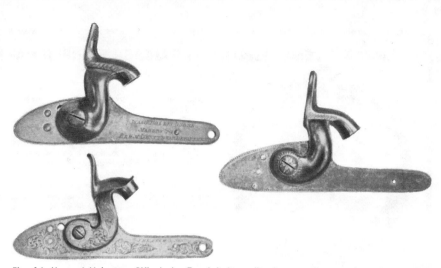

Fig. 14. Unusual Volunteer Rifle locks. Top left is smaller in over-all proportions than normal locks, and is lighter in weight. Markings are typical of one of the largest Birmingham arms manufacturers of the period. Bottom left is a sporting pattern lock as used on the Sporting/Military Short Rifles, being somewhat larger in size than ordinary sporting locks but of the same pattern. The lock on the right is by G.H. Daw and is typical of his Jacob rifles made on the Enfield pattern.

(at right) consist of three lines of engraving on the top tang of the buttplate (and elsewhere), and the example shown would read as the 201st rifle issued to the 1st Middlesex Volunteer Rifles. The "V" is for Volunteer, the letters on the left of the center line are for the county, and the figure on the right of the center line indicates the county unit number; the bottom line shows the number of the rifle issued to that unit. Occasionally there will be an additional letter in the center of the second line; these indicate, respectively, that the unit to which the rifle was issued was either Artillery (A), Engineer (E), Light Horse (L) or Mounted Rifles (M).

The mark at right would be read as the

$$V$$
$$Mx\ 1$$
$$201$$

27th rifle issued to the 4th Lanarkshire Mounted Rifles. Great stress was put upon the necessity for engraving, not stamping, these marks, which appeared also on the ramrod (just beneath the jag), the muzzle stopper and bayonet scabbard. The use of these marks was extended in 1862 to cover all issues to Colonial Volunteers, so that the multiplicity of abbreviated locations to be found is extremely lengthy. In connection with these markings it may be well to note that, in addition to the Long Enfields which were issued to the Rifle Corps, other Volunteer forces were armed from government stores. The Regulations of 19 January, 1861, called for the issue of Artillery Carbines to the Volunteer Artillery; Cav-

$$V$$
$$Lk\,M4$$
$$27$$

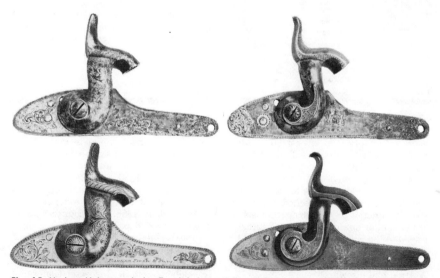

Fig. 15. Variant Volunteer locks. Top left is partially engraved type with basic scrolls on both lockplate and hammer; Enfield hammers bearing more than the usual double border-line and "flame" engraving are very uncommon. Bottom left, a fully engraved Enfield-pattern lock with elaborate scrolls on plate and hammer, leaf border on plate, and "fish-head" hammer nose engraving, in addition to feathering on spur and flower-head hammer screw. Locks on upper and lower right are typical William Greener Enfield locks, with "Belgian" style hammers typical of Greener's Volunteer rifles. The coat of arms and N.V.R.C. indicate the Newcastle Upon Tyne Volunteer Rifle Corps, while the crown and T.V.R.C. of the lower right lock are for the Tynemouth Volunteer Rifle Corps. These forms of lock marking are also typical of Greener's Enfields.

RIFLING SYSTEMS USED IN 577 CALIBER ENFIELD PATTERN VOLUNTEER RIFLES

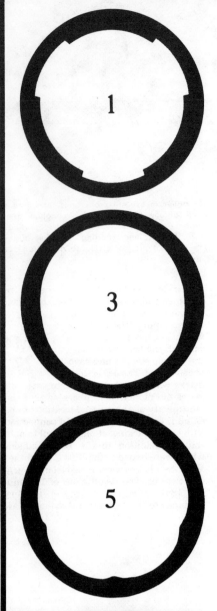

1. Government 3-groove. Standard for Pattern 1853 Long Enfield Rifle Musket and Pattern 1856 Short Rifles; most common Volunteer rifling system. One turn in 78 inches, early examples having uniform depth, later ones progressive in depth from .013" at breech to .005" at muzzle.

2. Government 5-groove. First adopted for the Pattern 1858 Naval Rifle, also used on Pattern 1860 and 1861 Government Short Rifles and Carbines, and on many later Volunteer Short Rifles. Found in heavyweight and standard barrels. One turn in 48 inches, progressive depth rifling.

3. Lancaster's oval bore. Cut with a gaining twist, average one turn in 36". Major and minor axes at muzzle, .593" and .577"; major and minor axes at breech, .598" and .580". Used on Royal Engineer's Short Rifle, and most Short Rifles for Volunteer Engineer Corps.

4. Jacob's 4-groove. Used by G.H. Daw, Reilly & Co. and others on Volunteer Short Rifles. Twists vary, but usually one turn in about 46 inches in Daw's Enfield Pattern Short Rifles.

5. Major Nuthall's 5-groove. Patented in 1859, and used primarily by Thomas Turner of Birmingham and Reilly & Co. of London on Volunteer Short Rifles. Also in 4-groove variety. Twist of one turn in 48".

6. Boucher's 6-groove. Shallow hexagon with well-rounded angles. Twist varies. Often mistaken for Nuthall's rifling when found in 5-groove version. Very few made.

alry Carbines to the Light Horse Volunteers; Lancaster Short Rifles to the Engineer Volunteers (the largest body other than the Rifle Corps), and Short Rifles to the Mounted Rifles. A sufficient number of such markings have been found on the rifles issued to such units to clearly indicate that in practice this schedule was not strictly adhered to. The arms themselves are of similar quality to the Long Enfields issued to the Rifle Volunteers, being older rifles of Birmingham and Liege origins, generally refurbished at London's Pimlico Arsenal and elsewhere.

Volunteers and Their Rifles

We left the development of the Volunteer Movement in mid-1858 to discuss in some detail the weapons with which they armed themselves. It is hoped that the reader may now be somewhat clearer in his mind as to the organization and classifi-cation of the many models and myriad variations of the Volunteer Enfield rifle. In order to present a complete view of the rifles and their owners a more general discussion of both will now be resumed.

Writing in 1860 the Boswell of the Volunteer Movement, Lieutenant Hans Busk of the Victoria Rifles, indicated that in November, 1858, the country would have been hard put to field 300 trained Volunteer riflemen. Judge of the degree of growth then, for by January, 1860, this number had increased to some 95,000! By November, 1860, the Inspector General of Volunteers gave their numbers as 130,000, which had increased another 10,000 by February, 1861. It is easy to see why contemporary writers called the phenomenon the Volunteer Movement of 1859, and it is equally clear that the vast majority of Volunteer Enfields was made during 1859 and 1860. It is during these two years that the demand for quality rifles of a military nature was the greatest, and during this period there was no let or hindrance from the government so long as the rifles conformed to quite basic requirements. After 1860 the growth of the Volunteers seems to have been more gradual, their numbers being given as 163,000 in May, 1864. Interestingly, the Regular Army numbered 146,800 of all ranks at the beginning of 1864.

Aside from the creation of a trained force of marksmen designed to augment the home defense arrangements of the Regular Army, and to allow larger numbers of Regulars to be sent overseas without weakening the home front, the most lasting result of the Volunteer Movement of 1859 was the establishment of the National Rifle Association. The British NRA was founded in 1859 to give permanence to the Volunteer Movement and to encourage the growth of rifle shooting in general.

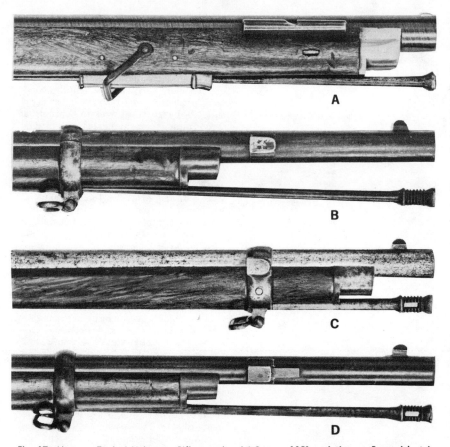

Fig. 17. Above — Typical Volunteer Rifle muzzles. (a) Pattern 1851 variation on Brunswick style with circular-section bayonet bar, key-fastened stock, brass ramrod pipes and button-head ramrod; swivel through stock and lug on bottom of barrel. Has a twist barrel and dovetailed brass foresight. (b) Patterns 1856, 1860 and 1861. The usual Short Rifle muzzle style; stock to within 5½ inches of muzzle, typical ramrod, foresight, bayonet bar for sword bayonet and barrel band. (c) Pattern 1858. Stock to within 1½ inches of muzzle, pinned front band with bayonet bar on side. Usual ramrod and foresight. (d) Pattern 1856 with Engineer's bayonet bar. Found on almost all Lancaster oval bore rifles and others intended for Engineer's use, and on other rifles of undetermined usage; often noted on Greener's rifles. Forward extension on bar gave greater rigidity to bayonet. Below — Unusual Volunteer Rifle muzzles. (e) 1854-dated Long Enfield by John Dickson & Son, of Second Model pattern with "swell ramrod" and band retained by spring. Note width of front band. Found on early Long Enfields by private makers and on some 2nd Class refinished rifles issued to Volunteers. (f) Short Rifle made to take pattern 1853 socket bayonet; very unusual as almost all Volunteer Short Rifles were made for the sword bayonet. Note also pinned foresight blade, a rare refinement. (g) Daw-Jacob muzzle, turned round to take standard sword bayonet, rest of barrel being egg-shaped with full-length top float or nocksform. Ramrod has deeply cupped bronze tip for Jacobs shell, and is serial numbered with the rifle.

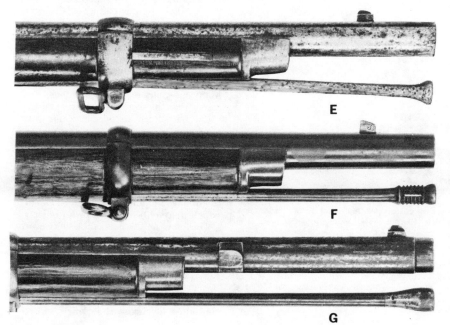

During the period under discussion the competitions for Volunteers were predominant at the yearly meetings at Wimbledon, and every encouragement was given to increase the proficiency of Volunteer riflemen. The entire program of the NRA was oriented to military shooting, and it has retained this flavor to the present day, emphasizing the accuracy of the rifle as it would apply under field conditions rather than under the precision conditions of pure target shooting.

The civilian support given to the National Rifle Association, and therefore directly to the Volunteer Movement, was immense. The press in general supported and encouraged the activities with detailed coverage and publicity; the columns of *The Times* and the *Illustrated London News* are fruitful sources of information on the Volunteer Movement, and a special journal, the *Volunteer Service Gazette,* was founded to deal with all manner of material concerning the Volunteers. The support given by the nobility and the upper classes was such that the Volunteer Movement became a definite social as well as a military development, and certain units became quite fashionable among the upper ten thousand. H.R.H. Prince Albert became the first patron of the National Rifle Association; Mr. Sidney Herbert, the Minister at War, its first president; the Earl of Wemyss (Lord Elcho), its first chairman. Titles abound in the names of committee members and other officials. It is surprising the numbers of the nobility who joined the Volunteer corps as privates, but of course they figured largely in the ranks of the commissioned as well.

Volunteer rifle shooting under NRA auspices was done at ranges from 200 to 1000 yards, but the firing beyond 600 yards, that is to say, 800, 900 and 1000 yards, was done with "small bore rifles"—primarily Whitworths—as the 577 service rifle was not considered sufficiently accurate for target shooting at such longer distances. This caused an almost immediate outcry, with demands for handicapping the small-bore to equalize it with the Enfield, but no satisfactory solution was ever found, and the Volunteers continued to use 577 rifles in all but special long range competitions. The offhand position was specified for 200-yard shooting, kneeling was used up to 600 yards, and beyond that the prone position. Some of the peculiar "no-artificial-rest" contortionist positions so familiar during the American Creedmoor matches of the 1870s originated at the Wimbledon meetings in these early years; some of them are still used today by long range shooters. The results obtained during the early years in particular were not outstanding, but the averages improved from year to year; by military standards they were more than acceptable.

February, 1861, saw the appearance of two War Office circulars which sounded the death-knell for what we largely accept today as Volunteer Enfields. The illustrations indicate to a fair degree the amount of variation possible within the basic government requirements, and the size to which the Volunteer forces had grown by this time inevitably had its effect upon the bureaucracy. It was therefore announced

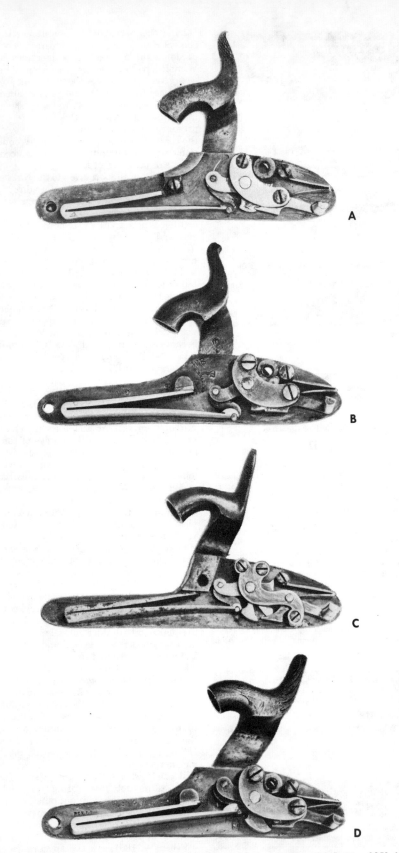

Fig. 18. Insides of typical and variant Volunteer rifle locks. At top — (a) Pattern 1851 lock conforms to usual design for this model except that it has a swivel mainspring. Compare form of hammer with lock at bottom (d); note long boss above screw retaining mainspring. (b) Early issue Enfield lock marked *Tower 1855*. J. Brazier was the lockmaker, WB was a finisher or filer, and the crowned letters and numbers are government inspectors' marks. Note similarity of form of hammer to lock above. (c) Daw-Jacob lock, has detented or "fly" tumbler; single bolt or lock screw; 3-screw civilian style bridle with pin-pivoted sear. (d) Parker Field fully engraved lock of later Enfield design, having a detented tumbler, otherwise typical in construction. *Field* is the lockmaker's name, other initials are workmen's. Note engraving on hammer nose and more robust form of hammer.

in the first instance that, for the sake of uniformity, all Volunteer Corps would be armed with the Government Enfield. Those who had bought their own rifles could either sell them to the government or keep them for private use. This first announcement, early in the month, must have produced some rather explosive results, for by the third week in February a second announcement had to be made temporizing upon the decisiveness of the first. Now a return was asked for of the number and description of privately-made and owned arms in the hands of Volunteers, and it was added that the purchase of privately owned arms by the government would not be carried into effect until the Secretary of State for War had examined and considered these returns. In the future, however, all newly raised Volunteer Corps, or augmentation of existing units, or those requiring replacement of arms, would be armed from government stores, i.e., with the Long Enfield 2nd Class arms shown in figs.2a and 2b.

In practice this pair of announcements worked out as a compromise; the Volunteers were in fact gradually re-armed with the Government Enfield, but there was no purchase of privately-made rifles by the government. Therefore, one of the primary objections of the Volunteers to the scheme was silenced; the government had only offered to pay the going price for a new Enfield—about £3.6.0.—whereas the normal Volunteer rifle had cost £5.5.0. and upwards, and had been bought when rifles were at a premium. This was a most unattractive forced retirement. But a fierce correspondence bloomed forth in the Volunteer press of the day, the gist of which was that there was no point in Corps armed with tired, worn-out refinished rifles competing for prizes against Corps shooting the new Government Enfield or a London Armoury Company Enfield; many of the new Corps formed in 1861 were so-armed, thus of course possessed a tremendous advantage. Permission was granted to exchange one's own rifle for a London Armory Company Enfield, or to have an Enfield or LAC barrel put into the stock of one's "rack rifle" for competing at the great Wimbledon meeting. Even this sop to popular agitation never really solved the problem satisfactorily, as it still left many Volunteers with the older weapons for the remainder of the shooting year, which in England is virtually nine of the 12 months. Many members of later Volunteer Corps came from the working classes, men who could not afford to purchase (for prize meetings) a London Armoury Company Enfield. In several Volunteer Corps it therefore became a practice to offer these rifles as Company prizes within the Corps, so that at the periodic shoots held by each corps, the members of each Company might have a chance to win a superior rifle, which thereby became his own property.

This move on the part of the British government did not by any means halt the production of "checkered Enfields," for officers of both the Regular and Volunteer forces still had the option of selecting their own arms. From existing specimens dating from this later period it is plain that they continued to choose the Enfield pattern

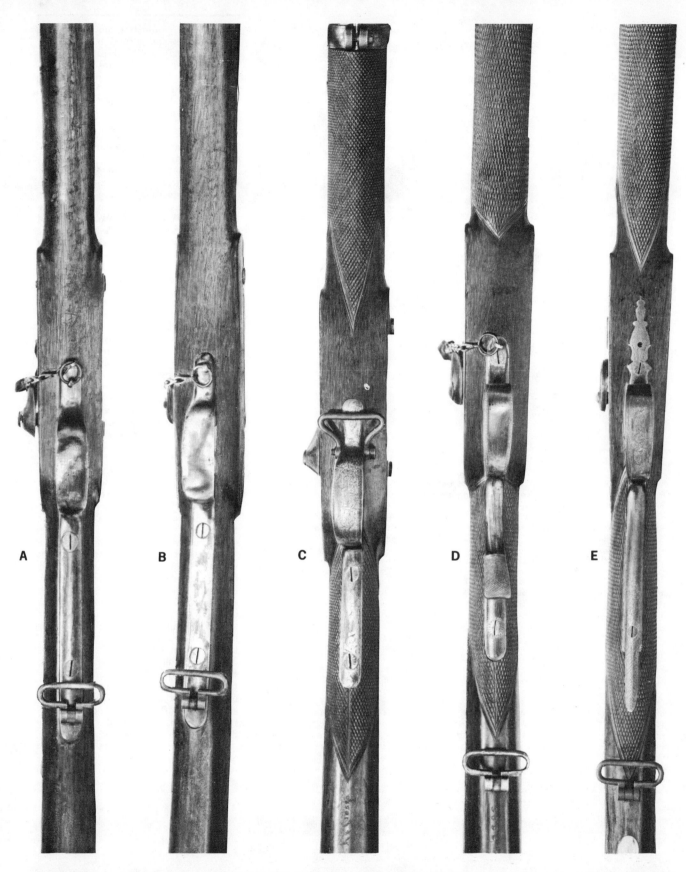

Fig. 19. Trigger guards and swivel mountings. Left to right. (a) Standard Short Rifle trigger guard and rear swivel mounting through rear of guard strap. Snap-cap fixture also standard. (b) William Greener Short Rifle. Note sharp undercutting of wood at forward edges of lock flats, typical of Greener Enfields. (c) Fully engraved Long Enfield; note short guard strap, swivel mount, basic scrolls and leaf border engraving on guard; flower-head screws are found on some rifles otherwise unengraved.

(d) Daw-Jacob rifle, showing common form of spur-guard or scroll guard with knurled extension acting as pistol grip. Note also rear swivel screwed into wood to rear of guard strap. Serial number of rifle stamped into wood to rear of guard strap on this rifle and one shown in (c). (e) Sporting/Military Short Rifle, showing normal sporting pattern trigger guard with hole for mounting snap-cap fixture. Escutcheon inlaid in stock to rear of butt swivel, which is also directly screwed into stock.

The writer would like to express his sincere appreciation to Messrs. E.M.N. Baldwin, J.B. Bell, M.H. Benn, E.J. Burton and M.O.A. Stanton for the use of rifles from their collections in the illustrations, and to Messrs. E. Holmes and S.F. Scorey for their superb photography.

Accessories used with Volunteer Rifles, circa 1861. The Volunteer Movement provided an immense outlet for commercial gadgetry. Gunmakers and riflemen were not long in bringing forward designs—which were then produced and used—in great numbers. The picture shows but a few of these items along with such essential pieces as cartridges and powder flask. 1. Packet of ten 577 Enfield paper cartridges for commercial sale (rather than military issue). 2. Judging Distance Gauge by Holtzapffel & Co.—used to determine the range of infantry or cavalry. The high trajectory arc of the 577 Enfield made precise judgement of range necessary in order to hit the target, and distance-judging drills formed as much a part of the Volunteer's training as did actual firing. By moving the slide down until the figure in question exactly filled the gap, with the instrument held 25″ from the eye by the cord attached, the range could then be noted by the calibrations marked on either side (one for infantryman, the other for mounted cavalryman) and the slide of the Enfield sight set accordingly. 3. Leather-covered German-silver topped rifle flask or "double-shutter" flask by Hawksley; a thoroughly efficient instrument for throwing the exact charges of powder necessary for accurate target shooting. 4. Vernier sight adjuster for use with Enfield type sights having no precise means of moving or setting the sight slide. By setting the slide of the sight against the bar of the Vernier, and then turning the screw, the slide is brought to the exact height desired, regardless of the crude divisions marked on the sight leaf—and the Vernier calibrations then read off and recorded. 5. Musket nipple key or wrench made for Volunteer use. Combines compartments for jag, ball-puller and spare nipples, one in either arm, with pricker down inside central shaft, and nipple wrench at bottom of central shaft. 6. Muzzle protector-rod guide of hard rubber by Silver & Co. for 577 Enfields; also made of horn, copper or brass, they were intended to prevent the steel ramrod of the Enfield from wearing the muzzle of the iron barrel. They were widely used by Volunteers. 7. Standard issue Enfield muzzle plug or tompion with cork body and brass top. 8. W.H. Blanch's combined "muzzle stopper, oil bottle and pricker" one of Blanch's many combination devices. 9. Dixon's combined muzzle protector and sight shield, which operates like a socket bayonet against the pressure of a coil spring in the body of the copper tube. 10. W.H. Blanch's combined nipple key, sight shade, muzzle protector and screwdriver—a device more ingenious in its design than efficient in operation: the screwdriver and nipple key do not have sufficient leverage for many situations, while the sight shade does not line up properly to be of real benefit; the muzzle is protected only around the sides, a separate tompion still being required (no doubt intended to be one of Blanch's as well!).
Writer's collection, photography courtesy of Tower Gun Works.

Short Rifle as the basis for privately-made arms. But certain it is that the numbers of privately-made Short Rifles diminished sharply from early 1861, and that the Long Enfield increasingly became the arm of the Volunteers.

It is possible that this check upon the manufacture and use of privately-owned Enfields may have produced a small outflowing of this type of rifle to America, and thereby account for at least some of the Volunteer Rifles found there with Civil War associations. But in general these rifles would have been ordered by individuals or possibly brought over by speculative merchants in small numbers—perhaps purchased in England from gunshops having stocks of rifles on hand at the time of the appearance of the government circulars. It was the regular issue Pattern 1853 Long Enfield which formed the great bulk of British exports to both sides during the

Civil War, and not the Volunteer Rifle as a class of arms.

The Volunteers continued to use the P/53 Enfield and various models of the Short Rifle until 1871, even though the breech-loading Snider rifle had been officially adopted in 1864. The War Office did not consider that there were sufficient Sniders in the hands of the Regular Army and in reserve to allow of rearming the Volunteers until this late date. Interestingly enough, 1871 saw the adoption of the Martini-Henry 450 rifle in place of the Snider for the Regulars, but the Volunteers did not receive the new small-bore rifle until 1885.

The Volunteer Rifle today forms a more numerous class of arms for the collector than even the various issue patterns. The P/53 and its variants suffered terrific destruction as the result of the American Civil War, the various colonial conflicts of the British Empire and the Franco-Prussian War in which large numbers were used up by the arms-poor French. In addition great numbers of Enfields were converted to the Snider system and many thousands of others doubtless suffered the fate of "an old Army rifle." Volunteer Rifles, on the other hand, being generally of better quality and more deserving of notice, and also from having started life in the hands of a private owner rather than as government property, fared better with the passage of time. These now present for the collector as well as the shooter of military weapons a fascinating combination of military and sporting features both in construction and history. For the social, political and military background of the Volunteer Rifle is quite as interesting and important as the rifles themselves, considering the contribution which they made to the development of military target shooting throughout the British Empire at its height of prestige and development. Some of these rifles saw use in all parts of the globe for a half-century, while others contributed to the improvement of the standard of military marksmanship; not least, it was for the benefit of the units armed with these weapons that the first nationally sponsored rifle shooting organization was founded in Great Britain. ●

Bibliography

Illustrated London News, a weekly, 1858-1866.
The Navies of the World, by Hans Busk, London, 1859.
Proceedings of the National Rifle Association, 1860-1871, annually.
The Rifle: And How to Use It, by Hans Busk, London 2nd ed. (1858), 7th ed. (1860), 8th ed. (1861).
The Volunteer's Book of Facts: An Annual Register by W. H. Blanch, 3rd ed., London, 1862.
Volunteer Rifleman's Magazine. London, 1860.
The Volunteer Rifleman and The Rifle, by John Boucher, 2nd ed., London, 1859.
Volunteer Service Gazette. London, October, 1859-1865.
Volunteer Times. London, 1862.
War Office Circulars, 1868-1864, Public Record Office, London.

Shooting for the market was at one time a way of life for thousands of America's skilled shotgunners, men who made small fortunes at . . .

TEN CENTS A DUCK!

by BOB HINMAN

THE YEARS 1880-99 found some 500 market hunters working their trade in Currituck County, North Carolina. Baltimore buyers waited on the beach with barrels and ice. One of them bought over 40,000 birds a year, and there were three or four other big buyers in the area.

The scene was much the same up and down the coast. The gunners would set up shop at the landing with the day's kill in sorted piles or hung by the feet to drain. They were bought and packed in flour barrels, awaiting pick-up by steamer for delivery to New York's restaurants and milliners.

Shore birds, whether for meat or feathers, brought 3¢ for the smaller ones, 8¢ for the bigger. Gulls and herons were a dime apiece, while a swan brought the lordly sum of a dollar. But the bread-and-butter bird of the market hunter was the duck—at 10¢ each!

The entire East Coast was market-gunned from Maine to Florida, and the same thing went on in the Mississippi and Illinois River Valleys. On a good day, an industrious shooter could take 200 ducks with a few geese tossed in. Snipe and other beach birds were gang-shot in "walks" with a daily kill of about the same number.

Something had to be done, many felt, and Connecticut led the way. In 1901 it closed the season from January through August, ending the spring hunting of waterfowl. There had been some local bans prior to this and a growing public concern to stop the spring slaughter of our migratory birds. Nevertheless spring and market shooting continued elsewhere for the first federal law of 1913 was declared unconstitutional.

In 1916 we entered into a treaty with Canada to protect waterfowl, but the agreement had few teeth in it, and the slaughter went on. It wasn't until 1918 that an "enabling" act was passed, affecting the sale of waterfowl. Even then, as now, it was another two years before the Supreme Court got round to approving it and enforcement began. It spelled the

---

Above—The sink-box, used mostly in the East, was a devastating device on canvasbacks and particularly on redheads. These last would "ball-up" to the point where several birds could be taken with one shot. (Photo courtesy of Milwaukee Public Museum.)

---

doom of mass market hunting, but it was almost too late.

An Old Trade

Marketing of game in America had been a way of life since the pilgrims had traded trinkets-for-turkeys with the Indians, but this country had never seen commercialism in waterfowl on the scale it did in the last quarter of the 19th century.

While we rightly condemn the old market hunters today, in the light of our better knowledge, it was not always thus. America had a long and great hunting heritage, with the game belonging to those who could take it —the supply would never run dry, almost everyone said.

The market hunter was both a scoundrel and local hero. He ran the social scale from the infamous Jake Groat, boasting he could "kill 200 ducks and a jug of booze a day," to gentlemen hunters such as Fred Kimble. The professional killed no larger bag than the sportsman, but he worked at it day after day, and individually accounted for vast numbers of birds. Most learned to keep their mouths and account sheets closed in

into the new century. If he got his hands on a breechloader, he loaded his own shells and often made himself coarse black powder of unstable quality.

The Eastern shooter bought Tatham & Bros. leadshot, while the midwesterner used the output of the Chicago or St. Louis Shot Tower Co. Bulk powder was whatever local brand was in favor at the time, its popularity based more on price than performance.

There were many famous powders to choose from—Hazard, DuPont, Acme, and Wizard. The more knowledgeable and affluent hunter preferred Laflin & Rand's Orange Ducking Powder. It could be had in 6¼ pound kegs and was thought to be less affected by dampness than other powders available. Grain sizes were 1 through 5, and it was considered the

Capt. Adam H. Bogardus, one of the greatest wingshots America has known. As a market hunter, he was a legend in his own time, and long held the title of "Champion Wing Shot Of America" at trap, glass balls and live pigeons.

This early flintlock punt gun weighed 50 lbs., had an 87" barrel and a bore of 2¼". Most likely made in this country in the early 1800s, but it has a British lock of earlier date. Such guns were used as late as 1900 or so, were not outlawed here until 1916. (Photo courtesy of Illinois State Museum.)

Game was plentiful and large bags were the rule before the great drought of the early 1930s. Before legal limits were set by state or government decree, many clubs set their own limits, some for only 50 ducks per day per gun! (Photo courtesy South Dakota Dept. of Game, Fish, and Parks.)

public.

As in all trades, some were more successful than others. The Chesapeake Bay battery shooter could average between $500 and $1000 a season with his ready market and high prices for wild celery-fed canvasbacks. But the average money-gunner was an unskilled, uneducated man with hungry kids. He fished in summer, trapped in winter, hunted spring and fall, and did odd jobs between.

Tools of the Trade

Equipment was only as good as he could afford—which often wasn't much. Many shot muzzleloaders well

An artist's version of a very early sink-box. Later models had a cockpit in the center which brought the gunner to almost water level. The retrieving boat is waiting to the right of the picture.

best of long-range medicine. It was *not* orange in color—the name originated from the old Orange Mills in Orange County, N.Y.

The late '80s saw a slow changeover to what was then called "wood" or white powder, new forms of smokeless propellants. The English Schultze and the American Wood Powder were best known. While giving little smoke and cleaner to use, all early nitro powders were unstable and thought by many to be slower and less powerful than black. It was the day of Damascus barrels, and our early market hunter continued to use black powder for many years after the advent of smokeless.

Whether using white or black powder, wads were rammed-in two sizes larger than the bore—8-gauge wads in a 10-gauge gun, and with reason other than preventing gas leakage. With the brass shells then much in use it was common practice to favor one barrel, usually the more-open bored one for the first shot. When one barrel was fired several times straight, the load in the other barrel was sure to loosen its wads, letting shot spill down the bore. This fault was less prevalent with paper hulls, but they were more expensive in the long run than brass; they didn't last as long.

Patent crimpers and indenters could be had for use with brass cases; these would have prevented normal-size wads from loosening.

Wadding could be anything at hand, or the usual "pink-edge" over-powder wads and one over-shot card wad. This thickish top-wad didn't seem to bother patterns to the extent we believe it does today, and there are many pattern records left to prove it.

The paper shell was gradually preferred by the professional, not only because it held wads tighter and could be crimped, but also because it was thought to be a poorer conductor of heat than brass. In heavy shooting, guns were often fired so fast the resin boiled from the soldered rib.

Capt. Adam Bogardus tells of this and other gun heating problems in his book, *Field, Cover & Trapshooting.** The great amount of game present in the '80s gave ample chance to warm a barrel. Listen to old Cap:

"Sometimes flocks of curlew and plover are so numerous and fly in such a way that a great number may be killed in a short time. I shot a place that had been burned over one afternoon, and flocks were coming in one after another. I killed 264 curlew and plover and got back to Elkhart (Illinois) at sundown. This was done with a muzzleloader. I believe I could have taken 500 with a breechloader."

Bogardus goes on to say he killed with his own gun over 6000 ducks, geese, cranes, plover and snipe in only three months' hunting, His favorite gun at this time was a 10 bore English double with 32" barrels. It weighed 10½ pounds and was loaded for ducks with 5 drams powder and only 1 or 1⅛ ounces of No. 6 shot. The load remained the same for geese except that pellets of No. 3 size were used.

*New York, 1891. First issue, New York, 1874.

Such light loads of shot may come as a surprise to many readers, but it was about the standard then, and was believed to give greater velocity and penetration. The standard 10 gauge field load of the time was 4½ drams of powder and 1 ounce of shot.

The modern wildfowler, using 12 gauge magnum loads with up to 1⅞ ounces of shot, throws a lot more lead at his birds than did the old market gunner, on average. Even the 8 gauge market shooters in the U.S. seldom used shot loads over 1½ ounces. On the other hand Greener—writing in 1892—considered an 8 gauge gun the ideal arm for the wildfowler. He strongly recommended his 15-pound double gun, with barrels 34-36 inches long and full choked, loaded with 2-2½ ounces of shot and 7 drams of black-powder. Shot sizes of 4 or larger were suggested for best patterning.

The 8 gauge was not rare—the British made much of it for fowling—but the American standard for the two decades preceding 1900 was the 10 gauge. It was thought to be the smallest gauge suitable for ducking and was as common in the blind then as our 12 is today.

Punt and Scull Guns

Nearly all past references to market hunting mention the punt gun. There are records of a few used on the Eastern shores, but there appears to be little evidence these monsters were widespread in America. Cost alone would rule out their use by the majority of working market hunters, the price being as much or more than two or three top-grade shotguns. Most punt guns were of English make. Both Greener and Holland & Holland, among others, made breech-loading punters—usually 1½″ bore and weighing close to 100 pounds. Some were chambered for brass shells 7 inches long and charged with 3 ounces (not drams) of powder plus 1½ pounds of shot. Both smaller and larger sizes were made and some behemoths were in the cannon class pushing up to 2 pounds of shot. A few were eliptical at the muzzle, spreading shot over a great area without thought to uniformity of pattern.

Most were rope mounted to the

Propelling force was obtained by working a stern-mounted paddle back and forth. It shoved the boat ahead as if pushed from the rear. The leather-wrapped oar, sometimes worked through a hole in the transom, was noiseless and only the faintest ripple sounded as the boat skimmed through the water.

Its bow was covered over and trimmed with willows, grass, smart weed, and in season, ice or snow. The bottom of the boat was padded with hay for the sculler to lie on his back or side and peer over the cockpit coaming. He would silently scull into a raft of unsuspecting ducks who saw

only a floating log, an ice floe, or a clump of brush.

As the hunter reached their midst, or felt close enough, he'd empty one gun at the flock on the water, then use another as they jumped and took flight. Often 20 to 40 birds could be taken with only the two guns. Then it was but a matter of finding another rafting flock.

Sink Boxes and Blinds

The sink-box was something else. Often called a sneak-box or "float," it was a wooden coffin-shaped affair about 6 feet long by 2 feet wide and only 1½ feet deep. Wooden wings or flaps, 6 to 7 feet wide, were hinged to the box itself, which floated with the movement of the waves. The box was sunk to almost water-level by ballast, and the box opening covered with brush. Decoys, placed about the outriders, were often made of cast-iron to help hold the flaps steady in rough water. The gunner crouched in the small cockpit and raised up to shoot his birds. He was tended by a retrieving boat that stayed at a distance. The sink box was a cumbersome device, often capsizing with the hunter during a blow. But it was an effective killer. Some authorities believe that more red heads and canvasback ducks were taken from a sink-box than there are living today.

A variant form of the sink box just described was some 5 feet deep, permitting the gunner to stand upright in it or crouched a bit. Coamings around

Above—It is doubtful that such fanciful swan boats were used to any extent. They would be unmanageable in a wind, and certainly they wouldn't have been as effective as a camouflaged scull boat. Right—shooting mallards from a scull boat on the Mississippi river.

boat, but some used a system of springs or rubber buffers to absorb recoil. Col. Peter Hawker and Sir Ralph Payne-Gallwey made them famous in England, but few of them were used here.

We preferred the scull-boat and a battery of two or three shoulder guns. In the '80s it was not considered unsporting to shoot sitting ducks—even by gentlemen hunters. Most commercial shooters thought it the *best* way, and sculling was the most productive method of getting within range of rafted birds.

The scull-boat was designed for bay shooting on open water and was practically useless around weeds or stumps. Low and flat in shape, it drew only a few inches of water, but the sculling oar needed some two feet of depth to work properly.

the perimeter helped to prevent shipping water, and these same sides were trimmed with local brush to give the shooters some camouflage.

Only the head and shoulders of the gunner appeared above water level when shooting started and, depending on its height and amount, the brush attached gave fair concealment.

Some sink boxes of this form were made big enough to hold two men, sometimes more.

A sort of grounded sink-box was the point blind, usually a large barrel or hogshead, sunk flush with the beach. The gunner simply squatted or stood in the barrel and pulled brush over the opening.

Line shooting was once popular along the coast and large bays. A string of boats would line up, about two gun ranges apart, while either power or sail craft would drive the birds over the firing line. A good score for such pass-type shooting was two "cans" for three shells, and bets were made down the line.

John Murphy's book, *American Game Bird Shooting** shows an etching of what was called a "Swan-boat," a rather large dory, shaped to resemble a gigantic swan. The idea, I imagine, was to float this strange contraption toward birds, leading them to think that it was the great-granddaddy of all swans! While such boats may have been used, I've never seen a mention of them elsewhere. An artist's whim, maybe?

In the name of commerce—or cupidity—ducks were netted, trapped, and taken on corn-baited trot lines. One printed report advised getting them drunk on distillery mash so they could be clubbed. The Indians looked on "fire hunting" as the surest and cheapest way of getting large bags. Torches were carried into the swamps where geese and swans had bedded for the night. The birds, mesmerized by the glare, waited to be knocked over with guns or clubs.

Night hunting was common in many

*New York, 1882.

places, most especially through the South, but most market gunning was pretty much the same type of hunting we know today, except for the size of the bag.

Shooting Contests

True, the early hunter ground-swatted many birds, but most were good wing shots through practice if nothing else. They took great pride in their shooting and local contests were held to determine the champion. The rules were simple: shoot for a certain length of time, and on return, the winner was the man with the most ducks.

Fred Kimble, who often traveled around to challenge the village champion, later remarked, "Those matches were interesting to me then—more interesting now, because nothing like them will ever again be possible anywhere in the world." Kimble hunted the Illinois River near Peoria in the fall and the flooded timberlands in the spring.

Perhaps best known for his claim to having invented the shotgun choke, Kimble was without doubt one of the greatest wingshots this country ever produced. Whether or not he invented the choke is open to argument, but he certainly deserves credit for making known its advantages in America, as Greener did in England.

Kimble experimented with the narrowed muzzle until he had a gun that would reliably kill at 60 yards instead of the 40 generally considered the limit for scatterguns of the day. He developed a muzzleloading choked 6 gauge of his own contriving and later had a gunsmith named Tonks make a 9 gauge muzzleloader choked down hard. Then he went looking for a duck shooting match. His first victim was Reese Knapp of Browning, Illinois, considered one of that state's finest wingshots. Knapp shot the "biggest duck gun in the country," a 4 gauge single barrel weighing 16 pounds, one said to have accounted for some 60 birds with one blast. At the end of the day, Knapp had only 37 mallards against Kimble's 128—and all of them had been flying birds.

Kimble followed his own advice that "The price of good shotgunnery is constant practice." He not only shot from 100 to 200 shells a day during duck season but was, like Bogardus, a well-known glass ball and live pigeon shooter. Shortly before he died, Kimble was quoted as saying he had never hunted ducks for the market. According to his diary, he killed many hundreds of ducks every season—I wonder what he did with 'em!

Well, the market hunters are gone now—legislated out of business long ago—perhaps to a Happy Hunting Ground of their own. Would they have believed the day would come—as it has—when the legal limit on ducks and geese is one or two birds? ●

Many market hunters turned to guiding and the making of decoys after the sale of wildfowl was banned. Charles Schoenheider of Peoria, Ill., made excellent hand-carved decoys, blocks that bring more money each from today's collectors than they did by the dozen when Charlie made them. (Photo courtesy of Chas. Schoenheider Jr.)

Johnny Gets His Gun

by LUCIAN CARY

J. M. Pyne, the great barrelmaker, put Johnny's rifle together, but that was after the youngster had shown his mettle in a dire emergency.

JOHNNY had to piece the story together from what they told him and what he overheard. His father and mother never told him any more than they could help. He heard his mother say to his father that she didn't want her son to grow up scared.

Johnny was eleven years old then. He knew a great deal more than they supposed he did. He knew those men had shot his father that day in Chicago because his father was the only eyewitness the state's attorney had. The two men in plain clothes who had been assigned to protect his father had died that day. One of the newspapers said they had died as bravely as policemen usually died.

Johnny's father had been in the hospital for months. The surgeons had taken four submachinegun bullets out of his father's body. But his father had got well.

Johnny knew what his mother feared most. If they ever caught the two murderers who had got away, his father would have to testify against them too. That was why the state's attorney had urged his father to go away somewhere. Johnny heard his father and mother discussing what they ought to do, when they thought he was asleep. His mother said they ought to pack up and drive to her father's place in the North Woods and stay there for a year.

"I suppose," Johnny's father said, teasing her—"I suppose you think I'd be safe there because your father would protect me. If anybody who looked bad came along, the old man would out with his trusty rifle and pot him."

Johnny's mother ignored the gibe. She was in earnest. "Father is seventy-five," she said. "I don't believe he shoots any more. I'd feel safe up there with him because it's so far from a city. I'd feel that city killers would never find their way up there."

"It isn't likely they'll ever try to find me."

"You know what the state's attorney said."

"The state's attorney believes in melodrama."

"Perhaps he does," Johnny's mother said. "But if you're afraid, you're afraid whether it's reasonable or not. I'm afraid."

"You'd be bored to death up there in the woods," Johnny's father said.

"I wouldn't. I'd love it. I'd love to see that father gets the right things to eat and that he doesn't work hard. And you'd like father. He's an artist too."

Johnny could hear his father get up and walk back and forth. He must be weakening.

"You'd get a lot of work done," Johnny's mother said. "With nothing to distract you."

"At least," Johnny's father said, "there wouldn't be any cocktail parties. There wouldn't be any rich women you have to flatter because they might buy something."

II

JOHNNY lay awake that first night at grandfather's in the dark loft over the sitting room and listened to the wind in the pine trees and the distant roar of the brook over the dam, and wished he hadn't asked to sleep there. He had asked to sleep in the loft because you climbed a ladder to get there, pushing up the trapdoor with your head.

Johnny listened to the strange sounds and thought he heard a car coming, and was afraid. He knew it couldn't be the men who had promised to get his father. He knew it was just the wind in the pine trees. But he was afraid. He knew pretty much how the men would look. He had seen the sketches his father had made from memory. His father did that sort of thing with a touch of exaggeration, so you knew the person quicker than you ever would from a photograph.

But after that first night Johnny forgot to be afraid. He was too much interested in his grandfather and his grandfather's shop. There was no school within twenty miles and no neighbor within ten miles. Johnny's mother taught him arithmetic and geography and English every morning, while his father painted. After lunch Johnny was free. Grandfather never came in to lunch, no matter what Johnny's mother said. He took a couple of sandwiches and a small tin pail of coffee with him when he went to work in the morning. After lunch Johnny ran the hundred yards down the road to his grandfather's shop. He usually stayed there until dark.

You wouldn't think much of the shop unless you knew. The shop stood beside the brook, below the little mill pond that furnished power for the lathe. The shop was one big room, with a bank of windows along one whole side over the bench, and a chimney in the middle. It looked as if it were full of junk. But if you were a rifle crank you knew better. If you were a rifle crank you knew it was full of treasures. If you were a rifle crank you knew that grandfather made the most famous rifle barrels in the world—match barrels.

He wore two pairs of glasses now, and used a magnifying lens in a brass mount

besides, when he wanted to read the micrometer. But he made match barrels, rifling them by hand, just as he had rifled them for fifty years, to meet the only test he had ever recognized. The test was the way they'd shoot in the machine rest.

If the rifle shot the kind of groups grandfather thought a rifle ought to shoot, he'd put his rifle in the vise and get out the die. He'd line up the die on the left side of the barrel, near the breech, and strike it a smart blow with the hammer. When he took the die away you'd see the name on the barrel, in small Roman letters, cut sharply in the steel:

J. M. PYNE

Sometimes, if it was a .22, it wouldn't shoot. Grandfather would threaten to wrap the barrel around the anvil. Grandfather would curse .22's. Grandfather would say with passion that he hated .22's. But he never did wrap the barrel around the anvil. When he cooled off he went to work on the action. He'd make a new firing pin. He'd change the mainspring. It was the ignition that made the trouble. Grandfather always worked twelve hours a day. But when he had a .22 that wouldn't shoot, he'd work seventeen or eighteen hours. He'd work far into the night under a battery of gasoline lamps.

Johnny learned to keep still when a .22 wouldn't shoot. Johnny would get one of the bound volumes of *Shooting and Fishing* from the stack against the chimney and curl up on the cot and read. One afternoon, in a volume thirty years old, he came on an article about a new world's record for a hundred shots at two hundred yards offhand. There was a picture of the target with the bullet holes in it. The name of the man who had made the record was J. M. Pyne.

Johnny took the volume and laid it open on the bench beside the vise and pointed to the target.

"You did that," Johnny said.

Grandfather looked at the target—a long look. Then he looked at Johnny over his glasses. Grandfather's beard was white and his shoulders were stooped with more than fifty years of bending over the work. But there were moments when his brown eyes sparkled with mischief.

"I used to shoot," he said.

"Don't you ever shoot any more?" Johnny asked.

"Not often," grandfather said. "My left wrist is half crippled."

"You can't shoot at all?"

"I wouldn't say that," grandfather said. "I can still pull one plumb if I have to. But I can't shoot hundred-shot matches any more. My wrist won't hold out for more than a few shots."

Grandfather bent again over his vise. He was working on the tip of a trigger where it engaged the sear, with a smooth, hard, oil stone. He'd take three or four strokes with the slip of stone and pause to look at the work through the magnifying glass.

"I wish I could see you shoot," Johnny said.

"I'd have to stop and cast some bullets for the .32-40," grandfather said, "but I could shoot a couple of shots with the hunting gun. I'd like to be sure it's sighted in.

A deer might come along this fall."

Johnny got a target and ran outdoors and down the range. He tacked the target on the frame in front of the log butt at a hundred yards. Grandfather had the spotting scope set up, and the shooting port open, and the hunting gun out when Johnny got back.

The hunting gun was a plain .30-40 single-shot rifle with an ivory bead in front and an aperture sight on the tang. There was a row of punch marks on the stock. There were twenty-two punch marks without a break. That meant twenty-two deer in twenty-two shots. The twenty-third mark was double. That meant it had taken a second shot to kill the twenty-third deer.

Johnny looked down the range. The black of the target was six inches in diameter and contained the eight, nine and ten rings. The ten ring was two inches in diameter. The black looked awfully small to Johnny. What if grandfather couldn't hit the black? What if he couldn't hit the paper? He was an old man now. He was thirty years older than he had been when he had made that world's record.

"You take the spotting scope," grandfather said, "and when I've called my shot, you tell me what I've got."

Johnny put his right eye to the spotting scope and watched grandfather out of the corner of his left eye. Grandfather raised the rifle and put his cheek against the stock, and his body straightened and the weariness went out of his shoulders. He held his head high as he peered through the aperture of the rear sight. The roar of the rifle startled Johnny. He hadn't known it would be so loud or come so quickly.

"I pulled it high at twelve o'clock," grandfather said.

Johnny looked wildly over the white part of the target above the bull's-eye. He couldn't find the bullet hole.

"It isn't in the white," Johnny said.

"No," grandfather said. "I didn't say it was a wild shot. It's a nine at twelve o'clock."

Then, staring through the scope at the black, Johnny saw the break in the ten ring at twelve o'clock.

"It's a ten!" he cried.

"It shouldn't be," grandfather said. "I pulled a nine."

Grandfather reloaded the rifle. This time Johnny watched through the scope while grandfather aimed, and when the rifle roared, Johnny saw the hole leap in the black, taking away part of the little white 10 in the center of the black.

"It's a ten!" Johnny cried. "What is it you call it when it's absolutely in the middle?"

"A pin wheel," grandfather said.

He put the rifle in the vise, with the leather clamps, and pushed a pledget of absorbent cotton through the bore with a cleaning rod.

Johnny watched him. He seemed pleased with himself, but not at all excited.

"Could I ever learn to shoot like that, grandfather?" Johnny asked.

"I had a bit of luck," grandfather said.

"Luck!" Johnny said.

"Yes," grandfather said. "I pulled the first one for a nine and I got a ten. That's luck. I pulled the second one plumb and got a pin wheel. It's always luck when you get a pin wheel. The rifle won't shoot that close. The rifle will just about stay in two inches at a hundred yards. So when you pull one plumb and get a dead-center shot, it's luck."

"I bet you could get a ten any time you wanted to," Johnny said.

"No," grandfather said. "But I can pull one plumb if I have to. I wouldn't be very far from the ten ring, if I needed a ten."

"Grandfather," Johnny asked again, "could I ever learn to shoot like that?"

Grandfather oiled a pledget of cotton and swabbed the bore of the hunting gun.

"I've always said that any man who had the guts could learn to shoot offhand," grandfather said. "But nowadays they haven't the guts. Nowadays they all learn to shoot lying on their stomachs and resting their elbows on the ground, all trussed up in a sling strap, military fashion. And when they try to shoot standing up and can't make more than half a score, they quit and go back to the prone position, so they can hit something."

"I'd like to learn to shoot offhand," Johnny said.

Grandfather took the hunting gun out of the vise and stood it up in the corner.

"The trouble is," Johnny continued, not without guile, "father thinks that I'm too young to have a gun."

Grandfather glared at Johnny. "What," he demanded—"what does he know about it?"

Johnny thought that was the moment to say nothing.

"I haven't a rifle in the shop that's light enough for you to shoot," grandfather said. "Even the hunting gun weighs close to ten pounds."

"I know," Johnny said, "I'll have to wait until father will buy me a light rifle."

"I'd rather trust you with a rifle right now than most of the men who go deer hunting. You know more about rifles just from being around my shop and asking questions."

He got his flash light and crawled under the long workbench. Johnny waited hopefully. It looked impossible to find anything in that shop, with everything piled hit or miss. But Johnny had never known grandfather to fail.

Grandfather emerged at last. He had a light rifle barrel in one hand.

He put the barrel in the vise and wiped it out. Then he took a soft lead slug and pushed it slowly through the bore.

He caught the bullet in his cap as it came out of the muzzle. He studied the slug with the magnifying glass and measured it with the micrometer.

"I'm two or three years behind with my orders," he said. "That's why I moved up here in the country. So my customers couldn't bother me. They have to write to me to complain, and I don't have to read the letters. And now I'm going to lose another week while I fix up something you can shoot."

"I know you oughtn't to do it," Johnny said. "Only—"

"Only you hope I will."

"I do want a rifle," Johnny said. "I want to learn to shoot."

"You needn't worry," grandfather said.

"You're going to learn right here in this shop, and nobody but you and me is going to know anything about it."

Grandfather cut a piece off the end of that light barrel where it had a tight place in it, and lapped out the bore, and rechambered, and fitted it to an action, and lightened the hammer and adjusted the trigger pull. He made a stock and a forearm, and found an old vernier peep sight.

After that, Johnny had a lesson in offhand shooting every afternoon. Johnny learned things about rifles through a long northern winter. Chicago seemed very far away.

III

JOHNNY'S father went to New York for two weeks in March about an exhibition of his pictures. The only train he could get back on stopped at Wood's Junction, forty miles away, at three o'clock in the morning. Johnny's mother planned to start out the evening before to meet him. The road was still frozen, but a good deal of it was so rough you couldn't drive more than ten miles an hour over it.

Grandfather had an ulcerated tooth. Johnny's mother decided she'd have to start after lunch and take grandfather to a dentist. They might get some sleep at Wood's Junction while they waited for the train.

She asked Johnny if he'd mind spending the night alone in the house. Johnny said of course he wouldn't. He was twelve years old now.

"We could take you with us," his mother said.

"Who would keep the fires going?"

"That's it," she said.

You had to feed wood fires.

"I suppose it's all right," she said. "We'll be back here by seven o'clock in the morning, unless the train is late. But if anything should happen to you, I'd never forgive myself."

"What could happen to me?" Johnny asked.

"The only thing I'm afraid of is fire," his mother said.

"I know how to tend fires," Johnny said.

"I know you do," she said.

Johnny saw that she had lost her fear of the men who had promised to get his father. They had been living at grandfather's for almost a year, and nothing had ever happened.

Johnny got no chance to speak to grandfather alone before they left. He wanted to ask for the key to the shop, so he could shoot his rifle, but he could not ask in front of his mother. He had to occupy himself carrying in wood after they had gone.

When it came on dark, Johnny lit the big oil lamp on the sitting-room table and put fresh wood in the chunk stove. He turned on the drafts in the kitchen stove and cooked himself a dish grandfather called yellow jackets. He cut up two cold, boiled potatoes and browned them in a pan with strips of bacon and broke eggs over them and stirred the whole. After supper he sat down beside the big lamp with Fremantle's *Book of the Rifle*. For once, he could stay up as late as he liked.

Now and again he looked up and listened. He wasn't afraid. He knew there was nothing to be afraid of in the North Woods. He bent again over his book. He read on and on.

Suddenly he found himself listening like a wild animal. He thought he had heard a car coming in the distance. Of course, it was just the wind in the pine trees outside. But he listened. And, listening, he knew it wasn't the wind. It was a car coming. He jumped up and went into grandfather's bedroom and looked out. It was dark in the bedroom and darker still outdoors. He saw the headlights of a car in the dark. The car was coming pretty fast, considering the road. The lights lurched from side to side.

The car stopped and turned in. Johnny watched with his nose against the cold windowpane. The car was a big sedan. Two men got out of the car. They came toward the house.

Johnny waited until he heard them on the porch. Then he opened the door and asked them in. They came in, stamping their feet. There was still some snow on the ground.

"Well, bub," the tall man said, his back to the chunk stove, "where's your folks?"

"They're away," Johnny said.

"They'll be back tonight, won't they?"

"No," Johnny said. "Not till tomorrow."

"The reason I'm asking," the tall man explained, "is that we're tired and hungry and we're lost. We thought we might get a meal here and put up for the night."

"I guess you can do that." Johnny said. You didn't turn strangers away in the North Country. Even if you didn't like them, you gave them a meal and let them stay the night. "I could give you ham and eggs and fried potatoes and coffee," Johnny added.

"Fine," the tall man said. He took off his hat and coat. He wasn't bald. The other man took off his hat. He wasn't bald either. One of the men Johnny's father had sketched for the state's attorney was bald. His hat had fallen off that day in Chicago and revealed him as completely bald.

Johnny found the ham and the eggs and peeled some cold, boiled potatoes. The short man cooked the ham and eggs while Johnny found bread and butter and set out plates and knives and forks on the kitchen table. The tall man got a bottle of whisky out of his overcoat pocket. They drank half a tumblerful of whisky apiece and poured out more, and ate like hungry men.

When the two men had eaten, they went out to their car. Johnny watched them from the dark bedroom window. The tall man had a flash light. He held the light while the short man got something out of the rear of the car. Johnny saw that he had a gun. He handed the gun to the tall man and got another gun. The tall man locked the door of the car. He tried the other doors to make sure they were locked too.

Johnny ran back into the living room. He was putting wood in the chunk stove when they came in. He took a look at those guns and tried not to betray his interest.

They put their guns in the corner of the sitting room. Johnny saw that one of them was a Springfield Army rifle and the other was what the Government called a light machine rifle, though it was twice as heavy as a Springfield and was only light when compared with a machine gun. You could come by a Springfield honestly enough, but the Government did not sell the light machine rifle to anybody. Johnny had never seen one before. But he knew the gun by the pictures he had pored over in grandfather's shop.

"We've been hunting," the tall man said. He nodded toward the rifles and smiled at Johnny.

It was all right to say you were hunting in March, if you needed the meat. No native would report you to the game warden for killing a deer out of season. But city men with a big car had no business hunting deer in March. And did they think he was so stupid as to believe that anybody would hunt deer with anything so heavy and clumsy as the Government's machine rifle?

"I guess," Johnny said—"I guess I'd better show you your room before I go to bed."

"All right, bub," the tall man said. Johnny noticed how tired he was. His eyes were bloodshot. He looked as if he hadn't slept for days. His face was a kind of dirty gray.

Johnny showed them the spare room. It had two beds.

"The stove doesn't heat much in here," Johnny said. "But there are plenty of blankets."

"You haven't got a telephone?" the tall man said.

"No," Johnny said. "The nearest telephone is at Johnson's."

"How far is that?"

"It's twelve miles," Johnny said.

The tall man nodded.

Johnny showed him how to turn off the drafts of the chunk stove before he went to bed, so the fire would smolder all night instead of burning out. Johnny said good night politely and climbed the ladder into the dark, cold loft. He found his flash light on the shelf beside his bed. He took off his shoes and rolled under the covers and listened.

The two men sat at the sitting-room table and talked. At first their voices were so low Johnny could not distinguish the words. He put his ear close to a stud at the head of his bed. He could hear a good deal better. The two men were drinking whisky, and as they drank, their voices grew louder. Johnny could hear every word they said. But some of their words puzzled him.

"This place would make a good refrigerator." Johnny recognized the short man's voice. He had hardly said a word all evening, but he was talking freely now.

The tall man disagreed. "You don't know country people, Al," he said. "They've got nothing better to do than watch a stranger. The country gets hot fast."

They got nasty with each other as they drank. They reminded each other of things. They had a long argument about where they would go in the morning. The tall man got impatient.

"Listen, Al," he said, "as soon as we bump this guy off, we're going to Buffalo—to Joe's."

Johnny lay there, his heart pounding. At last they went to bed. Johnny heard them arguing about the drafts in the chunk stove, and then they went into the bedroom.

Johnny waited. He had no way of telling time. He waited until he was sure he had waited an hour, and then he waited longer. He put his flash light in his pocket and crawled on his hands and knees toward the ladder. It was slow going because so many of the boards creaked. He opened the trap-door and listened. He could hear a snore. He listened until he was sure he heard two distinct snores. He went down the ladder backwards, in his stocking feet.

The corner where they had stood their guns was empty. They had taken their guns into the bedroom with them. Johnny turned the lamp low and stole to the open bedroom door and listened. He got the flash light out of his pocket and took a quick look inside the room. They had gone to bed with their clothes on.

They had each hung a .45 Government automatic pistol on a bedpost. The holsters were the kind that hang under your arm-pit.

Johnny stole back into the kitchen, and shut the door, and lit the bracket lamp. It was cold in the kitchen. Johnny turned on the drafts and, taking great pains not to make any noise, put some kindling on the coals. It was one o'clock by the alarm clock on the shelf. He ought to make Johnson's in three hours, even in the dark. Ole Johnson had a car as well as a telephone. He'd get word to Wood's Junction. The sheriff would form a posse. But somebody would get killed. His father might get killed.

Johnny thought it out. He might sneak in and get their guns without waking them up. But when they did wake up they'd know. They might have more guns in that car they'd locked up so carefully before they came in.

He might take the cartridges out and throw them away. But when they awoke they might look at their guns, opening them part way to make sure they were loaded and ready to fire. That was what men who were used to guns would do. And if they did that, they'd find out their guns had been unloaded. They might have more cartridges in their pockets. They probably had more cartridges in the car they had locked up.

Johnny thought of using lard. But he hunted through the cupboard, moving tins cautiously, until he found a coffee can half full of thin cakes of bullet lubricant. He had watched grandfather make it, trying out mutton tallow and straining it, putting in bayberry wax and a little cylinder oil, and stirring in finely powdered graphite. Johnny put a cake of the stuff in a clean pan and put the pan on the fire. When the lubricant melted, he set it to one side where it would keep warm.

He opened the kitchen door and listened. They were still snoring. Johnny stole across the sitting room. He located the machine rifle with the flash light and put the flash light back in his pocket. He took the rifle in both hands and walked as slowly, as softly as he could back into the kitchen. The gun was very heavy, heavier than grandfather's pet *Schützen* rifle. Johnny had to figure how to open it. But he did it. He made sure there was a cartridge in the chamber.

He stood the butt of the rifle on the floor. It was almost as tall as he was. He put a small funnel in the muzzle. He poured the bullet lubricant into the muzzle, a little at a time, so it would cool against the cold steel. He poured the barrel almost full. Then he carried the rifle back and set it up where he had found it and got the Spring-field.

He took the Springfield to the kitchen and opened the bolt part way and made sure there was a cartridge in the chamber, and then he filled the bore almost to the muzzle with the bullet lubricant.

It was ticklish, getting the two automat-ics out of their holsters. He had to stand in the dark, within a foot of the tall man's head, and work one gun gently out of its holster and then the other. He found, when he got back to the kitchen with the automatics, that the slides were very stiff. He had to pull and pull against the spring to get those guns open enough to make sure there was a cartridge in the chamber. And he had to be sure. If the chamber was empty, the bullet lubricant would fill it and the man wouldn't be able to get a car-tridge in and he would know something was wrong. But if the cartridge was in the chamber, the grease would only fill the space ahead of it. If the man opened the slide a little way to make sure it was ready to fire, he'd see the brass of the case and think everything was all right.

Johnny filled the barrels of the two auto-matics with bullet lubricant and got one of them back in its holster. The tall man stirred and turned over. Johnny waited, trying not to breathe, until he snored again. Johnny pressed the flash-light switch to see just where he was and where the holster was. He almost cried out. The tall man was bald. His thick hair had slipped over on the pillow while he slept. It was a wig.

Johnny got the gun into the holster and went back into the kitchen. He had left his shoes in the loft. He'd have to get them. He couldn't walk twelve miles over a rough and frozen road in his stocking feet. He climbed the ladder and crept down to his bed and got the shoes. He tied the laces together and hung the shoes over his neck so he's have both hands free, crawling back to the ladder and climbing down.

It was two in the morning by the alarm clock on the kitchen shelf. He'd have to hurry. He turned the wick of the bracket lamp low. He had his hand on the knob of the kitchen door when he heard one of the men stir. Johnny waited. The man sudden-ly came staggering out of bed and toward the kitchen. Johnny hadn't time to do any-thing. It was the tall man.

The tall man picked up a tumbler and looked about for water and saw Johnny.

He didn't say a word. He got his glass of water and drank it thirstily. He looked at Johnny.

"Where you going, bub?" he asked.

"Out," Johnny said.

The tall man grabbed Johnny by the col-lar and shoved him into the sitting room and over to the ladder.

"Up," he said.

Johnny climbed the ladder. The tall man followed him part way and pulled the trap-door shut. Johnny could hear him fum-bling with the big wooden buttom that fas-tened the trapdoor shut. He tried the door to make sure it was fastened. Johnny heard him going back to bed.

The window at the end of the loft was too small to climb through. He couldn't get out. He was trapped.

Johnny lay in bed, shaking with fear. He lay there for hours until he heard the two men getting up. They were starting up the kitchen fire. The tall man came into the sitting room and yelled up at Johnny.

"Where's the coffee, bub?" he demanded.

"I don't know," Johnny said. "But I could find it."

The tall man opened the trap. "Come on down," he said.

Johnny put on his shoes and climbed down and hunted in the kitchen cupboard. He had shifted things around the night before, hunting for the bullet grease.

The tall man had found the coffee can of bullet lubricant, but he didn't know what it was. He only knew it wasn't coffee.

Johnny sat in a corner while they ate their breakfast. It was nearly seven o'clock. Johnny listened for the sound of the car. He had to hear the car before they did. It was his only chance for warning his father and his mother and grandfather.

"I'd better put some wood in the chunk stove," Johnny said.

"All right," the tall man said.

Johnny went into the sitting room. He paused and listened and dropped a chunk in the stove. He listened again and dropped another chunk.

"Come on back here," the tall man said.

"I'm coming," Johnny said. He listened again. He heard the car. He waited for the right moment.

Johnny ran for the kitchen door. He got outdoors before they could stop him. The car was almost at grandfather's shop. Johnny waved his hands and yelled. The car stopped alongside grandfather's shop just as the tall man got Johnny by the col-lar.

The short man came running out of the house with the machine rifle. Johnny saw grandfather motion his father and mother to get behind their car. Grandfather went into the shop.

"Hold it," the tall man said. "Hold it until you can see a head."

The short man rested the barrel of the machine rifle on the hood of his car and trained it on the other car.

"Here comes the old man," the tall man said.

Grandfather came out of the shop. He had the hunting gun. He walked toward Johnny and the tall man. He was keeping a tree between himself and the man with the machine rifle as he walked. He reached the tree. There was no more cover. Grand-father had to expose himself to shoot.

"Now," the tall man said, and as he spoke he threw both arms around Johnny and held him up as a shield.

Johnny could feel the man's chin press-ing into the back of his head.

The machine rifle went off with a sound much louder and duller than a .30-06 usu-ally makes. The short man stood there with a piece of the stock in his hands and blood running down his face. The rifle had blown apart in his hands.

Johnny saw grandfather raise his rifle and point it straight at him. The tall man

held Johnny tightly. Grandfather hadn't much to shoot at above Johnny's head. But Johnny knew he had enough. Grandfather could pull one plumb when he had to.

Grandfather's rifle cracked and the arms around Johnny went suddenly limp and the man who held him slumped. Johnny ran toward his grandfather. As he ran he heard an explosion behind him. The short man had fired his automatic pistol. The short man was standing up still, but he reeled as he stood. His pistol was no longer a pistol. It was a twisted piece of steel.

"It's all right, grandfather," Johnny said, "I fixed their guns."

And then Johnny was in his mother's arms and she was calling him, "My baby! My poor baby!" and Johnny's father was saying how lucky it was that the short man's gun had blown up.

Grandfather snorted. "Lucky," he said.

"Lucky!" He turned to Johnny. "What did you do?"

"I used some of your bullet lubricant," Johnny said. "I melted it and poured it in while they were asleep."

His father and mother didn't know what he was talking about. But grandfather knew.

"Now they'll have to let you have a gun," he said. "Now they'll believe you know about rifles." ●

A thoroughly researched and detailed account of Lee's numerous contributions to firearms technology and advancement. New information and a long-lost model are offered here for the first time. *Part one.*

by LARRY S. STERETT

Above—James Paris Lee as he looked in 1899 at age 68. A rare photograph of one of the world's foremost but least known firearms inventors.

JAMES PARIS LEE was one of the most brilliant of all the inventors who contributed to the art of gunmaking. Born at Harwich, Roxboroughshire, Scotland, on August 9th, 1831, to George and Margaret (Paris) Lee, he migrated with his parents to Shades Mills (Galt), Ontario, Canada, in 1836. His education began at the old Gouinlock School in Galt, but was completed at Dickie's Settlement, Dumfries, under a Mr. William Telfer.

James' father, George Lee, was a skilful watchmaker and jeweler. When James was nearly 17, he entered his father's shop to learn the trade. His interest in firearms began to blossom about the same time, for one of his first experiments was to make a rough stock and fit it to the barrel and lock of an old horse pistol he'd been given.

When everything was complete the pistol had to be tested and, in his own words, "I got my brother Jack to touch the gun off with a spunk, the immediate effect of which was to blacken my face with powder and hurl the barrel about 20 yards in an opposite direction."

On October 15, 1847, George Lee recorded in his diary: "Jimmie has shot himself and will go limping through the world during life!" James had been hunting in Dickson's woods near Galt and was returning in the evening, cold and wearied, with his shotgun over his shoulder when it fell to the ground and discharged. The charge passed completely through the heel of his right foot from the left side, taking with it a piece of his leather boot and searing the flesh to the degree that profuse bleeding

The Rifles of
James Paris
Lee

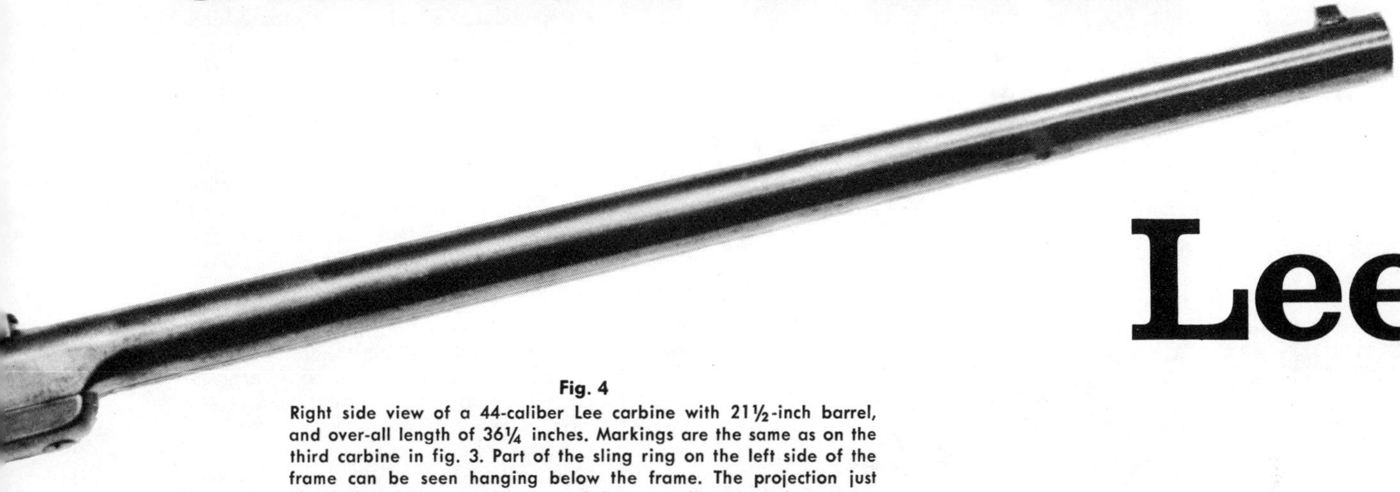

Fig. 4
Right side view of a 44-caliber Lee carbine with 21½-inch barrel, and over-all length of 36¼ inches. Markings are the same as on the third carbine in fig. 3. Part of the sling ring on the left side of the frame can be seen hanging below the frame. The projection just above the trigger guard is part of the manually-operated extractor.

did not occur. Dragging himself on his hands and knees through nearly 200 yards of brush to reach a road, he was found by a passing farmer and taken home. After nine months in bed, James Lee was again up and about, but it was nearly a year and a half before he was able to move about freely.

Having finished his work with his father, James traveled to Toronto to learn the practical side of the trade. After spending 6 months with a manufacturing jeweler named Jackson, on King Street, he decided to go into business for himself, and to open a shop in Chatham.

Boarding the Galt-London-Chatham stage one day in 1850, James Paris Lee set out on a journey that was to affect his life in more ways than one. Hardly had he settled in Chatham and put out his sign, when he met 16-year-old Caroline Chrysler, the second daughter of one of Chatham's most respected families. It was apparently love at first sight for both, but the marriage was delayed for two and one-half years because of her age. Said to have resembled Empress Eugenie, the famous French beauty of the period, Mrs. Lee was an amiable woman who accompanied her husband on nearly all his later journeys to Europe and in America, until her sudden death in London, England, in 1888, due to heart failure. The union produced two sons, both of whom later assisted their father in his work.

Remaining in Chatham for nearly 5 years, the Lees moved to Owen Sound for a brief period and then on to Janesville, Wisconsin. Shortly before the Civil War, James Lee was induced to move from Janesville to Stevens Point, Wisconsin, on the Wisconsin River, and to set up as a watchmaker and jeweler. (The 1860 Federal Census lists Lee as a resident of this town of 1533 inhabitants, his occupation, watchmaker.)

Early Venture

The Stevens Point newspaper, *The Wisconsin Lumberman,* credits Lee with being the "inventor and pioneer in the manufacture of...extract of hemlock." In the area the valuable bark of the hemlock was being left to rot. Its transportation was so costly that bulk shipments of the bark were unprofitable. Lee conceived the idea of extracting the tannic acid from the bark and shipping it out of the woods in condensed liquid form. In a letter dated July 27, 1898, to a friend, the Honorable James Young, Lee described this ill-fated experience.

"...It looks rather queer to sell tanbark at $40 per barrel. That experiment took me into the hemlock forests in their original beauty. Great hunting here! I wondered at the great wealth of hemlock bark, and why it could not be transferred to market in a more profitable form. Result was I got a small portable engine through a blazed way (there were no roads at that time), stationed it on the banks of a beautiful lake, erected a mill to grind the bark, and a long copper pan 4 feet wide and 50 feet long, to evaporate the leechings into a thick syrup, getting the tanning strength of eight cords into a 40-gallon cask. The first test of it succeeded in burning up the leather. They didn't dilute enough."

In any case, the end result was to seal the fate of the enterprise, proving unfortunate for everyone concerned.

The extensive lumbering operations indicated a very successful future for the area, but James Lee admitted that the abundance of game and the grandeur of the forests helped to attract him. Deer, bear and wolves were to be found around Stevens Point, and nearly all of his spare time was devoted to hunting or to the production of a repeating rifle to replace the old muzzle-loading models. Not content with three or four shots, Lee wanted to produce a 40-shot repeater and, after numerous attempts, he was successful. The well-made model, which showed much promise, consisted of a rifle with a hollow sheet metal buttstock containing a number of magazines, the cartridges in which were placed one above the other. After firing, and ejection of the empty case, a rod pushed a loaded cartridge into the chamber, and at the same time transferred a cartridge from one magazine to another nearest the chamber. Unfortunately metal cartridge cases were not readily available at this time and the mechanism would not operate properly with those available. As a result this rifle never was commercially manufactured, and whether one survives today is not known to the author. It did, however, embody a principle that was to appear later in the rifles of many nations.

While the 40-shot repeater was hanging fire (perhaps literally), Lee developed a successful method of converting the Springfield muzzle-loading rifle into a breechloader, followed by a single-shot cavalry carbine. On July 22, 1862, U.S.

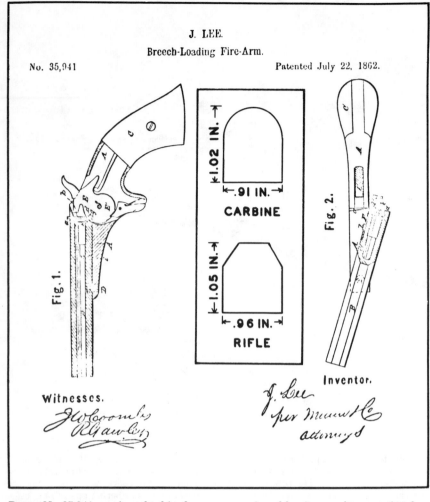

J. LEE.
Breech-Loading Fire-Arm.

No. 35,941   Patented July 22, 1862.

CARBINE
1.02 IN.
.91 IN.

RIFLE
1.05 IN.
.96 IN.

Fig. 1.

Fig. 2.

Witnesses.

Inventor.

The Honorable W.D. McIndoe, a Congressman and a friend of Lee, apparently saw some potential in the carbine. He helped Lee gain financial backing for the new firm, which was organized in Milwaukee on October 13, 1864[1]. Various sources list this firm as Lee Arms Company, Lee Fire Arms Company, Lee Firearms Company, Lee's Firearms Company and Lee's Fire Arms Company. However, the last form is the one appearing on the Articles of Association filed with the Secretary of State in Madison, Wisconsin, on November 2, 1864.

The Articles stated the objectives of the new firm to be "manufacturing in the City of Milwaukee Fire Arms of the pattern and form specified in Letters Patent and the Schedule accompanying the same, issued by the Government of the United States to James Lee, and also of other patterns if deemed advisable." Incorporation was approved on March 8, 1865. Capitol stock was valued at $100,000, in shares of $100 each. Of this amount only $10,000 was actually paid in. The firm was to be managed by 7 directors, elected on the first Monday of each year. The original 7 included:[2] Charles F. Ilsley, James Kneeland, James Lee, Thomas L. Ogden, Lester Sexton, Solomon Taintor and Daniel Wells Jr. Kneeland was elected president of the Board, with H.F. Pelton, Secretary. James P. Lee was appointed Superintendent of the Works. The Honorable W.D. McIndoe was not listed as being on the Board, possibly because a conflict of interest charge might be leveled in connection with a military contract.

The armory was established at 454 Canal Street in October, 1864, and the job of procuring materials and equipment began. (Canal Street is now Commerce Street in Milwaukee, and the 454 area is a part of the Joseph Schlitz Brewery complex.) A number of parts were presumably bought elsewhere in the finished stage, ready for assembly. These included sling bars and rings, buttplates, and front and rear sights, which appear identical to those made by the Burnside Rifle Co. of Rhode Island, and which are referred to as "Burnsides" by Col. McAllister in one report.

Barrels were supplied by E. Remington & Sons of Ilion, New York. A total of 1136 barrels were shipped to Milwaukee for rifling and chambering, and to be fitted with sights and extractors. This arrangement was ideal since the Remington firm was equipped to produce barrels, and government inspection and proof was taken care of by the Ordnance Department inspectors before the barrels were shipped to Milwaukee.

Contract Troubles

In April, 1865, the official order for the delivery of the carbines was issued by the Ordnance Department as follows below.[3] Note that caliber 44 is shown in this letter; caliber was not given in the letter of May 7th, 1864.

Patent No. 35,941, was issued to him for an "Improvement in Breech-Loading Fire Arms." While the patent drawing is for a pistol—only one model of which is known to exist today—mention is made in the specifications of " ... a rifle or piece with a long barrel," and this was the type later manufactured by the Lee's Fire Arms Co. of Milwaukee, Wis.

In March of 1863, Lee submitted one of his breech-loading alterations of the Springfield rifle to the U.S. Ordnance Department for trial. The rifle was not satisfactory, and in November a second type was submitted. This second model, and a later third model, were acceptable, but a contract for their manufacture was not forthcoming. However, a request for a breech-loading carbine for testing was made, and by April, 1864, Lee had produced one, based on his 1862 patent. This carbine was also acceptable, but some extraction difficulties were experienced. No doubt expecting a contract, Lee offered to provide 1000 of the carbine model for testing, with delivery to be within 6 months of the date of the order. The offer was approved, as indicated by the following communication:

Lee's First Contract

James Lee Esq.   Ordnance Office
Washington D. C.   May 7th 1864
Sir

Your letter of April 19th to the Secretary of War offering to furnish 1000 of your breechloading carbines at $18 has been referred to this office with authority to enter into such contract with you. Should you therefore present to this Department a carbine free from the defects mentioned in Captain Benton's report the contract will then be given you. The defect was "The cartridge case ejector frequently failed to start the case, the projection next to the case (on the ejector) appears to be too short to take a firm hold on the rim of the case." The carbine must be presented this or next month.
Respectfully
Your obt Svt
George D. Ramsay
Brig. Gen. Chf of Ord

Lee improved the extractor design without difficulty, and his request for permission to manufacture the gun frames of malleable cast iron instead of wrought iron was accepted. But he had no facilities for manufacturing the carbines in quantity, and his request for an increase in the contract price was rejected.

As for Lee's original plans for manufacturing the carbines, it is a matter for conjecture. He may have intended to have the carbines made elsewhere, under his name, or he may have intended to sub-contract the parts and to assemble the carbines himself, with workmen hired for his purpose. In any event, since the letter from Gen. Ramsay did not specify a time of delivery, Lee decided to form a company and make the carbines.

Fig. 3

Breech details of three Lee carbines, showing rear sight locations, trigger guard variations and markings. The crudely-marked top carbine is considered the first specimen made (No. 1). The middle carbine is unmarked, while the third carbine has the standard markings found on commercial production pieces. The two frame holes in the lower carbine are for attaching the sling bar. Note the higher standing-breech on the first two carbines, compared to that of the third. (No. 2183).

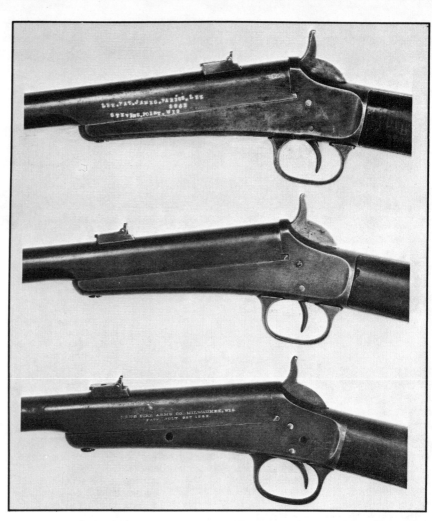

Mr. James Lee   Ordnance Office
Milwaukee, Wis   April 18, 1865
Sir

You will please deliver to the Inspector of Small Arms, the one thousand breech loading carbines Cal. 44 and appendages the order to furnish which was given to you on the 7th day of May, 1864 for which eighteen dollars ($18) will be paid for each carbine including appendages that is approved by the Inspector. Please forward to this office as soon as possible two (2) carbines to be used as standards in the inspection and reception of the above. These one thousand carbines will be packed in suitable boxes, for which a fair price, to be fixed by the Inspector will be paid.

Respectfully
Your obt Svt
A. B. Dyer
Brig Gen. Chf of Ord

Although the order called for two carbines to be used as standards, a single carbine was shipped to Ordnance for inspection on August 31, 1865. It was rejected. In so doing the following reasons were advanced by the inspector, Gen. W. A. Thornton:

The barrel, indicates rough rifling and to remedy which it has been leaded to such an extent that the edges of the lands are quite round. It is badly ringbored at the muzzle and the breech-chamber is roughly reamed. Front sight . . . can be readily pushed out by the fingers. The hammer has a corner broken from the middle notch. Notches roughly filed . . . The mainspring is apparently too weak . . . The breech piece is . . . very doubtful in strength through screw holes at points of junction to the barrel and in tang joining it to the stock. The stock is very roughly cut in bedding the main spring and too deeply cut for the tang of the breech piece . . . It is therefore liable to be easily broken. The butt plate has a seam in the material . . . The sear spring is broken . . .

In January, 1866, the two models originally called for in the order of April, 1865, as inspection standards, were finally furnished. After inspection they were reported on as follows:

Office of Inspector of Contract Arms
No 240 Broadway
New York, January 26, 1866

Maj. Gen'l A.B. Dyer
Chief of Ordnance

General

I have the honor to inform you, that I have inspected two model Carbines, furnished by James Lee Esq. of Milwaukee and respecting which I have to report that I find,

Carbine No. 1.

Frame—of Malleable Cast Iron and thin at front end where the screw connects it to the barrel.
Stock—Split at top butt screw hole.
Barrel—Chamber torn in rifling.
Connection Screw—Thread torn.
Butt Plate—Seams in material out side.
—Top Screw hole countersunk too deep.

Carbine No. 2.

Frame—of Malleable Cast Iron.
Barrel—Torn in rifling.
Mainspring—Crooked at Set Screw.
In all other conditions I consider these arms are well gotten up, and I respectfully recommend their acceptance as Models with the understanding that like Carbines furnished to the United States shall be equally as good in workmanship and free from defects.

Respectfully, I am sir,
Your obedient servant
W. A. Thornton

Even with the recommendation the Ordnance Department refused to accept the two carbines as inspection standards on the grounds of incorrect caliber. According to a letter to Gen. Thornton ". . . they (the carbines) gauge only .42 calibre while my order of April 13th 1865 calls for .44 calibre. Please see if the carbines will take the cartridge for Spencer carbine cal. .44; if so these may be returned for stamp as model carbines for the inspection."

Thornton apparently informed Lee that the carbines were unacceptable, due to an error in caliber, although Thornton had informed the Chief of Ordnance ". . . I did not verify them as to the size of their bore when I made their inspection." Lee immediately went to Washington to try and clarify the matter, but was unsuccessful. By mid-spring the two carbines had been returned to Milwaukee.

By this time Lee may have been convinced that the military were not going to accept his carbine, for one reason or another. It should also be remembered that the Civil War was now over, and the arms were not needed; the caliber may have been only an excuse to hedge on a contract. To recover some of the losses, Lee began to explore the civilian market. Unfortunately surplus arms were flooding the market, and could be bought at a fraction of the cost of the new Lee carbines.

Possibly in an attempt to help a local industry the *Milwaukee Daily Sentinal* published an article entitled: "HOW BREECH LOADING GUNS ARE MADE —A Visit To Lee's Arms Manufactory" on page 1 of the March 23, 1866, edition. (Note that the name of the firm shows still another form attributed to the Milwaukee enterprise.) The article appeared as follows:

We recently paid a visit to Lee's Arms Manufactory, situated on the Canal, in the sixth ward of the city, and were conducted through the various departments by the gentlemanly President, James Kneeland, esq.

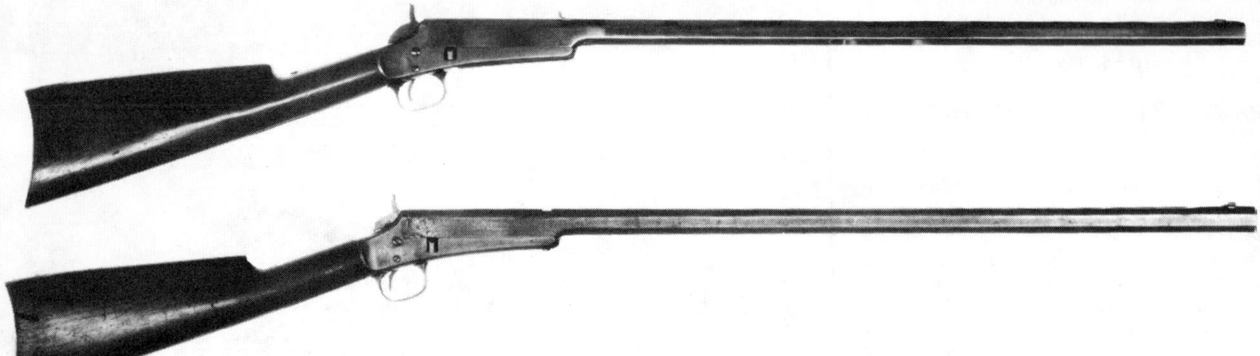

Fig. 5

Right side view of two 38-caliber Lee rifles with octagon barrels. The top rifle has the highest known serial number (2268) of Lee arms made in Milwaukee. The stock is well-figured, and the metal has a highly polished blue finish. Barrel length is 29⁹⁄₁₆ inches and it is 44⁵⁄₁₆ inches over-all. In addition this rifle has a frame-mounted floating firing pin instead of the usual hammer-mounted striker.

and the Superintendant and inventor of the arms, James Lee, esq.

Comparatively few of our readers are acquainted with the manner of making guns, and we venture to give a brief account of our tour of observation.

The barrels of the gun are purchased in the rough state and brought to the manufactory here. They are made of the best decarbonized steel. The first process is to mill the barrel down to its proper size and form. During this process it has to pass through 19 different operations. It is then taken to the rifling machine. In order to insure greater accuracy in firing the gun, the barrel has to be grooved or rifled, so as to give the ball, on issuing from the gun, a rotary motion, which like the motion of a top, keeps it unerringly on its course. It has been found by experiment that the shorter the twist in the barrel, the longer the range and the accuracy obtained. The twist in the Whitworth gun, which is acknowledged the best now to be known, has one turn in 20 inches. The twist of Lee's gun is one turn in 23 inches. The rifling machine, at each revolution, takes a cut of but one eighty-thousandth part of an inch. This apparently incredibly small cut is necessary from the fact that a larger one would be liable to tear the barrel and such an accident would render it useless. The shavings from the machine are as fine as the finest of wool. After rifling, the barrel is taken to the polishing room and a fine finish put upon it. It is then taken to the blueing furnace and beautifully colored. It is now ready for use. The barrel passes through 43 different operations from the forging to the blueing process.

The breech is then taken in hand. It is made from the best de-carbonized iron, requiring to be kept at a red heat for 16 days. It is first put through a milling machine, then filed, drilled, polished, and blued, passing through no less than 60 different processes from the forging to the blueing.

The lock is perhaps the simplest part of the gun, having only four pieces—a hammer, trigger, mainspring and trigger-spring. It is so simple that the most inexperienced could take it apart or put it together. Yet the hammer passes through 20 different and separate processes, the trigger through ten, the mainspring through six.

The stocks are made from Wisconsin black walnut, which from its hardness has been found to be the best material for the purpose. As the lock is situated in the breech of the gun, there is comparatively little work about the stock. It is made wholly by machinery; first grooved for the mountings, then formed into the proper shape, then sweated and polished, and lastly mounted.

Every portion of this gun is made by machinery and each part of every gun is the same. The advantage of this is in the fact that when a part of the gun is either lost or broken it can be replaced by another from the manufactory at but little cost. Every gun is subjected to a rigid test, and any imperfection, no matter how small, condemns it. All the machinery and tools used have been made expressly for the manufacture of the arm, and the company have been at an enormous outlay for the requisite machinery. The manufactory is now in excellent working order, and will soon be able to turn out a large number of guns daily, and will furnish employment to quite a number of men. None but the best of mechanisms are employed, however, as the variation of even so much as a thousandth part of an inch in any of the parts of the gun would spoil it for use.

The arm deserves a minute description, but with our imperfect knowledge of its mechanism, we cannot hope to do it justice.

It has many advantages over the ordinary rifle. There are only 8 pieces in the whole gun—less than half the number in either Burnside, Henry or Spencer rifles—and they are so simple that anyone can put them together with ease. It can be loaded and fired 20 times a minute by an expert sportsman, and can be used with one hand when occasion requires; it being light and almost self-working. Its penetration is truly wonderful. With but 23 grains of powder a ball was driven through an inch board, 6 inches of cotton, tightly compressed, and a body of water 6 feet in extent. The force required to accomplish this fact connoisseurs will appreciate. The arm is very light—the heaviest now manufactured being only eight pounds and six ounces. The effective range of the gun is about three-quarters of a mile and its accuracy at that distance is as great as that of any other arm in the United States.

The company is now manufacturing four different sizes of guns, an army carbine, weighing 5 pounds, 6 ounces, a light sporting rifle, weighing 6½ pounds, a heavy sporting rifle, weighing 8 pounds, 5 ounces, and one an ounce heavier.

The manufactory is now busy on a government contract for carbines. The demand for sporting rifles is greater than the supply, and the manufactory will have to be enlarged to enable it to furnish enough for the trade.

This arm has been commended highly by the chief of ordnance bureau and by many prominent sportsment and soldiers. As a sporting rifle it possesses great advantages over others and is fast superseding all rivals. Wisconsin inventors have introduced many useful improvements in every department of science, but none is more important than the invention of this breech-loading arm. Mr. Lee has made the construction of firearms a life study, and has succeeded in bringing perfec-

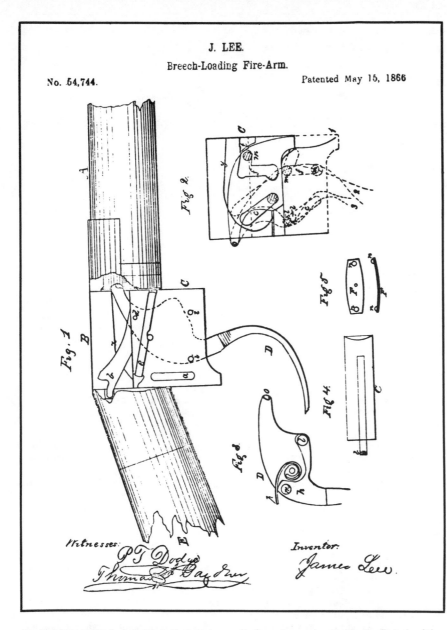

J. LEE.
Breech-Loading Fire-Arm.

No. 54,744.

Patented May 15, 1866

Fig. 1
Fig. 2
Fig. 3
Fig. 4
Fig. 5
Fig. 6

Witnesses:
P T Dodge
Thomas ... Gardner

Inventor:
James Lee.

Fig. 6
James Lee's patent 54,744 of May 15, 1866, was the basis for the actions shown in figs. 7 and 8. See text for details.

...." On December 20, 1866, after completing the visit, Col. McAllister filed his report.[4]

Lee's Claim Settled

In January, 1867, James Lee wrote to the Secretary of War, E.M. Stanton, requesting compensation for the expenses incurred while attempting to fulfill the contract for the carbines. In due course the request found its way to the then Chief of Ordnance, Bvt. Major General A.B. Dyer. In his reply to Stanton, dated February 18, 1867, Gen. Dyer stated that Mr. Lee had acted in good faith, and should be compensated. But instead of requesting that the contract be fulfilled for 1000 carbines at $18 each, he recommended a compromise. Assuming that Lee's total expenses at the date of McAllister's report were $20,350.15, the tools and equipment were worth $6,000, and that rifles and parts on hand could be sold for $6,175, the net loss would only be $8,175.15, which the government should be willing to share to the extent of $4,087.57. This method of settlement, according to Dyer, would thus save the government a minimum of at least $6,000.

A year later, the matter still not settled, Lee wrote to Washington protesting the unfairness of the suggested settlement. In turn Dyer stated that Lee had no claim other than the "one of damage which . . . could only be . . . properly acted on by legislative authority." This was in accordance with the Congressional act of March 3, 1863, and in December, 1868, "General Jurisdiction Case No. 3263: James Lee vs. the United States" was decided.

The verdict depended on whether the carbine was to have been 42 caliber or 44 caliber, which in turn depended on when the contract originated. Lee maintained that the letter of May 7, 1864, accepting the carbine evaluated the month before, constituted the contract, and the carbines submitted later followed this accepted pattern. The Government maintained the order dated April 18, 1865, calling for ". . . one thousand breech-loading carbines Cal. 44 . . ." was the actual contract.

Lee had asked $12,000 for expenses and $3,000 for damages. The Court awarded him $6,175 for damages only, since he ". . . still maintains his machinery and a large amount of material . . ." Interestingly, the Court held the letter of May 7, 1864, to be the valid contract and advanced the opinion, "When the carbines were needed the calibre was not a matter of serious importance; when they were not needed,[5] the calibre became the controlling element . ."

It is almost certain that by this time Lee's Fire Arms Company was no longer in business. The attempt to sell the civilian market had failed and only 102 carbines had been sold by December of 1866, and these at a loss of $4.50 each. The rifles and carbines were not advertised after November, 1866, and the firm is not listed in the Milwaukee city directories after 1867.

tion in this gun. We feel a pride in the success of the invention as should every resident of Wisconsin.

After reading this article, one begins to wonder whether it was written by a reporter for the newspaper or by an advertising agency. The facts do not bear out some of the statements made in the article.

Under the heading "Fire Arms and Ammunition" the same issue carried an advertisement that appeared periodically into November, 1866. It read:

Lee's Fire Arms Company on the Canal water power, Milwaukee, are manufacturing Lee's Patent Breech-Loading Rifle which the company now offer to the public.

The company own the patent and are the exclusive manufacturers of the Arm in the United States.

In offering to the public this Gun the company claim that it is more complete and perfect in every particular, and cheaper than any other arm in use. The superiority of **LEE'S PATENT BREECH-LOADING RIFLE,** consists in its simplicity of mechanism—it having only about one-half the number of pieces that other breech-loading guns have.

Its Superior workmanship, the Barrels of the finest Decarbonized Cast Steel. Rifled in the most approved manner in 6 grooves of equal width to the lands, sharp Whitworth twist, once round in 23 inches—its rapidity in firing over all others. It can be fired 20 times per minute, or from 10 to 12 times per minute with one hand. It has a greater Accuracy, Force and Penetration, with the same quantity of powder, than any other breech-loading rifle, and more than double the force and penetration of any muzzle-loading gun ever made. With 23 grains of powder (only about one-quarter the quantity the Berdan gun requires), it will throw a half-ounce ball of 44-100 of an inch calibre through 10 inches of green, or 12 inches of seasoned pine timber.

In November, 1866, one Lt. Col. J. McAlister visited the ". . . armory of Mr. Lee . . ." in order to ". . . examine into the progress that has been made, the expenditures incurred and the materials on hand for filling the contract, and report the same with such remarks and recommendations respecting a settlement of the case

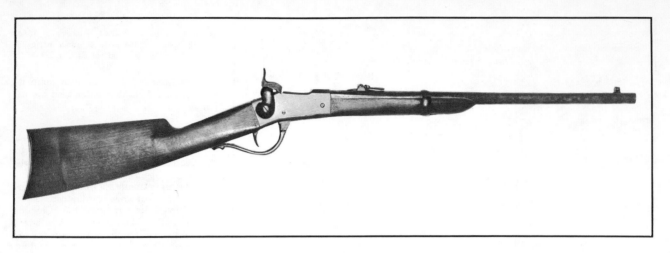

Fig. 7

A rifle based on Lee's 1866 patent. The interior design follows the patent specifications closely but not exactly. The frame is of bronze, other action components are of steel or iron. A number 5 appears on several parts, but the gun is unmarked otherwise.

There are many unanswered questions connected with James Paris Lee and his activities, not the least of which are the dates of his residence in various cities. When the Lee family left Stevens Point for Milwaukee is not exactly known. James Lee is not listed in the Milwaukee city directory until 1866, nor in Stevens Point after the autumn of 1864. It is probable, therefore, that the move took place at about the same time of the formation of Lee's Fire Arms Company. Lee doubtless had been in Milwaukee numerous times previously and would have made several contacts. The Lee residence is listed as 130 Prospect in the 1866 to 1873/74 city directories, although Lee is listed with Lee's Fire Arms Company only in 1866 and 1867. In 1900 a boyhood friend of Lee wrote that Lee had gone to Ilion, N.Y., to work at the Remington factory following the failure of the Milwaukee business. Lee had become acquainted with the Remingtons previously, having used their barrels for his Milwaukee-made carbines and rifles, and it was a tradition of the Remington firm at this time to invite inventors to use the facilities at the Remington Armory. Thus the Lee family apparently stayed in Milwaukee while James Lee worked in Ilion, at least until after May, 1874, when the *Milwaukee Daily Sentinal* noted that Lee had gone east to renew tests of his gun at Springfield (Armory).

The type of arm made at the Milwaukee factory was based on U.S. Patent No. 35,941. As previously mentioned, the patent model was for a single shot pistol having a spur trigger and a barrel which pivoted horizontally to the left. A tongue on the barrel breech prevented vertical play. The centrally positioned outside hammer was designed so that when it was in the half-cock position the barrel could be swung out for loading. But when the hammer was fully cocked the barrel could not be moved. Extraction of the fired case was done by a manual movement of an extractor sliding in a groove on the right side of the barrel. The rim of the case was acted upon in much the same manner as in double barrel shotguns.

The frame provided for a separate steel breech plate, indicating the frame was to be produced from a softer metal, and at least one brass frame pistol of this same basic design is known to exist. It is said to have a single 6 stamped on the breech of the 44-caliber barrel, which is 8⅝ inches long. Over-all length is reported to be 13 inches.

The Pilot Rifle

Of the long arms based on this patent—32 are reported to exist—none have spur triggers and the barrels all pivot to the right instead of to the left. Two different standing breech shapes exist, as shown in fig. 1. with the rifles having one shape and the carbines another; carbine breeches also vary slightly in height. The arms were apparently available chambered for three different rimfire calibers, although only two—44 and 38—were advertised, but for exactly which cartridges is a matter for debate. Herbert Uphoff has said that the 44 Henry and 44 Ballard Long cartridges will chamber in some of the 44 caliber arms, but the possibilities of others cannot be overlooked.

The 38 caliber cartridge may have been the 38 Extra Long, but the first mention of a 38 caliber appears in the 1866 advertisments, or about when the 44-caliber carbine was rejected for military use. Yet a recent Norm Flayderman catalog listed a Lee rifle with 1864 markings chambered for a 38 rimfire cartridge.

Several arms were no doubt made prior to the formation of Lee's Fire Arms Company, but only one specimen—a carbine—is known to exist today, unless the just-mentioned 38 caliber rifle is one, which is doubtful. Crudely made, this early carbine resembles the later models but has a differently shaped stock and front sight, and a slightly longer barrel, plus other minor differences. The barrel is very unevenly stamped, on the left side, near the breech, in three lines. The double S in "Pariss" is so stamped!

LEE. PAT. JAMES. PARISS. LEE
1862
STEVENS. POINT. WIS

The greatest difference between this carbine, stamped with a number 1 under the barrel, and the later models is the degree to which the barrel may be swung aside for loading—about 170 degrees to the right, compared to some 8 degrees for the later models based on the same patent. The patent provided for a barrel stop, but this particular carbine does not have one.

Uphoff thinks this carbine is possibly the sample submitted for testing as a standard in June, 1864, since it has the improved extractor on the bottom of the barrel, instead of the side-mounted type mentioned in the patent.

The sights on the carbines are of Burnside type—dovetailed front blade, and an L-shaped rear, secured to the barrel by a single screw, and having notches for 100 and 500 yards, with a notched aperture for 300 yards. The rifle has a dovetailed front sight, similar to those on the carbines, and an L-shaped rear sight, with a reversible slide having different notches, dovetailed into the barrel.

The carbines made in the Milwaukee factory, if marked, are neatly stamped in about the same barrel position as on the Stevens Point carbine, but in two lines, as follows:

LEE'S FIRE ARMS CO. MILWAUKEE, WIS
PAT.ᴰ- JULY 22 ᴰ- 1862.

Rifles were stamped the same way, but in a single line on the top of the barrel.

Carbines and rifle barrel lengths vary from those advertised, apparently because of very liberal manufacturing tolerances. Reported barrel lengths of known carbines range from 21 to 21½ inches, except for No. 1, which has a barrel of 21¹⁵/₁₆ inches long and all barrels are 44 caliber. Rifle barrels vary from 25¼ to 30¾ inches; the average 44-caliber barrel runs 29 inches, the 38-caliber barrels averaging 28¾ inches. This would tend to indicate that the two extremes may not have been standard rifles, but possibly special orders. The barrels were rifled as noted in the advertisment, except for the original sample, which has been reported to have five grooves and a gain twist.

Many of the carbines have sling bars and rings on the left side of the frame. Apparently all of the contract models were so intended, but only two of the known rifle specimens have sling swivels. Of these two rifles only No. 1659 is considered authentic; the front swivel is mounted on a base dovetailed into the barrel about 18 inches ahead of the breech, while the rear swivel is on a plate inletted into the stock 7 inches from the toe.

Here are many unanswered questions concerning the Milwaukee firm and the Lee carbines and rifles based on the 1862 patent. Why are no low number models known? The lowest number located—after the Stevens Point model—is 1247, a rifle. What happened to the rest of the 255 finished carbines, of which 102 had been sold, as reported on December 20, 1866? Were they numbered consecutively? Were the parts for the rest of the contract carbines destroyed, or were they used to produce civilian carbines and rifles to order? This suggests the reason for the apparent random numbering arrangement of the known rifles and carbines. Whatever the answers, Lee carbines and rifles do exist, but obviously Lee's Fire Arms Company of Milwaukee did not fare well.

Rare Lee Design

James Lee continued to work on a better rifle design, even while attempting to sell the 1862 design and attending to his work on Canal Street. On May 15, 1866, shortly after work had been suspended on the military carbines, U.S. Patent No. 54,744 was issued to "James Lee, of Milwaukee, Wisconsin." The specifications list the patent as an "Improvement in Breech-Loading Fire-Arms," but the drawing is for a "Breech-Loading Fire-Arm." The action of this arm comprised a rectangular breechblock of "iron," moving vertically in the receiver well, and operated by an under lever with an extractor at its forward end. The front of the breechblock was beveled on the upper edge to help force the cartridge into the chamber. A small metal bar was recessed into the top of the breechblock in such a way that when the lever was operated to lower the block "... the rear end of (the bar) is held up, while its front end is carried down with the block, thereby forming an inclined way extending from the lower side of the bore up to the top of the frame...up which the cartridge-shell slides when thrown out by the ejector." The whole affair resembled a merging of the Peabody design of 1862 and the Sharps design of 1848.*

Lee had mentioned to his friend James Young that while at the Remington plant he tried not only all kinds of experiments,

but that his thoughts, both day and night, became so absorbed with them that sleep often became impossible. Sleep may have been impossible, but ideas were not, for the 1870s were the most productive of Lee's inventive years.

On May 16, 1871, U.S. Patent No. 114, 951 was issued to "James Lee, of Milwaukee, Wisconsin, Assignor to Philo Remington, of Ilion, New York." This patent was also listed as an "Improvement ..." and consisted of a Martini-type action, with the breechblock hinged at the rear and tilted downward by the movement of a lever which served as the trigger guard. A centrally mounted outside hammer was used, the mainspring fastened to the lower tang. Although the breechblock was lowered by the use of the lever, the design was such that "... the hammer can be used for operating said block—as, for instance, in closing it as the hammer is drawn back to the full-cock."

Initial movement of the lever lowered the breechblock, with its concave top surface, to guide the cartridge into the chamber, and continued movement activated an extractor to withdraw the empty case. At the same time the lever movement forced the hammer to the halfcock position and retracted the firing pin. Chambering a fresh cartridge caused the breechblock to rise enough to hold the cartridge in place, after which the closing could be finished by the use of the lever or the hammer. This 1871 version apparently did not progress beyond the prototype stage, but it was the basis for some later Lee designs.

On June 20, 1871, U.S. Patent No. 116, 068, for another "Improvement ..." was issued to James Lee as before and assigned to Philo Remington. Again the design was for a Martini-type action with a centrally located outside hammer, but the under lever had disappeared and the breechblock was operated by the hammer alone. Examination of the patent drawings indicates that this was probably one of the rifles entered in the Army trials the next year, possibly rifle No. 54, having a solid

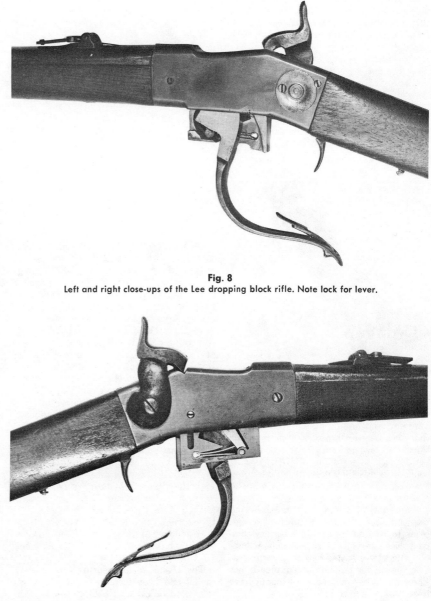

Fig. 8
Left and right close-ups of the Lee dropping block rifle. Note lock for lever.

*The only specimen of this Lee patent design to appear so far is owned by John T. Amber, editor of the Gun Digest. A Short rifle or carbine, it has a military style barrel of about 52 caliber, rifled with three broad grooves. The "small metal bar" mentioned above is pivoted in the top of the breechblock, near the middle. Its rear end is hooked to catch on the top rear of the receiver mortise, which is not as it appears in the patent drawing. Besides acting as an inclined plane for the ejection of fired cases, the slender steel bar also served as a loading tray or platform. The receiver is of brass, but all other action components are of iron or steel. As the illustrations show, there is a locking arrangement for the lever. The number 5 appears on several action parts, but the gun is unmarked otherwise. The exact cartridge called for is not certain, but one of the Spencer bottleneck types appears likely.

frame and a two-piece stock.

Pulling the hammer back to the half-cock notch caused a hook to retract the firing pin, and lowered the breechblock to the loading position. In the lowest position the breechblock would strike the tail of the extractor, causing it to pivot and throw out the empty case. The extractor then continued on around to catch on the front or free end of the breechblock, holding it in the lowered position. Chambering a fresh cartridge would shove the extractor forward, releasing the breechblock and allowing it to spring up into the closed position under tension from the mainspring. After this, ". . . the hammer may then be brought to the full-cock, and the arm fired."

Unique Mainspring

This June, 1871, design used a unique U-shaped mainspring, the only other spring in the arm being a short, flat, trigger spring. The mainspring ". . . is attached to and moves with the hammer, and has no fixed position . . . yet performs all the duties of an expansile and contractile spring . . . to raise the breechblock and to attach and detach a hook . . . to and from the breechblock." "The advantage of a . . . mainspring so hung is this: being support-

ed at the two ends on and moving with the hammer, and having no sliding bearings, there is no power lost in friction. It avoids the use of a swivel or other intermediate or extra piece to fasten to or with, as now used. It avoids the necessity of extending the guard-strap back to afford a point of attachment."

Excluding pins and a single screw the total number of parts in this 1871 design came to 10, and the action was very compact. Even so, the design was not acceptable when later tested by the government. The reason for the non-acceptance is not known, but the hook mechanism may have been susceptible to breakage.

Fig. 9
The M1875 Lee-Springfield rifle. Caliber 45-70, 32½-inch barrel, 49¼ inches over-all. Markings on tang of receiver are: U.S. PAT. MARCH 16, 1875. The tang of the buttplate is marked U.S. All three swivels are missing—the rear one found at the front of the trigger guard, and the two at the front band; one was for stacking.

On January 2, 1872, U.S. Patent No. 122,470 for an "Improvement . . ." was issued to Lee, this one also assigned to E. Remington & Sons. This improvement covered a cartridge extractor, trigger lock, and barrel band without swivel for a rolling block action. Apparently this patent covered no more than it said, indicating that Lee was working for the Remingtons at this time, at least to the extent of improving the Remington rolling block design. These were being manufactured in considerable quantities at this time.

January 16, 1872, saw the issuance of U.S. Patent No. 122,772 for yet another "Improvement . . ." to "James Lee, of Milwaukee, Wisconsin." Curiously this patent was not assigned to anyone or to any firm, and might indicate that Lee had returned to Wisconsin to work on his own designs, with the idea still of interesting the government in one of them. Like two previous arms, the 1872 design was for a Martini-type action, the breechblock hinged at the rear and free at the front. The mechanism was also hammer operated, but unlike the 1871 design.

The U-shaped mainspring of the 1871 model had been located below the hammer, and below and behind the breech-

block. The 1872 design used a V-shaped spring ahead of the hammer and directly below the breechblock. This spring ". . . in addition to its duty as a mainspring, also serves to keep the hammer and breechblock in their relative working positions, and to keep the firing-pin in the breechblock." The operation was now based on a ". . . two-part hammer with an articulated joint between them, . . . so that one part may have a slight movement independent of the other part, and so that the first movement of the upper part shall impart a backward movement to the under part to remove the hammer from the firing-pin." The first movement with the 1871 design had been to pull the hammer back to the halfcock position to lower the breechblock; with the 1872 design the first step was to press the thumb-piece of the hammer forward to relieve the pressure on the firing pin, with continued pressure lowering the breechblock. After a fresh cartridge was chambered, the breechblock was raised by pulling back on the thumb-piece ". . . as in the act of cocking, which will first raise the breech to a closed position, and by continuing that motion will cock the arm."

One other noteworthy feature of the 1872 design was its take-down. "The breechblock, hammer, and mainspring can all be removed together without disturbing their relative positions by taking out the pin that the breechblock swings on, which, for cleaning or repairs, is quite important."

The 1872 design, coupled with the extractor of the 1871 design, was tested during the government trials of 1872 as entry No. 61. Like the previous 1871 design, it used a solid receiver and a two-piece stock; the buttstock was secured by a throughbolt screwing into the base of the frame, in the same manner as the Peabody-Martini.

On June 6, 1872, Congress approved the

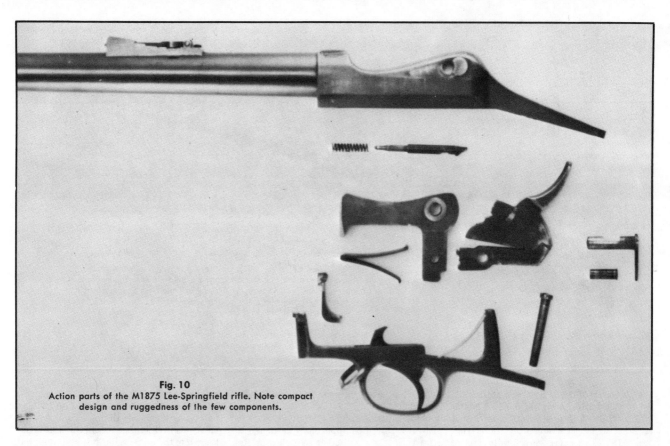

Fig. 10
Action parts of the M1875 Lee-Springfield rifle. Note compact
design and ruggedness of the few components.

appointment by the Secretary of War of a "Board for the Selecting of a Breech-System for Muskets and Carbines" to consist of one general officer, one ordnance officer, and one line officer each from the cavalry, infantry, and artillery. $150,000 were appropriated for manufacturing the arm selected.

1872 Trials

The Board met on September 3, 1872, and continued in session until May 5, 1873. During this time a total of 95 arms or models were examined and/or tested, including 9 arms of foreign manufacture and three designs by James Paris Lee.* The Lee arms were entries No. 53, 54, and 61, and all were listed as "Muskets, calibre .50." The Board stated that ". . . the service .50 calibre musket-cartridge was employed whenever possible . . ."

Firing tests were conducted at Springfield Armory and, after nearly 25,000 rounds had been fired, the tests were concluded. A total of 21 arms were then selected for more severe tests. Of Lee's designs, only No. 61 was among the semi-finalists; it was not selected when this group was later narrowed to the 6 arms that ultimately resulted in the selection of the Springfield "trapdoor" design—later to become the famous Model 1873.

The author has been unable to locate either the arm or the patent relating to entry No. 53 in the 1872 trials. This gun apparently used a sliding bolt in somewhat the same manner as the straight-pull design of 1895. However, a cam-lever at the

*Based on Lee patents and descriptions given in the Ordnance Board reports, entry No. 54 was constructed on Lee's patent No. 116,068 of June 20, 1871, and entry No. 61 is covered by Lee's patent No. 122,722 of Jan. 16, 1872.

upper rear of the bolt was used to lock and unlock the bolt by camming a lug on the underside of the bolt down into and up out of a recess in the receiver. This arm also had a one-piece stock and ejection of the empty cartridge cases was upward.

While the Springfield conversion design had been adopted by the Army, the search for a better one went on, and apparently the 1872 Lee model (No. 61 above) had made an impression, for in 1874 Congress approved the expenditure of $10,000 for further development of the Lee design.

On March 16, 1875, James Lee was issued U.S. Patent No. 160,919 for another "Improvement . . ." The application had been filed on May 9, 1874, the last time Lee is mentioned in the Milwaukee papers as being in Milwaukee, he having gone east to renew tests of his gun at Springfield.[6]

The 1875 model used a one-piece stock following the contours of the 1873 Springfield stock, with the barrel, bands, band springs, swivels, sights, buttplate and ramrod also following the 1873 pattern. It was only logical to use the Springfield parts, since the Lee and Springfield models were both being manufactured at the Armory, with the Lee rifle on a trial basis for testing.

The V-shaped mainspring of the 1872 model was retained in the 1875 model, and pushing forward on the thumbpiece of the hammer lowered the breechblock, causing its bottom edge to strike the extractor, thus ejecting the empty case and locking the breechblock in the loading position. (According to the patent specifications the mainspring, not the breechblock, struck the extractor to eject the case, but in the manufactured rifle it is the breechblock.) Shoving a fresh cartridge into the chamber moved the extractor out of the way, un-

locking the breechblock and allowing it to rise automatically, via the compressed mainspring. The gun could then be cocked and fired as usual. The entire loading and ejecting process could be done so rapidly that Lee said: ". . . I have fired 30 cartridges in about three-fourths of a minute, taking each cartridge by hand separately from the cartridge-box."

If the Lee was not to be fired immediately after loading the hammer could be moved back until a "click" was heard, which indicated that the breechblock was fully locked and the firing pin had been retracted. The rifle was "safe" in this position. When the rifle was to be fired immediately after loading the final locking of the breechblock was accomplished during the cocking of the hammer, not as a separate movement.

With a barrel length of 32½ inches and a length over-all of 49¼ inches, the M1875 Lee was still more than 2½ inches shorter than the issue Springfield with the same barrel length. This was due to its compact receiver, which also permitted it to be in-letted into the stock with a simple mortise.

Another feature of this Lee design was its unique take-down. A lip on the front edge of the trigger guard assembly, with attached trigger and trigger spring, slipped into a notch in the lower part of the receiver ring below the barrel, and a single bolt through the rear tang held everything together—simplicity itself.

Only 143 of the M1875 Lee-Springfield rifles were manufactured, according to the Ordnance Report for June 30, 1875, the appropriation having been expended. The design failed to dislodge the Springfield as the issue rifle of the Army; in fact the single-shot Springfield reigned supreme as

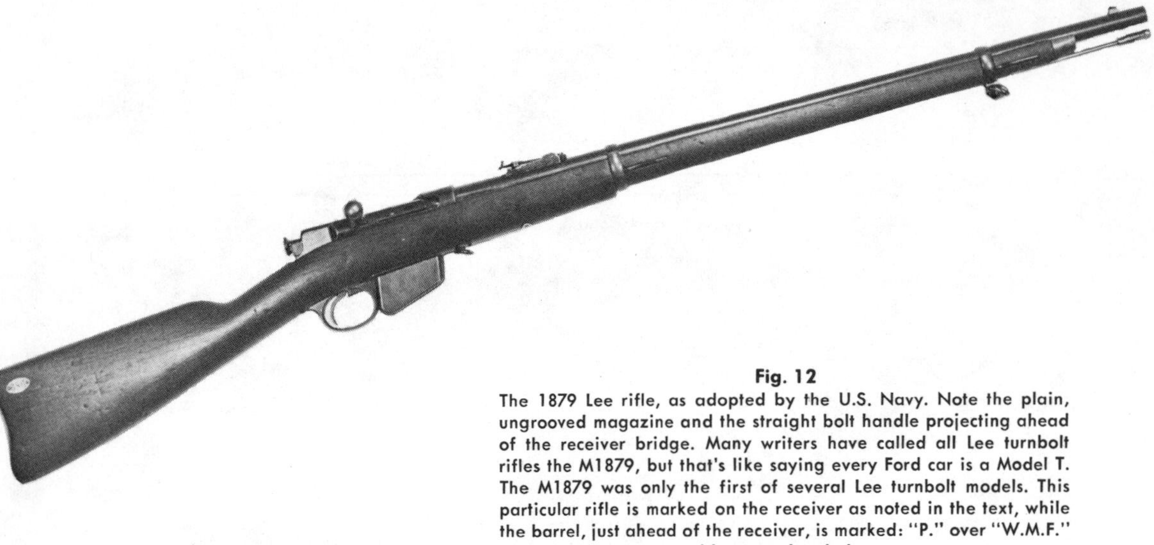

Fig. 12
The 1879 Lee rifle, as adopted by the U.S. Navy. Note the plain, ungrooved magazine and the straight bolt handle projecting ahead of the receiver bridge. Many writers have called all Lee turnbolt rifles the M1879, but that's like saying every Ford car is a Model T. The M1879 was only the first of several Lee turnbolt models. This particular rifle is marked on the receiver as noted in the text, while the barrel, just ahead of the receiver, is marked: "P." over "W.M.F." with an anchor below.

the choice (?) of the U.S. Army until 1892, many years after other nations had adopted breech-loading magazine rifles. Stored at Rock Island Arsenal after their trial, the M1875 Lee rifles were finally sold at one of the government auctions for $36 each.

1875 Design Fails

The March, 1896, issue of the now long-defunct English Arms & Explosives magazine reported that in 1875 Mr. James Lee had offered the British authorities a Martini-Henry rifle with the block operated by the hammer, instead of by the lever, and in various trials it had given some wonderful results in the rapidity of firing. Spare cartridges were carried in a single column type magazine, but not fixed to the rifle, which was a single shot. Instead, the magazine, which would hold 30 rounds, was hung from the left shoulder. Upward of 28 shots per minute were fired with the rifle, but it still did not satisfy the requirements of the British for a new rifle. The model offered the British was no doubt the solid-frame Martini-type based on the 1872 patent, rather than the model which was produced at the Springfield Armory about this time.

A vertical (Martini-type) action Remington-Lee rifle, which resembles the Springfield model but which would not chamber a 45-70 cartridge, was listed in Flayderman's catalog No. 70. It had a two-piece stock with full military fore-end and two bands. The barrel length was given as 32½ inches, with Remington markings on top. Minor manufacturing differences, such as frame contours, top of the breechblock, etc., indicate that this may have been an 1872 model of the type offered to the British.

On April 27, 1875, U.S. Patent No. 162, 481 was issued to Lee for a magazine box, but the specifications have not been located. It is therefore not known whether this is the magazine referred to in the British trials above.

Following his failure to interest the British in a rifle, Lee apparently returned to the U.S. to work for the Winchester Repeating Arms Co., for whom he is reported to have developed a refinement of their lever action Model 73. This was in 1877, and he was still attempting to perfect a rifle the U.S. government would accept.

On August 7, 1877, U.S. Patent No. 193, 831 was issued to Lee, "of Milwaukee . . . ," also covering an "Improvement . . ." The application was dated October 9, 1876. (Lee is not listed as being in Milwaukee after 1874, but three years later this address still appears on patent papers.)

The 1877 design was also based on a hammer-operated Martini action. The breechblock was lowered by shoving forward on the thumbpiece of the hammer, but the hammer was a one-piece type instead of the two-piece as previously. The new hammer was a rebounding model, only in contact with the firing pin during the firing cycle. The V-shaped mainspring, with spurs added, was the only spring in the entire action, performing all necessary acts required of a spring. Other improvements were in the shape of the firing pin, the pivot pin for the breechblock, and the sear, plus a slightly reshaped receiver and trigger guard assembly. Altogether there were only 15 parts in the 1877 design, including 7 pins. The design was simple, easy to operate, and apparently reliable, but the fact remained that it was a single shot at a time when repeaters were becoming the vogue.

In accordance with an act of Congress dated November 21, 1877, another Ordnance Board was convened for the purpose of selecting a magazine rifle. This time a total of 29 arms were examined, and No. 25 was one entered by James Lee of Hartford, Conn. (As noted above, the 1877 patent was issued to Lee at Milwaukee, but the rifle entered in the trials a few months later places Lee in Hartford, Conn. Later patents will include Ilion, N.Y., and again Hartford.) Which Lee model this was is not known to the author, but it is assumed that it is the 1877 design, possibly with the magazine mentioned previously. This opinion is based on Lee's statement that the 1877 design ". . . can be loaded and fired at the rate of 37 times per minute, . . ." Regardless, it was beaten out when the Board selected the Winchester-manufactured Hotchkiss, and recommended that $20,000 be spent toward obtaining a trial lot for field testing.

1879 Bolt Action

Returning to the Remington Armory in Ilion, Lee was provided a workshop by Philo Remington, and such assistance as he needed. His perseverance at last paid off, for in 1878 the Lee bolt action rifle, capable of firing 30 rounds a minute, became a reality. On September 6, 1878, application was filed for a patent, and on November 4, 1879, U.S. Patent No. 221, 328 was granted to "James Lee, of Ilion, New York," for a design that was to become the most famous of all Lee rifles.

Alden Hatch in his book *Remington Arms in American History* relates a curious tale about Lee. During 1878 and 1879, while Lee was working on his bolt action rifle, he was living in a room at the Osgood Hotel in Ilion. He frequently took his drawings and models back to his room to work on them at night. The room directly above his was rented by an enterprising German, who also worked for Remington. It has been said that the German bored a hole in the floor of his room and lay on his stomach for hours, his eye glued to the hole to watch what went on below. The name of the German? Franz Mauser, a brother of the inventors of the Mauser repeating rifle —Peter Paul and Wilhelm Mauser. Whether the watching was profitable or

Fig. 13
Another M1879 Lee, the bolt opened. Compare rear sight here with that shown in fig. 12—which appears to be a replacement and is on backwards from the normal arrangement.

not is debatable, as the Mauser rifles were not equipped with box magazines until 1886. However, the fact remains that Lee later sued the Mauser brothers for patent infringement.

Lee apparently wanted to manufacture his rifle on his own, so the Lee Arms Company of Bridgeport, Conn. was formed sometime in 1879 in order to do so.[7] The address of the firm, at the foot of Clinton Avenue, next to the New Haven Railroad, was the same as that of the Sharps Rifle Company, which was listed in the Bridgeport city directories until 1886. Apparently Lee's financial backers were also of the same group, for E.G. Westcott, president of the Sharps Rifle Company in 1879, was later listed as treasurer of the Lee Arms Company. Previous to 1878, Westcott was listed as president and treasurer of the Sharps firm, but in a rare Sharps folder dated 1878, and apparently intended for British trade, Westcott is listed as vice-president and treasurer, and A.W. Winchester is president. In 1881-82, after the Sharps firm had ceased operations, Winchester is listed as the Sharps treasurer. The backers apparently lost interest in the rifle manufacturing business shortly after the new Lee firm was formed. The last Sharps catalog consisted of an 1879 edition with a blue 1880 price list attached, and operations were suspended in October, 1880, after only a few of the Lee rifles had been manufactured.[8]

The Lee patents were taken over by Remington, a natural move since the rifle had been developed at the Remington Armory, and the manufacture transferred to Ilion under license. The rifles were produced by Remington for the Lee Arms Company, which continued to act as the selling agent, commercially advertising the rifle in the *Army & Navy Journal* from April 13 to November 27, 1880.

The 1879 patent was very simple and direct. It provided for a "... bolt-gun hav-

ing an opening through the bottom of its shoe or receiver, a detachable magazine ... with rear and of different lengths ... to allow the cartridges to lie therein in an inclined position, and with their flanges (rims) overlapping one another ..." It also provided for two other magazine modifications, including one that circled the gun stock, a firing pin with a knob on the end to allow the pin to be drawn back by hand or to the halfcock position, an extractor and a ".... curved sliding plate (cut-off) ... to allow the rifle ... to be used as a single-loader ..." The actual arm followed the patent specifications closely.

The first rifles were marked on the upper left side of the receiver:

**The Lee Arms Co. Bridgeport Conn.
U.S.A.
Patented Nov. 4th 1879**

This was followed by a serial number and an inspector's initials, such as W.W.K., W.M.F., and P. Rifles purchased by the U.S. Navy were also stamped with **U.S.** above an anchor.

The straight bolt handle projected to the right, just forward of the receiver bridge. The one-piece bolt cocked on closing. There were two locking lugs, consisting of the root of the bolt handle with its integral guide rib, and a small lug directly opposite which locked into the left side of the receiver. The cocking piece knob was small, flat, and smooth. The rotating extractor slipped into the front of the bolt and was retained by a hooked piece which fitted into the guide rib. The degree of rotation of the extractor was established by a groove in the bolt body just ahead of the guide rib.

The barrels, 29½ inches long, were rifled with 5 wide grooves. Over-all length was 48½ inches, weight about 8½ pounds.

A gas escape port was located in the left side of the receiver ring ¾-inch back of the forward edge, in the event of case failure. The firing pin could be drawn back to the

halfcock position to serve as a safety when carrying it with a live round in the chamber.

The M1879 stock extended to within three inches of the muzzle and had a nose cap. Two bands were used, both retained with conventional leaf springs. The upper band held a sling swivel; the lower swivel was retained by a front trigger-guard screw. A cleaning rod fitted into a groove in the bottom of the fore-end and extended to the muzzle. There was no upper handguard and the grip of the stock was straight. The buttplate was of steel, curved, in the same basic shape as on the Springfield M1873.

Two different rear sights have been observed on the M1879. The more common one is a folding tangent, graduated on the notched elevation slide to 500 yards, and on the leaf to 1200 yards. It is adjustable for windage by sliding the crossbar, which has "buckhorn" side elements.

The M1879 was chambered for the 43 Spanish, 44-77 (bottleneck), 45-70 Gov't. and 45-90 Winchester cartridges. The magazine held 5 cartridges and was plain, without grooves or corrugations.

Both sporting and military versions of the M1879 were apparently produced. However, the bulk of the production was the military model.

In 1876 the Navy Bureau of Ordnance had recommended that "... we should adopt a magazine gun, which for naval purposes is in every respect preferable." By 1879 a total of 2500 of the 45-caliber Hotchkiss rifles had been bought for testing. A year later, in the Annual Report of the Secretary of the Navy, mention was made that the Hotchkiss guns, along with 250 each of the Remington Keene and Lee guns—chambered for the 45-70 Gov't. cartridge—were enough to arm the 75 ships then in commission with repeating rifles, and to test the relative value of the three systems—magazine in butt, beneath the barrel, and detachable.

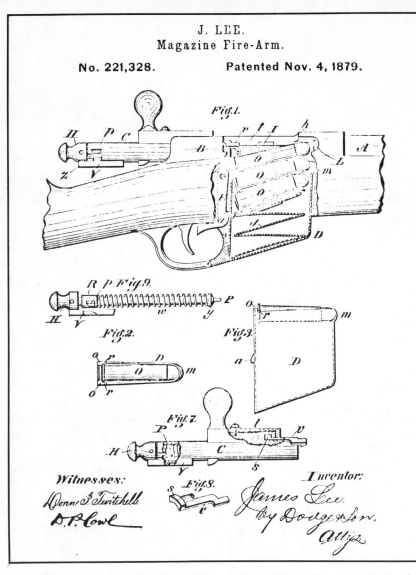

J. LEE.
Magazine Fire-Arm.

No. 221,328.   Patented Nov. 4, 1879.

Fig.1.

R P Fig.9.

Fig.2.   Fig.3.

Fig.7.

Witnesses: Fig.8.   Inventor:
Donn J. Turtchell.   James Lee.
D. P. Cowl   by Dodge & Son,
      Attys.

Fig. 11
One of the most important U.S. patents ever issued was that of November 4, 1879. Number 221,328 covered the invention of James Paris Lee for a rifle with a detachable box magazine.

with the "Red Jacket" revolvers; the main flaw is the apparent term of existence for the firm—1877-80. Gardner says Roland L. Brewer of Pittston, Pa., (1878-84) was granted U.S. Patent No. 239,914 on April 5, 1881, for a revolving firearm, the patent assigned to J.F. Lee, of Wilkes-Barre. The last name and the location are right for the Lee Arms Co. making revolvers. The same Brewer was later issued three firearms patents—assigned to the Colt. This would seem to indicate the maker of "Red Jacket" revolvers was J.F. Lee, not J.P. Lee. Possibly some reader has further information.

8. What may have been one of the first M1879 Lee rifles apparently produced at the Sharps factory used parts identical to those on the M1879 Sharps-Borchardt military rifle. The rear sight is the same as the Borchardt, the two bands are Borchardt-type (secured with wood screws through the bottom instead of with springs as on the later production) and the buttplate is of flat checkered steel —Borchardt design. The 43 caliber barrel, 32½ inches long is rifled with 6 grooves. Total length is 51⅝ inches. No markings appear on the wood or metal. The magazine holds 5 cartridges. The bolt is one-piece but the handle is behind the bridge instead of in front as on the standard 1879 rifles. Only one such rifle is known.

Bibliography

The Fuller Collection of American Firearms, Harold L. Peterson, Eastern National Park & Monument Association, 1967.

Digest of U.S. Patents Relating to Breech Loading and Magazine Small Arms 1836-1873, by V.D. Stockbridge. Reprint by Norm Flayderman, Greenwich, Conn., 1963.

Small Arms Makers, Col. Robert Gardner, Bonanza Books, New York, 1963.

The Breech-Loader In The Service 1816-1917, Claude E. Fuller, N. Flayderman & Co. New Milford, Conn., 1965.

Guns Through the Ages, Geoffrey Boothroyd, Bonanza Books, New York, 1961.

"Lee's Firearms Co.," Herbert L. Uphoff, The *Gun Report,* June and July, 1967.

The Lee-Enfield Rifle, Major E.G.B. Reynolds, Herbert Jenkins, London, 1960.

Suicide Specials, Donald B. Webster, Jr., The Stackpole Company, Harrisburg, Pa., 1958.

The Book of Rifles, W.H.B. Smith and Jos. E. Smith, The Stackpole Company, Harrisburg, Pa., 1963.

"Model 1875 Lee-Springfield," Gordon F. Baxter, Jr., The *Gun Report,* November, 1960.

"Remington-Lee Rifle," Ludwig Olson, The *American Rifleman,* April, 1966.

"The Rifles of James Paris Lee," Robt. H. Rankin, *Guns & Ammo,* March, 1964.

Remington Arms in American History, Alden Hatch, Rinehart & Co., New York, 1956.

American Gun Makers, A. Gluckman and L.D. Satterlee, The Stackpole Company, Harrisburg, Pa., 1953.

The Rifle in America, Philip B. Sharpe, Funk & Wagnalls, New York, 1947.

The Gun and its Development, 9th ed., W.W. Greener, Reprint by Bonanza Books, New York, 1967.

"James Paris Lee," James Young, The *Saturday Globe,* Toronto, Can., June 9, 1900.

The United States Navy Rifle, Calibre 6 Millimeters, Model 1895, Description and Nomenclature, P.R. Alger and N.C. Twining, Lockwood & Brainard, Hartford, Conn., 1896.

"The Lee Straight-Pull Magazine Rifle," E.G. Parkhurst, *American Machinist,* November 22, 1900.

Winchester, The Gun That Won The West, H.F. Williamson, The Sportsman's Press, 1952.

In 1881 it was reported that the "... 300 Lee breech-loading rifles are being manufactured at the Remington Armory." By 1882 the 300 "Lee Arms Co." rifles had been delivered and introduced into the service.

Other countries buying the Model 1879 included Spain, Argentina, and China. The Chinese purchase was the basis for a humorous comment attributed to the inventor some years later. The Chinese were well pleased with the Model 1879, and had used the rifles to defeat some French troops. Afterward an eminent Chinese gentleman named Yung Wing brought several young Chinamen to the United States to complete their education at eastern colleges. Being in the area he stopped by Hartford to see James Lee at his home, and to compliment him on his rifles. During the conversation Lee jokingly commented that he was never quite sure whether the Chinese Government had selected his rifle on its merits, or because they believed its inventor to be a Chinaman, his name being Jim Lee.   ●

References

1. "Lee Firearms Company in Milwaukee," Harry Wandrus, **Hobbies**—The Magazine for Collectors, December, 1949.

2. H.L. Uphoff lists 6 of the same individuals as shareholders. The exception is an Alexander Mitchell, instead of Thomas L. Ogden. He also lists the president of the Board as Charles F. Ilsley, with James Kneeland, Daniel Wells, Jr., Lester Sexton, and James Lee as directors.

3. This was the only Ordnance Department contract granted to a mid-western arms company.

4. Col. McAllister reported that Lee had on hand 202 carbines in various stages of completion, and that 255 had been finished, 102 of these last sold at $22.50. A full list of the parts Lee had on hand was furnished, their cost, etc., and Col. McAllister noted that Lee stood to lose some $6500 if he finished his contract. A compromise settlement was suggested by Col. McAllister.

5. The Civil War was over.

6. Mention has been made in one source that James Lee enjoyed the distinction among private inventors of being moved by the government from his home at Stevens Point, Wis., to Springfield Armory in Massachusetts to supervise the manufacturing of his rifle. This is doubtful, since only the 1862 patent carried the Stevens Point address, and succeeding patents up to this time carried the Milwaukee address, plus the fact that Lee is listed as residing at 130 Prospect Street in the Milwaukee city directories during the 1866-1874 period. Possibly the government agreed to move his family from Milwaukee to Springfield so that they could be with him.

7. During this period another Lee Arms Co. came into being. Whether it was connected with James Paris Lee is moot. Gluckman and Gardner both list the Lee Arms Co. of Wilkes-Barre, Pa., as makers of "Red Jacket" rimfire revolvers around 1877-80, and Gardner indicates "... possibly before and after" this date, and tacked on "James Paris Lee." Sharpe says that Lee moved to Wilkes-Barre after he had sold his rifle rights to Remington, and there formed a new Lee Arms Co. to make a variety of rimfire revolvers. Only Sharpe and Gardner mention James Paris Lee as connected with the Wilkes-Barre firm, and only Sharpe actually states Lee formed the company. Apparently very little is known about this firm and its organization, but if James Paris Lee was connected with it, it represents his sole departure into the handgun field—other than his 1862 patent for a single shot handgun. This time factor is about correct, as many Lee designs originated during the 1870s. The author's opinion is that James Paris Lee was not connected

Today's MADE-IN-SPAIN Pistols

by MAJOR GEORGE C. NONTE, Jr.

Time was when Spanish auto pistols were—not to put too fine a point on it—junk. Not so now, for Astra, Star and Gabilondo are of good fit and finish, they are accurate and reliable.

THE SPANISH arms industry has a long and illustrious history. Who hasn't heard of Toledo blades? With the coming of modern handguns at the turn of the century, business really began booming in the areas around Eibar and Guernica. Those northern Spain centers gave birth to all manner of small and large companies busily engaged in the manufacture of automatic pistols—not to mention copies of U.S. revolver designs.

The total number of firms involved probably cannot even be determined nor, often, can existing guns even be traced to the original maker. Competition usually improves the breed, but in Spain it had the opposite effect. By the 1920s the quality of Spanish handguns was generally considered about the worst in the world. A few firms made good quality arms, as can readily be ascertained by examining the products of Unceta, Gabilondo, and Echeverria. But there were scores of other makers of guns so crude they've been known to come apart with mild factory loads. Most were poor copies of basic Browning or similar designs, roughly finished and sloppily fitted and assembled.

A great deal of this may be traced to so-called "Cottage Industry" practice. Small shops, often in a home, indifferently filed and finished (?)

rough castings and forgings supplied by one maker. Another shop might take barrels from one maker, slides or frames from another, small parts from somewhere else, and assemble guns. Virtually no control existed over tolerances or quality.

Somehow, it seems that the worst of the Spanish autos found their way to the U.S.A. By the mid 1930s, they were so poorly thought of that even a fine Spanish pistol was hard to give away. It is unfortunate that the same attitude still exists to a large degree. The virtually uncontrolled system that produced the bad pistols was not permitted to operate so loosely after the bloody Spanish Civil War. Whatever you might think of Francisco Franco otherwise, he did clean up the Spanish arms industry. Iberian handguns of today are of good quality, and have been for quite a number of years. Only Star, made by Bonifacio Echeverria; Babilondo y Cia. (both of Eibar) and Astra Unceta of Guernica now produce automatic pistols. The latter two also produce revolvers, but we'll not dwell on them here.

All three companies suffered considerably during the Spanish Civil War. Most records were destroyed so it is difficult to determine exactly what went on prior to about 1939-1940. In some instances, specific models exist, but absolutely no information on them is available at the factories.

At least some models of each make are currently distributed in this country and can be bought across the counter—the new law of the land permitting! In addition, the past decade has seen many thousands of surplus military pistols of all three makes sold here at attractive prices. This prompts many questions by shooters who have been told "Spanish pistols are no good." So, let's take a brief look first at the three firms, and later a review of the frequently encountered models.

Astra is the trade name of Unceta y Cia. The firm, founded in 1908, at first produced only pistol parts for other makers. In 1912, it began manufacture of the new Campo-Giro 9mm pistol for the Spanish army. These guns were superbly made, establishing a level of quality adhered to in Astra products from that time onward. I've examined dozens of Astra specimens made in the 1920s, 1930s, and 1940s, and they invariably show very fine workmanship throughout.

Unceta produced many other models over the years, but the name Astra has become virtually synonymous with the tubular-slide Model 400 (also known as 1921 Military Model) developed from the Campo-Giro. Many Browning-type 6.35mm and

Today's MADE-IN-SPAIN Pistols

7.65mm blowback pocket pistols were also produced—some of them under other names, principally Victoria.

Unceta has prospered and today produces excellent pistols, some models of which are distributed by Firearms International.* It also has the distinction of producing the 25 ACP automatic sold as the Colt Junior. This in itself speaks highly of modern Astras.

Gabilondo y Cia is another old-line firm, founded at Eibar in 1904 to produce revolvers. Not until 1914 did it begin making auto pistols, a move which brought it good fortune. The Ruby 7.65mm blowback pocket pistol of basic Colt/Browning design, was the first to be produced. It proved immediately popular, being reliable and well made. The French army ordered great quantities of Ruby pistols for WW I use, demand eventually raeching 30,000 per month. Gabilondo couldn't meet the requirement so they contracted with several other firms to produce the guns under the Ruby name. Eventually, about a dozen companies produced Ruby and Ruby-type pistols. These guns were not always up to Gabilondo standards and account for the derogatory remarks sometimes heard about Ruby pistols.

Following WW I Gabilondo produced well-made copies of the FN/Browning M1910 pistol under the names Ruby, Bufalo, and Danton. Copies of the Browning 6.35mm pistol were also produced, but in 1931, the larger-caliber Colt/Browning locked-breech guns were closely copied and produced under the Llama name. This continues today. These same guns were also produced by Gabilondo under the names Tauler and Ruby. All were well made and samples I've examined performed quite well.

Star Bonifacio Echeverria apparently began producing automatic pistols in 1906 or shortly thereafter. Early records were destroyed during the Spanish Civil War. The first guns were apparently 6.35mm and 7.65mm pocket pistols of conventional design. A 9mm (380) design was added later.

Star importance began to rise when, about 1919, it decided to market an improved version of the Colt/Browning locked-breech M1911 design. The locking system was copied accurately, but the firing mechanism changed entirely. The models 1920, 1921, and 1922 culminated in the Model A, which was widely sold in Latin America in 9mm and 45 caliber. This very good basic design is still produced

* See our Directory pages for addresses.

Astra M-600, in 9mm Parabellum, is a development of the M-400 in 9mm Largo. The M-600 was supplied in quantity to the German government during WW II.

Astra M 3000 was chambered in 7.65mm (32 ACP) and 9mmK (380 ACP) calibers, several thousand of the latter were delivered to the German government during WW II. The M-4000, shown here, is designated the Falcon but not imported here at present.

Table 1   Astra Pistols
F.I., importers

Model	Cal.	Mag. Cap.	Wt./ozs.	Lgth./ins.	Bbl./ins.	Price
Cub	22 Short	6	13	$4\frac{1}{2}$	$2\frac{1}{8}$	$39.95
Cub	25 ACP	6	13	$4\frac{1}{2}$	$2\frac{1}{8}$	39.95
3000	32 ACP	7	22	$6\frac{3}{4}$	4	
3000	380 ACP	6	22	$6\frac{3}{4}$	4	
Constable	32/380 ACP	7	23	$6\frac{5}{8}$	$3\frac{1}{2}$	

The 5 models listed are in production, but only the Cub models are available.

today in the restyled models S, P and M, and the super S, the current Spanish service pistol. The Star locked-breech pistols all show very fine workmanship, especially the Model B 9mm guns made during and after WW II. The extensive line of Star pistols is distributed here by Firearms International.

Astra Models

Through the wartime destruction of records Astra Unceta y Cia. can't say precisely what models and quantities of pistols were produced before the 1930s. The original firm, Esperanza y Unceta, was formed in July of 1908 by an arms dealer of Eibar, one Pedro Unceta, and Juan Esperanza, a merchant of hardware and other things.

Parts for pistols assembled by other makers were the first products, followed by the Victoria pocket pistol which closely copied post-1900 Browning 25 and 32 models. In 1912, a move was made to a new plant in Guernica—necessary because additional facilities were required to produce the newly-adopted M1913 Campo-Giro 9mm Largo (Long) pistol for the Spanish government. Campo-Giro production solidly established the new firm, and its pocket pistols were widely distributed, also under such other names as Leston, Sat, Museum, etc.

The trade name "ASTRA" was registered in 1914, though probably used before that date. Other, but conventional, pistol designs were produced. During WW I, some 150,000 7.65mm Browning-type pistols were furnished to the French and Italian armies.

In 1921, the Astra M400 replaced the Campo-Giro as the official Spanish service pistol; from then until 1946, some 105,000 units are reported to have been produced. This was an unusual *blowback* design chambered for the 9mm Largo cartridge and was essentially an improvement of the Campo-Giro developed by Astra. Cartridges of such power are not generally considered suitable for use in blowback designs, but the M400 proved entirely satisfactory.

The basic M400 design was scaled

Astra Cub is a development of the original external-hammer version of M-200. Currently sold as the Colt Junior, as well as under its own name, it is available in 22 Short and 25 ACP.

Latest Astra model is the Constable in 7.65mm. Outwardly it is quite similar to the Walther PP and PPK, but it is much different inside—valuable double-action first shot capability and the hammer can be safely lowered on a chambered cartridge.

down and modified to form the M300 (300/1,2,3,4) in 7.65mm and 9mm (380) calibers in 1922. In 1944, an improved version was designated M-3000 and continued in production. During this time, several models based on modified Browning designs were produced in large quantities. By the end of WW II, these encompassed the M200, M100 Special, and others of which little record remains.

During the latter part of WW II, until 1946, approximately 60,000 M600 9mm Parabellum pistols were produced for foreign sales. This was the basic M400 slightly redesigned and made smaller to handle the 9mm Luger cartridge. These guns were very well made. They were followed by limited production in 1958-1960

of an exposed hammer version called the Condor and intended purely for civilian sale. Only 6400 Condors were produced, according to recent correspondence with Astra; they are, however, vague about whether production has permanently ceased.

By the mid-1950s, the old M200 had been superseded by the Astra Cub and Firecat, available in 25 ACP and 22 Short calibers. Both were modified Browning designs, the former with exposed hammer. Variations within models were produced. The M3000 was available in 32 and 380 ACP.

In 1957, the Firecat was revised slightly and has since been manufactured in Spain for sale by Colt's as the Colt Junior in 25 ACP and 22 Short caliber. It replaces the old Colt 25 Pocket Model discontinued in 1946.

At the present time, a few Astra models are available in this country: the Colt version of the Firecat mentioned above and the Cub imported by Firearms International. The 32 and 380 M3000 (now designated Falcon) and the new double-action Constable are in production but not generally available here.

All current Astra models are listed in the accompanying table. Workmanship is good in these guns. Personally, I'd like to see the remaining models available in this country.

Gabilondo Models

Perhaps prompted by the apparent

success of Star, Gabilondo introduced in 1931 a near-copy of the Colt/Browning M1911 pistol. Initially this gun resembled the Star more than the Colt and had the solid backstrap of the former and a modified firing mechanism. Some such guns were marked *RUBY*. It apparently became evident that if copying were to be done, it would be best to copy the highly-regarded Colt, and to do it accurately. This was during the time when the reputation of Spanish pistols was gathering speed on the downhill slope. "Just another Spanish gun" wouldn't be enough.

Consequently, the Colt 45 Government Model was copied line for line, measurement for measurement—so well, in fact, that often (not always) Colt parts will interchange. The name Llama was chosen for the new line, which was produced in 9mm Long, 38 ACP, and 45 Auto calibers. Minor variations were produced. For example, the Llama "Extra" barrel was approximately ½" longer, the slide ⅜" longer, than the Colt—leaving the barrel protruding farther from the bushing. Even so, a Colt barrel and slide could be fitted to the Extra. On some variations the grip safety was deleted, and the internal extractor replaced by an external claw let into the slide.

One Senor Tauler, large arms dealer of Madrid, ordered large quantities of Gabilondo/Llama pistols marked with his name. These guns are sometimes thought to be another make, but were identical to Llamas being made on the same assembly lines at the Gabilondo plant. They are usually marked "Tauler Mark P" on the left side of the slide, with "Military & Police" on the right. Usually the manufacturers name appears somewhere on the gun, subordinate to "Tauler." Some identical guns are reported to be marked "Ruby," but I've not examined a sample.

Primarily for export Gabilondo developed a smaller lighter pistol—the "Llama Especial"—in 9mm Parabellum caliber. It resembled the Star more than the Colt in that the backstrap was solid, deleting the grip safety. The trigger was pivoted, modified lockwork was fitted, an external extractor was used, and the hammer was rounded and pierced a la Colt Commander. I used an Especial extensively in Europe and found it an excellent gun. It was available in the 1950s in this country through Stoeger Arms, but no longer. This model was also made and marked "Mugica" for an Eibar arms dealer, one Jose Mugica.

The basic Colt/Browning copies remain in production today. Following WW II, Gabilondo introduced a 2/3d-scale version of the big autos, chambered for the 380 ACP cartridge. Mechanically identical to the 38 and 45 guns in every way, it is designated here as Model IIIA. The 32

ACP companion Model XA is identical in appearance to the IIIA, but dispenses with the locking system. It functions as a fixed-barrel, blowback design. An identical Model XV in 22 Long Rifle caliber is also made.

Also, since the war, small Browning-type blowback pistols in 22 Short and 25 ACP have been introduced as the Models XVII and XVIII respectively.

During the early 1960s, ventilated ribs were incorporated into the slides of all Llama models made for U.S. sale. Also, "accurized" versions of the 38 and 45 guns are now made. Called the "Match" model, they incorporate target-type adjustable sights and are carefully hand-fitted for maximum accuracy.

Star Models

Prior to the 1920s, Star pistols were all of elementary blowback design, chambered for the small 6.35mm, 7.65mm and 9mm short cartridges. In 1920 they introduced a large-caliber, locked-breech gun of military style and size. Called the Model 1920, it was offered in 7.63mm (Mauser) and 9mm Long (Bergmann-Bayard).

The M1920 represented the first attempt to this scribe's knowledge to improve upon the Colt/Browning swinging-link, recoil-operated locking system of the M1911 U.S. 45 Automatic. From the chamber forward the design copies faithfully the Browning locking system, as can be seen in the accompanying "exploded" drawing. Rearward of that point, the slide was changed to use a simpler and cheaper spring-loaded claw-type extractor (part No. 66) mounted in an external slot. At the upper rear of the slide was installed a rotating manual safety (see fig. 9). It did not block the sear or hammer, but when engaged rotated a steel block in position to prevent the hammer from striking the firing pin. Engaging this safety also retracted the rear sight into the slide.

The biggest difference from the Browning design was in the firing mechanism. The backstrap was made integral with the frame, doing away with the grip safety and separate mainspring housing. Instead, a simple recess was bored beneath the hammer to house a coil mainspring (part No. 09). This replaced 4 parts with 2, and eliminated several costly machining operations.

The Browning sliding trigger and intricately-shaped disconnector were replaced by a pivoted trigger, a stamped sear bar, and a simple flat

Gabilondo Llama series in 45ACP and 38 Super Automatic directly copies the Colt Govt. Model 1911-A1.

Llama 9mmK (380 ACP) is a reduced-size version of the big 45 and 38 pistols.

Llama models identical in appearance to the 380 series are available in 32 and 22 RF calibers, but function as unlocked-breech, blowback actions.

interrupter (disconnector) riding in a slot on the right side of the receiver. These innovations reduced costly machining operations and proved to be as durable and reliable as the Browning system. A simple, sturdy pivoted sear was used.

Externally the M1920 greatly resembled the Colt 45 auto, but had a clumsier appearance because of its abrupt stock/barrel angle and straight backstrap.

In this form the Star represented a significant mechanical improvement on the Colt/Browning, not a "cheap copy" as it has frequently been described. It could be produced more quickly at less cost than the Colt, yet possessed the same inherent reliability and durability. It had only one serious shortcoming; the safety did not block the hammer.

The M1921 was essentially the same gun fitted with a long grip safety pivoted near the bottom of the frame.

This feature was not considered worth the additional cost by Star customers, and the M1921 was not manufactured in large quantities.

Mechanically, the final form of the Star high-power design was achieved in the M1922. The slide-mounted safety was discarded and replaced by one pivoted on the left rear of the gun frame. Here again simplicity and low cost were achieved. This safety contains a notch on its shaft. When disengaged, the notch does not interfere with hammer movement, allowing it to fall and strike the firing pin when the trigger is pulled. When engaged, a solid portion of the shaft intercepts and bears down upon a "tail" on the hammer. The hammer cannot move, even though the trigger is pulled. This safety is quite positive and trouble-free in its action, yet is basically simple and easily produced.

The M1922, with only very minor modifications became the Star Model

A and was offered in 9mm Long. By April, 1934, approximately 80,000 had been manufactured in 9mm Long, mostly for the Spanish Guardia Civil (Land Police). The Guardia Civil guns were stamped "GC," for the benefit of collectors who like to know who used a gun.

First made in 9mm Long, the Model A was offered in 9mm Parabellum in 1932. The slightly enlarged Model M was offered first in 1924, in 45 Auto and 7.63 Mauser, both as a semi-automatic pistol and as a selective-fire machine pistol with detachable wood holster-stock. In 1925, the M became available in 38 Auto. When the more powerful 38 Super Auto cartridge was introduced, this same gun was used for it without change. By 1934 some 5,000 in 38 Auto (Colt) and 6,000 in 45 Auto had been manufactured. Production of 7.63mm Mauser pistols was apparently quite small.

By WW II the basic Star design had been somewhat restyled, but not changed mechanically. Stock angle and profile were changed, resulting in an appearance almost identical to the Colt 45. In this form the 9mm Long became the Model A; 9mm Parabellum, Model B; 38 Super Automatic, Model M, and the 45, the Model P. Identical otherwise, and with considerable parts interchangeability existing, the A and B are smaller than the P and M. Frames and slides of the latter two are wider and barrels are larger in diameter to accommodate the Colt cartridge. Weight is 1⅝ ounces greater. Dimensional differences are contained in the accompanying tables.

At the present time, all but the Model P are in production. A sample Model AS just received displays excellent workmanship. It functions perfectly with 9mm Long, 38 ACP and 38 Super Automatic factory loads. So long as proper bullets are used, it performs equally well with medium- and full-charge handloads in 38 Super cases. In regard to use of 38 Super Automatic ammunition in Star pistols chambered for the 9mm Long (normally marked "9mm/38") authorities say the guns are intended for use with *both* cartridges, and that they are proofed with loads developing 150% of 38 Super pressures.

Accuracy with this sample gun and with two 9mm Parabellum Model Bs has been excellent—equal to that of a new Colt 38 Super Automatic pistol with comparable ammunition.

The big-bore Star pistols became quite popular in Latin American countries. As a result, the Brazilian firm Hafdasa produced a nearly identical copy of the Model P in 45 caliber. It differs only in minor dimensions and in the use of the Colt/Browning firing pin and internal extractor design. This gun is known as the Ballester-Molina and was once a standard Brazilian Army service sidearm.

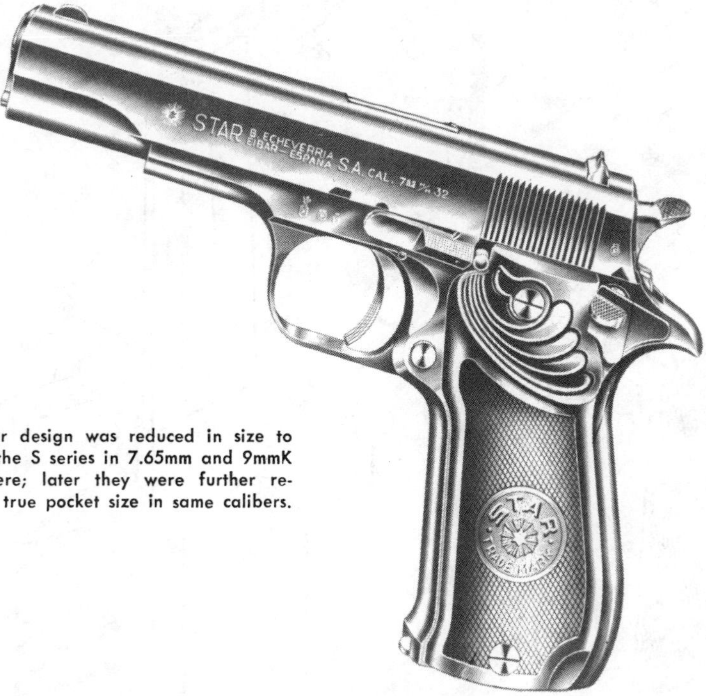

Basic Star design was reduced in size to produce the S series in 7.65mm and 9mmK shown here; later they were further reduced to true pocket size in same calibers.

Table 2 Llama (Gabilondo) Pistols
Stoeger Arms Corp., importers

Model	Cal.	Mag. Cap.	Wt./ozs.	Lgth./ins.	Hgt./ins.	Bbl./ins.	Price
XV	22 LR	9	21	6¼		4¼	$52.50
Exec.	22 Short	6	13½	4¾		2⅜	37.50
XVIII	25 ACP	5	13¾	4¾		2⅜	37.50
XA	32 ACP	8	21	6¼	4⅜	3¹¹⁄₁₆	52.50
IIIA	380 ACP	7	20	6¼	4⅜	3¹¹⁄₁₆	52.50
VIII	38 Super	9	38½	8½	5⅜	5	71.50
IXA	45 ACP	7	38	8½	5⅜	5	71.50
MATCH	38 ACP	9	38½	8½	5⅜	5	131.50
	45 ACP	7	38	8½	5⅜	5	131.50

Engraved, plated, specially finished and special grip models available at extra cost.

Cased presentation models available on special order at considerable delay. Models XV, XA, IIIA available as "Airlite" with alloy frames, weighing 4 oz. less, same prices.

All models listed are in production and available.

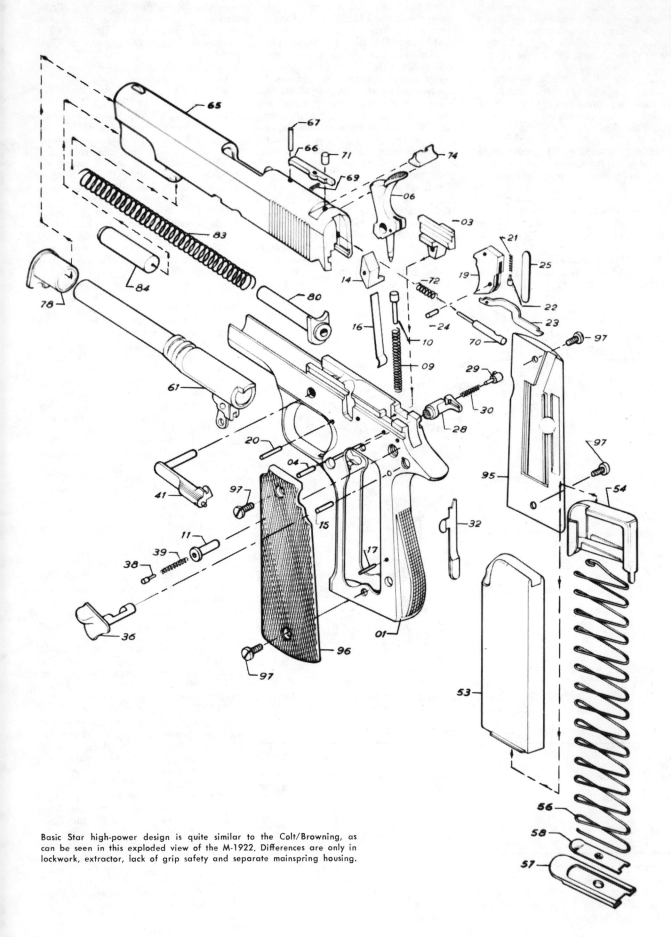

Basic Star high-power design is quite similar to the Colt/Browning, as can be seen in this exploded view of the M-1922. Differences are only in lockwork, extractor, lack of grip safety and separate mainspring housing.

Table 3 Star (Echeverria) Pistols
F.I., importers

Model	Cal.	Mag. Cap.	Wt./ozs.	Lgth./ins.	Hgt./ins.	Bbl./ins.	Price
F	22 LR	10	27½	7¼	5	4¼	$59.95
FI	32 ACP	9	27½	7¼	5	4¼	
F Sport	22 LR	10	29½	9	5	6	59.95
F Olympic	22 Short	6	28	9	5	6	
HK Lancer	22 LR	8	14½	5½	4	3	
CU	25 ACP	8	10½	4¾	3½	2⅜	59.95
DK	380 ACP	6	14	5¾	4	3⅕	69.95
SI	32 ACP	9	22	6½	4¾	4	69.95
S	380 ACP	8	22	6½	4¾	4	69.95
Super S	380 ACP	8	22	6¾	5	4	
B*	9mm Para.	8	37½	8½	5⅓	5	84.50
M	38 Super	9	39⅛	8½	5⅓	5	84.50
P	45 ACP	7	39⅛	8½	5⅓	5	
Super B	9mm Para.	9	35¼	8¾	5½	5⅕	
Super M	38 Super	9	40	8¾	5½	5⅕	

All guns listed are in production, but only those carrying a retail price are available.

*The Model AS (called in Spain the Model A) is identical to the Model B, but is said to function reliably with 9mm Largo or 38 Super cartridges. It is usually marked "9mm/38."

Impressed with the success of the large-caliber locked-breech guns, Star adapted the design to smaller pistols chambered for the 32 and 380 ACP cartridges. Significant among these is the "Starfire" Model DK, the smallest and lightest 380 pistol available today. Only 5¾" long and 4" high, it weighs 14 ounces. More conventional in size are the SI and S in 32 and 380 respectively. They measure 6½" long, 4¾" high, and weigh 22 ounces. Mechanically, these smaller guns are identical to the big military and police models. Star also produces small blowback-design pocket pistols in 22 and 25 caliber. Significant is the "Lancer" Model HK in 22 Long Rifle caliber. Virtually all other pistols this small are chambered only for the 22 Short or 25 ACP—both inferior in striking power to the 22 LR in High

Star of 1920 was an initial effort to produce an improved version of the Colt/Browning. Manual safety on the slide retracted the rear sight and interposed a block between the hammer and firing pin, but did not block hammer or sear.

Star Model M machine pistol in 45 ACP and 7.63mm Mauser calibers was intended to compete with Mauser's Schnellfeuer during the 1930s. Few were made.

Today's MADE-IN-SPAIN Pistols

Velocity, Hollow Point form.

The current Star line also contains other blowback models in 22, 25 and 32 caliber, most of which are available from F.I. The accompanying chart details the general specifications of all Star models for which we've been able to dig up the information.

The question most likely to be asked concerning any Spanish pistol (and I've received hundreds of letters on the subject) is "How good is it?" Star, Astra, and Gabilondo automatics (actually marked as such, not copies) are of good fit and finish, accurate, durable, and reliable, regardless of model or date of manufacture.

Functionally, they are equal to contemporary domestic guns and the better European makes.

In quality of workmanship, the above makes produced before WW II are excellent. Generally speaking, they can be rated (1) Astra, (2) Star, (3) Gabilondo. Fit and finish of Astra M400 and M600 are very fine, only slight deterioration having taken place during WW II.

Star models of the period are virtually equal in quality, with, in my opinion, Model B pistols of the late 1940s, being perhaps slightly nicer than some Astras. These particular guns have barrel and slide fitted with *less* play than even contemporary domestic models. This is particularly evident in the large lot of guns recently sold by Interarmco.

Gabilondo Llamas of the period are reasonably well finished, but not quite equal to comparable Star and Astra models. This is particularly evident, internally, at points like the ejector, extractor claw, disconnector, etc. Internal parts are rather rough com-

pared to the other two makes.

Regarding current-production guns, I rate them (1) Star, (2) Astra, (3) Llama, with the exception of the Llama "Match" which is carefully hand fitted and priced accordingly (over $130). It ranks at the top of the heap.

In regard to current domestic guns, say the Colt Government Model and S&W M39, Star very nearly matches them in both fit and finish, while Astra and Llama fall successively farther below.

Functionally, the several dozen specimens I've handled and shot are equal to comparable, current domestic models. As far as any personal preference is concerned, the Star B (9mm P) and AS (9mm/38-38 ACP) currently in use rank second only to my S&W M39. They are very closely fitted, nicely finished, and are both accurate and reliable.

After all this, I can honestly say that current Spanish pistols are good. One need not hesitate for a moment in choosing any of today's Astra, Llama or Star pistols. ●

Present Star configuration is typified by Model M shown here. A and B models are identical but slightly smaller. Super series has an added quick takedown feature.

Star of 1922 embodied all features of later models and became the Model A.

SPORTING ARMS
of the world

*Despite the gloomy predictions of the naysayers, and in the face
of an economy in general that is weaker than we like, the past several
months have seen the arms industry at large doing very nicely indeed.
This is, by far, our greatest review of new sporting arms and accessories
ever. Foreign and domestic firearms are covered, many in depth and
detail, including shooting reports.*

by LARRY STERETT, BOB ZWIRZ and the editors.

THE BIGGEST news in the U.S. sporting arms world for the past year must be the increased interest in black powder arms. Sales at the industry level for 1970 were estimated at $10 million, and the anticipated sales for 1975 have been predicted at $20 million. This represents a 15-20 percent increase per year, and many U.S. firms have suddenly realized that an untapped market in this field does exist. Firms such as Service Armament, Dixie Gun Works, and Replica Arms have been supplying black powder handguns, rifles, and even a few shotguns for several years, along with many smaller firms. These arms, generally copies of various U.S. or English guns of the early and mid-1800s, were almost universally manufactured in Italy.

Now, at least three, and possibly more, U.S. firms well known to shooters for non-black powder items have jumped on the soot-and-smoke bandwagon. One of these firms—Lyman Gun Sight—isn't really new to the BP field insofar as they have been producing bullet and ball moulds and sights for BP arms for many, many years. What is new is their introduction of actual arms—the first being two Remington-style revolvers, to be followed by a muzzle-loading rifle in two calibers. The second firm—Harrington & Richardson—may not be new either; this century-old firm may have produced a few BP arms a hundred years ago, but in 1971 they introduced a 58-caliber muzzle-loading rifle that is sure to gain followers. The third firm—Thompson/Center, manufacturer of the excellent Contender pistol—is a young firm compared to the other two, but definitely not a firm to drag its heels. They not only introduced one, but two muzzle-loading rifles—flintlock and percussion—in three calibers. A modern version of the old Hawken design, the T/C arms are strictly "Made in America."

The above mentioned arms, along with others, will be covered elsewhere in this report, with specific comments on each.

Centennials

If ever there was a year for centennials, 1971 would have to be up near the top. Not only did two sporting arms firms—Iver Johnson's Arms & Cycle Works and Harrington & Richardson—celebrate their centennials, but it was also the big year for the National Rifle Association. The NRA, now a million-plus strong, was founded on November 17, 1871, in New York state by a group of National Guard officers to help educate American citizens in the use of firearms—they had found citizen soldiers left something to be desired in times of crisis. Today the NRA is still dedicated to the education of public-spirited citizens in the safe and efficient use of small arms for pleasure and protection; to foster firearms safety and accuracy in law-enforcement agencies, among citizens subject to military duty and those in the armed services; and to further the public welfare and national defense. A few of the accomplishments of the NRA during the past century include the nationwide Hunter Safety Training and Home Firearms Safety Courses; acting governing body of U.S. competitive rifle and pistol shooting and member of the U.S. Olympic Committee and International Shooting Union, and parent organization of most civilian, military and police shooting clubs and marksmanship units. The list goes on and on. Without a doubt the NRA is the foremost guardian of the American tradition and constitutional right of citizens to "Keep and Bear Arms." (Every reputable American who owns or shoots a gun should be a member of the National Rifle Association. For information write Membership Division, National Rifle Association, Dept. GD, 1600 Rhode Island Avenue, N.W., Washington, D.C. 20036.)

To commemorate its 100th Anniversary the NRA authorized three firms to produce special NRA firearms—Daisy/Heddon, Winchester-Western, and Colt Industries. Each firm is manufacturing two such arms and every centennial model will have the official Centennial Medallion inlaid in the stock. Daisy is manufacturing a lever action BB gun of the 1894 style, and a BB handgun of the Colt M1873 style. The Colt commemoratives consist of a 45 Gold Cup National Match model and the classic Single Action Army M1873. Although there are only two Colt models, the SA Army will be available in two calibers—357 Magnum and 45 Long Colt—and three barrel lengths—4¾. 5½, and 7½ inches, making a total of six variations of the one model. The Colt handguns are housed in special walnut display cases lined with golden velvet. Winchester's commemoratives consist of two lever action long arms based on the M1894 action. One, called the NRA Centennial Rifle, resembles the popular M64 that was discontinued in 1957, while the second model, called the NRA Centennial Musket, resembles an arm that might have been manufactured around the turn of the century. (Winchester produced a Model 1895 NRA Musket back in 1905. But it was a box magazine repeater with an upper handguard, and does not bear much resemblance to the new Musket.)

Last Minute Notes

Most firms responded to our inquiries, but there were exceptions. Four letters and a phone call to Spesco produced nothing. Ranger Arms reported a change in the management, but the promised gun information failed to arrive. Adanac failed to send information on its imported shotguns. Intercontinental said they'll have replica Rolling Block rifles, they still have Dakota revolvers, and a line of black powder guns. Other firms mentioned in the 25th edition reported no changes in their current line or failed to reply. LS

Armi Fabbri

We live in an affluent time, certainly for the most part, despite the rise of unemployment this year of 1971, yet relatively few spend as much as $1000 for a new shotgun. Yet that sum, wisely spent for a gun of high quality and optimum usefulness, offers a far better ultimate equity than four or five times that amount exended on a new automobile. Need I mention the Purdey—a single Purdey sold in 1948 for $1000, and that same gun today, in nice used condition, will bring up to $4000.

What, then—granting the comparatively low sales volume of one grand smoothbores—do you think about a line of double guns that begin at over $2000? Not to mention one that will, when it's ready, be much higher! At this point, while you're stunned, I can't do better, I think, than print here part of a letter from the vice-president of Armi Fabbri, Mr. Leonard C. Puccinelli. His letter is slightly paraphrased, but it's entirely accurate:

". . . our small factory employs 15 craftsmen, dedicated to producing a limited number of expensive custom shotguns, made to special order only. We make only 6 guns monthly in order to maintain what we think is the highest quality shotgun built in the world today, at any price. Mr. Ivo Fabbri, our President, is in charge of production and domestic business. He works along with the men on every gun made. All export sales are handled by the writer, who also advises on technical matters and improvements based on his competitive shooting experience and his 15 years in the arms and ammunition field.

"Armi Fabbri, created in 1965, now offers over-under and side-by-side guns in 12, 20 and 28 gauges, these in 5 grades ranging in price from $2230 to $3230 in Brescia. Projected for 1972 is the Puccinelli 8000, a gun that will cost $8000. The most expensive shotgun ever built, its value will lie in technology and design, not in engraving and gold inlays."

Available this year is a matched pair of sidelock guns called "The Professionals," offered in over-under or side-by-side style. Both sets of barrels will fit each frame, thus avoiding break-down problems in the field or at the range. As will all Fabbri guns, these will be made to the customer's ideas and dimensions, chokes to his order, etc. Each of these guns will be supplied with a set of spare parts, tools and cleaning gear, all in a fitted, full leather trunk case. Priced at $5810 for the cased pair, only two or three such guns will be made yearly. Delivery time runs 12 to 24 months for all Fabbri guns.

Numerous extras are available, of course, among them spare barrels ($570 up), stainless steel locks ($92), hand-detachable locks ($146), matched pairs ($325) and if a self-opening side-by-side is wanted, $165.

If I were 10 years younger and $6000 richer I'd order those "Professionals." They'd be worth a lot more than a Cadillac, bought now, some few years hence. JTA

This is Armi Fabbri's Majestic Grade, shown here in over-under form, but made also as a side-by-side. The lockplates and receiver parts are elaborately inlaid with various precious metals. $3070.00.

Benet Arms/Gold Rush Gunshops

We've had a last-minute chance to look over several of Bill Edwards' recent arrivals—two of these were the so-called pocket auto pistols, made by Bernardelli. One was a 22 LR, the other the same gun in 380 ACP, both of these "USA" models upgraded to meet IRS/GCA68 requirements. Both are developments of the earlier VB 60, both are of blow-back type, the 3½-inch barrels fixed in position. Checkered black plastic grips were found on the 22, checkered walnut ($10 extra) on the 380. Identical in form, both are quite thick and have thumb shelves for a right-handed shooter. There's no shortage of safeties on these USA pistols—a manual type and hammer-blocking system are found on the left side, while a magazine safe prevents discharge when the clip is out of the gun. All worked well, too, as a brief functioning trial showed.

The 7-shot 380 was shot first, firing at 25 yards from a sitting position and using both hands. Five 3-shot groups averaged close to 4 inches, and there were a few semi-jams; fresh rounds failed to seat fully home in the chamber, requiring some hand help. Extraction and ejection of fired cases was faultless. The trigger pull tested 7½ lbs., with a touch of creep, neither of which helped the performance. The 380 slide stays open after the last shot.

The 10-shot USA 22 was targeted next, same conditions as above except that four 5-shot strings were made. CIL high-speed ammo was used, the average group running about 2⅝ inches. This pistol had a 3¼-lb. trigger, which was a relief! There were no feed/eject problems at all. The slide does not lock open after the final shot.

The third of the Benet-Bernardelli auto pistols tested was the M69, a target grade/weight version of the old M60 VB pistol also. This new 22 LR autoloader, intended

for "Standard" match shooting per ISU rules, has essentially the same mechanism and frame of the USA models described above. The barrel, however, is 5.9 inches long, its forward section carrying a one-piece combination barrel weight and sight rib. This unit remains fixed as the slide moves back and forth in firing, hence both sights are undisturbed, never out of alignment. Sight radius is 7.1 inches, the rear sight a square notch just wide enough to let a glimmer of light be seen at either side of the ¹⁄₁₀-inch Patridge-type front blade. I'd like it a bit wider. Two extra front sights are furnished—an ⅛th-inch blade and a round, flat-faced bead in the same size (all 3 of the sights are matt-black). Neither ⅛-inch sight is usable with the rear sight, however, though I suppose one could file the notch wider or make it semi-circular.

There are some other differences in the M69—the hammer-block safety of the USA models is not found, the other two are the same. The magazine follower forms a

Benet-Bernardelli USA auto pistol.

slide stop when the last round is fired, and the 10-round magazine has a longer bottom extension. The checkered walnut grips, much like the USA grips in general form, are nearly 2 inches thick.

Trigger pull on the M69 is a crisp, clean 2¾ lbs., no creep evident. I was puzzled for a moment over a light twangy sound heard at the letoff. This came from the long sight rib which, not being attached anywhere to the slide, vibrates when the hammer falls.

Functioning of the M69 was excellent, no bobbles of any kind, but I wasn't comfortable with that fat grip. Even with my size 10 mitt I couldn't manage a straight-behind-the-gun hold, though I don't think my groups suffered thereby. That was 2-handed shooting, elbows on my knees, but in offhand firing I'd want a slenderer grip. The front strap is grooved, as is the trigger.

Groups of 5 shots, again at 25 yards, went into an average of 3 inches, but there were fliers that I couldn't account for right away. There was at least one shot in every string that went out. Then, changing from the Brand X I was shooting to CCI high-speed 22s, the pistol started perking. My biggest string ran 2¼ inches, the smallest 1⅜ths, for an average of 1⅞ths. Proving once again that 22 rimfires can be fussy about their fodder.

The slides of all 3 VB pistols are very well fitted to the frame rails, only a tiny amount of lateral play evident. The VB magazines are stiff and of sturdy stock, the lips properly formed. The forward portion is round in section, not flat as is the case usually, this adding to rigidity and better feeding.

Two magazines, a screwdriver, barrel brush, oil bottle and sight wrench are supplied with all of these Bernardelli pistols at the quoted prices.

The USA/22 and USA/380 pistols sell for $79.50, and the M69 target lists at $99, including the checkered walnut grips.

The fourth firearm sent to us for a belated look was the Gold Rush Model 1873, a very close replica indeed of the "Gun that won the West." I guess that has to mean a W-nch-st-r, not a C-lt, because this is a 20-inch barreled carbine, caliber 44-40 WCF. The blue is well done, as is the oil-finished wood, while a point-by-point check shows a strong adherence to the lines and dimensions of the orginial. Even the cartridge carrier is of brass, and there's the traditional sliding trap in the buttplate. The sectioned cleaning rod, alas, is not present, nor is the sling ring and its stud. The folding-leaf rear sight shows its ancestry, too.

My only criticism—it takes a hefty effort on the lever to cock the hammer, but maybe that's because it's new and stiff.

The reproduction '73 has a full length magazine, weighs 7¼ lbs., and the tab is $169.

Edwards—via Benet Arms or other titles—is also importing lots of other firearms, old style and new: Colt and Remington caplock revolvers, percussion long guns, too. The full line of SIG (Swiss) auto pistols in 9mm Luger and 22 rimfire, other SIG arms, MAB (French) auto pistols, to name only a few. He'll gladly send full information.   J.T.A.

Gold Rush 1873 well-made replica, cal. 44-40 WCF, is fully shootable, simulates early Winchester 99.9%.

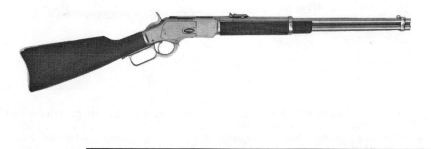

Browning Superlight 20 Gauge

It doesn't happen very often, or we'd all of us be more gun-poor than we are, but you know the feeling and the thought—unspoken or not—that hits you now and again when you pick up and shoulder a new gun. Suddenly there's that warm, pleasurable feeling, that instant knowledge that springs from an awareness of fit, balance, handling and sighting that makes you say, "Boy, I know I can shoot this one!"

By this time it's pretty obvious that I'm going to write about the new Browning Superposed spotlighted by our heading. Over the years I've owned three Browning shotguns, and I've shot several others for varying periods of time. The truly excellent quality built into all Browning arms is so well known and universally acknowledged that I won't belabor that aspect here —all of us have come to expect that sort of craftsmanship from Browning. The big surprise would be a second-rate Browning.

So, when I heard of the new Superlight, and saw it pictured, my reaction was predictable—"Well," I might have said "here's a variation of the Browning 20 over-under one with a straight-grip stock," and let it go at that. I couldn't have been more wrong, I'm delighted to confess, and I learned that right now as soon as my sample gun arrived and I'd torn off the wrappings!

This one, friends, is a new Browning 20, but it calls for handling, feeling and snugging it into that shoulder hollow, to sense the subtle differences that make it so. Sure, it looks very much like Browning's Standard or Lightning 20s (6¾ and 6⅜

pounds approximately), but in addition to its own particular specs and dimensions, it has—as far as I'm concerned—a very much different feel than do the other Browning 20s. Most of the weight—a scant 5¾ pounds—is between the hands, always a sign of good balance and good handling qualities. Most of the weight reduction seems to stem from the lighter, more-tapered barrels—though the buttstock takes off an ounce or two through the straight stock—which also means that the gun is a mite muzzle light. That's fine with me— this is an upland gun meant for the quail and woodcock thickets, and that's just where it should shine.

The thing that made it really right for me, though—and for that reason this new Browning may not suit you exactly—is the drop at the comb just 1¼ inches, and therby ⅛- to ³⁄₁₆-inch higher than the other Brownings I've shot, and measured. Other

Browning's light, delightful Super Light 20.

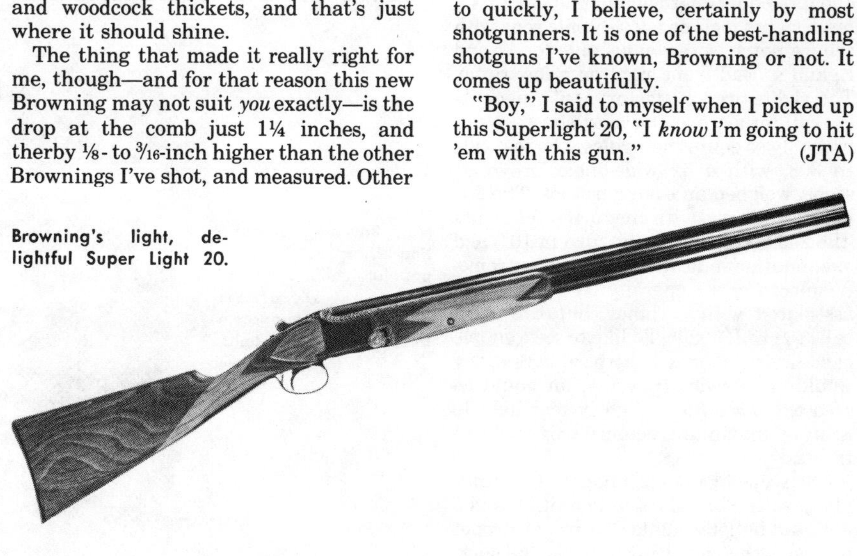

dimensions are about standard—2" (52mm) at heel, a pull to the single trigger of 14³⁄₁₆" (36 cm) and a pitch down of 1⅞" (48mm).

My cheekbones are high, so I need a higher-than-normal comb height if I'm to get any elevation. With this new Browning I'm seeing a good portion of the slender rib, the gun firmly into my cheek, instead of looking at the top snap as I usually do!

As I've said, this new Browning 20 won't fit everybody, and the muzzle light barrels may wave around a bit at first, causing a few misses, but it can be adapted to quickly, I believe, certainly by most shotgunners. It is one of the best-handling shotguns I've known, Browning or not. It comes up beautifully.

"Boy," I said to myself when I picked up this Superlight 20, "I know I'm going to hit 'em with this gun."   (JTA)

Browning Arms Co.

Browning Lever Rifle

It was some 5 years ago that Browning introduced their lever action rifle, but something went sour and the BLR dropped out of sight. Now it is back, but instead of being made in the U.S., as originally planned, the rifles are being produced in Liege (Belgium) at the home of the Browning bolt action rifles, Superposed and automatic shotguns. The quality is just what one expects of Browning, excellent. Currently available only in calibers 243 and 308, the BLR weighs a scant 7 pounds with iron sights, and it's nearly 40″ over-all. A rack-and-pinion arrangement operates the breechbolt and rotates the multiple-lug bolt head. The recessed bolt face encloses the cartridge head, ejection is to the side, and the solid receiver top is tapped for easy scope mounting. A detachable 4-round box

The Grade V center-fire caliber auto rifle is handsomely engraved, with game figures inlaid in 18K gold.

Browning Auto Rifle

Anyone familiar with these Browning sporting autoloaders knows that there's a great expanse of metal on the receiver sides, a broad area that simply asks to be engraved. Browning has done just that for 1971, and the rifle pictured—as well as several others so embellished—was seen in the flesh at the last NSGA show. Handsomely done, all of them, and I wish we had space to show more than the one we've

selected—that is the Grade V, with animals appropriate to the caliber inlaid in 18K gold, the rest a deeply engraved game scene.

Browning's new full-color catalog has just come, its format and content arrangement a new departure for them. Guns, archery equipment, clothing and boots, plus accessories are shown in rich colors, and that includes the various new-for-71 Browning products.   JTA

magazine, projecting a bit below the receiver, gives the BLR a slight bulky look, but it gets the job done. The wide-grooved trigger swings down as a part of the lever assembly—no more pinched fingers.

There is no safety as such, but none is needed. The safety is built-in via an exposed 3-position grooved hammer, an inertia firing pin, and a trigger disconnect system. A blow on the hammer will not drive the firing pin forward with enough thrust to fire a chambered cartridge, and when the lever is down the trigger disconnect system prevents firing until the breech is fully closed and trigger pressure is released and reapplied.

The select walnut stock has an oil finish, a straight grip, a recoil pad, and an ample amount of impressed checkering on grip and fore-end. Length of pull is about 13¾″. Issue sights include a low-profile rear with square notch, screw adjustable for W and E, and a bead front sight on a low ramp. The sights are satisfactory, but the calibers call for a scope and most shooters will probably so equip their rifles. The test rifle in 308, with a 5x wide-angle Browning scope, weighed an even 8 pounds. The 20″ barrel was rifled with one turn in 12 inches (the 243 is rifled with one turn in 10″) and examination indicated it to be an extremely smooth one. Generally 20″ barrels are associated with carbines, but Browning calls the BLR a rifle; I'd like to see a couple of additional inches on both calibers—they wouldn't cut swing-time any, but would decrease muzzle blast slightly and help to achieve maximum potential of the cartridges.

The scoped BLR was taken to the range along with 5 brands of ammunition and 3 different bullet weights. The brief workout indicates this new BLR is one of the slick-

est—if not *the* smoothest—lever action rifles this writer has ever worked with—a wet otter on a mud slide couldn't operate more smoothly.

For years shooters have been fed a line that rifles with 2-piece stocks are less accurate than those with one-piece stocks. In some instances this may have been so, but not with the BLR. From the bench the

largest 3-shot group at 100 yards measured just over 2½″ center-to-center; the majority of the groups—regardless of bullet weight—measured between 1″ and 2″ or considerably better than some bolt action rifles with one-piece stocks. The smallest 3-shot group went ⅞″, made with the 180-gr. New Zealand-made Hy-Score load. Yes, the BLR can shoot.

Browning-Made Ammo

Browning has also introduced U.S.-manufactured ammunition in 18 rifle calibers, ranging from the 222 Remington to the 458 Winchester Magnum, and in 11 handgun calibers, from the 25 ACP to the 45 ACP. Altogether there are 47 different loads available, but although development of the new line has been underway for over

3 years, no cartridges were available for testing as this is written (late March, 1971). When the ammunition does hit the market—well in time for the hunting season—it will be in black-and-gold colored foil-covered boxes with styrofoam blocks holding the cartridges separately. Unprimed brass and bullets will be available in 11 rifle and 5 handgun calibers.   L.S.

New Browning ammunition is made in most popular calibers, packaged in styrofoam holders, the handsome boxes black and gold.

Early in March (1971) Clayton Nelson, general manager of Champlin Firearms—and a top notch stockmaker as well—and I spent a pleasant afternoon together—a session during which I learned several interesting things about the 1971 improved Champlin action and how it's built.

A new and better bolt stop system is used, the release lever a small, unobtrusive piece of steel that appears at the top of the trigger guard, ahead of the trigger and conveniently to hand. More importantly, however, the new bolt stop lies below the bolt body, not at the side as before. The depth of engagement is now .120″ against the previous .090″, and the new bolt stop diameter has been enlarged from ³⁄₁₆″ to ¼″. Obviously a stronger and safer system. The new bolt stop location means, too, that the area just behind the left receiver wall is now clean and smooth, not that the small button there, a la Winchester M70 design, was ever obtrusive.

The '71 Champlin has an entirely new trigger-safety system. Canjar, whose excellent triggers have been standard on the Champlin rifles from the beginning, was asked to design a new trigger-safety that would be adaptable to the Champlin bolt, one that would let the safety lie on the top tang and would, when operated, lock both the trigger and the bolt. Canjar did just that and, in so doing, came up with a trigger that now fastens solidly to the bottom of the action—in previous Champlin rifles the trigger was attached via a pivoted pin, as in Mausers and Springfields. The new Canjar trigger is a "stock" item now, too, whereas the older trigger was a customized unit in effect. The new Canjar system will have complete interchangeability, not possible before. Please note, however, that the 1971 Canjar trigger-safety system is *not* exchangeable with the earlier design; the top tang safety-lever position rules that out.

In point of fact, through improved techniques of manufacture, *all* components of the Champlin bolt-receiver system are now interchangeable—in spite of several parts now being held to considerably closer tolerances than before! Prior to this time, every part of the Champlin action was custom fitted, but today—through closer, more rigid specifications and tighter quality control—any part of the action can be ordered by a Champlin rifle user and it will fit.

For an example of this new methodology, the 1971 bolts are much More tightly fitted than before, yet by this very fact they operate more smoothly, with an almost nil chance of binding or sticking. Bolt clearnace is now held to .005″, against a former practice that allowed .015″. This snug

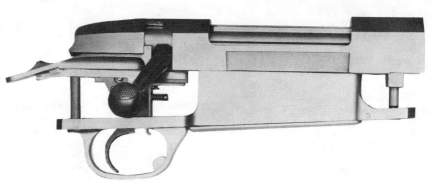

The 1971 Champlin action has new tang safety, bolt release, other improvements.

fitting results, in good part, because the latest bolts are fully ground, not simply machined and polished. A lot of polishing is still done, of course, as a glance at the Champlin bolt quickly shows—old or new—but the corners on the bolt body, two on either side of the three ribs and three lugs, can now be kept crisp and sharp. The net result—a better looking, more rapidly operated bolt, and virtually foolproof—a nice thing to know in a tight corner.

The 1971 Champlin firing pin has been notably improved. It is an entirely solid pin now, whereas before it was a collared affair (to hold the spring), and the new pin is shorter by about ¼-inch, hence it's stiffer. The older pin could, conceivably, become bent through a small misalignment of the bolt—though Nelson said they'd never had a complaint—so to avoid any such happening, Champlin went to the new one-piece firing pin desigh. A new, smaller-diameter, more-coils spring is used on the pin (Mauser-type springs were used previously), and the combination of the shorter firing pin plus the smaller coil spring has given an even faster lock time than before—the older lock time was pretty speedy itself.

Retention of the cocking piece on the firing pin is improved also, now by means of a Nylock-Allen screw in the bottom of the cocking piece. Previously two parts were used—a flat pin on the cocking piece and a stud going through the bolt sleeve to prevent its rotating. Otherwise the cocking piece is unchanged in form, but a different steel (8620) is now in use, resulting in a tough core and a case-hardened exterior. This insures freedom from cracking—which was a possibility, however remote, with the older cocking pieces.

A major change for 1971 concerns the fabrication of the bolt and the bolt handle. Up to now the bolt handle had been inserted into a hole in the bolt body, then heli-arc welded inside and out. Heat treating and tempering occurred after this job, of course, and it wasn't always easy to get the required differences in hardening at the bolt handle and cocking cam against the bolt body. In the new techinque an integral ring is formed as part of the bolt handle, this ring designed to be a hot, push fit onto the rear of the bolt body. Before joining the two parts, the bolt body is diamond-knurled for about .003″, thus making for an ever tighter fit. Locktite is also used as further insurance against slippage, and in severe tests the bolt handle bends—the bolt handle ring stays put, no rotation about the bolt body having been detected to date.

Because the bolt handle and bolt body are separate pieces, before assembly, it's now an easy matter to obtain the desired hardness in both elements—the bolt body is held to about 45 Rockwell, the bolt han-

The 1971 Champlin Rifles
Several important changes produce a better, smoother action.

dle and cam to about 55 on the C-scale. A highly desirable condition, of course—getting hardness differentially from a one-piece bolt was never all that easy.

Gas escape holes in the new Champlin bolt number three, each $3/16''$ in diameter, and venting downward, as before. The older bolts had an ovalized port some $3/16''$ by $3/8''$. Gas escape area is about the same, but the round ports are easier to make, and most people believe they look a lot neater.

Most, if not all, of the new Champlin action components are made by investment casting, a technique that's far more acceptable by the gun buyer than it was a few years ago. It's commonly realized today that investment castings, properly engineered, are as strong as forgings—in some respects even stronger. Nelson had two pertinent comments to make in this area—investment castings, even with Rockwell readings the same, don't have nearly the machineability of bar stock which indicates, to him, the greater toughness of the castings. He then pointed out a fact that is not generally understood or appreciated—bar stock, all too frequently, shows a considerably higher percentage of occlusions (defective areas) than investment castings reveal. As a further hedge against occlusions or other potential defects, every casting furnished to Champlin gets X-rayed—and the X-ray sheet goes to Champlin.

Clayton Nelson had brought to our meeting two complete new actions, plus a handful of component parts in various stages of fabrication. During our talk I'd been looking the actions over carefully, noting the several changes that Nelson described. Aside from the disappearance of the outside bolt release button and the obvious new tang safety, the only essential differences I could detect between the new actions and my 1968-made Champlin, a 338 Winchester Magnum, was in the closer fit of the bolt sleeve and the receiver. The mating of these pieces, with the bolt closed, is very good indeed—I don't see how the alignment, the jointing, could be any better. Manipulations of the bolt, however, quickly demonstrates the gliding smoothness that I've mentioned earlier. Both actions, by the way, weigh exactly the same, in spite of the several alterations and modifications I've described. The octagon-topped receiver and bolt sleeve have been kept, of course—that aspect of the Champlin actions has already become a ready identification mark for the company. I like it, but as an old single-shot rifle fan I suppose I'm prejudiced.

Nelson disassembled the two new actions as I watched, then gave me a modern-day Eli Whitney demonstration. He exchanged bolts, cocking pieces, firing pins, etc., showing that these latest Champlin actions are truly interchangeable in their components. To enforce the point, he told me that one of the actions had made up almost a month before the other!

Might a short Champlin action be in the cards? Possibly, Nelson said, but certainly not in the immediate future. They had made up a couple experimentally, using a new technique the company doesn't want revealed yet, so I'll leave it at that—and I'll leave you at this point.　　JTA

New Sharps Sporting Rifles — made by Colt

In early April of 1971, at the NRA meetings in Washington, D.C., Colt Industries introduced a modern Sharps-Borchardt single shot rifle of classic design. This writer field-tested a prototype of this rifle, made by the Sharps Arms Company of Salt Lake City, Utah, over two years ago. It was a gem. In April, 1970, Colt bought up the Sharps firm, since which time Colt has made improvements in the original design before offering a production rifle. The new rifle still has the same falling block action, breechblock moving at 90° to the chamber, and roller bearings that make movement as slick as an otter on a mud slide. The short-fall firing pin, of the inline type, gives very fast lock time. The safety, located on the breechblock on the left side, may be locked out of operation if desired; the Canjar-type set trigger is fully adjustable.

Fore-end attachment has been changed —a problem on the prototype rifles—but the buttstock is still held to the receiver by a through bolt for rigid lockup. Select-grade fancy walnut is used, the finish hand-rubbed, and checkering is a borderless 22-line fleur-de-lis pattern. The stock has a classic cheekpiece and solid rubber recoil pad, but no grip cap. A European 4-round cartridge well is inlet into the underside of the buttstock, between the rear swivel stud and the toe.

Barrels for the new Sharps come in two lengths—26 or 28 inches—and three weights—light, medium and heavy. Calibers will range from the 17 Remington to the 375 H&H Magnum. Weights will run

8¼-9 pounds. (The Utah firm had planned on reintroducing some of the old Sharps calibers with modern loadings, in new brass, plus a few wildcats, but Colt Industries has no such plans, at least not for the present.)

Price of the new Sharps is $750, complete with a velvet-lined, genuine leather, trunk-type carrying case and a host of accessories. The accessories include a special Colt-made scope mount with one-piece mount base, quick-detachable swivels and Shikar sling, a special screwdriver kit with assorted bits, a cleaning kit—patches, wiping cloth, etc.—and a stainless steel cleaning rod with various tips and brushes. The price may seem steep, but the new Sharps is a quality product. backed by an old-line firm that has been in the arms manufacturing business for 135 years. Larry Sterett

Sharps 22-250 Trial

A day after getting Larry's foregoing account on the Colt Sharps, a sample of the new rifle reached me. This one, serial No. CS2164, is what will be, I gather, the standard grade (Colt isn't going to turn over any of those $750 grades to the gun scribblers, looks like!). There's ample checkering on this 22-250, but it lacks the spare cartridge trap of the de luxe rifle, nor does it have the cheekpiece. Quick-detachable swivels (but no sling), are furnished for the studs installed, and the scope base was attached. The 26-inch barrel has no front sight, and there's no provision for mounting a rear sight on barrel or receiver. The leather

Your editor examines the Colt Sharps with Gordon Walker, former Colt president (right), at the 1971 NRA meeting. Russ Carpenter photo.

Close-up shows breechblock and safety of Sharps Sporting Rifle.

New standard grade 22-250 Sharps Sporting Rifle. The Telepacific chronograph is at right.

case and the 3 accessory kits are not included either.

I mounted a Redfield 12x varmint scope in Redfield rings—which the base on this rifle accepts—using the Alley collimator to put the crosshairs dead center but a trifle low. I grabbed a box of Norma cartridges—55-gr. semi-pointed SPs—and sat down at the 100-yard bench. I tried the trigger unset several times to get the feel of it. It was very light, some 2 pounds or less, I thought, with just a touch of creep.

My first 4 shots printed about 2 inches over the point of aim but some 3 inches right. They made a good tight cluster of less than an inch, but the 5th shot was 2 inches away! How'd that happen? Fortunately, I'd been putting the Sharps into position on the bags before pushing the safety off, holding it there firmly as I eased the safety forward with my left hand. With the 5th round in the chamber, releasing the safety also freed the firing pin, and the rifle went off! I was shook for a moment, of course, but the bullet hadn't gone all that wild—it had printed a couple of inches over the other 4.

Several trials of the empty rifle gave the same result—the cocked firing pin falling 3 out of 5 times or so when the safety lever was pushed forward. The Canjar(?) set trigger (which is of the push-forward-to-set type) mechanism revealed an Allen screw in its bottom, and a little fiddling with it gave me a safe pull, and only slightly heavier. What the original pull was I don't know, but it's now 2¼ lbs.

Accuracy, I thing, was very good for factory loads shot through a rifle just as received. Firing fairly slowly, those first 5 went into ⅞-inch (despite the shakeup), the next 5 were in ¾", and I put 10 shots into the last group, the spread 1 3/16" on centers. Of wind there was none, and the light was good. A 100-yard target came with the Sharps rifle signed (and perhaps shot) by Les Bowman, which showed 5 in .638-inch, a handload using 35 grains of 4320, the Sierra 53-gr. BRHP bullet, and Remington 7½ primers in Remington cases. I'll try that recipe next.

There is, I was a bit surprised to find, a fair amount of shake in the new Sharps action. The breechblock shows obvious lateral play in the receiver, and there's vertical slack as well. Whether a good snug fit

all round would improve the shooting qualities is moot in view of the factory target and my own brief shooting, but I'd have more confidence if the play wasn't there.

Bob Steindler appeared at Creedmoor Farm on May 16, bringing with him his own sample Colt Sharps, also in 22-250, and lugging along George Nonte's like rifle, this Sharps in 243 caliber. Neither of these rifles had been fired before, so we mounted scopes and put some 15 shots through each of them to get sighted in, to condition the barrels and warm 'em up.

Then, shooting for keeps, we got these 100-yard results from Bob's 22-250, a 12x Redfield aboard: 36.4/H380/CCI 200 and Sierra 53-gr. BRHPs went into 1.15" for 5 shots, with 3 in .380". Three more groups, using the same recipe, averaged 1.41", but two of them had 3-4 holes much tighter.

Using 35.0/4320/CCI 200 and the same

Sierras, the average for 3 groups was about the same, or 1.44". This is the load used at Colts to make a test target, measuring about .560", these furnished with each rifle.

Three more 5-shot groups, fired with Dean Lincoln's custom ammo (50-gr. Hornady bullets, no other data supplied), gave another 1.25"-1.45" average.

Nonte's 243 Sharps was then shot, the scope a 2-7x Redfield. Results were about the same as we'd got with the 22-250s, mine and Bob's, but the groups were a bit more round. Both 22-250s showed a tendency to vertical stringing

Canadian (CIL) 100-gr. soft points went into 1.38", with 3 in .870". Federal 80-gr. SPs did about the same—1.42", with 3 holes making .900". Sierra 75s and 85s, using 41.5 to 43.7 H380 and CCI 200s, averaged about 1.40", again with 3-4 shots going as small as .620". J.T.A.

Daisy/Heddon

This Arkansas firm usually isn't considered as a firearms manufacturer, although it is now such, but most shooters will agree that Daisy had a lot to do with the sporting ideals of many of today's riflemen and shotgunners. This writer, for one, grew up with a Model 40 Daisy Red Ryder Carbine made in the old Plymouth, Mich. plant. The newest model on the market at the time, it held 1000 BBs. Complete with a leather thong on the saddle ring, a walnut fore-end and Red Ryder autographed stock, it went on many trips afield. It accounted for an untold number of grasshoppers, holes in paper targets, plus sparrows, hollyhock buds and many other targets. Later, when the owner graduated to a rimfire rifle it was borrowed by an uncle who left it in the barn for dispatching sparrows. The year-round climate of a barn did nothing toward preserving the metal finish. When another generation showed some shooting interest, the carbine was retrieved.

With its coating of rust carefully removed via fine steel wool and Hoppe's, the Daisy started doing duty again. Today, having passed through four sets of hands on its second time around, the Red Ryder Carbine still provides many hours of enjoyment; its accuracy isn't quite what it was when new—or not as its original owner

remembers it—but it isn't too bad either.

Today, Daisy/Heddon doesn't make a Red Ryder Carbine, but it does manufacture a complete line of BB guns, including a couple this writer recently checked out. Several years ago Daisy started making "spittin image" models based on cartridge sporting arms. One of the first was based on the Winchester 1894 Carbine, and one of the latest is the Buffalo Bill Scout, based on this same design. The stock and fore-end are of brown, molded Cycolac; a Buffalo Bill medallion is inlaid in the right side of the stock, and a simulated silver receiver with Buffalo Bill's signature are special features. The underlever, buttplate, barrel band and ring are also simulated silver. The Scout has a two-way cocking mech-

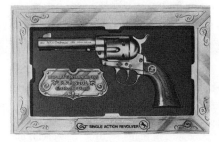

Daisy's NRA Centennial Single Action BB revolver.

anism which requires the underlever to be pulled outward until two clicks are heard, then pushed back into position. Cocking also moves the hammer to a half-cock (safety) position; thumbing the hammer completely to the rear permits the Scout to be fired. The Scout's magazine holds 40 BBs. Weight of the Buffalo Bill Scout Model 3030 is an even three pounds; it is 38 inches over-all, and has a step-adjustable rear sight. (A special version of the 3030 with NRA Centennial Medallion, etc., is available as a commemorative.)

The latest Daisy BB gun is the Model 86/70 Safari Mark 1. This 240-shot repeater measures 34 inches over-all, loads through a sliding port in the barrel, and weighs just over two pounds. It comes in a special case, complete with carrying handle and a 32 x 50-inch four-color poster illustrating and giving details on Africa and 10 species of big game. The Mark 1 still cocks via a lever, but the lever is concealed in the pistol grip and the lower end serves as the pistol grip cap. The result is a very streamlined appearing BB gun, but one that still has the appearance of a sporting arm, even to the extent of having a push-thru safety on the rear of the trigger guard. The stock and fore-end are of brown Cycolac, and the grip checkered; pull length is about perfect for a youngster. Sights consist of a ramp front with blade, and a non-adjustable open rear, satisfactory for short shots, at tin cans, etc.

Most recent additions to the Daisy line are the "5 Shooters," a pair of 177-caliber pellet guns. Labeled the 400 and 450, they have Monte Carlo hardwood stocks and beavertail-style fore-ends: the receivers have decorative engraving, and the 450 has a gold medallion on the stock. The 450 is the big boy of the pair, measuring 37 inches over-all and weighing 3.3 pounds, complete with rifled steel barrel. Weighing 2.6 pounds and 1¼ inches shorter, the 400 has a smoothbore barrel. Both models have post ramp front sights and adjustable rear sights—for windage and elevation on the 450, elevation only on the 400. The new feature is a revolutionary removable rotary clip located near the front end of the fore-end. After loading the clip and cocking the lever, the clip is rotated to place a pellet in firing position; during the cocking operation the trigger is disengaged and a sliding safety on the receiver goes "on."   LS

Daisy

Daisy has two products this year that honor the 100th Anniversary of the NRA—a privilege granted to no other BB gunmakers. One of these NRA Commemoratives is the Daisy "Spittin' Image" carbine, a look-alike for the rifle that won the West, even to the sling-ring. A lever action, of course, the Model 5894 Carbine has a 40-shot magazine, a positive safety, a side-loading port and its stock is made of ABS Cycolac. Price, about $23 retail.

The other NRA Commemorative is another spittin' image, this time of the Colt Peacemaker single action revolver. The Model 5179 holds 12 BBs, has special burnishing on the barrel and receiver, and lists at $12.   JTA

Daisy's NRA Centennial Carbine

Erma

The German-manufactured Erma handguns and 22 caliber MI Carbines were distributed in the U.S. by L.A. Distributors for several years, but as of late 1970 this was no longer so. However, a new distributor had not been appointed by the year's end, although several firms were being considered.

One of the latest arms to bear the Erma name is the EG-71—a lever action rimfire repeating rifle bearing the name "Wagonmaster" and resembling a cross between the Winchester M94 and a Marlin M336. The bolt is housed within the receiver, which has a solid top grooved for a tip-off scope mount. The operating lever, stock, barrel bands, and sights resemble those of the M94. Sights consist of a hooded ramp-mounted front blade with a standard open field-type rear adjustable for elevation. The stock and fore-end appear to be of beech, stained walnut color, and finished with some form of plastic; the wood to metal fit is excellent. The metal parts are finished glossy black, and well-polished. Weight of the test rifle—without scope—was 5½ pounds scant, about right for a rimfire rifle with a barrel length of 18⅝ inches. Over-all length measured 35¾ inches, making the EG-71 a very handy rifle for plinking or hunting.

Several brands of long rifle ammunition were used in checking the accuracy and functioning of the EG-71. Mounted with a new Weaver V22 scope set at 6X, 5-shot groups were fired from the bench at 25 yards, using sandbag rests under the fore-end and buttstock. (The tubular magazine below the barrel holds 15 rounds, thus three 5-shot groups could be obtained from each magazine filling.) Groups of less than one-inch were commonplace, the smallest measuring ⅝-inch—these were produced with both Hodgdon Standard Velocity and CIL Match cartridges. Herter's, Remington Golden and Western Super-X cartridges produced groups measuring only slightly larger—still less than one-inch—and one 15-shot group, fired with Herter ammunition as fast as the lever could be operated, measured only 5/16-inch.

The last price of the EG-71 was $69.95, but this is of course subject to change; the current price as you read this may be different. Prototypes of a second rifle—a pump action model called the "Rough Rider"—were being tested as 1970 came to a close, but production models were not available in early 1971. The Rough Rider uses the same basic design as the EG-71, but with a sliding fore-end to operate the action mechanism instead of the under lever; the magazine capacity, outside hammer, barrel length, over-all length and approximate weight will be the same as for the EG-71.   LS

Charles Daly, Inc.

This well-known firm doesn't have much new to report this year. Their side-by-side models have been discontinued—for the present at least—because of price increases felt to be out of line. A Browning-type long-recoil autoloading shotgun is being imported from Japan, but no information was available for release in mid-April (1971), and consideration was still being given to the Japanese-made Howa bolt action rifle, but nothing definite had been decided. (Howa produces the Weatherby Vanguard rifle, but original Howa rifles were almost exact copies of the Finnish Sakos.) In the over-under shotgun line there have been few changes—prices are up $20 to $60 on all models, except the Diamond Grade, still at $650. One alteration this writer welcomed was the Americanizing of the pistol grip—it is now flat on the bottom, instead of rounded as before, and the Superior models have grip caps. The Selexor ejector is available on some

Superior models—allowing either automatic or manual ejection—and Multi-Gauge Inserts are still available in 20, 28 or 410 bore at $150 per pair installed in any Charles Daly shotgun having 26" barrels. Snap caps and fitted gun cases are available for all Charles Daly shotguns, and Grand Slam riflescopes are available in 7 different models.   LS

The Daly Selexor system

Firearm Development, Inc.

This firm is new and so is the design of their first rifle—the Omega III—but designer Homer E. Koon, Jr., is better known. Formerly with Ranger Arms, he's the designer of their Texas Magnum. Entirely U.S. made, the Omega III is available in one model only—right or left hand version—at one price—$397.50. A choice of calibers—25-06, 270, 30-06, 7mm Rem. and 300 Win. Magnums 338 Win. or 358 Norma Magnums—22″ and 24″ barrels only—Monte Carlo, Classic or Thumbhole Varminter stock styles and Claro walnut, English walnut or laminated—are the options at no extra charge.

The unusual, to say the least, Omega III is a bolt action rifle with a 2-piece stock, the stock readily detachable for replacement with a differnet style, if desired; extra stocks, your choice of style and wood, are $97.50.

Heart of the new design is the round-bottomed steel action with flat sides and octagon-shaped bridge and receiver ring. Inside is a rotary magazine that holds 5 standard or 4 magnum cartridges. The follower delivers the cartridges to the bolt in almost a straight line with the chamber, instead of the tilt-up, slide-over position of cartridges feeding from most Mauser-type magazines. The usual detachable floorplate is absent from the Omega III, but a quick-release button on the rotary magazine allows the remaining rounds in the magazine to spin out of the loading port when the bolt is retracted, thus literally emptying the magazine in one flowing motion. Also new, and unique, is the octagon bolt body with square locking head; the bolt rides on the ridges or corners, the jeweled flats remaining untouched. Since the bearing area is so small, friction is kept to a minimum; the ridges tend to burnish themselves with continued use. The bolt face is enclosed, the cocking piece is shrouded, and the bolt handle has the shortest lift of any on the market—50 degrees. Safety features include 3 large gas-escape ports in the right side of the bolt—when in the locked position—and dual safeties; a twist type at the bolt rear can be given a quarter-turn to lock the firing pin, while a push-thru safety at the back of the trigger guard blocks the trigger. The safeties are independent: one or both can be used at the same time. The single stage trigger has counter-balanced springs to reduce over-travel, prevent creep, and allow full adjustment for a positive let-off.

A silver pistol-grip cap with a single gold initial is standard on Monte Carlo and Classic stocks, and a small gold shield is inletted into the underside of the fore-end to permit engraving or initialling. A recoil pad and swivel studs are standard.

The Omega III comes without sights, but accepts most scope mount bases—Conetrol mounts are an excellent choice. Every Omega III is supplied with a 3-shot test target, fired at 100 yards; the group must not exceed one inch, center-to-center.

(I examined the Omega III at the NSGA show in February, 1971, but found none of the several models on view in fully operating condition. What I did note—to my

Omega III rifle with Monte Carlo style buttstock. Note 3 gas ports in bolt, safeties behind trigger and at rear of bolt sleeve, the massive action.

considerable surprise—was the method of buttstock attachment to the receiver, though non-attachment might be a better word. There is no through-bolt, nor is any intended, said Mr. Koon. [Neither is there any recoil lug on the Omega III, of which more later.] The forward section of the wood is cut out centrally to provide an opening for the upper and lower tangs. [The buttstock, away from the receiver looks much like those for boxlock shotguns.] The twin forward edges of the wood, somewhat rounded, enter the openings on either side of the tangs, abutting against the metal, and held against lateral movement by flanges formed into the rear of the receiver side walls.

The buttstock is held to the receiver by a single wood screw entering via the lower tang, and by another [I think] threaded through the upper tang. Mr. Koon told me that the front portion of the buttstock was intended to absorb all recoil for, as I've said, there is no metallic recoil lug fitted otherwise.

It was pointed out to Mr. Koon that recoil, over some amount of shooting time, would batter the wood in contact with the receiver, would eventually drive it back and loosen it through compression of the fibers and/or shrinking. Such actions would also enlarge the tang screw holes, aggravating the condition, and drive the tang ends deeper into their recesses.

In that case, said Mr. Koon, the owner—or his agent—could remove the stock, re-inlet the tang [s] smoothly, thus taking up for wear, and re-assemble. ED.)

Garcia Corporation

Several new items appeared in the Garcia/F.I. line for 1971, including the Beretta Mark-II single shot trap gun, designed specifically for the American shotgunner. Priced at $395, the MK-II is available only in 12 gauge, and weighs about 8½ pounds, varying a bit on the density of the walnut in the stock, and on barrel length. (A 32- or 34-inch barrel is available.) Internal parts of the chrome-moly hand-engraved receiver are hand fitted and feature a special sear and trigger. The ventilated barrel rib is high, wide, and tapered to insure a near-perfect swing onto targets. Stock dimensions are 1⅜″ by 1¾″ by 14⅜″, at comb, heel and pull respectively; coupled with a full pistol grip, Monte Carlo comb and a long-tapered beavertail fore-end, the handsome result is what many people have been looking for in a trap gun.

Also new to the Beretta/Garcia shotgun line is the AL-1 automatic in 12 and 20 gauges. The AL-1 has all the features of the previously-available AL-2, except the ventilated rib and the engraved receiver. The receiver is still milled from a single block of aluminum alloy and the barrel is chrome-lined to help prevent leading. The AL-1 lists at $178 in a choice of 26, 28, or 30-inch barrels, with extra barrels at $78. The Beretta SO-6 and SO-7 double barrel sidelock shotguns are also available on special order, in 12 gauge only, with a choice of barrel lengths and chokes, double or single selective trigger, and other custom features. The price depends on exactly what is ordered. Other shotguns in the line remain the same as before.

(Other new Garcia-Berettas will be found in our 4-color section and in the catalog pages.)

New calibers have been added to the rifle line. The single shot Bronco is now chambered for the 22 WRM cartridge, the tag only $22. The Sako Finnbear is offered in 25-06 Remington caliber, introduced in 1970, plus the time-tested 375 H&H.

Garcia-Beretta SO-7

Interarms Star Gauge Shotguns

These Star Gauge guns have a well-done ventilated rib, offering an improved sighting plane for fast target tracking and helping to eliminate heat wave distortion in fast shooting. It's a low-slung rib, too, adding to the trim lines of this double.

Though basically alike in appearance, the Star Gauge guns came in two distinct models. The twin-trigger standard, at $149, has manual extractors. The de luxe version, with a non-selective single trigger, has ejectors. This model, made with an outstanding left-barrel inertial firing-pin system, virtually eliminates "doubling."

The barrels, chrome-lined, are assembled on the demiblock system. The receivers are color case-hardened, and lightly but tastefully engraved. The front sight bead is some sort of light-gathering material, probably Lucite.　　　　　　B.Z.

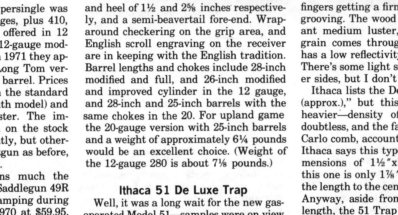

Bob Zwirz, head down hard on Interarms' Star Gauge double.

Ithacagun

In 1969 the Model 66 Supersingle was available in 12 and 20 gauges, plus 410, with the 66RS Buckbuster offered in 12 and 20 gauges. In 1970 the 12-gauge models were discontinued, but in 1971 they appeared again, including a Long Tom version with 36-inch full choke barrel. Prices have increased to $36.95 on the standard Model 66 ($41.95 on the youth model) and to $49.95 on the Buckbuster. The impressed checkering pattern on the stock grip has been changed slightly, but otherwise the 66 is the same shotgun as before, except for the walnut stock.

The rimfire line remains much the same, except the excellent Saddlegun 49R Repeater is slated for a revamping during 1971. It was available in 1970 at $59.95, but does not appear in the '71 catalog. Price increases have not caught the LSA-55 rifles yet, and they remain the same as in 1970. New is a longer action model called the LSA-65, in 270 and 30-06 calibers; available in standard and deluxe models at $174.95 and $214.95. Two additional calibers—25-06 and 7mm Remington Magnum—are slated for late 1971, or early 1972.

Most changes at Ithaca occur among the shotguns. The Perazzi MX-8 Trap and the Competition 1 Trap models have been reduced from $1500 and $825 to $1295 and $795 respectively, and a Perazzi Single Barrel Trap gun is available with 34-inch barrel for $795. The Perazzi Competition 1 Skeet model has cut from $900 to $875. The various 37 slide-action models remain the same, except prices have increased $10 each on the seven grades in the 37 series, and $5 on the M900 Slug Gun. The Model 600 and 700 Skeet Sets, with 20, 28 and 410 barrels, have gone up $100—quite a jump. Prices on other models have increased also, with the range from $4.95 on the 700 Trap and Skeet guns to $30 on the entire 600 series of over-under models. One new side-by-side—the 280 Grade—appeared in early 1971. Available in 12 or 20 gauge—the latter with 3-inch chambers—at $249.95, the 280 features the same action as the 200, but with an English-style straight grip stock having drops at comb and heel of 1½ and 2⅝ inches respectively, and a semi-beavertail fore-end. Wraparound checkering on the grip area, and English scroll engraving on the receiver are in keeping with the English tradition. Barrel lengths and chokes include 28-inch modified and full, and 26-inch modified and improved cylinder in the 12 gauge, and 28-inch and 25-inch barrels with the same chokes in the 20. For upland game the 20-gauge version with 25-inch barrels and a weight of approximately 6¼ pounds would be an excellent choice. (Weight of the 12-gauge 280 is about 7⅛ pounds.)

Ithaca 51 De Luxe Trap

Well, it was a long wait for the new gas-operated Model 51—samples were on view at the 1970 NSGA show—but it does look like the wait was worthwhile. The trial gun arrived yesterday, but it'll be Friday night, two days away, before I can do any trapshooting with it. Out here in the country we don't have fields that run daily, worse luck.

This "Featherlight Automatic" De Luxe Trap 51 is a handsome job—the wood is full fancy figured walnut—crotch grained—and the checkering front and rear is hand done and well done. The capped pistol grip (with the ubiquitous white spacer, and ditto between the butt and the solid red-rubber Pachmayr-type pad) has a smooth curve, if a trifle long. The semi-beavertail fore-end offers good control, the fingers getting a firm grasp in the shallow grooving. The wood is finished to a pleasant medium luster, not glazed, and the grain comes through nicely. The bluing has a low reflectivity, too, I'm glad to see. There's some light scrolling on the receiver sides, but I don't think it's engraving.

Ithaca lists the De Luxe Trap at "8 lbs. (approx.)," but this sample runs 11 oz. heavier—density of this fancy walnut, doubtless, and the fact that it has a Monte Carlo comb, accounting for the difference. Ithaca says this type of trap stock has dimensions of 1½"x1½"x2¼"x14½", but this one is only 1⅞"-plus at the heel, and the length to the center of the pad is 14⅜". Anyway, aside from needing a bit more length, the 51 Trap fits me well, so that's one alibi I won't have come Friday!

The gun reached me in two pieces—barrel assembly-forearm and buttstock-receiver. It went together quickly, without a hitch, and spare barrels will interchange without fitting. Further takedown—when gas-chamber cleaning is indicated—is also easy, and southpaws can readily reverse the safety themselves. (I just removed the gas piston— easily done—and Ithaca test-fired this gun all right, as the small amount of carbon showed).

An instruction booklet comes with the 51, giving clear details of takedown, cleaning, parts, etc.

The de luxe trap 51s may be had with 28" or 30" barrels, choked IM or F. The test

Top—Ithaca's Model 280 "English" double gun. Below is their Model LSA-55 De luxe centerfire rifle.

Ithaca Model 51 De luxe Trapgun

gun has a 30″ tube, but I can't locate the stamping for the choke designation anywhere, though a slip of paper packed with it reads "12-30—Full Trap Choke," so I guess that's it. I'll see if I can find a worn dime somewhere.

All 51s are 12 gauge, have 2¾″ chambers, and carry 3 shots, no more. Standard grades weigh about 7½ lbs., are made with or without vent ribs on 30″, 28″ and 26″ barrels, these choked Full; F., Mod. or Skeet, and Imp. Cyl. or Skeet respectively. One does not get the fancy walnut on the regular grades, of course, which is reflected in their lower prices. A table shown here gives stock dimensions of all Ithaca 51 variations and their suggested retail prices.

Stock Dimensions—Prices

Field/skeet	1⅝ x 2½ x 14
Trap	1½ x 1⅞ x 14¼
De L. Skeet	1½ x 2¼ x 14
De L. Trap	1½ x 1⅞ x 14½
De L. Trap/MC	1½ x 1½ x 2¼ x 14½

Field	$179.95
Field/VR	204.95
Skeet/VR	209.95
Trap/VR	214.95
De L. Skeet	234.95
De L. Trap	244.95
De L. Trap/MC	254.95

An old friend of many years standing, Jim Tollinger, designed a gas-operated system of the Ithaca 51. The breech mechanism has 3 locking lugs, not one, for greater strength and safety, the bolt rotating to the top to prevent dirt or debris being caught. The unique 2-piece gas system uses no washers, rings or whatever. One moving part, that small piston I've mentioned, actuates the ejection-loading mechanism. The piston is hardened and ground, so it should offer long, trouble-free service. However, in case there is trouble, the gas cylinder-piston unit is fully interchangeable, with no need to replace the entire barrel.

This new gas system is also self-compensating, so that automatic adjustment is made for various loads—a good feature. Recoil with the new 51 is minimal, too.

Receivers of the 51 are machined and milled from solid steel, ordnance grade, and the component parts are hand fitted as well for smooth functioning. I found that to be the case in preliminary trials—operation couldn't be faulted in that brief session, and recoil, as claimed, was soft. Nearly 8¾ lbs. of gun helped in that department, of course.

I met Jim Tollinger when he worked in the gunshop at Marshall Fields (Chicago), just after the war. Jim, who graduated from the University of Budapest (Hungary) with a degree in design engineering,

and had just left U.S. Army Ordnance, was even then busy designing and building new gun mechanisms, one out of many being a 10 gauge slide action that was of great technical interest.

Last evening Wayne Beggs and I went out to the local trap field with the M51, the light good and little wind. Because there was nobody else around, we decided to shoot a fire-and-fall-back game rather than a regular round. Starting at 16 yards we'd move back a couple of yards if we busted a bird there, and so on to 20, 22, etc.

Between us we put 100 trap loads through the M51, with nary a bobble—the gun functioned perfectly—and Wayne got as far back as 30/32 yards several times. Not me, though—the longest yardage I reached was 22, and that not very often. We were, of course, moving forward if we missed a clay.

Wayne and I agreed that the new M51 Ithaca was a climbing-bird gun, at least in this de luxe trap grade. We soon learned that we had to see the birds well over the front sight, otherwise we'd be over-shooting. Once that was discovered, we had no more trouble—well, Beggs didn't anyway, for he was breaking the clays 'way out there. JTA

Jana International

Importer of the excellent Parker-Hale rifles for the past several years, Jana is now handling the Spanish-made Laurona Model 67G 12 gauge over-under shotgun. Chrome-plated bores, ventilated rib, hand engraving, extractors, and automatic safety are standard. The main feature of the Laurona is the "twin-single triggers," which can be used to fire both barrels in succession with two pulls—front trigger fires the lower barrel first followed by the upper barrel with a second pull; pulling the rear trigger first fires the upper barrel, then a second pull fires the lower barrel. The arrangement works, and well, and while the Browning Superposed had the same design in the early 1930s, it hasn't been seen in recent years. Finish and metal-to-wood fit on the model examined were excellent. Weight, with 28-inch barrels chambered for 3-inch shells, was 7 pounds 2 ounces—a good compromise. LS

JBL Arms Co.

Dumoulin is an old name to European shooters, but these Belgian-made rifles have not always been readily available to U.S. shooters. Now they can be had from JBL Arms or, in Canada, from Ellwood Epps Guns, Ltd. Three bolt action models are listed; a 24-inch barreled rifle and a varmint model differ only in barrel weight, while the 20-inch-barrel carbine has a full Mannlicher-style one-piece stock. The standard rifle is offered with an F.N. Mauser Supreme or Finnish Sako action, button-rifled barrel, select French walnut stock with beavertail fore-end, hand checkering, rosewood fittings, grip cap inlay, recoil pad and QD swivel studs. Standard calibers range from 22-250 to 358 Winchester, including 25-06 and 30-06. Most Norma, Remington and Winchester magnums cost $15 extra. The several Weatherby magnums—and 300 and 375 H&H magnums—cost and extra $29. African calibers—404 Jeffrey, 416 Rigby, 425 Westley Richards, 458 Winchester, 460 Weatherby and 505 Gibbs— are $58 more. More extras —Presentation Grade French walnut adds $240; different checkering patterns tack on $15 to $51; six engraving grades can add up to $960—the best—for the oak leaf motif with gold inlays; antique silver finish, $20; and on and on!

Henri Dumoulin double rifles are available from JBL Arms in medium and heavy calibers, weights about 7¾ and 10 pounds respectively. Delivery time, 9 to 12 months, only through your local dealer. The actions are of Anson & Deeley type with triple Purdey locking, Holland type ejectors, and a choice of satin chrome or case-hardened finish without extra charge. Single or double triggers are available, but the safety is strictly non-automatic. Barrels are Krupp steel, 25½ inches long, with shallow-V rear and silver bead front sight; factory loads are required to group within about 3 inches or less at 65 yards. Extra barrels are $400 in medium calibers, $500 for the heavies. Stocks are French walnut with German-style or Monte Carlo cheekpiece, oil or glossy finish, beavertail or standard fore-end. Fine checkering is standard fore and aft, as is a pistol grip on standard and deluxe models. The deluxe heavy calibers have a pistol grip cap with a trap for a spare sight.

The medium caliber rifles are chambered for 7x65R, 30-06, 8x57, 8x60RS or 9.3x74R cartridges; the heavy rifle is available only in 375 H&H, 458 Winchester or 500/465 calibers. The medium caliber standard rifle goes at $1200; the standard heavy caliber rifle costs $1640. Deluxe grades cost another $176 and $220 respectively. L.S.

JBL/Dumoulin Double Rifle

Harrington and Richardson

Ted Rowe, Jr. (right), president of H&R, and Tom Wallace, director of the Springfield Armory Museum, look over an "Officers Model" Springfield. A limited number of these rare rifles have been recreated by H&R to commemorate its Centennial Year in 1971. The Springfield Armory Museum, which has an original "Officers Model" on display, is also celebrating its 100th birthday this year. In the background is an H&R handgun display that was on view at America's 1876 Centennial Exposition in Phil.

Despite price increases on everything, H&R had done an exceptional job of holding the line. The Topper line increased a maximum of $3.50, this on the 490 Topper Jr. The 14-model revolver line has only two increases: $3 on the 949 Forty-Niner and $1 on the 970 Starter Revolver. The 404 double barrel shotgun is still $99.95, without checkering, or as the 404C with checkering for $109.95. The 317 rifle is now chambered for two additional calibers—17 and 222 Remington—at no increase. The 760 and 755 single shot rimfire rifles have been discontinued. The 865 Plainsman and 750 Pioneer rifles are $5 higher, and two modified versions with Mannlicher-style stocks have been introduced as the 866 and 751 at $49.95 and $38.95.

The 4-caliber HK-4 pistol is no more. The 1970 model is available in 380 auto for $110, and for $37.50 more you can buy a 22 rimfire conversion kit. A special limited edition (2000 pistols) set is $160. This includes the HK-4 380 pistol and the rimfire conversion kit, all in a red velvet-lined wood presentation case. These sets have special numbers (HR 1 to HR 2000), a golden name plate on the slide, and a gold-plated trigger.

Brand new from H&R is the Harrich No. 1, a single barrel trapgun built by Sodia in Ferlach, Austria, to H&R specifications. For further details of this Harrich see the Testfire Reports elsewhere in this issue.

One of the new items from Webley & Scott, Ltd., offered by H&R is an over-under boxlock shotgun—the Model 900. The color hardened receiver is engraved with English scroll—naturally. Select French walnut is used for the semi-pistol grip stock and fore-end, and hand checkering is standard. Game and Skeet gun stock dimensions are: 1½" by 2¼" by 14¾"; for the trap model they're 1 5/16" by 1¾" by 14¾". Single selective or double triggers are available, and the safety is manual. The 26" or 28" barrels on the Game and Skeet guns are choked Imp. Cyl. and Mod., or both may be had with Imp. Cyl. bores. The 28" or 30" trap gun barrrels come Mod. and F or F and F. The 900 guns weigh about 7¼ pounds, depending on barrel lengths and wood density. At about $650 the 900 should find a home with many U.S. shooters. A de luxe version—the 901—has extra special French walnut, rose engraving, and letter-perfect finish, according to the spec sheet, plus a price tag bordering on $1000.

The Webley Hawk is a new air rifle for 1971, with interchangeable barrels. This break-action rifle will probably sell in the $50-$60 range, in 22 or 177 caliber, with the 2-barrel combination several dollars higher. The Hawk weighs under 6 pounds. Cocking the Hawk automatically puts it on safe, an unusual and worthwhile feature. The sights are adjustable, and the receiver is grooved for tip-off scopes. The pistol grip stock has a Monte Carlo comb with cheekpiece and recoil pad, the fore-end grooved for easier handling. The barrels are steel, button rifled, and easily interchanged.

H&R, celebrating their centennial in 1971, are doing it in a big way with a Commemorative Officer's Model Springfield rifle. Priced at $250, and chambered for the 45-70 cartridge of current manufacture, the Springfield is being "Made in America" as a limited production replica of the original—which bring upwards of $3000—when you can find one. While not an exact replica, it is an excellent re-creation using modern methods and materials to produce a shootable rifle.

H&R's Officers Model Springfield, a close replica of the rare and famous original made on the 1873 U.S. rifle.

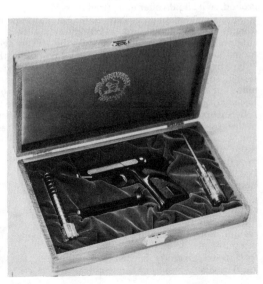

H&R's "Commemorative Auto Pistol Set" offers matched barrels and magazines in 380 and 22 LR calibers, these and the pistol specially serial numbered.

The most noticeable differences are the absence of the buckhorn sight on the barrel, the detachable pistol grip (found on the rifles made after April, 1877). The original globe front sight is now a blade. There are a few other minor changes—necessary in order to conform to modern manufacturing processes. The action parts are basically investment castings, which can be made to dimensions previously obtainable only by milling; they are equally as strong, if not more so.

The barrel length is the same—26 inches—and the oil finished walnut stock has one barrel band, plus being checkered on the fore-end and around the grip. The breech-block, receiver, hammer, lock, band, and buttplate heel have a limited amount of engraving, as did the original, and the fore-end of the stock is tipped with white metal—in the H&R model the metal is aluminum cast directly into the stock before finishing so it becomes almost a part of the wood. A decoration not found on the original is a large polished brass plaque, on the right side of the butt, bearing the inscription: *Officer's Model Springfield Rifle, Harrington & Richardson Centennial 1871-1971.*

The OMS is mainly a collector's item, but it is chambered for an available cartridge, which means it can be shot. We'd hoped to make a brief accuracy report, but a test rifle wasn't available in time (May 1, 1971).

At the NRA show in Washington the first part of April, H&R introduced another near-replica based on the single shot Springfield action—an 1873 carbine commemorating Springfield Armory. This one is strictly a collector's item, unless you enjoy shooting single shots with a $1000 price tag.   Larry Sterett.

Replica Arms

This Ohio firm has been handling black powder replica handguns and long arms for several years. For 1971 four new arms have been added. The first item examined, a replica M1862 Colt revolver in 36 caliber at $89.95, has a one-piece walnut stock, half-fluted and rebated cylinder, and barrel lengths of 4½, 5½ or 6½ inches. Really new is a 12 gauge muzzle-loading shotgun with 28-inch browned steel barrels—chrome-lined and choked modified and full. It has bar-action locks and the nipples accept size 11 caps. A French walnut stock and fore-end, hand checkered, are standard. The plain model is $139.95, the engraved version $160. (Wadcutter, nipple wrench and shot pouch, etc., may be available by the time you read this.) Replica has offered two excellent long arms—the Berdan and the Plainsman—for some time, but in early 1971 a third model—the Ohioan—was introduced. Available only in 45 caliber at $149.95, the new rifle has a Kentucky type full stock, single trigger (no set), and brass trim. The 6-groove 35-inch barrel is dovetailed for fixed sights (adjustable sights can be installed if desired). Bore

diameter is .452-inch, the grooves .006-inch deep. Over-all the Ohioan is 49½ inches long, weight about 6½ pounds.

RA's newest item is the M1875 Remington cartridge revolver mentioned in our 25th edition. Priced at $134.95, this modern 7½-inch barreled single action replica is chambered for 38 Special or 45 Long Colt cartridges.

The original Remington M1875 was chambered in 45 Long Colt, 45 Gov't. (*not* 45-70 Gov't.), 44-40 WCF and 44 Remington, had a blued finish, oil-finished walnut stocks and a lanyard loop at the bottom of the grip. The civilian version was usually nickel-plated, but the new replica will be like the blued Army version. Some 25,000 of the original M1875 Remington Army were made before it was replaced by the M1890 (only 2000 or so of the latter were manufactured, with 5½ or 7½ inch barrels in 44-40 only). The Remington was an excellent revolver, but the Colt M1873 had a head start and a name that was almost a household term for revolver. If the new replica proves as good as the original it will be something; a test model was not available, but if one arrives in time a report will appear elsewhere in this edition.   LS

Remington Arms Company

It had to happen, and it was almost a sure bet that Remington would introduce it—a commercial 17-cal. cartridge. In the 1950-1970 period 15 new cartridges, not counting the 444 Marlin, were introduced by one firm—Remington Arms Co., Inc. For 1971 the same firm brought out the 17 Remington. The new cartridge is unlike any of the 17-cal. wildcats currently existing, but it is possible that 17/222 rifles could be rechambered for the 17. Made by necking down the 223 Remington, the new 17 has the same case length, case diameter, and shoulder angle of the original 223 caliber. However, the shoulder on the 17 Remington has been moved back .087" to improve accuracy, it's said.

The new 17 is loaded with a 25-gr. HP "Power-Lokt" bullet of .1725" diameter. Muzzle velocity out of a 24" barrel is listed at 4020 fps, making it the fastest factory-loaded round in current production. Sighted in at 200 yards the drop at 300 yards is only 6.3", very close to the 6mm Remington for flatness. The new 17 will be available only in the Model 700 BDL at first. The 24" barrel has a twist of 1 turn in 9 inches, so factory ballistics should be realistic. The 17s have shown increased popularity the past few years, so the new 17 Remington should sell well.

The Model 700 BDL has been available as a heavy barrel "Varmint Special" since 1967. The 25-06 Remington can now be had in the HB version, its 24" barrel having a twist of 1 turn in 10 inches. The slightly tapered barrel similar to those used on the 40-XB rifles, has front and rear blocks for mounting a varmint or target-type scope.

The 580 series of rimfire rifles was introduced by Remington in 1967. The same

basic action was later used for the excellent Model 540-X target rifle. Now another version is available—the 580 Boy's Rifle, containing all features of the original 580 except that the stock has been shortened and specially tailored to young shooters. The length of pull is 12⁵⁄₁₆" a full inch shorter than the regular model. The barrel is still 24" long to provide a long sighting radius.

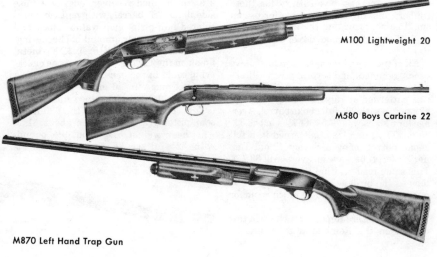

M100 Lightweight 20

M580 Boys Carbine 22

M870 Left Hand Trap Gun

Remington hasn't forgotten the shotgunners. January of 1971 saw the introduction of the M870 in 12 and 20 gauges with left-hand actions—exact mirror-image versions of their right-hand counterparts. Loading/ejection ports are on the left side of the receiver and left-handed safeties are standard. All other features, including the super smooth "vibra-honing" of the metal surfaces, remain the same. Three 12-gauge versions are available—a Field Grade with 30" full, 28" modified or 26" improved cylinder barrel, plain or with vent ribs; a Magnum with 30" full choke barrel, plain or with vent rib, and a Trap Grade with 30" full choke barrel, standard or Monte Carlo stock. The only 20 offered now is a Field Grade—28" full or modified, or 26" improved cylinder barrel, plain or vent rib. (NOTE: Barrels for the right-hand 870 will not interchange with barrels on the left-hand guns.)

Another new Remington is a 20-gauge Lightweight Magnum 1100 to supplement the regular 20-gauge Lightweight 1100 introduced in 1970. The Lightweight Magnum has the smaller frame and mahogany stock of the standard Lightweight, and will initially be made with a 28" full choke barrel—plain or with vent rib—chambered for 3" magnum shells. (The new barrel will *not* interchange with barrels on the regular Lightweight 1100 chambered for 2¾" shells.) The new Lightweight Magnum makes for 62 different specifications offered in the 1100; an impressive choice for an impressive shotgun.

Remington introduced a new 2½" 410 load in 1970, made with a one-piece plastic base wad and a larger-diameter No. 97-4 primer. For 1971 Remington incorporated these features into a 3" shell for improved patterns and reloadability. The choice of shot sizes will be No. 4, 5, 6, 7½ and 9, giving the 410 shotgunner a size for every job.

Bridgeport didn't forget the handgunner either. For 1971 three new handgun loads were announced, the result of continued 38 Special development. These new loads include the 9mm Parabellum (Luger) with a 115-gr. jacketed HP bullet, muzzle velocity 1160 fps from a 4" test barrel; a 158-gr. semi-jacketed HP 357 Magnum loaded to a muzzle velocity of 1550 fps (8¾" test barrel) and a 240-gr. semi-jacketed HP for the 44 Remington Magnum, loaded to 1470 from a 6½" test barrel. These new loads—the bullets will be available for reloading —provide increased versatility for these calibers, making them suitable for use on small game, providing the handgunner is skillful enough to make use of their potential.

All of the new Remington products have been examined, and several given a limited amount of testing. The new 3" 410 load was patterned at 25 yards using a Savage 77F pump with 26" full choke barrel. Average for 5 shots was 77.5% of 7½s in the 30" circle. The same load, patterned in a full choke barrel using a Savage "Four-Tenner" insert tube, gave an average of 63.7%. This same load on Blue Rocks was OK as long as the birds were taken quickly—¾-ounce of shot doesn't allow much room for error.

See my Testfire Report elsewhere in this edition on the Remington 25-06 and 17 rifles. L.S.

New Remington Rounds Since 1950
16—count 'em—16

Introduction of the 17 Remington centerfire cartridge is the latest in a long line of metallic cartridges developed by Remington Arms Company, Inc., over the past twenty-one years.

The total makes for an impressive list, with everything from varmints to North America's biggest game covered. Remington's goal has been, basically, to meet three primary objectives:

To give American hunters a wider range of calibers and ballistic performance for use on the great variety of game and hunting conditions existing in North America.

To improve the performance aspects of sporting cartridges available to Ameri-

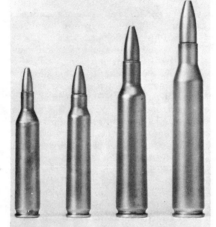

From left—17, 223, 6mm and 25-06 Remingtons.

Richland Arms

This firm's side-by-side and O-U shotguns —such as the 844—are fairly well-known, for they're the models listed in the Richland catalog and those usually reported on in various publications. Richland, however, also carries a line of shotguns that is not advertised, does not appear in the catalog, and is available only in limited numbers. Each year these various models are sold to dealers in early February; no retail price is set, so the dealer's prices may vary from those mentioned below. Included this year are the Models 117T, 812, 820, 108, 107, 109 and 232; the first 4 are over-unders, the last 3 side-by-sides. All have boxlock action and two triggers. The 117T has a satin-chromed receiver, engraved false sideplates, 28" barrels with vent rib, dark-colored half-pistol grip walnut stock and fore-end with a fair amount of checkering. Priced to sell for just over $200, metal finish on the 117T was good, but the checkering could have been better. The 820 is a 20-gauge magnum, 26" or 28" barrels, vent rib, straight-grip stock blued finish; $150 or less. The 108, similar to the 820 has a semi-pistol grip stock, price about $150. The heavyweight 812, about 9½ pounds with 32" full choke 12-bore barrels, is

can shooters via the development and introduction of new calibers.

To offer high performance ammunition and sporting arms, shooting equipment that is readily accessible at retail outlets throughout the country.

Here's the list of new calibers introduced by Remington since 1950. Even if these were the only ones in existence, the American rifleman/hunter would still be superbly equipped for all possible hunting situations available to him.

1950 - 222 Remington
1955 - 244 Remington
1955 - 44 Remington Magnum
1957 - 280 Remington
1958 - 222 Remington Magnum
1961 - 22 Remington "Jet" Magnum
1962 - 7mm Remington Magnum
1963 - 221 Remington "Fire Ball"
1963 - 6mm Remington
1964 - 223 Remington
1965 - 22-250 Remington
1965 - 350 Remington Magnum
1966 - 6.5mm Remington Magnum
1970 - 25-06 Remington
1970 - 5mm Remington Rimfire Magnum
1971 - 17 Remington

Of these cartridges, only a few have failed to make the grade. The 280 cartridge, an excellent one in its own right, and beautifully accurate in most Remington rifles made for it, was soon overshadowed by the more versatile 7mm Rem. Magnum. The 244, victim of its own bullet weight choice and the slower twist of the rifle chambered for it, is seen in the 6mm Rem., n identical envelope. The 22 Rem. Jet and the 221 "Fireball" are fading fast.

chambered for 3" shells. Double triggers, plain extractors, manual safety, plain blue finish, and a recoil pad are standard. The 812 is just over $200, or it may be bought with extra 26" barrels, choked modified and full for some $300, thus two guns on one action.

Side-by-side models include the 232 (12 or 20 magnum) with 27" or 25" vent rib barrels in the respective gauges. Plain blue metal, a straight grip stock are standard. Just over $100. The 107 (12, 20, 28 or 410) has a satin-chromed receiver with false sideplates, 28" barrels, straight stock, sells at about $150, without false sideplates something over $100. The 109 (12/26" or 28" and 20/22" IC and Mod.) sells for $150.

The really big news at Richland is their 10-gauge "Waterfowler" O-U 810. Made in Italy it lists at $320, has 32" vent-rib barrels with 3½" chambers. A walnut stock and fore-end, recoil pad and hand checkering are standard. About 10½ pounds, the 810 has two triggers, manual safety and extractors. The blued Kersten lock action has a small amount of engraving. Böhler steel barrels, choked full and full, have long forcing cones for maximum range and pattern density. The 810 should be welcomed by the confirmed goose hunter. LS

Richland Arms' 810 Over-Under 10 gauge has 32" barrels, takes 3½" shells, weighs about 10½ pounds.

Lyman Gun Sight Corp.

Lyman, now a member of the Leisure Group, has been busy the past year. New items introduced include Alox/Beeswax Bullet Lube, a Universal Case Trimmer, Stock/Bluing Kits, and a new edition (45th) of the *Lyman Reloading Handbook*. But the really big news is Lyman's introduction of replica and black powder arms. The first entry was a pair of revolvers—the New Model Navy and New Model Army in calibers 36 and 44 at $94.95 and $96.95 respectively. The Remington design was chosen because of its strength—the top strap on the solid frame also provides a base for adjustable sights. Target versions of both guns, with adjustable sights may be ready by the time this appears in print.

Two muzzle-loading rifles, scheduled for 1971, are based on the Hawken design. 45- and 58-cal. models should be ready by summer, in plenty of time for the 1971 hunting season. Lyman is also planning a full line of black powder accessories—powder flasks, nipple wrenches, target sights, carrying boxes, lubricants, and possibly even cast lead balls ready for shooting. A complete black powder kit for beginning shooters has been considered; this would include the rifle or revolver and everything necessary to shoot it—right out of the box. Other possibilities include a build-it-yourself kit for shooters wanting to assemble their own guns, special publications for black powder shooters, and Lyman-promoted black powder shoots. (A permanent trophy—the Lyman National Muzzle Loading Revolver Championship Trophy—has been presented to the National Muzzle Loading Association at Friendship, Indiana.)

The Universal Case Trimmer, used to trim some 17-cal. brass, was almost as fast as a power trimmer. Just place the case in the 3-collet chuck, push the lever to tighten, run the pilot in and start turning the handle. Its ball-bearing chuck takes un-

Lyman's new caplock sixshooter is made in 36 and 44 calibers.

primed rimmed, rimless or belted cases, and there's an adjustable stop, of course. Nine cavities at the rear of the trimmer hold spare pilots. The trimmer can be bolted to the loading bench, or to a block for fastening in a vise. A sheet of instructions, including a table of trim lengths for current rifle and handgun cartridges, comes with the trimmer.

One of the New Model Army 44 caliber revolvers was also examined and a limited amount of firing done with it. With an 8″ barrel, it measures 13½″ over-all and weighs 42 ounces. The instructions suggest use of a .451″ ball, the charge for which being 39 grains of FFFg with Alcan caps for a velocity of 995 fps, says the 45th Handbook. No FFFg was on hand at the time, but a Lee No. 167 dipper holds 38.4 grains of Curtis & Harvey F, which is finer than Du Pont FFg. Loads checked included the above, plus 26.0 grains of FFg thrown by a flask. At 25 yards, from the bench using a two-hand hold, repeated 5-shot groups measured just over 3 inches, with C&H grouping in the black, the FFg slightly lower. Alcan G11F caps were used and

lithium grease was applied above the balls to fill the chambers to the mouth. All loading was done at the bench with the aid of the MCK EZ-Loader.

Newest Lyman items include a 505-gr. scale—the Model D-7—and a powder dribbler; a 20x bench rest scope, and 9 styles of shooting glasses. The D-7, at $17.50, is black with easy-to-read white figures, and 1/10-gr. accuracy (plus or minus) is guaranteed; it has magnetic damping, and a lifter to raise the knife edge off the bearing—a worthwhile feature on all scales, but seldom seen on those under $30. The dribbler is $3.

The 20x scope is the compact style, with internal adjustments for windage and elevation. Only 17″ long, and weighing only 15⅛ ounces, the new scope has a 1″ tube and uses conventional mounts. It is parallax adjustable from 50 yards to infinity, and click adjustments are an optional ⅛″ or ¼″. Reticles include dot, crosshair, tapered post, or tapered post with crosshair. Designed for competition benchrest shooters, the price is $109.50. A lot of varmint hunters will probably buy it, too.   LS

Marlin Firearms

Marlin celebrated its centennial in 1970, but it definitely did not rest on its laurels. Instead, it started the second century by introducing more than a dozen new or modified sporting arms. Topping the list was the 444 Sporter. In answer to demands for a shorter version of this "big bore" Marlin chopped two inches off the barrel and added a pistol grip. Otherwise the rifle is the same as the regular 444 (except for the squared-up lever loop on the regular model), including the price of $145. The other centerfire modifications include giving the Glenfield 30-30 carbine a full length magazine, thus increasing its capacity to 6 rounds: the modification is labeled the 30A, the price $105. A slight change is apparent on the 336T, which has had the lever loop squared to the same shape as that found on the Model 1894 carbine.

For rimfire lovers there are 8 new models or modifications to choose from. The 49 has become the 49DL with a scroll-engraved receiver and a slightly changed impressed-checkering pattern on the pistol grip; the 99C now has impressed checkering on the pistol grip and fore-end. The

veteran Model 39 lever action rifle has become the 39D at $99.95, complete with pistol grip walnut stock and tapered round 20½-inch barrel. A few of the Model 39 Century Ltd. anniversary models are still available at $125, complete with tapered octagon barrel.

The National Rifle Association celebrates its centennial during 1971, and Marlin salutes the NRA with a pair of "Article II" arms based on the Model 39. These have tapered octagon barrels—20

inches for the carbine, 24 for the rifle, curved brass buttplates, walnut stocks, pistol grip for the rifle and straight grip for the carbine, and a "The Right To Bear Arms" medallion inserted on the right side of the receiver. The price? $135 for either, and production will be limited.

Marlin has gone to series models for their bolt action rifles, with the exception of the 101 single shot which has a new ramp front sight and a slightly different stock—minus pistol grip cap. The new

Top—Marlin's 39M Article II rifle carries the Right to Bear Arms symbol. Below, Marlin 444 Sporter with the M800 scope.

rimfire rifles are the 780 and 781 chambered for 22 Short, Long, and Long Rifle cartridges, with the 782 and 783 chambered for the 22 WRM cartridge. The 780 and 782 models have detachable 7-round box magazines; the 781 and 783 use tubular magazines. The all-steel receivers are newly designed, as are the trigger guards, and the one-piece walnut stocks, complete with fluted Monte Carlo comb, and impressed checkering on the grip, are decided improvements. The stocks all have white buttplate spacers, but the pistol grip cap and spacer have been dropped. Swivels and sling come with the magnum models, and all 4 rifles in the 700 series have grooved receivers for tip-off telescope mounts; the receiver surface is serrated for non-glare sighting. Over-all these new rifles form an excellent appearing group. But no firing has been done with any of them, thus nothing can be said about functioning or accuracy.

The L.C. Smith sidelock double barrel shotgun has been scarce—its production is limited—yet Marlin has gone a step further and introduced the Deluxe L.C. Smith at $400. For the extra $75 over the standard L.C. Smith you can not only receive the quality of the standard, but you receive select American walnut in the pistol grip stock and the new beavertail fore-end, along with a geniune Simmons floating ventilated rib.

The really big news in the Marlin camp is the 120 Magnum Pump Gun. (Would you believe the 120 receiver looks very similar

Top—Marlin's L.C. Smith in DeLuxe grade. Other gun is their Model 120, a single barrel pump.

to a discontinued shotgun with the same two first digits? The new 120 is entirely a "Made in America" arm, and its receiver is machined from a solid block of high tensile steel. All parts of the 120 action—operating or non-operating—are of steel alloys with no plastics or non-ferrous parts. The first 120s—due about the time you read this—will be in 12 gauge only, with a choice of 26-inch Improved Cylinder, 28-inch Modified, or 30-inch Full choke barrel topped with an all-steel floating ventilated rib having front and middle beads. (Barrels are completely interchangeable in seconds, and extra barrels are available at $50 each, complete with vent rib.) The 120 will handle regular 2¾-inch shells or 3-inch magnums. Double action bars provide a non-binding silky-smooth action, and a new-design slide-lock release that can be operated with gloves on, are desireable features. The stock and semi-beavertail fore-

end are of American walnut with impressed checkering; a fluted comb, pistol grip cap, and deluxe recoil pad are standard. Other features include an engine-turned bolt, big-head crossbolt safety in the front of the trigger guard, and a stainless steel follower in the 5-round magazine—3-shot plug furnished. Putting all of this in a $150 package is quite an accomplishment for the Marlin firm.

The Marlin scope line has remained the same, but there are two other items of interest to shooters. The first is the Veri-Fire—a precision optical collimator for scope on iron sight installation. It comes complete with 22 and 30 caliber spuds at $25, and extra spuds are $2-$2.50 each depending on caliber. The second item is a wall plaque of simulated woodgrain moulding carrying Article II of The Bill of Rights. About 10"x13¼", the plaque is available directly from Marlin for $5 postpaid. LS

Mauser-Bauer Corp.

The corporation is new, but the Mauser name is world renowned. Interarms distributes Mauser handguns, but M-B distributes Mauser long arms only, at least for now. The current line comprises 5 each of rifles and shotguns.

The M3000 and M4000 rifles have the same basic modified '98 action as the earlier M2000 handled by Interarms, except the M4000 is smaller and chambered only in 222 or 223 Remington. At $179.95, the 6¾-lb. M4000 has a folding-leaf rear sight and a hooded ramp front. The M3000 at $189.95 in standard calibers ($218 in magnums) is sightless—iron sights are $10 extra—but it's tapped for all popular scope mounts. The barrels, cold forged or "hammered," are 22" to 26", depending on caliber—243, 270, 308, 30-06, 7mm Rem. Mag., 300 Win. Mag. and 375 H&H Magnum. The unusual safety, on the right side of the streamlined bolt sleeve, blocks the firing pin, hence the bolt can be operated with the safety "on," and cartridges chambered or removed. The floorplate release, just ahead of the guard, requires holding the hand underneath to catch the cartridges—it takes some getting used to, but it works. (A left-hand M3000 is $239 for standard calibers. Actions, barrels, and barreled actions are available.)

The M660 Short Action Mauser rifle, $319 in 243, 270, 308 and 30-06, has an action only 4½" long, some 3½" shorter than the regular '98.

These short-action Mausers, with interchangeable barrel system, have been described at length in these pages previously, so they won't be detailed here, but a new caliber combo will be described.

A big game version—the 660 Safari at $399, is made in 458 and 375 H&H, weight about 10 pounds. Tapped for scope mounts, it also carries a bead front sight and an express-type rear on the barrel sleeve. The magazine holds 3 rounds (like the standard rifle), but the barrel is 25½" and the stock is simpler—no grip cap flare and the fore-end tip is more conventional.

The over-under rifle, $1200, is made in the same calibers as the standard 660. About 7¼ pounds, its 24" barrel has a tapered matted rib and open sights. The boxlock receiver, satin chromed with game scene engraving, has Kersten bolting and auto ejectors. The tang safety is non-automatic, and cocking indicators project from the stock flats. Two (adjustable) triggers are standard, and the trigger guard is horn, not metal. The wood, French walnut, is skip-line checkered fore and aft, and the stock has that slightly humpbacked curve and small cheekpiece so beloved by Germans.

Three over-under shotguns are available—the 620 International Champion, the

71E and the 72E. Lowest priced is the 71E at $315, made only as a 12/28" with chrome-lined barrels choked IM and F. Its action, color hardened, has a Greener crossbolt, selective ejectors, and manual safety. It features the twin single triggers now becoming popular. The front trigger fires the bottom barrel first, then the upper barrel, or the rear trigger fires the top barrel first, and so on. Each trigger can be used independently, if desired, as on a standard double trigger shotgun. The French walnut stock and beavertail forearm have ample hand checkering. The comb, rather narrow but not sharp, is unfluted.

The 72E at $399 uses the same basic action and stock of the 71E, but the receiver and guard are hand engraved in open scroll, and the finish may be glossy black, satin chrome, or color hardened. Field and trap grades are available with 28" or 30" barrels respectively, choked Mod. and F, plus a 28" Skeet gun. All have VR barrels. Skeet and trap grades have ventilated recoil pads. The 72E has a single selective trigger, the selector lever located on the upper rear shank of the trigger—very easy to operate. The 71E and 72E models weigh about 7½ pounds.

M-B's Model 496, a single barrel trapgun.

An excellent—if not new—idea, aside from interchangeability. Mounting the trigger(s) system on the guard offers greater strength via less cutting away of wood and metal in the action area. Cleaning, oiling, adjusting and repair are more readily done, too, with no fear of excess oil getting into the wood.

The triggers are adjustable for pull and travel, and all have a slight twist to the right to position the finger correctly.

The chrome-lined barrels of the test gun, 29 3/16″ long, are topped with a .425″ ventilated rib with muzzle and center beads. Chokes were F and IM, but F and M, or M and IC barrels are available in this length, while the 28″ Skeet model barrels have special chokes that combine a recess and a flare. The receiver is machined from a forging of chrome-nickel-molybdenum steel; a color hardened finish is standard, but an engraved model with satin chrome finish can be had on special order. Lockup, a modified Kersten bolting, is satisfactory, but tends to crowd the upper barrel area. Selective ejectors are standard.

The 620 stock and fore-end are of French walnut, hand checkered 26 lines-per-inch with a border; there were a few runouts on the grip area and some border-area diamonds were not complete. The wide, comfortable comb is fluted. Stock dimensions ran 1$\frac{7}{16}$″ x 1$\frac{15}{16}$″ x 14$\frac{5}{8}$″ to the single trigger. The beavertail forearm has finger flats—not grooves—on the upper sides, and inletting of the forearm iron is above average. The test gun weighs 7¾ pounds, and a recoil pad is standard.

The 620 was patterned with Winchester AA trap loads. Five-shot averages for the IM barrel was 61.4°, 76.2° for the full choke barrel. Results at trap were satisfactory, but the 620 doesn't point as naturally for me as some other over-unders. The price seems a mite high, too, for the quick-detachable-trigger Perazzi is $200 less.

The 580, the only side-by-side double in the M-B line, is a classic example of English styling. The action is a Holland & Holland type sidelock with double safety levers, and coil springs instead of leaf; the inner wall of the lockplate is engine-turned, the outside fully scroll engraved to match the satin-chromed receiver areas. The 28″ barrels are chrome-lined, choked IM and F, are chambered for 2¾″ or 3″ magnum shells. The top rib, anti-reflection coated, carries a silver-colored muzzle bead. The straight-grip French walnut stock is well figured, and 32-line hand checkered, as is the splinter fore-end. Stock finish may be lacquer or hand rubbed oil. The 6¾-lb. 580 is $850 with two triggers and selective ejectors or $935 with a single trigger.

The 496 is an 8¼-lb. single barrel trap gun at $399, made only as a 12/32″ with a full choke, vent rib chrome-lined barrel. The action has double underlugs, Greener-style crossbolt, an automatic ejector and there is no safety on the tang—a device seldom used on a trap gun since loading and closing are done just prior to firing. The engraved receiver is color hardened. The well-shaped Monte Carlo stock of select walnut has a trap-style pad and a graceful beavertail fore-end. Checkering on the fore-end and grip runs 24 line. LS

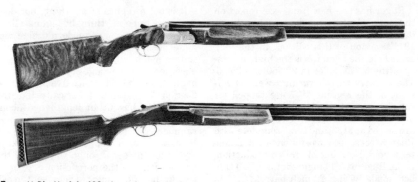

Top—M-B's Model 620, best in the line, has interchangeable trigger/lock-work assemblies. Gun below, their Model 72E, has twin-single triggers.

O.F. Mossberg & Son

This firm celebrated its 50th Anniversary in 1969. In 1970 they had several new models, including the Model 800 rifle chambered for the Remington short magnum cartridges—temporarily discontinued. For 1971 one new rifle was introduced and one shotgun reintroduced. The latter was the "New Haven" 600 in 12 and 20 gauge only with 25-inch modified-choke barrel. Except for the one barrel length and choke the 600 is almost identical to the Mossberg 500 as it was first introduced several years back—it is plain, but definitely an excellent shotgun.

The new rifle is the Model 810A, which at first glance appears to be a full length version of the excellent Model 800A. Priced at $124.95, the 810A is chambered only in 30-06 at present, but it's safe to assume it will be available later in other calibers. Weight with an 8-groove AC-KRO-GRUV 22″ barrel is just over 8 pounds, including the folding rear and ramp bead front sights. The Monte Carlo walnut stock has a fluted comb, a grip cap and rubber buttplate with white spacers, sling swivels. Checkering fore and aft is the impressed type. Over-all, woodwork on the 810A is better than on the first 800A rifles.

The action of the 810A is not simply an enlarged version of the 800A. Three or four changes are immediately noticeable without opening the bolt. The bolt handle of the 810A angles to the rear while the

degrees apart in two rows, and the bolt head is recessed so the lugs are the same diameter (.75″) as the bolt body. The 810A has two pairs of large opposing lugs—.95″ diameter compared to the bolt body diameter of only .72″—putting it more in line with the Mauser style, except for the extra pair of lugs. The extractors and ejectors of the two rifles are basically the same, although the strikers vary slightly. For most shooters the main differences are in the magazine area. The 800A has a synthetic trigger guard which houses the trigger mechanism, and is removed from the stock along with the barreled action; the stamped steel magazine shell, stock plate, and hinged floorplate are all separate pieces. On the 810A the entire trigger mechanism is pinned to the barreled action in a separate housing. When the barreled action is removed from the stock, the alloy trigger guard remains in the stock, along with the detachable 4-round magazine. Yes, a detachable 4-round magazine—the release is located directly ahead of the trigger guard and is operated by pushing forward. The magazine is easily operated and handy; designed to hold 4 cartridges, the model tested held 5 rounds, and all 5 would feed without difficulty, giving the 810A a 6 round capacity—including the one in the chamber.

To determine the accuracy capability of the 810A it was taken to the range for a limited session at the bench. No scope mount bases were available, and time was not taken to cobble any, so all firing was

800A angles forward; the 810A receiver ring is ¼-inch longer than that of the 800A, while the bridge is about .100″ longer and .070″ lower—meaning most scope mount bases for the 800A will not fit the 810A; the distance from the receiver bolt handle cut-out to the rear of the tang is over an inch longer on the 810A, and the tang shape is different; the safety or bolt cap is different on the two rifles, although the thumbpiece and action of the safety is the same. Removal of the bolts reveals other differences. The Model 800A has 6 locking lugs of varying sizes arranged 120

done with the standard open sights. Firing was done using sandbag rests, and consisted of a number of 3-shot groups using 3 brands of ammunition and two bullet weights—125-gr. and 150-gr. No group went over 5 inches at 100 yards, and most hovered around 3-4 inches—entirely satisfactory for open sights; with a scope sight the group sizes should shrink to at least half. With the Federal 125-gr. load groups went around 2 inches or slightly less—with open sights! The limited examination certainly indicates Mossberg has a real winner on its hands with the 810A. LS

Ruger has one new item—see report on the Ruger Caplock—and a few almost-new items, these covered in the "Handguns 1971" section of this edition. In the long arms field the big news is the high accuracy of the M77V rifles in 22-250 and 25-06. These heavy barrel (varmint weight) versions of the regular M77 are tapped for regular Lyman or Unertl target scope blocks. Both calibers have 24-inch barrels, are priced at $165, and come complete with Ruger steel scope rings for one-inch diameter scopes. New, but in limited production, is the Ruger No. 1 single shot in 45-70 caliber, made with a 22-inch barrel. Also in the works is an over-under shotgun, but no delivery date for production models has been given.

Ruger Caplock Revolver

The Ruger caplock revolver mentioned in the 25th Edition is well on the way to becoming a reality—possibly by the time you read this. A prototype model (No. 2), checked out in early 1971, appears to be the ultimate in percussion revolvers. The grip assembly and trigger are the same as on the Ruger Blackhawk and the feel is excellent—much better than found on replica or near-replica percussion revolvers. (The Ruger caplock can properly be termed the first modern caplock revolver

—it is not a replica of anything, nor does it profess to be anything but an excellent percussion revolver of modern design and materials.) The rear sight has a .10-inch square notch, adjustable for windage and elevation; the patridge-style ramp front has a .125-inch blade matted to prevent reflection. The frame is basically like the Ruger Blackhawk, but lengthened about ¾-inch to handle the loading lever and rammer assembly. The hammer—with the Blackhawk spur shape, but a Hawkeye style nose, passes through the rear of the frame to strike the percussion cap, or to rest in the safety notches between the cylinder nipples.

Takedown is the slickest found on any percussion revolver—at least any this writer is aware of. With the hammer at halfcock the slotted-head pin that retains the base pin, on the right side of the frame, is turned counterclockwise just over a quarter-turn; this can be done with the fingers without effort. The loading lever is now unlatched, permitting the base pin, loading lever and rammer to be slid out of the frame forward, followed by turning the cylinder out of the frame to the right. The process is simple and fast, requiring less than 10 seconds to complete.

The prototype Ruger caplock weighed 46 ounces. Over-all length was 13½ inches, barrel length 7½. The round barrel was

rifled with 6 wide, shallow grooves. The unfluted cylinder, of chrome moly steel, measured 1.680 inches in diameter, 2.00 inches in length, and weighed just over 12 ounces.

Prior to taking the Ruger to the range the trigger pull was checked, using fired caps to protect the nipples, and it broke at approximately 4½ pounds with only a slight drag. Some might feel this is a trifle heavy, but much shooting later failed to show any adverse effect on group sizes.

Weather conditions at test time were not exactly ideal—ranging from -4° F. to 42° F., and from cloudy to bright sunshine. With the thermometer hovering around zero, the first trial was a bust. Later, when the mercury had climbed above the freezing point, the caplock had 10 cylinderfuls put through it from 25 yards, using a sandbag forearm rest. Two ball sizes had been sent with the gun—.457" and .465".

Two types of black powder were used—Du Pont's FFg and Curtis & Harvey's F. (This latter powder, made in England, smaller in granule size than Du Pont FFg, is about like our FFFg.) A 44-caliber revolver flask was used part of the time, but it dropped a maximum of 26.0 grains of FFg or 29.3 grains of C&H, whereas the 45th *Lyman Handbook* recommends 37-39 grains of FFFg for .451" round balls, or 50.0 grains of FFFg for the 470" round

Sturm Ruger & Co.

From left—Top of new Ruger M77 long action shows rounded top for standard scope mounting and full-ball bolt knob. Latest 10-22 carbine, pistol grip and fore-end hand checkered, has sling swivels, is tapped for scope blocks or takes tip-off mounts. Ruger No. 1 S.S. rifle in carbine form, cal. 45-70, has new stock and lever. Ruger caplock 6-shot revolver, cal. 44.

ball in the 44 Walker. With this in mind various Lee dippers were charged with C&H black powder, struck off level, and the charge weighed on an Ohaus 304 scale. Lee's No. 129 dipper held 30.0 grains, the No. 141 held 33.3, while the No. 167 picked up 38.4 grains, all FFFg. During the first and second sessions 26.0/FFg and 30.0/C&H F were used alternately with both ball sizes, .457 and .465. The best combination proved to be 26.0/FFg with the .457 balls; the smallest group measured 2⁹⁄₁₆ inches center-to-center. The C&H F load with the .457s made one group of 3½″. All of these early groups could be covered with the hand, but the .465 ball groups averaged just over 3.0 inches.

Later on I used 33.0 and 38.4 grains of the C&H F with both ball sizes. The loading was done in sequence—charge all chambers, seat all balls, and then fill remaining space with grease. (Crisco and lithium lube were used.) With the lithium placed in a plastic squeeze bottle—a catsup dispenser works well—the entire loading process can be shortened to about 3 minutes with the aid of a revolver stand—such as the MCK E-Z-Load—excluding the capping. When the production Ruger caplock becomes available, an accessory kit including a straight-line brass capper would be an excellent idea.

Group sizes with the increased charges grew to over 3 inches; one 5-shot group did go into 2⅝ inches center-to-center, but the average measured 3⅜ inches. The smaller groups were made with 33.0/C&H pushing the .465″ balls, topped with lithium lube. A brief penetration test was also made with the above-mentioned load, shooting into water-soaked folded newsprint tied to give an 18-inch thickness; penetration averaged right at 3 inches at 15 yards.

The Ruger caplock is quite a revolver, and prototype No. 2 performed much better than some current production pieces made abroad. As with all prototypes there were a few bugs—one nipple appeared slightly oversize, making it difficult to remove the fired cap if it did not split on ignition, and there was a slight bolt drag on the cylinder. Otherwise the gun performed like a veteran. The production model will no doubt show some changes, with perhaps the chamber size reduced to handle .451″ balls—a more common size than the .457″. Another could be a slight decrease in the height of the front sight blade—the adjustable rear sight is excellent. I would like to see the loading lever web altered to a more graceful shape, but even if no changes are made, the Ruger caplock as is represents the ultimate in modern percussion revolvers.

New Ruger Arms

As this is written in late May I have yet to learn what super secret gun it is that Bill Ruger plans to spring on us come June 22, when a gaggle of gun writers gather together at Newport, N.H. It can't be the over-under shotgun Bill's building, for that gun's been already bruited about, and anyway Ed Nolan said that one ain't it. Here are the things I can tell you about, though:

There is to be a new version the No. 1 single shot rifle, this one chambered for the 45-70 cartridge only (at least so far). A few small changes will be made in the woodwork, I understand, to let the gun sell for a fair amount under the going price for the No. 1 Ruger, like $50 or so under!

A new sporting rifle version of the rimfire 10/22 autoloading Ruger is to be offered, and we'll also see the unveiling of Model 77 bolt action rifles with conventional, rounded-top receivers, permitting the use of standard scope mount bases—Conetrol, Redfield, Weaver, et al. There has been, of course, a considerable call for such receiver treatment, but Ruger will not, I think, abandon the integral-base action. As for me, I prefer the latter type—they're fixed, immovable and, in my experience, most satisfactory.

Savage Arms Company

Savage now offers some 69 models—yes, 69—priced from $26.95 for the M73 shotgun to $365 for the Anschutz Model 1413-L Target Rifle. These 69 are basic models, and that does not include the many different chamberings available, for example, in the Model 110-C—the 25-06, 7mm Remington and 300 Winchester Magnum. The Model 24 rifle/shotgun combo has been dressed up as the 24-D by separating the barrels—a la 24-V style—adding a muzzle barrel band with integral front sight, Monte Carlo stock with impressed checkering, and a satin-black metal finish—all for $77.95. A 22-inch barreled saddle gun version of the 99 has been added as the 99-A. It's available (by popular demand, according to the Savage firm) chambered for the Newton-designed 250-3000 Savage cartridge introduced nearly 60 years ago. The 99-A has the straight grip stock with a square loop lever and a slim Schnabel-style fore-end. The action is the modern version, with the top tang safety, the receiver tapped for scope mounts. The 99-A is $154.95.

One of the biggest hits of the '71 NSGA Show was a replica of the old Stevens Favorite rimfire single shot rifle; Savage doesn't call it a commemorative, but a serialized limited edition model. Priced at $75, complete with a small booklet on Joshua Stevens and his arms company, the new favorite has a straight grip walnut stock with curved solid brass buttplate, an inlaid brass medallion on the right side of the stock reading "Joshua Stevens—Father of 22 Hunting," and a slim fore-end with Schnabel. The receiver, color case-hardened, is inscribed on both sides in "gold" with *Stevens Favorite;* the hammer, underlever, and field-type rear sight elevator are

From the top—Stevens Model 71 Favorite 22 rifle, Savage 99A carbine in 250-3000, Savage Model 550 double barreled shotgun, Savage Model 30-T slide-action trapgun.

gold plated. The 22-inch octagon barrel carries a brass blade front sight. Over-all it's 37 inches, average weight about 4½ pounds.

In the scattergun department the best news—at least to this writer—was the redesigned selector on the Model 440 and 444 over-under shotguns. The ridiculous little pin sticking up through the left side of the upper tang has been replaced by a large button located in the center of the safety. Before, to shoot the upper barrel first it was necessary to push the selector pin forward each time; now you simply push the button to one side and it stays there until you decide to change it. The position is ideal, the button is large, easy to reach and operate, and not apt to be changed accidently. Shotguns equipped with the new selectors show a B after the model number, such as Model 444B.

A new side-by-side tabbed the Savage 550 was introduced in 12 and 20 gauges. It has selective auto ejectors, a wide ventilated rib with center and muzzle beads, a well-shaped tang safety, single non-selective trigger, a walnut stock with white spacers under buttplate and grip cap, and a beavertail fore-end. Except for the impressed checkering design and the stamped birds (?) on the receiver the 550 appears very similar to the Fox B-SE model. $172.95.

The 330 is now available in 12 gauge with an interchangeable set of 20 gauge barrels for $287.95. The idea is excellent, and the price is not out of line. The other new shotgun is the field grade Model 30 in 12, 20 and 410, priced at $95.95. ($99.95 for the same shotgun with an adjustable choke.) A steel receiver large enough to handle magnum chamberings, interchangeable barrels, top tang safety, and fluted beavertail fore-end are the main features, and 12 and 20 gauge slug models with rifle-type sights are available. (The slug barrel can be bought separately for $28.25, and plain or ventilated rib barrels are available for $21.75 and $43.25 respec-

tively.) A deluxe version with ventilated rib is also offered, plus a special trap model with Monte Carlo stock.

Another Anschutz air rifle has been added to the Savage line. This one—the Model 335—is slanted for use in the NRA's 333-program, but is suitable for all target shooting. Basically it is a 177 caliber break-action model with adjustable open sights at $58.95, or with micrometer sights at $81.00.

Universal Firearms

Several scopes and the 38 Special revolvers have been dropped from the Universal line, while the 12 gauge Auto-Wing shotgun will now be available only with a 26″ barrel at $159.95. There is a possibility that a rimfire rifle and pistol may be added later, but the present Universal line of 256 and 30 carbines, Mauser rifles, "Wing" shotguns in 10-, 12-and 20-gauge models, scopes and mounts remains much the same as covered in our 25th edition.

Thompson/Center's Hawken Muzzleloaders

As many of our readers know, the T/C firm has, over the past several years, become well known indeed for their single shot pistols, made in a wide range of calibers, and all usable on the same frame via quick and easy interchangeability of barrels.

T/C has just started delivery of a new firearm—a rifle that's a near-image of the frontier rifle made by the famed brothers Samuel and Jacob Hawken in St. Louis, Missouri, from about 1815 until 1862. Hawken rifles—first in flintlock form, then as caplock—were the prime favorite of such mountain men as Jim Bridger, Kit Carson, Jed Smith and numerous other trappers roaming the then little-known West.

The new Hawken—offered in 45 and 50 caliber, and in flintlock (later on) and percussion—is not an exact duplicate of the old Hawken rifles, but it comes close. It is, as well, highly attractive in its own right, and it should shoot.

There's been no chance to try it out so far, but if weather permits before press time, we'll report.

The barrel and breech-plug of the T/C Hawken are made of modern, tough alloy steels, and the "hooked-breech" system is used. This permits easy barrel removal for efficient cleaning. The graceful yet sturdy hammer is powered by a coil spring, for long-time reliability, and double-set triggers are standard equipment. The gleaming, solid brass trim or "furniture," as seen in the buttplate, graceful reverse-curve trigger guard, fore-end cap, ramrod thimbles and patchbox, make the 1971 Hawken a handsome rifle.

Our specimen Hawken is 45 caliber, the full octagon button-rifled barrel cut with 12 right hand grooves making one turn in 36 inches. The 28-inch barrel is ¹⁵/₁₆-inch across the flats at the muzzle, carries a bead front sight and a U-shaped rear sight that's adjustable for elevation and windage. Sight radius is 21 inches.

Hammer, lockplate (both engraved, too), and guard are color case-hardened, the latter with a second-finger curl.

Take down is simple—turning out one screw releases the bar lock, while pushing out the single fore-end key permits removal of the barrel.

The brass buttplate has a moderate curve, not a deep crescent form—which should ease felt recoil—and the walnut one-piece stock carries a cheekpiece typical of the period.

The T/C Hawken is available alone (with brass cleaning jag) at $175. An accessory pack, bringing the price to $193.50, includes a Lyman round ball mould, with handles; four powder scoops; a short starter; a spare nipple or cone and nipple wrench; 100 special T/C shooting patches and a bottle of Hoppe's black powder solvent. This same kit can be bought later for $18.50, a several-dollar saving compared to the unit prices.

Here are suggested charges—black powder only—by T/C for the .440″ round ball cast by the Lyman mould, assuming reasonably pure, soft lead:

50	grs	FFFg—	MV	1450	fps
55	,,	,,	,,	1520	,,
60	,,	,,	,,	1590	,,
65	,,	,,	,,	1650	,,

T/C suggest the following charges for use with Lyman's 45 Minie ball (mould #445599) of 250 grains. Note that FFg is used, not FFFg. The former seems to give more uniform results, better accuracy.

55	grs.	FFg—	MV	1190	fps
60	,,	,,	,,	1270	,,
65	,,	,,	,,	1300	,,
70	,,	,,	,,	1350	,,

Weatherby, Inc.

Introduced at the 1970 NSGA Show, the Vanguard rifles didn't reach the market until the fall of 1970 in time for the hunting season. Priced at $199.50 and available only in standard (non-Weatherby) calibers, the Vanguard barreled action is made in Japan by the Howa Mfg. Co., and stocked in typical Weatherby style in South Gate, Cal. with select American walnut, a rosewood fore-end tip and pistol grip cap. Detachable sling swivels are standard. The action is a Mauser design of the Sako type. (Howa made rifles for another firm a few years back that were almost identical to the Sako—complete with male dovetails on the receiver ring and bridge.) The smooth-top receiver is tapped for conventional scope mounts. The safety lever is large and excellent for use with gloves. The most noticeable feature of the Vanguard is the bolt sleeve; completely enclosed at the rear it prevents any gas leaks from reaching the shooter's eyes. Vanguard barrels are "hammer-forged," and on the rifle tested—a 308 with 22″ barrel—the result produced some excellent groups. Mounted with a Weatherby Imperial 4 x 81 scope, the test rifle weighed 8¾ pounds, unloaded and without sling.

Seven brands of ammunition were used in bench testing the Vanguard, and bullet weights ranged from a tiny 108-gr. to 180-gr. soft points. Three-shot groups were fired, none going over 3″ at 100 yards; many were around one MOA. The surprise was Sako's 108-gr. load; the Vanguard shot into less than one MOA with this load, and one 3-shot group measured ½″ center-to-center. The Vanguard also seemed to like the 180-gr. bullet, with Federal Hi-Shok and Hy-Score loads producing 3-shot groups of ⅞″. With the right ammunition the new Vanguard can lay them in the black.

Sauer, the German firm that makes Weatherby rifles, also manufactures shotguns and shotgun/rifle combinations. Weatherby is the exclusive U.S. distributor of these. The current line includes three side-by-side double barrels, two over-under models, and two combination guns. The Sauer "Royal" double has the Anson & Deeley action with Greener cross bolt, double under lugs, single selective trigger, auto safety, side cocking indicators, and fine hand checkering on the walnut stock and semi-beavertail fore-end. Available in 12 gauge with 30″ or 28″ barrels, and in 20 gauge with 28″ or 26″ barrels, the "Royal" lists at $445. The "Artemis" double, made only in 12 gauge with 28″ barrels, features Holland and Holland type removable sidelocks with double sear safeties and automatic selective ejectors. Greener cross bolt, double under lugs and SST are standard. Two "Artemis" grades are available, differing in the type of engraving—fine line or full English arabesque. Prices, not yet set, will be around $2000. The third lateral double is the Sauer-Aya Model 65. Available in 12 gauge only at $270.00, no further information was available at the time of this report. The Sauer "66" over-under is offered in

Field, Trap, and Skeet models, with three grades of engraving. Made in 12 gauge only at present the "66" is based on the Purdey System with H&H type removable sidelocks, selective automatic ejectors, and a SST. The Krupp Special steel barrels have a wide ventilated rib with muzzle and center beads, and are available in 28″, 30″ and 26″ lengths according to the respective models. Stocks and fore-ends are of select walnut with a ventilated recoil pad. The trap and Skeet gun fore-ends are ventilated to permit faster cooling of the barrels. The Field Model is $685, $755 for the trap and Skeet Models; the top grades with full English arabesque engraving are $600 higher.

The Sauer Drilling 3000 E consists of double 12 gauge barrels over a single rifle barrel in a choice of 222, 243, 30-06, or 7x65R calibers. The 25″ barrels have a matted top rib and an automatically operated folding leaf rear sight for the rifle barrel. The 3000 E uses a Blitz action with Greener cross bolt, double under lugs, separate extractors, and cocking indicators on the upper receiver tang. A Greener side safety is standard, and the front trigger acts as a set trigger for the rifle barrel. Weights vary from 6½ to 7¼ pounds depending on caliber, and the standard model is $830. A deluxe model, with more elaborate engraving is $945. The BBF over-under consists of a 16-gauge shotgun barrel over a choice of 30-30, 30-06, or 7x65R rifle barrel. A Blitz action with Kersten lock is used, and a conventional shotgun type slide safety on the tang is standard. The BBF has double triggers— the front for the rifle barrel can be set, while the rear trigger fires the shotgun barrel. List for the standard BBF is $735, with the deluxe model at $845.

Both the 3000 E and the BBF have select walnut modified Monte Carlo stocks with pistol grip and cheekpiece—European

style. The standard models have fine-line hand checkering, with skip-line checkering on the deluxe models; sling swivels are standard.

There is also a shotgun bearing the Weatherby name. Prototypes of this new over-under were seen at the NSGA Show a couple of years ago, but it wasn't until mid-1970 that production models actually became available. Called the Regency, this new Weatherby is made in Gardone, Italy, by Angelo Zoli (not Antonio) and beautiful is the only word for it. Featuring a boxlock action with Greener cross bolt and sidelock style plates to enhance the elaborate engraving, the new shotgun has a mechanically-operated single selective trigger instead of the usual recoil-operated variety. This means an automatic switch-over to the second barrel if faulty ammunition should cause a misfire. The selector lever is located on the front top of the trigger so the choice of which barrel fires first can be instantly made with a flick of the trigger finger. Auto ejectors and a ventilated rib on the 28″ barrels are standard. At $595 in gauges 12 and 20 (3″ chambers), the Regency is an outstanding O-U shotgun. The fully engraved silver-grey receiver, coupled with the polished blue barrels and the high luster American walnut stock, would made it welcome anywhere but the Regency is a working shotgun. Three choke combinations—Skeet and Skeet, modified and improved cylinder, modified and full—are available, and the weights of slightly less than 7 pounds (20 gauge) to about 7½ pounds (12 gauge) are about right for most field or clay bird shooting.

On the Regency tested fit and finish of metal and wood were excellent. Wood was well figured, the fluted wide comb comfortable. However, the checkering was something else; there were no run-outs—only minor nicks—but flat diamonds were common instead of the good sharp diamonds expected on a shotgun of this price. There were some extremely deep grooves and several tears on the fore-end apparently due to soft wood or a dull tool.   L.S.

Top—Weatherby's Regency grade over-under shotgun. Below is Weatherby Vanguard centerfire rifle.

The big red W didn't offer any new calibers in 1971, but they did introduce several model changes, new 22 rimfire bolt action rifles, and some new loads. The old 94, one of the bread-and-butter rifles of the W-W line, shows several modifications. There are screws visible that were not on the old 94s, the hammer spur is now grooved, not checkered as on the old-timers, and it is a mite wider. Wood-to-metal fit isn't quite what it used to be, and the wood reveals scratches, rasp marks, etc. However, some changes have been for the better. A new steel carrier, of inherently sturdier block design, has replaced the lighter weight version introduced a few years back, thus providing smoother, more positive cartridge feeding. An improved loading-port cover facilitates more rapid loading of cartridges into the magazine, even with gloves on. Improved linkage—via a redesigned lever camming slot—makes the new 94 easier and more rapidly operated than any previous model. Progress costs, and the new 94 in 30-30 and 32 Special only is $99.95, or in 44 Magnum at $109.95.

In tribute to the NRA's 100th year, and with that organization's authorization, W-W is producing two limited-edition commemoratives during 1971. The M1894 NRA Musket has a 26-inch tapered round barrel cradled in a full-length stock of American walnut (enclosing the 7-round magazine) tipped with a black-chromed fore-end cap. A chromed barrel band with non-detachable sling swivel completes the militaryish look. The matched walnut buttstock has a black-chromed curved buttplate, squarish comb, and a special silver-colored NRA medallion inset into the right side, plus a sling swivel near the toe. Sights consist of a high blade front dovetailed into the barrel, and a folding rear similar to the pattern used at the turn of the century, and calibrated from 0 to 20 on the leaf; 200 yards doesn't seem to fit the adjustment range, and 2000 yards is a mite far for the 30-30 cartridge.

The second NRA commemorative is another 94 rifle, reminiscent of the highly popular, but discontinued, Model 64. The new rifle has the same semi-pistol grip stock and forearm style, with a contoured lever to fit the pistol grip curve. The forearm has a blued steel cap with a stud for quick-detachable swivel, and the half-magazine, extending just past the fore-end, holds 6 rounds. The 24-inch tapered round barrel is fitted with an adjustable semi-buckhorn rear sight, and a hooded ramp post front.

About 7 pounds 2 ounces and 6½ pounds respectively, the receivers are black chromed. The left side is inscribed with the letters "NRA" encircled by a scrollwork design and flanked by the dates: 1871 and 1971; the right side of the receiver has two scrollwork designs of a similar pattern. The tangs bear the inscription: *Model 1894 Winchester*, and the barrels are marked either *NRA Centennial Musket* or *NRA Centennial Rifle*. These Centennials incorporate the same improvements made in the regular 94 design, but are finished to be both functional and useful. They're $149.95 each, or in matched sets with consecutive serial numbers, the pair is $325.

While buyers of the M1894 NRA Centennials will no doubt hang them on the wall, or use them as conversation pieces, they are modern rifles, useful for hunting. If I had to stick with one 30-30 lever action rifle the new NRA rifle would be it—it just plain feels good and when the butt touches the shoulder the sights are on the target.

The NRA models were shot from the bench, 3-shot groups made at 100 yards. Only the issue iron sights were used.

The Musket didn't favor any particular load or bullet weight. Groups ranged to just over 9 inches, the group centers some 5 inches to the right of the point-of-aim. Such average accuracy is satisfactory enough to hit deer-size game at 100 yards. The smallest group was 3⅝ inches, using Federal 170-gr. Hi-Shok bullets. Shooting was done out-of-the-box, no attempt made to change barrel bedding, so accuracy may possibly be improved with some slight additional effort.

The rifle seemed to prefer the various 150-gr. loads. Disregarding one wild group, the average of all groups, including 150- and 170-gr. loads, was 2⅛ inches. The smallest ran 1⅝ inches, made with Dominion 150-gr. "Pneumatic" bullets. The Gevelot 150-gr. load did almost as well, one group measuring 1¾ inches. Surprisingly, the rifle preferred Canadian ammo to U.S., though the Winchester 150-gr. SP and HP loads were under 2½ inches, as were Speer/DWM 170-gr. and Herter 150-gr. loads. The NRA Rifle proved exceptionally accurate for an out-of-the-box model with iron sights; one notch on the elevator put them in the black.

During the 40th World Shooting Championships at Phoenix, Arizona, during Oc-

Winchester-Western

tober of 1970, seven of the top 12 shooters in the Army Rifle 3-position event used a new rifle, the Winchester Model 70 International Army Rifle. In 1971 this rifle became available to civilian shooters on special order at $399.95, in 308 only. The rifle weighs about 11 pounds, and is 43½ inches over-all with a 24-inch slightly tapered barrel. The receiver is tapped for standard M70 sights, and both barrel and receiver are coated with a special non-glare finish. The oil-finished stock is welded to the receiver with a special glass-bedding process to insure perfect fit; the very deep forearm has a rail that extends almost to the trigger guard. It's unusual in appearance, but the results speak for themselves—this new rifle can shoot, and that's the name of the game.

The new rimfire rifles are made in 3 versions—the 310, 320 and 325, a single shot and two 5-round box magazine repeaters, priced $44.95, $57.50 and $62.50 respectively. The first two handle 22 Short, Long, or Long Rifle cartridges, the 325 using 22 WRM loads. All three have 22-inch barrels, are 39½ inches over-all, have about 13½-inch pulls and weigh about 5⅝ pounds. The American walnut stocks have Monte Carlo fluted combs, an ample amount of impressed checkering on pistol grip and forearm, sling swivels and black plastic buttplate. The "new" receivers are grooved for tip-off scope mounts, tapped for receiver sights, and matted to reduce glare. The trigger, wide and serrated for positive grip, measured 4½ pounds and clean. The safety is positive, located directly behind the bolt handle for easy access. The box magazine has a cylindrical section

on front which mates into an aluminum magazine housing, making misalignment almost impossible. (The stamped trigger guard is entirely functional but displeasing in appearance. Were it an investment casting or a machining it would be worth an extra buck or more.) The standard sights are a ramp-mounted front bead, and an adjustable rear of the regular field type.

A Model 320—mounted with a Weaver D6 scope—was bench tested with the new T22 ammunition, at 25 yards. 5-shot groups ranged from ⁷⁄₁₆-inch to 1 inch. One group had four shots in ⁵⁄₁₆-inch. With a receiver sight, and some slight bedding changes and/or ammunition, the M320 will make an excellent low-priced small-bore target rifle, capable of shooting possibles.

For shotgunners Winchester now has the M1200 Monte Carlo slide action and the M1400 Monte Carlo Mark II automatic, each with Winchoke barrels. The new versions list at $219.95 and $239.95 respectively, made only with 28″ vent rib barrels.

Winchester-Western, pioneers in the production of compression-formed plastic hull shotshells, now make a new shell, the "Upland." The new load is dependable, virtually immune to the effects of weather, and may let the reloader get up to 300% more reloads per shell. The Upland loads, available in 12, 16 and 20 gauges, range from 1 to 1¼ ounce of shot in 12 to ⅞- and 1-ounce loads in the 20, with shot sizes from No. 4 to No. 9. The Mark 5 plastic shot collar is used to protect the shot pellets from barrel distortion, and a special gas-chamber seal insures against patchy shot strings. The 12- and 20-gauge Upland

loads were patterned in several shotguns mentioned elsewhere in this edition, plus being used at the trap range—no game was in season. The results were entirely satisfactory.

The small-bore shooter hasn't been forgotten. Regular and HP 22 LR cartridges are now available in a new pack, and there's a 22 LR called the T22 (T for "Target"). Short and LR sizes will be priced the same as regular standard velocity ammunition. The new cartridges have specially contoured bullets coated with a dry lubricant that is clean, but remains stable and prevents leading.

There are also a few changes in some of the older W-W models, including the M70 in 25-06 caliber, along with 25-06 cartridges. (The 770 will be chambered for the 25-06 later—possibly by the time you read this.) A special "police" version of the 770, offered in 308 and 30-06, has a sand-blasted metal finish. The 670 has a revamped stock finish, and minor improvements have been made on the 1200 and 1400 shotguns—shell carrier, hammer stop, trigger, etc.—and on the ventilated rib of the M101 over-under.

While it hasn't been announced, W-W is at least considering the reintroduction of the 220 Swift cartridge in an up-loaded form to give a muzzle velocity of around 4325 fps. This would be the "world's faster commercial cartridge"—the new 17 Remington cartridge now holds the title—and with the M70 and M770 rifles chambered for it, the New Haven firm could have an advertising field day—at least until some firm decides to introduce a cartridge topping 5000 fps.   LS

Winchester-Western

Pachmayr Gun Works

PGW is owned and operated by Frank Pachmayr, designer and patentee of the famed White Line recoil pads, to say nothing of numerous other products for the shooter/hunter. Pachmayr butt pads, for rifle and shotgun, are made in almost a bewildering array of styles, thickness, colors, etc., but there's only one quality—the best.

Other PGW products are just too many to list here in their entirety, but here's a sampling—pistol grips, decoys, stock blanks, pistol-grip caps, flush-mounting sling swivels, cases for match pistol shooters, and not least by any means, his Lo-Swing scope mounts. These permit the near-instantaneous switch from scope to iron sights, a desirable facility in short-range woods country, and particularly handy anywhere rains and heavy snows might be expected—or where dangerous game is hunted in thick cover.

At this point the question usually arises, "What accuracy can be expected from a rifle topped by a rotatable scope? Does it go back to its original point of aim after being swung out of position?" The Lo-Swing user can expect just as good accuracy as from any other mount, assuming scopes of like power. Many tests have proven this to be true—including several of my own. As a matter of surprising fact, the Lo-Swing mount is so engineered that the scope mounted in it lies parallel to the rifle's bore even when the scope is rotated out of position! Shooting tests made with the Lo-Swing mount positioned as much as an inch or so away from its normal position gave groups that printed right on top of shots made with the mount-scope firmly down! Pachmayr told me during a visit with him at the 1971 NSGA show, that he'll soon be offering a new design of detachable comb/cheekpiece that will have high interest for target and varmint shooters. This device will, Frank said, be just about universally adjustable—up and down, angled, canted, you name it. PGW has numerous brochures and pamphlets describing its many good products. They're free for the asking.   JTA

Schwab Release Triggers

What's a release trigger? I didn't know either until a few years ago, but they've become a big item among competition claybirders in recent years. The idea is simple enough—when a release trigger is pulled, nothing happens! Well, that isn't exactly correct, because pulling on this kind of trigger cocks or sets the mechanism, the gun then firing as the trigger is released.

Release triggers are said to be big medicine for ailing, and complaining trapshooters. Cures their flinches and fidgits, brings 'em out of a slump, you name it. They do seem to work, at least sometimes, as you'll hear. At worst, they give the cure-seeking shooter something else to try instead of having a new stock made, having the comb on ole Betsy raised—or lowered—an eighth-inch, or quitting the damn game forever.

Be that as it may, M.L. Schwab (Schwab's Gun Shop, 1103 E. Bigelow Ave., Findlay, Ohio 45840) makes a good one, by all accounts. His biggest seller appears to be one made for Remington Models 1100 and 870, these built up using brand new factory trigger assemblies, as are his other types as well. They're impossible to "pull through," it's claimed, and they work from the original sears—no cuts are made in the hammers. A new type action bar is installed, letting the "set" trigger be deactivated safely, in the event of a broken bird, etc. The Schwab release triggers can be re-set whether the action is open or closed.

Wayne Beggs, a local trapshooter with a 23-yard handicap, has been using the Schwab release trigger for some three weeks now, fitted to his own M1100 Remington 12 bore. He told me that he'd picked up one or two birds on his first rounds with the new trigger, breaking 25 on the first string. Whether that will last is anyone's guess, but he wants to keep it for a couple of months! That says something.

Installed or removed in minutes on a Remington M1100 and M870, the Schwab RT for those shotguns sells for $50, guaranteed one year "if not tampered with." Models for Browning singles and superposed are $55 and $50; a Krieghoff type costs $65, and one for the Model 12 Winchester runs $35.   JTA

Trail Guide Products

A very useful item for shooters is their Speed-Sling, made of nylon webbing with steel fittings, in a choice of black or red colors. Priced at $9.95 it comes completely assembled with a set of illustrated instructions for installation. Weighing 5 ounces and tested at 4000 lbs. tensile strength, it adjusts from one position—taut to hasty-shoot to a two-shoulder carry—in one second. They're said to be weatherproof and resistant to stains. Using a Speed-Sling on a Remington M700 for several months verified all the claims made for it.   L.S.

Triple-K

Here's a unique service for shooters. Triple-K manufactures magazines and other small parts for over 400 handguns and rifles, the magazines guaranteed to fit. Magazines will also be custom made for models not listed, at a charge of $10.00 for the first magazine and $6.00 each thereafter. Large capacity models are available too, along with standard size models. Many firing pins, springs, and even a few shotgun parts are available. Triple-K is also expanding with a line of leather goods. An excellent, illustrated catalog is available for $1 showing the various parts available, and usually the arm it fits. For the collector or shooter having a rifle or handgun with the magazine missing-such as a Savage Model 23 or Savage Super Sporter—Triple-K may well have the answer.   LS

Thomas F. White

The well-detailed map horn pictured nearby shows White's excellent work at its best—and most expensive. He is now building plain horns also, for shooters and hunters, priced in the $12-$16 range, and small priming horns for the flintlock shooter.

White will also be making complete Kentucky rifles, with carved wood and engraved metal, before long. I saw one of these at the NRA meeting, and a very fine job it was. Write to White for further data.

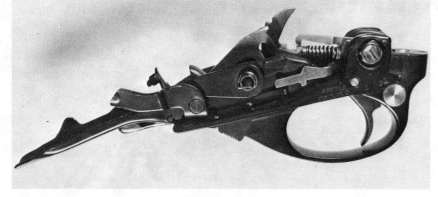

Schwab's Release Trigger proved fully reliable, an excellent aid for the claybirder.

ODD-BALL HARD-BALLS

For well over a half-century we have been blessed—or bemused—by the 45 ACP, so there's little left to say about it, right? Wrong. This collector describes in detail a number of unusual GI 45s, guns few shooters know exist

MASON WILLIAMS

IN SHOOTERS' parlance "hardball" refers to the GI cal.-45 Colt automatic pistol that fires GI ammunition — loads with full metal jacket bullets. Usually these handguns are pretty much as-issue jobs, or else they are the finely finished Match Target pistols available from the Director of Civilian Marksmanship via the National Rifle Association. Seldom has a better dollar value been offered the American handgun shooter. This article, however, is not about match target handguns, regardless of their capabilities. Rather, I would like to ramble on about some of the goofed-up 45 ACP pistols that I have run into.

In most businesses it takes a lot of brains and initiative to foul up on a production piece, and when such happens the result is customarily sold at a premium price as a "one in a million" item. The rate of goof-ups in the arms industry, I believe, ranks as one of the highest in the world, particularly during wartime when the primary object of production lines is to get as many pistols as possible into the hands of our men. When the scrap is all over, Ordnance sits down and sorts through those which remain, then picks out the unusual items and does something with them. Now and then one gets through them, though, and that is what this article is all about.

Now, I'm sure that somewhere among my readers there lurks an over-zealous policeman or Federal officer who wants to get a Medal of Commendation. Let me state for the record that all the oddballs mentioned here

are strictly — but strictly — legitimate. So relax and forget about the medals. Also, at this point, a word to collectors. None of these is for sale. If anyone has a real oddball I sure would like to hear about it. I'm not an avid collector but when an unusual Model 1911 cal. 45 ACP comes my way, I buy it if it will add to my basic collection and to my over-all knowledge of 45s. Many 45s that have been reblued, altered, etc., have no value to me. I am interested only in the more unusual "as-issue" oddballs. The thing that fascinates me is how these pistols get through the countless Government checks, inspections, etc., to finally fall into the hands of the American shooter. A lot of these pistols are simply *curiosa,* while others are genuine collector's items. Often it is difficult to draw the line. I will not attempt to do so.

I must be vague about certain details here, because the entire history and background of the 45 ACP pistol is filled with grey areas. Records no longer exist or have been lost. Many of the men who worked on the original 45s are no longer with us. Much of the information is secondhand. So please do not be too critical if I appear to sluff off some details. Most of the time I will come right out and say I just don't know. Bear with me and let's have some fun trying to figure out some of the goofs that I know about.

Rem-UMC

Let's start off with one I purchased from the Director of Civilian Marksmanship. Now the DCM is about as

official an agency of the Government as one can find — and anything that is officially an agency of the U.S. Government dislikes anything that does not fit the prescribed specifications. Let me try to trace — theoretically of course, because no one really knows—the origin of this particular 45 Model 1911 and/or Model 1911A1.

Way back around 1917 the U.S. Army needed 45s, so among other contractors they authorized Remington-Union Metallic Corp. to manufacture as many 45s as they could. Remington-UMC was given a block of serial numbers entirely separate from the regular run of numbers. These commenced with number 1 and ended with number 21,676. This much is known.

The frame of this 45 meets every requirement as one of the Remington-UMC frames, starting off with the inspector's initials, "EEC," just above the magazine release on the left side of the receiver. The phrase "United States Property" is in the correct place (for this specimen) on the left side of the frame ahead of the trigger guard. So far all is well.

The numbers on these pistols should be stamped just above the trigger on the right side of the receiver. Mine has No. 1545 all right, which is correct for a Remington-UMC. Two Ordnance bombs are stamped side by side partially over and partially below the "No." preceding the serial number. Directly below these ordnance bombs and a bit to the left is stamped 10210, in slightly smaller numerals. This is the only instance I have ever run into

ODD-BALL HARD-BALLS

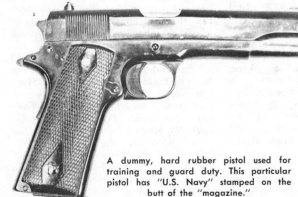

Right side of the double-numbered pistol, grips removed to better show double numbers and the two Ordnance bombs, the latter stamped in the correct location. The two numbers fall within the numbering block assigned to Remington-UMC.

of a firearm carrying two numbers. The interesting point is that both numbers fall well within the numbering series assigned to Remington-UMC back in 1917.

My thought on this double numbering is that this receiver came off the line for issue, and then for some reason was held out and possibly used as an instruction control receiver. This could well have been the case because the low number 1545 shows this was one of the first production receivers off the line. Later on, pressure for more and more pistols could have forced the company to re-number the receiver and re-issue it for service. This is all guesswork. I don't know. I have examined all the stampings under a glass and they appear to be of the same approximate vintage. This receiver came to me completely equipped as a Model 1911 frame with the short safety spur, flat mainspring housing and every indication that it was original throughout.

If you think one error is plenty for one pistol — hold on to your hats. The slide is standard, of Colt manufacture, and meets all specifications of the Model 1911A1 slides. On the other hand, all slide parts appear to be Model 1911 type. The left side carries all the correct stampings for such a slide, but there is absolutely nothing on the right side of the slide — not even serrations, despite the fact that the left side does carry serrations. I have miked the slide and it meets specifications. Obviously someone failed to put this slide through the final

stamping on the right side, but how the serrations were left off remains a mystery. It's a weird looking pistol viewed from the right side.

This pistol was obviously brought in after World War II for rebuilding. The finish, a relatively new and perfect parkerizing, is clean, light and unused. Plastic grips were added. How such an odd combination ever got through without someone picking it up I don't know. As I mentioned above, this pistol was purchased by an NRA member from the DCM just a couple of years ago. No other pistol that I own has so many oddball things wrong with it.

45 Dummy

Compared to this one-in-a-million pistol let's look at another weird 45. To confuse the issue even more, this 45 is not a pistol at all. What is it? It's a dummy 45 pistol made of hard rubber, plus solid lead, to give it weight so that it duplicates the hang and feel of the conventional 45 ACP. The butt is stamped U.S. Navy. I spent four full years in the Navy during the Second World War and I saw just one of these pistols. It was kept by the Executive Officer for training purposes. Every now and then some fortunate seaman would be permitted to drop it into his empty holster and go on guard duty. I have heard men speak of these dummies, and I understand many were used for hand-to-hand combat training during the war. As far as I am concerned these dummies are so realistic that if the lights were low or visibility bad I

certainly would not argue with a man shoving one at me. Despite the fact that they cannot fire they make an excellent blackjack or pacifier. I would hate to be clobbered by one. One of my friends back from China in 1947 gave it to my son to play with. One day he and a friend were repulsing Indians — the odds were something like 6000 to two — and he threw it at the screaming savages. I happened to witness this and, on picking it up, realized what it was. Unfortunately, the hammer broke off during the breaking up of the Indian charge. Since then it has been carefully protected. Being martially marked it will remain in my collection of 45 ACPs.

Lunch Pail 45

I now come to a real fouled-up 45 ACP — one that I have named my "lunch pail" 45. This pistol also started out in life as a Remington-UMC handgun — at least to the best of my knowledge. The slide meets every requirement of that brand, including all component parts of the slide assembly.

The odd thing about this pistol is the receiver. It has the customary "United States Property" stamping on the left side of the receiver, ahead of the trigger guard, but that is the only mark on the frame. No serial number, no inspector's initials, no marks of any kind appear. Again the receiver has been assembled with parts that meet the specifications of a pistol of that manufacture and age.

The outside shows considerable holster wear, a police officer having car-

A dummy, hard rubber pistol used for training and guard duty. This particular pistol has "U.S. Navy" stamped on the butt of the "magazine."

This Remington-UMC pistol has no serial number and is without any inspector's stamps, assembler's stamps or other markings—a real "lunch pail" pistol.

The Savage Arms "slide" pistol, rarely seen today. To the author's knowledge, Savage Arms did not produce complete pistols.

ried it for nearly 30 years. I doubt if it has been fired more than a hundred times. The inside parts show little or no wear and they all appear to be original.

The slide and the receiver assembly appear to have been together for a good many years — in my opinion they are the original assembly. I can't be certain, of course, but I imagine this receiver was "borrowed" from the line after completion but prior to final acceptance and stamping. The parts were probably also brought home piecemeal in the lunch pail every evening. With the millions of parts then coming off the line each day it's a wonder more of this style don't turn up. If you ever run into one I suggest you take it to a local authority and ask them to assign it a number; then you will be in the clear. A lot of these pistols — so I am told — were given to foremen and heads of departments after the war as a token present or as a momento so don't assume that every one was stolen.

Savage 45

Another oddball that you will run into occasionally is the "Savage" variation of the Model 1911 45 pistol. Now this has nothing to do with the Savage Arms Corp. in Westfield, Mass. In 1917-1918 the demand for 45 pistols was so great that the government gave contracts to any firm which could produce them. The records are a bit fuzzy but it appears that the A. J. Savage Munitions Co. of San Diego, Calif., was given a contract to manu-

facture complete Model 1911 pistols. From what I can find out they only made slides before the contract was cancelled in 1919. It would appear that these slides, or at least some of them, were accepted by the government so that, after the war, these slides were incorporated into rebuilt pistols. You can identify these Savage slides by the lettering, all in one block, on the left side of the front part of the slide. This reads:

Patented Dec. 19, 1905
Feb. 14, 1911, Aug. 19, 1913
Colt's Pt. F. A. Mfg. Co.

Directly to the rear of this lettering is a flaming bomb with a large S inside the bomb circle. The right side of the slide carries the standard stamping "Model of 1911 U. S. Army." While this variation may factually be considered a "production" model they are seldom encountered. Few people have ever seen one.

X-Number 45s

Another seldom-seen variation is the X number pistol. As I understand it these pistols were brought back into certain government armories, stripped down and rebuilt. From what I can determine all of the receivers were machined flat and cleaned on both sides to remove all lettering and numbers. After blueing the receivers were stamped on the right side with an X followed by a new serial number. Those serial numbers I have seen were low, mine being 1923. This new number is found above and behind the

trigger. Above the number is the phrase "United States Property."

On the left side of the receiver — at least on my pistol — is a sitting eagle. Below this is S17. The eagle and the lettering are quite small and you need a good glass to make out the details. They are located directly above the magazine release, slightly higher than the spot where the regular inspector's initials are customarily found.

I have seen these pistols with the receivers machined so much that the naked eye can readily see the difference between the thickness of the X frames and a new frame. If you run into one of these X numbered 45s, examine the slide for machining — it might well be original and legitimate.

Low Number 45s

Every now and then you will see one of the original low number Model 1911 pistols. The first 50,000 or so were superbly finished. They stand out like a flashlight among candles. The very early ones, carrying numbers down around 10,000 or lower, are beauties — too good to shoot, in my opinion. So far I've seen only one with a misplaced serial, that one number 6324, so-stamped far ahead of the trigger guard. This on the right side of the receiver, of course, directly opposite the legend "United States Property" stamped on the opposite side.

I have run into quite a few of the old World War I pistols carrying serial numbers that date them back to 1916, 1917, 1918 and 1919, which have been entirely re-finished, parkerized and given new inspector's initials. I don't know when this was done, but from the looks of the finish I'd guess sometime after World War 2. Those I've examined closely show little signs of wear, indicating that the work must have been done fairly recently — or the pistols released lately. These are good buys for the man who wants a rugged handgun.

In conclusion I'd like to point out that many 1911 and 1911A1 pistols may be found in variations that add considerably to their value for collectors. If you find one of these oddballs ask a collector about it — it may be of some worth. ●

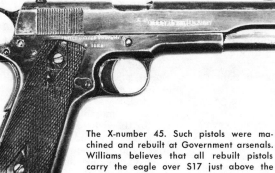

The X-number 45. Such pistols were machined and rebuilt at Government arsenals. Williams believes that all rebuilt pistols carry the eagle over S17 just above the magazine release on the left side of the frame of the pistol.

One of the original 1911 pistols with the short spur used before the Cavalry re-designed the hammer. Note location of the serial number. Only the first few pistols had the number in this place, Williams believes. By serial number 10,000 the number was back over the trigger.

TRAP, SKEET and the HUNTER

Fast moving, challenging clay target games hone wingshooting skill afield. Here's a deep and helpful essay on how it's done and how to do it.

by ALLEN F. RUFFIN, JR.

MINUTES AFTER the chill morning air became alive with the thrilling sound of a hundred thousand or more Canada geese leaving the marsh for feeding fields, a hunter crouched nervously in a field pit. He stared fixedly through the grass screened 6-inch slot between the earth and the pit cover as a small flock of Canadas glided in to the silhouette decoys.

Now his partner, quitting the use of the call slung round his neck, groped along the forward pit wall for his shotgun. Just as the leading geese put their feet down and whiffled from side to side for landing position, he said, "Let's take 'em."

Together they threw back the pit cover. They rose, only heads and shoulders above the level of ground, shouldered Browning 5-shot magnum 12 gauge guns, and swung—one to the left, the other to the right—as the geese furiously beat the air with their wings while thousands more passed high over and around the cornfield.

Three times each hunter fired. In less than a minute, 5 big geese were on the ground, while a sixth suddenly ceased his efforts to rejoin his brethren and fell, 200 yards away.

Not yet mid-morning, these hunters had their limits, were ready to see to the cleaning and picking of their game, a cozy lunch in a waterman's restaurant, and a leisurely drive home. Time after time, over the years, these two have repeated this performance while other waterfowlers, cursing their missed opportunities, spent the entire day shivering from the damp cold in the pits, or the biting wind in water blinds.

Luck? Not a bit of it. Skill, and hunting know-how were responsible.

How did they get that way?

Practice, and lots of it.

But today, few nimrods are able to get the abundant practice on wild game that gave our forebears their great skill with scatterguns. We must develop our ability by other means. Trap and Skeet shooting provide those means.

Both games are today so popular that they've become sports in their own right — many participants care

little or nothing for hunting. They are good fun, fast, exciting, challenging and healthy outdoor pursuits that can capture a man's attention to the exclusion of all else.

It is difficult to say just how trapshooting got started. Perhaps it was something like this:

Some 570 years ago, two soldiers stood alongside a river taking alternate shots at bits of driftwood floating by. One of them, a bit weary of playing this game with their clumsy matchlock guns, picked up a clod of earth.

"I'll wage a bumper of hock thee're not man enough to strike this with your charge should I throw it, Peter," he said.

"Throw," answered Peter, "and can I hit thy clod and thou cans't hit mine, then it's two bumpers thou shalt buy."

Bored soldiers with guns and ammunition available still play such games today.

In time matchlock ignition gave way to the wheel-lock, this in its turn soon superseded by the snaphaunce and miquelet, in which flint was struck against steel by a spring upon release of the trigger. This development had been rapid, taking place within some hundred years from the first use of a gun as such—as distinguished from the hand cannon. The time was ample, anyway, for shooting contests of all kinds to be developed. With the passing of another hundred years, the flintlock came into being. Its lock mechanism was so highly refined that it was to remain champion for nearly 250 years.*

During this period, many flintlock guns were made for sporting rather than military purposes, among them some extremely fine large-bore birding and fowling pieces. It is impossible to think of any gentleman owning such a gun who would not have instantly rose to a challenge of his marksmanship. That is, of course, as long as the challenge had been made by a social equal.

The first mention of anything resembling trapshooting was in the English *Sporting Magazine* of 1793. By 1810, the first club was organized. Of course, their targets were live birds—pigeons—held in a trap until released. The name was taken up for the target we shoot at when it was introduced by George Ligowski in the early 1880s as a replacement for wood blocks, glass balls, or other targets that hardly flew well enough to be any challenge. The Ligowski clay target gave trapshooting the impetus needed to become a popular sport.

Clay target shooting today is less snobbish. It is anyone's game—farm-

*The lock design, in fact, has not changed greatly even today. The caplock merely substitutes a cap-striking hammer for the flint-holding-jaw type, the internal design remaining virtually the same, if subsequently refined.

ers, physicians, lawyers and policemen, happy to be in the company of others interested in shotgun marksmanship.

But, what about Skeet? Isn't that a curious name?

Up in the old New England state of Massachusetts in the days of raccoon-skin coats, open touring cars with twin windshields, hip flasks and flappers, a few not-so-poor gentlemen found themselves bored with the stylized conventions of trapshooting. They had had a few belts of soul-saver one evening, a practice widely followed by sportsmen everywhere as a precaution against the Devil entering the body, and their conversation turned to clay targets and how poorly such shooting suited their needs as practice for grouse and woodcock gunning.

Out of this grew a new game. It had a single trap placed at 12 o'clock on the rim of a 25-yard circle, with 12 shooting stations spaced equally apart around the rim. Targets were thrown over the 6 o'clock position. This gave a great variety of angles at close range that better duplicated their field shots.

These Baystaters called their game "shooting around the clock." It didn't stay that way for long. Just about the time they had built up an enthusiastic following among local scatter-gunners, trouble loomed on the horizon. A chicken farm.

For each size of shot, there is a maximum distance of travel. Even when shot size is restricted—which is almost impossible to enforce because of the desire of occasional shooters

to try out their hunting loads, something more than this distance for the largest shot must be allowed for a safe-fall area. The chicken farm's new facilities encroached on the safe-fall area on one side of the big circle.

So the enterprising gentlemen in Massachesetts merely restricted shooting in that direction by cutting their circle in half. They placed a trap on each end of the diameter. Seven shooting stations were spaced around the semicircle, and an 8th place midway between the two traps. Eventually the left trap was elevated. After some fiddling around, they formalized rules calling for a single shot fired from each station at a target from each of the two traps, one at a time, followed by a return to stations one, 2, 6, and 7 to shoot at doubles—pairs of targets thrown from each trap simultaneously. This consumed 24 shells from a box of 25. When a man missed a target, he tried it again with his extra shell. If he got them all, he shot the extra at a target from the trap and station of his choice.

In those days, no one shot straight very often. Typically, the guns were field type side-by-side doubles with

In trap, 5 shots are fired from each station by each shooter, and then all hands shift station. The shooter on station 5 comes around the rear to station one. The ATA's home grounds at Vandalia, Ohio, border the runways of the Dayton Municipal Airport, where the coming and going of big aircraft bother some shooters, but the scores rarely show it.

TRAP SKEET and the HUNTER

Doubles at the Grand, with two targets in the air. Note shell-miser pouch on the belt of the shooter (left) in which he collects his own empty shells for reloading.

modified and full choked 30″ barrels with twin triggers. In the ready position, the shooter held his shotgun in both hands with the buttstock down by his hip. After his call, the release of the target could be delayed up to three seconds. None of this made for easy hitting.

What about that crazy name?

What's in a Name

One of the gentlemen who invented this form of shooting was an editor of a respected, but now dead, outdoor monthly. He gave the new game several mentions in his publication, which stimulated nationwide enthusiasm. So much so, that he sponsored a contest to find a name for it through his magazine.

Mrs. Gertrude Hurlbutt of Dayton, Montana won the $100 prize with the name "Skeet." She claimed that this meant "to shoot" in an old Scandinavian tongue. Indeed, I have been able to learn that it does have a parallel meaning in Old Icelandic, but probably related more to the bow and arrow than to the shotgun. Curiously, in modern Swedish, a word pronounced similarly to "Skeet" means "dirty." Dirty you are, too, from target bits and powder residue after a few rounds, as a course of 25 shots is called.

Guns, Loads and Rules

The two games, trap and Skeet, are completely different in rules, shooting techniques, and equipment. Since it is a newer game, let's look first at Skeet.

Today, the game is played in much the same way as when first developed. It is no longer necessary, however, to hold the gun at the hip. It can be shouldered and sighted before each shot. Targets are thrown after the call as soon as the puller can push the electric release button. (However, while the United States has changed its rules, the rest of the world has followed the original low-gun, delayed release formula. This is the way Skeet is still shot in International and Olympic competitions, with a stronger, faster target that travels farther and faster than the target used in U.S. Skeet. In my opinion, the Olympic style makes for a far better game.)

You can shoot Skeet alone, but it

is more fun with company. Shooting informally for practice, you make up squads of shooters who are ready to shoot at the same time you are, and your names are entered on the squad sheet. Each station is shot in order as numbered. Get your loads, No. 9 shot —any gauge. You won't find 10-gauge shells at clay-target clubs, but they will have almost anything else popular in the U.S. In Skeet, there are separate events for 12, 20, 28 and 410 gauge so you can shoot any of these, and even 16 gauge loads are available at many clubs. In the different gauges, the shot weights are 1⅛, 1, ⅞, ¾ and ½ ounces. You may shoot 3-inch ¾-ounce loads in a 410 in 28 gauge competition. Handloads are permitted almost everywhere except at the yearly national championship. Shoot heavier loads if you wish, even with big shot, but expect to get a little ribbing from your friends.

When you get to the field—*your gun open and unloaded, please*—it is customary to introduce yourself to anyone on the squad with whom you are not acquainted. The game *was* originated by gentlemen.

While the trap puller gets himself organized, put on your shooting glasses and ear plugs or muffs. You will find a number of Skeet shooters who wear one or a pair of light gloves in warm and cold weather. This is not foppery, they believe it gives them better control of the gun. Skeet shooters do tend to be dudes, though, so you'll feel more comfortable if you wear an appropriate outfit before turning up to shoot. The photos give an idea of what is worn.

When everyone is ready, the first man on the squad steps into the Station 1 shooting box. He may have his feet partially out of the boundary, but you might as well start correctly if you ever think you'll be going to the Olympics. Keep both feet completely within the box.

The squad leader then will call to see preliminary targets from each trap. In competition, he may ask that the traps be adjusted to throw the clays to the correct angle and distance, but in practice hardly anyone bothers with this. This procedure gives an idea of where the clays are going.

Note that not until this point does the squad leader put a shell in his gun. He may load two.

He will then shoulder his gun and call for a target. The first target comes from the high house at the left of the field. This goes for the other stations as well. If he misses it, he tries another high-house bird. Then he may shift his foot position and call for his low-house bird.

Don't get agitated if he stays right there and calls again. Then he will get his doubles. This is the "speed-up" system of shooting to make the squad go a little faster.

While he is shooting, other squad members remain well away from the station and keep silent. Before and after the shots, however, there is often a lot of good natured wisecracking back and forth.

When the leader is finished, he leaves the station and the second man on the squad replaces him. Only the leader gets to call for sample targets. Those who follow must load up, ready to fire.

When all squad members have fired on Station 1, the group shifts to Station 2 and again follows the leader in order. This routine is followed through Station 7. At Station 8, each squad member fires in turn at the high-house targets while the others wait behind him. This is for obvious safety reasons, and also keeps those not shooting out of the way of clay target fragments. Still, one must keep a sharp eye. After everyone has shot a high-house bird, the group shifts around toward the other side for low-house targets.

That is all there is to it—except

hitting the targets. Careful instructions for this fill a book—and have filled several—and there is hardly space for such detail here. A couple of really good ones are *Hartman On Skeet* by Barney Hartman (Van Nostrand, N.Y.C. 1967, $8.95) and *Skeet Shooting With D. Lee Braun* edited by Robert Campbell (from Remington dealers, $4.95). Both are excellent, and are written by top-flight Skeet shooters with plenty of coaching experience. However, what you have learned here is sufficient to be able to understand the pattern of Skeet shooting, and anyone with a modicum of understanding of shotgunning will soon pick up many of the refinements from more experienced squad members.

Because the ranges are close, open choked shotguns are the only satisfactory choice for Skeet. Just about every make and type excepting the bolt-action and single barrels will suffice if appropriately choked. (The exceptions obviously because of their limitation for doubles.) However, in 1970, if one wants to buy a shotgun for Skeet one single make and model is about tops.

Guns for Skeet

There is no question that the Remington Model 1100 gas-operated autoloader is preferred by top Skeet shooters around the country. The nature of its gas mechanism helps to tame the recoil one feels, which is important in a prolonged match. These can run to 250 regular targets with as many as 800 more having been once needed to shoot off ties. It has the handling characteristics wanted for Skeet, is available in all Skeet gauges, and is attractively styled.

While the former champ, the Winchester Model 12, is now only available in the expensive Pigeon grade, used M12s are in much demand among clay target shooters, consequently are rising in price. If one can handle a slide-action without awkwardness, the Remington 870 also is a good choice and is made in all Skeet gauges.

Lagging behind the autoloader, but with a dedicated following, is the over-under double. Without doubt, the Browning Superposed is king but the Japanese-made Charles Daly over-under guns are giving it stiff competition. Krieghoff over-under Skeet guns are highly refined and elegant, and I once fell quite in love with a San Remo grade that I could not afford but which shot exceptionally well. As yet there are not too many Krieghoffs around so don't judge their quality on that basis.

A double gun for Skeet is best fitted with a single trigger, selective or otherwise, although the selective version is preferred. (Twin triggers can be used, but many shooters find it awkward to shift their trigger finger when shooting doubles. As an old hand with side-by-side doubles in the field, how-

Above—The annual championship of the National Skeet Shooting Association is shot at different clubs around the country from year to year. In 1968, at Kansas City, Tommy Heffron, seen here, broke 250 targets straight in the 12-gauge event to tie, and then set a record with another 800 straight in the shootoff with Allen Buntrock without breaking the tie. They were named Co-Champions.

Left—Trap and Skeet are liked by the ladies, too. Loral I Delaney—attractive, personable and professional trainer of hunting dogs and a trapshooter—can put down many a man with her Model 12 Winchester.

ever, I do not find twin triggers a handicap, but then I am not in top Skeet competition either.

Several other over-under shotguns will be found on Skeet fields, including the Winchester 101, Savage, Ithaca, Beretta, and others of foreign make carrying the names applied to them by their importers. Among the got-bucks generation, you will find Merkels, Woodward/Purdeys, Dicksons, and other revered names. Occasionally a Parker side-by-side Skeet gun is seen in the hands of a fond owner, and there are many no-longer-made Remington 32s, practically identical to the Krieghoff, still shot at Skeet.

Still, just for shooting practice, any shotgun capable of shooting two shots in quick succession will do. The refinements are for the experts, not for the occasional Skeet shooter who wants only to get his eye in for hunting season. So, while 26″ barrels are widely used for Skeet, sometimes 28″ on over-

unders, if your own gun has 30″ tubes choked modified and full, use it anyhow. It will make hitting a little more dependent on accurate pointing, but isn't that what you're out there for? If your barrel is fitted with an adjustable choke device, with or without vented recoil reducer, open it up to improved cylinder and shoot away. They are acceptable on the Skeet field, and Lyman's Cutts Compensator is much liked by some top shooters both for the balance it gives the gun and for its recoil-reducing characteristics. I shot one myself for many years, using the spreader tube, which got me many a 25 straight.

You will soon notice that most Skeet shooters would feel more undressed if their shotguns lacked a ventilated barrel top rib, than if they had forgotten their shooting glasses. In my opinion, the glasses are essential but the rib is not. Its purpose is to change the pattern of heat waves rising from a barrel heated by shooting so that the view of the target over the barrel is not distorted or misplaced by refraction of the light rays through changing air densities. Often, however, vent ribs are too narrow, too close to the barrel, and fail to fully perform their intended function. These are more decorative than functional. However, vent ribs are in, and you will want one ultimately.

It is quite practical to improve the quality of a field grade gun for Skeet shooting by having a vent rib added to a plain barrel. Simmons Guns Special-

TRAP SKEET and the HUNTER

ties, Herters, Polychoke and some custom gunsmiths will do this work. The service departments of some bigger manufacturers are able to do this work as well, and for almost all guns popular for Skeet extra barrels with vent ribs and Skeet choke are readily available.

Shooting glasses are a story in themselves. Popular brands are American Optical and B&L, especially in the Bud Decot pattern, Willson, Mitchell, and Hy-Wyd (which are sold by Bud Decot as well as the B&L pattern). Other brands come and go and are also suitable. The important thing is *eye protection,* achieved by hardening the lenses. These must be at least 2.5mm thick, preferably 3mm. These glasses can be mail ordered, but are better obtained from an eye specialist who can determine if prescription grinding is required and fit the frames to the special demands of your own head size and shape. For an all purpose glass, choose a light-grey tint. Avoid weird colors such as pink, gold, or blue.

Any eye cover, however, is better than nothing at all. Wear cheap plastic sunglasses, if nothing better is at hand, but wear something. Even if your own equipment works just fine, there is still possibility of eye damage no matter where you are on the shooting field. I have seen spectators sitting at the edge of the field struck by single shot pellets having enough velocity to break the skin and bruise. These pellets either exited through the slots of a muzzle device, which is unlikely, or were rebounds from the target. Vision is priceless. Protect it.

Trapshooting

One starts off trapshooting in about the same way as he does Skeet, by getting on a squad. Then everything changes.

Trap is a more purposeful game than Skeet, and those who find it more satisfying are responding to its greater demand on shooting skill in comparison with the athletic ability required by Skeet. Trapshooters as a group tend to be older, less flamboyant men than Skeet shooters and pursue their game with greater dignity. There is far less talk on the field until the last shot has been fired. A nervous

or mouthy shooter soon finds that he has difficulty finding anyone to shoot with.

Trap is shot by a 5-man squad shooting from 5 stations, the minimum distance 16 yards, firing at clays thrown from a single trap. The stations are on lines drawn through the trap to the rear in a fan-like layout. One form of the game is shot exclusively from the 16-yard positions, which is the best game for the beginner. Shooting positions move farther back, in half-yard steps, to 27 yards, for handicap competition. A shooter is assigned his handicap yardage (by the A.I.A.) on the basis of his scores on registered targets. Another version shot from the 16-yard mark is doubles, where two targets are thrown at once.

The machine that throws trap targets moves the throwing arm from side to side, whereas in Skeet, the trap arms are fixed. This gives trap targets different angles of flight to the sides, normally within 22° to either side of center, but legally within 47°. Target elevation is fixed.

The squad takes position on the 5 stations according to the order named on the squad sheet. The man on the first (left) station may ask to see a target or two to gauge angle and speed. He then loads a single cartridge, shoulders his gun, calls for the target, swings and fires.

While there are variations in technique, a good beginning is to point one's gun about a foot above the forward edge of the traphouse. If on stand 1, aim above the left corner of the trap house, from stand 2 halfway from left to center, from position 3 over the center, from 4 over the right corner, and from No. 5 about two feet to the right of the right corner. Position your feet with the toes along a line parallel to the greatest angle of target flight to the left if you are right handed, or to the right if you are a southpaw. This seems a little awkward at first, but favors swinging on targets with sharp angles to the trigger-hand side. If one faced the traphouse more squarely, which seems normal, when swinging on a sharp angled target to the right for a right hander the muscles will become taut, which both slows the swing and tends to elevate the gun.

Stand up squarely, both feet spread apart a comfortable amount. Don't crouch, but lean into the gun a bit if this seems comfortable. A relaxed, erect stance is desirable. Put the gun up to your shoulder, clamp your cheek to the comb of the stock like it was glued there, and make what little adjustments are required to get the correct sight arrangement. You should be able to see the bead just a bit above the breech or receiver front. If your gun is ribbed and has two sight beads, the correct view shows the front bead sitting just on top of the mid-rib bead

in a figure-eight configuration.

Now point the gun over the traphouse as described. Cast your eyes out about 15 feet forward of the trap center and get them focused there. Don't focus on the gun. Call for the target. Just as it appears in your vision, pause for an instant before swinging to define its direction of flight. Then swing after it with the gun. Go after it good and fast, and fire when you have swung about 6" or so past it, if it is an angling target, and you won't have to worry over differing leads for differing angles. Delay until the target is about to hit its apex, though, and you will have to worry. Some very good hunters are deliberately slow, but they had one devil of a time learning leads when they first began shooting. I used to be among 'em.

I borrowed these tips from Lee Braun's excellent book on trapshooting, and adopted my own technique to them with a steady increase in my scoring. I once instructed a young man who had never before shot at a clay target this way for about 10 minutes, and he immediately began busting about 10 out of 25 birds. Six months later, he broke his first 25 straight, so excited that he 'phoned to give me the news. So I believe these instructions are about all a beginner needs. If you want to learn more of the refinements, buy Braun's worthwhile book.

Trap Guns

Except in doubles and International Clay Pigeon, only a single shot is fired at each target, so there is more variety among trap guns than in Skeet guns. In contrast to Skeet, however, recoil-reducing muzzle attachments are taboo. Shooting in a line, trapshooters object to the loud noise they make.

Trap is a 12-gauge game. Practice shooting, however, is all right with any gauge. Appropriate loads of No. 7½ and No. 8 shot are sold in 12, 16, and 20-gauge at most good clubs.

For many years, a full-choke barrel was considered the only one for trap, but modern improvements in shotshell performance, during the past decade, have changed this. If one shoots plastic shells with plastic shot-protecting collars or wads—factory or handloaded—he will do better from 16-yards with a more open boring. Modified is perhaps the best all-round choice for shooting from 16 to 20 yards, improved modified from 20 to 24, and a full choke back to 27 yards. If, however, you handload with the old standard card over-powder wads and felt filler wadding, without a shot protector, go up one degree in choke.

To maintain follow-through without conscious effort, which is just as important in trapshooting as it is in golf, tennis or baseball, a long barrel is desired. Thirty inches is pretty much standard, but fast shooters can use

28". More deliberate shots may use a 32" tube effectively, and some 34" guns are liked at the longer handicap yardages.

The ventilated barrel rib is, as in Skeet, a must with trapshooters. Not that it is needed by a beginner, for he can do just as well with his plain-barreled bunny-gitter. When properly fashioned, however, the vent rib can aid a seasoned trapshooter. Pointing is important in trap, and the guide to the eye that the shadows alongside the rib provide are a help to pointing accuracy without the need for the eye focus to leave the target.

Probably the most popular all-time trap gun is the Model 12 Winchester slide-action, but among trapshooters today who appreciate that lessened recoil might aid scores over a long match, the gas-operated Remington Model 1100 is finding favor. Their Model 870 slide-action also is a fine trap gun. With the more decorative figure in the C-grade wood, both can be pretty guns as well. Many other guns, such as the Savage slide-action and the Hi-Standard slides and autos, Mossberg, Harrington & Richardson, and Stevens pumps may be used effectively at trap. Foreign-made autos, on the long-recoil principal, also do well, such as Franchi, Breda, Ithaca, et al. In fact, just about any gun type can be shot effectively if the shooter has the time to become accustomed to it —even the single-shot hammer guns and bolt actions, although none of the magazine guns have achieved the popularity of the two Remingtons and the Winchester named above.

Winchester has a pair of magazine guns, the 1200 slide-action and the 1400 gas-operated autoloader, which are wholly suited to trapshooting but have not caught the fancy of most regular shooters. Trap is a faddish game.

One can dream up a dozen reasons why one gun or another lacks popularity, but they're guesses. No one really knows the answer. Two very worthy guns that have not caught on with trapshooters are the superb Browning Auto-5 long-recoil autoloader, which is highly popular as a field gun, and the Ithaca Model 37 slide-action. I've often pondered why this should be so, but I've never found a wholly satisfactory explanation; and, in the many years that I have shot, competed, and written about trapshooting I think I have heard of them all!

As in Skeet, the over-under is the favored child of the post-WW II period. Browning's Superposed is king, with their extra-wide Broadway ribbed model currently much liked. The likely second is the Charles Daly. The Selexor feature of the Daly guns (little buttons on the breech sides that defeat the selective ejectors) is especially worthwhile to handloaders who save their empties—trapshooters are enthusiastic consumers of handloads. The Winchester 101 is competing hard for a place here, as are the Ithaca SKBs. Krieghoff over-under trap guns are very much liked by their owners, but as yet there are still not many around—they're not exactly cheap. The others, Savage, Beretta, and other imports, also make fine trap guns.

A comer in this field is the Perazzi line of over-under trap guns distributed by Ithaca. These feature quick-change trigger/lock assemblies and interchangeable stocks as well. They're quite expensive, but are highly refined for competition. I suppose winning is all the sweeter if it is done with a multi-hundred dollar shotgun, but a win is a win whether shot with a super-duper wonder gun or an old single-barrel squirrel special. As for

me, I'd get a terrific boot out of going 200 straight with the latter, but there is such a thing as pride of ownership. That explains the occasional Woodward and Merkel seen on the trap fields, not to say the side-by-side Greeners, Purdeys, and other aristocrats.

Side-by-side shotguns still have a distinct place in trapshooting. Many still prefer them for doubles, and the old Parker, Winchester Model 21, Fox, Lefever, and Iver Johnson specialized trap shotguns can drag some fancy money out of the wallets of trapshooters who decide they have just got to have one. The last two, of course, are hardly ever seen today and their prices are markedly lower than prices of the Winchester and Parker guns.

No matter which way the twin barrels are oriented, for trap a single-selective trigger is preferred. They're not really needed except perhaps in doubles and International, as only one shot is fired at a single target and the shooter can easily arrange his trigger finger on the proper twig well before calling for the target. A single *non-selective* trigger, of course, means that the shooter has no choice over which barrel is going to be fired first; if he has a conventional modified choke in the first barrel he's limited to about the 20-yard position at handicap.

Trapshooters want selective ejectors in the doubles also. This is a curiosity since most of them handload and never let their empties touch the ground. They need the ejectors as much as

There's nothing wrong with side-by-side doubles at Skeet, though they have lost favor with some shooters. Just to show that he lives and is well, here's the writer trying out a double at the Loch Haven Skeet and Trap Club.

TRAP SKEET and the HUNTER

they need a third shoelace, but they want 'em and they get 'em! Don't let their lack in your own Fox Model B or Beretta double disturb you for one moment. Go right out and shoot. Get used to the game and your own gun, and before long you can be right up there with the top money winners without having to invest in any expensive ordnance.

Trapshooting has spawned an unusual and highly refined type of shotgun that is little suited to any other use—the single-barrel. While single-barrel adaptations of over-under shotgun actions are available in Winchester 101, Charles Daly and Krieghoff guns, these are stepchildren to the true single-barrel trap gun. This gun is made on an action designed especially for single-barrel use. They have been around for a long time, and one sees quite a few Parker and Charles Daly guns from the older, pre-war era at the Grand American Trapshoot, the annual national championship of trapshooting held each summer at Vandalia, Ohio.

There are some high-priced imports in single-barrel configuration, such as Stoeger's Model 27 at $449.50, the Abercrombie & Fitch at $395, and the Parkland Sodia at $1450. The highly prized Ithaca 4E and higher grade singles, made wholly in the U.S., are much desired but long delayed in new delivery. They start around $1500. The only other U.S. made singles are the Ljutic Mono-Gun at $1795 and Dyn-A-Trap at $998.50.

Browning's new Japanese-made BT-99 single-barrel trap gun has only limited availability in 1970, but is a fine shotgun, and at $295 is bound to make quite an impression among trapshooters.

However, all the single-barrel trap shotguns are for specialists in the American form of trapshooting 16-yard and handicap, and are little suited to any other type of shooting.

International Shotgunning

There is another form of trapshooting, shot worldwide and in important International and Olympic competition. This is Clay Pigeon, which requires a very expensive 15-trap trench setup, of which less than 20 exist in the U.S. Six men take the field in this game, and they shoot from 5 stations at 16 meters (about 17½ yards) behind the traps. In front of each station is a group of 3 traps, each fixed at different angles, both vertically and horizontally. When he calls for a target, a shooter doesn't know from which of the 3 traps the target will come. He could get a ground-hugging straight-away, an almost vertical target, or a weird sharp angle.

The targets are thrown a lot farther and faster in Clay Pigeon than in American trap. To resist breakage from the greater throwing force of the trap, the targets are made tougher. The rules permit 1¼-ounce shot loads, in comparison with the maximum 1⅛-ounce loads permitted by domestic rules. These heavier shot charges favor better breakage of the tougher targets, and so do the two shots allowed at each target. First, you have got to get on them—and that, friends, is tough.

The shooters shift position to the right after firing at each target. The 6th man on the squad comes around behind while the other 5 are on station. I have shot this game over a couple of 300-target programs and learned that there is just about enough time to shoot, clear the gun if the second shot was not fired, get off station, get on the next, and reload before it is time to shoot again. Any little thing that is disturbing will break the shooter's concentration momentarily—and that is all it takes to cause a miss.

Because of the pounding the shooters get from the 3¼- or 3½-dram, 1¼-ounce loads, with two shots almost invariably fired at each target—the second shot is often fired at a chip if the target breaks with the first shot just to keep up the rhythm—only 100 targets a day are shot in most competitions. I can tell you that this is about all one wants!

I consider Clay Pigeon to be the most challenging, the toughest, and the most fun of all clay target shooting sports. It is important, too. The United States fields teams in Olympic, European, International, and Pan American Championships, in which winning has significant political importance little appreciated in the U.S. If we win in these events, we gain much face abroad. If they lose, the iron curtain nations lose face.

A lot of experience is needed to do well, and this means practice. With the cost of a single International Clay Pigeon field between $20,000 and $30,000 and going up, practice is hard to come by.

Skeet, Trap, and the NRA

This is one reason why the National Rifle Association has entered into an area that properly belongs to the Amateur Trapshooting Association and the National Skeet Shooting Association, the governing organizations for domestic trap and Skeet. The NRA is charged by the International Shooting Union with responsibility for all forms of International shooting in the U.S. This responsibility carries with it the implied requirements for

Skeet and the young do very well together. Skeet can create a closer relationship between youngster and parent than almost any other endeavor except hunting. Note ear protectors and shooting glasses, which are essential to avoid potential vision and hearing damage that can be caused by shooting.

training, practice, and development among U.S. shooters in all forms of International competition.

Years ago, when there were no developmental programs in International Skeet or Clay Pigeon, the NRA started them. There was no thought then of usurping the rights of the other associations, but someone had to assume this responsibility, manage tryout shoots, and put up the money. Now, after some pretty nasty accusations and recriminations from the regular Skeet and trap people, it appears that the program is showing initial success. More and more non-military shooters are developing skill in these sports, and our teams seem to do a little better every time they compete.

Since the Clay Pigeon facilities are so much more complicated and expensive than International Skeet needs, which requires only a longer target throw and a timer for delayed target release after the call, it seemed impossible to develop enough Clay Pigeon fields for widespread practice.

A man who is today the NRA's Director of International and Shotgun Competitions, Mike Tipa, developed a relatively simple modification of a standard Winchester trap that enables the trap to throw targets in changing vertical as well as horizontal directions. This trap solved the problem. Mike is a personable, multi-lingual and decorated (by foreign governments) shotgunner with wide International experience. He is also Chairman of the International Shooting Union's Technical Committee. He has complete plans and specifications for this trap field as well as an International Skeet field that anyone can get by writing to him at NRA Headquarters, 1600 Rhode Island Ave., N.W., Washington, D.C. 20036. The modified trap is available now from Winchester, and existing traps can be altered at nominal cost. Mike and his crew will also give whatever assistance they can to a club that is interested in starting International shotgun programs.

Where to Shoot?

All right, now you know all there is to know about clay target shooting—with one exception that bothered the hell out of me when I was young, and just beginning to shoot seriously—how do you find shooting grounds?

Write to the NRA's Training, Competitions, and Facilities Division and ask for a list of clubs in your area if you are, as you should be, an NRA member. These are primarily rifle and pistol clubs, but many have shotgun facilities. If they don't, doubtless some of the shooters there will be able to put you on the right track. Ask salesmen in gun shops. Look in the yellow pages. Write to the NSSA at 212 Linwood Bldg., 2608 Inwood Rd., Dallas, Tex., 75235, and ATA, Vandalia, Ohio, 45377, and ask for copies of the pages from their annual records publications that list gun clubs in your state, and for the names and addresses of the state association secretaries so you can telephone them if necessary. Lastly, if you live so far from a club that shooting seems nigh impossible, start your own club. NRA has guidelines on this, too, available for the asking.

Blackpowder enthusiasts are not forgotten either. The National Muzzle Loading Rifle Association, P. O. Box 15, Friendship, Ind., 47021, conducts trap shoots for muzzle-loading shotguns at its regular semi-annual shoots on the home grounds. Many local blackpowder clubs have trapshoots also. Write to the NMLRA for information on local organizations and the home shoots. But, don't bring your front-feeder to a regular trap or Skeet club as I once did. Even though only practice was being shot, I only got off two barrels before the regulars formed a committee and passed a resolution. They ruled than Ruffin was going to put that dirty thing away if he was going to shoot with them.

One final tip. The U.S. Army Marksmanship Training Unit clay pigeon shooters at Ft. Benning agree that there is one supremely important factor in good scoring. See the target. Concentrate on it. Concentrate so hard that the individual rings can be made out. It sounds difficult, and it is, but it can be done. It is also good advice no matter what form of clay target shooting is done.

Now, go get 'em and break 'em all —but wear ear and eye protection while you do. Ball it up, and unless you're already as good as I am, your success with birds and waterfowl can't help but benefit. ●

Typical U.S. Skeet range layout. The crossing dotted lines indicate travel path of clay targets.

Arnold Griebel
1890   1970

**One of the world's great artists in metal, he was
completely committed to his demanding, difficult craft.**

by JOHN T. AMBER

ONE OF THE world's great engravers died on September 13, 1970. He was 79. If Griebel had a special talent, it was in his magnificent relief sculpturing of animal and bird figures. His drawing of these, his command of foreshortening and perspective, his rendering of musculature, was, in my opinion, unsurpassed by anyone of his field—and equalled by few. Some several years back, he spent two years at the Art Institute of Chicago, studying anatomy.

Griebel learned his craft at Suhl (Germany), a great gunmaking center, but also a place where gun engraving—and the development of that skill—flourished. In those days most firearms received some engraving, almost regardless of their cost—and the best European guns carried a considerable amount. Most of the sporting guns of that day, shotguns and rifles, were made on break-open actions, and most of those were hand-made in the Suhl area.

The machine-made bolt action rifles were not yet anything like as popular as they were to become.

Griebel came to the United States in 1928, but there was little demand here then, or in the depression years that followed, for embellished firearms—or for little else that cost extra money. Griebel worked during those lean years as a die engraver here and there, until, in 1939, he became a full-time employee of a Chicago house making engraved stamps and embossing dies. His gun engraving was a spare-time thing, done at home, until his retirement in 1951.

Times had got better, too, and as his reputation grew, the demand for his engraving increased so much that he usually had a year or two of work ahead of him.

Bruce Grant, writing in our 6th edition, prepared in 1951, said that Griebel was, "in the opinion of many, the finest artist in metal in the United States." The GUN DIGEST was, I believe, the first publication to feature gun engraving, and over the years we have displayed Arnold Griebel's superb work many times. I like to think that our efforts may have had some part in the growing appreciation of good engraving in metal.

I knew Arnold Griebel for some 30 years, and a more charming, gracious gentle man it would be impossible to find. He worked under conditions that many would have found appalling, his bench a small table in his little kitchen! The light was good—if that's the word—for only a few hours a day, yet in our many conversations, he never voiced a complaint.

Arnold Griebel is survived by his wife, Lydia, a son, Paul, and 2 grandchildren.

The world has lost an outstanding artist, and I've lost a good friend. ●

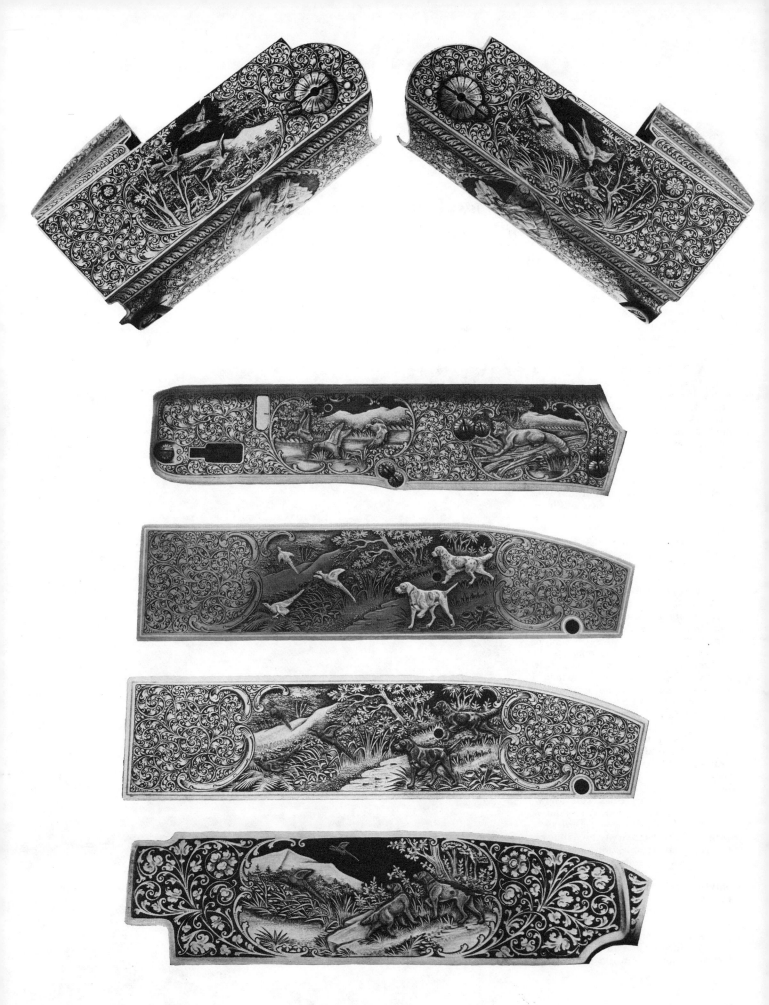

Age of the AUTOLOADER?

It takes years — sometimes a lot of them — for almost any kind of rifle to get all the bugs ironed out, for a truly first-class model to reach production. It's been that way with the big game autoloader, but now — glory be, says this Tejano — its day has arrived!

Hayes studies distant deer in vain search for antlers. With the Redfield receiver sight replaced by the Weaver K4 scope, as shown, the 30-06 autoloader is satisfactory for long-range big game hunting, though author would not try such a shot from offhand position.

by **TOM HAYES**

IN A RECENT issue of a sporting magazine, I ran across the thought-provoking statement that the popularity of the self-loading rifle might easily equal that of the bolt-action among our big-game hunters except for one glaring shortage: no bold, forthright warrior had as yet appeared on the American literary scene to champion the autoloader's cause. Well, here I come, hackles raised and eyes ablaze, and I warn all mice and foxes to get out of the way—I'm loaded for *bear!*

Let me say right here that there are autoloaders and there are autoloaders; they vary among themselves as greatly as do field dogs and six-shooters. Among them will be found clunkers as well as champions. There are available certain autoloading rifles which I wouldn't recommend for saluting the "Fourth," much less as serious hunting weapons. (The same may also be said for various lever-, pump- and bolt-action rifles, a number of which I shouldn't like to be found dead with.)

It takes time—many years, often—to eliminate the "bugs" from a gun design and produce what might be called a perfected action. The shoulder-supported single-shot firearm, for example, appeared in the 15th century but wasn't perfected for several hundred years. Exposed-hammer, lever-action repeating rifles were known prior to the Civil War, but relative perfection wasn't achieved until 1886, with the introduction of the Winchester rifle having that model number. The concealed-hammer lever action—introduced in 1899 by Savage — was only recently perfected here by the incorporation of a crisp trigger and, some 60 years overdue, a handy thumb safety.

The ancient turn-bolt repeater, brilliantly improved by Paul Mauser after kicking around the world for 30 years

Big-racked Texas white-tailed buck fell to Hayes' autoloading '06 on December 25—a fine Christmas present!

or more, is generally stated to have been perfected in 1898 although our latest models—having adjustable triggers and silent sliding safeties — expose this statement to serious question.

A pump rifle for big game appeared in 1885 for some older cartridges, such as the 38-56, 40-60 and 50-95; another one, for a series of more modern centerfires, came out in 1912. This action, too, slowly is approaching a perfected state.

Now, let's discuss the autoloader—sometimes wrongly called the "automatic"—as chambered for centerfire calibers suitable for hunting our larger game.

Advent of the Auto

The first domestic, production-model, self-loading, centerfire sporting rifle was the Winchester model of 1905. This was soon followed by the Model 07, which took its model number from the year of introduction—1907. This well-made rifle, unfortunately, had several failings of a congenital nature, and the arms writers of that bygone day — like unto their current counterparts — immediately outdid each other in heaping vitriolic diatribes on this "ugly duckling." All of the 07's troubles stemmed from Winchester's employment of a straight blow-back breeching system, necessitating the use of relatively low-powered cartridges which, even in those days, fell far short of universal acceptance as "big game" calibers. The 07's design required a heavy, sliding breechblock which added unfavorable weight, detracted from the rifle's balance, and produced during recoil a peculiar, weight-shifting "double-shuffle" which many shooters found disconcerting. I never liked the 07 enough to want one, but I haven't found it nearly so bad as it's been painted. Actually, most of the "poor" balance

exists in the minds of the 07's rabid detractors, and the weapon-weight, though substantial, is hardly excessive. The double-shuffle experienced during recoil doesn't bother me at all. The only feature I find worthy of serious censure is the lack of suitable calibers. It's interesting to note that, despite its shortcomings, the Model 07 outlived the majority of its early detractors, having been in production until about 1958.

Following the 07's introduction, the shooting press managed to work itself into such a mass-hysteria that not only was this model adjudged a blight on the existing sporting arms picture, but autoloading rifles, per se, were solemnly pronounced to be henceforth and forever unsuited to sporting use. Thus the big-game autoloader's case was closed before it had hardly been opened, and woe betide the brazen upstart who should ever publicly dare to challenge the Official Verdict. This was the atmosphere which in 1908 greeted Remington's fine big-game autoloader, the John Browning-designed Model 8, when it first saw the light of day.

The name John Browning, in connection with firearms design, may mean little or nothing to today's poorly informed (but highly indoctrinated) shooters, so let me tell you this: John Browning was the all-time great of modern gun designers. He never released a model for production until it functioned flawlessly. His weapons were above intelligent criticism by all but a few of his contemporaries because his genius and design-knowledge were superior to their own. The arms press of that bygone day had so far exceeded the point of no return in its blanket condemnation of big-game autoloaders, however, that few writers bothered to explore the Model 8's astounding capabilities — and even fewer found the courage to lift a

feeble voice in its defense. In fact, a couple of insignificant and irrelevant features of the Model 8 provided a tooth-hold for the critical "experts," and these worthies wasted no time in chewing this outstanding firearm to pieces.

Model 8 Remington

To use adequate big-game calibers without the prohibitive gun-weight required by an equally powerful arm employing a simple blow-back design, the Model 8 utilized the long-recoil breeching system. In this, the barrel and breechblock are locked together at the time of firing, and *both* recoil in this locked condition. The long-recoil system, therefore, requires that the entire barrel be free to move several inches in an axial direction. Browning wound the powerful recoil spring—which resists and softens the force of the recoiling barrel and then returns the barrel to its original position — around the barrel itself, and encased this spring-wound barrel in a stout steel tube having a front bushing for the barrel's muzzle and being rigidly attached to the receiver at the rear.

The Model 8's ingenious barrel-within-a-barrel effected the world's first practical high-power sporting autoloader—a rifle of astonishing accuracy which demonstrated a consistency of zero that the writer has yet to see surpassed. The Model 8's monumental "fault" was really only a misfortune; it happened to look more like a short-barreled shotgun than a big-game rifle, and the esthetic senses of the already prejudiced arms scribes were severely jarred. Though the Model 8 was quick-pointing, adequately balanced, and of near-ideal weight, its rather clumsy *appearance* was immediately accepted as good and sufficient proof of its *suspected* clumsiness.

If you should happen to thumb

Remington 81 Woodsmaster became a favorite of the author for whitetails after stock comb was lowered and Redfield sights added.

through the yellowed pages of some pre-war gun magazine and run across one of those typical articles anent the Model 8, you would probably be amazed by the following statements: It was so heavy, bulky, clumsy and out of balance that its user was predestined to abject failure. It was so deadly on game that its use as a sporting weapon should be prohibited. It was such an ugly conglomeration of machinery that no gun-wise person would even consider its use. It was rapidly becoming a favorite with such gun-ignorant persons as market hunters, poachers, and professional guides. I'm not kidding; this absurdly contradictory theme was played to death for 50 years.

The terms "perfected firearm" and "perfect firearm" must not be confused; there are a goodly number of perfected guns floating around, but the perfect one is not yet with us. Every firearm ever made has possessed features which were subject to criticism, and the "perfected" Model 8 was no exception. Its safety-lever was unhandy — almost as bad as that of its press-praised contemporary, the early Savage 99. The protruding magazine, resembling that of the press-lauded Winchester 95's, did nothing to enhance the Model 8's appearance, and it did force the carrying hand a trifle forward of the rifle's balance point. Aside from these minor inconveniences, and provided the action wasn't gummed-up with a stiff oil in cold weather (the user's own fault), the old Model 8, in the touch-and-go business of whitetail shooting in typical cover, was the most reliable venison producer of its day; and those chambered in caliber 35 Remington made themselves a reputation as elk and big bear tranquilizers within the 200-yard limit of this cartridge's effectiveness.

During the early WWII years, I discovered that Tom, Jr's advanced age of 15, coupled with his recent feat of having killed his first buck (*running*, at 75 yards, with my Krag sporter) entitled him to a deer rifle of his own. I also discovered that new rifles were unavailable, and used ones practically so. In desperation, I laid out 60 uninflated dollars for a battered relic of a Model 8 and sent it to Remington for overhaul. A late model, enlarged fore-end was installed, and I replaced the original sights with Redfield's Sourdough front and aperture rear. Expecting little in the way of performance from this oldtimer, I kept it for myself and passed the prized Krag on to its young admirer. It didn't take me long to develop a

high regard for this weather-beaten rifle, and a lesser regard for its "learned" detractors. All this rifle ever asked of me was just to show it a deer, and over the years I've shown it quite a few.

When I returned home at the war's end, young Charles, too, was ready for his own deer rifle, and the Model 8 became his possession. He still owns it, it isn't for sale, and he gets mighty tired of our borrowing it at every opportunity.

Model 81 Remington

Having parted reluctantly with this Model 8, I kept hankering for a duplicate replacement. Finally, I found a used Model 81, the almost-identical successor to the Model 8. This rifle was in nearly new condition, and the moment I raised it to my shoulder I discovered the reason: *the sights couldn't be aligned on a target.* Believe it nor not, the makers had provided a thick, fat, overly high monstrosity of a stock clearly intended for use with a necessarily *off-set* telescope sight! A woods rifle forced to be burdened with a telescope sight? I could hardly believe my eyes. A woods rifle deprived of iron sights isn't a woods rifle, and a telescope sight without a precision, long-range rifle under it isn't much of anything. It's no wonder the original owner disposed of this gun at considerable financial sacrifice, and I'll bet he clobbers the next innocent sales clerk who even mentions the word autoloader.

I couldn't wait to get home with the 81 and attack that chunk of timber with rasp and sandpaper. I whittled off almost enough wood to build a fence around any ranch in Texas; honestly, the pile of chips and shavings I made constituted a distinct fire hazard. I thinned the grip down to where it fitted a normal hand, and lowered the point of the comb nearly half an inch. The butt was left intact except for a couple of large, deep holes under the buttplate, and the entire stock was thinned from grip to butt. The now-handsome, perfectly fitting stock was then refinished. Redfield Sourdough and aperture rear sights were installed, and I owned the best 35 Remington Model 81 in the whole wide world. In fact, I still own it, and will continue to do so until death do us part.

Most authorities maintain that the Model 81 "died." I claim that Remington killed it with that godawful

stock. This point, however, is completely academic; the fact remains that the Model 81 was dropped from production, and for the following Remington-stated reasons — all undoubtedly true; it cost too much to manufacture; it wasn't adaptable to the hot long-range calibers; it wasn't suited to the accommodation of a telescope sight.

Why anyone excepting a person with failing eyesight would hobble a woods rifle with a telescope sight, is beyond me; and regarding high-velocity loadings in a woods rifle, even the experts have been reluctant to recommend these. At any rate, the press-promoted "scope-everything" and "featherweight rifle" crazes had the gallant 81 on the ropes, and the rifle's maker polished off the old warrior with that ungodly "telescope" stock which left long-range-minded scope users completely cold and thoroughly alienated the woods-rifle clique as well.

In addition to a better stock, the 81 needed several improvements — a handier safety, removal of that pot-bellied magazine, and adaptation to the more powerful 30-06 cartridge for inveterate elk, moose and big-bear hunters. A more streamlined appearance would have helped, too. But getting all these things in the 81 was impossible. What were we dyed-in-the-wool autoloader fans to do?

Remington 740 Auto

Just as everything looked darkest, Remington announced their revolutionary Model 740, a handsome, streamlined, gas-operated light weight 30-60, having a handy safety and *non*-pot-belly magazine! Another improvement of definite worth considering the ranging capabilities of the '06 load, was the 740's adaptability to scope use. Here, for the first time, was an autoloading woods rifle that showed promise of serving reasonably well in place of a well-tuned bolt-action weapon for that occasionally encountered long shot. An additional bonus was the gas-operated action which reduces recoil effect to the extent provided by at least 12 ounces of additional gun-weight. In other words, the 7½-pound

740 seems to kick no harder than an 8¼-pound bolt-action of identical caliber.

The 740's announcement c r e a t e d quite a stir in arms circles. Before long, however, somewhat unfavorable reports on it began to circulate, and my burning desire to own one began to cool. The Model 740 reportedly didn't give the accuracy of which the cartridge was capable. Outsize groups were believed caused by variations in contact pressure between the receiver and the fore-end as the barrel heated up in firing, and the point of impact would vary unless the barrel was allowed to cool completely between shots. (Incidentally 740 owners can obtain an "accuracy block" designed to eliminate this trouble from Williams Gunsight Co.).

The standard grade 740 had a stock quite satisfactory for iron sights, but too low at the comb for best scope use. The de luxe model stock was correct for scope use but too high for the factory-equipped front sight. Neither model, therefore, was entirely satisfactory for a quickly interchangeable sighting system — a necessary requirement for any gun deserving to be called an "all-round" rifle. The de luxe model was equipped with fixed sling swivels — an abomination on a woods rifle, but easily removed.

Because the 740's rotating locking-lugs were cut at a steep angle, it is slightly difficult to open the action by hand. This becomes more than a minor inconvenience on certain rare occasions when the operating handle is accidentally pushed rearward a trifle, thus disengaging the sear, and then fails to move fully forward despite the bolt-return spring pressure. In this situation, the rifle can't be fired. 740 users soon learn to check this handle's position periodically, thereby avoiding this trouble.

Incidentally, most functioning failures involving any autoloading weapon stem from one of three principal causes: the use of dented, dirty, or corroded ammunition; failure of the user to let the bolt slam down solidly on the cartridge being chambered, or use of a lubricant which stiffens in cold weather and ties up the action. All are easily avoided.

Self-loading rifles require a reasonably clean, rust-free chamber; gas-operated rifles are particularly demanding in these respects. Manually operated weapons, by the excessive force required to chamber or extract a cartridge or case, indicate when the chamber needs attention; the self-loading rifle gives no hint that something is amiss until it suddenly refuses to function.

However, in any situation requiring more than one shot, the properly maintained autoloader is much less subject to firing failures than any manually operated rifle. This is a fact, not an opinion. We have used three different Remington big-game autoloaders for an aggregate period of 30 years, *and we've never experienced a malfunction.* We don't pamper our guns one bit; we give them only the minimum care and attention that any respected weapon deserves.

Although I couldn't work up enough desire for the 740 to trade in my fine 81, I still believe that every 740 purchaser got his money's worth. Literally thousands of these guns are performing yeoman s e r v i c e for their owners, with never a hint of malfunction or other failure.

Remington 742 — Ultimate Auto

Still, it was possible to improve it, and it is my opinion that 1960 will go down in arms history as the year in which the high-power sporting autoloader was perfected. Remington, in that memorable year, unveiled their magnificent M o d e l 742. Practically identical in appearance to the 740, only three minor mechanical changes differentiate the 742 from its predecessor; but what a difference these "minor" changes make!

Firstly, the interrupted locking-lugs threads are cut at a slightly less abrupt angle, eliminating the bolt's tendency to rest in a partially unlocked position. This also makes the bolt more easily retractable by hand. Secondly, a new method was adopted for fastening the fore-end to the barrel; now there is no direct contact with the receiver. This has resulted in such impressive accuracy that even the autoloader's most rabid detractors have been subdued. Thirdly, the 742's s t o c k is made with a comb high enough to work with a scope sight — and the excellent open iron sights have been made high enough to work with this stock! Such a simple solution to the problems connected with interchangeable sighting s y s t e m s leaves us wondering why it was so long in coming, but the fact remains that Remington was the first domestic rifle maker to see the light.

The 742 retains all of the 740's virtues: streamlined beauty, perfect balance and snapshooting pointability, ideal length 22″ barrel, 30-06 cham-

bering, highly satisfactory trigger pull, and its rock-bottom weight — for any powerful, seriously intended hunting rifle — of only 7½ pounds. Incidentally, a hunting rifle of any power having substantially lesser weight than the 742 will be difficult to hold steadily for exacting, offhand aim, and the recoil will be quite disturbing if the weapon is chambered for a powerful caliber such as the 30-06.

I happened to have 13 firearms in my gun closet when the 742 hit the market, and it suddenly occurred to me that that was a very unlucky number which demanded immediate rectification. It never occurred to me that this crisis could have been resolved by selling a firearm, so I bought a Model 742.

The moment I laid eyes on that high sight-line I saw tremendous possibilities for dual sighting; later, when I laid the Weaver Q.D. scope base on the receiver and found that it in no way interfered with the use of the iron sights, I decided to make it a permanent fixture if the rifle's accuracy proved worthy of a scope. The mount was quickly screwed to the receiver, the Weaver K4 attached, and off I galloped to the rifle range.

I set up a target at 100 yards, laid the rifle over a sand bag, and happened to get the first shot well on the paper. I fired two more, and when I peeked through the spotting scope I could hardly believe my eyes. Each of those three shots would have cut a dime, and all can be hidden under a quarter! I kept this group for a souvenir, and it remains tacked to my den wall to this very day. The ammo? Over-age G.I.!

The factory sights have been removed from my 742, and the muzzle end sports — you guessed it — a Redfield sourdough. The inconspicuous scope base and the base for a removable-slide aperture sight are permanently attached to the receiver. I can change from iron sights to telescope, or vice versa, in less than 60 seconds. I've taken 5 deer already with this wonderful gun, and you can bet I'll hang on to it until a better autoloader comes along. I have a feeling, though, that I'll have this rifle for a long, long time.

●

FLYING SHOTGUN

... the Nazi Air Force 3-Barrel

by D. C. Cole

AMONG THE MOST unusual of military small arms is the M30 Drilling, issued in limited numbers as a survival gun to special units of the Luftwaffe early in World War II. Until 1941 the air forces of the Third Reich were involved in operations of such nature that a survival gun was not considered necessary. Survivors of forced landings in Western Europe and the English Channel were within hours, if not minutes, of rescue or capture. Weapons carried by airmen in 1939 and 1940 were mainly automatic pistols. On occasion submachine guns and, rarely, Mauser military rifles were carried.

In 1941 the nature of terrain covered by Luftwaffe operations changed abruptly. Air crashes in the Balkans, North Africa and Russia placed airmen in rough country far from habitation and exposed to some danger of starvation. A survival gun became necessary.

The drilling offered a number of advantages over other arms. This versatile German gun met a wide variety of requirements. In one lightweight package it presented a double barrel shotgun for handling pellets or heavy slugs and a powerful rifle barrel for long range shots. Disassembled, it could be stored in a small space; it had ruggedness, simplicity and, finally, as the traditional German hunting weapon, familiarity. Its chief disadvantages were high cost and limited production facilities.

The internationally known firm of J. P. Sauer & Sohn, Suhl, was chosen as the manufacturer. The Sauer drilling designated M30 was a solidly constructed gun. Built on a Blitz action,

When shot-down Luftwaffe pilots needed survival guns during World War II, it was only natural that the traditional German drilling be adopted. Here's the lowdown on the model chosen — the Sauer & Sohn M30

it was equipped with double underlocking lugs, Greener cross bolt and sideclips. This secure lockup was desirable, considering the selection of the powerful 9.3x74R cartridge for the rifle barrel. The smoothbore barrels were chambered for the 12-ga. 65mm shotshell which enjoyed a world-wide distribution in the 1930s and was highly regarded in Europe and Africa. The left barrel was regulated to fire the Brenneke rifled slug over sights to point of aim at 35 meters. Brenneke slugs were and are highly regarded for stopping heavy thin-skinned game at close range.

Outstanding Cartridge

The 9.3x74R rifle cartridge is one of the world's great medium-bore loads. Its versatility places it on a par with the 375 H&H rimmed, with which it competed for pre-war African sales. The M30 was issued with RWS cartridges loaded with 257.7-gr. H-

mantel bullets.* At 2,650 fps from the 65cm (25½") barrel, the bullet delivered 4,000-plus fp of muzzle energy. Flat trajectory and great power made this cartridge more than sufficient for one shot kills on any game likely to be encountered in survival situations.

The drilling barrels were constructed of high grade Krupp barrel steel. M30s were proofed under the German Proof Laws of 1939 which called for an 80 atm. (over 12,000 psi) test for 65mm shotshells, and a 30% overload for rifles (about 54,000 lbs. in 9.3 x 74R). In addition to proof marks on the action and barrel flats, the barrels carry the rifle caliber designation on the matted rib just forward of the rear sight. Proofhouse acceptance marks of Eagle and Swastika are found on the right barrel at breech and the butt near the plate.

Separate extractors for the shot and rifle barrels are fitted, with the rifle case being raised higher for ease of removal. An indicator pin for each barrel rises on the tang when it is cocked, falls on firing. A sliding button on the tang is moved forward to prepare the rifle barrel for firing (at the same time raising a single leaf, 100-meter open sight on the barrel rib); the rifle barrel then can be fired by the forward trigger. Safety is a sliding button on the left side of the small of the stock.

Stocks are of medium to high grade European walnut, oil finished. Some have brass reinforcing pins through the pistol grip, as the recoil of the

---

*H-Mantel bullets are an RWS design in which the jacket is folded inward at about the midpoint of the bullet's length, forming a partial partition intended to prevent excessive bullet deformation in high-velocity cartridges.

Close-up of the M30 action shows the side safety, barrel selector on the tang, Greener crossbolt and sideclips and underlocking lug. These latter items make for a strong solid action, a necessity with the powerful cartridge used in the rifled barrel. Pins visible near the front of the opening lever indicate which barrels are cocked; they fall on firing. Front trigger fires the rifle barrel when the selector button is moved forward; it can be "set" by shoving frontward, then gives a letoff of only several ounces.

The 9.3x74R cartridge, for which the M30's third barrel is chambered, is currently available from both Norma Projektilfabrik and RWS. A rimmed case some 2.93" long (3.47" over-all), it has plenty of capacity to drive heavy bullets at good velocity. Current Norma loads include a 232-gr. bullet (hollow point or full metal jacket) at 2634 fps for 3550 fp energy, and a 286-gr. round nose softpoint or full jacket at 2362 fps for 3544 fp. This is enough power for the world's largest game under normal hunting conditions.

9.3x74R was apparently hard on stocks here.

The fore-end is removed by a lever release similar to those in better grade shotguns. Action, trigger guard and even screw heads carry considerable scroll engraving. Sling swivels are fitted to barrel and butt. Compact and portable, the M30 measures 42" over-all and weighs 7½ lbs.

The M30 was issued in a special aluminum compartmented case, painted olive drab, measuring 27"x7¼"x 4½". Wooden compartment bulkheads and felt barrel pits protected the gun. A coarse felt gasket sealed the case against moisture. Stenciled inside the lid was a list of the issue contents, which included: barrels, fore-end and buttstock; cleaning kit; sling; 25 rounds of 12-ga. shells with 3½mm shot; 20 rounds of 12-ga. Brenneke slugs; 20 rounds of 9.3x74R H-mantel rifle cartridges, and a 32-page instruction manual. Not listed but included was the official proof paper. Weight complete was 32 pounds.

Production Records Missing

My attempts to determine exact production numbers of the M30 have been fruitless. Letters to Sauer & Sohn, Köln, brought the information that records were abandoned to the Russians in 1945. Letters from VEB Ernst Thalmann Werke, Suhl, the East German firm now occupying the old Sauer plant, stated that pre-1945 records were destroyed during the heavy fighting in Suhl in 1945.

All guns examined by the author have carried serial numbers in the 334,000 to 339,000 range. All bear proof marks established by the Proof Law of 1939. This did not become effective until 20 April 1940. Late in 1941 armament plants were assigned code designations for marking guns produced for military and later for commercial requirements. Sauer was assigned code "ce." This marking subsequently appears on weapons manufactured by Sauer & Sohn, but no M30 reported to the author has carried the ce mark. This indicates that the M30s were taken from guns manufactured or proofed between May, 1940, and the end of November, 1941. The instruction book does carry the ce code mark on its last page and is dated "Edition of June 1941."

Commercial drillings are found in the same serial sequences as the M30 numbers. Apparently the Luftwaffe contract was carried out in conjunction with regular commercial production schedules. Peculiarly, the present Sauer firm estimates that guns in the 338,000 range were produced in early 1939; however, #334,660 carries "25 September 1941" on its official proof papers.

Possibly the Luftwaffe was supplied with commercial drillings originally intended for Scandinavian or African trade but which remained unassembled and unproofed in 1939. Such guns may well have been held for proof under the new law.

If production 1938 through 1940 guns were so acquired, several thousand might have been made. On the other hand, if December, 1941, marks the close of production and June, 1941, the opening of the series, then perhaps as few as 200 were produced. Sauer employees have no recollection of *any* large batch of M30s being produced at any time. A run of 1000 or so guns of identical type in six months surely would have left an impression. Probably fewer than that were produced; cost has been estimated at ten times that of a military Mauser rifle.

Approaching the problem from another direction we find that the M30 was intended for issue to "high ranking" Luftwaffe officers. Adolph Galland states that there were "about 400" Luftwaffe generals in 1943.* Air Sea Rescue units, special reconnaissance units and some air transport units may have been intended to receive M30s. Yet in all the mass of written materials examined — memoirs, diaries, histories and accounts by Luftwaffe personnel — not once is the M30 mentioned. Other equipment from flare guns to coveralls is described in detail, but the M30 drilling is conspicuous only by its absence. Of the few such guns appearing in the U.S. the majority seen by the author are in very good to excellent condition.

Most M30s undoubtedly were destroyed in combat or wastage, the remainder finishing the war in storage or aboard transport planes assigned to important Reich officials. Numbers have been sufficiently reduced by attrition to make the M30 one of the world's rare martial arms. About 20 have appeared in American advertisements in the last few years at prices of $300 to $700. The extremely practical nature of these fine weapons as well as their great rarity make them one of the most desirable pieces available to collectors of modern weapons. ●

*Adolph Galland was a famed general in the Luftwaffe, one of their leading combat pilots.

U.S.

★ ★ ★

Hand

The Tompkins pistol

A fully-detailed and critically-oriented survey of the American handguns that appeared — some to soon disappear — over the past quarter century.

by DeWITT E. SELL, Ph.D.

ANYONE ABOUT to read a non-fiction article or book should ask this question: "What are the author's qualifications for dealing with the subject he is writing about?" Since there are no formal academic courses available in the subject matter of this article, knowledge can be acquired only through the twin channels of personal experience and researching the experience of others who have set them down in print.

The writer is a psychologist by vocation. For the past two decades his consuming avocation has been American cartridge handguns. During that period he has read the major contributions of the acknowledged authorities in the field; has attended innumerable gun collector's meetings around the country; has been a Director and Historian of the world's largest gun collectors association (Ohio GCA); has written extensively for the leading firearms publications of the U.S. and has authored two comprehensive books on American cartridge handguns.

In addition he has bought, traded, or sold in excess of 300 various models of American cartridge handguns—there is only a minute percentage of known and verified U.S. handguns manufactured since 1857 that he has not handled and carefully inspected (if not possessed) at one time or another. This preamble was deemed advisable in order that the reader might have some basis for judging the merit of the opinions expressed in this review.

There has been a phenomenal growth of interest in firearms in general since the termination of WW II. State and regional gun collectors associations virtually blanket the country, there being scarcely a weekend that one could not attend a gun show somewhere in the U.S. Interest has not been confined to collectors, but is widespread among competitive shooters, hunters and casual plinkers as well. The National Rifle Association, which more than any other organization represents the firearms fraternity, is celebrating its centennial anniversary in 1971. It has enjoyed its most accelerated expansion in the past quarter-century, and now numbers over a million members.

I. Production Versus Demand

How well has the American firearms industry met the demand of consumers who desire to own and use handguns for various purposes? Certainly during the past 25 years there has been no lamentable shortage of revolvers of all lengths, actions, calibers or styles. It is a somewhat baffling fact, but the revolver has remained the favorite type of handgun in America—despite the fact that semi-automatic pistols of excellent design and function have been available since the early 1900s. In some respects it is analogous to preferring stick-shifting to an automatic transmission. There are obvious features of the revolver that are not common to the semi-automatic, and vice versa, but I am not going to resurrect at this point the interminable debate on revolvers vs. automatics! Both

types have their special advantages and special uses, and these should determine which you should buy or use upon a given occasion.

By 1950, many of the revolvers that had gained favor prior to firearms factories converting in the early 1940s to military production were back on the market. Most were revived initially with only minor, if any, modifications from their pre-war versions—the idea being to get back into civilian commerce as quickly as possible. None of the major pre-war handgun manufacturers failed to resume production following the termination of hostilities, but there were quite a few models which were permanently discontinued. In this writer's opinion there were some mistakes made in dropping certain models, and this will be touched upon later. However, a wide range of selections made their appearance—from the Cadillacs to the lower quality Fords. There were dependable "six-shooters" (actually chambers varied from 5 to 9) available for any purpose and most any size pocketbook.

With one exception, hammerless revolvers failed to be revived after 1945, whereas during the first half of this century the hammerless revolver had been available in a number of makes and models. Their virtual disappearance is not readily accounted for. For instance, Smith & Wesson's Safety Hammerless models in 32 S&W and 38 S&W are quickly saleable items at gun shows—attesting to their continuing popularity from a utilitarian and historical standpoint. Smith & Wesson

guns Since World War II
an Evaluation in Retrospect

still list the only exception, their Centennial model in 38 Special, which made its debut in 1954. Smith & Wesson also produce the Bodyguard with integral hammer shroud, while Colt has an optional hammer shroud attachment available for several of its models. These models so equipped can be carried in the pocket without undue concern over the hammer becoming entangled.

No, the firearms industry cannot be faulted for failing to meet consumer demand over the past quarter-century where revolvers are concerned. With the advent of the 44 Magnum in 1955, the revolver became capable of downing anything that moves on the American continent when necessity dictates.

American automatic (actually semi-automatic, but the more commonly applied designation will be adhered to) pistol production does not rate as high an accolade as does revolver production for the period under review. Some notable achievements mark this era, which will be cited in Section II of this article, but there has also been some defaulting in meeting consumer demand for certain types of automatic pistols.

The highly-regarded Colt pocket models in 25, 32 and 380 ACP never made it back to the production line after WW II, nor did the superb Ace 22 RF in its two versions. As a matter of fact, no U.S. manufacturer has made quality pocket automatics available in 25, 32 or 380 calibers during the period of this review.

It was gratuitous, perhaps, to attribute the disappearance of these small automatics to altruistic motives on the part of American manufacturers, as did the late Julian S. Hatcher (*Official Gun Book*, Crown, 1950, p. 46), who wrote: "They are looked on with disfavor by law enforcement agencies and by such forward-looking organizations as the National Rifle Association. The leading firearms makers of this country have taken the same view and, in spite of the loss of revenue involved, they have discontinued the manufacture of 25- 32- and 380-cal. pocket-sized

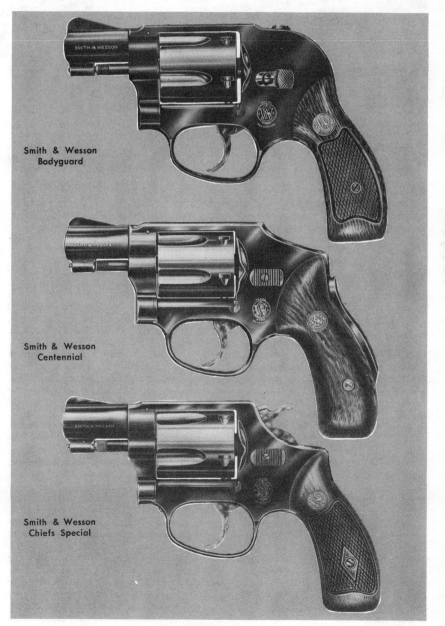

Smith & Wesson
Bodyguard

Smith & Wesson
Centennial

Smith & Wesson
Chiefs Special

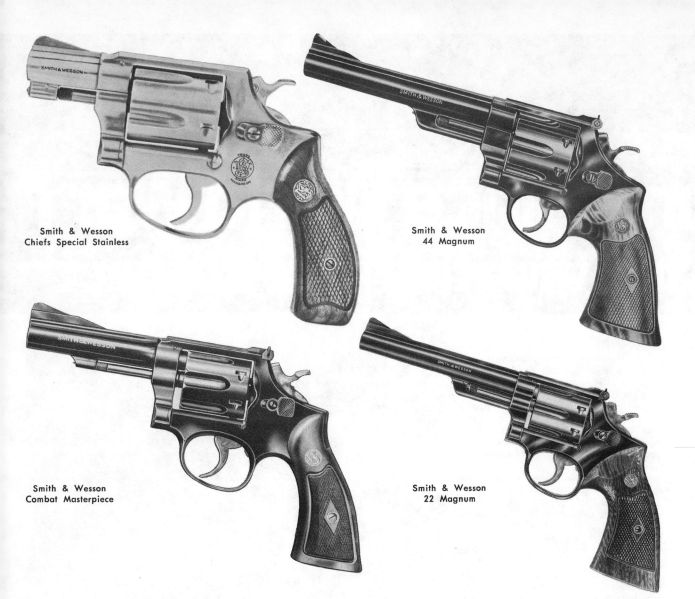

Smith & Wesson
Chiefs Special Stainless

Smith & Wesson
44 Magnum

Smith & Wesson
Combat Masterpiece

Smith & Wesson
22 Magnum

semi-automatic pistols."

Browning, Belgium-based, has long been selling its ultra high quality 25 and 380 pocket automatics in the U.S., and this writer has never heard this firm criticized for doing so nor seen Browning condemned in print. In addition to Browning, makers such as Walther, Astra, Star, Llama, Beretta, Bernardelli and Unique—as well as other foreign firms of lesser prominence —were doing a steady business in this country by supplying their pocket autos in 25, 32 and 380 calibers. Automatics in these calibers have at times been deprecated as either criminal weapons or inadequate for self-defense. While this writer does not wish to go on record as recommending them for either purpose, nevertheless they are decidedly lethal and possess the twin virtues of compactness and lightness—thus serving admirably as a hideaway weapon where such measures are warranted for self-protection. The way crime continues to rise, such measures appear more warranted with every passing day. Women, too, can generally handle these satisfactorily, whereas they might find it awkward or impossible to defend themselves with arms of larger size or heavier caliber.

There seems little question that American handgun entrepreneurs missed the boat in this connection. There has been a constant demand over the past two decades for these foreign automatics, which has only recently been curtailed by the Gun Control Act of 1968.

Both Colt and Smith & Wesson have provided competitive shooters with target model automatics chambering the 38 Spl. wadcutter cartridge. This need has now been well-satisfied. We have witnessed during the past 25 years a plethora of automatic pistols in 22 RF caliber of all makes, styles and uses. There seems to be no unfulfilled need here. However, Colt still has no competition in the 45 ACP automatic, and it remains an enigma why Smith & Wesson, High Standard, or some other maker has not come out with a match grade competitive model.

Someone—I seem to recall it was Walter Roper—read an epitaph for the single-shot pistol following WW II and laid it respectfully to rest. Apparently *rigor mortis* had not fully set in at the time of its burial, for it has arisen in at least 12 forms since 1945! Perhaps it is difficult to make out a good case for the single-shot pistol in modern times, nevertheless they continue to

make their appearance in new forms and calibers from time to time and enough people must buy them to keep their makers in business—at least for awhile. Some of them will be cited in Sections II or III.

As everyone is well aware, the U.S. economy has experienced a steady inflationary trend since WW II. This has militated against holding manufacturing costs and unit prices at pegged levels for extensive periods. Handgun makers have been obliged to be ever on the lookout for means of reducing costs of the many steps involved in finishing and assembling. The biggest single cost factor in virtually any manufactured product is that of the human labor involved, and over the past 25 years of handgun production there have been continual efforts to reduce or eliminate milling and hand-finishing operations. While virtually all U.S. handguns currently produced by our established firms function reliably and possess construction strength above minimal safety standards, nevertheless they do not measure up over-all to pre-WW II models in precision of fit, smoothness of function and esthetic appeal. This has been true of some makes and models more than others, of course. Pre-WW II Colts, for example, are

Great Western
Double Derringer

Colt Frontier Scout

Colt Cobra

Colt Civil War Centennial

avidly sought by knowledgeable handgun fanciers in preference to many post-WW II versions.

Certainly all modifications in models, materials and manufacturing methods introduced since WW II cannot be labeled "progress" in the sense that this term is synonymous with "improvement." Frequently model modifications have been for the benefit (profit) of the maker rather than the consumer. True, the inflationary economy has exerted a downward pressure on over-all handgun quality, but this may be too facile an alibi for the convenience of corporate managers who would be hard pressed to justify, on this sole basis, some of their manufacturing and pricing policies. One glaring example of the latter that comes immediately to mind applies to Colt's Single Action Army revolver. The retail price of this model as of October 1, 1941, was $38.50. When it was returned to production in 1955, it was priced at $125—3¼ times its pre-war price. Since 1955, it has risen an additional $65 to $190 as of 1969, or approximately 5 times its 1941 price!

By contrast, Ruger's popular quality-constructed Single-Six, introduced in 1953 at $63.25 with hard rubber grips, listed in 1969 at $64.25 with walnut grips—a dollar higher after 16 years of inflation which the grips alone could account for!

A good part of the explanation for such wide variation in pricing policies and/or quality control lies in "who's running the store," and with what motives. The Colt firm has passed through several corporate ownerships since WW II and for some years now has been enjoying big—and probably lucrative—government military contracts. Concentration on these has fostered an indifference on the part of Colt top management, I feel, as to whether their commercial handgun models sell in any quantity or are competitively priced. It appears to me that at least since 1945 the name Colt has been depended upon to sell their products rather than equitable value.

Again by contrast, Sturm, Ruger & Co. remains in the hands of its principal founder, Bill Ruger. The *esprit de corps* within this organization must account for its continual attention to quality control as well as resistance to price increases. These people obviously like what they are doing and apparently are content making a reasonable living from their efforts. Actually, Ruger and Iver Johnson's are the only major U.S. gunmakers still controlled by

the founder or his direct descendants. The day of the individual entrepreneur who took great pride in the creations that bore his name, and was able to instill this pride in his workers, has all but vanished from the American industrial scene nor is it likely to again dawn in a forseeable future dominated by conglomerate ownership of mass-production facilities.

The prolonged conflict in Viet Nam, which has been dragging on now since 1961, has had a marked effect on diminishing the supply of civilian handguns. This seens to have been most evident in the case of Smith & Wesson. Their products, particularly certain most-wanted models, have been in short supply for several years. This shortage has created a scalper's market, with certain models selling at times well above the manufacturer's suggested list. The writer personally observed a gun store owner pay in excess of list for a Smith & Wesson Combat Masterpiece in 22 RF caliber! The writer has never been able to discover where most of Smith & Wesson's production is being filtered off. Most models of the other major U.S. handgun producers are obtainable, although you may have a waiting problem involving weeks.

II. Innovations of Note—Revolvers

Perhaps it is redundant to point out that it is beyond the scope of this review to evaluate every model of U.S. handgun that has appeared since 1945. As these handguns have been introduced over the past 25 years, they generally have been discussed in some detail in the appropriate annual issue of the GUN DIGEST. As has already been contended, not everything NEW necessarily means *better*. We'll limit ourselves in this section to citing those innovations considered noteworthy, and why they merit, so to speak, honorable mention. For a complete listing of new models offered the public since 1945, see the appropriate tables.

Since revolvers are still foremost in popularity with U.S. handgunners, it seems appropriate to lead off with those models that have been placed on the market which are of singular significance to the revolver fancier. To avoid jumping around from one maker to another, thus creating confusion rather than clarity, the notable offerings of one firm will be cited before focusing on those of another.

Colt, the oldest handgun producer in the U.S. still operating under its original trade name, will be taken up first. In 1950, Colt introduced the first of its lightweight revolvers, these featuring alloy frames with steel barrels and cylinders. Dubbed the Cobra, the 2-inch barrel version of this model weighs 6 ounces less than the all-steel Detective Special it resembles. An optional hammer shroud for the Cobra is intended to prevent the hammer from catching in clothing wherever concealed, and to permit double-action firing from a coat pocket. Colt's Agent, brought out in 1955, is another alloy-frame belly-gun virtually identical to the Cobra but with a more compact handle.

While Colt chambered their Single Action Army, New Service and Shooting Master revolvers for the 357 Magnum cartridge prior to WW II, their first post-war revolver to chamber this powerhouse (1953) was simply called the "Three-Fifty-Seven." Intended as a combination service and target revolver, it could be obtained with standard hammer and stocks or target hammer and stocks. That year (1953) also saw the debut of the Trooper, which resembles the Three-Fifty-Seven, but was initially chambered in either 38 Special or 22 RF with 4-inch barrel only. In 22 RF, it provided an economical training arm for police departments. By 1969, a Trooper MK III was available in 357 Magnum, but the 22 RF version had disappeared.

Perhaps the most prestigious handgun Colt has produced since WW II is the Python, which Colt claims is "the finest revolver made." Colt is certainly entitled to name any of its models as the finest they make, but to state categorically that any one model of theirs is *the* finest made is patently debatable. This Cadillac of the Colts is admittedly de luxe in styling, fit and finish. Outstanding features of the Python 357 Magnum are its integral ventilated-rib barrel, floating firing pin in the frame, wide-spur target hammer, ejector-rod housing under barrel, walnut target stocks and rich Royal Blue finish. Colt's

Colt Python

TABLE ONE

U.S. HANDGUN MODELS AS OF 1940/REVOLVERS

MAKER	MODEL	CALIBERS
COLT	Official Police	38 Spl.; 32-20; 22 RF
	Police Positive	38 Police Pos. (NP)
		32 Police Pos. (NP)
	Police Positive Spl.	38 Special
		32-20
	Police Positive Target	22 RF
		32 Police Pos. (NP)
	Pocket Positive	32 Police Pos. (NP)
	Officers Model Target	32 Police Pos. (NP)
		38 Spl.; 22 RF
	New Service	38 Spl.; 357 Mag.; 38-40; 44 Spl; 44-40; 45 Colt; 45 ACP; 455 Eley
	New Service Target	44 Spl.; 45 ACP
		45 Colt
	Shooting Master	38 Spl.; 357 Mag.; 44 Spl.; 45 Colt; 45 ACP
	Detective Spl.	38 Spl.
	Bankers Spl.	38 Police Pos. (NP)
		22 RF
	Single Action Army	32-20; 357 Mag.; 38 Spl.; 38-40; 44 Spl.; 44-40; 45 Colt
HARRINGTON & RICHARDSON	22 Spl.	22 RF
	922	22 RF
	Eureka Sportsman	22 RF
	Sportsman (SA & DA)	22 RF
	Trapper	22 RF
	Young America	22 RF; 32 S&W
	Vest Pocket	22 RF
	American DA	32 S&W
	Model 4	32 S&W; 38 S&W
	Model 5	32 S&W
	Model 6	22 RF
	Premier	22 RF; 32 S&W
	Automatic Ejecting	32 S&W; 38 S&W
	H'less (small frame)	32 S&W
	H'less (large frame)	32 S&W; 38 S&W
IVER JOHNSON	Supershot Sealed 8	22 RF
	Protector Sealed 8	22 RF
	Safety Hammer Automatic	22 RF; 32 S&W; 38 S&W
	Safety H'less Automatic	22 RF; 32 S&W; 38 S&W

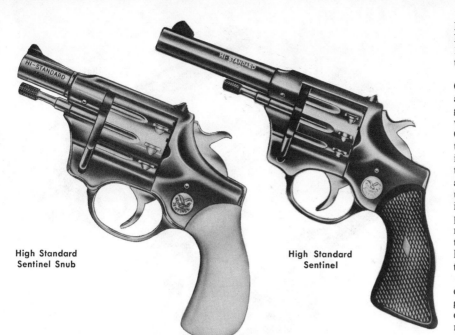

High Standard Sentinel Snub

High Standard Sentinel

TABLE ONE (Cont.)

U.S. HANDGUN MODELS AS OF 1940/REVOLVERS

MAKER	MODEL	CALIBERS
SMITH & WESSON	32 Hand Ejector	32 S&W
	38/32	38 S&W
	Military & Police	38 Spl.
	Safety H'less	32 S&W/38 S&W
	357 Magnum	357 Mag.
	38/44 Outdoorsman	38 Spl.
	M&P (K-38) Target	38 Spl.
	K-32 Target	32 S&W
	38/44 Heavy Duty	38 Spl.
	1926 Model 44	44 Spl.
	1926 M44 Target	44 Spl.
	1917 Army	45 ACP/45 AR
	K-22 Masterpiece	22 RF
	22/32 Kit Gun	22 RF
	22/32 Target	22 RF
	Regulation Police	32 S&W; 38 S&W

U.S. HANDGUN MODELS AS OF 1940/AUTOLOADERS

MAKER	MODEL	CALIBERS
COLT	Ace	22 RF
	Ace, Service	22 RF
	Pocket	25 ACP
	Pocket	32 ACP; 380 ACP
	Super 38	38 ACP HV
	Super Match	38 ACP HV
	Gov't Model	45 ACP
	National Match	45 ACP
	Woodsman, Target & Sport	22 RF
	Match Target Woodsman	22 RF
H&R	Self-Loading	32 ACP
HIGH STANDARD	B or H-B	22 LR
	S-B	22 RF Shot
	A or H-A	22 LR
	C	22 Short
	D or H-D	22 LR
	E or H-E	22 LR

U.S. HANDGUN MODELS AS OF 1940/SINGLE SHOTS

MAKER	MODEL	CALIBERS
STEVENS	"Off-Hand" Target	22 RF
COLT	Camp Perry	22 RF
H&R	U.S.R.A.	22 RF

Diamondback is a less bulky brother of the Python, which it resembles. Brought out in 1966, this lighter version is chambered for the 38 Spl. or 22 RF.

The only other post-WW II revolver of Colt's worth noting is their Frontier Scout, a lightweight version in 22 RF of the Single Action Army. Noting Ruger's success with the Single-Six western-style revolver, Colt decided rather belatedly to cash in on the trend in this direction by first returning their discontinued Single Action Army to the production line (1955). Their look-alike Frontier Scout didn't make the scene until 1958. In 1962, Colt offered this model in a heavier frame version at a higher price. The Frontier Scout is the principal model featured in the many commemoratives that have been put out by Colt in the last decade, these to be dealt with collectively in Section III.

Smith & Wesson, now well into their 2nd century of continuous production of handguns, have offered the greatest variety of quality handguns in both centerfire and rimfire of any U.S. maker.

One of the first noteworthy things S&W accomplished following WW II was to equalize the loaded weights of their Masterpiece series—the K-38, K-32 and K-22. Since the frames of these K revolvers are identical, matching of weight is accomplished by variance in barrel diameter to compensate for variance in amount of metal removed in boring for the three calibers. Of course, over-all allowance must be made for the cylinder-weight differential in these calculations. The Masterpiece series also returned post-WW II with matted-rib barrels and Magna grips, among other modifications. In 1949 the Combat Masterpiece was introduced, offered in 38 Special or 22 RF. This 4-inch barrel target-grade holster gun was aimed at law enforcement officers for the most part. It differs from regular Masterpieces only in barrel length and front sight—the latter a Baughman Quick Draw on a plain ramp. The 22 RF version of this model has today become, perhaps, the most sought after modern revolver in this caliber.

Smith & Wesson's best-selling snub-nose 38 Special for the past two decades has been the Chiefs Special. Introduced in 1950, it can be had with either a 2- or 3-inch barrel. In 1966, this popular snubby was brought out in a stainless steel version, which represented a genuine breakthrough in the machining of such tough metal. While these have been in short supply, and selling at scalper's prices, they're continually sought.

Smith & Wesson have offered since 1955 what the writer (and many others, you can be sure) regards as the top 38 Special snub-nose revolver made. It was named the Bodyguard by the Chief of Police in Marshfield, Wisconsin, in a contest staged at the IACP Conference (Philadelphia, Penna., 1955). The writer had adopted this model in the all-steel version as the bodyguard for him and his family! With integral hammer shroud, which prevents entanglement, yet permits quick cocking when single action use is desired, it is "truly a dependable and formidable weapon for personal defense," as Smith & Wesson contended in an advertisement. S&W's snubbies are all 5-shot, while Colt's like models have what they claim is "that all important extra shot—the 6th one." This writer believes that if you don't get your criminal in 5 shots or less, you are unlikely to be around to get off the 6th one!

A home-defender almost equal to the Bodyguard is S&W's Centennial model, brought out in 1953. This is the only hammerless (concealed hammer) centerfire revolver produced in the U.S. since Iver Johnson's dropped its hammerless Safety Automatic revolvers in 1950.

Articles have been written in popular newsstand magazines with such titles as, "Do You Need A Gun In The House?" There is only one answer to such a question; an unqualified "Yes!" With the crime rate constantly rising faster than the population rate, the threat of this social cancer appears more insoluble than ever, and each one of us to a certain degree is obliged to assume responsibility for the protection of our persons and our property.

S&W's 1955 45 Target is a truly premium-grade DA target revolver, and the only one of its kind currently "available" chambered for the 45 ACP or 45 Auto-Rim. It sports an extra heavy 6½-inch barrel, and total weight is 45 oz. For anyone preferring a revolver to an automatic in 45 competition, this model has got to be it.

It seems incontrovertible that the most sensational handgun development of the past 25 years was the 1956 announcement of the 44 Remington Magnum cartridge and the revolvers designed to use it. The 44 Magnum exceeds the previously most powerful handgun cartridge, the 357 Magnum, by nearly twice the amount of muzzle energy. The S&W 44 Magnum is undoubtedly the world's most beautiful high-power revolver! In addition to superb fit and finish, it excels in trigger pull and lockwork. Tests have shown that the 44 Magnum is as accurate with the lighter-loaded 44 Special cartridges (which it also handles) as target revolvers especially made for the latter cartridges. If controlling a tremendous amount of shocking power is your bag, and you can withstand abhorrent (or so it seems to this writer) recoil, then the 44 Magnum is your baby.

Sturm, Ruger & Co. is the only firearms manufacturer beginning operations after 1945 to have achieved major status as of 1970. Launched more with faith than capital, this firm did the unexpected—it prospered to the extent that a modern new plant was needed and acquired in 1959, just one decade after its first handgun model was introduced. While their first handgun was a 22 caliber automatic pistol, Ruger was not long in developing a line of revolvers that swept them to an unprecedented success. The first of them (1952) was the now famous Single-Six 22 RF, which simulated the traditional western single action six-shooter that dates back to 1873. It is hypothesized that western movies and TV whetted the public's appetite for these single-actions, and that Bill Ruger was the first to recognize the trend and capitalize on it. In any event, the Single-Six went over with a bang, leading Ruger to put out single action centerfire revolvers beginning in 1955 with the Blackhawk 357 Magnum. This was fol-

High Standard
Double-Nine

Harrington & Richardson
Ultra Side-Kick

Savage 101 Safety

TABLE TWO - A

CENTERFIRE REVOLVERS INTRODUCED FROM 1945 to 1970

MAKER	MODEL	CALIBERS	INTRODUCED
CHARTER ARMS	Undercover	38 Spl.	1966
COLT	Cobra	38 Spl; 32 NP	1950
	Trooper	38 Spl.	1953
	Trooper MK III	357 Mag.	1969
	Three-Fifty-Seven	357 Mag.	1953
	Marshall	38 Spl.	1955
	Agent	38 Spl.	1955
	Courier	32 NP	1955
	Python	357 Mag.	1955
	Buntline Spl.	45 Colt	1957
	Diamondback	38 Spl.	1966
DAN WESSON	Model 12	357 Mag.	1970
DARDICK	Series 1100	38 Dardick Spl.	1959
	Series 1500	22 RF	
GREAT WESTERN	Frontier	22 RF; 38 SPL.; 44 Spl.; 44-40 45 Colt; 45 ACP 357 Mag.; 44 Mag. 22 Hornet	1954
	Deputy	22 RF; 357 Mag. 38 Spl.	1955
	Buntline	45 Colt	1956
H&R	Guardsman	32 S&W	1954
	Defender	38 S&W	1964
RUGER	Blackhawk	357 Mag.; 9mm; 41 Mag.; 45 Colt; 45 ACP; 30 US Carbine	1955
	Super Blackhawk	44 Mag.	1959
	Security-Six	357 Mag.	1970

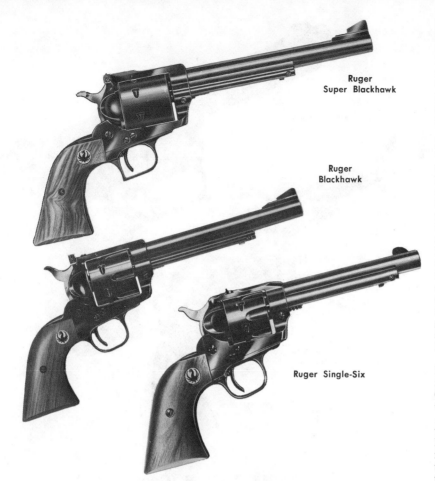

Ruger
Super Blackhawk

Ruger
Blackhawk

Ruger Single-Six

TABLE TWO - A   (Cont.)

CENTERFIRE REVOLVERS INTRODUCED FROM 1945 to 1970

MAKER	MODEL	CALIBERS	INTRODUCED
S&W	Combat Masterpiece	38 Spl.	1949
	Chief's Spl.	38 Spl.	1950
	Chief's Spl. Stainless	38 Spl.	1966
	1950 Target	44 Spl; 45 ACP	1950
	1950 Army	45 ACP	1950
	Centennial	38 Spl.	1952
	Highway Patrolman	357 Mag.	1954
	1955 Target	45 ACP	1955
	Bodyguard	38 Spl.	1955
	44 Magnum	44 Mag.	1955
	357 Magnum	357 Mag.	1956
	22 Magnum	22 Jet	1961
	41 Magnum	41 Mag.	1964

TABLE TWO - B

CENTERFIRE AUTOLOADERS INTRODUCED FROM 1945 to 1970

MAKER	MODEL	CALIBERS	INTRODUCED
AMERICAN FIREARMS	Stainless Steel	25, 32, 380 ACP	1970
COLT	Commander	45 ACP; 9mm; 38 Super	1950
	Gold Cup N.M.	45 ACP	1957
	Gold Cup N.M.	38 Spl.	1961
HIGH STANDARD	G-380	380 ACP	1947

lowed in 1956 by the Blackhawk 44 Magnum; the Bearcat (1958) 22 RF, a 17-oz. version of the Single-Six with 4-inch barrel; the Super Blackhawk (1959) 44 Magnum; the Single-Six Convertible (1961) featuring two cylinders—one in 22 RF and another in 22 WMR—and the Super Single-Six Convertible (1964), a target grade version.

Never satisfied to rest on his laurels, Ruger unveiled his first double action revolver in 357 Magnum at the 1969 NRA convention. According to a Testfire Report by John T. Amber, this DA is destined to be a winner. The influence of Harry Sefried in the design of this handgun is readily apparent. Sefried, formerly with High Standard, was primarily responsible for development of the H-S Sentinel. This new Ruger has the following features in common with the Sentinel: western-style grips with flared butt, solid frame with no sideplate or screws, composite function of few parts, easy disassembly. This new model deserves to be classed among the most novel handguns of the past quarter-century, and should prove a basic commodity in the Ruger line.

Incidentally, Ruger is furnishing Blackhawks in such other calibers of 41 Magnum, 30 U.S. Carbine-9mm and the 45 Colt-45 ACP—the latter two convertible via special cylinders.

High Standard introduced their first revolver in 1955, the Sentinel, which Wm. B. Edwards (*Guns,* June, 1955) hailed as "the first new revolver in 50 years." Actually, the major new features of this revolver are the engineering tricks employed to reduce the cost of production! Things like a drilled-hole ratchet rather than a milled one, a cast-aluminum anodized frame without sideplate or screws, and the combination functioning of fewer internal parts. These measures prove of great benefit to the profit-minded manufacturer, but give no reason for jubilance on the part of the consumer. The Sentinel is cited because it is an innovation of note—if more for the maker than the buyer.

More noteworthy as new is High Standard's Double-Nine (1958)—a clever adaptation of the Sentinel action in an alloy frame, simulating a western style single action. While it can be fired both single or double action, its cylinder swings out for loading or ejecting; the extractor rod is only a dummy. Shortly after introduction, the Double-Nine exceeded all other models in sales. It has the visual qualities of the single action with the speedy operational qualities of the double action.

Harrington & Richardson are celebrating their centennial year of operation in 1971. They have supplied low-cost handguns of good quality over these many years and, while few have created a stir in the trade, few warrant condemnation. The only handgun which this firm introduced in the past 25 years which merits citation is the Ultra Side-Kick of 1958. This model (along with the older Sportsman 999, and the USRA 22 RF single shot) represents the top of the line of current H&R revolvers. Featuring a ventilated-rib barrel, the Ultra Side-Kick has a Safety Lock incorporated in the base of the grip frame for locking the action with a key. Stocks are walnut with proper thumb rest. At one time, the swing-out cylinder release was built into the rear of the hammer, but this feature was later discontinued, probably because of the cost factor. The idea was not only novel, but good!

Iver Johnson's are also marking their centennial anniversary in 1971. Few today are aware that at one time I. J. made more handguns than any other U.S. maker—and no firearms maker ever did more to foster public consciousness of the safety factor in handling handguns than they did with their "Hammer the Hammer" publicity. That slogan became a household commonplace not long after the turn of this century. While Iver Johnson's has been steadily fading from their former eminence in the trade, they're apparently still meeting a need for economical but reliable sidearms. IJ's most noteworthy handgun contribution since WW II has been their Trailsman (1958) and Viking (1964) models, which are actually identical externally. The former has a rebounding hammer, while the latter incorporates the famous "Hammer the Hammer" action. Barrels are chrome-lined and cylinders have patented Flash Control.

A new firm with a venerable name is expected to take its place among the elite of handgun manufacturers. Daniel B. Wesson IV, great grandson of one of the original partners of the famed Smith & Wesson firm, has gone into business for himself under the trade name of "Dan Wesson Arms" at Monson, Mass. A Test Fire Report of Dan Wesson's first handgun, the Model 12 357 Magnum, will be found in the 24th edition of GUN DIGEST. It has a number of features novel to revolvers and should create quite a reaction among handgun enthusiasts. In a personal letter to the writer, Dan Wesson expressed confidence that his revolutionary revolver would be available commercially by Mid-1970.*

Automatics

So much for revolvers since 1945. Now, let us look more cursorily at the post-WW II picture relative to U.S. automatic pistols. While U.S.-made automatic pistols have been with us since 1900, they have never found as much favor with Americans as have revolvers. Automatics in 22 RF are, perhaps, an exception.

High Standard has been foremost among producers of automatic pistols in 22 RF over the past two decades. They began production of 22 caliber autos in the depths of the depression (1932), and managed to survive during those hard times for two good reasons—their products offered high quality at a low price. Not long after the close of WW II, High Standard was busy retooling for civilian production, and in 1949 launched their G-series of advanced design 22 RF automatics which, by 1950, included the Supermatic, Olympic and Field King. In 1958 High Standard radically redesigned the Supermatic, offer-

*At this time (March, 1971) that intention was not fulfilled, so the Dan Wesson revolver will have to be considered a borderline case as far as announcement - production dating is concerned. ED

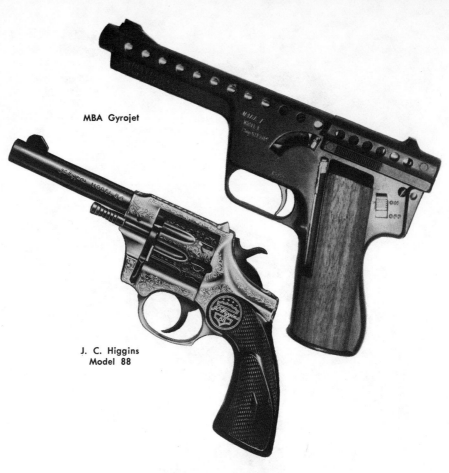

MBA Gyrojet

J. C. Higgins Model 88

TABLE TWO - B (Cont.)

CENTERFIRE AUTOLOADERS INTRODUCED FROM 1945 to 1970

MAKER	MODEL	CALIBERS	INTRODUCED
KIMBALL	Combat Target	30 U.S. Carbine	1958
SMITH & WESSON	Model 39 DA	9mm	1954
	Model 44 SA	9mm	1955
	38 Master	38 Spl	1961

TABLE THREE

RIMFIRE REVOLVERS INTRODUCED FROM 1945 to 1970

MAKER	MODEL	INTRODUCED	NOTES
CHARTER ARMS	Pocket	1970	Scheduled for 1970 production.
COLT	Trooper	1953	Disc. in 22 RF
	Courier	1955	Disc.
	Frontier Scout	1958	Basic model for commemoratives
	Buntline Scout	1959	9½-inch barrel
	Diamondback	1966	Also in 38 Spl.
FIREARMS INTERNATIONAL	Regent	1966	Cheapest U.S. 22 RF revolver
HARRINGTON & RICHARDSON	622	1956	Solid Frame
	Side-Kick	1956	First H&R model with swing-out cylinder
	Ultra Side-Kick	1958	Safety lock in butt, vent-rib barrel
	Forty-Niner	1959	Western style DA
	Gunfighter	1960	Western style DA
	Snap-Out	1962	Solid frame

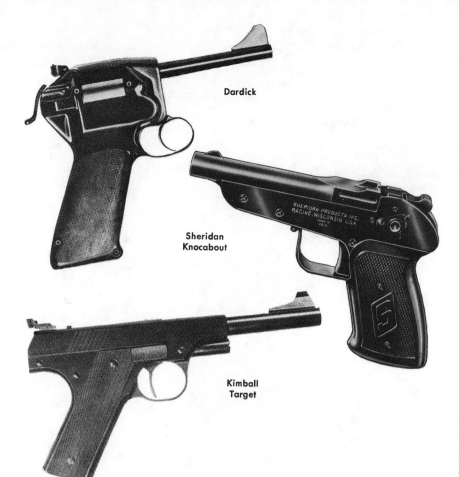

Dardick

Sheridan
Knocabout

Kimball
Target

TABLE THREE (Cont.)

RIMFIRE REVOLVERS INTRODUCED FROM 1945 to 1970

MAKER	MODEL	INTRODUCED	NOTES
IVER JOHNSON	Supershot	1954	Tapered rib barrel, top-break, DA
	Armsworth	1955	Tapered rib barrel, top-break, SA
	Target	1955	Solid frame
	Cadet	1955	Solid frame, 2½-inch barrel
	Trailsman	1958	Rebounding hammer
	Sidewinder	1961	Western style DA
	Viking	1964	Famous "Hammer the Hammer" action
HIGH STANDARD	Sentinel	1955	Swing-out cylinder—Imperial version issued 1961
	Sentinel (colors)	1957	Ladies snub-nosed in gold, turquoise and pink
	Double-Nine	1958	Western style DA—Longhorn, Natchez and Posse models are variations of Double-Nine
HIGGINS, J.C.	Model 88	1955	Made for Sears, Roebuck by High Standard. Disc.
	Ranger	1959	Made for Sears, Roebuck by High Standard. Disc.
RUGER	Single-Six	1953	Convertible models available for 22 WMR
	Bearcat	1958	Pocket-size Single-Six
	Super Single-Six	1965	De luxe target version of S.S.; adj. rear sight
SMITH & WESSON	Combat Masterpiece	1949	4-inch barrel version of K-22 with Baughman Quick Draw front sight

ing it in three versions: Trophy, Citation and Tournament. As of 1962, High Standard asserted that their line of firearms consisted of 114 different models, or model variations. The great majority of their firearms are 22 caliber handguns, and no one has seriously challenged their title—King of the 22s—since at least 1958. There have been just too many H-S 22 automatics in various modifications since WW II to cite them individually. Suffice it to say that I have never seen, nor heard of, a "lemon" to date. In case any readers are interested, the writer's choice of H-S 22 autos, if limited to one, would be their ISU Olympic model (22 Short RF).

Colt has produced no new noteworthy automatics in 22 RF since WW II—the Woodsman series all antedate that clash of arms and ideologies.

Smith & Wesson electrified the handgun world in 1957 with the emergence of their elegant Model 41 autoloader. Produced by S&W in 22 caliber it was justifiably featured on the cover of the 12th edition (1958) of GUN DIGEST, and was without doubt 1957's "firearm of the year." The Model 41 is currently available (if your're lucky enough to locate one) in a heavy barrel version with extendible front sight. The S&W Model 46, somewhat less de luxe, is a cheaper version of the Model 41.

Sturm, Ruger & Co. gambled on success or failure when entering business in 1949 with their initial offering—a unique but attractive 22 RF automatic known only as the Standard model. It became an immediate success and the reasons are manifold: it possesses appealing lines similar to the Luger; hangs and points naturally; uses no frame screws; incorporates coil springs throughout and, best of all, sold originally for $37.50 (it's still under $50 after 21 years of inflation!). A target version of this automatic appeared in 1955 as the Mark I Target.

Now let's focus on some U.S. automatics which consume heavier fodder than the 22 RF. Colt made a notable break-through in 1950 by evolving a lightweight centerfire automatic with an aluminum alloy frame. A look-alike in comparison to Colt's Government 45, this new Commander model has a slide and barrel ¾-inch shorter. These modifications reduced the Commander's weight to two-thirds that of the regular 45, yet did not unfavorably affect dependability or shooting comfort. The Commander has been chambered in 45 ACP, 38 Super and 9mm from the start.*

Colt's Gold Cup series merits mention, since they are highly refined target autos. While there was a 45 ACP National Match prior to WW II, the Gold Cup of 1961 was the first on the post-WW II scene which could function with 38 Special mid-range wadcutter loads. While virtually identical in external appearance to the Gold Cup in 45 ACP, the 38 Special has considerably different innards; particularly a "floating" barrel (not mounted on a link), which is free to recoil straight back with the slide for a short distance. It had a number of "bugs" during its commercial infancy, but these appear to have been corrected to the

---

The Commander is now available with steel construction.

satisfaction of most users of current specimens. Both Gold Cups are identical in weight, 37 oz., a desirable aspect where one intends to use both calibers.

1954 saw the introduction of Smith & Wesson's first post-WW II automatic pistol, and it lived up in every way to what the world had come to expect from this venerable firm. The S&W 9mm Automatic, Double Action Model 39 has the distinction of being the first double action auto pistol made in the U.S. Charles Askins contended (in 1961) that the Model 39 is the only modern centerfire automatic pistol made in the U.S. and, "very probably," the best centerfire pistol in the world! The angle of handle to barrel and the contours of the stock make for natural pointing and excellent fit in the average hand. Its double action rivals the revolver in readiness for instantaneous use. The S&W Model 39, using an alloy frame and mainspring housing to reduce weight, is designed for the most rugged service and may one day become, in its present or a modified form, the ultimate successor to the hoary Colt Government 45.

Two years in the developmental stage, Smith & Wesson by late 1961 was ready to offer the big-bore competitive handgunner a rival in 38 Special (wadcutter) to Colt's Gold Cup in this caliber. The S&W 38 Master, in exhaustive and impartial tests, more than met the exacting criteria of functional reliability, precision accuracy, fine trigger action and correct balance for efficient handling. Using a locked breech and moving barrel system, the 38 Master can be dry-fired without damage when the manual safety is on. It looks like this most expensive of S&W's target autos is here to stay.

It is time to give brief consideration to a number of miscellaneous innovations of note—some single shot and multiple-barrel pistols that have had an impact on the handgun world since WW II.

Although the single-shot pistol has been declared by some writers to be as defunct as the passenger pigeon, the last of these Mohicans seems a long way off yet, judging by the post-WW II market. There have been at least 12 varieties of U.S. single shots made since 1945. First on the scene was the 22 RF Tompkins Target of 1947. With a one-piece walnut stock that extends from butt to muzzle, it is reminiscent of a 19th century dueller. When the late Walter Roper evaluated the Tompkins, he said emphatically that the Tompkins pistol had the most remarkable trigger pull and mechanism ever put on any pistol or rifle he'd seen or heard of. The writer has examined the Tompkins and will endorse Roper's high estimate of its trigger action. A remarkable handgun indeed, but by the early 1950's it was already a collector's item!

Sheridan's 22 RF single shot appeared on the market in the first half of 1953. Aptly designated the Knocabout, this rugged, well-engineered pistol could withstand considerable banging about without significant damage or danger to the owner. Built on a tip-up principle, its fixed breech-block contains a floating firing pin. An oversize rotary-bolt safety serves to block the hammer effectively when on "safe." At

Smith & Wesson Model 52

Smith & Wesson Model 39

TABLE FOUR

RIMFIRE AUTOLOADERS INTRODUCED FROM 1945 to 1970

MAKER	MODEL	INTRODUCED	NOTES
COLT	Challenger	1950	Disc.
	Huntsman	1956	No automatic slide-stop; both sights fixed
	Targetsman	1960	No automatic slide-stop; adjustable rear sight
HIGGINS, J.C.	Model 80	1956	Made for Sears, Roebuck by High Standard
HIGH STANDARD	Model G-B	1949	Push-lever take down
	Model G-D	1949	Push-lever take down
	Model G-E	1949	Push-lever take down
	Olympic	1949	22 Short target
	Supermatic	1950	22 LR target
	Field King	1950	Std. wt. target
	Sport King	1952	Lt. wt. 22 LR utility
	Flite King	1954	Lt. wt. 22 S utility
	Dura-Matic	1954	Std. grade utility
	Supermatic Trophy	1958	Highest grade target
	Supermatic Citation	1958	Lesser grade target
	Supermatic Tournament	1958	Lesser grade target
	Olympic Citation	1958	22 S target
	Olympic ISU		22 S target
SMITH & WESSON	Model 41	1957	Highest grade target
	Model 46	1959	Lesser grade target
	Escort	1970	Pocket-size
STERLING	Cup Series	1970 ?	Announced
STOEGER	Luger 22	1969	First U.S. made "Luger"
WHITNEY	Lightning (Wolverine)	1955	Alloy-frame utility
RUGER	Standard	1949	First Ruger model
	Mark I Target	1955	Target version of Standard

Smith & Wesson Model 41

Smith & Wesson Escort

TABLE FIVE

SINGLE SHOT AND MULTIPLE BARREL PISTOLS INTRODUCED FROM 1945 to 1970

MAKER	MODEL	TYPE	CALIBER	INTRODUCED
TOMPKINS	Target	S.S.	22 RF	1947
S-M	Sporter	S.S.	22 RF	1953
SHERIDAN	Knocabout	S.S.	22 RF	1953
WAMO	Powermaster	S.S.	22 RF	1956
SAVAGE	101 Safety	S.S.	22 RF	1959
COLT	No. 4 Derringer	S.S.	22 RF	1959
	Civil War Cent.	S.S.	22 RF	1961
REMINGTON	XP-100	S.S.	221 Fireball	1962
RUGER	Hawkeye	S.S.	256 Mag.	1962
SVENDSEN	Little Ace	S.S.	22 RF	1960
THOMPSON/CENTER	Contender	S.S.	various	1967
MERRILL	Sportsman	S.S.	various	1970
GREAT WESTERN	Double Derringer	2-shot O-U	38 S&W 38 Spl.	1955
BUDDIE ARMS	Double Deuce	2-shot O-U	22 RF	1960
HIGH STANDARD	Double Derringer	2-shot O-U	22RF; 22WMR	1963
CHICAGO	Derringer	4-barrel	22 RF	1964
SVENDSEN	Four Aces	4-barrel	22 RF	1965

24 oz., it is not a burdensome comrade. Despite the need for such a utility single shot in 22 RF, Sheridan's president informed the writer it was discontinued in 1960 since it did not fit in with Sheridan's emphasis on pneumatic arms.

Savage re-entered the handgun field in 1959 with a "unique" single-shot pistol in 22 caliber. Styled like a western six-gun, its dummy cylinder is actually part of the barrel unit, which swings out of the frame to the right far enough to permit loading and extraction of empties via an ejector rod. In reality, the mechanics of this model are not really unique, as might appear to one unacquainted with antique pistols. The Savage 101 Safety single shot is obviously similar to Daniel Moore's cartridge revolver patented September 18, 1860! This little Savage admirably serves the utilitarian need for a low-priced plinker, training handgun or camper's friend.

While Remington's XP-100 is generally listed as a single-shot pistol, it is in reality a hand rifle similar to the Pocket or Bicycle rifles made by Stevens and others that could be fired using one hand. While it is cited here, the author does not regard it as particularly noteworthy.

While it has yet to make it to the commercial market, High Standard in 1960 had an experimental 22 rimfire "free" pistol that is worth noting. It featured an electric trigger which had no connection with, and thus did not directly actuate, the sear. This design was hailed at the time as revolutionary, and one which might one day put the U.S. in the spotlight at international free-pistol matches. This writer does not know why this new light on the handgun horizon faded before it could fulfill its promise.

The Thompson/Center Contender, a post-WW II single-shot pistol, looks like it will be around for some time to come as it has eliminated a number of objectionable features in advance. All metal parts are of steel, and all wood parts are of selected good-quality walnut. Grip angle is the highly favored 31 degrees. But what has made the Contender a seller in addition to its commendable qualities is that it features interchangeable barrels in a large selection of calibers. It even incorporates a selective firing pin; by means of an off-set screw on the face of the hammer the firing pin can be rotated so that it will function equally well with rimfire or centerfire cartridges. Changing barrels, and thus calibers, is easily accomplished. Here is a truly unique, quality-engineered single-shot handgun that should satisfy those who favor the type.

Great Western, in 1955, was the first to produce a replica of Remington's famous Double Derringer for a centerfire cartridge. It was a virtual duplication of Remington's Gambler's Special. Of course, the GW was made of chrome-molybdenum steel rather than cast iron and incorporated coil rather than flat springs. In either 38 S&W or 38 Special, this derringer can only be considered a very lethal extra gun that may make a big difference in an emergency.

The only other U.S. derringer made since WW II that can be judged practical is High Standard's of 1962, which serves ade-

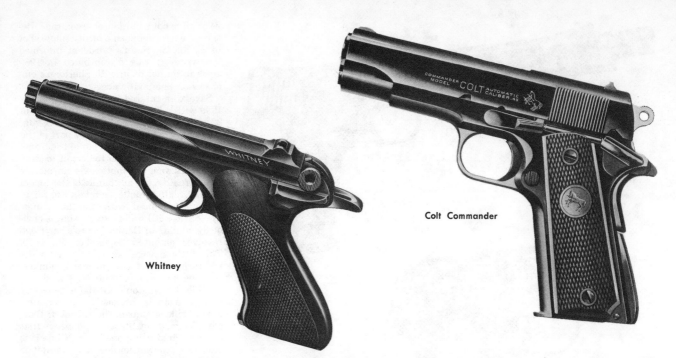

Colt Commander

Whitney

quately in the role of a second-string hideout weapon. This compact arm has two commendable features: it is hammerless and it is double action. Both features mark firsts in cartridge derringers. Loaded with high velocity hollow-point 22 Long Rifle cartridges (Model D-100) or 22 WMR cartridges (Model DM-101), this 11 ounces of prevention is worth pounds of reassurance.

At this point, some readers may be prepared to give the author Hell for failure to mention as praiseworthy their favorite paper-puncher, snake-dispatcher or home-defender. Before any reader so inclined dwells upon such uncharitable thoughts, he is kindly requested to scrutinize carefully Table I, listing U.S. handgun models available prior to WW II, to determine if his pet shootin' iron is not to be found there. Many pre-WW II models were returned to production after 1945, and quite a few are still available. Even though these handguns may have undergone modifications in the post-WW II years, if they basically antedate 1945 they do not fall within the scope of this review. For example, Colt's Officers Model Match of today was known as the Officers Model Target prior to WW II and as Officers Model Special during 1949-53. The current S&W K-38 is structurally the pre-WW II Military & Police 38 Target.

Be assured that the writer has the greatest admiration for many U.S. handguns introduced prior to 1945 which would be included in any list of all-time greats, but these fall outside the range of this article.

III. Duds and Frivolities

Two classes of handguns are discussed in this section. "Duds," as used here, is synonymous with commercial failures and is not meant to impugn necessarily the quality or ingenuity of those handguns which unhappily qualify for this classification. "Frivolities," on the other hand, may have enjoyed a great deal of commercial success, but are nevertheless either of little value

or importance, irrelevant or impractical. Quite a few handguns have fallen under each of these categories since 1945. We'll start with the "Duds" in alphabetical sequence in an attempt to avoid bias, or at least reduce its obviousness.

Cody Thunderbird

In 1957, the Cody Mfg. Co. of Chicopee, Mass., began manufacturing a 6-shot 22 RF revolver that, with the exception of plastic grips, some few parts and a steel barrel-liner, was all aluminum. The 4-inch barrel version weighed 22 oz., less than 1½ pounds! This arm was supplied in two finishes—Hybrite (polished aluminum) or Brylite, a lustrous black. Prior to this enterprise folding steel cylinders had been substituted for aluminum, but to no avail.

While the Thunderbird was not an impressive handgun judged by usual criteria, this writer cannot refrain from testifying, from personal experience, that it possessed a crisp, creep-free trigger let-off when fired single-action, a feature frequently absent in revolvers of better repute and higher cost! An unusual feature was a safety lever, in lieu of a rebounding hammer, which locked the action and prevented the hammer from reaching the cartridge rims when carried loaded.

Dardick

The Dardick of 1959 was in all probability the most radical development in cartridge handguns of the past 25 years. Hard to definitively classify, this arm comes closest to being a double-action "automatic" revolver. Named after its inventor, David Dardick, it employs a cylinder with three open chambers which pick up triangular cartridges (or "trounds") from a spring-loaded magazine holding 11 (Model 1100) or 15 (Model 1500) of these trounds. These cases were made of Fortiflex, a polyethylene plastic. The bullets themselves were 38 Special while adaptors permitted switching to 38 wadcutter, 9mm or 22 RF by changing barrels. The gun's silhouette

can only be described as grotesque and the fate of this dud should serve as a grim reminder that commercial success depends on much more than mechanical feasibility. A law of economics states that a purchase is made when the subjective value (potential customer's appraisal) reaches or surpasses the objective value (retail price). The Dardick ignored esthetics and suffered the consequences.

Great Western Arms

Great Western Arms, a California-based enterprise, began operations in 1954. About this time, the demand for single-action revolvers was great for use in western movies and TV which, in turn, stimulated demand for this type of handgun among viewers. In an effort to speed up production, Great Western failed to fit and finish their single-action revolvers in a manner which impressed potential customers, or convinced them they were getting their money's worth. By 1955, Colt had their Single Action Army back in production—a well finished weapon of precision functioning that, while high-priced, cut drastically into Great Western sales. During 1959, Great Western moved to a new factory in North Hollywood and were well aware of the necessity for exercising greater quality control, but by that time the damage to their name was already done. By late 1962 the firm was fading fast.

Kimball Arms

The J. Kimball Arms Co., Detroit, Michigan, put into limited production during 1958 an automatic pistol which Kimball designed to use the 30 U.S. Carbine cartridge. It was to have been available in a 3-inch barrel Combat model with fixed sights and a 5-inch barrel Target model with Micro sights. Impartial tests revealed dangerous structural weaknesses in the design of the Kimball, and the venture failed while a U.S. patent claim was still pending. This writer feels that the

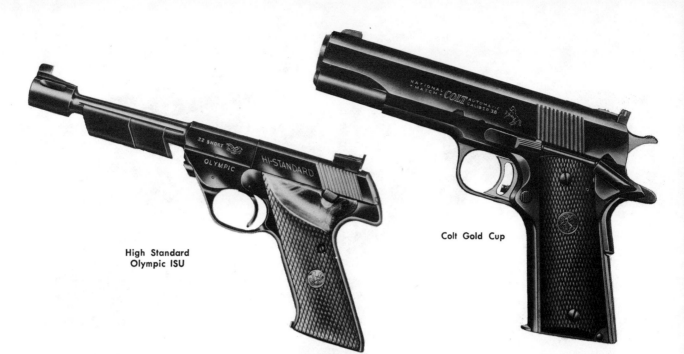

High Standard
Olympic ISU

Colt Gold Cup

straight-cased 30 U.S. Carbine represents a desirable prospective caliber for an automatic pistol and predicts that one day the "bugs" in producing an automatic for this cartridge will be overcome.

MBA Gyrojet Rocket

First reported on in the 1967 GUN DIGEST, the MBA Gyrojet Rocket pistol was encountered by the writer in September, 1965, at a Sahara (hotel) gun show in Las Vegas, Nevada. It is indeed a weird innovation in handguns. This Space Age arm has a hammer which strikes the nose of the cartridge, or rather rocket projectile, and whose unrifled "barrel" is really only a launching tube. Its self-propelled unguided rockets contain solid fuel and a percussion primer. Canted ports in its base impart a stabilizing spin to the projectile. Its standard 13mm rocket has half again as much velocity as does the 45 ACP and nearly twice the energy. Here again, esthetics were ignored: the MBA neither looks nor feels like a traditional handgun. The models this writer saw were cheap-looking stampings drilled full of holes, roughly finished and of unshapely lines. It is no wonder they've been commercial duds so far. However, their ultimate destiny is not yet clear, and one should be hesitant to dismiss this development in a cavalier fashion.

Ruger Hawkeye

Ruger had been contemplating for some time a long-range single-shot pistol. He finally decided, following development of the hot 256 Magnum cartridge, to chamber his first single-shot pistol, the Hawkeye, for this cartridge. It was an unfortunate decision. The 256 Magnum did not take in rifles either, and is now virtually obsolete. Almost without exception, handguns chambered for tapered-case cartridges have been commercial failures, although this may be circumstantial rather than directly causative. A beautifully-engineered handgun with a solid, swing-out breech-block, Ruger's 1962 Hawkeye deserved a

longer life and might have enjoyed one in another caliber (30 U.S. Carbine?).

Smith & Wesson 22 Magnum

Already a collector's item, this revolver was billed as "1961's most exciting handgun news" and was featured on the cover of the 16th edition of the GUN DIGEST. The 22 Magnum uses a convertible hammer nose for firing either 22 RF or 22 Jet CF cartridges with the flip of a thumb. The secret lies in two separate firing pins. Initially furnished with 6 chamber inserts to take 22 Long Rifle cartridges, an auxiliary cylinder could also be ordered fitted at the factory. This model used the "K" frame, plus an ejector-rod housing beneath the barrel. Users report a devastating muzzle blast, loud enough to put unprotected tympanic membranes out of business!

Whitney Firearms

It grieves the writer to call the Whitney 22 RF automatic pistol a dud. "Streamlined for feel and beauty; made of the highest tensile strength alloys and steel—it's really tomorrow's pistol today," reads a 1958 blurb for this brainchild of an ingenious designer, Robert L. Hillberg. The quote may also contain the clue as to why the Whitney didn't make it commercially. Perhaps it *was* tomorrow's pistol and the public was not ready to take seriously a handgun which seemed to be a copy of ones seen previously only in space comics, TV or movies. In any event, this natural-pointing lightweight was knocked out by 1962.

Now for the "frivolities"—again in alphabetical order.

Buddie Arms Double Deuce

In Fort Worth, Texas, an industrialist by the name of Hibbs has been assembling the "Double Deuce" derringer in 22 rimfire since 1960. The writer has been furnished satisfactory proof by Mr. Hibbs that all of its parts are made in the U.S., and the arm should rightfully appear on any complete check list of U.S. rimfire handguns. It was

the first post-WW II double derringer in 22 rimfire of U.S. manufacture—the only other one to date is High Standard's. The Double Deuce is essentially well-made, but could be better finished for more esthetic appeal. Since it is single-action, cumbersome, with exposed hammer to hang up inside clothing, it must be classed as more of a nostalgic frivolity than suitable for any practical purpose.

Chicago Derringer Corp.

The Chicago Derringer Corp. of Bensenville, Illinois, brought out in the early 1960s a 4-barrel derringer in 22 rimfire. Made with a solid bronze frame, this well-made multiple-barrel conversation piece was not, repeat, was *not* intended to be an exact replica of the Sharps or any other derringer. To be perfectly frank, the writer does not know for what purpose it was intended, but perhaps it was meant for those who thought they couldn't live without one. The writer owned one once, but eventually decided that since it served no rational purpose he could live without it!

Colt

No manufacturer has been more active in the "field of frivolity" than Colt. First to see the commercial pots of gold awaiting the promoting of fancied-up handgun models commemorating historic events, Colt has been deluging the market with umpteen versions marking significant, as well as trivial, events of the past.

The majority of Colt's commemoratives have been made on their 1962 22 rimfire Frontier Scout frame. Variation is attempted through mix-matching finishes and grips, but the only real difference, if it can be called that, consists of one line of lettering on the barrel indicating the event commemorated. Why are these commemorative Frontier Scouts frivolities? Here's why: it is a well-known fact of economic life that when one plunks down his initial payment on a new car and drives it out of the showroom, the value has dropped by 20% or more depending upon

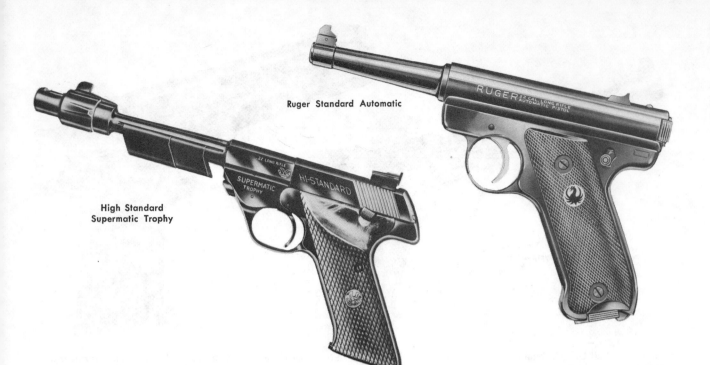

Ruger Standard Automatic

High Standard
Supermatic Trophy

the original cost. So, too, if one pulls the trigger on a live cartridge in one of these duded-up commemoratives, he must be prepared to sacrifice between a third to a half of the retail cost for his rashness. There is nothing so hard to sell as a fired commemorative! So take your choice: Use one as any other handgun and lose substantially on your investment, or keep it safe and snug (unfired) in its own little bed (case).

Kent Bellah (GUN DIGEST, 1961) called Colt's No. 4 Derringer in 22 Short "a genuine Colt." At the time of its appearance, the writer heard Colt was having these derringers made in Spain, but never confirmed this rumor. The first time the writer tested one, he cocked the hammer and pulled the trigger 3 times before ignition was achieved! Cute they may be, but frivolous they've got to be. Not recommended for use with high-velocity ammo, they should not even be regarded as a last ditch protective measure with standard ammo since ignition is far from reliable. Despite their fallibility, no doubt these replicas of a past era made a lot of money for Colt, as Americans have a soft spot for the nostalgic, and often the impractical as well.

With the obvious idea of cashing in on the 100th anniversary of the War Between The States, Colt produced in late 1961 a scaled-down reproduction of their once-renowned 1860 Army model. Apparently with an eye toward the mass market rather than the connoisseur, Colt employed a cheap alloy equivalent to pot-metal in constructing this replica (other than barrel-liner and small parts), and then covered the barrel and dummy cylinder with Royal Blue while the frame and trigger guard were gold-plated. A 22 Short single shot requiring disassembly for loading and shell extraction, it is incontestable that this Civil War Centennial model constitutes nothing more than a frivolity.

High Standard Sentinel Snub-in Color

The writer might be challenged for listing the H-S Sentinel Snub in Gold, Turquoise or Pink among the frivolities and if it makes anyone feel better, go ahead! I'll grant you the 22 Long Rifle high-velocity bullets come out of the muzzles in these hues just as fast as they do in barrels of equal length in traditional blue or nickel. Many conservative handgunners were aghast when they first beheld these revolvers in colors to match milady's wardrobe! Not so the ladies, many of whom insisted on owning one, and had previously evinced little interest in such a possession. At any rate, the fad for these frivolities lasted from 1957 to 1963. The reason for their discontinuance is not known, but, presumably, sales fell off when the novelty aspect diminished. Shall I let you in on a secret? I've got a Sentinel Snub in "shocking pink" tucked away in my collection!

E. Svendsen "Little Ace" & "Four Aces"

In Itasca, Illinois a competent Swedish gun designer claims to be producing the "world's smallest real derringer" and the "world's smallest 4-barrel derringer." This writer is prepared to give credence to these claims. This is the same Erl Svendsen who started out to make western single-actions in the 1950s, but ran into who knows how many obstacles and never overcame them. Perhaps he's on the right track, as there is little U.S. competition in the derringer field. These derringers are entirely and nicely fabricated of steel and bronze and chambered for 22 Short only. Since use of high-velocity cartridges is not recommended in these derringers, plus the fact they are single action, they scarcely serve any utilitarian function. Cute, perhaps even desirable frivolities, but nonetheless frivolities.

IV. A "Guesstimate" as to the Future of Handguns in the U.S.

The handgun is at the crossroads today in the United States. I am certain no reader will contest this assertion. Gun opponents appear to be as indefatigable as they are irrational. The handgun remains the prime whipping boy of firearms for the crime problem in general. While commissions and do-gooders are busily engaged in devising ways and means of divesting U.S. citizens of their constitutional right to keep and bear arms, they are not obliged to rack their cerebrums to come up with realistic solutions to the problems of how to prevent felons from committing crimes in the first place, and prevent them from avoiding the penalties for doing so in the second place. As we who prefer reason to emotion keep pointing out, "Guns don't kill people—people kill people!" But I'm afraid anti-gun folk are impervious to logic.

The emotional hysteria which followed the assassinations of President Kennedy, Martin Luther King and especially Senator Kennedy was cunningly capitalized upon and exploited by the foes of an armed citizenry as a means of convincing Congress to finally pass the ill-conceived Gun Control Act of 1968. Not content with this achievement in perfidy, the National Commission on the Causes and Prevention of Violence, appointed by gun-foe President Johnson and chaired by ultra-liberal Milton S. Eisenhower, had the temerity to advocate virtual confiscation of all handguns in the hands of U.S. citizens with singularly few exceptions! To quote this brother of a first-rate military man who rose to become President of the United States, "The day is coming—it ought to be here today, but isn't—when we are going to have to have a system of restrictive licensing so those guns must be taken away from everyone except those who need them."

If we were to accept this Commission's interpretation of "need," about 95% of us would be eliminated as having any. If you prefer a realistic common sense interpretation of "need," every householder who loves his family as well as himself needs a gun in the house. Famed English mystery writer, Edgar Wallace, who was quite familiar with the criminal classes of Britain and recognized as an authority on them said: "Burglars, by the way, are a very timid class. Their nightmare is the vision of a householder armed with a revolver. There is not one burglar in a hundred who does not go through life with this horror hanging over him." With as many mentally deranged and otherwise psychopathic persons running around loose as there are today, we would be naive to believe that police protection will always be immediately available when required. There are other human needs which handguns legitimately serve, of course, but personal and home defense is assuredly a paramount one. The National Commission on the Causes and Prevention of Violence has turned in its final report and presumedly will be disbanded. Let us trust that President Nixon will let it rest in peace!

The two most persistent and relentless anti-gun proponents in Congress during the past decade were Senators Dodd of Connecticut and Tydings of Maryland. More than any other pair, these Senators were constantly clamorous in misleading the public as to the role of firearms in crime and in fostering the enactment of restrictive legislation with respect to firearms.

The elections of 1970 were, in one sense, a barometer as to where the public stood on the firearms issue, and on what the future held for the continued existence of firearms in the hands of the citizenry. Happily for the firearms fraternity, and for the welfare of our form of government for that matter, these two blatant foes of an armed citizenry went down to a resounding defeat as did another of their ilk—Senator Gore of Tennessee.

Responsible firearms owners, whether collectors or active sportsmen, can take satisfaction that they rose to the occasion when a vital aspect of American freedom was being seriously threatened!

The political demise of these former U.S. Senators just may put a little fear, if not common sense, into the heads of other anti-gun congressmen—resulting in a moratorium, or damper, on further hamstringing legislation as well as spurious allegations directed at American sportsmen or reputable associations such as the NRA.

We must not dismiss it lightly, the anti-gun people scored a significant victory with the Gun Control Act of 1968, and the sweet smell of success will no doubt spur them on to propose more inane measures. Anyone desiring to buy ammunition designed for use in handguns must now "sign up" for it—virtually registering the fact that he owns, or has access to, handguns using ammo in the calibers purchased. Dealers can no longer sell firearms at gun collector's shows nor, for the most part, to residents of other states. Tourists are forbidden to buy firearms made after 1898 in their travels about the country. How the compromise date of 1898 was arrived at for the purpose of demarcation between legitimate collector firearms and modern firearms, the writer is at a loss to clarify. I suppose the non-dealer is expected to be grateful he has salvaged legal permission to collect, buy, sell, trade or ship interstate pre-1898 guns. If a firearm 70 years old (1898-1968) constitutes an antique, obviously there should be efforts made to get this arbitrary date of 1898 moved up as time goes by.

The National Rifle Association would be remiss in an obligation to its members if it failed to stand up for their right to own handguns as much as any other type of firearms. It is therefore heartening to note that in the January, 1970 issue of *The American Rifleman*, a full page editorial points out that the vast majority of handguns owned by U.S. citizens are used for recreational purposes, and that we must protect our right to own handguns to safeguard our right to own any guns! May the NRA never retreat from this position.

It is difficult to be highly optimistic about the handgun picture, but on the other hand we must avoid becoming indolently pessimistic. The future of handguns in the United States in the last analysis depends upon each one of us who owns as much as one handgun, and who desires to continue doing so. We must stand united and not allow ourselves to become a silent majority. We must demand that our sportsmen, shooter's and collector's associations speak up and take whatever action lies within their power to prevent or remove senseless legislation. The price of freedom to own handguns is the same as the price of all other freedoms: eternal vigilance! We must meet every measure conjured up by the anti-gun element with counter-measures of superior brilliance and force. If we follow this philosophy unremittingly, many future generations may be enabled to enjoy handguns in these United States of America.

Assuming that handguns will continue to be produced in the U.S. during the remainder of this century at least, and that any citizen of sound mind and clean record may continue to purchase them, what changes can be anticipated?

The writer has already revealed in Section III his reaction to the MBA "Gyrojet Rocket" handguns and rifles. While far from being attracted to these handguns on the basis of esthetic appeal or any other basis, he was tentatively resigned to face the coming close of the conventional cartridge era of ignition. Here was a handgun that launched 13mm self-propelled "rockets" which traveled at considerably greater velocity, and were approximately twice as powerful, as the cartridge which has remained the U.S. military standard in side arms since 1911, yet with recoil about one-tenth that of the 45 ACP cartridge.

Since this is the Space Age, one could naturally assume that handguns would eventually follow suit and use the principles of the rocket and solid-fuel propellant. Yet more than 5 years have gone by as I write this, and so far no "Gyrojet Rocket" pistols are to be found in retail outlets and no bankruptcies have been reported by our established conventional cartridge handgun makers. Could our government have secretly acquired all rights to these rocket launching small arms to keep them out of the hands of civilians or other nations? Your guess here may be better than mine.

Daisy, of air-rifle fame, spent some 5 years developing a rifle to use caseless, primerless ammunition, but so far no attempt has been made to adapt this ammo to a handgun, nor has the Daisy V/L rifle caused a stampede to the gun shops by the shoulder arms gentry.

The cartridge era has been with us now for well over a century, and the writer ventures a prediction that it will continue as the prime system for the remainder of the 20th century.

If a frivolity has been correctly classified as such, it will remain a frivolity forever. But what proved to be a dud yesterday may, in modified form, be the big bang of tomorrow!

The writer may not have told it like it is in every instance, but he's told it the way he sees it from this vantage point in time based on his experience. His hope is that every reader will find some benefit from this essay, and that no one will be the worse for having read it. That some of the writer's observations and pronouncements will be challenged is to be anticipated. But then, this is America—the land of the free and the home of dissension! ●

J. C. Higgins Model 80

A History of

This is the 5th installment of the new and fully up-to-date series "History of Proof Marks" initiated in our 22nd edition. The author, Mr. Lee Kennett, is highly qualified to have undertaken the definitive research required, and we feel certain his comprehensive and detailed work will prove reliable, interesting, instructive and valuable.

While Mr. Kennett used the framework of the late Baron Engelhardt's "The Story of European Proof Marks" as a structural guide, he personally visited and talked with Proof House officials in many countries in his research. He will continue to do so until all nations in the survey have been covered. When that time arrives, we will publish the complete book.

With this issue we present "Proof Marks in Italy." The completed and published book will carry a full account of the origins and historical back ground of proof marks.

PROOF IN ITALY

ITALY PLAYED an important role in the evolution of firearms in Europe. Some Italian gunmakers, like the Cominazzo family, for example, enjoyed a Europe-wide reputation as early as the 16th century. According to some authorities the Italian city of Pistoia gave us, by derivation, the word "pistol." The northern city of Brescia, and the nearby town of Gardone Val Trompia, soon became the chief centers of arms production. Considering the importance of Italian arms production from quite early, one may wonder why no compulsory national proof system was devised before the 20th century. A partial explanation lies in the fact that Italy, and Germany as well, did not become unified nations until barely a hundred years ago.

Proof of firearms by makers and by municipal authorities was practiced widely. There was a privately operated proof house at Brescia in 1910, and probably for many years before.

The Italian government took the first step toward a national proof system when it opened a proof house at Gardone in 1920, and at Brescia in 1921. The proof offered was optional. Provisional proof of shotgun barrels in the rough was made at 14,700 psi and designated by mark no.1. A second set of proofs was available for finished smoothbore barrels *and* for finished shotguns. The combined second provisional-definitive proof with smokeless powder was done at 9000 psi and represented by mark no.3. A supple-

mentary mark, no. 4, was applied to shotguns undergoing definitive proof in completely finished and blued state. This mark was always found in conjunction with no. 2. or no. 3. Obviously the system anticipated the coming into effect of the international rules formulated at Brussels; the definitive proof of smoothbores, with black powder or smokeless, was described as "official international proof." Moreover, rifled arms were proved at 30% excess pressure in completed state, this proof being designated by mark no.5. A final provision of the 1920 system permitted the proof of arms already manufactured but apparently not yet sold. These could be submitted until 1 September 1921, and were to bear, in addition to the usual proof marks, the letters "BPD" as well as the year of proof. Though the law was a good one, work was begun almost immediately on a compulsory system. The legislation necessary was signed on 30 December 1923, and the implementing decree appeared on 10 October 1924. The new system went into effect on 8 February 1925.

It is quite clear that the Italian government in the 1923 rules intended to enforce to the fullest the conditions of the Brussels Convention. The law required that all arms submitted to proof bear factory marks and numbers, and exact information as to caliber was required. For shotguns, chamber and bore dimensions had to fall within international standards; even the dimensions of the shell rim seat were specified. All arms successfully proved bore the distinctive house mark of the proof house. There were three

Proof Marks

Gun Proof in Italy

by Lee Kennett

of these in 1925, at Gardone, Brescia, and Camerlata (marks nos. 7, 8 and 9).

The law originally offered to gunmakers two separate provisional proofs for shotgun barrels. Single barrels in the rough were given a black powder proof at 15,600 psi, symbolized by a crown (mark no. 10). Barrels could also be proved in the finished, filed state, joined if intended for doubles, and lacking only chambers. These were proved with black powder at 12,800 psi, designated by two crowns (mark no. 11).

Definitive proof of shotguns was of two types: black powder or smokeless. The black powder proof developed 8800 psi, and was identified by mark no. 12. The letters "PN" stand for *polvere nera* or black powder. The smokeless proof, known as the "international smokeless proof," generated pressures of 12,000 psi. It was represented by mark no. 13. The letters "PSF" stand for *polvere senza fumo*, smokeless powder. Shotguns could be submitted to these proofs either "in the white" or completely finished. In the latter case marks 12 or 13 were accompanied by mark no. 14; the word FINITO, meaning "finished." Shotguns with chambers longer than 70mm (2¾") were proved with extra heavy charges, as were punt guns, charges in these cases apparently being fixed by the proof master.

Rifles, pistols, and revolvers were proved in a finished state with 30% excess pressure over the strongest commercial loads, whether black powder or smokeless. For this proof mark no. 15 was assigned. Revolvers were tested in each chamber; automatic pistols were tested with the proof round, then with as many commercial cartridges as the magazine would hold.

As a rule, guns were stamped with the year of proof. Shotguns were stamped with barrel weight in kilograms, bore diameter and choke diameter in millimeters, as well as chamber length and diameter of shell rim seats.

Proof rules were amended slightly in 1929, the changes going into effect on 7 August of that year. Shotguns of smaller than 16 gauge now underwent a slightly higher definitive smokeless proof at 14,700 psi. Pressure for 16 gauge and larger were not changed. A second alteration was the dropping of mark no. 15 to indicate proof of rifled arms. These henceforth received mark no. 12 or mark no. 13; pressure requirements remained the same.

In 1930 the house mark of the Brescia proof house was dropped, the operations of this establishment being merged with those of Gardone. The Camerlata house and its mark had been abolished in 1926, after only a few months in operation. The Camerlata mark is very rarely seen, being found on the guns manufactured by the Armi Lauria Company and a few foreign weapons. Although some publications on proof show the Brescia house mark as current as late as the 1950s, Italian proof authorities state quite formally that since 1930 only the Gardone house mark has been used.

There were no further major changes in the proof system until 14 September 1950. Since Italy at that

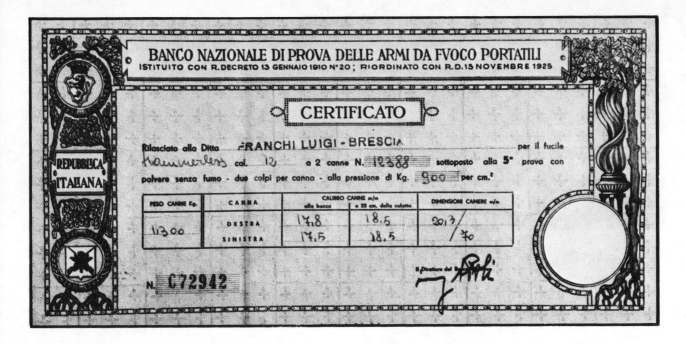

BANCO NAZIONALE DI PROVA DELLE ARMI DA FVOCO PORTATILI
ISTITUITO CON R. DECRETO 13 GENNAIO 1910 N° 20; RIORDINATO CON R.D. 15 NOVEMBRE 1925

REPUBBLICA ITALIANA

CERTIFICATO

Rilasciato alla Ditta **FRANCHI LUIGI - BRESCIA** per il fucile
Hammerless cal. 12 a 2 canne N. 12388 sottoposto alla 5° prova con
polvere senza fumo - due colpi per canna - alla pressione di Kg. 900 per cm.²

| PESO CANNE Kg. | CANNA | CALIBRO CANNE m/m | | DIMENSIONI CAMERE m/m |
		alla bocca	a 22 cm. dalla culatta	
1300	DESTRA	17,8	18,5	20,3 /
	SINISTRA	17,5	18,5	/ 70

N. C72942

Above—Proof certificate for a 12 gauge double barrel shot gun made by Luigi Franchi, proved at Gardone val Trompia. Below—Bottom view of an Italian superposed shot gun recently proved at Gardone val Trompia. See facing page for an explanation of numbered proof marks.

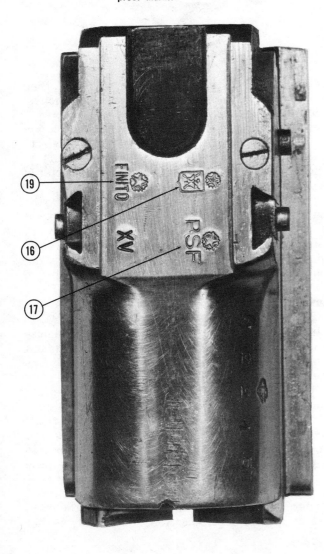

(19) FINITO
(16) XV
(17) PSF

time abolished the monarchy and established a republic, the royal crowns on the proof marks were replaced by the star in wheel symbol of the republic (marks 16-19). At the same time, the number of marks was reduced, so that now first provisional proof, second provisional proof and definitive smokeless proof are all indicated by the same mark (no. 17).

On 2 November 1962 rules were again changed in minor points. A superior smokeless definitive proof was introduced (mark no. 20), requiring pressures of at least 17,600 psi. This is optional for shotguns with standard chamber length of 70mm, but obligatory for those with longer chambers. Another provision requires that all automatic or self-loading arms be tested for correct functioning with as many commercial cartridges as their magazines will hold. Finally, a set of marks has been devised to indicate degree of choke (marks 21-25). The relevant mark is placed on each barrel well forward of the flats.

In conclusion, it can be said that proof in Italy has conformed to the Brussels standards since its inception. The present director of the proof house adds, however, that in practice, "from 1925, when the proving became compulsory, we use smokeless powders for the breechloading arms and black powder for the muzzleloaders." ●

Bibliography

The main elements of this chapter were drawn from the text of the relevant laws and information supplied by letter from the authorities at the Banco Nazionale di Prova at Gardone Val Trompia. The author would like particularly to thank Ing. Domenico Salza, its director, for his help. Two recent works on firearms might also be cited: Letterio Musciarelli's _Storia universale delle Armi_ (Universal History of Arms), Brescia, 1963; and Federico Negri, _Il Fucile da Caccia_ (The Hunting Shotgun), Florence, 1964.

Italian Proof Marks 1923-1967

In this table the mark numbers at left are those assigned by the author, and keyed by him to the text for reference. The 2nd column shows the true form of the proof mark and gives the period of its use. The last column tells of the marks' significance.

Optional Proof System of 1920

1 · 1920-1925 · Provisional proof of shotgun barrels in the rough at 14,700 psi.

2 · PSF · 1920-1925 · Second provisional and definitive smokeless powder proof of shotguns at 12,500 psi.

3 · PN · 1920-1925 · Second provisional and definitive black powder proof of shotguns at 9,000 psi.

4 · FINITO · 1920-1925 · Supplementary mark indicating definitive proof administered to completely finished arm.

5 · 1920-1925 · Definitive proof of rifled arms at 30% excess pressure.

6 · B.P.D. · 1920-1921 · Supplementary mark indicating proof of arms already completed when the proof rules came into effect.

Compulsory Proof System, 1925-

7 · 1925-1950 · House mark of the Gardone Val Trompia Proof House.

8 · 1925-1930 · House mark of the Brescia Proof House.

9 · 1925-1926 · House mark of the Camerlata Proof House.

10 · 1925-1950 · Black powder proof of unjoined shotgun barrels at 15,600 psi.

11 · 1925-1950 · Black powder provisional proof of joined shotgun barrels at 12,800 psi.

12 · PN · 1925-1950 · Black powder definitive proof of shotguns at 8,800 psi. After 1929 used also for black powder proof of rifled arms at 30% excess pressure.

13 · PSF · 1925-1950 · Smokeless powder definitive proof of shotguns at 12,000 psi. After 1929 used also for smokeless proof of rifled arms at 30% excess pressure.

14 · FINITO · 1925-1950 · Supplementary mark denoting definitive proof of arms when completely finished and blued. Used in conjunction with marks 12, 13, or 15.

15 · PD · 1925-1929 · Definitive proof, smokeless or black, for rifled arms at 30% excess pressure.

16 · 1950- · Replaced mark no.7.

17 · PSF · 1950- · Replaced marks 10, 11 and 12.

18 · PN · 1950- · Replaced mark no. 12. Used only on muzzleloaders and heavy duck guns.

19 · FINITO · 1950- · Replaced mark no. 14.

20 · PSF · 1962- · Superior definitive smokeless proof of shotguns at 17,600 psi or more.

21 · ☆ · 1962- · Mark indicating full choke (.9 to 1.1mm constriction)

22 · ☆☆ · 1962- · Mark indicating ¾ or improved-modified choke (.7 to .8mm constriction).

23 · ☆☆☆ · 1962- · Mark indicating ½ or modified choke (.4 to .6mm constriction).

24 · ☆☆☆☆ · 1962- · Mark indicating ¼ or improved cylinder choke (.2 to .3mm constriction).

25 · CL · 1962- · Mark indicating cylinder bore (.1mm or less constriction).

NOTE: Those periods not showing a closing year indicate continuing use of the mark indicated, up to the time of publication of this book.

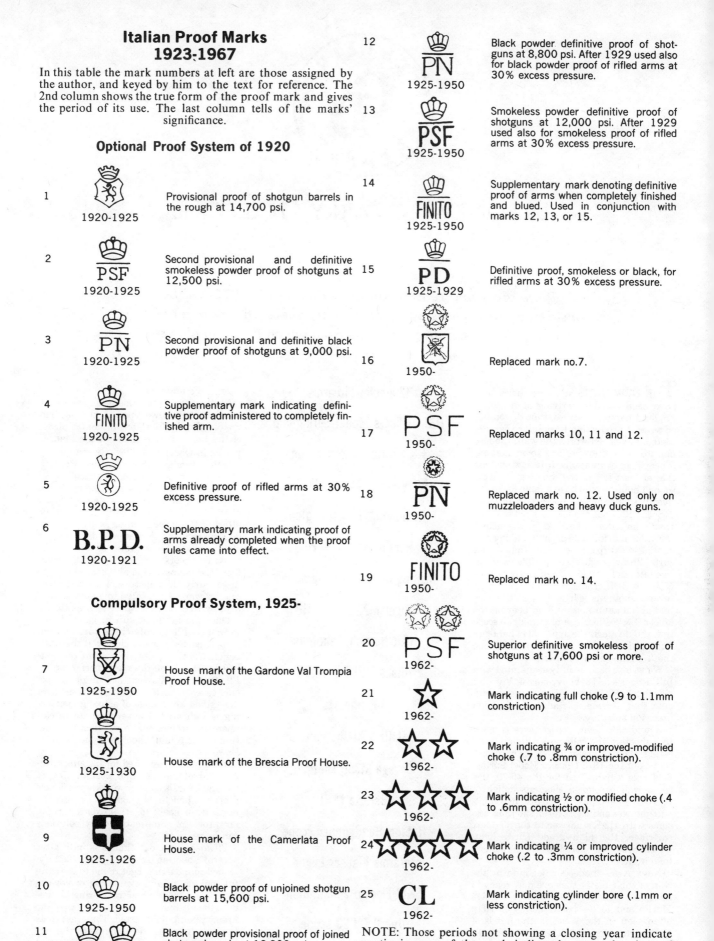

TESTFIRE GD REPORT

by BOB ZWIRZ, LARRY STERETT and the editors

*There are sound reasons for believing that 1971-72 will be
considered bonus years by shooters everywhere. There's a very wide
range of new shooting products from which they can choose.*

THE NEW GUNS and accessories that have been steadily arriving at my New England testing facilities, though coming off several production lines later than expected, have been worth the wait, the last minute rush they put me to in making proper field evaluations. It is now obvious that at least two of the shooting products we had hoped would be available for inclusion in this issue will not arrive in time.

So far 1971 has brought us a hot new duo from Remington—the 17 Rem., the factory cartridge moving a 25-gr. bullet along at a sizzling 4020 fps, plus a rifle that is, not surprisingly, highly compatible with it. The latter, of course, is their justly famous M700 in BDL grade. We'll also report on several shotguns worth their salt, a new line of handgun ammunition bearing the label of S&W-Fiocchi, and a handgun scope that should merit the approval of handgun hunters looking for an optical assist, one that's significantly compact, too.

We've also become fully acquainted with Bill Ruger's M77 heavy-barrel Varmint rifle in 22-250; in so doing we came up with data that, for me, has added up to truly precision shooting.

Rounding out our report there is much that shooters and collectors will find interesting about Harrington & Richardson's replica of the 1873 Officers Model Springfield rifle. Chambered for the 45-70, this could well become a shooter's delight/a collector's keepsake. We've also had limited time to conduct several shooting sessions with H&R's answer to the 17 Rem. cartridge, the high grade Ultra lightweight rifle chambered for the new Remington factory load.

Navy Arms made our deadline by the skin of their teeth; they are now ready to introduce a replica Rolling Block—in 444 Marlin and 45-70—based loosely on rifles often seen in the West, in the hands of buffalo hunters and other professionals. Target grade rolling block Remingtons were also popular at Creedmoor and other

Champlin Firearms

H&R Officers Model Springfield

H&R Ultra 17 Remington

Navy Arms Rolling Blocks

Remington 17 Remington

Remington 25-06 HB

Remington 17 Chronographed

Ruger M77 22-250 HB

H&R Harrich I shotgun

Ithaca M280 shotgun

J-K Imports

LAD Erbi shotgun

Savage M330 shotgun

Beretta M90

Hutson Handgunner scope

Interarms Mauser Luger

S&W Fiocchi ammunition

Unertl BV 20 scope

John Dewey Tools

long range matches.

Lastly, from Interarms, Ltd., we'll take a look at their newest import, the German Pistole Parabellum—an authentic model of the Luger that is made at the Mauser Works in Oberndorf, West Germany.

While reading this "Testfire Report" you'll soon note that I use a specific technique when field testing shooting products. With rifles, shotguns or handguns I do all of my initial shooting without tuning or altering the firearm in any way. By conducting tests in this manner I discover just about what the average shooter finds, when he shoots the gun, just as it arrives from the factory. This also, frankly, gives me a fairly clear picture of the degree of quality control allocated to a specific firearm by that manufacturer or importer.

Once I'm familiar with its general performance, I'll usually check various component parts far more closely at the work bench. At this point, if not entirely satisfied with its "off-the-shelf" performance, I'll often try a bit of custom tuning. In specific cases, where special tools or a more diversified knowledge of actual gunsmithing is indicated, I never hesitate to call upon the professional services of my long time friend and shooting cohort, John Dewey.

John, justly respected for his gunsmithing, barrel-making, and custom line of loading tools, is equally well known for his precision benchrest shooting. Usually, by putting our heads together over a particular problem, some satisfactory solutions can be reached.

I'll also point out that it is only after several shooting sessions, using factory-loaded rounds, that I get round to the careful cooking-up and evaluating of various handloads, loads which may bring us closer to the ultimate accuracy-potential of the firearm being field tested. The grass-roots testing, however, is done with factory loads, for these are what most shooters/hunters will use.

Bob Zwirz

H&R 17 Caliber Ultra Rifle

Shooting sessions with the new 17-cal. Remington factory round, in a Remington 700 rifle, were barely completed when along came H&R's 317 rifle chambered for the very same case.

Over the past several years I've had ample opportunity to shoot and hunt with two different H&R rifles chambered for the 17/223 wildcat. Both delivered satisfactory accuracy using a 25-gr. HP with 19 grains of 4198. For that reason I welcomed the change to shoot their newest version, chambered for the new factory-loaded Remington 17.

What I can tell you here about the performance of the new H&R combo is limited to my shooting of it without any special tuning—right out of its box. The only item I checked was the trigger pull. Finding it factory-set at a shade under 3 pounds, I decided not to lighten it, at least not for my first shooting.

The only additions to the basic package are the 2-piece Conetrol bases I installed, Conetrol Gunnur rings, and Redfield's newest scope, the "Widefield" variable (4P CCH, 3x-9x).

All shooting was done at 100 yards, from benchrest. Temperature was 61°F. with intermittent 8 to 10 mile wind gusts, striking

H&R's Sako-actioned lightweight sporter, now chambered in 17-Rem. caliber, among others.

at about a 60° angle, down range.

The scope was set at 9 power, light on the target was excellent, and very little mirage was evident. The fact that it was slightly overcast, though bright, helped considerably.

After firing 15 shots to familiarize myself with the 317 I started shooting for real. My first two 5-shot groups printed into 1⅜" and 1½", after which the difficult-to-judge wind gusts calmed down for a spell. Out of eight 5-shot groups fired during this period, the 3 best measured 1", ⅞", and ¾"—exceptionally good considering that nothing was done to the rifle in the way of tuning.

Accuracy of this kind, combined with the 17's hydrostatic stock power inevitably adds up to the clean kills varmint shooters want. In any case, it's good to see such precision shooting from a rifle that is just as it left the factory. Certainly the Sako action used by H&R has always delivered good results, in my experience and, according to the grapevine, the Douglas 17 barrels used on these new rifles were painstakingly made. If this is indeed true Douglas gets a tip of my hat for their fine quality.

The 317, along with a 17-cal. brass 3-section cleaning rod, brush and tip—$249. Presentation Grade, $450.   Bob Zwirz

H&R "Officers Model" Springfield

As part of its 100th anniversary Harrington & Richardson has recreated one of the most highly prized variations of the '73 Springfield rifle, the "Officers Model."

It was just a century ago that Gilbert Harrington, co-founder of Harrington & Richardson, invented the world's first shell-ejecting revolver. Shortly thereafter the United States government began making the nation's first general issue breech-loading rifle, the 45-70 Springfield Model 1873. It was to see service for more than 40 years.

Over these years there were numerous variations in the standard infantry issue rifle and the cavalry's well-loved carbine.

However, the most highly prized version, sought after by world collectors, has been the "Officers Model" of the '73. To this day it remains one of the most handsome rifles ever produced by a military armory. This availability in a bygone age lasted for only a few years, starting in 1875. Less than 500 units were produced.

As now decreed by H&R the replica Springfield will be limited to a total production of 10,000 rifles. Those rifles bearing serial numbers to 1500 will sell for $300, from 1501 to 3000, $275. Rifles with serial numbers 3001 through 10,000 will be $250. H&R recommends the use of standard low-intensity 405-gr. commercial

45-70 ammunition only.

While talking about this truly handsome rifle with Joe Widner, an H&R executive, he pointed out that this centennial commemorative, entirely U.S.-made, is in every way an authentic recreation of the original. Each officers Model will carry the distinctive H&R 100th Anniversary plaque and the same attractive engraving found on the original model. This engraving appears on the breechblock, receiver, hammer, lockplate, barrel band and heel of the buttplate.

No matter how I view the exterior metal work, the treatment of wood surfaces and the over-all appearance of this replica, I

H&R's latest, the 45-70 Springfield Officers Model—a handsome rifle, handsomely executed, and a very close copy indeed of the rare original even to the tasteful engraving, case-hardening colors, folding tang sight and more.

can only report that the entire project of reproducing this elegant rifle has been a success. The hand checkering, as an example, has been carefully executed, with nary a run-over. The famous "trap door" breech, the hammer and trigger assembly, all look so genuine that they appear to have been taken from a "mint" original Springfield "OM." Even the ramrod is authentic, having the same male/female locking device you'd find on the real McCoy.

The 26" barreled rifle weighs about 8 pounds, depending on wood density. The rear sight is a folding Vernier-type mounted on the wrist, with windage and elevation adjustments. The front sight is the standard blade type. With the peep disk set at the bottom of the slide the rifle is sighted-in for 50 yards; when raised to the top of its travel it is adjusted for a range of slightly less than 700 yards. In actual test firings the '73 Springfield proved accurate at ranges of over 500 yards.

Because this H&R "Officers Model" was placed in my hands only hours before this "Testfire" material was due, I was able to shoot a mere 20 rounds of 405-gr. cartridges. During this brief session I twice fired 5 rounds at 100 yards, using the disk in its lowest position. Those two strings averaged 1.75 inches, though one of them put 4 shots into one ragged hole. The glass showed 59°F., with wind gusts coming from behind my bench at about 9 to 11 miles. The last 10 rounds—two 5-shot groups—measured closer to 2 inches. With another hundred rounds through the barrel to break it in, and with that much more familiarity, I'm sure the rifle will do better.

All in all this is a top quality replica, one which can be considered a delight to own, a challenge to shoot.   Bob Zwirz

Zwirz isn't really about to shoot the H&R 45-70 O.M., not with that buttplate inches away from his shoulder. He's just getting used to a folding "tang" peep sight.

Navy Arms Rolling Block Rifles—444 Martin and 45-70

At practically the last possible moment Val Forgett delivered, for inclusion in this Testfire Report, his latest in a long line-up of replica guns—a modern interpretation of the justly famous Remington Rolling Block.

The original old RB Remington rates historically, as the most popular single-shot action of its day—and one of the best. Not only a favorite military arm, it was in great demand by professional hunters, sportsmen and target shooters. The same action was also incorporated into pistols, used by the Army and Navy, as well as by civilian shooters. The RB action, as we know it today, appeared in 1871, an outgrowth of Leonard Geiger's split-breech design of 1863. Joseph Rider was, in the main, responsible for the famed RB's ultimate development, though various changes occured over the years after 1871.

Val sent me two RBs, not one—a rifle and a carbine, plus a note telling me that 4 models in all would be offered—a standard model with full octagonal barrel, in rifle or carbine length, plus a Creedmoor type with a half-round, half-octagonal barrel, rifle or carbine. (A Creedmoor carbine?) All will be offered in 45-70 or 444 Marlin.

The two Navy Arms RBs I've been testing are, to a reasonable degree, authentically reproduced. Modern steels are used, of course, the barrels made by Numrich Arms. These are "hook rifled," wherein each groove is singly cut. The actions are attractively color case-hardened, and the guard, barrel band and buttplates made of solid, highly-polished brass.

A postscript to Val Forgett's note explained that these two test rifles had been deprived of any stock finish. That figured, for the first thing I'd noticed was that the light walnut in the fore-end didn't go at all well with the dark tone of the stock.

Now, having lived with these RBs for several days, I find there's one particular item that irritates me. Why couldn't the original open rear sight have been faithfully copied, too, instead of the Mickey Mouse rear sight that is installed? The original military/hunting sight was quite all right, the Creedmoor-type target sight even better.

The original rolling block breech was as simple, fast-to-operate and trouble-free as anyone could wish—as long as it was kept clean. Extraction power was not a great RB feature. During my own test sessions with these replicas I soon learned that smooth operation came easily. After cocking the hammer you simply thumbroll the breechblock back and there's the open chamber. If you had previously fired a round, this simple procedure also extracted the empty case.

In the original rolling block a fresh round could be inserted without fear of accidental discharge; while the breech was open, the hammer remained automatically locked. The same feature, of course, is found on the Navy Arms offerings.

Rather than judge the accuracy of these replicas via the factory iron sights (especially those sights), I tapped the barrel to take a scope base. A 6× fixed-power Leupold was mounted on the rifle. All shooting was done with Remington or Winchester 405-gr. soft points, both brands grouping about alike—5 shots at 100 yards into 1.75 inches. Handloads might well do better, of course, but not at all bad, I think, for factory cartridges.

(Years ago I owned an 86 Winchester 45-70 that would print 5 factory rounds within a minute of angle. Over the several years I owned the 86 it accounted for several black bear and a moose.)

Apart from the Numrich barrel, the Navy Arms Rolling Blocks are made in Italy, at Brescia, cost $150.   Bob Zwirz

Zwirz fixed a scope to Navy Arms' replica Remington RB for more precise aiming, one with very long eye relief, apparently!

Remington 17 Caliber Rifle Chronographed

A chance came today to see what the 17 Remington would show on the home chronograph. The new Telepacific unit (described at length elsewhere in this issue) was selected for checking the Rem. 17's speed. The instrument had been here for some time previous, but the long, cold winter had prevented our use of it.

Ten shots were fired, the readings taken at 7½ feet via screen spacing of 5 feet. Except for the final shot, none of the others reached or exceeded 4000 fps. The 9 shots averaged 3919 fps, the high reading of these 9 being 3968; the low was 3861, a fair spread. By including the last shot, at 4049 fps, the average for the 10 went to 3932. Allowing even a generous 25 fps to offset the muzzle-to-screen distance would increase the 9-shot average to 3944, the 10-shot figure to 3957, neither of which reaches the claimed 4020. I regard the 4049 shot as non-typical in view of the velocities the other 9 gave.

I talked to Bob Steindler last night, learning that he also had chronographed the 17 Remington. His average for 10 shots, the figures taken on an Avtron unit, were about the same as mine, but a bit lower.

If time allows, another speed test will be made, using another chronograph, but I can't fault the Telepacific in any way. It functioned perfectly, and all 10 shots were put through the same pair of multi-shot screens.   JTA

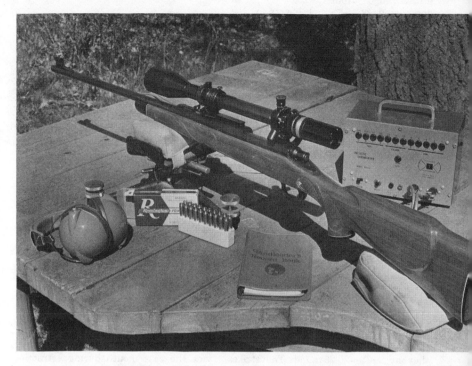

Unertl's new benchrest-varmint scope, the BV20, is compact, lightweight, and mounts over the receiver via an extension front base, giving ¼-inch adjustments for windage and elevation. Range focussing is at the rear, handy and convenient. Rifle is Remington's 17-cal. Model 700 BDL.

17 Remington Rifle and Cartridge

Billed as the "world's fastest commercial cartridge," the new load is indeed a hot little number. (Norma still supplies 220 Swift cartridges, at 4111 fps, so perhaps "US" should be inserted into that claim.) Obviously Remington realized that many shooters/varmint hunters had become seriously interested in 17-cal. wildcats generally. These same people, though, had learned, some of them the hard way, that really reliable 17 rigs—especially barrels —weren't at all that easy to come by.

Various wildcat 17s have been with us for many years, off and on, but P.O. Ackley, some years ago, introduced a couple of 17s: the 17 Bee and the 17 Hornet, that were quite popular, as was the A&M 17 Javelina later on. A&M 17-cal. barrels, by the way, were excellently made, really smooth. Nevertheless, the big problem with the 17s was unsatisfactory barrels, usually.

In late 1967 Winslow Arms offered rifles in 17/223, 17/222 and 17/222 Rem. Mag. calibers. At that time I was sure that the 223 case would find the greatest acceptance as a 17 because of the easy availability of military brass. Soon afterward H&R introduced their Model 317 rifle, cham-

John Dewey's drive-in type necksizer also expels spent primer as case is removed.

bered for the 223, and the 17/223. This is the same Sako-actioned rifle H&R has just chambered to accomodate the 17 Rem. factory load.

The 317 will, however, still be offered in 17/223 for those who would prefer to hand-load, in 222 or 223.

Remington has not only improved the efficiency of the 17 case, but has come up with a barrel far superior to many previously available. The 17 Rem., please note, is not a duplication of previous 17 wildcats. Remington's R&D department necked down the 223 case to 17 caliber without any change in case length, diameter or shoulder angle. However, the shoulder itself was moved back .087" from the mouth. Intensive testing by Remington showed conclusively, they say, that accuracy is decidedly better with the longer neck.

A chlorophen test on several counterbored screw holes in my 17 Rem. barrel show that stainless steel barrels are being used. It also became obvious, after a good deal of shooting with it, that the finishing of the 17 bore left mighty little to be desired. No small accomplishment when running tools through that minuscule hole.

Once a few test rounds were fired from the rifle, as shipped, the iron sights were removed and a 10x Leupold scope installed, using Conetrol's one-piece Custum base and their excellent Gunnur split rings. These last allow fast installation or removal.

Factory trigger pull, set for a crisp 3½ pounds, was later reduced to a safe 1-

pound pull for better performance at the bench. During our initial shooting temperatures ranged around 30° to 40°F., with gusty winds of 15-18 mph harrassing the range. Needless to say, those breezes gave the 25-gr. bullet more lateral dispersion than we cared to see. Even with the wind bugging us, John Dewey and I managed to hold all groups to just over an inch, maximum. We did, however, come away from all but a single shooting session with 5 groups of 5 shots each measuring, as a fair example, .741". No matter how you judge, such groups are satisfactory for a factory varmint rifle/cartridge combo.

A number of others who've been shooting the new 17 duo have told me that many of these rifles, if not all, are making groups a little less than minute-of-angle, using factory loads. Under optimum conditions some of these 17 Remingtons will perform closer to the ½" mark—but I've not been able to find the right weather yet.

Cleaning, which was usually a critical factor in earlier 17s, at times became such a bugaboo, especially in less-than-desirable-barrels, that scrubbing the bore after every 5 shots became a must—unless you craved pressure problems and a noticeable loss of accuracy. Now, according to Remington, their 17s need no more cleaning than other varmint rifle calibers—which, they say, is after 20-25 rounds. That strikes me as a bit contradictory—cleaning after 20-25 shots is fairly frequent, I'd say. Cleaning requires the wire brush treatment, and for long chamber/barrel life a product such as Dewey's "Bore Saver" is a wise investment. Dewey now has, too, a quality rod, sheathed in Du Pont Surlyn, and other 17-cal. cleaning items.

Next, having adjusted the trigger to a 1-pound pull we began thinking about handloads. But first we did a simple task

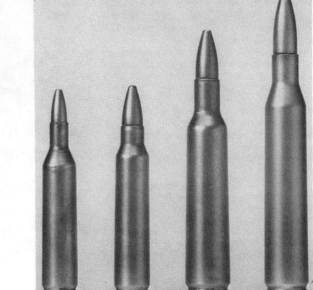

17 REM.   223 REM.   6mm REM.   25-06 REM.

that should interest the reloading fraternity. Remington 700 rifles have a strong, positive ejector, great for hunting and for those who toss empties away, but it flattens the case mouth during extraction. The remedy? Remove the ejector pin and spring, clip off exactly 7 turns of the ejector spring. Once reassembled, no more violently thrown cases.

Remington strongly urges handloaders to use their 7½ primers with the 17 Rem. case, a matter of performance and compatibility. the 17 Rem., they say, was developed and designed for the 7½ primer. Safety, you can be certain, is never a problem with the 700 action. Unfortunately,

none of Remington's 25-gr. Power-Lokt bullets had been received, but by using another bullet of the same weight, and moving up to 22 grains of H-380, our all-too-brief trials resulted in groups that about matched the factory-load performance. I'll also be anxious to try 4198 (probably 19 grains) with the Power-Lokt bullets when they arrive.

The new 17, available only in the M700 BDL grade, at least so far, is $184.95. This combo's low noise level, safe bullet characteristics and satisfactory accuracy should make it a popular choice, especially in built-up areas or thickly-settled rural areas.
                        Bob Zwirz

The 25-06 and 17 Remingtons

Accuracy testing of the 25-06 Model 700 Varmint rifle consisted of firing several 3-shot groups at 100 yards from the bench. The barrel scope block was tilted 5 degrees to the left of center (who says test rifles are specially selected?) so the factory blocks were removed and replaced with a set of action bases for the Remington 20X BR scope. (The original BR scope used Unertl mounts, but the latest models have different mounts—more massive, with different base and adjustment locking screws, housing knobs, and different click adjustment values—and they won't fit every brand of target scope blocks.)

Because time was short, the only factory load checked was the 87-gr. Remington Power-Lokt. Shots were fired every 60 seconds, and groups consistently ran about ½ minute of angle. This particular rifle and scope, then, coupled with factory loads, is an excellent choice for taking larger varmints—and other 25-06 HBs should perform about as well, maybe better! As a check the same scope, and cartridges from the same lot, were used with a regular M700 in 25-06 caliber. Larger groups resulted, ranging from less than one inch up to two inches—but accuracy was still bet-

ter than many factory rifles used for hunting, and with more time to check bedding and do some tailoring of a handload to the rifle, the regular 700 may also shoot less than 1 MOA. RCBS has loading dies, Sierra has two new boat-tail bullets designed specially for the 25-06—a 90-gr. and a 120-gr.—and Hornady has a new 120-gr. that should be ideal for big game.

Some time was spent checking out the Sierra 90-gr. in the 25-06 Varminter. This new bullet, a hollow point boat-tail, is about .903" long, and the point has four notches spaced 90° apart to produce maximum expansion. The once-fired R-P cases were neck sized only, then recapped with RWS primers. Four different powders were selected, all charges weighed. Seating was set to give an over-all length of 3.093". Loads were near maximum, but two of them equalled the accuracy of the factory 87-gr. load, shooting 3-shot groups of ½ MOA or less. These two loads consisted of 39.0 grains of Rx-11 and 45.0 grains of H-57

—a Hodgdon powder using 4320 data. Two other powders, Hodgdon's H-450 (55.0 grains) and H-380 (47.0 grains), gave groups just over one inch. Regardless of whether factory loads or handloads are used, this new M700 varmint rifle is accurate.

Tools used were RCBS dies, Ohaus 304 scale and Lee priming tool.

For lighter varmints the new 17 Remington cartridge is proving to be a real winner. The M700 rifle in this caliber weighs 7¹⁄₁₆ pounds with open sights, but with the rear sight removed and a Remington 20X BR scope installed the weight jumps to 8⅜ pounds. The resulting combo shoots those little 25-gr. HP bullets into ½ MOA or less almost every time. Bullet blow-up is complete—ideal for populated rural areas—and while the crows and ground squirrels were not very cooperative, the hydrostatic shock performance was checked. One-gallon screw-top containers were filled with water to overflowing, then tightly capped.

These cans are 4" deep, front to back. Firing was done at 20 yards with factory loads. Entrance holes were just over 17 caliber, with the metal turned in, but the bullets never reached the rear wall. A few dents did appear in the real wall, but no cracks or penetrations; the containers were split open, almost flattened, and careful examination revealed dust-size particles of lead and copper in the seam edges—blowup was complete and instantaneous.

Handloading the 17 Remington presents no major problems. The Remington bullets are available as separate components, while Hornady has an excellent 25-gr. bullet, as do several independent bullet makers, such as Baker and Williams. RCBS has reloading and forming dies, so factory brass or 223 Remington cases can be used. Forming is simple, requiring 3 dies—form, trim and ream—and the end product cannot be told from original 17 Remington cases.

The only problem is primers, and here's what Remington has to say: "... we recommend strongly that you use *only* Remington No. 7½ primers with the 17 Remington case. This is not an attempt to promote primers of our manufacture ..." We recognize the quality of other, competitive primers. However,...all other primers tested showed them to be incompatible with the specific characteristics of the 17 Remington cartridge... the 17 Remington was designed for compatibility with the Remington No. 7½ primer...other primers tested... are not close enough to...the Remington No. 7½ primer to produce comparably acceptable results."

As the deadline for this edition approached, Remington No. 7½ primers could not be located in time. Therefore, only a little hand-loading was done—with 223 brass reformed in RCBS dies, and with the once-fired 17 Remington brass—and this much only to get an idea of what might be suitable for checking later. To achieve maximum effect with the lightweight (25-gr.) 17-cal. bullet, it is necessary to push the velocity up and still try to retain accuracy. With this in mind powders which had proved suitable in the 17/223 were selected and non-maximum charges weighed out. Considerable work remains, and none of the loads were chronographed, but one which shows promise is 21.0 grains of Reloder 11 (now discontinued, along with Rx 7 and Rx 21) with the 25-gr. Hornady bullet.

The ultra-small bore calibers are usually considered to be subject to extensive fouling problems. Remington has this to say on the subject:

"... Bore fouling has proven to be no more of a problem with the 17 Remington than that experienced with other varmint calibers. For maintenance of maximum accuracy, however, we recommend wire brush cleaning of all varmint calibers at least every 25 rounds."

As has been its tradition, Remington continues to be a progressive firm—constantly working to meet the demands of today's shooters with new and improved products. Few commemoratives, and no black powder arms, but excellent, modern-design firearms.   (LS)

Ruger M77 HB Varmint Rifle—cal. 22-250

Due to extremely cold and oft-times snowy weather virtually all of my testing with Bill Ruger's M77 Varmint was done from the bench at 100 yards. Certainly no self-respecting chuck could be expected to venture out in the weather that hit us in my New England haunts.

My caliber choice for the heavy barrel M77 was the 22-250. The barrel, 24 inches long, comes tapped for a target scope block, as is the front scope base on the receiver. Their other HB rifle, the 25-06, comes similarly equipped, and both are shipped with Ruger's 1" steel tip-off mounts.

For initial sessions with the 22-250 I mounted a Bushnell Scopechief (3x-9x) using the Ruger mounts. After more than two hours familiarizing myself with this combo, and while firing standard factory 22-250 rounds, it became fairly obvious that not a single 5-shot group would measure under 11/16". Temperature was 19°F., wind gusts of around 12 mph, definitely not optimum conditions. However, the groups fired, while not that great for this caliber, were not unexpected from factory ammo.

Changing ammunition brands didn't help appreciably, even though the wind let up during the last hour of shooting. Later, a detailed check-out of inletting showed that this facet of production had received kind care at the Ruger factory. The trigger, a bit on the heavy side, was crisp and free of creep.

I should point out here that groups of 1", or a fraction more, should be satisfactory to most shooters buying a production line rifle and using factory ammo. Unfair though it may have been, my tests with the M77 were based on "known values," experiences with several finely tuned 22-250 rifles. I wanted to find, of course, that magic button which would bring out an accuracy potential I know to be inherent in most guns bearing the Ruger symbol.

The first tuning step was to adjust the trigger to the 1-pound pull I prefer for varmint shooting. Next, I switched to a Redfield M3200 target scope to see how much 20x magnification would help. Now it was time to see what could be done with handloads.

Dewey and I agreed that a good start might well be 36 grains of H-380, a slow-burning powder, and Sierra's 52-gr. BTHP bullet. Even during lulls in the wind, groups never tightened beyond 1½". With our fourth loading, at 39 grains, groups improved. (37 and 38 grains hadn't helped much.) At 40 grains, using a Sierra 53-gr. HP bullet, we got marked improvement. Flyers, which had been far too frequent with the lighter loads, became a rarity.

Regarding our next recipe for the 22-250, please note that had our experiments taken place during summer's heat you can bet we wouldn't have ventured as high as 41/41½ grains of H-380, our ultimate loads. True, they were OK, even on the hottest of days, but I cannot recommend them. However, with 40/H-380, and using the 52-gr. Sierra BTHP bullet, CCI-Mag. primers, Dewey and I fired a satisfactory number of 5-shot groups averaging ⅝". For the record, using that 41½ grains of H-380, plus the same components, we managed groups measuring a nice, soul-satisfying ½" at 100 yards—not bad for a production rifle!

Either way a man can collect a mess of chucks. With the factory loads this specific rifle is fully adequate. With the handloaded rounds—superb.   Bob Zwirz

Ruger's M77 heavy-barrel 22-250, Redfield's 3200 target-varmint scope up, Zwirz now shooting.

Beretta M90 Test

Raymond Caranta, our European editor, had an opportunity recently to fire the new M90 Beretta, cal. 32 ACP—which double-action/single action gun we reported on in this space last year (25th ed., p. 151).

Caranta wrote that the grip felt well in his medium-small hand, the trigger giving 5-6 pounds of pull in single action, with some creep, but nearly double that fired DA. The thumb safety felt a bit stiff. He fired 150 rounds of Fiocchi and FN-Belgian ammo, SA and DA, and here's what he said about it:

" . . . no misfires or jams. This pistol is pleasant to shoot, very accurate for a pocket model. At 25 yards, 4-inch groups could be easily obtained when shooting from a rest, but accuracy potential is greater than that.

"Fired off-hand, 5-shot groups were all in the black of the ISU standard target (8" dia.) at 25 yards.

"The new Beretta is well made, reliable and accurate, its stainless steel barrel a great idea." (R.C.)

Beretta M90 take down: Remove magazine, pull slide rearward. Pull and raise front end of slide lock, in front of receiver, under barrel. Raise slide, let it go forward until free of barrel.

Interarms' Mauser/Luger

For over 10 years the rumor has run rampant that, after more than 30 years off the production line, Georg Luger's all-time classic, the Parabellum, was being readied for a return engagement.

Now it's all come true' I've just finished shooting and field-stripping a new, "mint" 7.65mm Parabellum. According to the factory target (⅝" at 15 meters) included with the pistol and its accessories, it was tested for accuracy on 19 Jan. 1971 at the Mauser Werke in Oberndorf am Neckar, W. Germany.

This pistol, I must point out, is the *true* article. Don't for a second confuse this bonafide Parabellum with any past, look-alike facsimiles, from any source. This model, fully authentic and faithful to Luger's design, has been produced using the original tooling, and it's made of forged and machined steel.

The Parabellum can be considered a fairly difficult and costly pistol to manufacture, so much so that several arm-chair production experts insisted it would prove too expensive to be machined at today's costs. Many, when asked about a possible retail price, said it probably would run around $500. Apparently Interarms, working with the Mauser staff, had different ideas.

The latest Parabellum is the authentic 1929 Swiss Model, one which has the thumb-safety positions reversed from the more common models. The receiver is etched, a distinctive symbol of the American Eagle, while on the toggle action there's the famous Mauser "banner."

This Swiss model, chambered for the 30 Luger cartridge, has doubled safety features—the standard manual thumb-safety plus a grip safety. Many of us thought a 9mm Parabellum would be released first but that's somewhere in the future. Interarms says that not only will the 9mm be offered, but so will some other models of the Parabellum, plus a choice of barrel lengths and other options, including engraved presentation pieces. The price ($265 today), they tell me, will be the same for all basic models, either caliber, and all barrel lengths.

In this necessarily brief report I won't attempt to examine all the features of this will-not-die pistol. Most everyone these days has handled, seen, or read about the "Luger." I can say that my test Parabellum performed perfectly with all the loads I ran through it. Mechanically it matches the reliability of several Lugers I'm familiar with.

I did notice that the original-issue checkered grips on my long-owned, personal pistols were more delicately shaped, the checkering slightly cleaner. Mauser Werke has also made two other little changes. First, with a round in the chamber, the pistol's extractor has always raised to show, clearly marked on its port side, the word *Geladen.* This tells you, visually as well as by feel, that it's ready to be fired. This new Mauser has "Loaded" printed on the extractor. On the thumb-safety, where it had always been previously inscribed *Gesichert,* the new pistol says "Safe."

Maybe the Mauser people felt they were doing a service for the American market, but I liked it the old way—just stubborn, I guess.

Length of the new Parabellum is 10½", height 5¼", width 1⅞", barrel length 6". It weighs 32 ounces empty, and the magazine holds 8 rounds. Bob Zwirz

Hutson Handgunner Pistol Scope

This optical product has been designed and produced by the Hutson Corp. of Arlington, Texas. I asked Neil Hutson, president of this well-known optical firm, to send me two units.

The first sample was installed on a Ruger 44 Magnum Super Blackhawk, a real blockbuster and a good choice when the shooter wants to subject a scope to real punishment. The Handgunner is a true pistol scope, not an adaptation of rifle scope. Exceptionally light and small, it weighs just under 3 ounces and is only 5¼" long.

The Handgunner has a 25" eye relief, and at this time is available in 1x power only. Why only 1x or unit power? Several reasons. Without magnification the scope can be brought on target quickly, with both eyes open. The image won't jump around as it normally does when scopes have any magnification. With the Handgunner's 1x you're able to view the area around the target while, at the same time, you are actually sighting through the scope. Such viewing is possible only when target and surrounding area are in the exact same magnification—or lack of it.

Hunters, particularly, will appreciate this glass in those situations where game tends to fade into the background. With the Handgunner the shooter can spot his

Zwirz checks out the Hutson Handgunner pistol scope on the Dan Wesson revolver.

game clearly, point, aim, and fire in one unbroken motion, never interrupting his view of the quarry.

The second test scope was sent to Dan Wesson Arms so they could decide on the best method of installation. At that time no commercial base was made for the Wesson revolvers, but the answer, as worked out by the Wesson staff, is a real winner. They installed it on the actual ramp which runs along the removable shroud. Thus, if you want to use the Wesson without the scope all you need is a spare shroud. Interchangeability of barrels/shrouds takes less than two minutes, using the simple tool supplied with each Dan Wesson gun. The installation proved rugged and highly practical. At no time, during long sessions

of evaluating various 357 factory cartridges and handloads, did I have any problem with the mounts or the scope itself.

However, in poor light conditions, or where brush or deadfalls provided a cluttered background, I found myself wishing for thicker crosshairs. For target shooting, though, it proved just right.

The Handgunner is priced at $35, the adjustable mounts $14.95, extra base adaptors $9.95. The units I used had 2-minute wide crosshairs. The tube is of rust-free aluminum, objective diameter is ⅞", the field of view about 4 feet at 50 yards.

Neil Hutson told me that a second Handgunner scope, to be ready by late summer of 1971, will have 1.7x magnification, for those who feel the need.   Bob Zwirz

Smith & Wesson-Fiocchi Ammunition

Some time ago S&W acquired the well-known Alcan Company, located in Alton, Ill. As a result we now have a new brand of factory-loaded centerfire ammunition.

The first three offerings, all in 38 Special, were: a 110-gr. Jacketed Hollow-Point, a 158-gr. Round Nose, and a 148-gr. Wadcutter. The Dan Wesson Model 12, with 6" barrel, was used for the major portion of chronographing and target work. Additional shooting was done with a Charter Arms 2" revolver, a custom-worked Colt with a heavy 2" barrel, and a S&W Highway Patrolman with a 4" barrel. No big surprise, even at 25 yards, accuracy was best with the longer barrels. Chronograph and target shooting sessions produced the following data.

The 110-gr. JHP loads (#S38HP1) ultimately gave us an average chronograph figure of 1234 fps, about average for that bullet weight. There are, of course, faster-moving like loads; with Norma's 38 Special "High Speed" I've obtained 1539 fps from the same 6" barreled Wesson. Super Vel's 110-gr. HP chronographs at 1370 fps from the same gun.

At 25 yards, from sandbag rest, 1⅞" groups were average (10 targets, 50 rounds), though some tighter groups were fired with the 110-gr. JHPs and the long barreled Wesson. There are expert handgun shooters who could better my scores, but these groups with the new 110-gr. HPs must be termed satisfactory.

Their 158-gr. RN 38s (#S38RN) chronographed an average of 847 fps; close indeed to the listed velocity figure for Reming-

ton's 158-gr. RN. Accuracy, at least for this shooter, was not nearly as good as the 110-gr. bullets gave. Groups averaged closer to 2⅝", again at the 25-yard range. Conditions weren't good—extreme cold and occasional stiff breezes—so it is quite possible these affected the results to some degree.

Based on my findings, the RN loads can be placed as about "average" for the industry. Further accuracy comparison, if judged against the excellent 148-gr. Federal RNs, could be tough. Particularly since the Federal stuff produces 1" to 1½" groups at 25 yards, while moving at 750 fps.

Shooting with S&W-Fiocchi's 148-gr. Wadcutter (#S38WE), I wasn't surprised to find that, as of this date, I've yet to see one wadcutter perform differently than another. The shooting quality of wadcutters seems to vary noticeably from one company to another, one lot to another. The S&W loads chronographed at 769 fps, very close to Remington's 148-gr. Wadcutter ammo—770 fps. As for accuracy, the best that three shooters could produce were groups just a hair under 2⅞". Averages came closer to 3". Again it could have been partially the result of the extreme cold.

Moving back to the 15-foot range I did manage to fire two targets, using the S&W-F Wadcutters. One went 1⅜" (on centers) for 6 shots; the other (5 shots) 1½". A single flyer hurt this group. Four shots were around 1", but by this time I was too chilled to perform with full effi-

ciency.

While accuracy could be termed average for the RN and the Wadcutters, the 110-gr. JHP loads can be classified as highly accurate. Not a single misfire was encountered during testing—all in all a good combination of components.

Final note—just before this "Testfire" report had to be wrapped up, a second shipment of S&W-F ammunition reached us. Included were the following brand new loads: 357 Magnum, 158-gr. JSP and 125-gr. JHP, 9mm, 100-gr. JSP and 115-gr. JHP.

There was no time for chronographing or target work, but one of these latest loads was used during a fast 3-day hunt for Florida boar. Using the target sighted 6" Wesson Model 12, my hunting companion dropped a 240-pound boar with two fast shots. The first went into the chest cavity; the second, at closer range, through the side of its head.

At my request he had loaded the Wesson with—his personal choice—the 125-gr. JHP 357 loads. From what he told me, plus what I observed, it was clear that he had no problem with accuracy. It was also easy to see that bullet performance was highly satisfactory on this extremely angered animal. He had already slashed a boar dog right through the lower jaw, and had convinced another one to keep his distance.

It is unfortunate that the results of chronographing and target shooting with these new 357s and 9mm rounds can't be included in this report, such pertinent data will soon appear.   Bob Zwirz.

The Erbi Double

These new side-by-side double guns, Spanish made, are offered in 12, 20 and 410. Having shot lots of clay birds and some quail with two of them, I honestly feel that these Erbis, at their price, are nothing short of amazing. At anything over $175 no, but they're only $109.50!

The shotguns used for field testing were a 28″ 20, bored modified and full, and a 12/26″, choked improved cylinder and modified. All of these Erbis, by the way, have two triggers and manual extractors.

The lack of single triggers and ejectors doesn't bother me one bit, for I learned to handle a double-trigger long ago. Shotshell reloaders, of course, consider non-ejectors a blessing.

These Erbies have several pleasing attributes—the automatic tang safety, for example, is well-designed functionally. It is unusually wide, deeply serrated, and has a high-sloping contour for the shooter's thumb.

The guns are cleanly made, allowing fast, problem-free takedown and reassembly. Metal to metal fitting is good, as good as I've noted on other guns, costing some 50% more. Spanish walnut is used, the natural color and texture showing through the finish quite clearly; nowadays that's something for which to be thankful. The finish appears to be an oil-type, to a degree which could be classified as medium luster.

The beavertail fore-ends are sensibly scaled to the particular gauge/barrels of the gun, the general stock style is pleasing, and the 20-line checkering is deep and functional. Case hardening and engraving are also part of this package.

In deference, I suppose, to presumed American tastes, or through ill-considered

Bob Zwirz about to nail a fast flying quail with the Erbi double.

advice, the Spanish makers felt the need to offer pistol grip stocks. The same reasoning, probably, made them use white line spacers (what else?) at the grip and the recoil pad. The pad, certainly, could well have been left off the 20 and 410.

LAD says the Erbi guns will be available in 12, 20 and 410; 26″ barrels in IC & M; 28″ in M&F; 30″ in F&F.

Looking at everything, the Erbi is an attractive package. In fact, at the price being asked—truly remarkable.　　Bob Zwirz

Greener-Martini Trapgun

H&R has another trapgun—a Greener on the Martini action. In 1971 H&R took over distribution of the British Webley line of fine arms, including their several side-by-side shotguns, air rifles and pistols, and the Greener trapgun. Based on the Greener-modified Martini action—the basic action was patented in the U.S. in 1862 by Peabody—the Greener 12 lists at $250 with a 32″ or 34″ full choke barrel chambered for 2¾″ shells. The test gun weighed 8 pounds with the 32″ barrel. Length of pull was 15 inches, and a Monte Carlo comb and Pachmayr trap model pad are standard fixtures.

The pivoting-block Martini action is lever operated. A shell is dropped on the tilted concave top surface of the block and chambered with the thumb, then the block is raised by swinging the lever back and up. After firing the lever is swung down, causing the block to strike the rear edge of the L-shaped extractor, either extracting the empty for final removal by hand or completely ejecting it—depending on the striking force given the block.

The Greener was patterned at 40 yards with Remington "Power Piston" Target loads, and Federal International Target and Flyer loads (3¼/1¼/7½). Five rounds averaged over 78% and 77% respectively, the centers about 6 inches above the aiming point—exactly where this writer likes to see the birds relative to the barrel muzzle. Later, when these loads were used on clays the Trap Gun performed almost like a machine, the whirling disks disappearing in a cloud of black dust. With an idea that this Trap Gun with its long sight radius and tight choke might make an ideal goose gun, it was patterned with Super-X Double X Magnum shells loaded with 2s. Five shots averaged 90.4% in the 30″ circle, with most of the load within a 20″ circle; not bad.　　L. Sterett

Ithaca SKB 280 English

Newest member of the line is the Model 280, dubbed the "English" for sound reasons. Designed in that tradition, the new double is a straight-stocked side-by-side field gun.

(Some of the first SKB guns I had looked at, in 1968, showed too much of the "modern miracle" approach to wood finishing. The wood was so heavily coated with their particular miracle that it was impossible to see the grain. This has been corrected.)

As many shooters know, Ithaca some time back called upon the resources of Japan's SKB gun plant to work with them on an extensive line of shotguns for the American market. This has come to include autoloaders, side-by-side and over-under double guns.

From what I've seen, these smoothbores appear to be good buys for the customer wanting reliability at prices between $190 and $300.

Stock and semi-beavertail fore-end are cleanly hand-checkered (raised, not impressed) at 18 lines to the inch. The finish is still of the high-gloss type, and it's still impervious to all the bugaboos gunmakers warn us about, but it has been put on without screening out the wood. The grain shows clearly, is quite decent in appearance, and the over-all effect is of highly polished wood, not an orange-hued horror.

The 280 is a handsome shotgun, one

developed specifically for the shooter who has long had a love affair with the pleasing lines of old English double guns. The lines, kept basically English, are evidenced by the straight-grip stock, though the rules were relaxed when the semi-beavertail fore-end was selected over the older splinter-type wood. If you haven't shot with a straight-grip gun, I think you have a surprise coming. In a field gun, especially, I find it comfortable to shoot and unaffectedly handsome.

The 280 has a single selective trigger rather than the two triggers a straight-hand stock implies. Whether a shooter likes this or not is a highly personal matter. For those who normally fire their barrels in the standard order, there is nothing all that new with which to become familiar. Where barrel selection must often vary, feeling is that a shooter's finger can find the other trigger faster than it can locate and push a selector button. Still, for everyone sharing my opinion I'm certain there are just as many who'll favor the selector. This is certainly true of Skeet and trap shooters. In any case, Ithaca wisely provided a spacious trigger guard. It makes the wearing of gloves no nuisance at all.

The 280, at $249.95 in 12 or 20 gauge, is offered in a wide selection of chokes and barrel lengths. Ejectors are standard. For this field test I chose the 3" chambered 20, its 28" barrels bored full and modified. I particularly like the Raybar front sight and the center bead. Some may not abide by its conspicuous presence, but I like its help on dirty days afield. No matter how you feel about this little globe of light, this is certain—you can't miss seeing it.

All single trigger Ithaca-SKB doubles have inertia (recoil) trigger mechanisms. These automatically cock the trigger for the second shot *following* the firing of the first barrel. The gun will simply not function when dry firing, though sometimes banging the butt against the hand may simulate recoil.

The barrels, chrome-lined and roto-forged, are nicely finished. By examining them under strong light, helped by a good loupe, it can be seen where they enter the mono-block breech. Who cares? The mono-block method of joining barrels and breech sections is a thoroughly reliable one, long since proved in practice. Some of the world's costliest shotguns are so made. Chrome-lined barrels? A boon, possibly, to those not overly diligent about cleaning after shooting or for those who frequent the salt water scene. Chrome-plating is also found on several of the 280's working parts, including ejector locks.

Patterning the 280 at 40 yards was hurriedly done (deadlines again), but the re-sults were quite satisfactory with typical bird loads—6s, 7½s and 8s. The full choke barrel averaged 71-72% with the smaller shot in the 30" circle. That's tight for a 20. The modified barrel threw 54% at the same range, a trifle loose.

The fact is, of course, that widely-varying percentages could have been obtained with this gun, as with most others, by shooting several brands—and various shot sizes. More important to me, though, was that the patterns showed themselves to be all that was needed to powder an appreciable number of clay birds. During this target shooting the 280 demonstrated good balance, fast pointing.

Stock specs for the 280 are: 1½"×2⅝"×14". My 20 went 6½ pounds, while the 12-gauge 280 weighs about 7⅛. I wish they'd stuck to a nice conservative scroll or foliated engraving on the receiver, but thereon is, I am led to believe, quail in flight. I particularly like the 280's fore-end release, a push-button type, and most convenient. I'm also pleased to see an automatic tang safety. A worthwile feature in my book, though many disagree.

The 12-bore 280 comes with 26" or 28" barrels (2¾" chambers) bored F and M or M and IC. The 3" 20-gauge barrels (25" or 28") may be had with F and M or M and IC chokes.

Bob Zwirz

H&R's Harrich No. 1 Shotgun

For the past three years H&R has been working out the final details for a competition grade trap gun with world-famous Austrian gunmaker Franz Sodia. It is a lot of shotgun, as indeed it should be. For two reasons. The men of Ferlach are fine gunmakers, and the price of this gun is mighty steep.

The introduction of several new, top-quality shooting products by H&R is part of its 100th anniversary year being celebrated during 1971. Their replica of the Officers model Springfield rifle and a commemorative pistol set are just part of their stepped up plans for 1971-72.

Regarding the Harrich No.1, H&R and Sodia people have not only talked among themselves, but have been wise enough to consult with several of our nation's outstanding trapshooters. The result of these combined efforts? A trapgun that is certainly to be rated one of the finest quality single-barrel "competition guns" ever offered to American shooters. It is in every sense a handcrafted gun, from its massive full sidelock action to its barrel, with equally heavy walls and chamber. The latter feature minimizes heat expansion effects, provides better balance and pointing qualities.

The locking system of the Harrich is the long-proven Anson & Deely type, with Kersten top bolting and double under-locking lugs. Its barrel is of Bohler Rosant steel, precision machined. A high-line, ventilated rib with full length, two dimensional taper helps overcome sighting plane distortion to a degree that H&R/Sodia feels has never before been attained.

The buttstock and fore-end of high grade European walnut, obviously chosen for its straightness of grain, insures the strength and dependability of the gun's wood-to-metal fitting. The standard stock design shows a conservative Monte Carlo comb, with a finely checkered, modified pistol grip. The front handle is a long, man-size beavertail, checkered over 80% of its surface.

The Harrich No. 1 exhibits tastefully executed hand engraving; on the left sidelock plate there's a fine-line field scene of a hunting dog and flying pheasants. On the right side the well-balanced engraving shows ducks in flight.

The Harrich, in 12 gauge only, of course, is chambered for 2¾" shells, and is available in full choke only. The stock, carrying a top grade recoil pad, has a drop at comb 1¼" by 1¼", the heel drop 2". The pull is 14¾". A 32" or 34" barrel is optional. Our test gun was a shade over 8¼ pounds. Special stock dimensions can be ordered at extra cost, and for those with a flinching problem a selective release-pull trigger can and does help.

As a trapshooter myself, I was anxious to shoot a few rounds with a smooth-moving squad. I had this opportunity when I brought the Harrich down to Florida's famous Remuda Ranch, where I hoped our test gun would give me a little edge over the local competition—of which there is plenty. Two guns I'd previously been shooting at trap, an Ithaca 4E Grade and, to a far lesser extent, their MX-8 (Perazzi), have allowed me to shoot about as well as I ever shall. Nonetheless, though the Harrich was new to me, scores averaged about the same as I get with my old time favorite, the Ithaca 4E.

Several other trapshooters shot the Harrich while I was at Remuda, practically all of them agreeing that it is to be rated among the top trapguns available to serious shooters. It has the proper weight, balance and feel to fulfill the most rigid requirements of both 16-yard and handicap shooting.

Over-all appearance, functioning and quality show it to be a real thoroughbred. The basic price is $1500.
Bob Zwirz

J-K Imports

Many shotgun importers carry models that fall pretty much within a certain price range—usually in the $200-$300 vicinity. Not J-K Imports. Depending on your needs (and pocketbook) you can get a "Field Grade" over-under 12 with chrome-lined barrels, case-hardened or chromed receiver, ventilated rib, coil mainsprings, double triggers, manual ejectors and a hand checkered French walnut stock in your choice of style and dimensions for $177. Or, an elaborately de luxe "S.105 Gran Prix EE LL" double with genuine sidelocks for $1500. If your choice falls somewhere in between, you can have the H&H type sidelock "Montreal" double in 12 or 20 gauge with triple Purdey lockup, fully hand-engraved receiver, French walnut stock, chrome-lined barrels, etc., made up to your individual requirements. These start at $343 with a host of such extras as your initials in gold for $20. Double triggers and manual extractors are standard, with single trigger and ejectors being extra. (This model outsells the less expensive boxlock models by three to one.)

A solid boxlock double "Saba" is available at $179 in 410, 28, 20, 20 Magnum, 16, 12 and 12 Magnum gauges, with Purdey-type lockup, chrome-lined barrels, and choice of silver, blued or case-hardened receiver with hand engraving. The customer has a choice of stock styles—pistol grip or straight—barrel lengths, and chokes without extra cost. The "Sirio," a fully hand-engraved 12 or 20 boxlock, is built to the customer's specifications, starting at $210.

The "Olympic Trap E L" is the firm's 12 gauge special O-U trap model. Built to the customer's specs, it starts at $475, and has a double underlug action, gold-plated trigger, chrome-lined barrels with wide vent top rib and a vent rib between the barrels, choice French walnut stock with hand checkering, semi-beavertail fore-end, and recoil pad. The "Olympic" gun sells for $265 in 12, 16 and 20 gauges.

The "Condor" is a boxlock O-U with dummy sideplates and fully engraved receiver, made in all popular gauges. Two triggers and manual extractors are standard. Lockup is by double side lugs and Greener crossbolt. Choice of stock styles, dimensions, barrel lengths, chokes, are all available, and for only $265. Without the dummy sideplates the same basic shotgun, called the "Airone," is $224.95.

For the shooter wanting something a little different, the "A.S.L. 206" at $347 may be the answer. Available only in 12 and 20 gauges, standard or magnum chamberings, this O-U has "double multi-triggers." (The front trigger fires the lower barrel first, then the upper, while pulling the rear trigger first fires the upper barrel, then the lower.) Ejectors are standard. Locking is via twin side lugs, two under lugs, and a Greener-type crossbolt. Options are: pistol grip or straight-hand stock, standard or beavertail fore-end, made to order, plus choice of barrel lengths and choke combinations. Chrome-lined barrels, fully hand-engraved receiver, and a handsome hand-checkered French walnut stock are standard. An interchangeable SST is only $30 extra.

J-K shotguns are made in Italy by Mario Beschi. Estimated delivery time on the custom-built models is 90 to 120 days. The customer has a choice of dull oil or glossy finish, styles, and dimensions, at no extra cost. (For $20 extra a special selected chunk of walnut will be used.) The amount of engraving varies with the price of the individual model. Stock through-bolts on all over-under models are standard. Manual safeties are standard on most models, but automatic safeties are available on request—usually at no extra cost. Extra sets of barrels are available for most models, but they must be ordered with the original shotgun and the price depends on the model.

According to Ken Madden of J-K, there seems to be a trend toward double triggers

J-K Imports "A.S.L. 206" over-under (top) has fully engraved sideplates, "double multi-triggers," very comfortable fore-end. ● J-K's "Condor" over-under (center), offered in 12, 16, 20, 20 Magnum, 28 and 410, has fully engraved frame, weighs 5¼ to 7¼ pounds. ● J-K's "Montreal," a true sidelock double, is fully engraved, comes in 12 or 20 only, has triple Purdey locking. $343 up.

and plain extractors. Nearly 70% of their custom-ordered shotguns last year were so-made. About a third of these orders included extra sets of barrels, and a high proportion were for 28s and 410s.

The "S-100," a single barrel folding gun is available in all gauges at $51 and J-K also carries an excellent line of leather goods for shotgunners. There's a 25-round shell belt, "Leg-O-Mutton" cases for barrels up to 32 inches. Cases range from $19.95 for a canvas/leather model, up to $34.95 for a tanned goatskin version.

An "A.S.L. 206" 12 gauge was checked out. It weighed 7½ pounds, measured 45⅞" over-all, the barrels 28⁷⁄₁₆". Stock dimensions are: 14⅝" (to front trigger) by 1⅝" by 2¼". This shotgun had those "double multi-triggers" described earlier.

The false sideplates of the "A.S.L. 206" give it the appearance of a sidelock. These sideplates add some strength to the stock, and offer an area for the elaborate engraving that puts this shotgun several steps above plain models. The engraving, consisting of floral scrolls with stippled background over the entire receiver and sideplate area, is good. The receiver and sideplates are satin-silver, the rest of the metal a deep blue-black; the excellent metal finish shows no file or machine marks on external parts. The wood is light and dark streaked French walnut, the glossy finish very smooth, no scratch marks evident. The grip carries a black plastic cap, and a ⁷⁄₁₆" ventilated brown recoil pad is fitted. The fore-end, flat on the bottom with only a slight curve, is wider below for a comfortable semi-beavertail. It is narrow at the top to provide room for the thumb and fingers. Checkering is 20 line with a narrow border; the quality is good but shallow, and there are a few run-outs. However, the finish was applied over the checkering, the result more decorative than functional.

Vent rib is .310" wide and matted. The manual safety is matted, but so finely that it is almost smooth. Guard, top lever, fore-end iron, even the fore-part of the safety, are simply engraved, as are all the screw heads—the upper tang screw even has an engraved guard screw, a feature not often seen on shotguns.

The 206 was patterned with two different loads in its full and improved modified barrels. Using Federal Champion loads (3/1⅛/7½), the full choke barrel averaged 69.5% for 5 shots in the 30" circle at 40 yards, while the IM barrel averaged 67.0%. Using Winchester's new Upland loads (3/1/6), the full choke barrel averaged 61.3%. Then an assortment of shotshell loads in various shot sizes were used during several sessions. Two shots were fired at each bird, mainly to test the "double multi-triggers." Regardless of which barrel was fired first, a second pull on the same trigger fired the other barrel; the triggers were also used as standard double triggers, and no difficulty was experienced at any time. Special attention was also paid to the selective ejectors; with one shot fired, opening the 206 would eject the fired case, leaving the loaded shell drawn out about ⅜". Fit of the 206 was excellent, and any Blue Rock appearing above the muzzle could easily be broken; part of this success no doubt resulted from the choking, slightly more open than some current shotguns.

Savage 330 Over-Under

Valmet of Finland, along with the Savage people, may take a bow over the timely introduction of this rugged and somewhat unusual over-under shotgun. What's the big news? Just this—the Model 330 12-gauge gun may be bought, optionally, with a quickly interchangeable 20-gauge, 28" barrel set, choked modified and full. The same fore-end fits both barrel sets, and changing tubes takes only a couple of moments. (An earlier Valmet 330, sans the fast-switch barrel feature, was introduced in July of 1969.)

The new 330 can be bought as a set, along with a good looking soft black gun case that has an attached pocket for the extra barrels, or he can wait until the mood strikes him, then order the 20-gauge barrels separately. In this instance he must return the complete shotgun to the Savage plant in Westfield, Mass.

I don't claim to be a member of the one-shotgun fraternity—I can't. I'm pretty much duty-bound to test various shooting tools afield, practically throughout the entire year. This includes hunting forays as well as frequent sessions on clay birds. Even when not on field assignments I am heir to such a gaggle of shotguns that all loyalties to any specific gun tend to become blurred. I know exactly what the experts say about sticking with one well-fitted smoothbore, but try as I may the wild desire to savor each one afield is at times uncontrollable.

But—if I were looking for a one-shotgun concept at a manageable price, I'd take a long look at the Savage/Valmet 330. Most every hunter has, at one time or another, felt that he might enjoy his sport more fully with a gauge other than the one he was then carrying. Certainly we've all wished, on occasion, that we had different chokes ready to hand.

The basic 12-gauge 330 comes in three barrel lengths; 26", 28" or 30", one or another of them a good choice for upland game, waterfowl and about all of the furred varieties taken with the smoothbore. The 12-gauge 26" tubes (which I requested) are bored improved-cylinder and modified. The 28" and 30" pair are choked modified and full, the 30s for those who

crave the longer tubes. Stock dimensions, about average, should please and fit most shooters—14" pull, 1½" drop at comb, 2½" at heel. Removal of the barrels from the 330 receiver is quite unusual, perhaps even unique. With the gun empty (natch), pull the trigger twice. Now move the top lever right, to open position, but do *not* break the gun. At this point raise the barrels straight up and out!

You will find that holding the trigger back keeps the stirrup trunnion from swinging when you go about replacing the barrels. You'll soon get the "feel" of this operation if you try it first with the trigger released, then without pulling the trigger.

The 330's mechanically operated single trigger doesn't require the effect of recoil action. Thus Savage's "Four-Tenner" tubes can be used, when the lighter gauge fills some particular need, or if you want to have a go at Skeet with the 410.

The barrel selector is located on the trigger assembly. This may cause some fumbling for a short time, but it will become familiar. The lock-up system of the 330, also unusual, is something like the system used on the Czech BRNO over-under doubles. Rails on the monoblock breech are engaged by a locking shield forward of the top snap lever, which snaps forward as the gun is closed. This safety shield overlaps the breech for added strength. The 330 has a top tang safety in the conventional spot.

The Savage/Valmet 330 has simple extractors, no ejectors; these last would cost substantially more. Extraction of hand-loaded and factory hulls was positive, offering no problems. In fact, it is assured by means of a simple cam action as the gun is opened.

The wood on our test gun is oil finished European walnut and, for that custom look, comes through with traditional side panels, as well as fleur-de-lis checkering at the pistol grip and fore-end. Workmanship, in and out, is well-above average, as is the bluing and the decorative design worked into the frame.

This is, I feel, one of the better-engineered guns to come along. There is something "natural" about shooting with it, it handles and balances nicely. Bob Zwirz

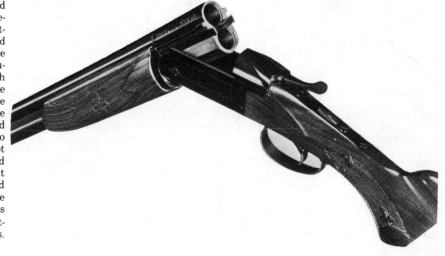

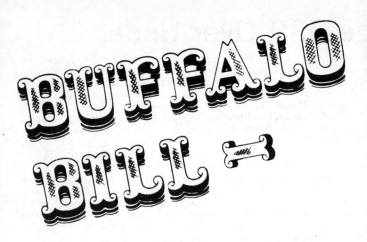

BUFFALO BILL —

Good Man With A Gun

A close look at the many guns,
the colorful exploits of William Cody,
his friends and associates.

by JAMES E. SERVEN

IN CODY, WYOMING, there is now one of the great centers of western art in America. Named for the famous scout and showman, William Frederick Cody, the town of Cody, a short distance east of Yellowstone Park, is fast becoming a shrine for thousands interested in the American West as portrayed by Frederic Remington, Charles Russell, Charles Schreyvogel and Edward Borein, along with other talented artists and writers. Here the Whitney Gallery of Western Art and the Buffalo Bill Historical Center, under the capable direction of Dr. Harold McCracken, contain gems of western art and pioneer history which amaze and delight the visitor.

Approximately a half-century after Colonel Cody's death in 1917, the Winchester Company has placed on the market a "Buffalo Bill" commemorative rifle and carbine built on their traditional 94 action in 30-30 caliber. The first 300 rifles have been cutomized as special presentation models, put up in a velvet-lined solid mahogany case, and donated to the Buffalo Bill Memorial Association at Cody for fund-raising purposes. Similar "Buffalo Bill" commemorative guns without the presentation features and numbered

subsequent to 300 may be purchased through arms dealers. This gesture is well warranted, for during Colonel Cody's showman days and for a short period during his scouting activities, Winchesters were his favored rifles.

The resurgence of interest in Buffalo Bill Cody, sparked by growing recognition of the town of Cody as a center for western art, brings with it an increased curiosity about this Iowa farm boy, transplanted to Kansas, who became the male head of a family at eleven, a Pony Express rider three or four years later, proceeded into an adventurous and heroic life on the frontier, and finally became one of the greatest showmen ever to excite audiences around the world.

My interest in "Buffalo Bill" was aroused when, as a very young boy, I witnessed his Wild West Show in the old Madison Square Garden, New York City. I recall Colonel Cody vividly as he made an impressive entrance into the arena on his famous white horse. Years later, in 1931, I visited Colonel Cody's grave on Lookout Mountain west of Denver, and later that year interviewed Cody's niece, who operated the Irma Hotel in the town of Cody. This hotel was then richly endowed with

paintings and other interesting objects associated with the great scout and showman.

When I recently decided to do serious research on William Cody, I found my library contained eight books devoted exclusively to his exploits, and as many others which contained interesting Cody references. These books appeared to be a rather extensive source of information, but much of the material they contained proved questionable.

Published earlier than these books were the Beadle & Adams paperback "dime novels." Prolific writers in this medium were Col. Prentiss Ingraham and Ned Buntline. If historical accuracy is found in these thrillers it is wholly accidental. To a lesser degree, many of the hard-bound Cody books contain inaccuracies, excursions into fantasy and contradictions. One minor instance is a picture of young Cody with a Model 1873 Winchester rifle; the caption under the picture reads "Taken

Above—Cody the buffalo hunter leaning on the muzzle of his famous 50-70 Springfield rifle "Lucretia Borgia."

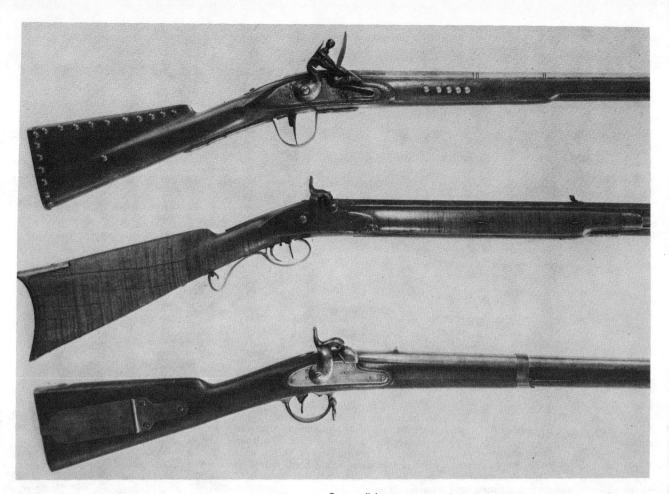

Guns well known to young Cody during his early days in Kansas were the flintlock Indian trade gun (top); the Hawken caplock rifle made in St. Louis (center), and the U.S. Model 1841 "Mississippi Yager" (bottom), said to have been the kind of rifle Cody used to kill his first Indian.

Appearing in an early program of the Wild West Show, this drawing from a dime novel pictured the death of Yellow Hand and Cody's "First scalp for Custer."

On the 17th of July.

1869 at Fort McPherson." This was four years before the Model 1873 rifle was produced! More critical deviation from fact found its source in the fertile mind of Major John M. Burke, sometimes known as Arizona John, who was probably the greatest all-round press agent of his time. Much of the Cody legend of endless heroics was built through the deft manipulations and persuasive charms of Arizona John Burke. The legend was promoted in many ways, not the least being the Prentiss and Buntline dime novels, ghost-written books by Cody or his family, and other publications which pictured Cody as not only the greatest hero who ever lifted an Indian scalp, but a gentle, peaceful soul who loved children and womanhood. This personable young plainsman was the fertile seed which his exploiters nursed into a great flowering of national prominence. The part-truth and part-fiction which has surrounded Bill Cody's role is aptly called "Buffalobilia."

Richard J. Walsh, author of the very creditable book *The Making of Buffalo Bill*, undertook one of the most exhaustive and accurate studies of old records, newspapers, government files, family papers, etc. Walsh sifted much of the chaff from the wheat but found meager provable evidence of young Cody's life until he was 18. However, it is known that William Frederick Cody was born on February 26, 1846.

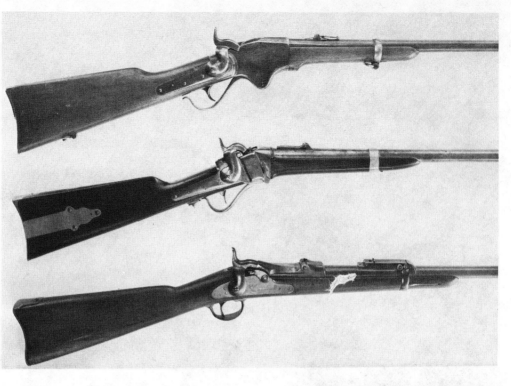

By the 1870s horsemen on the prairies had established as favorites the Spencer carbine (top), the Sharps (center) and the "trap-door" Springfield (bottom).

His father, Isaac Cody, was killed in 1857, leaving the Cody family in difficult circumstances.

Seeking to improve the family fortunes, the 11 year old boy obtained employment as a messenger through the kindly Alexander Majors of the great freighting firm of Russell, Majors & Waddell, who later also operated the Pony Express.

During this youthful period it is claimed that young Bill killed his first Indian, having chanced to see the warrior stalking other members of the party with whom he was traveling. It is interesting to gun-minded readers that Cody stated in later years that he used on this and other occasions a "Mississippi Yager." This famous Model 1841 military rifle in 54 caliber was sometimes furnished by the government to emigrants and frontiersmen. Sixty rifles of this model were supplied from Camp Floyd in July of 1860 to arm station attendants along the route of the Pony Express.

The next important event in the life of young Cody was his elevation from messenger to Pony Express rider. Life on the frontier had developed and toughened him. Although the youngest of the Pony Express riders, he made an emergency ride of 320 miles in a little under 22 hours, establishing a record for the longest Pony Express ride without a formal rest period. He was then in his fifteenth year.

In 1864, when he was 18, Cody joined the Union Army as a teamster. Possibly the most important thing that happened to him during this military service was his meeting with Louisa Frederici in St. Louis. They were married March 6, 1866, a week after Cody's twentieth birthday.

Several business ventures followed his discharge from the army proved unsuccessful, and Bill then turned to a pursuit he knew best. The years on the frontier had made him familiar with the prairie as few knew it, and he had developed into one

of the best marksmen in the West. These qualifications made him an ideal choice as a hunter for the Kansas Pacific Railroad then building toward Denver. They needed meat, lots of meat. Great herds of buffalo were near at hand; Cody was the man to harvest them.

Bill Cody went to work for the Kansas Pacific in 1867, and within 17 months downed over 4000 buffalo. Besides Cody the chief actors in this drama were his great buffalo-running horse Brigham and the 50-70 breech-loading Springfield rifle he called "Lucretia Borgia."

Earlier in Cody's career he had relied on the Mississippi Yager caplock rifle mentioned earlier, a caplock Colt 44 Dragoon and 36 Navy revolvers. No doubt he had also used the Sharps carbine, a popular arm with Pony Express riders, and later the Spencer repeater.

After the War between the States, the federal government had converted their Springfield rifled caplock muskets by means of the Allin trapdoor or hinged-breech system into 50-caliber breechloaders, sometimes called "needle-guns" because of their long firing pins. These used the 50-70-450 metallic cartridges—70 grains of black powder and a 450-gr. lead bullet. Apparently Cody shot up quite a few cases of this ammunition. One of the workmen on the railroad is said to have composed this jingle:

"Buffalo Bill, Buffalo Bill,
Never missed and never will;
Always aims and shoots to kill,
And the company pays his buffalo bill."

Cody's skill in providing buffalo meat for the big work force of the railroad gained him some fame. This was enhanced by a

Buffalo Bill Cody in the 1880s shown with a rolling block Remington rifle and his pair of ivory handled single action Colts.

well-publicized buffalo-killing match with Billy Comstock for a purse of $500. The shoot was staged 20 miles east of Sheridan, Kansas, and the final score showed Cody with 69 killed against 49 for Comstock. Cody used the same "Lucretia Borgia" Springfield rifle while Comstock used a 44 Henry repeating rifle.

When construction on the Kansas Pacific was suspended Cody, now having fairly won the sobriquet "Buffalo Bill," went to Fort Larned where he worked for the quartermaster. Soon afterward, he made a spectacular ride through hostile Indian country to bring a message to Gen. Phil Sheridan, starting a chain of events that elevated him to Chief of Scouts for the Fifth Cavalry. Although he well deserved that title, his press agents in *True Tales of the Plains*, published in 1908, described him as a "Frontiersman and late Chief of Scouts, U.S. Army," a title he had not possessed.

Considerable literary effort was expended to immortalize Bill Cody's scouting service with the Fifth Cavalry. His sister, Helen Cody Wetmore, gave her name as author of a book titled *Last of the Great Scouts*, published in 1899. Zane Grey was induced to add his name to that of Mrs. Wetmore and write a short chapter for a reissue of this book in 1918.

Typical of Buffalo Bill fiction, this story had Cody dashing into a band of Indians "his revolvers ringing out death knells at every shot."

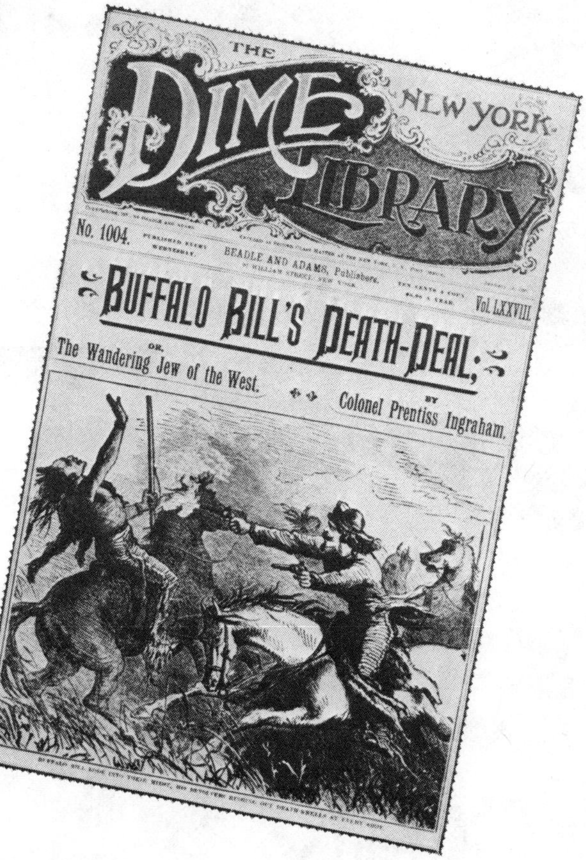

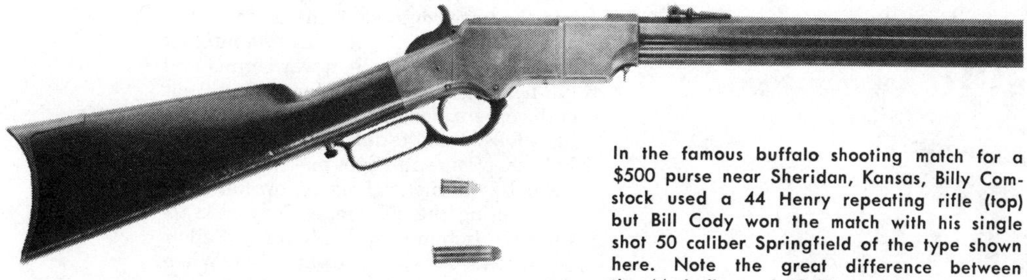

In the famous buffalo shooting match for a $500 purse near Sheridan, Kansas, Billy Comstock used a 44 Henry repeating rifle (top) but Bill Cody won the match with his single shot 50 caliber Springfield of the type shown here. Note the great difference between the 44 rimfire and 50-70 centerfire cartridges.

The undeniable good qualities of this young scout for the Fifth Cavalry were his great endurance, excellent horsemanship, keen knowledge of the prairie terrain, an understanding of Indian character, excellent marksmanship, and a fearless disregard for danger. He served the Army well, if not spectacularly, until his big moment of glory came on July 17, 1876.

Before describing the events of that day, it should be mentioned that Buffalo Bill Cody, as a civilian scout, served the Army only at intervals. He found enough off-duty time to serve as a hunting guide for such prominent men as James Gordon Bennet of the *New York Herald*, who described Cody as "the beau ideal of the plains." In 1872 he was a guide in the famous buffalo hunting party of the Grand Duke Alexis, Gen. George Custer and Gen. Phil Sheridan. In that same year he had been induced by Ned Buntline to appear with Texas Jack Omohundro and Buntline in a corny melodrama called "Scouts of the Prairie." On hearing that Buntline had penned this play in four hours, critics wondered why it had taken so long! Ned Buntline was a notorious but persuasive rascal with a flair for the sensational.

At this period in his life Cody had the good fortune to form a friendship with Major John M. Burke, a friendship that was to endure with mutual respect and profit for 44 years.

Bill Cody's final and most sensational exploit on the frontier followed by few years his return to Kansas after his disappointing debut as an actor with Buntline. In 1876 he rejoined his old army friends as a scout, again with the Fifth Cavalry. He was, at 30 years of age, in the prime of life. Which brings us to July 17, 1876.

The Fifth Cavalry, stationed in Arizona after 1871 to fight Apaches, had been ordered back north to give their support in the 1876 war with the Sioux. The tragic news reached them that about 265 men of

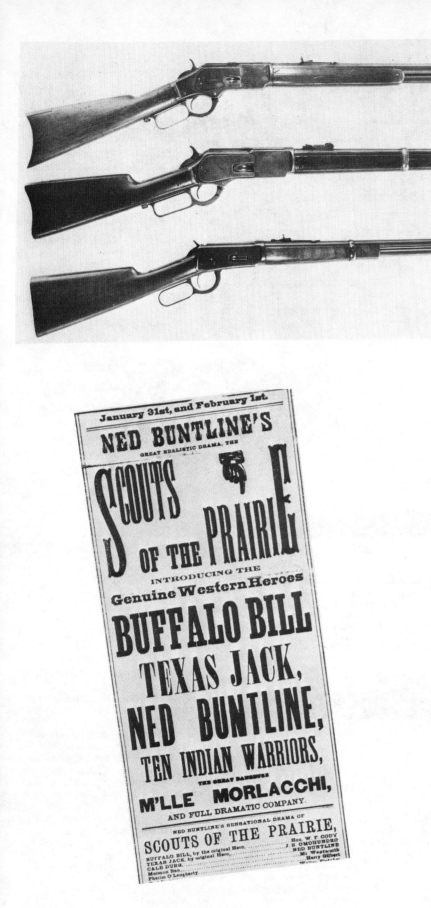

After 1873 Winchester rifles became almost constant companions of Buffalo Bill Cody, not only for hunting but to an even greater extent for the exhibition shooting in his Wild West Show. Pictured here are the Model 1873 (top); the Model 1876 (center); and a typical carbine made on the 1894 action.

Ned Buntline persuaded Cody to play a part in this blood and thunder drama, which opened at Chicago in December, 1872.

the Seventh Cavalry under Custer had been killed, scalped and mutilated on June 25 on the Little Big Horn. Intelligence also reached Colonel Merritt of the Fifth, to whom Cody was assigned as a scout, that 800 Cheyennes had left the Red Cloud Agency intent on joining the Sioux and other Cheyennes under Sitting Bull. Immediately Colonel Merritt selected 500 troops and set out on a forced march for War Bonnet Creek, the most advantageous place to intercept the "hostiles."

At daybreak on July 17, Cody caught sight of the approaching Cheyennes. He hurried back to Colonel Merritt, whose cavalry was well hidden behind a butte. Three miles to the south the supporting army wagon train, plus many soldiers, was approaching. From a rise, behind which Cody and 15 cavalrymen hurried to observe the Indians approach, it became apparent that the wagon train could not see the Indians but the Indians could see them. As Cody and his companions watched, two dispatch riders left the wagons and galloped forward to join Colonel Merritt's mounted force. Seeing this, a small party of Cheyenne braves swept into the valley to attack the two riders.

Without hesitation, Cody and his 15 companions rode down to the rescue. Surprised, the Indians drew up their horses and the two groups confronted each other at a safe distance. A young Cheyenne chief named Yellow Hand, in a war bonnet and full fighting regalia, rode forward in front of the others. Seeing Cody's flowing blonde hair, he shouted tauntingly, "I know you, Pahaska. Come and fight me!" (Pahaska or Pa-ho-has-ka meant long yellow hair.)

Accepting the challenge, Cody rode toward the Indian at full gallop and Yellow Hand headed his horse toward Cody. When they were about 30 yards apart Cody, accustomed to shooting a buffalo from a galloping horse, raised his rifle and fired. The ball thudded into Yellow Hand's horse, sending the horse and rider to ground. At the same time Cody's horse stumbled over a gopher hole, throwing Cody from the saddle. Both combatants quickly regained their feet. A ball from Yellow Hand's rifle whizzed past Cody's head, but Cody's second shot caught Yellow Hand squarely in the chest, knocking him down. Rapidly closing the distance between them, Cody drew his bowie knife and plunged it into his rival. Quickly he jerked off the war bonnet and took the topknot scalp. Shaking it in the air, he shouted: *The first scalp for Custer!*

The record remains unclear as to the exact rifle Cody used in this famous duel. When Colonel Cody was dying he gave his last interview to a newspaper friend, Chauncey Thomas. In answer to Thomas' question as to what rifle the old frontiersman liked best Cody, his answer no doubt influenced by nostalgic memories, replied: "Lucretia Borgia . . . I liked it better than

the Sharps, and with it I killed 4250 buffalo besides deer and antelope for the Kansas Pacific builders." Asked if he always used the same gun Cody said, "Practically so. The barrel of Lucretia Borgia is now on elk horns at the ranch, with the knife with which I killed Yellow Hand. I don't know where the stock is." Lucretia Borgia was, of course, the same 50-70 Springfield rifle so closely associated with many of Cody's exploits in the late 1860s and early 1870s.

Another rifle that might have been used in this duel was a Winchester. Cody sent a letter to the Winchester Company praising their 1873 model, a letter that appeared in the 1875 Winchester catalog. Cody mentioned, however, that it had taken 11 shots from this gun to down a bear. One shot from a gun of this caliber (44-40) would have had to have been precisely placed to drop Yellow Hand's horse.

In the military encounter that followed Cody's duel with Yellow Hand, the Cheyennes were driven back to the reservation and quickly quieted. However, Sergeants Richardson and Blaut, along with Capt. Charles King, had witnessed Cody's bravery. Realizing the psychological influence it had had in turning the Red Cloud Cheyennes from their hostile adventure, they were far from quiet in praising their Chief Scout's prowess. The story quickly spread over the wires to the East and was featured in the *New York Herald*.

This dramatic example of personal bravery was a fitting end to Bill Cody's fighting days on the prairies. The entertainment world, with its glitter and promise of easier living beckoned—and Arizona John Burke was at hand to guide Buffalo Bill Cody into a hero's role. Burke, of course, had to have suitable material to mould and Cody had the basic qualities. Quick to learn the amenities, courtly in manner, handsome in appearance and of admirable physique, Cody looked and acted the part he was to play for the next 40 years.

At this point Buffalo Bill Cody was given the more dignified title of Colonel William Cody. Inasmuch as Cody received a colonel's pay as Chief of Scouts for the Fifth Cavalry, his press agent felt the use of Colonel reasonable. Twenty years later the Nebraska National Guard voted Cody a commission as an "Honorary Colonel," giving Cody more justification for the use of the title.

Only one more call to military duty came to Cody after he had embarked on his career with the "Wild West Show and Congress of Rough Riders of the World." Indicative of the high regard the government placed on the old Scout's influence with the

The only firearm authorized by the Buffalo Bill Memorial Association, the new Winchester Buffalo Bill Commemorative lever action repeater will provide a royalty to the association for each unit sold. Available in both rifle and carbine styles, the two models are reminiscent of the show guns of Buffalo Bill's era.

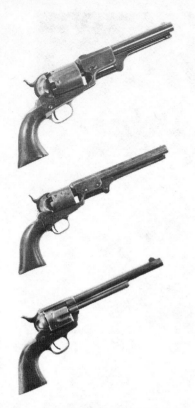

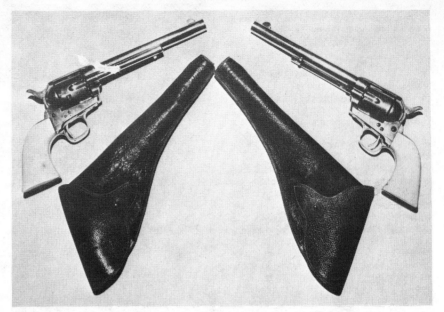

Above—Colonel Cody's favorite pistols, a pair of Colt Single Actions made by Colt in 1880, caliber 44-40. Now on display at the Buffalo Bill Museum in Cody, Wyoming.

Left—During Bill Cody's life on the prairies the Colt 44 Dragoon revolver (top), the 36 Navy model (center), and the 44 or 45 single action "Frontier" six-shooters were favorites.

Indians, General Miles sought his help in negotiating with Sitting Bull during the Sioux rebellion of 1890-91. The call came too late, however, for before Cody could proceed from the Standing Rock Agency, Sitting Bull was killed by the Indian Police.

It is not the place here to detail Col. William Cody's successes in the entertainment world. Many vivid accounts had been written of life on the American frontier, but Cody brought to audiences in America, Europe and Great Britain the real thing—Indians, cowboys, prominent frontiersmen, such great marksmen as Adam Bogardus and Annie Oakley. The "Wild West Show" was the forerunner of the rodeo, more exciting than the circus, and performances were never forgotten by those who saw them. Buffalo Bill gave to American youngsters their exciting games of "cowboys and Indians."

In addition to his faithful advance man and publicity agent, John M. Burke, Cody had able support in his partner Nate Salsbury. Cody was the shining star whom people came to see. He was immortalized on canvas by Rosa Bonheur and Frederic Remington. He was feted by nobility. Behind the scenes Burke and Salsbury kept the show on the road, for the show needed steady guiding hands. Their great star was one of the profession's heaviest two-fisted drinkers, generous to a fault, and one of the world's worst poker players, huge sums melting away while he waited for his luck to change.

Turning back to Cody's guns, during his interview with Chauncey Thomas a short time before his death, Colonel Cody recalled, "Our term of service on the plains covered so many years, and so many different kinds of guns came into use that we tried out this one, then that one. The 73 Winchester was well liked, as was the

Spencer Carbine, especially on horseback, but they could not shoot alongside of the needle-gun (50-70 Springfield)."

When asked about the heavy Sharps buffalo rifles, Cody had little to say about them. As he had done most of his buffalo hunting on horseback, the heavy Sharps rifles were unsuited for that kind of work.

A question about handguns brought the reply, "Like the rifles, new kinds and sizes came in and put others out. So we used all kinds, and sometimes any kind we could get. (First) it was the cap-and-ball Colt, then the metallic cartridge six-guns came on the plains, and they saved us a lot of trouble, especially in wet weather or on horseback. The only way we could load a cap-and-ball on horseback was to have extra cylinders and change from an empty to a loaded one, and then reload the empty cylinders when we had a chance. But with wet clothes, wet hands, and everything wet, that was often hard to do, and sometimes we could not reload at all. A muzzle-loading rifle or shotgun were different because we could keep the muzzle and loading things covered better. So the metal cartridges were a great thing."

Asked what kind of knife he had used in his duel with Yellow Hand, he said, "Just a big heavy bowie blade." Then he added, "For skinning and cutting up meat, of course, we used common butcher knives; no particular kind."

During his years in show business Cody was the recipient of many kinds of firearms. Winchester lever action carbines were the type he usually employed in his spectacular act of breaking thrown glass balls. The Winchester Company made up special 44-40 shot cartridges for this purpose employing 20 grains of black powder and one-half ounce of No. 7½ shot.

A surviving photograph pictures Cody, while still a relatively young man, holding

a Remington rolling block rifle. Another photograph shows him with what is apparently a Colt lever action rifle. Certainly he liked guns and owned many kinds. Some years ago I purchased a Long-Range Ballard rifle with convincing documentation that it had been part of a trade negotiated by Cody when he swapped a team of jaded horses and the rifle for a fresh team when his show was at Salt Lake City. This rifle is now a part of the firearms exhibits at Harold's Club in Reno, Nevada. You will find many other guns once used by this great rifleman at the Buffalo Bill Museum in Cody, attractively displayed under the supervision of Curator Richard D. Frost. Among these are Cody's favorite pair of ivory-handled Colt single action Army revolvers.

The over-glorification of Buffalo Bill Cody's varied roles in life might have left a sour note as his record hardened into history, but through the glitter and the ballyhoo emerged sound, sterling qualities in the man that needed no exaggeration. Through his career there were bad times and good. In final analysis, there was much to admire.

Among the many tributes paid to William Frederick Cody, the words of James Barton Adams found in the May, 1917, issue of Outdoor Life seem to be especially appropriate for a note on which to conclude this story of one of the West's most colorful sons.

"When came the final call and he drew near
   The trail that into death's deep darkness led,
His brave, heroic spirit knew no fear
   Of unseen mysteries that might lie ahead.
As fearlessly as when he started out
   Upon the trail of savage Indian band
Who sought rapine and murder, the old scout
   Faced the inevitable summons, and
With smile upon the face, pain drawn and pale,
Passed into the dark shadows of the trail." ●

EXTRACTORS and EJECTORS

—— a Century of Revolver Systems

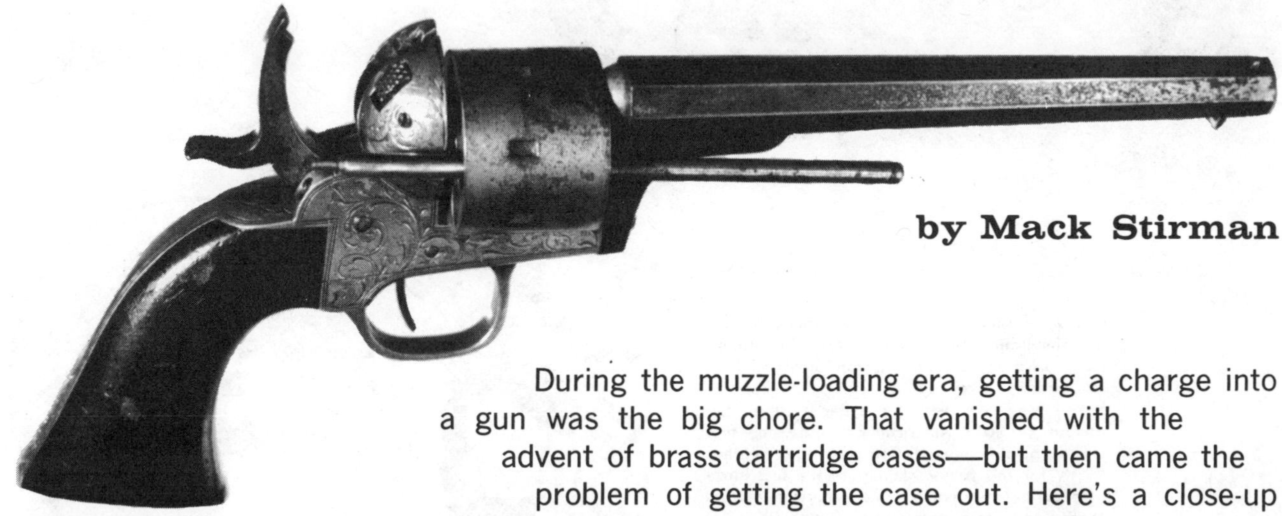

by Mack Stirman

During the muzzle-loading era, getting a charge into a gun was the big chore. That vanished with the advent of brass cartridge cases—but then came the problem of getting the case out. Here's a close-up study of numerous extraction systems

Fig. 2 — (above) Moore 7-Shooter with detachable rod under barrel. This 32-cal. rimfire, brass-framed revolver was popular during the Civil War. The 7-chambered cylinder and 6-inch barrel pivoted to the right just far enough to use the spring-loaded extractor-rod. The one-piece walnut grips are similar in shape to Colt's, and are secured in the same manner. Mack Stirman Coll.

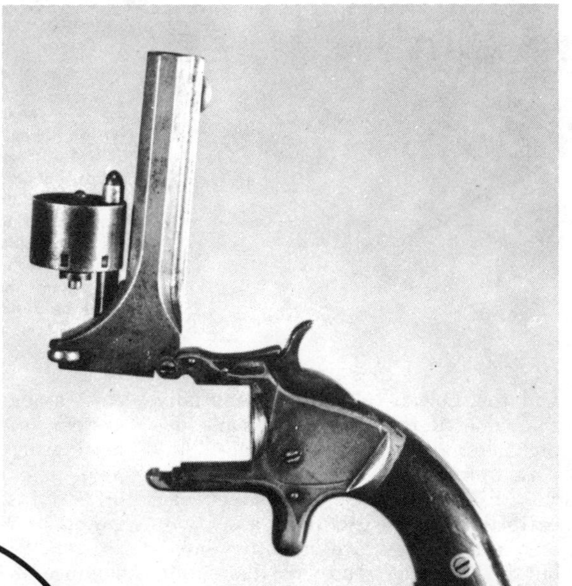

Fig. 1 — Smith & Wesson 1st Model, 2nd Issue, with primitive but efficient extractor. (Yes, we know the photographer put the cylinder on the ejector upside down!) This model has 3 3/16" octagon-ribbed barrel and 7-shot 22-cal. cylinder. Grant Chandler Collection.

PROGRESS MULTIPLIES problems which Progress solves.

Extraction was no problem with flintlock or percussion arms. Everything blasted down the bore! When Progress (in the person of Daniel B. Wesson) developed a self-contained, metallic cartridge, she was faced with the double problem of a revolver to accommodate it and extraction of the fired case. The Smith & Wesson Model 1, First Issue (first manufactured Nov. 1857), was the solution. In this instance Solution seemed to be as congenial a partner to Progress as Smith was to Wesson—both the revolver and the cartridge occurred about the same time! When the cartridge had been fired, the spent case had to be poked out of the chamber. The S&W revolver had an extractor rod permanently fixed in the handiest possible location: under the barrel. This was the "poker-outer." The barrel-unit was tipped up to expose the cylinder, which was then removed by hand and each chamber was pushed down over the end of the rod to extract the fired case. This was such an efficient, yet simple, method of extraction that it was used through a number of models (as Fig. 1), and manufactured as late as 1874.

This simple solution to the problem was copied in principle (but varied in application) in other revolvers; the Moore 32-cal. Seven Shooter was pat-

Fig. 3 — Plant and Eagle front-loading and extracting revolvers. The 42-cal. is marked *Plant's Mfg. Co. Newhaven Ct* on the top of the ribbed octagon barrel, and *Merwin & Bray. New York* on the left flat. The 28-cal. is marked *Eagle Arms Co. New York* on the top rib. Notice the cupfire cartridge being extracted to the front of the cylinder. Mack Stirman Coll.

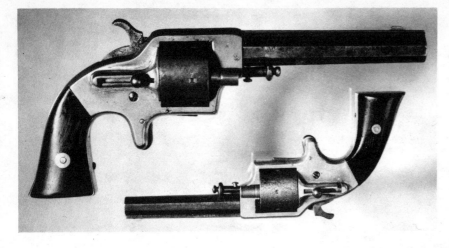

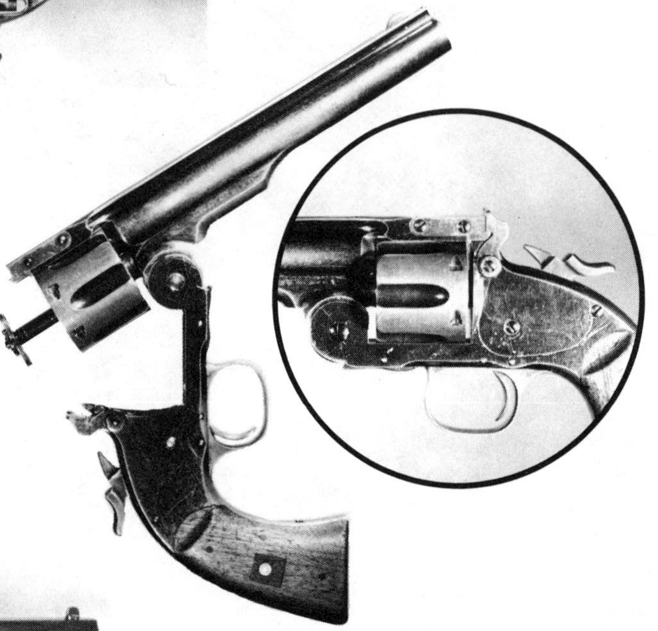

Fig. 5 — Smith & Wesson 44 American. The first simultaneous-extraction system was patented by Charles A. King; the top-latch and barrel-assembly pivot by W. C. Dodge. The 8" barrel and 6-chambered cylinder used the famous 44 S&W American cartridge, the first U.S. large-caliber centerfire cartridge. Another "first" for this famous handgun: the first large (44) caliber revolver on the American market that was not a conversion. Grant Chandler Collection.

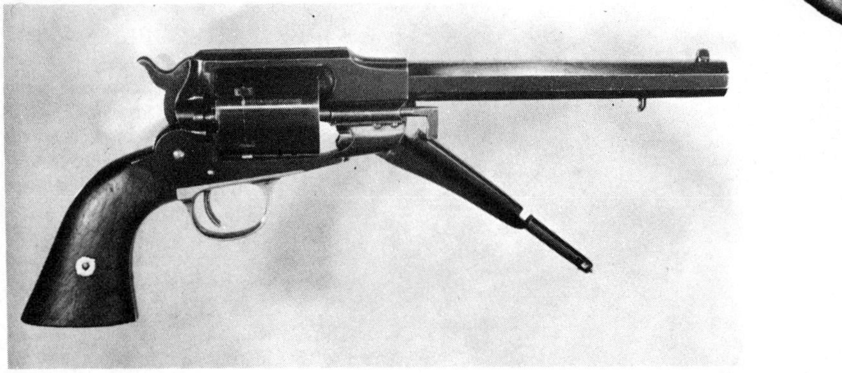

Fig. 4 — Remington 44 Army Percussion Conversion. Numerous conversions were devised, both by the factories and by private gunsmiths, yet in nearly all of them there was a similarity to this example. A new cylinder was provided, a loading groove was milled into the recoil shield, and an extractor rod was added. The notch in the rammer holds the rod against the barrel when not in use. Many could be restored to percussion by replacing the original cylinder. Grant Chandler Coll.

ented in 1860, and also provided a poker-outer under the barrel (see Fig. 2). However, instead of the barrel tipping up, this was a pivoting arrangement that moved the cylinder barrel unit aside far enough for cartridges to be loaded into the chambers without removing the cylinder from the frame. After firing, the cylinder was again pivoted to the right, the extractor rod was removed from its holder under the barrel and the cases were extracted separately by hand. One of the little refinements of Progress was the spring-loaded tip in the end of the detachable rod that held it securely in its place under the barrel. (Oh, yeah? Progress? The description of the remaining specimens usually reads, "Extractor rod missing!") Other revolvers, such as the Cone, the Grant and the Lower (all three essentially the same design), used the same detachable-rod extraction system.

In self-defense I should mention that I know the difference between extraction and ejection, and that, technically, they are not the same; but in this brief study no distinction is made. Also, this article does not claim to include all the different systems or modifications that have been manufactured. Those covered are listed because some were popular, and because some specimens are available for illustration. Others are included for the spice of novelty and nightmares!

Please notice that most of these revolvers are from the collection of Mr. Grant Chandler, of La Grande, Ore. For more than 40 years he has been a close student of the handgun revolver system, and claims it is the most fascinating research in the firearms field—and not for lack of interest in other arms. He has one of the most varied and extensive collections in Oregon. I further acknowledge his assistance in this bit of research. For any lack of quality in the pictures I must bear the criticism, since I was the photographer.

Rollin White Patent Evasions

Smith & Wesson controlled the vital Rollin White patent of April 3, 1855, on a bored-through cylinder, which permitted cartridges to be loaded from the rear. During the life of this patent a number of ingenious evasions were manufactured, many of their extraction systems being novel, to say the

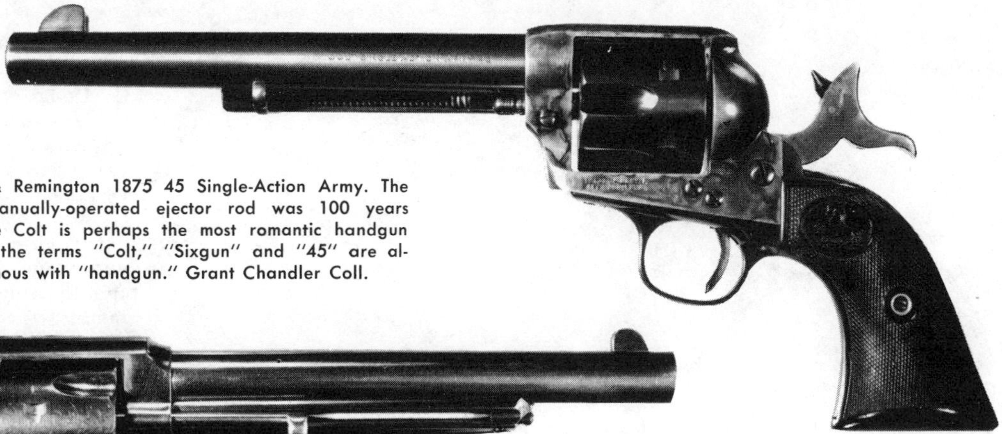

Fig. 6 — Colt & Remington 1875 45 Single-Action Army. The spring-loaded, manually-operated ejector rod was 100 years old in 1963! The Colt is perhaps the most romantic handgun ever made, and the terms "Colt," "Sixgun" and "45" are almost synonymous with "handgun." Grant Chandler Coll.

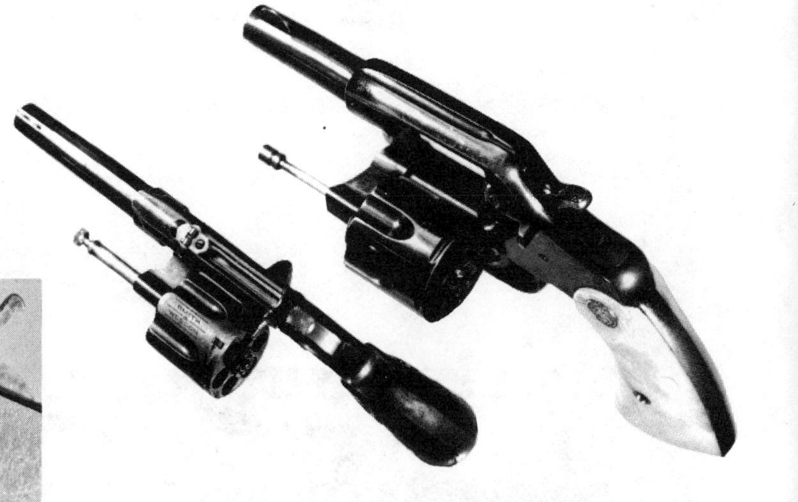

Fig. 7 — Hand-Ejector Colt and Smith & Wesson. The solid-frame, side-swinging hand-ejector appeared first on the Colt 1889 38-cal. Navy Double Action (top) and Smith & Wesson's 1896 Model I, 32 Hand-Ejector, First Issue (bottom). Note the name and patent dates stamped on the Smith & Wesson cylinder. Grant Chandler Coll.

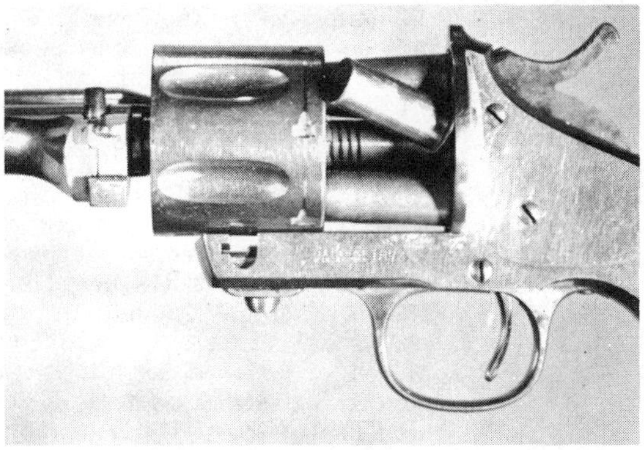

Fig. 8 — Selective-Simultaneous-Extraction. Merwin & Hulbert Pocket Army 44 illustrates the extraction of a fired case while unfired cartridges are held in place by the extra length of the bullet. The 3¼" barrel and crested birdshead grip are typical of the M&H Pocket Army. Mack Stirman Coll.

least. Plant Mfg. Co., New Haven, Conn., made a brass-framed, 6-shot 42 caliber "front-loader" that bore patent dates of July 12, 1859, and July 21, 1863. A special cartridge was devised that could be loaded in the front of the cylinder, fired, and ejected out the front. This cartridge had a cup-like depression at the base, instead of the usual rim. It took little imagination to name it a "cup-primer" cartridge! Fulminate was placed in the rim of this cup, as in the conventional rimfire cartridge. Powder came next, then the bullet was seated completely within the case. There was a slight flare at the rim of the mouth which helped to hold the cartridge secure in the chamber. A *small* hole in the rear of the chamber permitted the long, hook-nosed hammer to strike the in-

side rim of the cartridge and fire it. It was necessary for the ejector to be positioned behind the cylinder, in order to expel the fired case toward the front. Fig. 3 shows the small but efficient front-ejector. A smaller version of this same gun is also pictured, bearing the same patent dates on the cylinder and marked, "Eagle Arms Co., New York." It was made in 28 caliber cup primer, and had the front-ejector.

At the close of the Civil War people were greatly interested in the new cartridge revolvers of Smith & Wesson. Other manufacturers had stocks of percussion revolvers they could not sell and various methods were used to convert these cap and ball guns to metallic cartridge arms. In such a conversion (as shown in Fig. 4) the

percussion "rammer" or loader, under the barrel, was frequently altered to secure an added extractor rod, which was much handier than using a nail, a pencil or some such. It had the added advantage of being permanently attached to the gun and not easily lost.

The Rollin White patent expired in 1869, but the company met the challenge by introducing the Model No. 3 American, in 1870 (see Fig. 5). In May of the following year a contract was signed with the Russian Government which called for 20,000 revolvers of the Russian Model, and subsequent contracts raised the total to about 150,000 revolvers. These contracts were not completed until 1878, and a New Model No. 3 was developed the same year. With the appearance

Fig. 9 — Merwin & Hulbert Twist-Apart Construction. This odd arrangement was based on the sturdy cylinder pin, upon which the barrel-and-cylinder unit twisted and pulled forward. A hardened pin on the side of the barrel lug worked in an inclined groove cut in the cylinder pin, providing a camming action to extract swelled cases. The Army model had a 7" round barrel, with either frontier or crested birdshead grips, in 44 Single or Double-action. Note the folding hammer-spur, to be found on all calibers. Mack Stirman Coll.

Fig. 10 — Instantly-Interchangeable Barrels of Merwin & Hulbert. In its original factory box, this new and unfired set features two 38-cal. barrels (5½" and 3½"), hand-fitted to the same frame and bearing the same assembly number. The box is marked "Ivory," showing that the grips are also original. The twist-apart extraction was efficient with either the stub-trigger or the regular trigger guard. Mack Stirman Collection.

Fig. 11 — The English Thomas Patent 32 Caliber. The 4 3/16" barrel and 5-chambered cylinder are released by a latch just ahead of the cylinder; the barrel is turned 180° and then pulled ahead, much like the Merwin & Hulbert. The top strap is marked *John Potter Lynn*, and the barrel and cylinder bear English black-powder proofmarks. A loading gate is hinged on the right frame, and the safety is on the left frame at the top of the grip. The typically English one-piece walnut grips are finely checkered. Mack Stirman Coll.

of the Model No. 3, the plot quickens. Charles A. King and William C. Dodge were both contributors to its tip-up, simultaneous-extraction system. During these years the system was revised and improved, yet the principle remained the same. If the efficiency of the original poker-outer was confirmed by its 17-year tenure, be it noted that this simultaneous-extraction system was manufactured in substantially the same form in the S&W 32-cal. Double Action, as late as 1919—49 years after its introduction.

While Smith & Wesson was busy in another area, the Colt Peacemaker was establishing itself in the affection and legend of a nation. The beloved and time-honored Single Action Army revolvers, both Colt (1873), and Remington (1875), used the same type of extractor, as pictured in Fig. 6. It was slow, but for simplicity and efficiency it was hard to beat. The Colt Single Action, with this same extractor, is still being made today, and it is folly to argue with success!

Hand-Ejector System

There was neither weakness nor fault with the simultaneous-extraction system of the superlative top-break Model 3. The weakness was in the frame latch, and the need was a solid-frame revolver. The Hand-Ejector system of Colt and Smith & Wesson (Fig. 7) was the answer, and it is a worthy successor. It made its appearance with Colt's new Navy 38 Double Action, Model 1889, and S&W's 32-cal. Hand Ejector in March of 1896. It is still the most popular extraction system in revolvers. That means nearly three-quarters of century, which proves it is good! When the cylinder has been released and swung aside on its yoke, a plunger is manually operated to simultaneously eject all cases.

Sometimes it is desirable to extract a few fired cases from a cylinder, but retain the unfired cartridges. The Merwin & Hulbert is the only American revolver that has offered selective-simultaneous extraction. Fig. 8 shows how the unfired rounds are held in their chamber by the extra length of the bullet, while the shorter, fired cases fall away with a gentle shake. The gun is then closed, and the empty chambers are loaded through the loading gate on the right side. The strange twist-apart feature of the Merwin & Hulbert is seen in Fig. 9. The release button just forward of the trigger guard permits the barrel-and-cylinder unit to be twisted a quarter-turn to the right, then pulled forward to complete the extraction.

Just as Smith & Wesson's top-break revolver succumbed to a weak latch and an increasingly powerful cartridge, the Merwin & Hulbert also faced the same irresistable advance of Progress. After firing, the early-day copper case frequently swelled and stuck in the chamber, requiring unusual force to extract it. The M&H was especially efficient in such an emergency, since its twisting, camming action was designed to exert tremendous force in primary extraction. When brass cases were developed and improved, this difficulty was largely eliminated and one of the greatest advantages of the M&H was no longer needed. This unfortunate combination of circumstances contributed to the death of this great American product at about the turn of the century.

This high-quality handgun was available in 44, 38, and 32 calibers, and various barrel lengths. It bears the further distinction of being the first American handgun that was offered in an instantly-interchangeable, two-barrel set, as seen in Fig. 10. The long barrel (Belt Model) could be slipped off the cylinder-pin and be replaced by the short (Pocket Model) barrel in a matter of seconds!

Addenda

While some of the Rollin White patent evasions depended upon a new and novel cartridge with "cups" or "teats," the Slocum revolver attacked the problem differently. At the time of the patent (1863), the rimfire cartridge was the most popular, so the Slocum was designed to use it, but a different cylinder was devised. Instead of the cylinder being "bored through," five troughs were cut in the side of the cylinder, to accommodate five sleeves. To load, slide the sleeve forward, drop in a rimfire 32 Short cartridge and slide the sleeve back over the cartridge. Not only is the cartridge thus held in its proper position, but the rim is held firmly to the back of the chamber for the blow of the firing pin. The extractor is the stationary pin just ahead of the cylinder. When the sleeve is pushed forward over this pin, the fired case is pushed out the back of the sleeve, and with a shake it will fall free of the chamber. Although White sued many companies successfully in defense of his patent, he never brought suit against the Slocum evasion. It is also notable that the Slocum was well-made, on good sound mechanical principles, and satisfactorily accommodated the early rimfire cartridges it used.

European Systems

The Thomas revolver (Fig. 11) is an English product* of about 1870; its extraction system resembles that of the Merwin & Hulbert because the cartridges are held by their rims at the standing breech and the cylinder pulled away from them. The little knob under the barrel is simply to supply leverage for primary extrac-

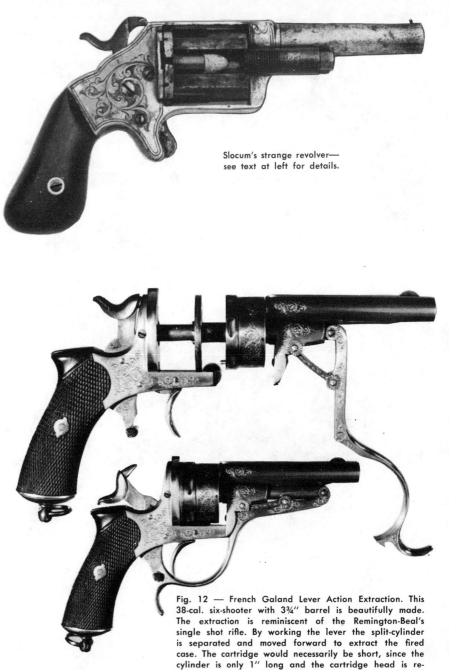

Slocum's strange revolver—see text at left for details.

Fig. 12 — French Galand Lever Action Extraction. This 38-cal. six-shooter with 3¾" barrel is beautifully made. The extraction is reminiscent of the Remington-Beal's single shot rifle. By working the lever the split-cylinder is separated and moved forward to extract the fired case. The cartridge would necessarily be short, since the cylinder is only 1" long and the cartridge head is recessed. Mack Stirman Coll.

tion as the barrel is turned 180 degrees, then pulled forward in its way, which in turn pulls the cylinder forward. It is marked on the left side of the frame beneath the cylinder: *Thomas's Patent No. 779,* and under this: *No. 128.* I can only surmise that this was the 128th manufactured.[†] It shows excellent workmanship throughout, and is one of the few revolvers with a safety. (Just beneath the hammer on the left frame).

The Galand (Fig. 12), of about the same period as the Thomas, is marked *Paris.* There were also factories in Belgium and England. This gun is engraved, and it is difficult to tell if a line is the joining of metal, or the engraving. Superior workmanship. The

ingenious method of extraction is positive, neat and practical, and the chamber was recessed to enclose the rim of the cartridge. This and the rebounding hammer made it quite advanced for the 19th century.

The variety of extraction systems

*Wm. C. Dowell, 119 Watford Rd., North Wembley, Middlesex, England (author of *The Webley Story*), a student and collector of firearms since 1914, has a vast fund of gun information. He graciously supplied information on the English revolvers I mention, and it is with sincere gratitude that I recognize his scholarship in the field.
† (According to general British practice in those years, the larger number would indicate that this was the 779th usage of the Thomas patent, with 128 being the maker's serial number. This inconsistency could be explained in a couple of ways, at least: one, the Thomas patent was in use on other than the model or type described, or two, in use by another manufacturer. ED.)

Fig. 14 — An interesting English Twist-Apart. Like the Merwin & Hulbert action, this also has twist-apart extraction. Mr. Dowell reports that this 450-cal. gun, marked Victor, serial number 1047, was in his collection until he sold it in October, 1962. There are 5 chambers, the barrel is 6¾" long, and the barrel is freebored about ¾". Grant Chandler Coll.

Fig. 13 — English Hill's Patent Self-Extractor. This 450-cal. revolver has 6 chambers. The barrel is 6¾" long with 5 narrow lands and 5 wide grooves. Double-action. Grant Chandler Coll.

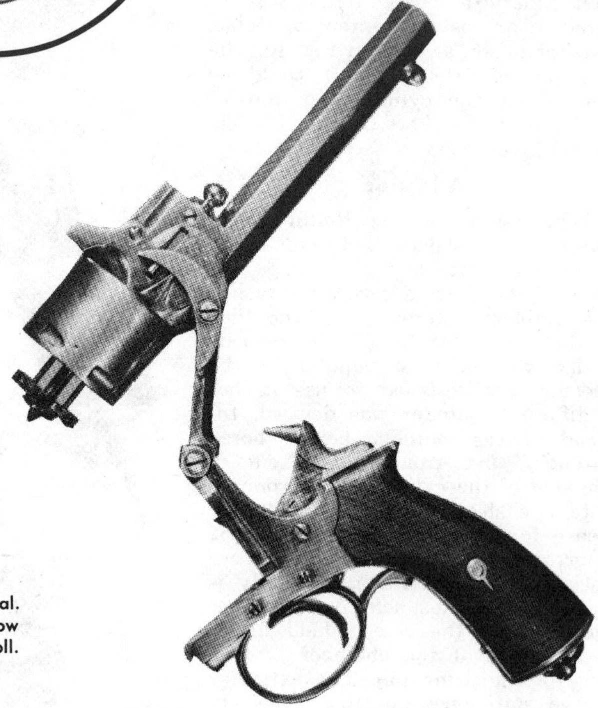

that were spawned from 1865 to 1880 indicates the common difficulty with early metallic cartridges, made of inferior material and sometimes poorly constructed; extraction of the fired case that had stuck! Notice again, the principle of anchoring the head and pulling the cylinder away from the cartridge. A lever-action extractor as in the early single shot, lever-action rifles.

Hill's Patent Self Extractor appears on the barrel-rib of another English product (Fig. 13). This was William James Hill, a London gunsmith of 1872-1879. The barrel/cylinder unit is tipped up and extraction is effected at the very peak of its upward swing. It is easy to imagine the great force that is exerted by such leverage. It is interesting to note that this inventor obtained an English patent for a re-

bounding hammer in 1878. Daniel B. Wesson and James H. Bullard secured their American patents for the same feature in 1877.

Fig. 14 shows a gun which is engraved along the top rib with the name of the inventor, James Mc-Naughton, George St., Edinburg, who was also lodging patents relating to shotguns from 1867 to 1879. The bore has 12 lands and grooves, with the top of the land flat, and the bottom of the groove rounded. The breech is freebored for about ¾".

The gun collector derives pleasure from his hobby in numerous ways. Every gun is a monument to the romantic past, and history is the record of that romance. Every collector becomes an historian, and the greater his interest, the greater his pleasure. Few collectors would qualify as me-

chanics or engineers, and some of us are baffled by the intricacies of the pouring spout on a pitcher. Yet with a little application we can learn the basic principles of gun design, and most of us can understand and appreciate the varied applications of those principles. Suddenly we discover a new and absorbing interest in our hobby, and a greater pleasure is our reward. Study the interesting mechanics of your guns. Perhaps you think the single-shot rifle is the simplest of all cartridge guns, but an examination of those submitted for Army trials during and after the Civil War shows that many variations were devised! Learn how your firearms work and you'll enjoy a double pleasure from your collection—you'll double your fun at no extra expense. •

STEVENS 20 GAUGE PUMPGUN

Cataloged weight of the gun was 6 pounds; mine weighs 5¾. Barrels could be from 26 to 32 inches. Made in field grade only, the 1911 cost was $27.50.

A detailed and comprehensive history of the rare and ingenious Model 200, America's first 20-bore repeater. Illustrations by the author.

by D. F. BREEN

FROM COLONIAL DAYS to the present era, firearms have been a vital necessity to our nation's growth and way of life. Many of us have become infatuated with these implements of sports, these guardians of our domain. They helped create the heritage that inspires us to relive our legends. Their traditions incite us to search the past for hidden gun lore, to rummage through musty tomes for firearms information. Our curiosity is relentless, as a result the American Gun is now a prisoner, confined in a house of glass with no place to hide.

Admittedly; if there is no place to hide — there is little danger of becoming lost. But wait . . .

Only a few decades ago, an American-made firearm of rare distinction actually vanished in that transparent geodesic dome that houses our gun world! If you doubt that this was possible, read the following obituary:

"The *first* repeating 20-gauge shotgun was born at the Stevens Arms factory in 1911, lived briefly, died mysteriously, and now lies buried in a weed-covered grave . . ."

Surely, Destiny has never been more ungrateful to the memory of a pioneer.

This 20-gauge multi-shooting forerunner possessed refinements that were modern by today's standards. Its most unusual feature was 50 years ahead of its time. One ingenious aspect of its construction might yet become invaluable to shotguns in the future. Nevertheless, despite these outstanding endowments it sank into obscurity. Others of lesser merit gained renown.

The year was 1911. The factory was the J. Stevens Arms and Tool Company of Chicopee Falls, Mass., specialists in target pistols and rifles from 1864. In 1911 the company had expanded to a complete line of firearms, including a 12-gauge pump shotgun designed by John Browning. This one, known as the Model 520, had appeared in 1904, and was the first modern-look hammerless repeater offered to the shooting public.

Advent of a New Model

It was during this calm and pleasant era that Stevens launched another "first" upon the gun world. It introduced a newly-fashioned 20-gauge pump shotgun. It weighed less than 6 pounds, and was chambered (unbelieveably) for shells up to 3 inches in length! This little pioneer reigned unchallenged for a year and a half as the only 20-gauge shotgun capable of firing five quick shots without reloading. Unfortunately, its life-span was brief — about 3 years. Following its disappearance, a half-century elapsed before America produced another 20-gauge repeater handling a 3-inch shell.

Stevens called their new gun the

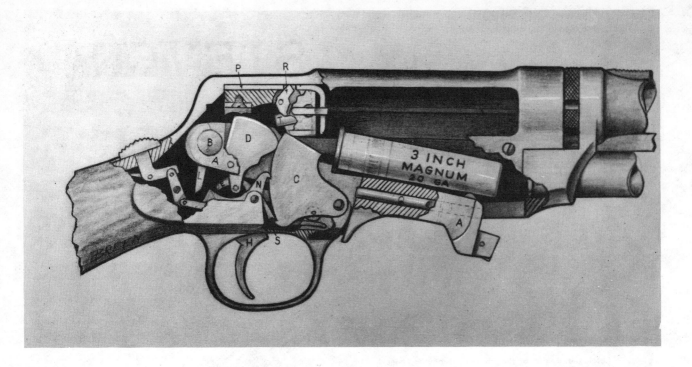

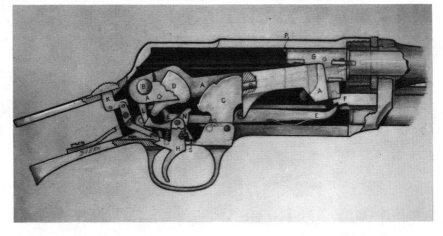

Above, the Stevens Model 200 with breech open. The unusual shell ejector (P) was taken from the repeating rifle designs of Andrew Burgess. Note the recoil weight (D), and dog (N) holding hammer (C) in locked position.

Stevens 200 at moment of firing. Recoil weight (D) has been thrown forward by recoil of the gun. A stud on its lower end raises rear end of locking bar (E), depressing front end, and disengaging slide action bar at (F), thereby unlocking action. On final closure of the gun, a projection (L) in rear of locking-bolt (carrier) (A) bears on rear of dog (N) lifting it out of notch in hammer (C). The hammer moves forward a fraction of an inch until caught by sear (S) in cock-notch.

Model 200. Its first notice appeared in the second issue of their 1911 catalog. As noted in the illustration this gun would handle shells from 2½ inches to 3 inches long, the former being standard at that time. 3-inch shotgun shells, brass or paper, were available in all gauges up to 20 as far back as the turn of the last century, but were intended for use only in break-open double guns. The Model 200 repeater was designed to accommodate the entire gamut of shotshell loadings from mild (⅝ oz.) 20-gauge to the standard charge (1¼ oz.) for 10-gauge guns. Weighing under 6 pounds, it combined the carrying ease of an upland double with the far-shooting talents of a long-tom wildfowler. No armsmaker before that time had offered so much versatility in so small a package.

The reasons for producing the Model 200 can only be guessed at now.

Why, for example, did Stevens, in 1911, reject a 20-gauge version of their esteemed breadwinner — the 12-gauge Model 520? In that era, the shooting majority was not sympathetic to the undersized 2½-inch 20. These stalwarts considered the little load adequate only for small boys or ladies. It may well be that the ability to make and market a 3-inch 20-gauge repeater tipped the scale.

The solution to their problem came from an obscure and unexpected source. Early in 1908, Mr. Charles Young, who modestly gave his address as "somewhere near Enon, Ohio," had designed a repeating shotgun in which shells up to 3 inches — or longer — would function in an action made *shorter* than those customarily designed for 2¾-inch cases. This he accomplished by the use of a short (1½ inches long) breechblock and a novel

method of sealing the void left behind it when the gun was closed.

Although the receiver mechanism would require extensive machining, Stevens chose this gun in preference to a cut-down replica of their less-complex Model 520. The possibilities associated with a light 20-gauge repeater shooting a long 3-inch must have seemed attractive at the time, and this unique facility might well have influenced the company's approval.

The most patentable feature of Mr. Young's invention dealt with two thin steel blades, rotating within the receiver. One blade, swinging upward, guided the shells into the chamber. The other swung into position behind the short breechblock, closing the opening in the ejection port. The design was simple, yet, to function properly, these two parts (together with a host of others in the receiver) had to

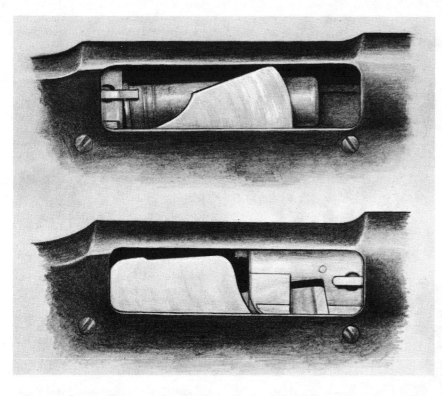

Here are the two all-important features that made the Model 200 possible. In the top illustration the cartridge guide (used before in other guns) rises into position as the breechblock moves forward. It is depressed by the breechblock after completing its function. Without this guide, the 2½ inch shell would jam or roll out of the receiver. The lower view shows closure blade swinging upwards to mask the opening behind the short breechblock.

This drawing shows the long 3-inch ejection port and knurled locking ring on the barrel. Turning this ring required a special spanner wrench, which was cleverly housed and locked in the front end of magazine tube when not in use. Gun is in ejection position.

be machined and fitted with the utmost care. Needless to say, Stevens Arms Company met the challenge. No other repeating firearms made in America has surpassed it in excellence of manufacture.

The number of milling operations, routings, broaching and profiling cuts in the Model 200 would stagger the aplomb of a production foreman in a modern-day arms factory. There were 36 metal parts (exclusive of pins, springs and screws) that required from 6 to 41 separate machining operations: many were finished to a mirror-like surface.

Mr. Ray Omerod, employed at the factory during the last 38 years, is perhaps the only man left who remembers the older methods of gun manufacture. Discussing the Model 200 with its maze of intricate parts, Ray said:

"Milling machines were the heart and soul of the old-time gun factories. The operators on the millers and pro-

filers took pride in their work. No one was hurried. There were lots of little parts in those old guns, and since they had to interchange and work to perfection, every operation was gauged and held to close tolerances. Today, guns are made in a more simple manner. Intricate parts can be stamped, bent and twisted with one blow of a drop hammer. A single part sometimes does the work formerly done by two or even three. Surprisingly, modern guns work as well, or even better, than those made in the days when the milling machine was boss of the gun factory."

Model 200 Features

The Model 200 was the first hammerless repeater to locate the safety on the top tang, a la double gun. This feature came into use on later pump guns, continued for about 20 years and disappeared in favor of the cross-bolt-in-trigger-guard system. Recently it has been revived on at least two American-made shotguns. Many hunters hold firmly that a thumb-operated safety is the best for quick action in the field.

Two other safety features appeared on the Stevens 200. One locked the hammer in a cocked position until the gun was closed; the other was a two-piece firing pin that became operative only when the action was closed and ready to fire. Although these important safeguards were used on earlier slide-action firearms, they were crude and not wholly reliable. Stevens, with the aid of Browning, brought both to a high degree of perfection, and they have since become standard equipment on all repeating smoothbores.

On the other hand, the Model 200 was burdened with the dubious, much-debated "hang-fire" safety. The purpose of this device was to prevent the gun being opened in case of a hang-fire or misfire. In the Stevens 200 arm this was achieved by using gun-recoil in a manner similar to that which operates the single trigger mechanism of some present-day doubles. Shotshell performance at that period must have warranted its inclusion, but it is odd that some manufacturers considered this device a necessity, while others deemed it useless. Remington (a maker of ammunition) disdained the notion that there was danger involved, and never used it. Today it is obsolete.

The Stevens 20-bore repeater possessed a minor defect that was really a blessing in disguise. Its take-down arrangement was the weakest feature of an otherwise excellent little gun; removing the barrel was an awkward procedure. To maintain rigid contact between barrel and frame a threaded lock ring was used, and this also served to provide for interchangeable barrels without factory fitting. This last, of course, would also dispense

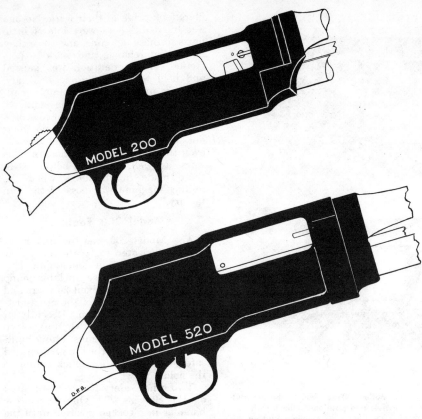

This view shows compartive size of the Model 200 (top) and its older brother, the Browning-designed Model 520. While the Model 200 would handle longer shells, note that its receiver length is considerably shorter.

with the added cost of an extra fore-end and magazine tube. Other pump guns of that period did not provide this luxury. Today it would be un-thinkable for a manufacturer to at-tempt the sale of repeating shotguns without this feature.

Thus it can be seen that the Stevens Model 200, produced in 1911, was distinguished by many refinements classed as modern-day innovations. At least, they have not been improved upon. Most important of the Model 200's attributes was its capacity to handle 3-inch shells, a feat only re-cently common with American-made pump guns. The term "20 gauge Mag-num" is new to the present genera-tion, yet the only thing really new is the word "Magnum."

Shortest Breechblock

This brings the spotlight to focus on what might be the most significant detail in the construction of Stevens' little pioneer — the shortest breech-block on record. Actually, the breech-block proper was only a half-inch long, although an extention was added to facilitate smooth travel without bind-ing. Had Stevens incorporated the double action bars of the earlier Spen-cer and Union pump guns, this exten-

tion would have been unnecessary; the square-backed frame could have been streamlined and its length shortened.

No one will deny that the pump gun is overly long because of a receiver that extends 7 inches behind the bar-rel breech. In a double gun this length is only 1¼ inches. Many feel that this difference contributes to the quicker handling and better balance of the dou-ble gun. Since 1893, the pump gun's receiver has been growing longer, though this is offset somewhat by a trend towards shorter barrels. The construction of the Stevens Model 200 proves that a short breechblock is practical, and, with double action bars, a pump gun's frame could be short-ened by ⅓ of its length. Cutting it back ought to make for a lighter, bet-ter pointing gun. At least it would provide a new look, and a "new look" has sales appeal. Someday, perhaps, an enterprising gun designer may de-cide to swing the pendulum the other way, reducing both receiver and all-over gun length. In this event, the unusual aspects of the Stevens Model 200 might prove worthwhile considera-tions.

Records of the Stevens Arms Com-pany seem to be no longer available. The original organization passed into other hands during the first World War, and after 1920 became part of the Savage Arms Company. With the years, the old firm's identity has gradually slipped away. When peace was resumed after WW I, several of Stevens' excellent firearms were dropped from the catalog, among them the 20-gauge Model 200 repeater.

Historical details of this fine little shotgun are seemingly lost, the men who might have told its story long departed. No one knows how many were made or the exact reason that ended its career. Today, Savage knows of only three lonely specimens which still endure. These, together with a yellowed page from an old gun catalog, mark the only evidence of this little gun's existence. ●

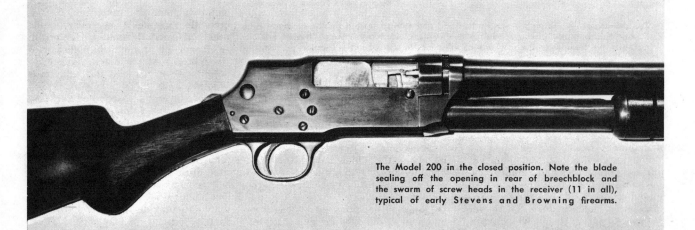

The Model 200 in the closed position. Note the blade sealing off the opening in rear of breechblock and the swarm of screw heads in the receiver (11 in all), typical of early Stevens and Browning firearms.

BEING LOST in a wilderness and having to survive off the land is exciting to think about, but no doubt would prove frightening to most. Nevertheless, these situations occur, even today, as the result of airplane crashes, shipwrecks, or the loss of horses, canoes, etc. Any such event can place an individual in a real predicament.

Under these conditions a gun would

a lot of ammunition when used sparingly. The 22 Short is almost as good for small game and offers an even further reduction in weight and bulk. The 22's faults, aside from limited power, are that cartridges are not nearly as durable, waterproof and oilproof as are larger rounds, because only the soft heel of the bullet is crimped into the case and it is easily

metal patch bullet is available. Also, the old 22 WRF or 22 Remington Special (lead bullet, inside lubricated) can be fired in the magnum chamber. They are probably even better for small game.

In looking at the 22 rifles themselves it's obvious that the present mass market demands low-priced guns loading action, the 22 WRM in bolt

GUNS FOR SURVIVAL

be invaluable for taking game for food. While few guns have been designed purely as survival arms, we have so many types available that several should be adaptable. The relative merits of the different designs will be discussed here in an effort to determine which would be most useful in the wilderness.

A survival gun should be simple, light, compact, dependable; it should have good sights and be easily disassembled for cleaning. This last is important for the best of guns can fail quickly if not properly cared for and our man in the bush will have, at best, only a few tools. Also, it should be usable on a variety of game.

We are not likely to find all we want in any one gun, especially in regard to an all-round caliber, so it becomes a matter of seeking out the best compromise.

Rifles

The first rifle that comes to mind is one chambered for the 22 Long Rifle. This cartridge's usefulness on small game as well as its popularity with deer poachers is well known. Small size and light weight are its most favorable points. Several hundred rounds can be carried easily—

by Glenn I. Berns

It takes only a moment
for a plane crash, a car
breakdown, a canoe sinking
—in the wilderness or
somewhere off the beaten
path—to put you into a
survival situation. Whether
you live or die can depend
on your ability to overcome
a strange and harsh
environment—to live off
the land. One of the guns
described here could
make the difference

damaged.

The 22 Winchester Rimfire Magnum is a great improvement. It eliminates the faults mentioned above and is a much more powerful cartridge in an only slightly larger case. It is not big enough to qualify as a sporting round for deer-sized game but will certainly do in a pinch. The hollow point bullet is actually too destructive on edible small game, but a full

action, pump and lever. Each is avail-for plinking. While the manufacturers provide good value for the money, these guns leave a lot to be desired. Few 22 rimfire rifles exhibit the quality of workmanship apparent in even modestly priced centerfire rifles. This is too bad, as the little 22 is about the only choice these days in a small game rifle. The standard 22 comes in single shot, bolt, lever, pump or autoable in the Savage M24 combination gun.

Most manufacturers produce bolt action 22s. Many have stamped parts which don't help appearance, but the better ones shoot well and give little trouble in normal service. The strong point of bolt guns is that they are the easiest to clean and care for and are perhaps a bit more accurate than other types.

Excellent quality pump action rifles are made by Winchester, Remington, Savage, High Standard and others. Pumps are necessarily a bit on the complicated side. Their designs permit routine cleaning of accumulated powder residue and bullet wax — all that's usually needed — but any further disassembly is almost a shop job. This comment extends to the autoloading group as well, and in the in-

Air Force M4 survival rifle has a collapsible wire stock, 13¾" barrel, weighs only 4 lbs. Chambered for the 22 Hornet cartridge, it will handle deer-size game in emergency. Box magazine holds 5 rounds. Not available commercially.

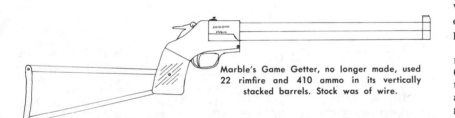

M6 Survival Rifle/Shotgun, an Air Force over-under, uses Hornet ammo in rifled barrel, 410 shotshells in smoothbore. Folding stock has ammunition compartments. 28" over-all, with 14" barrels, it weighs 3¾ lbs.

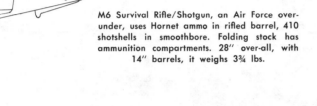

Marble's Game Getter, no longer made, used 22 rimfire and 410 ammo in its vertically stacked barrels. Stock was of wire.

expensive models these are sometimes lacking in accuracy, balance and other fine points.

Two 22 rifles we especially like are the lever action Marlin 39 Carbine and the Ruger 10/22 Autoloader. Both of these short, light rifles take down quickly and easily, are accurate and sure functioning, and are among the best models we have. The Ruger is even tapped for a *quality* telescope sight, something we would like to see on more 22s. The inexpensive scopes are fine for plinking, but I'd prefer a high-grade glass on a survival gun. These rifles cost more than the run-of-the-mine 22, but are well worth the price.

As it happens, Weaver can supply his Tip-Off mount with 1" rings, and Redfield makes 1" rings with special bases to fit grooved-receiver 22s, thus attaching a quality scope is not difficult.

I remember one authority stating that his idea of a survival gun was a high power rifle, reasoning that one should live off the largest game in the area. This man spent much time hunting in the far north, Canada and Alaska, where big game is comparatively plentiful. Here, the scope-sighted, magnum rifle is just the ticket. However, many places do not contain any large game, and even where it does exist smaller animals are invariably more plentiful.

Of course the centerfire rifle can be handloaded down for small game shooting, although the ammunition is still just about as bulky and heavy as the full power rounds. You will also require different sight settings in most cases, but it can work out pretty well. We've had good luck with the 30-30 using the 110-gr. Hornady round nose bullet designed for the M1 Carbine ahead of 12 grains of 4759. This gives about 1300 fps, which is not enough to expand the bullet (it was intended

for much higher velocity), but it is still more potent than the 22 LR. In my gun I can use the top of the front sight for the factory load and the center of the bead for the light loads at short range with no other sight adjustment. Lyman's *Ideal Handbook* lists hundreds of cast bullet loads for rifles, and at low velocities lead bullets do as well as jacketed. Try the lighter flat point types; they are easier to stabilize at low velocities and are more effective on small game than spitzers.

At one time Marble Arms of Gladstone, Mich., manufactured auxiliary chambers for many centerfire rifles. These permitted the use of certain pistol cartridges in rifles. The 30-cal. rifles could use the 32 S&W cartridges and the 35s used various 38-cal. cartridges.

If a centerfire rifle is chosen — and it's a standard item on many expeditions into remote places — we'd recommend one of the old military bolt actions, the '03 Springfield, the '17 Enfield and the '98 Mausers in particular, for obvious reasons — reliability and ease of maintenance. These rifles were built for hard service, are as foolproof as anything we have, and are relatively inexpensive. Many are available in excellent condition and can be altered or restocked to suit any preference.

If price is unimportant and a new centerfire bolt gun will be chosen, then Winchester, Remington, Savage, et al, offer a variety of models and calibers, particularly in sizes other than 30-06.

Nothing larger than the 30-06 is needed, and the 257 or one of the 6mm's might be better as ammunition is lighter and these cartridges are adequate for all medium size game. Also, smaller cases are generally superior for reduced loads as they burn light charges better. We can approximate the ballistics of the old 25-20 and 32-20, small game favorites of years ago, and still have a reasonably powerful full load available. For instance, 9 grains of 2400 will give an 85-gr. 6mm bullet some 1450 fs, while 20 grains of Norma 200 gives a 150-gr. gascheck 30-cal. bullet 1400 fs.

A new caliber, the 5.6x57mm, may soon be available in a bolt action rifle to be made by Krico of West Germany. Similar in form to the Krico rifles now made in 22 RF and 222 Remington, the new one will offer a cartridge most interesting from the survival-gun standpoint. The new 5.6x57 will be sold with either or both of two adapter cartridge cases, each with its own firing pin, etc. One will be for the 22 WRM, the other for 22 Hornet. With a few of these adapters in his pocket the user of the Krico 5.6x57mm is well-equipped for any game from deer on down.

Ballistics of the 5.6x57mm are im-

Savage M24 Deluxe is a top choice among survival guns, giving instant selection of bullet or shot load for furred or feathered game. Rifle barrel can be had chambered for 22 LR, 22 WMR or 222 Remington, shot barrel for 410 or 20 gauge.

pressive, at least on paper. A 75-gr. bullet is given a muzzle velocity of 3400 fps. Zeroed at 200 yards, the mid-range point of impact is about one inch.

The Air Force today has a centerfire survival rifle designated the M4. This is a bolt action 22 Hornet with a 5-shot box magazine and a collapsible wire stock. Weighing just 4 pounds with a 13.75″ barrel, it is too short to be legal under the National Firearms Act even if the model were commercially available.

Shotguns

Shotguns are suited to a variety of uses, since shells loaded with buckshot or slugs are available, as well as small shot. The drawback here is obvious: shotshells are so heavy and bulky that only a few can be carried. In fact, the weight problem rules out all except possibly the 410, and even these, with ¾ oz. of shot, weigh up pretty fast. Oddly enough, the 410 slug load weighs just 87 grains (1/5 oz.) and possesses just enough energy to be considered dangerous.

Ignoring the ammunition problem for the moment, we can see instances where a shotgun will score when no man with a rifle could, except by luck. For instance, shooting birds on the wing or small game on the run (although we would do precious little of this type of shooting if it could possibly be avoided). Another example is under poor light conditions where the game or the sights are barely visible. Still another case is an individual who is either injured or so fatigued that he simply cannot shoot accurately with a rifle or pistol. Similarly, for a person

unskilled in the use of any firearms, a shotgun will offer the best chance. So we cannot ignore this type entirely.

The double barrel shotgun is the best choice among smoothbores. It is actually two guns on one stock, with a separate lock for each barrel. Both aren't likely to fail at one time. This is one reason double rifles are the first choice of many African white hunters. Also, you can load a slug in one barrel and shot in the other, and thus be prepared for large or small game.

Combination Guns

Multi-barreled arms featuring both smoothbore and rifled barrels have long been popular for European hunting. Three-barrel designs, which usually have twin shotgun barrels above a rifle barrel, are called drillings, while four-barrel combinations are known as vierlings. The three most common shotgun gauges are made, though 16-gauge is most often seen. Many rifle calibers are available, making these drillings versatile and suitable for almost any hunting. The catch is that they are expensive; they also possess complicated and sometimes delicate lockwork.

A simpler combination gun would be better for a survival weapon, and one is available in the U.S. This is the Savage Model 24. It is an over-under with either a 22 LR or WRM barrel on top and a shotgun barrel of either 410 or 20 gauge underneath. The Savage 24V is made in 222 Rem. and 20 gauge. This is a simply constructed, well made little gun, quite useful just as is. Improvements might include a brazed-down frontsight with a colored insert, a little better trigger pull and a

trapdoor buttplate. These modifications can be accomplished with a small amount of custom work. The basic gun is there and it's a good one.

The Air Force must have had a similar gun in mind when designing the M6 Survival Rifle/Shotgun, an over-under using 22 Hornet and 410 barrels. This gun has a folding stock which contains compartments for ammunition and cleaning supplies. It weighs 3.75 lbs., has 14″ barrels, and is about 28″ over-all.

This gun is not available commercially. We mention it to give some idea of the military's thinking on the matter. Note that they picked something a little more powerful than the 22 LR for the rifle barrel. Today I believe they could do as well with the 22 WRM, which should about equal the Hornet's ballistics in so short a barrel.

A similar gun is the 22/410 over-under Game Getter put out years ago by Marble. It was a sort of oversized pistol with a wire shoulder stock. This is now an illegal firearm. Too bad, as it is an interesting gun and no doubt would be very useful.

There is one more alternative, the rifled Krieghoff insert designed for 12, 16 or 20 ga. break-open shotguns. Some 9″ long and weighing 5 ozs., it is made for either the standard or magnum 22s. The premium priced version is said to group in an inch at 50 yards. I haven't tried one, but hear they are as good as claimed.*

---

*When tested by the GUN DIGEST staff, a Krieghoff insert in 22 WMR averaged ⅜″ for a number of 5-shot groups at 50 feet.

Berns' favorite centerfire rifles for remote country use, because of their reliability and ease of maintenance, are the military bolt actions such as the 1917 Enfield, 1898 Mauser and, shown here with type C stock, the 1903 Springfield.

Certainly the idea is good. These inserts have adjusting screws which allow alignment of the insert in the shotgun barrel, and sighting in is accomplished in this manner. Theoretically then, you can get the 22 insert in one barrel to shoot to the same point as a slug from the opposite barrel, and that is what's so interesting about the whole idea. With even a 20-ga. gun the 273-gr. slug has real big game potential and you have the 22 available for rabbits, etc., at the same time.

Handguns

We have just as large a selection of handguns to choose among as we have rifles or shotguns. Before discussing them, here are a few general observations.

First, handguns are much more compact and considerably lighter than

to shoot well. Even under the conditions most favoring the handgun, any decent rifle is at least three times as good. Still, if you can shoot one well enough to stake your life on it, we can go ahead and consider some of the better guns.

There is no shortage of fine revolvers. Smith & Wesson, Colt and Ruger produce medium-frame revolvers of exceptional quality in 22 caliber and centerfire models. The single action models are far simpler in design and operations than the double actions and much easier to take apart and assemble; however, the removal of the

the 357 factory ammunition or equivalent handloads have taken much large game. Certainly a heavily loaded 44 or 45 is superior for the latter purpose, but remember that this ammunition weighs up to 50% more than the 357 round. Being able to carry half again as much ammunition is the big point in favor of the 357. If the smaller round can do the job there is little use in carrying all the extra weight just for the sake of overkill.

One trouble with the 357 is that light and heavy loads don't want to shoot to the same place. With 44s or 45s, so long as the same weight bullet

Among commercial bolt action centerfires, new Winchester 670 carbine with 19" barrel, 6¾-lb. weight, would be an excellent survival gun in 243 caliber.

rifles — important considerations. If a man must travel much on foot every ounce is a burden, thus a handgun rates consideration as a survival gun. It is more easily carried and is better protected in a holster than would be a long gun carried in the hand or slung from the shoulder, and in some respects it might even be considered safer as it would be handled only when actually used for shooting. Secure in its holster, it is also less likely to be lost or out of reach when needed most. Furthermore, it can be fired with one hand, important if one hand should become disabled thru accident.

This last fact pretty much rules autoloading pistols out of consideration for our purposes. It is almost impossible, using only one hand, to load a magazine, insert it in the gun and work the slide to chamber a round in any of our popular auto pistols. Loading and firing a revolver, though, either single or double action models, with one hand is no trick at all. Revolvers also handle a wider variety of ammunition than autos and possibly are safer.

Offsetting most of the handgun's advantages is the fact that it is so difficult

sideplate on the double action gun exposes all the working parts which are then easily cleaned and lubricated — all that's usually ever needed. In materials and workmanship there is little to choose between them.

As they come from the factory, double action guns almost invariably have better trigger pulls and are probably a bit easier to shoot accurately than single actions. The single action guns have less apparent recoil. These few generalities sum up the practical difference between the two types.

The Smith & Wesson K-22 and the Colt Officer's Model Match are easily the best of the 22-cal. revolvers, (both are also made in 38 Spl.), with Ruger's Convertible Single Six, having good adjustable sights, a close competitor. The 22 WRM chambering, offered in the Ruger and S&W, is a better choice than the 22 LR, because of its greater power. Smith & Wesson's 22 Jet provides even more energy, but the 22 WRM is almost as good and its ammo is lighter and less bulky. Chamber inserts allowing use of the 22 LR are available for the Jet.

Many people will insist that any 22 just isn't enough gun. Perhaps they are right, and for them the 357 Magnum is ideal. Both single- and double action models are made. 38 Spl. wadcutters and the standard 38 service round are ideal for small game, and

is used, the powder charge seems to make little difference in the sighting, light or heavy loads often shooting to the same point. The 38s usually shoot to one side or the other. Naturally we don't claim to have tried this in all makes of revolvers and in all barrel lengths, but you will find the above generally true. There are two partial solutions: sight in for the light load (it will require the most accurate bullet placement) and hold off for the heavy one, or for a "light" load simply use a round nose bullet which will be less damaging ahead of the same powder charge in both loads. Constantly changing sights in the field is out.

If you want shotshells in a pistol, you almost have to go to a 44 or 45. The armed forces have a 45 ACP shot cartridge loaded with #8 or #9 shot, so they apparently think the idea has some merit. This 45 ACP loading is a weak sister compared to larger cases. Shot patterns from rifled barrels are none too good at best so we certainly don't want to be handicapped by severely limited capacity. The 44 Magnum and 45 Colt are both quite a bit larger. Alcan loads a plastic shot cartridge with #9 shot for the 45 Colt, and Shooters Service of Clinton Corners, N.Y., and probably others, will load any caliber to your specifications. The handloader can do just as well for himself, of course.

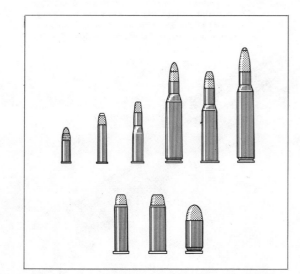

The author's first choice in defense handguns is this Smith & Wesson M1950, chambered for the 45 ACP cartridge. Not only is this load efficient, but its large bore also has a psychological effect that could well make it unnecessary to actually use the gun.

A handgun is the least bulky defense gun. We prefer the revolver to any auto, and feel that the double action in 44 Spl. or 45 ACP is best of all. With standard loads these heavy frame guns do not recoil much more than medium-frame 38 Spl. revolvers but are far more powerful. The 357 Magnum is in the same class as these bigger calibers but there is an undeniable psychological advantage in the larger bore. The mere sight of a cylinderful of 45s is enough to convince anyone in his right mind that you don't have anything that he really wants after all. The 41 and 44 Magnums? They have more power than needed and kick too much for the average person.

It is doubtful that many criminals understand much about firearms or they would not insist on choosing the cheap, small-caliber types they usually do. How many times have you heard of someone who is still alive because the hood's gun misfired? Likely he is even scared of his own gun, but feels it will give him the advantage over his unarmed intended victim.

Even the best revolver shotshells are nothing to write home about. Using the Alcan 45 Colt load, which is typical, we have found 10 yards is the outside limit for any sort of pattern. At 7 yards they work quite well. Obviously, this is a short range proposition suited only for small birds and the like.

Sights

There is no doubt that a telescope sight is a great asset on a rifle. A low-power scope with good light gathering ability and post or large dot reticle is usable under light conditions that would make iron sights hopeless. High powers and fine crosshairs are too specialized for all-round use. A rifle should also have sturdy iron sights, open or peep, and the scope should be mounted in a detachable or swing mount that allows quick use of the iron sights.

The Redfield Sourdough is a good front sight that will take a lot of knocks. A protective hood is recommended if the front sight chosen will accommodate one. Open rear sights do not interfere with scope mounting and are satisfactory for many situations.

Scope sights on revolvers are something else again. With one you must give up iron sights completely as most mounts replace the rear sight or block iron sight use. A scope makes the handgun bulky and unwieldy and thereby eliminates its most attractive features.

In standard iron sights the Patridge design is now almost universal. The only common variation is the red insert in the front sight and the white outline rear notch often seen on Smith & Wesson revolvers. Colored sights show up better in poor light. However, you will almost always shoot better with plain black sights as it is easier to maintain exact sight alignment.

Defense Guns

We are faced in this age with the possibility of another type of survival situation, that following a nuclear attack. If you should escape the blast it is not likely you and your family would be forced out of your home and so far back into the boondocks that you would have to hunt game for food. Rather, in all probability, it would be more a matter of self-protection, if not from invading forces then from looters and plunderers.

In Conclusion

In a final analysis it would appear that for general use as a survival gun a combination rifle/shotgun would be top choice. A good bolt action centerfire rifle of about 25 caliber, using light and heavy loads, would also be excellent.

Ultimately, the big considerations are the area you live in (or would be traveling through), your individual capabilities and, finally, your personal preferences. The watchwords are lightness and simplicity. There is no reason why a handgun could not be carried as an auxiliary to the shoulder arm.

In the matter of a defensive handgun we feel that the Smith & Wesson 1950 and 1955 Target in caliber 45 ACP are outstanding. They are fairly easy to shoot well, adequately powerful, usable with either hand, quick to reload (with 3-shot clips) and provide unquestionable reliability. The ultimate choice of course belongs to the individual. ●

Cartridges useful in survival guns, according to the author, include (top row from left): 22 LR, 22 WMR, 22 Hornet, 257, 30-30, 30-06; (bottom row) 357, 44 Magnum, 45 ACP.

Weights of Various Cartridges

Caliber	Bullet Wt. (grs.)	Wgt./C (lbs.)
22 Short	29	.53
22 Long Rifle	40	.75
22 Long Rifle (Shot)	—	.60
22 Magnum	40	.96
22 Hornet	45	1.77
6mm Remington	100	4.36
257 Roberts	100	4.36
30 US Carbine	110	2.86
30-30 Win.	150	4.60
30-06	150	5.57
38 Special	158	3.24
357 Magnum	160	3.67
44 Magnum	240	5.30
45 ACP	230	4.61
410 3" Shot.	¾ oz.	6.46

Rifle by Al Biesen

I've been a part of the gun world long enough to have learned that the craftsmen in it cannot be expected to do the 9 to 5 bit, to punch a clock, to get the jobs out as promised. That's particularly true, I think, of the men who do the best of stockmaking and metalsmithing. They're artists, many of them, in the best sense of the word, and like their kind—perhaps always and forevermore—they are temperamental fellows often, sometimes giving the client the kind and style of work they believe he should have, never mind that the end result doesn't quite match the customer's ideas or design! It's an entertaining and edifying thing, frequently enough, to listen in on a wrangle between the man who has set out quite clear thoughts on what he wants in this, his fourth or fifth custom stock, and the gunmaker, supremely confident that he knows—no question about it—just how the stock should be made. More than once I've heard Henry Vogt—for many years a first class stocker, and as good a general gunsmith as I've known—raise his voice and tell the complaining customer: "I make it the shtock the vay it should look und fit, goddamit!" He was right, too, nine times in ten. Henry was a devoted traditionalist, and no one was going to get a stock he'd made that was anything but right, as he saw it. They didn't, either.

Early in 1965 I talked myself into ordering a rifle from Al Biesen—who needs little introduction to those interested in custom gun work. For the others, Biesen is justly considered a ranking member of a highly restricted clan—the dozen-odd or so men in the U.S. who are genuinely makers of rifles to the customer's wishes and dimensions. No rough-turned, pre-inletted stock blanks for these workers—they'd rather do it themselves!

At the same time I sent a pre-1964 Model 70 Winchester, in 264 caliber, to Fred Huntington of RCBS, asking him to remove the 6.5mm barrel and install one chambered for the 7mm Remington Magnum, a new barrel that Bill Hobaugh had just made. I'd seen some fine looking walnut blanks at Frank Pachmayr's shop in Los Angeles, and one of these, in a handsome swirly figure, went to Al Biesen also. I gave Al quite complete information on dimensions, metal work wanted, checkering and so on, and he said he'd have it ready for me in about six months or so.

Six months went by, a year, another several months, but I steeled myself—I didn't bug Biesen once until some two years had passed. During the next couple of years I wrote to Al once or twice, phoned him once, but no rifle. He said he'd been awfully busy. Then, during a trip to Utah in August in 1970, I phoned Biesen again. I said that I thought I'd been pretty patient, that I'd like to have the rifle for the fall hunting, and for a picture in the issue you're reading.

I didn't hold my breath, of course, but the completed rifle arrived in October of last year, some five years after I'd sent Al the makin's! Worth waiting for, though the illustrations won't do it justice. It is a handsome piece, I believe you'll agree—the crotch grain in the buttstock curls and twists attractively, though the contrast is too low to reproduce well. The wood is beautifully smooth, a low-luster oil-type finish giving it a rich sheen. The multipoint checkering is well cut indeed, the fore-end generously covered from top to top. The cheekpiece, full enough to be truly useful, fairs forward gracefully, tapering off just at the rear edge of the grip checkering. The comb nose is on the full side in typically Biesen style, but that suits my face and cheek fine. The rounded radius of the comb nose flares smoothly down into the matching radius of the hand hole. The ovalized pistol grip is on the trim side, 4½ inches in circumference, and it's capped by Biesen's handmade, sharply-checkered steel cap. The lightly-concave shotgun style butt has Biesen's matching checkered steel plate, in this instance carrying a hinged trapdoor. Al also checkered the bolt knob, a very well done job, and he altered the floorplate release by putting the release knob in the guard. I'd sent Al a one-piece Conetrol base—a scope mount design I'm fond of—which he cut in two, making the separate pieces just long enough to cover the receiver ring and bridge exactly. All of the metal carries a soft, semi-matte blue, the bolt and raceways nicely engine turned.

How does it shoot? Quite well, I think, in view of my having put only some 80 rounds through it so far. I didn't get to take it hunting, and it's been a cold winter. Groups at 100 yards—with good-bullet handloads have done about an inch; factory loads have averaged about 1½ inches at the same distance. One aspect has been gratifying—just about all full loads have printed to nearly the same point of impact at 100 yards, whether 125-gr. or heavier weights were shot. Lateral dispersion was completely negligible.

It's pretty obvious that I'm pleased with the new Biesen rifle, and there's only one minor fault—the barrel is not inletted to its full-diameter mid-line. That lies slightly above the wood.

Still, the way prices have been rising, I wonder what the work would have cost me some four years ago, had Biesen delivered it to me as promised? JTA

Al Biesen did all metal and wood work except for the RCBS chambering on this Winchester 70 rifle. The bolt knob is checkered, the bolt body, extractor and raceways are damascened. Grip cap and trapped buttplate are checkered steel, made by Biesen. With Browning 2-7x scope and 2-piece Conetrol mount, rifle weighs 9¼ lbs.

Checkering is new Jack O'Connor
pattern, has everything—fleur-de-lis
points and ribbon, good coverage.

Dale Goens—
Custom Gunsmith

Floorplate of the Col. Wiley
rifle; animals are in gold, all
engraving done in Belgium.

This handsome M70 Winchester rifle,
made for Col. W.C Wiley (USAF, ret.), carries a new checkering pattern named for
Jack O'Connor. It combines fleur-de-lis,
multi-points and a ribbon. The engraving
seen on the floorplate and scope base/rings
was done in Belgium. There is also an engraved matching grip cap, not visible in
the photos.

The new checkering design can be seen
in good detail in the fore-end photograph—
where it will also be noticed that Goens'
checkering is borderless, without runover
—the marks of a first rate job.

Richard Hodgson
New Master

I saw the rifle pictured here at the NRA meetings in Washington—and I wish you could have. The photograph of it is an excellent one, crisp and sharp, the tone values broad and revealing, but it can't possibly do justice to the truly superb—no, magnificent—craftsmanship that distinguishes this chastely handsome rifle, elegant in its simplicity. The joining of wood to metal is perfection itself, as I've seen. The checkering is well-cut indeed, the long aspect diamonds uniform throughout and cut to crisp points.

What the illustration cannot show is Hodgson's beautiful metalsmithing—the new trigger guard, made more slender and graceful, cut from the solid steel; the fine-checkered sliding safety lever, his own concept of a lever-release floorplate.

I must have brought a dozen-plus men over to Hodgson's small space at the exhibit hall, most of whom I knew to have a critical eye, yet every one of them found his work praiseworthy indeed.

If I sound pleased and enthusiastic over the appearance of another dedicated craftsman—I am, and our world is the better for his skills and discipline. JTA

John E. Warren—
Master in
Wood and Steel

I think the rifle pictured here, both full length and in detail, is a most handsome piece, a pure example of classic styling at its best. I'm prejudiced, of course, for I believe John Warren ranks high among the finest stockmakers of all time. I don't know of anyone whose work is better.

I have sad news, though, for those who might have wanted Warren to build a stock for them. While the light rifle shown here was probably not John's very last stock, it was one of the final few. When I visited him to collect this 6mm Remington he told me he'd had to leave off whittling; he had then, he said, some 3 years of engraving work ahead of him, jobs he could complete in that time only if he gave up the wood rasps and the checkering tools.

John was lavish with his skills on this little rifle. The Sako action—now without a floorplate—is scroll-engraved all over, as is the bolt sleeve and the knob. The knob, combining engraving and checkering, is part of a new bolt, gracefully swept back, that John made and fitted to the bolt body.

The shotgun style guard, grip cap, fore-end cap, the shaped forward swivel and the skeleton buttplate, all were made by Warren from the solid steel, and all are engraved with taste and restraint. The end grain inside the buttplate outlines is checkered, the diamonds flattened in the English manner.

John also added a top tang to the receiver, then fitted there a sliding safety that works smoothly and silently. The words SAFE are inlaid in gold.

The wood is not fiddleback maple, which it much resembles, but yama wood, from Japan. It is extremely dense, yet not overly heavy, and it is without pores, at least as far as I can see. It is very light colored, too light really, but it's already darkening, even in the few months I've had it.

John Warren shoulders the Sako 6mm light rifle, his Cape Cod workshop in the background. At left, engraving details of the muzzle cap and outline buttplate. Lower left, close-up of the new bolt and tang safety, both additions handmade by Warren.

The excellent checkering—there's not a miscue anywhere—doesn't show well in the photographs, but the pattern is the multi-point style I like and had asked John to cut. The checkering runs fully around the fore-end, and there's an ample amount of it. The comb-nose fluting is perfectly done, blending smoothly into the reverse curve of the cheekpiece.

The 20-inch stainless steel barrel is one of Ed Shilen's, the muzzle diameter .492-inch. Without sights, the rifle weighs 6.25 pounds.

How does it shoot? In the beginning, quite good and, at the same time, not so good, but it has been getting better as I put more bullets through it. This is, obviously, a hunting rifle, so that first, all-important shot should be on the mark. At the outset the rifle wouldn't do that—the first shot or two, the barrel cold and dried, went some 3 or 4 inches high. Then it would settle down and, with good handloads, groups of 5 would make an inch often enough, though the over-all average was closer to 1.35 inches.

I thought at first that this kind of shooting might have been caused by the steel fore-end cap, which goes all around the muzzle, but shooting without the cap seemed to make no difference. As I've said, the rifle is showing improvement—now the first shots print only an inch or two over the warmed-barrel groups, using the 100-gr. bullets I want for a game load. Bullets of 75/85 grains do much better, but I want the heavier weights.

John Warren is a busy man, with no help of any kind, so his work moves a bit slowly, especially when the gun is to benefit from all of his superb skills—engraving, woodworking and metalsmithing. I had to wait a while for the beautiful little rifle, but it was worth every minute of it.

JTA

COMBAT SHOOTING...

The theory and practice of two-handed combat shooting, intended for adoption by police and other law-enforcement agencies in the British Isles.

THE SUBJECT of combat shooting is of immediate importance to those handgun shooters whose weapons may have to be used under practical conditions. To other shooters it may be a matter of academic interest only, yet even among those the subject frequently arises. Various "experts" are likely to expound at length on the merits or demerits of different combat shooting techniques, and opinions are frequently influenced by experience (often secondhand and exaggerated), by the methods taught in a particular Police or Army unit, by the books and articles on the subject and, unfortunately but not infrequently, by films and TV. This being so, it might be interesting and possibly useful to examine the problems involved in taking the first steps toward combat shooting and to test some of the theories put forward against what the writer fondly thinks is a logical study of the problem.

Combat shooting is usually taken to cover the use of a handgun, offensively or defensively, in situations where the target is shooting back. Such situations arise without forewarning, in difficult locations, frequently in bad light and when the shooter is literally caught on the wrong foot. In short, conditions which are very far removed from the target range. Highly refined target arms will have little place under such circumstances, and it is an oft-repeated view that target shooting techniques with all their refinements have no place either. However, this matter should be considered with care.

Combat shooting techniques usually regard the distance from shooter to target as the prime consideration in the choice of method employed. The shorter the range, the faster the method of delivering the shot has to be; conversely, the longer the range, the more precise the method of delivery must be. It is obvious that in some combat situations speed is essential, yet speed always tends to work against accuracy. The larger the target, the less precise the delivery need be, but speed should never be allowed to negate accuracy. There is little point in getting off a fast shot which misses your opponent while he is a fraction of a second slower, but hits. The various schools of thought in combat training almost all start with an instinctive or semi-instinctive technique at short ranges, then move through pointed shots at medium ranges to aimed shots at long ranges. Most fix the maximum range for instinctive shooting at around 20 feet, varying the other styles on a sort of sliding scale toward the longer ranges.

Instinctive styles at ranges of 20 feet or less presuppose a need for speed, with both parties in the open and cover not readily available to the shooter. The distance is short, the target relatively big. Assuming that hits in the torso are the objective, the target will be around 30 inches high by 18 inches wide. It goes without saying that, if a shot is to be a hit, the barrel must be aligned with the target when the bullet leaves it. Accepting that the point of aim is the center of the target, the torso allows for a vertical error of up to 15 inches or a lateral error of up to 9 inches; the latter, therefore, is more critical.

A pointing error can arise in two ways. Firstly, if the pistol is properly aligned, both vertically and horizontally, it can actually be pointing at a spot 8 inches from the center and still be a good hit. However, any misalignment of the muzzle in rela-

Correct grip and a too low grip. Arrow shows direction of recoil and line shows fulcrum made by top of hand. Differences in these will cause a substantial change in point of impact.

...a Logical Start

in two parts
complete
in this edition

by
COLIN GREENWOOD

all photographs by Kenneth Marsden

tion to the grip will be magnified in direct proportion to the distance from muzzle to target. If a 4-inch barrel revolver is used the distance from grip to muzzle will be around 6 inches. If there is an error of alignment of ¼-inch, that is, if the gun is held with the *hand* pointing towards the target, but the *muzzle* is ¼-inch off to one side, the error will be multiplied 40 times at a range of 20 feet and the shot will be a miss.

The Perfect Grip

There is only one way to ensure correct alignment of the pistol every time, and that is for the shooter to take up a perfect grip. This has to be taken up quickly and instinctively, but nonetheless perfectly, and the only way to achieve this is first to learn the correct grip and then work at it until the hand is incapable of an incorrect hold. The correct grip for practical or combat shooting is basically the same as the correct grip for target shooting, the only variations being in the tightness of the hold, and possibly the location of the thumb. The center of the backstrap must be located in the center of the V formed by the thumb and forefinger, and the alignment of the barrel from rear sight to front sight must be a continuation of the alignment of the arm from shoulder to wrist, so that if the arm were brought up into the target shooter's stance, there would be one continuous line from shoulder to front sight. No matter how tight the grip for combat shooting, the pressure of the hand must still be predominantly fore and aft on the pistol, and the weight of pressure of the individual fingers should progressively decrease from ring finger to little finger.

The question of grip is also vital in connection with recoil which affects pistol shooting in two ways. Most of the recoil occurs after the bullet has left the barrel, but it can still affect the shooter both physically and psychologically; recoil can quickly make an inexperienced shot frightened of his gun, causing him to flinch badly in anticipation of the recoil. Flinching is a pretty certain way to ensure missing any target in either combat or target shooting.

The cause of recoil is quite simple. The burning gases under high pressures exert themselves equally in all directions, and only the bullet is free to move. The opposite and equal reaction to this is the backward movement of the gun in recoil; if it were able to recoil freely its movement would be exactly in proportion to the

movement of the bullet and the products of combustion. Supposing the total weight of the bullet and the products of combustion to be 200 grains and the weight of the pistol to be 2 pounds (14,000 grains), the velocity and the energy of the recoil will be just one-seventieth of the velocity and energy of the bullet at the muzzle. However, the pistol does not recoil freely when held. If the pistol is properly gripped, the hand firmly in contact with it, part of the weight of the body can be added to the weight of the pistol to represent the mass which is opposing the bullet, thus reducing the actual recoil of the weapon. A perfect grip is therefore essential in controlling recoil and combatting any tendency to flinch.

Recoil Effects

Most recoil movement occurs after the bullet has left, but it starts to operate while the bullet is still travelling along the barrel, which results in a lifting of the muzzle before the bullet leaves. Provided this movement is consistent, it has no significance and can be compensated for by the sights. Any skeptic may test these

theories by checking the difference in height above the barrel line of the front sight and the rear sight of a revolver; or he can take a break-open revolver (such as the Webley) and fix the barrel in a vise, bore sighting it at some mark. If the grip is now brought up to close the gun, checking the sights will show them pointing appreciably higher than the mark on which the barrel was bore sighted. This means that the sights are actually directing the shot low at the time of the trigger release so as to allow for the rise of the muzzle caused by recoil. A further test can be made by shooting two different bullet weights from the same pistol, for example the 145-gr. and the 200-gr. bullet in the 38 Smith and Wesson. It will be found that the heavier bullet strikes higher than the lighter—a result of the heavier recoil which the heavier bullet induces.

The recoil acts directly in line with the barrel and, of course, the hand is well below the line of the barrel. Thus the recoil acts as a lever, the fulcrum of which is the top of the hand. If the location of the hand on the pistol is allowed to lift or drop from

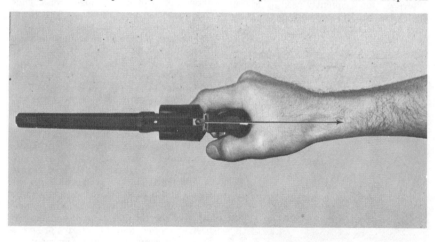

Top view of correct grip and off center grip. Arrow shows direction of recoil. Using off center grip, recoil will cause twisting of pistol and a substantial lateral error.

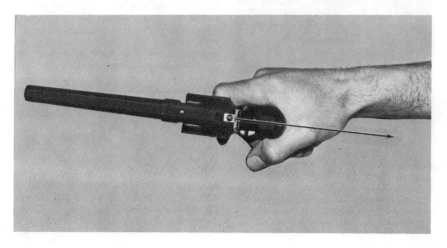

26TH EDITION, 1972 **171**

shot to shot, the leverage asserted changes substantially and the point of impact will be changed in the vertical plane. For all practical purposes, the recoil acts directly to the rear. If the pistol is correctly centered in the hand with the proper alignment from front sight to shoulder, the recoil is transmitted in a straight line to the arm and the body, where much of it can be absorbed, and there will be no lateral disturbance caused by recoil. However, if the grip is not perfect and the pistol is off center in the hand, the recoil will cause the hand to twist before the bullet leaves the barrel. This force can produce a substantial lateral error of alignment.

The force of recoil cannot be overcome by the shooter, but it can be controlled so that it does not adversely affect the shot. This can only be done with a perfect grip.

Another factor likely to cause the fatal ¼-inch of misalignment in instinctive shooting is trigger control. To see just how far bad trigger control can deflect the muzzle of a pistol, get someone inexperienced to try a fast double action shot with an empty revolver, and watch the muzzle swing out much more than ¼-inch, usually high and right. An educated trigger finger is needed to get a shot off quickly from an instinctive position, particularly with a double action revolver. Only excellent trigger control will allow the trigger to be drawn back until the shot breaks without any disturbance of alignment. The term "squeeze," too-frequently used in describing the method of releasing the trigger, is very misleading. The correct method involves pressing the trigger directly backwards without any pressure or deflection sideways and using only the trigger finger without any change of pressure from the other fingers on the grip. This is the type of trigger control required in good target shooting as well as in combat shooting. The problem of trigger control is also closely connected with the problem of grip. If an off-center grip is taken, it will be extremely difficult, if not impossible, to press the trigger straight back, and this will cause a serious lateral error of alignment. Short range, instinctive combat shooting is the form of pistol shooting furthest removed from the target shooter's art, and yet it will be seen that two of the most important factors are common to both.

Instinctive Shooting

Instinctive shooting is limited to the shortest ranges, and most accepted styles indicate that the pistol is held either just outside or just within the fringe of vision. No attempt is made to align the pistol visually. At ranges beyond 20 feet, most systems use a pointing method of alignment, where the pistol is brought well into the field of vision, but both eyes are kept open and focused on the target. No attempt is made to use the sights, but alignment is visually aided by looking along the barrel. As the range increases, the amount of error which can be tolerated decreases in direct proportion, so that at 40 feet a lateral error of ⅛-inch will cause a miss. Thus the point-shooting method is strictly limited in its effective range, and beyond 40 or 50 feet the sights must be brought into use if accurate shots are to be made. The reduction of permissible error in medium-range point shooting increases the importance of perfect grip and trigger control, and any shooter who is to perform well must first master these elements.

At longer ranges, any combat technique must involve the use of the sights if it is to be effective, and any use of handgun sights immediately raises the problem of where the focus of the eyes should be fixed. No eye is sufficiently flexible to permit both the sights and a target 25 yards away to be clearly in focus. The over-riding importance of correct gun-hand alignment has been explained, and if the terms previously used in connection with alignment are applied to the use of sights at longer ranges, the relationship between a sighting error and the resultant error on the target can be established. Using the same 4-inch barrel revolver the sight base will be about 5 inches, and a range of 25 yards represents 180 sight radii; therefore any error of sighting in these conditions is multiplied 180 times on the target, and a sighting error of a mere .010-inch will cause an error of 1.8 inches on the target, while a lateral error of .050-inch or 1/20-inch will cause a miss at 25 yards.

The combat shooter faced with a target at longer ranges will frequently be required to choose between focusing on the target and accepting the inevitable loss in accuracy which must result, or obtaining fine accuracy by focusing on the sights and having a less clear picture of his opponent. In practice, this decision rests on the range involved and the amount of target ex-

Typical target stance. To experienced shots, this is more accurate than any combat stance. Its value to combat shooters lies only in the ease with which errors can be diagnosed.

posed. At ranges just beyond the maximum for point shooting, the focus remains on the target and the sights are permitted to be somewhat out of focus. This gives a better alignment than the pointing technique. At long range, or where the target is only partially exposed, it will be necessary to fall back on the target shooting technique of focusing on the sights and allowing the target to be blurred. This technique is by no means easy to master and many experienced shots find difficulty in maintaining a concentrated focus on the front sight. Yet this is essential in target shooting and in those combat situations where fine accuracy is needed.

Target Shooting

The essentials of target shooting can be listed as:

1. Correct stance.
2. Perfect grip.
3. Correct sighting techniques.
4. Perfect trigger control.

It will be seen that grip and trigger control figure in all combat shooting, while sighting techniques are vital at all but the shortest ranges. At first glance, it may seem that the target shooter's stance, which has to be so carefully and precisely adopted, has absolutely no relevance to combat shooting and, indeed, it must be conceded that this stance would be quite ludicrous in most combat situations. The stances and positions adopted in various forms of combat shooting vary considerably, but all are quite different from the target shooter's stance. To be of value, a combat position should offer:

Two handed double action grip with stance suitable for pointed or aimed fire at longer ranges. This grip helps reduce effects of errors in technique but also makes it difficult to diagnose them.

1. Speed of movement in bringing the gun into action and in changing targets.

2. Control to maintain the gun within the limits of the target, and prevent overswing on any change of target.

3. Adaptability to any conditions of terrain and circumstance.

4. Holds which minimize any errors of technique which may arise in the heat of the situation.

This last point provides one of the stumbling blocks in teaching combat shooting. Although a good combat position will reduce any errors of technique, it will not eliminate them and it may well leave them to develop to the point where they are almost impossible to correct. Although errors may be minimized, they will still produce less reliable shots, and will inhibit progress toward proficiency in any type of shooting. No error can be corrected until it has been properly diagnosed, and the use of combat techniques in the first stages of training makes diagnosis virtually impossible.

It is often suggested that errors in technique can be diagnosed by "reading the target," and many shooters will be familiar with a segmented target, with a particular error shown in each segment. Firstly, they cannot explain what error might be present if there are shots scattered all over the target, as is frequently the case with a novice. Secondly, their very simplicity is dangerous and misleading in the extreme. Most of these targets show that shots falling in the 6 o'clock segment are the result of allowing the front sight to fall below alignment with the rear sight. This *may* be so, but the cause might equally be in a changed height of grip, excess pressure with the little finger, pushing forward the whole hand at the time of releasing the trigger, or indeed, by a combination of various faults. To suggest that the problem is as simple as these charts indicate is nonsense.

The combat shooter must, however, ensure that he has mastered grip, trigger control and sighting techniques, and eliminated any errors which may have arisen,

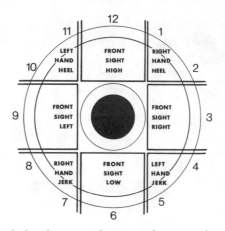

before he can make any real progress in combat techniques. If the combat positions make these first steps difficult to check, and the target does not offer a sufficiently accurate guide to any faults which may develop, the shooter will have to look elsewhere for the most suitable way of learning and checking these basic essentials. The offhand stance adopted by target shooters offers a method in which grip, trigger control and sighting can be taught clearly and in which any errors can be detected and corrected before moving on to combat techniques. An experienced coach, watching the movements of the shooter firing offhand, will be able to spot most errors, and "dry firing" (without ammunition) is frequently useful in tracing faults. However, the inexperienced shooter will be affected by knowing that his pistol is not loaded and, if flinching or trigger snatch were serious problems, he may not show these in dry firing. Possibly the best method of detecting faults in technique is "skip shooting," in which the coach loads a revolver (preferably in 22 caliber) with three live and three fired rounds in an irregular sequence. The shooter does not then know whether a live round or a spent case will be presented and any reaction to recoil or any faults which can be disguised by the effects of recoil can easily be spotted when the spent round is presented. The shooter as

well as the coach will then see, not only the error, but the effect which the error has on alignment. *If a shooter can see for himself what is going wrong, he is well on the way to correcting it.*

A logical study of the problem, therefore, indicates that the first step in learning combat shooting is best taken by following target shooting techniques to the point where the basic elements have been well learned. It is not necessary to go beyond this point in the strict context of basic combat training. However, any organization responsible for training men in combat shooting might well believe that practical measures taken to encourage target shooting as a sport represent an investment which will be repaid a thousand fold. If a real effort is made to encourage trainees to take up target shooting, even if only a small proportion do so, the organization will benefit from the fact that these men will maintain their mastery of the basic elements of shooting in their own time, probably at their own expense. Further, such interest in handgun shooting generally is likely to increase the amount of interest taken in combat shooting, and lead many of them to devote their time and efforts to improving their efficiency in this field also. In purely economic terms, therefore, such an investment must pay off.

The basic elements of combat shooting are the same as those of target shooting, and the art of pistol shooting can, perhaps, best be thought of as a tree. The trunk consists of the basic elements of grip, trigger control and sighting and, once these have been mastered, the tree forks into the two main branches of combat shooting and target shooting. Each of the main branches has smaller branches which represent the different forms of shooting within each branch. No matter how far he has progressed along the target shooting branch, an experienced target shooter has only reached the fork of the tree when he comes to apply himself to combat shooting. The novice, starting at the foot of the tree, cannot reach either branch until he has mastered the main trunk problems. ●

Combat Shooting—a Logical Start Part II

PART ONE of this article demonstrated that skill in any aspect of handgun shooting can only be based on mastery of grip, trigger control and sighting. The second part proposes to take the arguments a stage further; converting the theory into practice, looking at the problems of the individual who wishes to learn combat shooting, and at the organizations which have to teach it.

The teaching of combat shooting should progress through four distinct stages, each of which provides a logical step forward and each of which is a full, sound base for the next step. The four stages are:

Introductory Dealing with safety; functioning, care and maintenance of arms and ammunition; potential dangers from extreme range, penetration, ricochets, etc.;

laws covering carrying and the use of handguns.

Elementary The theory of pistol shooting; grip, trigger control, sighting, position and breath control.

Practical Adapting the basic elements of pistol shooting to positions likely to be of value; different positions from prone to standing; use of rests and support; making rapid changes of target; dealing with moving targets.

Tactical Fitting the practical methods into the tactics likely to be involved; taking cover and making the best use of it; shooting from behind cover; shooting in the dark; fast draw; methods of approaching opponents in widely differing situations.

The introductory stage is not fully covered here, but clearly safe gun usage and a full understanding of the guns and their potential are essential. The standards of safety cannot be anything but the highest, and the handling of a firearm must not cause the slightest danger, nor even the slightest feeling of uneasiness, to anyone whom it is not intended to endanger. A proper understanding of the handgun, how it works and how to care for it, is necessary for safety and for the efficient use of the gun. This must be taught to the stage where everything that happens between picking up the gun and firing the shot is fully understood. The potential of the ammunition in terms of maximum effective range, extreme maximum range, penetrating powers and ricochet dangers affect the

Two handed grip on revolver when firing single action. The thumb of the left hand is used for cocking and allowed to rest on top of right hand. If revolver is to be used double action, the thumb can rest along the top of the right thumb.

He must hold his aim, keep looking at the front sight while the shot breaks, then he will see the blade dancing all over the place as all the different pressures tend to wrench it out of alignment. Now he sees the problem; he should stay facing his blank wall until he can take his aim, break a single action shot and still have a near-perfect sight picture a full second afterward. When he can do that he is fit to show his face on a range, but not before.

The first gun to be fired on the range should be a 22 revolver—for a number of reasons. The revolver is the only handgun which can easily be used for skip shooting with alternate live and dummy rounds—there is no better aid to learning the basic principles than this. The revolver is a little simpler than the auto, is less likely to distract the novice at this stage. A novice is always apprehensive about the first few shots and the use of a heavy caliber revolver could make him gun shy, a problem difficult to overcome. There is no real difference between shooting a 22 and shooting a 357 Magnum until the recoil comes, and mastery of recoil follows mastery of the correct grip. Finally, 22 ammunition is cheap and a substantial amount can be allocated to this stage of training without unduly straining the budget. No matter what gun the shooter will eventually use—revolver or auto—and no matter how much centerfire ammunition is available for training, start him off with a 22 revolver.

First Range Shots

The object of the first series of shots is merely to demonstrate to both student and instructor that the lessons against that blank wall have been properly learned, and that grip, sighting and trigger control problems are being overcome. The first few shots will undoubtedly be affected by nervousness, so there should be nothing about the practice which will add new problems or distractions; they should be fired in exactly the same way as the snapping at the blank wall was done. No targets, just a large backstop, but this is not just blasting off half a dozen shots to get the feel of the thing. Each shot must be carefully deliv-

safety problem, but they also have a direct bearing on the use of the gun and the later stages of training. The man who knows the penetrating power of a large caliber revolver is not going to take cover behind a thin wooden screen. Similarly, such a man faced with an opponent partly hidden by a thin timber screen will know that he can take his opponent out by shooting through the wood instead of trying to hit a small exposed part.

Any agency required to provide men with arms and train them, and any individual who takes it upon himself to use a firearm, must know more than just how to fire it. He must know when to fire it or, more to the point, when not to fire. Time spent covering the law on this subject could save a great deal of trouble later.

Classroom stuff, all this stage one, but it must never be boring lecture material. The rules of safety have to be taught until they are second nature; range, penetration and ricochet problems require talk in terms of yards and miles, of feet per second, and of feet or inches of penetration in a particular material. All this will make more sense and be better retained if the talks and lectures are backed up with visual aids—visual aids which will register. Instead of simply saying that a 38 Special bullet will penetrate "X" inches of timber at "Y" yards, produce the timber with the bullet still bedded in it or, better still, shoot through the piece of timber and let everyone watch. Shooting at sealed cans of water or at an orange may be pretty old hat, but it does impress. When it comes to impressing people that bullets actually kill and that safety is important, try a color slide of a particularly messy bullet wound—strong stuff, but it impresses.

Theory and Practice

The theory of the elementary stage was the subject of Part I. Now we should see how this theory can best be put into practice. A good coach for each shooter will greatly ease many of the problems, but few shooters will be able to monopolize a good coach, even if they can find one, and no police agency can afford so many instructors. The problem can be eased a little by pairing off the students so that one can carefully watch the other while all are under the eye of an instructor. This helps in three ways. Firstly, the amount of dead time, when members of a class are simply waiting their turn to shoot, is reduced; secondly, the "coach" can learn a lot from his partner's mistakes; thirdly, the shooter is helped by someone who can watch all his moves at a time when he can only see his handgun.

The pairs of students take their first steps, still in the classroom, by developing grip, sighting and trigger control techniques. Revolvers loaded with empty cases, or preferably with snap caps are used and, of course, both guns and cartridge cases must be checked by each class before starting. The "target" for this stage is a blank, light colored wall—any wall with nothing on or near it to distract the shooter's attention from his sights. When he fully understands the proper sight picture and has, with a little coaching and correcting, got a good grip on the pistol, the shooter takes up the correct offhand stance used by target shooters. Then he concentrates on his sights and keeps concentrating on them while he tries his as-yet-uneducated trigger finger in breaking a single action shot.

Two handed grip for autos. This grip can also be used with revolvers when firing double action.

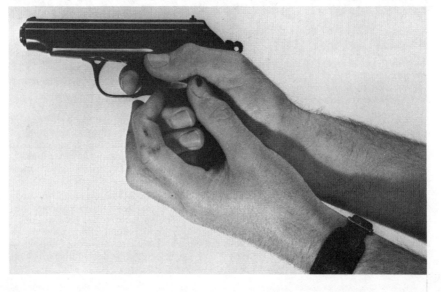

Prone position. Full two handed grip is used. Gun and body position are kept as low as the terrain will allow.

ered and then followed through by allowing the pistol to come to rest after recoil and checking the sight picture again. This follow-through sight picture should look pretty much like the sight picture did before the shot was fired.

The next step is to introduce a target, to see whether the early lessons are paying dividends. Arguments about the type of target which should be used for combat training have ranged far and wide; targets currently used vary from the standard round bull competition target to complicated figure targets with odd-shaped scoring zones. These targets all hinder the shooter in attaining his current object, no matter what value they might have in later stages of training. That round black aiming mark on the competition target draws the shooter's eye like a magnet away from his sights and the scoring rings tend to be very discouraging in the early stages. The same can be said of the silhouette targets in common use. What is needed at this stage is simply a plain rectangle of paper, preferably a matte, off-white color, with no aiming mark to distract the shooter's eye from his sights. Progress at this stage is measured simply by group size; as the shooter's grasp of the basic skills increases, the group size will decrease. A positive method of measuring this progress is needed, so the plain white target should have grouping circles drawn *on the back* where they will not distract, but will clearly indicate group sizes. Standard competition targets could be used for this provided they are put up with their reverse side toward the shooter, and provided that no account is taken of the score indicated on the back; the scoring rings used only to check the group size. The shooters should start at a range of 30 feet, with a target about 15 inches square. They should be told to shoot for the approximate center of the square, concentrating all their efforts on a good sight picture, a good trigger release, and following the shot through to check the sight picture.

At regular intervals skip shooting should be introduced into the program, with the "coach" loading the revolver for his partner and checking the follow-through position particularly carefully at each blank round. Until a shooter can regularly group within a 6-inch circle or less at 30 feet, he should stick to this stage

of the game. Once this standard has been reached, the shooter should be faced with a round bull target for a few shots to check that an aiming mark will not distract his attention from the sights. Throughout the course the shooter should be returned to the blank wall and target shooting practices at regular intervals to make sure that no errors have arisen. Then, when he has reached the stage of finding man-sized targets pretty easy to hit, to cut him down to size a little.

Combat Stances

The move to the practical stage must start with the adoption of a combat shooting position upon which the variations necessary to meet differing circumstances can be based. The necessary ingredients of a good combat position were stated in Part I to be:

1. Speed of movement in bringing the gun into action and in changing targets.

2. Control to maintain the gun within the limits of the target and prevent overswing on any change of targets.

3. Adaptability to any conditions of terrain and circumstance.

4. Holds which minimize any errors of technique which may arise in the heat of the moment.

No one position will fill all combat needs —these could vary from an ultra-short range shot delivered at lightning speed to a very precise shot at long range, with ample time. However, combat shooters the world over are now turning to the free standing two-handed position as the most useful basic combat method. It fulfills all the requirements listed above and is relatively easy for the novice to master. There are many variations of the two-handed grip, but two are put forward here as being more useful than any others. In both cases the pistol is gripped correctly by the shooting hand, a grip that does not vary in any way from that taught in the elementary stage. If the gun is a revolver, the shooting hand is then gripped by the free hand, with the little finger beneath the grip, the other fingers curled around the shooting hand. If the revolver is to be fired single action, cocking can be done with the thumb of the weak hand; for double action shooting the thumb can lie loosely on top of the thumb of the shooting hand. If the weapon is an auto, this style of grip can result in the loss of a little flesh from the top of the thumb as the slide slams backwards, and it will be far better to cup the weak hand beneath the shooting hand with the fingers around the front of the grip.

In both variations, the shooter faces square to the target. The arms are kept straight, the shooting arm pushing outwards, and the weak hand pulling inward to form a rigid triangle with the gun at its apex. The pull of the weak hand must be to the rear only, with no sideways pressure. From this position moving targets or changes of target are dealt with by swinging from the hips, keeping the triangular support for the pistol firm and controlled.

Kneeling position. By using the type of two handed grip recommended for autos, the pistol shooter is able to take up the same kneeling position as a rifleman would use. The supporting elbow is positioned just off the knee.

Any position will need to be modified to suit the cover or the terrain. The kneeling position is easily modified to take best advantage of the cover afforded by an automobile.

Targets well to the side are engaged by moving the feet round to face the target, not by swinging too far out of square. This free standing position should be taught and practiced at a range of about 20 yards, using plain silhouette targets and allowing deliberate fire until the position is mastered. The whole process should then be speeded up until the student can raise his pistol from an angle of about 45 degrees to the ground and fire an accurate shot in less than two seconds. From this point onward the moves through the various positions become much easier. The prone position uses the two-handed grip in exactly the same way as the standing position, the elbows being rested on the ground to give the minimum lift for a clear shot. In the kneeling position, the type of grip recommended for autos can be used in a position similar to that for rifle shooting. When the use of rests and support is taught, the basic two-handed grip will have to be varied except when shooting over the top of cover—a situation to be avoided whenever possible. In all cases, the gun should be kept clear of the cover and support should be obtained by resting the hands or arms against the cover.

Short Range Shooting

Dealing with fast, short-range targets should be left to the end of the practical stage to give the shooter as much training and experience as possible. The range at which the requirement for speed begins to take precedence over fine accuracy cannot arbitrarily be fixed. It must vary according to the skill of the shooter, the size of the target exposed and the time the opponent will take to get off his shot. At ranges of around 20 feet, when a rapid shot on a fully exposed target is called for, the two-handed grip should be used and both eyes should be kept open, with the focus on the target. If the initial stages of training have been properly carried out, the shooter will still see the sights and produce good alignment without wasting time on the process.

Pure instinctive shooting, with the pistol only just within the fringe of vision, must be restricted to the shortest ranges—10 feet or less, and to fairly large targets. The most experienced pistol shots have to work hard to master this technique, which is only used in those real emergencies when there is nothing else for it. *The most common mistake made in combat shooting is in trying to use instinctive shooting at hopelessly long ranges.* If the very slight amount of error of alignment needed to produce a miss is recalled, the limits of instinctive shooting are better appreciated. If your man is almost leaning on your gun, instinctive shooting works; beyond that you want to see what your gun is doing before you let off a shot.

Colin Greenwood, 38 years old when this article was written, has been an English police officer since 1954, rising in the years since to sergeant, inspector and, his rank today, Chief Inspector. He has participated in the shooting sports generally, including shotgunning and rifle shooting, but his main interest was, and is, in handgun shooting. He won the British Police Championship twice in ISU centerfire matches, placed several times in those and other handgun events, and was twice a member of the British Team competing for the European Police Shooting Championships. Mr. Greenwood's articles have been published in the (English) *Forensic Science Journal*, in several British police journals, in *Guns Review*, et al. His latest book, *Tactics in the Police Use of Firearms*, is an excellent work that deals with all phases of the police use of guns and related equipment.

Mr. Greenwood is (if he doesn't mind the term) an enlightened policeman, one who does not believe, *ipso facto,* that stringent gun controls mean an automatic reduction in firearms crimes. Last year Mr. Greenwood was granted a Fellowship at Cambridge University to reaseach and report on the effectiveness of firearms controls in England. That study has now been completed, and here is what Mr. Greenwood had to say, in part, about his findings: "...firearms controls have done little or nothing to combat armed crime. It can be shown that, when firearms were completely free from control (prior to 1920), there was less criminal use of firearms than there is now!"

For Mr. Greenwood's further thoughts on this subject, read his "Are Firearms Controls Effective," appearing elsewhere in this edition.   JTA

Once the first step in the practical stage has been completed, shooting should always be against a time limit except for the periodic return to the blank wall and grouping stages. The difficulty in providing turning or pop-up targets to work to short time limits has led some mathematician of long ago to work out that firing two shots in two seconds is the same as firing 6 shots in 6 seconds. Six seconds is easier to time than two, so pistol training in many parts of the world, not only in America, has been blighted by the "6 shots in 'X' seconds" bugaboo. Six shots in 6 seconds is certainly not the same as two shots in two seconds. Apart from the failure to allow for time to come on target, those responsible for this suggestion seem to have forgotten that no one is going to stand still while 6 shots are fired at him. Combat shooting in this way makes the shooter fire 6 shots each time he draws his gun, and there is every chance that such training will take hold when he finds himself in a real live combat situation—he will promptly empty his revolver at the first target to appear, a very dangerous habit. An empty revolver is of little use when the opponent can fire one aimed shot and end the matter. If, under combat conditions, a shooter has not hit his opponent with his first shot, or at worst with his second shot, he might find it more profitable to start on his prayers rather than trouble with the third shot. In training, the maximum number of shots to be fired at each exposure of a single target should be two, and the absolute maximum time allowance should be three seconds.

Final Stages

The final stage of training is beyond the scope of this article, which deals with making a start on combat shooting. In the tactical stage the techniques which have been learned have to be fitted into the conditions likely to be found in combat. This requires a lot of thought and research into the best methods of approaching a particular situation, whether it be taking out a criminal barricaded in a building or defending oneself against a sudden surprise attack. Fast draw falls into this stage of training—almost post-graduate stuff. All too often half-trained police recruits are asked to master the fine art of delivering an accurate, fast shot from the leather without having had the essential grounding in accurate shooting. The results are frequently tragic. No training system is complete unless it includes some tactical training in its finer forms, such as moving-film targets or a "Hogan's Alley" type of thing, where the shooter is faced with problems requiring quick and correct reaction as well as good shooting.

Combat shooting is not something which can be learned casually by reading a couple of books and watching western or detective movies. It is a science in which the basic lessons have to be well learned before proficiency can be attained. It may well look pretty easy when a practiced combat shot demonstrates his skill, but this is carefully studied ease, the result of training and practice. The novice will need to work hard at this, but if his training follows a logical sequence his progress will be more rapid and certain.   ●

Scopes & Mounts 1971-72

by BOB BELL

A penetrating and critical review of all the new and interesting glass sights, mounts and accessories.

SOMETIMES one shot is the convincer. Back in 1947 I was working in the woods near New Meadows, Idaho—low man on the totem pole in a logging operation, but that still made it possible for me to get into elk country regularly. On Sunday Dick Balbach, his brother Bob, and I were loafing around a small lake in the high country. We had our rifles along, of course. Mine was an Ackley-barreled 257 on a M98 Mauser action, bedded airtight in a dense walnut blank by Bump Lynn, a pattern-maker who, on rare occasions, used to whittle stocks. It wore the then-new Edward V (for Varmint) model 10x scope, and with handloads would stay under an inch at 100. Dick, who had gone through WW II with me, and Bob had M94 Winchester 30-30s.

A large bird, probably a heron, landed on a snag sticking out of the far end of the lake. I said I was gonna take a shot and asked how far it was. They agreed the range was about 500 yards. To me, still unused to that gin-clear Idaho air, it looked about 350, and that's what I held for. A ponderosa log made a useful rest and I got a good letoff. The 100-gr. Collins bullet, pushed by a near-caseful of 4350, hit directly in line but about 18 inches low. The bird took off, circled, and obligingly sat down again on the same stub. My second shot splattered feathers all over.

Neither Dick nor Bob said much, and I didn't give much thought to the happening myself, but the following spring, when I got back after spending a few months at home in Pennsylvania, both brothers had scope-sighted 270 Mausers built by Charley Evans, whose shop was just outside of New Meadows. That one shot convinced them that a scoped, high-velocity outfit could do things a 30-30 couldn't dream of.

Dick and Charley are gone now, and life

isn't quite the same without them. Even the 257—my first built-to-order gun—is gone, and the 10x Edwards had disappeared too. But that's enough looking backward. The friends will never be forgotten, but guns—and scopes—are easily replaced, and I've used many dozens of 'em in the years since. Here are some observations on this year's crop of glass sights. They may not be perfect, but, everything considered, they're quite likely the best ever offered to shooters.

⊕ **American Import Co.** continues to market the L.M. Dickson "Signature" line of hunting scopes—three straight powers and three variables. At $28.95 to $55, these are about in the medium price bracket. They have quite a following among Pennsylvania deer hunters, a number of whom have told me how pleased they were at the way the Dicksons stand up under bad weather conditions—notably rain. Full specs are listed in the catalog section.

⊕ **Bausch & Lomb** has a number of new products on the drawing boards, according to product manager Howard Palmer, but no new scopes or mounts this year. An understandable situation, in view of the two high quality lines of hunting models now offered by this company—the Custom and Trophy models. I've been using a 2½-8x Trophy B for a couple of years on a favorite long range rifle, a 7x61 S&H Magnum built on a lengthened FN action, and it has proven to be a durable, crystal-clear glass. Optically it does anything I can ask, the internal adjustments have continued their accuracy over this time period (some scopes perform well when new but deteriorate with use, as recoil and general hard handling get in their licks), and it's a size that looks well on an average hunting rifle, I feel. I guess such performance is to be expected from B&L though. Several friends who got original Balvar 8 variables when they came out in the mid-50s, are

Bob Bell with Thompson/Center's Puma 1½x handgun scope, here mounted on the T/C Contender in 357 Magnum. With 38 Spl. wadcutters, ragged-hole groups at 25 yards are easy.

still using them with full confidence and success.

Perhaps this ability to hold up over a long period of time has not been commented upon enough. Many scope users take time to test their outfits when new, and assume that their performance, if suitable, will continue forever. This isn't always true. In fact, with some cheap imported models it's rarely true. Scopes take a beating when mounted on high power rifles, and some mechanical designs simply can't stand up to it, though when you examine their optics just after purchase they seem as good as almost anything. Continued recoil can loosen lens mounts, affect adjustment mechanisms, even cause compound lenses to separate. When things start moving around inside a scope tube—even a few ten-thousandths of an inch—accuracy and reliability go out the window. High price doesn't guarantee an absence of such problems, but it's only common sense that top-quality materials, design and workmanship have to be paid for. So don't expect a $19.95 scope to match a $100 one. If you expect to keep a given glass on a gun for many years, get the best you can afford from a reputable maker. There are such people around—including Bausch & Lomb.

⊕ **Bridge Mount.** The firm of this name (Box 3344, Lubbock, Tex. 79410) offers a one-piece aluminum alloy base of extension form for Remington 40X and 700 short actions, using the factory tapped holes on those rifles. ¾" wide by ⁷⁄₁₆" high, the new base is 8½" long and very rigid. Designed to take the Redfield 3200 or Unertl Posa rings only, so far, mount separation is fixed at 7½" for minute-of-angle (near enough) adjustability with those scope mounts. The Bridge Mount is *not* usable with earlier (Lyman, Fecker, Unertl) target mounts and, as it is aluminum, mount rings carefully or the rounded cuts can be chewed up. Weighing only 4 ounces, with its 4 screws, the unit should be welcomed by competition benchresters, not to speak of varminters. $14.95 postpaid.

⊕ **Browning Arms** has added one new scope to its line this year, a 2½-8x wide angle which has a field ranging from 44 to 16½ feet. This scope is under 12½ inches long, weighs 12 oz. and has a clear objective lens of just under 30mm, which makes for a compact glass. Internal adjustments are half-minutes. Price, $109.95 with crosswire, post or 4-Plex, $10 more for a dot.

Browning continues to supply two other high grade scopes, a 5x wide angle and a 4x built on a ¾" tube for 22 rimfires, and solid bridge mounts.

⊕ **Buehler, Inc.,** manufacturer of one of the country's most popular scope mounts, constantly updates their line to fit new rifles as they become available. A note from manager Bob Ray indicates that Savage's M170 slide action rifle is fitted by the Buehler Code 60 one-piece base, while two-piece bases, Code 8-9, fit the Husqvarna 8000 and 9000 model rifles. The Weatherby Vanguard rifles—the medium-priced line from South Gate—are accommodated by the same Buehler bases that fit the popular Mark V Weatherbys.

Bushnell's Scopechief IV-DM scope-mount combination uses standard bases (Weavers shown), permits increased fore-and-aft adjustability.

⊕ **Bushnell Optical Corp.** announced their 4x Lite-Site Scopechief V last year, but few were distributed, perhaps because a worthwhile modification was approved just before production began. At any rate, they're now available, we have one.

The Lite-Site offers an advanced method of making a scope reticle visible under extremely poor light conditions. The normal approach to this problem has often been to enlarge the objective lens (thus transmitting more light) and make the reticle coarser, easier to see. The Lite-Site literally throws a little light on the reticle, in effect a "center dot" of light via a self-contained #640 1.4-volt battery. The power supply is activated by making a one-third turn of the cap which seals the battery turret, said turret being immediately aft of the elevation adjustment. The cap works stiffly, so accidental movement is unlikely. Battery life is reportedly about 10 hours, which amounts to quite a few dawn and dusk sessions in the bush.

Seeing that spot of light glowing against a dark background is certainly another unusual sight for a feller who can remember when seeing *any* sort of aiming point, even at high noon, was something of an accomplishment in scopes. But see it you do. Rough checking indicates the light dot covers about 5 MOA, which seems a reasonable diameter considering the distance at which game is normally seen in bad light.

No chance yet to use this scope on game, but I've studied its visibility on targets, domestic animals, tree trunks and other assorted objects. I can report that you definitely can aim with acceptable accuracy long after it's too dark to see any detail with the naked eye.

The light bulbs have a life expectancy of 100-plus hours and are easily replaced. Filters are available to cut down the bulb's intensity—which some users prefer after the novelty of the big bright dot has worn off a bit.

In operation, the light is seen on the focal plane of the scope via an internal pellicle. Light reflection reportedly amounts to less than 10% of the light transmitted through the scope. While the mechanical switch isn't claimed to be waterproof, the pinhole light aperture under the switch has a water-tight seal, so a fog-free condition should be maintained. Our sample scope came with an extra battery and a lower-silhouette turret cover, for use when the Lite-Site is not needed.

The new Lite-Site weighs 11.9 oz., has a handsome black finish, and the rear of the tube is capped with soft rubber to lessen the possibility of split eyebrows resulting from improper gun mounting.

Also new from Bushnell this year are the Scopechief IV-DM models. These feature an unusual—possibly unique—detachable mount. A male dovetail rail, an integral part of the bottom of the aluminum alloy tube, eliminates all need for mount rings. Detachable mounts (half rings) lock onto the rail, while the bottom portions fasten securely to conventional bases on the receiver bridge and ring. The rear of the rail is cut with several notches, which permits sliding the scope forward or back a reasonable amount to adjust for eye relief. The engagement of a cross stud in the rail notches prevents scope slippage.

This scope-mount is available in the 1½-4½x, 2½-8x and 3-9x variables, and the 2¾x, 4x and 6x straight power Scopechief IVs, from $62.50 to $102.

Bushnell's excellent and low-cost Banner scopes now have the eye-protecting neoprene shock absorber, attached to the eyepiece and replaceable, found so valuable on their Scopechief models. Banner scopes are now hard-anodized for longer lasting, more scuff-resistant finish, and have the same streamlined appearance of the top-line Scopechiefs. The medium-price Custom-scopes are also available now in the DM-mounting system described above, we've just learned, priced $42.50 to $69.50.

⊕ **Conetrol** scope mounts come in three price ranges, $32.85 for the Custum, $25.85 for the Gunnur, and $20.85 for the Huntur, though interchanging bases, rings or whatever can affect this. These are very slick looking mounts, with no projections whatsoever, and are made for most rifles that take a coventional screw-attached top mount on the receiver. Included are the lefthanded versions of the Weatherby Mark V, Savage 110 and Texas Magnum, as well as the dovetailed Sako, BSA and Ithacagun actions. Both solid and split rings are made for one-inch and 26mm tubes, while the medium and high rings are offered for 26.5mm tubes in the three grades. For those who want them, semifinished base blocks are offered in the Huntur range, bridge or two-piece.

Conetrol mounts also are made for the Thompson/Center Contender handgun, a rig we've been using awhile now—a Custum base with low Gunnur rings on a 256 Winchester barrel, bedding a Leupold M8 2x glass—and the way it shoots has to be seen to be believed. Working over chucks at a football field's length with this outfit is as much fun as quarter-mile shooting with a hopped-up rifle.

⊕ **Davis Optical Co.** (formerly R.A. Litschert) puts out a pair of target scopes called the Spot Shots and objective lens units which either boost the power of hunting scopes or increase their eye relief via new eyepieces so they can be used on handguns.

The top Spot Shot sells for $89.50, has a 1½″ objective lens and comes in powers from 10x to 30x. It has a ¾″ tube, quarter-minute external mounts, and weighs 20 oz. Focusing is done by moving the non-rotating objective unit out or in. The other Spot Shot has a 1¼″ objective, powers from 10x to 20x, price $69.50. Recoil spring is $3.50 extra with either scope. Just after WW II I had one of these, then under the Litschert name, and used it for several years for indoor match shooting and varmints, with good success.

Davis makes his Targeteer attachments with 1½″ objective ($29.50) and 1¼″ ($25) for many one-inch-tube hunting scopes, and the Varmint Master ($18) for such older ¾″ scopes as the Weaver 330 and J2.5. These complete objective-lens units use existing threads inside the front end of the tube for attachment, thus can be installed by the user. By increasing the focal length of the scope, they boost power to 6x or 8x, making a big game scope usable in the off months as a varmint glass. The field of view is reduced, of course, but eye relief remains about the same.

The long eye relief pistol eyepiece interchanges with the regular eyepiece on many American scopes, permits gun to be held at arm's length. It cuts power about in half. $15.

⊕ **Herter's Inc.,** continues to offer a large number of hunting scopes in both straight and variable powers. We had a pair of variables this year, a 3-9x and a 4-12x. Made in Japan, these had an attractive dark-glossy finish and, interestingly, had screw caps to protect the lenses when not in use.

These scopes—the Mark I and Mark VIII—had Herter's Rangefinder and Point of Aim reticle. This is a crosshair embellished with horizontal lines intended to give points of aim for 300, 400 and 500 yards when the center intersection is in zero at 200. In addition, there are four circles, each acting as a rangefinder at the various intervals mentioned, where they subtend that 18-inch circle so popular on all rangefinder reticles. In other words, if you assume that a big buck's withers-to-brisket measurement is 18 inches, and he fits just inside the 400-yard circle, that's the range; you then put the proper horizontal line (the one bisecting that circle) on his gizzard and squeeze off.

This reticle was computed on the basis of a 150-gr. bullet loaded to 2700 fps, such as in the venerable 30-06 and approximately so in the 264, 270, 280, 284, 300, 308, 8mm, etc., according to the literature accompanying the scopes. This also gives rather good information on zeroing-in procedures for these scopes, recommends close checking at measured ranges up to the 500 yards noted, and suggests how to adapt minor

trajectory variations to the reticle by juggling the basic 100-yard point of impact.

For hunters who like this kind of approach and don't mind what to me seems a cluttered aiming point—and the Lord knows there are many such guys—this could well be highly satisfactory.

⊕ **J.B. Holden Co.'s** "Ironsighter" scope mount, which permits use of iron sights beneath the scope, has been around long enough that it's available for most common rifles, including models such as the M1 Carbine, Ruger 10/22 and Savage 24V, which aren't always thought of in connection with such rigs. The newest rifle fitted is the M94 Winchester carbine. This one mounts a long-eye relief scope, such as the 2x Leupold, ahead of the action, and has an integral open rear sight. It requires tapping one or two holes, depending on caliber. Price is $19.95, five bucks more than Ironsighters for other centerfires.

Jerry Holden was kind enough to send a sample of this mount for inspection, and the workmanship and appearance are fine, but it's been many years since I owned a M94 so I had nothing to latch it on to.

For shotgun scope mounting, the #350 Ironsighter will fill the bill. Receivers must be tapped, so don't try it if yours isn't steel.

Also soon due is an Ironsighter for 22s with grooved receivers, to handle tubes of ¾″, ⅞″ or one inch. $6.95.

⊕ **The Hutson Corp.,** makers of the 1x Hutson Handgunner pistol scope, is offering a new type of spotting scope, the unusual Chromatar 60. New in that it's the first time a mirror-type or catadioptric-system telescope has been made available as a spotter, I believe, and quite different in that it's about a third smaller and lighter than comparable-powered glasses. Only 8 inches long by 3 inches in diameter, it weighs a mere 24 ounces.

Despite its small heft and size, the Chromatar 60 has an effective aperture of 59mm, said by the makers to be capable of a resolution higher than that offered by a standard 63mm lens. We have no means here of verifying that via an optical bench or the like, but our sample Chromatar 60, with a 22½x eyepiece, has performed well with one minor exception—and that may have

Hutson Corp., P.O. Box 1127, Arlington, Texas, 76010, is an outfit I'd never heard of in the optical field until last summer. I was talking with pistol grip maker Steve Herret and gunwriter Hal Swiggett at the Outdoor Writer's Association of America conference in Idaho, when Hal trotted out the smallest scope I'd ever seen, the Hutson Handgunner.

I examined his closely and made arrangements to get one myself. It's a very interesting scope, just 5¼ inches long, of unit power, with some 25 inches of eye relief. This means most shooters can extend a handgun at arm's length and get a full field. The tube is small, the ocular and objective ends enlarged. Adjustments are in the mount, currently made for quite a few popular handguns. Most revolvers require tapping one or two 6/48 holes, though the Thompson/Center gun works as is. The 45 ACP mount replaces the left grip, being anchored by a pair of screws. Dunno how that works on the old GI warhorse ... seems a shame to subject any scope to its complicated shuffling recoil. A 1.7x version of this scope is due out about the time this issue of GD hits the stands. Scope price, $35, mounts, $14.95.

⊕ **Paul Jaeger's** last letter says there's little new in his mount line, but he's still making the side mount ... which means that anyone who wants this style of mount

been because of the weather conditions prevailing during the brief test.

The skies were heavy and gray on that March day. While 22 caliber holes could be located in the black bull without much trouble (our old 20x scope demanded a little more searching-out), the general illumination or brightness level seen through the Chromotar 60 was not quite as high as the old glass showed—the image was just a bit darker, it seemed.

Next, under the same gray skies, we tried the new scope at 300 yards—the 200-yard butts were down temporarily. While 22 holes in the black couldn't be found except now and then, 7mm and 30-caliber holes were located with fair regularity.

I should mention that the backstops here at Creedmoor Farm don't let any light come through the targets from the rear, so any spotting scope is at a disadvantage.

The standard Chromatar 60 will sell for $109, with a choice of 15x, 22½x or 45x eyepieces. A small tripod, not adjustable for elevation, is $19.95, but I don't think it is a good support for a spotter. $20 or so will buy a Freeland stand, a better and more versatile unit, and one that includes a cradle for the glass. Hutson's cradle is $4.95, the scope held tautly by a strip of Velcro, that patented stuff that clings tightly to itself. It works well, being quickly loosened or tightened, yet holds the scope securely.

Eyepieces on the Chromatar 60 are set at 45 degrees, and they're $22 each separately. Later on a 20-45x variable-eyepiece scope will be made available, price as of now about $119.

All in all, a fine glass, the Chromatar 60, and if you already have a Freeland stand or some other, no more is needed. (JTA)

can still get as good as there is, for it's long been a classic. Jaeger is also making a few handgun mounts but nothing on a production basis yet.

⊕ **Jason Empire** has a fairly extensive line of big game scopes—2½, 4 and 6 powers with 32mm objectives; 4, 6, and a pair of 3-9s with 40mm objectives—while new this year is a 1½-5x with 40mm lens. This is a big objective for such a low power variable, but it will give a very large exit pupil —8mm even at top magnification—for fast work in the woods. Two 4x scopes for rimfires and one 3-7x complete the line.

⊕ **Kwik-Site** "See-Thru" mounts are made for many popular rifles, including

Kwik-Site's new Kwik-Mount/94 for the Model 94 Winchester.

now the M94 Winchester. On the 94 the mount is fastened to the left side of the action, the scope offset somewhat. The base uses factory holes so no drilling is necessary. This version (not a See-Thru type) sells for $19.95, compared with $14.75 for other rifles. The See-Thru refers to the figure 8 style rings, which lift the scope high enough to permit aiming with iron sights. When I was a kid many shooters wanted such a mount, but the idea died out as time went on. Now things seem to have come full circle, with renewed interest in such designs.

However, low-profile Kwik-Mounts, without the See-Thru feature, are also available for most rifles.

⊕ **Leupold & Stevens, Inc.,** now of Beaverton, Oregon, has a reputation second to none in the scope field. A full line of hunting models—stretching from the long-eye-relief 2x, which can be mounted ahead of the action on top-ejecting M94s, through 3, 4, 6, 7½, 10 and 12 powers—is offered, plus a pair of variables in 2-7x and 3-9x.

For a couple of years now I've been using a Leupold 12x on various varmint rifles, most often the HB M700 Remington 22-250; a 10x on a 40XB-BR 222 bench rifle, which I use for medium-range chucks (and try to shoot 'em in the ear!) and, more recently, a 2x on the 256 Winchester barrel —one of three tubes the Thompson/Center people sent along with their hotshot Contender handgun. One or another of these outfits is suitable for chucks at any range up to a strong quarter-mile, and beyond that I'm not in favor of shooting.

My 12x has the Duplex reticle, introduced by Leupold in 1962, a design that's become my favorite. The fine crosswires at the center permit precise aim, while the heavier portions extending outward from near the center make for a conspicuous reticle, one easy to find in a hurry. The distance between opposing heavy posts can also serve as a rangefinder, if the target's size is known with fair accuracy—and it remains motionless long enough for you to make your calculations—for this distance is listed by L&S as follows, at 100 yards: 2x, 24", 3x, 22", 4x, 16", 6x, 10", 7½x, 8½", 10x, 7", 12x, 5", 2-7x (at 7x) 10", 3-9x (at 9x)7".

Of special interest this year is the 6x Leupold "Golden Ring." Its size and weight are just about that of a standard 4x, making for a compact glass on a long-range rig, particularly a mountain rifle, where the extra power can be useful but where minimum bulk is important. It should do much

toward reviving interest in a magnification which once had considerable following but somehow got lost in the shuffle. Hunting pal Andy Hufnagle has for years been using a 7½x Leupold on a lightweight 243 Sako for all his deer hunting, be they whitetails in Pennsylvania brush or mule deer in Wyoming's sage country, and his results have been good, as he can handle a scoped rifle. However, for average use under such conditions, I believe a 6x would be preferable, because of its bigger field and adequate power, and this new Leupold should fill the bill.

⊕ **Lyman Gun Sight Corp.** is another highly respected scope builder, and they've just announced what has to be one of the top new items of the year—a 20x addition to the All-American line.

Bench shooters for years have hollered for short, lightweight scopes of high optical quality. They want to mount them on the action only, to eliminate any possible problem that might result from adding weight at one point on the barrel, and by keeping weight down they can add the amount saved to the barrel and still stay within the specified competition limits. The same arguments hold for varmint shooters, even though as a group they might not extend their equipment investigations as far as the benchresters. A few technically minded individuals have gone so far as to build their own scopes, or alter existing models (often the 10x All-American) to increase

magnification, and some of the better known shooters have been able to talk a manufacturer into creating a one-of-a-kind for them.

The 20x All-American is 17⅛" long, weighs 15¼ oz., is built on a one inch tube, has a field of 5½', eye relief of 2¼", and offers a choice of internal adjustment values—⅛ or ¼ MOA. Mounting is solid. It can be focused for range, of course, and its reticle is permanently centered. Some 7" shorter and 10 oz. lighter than the famed Lyman Super-Targetspot, itself a light-weight scope among target models, this new All-American should find favor with many shooters. Crosswire, tapered post and crosswire with tapered post are standard reticles. Price, $109.95.

Lyman now offers three more reticles without charge in the AA line—center dot, Center-Range III (vertical tapered post with horizontal posts connected by a thin wire), and Center-Range IV (what other manufacturers call Duplex, Dual-X, etc.).

Some years ago we obtained a full line of Lyman hunting scopes, and since then we've been using all of them on various rifles—switching them around as fancy suited. They've been afield in all sorts of weather—rain, snow, what have you—on rifles from the 222 to the 338 Magnum. Never has one let us down. We have a lot of faith in Lymans. One thing to keep in mind when zeroing in—Lyman click values differ from those of other scopes, so check the literature or tape the info on the tube before shooting. It'll save you some ammo. The adjustments are consistent, indicating precise machinery.

⊕ **Marlin Firearms Co.** has a fairly extensive line of scopes—a pair of fixed powers in 3x and 5x, variables in 1¾-5x, 2-5x and 3-9x, and three rimfire models—two of 4x and one 3-7x. In addition, there's a 4x Glenfield to go with the rimfire rifles of that designation.

The big game models are interesting in that all except the small 2-5x variable have 40mm objective lenses. This makes for a fairly big scope (outside diameter (1⅞"), but does give a good size exit pupil— 4.5mm even at 9x, which provides all the light the human eye can use and also makes for fast alignment. Combined with the conspicuous Tri-Post reticle, these scopes are right at home in the woods, which could well be deliberate since the Marlin lever guns fit very well into this environment also.

This year Marlin also is offering a Veri-Fire collimator for quick sight alignment. It comes with 22- and 30-cal. studs for $25, with extra studs at $2. Such items are fine for making sure your first shot will be on the paper, but don't expect them to give you precise zeroing. It happens on occasion, but only by chance. The way you absorb recoil, etc., usually makes a noticeable difference in point of impact, so check

Lyman's new All American 20x.

the collimator's setting by actual range firing.

Another item from Marlin—neither scope nor mount, but of interest to shooters—is a moulded wall plaque about 10x13 inches bearing Article II of our Bill of Rights. A worthwhile reminder of our country's beginnings and the importance of citizen-owned arms to its existence. $5 postpaid.

⊕ **Numrich Arms** has redesigned their 30-cal. Carbine mount to fit all original GI versions and such commercially made carbines as the Universal, Plainfield and Erma M22 rimfire. Rings take one-inch tubes, mount the scope over center, with a deflector to handle ejecting cases. $6.95.

⊕ **Pachmayr Gun Works'** famed Lo-Swing scope mount is quite likely the best known rig for hunters who deliberately head for areas where the weather is likely to be super-soggy, most shooting distances short, and game the kind that bites back—as for instance southeast Alaska's bear country. A scope is sometimes a hindrance here, but sometimes exceedingly useful. The ideal situation is to have it there when it's needed, be able to get it out of the way when not wanted. These requirements led to the development of this sophisticated

mount which, in a fraction of a second, can be flopped out of the way to make the short-range irons sights available. When swung back into aiming position, the scope is in precise zero. It takes topnotch design and workmanship to achieve this, but as many years of use by many hunters have proven, the Lo-Swing works.

The Lo-Swing is made for most rifles, including the lefthanded versions of the Savage 110, Remington 788 and Weatherby Mark V, and for scopes with 26mm, one inch, ⅞- and ¾-inch tubes. It can also be had for such military rifles as the M1 Garand, Krag, Springfield, Lee Enfield, Mauser, Enfield, 30-cal. Carbine, etc. The top mount version, which fits factory holes, sells for $25; the side mount, which should be installed by a gunsmith, is $20.

⊕ **Realist, Inc.** continues to offer the interesting and useful Camputer Auto/Range scopes in fixed power 4x and 6x, and variables in 1½-4½x and 3-9x. We've had a chance to use the 6x in extended tests and the 3-9x for a lesser time, and can report that both work as specified. That is, when zeroed in with the specified load at 100 yards, the hunter turns a "range ring"

until a set of parallel horizontal wires brackets an 18″-target. At the same time the scope tilts up or down a predetermined amount to compensate for bullet drop, letting you hold precisely where you want to hit at any sporting range. The trick, of course, is getting a wild critter to stand still long enough for you to perform the necessary bracketing. However, even if this isn't possible, you are no worse off than with any other scope, and if you can make the adjustments you're way ahead. The Camputer scopes come with mounts.

Realist also manufacturers 2½x, 4x and 6x, 1½-4½x and 3-9x big game scopes and the 4x and 6x Apaches for rimfires.

⊕ **Redfield Gun Sight Co.** has several new offerings this year, notably the changeover of their medium-size variables, the 2-7x and 3-9x, to Widefield versions. As reported last year, a new optical design of the ocular lens system, which changes the scope's field of view from a circle to a horizontal oval, at the same time materially increasing the horizontal dimension of the field, has been developed by Redfield. Offered originally in straight-power models, it now is incorporated in these two highly useful variable designs. Original field in the 2-7x was 44-16 feet. This now is upped to 49-19 feet. In the 3-9x, it's increased from 37½-12½ to 39-15 feet.

I've long felt that the 2-7x was the most useful variable for all kinds of big game shooting, so I asked to see a sample in this size with the new Widefield feature. It came in some months ago with the 4-Plex reticle and it certainly is an impressive glass. Image is brilliant, details are sharp and crisp; the power adjusting ring moves smoothly through its full range, internal adjustments match quoted values, and dunking in hot water reveals no leaks.

I must admit that I still haven't got completely used to seeing a modified rectangular field of view instead of a circle, this despite the fact that I've had a 6x Widefield for over a year. But this is little price to pay for the increased field, which obviously is an advantage in brush or woods country. It just isn't possible to get too much field for these conditions.

All the usual Redfield reticles, including Accu-Range, are offered in the new Widefields. The optical redesign of these scopes, incidentally, necessitated a slight forward shifting of the adjustment turret, so to insure proper eye relief under any mounting condition, a new, longer extension front mount ring was made. A few of the JR mount bases were altered to change the location of the front ring also.

I haven't yet had a chance to shoot any game with this new Widefield, but it's mounted on my pet 338 Magnum, replacing the original 2-7x Redfield, which served so well for range testing. Hope to really break it in this fall.

The 6x Widefield also has experienced some redesigning, becoming a bit more compact in the process. Clear objective lens diameter is down 2mm from last year's 41mm, length is down ¾″ to 12¾″. At 24 feet, field is a foot less, while eye relief has been increased somewhat to 3½″. A 6x is a fine choice for antelope, long range deer hunting, etc., and this is a good one.

Another new Redfield item is a 15-45x spotting scope, a companion to the earlier 15-60x. The same size physically, the new model seems to me a more logical choice for shooters. There may be times when a 60x can be used on a range, but I've never seen them ... mirage just doesn't permit it. The 15-45x sells for $99.95, too, which is quite a reduction from the more powerful model's $149.50. Both have long eye relief —.80″—which makes it easy to use them while wearing shooting glasses.

For several years now I've been using a 24x Redfield "3200" target scope on my Hart-barreled 308. The last time I fired it from the bench, it gave several consecutive 5-shot groups under a half-inch at 200 yards. That's quarter-minute-of-angle accuracy, closer than I hold as a regular thing, but this big scope let me see every bullet going into those ragged holes—which didn't make the fifth shots any easi-

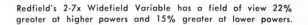

Redfield's 2-7x Widefield Variable has a field of view 22% greater at higher powers and 15% greater at lower powers.

er! The load, by the way, was the 168-gr. Sierra International and 42/4895.

Redfield has just announced a new line of scope mounts that are at once rugged, well made and attractively priced. I examined these FRontier Mounts at the NRA meeting, and the design and execution was impressive.

The rings are made from a tough, hardened aluminum alloy, the screws and dovetail clamps of steel. This makes for a lightweight mount, but Redfield says they're strong enough for the biggest magnum rifles, and that no slippage will occur.

Each base has dovetail grooves—one on each side—plus an integral cross-slotted stud. These insure that the rings will be located exactly the same each time they're removed and replaced, and this unusual setup also means that the scope will shoot to the same zero—within average hunting requirements—following removal and replacement.

Made for virtually all popular centerfire rifles, the new FR ring sets cost $9.95, the pair of bases $1.95.

⊕ **Sanders Custom Gun Service** is the exclusive importer of the MSW Wetzlar line of high-grade German scopes. Most are of all-steel construction with 26mm tubes. Now available are a 3x straight-tube model with 22mm objective, a 4x30, 4x36 and 6x42, as well as 2-6x and 2¾-8x variables. Prices range from $60.50 to $107.50. Some models are available in light weight alloy tubes with integral mounting rail on special order. The typical German 3-post reticle is standard, with five others offered at $10 extra. All offer a choice of both w. and e. internal adjustments, or simply elevation alone. Two new scopes this year are a 7x50 ($98.50) and 8x50 ($104.50).

Sanders also imports the Japanese-made Bisley scopes in all standard powers from 2½ to 10x, as well as four variables.

⊕ **Savage Arms** is primarily known for their extensive line of rifles, shotguns and Savage/Anschutz target rifles. However, they do market a pair of scopes for rimfires and four centerfire models, straight powers in 2½x and 4x, and 1½-4x and 3-8x variables. We've had occasion to use both variables over quite a length of time, with fine results. The small one, combined with the new M99-A lever gun in the longtime favorite 250-3000 Savage caliber, should make a honey of a whitetail gun, as well as an all-round outfit for today's cowboy who is as likely to be riding a Jeep or pickup as a horse.

⊕ **Stoeger Arms** has several new scopes this year. One is a straight 2½x, another is a 1½-4x variable, and both are built on inch tubes and intended for high-powered rifles. There's also a second 3-9x, of slightly different specs than the one offered last year (and still supplied). They also now have a 4x Junior model for rimfires, built on ¾" tube and having internal adjustments. It sells for $9.95, while the big game scopes are $25.95 for the 2½x, $38.95 for the 1½-4x, and $46.95 for the 3-9x.

Still available are the 4x, 6x and 8x big game scopes, all on one-inch tubes with half-minute internal adjustments.

⊕ **S&K Mfg. Co.,** builder of the popular Insta-mounts, has two new ones for 1971, according to Sid Haight. This mount, as most readers probably know, is intended primarily for use on military rifles converted to sporting use. Already made for a dozen-plus GI models, the new ones make it possible to get a glass sight on the German semi-auto M-43 ($30 for base, plus $8, $10 or $11 for S&K rings), and the A-R 180 ($20 plus rings).

⊕ **Tasco,** at last count, had 15 big game scopes, six for rimfires and a pair of target models, one of the latter a 6-18x, the other a straight power design in 12, 16, 20 or 24 power. These target jobs have external mounts, 40mm objectives, weigh 34 and 36½ oz.

(An attempt was made in 1970 to use the 6-18x and the 20x fixed-power Tasco target scopes, but because of deficiencies in the mount clamping system no shooting with them could be done. Perhaps this fault has been fixed by now, but we've had no such indication from Tasco. ED.)

Ted Levine writes that a new wide-angle scope called the .Omni-View also will be marketed soon, but we hadn't seen a sample at this writing.

⊕ **Thompson/Center Arms** now offers a 1½x handgun scope called the Puma.

Made in Japan, this little glass has internal adjustments, crosswire reticle, and an integral male mounting dovetail running the full length of the tube body except for the enlarged eyepiece. Its mount screws into the factory holes which normally secure the iron sight. A pair of Allen screws lock the mount to the scope tube.

We've been shooting one of these for some months on the 357 Magnum barrel of the T/C Contender, with excellent results. By "excellent," we mean that the scope has withstood the recoil which full power Super-X 357 loads dish out, and the mount has not moved since installation (we Loc-Tited the screws and base—standard procedure anymore with all scope mounts). It is fast and easy to use at arm's length, and it even gives the appearance of belonging on this somewhat different looking handgun—perhaps because of its unusual tube, which isn't round but rather is made up of about a dozen narrow flats.

Firing from rest at 25 yards, groups with full 357 loads were not too impressive, all running about 2½ inches. However, when we switched to Remington 38 Special Targetmaster 148-gr. wadcutters, we immediately got successive one-hole groups. Thinking perhaps my holding was at fault, I asked Jim Bashline to try them both. His results were practically identical.

Unertl BV20

There are two short-tube target scopes on the market now—the Remington 20XBR, introduced a couple of years ago, and the newer BV20. As you read this another lightweight high power glass will have appeared, the Lyman 20x, also a stubby one, but with internal adjustments, not external as they are on the Remington and Unertl scopes.

We've been using the BV20 on a Remington 17 caliber rifle for a spell and, except for a couple of minor criticisms, it's been eminently satisfactory. Our sample is the De Luxe type, which means that Posa-type split mounts, a magnum clamp and a return spring are supplied. The price is now $159.95, result of a recent increase. The standard BV20 has regular mounts and clamp ring, is without the recoil spring, and sells for $148.00. Both are identical optically and otherwise, but the De Luxe BV20 weighs 21¼ ozs., with the standard at 19 even, both without their steel lens caps. Both are 17⅞" long, have 43mm free objective lenses, and field of view at 100 yards is 94".

The most unusual feature of the BV20 is the provision for range or parallex adjustment. This is located just in front of the eyepiece, ready to hand—no reaching up

and over to get at the front end of the glass. The entire ocular element is moved back and forth in this new—and patented—system. Because of its short over-all length, the BV20 can be mounted wholly on the receiver, though receiver-barrel siting can be managed also. However, that's not being done to any degree, for the chief reason behind the short-tube design is to permit mounting *on* the receiver.

John Unertl sent along an extension-type Posa-style front base, which lets the rings be 7.2" apart for ¼-inch adjustment values. (We'll risk repetition—7.2" does *not* give quarter-minute increments, but 6.86" does.) Using this extension base setup, some slight rotational movement of the scope tube seems to exist, but it has not, it would appear, affected the shooting. This slight movement—if it is indeed such—derives from the extension front base, we'd guess, perhaps because of some torsion effects.

With the tube of the BV20 pushed forward in the rings as far as I can get it, that is, without letting the range-adjustment ring hit the rear mount, the eyepiece is too close to my eye. That makes for an uncomfortable shooting position, at least for me—I have to haul my head back to get the full field of view.

My other small point concerns range ad-

Unertl's BV20 Target Scope.

justment itself, which is critical. Only ¼-turn of the sleeve changes the range from 100 to 200 yards, which changing back and forth the benchrester does frequently in competition.

Nevertheless, the Unertl BV20 is a beautifully built instrument, optically and mechanically, as are all other Unertl scopes we've known.　　　　　JTA

⊕ **E.D. Vissing's** Supreme lens covers sell for $4.95 per set, and when the weather is bad—which is to say normal for hunting—they're worth an awful lot more. They protect the lenses from snow, water, dust, etc., yet flop open instantly when you touch a release button. They're made for every scope I ever heard of, but because of the variation in tube diameters—manufacturers seem to change the enlarged-end measurements more often than anyone realizes—the simplest way to order is to trace each end on a paper, mention the make and model, and mail to Vissing. He can fit whatever you've got.

⊕ **W.R. Weaver Co.** has lengthened their already extensive and highly popular line with a pair of Classic variables, the V700 and V900, to go with the 3x, 4x and 6x Classics introduced last year. In the long-accepted 2-7x and 3-9x sizes, these feature a high-gloss finish for hunters who like glossy guns and want scopes to match, rather than the dull, less reflecting finish of the earlier K models. More important, to my mind, each scope has a minimum number of threaded joints, each of which is compression sealed with a neoprene O ring. These are checked by submersion in hot water. In addition, eyepieces are permanently installed. These factors are important in making a scope weatherproof.

The Classic V900 has an objective unit that is adjustable for range, thus parallax can be removed for the last bit of accuracy when bench shooting, etc. The smaller V700 does not have this arrangement. Tubes of all Classics are aluminum, which saves several ounces compared with their counterpart K models. Five reticles are offered in all Classics—crosswire, Dual X, post, rangefinder, and (at extra cost) center dot.

Last year we discussed the then-new straight power Classics—which have now been given a workout by several shooters. The 3x went to an outfitter friend in Idaho, the 4x to a rough'n tumble whitetail shooter in Pennsylvania's Kinzua Country, and the 6x to a hunting pal in Coeur d'Alene, Idaho—a hotshot rifleman whose favorite sport is puncturing running jackrabbits in the sage country down around Challis. His pet rifle for this is a standard-weight 222 Sako, preferably with a 6x glass aboard, which is what made me think he'd appreciate this Classic . . . as he does. I've been shooting scoped rifles for well over three decades, but this guy's efficiency gives me an inferiority complex. Anyway, these friends have been able to subject the "old" Classics to a considerable amount of hard use, and they've come up smiling. I fully expect the new variables will also show their toughness, and hope to be able to report on that aspect of them next year.

Another new product from Weaver this year is the Qwik-Point sight, made in two

⊕ **Williams Gun Sight Co.** introduced their Guide Line scopes a year ago (4x, 1½-4½x and 3-9x), after many years as a leading scope mount manufacturer. Boyd Williams tells me that a second series of scopes, called the "Twilight" models, will be available by this summer. On the schedule are a 2½x, 4x, 2-6x and 3-9x. These will have the TNT (Thick 'n Thin) reticle, with the same scopes slated for crosswire and Guide reticles in 1972. Prices aren't firm yet, but they will be priced well below the Guide Line, somewhere in the $30-$60 range.

By the time you read this Williams will have on hand a new scope line, the Twilight series, these to be offered in 2.5x, 4x, 2-6x and 3-9x, all with their TNT (Thick and Thin) reticle—an aiming point quite like the dual-X or duplex type of other scopes. Prices haven't been fully set on the Twilight scopes yet, but they'll probably range about $30 to $55.

Williams has a new rear barrel sight as well, the elevation-adjustable Dovetail Open Sight, that makes possible—at long last—the installation of a dovetail-base sight without banging it into the dovetail cut in the first place—or hammering it later to get a windage change. The secret? A set screw in the sight top. Just insert the

DOS into the opening, turn the screw, and a gib is cammed into contact with the dovetail opening.

Simple and effective, the DOS looks good, too, and it's made in 4 styles (square, U or V, and very shallow-V) and 4 heights —³⁄₁₆, ¼, ⁵⁄₁₆ and ⅜". $3.95 complete, extra blades $1.25.

Another new—and much improved—product is the Williams trigger shoe line. Boyd Williams told me that he'd long been unhappy with some existing shoes—loose fits were common, so much so that the indicated model could hardly be kept on the trigger. The Williams triggers, to be ready about July 1971, will fit properly, he said—just order the model number wanted. Some 23 types will be offered, $2.95 each.

Williams big new catalog for 1971, full of good gun stuff, is yours for the asking.

---

models, the R-1 for rifles and the S-1 for shotguns. The Qwik-Point mounts like a scope and projects a bright luminous red dot onto the target or into the sky. It does not magnify, which simplifies shooting with both eyes open and in effect gives a limitless field.

Some six inches in length and about 8½ oz. in weight, the Qwik-Point has adjustments (¼" at 40 yds.) for proper zeroing of bullet or pattern. The body is anodized aluminum.

Built in a sort of double-decker design, with the reticle-creating tube above a sighting tunnel, the unit is fairly high, which makes it impossible to wrap your hand around the action for carrying, though it doesn't interfere with any two-handed carry.

This could well be useful for big game shooting in the woods, but I don't think I'm the one to write about such an outfit on shotguns. I never actually aim a shotgun on grouse, pheasants, rabbits or similar game, but simply swing and shoot. On those occasions when I catch myself trying to aim, I invariably miss. Perhaps I could use a Qwik-Point on passing ducks or even long-range dove shooting, but most of my scattergunning is the kick-'em-out-and-bust-'em-now variety, so I don't get much practice at the longer range stuff. If you're the more precise type, you could well go for this item. These sell for $39.95, complete with base and mount for most pump and auto shotguns, bases extra for rifles. Special bases #77 and 78 allow mounting on the M94 Winchester.

Weaver's latest, the Qwik-Point, is made for shotguns and rifles.

DAMASCUS
— beautiful
Their history and construction,

"Uncle" Bob Edwards, the only man who ever successfully made twist barrels in the U.S.

THE DISTINCTIVE patterns of the Damascus barrel are a familiar sight to gun enthusiasts. The knowledgeable collector knows they are composed of strands of iron and steel twisted together to form the characteristic figure. He also knows they passed out of fashion with the coming of the 20th century (or a few years beyond), and that their use with modern loads is generally condemned. Behind these assertions there lies a fascinating history and a good bit of legend.

To begin with, the term "Damascus steel" is something of a misnomer when applied to these barrels. True Damascus steel, whose history goes back well over 1000 years, was essentially a material for sword blades developed originally in the Orient; the city of Damascus, in Africa, was one of several centers of manufacture.* True Damascus steel was carefully forged from a cake or ingot containing elements of both iron and steel. Blades of this metal possessed extremely fine qualities of hardness and resilience, but the manufacture was difficult and probably a closely guarded secret. The 19th century Russian metallurgist Chernov† theorized that other smiths, unable to produce the true Damascus, hit upon the technique of twisting and welding strands of iron and steel. This composition, says Chernov, should properly be called "welded Damascus" to distinguish it from true or fusion Damascus.

True Damascus steel did not lend itself well to the making of gun barrels. Barrels of welded Damascus, however, were made in the Near East in the 17th century and probably before. By the late 18th century a few were made in Europe, where they seem to have been regarded as curiosities. It was not until the early 19th century that the "twist" barrel came into its own. It is quite probable that Napoleon had a hand in popularizing them. His famous Egyptian campaign of 1798 was a military failure, but it roused great interest in the Near East and its products. Along with the Rosetta Stone French soldiers undoubtedly picked up many of the curiously patterned arms. A Paris gunmaker named Nicolas Bernard began the commercial production of Damascus barrels in 1804. The Spaniard Melchior Alvarez and the Englishman J. Jones are credited with introducing them in their respective countries at about the same time. Damascus barrels began to be produced in Belgium in sizeable numbers about 1830.

In the second half of the 19th century the production of Damascus barrels became an important industry in the arms centers of Liège, Birmingham, St. Étienne, Suhl, and Brescia. Some were also produced in Czarist Russia, in the towns of Izhevsk and Tula. The craft was always primarily a European one. Few if any were ever made in the United States. The Ithaca Gun Company claimed that their master gunsmith, "Bob" Edwards, was the only man to make Damascus barrels successfully in this country. Production began to decline in the 1880's with the appearance of smokeless powder and excellent steels. The high cost of production was also a factor. By the 1930's only one barrel maker was still producing them in Belgium. To my knowledge the only firm still making Damascus steel today is the J. A. Henckels Zwillingswerk in Solingen.

Originally a distinction was made between "twist" and "Damascus," though the terms are used interchangeably today. Technically, a twist barrel was one formed by wrapping of metal in a spiral fashion. A very early barrel of this type was the *canon tordu,* made in France and Spain in the last half of the 18th century. The gunsmith began with an ordinary barrel, one formed from a rolled piece of iron with a weld seam running straight from muzzle to breech, something like the paper tube

BARRELS

but deadly

their faults and virtues

by LEE KENNETT

of a cigarette. This barrel was heated and twisted, on its axis, so that the weld seam became a spiral running around the barrel. This was a tedious and expensive process, but the twisting did reveal imperfect welds. Such barrels were not much seen after 1800. Another early type of twist barrel was the "plain ribbon." A plain strip of iron was wrapped in spiral fashion around a mandrel and welded. This may be regarded as the direct ancestor of the more elaborate barrels which began to replace it around 1830.

The most popular type of barrel in the early 19th century was probably the famous "stub twist," so-called because its chief ingredient was the stubs of old horseshoe nails. The use of these stubs in gun barrels had actually been attempted by Spanish gunmakers as early as the 17th century. Early barrel makers attributed superior qualities to these stubs, some in the belief that contact with horses' hooves gave them a mysterious strength; others claimed their excellence was the result of their being smelted with charcoal. For a number of years the popularity of stub twist produced a lively demand for the discarded nails. The name survived long after stubs ceased to be used as an ingredient.

In its original form stub twist was made by heating the stubs with chopped steel coach springs until the mass was fused into a "bloom." The bloom was then beaten or rolled out into long strips in which the particles of iron and steel formed a series of roughly parallel lines or striations. When coiled into a barrel these lines create a striped or barber-pole effect.

Skelp barrels were made in the same way, but from materials other than stubs. Files, scythe blades, barrel hoops, and horseshoes were some of the popular ingredients. The pattern was essentially the same as that of the original stub twist. Another type of twist was English ribbon or *torche*. Here the barrel maker began by stacking iron and steel plates into a faggot or *masse*, as it was called in Belgium. This was welded together and worked out into long strips. Before 1830 the metal was worked chiefly by hammering, and the striations were less uniform and regular. After this date rolling mills were used and the pattern in later barrels is more uniform. Whether stub twist — in its original meaning, or skelp, or *torche,* the pattern was the same series of parallel lines. All of these barrels were sometimes called "plain twist," to distinguish them from the more elaborate Damascus.

The metal for Damascus barrels—as the 19th century used the term—required more involved procedures. To begin with, the faggot was composed of more pieces of iron and steel. One Belgian maker used 300 bars and plates in his faggot. Once again the faggot is rolled out into strips or *baguettes* about 3/8 inch square. In cross section these retained the same compositions as the original faggot, but in highly reduced scale. Each rod or strip was then heated and twisted, usually to about 8 turns to the inch, reducing the length by about a third. In some of the more elaborate Belgian barrels the rods were given as many as 18 turns to the inch, so that they became completely round and resembled a long threaded screw. It was this twisting of the rods that distinguished the Damascus barrel. As W. W. Greener put it: "All Damascus barrels must be made of twisted rods, while plain twist or skelp barrels are made from plain straight rods." The usual practice was then to weld together three of these rods to form the ribbon which in turn was coiled into a barrel. This was known as 3-band or 3-iron Damascus. One and two bands were also used; French barrel makers often used 5-band, and in Liège 4 and even 6-band Damascus was made.

The variety of patterns that could be produced was almost infinite, depending on the proportion of iron and steel in the faggot and their arrangement, the number of bands, and the degree to which the rods were twisted. Pattern also varied as the barrel (sometimes) was turned on a lathe and succeeding layers of metal revealed. One French barrel maker named Ronchard-Siauve made 18 different types of Damascus! Some barrel makers developed a particular pattern as a sort of trademark and kept the composition of their faggots a secret. A man who knew his Damascus could identify at a glance the number of bands and the pattern. A real connoisseur could even tell the forge where a particular barrel was made. The more popular patterns were Boston, Washington, Diamond Twist, Chain Twist, Zèbre, Crollé, Moiré, Rose, Laminette, Frisé, Turkish, and Bernard.

Types such as Laminated Steel, Silver Steel, and *Ruban Acier* contained higher proportions of steel, from 70 to 80 percent; in general the proportion in Damascus barrels was from 40 to 60 percent.

Which nation made the best Damascus barrels? There was always a great deal of debate over this question. English barrels were often said to be the sturdiest, if not the most ornate. W. W. Greener claimed that foreign barrels might look best, but that English ones shot best. Probably the Belgian masters enjoyed the greatest

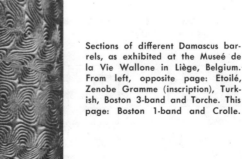

Sections of different Damascus barrels, as exhibited at the Museé de la Vie Wallone in Liège, Belgium. From left, opposite page: Etoilé, Zenobe Gramme (inscription), Turkish, Boston 3-band and Torche. This page: Boston 1-band and Crolle.

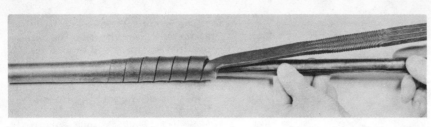

Here are the several steps in the manufacture of one type of Damascus barrel. From right: the hands are holding a mandrel used in forming a barrel. Three rods, measuring approximately ¼", are twisted individually to form those outside threads shown. The rods, now placed side-by-side, are hammered into a solid steel strap. The strap is then forced around the mandrel and the joints of the wrappings are welded together by heating and hammering to form a smooth barrel.

reputation internationally. By the late 19th century they were producing about a third of a million barrels per year; a great many of these were exported in the rough state, to be finished and fitted up abroad.

If anyone ever collects varieties of Damascus, he will have a challenging task. Some types are as rare as they are unusual in design. One that is seldom seen is Serpentine, composed of four bands of Damascus and one of plain steel. Also rare is straight Damascus, in which the pattern runs straight down the barrel instead of around it. A French maker named Breuil-Glaise made Crossed Damascus and Ribbon, characterized by a checkerboard pattern of alternating squares of Damascus and plain metal. Double wrapped Damascus, which was extremely expensive, was made by two layers of Damascus, one wrapped to the left and the other to the right; this was supposed to be much stronger than a single wrapping.

Incredible as it may seem, a few especially skilled barrel makers were able to produce barrels in which a name or monogram appeared over and over again as an integral part of the pattern. Exactly how this was done I have been unable to determine; such barrels may rightly be regarded as the supreme achievement in the art of the Damascus barrel. As one might suspect, most of them were made in Belgium. The Musée de la Vie Wallonne in Liège possesses some beautiful examples of these rarely-seen barrels.

Welding the Damascus barrel was a very demanding task requiring two or three skilled workers. In England a common practice was to "jump or butt-weld the short section together, then insert a mandrel into the tube and form the inside by hammering.* On the continent the ribbon was wrapped and welded simultaneously. In this case the ribbon was not coiled directly around the mandrel, as is sometimes asserted. A thin iron sleeve or *chemise* was first wrapped around the mandrel, and the ribbon was then wrapped around and welded to this chemise. The chemise was completely removed when the barrel was bored out to gauge. In welding, the ribbon was heated only a few inches at a time, as many as three hundred welding "heats" being required for a single barrel. The master barrelsmith would tap with a small hammer the precise spot his assistants were to strike. A ribbon of manageable length was not long enough to wrap a complete barrel; two or three had to be used, sometimes more. These were lapped or joined with great care so as not to interrupt the pattern. Even so, the best barrels were put together so that these joins were hidden between the ribs. French gunmakers got around this difficulty by drawing out ribbons of 16 feet and coiling them on themselves so that they were manageable. Though this saved making joins, it does not seem to have been used in other countries.

The forging was fraught with difficulties. Overheating could produce a barrel so brittle that it shattered on being dropped. Surface imperfections, called "greys," could ruin the pattern. The chief problem was to achieve a perfect weld. In some cases a faulty weld could be corrected after cleaning the surfaces with a fine file. Sometimes a section would have to be re-moved and replaced with a "patch," always taking care not to interrupt the design. The problem was a serious one, for the barrel was a mass of welding. A barrel of 3-band Bernard, for example, was composed of about 500 separate strands of iron and steel. There was also a large amount of waste involved. According to W. W. Greener, it took 18 pounds of prepared gun iron to make a pair of barrels weighing 4 pounds. Some Spanish gunmakers began with as much as 40 pounds of metal.

Once the barrels were forged, they went through finishing operations similar to those for plain barrels, with the exception of the treatment with acid, which brought out the figure. Damascus barrels were usually given some sort of browned finish, since this once again showed the figure best. A rich reddish-brown finish or one called plum-brown applied by English makers was particularly admired. Ordinarily the barrels were exposed to acid only long enough for the contrasting light and dark areas of steel and iron to appear. Sometimes, however, the acid was allowed to eat into the iron, leaving the more resistant steel standing out in low relief. In this case the pattern can be felt as well as seen. This was usually done with Belgian barrels of very fine figure.

Occasionally the identification of Damascus barrels presents a problem. If carefully polished and blued, their pattern tends to disappear. On the other hand plain barrels were sometimes given a Damascus finish by selective etching, a practice which William Greener indignantly called "sham damn." The barrels to be etched were usually wrapped with lithographed paper and then moistened with acid. The acid penetrated the uncoated portions of the paper much as ink penetrates the uncoated parts of a mimeographed stencil. In cases where one is unsure whether a gun has Damascus barrels, the best procedure is to submit the barrels to the acid test. An unexposed part of the barrel is cleaned of all finish and a drop of sulfuric acid applied. If the barrels are Damascus the characteristic pattern will appear. Another somewhat deceptive practice was to

Cross sections of four faggots showing the proportion of iron and steel and their disposition; the shaded areas represent steel. From left: Washington, Bernard, Crollé and Etoilé.

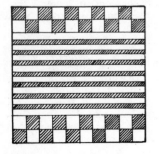
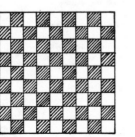
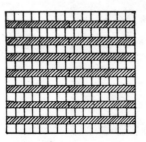
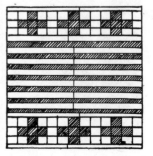

wrap a plain iron barrel with a thin Damascus covering. This is often seen in pistol barrels, and in such cases the "join" of the two metals can sometimes be seen at the muzzle. Toward the end of the Damascus period, plain steel barrels were covered with decalcomanias, simulating the genuine.

Twisting the rod or *baguette*.

The tremendous popularity of Damascus barrels resulted partly from aesthetic appeal. They were also a visible sign of quality—the finer and more intricate the pattern, the better the gun.** Oddly enough, they were also credited with greater strength. W. W. Greener wrote as late as the 1880s that "plain iron and steel will not stand so great a strain as the twisted metal." Devotees of Damascus argued that, like a rope, it was stronger because of the twisting. Others claimed that superior strength resulted from the lateral arrangement of the "fibers" in the metal. In this connection a considerable amount of myth arose. Many American hunters swore that their twist barrels would simply bulge under excessive pressure, rather than burst. This bulging was actually a sign of danger rather than of safety, since it indicated a low elastic limit. By the same token a belief has persisted in England that when a Damascus barrel gives way under excessive pressure, instead of bursting, it will "unwind" in a spectacular but harmless fashion.

The question of the safety of Damascus or twist barrels has been examined by experts many times, and they have almost unanimously condemned their use. Yet hunters continue to take them into the field and use them with apparent impunity. As an extreme example, I have an acquaintance—a gun dealer with hundreds of arms at his disposal — who uses the Damascus barrel from preference. After 30 years of this he still has all his fingers. It is also true that Damascus barrelled guns are occasionally turned up with nitro proof marks. Indeed, most European proof houses still accept them for such proof if they are in good condition—not that

they will, necessarily, pass the proving.

A Damascus barrel, like a chain, is no stronger than its weakest element, whether it be a faulty weld, soft or brittle metal, or a hidden slag incursion. Proof firing did not always reveal these defects. Indeed, there is room for suspicion that proof firing could open tiny fissures invisible to the eye. These would slowly be enlarged by corrosion and the strain of continued firing. This undoubtedly explains the instances in which Damascus barrels hold up for years with magnum loads, and then burst with a light field load. This treacherous sort of behavior should certainly be noted by those who use only black powder loads in such guns.

Even if one could be sure that his Damascus shotgun is as sound today as when it was made, there would still be a distinct risk. While the gun might not have changed, shotshells

Welding the rods together for 3-band Damascus.

certainly have. The heavier magnum loads today develop pressures approaching 12,000 psi, far above those generated by black powder or early smokeless loads. In fact the modern magnum produces a pressure that exceeds by 2,000 psi or more the definitive proof pressures used in some European countries before 1900! Then too, modern progressive powders maintain strong pressures farther down the barrel than was formerly the case. Hence the numerous bursts in twist barrels several inches forward of the breech, in unpleasant proximity to the shooter's hand. As if this were not enough, many of the older shotguns were chambered for shorter cases than those in use today. Firing a 2¾ inch shell in a 2⅝ inch or 65mm chamber may well produce higher pressures, for the crimp must unfold in the constricted area of the forcing cones. The practice is unwise with modern steel barrels; with Damascus ones it borders on recklessness.

For the prudent hunter who wants to shoot his old twist barrel gun, there are two possibilities, both of which have drawbacks. The gun may be rebarrelled by the sleeving process. The

cost is something over $100, and of course most of the beautiful figure must be sacrificed. The procedure seems to be safe if well done, though some European proof authorities are not enthusiastic about it. The second procedure is to use barrel inserts, which are inexpensive but reduce the gauge rather drastically and add weight. A 410 which has 32 inch barrels and weighs eight pounds has only a limited usefulness. All in all, perhaps the wisest course is to appreciate Damascus barrels for what they are—ingeniously constructed relics of a bygone era—and to accord them an honored retirement.　●

*There is a connection between Damascus barrels and the laminated sword blades of Japan. While a treatise on Japanese blade making would run to many pages because of the variations in forging that took place over the centuries, in essence the blades were hammered out into bars which were turned on themselves as many as dozens of times and more. This resulted in hundreds of layers of metal, the edges of which could be seen with controlled polishing and etching. In many instances this well-beaten core of softer metal was laid into a rough V-section of harder steel, the two then forged to form the blade. Again, proper polishing and etching would reveal the line of demarkation between the hard and the softer steel components.

†See *D. K. Chernov and the Science of Metals,* N. T. Gudtsov, *ed.* (Leningrad 1950).

**Wm. Greener (father of W. W. Greener), in *The Science of Gunnery* (London, 1841) and in *Gunnery in 1858* (London, 1858), is quite vehement in his condemnation of those Damacus barrels showing an excessively ornate twisting or figure. He said of such metal "It looks pretty; but certainly does not possess either the strength or tenacity of wire-twist iron. It is well known that the strength of a rope may be destroyed by twisting it too much: so is it with this sort of iron."

Wrapping the ribbon around a mandrel. Photos courtesy Musée de la Vie Wallone, Liege, Belgium.

Bibliography:

Anciaux, Maurice, *L'industrie Armurière Liégeoise* (Brussels, 1899).

Greener, W. W., *The Gun and Its Development* (London, 1881).

Laport, George, *La Fabrication des Canons de Fusil en Damas* (Liége, 1931).

Lenz, E. von, "Uber Damast" in *Zeitschrift für historische Waffenkunde,* vol. V (1906-1908, pp. 132-42.

Ronchard-Siauve, *Traité du canon de fusil* (St. Étienne, 1865).

Smith, Stanley Cyril, *A History of Metallography* (Chicago, 1960).

W. Greener on Damascus Barrelmaking

The rods are twisted by means of two iron bars, the one fixed, the other loose. In the latter there is a prong or notch to receive one end. When inserted, the bar is turned by a handle. The fixed bar preventing the rod from going round, it is bent and twisted over the moveable rod like the pieces of leather round the handle of a whip. The loose bar is unshipped—the spiral knocked off, and the same process recommenced with another rod. The length of all the spirals depends on the breadth of the rod; for instance, the stub twist has sixteen circles in six inches long; a rod five feet will make a spiral of only seven inches, while iron, of an inch in breadth, will make a spiral of as many inches long as there are twists, and hence the reason best barrels have more joinings than common ones of equal length.

The Damascus being rolled into rods of 11/16ths broad, form a spiral with the appearance of the accompanying wood cut.

The fancy steel barrels and others, where the rod is formed of more than one piece, such as the stub Damascus, etc., etc., etc., is of rather greater breadth, like unto the representation below.

The iron made from stubs, and steel, and plain fibrous steel, is invariably rolled down into rods of 6/16ths broad, forming a spiral, as below.

The spirals being thus formed, the welders commence their day's work. The batch consists of a foreman, one on whose skill all depends, and two subordinates, whose duty it is to blow the bellows, strike, etc.

They now commence the welding of twist barrels. Spirals that are intended for the breech end, are heated to a welding heat for about three inches, removed from the fire, and jumped close by striking the end against the anvil. Again they are heated, and again jumped, to ensure the perfect welding. They are then beat lightly in a groove, to make them round. The neatest part of the process consists in the joining of the two rods so as to make the barrel appear as if it had been twisted out of one rod. The ends of the two rods are a little detached, brought from the fire, and applied to each other. A gentle tap is then given, and the union is perfect in an instant. The rapid dexterity with which this is accomplished, ought to be seen to be duly appreciated. This trouble is only taken with the best barrels. In the manufacture of barrels of an inferior description, the ends of the rods are cut in a sloping direction, which, when welded together, become quite square at the part where the pieces are joined. In a finished barrel the points of junction are easily recognized. By tracing the twist, a confusion will be found to exist for about an eighth of an inch every 6 or 7 inches. From this appearance you may conclude that, for a barrel so joined, the welder had not the best price. Having joined the whole of the spirals, three inches are again heated to a welding heat, the mandril (sic) is introduced, and the tube hammered, in a groove, to the size required. This operation is repeated until the whole length is finished. This being done, then follows hammer-hardening, that is, beating the barrel in a groove in the cold state, with light hammers, for the space of half an hour. This is a most important part of the process. It closes the pores, condenses the texture of the metal, compresses a greater substance into less bounds, increases greatly the strength of the barrel, and renders it more elastic. This, however, is seldom done, unless spe-

cially requested, and then a gratuity is, of course, expected, either of money or beer, and I believe a few pots of the blood of Sir John Barleycorn will infuse more strength into your barrels than you could purchase for ten times the amount in money, as it has the effect of making the hammer descend with increased velocity.

The Birmingham workmen, if well paid, and well looked after (to counteract the bad habits they have acquired from being employed in the manufacture of so large a quantity of goods of an inferior quality) would produce an article superior to any that could be produced at the same cost in any other part of the world.

The deceptions practiced in this branch are numerous, and injurious to the trade. For instance, if you wish to have a single barrel made from Damascus, or any of the best irons, and you send to the manufacturer the weight of iron required, the probability is, that unless you superintend the manufacture yourself, iron of an inferior quality will be introduced into the inside of the spirals. By this fraud they obtain iron worth three-pence a pound more than that which they knavishly insert into the barrel. I had been repeatedly told of this practice, but I was incredulous.

It will scarcely be credited. I shall, I doubt not, be accused of throwing the hatchet, when I assert three-fourths of the barrels welded in Birmingham at this time, which claim to be twist barrels, are all plated, "veneered," from the Damascus to the humble twopenny or Wedgebury skelp,

a vast proportion certainly, but no exaggeration, it is true as that I have printed it. The method of accomplishing this is by having the iron required rolled down into ribbons of a thin description, and these are twisted spirally round a tube of common iron having the fibres running length way or parallel with the bore. The accompanying cut will convey the idea. (From *The Science of Gunnery* [London, 1841]).

Author Wildgen shown with part of his collection, including the fabled Lewis Gun.

GUNS OF WW II

by George L. Wildgen

MY FIRST GUN, a handsome English flintlock acquired 20 years ago, was purchased for me by a friend. The Dallas pawnshop would not sell a rifle to a 12-year-old, even though I had worked hard to come up with the $5 price.

Since then I have added about 75 pieces to a respectable, albeit less than spectacular, collection. My pride in this collection is justified, I believe, because it has involved a great deal of scrimping, scrounging and some tall "hoss-trading." Trying to get through college and then establish a place in the business world made a gun budget a luxury only to be dreamed of. I bought, sold and traded guns at every opportunity, getting many bargains, missing many more. It was fun and it was interesting.

A couple of years ago, however, I concluded I should channel my collecting activities to a more defined goal. I selected the area of military small arms of World War II. My reasons were three: sentimental, financial, and the interesting variety of WW II weapons. Perhaps an explanation of these will guide other gun enthusiasts who feel a strong yen to collect, yet have little cash to expend.

As an impressionable youngster I was intrigued by the war which was raging far away. The exciting action and grand heroics were depicted each Saturday afternoon at the local cinema where I watched John Wayne win the war in the Pacific with the limitless and devasting firepower of his tommy-gun.

The tommyguns, M-1s and Carbines fascinated me as much as Roy Rogers'

handsome Colt Single Actions (also possessed with limitless firepower!). I could hardly wait to join the neighborhood kids in re-enacting the capture of Iwo Jima with the crude guns we laboriously sawed and whittled from wood scraps.

My fascination continued after the war, and eventually made me a collector. Fortunately, my knowledge of firearms increased more rapidly than my collection, thanks largely to the kindness of the finest gunsmith I have ever known, Gordon Bess of Canon City, Colo. What I learned through many conversations with Bess provided me with an invaluable base that is fundamental to any successful collector—knowledge in his field.

Admittedly, my interest in martial arms was whetted by the movies, but this isn't as silly as it sounds. The old purist collector can "humph" all he pleases about the effect of movies and TV on the gun market, but the evidence is undeniable. The strong interest in Colt revolvers of the frontier era, far out of proportion to their scarcity, must be attributed to the obsession with the American cowboy hero as popularized by Hollywood. As another case in point, following release of the movie *Winchester 73*, the market took a sharp jump and a lot of folks went scurrying up to the attic to see if grandpa's old lever action had "One of One Thousand" engraved on it. Even more recently, interest in de-activated Thompson submachine guns rose as viewers become intrigued with

the blazing choppers seen on TV's *Combat* show. Now, lo and behold, dealers around the country report that the value of the little Walther PPK automatic has increased 50% as a result of the late Ian Fleming's decision to make it the mainstay in the formidable armory of his fictional hero, James Bond!* If there are such things as WW II combat aircraft collectors, I'm certain that, with the success of *Twelve O'Clock High*, B-17s are now sky high! (Pardon the pun!)

My second reason for concentrating on WW II military small arms is that the barometer in the trade indicates an accelerating trend in this area; and as interest rises, so do prices. In fact, the impact in just a few years has been awesome. The German Luger pistol illustrates the point. Not many years ago every pawnshop had a stack of Lugers they would have been delighted to move at $25 each. I have no idea where all the Lugers have gone, but comparatively few are left and these start at about $45, even in frightful condition. The same is true of certain Mauser military pistols, the 45 ACP and many other guns.

Therefore, if one is inclined toward this field, now is the time to get into the act. Fortunately, the prices on most items are still within reason and relatively much lower than in the specialized collecting fields of Colts and Winchesters. This current market situation gives the young guy with a limited income a good shot at an interesting facet of the gun world.

*If memory is correct, the inimitable Bond, at one time in his career, also used a 25-cal. Beretta. We wonder if this has had any effect on the value of this tiny Italian auto—ED.

As another appealing factor, the WW II category allows wide variety, plus a choice of specialities within a speciality. So many variations of weapons were developed throughout the war that it would be impractical to go after them all. The novice collector might well concentrate on his area of greatest interest. This could be, for instance, the variations of the Luger (there are over 100!). I have a friend who is trying to acquire one of every handgun developed for the 9mm Parabellum (Luger) cartridge. Another collects Mauser rifles, still another, automatic weapons.

Personally, I have concentrated on assembling representative primary small arms of the major nations involved in the war. The adjectives "representative," "primary," and "major" are intended not as strict limitations, but more as guidelines in order that I won't become bogged down with myriad variations of basic guns or a multitude of secondary weapons.

To illustrate this, the following are my suggestions to those interested in building a collection of this nature.

First, limit the field to arms of the United States, United Kingdom, U.S.S.R., Germany and Japan. These were the major powers. By representative small arms, I mean the first-line rifles, carbines and handguns of the chosen countries. These could be supplemented by especially interesting, second-line arms or by deactivated automatic weapons. More will be said about this later.

A coffee table display case with weapons of the German Wermacht. Resting atop a Nazi flag is the famous MP 38/40 Schmeisser submachine gun. The pistols are: artillery model Luger, standard Luger, P38, Walther PPK, Mauser HSC, and Mauser Military Pistol.

United States

The fundamental weapon familiar to every U.S. foot soldier and a "must" for such a collection is the U.S. Rifle, Cal. 30 M1 (the Garand). For the most part, the M1 was superior to other semiautomatic rifles which saw extensive use during the war. Its dependability and firepower gave the GI an advantage over adversaries armed with their nation's first-line rifle. The second U.S. rifle was the 30-cal. M1 Carbine. This lightweight weapon was quite popular but somewhat of a disappointment as a military weapon because of its limited power. Both the Garand and the Carbine are readily available on the open market, but many of these M1s are arsenal reconditioned jobs. This might make a difference to the collector who wants his items absolutely original. The M1 sells for about $75, the Carbine for about $60.

Although not used extensively during WW II, the Springfield and Enfield bolt action rifles in 30-06 caliber are fine weapons and played an important part in the early days of the war. These usually run from $25 to $35.

Fundamental to any military collection is the U.S. Pistol, Cal. 45, Model 1911 or 1911 A1—the mainstay of the GI handgun department through four wars. This pistol has probably been both cursed and praised more than any other. The few who can master it seem to do so superbly; the many who cannot often malign it as a jolting, bucking ear-shatterer which makes a pretty good club in a gang fight. Whatever your personal evaluation, the "forty-five" has proven itself an effective manstopper and great morale booster for over a half-century. A good GI-issue 45 costs around $50 nowadays. A variety of Smith & Wesson and Colt revolvers was also used by the U.S., but in relatively small quantities. The Model 1911 45 will do just fine in filling the bill for a representative U.S. handgun.

United Kingdom

Great Britain has not recently been noted for startling innovations in the military small arms field, and her WW II weapons offer few exceptions to this observation. Britain's basic army rifle was the No. 1 Mark III, popularly known as the S.M.L.E. or 303-cal. Short Magazine Lee Enfield. A few refinements of the old Enfield were made from time to time, including a shortened, lightweight jungle carbine, but basically the rifle was the same as that adopted a decade prior to World War I. The British never developed a successful semiautomatic rifle. However, their Sten submachine guns and Bren light machine guns were excellent automatic weapons. The British used the U.S. M1911 automatic pistol modified to handle

the 455 Webley self-loading cartridge. Other than slight differences due to the cartridge, the weapon is identical to the American pistol. The Webley 455 Mark VI and the Enfield 380 revolvers are rugged and interesting handguns which saw extensive service with British military forces through both big wars and are worthy additions to a collection. The British also made considerable use of the Smith & Wesson Victory Model revolver. Usually found in 38 S&W caliber, it was manufactured on the standard Military & Police frame and had a parkerized finish. Many have been converted to use the more powerful 38 Special cartridge.

Most British weapons are still inexpensive. Rifles and revolvers range in price from $13 to $35.

U.S.S.R.

Russian weapons vary sharply in both quality of design and of manufacture. The first-line infantry rifle was the Tokarev 40 semiautomatic in 7.62mm. This is a somewhat unwieldy rifle, about a pound lighter than the U.S. M1 and not nearly as rugged. The Tokarev replaced the 7.62mm bolt action Moisin-Nagant rifle. The Moisin was remarkably accurate and is a good buy on today's market for as little as $10. The Tokarev runs about $35. The basic Russian pistol was the Tokarev 7.62mm autoloader. This gun was essentially a simplified version of the Browning patent upon which the U.S. service handgun is based. The Tokarev is relatively hard to find these days, especially in good condition. Most sell in the $25 - $35 range.

Japan

The most distinguishing qualities of late-production Japanese small arms are the simplicity of design and the crudity of manufacture. (Many early items were nicely finished.) Like the British, the Japanese never developed a semiautomatic rifle in great quantity; nor did they use submachine guns to any extent. Their basic infantry weapon was almost exclusively the Model 99 7.7mm bolt action rifle which replaced the very similar 6.5mm Model 38 (Arisaka). This rifle, with its very strong Mauser-type action, proved to be an efficient military weapon. However, its firepower limitations, compared to the automatic weapons of opposing forces, put the Japanese soldier at a disadvantage in intensive, close-range combat situations.

The Japanese light and heavy machine guns were of excellent, although seldom original, design and are among the finest weapons of the war. Their quality was a real factor in providing the firepower which was lacking because of the absence of automatic rifles or submachine guns.

The basic Japanese handgun was the Nambu Type 14 8mm autoloader. Another auto was the freakish and crude pistol known as the Model 34. Believed developed primarily for aviators, it is an interesting collector's item.

Japanese weapons are also still low in price, the rifles going for from $10 to $25, the pistols about the same. Occasionally one will run onto variations of Japanese guns which are valuable collector's items. Among these is the Baby Nambu, a small version of the early Nambu pistol. The Japanese also manufactured, in small quantity, a close copy of the U.S. M1 rifle. This is a choice find for any collector.

Germany

In my opinion, the finest group of weapons developed for and during WW II was that of Nazi Germany. The designs, workmanship and innovations were unsurpassed. Quality remained high until their manufacturing facilities were systematically destroyed by Allied bombing and invading forces. Even so, the drastic innovations in gun design and manufacture occasioned by the mounting crisis have been closely studied by military arms designers and manufacturers since that time.

The front-line rifle which predominated throughout the German Wehrmacht was the Mauser Kar. 98 k in 7.92mm (8x57mm) caliber. This classic Mauser action is still regarded by many as basically the finest bolt action ever developed. The rifle is sturdy, reliable and accurate. With minor variations, it has been used extensively in military service by many nations during the 20th century.

The Germans recognized the value of a good semiautomatic rifle soon after the American forces, with their M1s, entered the war. As a consequence, a series of semiautomatic rifles was developed. The best were the Gewehr 43 and the Kar. 43, the same arm except for minor variations. However, by the time good production was reached, the tide of the war had changed and Germany was gradually, but certainly, losing. Production short cuts reduced the quality of this well-designed gun. Die stampings and castings were utilized instead of machined parts. The result was a crude appearance but, nevertheless, an efficient semiautomatic military rifle. The progress of the war prevented the Kar. 43 from being issued in great numbers, so the gun is a fine collector's item and, incidentally, a joy to shoot.

A good Kar. 43 is worth about $75. The Mauser rifles of German manufacture range in price from about $30 to $45. Arsenal reconditioned rifles are readily available at slightly less cost. These rifles are generally refinished and have new stocks. They

First line rifles of WW II, from top: U.S. 30 cal, M1 (Garand), and Carbine, British 303 cal. SMLE Mark III, German 8mm Kar 98, and Kar 43, Japanese 7.7mm Model 99, Russian 7.62mm Tokarev Model 40.

are likely to be made up from a collection of parts; those with matching serial numbers are rare.

One German weapon which bears mentioning is one which also defies categorizing. It is not really a submachine gun, nor is it a rifle or carbine in the usual concept of the terms. The gun was known as the MP 44. The initials stand for "machine pistol," German terminology for submachine guns. (Throughout the United Kingdom, submachine guns were known as "machine carbines.") The MP 44 might be more accurately described as the first successful "assault rifle," and toward the end of the war its designation was changed to Sturmgewehr 44 which, freely translated, means just that. It was an intermediate arm between the autoloading rifle and the submachine gun. Although a rather heavy and thoroughly grotesque looking weapon, the MP 44 succeeded in doing what the M1 Carbine never quite achieved. It offered

great firepower and versatility, being capable of both single shot or full automatic fire—a feature on most combat rifles developed since World War II.

The cartridge used in its 30-shot magazine was something of an innovation. A shortened version of the standard 7.92mm rifle cartridge, it had a 120-gr. bullet loaded to about 2250 fps, thus offered more power than our carbine round. This was the forerunner of the current all-purpose 7.62mm NATO cartridge. Because of this significant cartridge development and the improvised techniques used to cut manufacturing time, costs and problems, the German MP 44 must be regarded as one of the most important shoulder weapon developments to find its beginnings as a product of wartime expediency.

The German Wehrmacht used a variety of handguns, many being of outstanding design and quality. The patriarch of all military autoloaders is the Pistole 08—commonly known as the Luger. If one were to select a single handgun for an entire military collection it would probably be this weapon. The Luger was based on the design of an American, Hugo Borchardt. It was adopted by Germany in 1908 and manufactured until the middle of WW II. Its most commonly found caliber, 9mm Parabellum (Parabellum means "for war"), is regarded by many as the best all-round auto pistol cartridge. It also proved to be a superb submachine gun load and was chosen for such use by a majority of the nations involved in the war, including Great Britain. The Luger possesses excellent pointing qualities, important to the instinctive shooting characteristics of a combat weapon. Its exquisite lines have a lethal beauty which destines the weapon to a cherished position among gun fanciers, not unlike that of the renowned Colt Peacemaker.

The pistol which succeeded the Luger as the German standard was the Walther P-38. This gun was less expensive to manufacture than the complex Luger, and it also pioneered some innovations, including a double action feature which permitted carrying the pistol chamber-loaded with hammer down, and fired merely by pulling the trigger. Also, in case a round fails to fire the first time it's struck by the firing pin, another pull on the trigger repeats the blow, often discharging the load. This is quicker than the two-handed operation of retracting and releasing the slide in the event of a misfire. Of course, if a round is a complete dud it must be ejected in this manner, as with the 45 ACP.

A regular cult of Luger collectors diligently searches out the many variations of this pistol. Consequently, many factors, such as model, manufacturer and date, can cause sharp variation in the value of a Luger. A "plain vanilla" Luger—that is, an original, standard military issue which is *not* a naval model, artillery model, Swiss model, or one of about 100 other variations—will sell for some $50 in average condition. A "mint" Luger is worth about $100. P-38s go for about $15 less.

Another German handgun which bears inclusion in a collection is the strange looking Mauser Military Pistol, which is often referred to as the "broomhandle model," because of its peculiar grip shape. It is usually found in the powerful 7.63mm Mauser caliber but it was also chambered for other loads, including the 9mm. This pistol was sometimes used as a carbine. In certain models, its wooden holster could be attached to the gun and used as a shoulder stock. Some models were full automatic. Although this interesting pistol was primarily a subsidiary weapon in the German

army, it was used extensively by many nations during the war, especially China and others throughout Asia. These guns are worth from $40 to $150, depending on condition and manufacturer.

The Germans also used a goodly number of pocket automatic pistols, usually in 7.65mm. Several were of advanced design and excellent workmanship. These include the Mauser HSc, Sauer and the Walther PP and PPK. These popular little automatics sell from $25 to $65, the PPK bringing the highest price.

There is one pistol which must be considered for any military collection; however, it is difficult to place under any single nation. This is the 9mm Browning Hi-power. This excellent pistol was the last patent of John M. Browning, probably the greatest firearms inventor of all time. The finest of these were manufactured in Belgium, by the Fabrique Nationale d'Armes Guerre, S.A., of Herstal, Liege. When German forces occupied this country, the plant was taken over and weapon production channeled into the Wehrmacht forces. However, the Browning's greatest reputation came form its extensive use in the British and Chinese armies. (The gun was also manufactured in Canada by the John Ingles Co.). The excellent Browning design and its 13-shot magazine capacity made it a formidable and highly popular handgun. The current successful commercial model attests to its quality.

Automatic Weapons

This discussion has, thus far, included little comment regarding the collecting of dewats. "Dewat" is jargon which translates "deactivated war trophy." According to the regulations of the Alcohol and Tobacco Tax Unit of the U.S. Treasury Dept., fully automatic weapons must be registered and a $200 transfer tax paid when they change hands. (This regulation does not apply to law enforcement agencies.) This effectively keeps machine guns and submachine guns out of the hands of the general public. However, such weapons having been deactivated or rendered unserviceable to the satisfaction of the Alcohol and Tobacco Tax unit are perfectly legal. The deactivation process usually involves permanently plugging the barrel and welding the barrel to the frame. The gun can then never be fired; however, all internal parts will function normally and the gun can be dismantled and admired, as its general appearance is unchanged.

A number of automatic weapons from WW II are creditable assets to a collection. This field has the advantages of strong interest (dewats are marvelous conversation pieces) and the possibility of a complete and meaningful collection. It also has

drawbacks, not the least of which is price. Dewats are often outrageously expensive. This has persuaded many a collector to leave them alone. Undoubtedly, there must be a strong rationalization present to plunk down a sizeable amount of cash for a gun which can't even be fired. Nevertheless, interest in these pieces is definitely increasing and justifies inclusion in this discussion.

For all practical purposes, one can discount anything above the light machine gun class. In fact, with a couple of exceptions, the only items which bear mention are a few submachine guns. The reason is simple. A heavy machine gun is just that—heavy. Real heavy! Pay the express bill on one sometime, and you'll know. They are also bulky. A tolerant wife may well permit a reasonable number of rifles and pistols nicely mounted on the walls of the family den or in a handsome gun case; but a wheel-mounted, 150-lb. Russian Maxim heavy machine gun taking up the entire area where the couch used to be—that's something else!

I might mention two possible exceptions in the light machine gun class. The German MG 42 is perhaps the finest automatic weapon of the entire war. The gun is remarkable for many aspects, including simplicity, reliability and cheapness of manufacture. They threw away the book when they designed this gun, and the several then-radical innovations incorporated into it, notably the quick barrel change method, have since marked it as a prototype of machine guns developed thereafter. The last MG 42 I saw sold for over $200. If one has this kind of money for an inactive weapon, he couldn't pick a more significant one in this category.

One grand old weapon which should be given serious consideration is the Lewis light machine gun. Few weapons have earned such a widespread and colorful reputation as the Lewis Gun. It is, perhaps, the foremost conversation piece in my personal collection. The old stovepipe barrel and drum magazine attract the avid attention of even the most casually interested visitor. A reporter friend became so intrigued he did a feature story on the gun for a local newspaper. The Lewis was used through both world wars by at least a dozen countries. Its countless credits include its being the first machine gun to be fired from an aircraft. It is a thoroughly interesting and historic item. A deactivated Lewis Gun is a worthwhile investment at about $75.

The main interest in dewats is in the submachine gun line. The American Thompson is still the pièce de résistance of this category. The main military models—the 1928 A1, the M1 and the M1A1—were used by almost every Allied nation through

WW II and Korea. A few are even showing up in Viet Nam. This weapon, developed in the 1920s, garnered a bloody and somewhat romanticized reputation for its use in the gangland blood baths which took place from time to time during that era. Deactivated Thompsons bring a premium— from $95 to $180. Its successor, the U.S. M3 "grease gun," brings about half as much.

The 30-cal. Browning Automatic Rifle is certainly an important weapon which has seen a lot of combat use. Strangely, there is relatively little interest in the BAR, possibly because few are around, and those available are in the $150 price range.

Again, the Germans developed a superb submachine gun in the Schmeisser MP 38/40. Originally intended for use by armored vehicle crews and by paratroopers, the popular MP 38/40 supplanted earlier models and became the first-line, standard submachine gun of the German army. Simple and inexpensive, this widely-sought weapon is another German prototype which has been widely copied. A good Schmeisser will easily cost $100. As previously mentioned, the MP 44 assault rifle is an important weapon in the automatic line.

No nation used the submachine gun more extensively than did Russia. Most of the notorious burp guns were rather crude, but incorporated large magazines which gave a foot soldier good firepower for close-quarter work. The Model 41 PPSH (71-round capacity) was the most widely used submachine gun in WW II and Korea. It usually brings about $75.

Another fine submachine gun is the British Sten. This neat little 9mm machine carbine is an outstanding example of just how cheaply and simply an efficient automatic weapon can be manufactured. A Sten cost about $9 to manufacture, compared to some $200 for a Thompson. A deactivated Sten will sell for approximately $50 today.

I'm certain that by this point many collectors and enthusiasts are incensed that I have, perhaps, neglected a favorite weapon of theirs which played a part in WW II. The criticism may be valid as I have not attempted full coverage of the field of martial arms of this era. I do believe, however, that the weapons discussed are significant to a representative collection which aspires to be just that.

One important fact should not be ignored. Most WW II trophies need not be relegated to a position of dust-catchers on the wall or the gun rack. Many of these guns make splendid shooters for a variety of purposes. Probably no better big game rifle action than the German Mauser has been developed. The U.S. Springfield and Enfield actions also make excellent hunting rifles. The Lugers, P-38s and Colt 45s are potent manstoppers and can be a lot of fun to take out on the range to punch some targets or just to perforate tin cans. These guns are safe to shoot if the correct ammunition is used and the arm is in good working order. If there is any question on either count, a check by a good gunsmith is a sound idea.

There is one thing the novice collector who is interested in this field must acquire quickly, and it can largely determine the eventual success of his efforts. This is a good working knowledge of the guns involved and their current market values. These values vary, but the trend is definitely in an upward direction. The prices I have quoted are by no means "official." They are my best estimates from what I have seen at gun shows and in the various trade publications. A great many war trophies are still available from private individuals. These items may—or may not—be bargains. A man wanting to collect on a minimal budget must know not only the general value of these guns, but also the subtleties which can affect these values. For instance, a good Model 1911 45 automatic can be bought or sold readily in the $50 range. However, should one find one of these pistols manufactured by Singer Sewing Machine Co., the gun might be worth ten times this amount.

Conscientious study of trade publications advertising these firearms and judicious shopping around at gun shows are the best ways to learn their values and price trends. For general information on the guns themselves, a few good books are helpful. One of the best is *Small Arms of the World* by W. H. B. Smith, first printed in 1943. Now in its seventh edition, it was revised and expanded in 1962 by Joseph E. Smith.

A final word about the previously mentioned importance of timing in beginning a collection of this nature. Chances are, your local sporting goods or hardware store is not crowded with WW II firearms. The best ways to fill gaps in a military collection are at gun shows or from ads in magazines and trade publications. Currently there is strong pressure in the Congress of the United States to legislate against the mail order sale of firearms. This would badly cripple the private collector's efforts, as well as those of the 99.9+% of the shooters and enthusiasts who purchase guns for legitimate purposes. That it would inhibit the criminal is highly questionable. However, that is another issue and not to be debated here. It does suggest that these guns will be harder to come by and more expensive in the future. Unlike money invested in most hobbies, in which there is usually a depreciation factor, investment in these guns probably will appreciate, and at a rapid clip. Therefore, the timing is right, as are the prices, so give a thought to collecting WW II weapons.

I wish you well. ●

Author is holding two widely used submachine guns, the Russian Model 41 PPSH (right hand) and the German Schmeisser MP40. The U.S. submachine guns on the rack are (top to bottom): Reising Model 50, the Thompson Model M1, and the Thompson 1928 A1.

No pistol ever made has caused more argument and speculation than the legendary Luger. No one will ever know its whole story—though books have been written about it—but here's more grist for the mill

THE FAMED LUGER
OF FACT AND FANTASY

by HARRY M. CAMPBELL

V ERY FEW GUNS have gained the prestige accorded the Luger pistol, the early autoloading weapon which would be more properly designated the Borchardt-Luger, in commemoration of both gun designers whose talents combined in its creation and exploitation.

Enthusiasts have called the Luger the finest automatic pistol ever made, which possibly it was. Many other exaggerated claims often made for it, however, have little if any factual basis; it was neither the most powerful nor the most accurate pistol of its era. Although not considered quite suitable as an American military sidearm —it was rejected by our government— the Luger was adopted by the armed services of more nations and used longer than any other pistol in firearms history. It was not the ideal military weapon by comparative standards; this was proven by several exhaustive tests made by ordnance authorities, yet many Americans have shown marked preference for it over all others.

Actually, the Luger was in a class by itself. Its story needs no embellishment, for it has earned its own special niche in firearms history. It is secure among the immortals. Its name now calls to mind a standard of constructional excellence which has all but disappeared in firearms, along with the highly skilled handcraftsmen of its era, and both are now another page in gun history.

Lugers, in all probability, will never again be made—but, fortunately for us, a great number of them *were* made.

Increasing Collector Interest

While choice Luger specimens remain fairly plentiful today, we note that collectors are showing ever-increasing interest in them, and we can be sure there will be far greater interest in the future as availability decreases.

Prices have advanced considerably, especially during the past decade, in proportion to a growing demand for the less common models. Today's beginning Luger collector should have little difficulty, however, in finding good selections among the various models now available at reasonable prices. Prices vary somewhat in different localities, according to demand, but so far the market appears quite stable. An average low-demand-grade souvenir Luger, in shooting condition, may be offered for around $50, perhaps, while one of the rare "U.S. Eagle" M1900 specimens would probably bring four or five times as much. It is still possible, though, to find real bargains—even among the more choice pieces.

Such an opportunity is, of course,

Luger Carbine M1904 cal. 7.65mm, one of several combination models made by DWM, most of which were sold abroad as sporting arms. This model has the long barrel, wooden fore-end and sights adjustable to 300 yards.

Borchardt M1893 autoloading pistol, cal. 7.65mm, a variation of the first Borchardt which was chambered for his 7.63mm cartridge. The original was the first pistol having a magazine in the grip. It employed the toggle link locking mechanism later incorporated into the Luger.

quite rare; but when it occurs it is one of the top thrills of this fascinating hobby. It happened to a friend recently in a small Southern city. Rummaging through a pile of junk guns in a pawnshop, this man came upon an old, rusty, rather beat-up 7.65mm Luger. Admittedly it was a sorry looking piece, apparently hardly worth the few dollars the pawnbroker had loaned on it several years before. To the average gun fancier it was worth little, perhaps, but this man was a Luger collector. He recognized certain earmarks and risked $25 on his own judgment, for this old Luger had a thin 4¾" barrel and imprinted above the chamber was an American Eagle —the Great Seal of the United States; also, it bore a four-digit serial number without a letter. Maybe . . . just maybe . . . it was one of the 1000 such pistols purchased by Uncle Sam in 1901. Happily, it was!

As in any other field, the gun collector must know the game. He must be able to recognize various models on sight, as well as certain features which make some pieces far rarer than others. He must know comparative values within his own field, and, for a better understanding of these values, he should have a thorough knowledge of the reasons behind these various gun models — know why some were considered better than others bearing like date markings, perhaps. All this and much more is essential to the

The American Eagle — U.S. Army Luger M1900 cal. 7.65mm — was issued mainly to cavalry units. After a short period it was withdrawn and sold as surplus. Now it's a collector's item.

collector if he is to gain the proper perspective to really enjoy this many-faceted game.

The Luger's Borchardt Origins

The Luger was not merely another automatic pistol during that period when such guns began to attract attention; rather it was the end result of an evolution begun some years earlier and in a considerably different form as the Borchardt. In fact, the original Borchardt was also the forerunner of our present day machine-pistol, some few reservations considered.

To get a better understanding of the Luger, we should first take a look

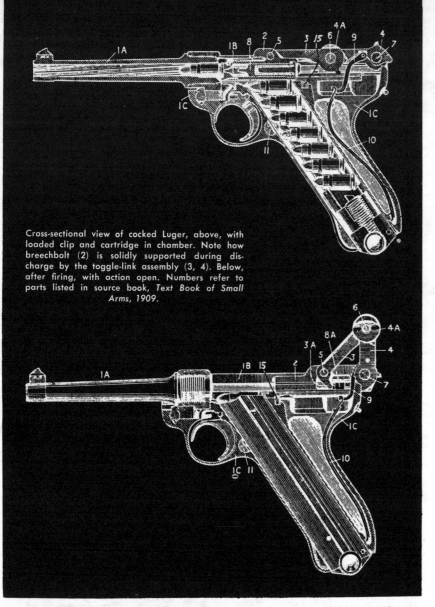

Cross-sectional view of cocked Luger, above, with loaded clip and cartridge in chamber. Note how breechbolt (2) is solidly supported during discharge by the toggle-link assembly (3, 4). Below, after firing, with action open. Numbers refer to parts listed in source book, *Text Book of Small Arms, 1909.*

at the Borchardt. It was an awkward appearing gun, having a rather long barrel and featuring the now famous link-toggle mechanism. This was enclosed in a bulbous housing extending several inches behind a near-vertical gripstock, which contained the magazine. It was a rather freaky design, but it attracted more than its share of attention. Repeated demonstrations proved its action was both reliable and amazingly fast, producing results far advanced for the period.

This was but one of several guns designed by Borchardt, a tool-and-die maker whose inventive genius extended into several fields, enriching many others but never himself. He was responsible for the Sharps-Borchardt, a hammerless single shot rifle that was decades ahead of its time.

We find ample evidence of this in America, where he was employed in various capacities for well over a quarter-century, amassing an imposing record of inventions and obtaining patents on various items ranging from sewing-machine parts to ammunition and, more especially, in the field of firearms designing. There may be some logic, perhaps, in the supposition that the famous toggle-link principle which he later employed in his pistol

was an outgrowth of his experiments while employed by the Singer Sewing Machine Co.*

Borchardt's later life is well known, particularly those years following his return to Europe. It has been said he was associated with Ritter von

*Datig mentions that Borchardt worked for Singer, but adds nothing about that employment giving Borchardt any ideas for a toggle-link system.

Lacking documentation on this aspect, it seems more likely that Borchardt became acquainted with the toggle-link design of breech-block closure patented by Smith & Wesson in February, 1854. This now famous system was used successively on Smith & Wesson, Volcanic, New Haven, Henry and Winchester arms, in that order, culminating in the 1873 and 1876 Winchester rifles.

Working on the Eastern seaboard in the 1870s, notably at the Sharps factory, Borchardt was easily in a position to become acquainted with any of these guns.

W. H. B. Smith in *Small Arms of the World* (Harrisburg, Pa., 1962), pp. 96, 97, notes that Hiram Maxim ". . . drew heavily on the toggle lock of the Henry-Winchester . . . for this automatic design," and shows an illustration of an 1866 Winchester rifle modified to operate automatically via recoil. This relatively crude system was patented by Maxim in 1883, but it was his 1884 patent, using an inverted toggle-link design, that became the basis for the many Maxim machine gun developments.

Jones relates (p. 26) that "This (Maxim's) toggle action was copied for the breech locks of the Borchardt and Luger pistols." This may have been the case certainly, but it seems to us more likely that Borchardt saw one or another of the Maxim predecessors, as noted above.

Mannlicher in Hungary, and that while employed in a government arsenal there he perfected his odd-looking handgun and patented it, first in Austria-Hungary, then in the United States and Belgium.* Later, while associated with Ludwig Loewe in Berlin, his gun was produced and put on the market in 1893.

The first model was chambered for a special cartridge known as the 7.63mm Borchardt, not to be confused with the smaller-cased 7.65mm (30-cal. Luger), for which later models were chambered.

The first detachable shoulder stock for the Borchardt was an American innovation, providing dual purpose usage. Loewe manufactured these guns in kit form with the wooden stock and accessories and a choice of barrel lengths for about $30. Despite this high price, many kits were sold abroad, principally in southern Africa and South America, but also in the United States, where they became fairly popular saddle guns.

Georg Luger

Georg Luger's contributions to the newly formed DWM (Loewe) organization is a story too well known to require repetition, for he was a man of many talents, including a high degree of shooting skill. He was a salesman with a flair for publicity, but he also knew the value of a subtle approach; he was also an organizer, with plenty of hard business ability and judgment. Despite all this, he is best known for the pistol he designed.

Luger saw certain possibilities in Hugo Borchardt's gun, but recognized the need for a smoother, far better balanced pistol, one more pleasing to the eye. He knew an awkward design such as the Borchardt's would soon be supplanted by one combining its superior mechanical features with more pleasing lines. Borchardt was reluctant to make any such changes in his gun, but Luger convinced Loewe of the necessity for them and did the job himself. This resulted in a transition form patented October 3, 1898, in Germany. This differed only slightly from the now world-renowned Parabellum, or Luger pistol, more properly known as the Borchardt-Luger.

The Swiss government was the first to officially adopt the weapon, following two series of tests during which competitive pistols were eliminated. Luger's first big contract was for 3000 pistols of new improved design with a grip safety device, known as the "Parabellum Automatic Pistol, Borchardt-Luger System, Swiss M1900." Serial numbers for this contract ranged from 2001 to 5000, without let-

*See Datig, pp. 37-38 and 217, *et seq.* It has not been clearly shown that Borchardt completed his pistol design in the U.S. or in Europe, nor that he was actually associated with von Mannlicher.

The stamping over the chamber indicates that this DWM-manufactured M1900 Luger is one of the famed "American Eagle" pistols, the first of which were sold to the U.S. government.

ter symbol. These were the only German-made Swiss Lugers sold on contract; all other so-called "Swiss models" are designated "commercial."

Luger's second government contract came from the U.S. Army, a trial order for 1000 cal. 7.65mm M1900 pistols, purchased by the Ordnance Department in April, 1901. Evidently the DWM company expected to sell our government many more, for they turned out some 6000-8000 pistols bearing a like stamping — the Great Seal of the United States—over the chamber. These hopes never materialized, as it was deemed after a short trial period that the Lugers were not sufficiently rugged for U.S. troop usage and were prone to develop repair problems because the precisely hand-fitted parts were not interchangeable.

This was the first of several so-called "Eagle" models. Unfortunately, no record of serial numbers can now be found, but we know these ran in series of 4 to 5 digits, with no letter. (Jones lists 2004 as the lowest number known to him of the 1900 cal. 7.65mm type. He gives 22405-23457 as the approximate range of the cal. 9mm 1902 model, but this also includes the "commercial" pieces.) This gun was used for about one year, issued mostly to selected cavalry troops in New England, the West and Southwest, and then was withdrawn and placed in storage. Ordnance records indicate some were sold to the public at $5 each, plus 50 cents handling charge. (Datig says that in 1906 the New York firm of Francis Bannerman purchased many if not all of these—price unspecified—and sold them at $19.85, with holsters at 95 cents.)

From around 1904 until shortly prior to the outbreak of WW I, thousands of Eagle Lugers were exported to the U.S. These were commercial versions of several models, some of which are now rare. The M1902 Eagle, for example, was the first 9mm commercial and it had the now familiar 4" "heavy" barrel. Only about 700 of these were exported to the U.S.

Seven Recognized Makers

Although collectors recognize only seven manufacturers of authentic Luger models, odd specimens turn up occasionally and touch off considerable controversy. Some bear evidence of "wildcat" ancestry, such as Chinese, Japanese or Afghan marking, and are generally forgeries. However, a few authentic DWM-made Lugers bearing the Japanese Imperial Chrysanthemum crest still are to be accounted for. Also, a few WW II souvenirs bearing Japanese proofmarks and chambered for the 8mm Nambu cartridge are found. These are reworked Lugers, usually of DWM, Vickers or Mauser manufacture.

Besides the original DWM script monogram, that familiar trademark which appears on the toggle of all older models, six other makes of the Luger are officially recognized: Erfurt, Simson, Krieghoff and Mauser of Germany; Vickers Ltd. of England and Waffenfabrik Eidgenössische of Bern, Switzerland. Additionally, some few P-08 military specimens bear the toggle markings of the Spandau arsenal, probably having been reworked there.

Many Luger collectors specialize; some are interested only in the various military weapons, while others prefer the better finished models, such as are usually found among some commercials — that deep, rich blue-black oldtime finish. Various combination models are also popular, especially such longer barreled military models as the 1904 Navy or the so-called 1914 Artillery, designed for cavalry usage but later issued to field artillery units.

Military collectors are particularly interested in older specimens bearing unit designations, usually hand stamped on the butt, or sometimes on the frame under the barrel. Naval arms might be stamped "3U-39" perhaps, or "5ns-12," code marks indicating issue to personnel of a certain ship, a naval service unit, or base guard unit. Occasionally one might even find an old DWM relic of pre-WW I days bearing such markings as "10-U-4," which signifies original issue to the old Black Knight troop of the 10th Uhlan regiment. This is but one of the more romantic aspects of the Luger collector's game.

The American collector should also familiarize himself with certain federal laws, particularly those in the "other guns" category. These require a special license and very high annual tax, applicable to many carbines and detachable stocks, including some of the choice Luger models. While obviously intended to serve other purposes, these and many state laws do impose drastic restrictions on collectors. Efforts have been made to exempt bona-fide collectors from unjust tax provisions, but without far better planning and revamping of such restrictive laws, American citizens may soon find themselves further handicapped.

Much to be Learned

There is much to be learned about Lugers, so much that no collector can hope to thoroughly explore all their facts in a lifetime, perhaps. But it's fun trying. Several fine books are available (see Bibliography), these telling the Luger story or parts of it from various angles and all well-worth buying and studying. From each we can learn new and interesting facts which add much zest whether our Luger collection be large or small.

Although, generally speaking, souvenir Lugers of WW II may not have much collector interest, don't fail to inspect closely those specimens that come your way. One of them *might* just happen to be a rather choice piece. Some GIs were fortunate enough to acquire an early model Krieghoff, for example, made for the Luftwaffe; or, maybe, even one of the older DWMs in mint condition.

Most WW II Lugers were made by Mauser, between 1934 and 1942. Some 10 models in all, these range in quality from very good to only fair. Code dates K or G indicate pre-war manufacture, while those marked S/42 might have been made at any time between 1936 and mid-1940. The M1934 Mauser Banner specimens vary in workmanship also, but these retain considerable popularity among collectors.

Older DWM contract arms bearing the imprint of other nations are especially prized specimens, such as the M1908 Bolivian or Portuguese. Some later models, such as the Mauser 1934 made for Persia, Japan, or one of the South American republics, are also in demand. Their prices are understandably high when in good condition.

Yes, better grade Lugers cost a lot of money these days, but so does everything else we buy—and, we may be sure they will cost a lot more in the future. During the next few years we'll see a decline in availability, and even now the more choice specimens are going fast.

For more than half a century the Luger was a controversial weapon; millions extolled its virtues while just as many condemned it. However, now that it has passed into history, most of us admire it for one reason or another. The Luger was something very special in firearms. There will never be another gun like it. ●

Bibliography

Luger Variations, H. E. Jones, publ. by the author (Los Angeles, Calif., 1959).

The Luger Pistol, F. A. Datig, 4th prtg. (Hollywood, Calif., 1958).

Textbook of Automatic Pistols, R. K. Wilson (Plantersville, S. C., 1943).

The Book of Pistols & Revolvers, W. H. B. Smith, 4th ed. (Harrisburg, Pa., 1960).

Joseph Rider at his exotic best; the "Magazine Pistol" of 1871-1888. A fascinating, if anachronistic, piece of work.

THE REMINGTON RADICALS

by Louis William Steinwedel

The Remington Rebellion produced a longer string of oddities, non-conformities, new designs and downright weird firearms than any other American gunmaker. Here they are.

THE STORY of Remington guns begins with a charming Horatio Alger tale of an enterprising pioneer-stock lad who hammered out his first gun at the family forge. He trudged across thirty miles of 1816 New York wilderness to have the barrel rifled, then started a modest gunsmithing business and built it into a great arms complex. It is a publicist's dream (and conveniently true), but the real image of Eliphalet Remington, Jr., an unbearded and rather short-haired rebel born in 1793, is not too far from that of some contemporary personalities who find the status quo anathema, suspect established ways of doing things, and constantly seek the new and bizarre. From these classic origins, the "Remington rebellion" spawned a longer string of oddities, non-conformities, new designs, and downright weird firearms than any other American gunmaker.

Young Remington's romantically conceived first rifle was also the first in the collection of radical Remingtons. In appearance, the carefully handmade rifle resembled a cross between a typical sporting weapon of the day and the U.S. Model 1814 "Harper's Ferry" rifle. It is logical to expect that the original Remington, vintage 1816, would have been a flintlock. In fact, the "first Remington" in the company's own collection *is* a flintlock, conveniently reconverted for demonstration from a later percussion gun.

The Scottish minister of Belhelvie in Aberdeenshire, Alexander Forsyth, found in 1807 that he could fire a gun with shock-sensitive fulminate compounds instead of flint and steel. He devised a system for dispensing a sufficient amount of loose powder made of this compound to fire each shot. Later inventors rolled the unstable powder into little balls for use with safer and more convenient "pill-lock" guns. A few adventuresome gunsmiths built pill-

lock arms; some, like Porter and Billinghurst, even evolved elaborate repeaters.

In his *Civil War Guns,*[*] William B. Edwards offers a convincing and scholarly argument that young Remington adopted the avant-garde percussion pill-lock ignition system for his early rifles, and that there never was such an animal as a flintlock Remington. There seems much to support this idea (so far no one has found an original flintlock Remington altered to percussion). It would appear that Remington was a rebel from the very beginning.

For the next few years Remington concentrated quite enterprisingly in building his business by making very good rifle and pistol barrels and substantial quantities of complete good-quality sporting rifles. Prosperity came, and with it another touch of minor unorthodoxy; a side-by-side combination rifle and shotgun.

The Jenks

About this same time Remington took up another peculiar project; to complete a contract (held by N.P. Ames of Chicopee Falls, Massachusetts) to build a breechloader invented by William Jenks for the U.S. Navy. The Remington-Jenks was an odd and unconventional weapon, but not an impractical one. The breechloading mechanism was operated by raising a hook-shaped lever at the breech which caused a sliding breech bolt to move back, allowing the chamber to be loaded. The oddity was that the gun was built with a "mule ear" type side hammer which snapped against a nipple mounted at the *side* of the barrel. This had the advantage of directing the percussion blast and any stray bits of cap away from the shooter's face. To the basic Jenks invention Remington added the further novelty of the May-

---

[*]Harrisburg, Penn., 1962.

Eli Remington's first rifle, possibly, though this flintlock was in percussion cap form before 1916.

An interesting Remington combination gun of about 1846, a side-by-side rifle-shotgun. Remington's early success was based on sporting rifles of similar pattern.

An early example of Remington's penchant for the unconventional; the Remington-Jenks breech-loading Navy carbine with unusual "mule ear" sidehammer.

Remington's first military percussion revolver, designed by Fordyce Beals, was patented in September of 1858. This one is the Navy 36 caliber, but an identical 44 caliber model was also made for Army issue.

Remington's first percussion revolver, a 31 caliber pocket pistol designed by Fordyce Beals. Significant identifying features are the strengthening top strap, unusual outside-mounted pawl, and one-piece "gutta percha" grip. About 2500 of these were made.

Joseph Rider's double action revolver in original percussion form is easily recognized by its characteristic "mushroom" cylinder. The double action mechanism design brought Rider's prolific genius to Ilion just before the Civil War.

Left—Remington New Model Belt revolver, caliber 36.

Center—Remington New Model Belt revolver, converted to 38 rimfire caliber.

Right—Remington New Model Pocket revolver, caliber 31, with spur trigger.

nard automatic tape primer. As a result, the final Remington-Jenks carbine was a rather esoteric piece of merchandise for 1847. Perhaps the greatest novelty of all was persuading the arch-conservative military to accept it.

A few years later, in 1854, Remington undertook another peculiar and incongruous government contract. At that time the Army had on hand thousands of outdated flintlock muskets, mainly of the 1816 pattern, which it decided to update instead of replace. The job and 20,000 muskets were handed over to Remington. The 69 caliber smoothbore barrels were to be rifled and the ancient flintlocks were to be converted to the faddish Maynard tape primer. The guns saw service in the Civil War, possibly in the siege of Vicksburg, where Union soldiers complained of "conversion guns" which often were older than their users.

In 1857 Remington introduced its first revolver, a 31 caliber pocket arm designed by Fordyce Beals, a name to be closely linked with Remington over the next few years. Predictably, it was not an ordinary revolver. The pawl, or cylinder-activating mechanism, which turned the cylinder when the hammer was cocked was, curiously, hung on the outside of the frame, and so seemed unecessarily vulnerable. This odd design was carried through three versions of the Beals pocket revolvers (in modified form on the second and third models) for a total of about 5000 pistols by 1860. As one more deviation from the norm, these Beals pocket guns were fitted with the then-novel hard rubber or "gutta percha" grips. Despite its honest execution by the artisans of Ilion, the advertising claim for the Beals pocket revolver as "a superior article" is open to some debate.

Fordyce Beals

Fordyce Beals is, of course, well known to collectors for his early single action 36 and 44 caliber Navy and Army revolvers of Civil War vintage. The Remington-Beals was a strong, well-made revolver which, like the pocket revolvers, used a top strap over the cylinder to strengthen the design. The Beals, and its 1861 and 1863 successor models designed by William H. Elliot, were unusual in that they were certainly the most modern and efficiently made percussion revolvers of the Civil War era. Despite their points of superiority over the 1860 Colt open-top Army 44, 130,215 Remington military revolvers were sold to the government at virtually bargain prices; $12.00 to $15.50 apiece as compared with up to $25.00 for the Colt. Remington was the most reasonable and reliable of all the Civil War arms contractors in a seller's market situation, when most of the Yankee arms merchants played fast and loose with Washington. Remington Civil War revolvers were not unique—there was, in fact, nothing patentable in most of them.

Civilian versions of the Civil War percussion revolvers were also made by Remington. Again, some interesting departures are found on them. The civilian revolvers can properly be traced back to Joseph Rider's 1860 double action 31 pocket revolver, a new self-cocking design which caught the Remington fancy and prompted the company to import Rider from Newark, Ohio. There was foresight in this move, for Rider proved a valuable asset at Ilion, and his little pocket revolver—easily recognized by its flared "mushroom" cylinder—became very popular and over 100,000 were sold. The Rider double action

31 was supplemented by a 36 caliber "Belt Model," essentially a scaled-down Navy, which was, interestingly, offered in both single and double action versions. The civilian line was completed by a 31 caliber single action pocket revolver built on the lines of the bigger military revolvers but with a spur trigger for compactness. It was, incidentally, one of the best balanced and handiest "feeling" small revolvers ever built.

The great arms complex at Ilion, of course, made the standard Civil War arm, the muzzleloading 58 caliber rifle-musket. But once again, the Remington penchant for non-conformity intervened. While most contractors built exact duplicates of the regulation U.S. Springfield with strictly interchangeable parts, Remington's trip hammers, grindstones, and stock-cutting machines turned out the most individual and attractive "irregular" regular-issue rifle of the Civil War, the celebrated "Zouave." This quite elegant brass-trimmed rifle, complete with inlaid brass patchbox, had almost the finesse of a sporting rifle. The Zouave was more closely related to the old U.S. Model 1841 "Mississippi Rifle" (so named for Jeff Davis' regiment in the Mexican War), a gun which Remington had once built on Government contract, than it was to the more "contemporary" 1861 and 1863 Springfields.

During the Civil War, Remington built a breech-loading carbine designed by Leonard Geiger. This gun, known as the "split-breech carbine," was never issued for Civil War service. In the postwar slump, Remington's prolific designer and plant superintendent, Joseph Rider, undertook to perfect the Geiger design. What Rider created was, of course, the famous "Remington

Originally a 50 caliber Remington rolling block Army pistol, this one was converted to 22 rimfire somewhere along the way.

A 20th century rolling block target pistol, the Model 1901. 700 were made in 22 LR, 22 Short, 25-10 Rimfire and 44 S&W Russian. The superb balance and feel of the Remington rolling block target pistol has kept it a favorite across several generations. Many custom rebuilding jobs have been done on basic rolling block pistols.

Rolling Block," possibly the simplest and best single shot breech-loading mechanism ever conceived. Remington rolling blocks in sporting, military, and pistol form were produced by the tens of thousands and exported all over the world. The rolling block crossed the barrier from black to smokeless powder, and military models were still being sold as late as the pre-World War I era. In fact, many a Frenchman marched to the trenches with a 9mm Remington on his shoulder.

Rider's Rolling Block

The Rolling Block played a part in perhaps the weirdest American arms purchase of all time. In 1865 Remington developed a 50 caliber rimfire pistol version of the Rolling Block; a hefty 36-oz. handcannon with a massive 8½-inch round barrel. Despite the fact that the Civil War established the revolver as an indispensable military tool and made the single shot martial pistol as passé as powdered wigs and knee breeches, Remington went ahead with the development of this formidable

Far left—Most Civil War musket contractors built exact duplicates of the standard U.S. Springfield 58 muzzleloader. Remington made the so-called "Zouave" rifle, which resembled the old 1841 "Mississippi" rifle. This elegant brass-trimmed rifle with inlaid patchbox has almost the finesse of a sporting rifle. Left—The ancestor of the famous Remington rolling block was this "split breech carbine" invented by Leonard Geiger. Built and delivered during the Civil War, they probably never saw any action. Postwar, Joseph Rider developed the idea further and perfected the familiar rolling block action.

anachronism and the Navy went ahead and bought it. Just how many the Navy acquired is uncertain. Charles Lee Karr, Jr., in his *Remington Handguns* suggests 500, although he records that "well over a thousand" were built. A second model of 1867, with a 7-inch barrel and using a 50 caliber centerfire cartridge, was also made. It remained in production until 1875, with a run of about 7000 pistols. An Army model designated the "Model 1871 Army" grew out of the less than judicious judgement of an Army Ordinance board called "The St. Louis Commission." Over 6000 of these 50 caliber pistols were made. Karr records that a final "Model 1879 Army" was developed but "never received actual trial." So ended one of the most curious examples of military ordnance judgment on record.

Despite its obvious unsuitability as a military handgun, the Rolling-Block pistol made a superb target weapon with very fine balance and natural pointing qualities. Remington finally got around to the obvious with the Model 1891 Target Pistol, of which only a hundred were made. Another target Rolling Block, the Model 1901, was built in calibers from 22 short to 44 S&W and sold for $16.00.

One of the most inexplicable of the Remington anomalies was its revolving rifle which appeared, rather well out of its era, in 1866. Colt had considerable experience with revolving rifles, and most of it was unfavorable. The Union bought 4612 of them during the war, but they seldom found favor with troops who found them heavy, unbalanced, and dangerously prone to "chain fire" if loaded hastily. With the superiority of repeating rifles like Winchester's well established, the concept of introducing a revolving rifle in 1866 is mildly incredible. Even more astonishing, Remington kept it cataloged until 1879, by which time they had managed to dispose of nearly 3000 of them, presumably at the substantial catalog price of $25.00. The cap lock revolving rifles were made in 36 and

Remingtons' Revolving Rifle.

Remington's revolving rifle was already an anachronism when it was introduced in 1866. The gun would take either metallic cartridges or "loose ammunition."

44 calibers, and were also available in converted form to take 38 and 44 caliber metallic cartridges.

The height of Remington non-conformity can be found in a series of fascinating pocket pistols in production roughly from the Civil War until 1888. In that year Remington was bought out by Hartley and Graham, and much of the handgun manufacture was discontinued. Chronologically, the first of these (after Joseph Rider's little double action 31) was his 17 caliber percussion derringer, more toy than firearm, and certainly one of the most inexplicable guns ever made in America. To load this petite (5⅝ ounces) brass-barreled gun, the shooter opened the breech pin, inserted the tiny ball, and placed a percussion cap behind it. That cap provided the propelling force—no powder was used! This quaint curiosity fell by the wayside in 1863 when gunsmithing talents at Ilion found more pressing needs.

The Vest Pocket

A vaguely similar but different 22 caliber derringer based on William Elliot's patent came out in 1865, retaining the same odd—and awkward—grip shape. Despite a rather non-competitive price of $3.25, the Remington 22 "vest pocket," as it was labeled in the catalog, stayed on until 1888 and sold a surprising 25,000 copies. The vest pocket 22 was similar in appearance but mechanically different from its big brother, the 41 rimfire caliber, based on Rider patents. Its production and sales record paralleled the 22.

In 1861 Remington marketed its first cartridge pistol, the Elliot-designed "Zig-Zag" derringer—a masterpiece of the bizarre! The "Zig-Zag" was a 22 caliber 6-shot hammerless pepperbox-type pistol which was cocked by pushing forward on a peculiar ring trigger. The gun effectively

skirted the Rollin White-Smith & Wesson patent on the bored-through revolver cylinder, but it was an awkward, unendearing little contraption. It was discontinued the following year with less than 1000 copies made.

Remington, however, was not ready to abandon the old "clustered barrel" technique of making a cartridge-firing repeating pocket pistol. In 1863 the company tried again with a revised version of the Elliot multi-barrel derringer which appeared in two different forms. This time there was a 22 caliber 5-shot pistol with the barrels bored out of a fluted cylinder, and a 32 caliber 4-shot with the barrels grouped in a box, like the Sharps pepperbox derringers. The complex mechanism was much the same as in the "Zig-Zag;" a ring trigger was pushed forward to cock the gun, and pulled back to fire it. The advantages of this lever action mechanism

An oddity among oddities, the Remington 17 caliber vest pocket derringer. This tiny brass barreled pistol fired a 17 caliber ball propelled solely by the power from a percussion cap. Less than 1000 of these intriguing little pistols were sold.

Remington's "Vest Pocket" 22 caliber pistol based on Elliot's patents, in which the hammer also serves as breechblock. Gun sold for $3.25, a stiff price amid the hot competition of the 1870s.

Elliot's patent 22 6-shot "Zig-Zag" derringer, built 1861-62. This unusual pistol was operated by pushing the ring trigger forward, which rotated the pepperbox barrels and cocked the weapon; pulling it back fired it.

An Elliot's 32 rimfire "ring trigger" pepperbox derringer, current 1863-1888. The finger lever was pushed forward to cock, back to fire.

Elliot's 41 caliber single shot derringer was utterly simple, had only three principal parts—hammer, trigger and mainspring. Note combined hammer and breechblock.

as compared with the more conventional hammer-cocked Sharps (which used a revolving firing pin on the hammer) are unclear. Perhaps even more obscure is how Remington managed to sell 50,000 of these strange little pistols between 1863 and 1888.

The 41 Derringer

After his multi-barreled guns William Elliot magnificently redeemed himself in 1866. He left his mark as a classic gun designer with his famous and long-lived "double derringer." The handy little 41 rimfire over-under was the natural descendant of English twist-action 2-shot pocket pistols of the 18th and early 19th centuries, and was an ace-in-the-hole for Reconstruction Carpetbaggers to World War II spies. The over-under derringer is so well known that it hardly needs description. It was one of the top selling Remingtons with over 150,000 made. That it was available until 1935 is no less than astonishing, and a great compliment to its simple, effective design. Even after its discontinuance, Elliot's century-old design received a new lease on life in the thousands of modern-made replicas.

It seems mildly incredible that the same mind which devised something as brilliantly simple as the Rolling Block could have created another gun so unduly complex as the "Remington Magazine Pistol." In 1871 Joseph Rider invented the leading candidate for the most radical Remington of all. Rider's oddball pocket pistol was a sort of mini-model of a Winchester lever-action rifle—without the lever—which carried its five 32 RF "extra short" cartridges in a spring-loaded tubular magazine under the barrel. At first glance, the pistols appears to have *two* hammers, but closer inspection reveals that the larger of the two is part of the carrier mechanism which feeds cartridges from the magazine into the breech and ejects the fired case. To operate the Rider pistol, you pulled back on the larger of the "hammers," which served to cock the second or real hammer, and at the same time fed a cartridge from the magazine into the chamber. In effect, the large hammer served the same purpose as the finger lever on the lever-action rifle.

Invented two years after there was no longer any legal prohibition against any-

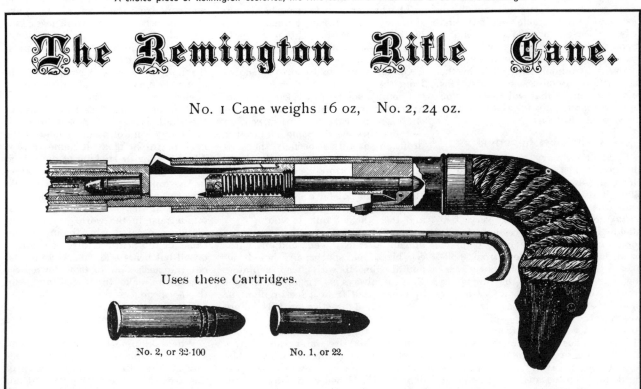

Remington can still wax radical even in modern times. The Model 66 is a 22 caliber autoloader with nylon stock and their bolt action, single-shot center-fire handgun chambered for the 221 Fireball—the Remington XP-100—are current-production radicals.

one making cartridge revolvers, the *raison d'etre* for the Rider magazine pistol is at best nebulous. Mechanically complicated, it was expensive to produce and sell—$9.50 as against $7.00 for a fine Remington "New Line" 38 revolver; its sheer unorthodoxy probably frightened off many prospective buyers. However, despite price and disregard for convention, Remington produced about 15,000 "magazine pistols."

The Rifle-Cane

If the magazine pistol wasn't sufficiently esoteric, the gunsmiths of Ilion had one more surprise up their collective sleeves. This one, which would probably strike hor-ror into the hearts of Treasury Department enforcement people, looked like an innocent walking stick with a dog's head carved into the handle. Actually, it was a 22 or 32 caliber rifle cane which could be carried inconspicuously and swung up on a dark street to ward off an attacker with a surprise shot.

In 1886 control of the Ilion institution passed out of the Remington family's con-trol and into a series of corporate re-organizations. Most of the offbeat handguns were dropped by the new directors in 1888, although the double derringer, a very good "frontier" 44, and some Rolling Block pis-tols were continued. Even with corporate disinterest in handguns, a new and very advanced automatic pistol, in calibers 32 and 38, and designed by John Pedersen, was brought out in 1918. The gun had ex-cellent balance and feel and was laden with safety features which overcame most objections to self-loading pistols. Curious-ly, it had three safeties, one of which pre-vented the gun from firing if the magazine was out. All Remington handguns disap-peared in 1935 shortly after Du Pont ac-quired the company, but now and then Remington can still wax radical. Who else would have the courage to come out with a 22 rifle with a nylon stock and get away with it? Or that long-barreled 22 centerfire bolt action pistol, the model XP-100, or is it a short-barreled, Mini-rifle?   •

A choice piece of Remington esoterica, the rifle cane which fired a 22 or 32 rimfire cartridge.

The Remington Rifle Cane.

No. 1 Cane weighs 16 oz,   No. 2, 24 oz.

Uses these Cartridges.

No. 2, or 32-100   No. 1, or 22.

CARE OF BIG GAME TROPHIES

After spending much time, money and effort to collect that big prize, will you have nothing to show for it because of poor preparation afield? A veteran taxidermist tells how to avoid trouble

by JERRY McNAMARA

WE ALWAYS HEAR ABOUT "the one that got away," but how often do we hear about the one that rotted away? I would venture to say that more big game trophies are lost through careless handling and uninformed preparation than by actually missing with the trusty old cannon.

In my profession of taxidermy I see great numbers of trophy animals in poor and in irreparable condition, and it is a never-ending source of wonderment to me that a hunter will spend his yearly savings for a hunt and then ignore the animal after it is in the bag. I therefore offer some suggestions and procedures that will enable you to save that trophy for the bare spot above your fireplace.

Cleanliness Important

It is of primary importance that the taxidermist receive the animal as clean and as nearly fresh as possible. Since hunters cannot always reach the mounting shop in a few hours, or drag a taxidermist along on every trip afield, it becomes necessary to do something to save the cape (skin of head, neck, and shoulder) from spoilage. If the temperature is above freezing, one cannot allow the animal to remain unskinned or unfrozen for more than a day or so. In warm weather the hair will "slip" or start to pull out very easily from the skin. If this happens the specimen is spoiled and the cape or hide cannot be tanned for mounting. Bears are especially hard to keep because of the great amount of fat on the hide, and they

will slip and spoil very soon after death if not properly cared for.

Therefore, if you have access to a locker plant or freezer and do not wish to undertake the skinning of the head, the entire head and cape should be deep frozen and packed in a box with dry ice for transportation home, the same as with the meat.

The hunter who transports his unskinned and unfrozen animal on top of the car in warm weather not only will lose the meat, but also will surely lose the trophy—and will have to use a gas mask just to remove the horns from the head.

If on a pack trip in rugged, remote areas, the trophy must be skinned, including—particularly in warm weather—the entire head. Some guides are proficient at this, especially the serious-minded men who understand the importance of trophy care. However, there may be times when you have no guide, or do not have one who is entirely familiar with this procedure, and then the job falls to you!

Actually, skinning is not nearly as difficult as it may seem, and any earnest big game sportsman should acquaint himself with head skinning. You can always get an unwanted deer or other head from a locker plant or a buddy and practice on this before the big trip comes along. In the field, before starting to skin, clean all blood from the hair. Use water, snow, leaves or rags—whatever may be available. Never wet the hair excessively; just dampen the blood and wipe it off. White sheep and goats are especially

bad in that they will be stained by the blood if it is not removed. A good fur dresser can bleach the hair on these trophies white again, but it's better to have them clean to start with.

Making the Cuts

The next step is to remove the head and cape from the body. Always make the cut in back of the front legs. This will allow plenty of cape for a shoulder mount, which is the most impressive way to display a head. Cut through the skin and completely encircle the body. The skin then can be peeled down over the neck and the neck meat cut off close to the base of the skull. Never — I repeat, never — make any kind of a cut or hole in the neck or throat of a big game trophy. The bleeding or sticking of an animal in the neck is one of the biggest farces in the hunting world. Neither should the throat be cut in the skinning process. If the throat is cut, the best taxidermist in the world cannot completely conceal it when mounting because of the brittle nature of the hair on all but bears and cats. If you must cut the neck skin to peel down over the meat, make the cut straight up the *back side* of the neck. The head and cape then can be taken into camp and further skinning done in a more convenient place.

When skinning out the head, begin at a point behind the horns and midway between the ears on the back of the neck. Make one long straight cut from this point down the full length

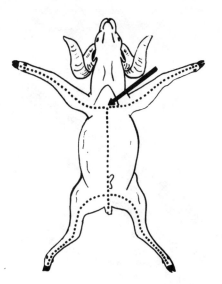

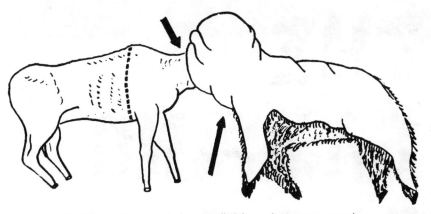

Fig. 1 — Opening cuts for animals such as sheep, deer, elk and moose are indicated by dotted lines. The belly cut never should extend beyond point indicated by arrow if a head mount is wanted. Neither should the throat be cut. If only a head-and-shoulder mount is wanted, cut the hide at point shown by dotted line in Fig. 2; cut all the way around the body *behind* the front legs.

of the neck to the rear. Next, make a cut from the starting point to the base of each horn on each side and peel the skin away from the bone at base of horn. On horned game (such as antelope, sheep and goat) you will need to cut through the skin to the bone, completely around the base of the horn. Be careful not to cut off the hair. On antlered game (moose, deer, etc.) you can pry the skin away from base of antler with knife or with screwdriver and hammer or block of wood.

When the skin is removed from

Fig. 3 — To skin out head, make cuts shown by dotted line on back of neck. Never cut front of neck skin. Delicate touch is required to free eyelids, nose and lips of trophy without damage. Ears must be turned inside out and salted.

around the horns, you can start to work it down over the face, turning it inside out in the process. Use great care when you reach the eyes so the eyelids are not cut. Placing the finger inside the rear part of the eyelid will serve as a guide when you reach that point. Better to cut your finger than the eyelid—the finger will soon heal, but the cape can be ruined forever!

Peel the skin away from the neck and face, cutting as necessary, until the nose is reached. At this point, sever the nose from the inside—leaving the nose on the cape, of course! Remember to cut close to the bone at all times and avoid cutting through the skin. When nose is cut through, sever the lips on both top and bottom, also leaving them on the cape, and the entire cape, in one piece, will be free of the skull.

The cape may then be deep frozen and brought or shipped to the taxidermist. If cape cannot be frozen, you must *turn the ears* and salt the entire cape. Turning the ears is the part that discourages most would-be skinners. To save the cape the salt must penetrate into the inside of the ear. You can be sure it does by separating the front and back parts of the ear. This is done by finding the base of the ear on the inside of the cape and shoving a blunt stick or spoon between the inner cartilage and the outer skin of the ear. Salt must penetrate the ear from the inside as it will not cure the ear from the outside. It does no good to skin out the head and leave the ears untouched, as they will slip hair—and big game trophy heads look awfully strange without ears! Ears need not be turned if kept frozen, however. Having your local taxidermist show you the proper procedure for handling the ears will help you to completely understand this phase.

Salt is the great savior of a skin or cape. Use it plentifully—you cannot use too much. Rock salt is no good. Use the finest grade of salt available, preferably common table salt. Spread it on all parts of the cape and be sure

the skin has no folds that aren't covered.

Roll up the cape with its fur side out and the salt inside. The cape will then keep until you rush to the Mountin' Man.

The skull with horns or antlers may be left intact, or to save on weight you may remove the top of the skull plate with horns attached. Saw hori-

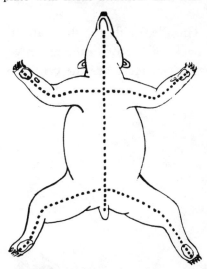

Fig. 4 — On animals such as bears and mountain lions, intended for rug mounts, opening cuts are indicated by dotted lines above. Be careful to make them symmetrical so that both sides will match. Extend leg incisions through pads. Head and feet must be skinned out quickly to prevent spoilage.

zontally through the skull in a straight line from front to back, through the center of the eye sockets. Remove the top of the skull with the horns in one piece.

You must remember that the taxidermist is not a magician. He cannot produce a good job from a bad skin. It is your job to insure that the skin or cape is taken care of properly. As you can see by the ideas set forth here, it is not usually much of a job to do so. The finished product will be well worth the effort. Remember—a little care goes a long way. ●

THE CAMPING RIFLE

by Jack Fairclough

Pet camping rifle of the author is this M61 Winchester pump in 22 rimfire magnum. He cut the barrel to 21", fitted a Lyman M66 peep sight, bored a hole in the buttstock to take spare ammo and matches, among other things.

The ideal rifle for the trail hiker, the back-packer or canoeman must meet special criteria. Here are the critical suggestions of an experienced outdoorsman.

The Ruger 10/22 Autoloader, here in Sporter form, would make a good camping rifle, as would the Savage 24S, the bottom barrel of which may be 410 or 20 gauge, the top tube in 22 LR. See our catalog pages for numerous other autoloading 22 rimfires, too many to display here.

MOST OUTDOORSMEN go camping whenever they have a chance. Just getting out into the bush has an effect on us all — the freedom that only this kind of living can give. Ingenuity usually used in closing an important business deal or machining a piece to the most exacting tolerances now becomes woodsmanship, the true test of a man's ability to take care of himself afield.

The prime importance in planning such outings is, of course, food, shelter, clothing and equipment. But what about the camping rifle? What is the *right* rifle to take with you when you go afield? Of course, any rifle *will do*. However, in this age of specialization, I believe the informed shooter should and would like to carry a rifle well suited to the task, rather than "make do."

If you plan a long back-packing trip, where every ounce counts, it would be foolish to carry a 9-pounder using banana-sized cartridges. Under such circumstances portability is the most important requirement. This may mean the sacrifice of other attributes, such as extreme accuracy or ex-

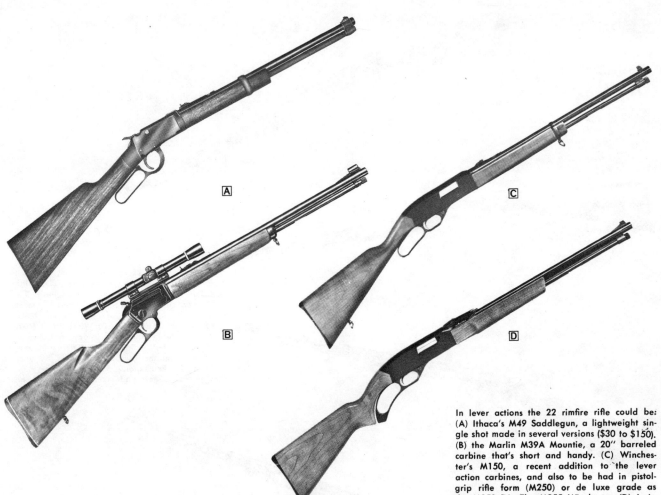

In lever actions the 22 rimfire rifle could be: (A) Ithaca's M49 Saddlegun, a lightweight single shot made in several versions ($30 to $150). (B) the Marlin M39A Mountie, a 20″ barreled carbine that's short and handy. (C) Winchester's M150, a recent addition to the lever action carbines, and also to be had in pistol-grip rifle form (M250) or de luxe grade as the M250 DL. The M255 Winchester (D) is in 22 rimfire magnum caliber.

treme power. Rifles chambered for the 22 Long Rifle and the 22 Winchester Rimfire Magnum are ideal for the back-packer. This is due to low report, sufficient energy and little ammo bulk and weight in relation to the number of rounds carried.

Most situations are covered very well by the 22 LR cartridge. However, great interest was shown when the 22 WRM was introduced. More powerful than the LR without the noise and expense of larger centerfire rounds, it sends a 40-gr. jacketed hollow point (HP) bullet at 2000 feet per second (fps) muzzle velocity with 355 foot pounds of muzzle energy. The LR's 37-gr. HP non-jacketed bullet has 1335 fps and a ME of 149 foot pounds. At 100 yards the maggie delivers a remaining velocity and energy of 1390 fps and 170 foot pounds respectively, compared with 1040 and 86 for the LR. The magnum cartridges cost about 2½ times as much as the LR, but have a decided edge on power, so the choice depends on your individual needs. Maximum effective range is considered to be about 75 yards for the LR and 125 yards for the WRM. I suggest that either caliber be used with solid bullets for pot shooting to avoid exces-

sive tissue destruction. For varmints, where this is not a factor, hollow points should be used.

The camping rifle may be called upon to dispatch a rattlesnake that is sunning in the trail or pick a crow out of the pine 50 yards across the meadow. With luck, you might get a shot at the bobcat that has been reducing the grouse population or the satisfaction of ending the depredations of a snapping turtle in a nearby pond. The list of possible situations is endless.

Many campfires ago, after carrying various makes, models, calibers and sight combinations into the woods, I had a pretty good idea of what such a rifle should be. Several good choices are available on both the new and used markets. Some "obsolete" used guns are almost classic examples; the Winchester 52 Sporter or Model 62 and Remington 121 Fieldmaster in 22 LR to name a few. They are no longer made, but a few may be found in good condition and should be considered. Currently produced models, of course, offer the largest selection. All action types are represented including an over/under, the Savage 24-S with a 22 LR or 24-MS 22 WRM barrel over a 410 or 20 ga. full choke

tube. This combination gun does the job well but has the disadvantage of requiring bulky shotgun shells. Rifle accuracy is very good, due in part, at least, to the stiffening effect of the two barrels being brazed together. The rifle barrel will probably be used most, but the smoothbore may be brought into play by shifting the barrel selector.

A repeater is usually desirable, but a good single shot is the Ithaca 49 with a lever-activated Martini-type action. At only 34 inches over-all and with a choice of both standard and magnum loads, this is the smallest of the lot. The 49 is reminiscent of the Stevens Favorite, though somewhat different in appearance. It is especially good for young campers and newcomers to the sport, for safety reasons.

Ruger's 10/22 and the Browning Grade 1 are excellent choices for the semi-auto fan. Both are chambered for the 22 LR. About $30 separate the two, which accounts for the Browning's better finish and take-down features, but both are light, fast and dependable. The Ruger has a detachable rotary box magazine and a loaded spare may easily be carried in your pocket. The Browning uses a

Four slide action 22 rimfire rifles, any of which would serve well as a camping rifle. High Standard's Sport King (A); Remington's 572 (B), here in plain grade, but made in BDL grade also, checkered fore and aft, etc. Next, the Savage 29 (C) and (D) Winchester's M62, neither rifle in production today, regrettably. If you're a bolt action fan, one of the 22 rimfire rifles on the facing page could be your choice. (E) Remington's 512X, a tubular magazine no longer made, but often found on

butt-loading tubular magazine and with its checkered stock, offers a non-slip grip.

For man-sized bolt actions, the Remington 512X provides the shooter with a 22 LR that has the familiar feel of a high power. The Mossberg 640K does the same with the magnum load. They are known for their accuracy, and though plain in finish, the simplicity of their actions makes them dependable. Both take scopes readily, as do the other rifles mentioned, but for camping a scope is not usually necessary.

The new Browning T-bolt rifle, a straight-pull type in 22 LR, is now available in a left-handed version for south paws—at no extra cost—in standard or deluxe quality.

Many other bolt actions, in less than man-dimensioned models, are of-fered, of course.

Don't fail to look over the new Remington rimfire bolt action, their Model 580. They're exceptionally sturdy, and the accuracy they are giving is excellent.

For a time tested slide action 22 LR, the Savage 29 is hard to beat. Short and light, this little pump gun is as solid as a rock, though considerably more accurate. In production since 1929, it is still one of the best values available today.

Shooters who prefer a hammerless lever action may well choose the Winchester Models 250 and 255, in LR and WRM respectively. They are modern in design and their appearance may be a shock to those who favor the more traditional. But don't let it scare you. This line was recently field tested in the jungles of

Central America and functioned perfectly. They will stand up to anything a stateside camping trip will give. This action is easily operated without removing the rifle from the shoulder as the trigger mechanism moves with the lever. There's now a brand new Winchester lever action 22 rimfire, the Model 150, and this one is relatively low-priced.

For those more comfortable with exposed hammer lever action rifles, there is the fine Marlin 39A, 22 LR, with workmanship and quality in the old tradition. It takes down by means of a coin-slotted screw on the right side of the receiver. I've owned one for 15 years and can testify to its value and dependability.

My own choice as the ideal camping rifle is the hammerless slide action Winchester 61 in 22 WRM. In

used-gun racks. Remington's latest, the M580 (F), a single-shot, but also available as a clip repeater (M581) or the M582, a tubular magazine type. (G), Mossberg's M640K Chuckster, in 22 magnum rimfire, a 5-shot clip repeater. (H), the Browning T-bolt clip repeater, an excellent man-sized rifle. Last (I), one you may never see—the famous M52 Winchester Sporter, out of production for many years, more's the pity.

production since 1932 as a 22 LR, it was revamped to chamber the WRM in 1962 and discontinued in 1964. I bought mine new and immediately had the barrel shortened to 21″ for the sake of handiness. Normal use and a nonscheduled flight down a Vermont mountain have proven its ruggedness.

After changing to a white bead front sight, a folding leaf sight was installed in the barrel dove-tail to act as a necessary, but seldom used, auxiliary. The Lyman 66 receiver sight lines up quickly and has given perfect service. One word of caution: Make sure that both primary *and* auxiliary sights are zeroed in. I go one step further and occasionally remove the 66s slide and install a Weaver J4 scope. The rifle's receiver is grooved for tip-off mounts, so this

is accomplished easily. A QD swivel stud in the buttstock and Judd's barrel band swivel near the muzzle enable the sling to go off or on in a few seconds. Thus, it may be hooked around a branch or canoe thwart when desired. This rig slings the rifle low, with the muzzle at shoulder level, preventing the muzzle from getting hung up when ducking under a branch or overhanging rock.

The hole in the buttstock, bored to facilitate fastening the stock to the receiver, can be put to good use. It can hold a full load of 14 cartridges in a waterproof wrapping and some waterproofed matches. All will fit nicely with room to spare. Both items are handy to have in an emergency.

Of course, if you do your camping in areas where potentially dangerous game is plentiful, common sense dic-

tates the carrying of a heavy-caliber rifle, supplemented by a take-down 22 rifle or handgun for camp chores.

Although camping rifles are fine for small game shooting, we will not discuss game hunting trips here. This leaves us with unprotected species of animals and birds (check your local game laws) and plinking targets limited only by the rules of shooting safety and your imagination.

And there you have it. Rifles that are ideal for camping as any around. They fit perfectly into that category of "friendly" rifles. They can become a part of their owners and give many years of dependable service.

Here's hoping you will "rediscover" the 22 rifle and its many benefits. Be your trip long or short, a camping rifle will serve you well in the wilderness. ●

ARE FIREARMS CONTROLS EFFECTIVE?

Abundance of Illegal Weapons Dictates New Approach

by COLIN GREENWOOD

Reprinted from the *Security Gazette*

OVER THE PAST few years there has been a tremendous increase in the use of firearms by criminals. The statistics issued by the Home Office show an alarming state of affairs and anyone with experience in the field will realise that the true figures are considerably greater. The statistics relate to the known crimes in which firearms were involved. To the figures must be added an indeterminate number of crimes in which firearms were carried, but the fact has not come to light.

For example, many housebreakers now carry firearms habitually, but the fact is revealed in only a small number of cases. The purpose of this article is to examine the rise in armed crime and to speculate about why the present rigid and strict system of firearms controls has failed in its primary purpose, for failed it has, as the figures will show.

The Statistical Background

The number of indictable offences known to the police in England and Wales in which firearms were involved is reported as:

1961	552	(107)
1962	588	(122)
1963	578	(144)
1964	731	(215)
1965	1140	(318)
1966	1511	(404)
1967	2337	——
1968	2500	——

The figures in brackets indicate the number of those offences in which the weapon used was a shotgun, sawn off or otherwise. Regrettably, the figures do not appear to have been broken down further. Undoubtedly air weapons, which are virtually free of controls, have featured in some recorded crimes. Clearly, pistols form a substantial proportion of the weapons used and rifles can reasonably be said to be the least used class of weapon, although they too have featured in some cases. It is unfortunate that no distinction appears to have been made between normal shotguns and sawn off shotguns, the latter having been subjected to a firearm certificate procedure for many years.

Certificate Application Procedure

The system of controls varies according to the class of weapon involved. Broadly speaking rifles, pistols and sawn off shotguns are subject to the very strict firearm certificate procedure in which an application to possess weapons is made to the Chief Officer of Police and, if the certificate is granted, full details of all weapons and ammunition are entered in the certificate. Sales of weapons are notified to the police.

An applicant for a firearms certificate must show that he has good reason for requiring the weapon and is subjected to the closest scrutiny. Shotgun controls are less stringent. An applicant for a shotgun certificate merely has to satisfy conditions about his character and antecedents. No record of weapons is shown in the certificate and no notification of sales need be given to the police. In this context it is important to note that a shotgun with barrels less than 24 inches in length is deemed not to be a shotgun for the purpose of the controls, but is subject to the firearm certificate procedure. With the exception of a very small number of the most powerful weapons, air weapons are virtually free from controls.

Colin Greenwood, 38 years old when this article was written, has been an English police officer since 1954, rising in the years since to sergeant, inspector and, his rank today, Chief Inspector. He has participated in the shooting sports generally, including shotgunning and rifle shooting, but his main interest was, and is, in handgun shooting. He won the British Police Championship twice in ISU centerfire matches, placed several times in those and other handgun events, and was twice a member of the British Team competing for the European Police Shooting Championships. Mr. Greenwood's articles have been published in the (English) *Forensic Science Journal*, in several British police journals, in *Guns Review*, et al. His latest book, *Tactics in the Police Use of Firearms*, is an excellent work that deals with all phases of the police use of guns and related equipment.

Mr. Greenwood is (if he doesn't mind the term) an enlightened policeman, one who does not believe, *ipso facto*, that stringent gun controls mean an automatic reduction in firearms crimes. Last year Mr. Greenwood was granted a Fellowship at Cambridge University to reasearch and report on the effectiveness of firearms controls in England. That study has now been completed, and here is what Mr. Greenwood had to say, in part, about his findings: "...firearms controls have done little or nothing to combat armed crime. It can be shown that, when firearms were completely free from control (prior to 1920), there was less criminal use of firearms than there is now!"

Pistols in School

Controls on pistols were introduced in 1903 but in their present form they, along with controls on rifles and sawn off shotguns, date from 1937. For 32 years pistols have been subjected to the strictest controls and yet it is an indisputable fact that a confirmed criminal, even though he may be prohibited by law from possessing firearms, can and does buy whatever weapon he wants with the greatest ease. There are countless examples to illustrate the point. Go back to 1952 and the well known case of Craig and Bentley who were convicted for the murder of P.C. Miles. Only a year earlier Craig, who allegedly fired the fatal shot, had been fined for possessing a 455 Webley revolver without a certificate. At his trial he said that in the previous five years he had had between 40 and 50 firearms through his hands. Where had he got them? Swapped or bought them from boys at school. He also said that he had made two of the weapons himself. And this was a boy of 16, prohibited by law from acquiring weapons.

Harry Roberts, who was convicted for his part in the Shepherd's Bush murder of three police officers in 1966, was found to have a small arsenal of weapons. According to the evidence at his trial, his previous record was such as to make him prohibited for life from possessing firearms. Where did he get them? In 1967 a Greek Cypriot was convicted of selling three pistols, a Luger, a Colt and an Enfield to Roberts. Needless to say, this man also held them illegally.

A Televised Gunman

In July 1968 a man appeared in profile on Independent Television, setting himself up as a killer available for hire. He produced a Luger pistol and ammunition to support this. Unfortunately for him he was recognised by a police officer who had previously dealt with him. At his trial he was said to have 14 previous convictions including one in 1947 when he was sent to prison for 14 years for shooting with intent to resist arrest. Where did he get his gun? According to his own evidence he had been approached a few days before the programme and he had simply gone into a West End club and bought the gun for £30 —literally over the bar. It is of some significance that, despite his record, this man was fined £50 and given a suspended six months prison sentence. There may have been special features in this case, but such a sentence is hardly likely to make other criminals surrender their guns for fear of retribution.

Some Illegal Sources of Supply

Where did these and the thousands of other firearms illegally in circulation originate? The answer can only be speculative, but they certainly did not come directly from the holders of firearm certificates whose weapons are checked regularly by the police. Many are wartime souvenirs which have not been surrendered in the various amnesties (note how frequently the Luger features). There is no doubt that substantial numbers of weapons are illegally brought into this country from abroad and dockside areas are a good place to start if one wishes to buy a weapon "off ticket."

Some weapons are stolen from military sources and a limited number are stolen from dealers and private individuals, but these latter thefts may not present a true picture. Frequently the weapons stolen from gunsmiths or private houses are very valuable, shotguns valued at over £1,000, and many are stolen for their cash value rather than for use as weapons. Whatever the source, these illegal firearms are quite freely available to the criminal who has a little cash and the right contacts.

Amnesties No Answer

Since the war, over 186,000 weapons have been surrendered in various amnesties, but this represents only a small part of the illegal weapons in circulation. Surely no one is so naive as to think that the hardened criminal is going to surrender his weapon in an amnesty? Those who took weapons along to the police were, by and large, perfectly respectable people. The criminals and less respectable element were not tempted by the magnanimous offer to relieve them of a possibly valuable and frequently valued weapon. Undoubtedly many such weapons remain in circulation.

Sporting Guns

Shooting sports tend to remain out of the public eye, probably as a result of the absence of spectator appeal, yet they form a substantial national and international sporting activity. At a conservative estimate some three-quarters of a million people in this country take an active part in one type of shooting or another. Ownership of firearms by these people, who have had to prove their eligibility for certificates and have been subjected to the closest scrutiny by the police, presents no problem at all. The mere fact that a person applies to the police for a certificate is evidence of his good intentions. There is no case on record of anyone applying for a firearm certificate to enable him to commit an armed robbery and it is submitted that there is not one shred of evidence to suggest that the absence of a firearm certificate prevented a single criminal carrying a gun.

Shotgun Certificate Anomaly

In addition to the burden of firearm certificates the police and the shooting public had the questionable burden of shotgun certificates thrust upon them in 1967. Examination of statistics shows that shotguns featured in under one third of the cases during the period when they were completely uncontrolled.

Strict controls on the legitimate purchase of pistols for some 30 years have not in any noticeable way prevented criminals from obtaining and using them, yet there appear to be those who hope that the less stringent and more easily evaded shotgun certificate procedure will materially affect the criminal use of that class of weapon. At least two chief constables expressed their doubts on this score in their last annual reports and the Home Office itself had very considerable doubts at least until 1965 when the then Home Secretary, Sir Frank Soskice said, "There are probably at least half a million shotguns in legitimate use throughout the country and the burden which certification would put on the police and the users would not be justified by the benefits which would result." However, by late 1966, the Home Office had changed its tune, though one can see little factual justification for such an about-face, and Mr. Jenkins was introducing shotgun controls in the Criminal Justice Act. The 600,000 shotgun certificates represent a tremendous amount of police time and effort and a lot of inconvenience for honest, respectable citizens, for it is only these who have applied for certificates. There are undoubtedly thousands of shotguns in the hands of persons who do not hold a certificate and the police effort involved in issuing certificates has not affected them.

Honest Disposal Made Difficult

It must be accepted that the hardened criminal who has armed himself is unlikely to surrender his gun voluntarily: it has become one of the tools of his trade and one which has made his job easier. However, consider for a moment the man who brought home a Luger at the end of the war (and there are many of these still about). He has it illegally and has failed to surrender it in the various amnesties. He knows that if he goes to the police the gun will be confiscated and he will probably be prosecuted.

If the pistol is in good condition it is worth around £20 and in any event he probably has rather an attachment to it. However, if he is short of money, he may be tempted to sell it, and if it is stolen he cannot report the fact to the police. It would be far better to make it clear that any application for a firearm certificate would be sympathetically dealt with and if, for some good reason it was impossible to grant a certificate, he would be permitted to sell it to a dealer for its full market value. Once the pistol is on record, either in a firearm certificate or in a dealer's register, illegal dealings become very difficult if the proper police checks are made.

Controls Misdirected

The proposition raised here is that the problem does not lie in the lawfully held weapons, but in those illegally held despite the controls. Yet almost the whole of the police effort is directed to getting the countless forms filled in by honest citizens. In considering the rate of armed crime in relation to the numbers of weapons in legitimate hands, it is interesting to note the situation in Switzerland which has the largest number of firearms in relation to population of any country in the world (including the U.S.A.). Virtually every male Swiss is a member of the armed forces and keeps his weapons at home. Guns in every home, and yet a recent enquiry elicited the information that armed crime was so rare that it was not recorded separately in the very comprehensive criminal statistics. Was not this the case in this country not too many years ago?

Each rise in the rate of armed crime has led to calls for the further tightening of existing controls on firearms. This appears to be a simple solution to the problem, but even a cursory examination shows that it is no solution at all. To direct all the legislative and police effort toward the legitimate firearms user is not only ineffective, but dangerous, in that it tends to hide the real problems under the veil of a simple solution. A hardened criminal found in possession of a firearm whilst prohibited by law faces no greater penalty than does the otherwise decent person who has retained a wartime souvenir and frequently the penalties imposed by the courts show that they have treated the case as a mere technical breach and not as the serious matter that it really is.

An examination of the tabulated figures show that 1964 was the start of the real escalation. Why? Certainly it had nothing to do with any firearms controls which remained unchanged since 1937 (though they were to be tightened slightly in 1965). Certainly it had nothing to do with any sudden increase in the availability of illegal firearms. The guns had always been there, but the criminal had previously carried them only rarely. Could it be that in 1964 the campaign to abolish capital punishment was at its height and that executions had, in effect, already stopped even though the legislation did not get through Parliament until the following year?

Rationalisation Needed

There can be no doubt that reasonable firearms controls which are acceptable to the shooting community can help reduce the casual use of firearms in crime and may help reduce the number of accidents with firearms (though these are not frequent in any case). However, it must be accepted that controls on the legitimate firearms user will not prevent the determined criminal from acquiring a gun. Harsh firearms controls may well have a reverse effect if otherwise decent people who have an interest in firearms feel disposed to retain illegally held weapons and so swell the already large black market. Whatever the answer to the armed criminal might be, it does not lie in providing forms for reputable citizens to complete and there are great dangers in the sort of thinking that tries to reduce armed crime by measures like the present shotgun controls.   ●

HANDLOADING

A timely review of the latest tools, components and accessories.

by the Technical Editors

B-Square Chronograph

Part 1—Equipment

B-Square Co.

Dan Bechtel, owner-operator of this outfit in Texas (P.O. Box 11281, Ft. Worth 76109), showed me his latest chronograph at the NRA meeting, and it has several new and unusual features. Crystal-controlled, of course for high accuracy, the Model 71 has nickel-cad batteries, a built-in battery charger and it's automatic—just plug in and shoot, no turn-switches to read. As our photo shows, the read-out numbers are at the top, easy to see and jot down. When you're through with it, plug it into the 110V line and it charges overnight—nor is there any danger of overcharging. Any standard screens can be used with the M71, but it comes complete—screens, holders, cables, brackets and instructions, all for $149.95.

Dan had a bunch of other stuff with him, good items for the shooter or gunsmith. His T-C scope Mount Base fits the Thompson/Center pistol, uses Weaver Tip-Off rings, sells for $5.20 postpaid. Despite the low price, it looked good. Ever have trouble with Redfield and Weaver scope screws? Dan has a T-handle wrench for these, each $4.20 PP, and each fitting the screws exactly. Dan's Screw Holder accepts 6x48 and 8x40 scope base screws, holds them firmly for power grinding when you need to shorten one. Also $4.20 PP. Two other items for the professional gunsmith are: a Recoil Pad Jig ($18.45 PP) which lets any pad be exactly fitted to the stock, including the toe angles, *off the stock*—no chance of damage to a fine finish. Still in the wood division, Dan's Swivel Jig is a precision drill guide that prevents off-center, crooked, mislocated swivels; $7.20 PP.

Getting into the higher money area now, there are 3 B-Square tools for the precision rifleman. Their Cartridge/Bullet Spinner is the best-designed of these I've seen. Rather than rotating the loaded round on a center holding the bullet, with the case supported by rollers, etc., this tool has two ground round bars on which the case rides, the neck and the bullet floating freely. The dial indicator included (.0005″) quickly detects neck or bullet runout. The "center" type of spinner can't do that if there is any eccentricity in the bullet—and there often is, unless the bullets have already been spun separately and the duds discarded. $35.95 PP.

The B-Square Case Neck Thickness gauge is different, too. The case, pushed into a holed piece of round stock, is firmly held against a ground arbor by two spring-loaded "pushers." Runout of the neck wall is read from a .0005″ D.I. $38.95 PP. B-Square's Bullet Spinner Gauge, the body a well-machined steel piece, holds precision-coned centers, fully adjustable to check runout anywhere on the bullet. The D.I. furnished is a jeweled type, reading to .0001″. $45.95 PP.

B-Square offers many other useful items, especially for the gunsmith—write.

Bill Ballard

That seems a likely name for a man making the stuff he does, and we're glad to welcome another craftsman to these pages. His numerous products are intended for those who shoot the older firearms, especially the old single shot rifles.

The Long Range Vernier-scale tang sight illustrated nearly duplicates the scarce originals exactly, the one shown intended for the Peabody-Martini, and selling at $40. He can and will make the same basic sight for other rifles—Sharps, Ballard, et al—the price varying a bit. These Vernier sights are nicely made indeed; full color-hardened (except leaf spring) and the elevation rod is double-threaded to speed changes from one range to another. Our sample showed fine construction.

Ballard hand makes the brass cases illustrated, those shown are only a few of the calibers and types offered. The Burnside (A) is $1.50; the Maynards, 50-50 and 35-30 calibers in the 1866 type (B and F) are 75¢ each; the 50-110 (C) is $1 and the 45-3¼″ (D) is $1.50. The small case (E) is a reformed 25-20 SS, these 40¢ each. There's a reduction if cases are ordered in lots of 10 or 20 pieces.

Bullet swages take a cast lead bullet or slug, without grease grooves, the user then hammering the plunger to produce a smooth, well-formed bullet, of a quality and dimensional tolerance a mould cannot make. Swages were a standard item in the kit of those shooting target-grade muzzleoaders, the "slug" rifles, as they're called today. Ballard's swages (illustrated) are made a bit differently, but they work excellently, and he's sold lots of them at $20. The base interchanges, so further calibers are $15. These Ballard swages are held to plus-or-minus .0005″, indicating tight control and good workmanship.

Ballard has been making a close copy of the old Lyman paper-patch cylindrical bullet mould for some time, selling at $22.50 complete for one caliber. Extra cavities are $12.50. Such moulds cast a smooth bullet, variable in length and weight, to be used in the swage described. Almost any caliber is available, the bullets all being round nosed and flat based. Recently Ballard has begun making 2-piece smooth-bullet mould blocks, meant for use in Lyman handles. These produce a flat-pointed, hollow-base bullet, also adjustable for length, cost $25.

Ballard makes a Pope-style re- and decapper at $15, the case heads and pins interchangeable, most calibers available. His breech bullet seaters (2 styles) are about $7.50, and he has straight-line bullet seaters at $10.

Ballard can, he says, ship unprimed metallic cases to anyone, and he'll send you his little product booklet for 20¢.

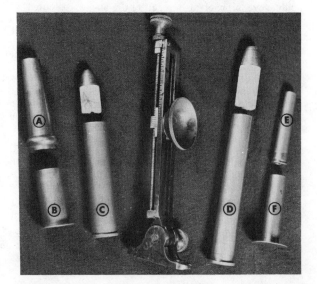

Some of the numerous items Bill Ballard makes.

C-H Tool & Die

At long last an idea I had some 10 years ago has become a reality. I'm referring to the new C-H Pro-Hex rifle cartridge die sets ($16.95), and their use of a tungsten-carbide expander button or ball. No more need to inside-lube the case neck, a tedious and rarely satisfactory chore, because really adequate oiling or whatever meant the necessity for removal of same. Efforts will be lessened, too, and I wouldn't be much surprised if case-neck elongation is lessened to some degree. The carbide button isn't going to wear down, either, and it's part of a new expander unit that carries a heavy-duty decapping pin for use on crimped-in primers.

Made entirely in the C-H shop, the Pro-Hex dies are hand polished and lapped; double locking rings permit finger-tightening of the dies in the press, but a set screw in the upper ring may be turned down for additional tightening if desired. The hexagon form of the die body also allows an open end or crescent wrench to be used on them rather than pliers.

Carbide Expander balls are available separately as well, these threaded 8x32 for 6.5mm and under, or 10x32 for 270 and bigger, thus usable in such other die bodies as RCBS, et al; these are $5.50. For the RCBS expander unit a complete rod, including the carbide ball, is offered at $6.50.

New C-Hampion Press has compound leverage, handles bullet swaging, resizing chores easily. C-H Pro-Hex die sets (below) feature T-C expander balls.

Our sample set of Pro-Hex dies, in 7mm Rem. Mag. caliber, worked well indeed. Cases came out of the size die nicely polished, no scratches of any kind, and the decreased effort in pulling the carbide button through was a lot less.

The latest—and sturdiest—C-H press is their Champion, an O-type that weighs 26 pounds. A large-diameter (1.185″) ram is used, giving some 16 square inches of bearing surface, and an equal-size hole is in the tool top. A ⅞-14 bushing is supplied, but with the bushing removed, bullet-making dies can be used as well. (We understand that the compounded-leverage system used on the Champion press is based on Fred Huntington's U.S. patent No. 2,847,895.)

C-H has a new bullet swaging die in the works, one that will make 3/4-jacketed handgun bullets in any heavy-duty press. As most of us know, home swaging of $4-jacketed bullets has pretty well disappeared. Leading, at the higher velocities one expected, was an all-too-common experience, nor was accuracy as good as it ought to have been. If these new C-H dies will produce bullets that look and act like Super-Vel's, for example, we can well expect a resurgence of interest in homemade handgun bullets with gilding metal envelopes.

C-H has many more interesting items for the handloader—send for their illustrated catalog.

Case-Gard 50

I'm not much of a plastics man, but I have no hesitancy in saying that these new 50-round ammo boxes by MTM Molded Products (P.O. Box 14092, Dayton, O. 45414) are easily the best I've seen. Made of a heavy-gauge polypropylene, the integral hinge (same material) is guaranteed for 1,000,000 openings or 5 years—whichever comes first, I guess. There is a clever latch that snaps closed when the lid is pushed down, yet opens instantly, and the cartridges won't lose their position even if the box is turned upside-down. There are 3 heights offered—Small (222 Rem. and similar cases); Medium (22-250, 243, 308, etc.) and Large, which takes all the Magnums, 30-06 and the like. $1.95 each, and worth it.

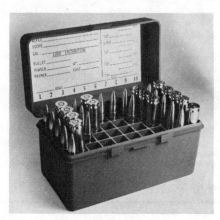

John Dewey Gun Co.

Dewey continues to offer his excellent Bullet Spinner, with or without a dial indicator ($38.50 to $67.00), plus other items too many to describe here, but his new stuff includes several things that I've found useful—and well made:

His benchrest quality Neck Sizing Die is the drive-in type, serving also as a primer decapper. The decap rod is included at the low price, but as these are custom made, four fired cases must be sent with the order. These cases should be of the style being shot, that is, reamed or neck-turned if that's your method. $10.00 for this NS Die, (plus $1.00 postage) or $30.00 postpaid for it and a matching Straight Line Seater. The latter is $19.00 separately, plus $1.00 shipping cost. Calibers available—17 on up.

The latest Dewey tool for precision shooters is Dewey's Neck Turner, a small, portable unit that does a first class job of shaving case necks to a uniform wall thickness. A long-life tungsten carbide cutter, fully adjustable, does a smooth job quickly. Price, $18.00, with an adjustable case holder at $2.75. Extra spindles are $3.75. Fired cases, several of them, should also be sent to Dewey when the Neck Turner is ordered.

John is back in production on several other items, notably his Cleaning Rod Guide for bolt action rifles ($7.00), a tool that's truly a "bore saver," especially in the throat section. He can also furnish his Colt Scout Base Pin Latch ($2.00—$2.50 in

nickel), and a Trigger Stop for all Ruger Single Action revolvers ($3.00).

J.D. also sent me other 17-cal. tools—a mandrel for use with his Outside Neck Turning tool, a Straight Line Bullet Seater and another 17-cal. cleaning rod (with brass brush and Belding & Mull-type tip for holding patches). The Dewey 17-cal. rods, of course, are usable in bores up to 6mm/243, and at the quoted price ($5.50, including a brass brush, plus $2.50 for packing and shipping) a strong plastic case is furnished, an excellent container for rod storage or transport.

His 17-caliber cleaning gear will be ready when you read this (I hope!), including rods, brushes, etc. Also new is a bore cleaning agent that John Dewey says is "more efficient than anything." $1.00 for 4 ounces.

Ask for the latest Dewey literature—it's free.

The Fergusons

In addition to the cartridge spinner and the recapping tools shown here—both very well made—this firm makes a case neck-turning tool at $18 for any two calibers; a bullet spinner that sells for $55 including a .0001″ dial indicator ($35 minus the D.I.), and a small arbor press, rack-and-pinion type, at $40. The latter tool serves well for straight-line bullet seating, and for pushing cases into neck-size dies and then driving 'em out.

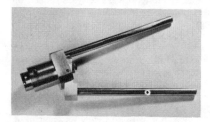

The Fergusons also make up a Neck Sizing unit, the type usable at the bench via a mallet or arbor press, and in which the used primer is ejected as the sized case is pushed out. The buyer furnishes 4 fired cases, just as they come out of the rifle, because this type of die is tailored to the customer's brass. Delivery time is about 3 weeks, the price complete for one caliber, $18.00.

All Ferguson tools are precision ground, lapped and polished where called for, and they all carry a lifetime guarantee to the original owner, barring abuse or obvious neglect. Even so, they'll be repaired at no cost! Their address is 27 W. Chestnut St., Farmingdale, N.Y. 11735.

New Lyman Products

The old Middlefield firm (now a part of the Leisure Group) has several new and interesting items for the handloader/shooter this year, and all were seen and examined at the 1971 NSGA show in Chicago.

The new short-tube 20x All-American target scope—just over 17″ long, and offered with the serious bench rest shooter in mind—won't be gone into here in detail. See Bob Bell's Scopes and Mounts story elsewhere in this edition for full information.

Lyman's new $17.50 powder scale, the Model D-7, shows a number of advantages over some other makes and types. The main casting is quite heavy, making for better stability and decreased vibration. The capacity is high—505 grains—with the graduations white on black for high, mistake-free visibility and setting. The knife edges and bearings are made of tungsten carbide—a notably hard material—for extra long life and sustained sensitivity, hence increased accuracy as well. Magnetically damped for faster reading, the D-7 is guaranteed to give 1/10-gr. plus-or-minus accuracy. A new type of beam lifter, actuated by a handy button, eliminates wear and tear on the bearings when the scale is not in use. The D-7 scale pan, with a good form of tapered spout for easier pouring, is positively positioned every time, a last assurance of enhanced—and constant—uniformity, which is the open secret of good handloads.

We announced the advent of Lyman's Universal Trimmer (for all metallic cases) in this department last year, but good production didn't get under way for some months, and a sample of the tool was not seen and tested until recently. It has proved to be a sturdy, well-designed case trimmer, one that not only works smoothly and efficiently, but rapidly. It uses a rotating collet system, unique in this field, that firmly grasps and holds any and all cases from the 17 Remington to the 458 Magnum. Pilots are available in 25 sizes (90¢ each), and those are the only extras needed. Length adjustment is critically controlled via two knurled rings (one coarse, the other fine), and the cutter shaft runs in an oil-impregnated bronze bearing. Pilots and cutter heads are of tool steel, fully hardened; the cutters are replaceable, of course, but they should last for years.

The bench-type Universal Trimmer, one pilot included, is $22. Another version, designed for drill press operation where quantity trimming is desired, is $14, including a pilot of your choice.

The last new Lyman item is the least item—though they're mightly useful gadgets—a Powder Dribbler, at $3, that is made with a wide (2⅞″) non-tipping base.

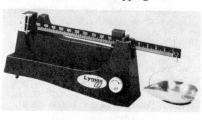

R. W. Hart & Son

Bob Hart—well-known to the bench rest clan—introduced an excellent rifle rest last year, which we commented on in GD 25, and favorably. Now he's offering several new tools for the precision handloader-shooter—first there's a straight-line bullet seater, adjustable for depth, of course, that is available in 222 Rem., 222 Rem. Mag., 6×47, 6mm Rem., 25-06 and 308. Price, $18. Next, a drive-in/drive-out neck sizing die in the same calibers (the knock-out rod decaps the case at the same time) at $35. The rawhide mallet to do the driving is $2.25. Last, a compact, short-lever sensitive primer seater that handles large and small caps, via an adaptor, that is $42.50. We haven't tried any of these items, but we do know Bob's quality—he can't do a bad job! Send order to Robert W. Hart & Son, 401 Montgomery St., Nescopeck, PA. 18635.

Bullet Gauge

A couple of years ago I received a mixed bag of bullets and that's the right term. Some 6-7 calibers were in the lot—all mixed together, and nearly 2000 of them! The cartons had broken up from rough handling or something.

I wish I'd had then the gadget I'm looking at now. This potential time-saver is a sturdy (.062″ thick) piece of stainless steel of just about the same shape and size of a Starrett Drill Gauge, nor does the similarity end there. However, instead of twist drill hole sizes, the new Reynolds gauge offers 16 precision-made holes for checking bullet diameters—223, 224, 243, 257, 264, 277, 284, 308, 311, 323, 338, 348, 358, 375, 429 and 458.

Don't wait for one with 217 and 234 holes, either— when they are gone, that's it.

B.T. Reynolds, 835-B Arcadia Ave., Arcadia, Calif. 91006, sells this useful and well-made device for $4.75, but his supply is limited.

Pindell Bullet Spinner

Ferris Pindell, another famed BR shooter, and formerly with Sierra Bullets, offers a bullet spinner he calls "new and better." At $129.50 it better be better, and indeed it sounds so—a .0001" dial indicator is included, and bullet run-out can be determined at any place on the bullet, including the base, boat-tail, etc. Pindell's location is Connersville, Ind. 47331.

Precision Accuracy Tool

C.C. Seitz, well-known benchrest shooter, has a small arbor press (5"x6" base of steel, 9" high, 4¾" clearance between ram and base) that operates via the usual rack-and-pinion arrangement. Nicely finished, the press offers controlled, smooth manipulation of straight-line sizing and seating dies. Order from the Pendleton Gunshop, 1200 S.W. Hailey Ave., Pendleton, Ore. 97801.

New Saeco Lead Tester

SAECO

A strong, well-trained thumbnail was an important adjunct to handloaders back when I started refilling cases with cast lead bullets. That was in the years when many of us—if not most—scrounged for lead, adding to the pot whatever we could find—battery plates, lead dug out of backstops. Some bullets were shot as many as 6 times and more—we couldn't afford to buy lead, at least I couldn't. Tin? A good source was toothpaste tubes.

Our mix, then, was an unknown thing, so the first few bullets cast got the thumbnail test—if a fair indent could be made, that was too soft for stiff handgun loads, about one to 25 or so, said our thumb. If we could just barely scratch the bright surface, perhaps that meant 1-10 or so.

This year there's a gadget that removes all the guess work. Saeco—justly-famous for the excellent quality of its numerous items for the reloader—offers a lead hardness tester that is at once unique and useful. About 6 inches long, the Saeco Tester measures the penetration (or indenting) of *your* bullet by applying a known force to it, then reading the relative hardness of the bullet from a vernier scale. Readings of 0 to 1 indicate pure or near-pure lead, 3-4 equals a 1-to-10 alloy, while a 6-7 readout shows linotype-metal hardness.

At $28.50 this useful item won't sell like ice cream cones on the Zambezi, but it could save the lead bullet man money (using scrap lead, adding hardeners as indicated) and give him more uniform—thereby more accurate—bullets. Perhaps best of all, the Saeco Tester will allow small hardness variations experimentally—up or down the scale—trials heretofore difficult to achieve.   (JTA)

Sundtek

Sundtek (Box 744, Springfield, Ore. 97477) is making two new chronographs, one of them quite sophisticated in design yet moderately priced for what it offers—a direct readout in feet per second. Five numeral-display tubes are used, the velocities on the standard Model 1500 measurable from 775 to 9999 fps. A low-cost option ($25) permits readouts from 77.5 to 999.9 fps. Time readings may also be taken, optionally, by flipping a switch. Accuracy is at least one foot second at 5000 fps, the time base (normal) being 10 million pulses per second. The "10 and 1" option operates at 1 MHz (1 million cycles). 10-foot screen spacing is required, though other separations may be had at extra cost. Operation is 117 VAC as cataloged, but a 6 VDC option may be arranged for. The Model 1500 is compatible with any mechanical and most electronic screens, but again older photo-eye screens and microphone trigger systems can be adapted. Base price of the Sundtek 1500 is $875; 100 paper screens, holders and coaxial cables (which prevent false readings) are $25. The instrument is compact and light—3.5"x9" wide x 8" deep, weight 6 lbs.

The Sundtek Model 150 is exactly the same as the 1500 except that time readings only are presented (also to 5 places), and the same optional aspects are available. Operation is by 117 VAC or 6 VDC as furnished (a car or other rechargeable battery is suggested) at the $450 price, which includes screen holders, 100 paper screens, coaxial cables, time-velocity tables and instructions. Dimensions are the same, the weight one-half lb. less. All of the foregoing data is taken from factory literature, plus a phone talk with Mr. Ivan L. Sundstrom, Sundtek's sales manager.

There has not been time, so far, to test either chronograph, but the information supplied sounds highly impressive, and I've learned that several Model 1500s are now in use at military installations and by some ammunition makers.

The Sundtek Model 1500 reads directly in foot seconds or, at the operator's option, in time of flight.

Left—Texan FW press, the LT above.

Texan Reloaders

Texan has recently introduced two new shotshell reloaders, one at a very attractive price. Called the Texan LT (or Little Texan) it was designed with the casual reloader, the novice or hunter in mind. Despite its low cost ($39.95 in 12, 16 or 20 gauge) it offers full length sizing, self-aligning crimp starter, a tapered final crimp and twin steel columns for good rigidity. Interchangeable powder and shot bushings are used, no charge bar changing needed, and high or low brass, high or low base cases are handled without adjustment. The wad guide fingers never need replacement, and the primer seating system won't cup shell heads. If the LT is wanted in 28 or 410, the price is $5 higher, or $44.95, and conversion kits are available, too.

The other new Texan shotshell loader is the Model FW, a sample of which we've been using for several months with every satisfaction. The test FW came to us in 20 gauge, its production intended in the main for use in the new Browning Super Light over-under. While the FW does all of the basic jobs mentioned in connection with the Texan LT, it is a sturdier, heavier press, and has features the low-price LT lacks—all component parts are fully machined castings, for example; a new wad ram eliminates any possibility of wad pull-out, while the FW wad guide automatically lowers and raises for fast and easy insertion of the wads. Certainly it is a fast, smoothly-functioning loader, and we've now put through it some 2000 loads without a bobble.

One small change was made in the FW because its output was meant for the new Browning 20 mentioned—which sometimes require a shell to be head-sized down a few thousandths more than standard. The tighter sizing ring took only a moment to install.

Because of the better performance of the sizing die developed for the FW press, Texan now offers a kit for converting their DP-I and DP-II loaders to the FW system. These kits, with clear instructions for their use, sell for $6.98.

The Texan FW, in 12, 16 or 20 gauge, with 6- or 8-point crimper, is $74.95; add $5 for 28 or 410, a 6-point crimper included. Conversion kits are available also.

Redding

Redding-Hunter recently announced the Model 23 Self-Indexing Star Crimp starter, made for 12, 16 and 20 gauge in 6 and 8 point type; in 6 point only for 28 and 410. The impact-extruded head, rotating on steel ball bearings, is specially hardened for a lifetime of use, say the makers. How its self-indexing is done isn't described—there is no external feeler visible in the picture—and it is not known whether the M23 unit is usable on shotshell loaders other than Redding's.

Sierra Loading Manual

Sierra, famous bullet makers, have just announced for July release a new *Sierra Bullets Reloading Manual.* Extensive data on loading Sierra bullets will be furnished,

of course, but the big, 3-ring binder book (for ready insertion of subsequent data sheets) has several other unusual features:

Trajectory figures, out to 1000 yards for long range competition and hunting calibers, were both calculated and field checked via actual firings.

A complete reference section, with index and glossary, plus fill-in sheets the owner can use for his test data, are included.

Price of the new manual in standard form is $4.85, but a limited and numbered 1st Edition (2000 copies) specially bound and signed by Bob Hayden, Sierra's operations manager, will be $15 each.

No advance copy has been seen, and we have no information yet on size or number of pages.

The Sierra manual has 352 pages, and is 7½"x 9".

RCBS

While Fred Huntington hasn't announced any major products for 1971-72, there are several new items for the handloader of metallic ammunition—especially for the 17-caliber shooters.

Foremost among all of these is a sensitive, low-leverage priming tool that offers smooth, uniform seating of primers. With this new "Precisioneered" tool, the primer can be felt going home into the primer pocket, which means that a loosened or over-tight pocket can be readily detected. In addition, the pockets can be easily checked before seating the primer.

An auto primer feed is also supplied with the RCBS Priming Tool, but if the reloader already has RCBS Auto Primer Feed Tubes and RCBS Shell Holders, he can get the new Priming Tool for $21.95, including both large and small Primer Rod assemblies, plus the Auto Primer Arm. For $3 more he gets the Primer Feed Tubes. RCBS shell holders are still $2.40 each.

Now that Remington 17 caliber rifles and ammo are readily available, RCBS will doubtless see a splurge in sales for their 17-caliber equipment—which they've had for some little time, for Fred wasn't to be caught napping on the mighty midget!

The 17-caliber tools include a Funnel ($1.20), a Case Neck Brush (60¢), a Drop Tube ($3) for the RCBS Uniflow Powder Measure, and a Burring Tool at $3. RCBS has, of course, loading dies for the Remington 17, as well as die sets for many older wildcat 17s.

Other new RCBS items are: Plastic-cased lube pads, the foam pads removable for cleaning, cost $3, and plastic handles ($1) for their case neck brushes—the latter at 45¢ for all calibers but 17. These new handles also take the RCBS Primer Pocket Cleaner Blade (which handles large or small pockets) at $2.40.

RCBS has a big 1971-72 catalog available for the asking, and the *RCBS Reloading Guide* has been revised and updated, the price still $1 postpaid.

Another RCBS publication, *Handloading Rifle and Pistol Ammunition,* a work of love by John (the Beard) Jobson of *Sports Afield,* is a 10-page booklet that shows graphically how to begin home loading. Fred will be glad to send you a copy, and it's a valuable work for the novice.

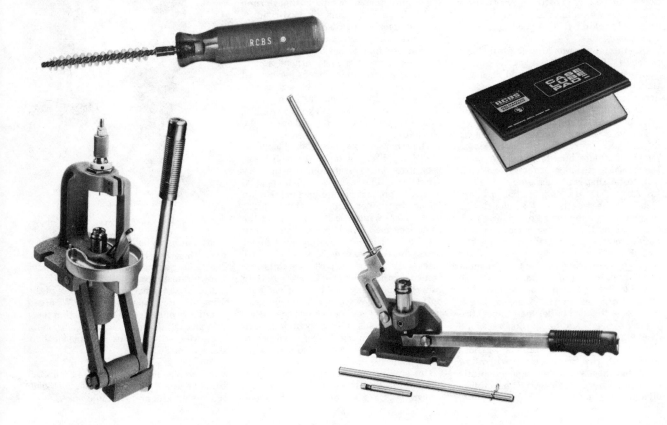

Telepacific Chronograph

Battery-operated, low-cost instrument performed excellently, with a bonus of multi-shot screens.

by BURTON T. MILLER

SOME 12 MONTHS AGO I acquired one of the first ballistic chronographs made by Telepacific Electronics Co., Inc., 3335 Orange Ave., Anaheim, Cal. 92804.

In the meantime I've come to appreciate what a convenience and education such an instrument can be. In the past year I've chronographed literally hundreds of rifle loads, air pistol projectiles and surprisingly enough, reloaded shotshells! Add to this the capability of chronographing rifle loads at distances up to 300 yards and it can be readily seen that this is a very versatile piece of equipment—and for just $135!

A crystal-controlled clock insures the accuracy of an expensive laboratory instrument. Operation is by two $1.35 batteries on separate circuits. If one begins to weaken they can be reversed and the unit will continue operation. No worries about being unable to complete a test program through lack of power when afield, no dependence on 115V power, no lengthy extension cords, thereby reducing the bulk of the equipment.

The 9" x 5½" x 7½", 6-lb. TPB-01 comes from the factory with two aluminum frames and 5 pair of screens, velocity tables and two cables, 15 and 20 feet long. These cables permit placing the readout unit alongside the shooter, in full view and reach at all times.

The front or first screen is 3" x 4", the far screen is 5" x 7". To assure a hit on the rear screen, the shooter centers the front screen so that the entire periphery of the rear screen is in view; thus, if you hit the front screen there is no way to miss the rear one!

The major advantage of these screens is that they can be used for 10 to 30 shots per pair, without getting up!

For normal use in determining "muzzle" velocity, the only extra needed is a piece of 2x4 lumber of about 64 inches long. The two screen frames provided are mounted on this 2x4, separated by exactly 5 feet.

Once set up and the circuits checked, the shooter fires, reads the velocity from the tables as indicated by the panel lights, records the velocity, pushes the reset button and continues firing.

One man can do everything necessary without help, and he can probably chronograph 10 times faster than can be done with the one-shot, replaceable-screen chronographs. With the TPB-01 he doesn't even have to get up—at least not for 10 or more shots.

My extensive testing shows that velocities attained were highly accurate and as consistent as those obtained with much more sophisticated instruments.

It is well recognized that some variance from published data will always exist for several reasons, for any given load—the inherent differences in individual firearms of the same caliber, temperature, humidity, powder lot, variations in case dimensions, primers used, etc. These things can't appear in the various manuals, but with these unknowns identical readings can hardly be expected!

To give an example of Telepacific performance, I first checked USAF velocities attained during a 10,000 round endurance test of ten M16 5.56mm rifles and ten AR18s of the same caliber. The velocity averages were taken from ten 10-round series from each rifle using mixed lots of G.I. ammunition:

M16	AR18
3138 fps	3095 fps

Barrel length of the M16 is 20", of the AR18, 18¼". Thus a higher average would be anticipated for the M16.

The TPB-01 gave 3128 for Winchester ammunition and 3138 for Remington in a new AR18—very close to the over-all Air Force averages.

Using one of the current manuals showing 223 velocities for the AR15, with its 20" barrel, the following reloads were fired for comparison:

Powder/grs.	Bullet/grs.	Average Velocities Manual	TPB-01
B1-2/26.5	Speer/55	3276	3263
RL-11/25	Speer/55	3272	3200
RL-11/25	Speer/HP52	3289	3247
RL-7/22.5	Speer/55	3231	3209
H335/27.5	Speer/HP52	3419	3364
4895/26.5	Speer/HP52	3239	3165
4064/23	Speer/70	2900*	2681

*Bob Hutton's Rifle Ranch 26" barreled rifle.
NOTE: Based on the above USAF official figures, the AR15 should average about 40 fps higher than the AR 180.

Recently we "manufactured" a frame from scrap 2" x 2" suitable for attaching long TPB screens to allow room for shot charges to pass through, the same frames afford space for 22" x 22" screens for up to 300-yard chronographing of rifle bullets.

Using Federal 12 gauge cases and Federal primers, here are a couple of typical load results:

30 grs. Herco	19 grs. 700X
1½ ozs. 6s	1⅛ ozs. 7½s
1317 fps TPB*	1217 TPB*
1330 fps (manual)	1290 (manual)

*About 12 fps should be added to the TPB figures to correct for distance from muzzle to center point between screens.

Pete Cooke, president of Telepacific, recently told me that a new TPB-02 model, even more convenient to use, will be out very soon. It will read out the exact velocity, with no reference to tables required; just record the velocity, reset and fire again!

This unit will have the same general dimensions, uses the same screens, etc., as the TPB-01 and, surprisingly, the cost will be only $197.50. Considering the convenience, the small $62.50 difference would appear most reasonable.

Soon to be announced also are Telepacific's "Electroscreens," an optional extra for both chronographs. Each new screen comprises a pair of short, vertical rods between which the bullet passes; the convenience of expensive and cumbersome photoelectric screens is obtained through two units measuring only 6" x 3" x 2", and they operate from the same internal batteries in the chronograph. Owners of the TPB-01 instruments need have no fear of obsolescence, for Pete Cooke says that these new screens will adapt to all TPB units in use without any modification. The Electroscreens, (Model TE-01) will sell for around $30 per pair.

The value of a truly functional chronograph to the amateur handloader was demonstrated very clearly recently when Pete Cooke set up a TPB-01 system at a local rifle range one Sunday morning, and offered its free use to any of the shooters present. Although most of the shooters—lined up at the chronograph until late afternoon—had been rolling their own for many years, this was the first time for most of them that the results of their labors had been anything but a matter of wild conjecture! Many were the smiles and many were the disappointed faces as those figures came rolling in, but on two questions they were all agreed: "How can a guy pretend to know anything about handloading without the use of a good, reliable chronograph?" and "Hey Pete! You gonna be out here again next Sunday?" Pete says that he hesitated to answer that second question in the affirmative as he visualized those "pet loads" arriving by the box car! ●

Telepacific's chronograph uses these multi-shot screens, permit 10-20 shots without changing.

Part 2—Components

Blondeau Slugs

Michael's Antiques (Box 233, Copiague, N.Y. 11726) can now supply Balle Blondeau slugs. These are the French-made solid steel slugs that gave the good results reported in Larry Sterett's article in our 1969/23rd edition.

Of modified diabolo shape, these cannot harm the bore in any way because of the soft lead bearing areas covering the circumference of each end. Boxes of 10 slugs (12, 16 or 20 gauge) will retail at $3.10, with full loading data included.

Markell Ammo

Markell Precision Cast Bullets (4115 Judah St., San Francisco, CA. 94122) has been a large-scale producer of top-quality lead bullets for many years, particularly handgun bullets in a wide variety of calibers and bullet weights. I've shot many hundreds of them during various test projects we've published, and thousands of Markell bullets have been used by a number of our contributors. These are excellent bullets, with no short cuts in their manufacture. In fact, the quality of Markell bullets recently received is better, if anything, than it was years ago.

Now Markell is making fixed metallic-case cartridges, at this time in handgun calibers only. Three types were delivered to us last week (mid-April), and it's good looking ammo. The new gold and red cartons—carrying 60 rounds each, not the usual 50—are imprinted "Markell Super Accuracy," which aspect of the new loads we're going to check at first opportunity! (More on that later). The cartridges are held separately in a styrofoam block, a touch that handloaders will welcome. The brass (non-plated) cases are headstamped MARKELL - 38 SPECIAL—new cases, of course.

His 148-gr. wadcutters, of course, are competition loads, their muzzle velocity 770 fps. One type (No. 03801) is for use in cylinder 38s, the other, with flush seated bullets (No. 03802) is designed for auto pistol use. They're accurate, all right—a California Highway Patrolman recently shot 1497x1500 in a combat match, including targets 50 yards away.

Markell's special police load (No. 03806) is of moderately high speed—160-gr. Keith type semi-WC at 1020 fps, which Markell says is thoroughly safe in any 38 Special, including 2″ guns. These have penetrated ¼″ steel plates, car doors, etc., in many tests.

Barnes Bullets Sold

Two gentlemen—Richard Hoch and R.W. Cook—have bought out Barnes Bullets; they'll continue to make and supply the Barnes line plus in the future offering some items of their own. The new firm will be Colorado Custom Bullets, Route 1-Box 5076, Montrose, Colorado 81401, and a new price list is now available.

Fred Barnes' main specialty was making bullets of decidedly heavier-than-normal weights for the calibers—125-gr. 25s, 200-gr. 7mms, 250-gr. in 30 caliber, and many others on up to the 600 Nitro Express.

Hornady Bullets

Bulletmaker Joyce Hornady now owns Pacific Gunsight of Lincoln, Neb. Hornady noted that "Precision bullets for reloading and precision equipment to reload them with are a natural combination. It has always been our goal to provide the shooting fraternity with the very best product we are capable of producing. We intend to continue the same high quality in our reloading tools and accessories that we have maintained in Hornady bullets."

Pacific will continue to operate at 56th and Colfax in Lincoln, with Bob Deitemeyer remaining as General Manager.

Hornady is the nation's largest independent producer of bullets for handloading. More than 86 different types are produced in the firm's Grand Island plant.

Du Pont Handloader's Guide

The 1971-1972 issue of this invaluable booklet is now ready—yours for the asking at your dealer or from the company—and it's well worth having. The proper selection and use of Du Pont powders has been revised and updated, while the shotshell loading data—14½ pages of it, no less—has been completely revised, with as many different types and makes of shotshells included as could be managed. All popular gauges are covered, including 10s and 28s, but most emphasis is on 12, of course.

The handgun section now shows 9mm Luger loads, and there's been a re-evaluation and revision of 38 Special loads.

Most popular calibers—and some not so popular—are shown in the rifle section, from the 22 Hornet to the 458 Win. Mag., but this division has not been revised, nor is there any 17 Remington load data.

Bound into the new Du Pont booklet is a valuable pamphlet, *Properties and Storage of Smokeless Powder*. Every handloader should read this material and be guided by it, for observing its precepts will help him avoid problems and troubles. Get a copy.

Jim's Loading Machine Grease

Jim Normington (Rathdrum, Idaho 83858), maker of Jim's Powder Baffles, is marketing a specially-formulated lube that, he says, not only makes all loaders work easier, but old grease gets dirty, needs re-newing. Put up in ¾-oz. snap-cap plastic bottles, the cost is $1, postpaid and insured.

Bitteroot Bullet Co.

Production of Bill Steigers' BBC bullets has been slower than Bill would like, and for two reasons. In the first place, their special construction takes more time, and then the operation has been a part-time thing. For some time BBC bullets have not been available in any big variety of calibers or weights, but that's going to change. Bill has decided he'll devote full time to bulletmaking. Because BBC bullet design doesn't allow high speed production, we won't be seeing the new calibers/weights overnight, of course, but they'll be along. Steigers has a free descriptive list, with prices.

Hodgdon Powder Co.

No, Bruce Hodgdon didn't invent or discover 4831 powder (did he?), but it's amounted to about the same thing. More of it, for the past 25 years or so, has been used than any other single powder, certainly, for magnum case reloading. I suspect that 4831 has out sold several other popular powders combined, and I know positively that it's the *only* powder a lot of guys use, whether they're loading magnum cases or not!

Well, Hodgdon has come a long way since, and at this time he offers 16 different smokeless powders; 5 of them for shotshell/handgun loading, the rest for rifle use. Most recently, Hodgdon began importing from Scotland a cleaner-burning, more uniformly-grain sized black powder, made by the famous old firm of Curtis & Harvey. Available in Fg, FFg and FFFg, the new Hodgdon-C&H black powder sells for $2.25 for a 16-ounce canister.

Hodgdon has two other products for black powder shooters that are new this year—Spit Ball and Spit Patch, both designed to ease the often-hard task of loading and cleaning cap and ball revolvers and rifles. More shots without full cleaning and final easier clean-up are the big advantages, but both are said to prevent rusting and to improve accuracy.

Hodgdon offers numerous other good products for the shooter-hunter, too many for this space. Ask for their catalog—it's free.

Sailer's Exotic Ammo

How badly do you need some 275 H&H cartridges, or a batch of 8x72R rounds? Maybe you've got a 40-90 Sharps you want to shoot, the one with the bottle-neck chamber? Anthony F. Sailer (P.O. Box L, Owen, Wisc. 54460) not only has these few but many more—far too many to list here, but his list shows 99 different centerfires offered, including several current cartridges in custom loading, plus a few obsolete rimfires and black powder-loaded 12 bore cases, these with No. 6 shot. Yet this is only a partial list, Sailer notes, and he's prepared to make cartridges in virtually any caliber on special order.

Most calibers listed are made from new brass, smokeless powder and jacketed bullets are used in the majority (black powder can be substituted on request) and minimum quantities are 20 rounds for rifle calibers, 50 for handguns. Factory ballistics are duplicated. Here are some price samples: 22 Savage Hi-Power, $6; 33 Winchester, $8; 9.3x72R, $10, and 45-100 Sharps, $13.50. Available only through your dealer, unfortunately, but this is an excellent source for obsolete calibers, foreign and domestic, plus custom loading of current calibers at competitive prices.

Whitney Shotshells

An unusual system of shotshell making is in operation by the Whitney Cartridge Co. (Box 5872, Pasadena, CA. 91107). All plastic, the Whitney system comprises a body tube threaded at the base to take a shell head—the latter are reusable numerous times, it's said, though the company suggests that reloaders use the case bodies and the base wads only for one firing.

Besides components, Whitney will be offering fully loaded shotshells, 12 gauge only so far, at highly competitive retail prices. Full information and loading data will be furnished.

Ken Waters on the New Bullets

Hornady

Hornady now offers 13 bullets—11 jacketed and 2 lead numbers—against his 7 of about a year ago. Added were a 38-cal. 110-gr. HP, a 41-cal. 210-gr. HP, a 44-cal. 200-gr. HP and a 45-cal. 185-gr. special target bullet with truncated-cone nose for the 45 ACP. The 2 new lead bullets are 38s—a 148-gr. hollow-base wadcutter and a 158-gr. RN service bullet—both said to eliminate some of the problems stemming from non-uniform lubrication. The writer hasn't been able to check this out yet, but they look good.

We have been shooting Hornady's 250-gr. HP for the 45 Long Colt, announced last year, and it's a dandy, grouping 5 shots in 4½" from a Colt Single Action at 50 yards, and expanding up to half-again its

Hornady's new 120-gr. HP 25-06 bullet.

original diameter when used with full power loads.

I was especially glad also to see the new 44 Magnum 200-gr. HP which, while labeled a handgun bullet, will, I predict, find much use in the popular 44 carbines. Folks who don't care for the strenuous bucking a 44 Mag sixgun produces with regular ammo are bound to appreciate the lessened recoil of this lighter slug. Hornady's loading data for this bullet indicates that muzzle speeds up to 1400 fps can be realized from a 7½" revolver barrel with 23.5 grains of 2400.

Riflemen can't help but like the beautifully streamlined Hornady 25-cal. 120-gr. HP bullet produced with the 25-06 and other big case 25s in mind.

Colorado Custom Bullets

The well-known Barnes Bullets are no more, but they'll continue to be marketed by Colorado Custom Bullets, RR #1, Montrose, Colo. They'll furnish the old Barnes line, all the way from 17- to 600-caliber, plus a few additions of their own, including a 200-gr. RN solid in 7mm, a 180-gr. RNSP for the 351 Winchester, a .366" 250-gr. spitzer, a pair of new 375s—one a 300-gr. spitzer SP, the other a 350-gr. RN, plus a 750-gr. RNSP for the 577 Nitro.

Particularly good news is that all their bullets will be priced to include postage. Since they must be ordered through a local dealer, it is a big help to know in advance the total amount of money that must be sent. This is a great source for those hard-to-get jacketed bullets.

Sierra

An especially newsworthy development has been the expansion of Sierra's line (now a part of the Leisure Group) into the field of handgun bullets. Long noted for the quality and consistent accuracy of their rifle bullets, it will be interesting to see if the new handgun slugs measure up.

New calibers include 9mm, 38, 41, 44 and 45. First to appear was a quartet of 38s—110-gr. JHP, 125-gr. JHP, 125-gr. JSP and 158-gr. JSP. Sierra calls their hollow points "hollow cavity" bullets because the hollow inside (behind the nose, that is) is wider than the frontal opening. This leaves the walls thin at the nose, producing an even more prompt and vigorous expansion than a traditional hollow point design gives. At the velocities possible with these new jacketed bullets, the 38 Special cartridge has been treated to a whole new lease on life!

A pair of 9mm bullets of traditional truncated-cone form but with the new hollow cavity feature in 90- and 115-gr. weights, followed. These .355" diameter slugs can be used in loading for the 380 Auto and 38 Super, as well as all the various 9mm Parabellum/Lugers. Jackets turned in at the nose prevent their lead cores from contacting the ramps or breech faces of auto pistols, thereby forestalling a most common cause of jams. Velocities possible with the 90-gr. are getting up into

Remington

Following up on the excellent and highly effective 38 Special 125- and 158-gr. HPs introduced last year, Remington has lately announced three additional handgun bullets—a 158-gr. semi-jacketed HP for the 357 Magnum, a 115-gr. JHP 9mm Luger, and a 240-gr. semi-jacketed 44 Magnum HP.

The purpose here, as with similar bullets, is to improve expansion, thereby increasing effectiveness. If these newest numbers are as successful in achieving this objective as were last year's 38s, we've got something to look forward to.

In line with Remington's policy of offering to handloaders the same bullets which are loaded in their factory ammo, the new 17-cal. 25-gr. HPs will also be available.

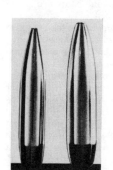

Sierra 6.5 and 7mm boat-tail bullets.

the magnum range.

41 Magnum fans will welcome two more new bullets—one in "standard" 210-gr. weight, the other a fast-moving 170-gr. These have likewise been given the full-jacketed hollow cavity treatment, hence should stand hard driving without fouling.

For the 45 shooter, there is a .452" slug of 185 grains intended for the 45 ACP; another of so far unspecified but heavier weight is scheduled to follow, probably available by the time you read these lines.

The final pair, in 44 caliber for both rifles and revolvers, measure .429" and come in weights of 180- and 240 grains. These two have the same hollow cavity design, but have been given a crimping groove and jackets are not turned over the nose edge. No opportunity to test them yet, but common sense tells me they'll be extremely deadly bullets.

Sierra hasn't neglected rifle projectiles either. There are, for instance, exciting new 6.5 and 7mm boat-tails that have already begun to set accuracy records. Beautiful just to look at, the 168-gr. 7mm Matchking (.284") and the 140-gr. 6.5mm Matchking, both hollow points, feature a long bearing shank which, together with the boat-tail bases, serve to provide maximum accuracy over long ranges. The 6.5 has an especially graceful ogive contour, but I'm betting on the 7mm to continue carrying off the honors as it's already done in three target competitions.

There is, too, a new 30-cal. .308" hunting bullet, a 165-gr. HPBT designed to minimize air drag and flatten trajectory over long ranges. This is an optimum weight in 30-caliber, balancing good weight with high velocity, and Sierra has added the fine accuracy so vital to a successful long range bullet. It should be a prime choice for either 308, 300 Savage or 30-06.

In 22s, Sierra has a new 52-gr. HPBT bench-rest bullet (.224"), that set a new record—a .138" group of 10 shots at 100 yards. I'm not entirely sure why this little bullet has a boat-tail, but certainly they'll be easier to start in case necks, and why argue with success? If they'll do that well

for the pros, they'll also work well in our varmint rifles.

Last, but decidedly not least, are a pair of sparkling new 25s (.257") in 90- and 120-gr. weights, both hollow point boat-tails like the others. Sierra says they were designed especially for the 25-06 and a 257 Improved as well, as I imagine plenty of other shooters will. The 90-gr. number should also adapt well to the 250 Savage.

As a parting shot, this writer still wishes Sierra would produce bullets larger than 8mm. Plenty of 338, 350 and 375 owners would like to be able to use Sierra bullets in their favorite big bores.

Speer

Speer caused a sizeable stir with their 70-gr. semi-spitzer .224" bullet, intended to make deer and antelope rifles out of the larger 22 centerfires.

Speer stipulated that muzzle velocity be kept above 3000 fps when using this bullet in barrels having a 14" rifling twist, in order to maintain stability in flight. Overly-long ranges should consequently be avoided so velocity stays high. Accuracy has been good, especially in the 22/250, and the 70-gr. bullet at 3400 fps shows nearly 1800 foot pounds at 100 yards, not at all bad.

A second interesting new rifle bullet is Speer's 30-cal. 180-gr. Magnum SP. This bullet is like a spitzer with its pointed lead tip cut off, perhaps best described as a semi-pointed bullet with small flat nose. I assume this has been done to keep the bullet from expanding *too* quickly at magnum velocities.

In 38-caliber Speer has a 158-gr. RN lead (.358") bullet for the old "standard" velocities; a new 158-gr. JSP of the same shape with just the right amount of lead exposed for good expansion without barrel leading; a 140-gr. JHP that looks like a combination of round nose and flat point, but with its hollow point and medium weight is one of the dandiest compromises this writer has seen between velocity and weight. It's already a favorite!

Most recently, samples of Speer's newest 110-gr. JHP and 158-gr. JFN have arrived for testing. The 110-gr. will answer current demands for a lightweight 38 Special bullet at magnum velocities, while the big flat-nose is most likely intended to satisfy those shooters who prefer that shape to the blunt round nose. These additions have given Speer a complete coverage of the 38-357 field.

New Speer handgun shot cartridges, loaded with 135 No. 9s at 1140 fps. The empty capsules are available to the handloader as well.

There is also a new .451" diameter RNSP of 200 grains, made with a shallow groove to receive a taper crimp, that seems destined to insure jam-free operation of 45 autos. Finally, there are the pair of 44-cal. jacketed bullets—one a 240-gr. flat nose with rounded ogive, the other a 200-gr. HP. Both are listed as "Magnums," but I simply had to try the lighter one in a favorite 44-40 Winchester 1892.

Somewhat oversize (.429") for many 44-40 bores, it will do well in others (better slug and measure your bore first); weight is exactly right for the 44-40, and that hollow point should augment killing power, especially since 44-40 velocity from carbines and rifles is higher than the hottest 44 Magnum revolver loads. Accuracy has been fine, and I can't conceal my enthusiasm for this new bullet.

Speer 38-357 Shotshells

It's taken a while, and many combinations of materials and forms were tried,

but now the Speer plastic shot cartridges for handguns—plus the empty capsules—should be available when you read this.

Dave Andrews, Speer Ballistician, suggests using No. 9 shot in loading the empty capsules, which hold about 103 grains or 135 pellets. No. 7½ or 8 can be used, but both reduce the pellet count, and should not be used. The standard Speer load of chilled 9s throws about 96% into a 16" circle at 15 feet from a 6" barrel, with muzzle velocity 1140 fps. Shorter barrels? OK, but less MV and more open patterns—a 2" barrel gives good, even patterns at 10 feet, Dave said, and the No. 9 shot is adequate for snakes, rats, et al.

Load data is printed on the capsule/base wad package—5.0/7625 and 6.0/Unique, maximum charges in the 38 Special case. There is no advantage in using 357 cases and heavier charges of powder, because poor patterns will result.

Speer loaded shot cartridges, 6 to a box, are $1.49, while the empty capsules and base wads are $1.95 for a box of 50.

Speer's new Bullet Display Board, their 6th to date, shows a scene at Promontory Point, Utah, by artist Jack Woodson. All Speer bullets are displayed—19 handgun and 63 rifle. As before, the display is framed in hardwood, and there's an easel back for convenience. Price is the same, too, $9.50 prepaid to FFL holders or through your dealer.

Speer has a new .257" bullet also, this a 100-gr. hollow point designed for varmints in rifles of the 25-06 class. The big open point means an explosive blowup on the smaller game, and accuracy is said to be superb—first trials by Speer *averaging* well under a half-inch for 5 shots at 100 yards. Sectional density is .216, ballistic coefficient .328, cost is $5.35 per hundred.

Speer's 1971 Bullet Display Board

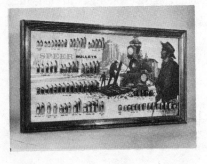

Winchester

Winchester unveiled a new bullet design last December called PEP, standing for Power Expanding Point. Initially these 25-cal. hollow points, without a cannelure and looking quite unlike other Winchester bullets, come in 90- and 120-gr. weights. Intended for the 25-06, they'll also be available in factory ammunition. Everybody's climbing aboard this 25-06 bandwagon. None to try so far, though.

Speer 357/158, 451/200 and 22/70 bullets

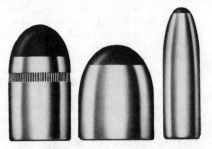

SAFETY PINS

We don't mean those nickel-plated stickers used in diapers, but rather the safety inherent in the 45 Automatic Colt Pistol because of its inertia-type firing pin. It works

by Arthur W. Sear

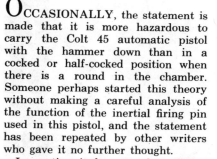

OCCASIONALLY, the statement is made that it is more hazardous to carry the Colt 45 automatic pistol with the hammer down than in a cocked or half-cocked position when there is a round in the chamber. Someone perhaps started this theory without making a careful analysis of the function of the inertial firing pin used in this pistol, and the statement has been repeated by other writers who gave it no further thought.

I question it because the relative position of the firing pin with respect to the primer is not greatly different whether the hammer is up or down. When the hammer of my 45 is cocked, the rear end of the firing pin protrudes some .032″ through the firing pin retainer plate. When the hammer is resting on the retainer plate, the point of the firing pin is still .032″ below the surface of the breechblock. To detonate the primer, the firing pin crushes into it an additional distance of .035″. (These measurements may vary somewhat from one gun to another; however, they are probably accurate enough for this discussion.)

The firing pin is shorter than the length of the hole through the slide and retainer plate, so that the hammer cannot directly push the firing pin into the primer. In normal firing, the hammer strikes the firing pin, imparting enough velocity that the pin ignites the primer. Primers are quite strong and the firing pin must do an appreciable amount of work in deforming the primer cup and detonating the priming compound. The amount of work, in foot-pounds (fp), necessary to detonate the primer was determined by simple experiment. I removed the firing pin and firing pin spring from my 45 and returned the firing pin to its normal position, without installing the spring and the retaining plate. Next, an empty primed case was inserted into the chamber and the slide closed. I then placed the muzzle directly downward on the platform of a bathroom scale and applied pressure to the rear end of the firing pin with a piece of brass rod. The pressure was increased in small increments and I examined the primer before going to the next higher load. At a force of 50 pounds, a small dimple was visible. At 80 pounds the dent was similar to that produced by normal firing—perhaps not quite as deep. I decided that a fair estimate of the work done in deforming the primer would be equal to that done by a force of 80 pounds acting through a distance of .035″. Calculation shows this work equal to:

$$\frac{80 \times .035}{12} = 0.233 \text{ fp}$$

Incidentally, this mistreatment of the primer did not cause ignition, probably because of the lack of shock and the relatively long time period over which the force was applied, allowing the heat to dissipate.

The initial kinetic energy (KE) of the firing pin is completely expended in mashing the primer, except for the insignificant amount used to compress the firing pin spring. Kinetic energy is expressed by the formula:

$$KE = \frac{1}{2} MV^2$$

If the kinetic energy is to be in fp, the velocity, V, must be in feet per second (fps), and the mass, M, in slugs. The mass in slugs is equal to the weight in pounds divided by the acceleration of gravity in fps, thus:

$$M = \frac{W}{32.2}$$

The weight of the firing pin was determined to be 68.5 grains. Since there are 7000 grains in a pound, the numbers put into the formula and set equal to 0.233 fp give us:

$$0.233 = \frac{1}{2} \times \frac{68.5}{7000 \times 32.2} \times V^2$$

Solving for V, we find that the initial velocity of the firing pin must be 39.1 fps.

The firing pin normally is given this velocity by the impulse it receives from the hammer. The same relative velocity between the firing pin and the primer can be brought about if the whole pistol is moving forward at 39.1 fps and the pistol suddenly stops. Then, since the firing pin is free to slide forward, it will continue at this velocity until it strikes the primer and detonates it.

A velocity of 39.1 fps will be attained by an object falling free for a distance of:

$$S = \frac{V^2}{2a} = \frac{1530}{64.4} = 23.8 \text{ ft.}$$

From this calculation, it appears that if a loaded pistol fell approximately 24 feet and struck a concrete roadway with the barrel pointed directly downward (so that the velocity of the firing pin would also be 39.1 fps directly toward the primer), the pistol would fire. If the barrel were tilted when the pistol struck the concrete, the velocity of the pistol would have to be greater to make the gun fire, since it is the component of velocity of the firing pin in the direction of the primer that must be great enough to mash the primer. If the pistol struck on its side or with the barrel pointed in a direction above the horizontal, the firing pin would have no velocity in a direction toward the primer and there-

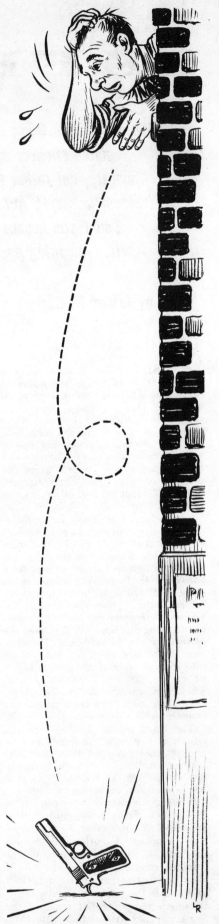

fore could not discharge the pistol.

It is the kinetic energy available in the firing pin as a result of its velocity that detonates the primer; therefore, the distance of the firing pin from the primer during the fall is not a factor. The fact that the pin travels an extra .032″ before striking the primer is not pertinent. The firing pin spring is not a factor in holding back the pin because the spring almost certainly will be compressed by its own inertia when the pistol strikes the concrete. So, hammer down, half cocked, or fully cocked, the inertia of the firing pin is equally capable of discharging the pistol under the conditions described above.

If the loaded pistol is dropped, or thrown, and it lands with the hammer striking the concrete, the consequence will certainly be affected by the initial position of the hammer. If the hammer is down and in contact with the firing pin, but resting against the firing pin retaining plate, the force of the hammer will largely be taken by the retaining plate and a relatively small amount of energy will be transfered from the hammer to the firing pin.

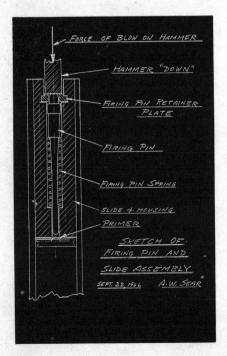

FORCE OF BLOW ON HAMMER

HAMMER "DOWN"

FIRING PIN RETAINER PLATE

FIRING PIN

FIRING PIN SPRING

SLIDE & HOUSING

PRIMER

SKETCH OF FIRING PIN AND SLIDE ASSEMBLY

SEPT. 22, 1966   A. W. SEAR

If the hammer is fully cocked and the weapon is dropped, it might land on the hammer with enough force to break the sear, thus releasing the hammer. In this case the mainspring will drive the hammer forward to discharge the pistol. Furthermore, if the pistol fires in this manner, the bullet will be pointed above the horizontal and will be more apt to inflict serious injury to anyone in the vicinity than will a bullet discharged downward as a consequence of firing pin momentum.

It seems a little silly to discuss dropping a loaded pistol 24 feet onto a concrete floor; however, something as hard as concrete is required to discharge the pistol. Landing on a soft or resilient surface, perhaps even a wooden floor, will not discharge the pistol because, during the initial deceleration of the pistol, the firing pin will come in contact with the primer before the relative velocity between the pin and primer reaches a value that can be hazardous. Once the firing pin is in contact with the primer, the whole pistol must be accelerated at a rate great enough to produce a force of 80 lbs. between the firing pin and primer. In order for the firing pin to exert this force on the primer, it must be undergoing an acceleration or (as in this case) deceleration of:

$$a = \frac{F}{M} = \frac{80 \times 32.2 \times 7000}{68.5} = 26{,}3000 \text{ fps/s}$$

or 8170 g's. The force required to decelerate the whole pistol at this rate is:

$$8170 \times \frac{37}{16} = 18{,}900 \text{ lb.}$$

A force of this magnitude would perhaps only take a chip out of the concrete but would make quite a dent in a wooden floor.

After considering the preceding exposition of the problem, it seems that the safest way to carry a loaded 45 ACP is with the hammer down. As another safe alternative, I have seen holsters for this pistol made so that a strap secures the pistol, fitting into the space between the rear of the slide and the fully cocked hammer. Thus, with the safety on, the pistol can be brought into action quickly without danger of premature firing.

Certainly the greatest degree of safety is obtained by carrying the pistol with the chamber empty and a loaded magazine in place. However, if a quick shot should be needed, you're in trouble, as operating the slide takes two hands. This is noisy as well as slow. The safest, quietest way is to have the pistol chamber-loaded with the hammer down. Then, with the trigger held back, the hammer can be cocked with the left thumb and the trigger released. This is much quieter than taking the safety off— but don't let your thumb slip off the hammer!   ●

garcia

Two new Beretta shotguns have been added to the long and distinguished list of Garcia Sporting Arms Corporation imports. On the left is the new Beretta Mk II single barrel trap gun, on the right is the new Beretta SO-7, a side-by-side double.

Sturm, Ruger & Co., Inc., Southport, Conn. is the manufacturer of handguns and rifles that have earned high regard among shooters everywhere. Pictured here are (from left to right): the 10/22 Carbine; the newly introduced 10/22SP with checkered stock; the Blackhawk revolver with extra cylinder; and the Standard Auto Pistol.

Ruger's ever-increasing line of guns includes: the 44R Carbine (left); the 1-H Single Shot Rifle; the Security-Six revolver (top); the newly-introduced Black Powder Revolver (center); and the Super Blackhawk revolver.

RCBS, Inc., of Oroville, Calif. is the manufacturer of a full array of centerfire cartridge reloading equipment and accessories. Included here are the J.R. "Reloader Special" Press, Uniflow Powder Measure, Powder Scale, Case Lube Kit, Die Sets, Burring Tool and Powder Funnel.

Remington

Pictured are the Remington Model 742 gas-operated Automatic Rifle and the Remington Model 760 Pump Action Rifle. From left to right: Model 742, Model 742 BDL Deluxe, Model 760 in 308 Win., and the Model 760 BDL Deluxe. All 742's and 760's are available in a variety of popular calibers.

Remington
AUTOLOADING RIFLE

THE RIGHT OF WAY

**THE RAPID FIRE RIFLE — LOADS ITSELF
BIG ENOUGH FOR THE BIGGEST GAME**
REMINGTON ARMS COMPANY
ILION N.Y.

DIXIE GUN WORKS

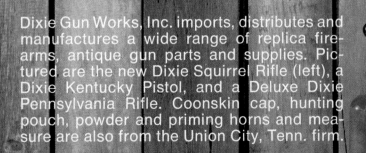

Dixie Gun Works, Inc. imports, distributes and manufactures a wide range of replica fire-arms, antique gun parts and supplies. Pictured are the new Dixie Squirrel Rifle (left), a Dixie Kentucky Pistol, and a Deluxe Dixie Pennsylvania Rifle. Coonskin cap, hunting pouch, powder and priming horns and measure are also from the Union City, Tenn. firm.

Brownell's Inc., Montezuma, Ia., distributes a wide variety of high quality tools, equipment, parts and supplies for the gunsmithing trade. The firm also publishes books and catalogs for gunsmiths and hobbyists.

WINCHESTER®

To honor the National Rifle Association on its 100th Anniversary, Winchester has produced two firearms that reflect the heritage and high standards of the NRA. The Winchester NRA Centennial Model 94 Musket (left) is patterned after the military-style 1895 musket that Winchester designed for NRA requirements. The NRA Centennial Model 94 Rifle is styled after the famed Winchester Model 64.

Poly-Choke

The original adjustable shotgun choke—the Poly-Choke is one of the very few exclusively American firearms developments, it provides a shotgunner with a variety of choke constrictions ranging from Cylinder Bore through Extra Full. Pictured, the Deluxe Ventilated Model and Poly-Choke's ½" Ramp Ventilated Rib the accessory that turns any field grade shotgun into a look alike for its more sophisticated (and more expensive) brothers. The rib is also available in standard 5/16" ramp.

Twenty-two caliber versions of two famous Colt single action revolvers help round out the company's line this year. The New Frontier 22 (left) boasts a ramp front and adjustable rear sight and color case hardening. The Peacemaker 22 (right), all-steel version of the famed 45 caliber Peacemaker, has a color case hardened frame.

Plans are well underway at Colt to introduce the Colt Sharps single shot rifle. Drawing upon the classic Sharps-Borchardt rifle for inspiration, the new Sharps is shown here in plain and deluxe grade.

To commemorate the 100th anniversary of the National Rifle Association, Colt has introduced "The Magnificent Seven", consisting of six Single Action Army revolvers and a Gold Cup National Match automatic; each carries a gold NRA medallion in the grips, is inscribed in gold and comes in a velvet lined presentation case.

The Magnificent Seven

COLT

To commemorate the 100th anniversary of the founding of the National Rifle Association and its service to the American shooter, Colt's presents

New from Colt this year are two lines of outdoorsmen's knives. Consisting of eight knives the lines include: (from top to bottom) the Trailblazer, the Mountaineer, the Plainsman, the Trapper, the All-Purpose-5½", the Trout and Bird Knife, the All-Purpose-4" and the Tuckaway Hunter.

Shadow
FIRST NAME IN FIREARMS

CASPOLL INTERNATIONAL, INC.
7-20, 7-CHOME, MINAMI AOYAMA, MINATO-KU, TOKYO 107, JAPAN

The Shadow line of under & over shotguns, manufactured by Caspoll International, Tokyo, is distributed in the United States by Tradewinds, Tacoma, Washington. Pictured are (from left to right) the Gold Shadow (a custom order gun), the Shadow Indy and the Shadow Seven.

SHERIDAN

The burgeoning interest in pellet guns is due in part to th[e] pneumatic rifles produced by Sheridan Products Inc. Pi[c]tured here are (from left to right) the Sheridan Blue Strea[k] the Blue Streak with Bushnell 4x scope, and the Sherida[n] Silver Streak with Sheridan-Williams Receiver Sigh[t]

Garcia Sporting Arms Corporation imports the famed Sako Rifles from Finland in a variety of models and styles. Pictured is a representative selection (from left to right) of: the Vixen Sporter, the Forester Heavy Barrel; the Finnbear Deluxe Sporter; and the Finnwolf Sporter.

garcia

Classic examples of the shotgun maker's art, these Berettas from Italy are imported by Garcia Sporting Arms Corporation. They are (from left to right): the SO-3, the BL-5, the BL-3 and the BL-4.

Hawes Firearms Company, Los Angeles, Calif. imports a number of popular revolvers that include (clockwise from top left): Silver City Marshall; J.P. Sauer "Trophy"; Western Marshall; Chief Marshall; Remington 1858 New Army; and J.P. Sauer "Medallion."

MARLIN

Marlin's new Model 120 Magnum pump shotgun features an all-steel action, fully interchangeable barrels, unique new slide lock release, steel ventilated rib, double action bars, engine-turned parts, walnut stock and forearm handsomely checkered and is entirely made in Marlin's new factory. The gun is available in 12 gauge with several barrel variations. This new, quality gun will be available in limited quantities in 1971, with full production in 1972.

The receiver of Marlin's new pump gun is machined from a solid block of high tensile steel. This all-new action also features large, positive cross-bolt safety (A) and new, unique action release bar (B) that lets you remove unfired shells even with gloved hands.

Marlin's new pump design features fully interchangeable barrels—you can buy a new barrel anytime. Install it in seconds right in the field. (It is not necessary to return gun to factory.) Extra barrels with rib $50.00* each.

*Suggested retail price, slightly higher west of Rockies.

Weatherby

Weatherby is the famed manufacturer and distributor of high grade rifles, shotguns, scopes, ammunition, gun cases and reloading dies. Pictured here (from top to bottom) are the: Regency Shotgun, the Mark V rifle with Imperial scope, the Vanguard with 3-9x Premier scope, and the Mark XXII with Mark XXII scope.

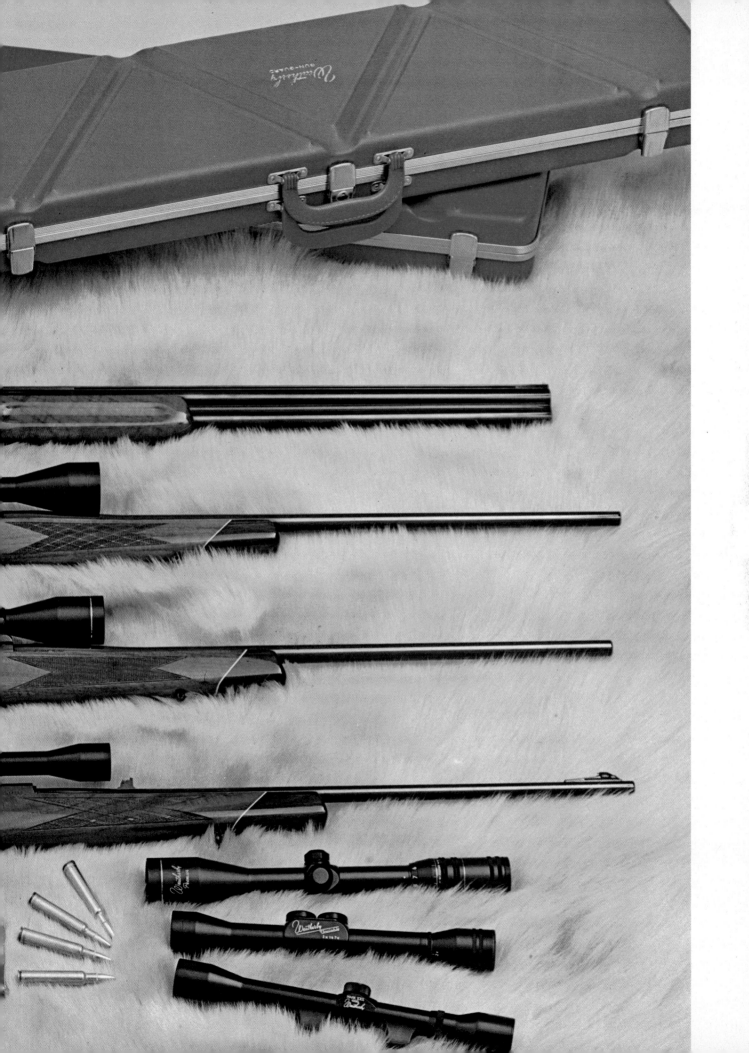

100th ANNIVERSARY
H&R
1871 – 1971

The first
H & R Shotguns...

At the turn of the century, Harrington & Richardson decided to design and manufacture its own shotgun. On February 27, 1900, a patent was issued on the new Model 1900 that had many unusual design features, including automatic ejection.

The shotgun was such an instantaneous success that the demand required further additions to the factory, one in 1900 and still another in 1901.

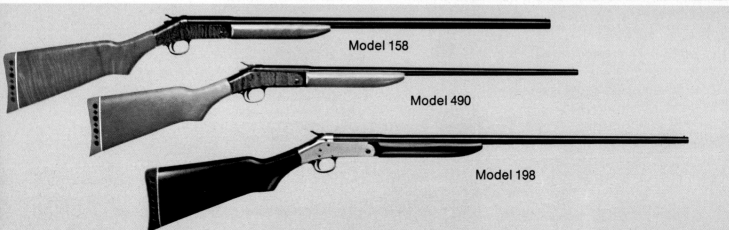

Model 158

Model 490

Model 198

100th ANNIVERSARY
H&R
1871 — 1971

Recognition awards...

During World War II, Harrington & Richardson produced hundreds of thousands of firearms for the armed services. For its excellent wartime production record, the firm was given the Army-Navy "E" Award for excellence five times, as well as a special commendation from the Marine Corps in recognition of the company's contributions to victory.

Harrich Model #1

Ponsness-Warren's highly acclaimed, extremely efficient Size-O-Matic and Du-O-Matic shotshell reloaders.

Firearms Import and Export Corp., of Miami, Fla. manufactures handguns and imports handguns, shotguns and replicas for the U.S. market. Pictured here is a representative array of the guns F.I.E. offers—the BR2 Double Barrel Shotgun and (from top to bottom) the G32 Guardian revolver, the new F38 F.I.E. Revolver, and the E27 Titan automatic.

Sloan's Sporting Goods, New York City, part of the Charles Daly organization is the distributor of a wide line of modern and replica firearms and accessories. Pictured here are the Pride-Of-Spain double barrel shotgun, the Auto-Pointer auto-loading shotgun, the Brown Bess flintlock pistol replica, the Bernardelli auto-pistol, and the Charles Daly Gun Case.

Four Charles Daly shotguns that display the Daly mark of excellence (from left to right): the Diamond Grade Trap, the Superior Grade Single-Barrel Trap, the LTD Field Grade, and Superior Grade Skeet.

LA DISTRIBUTORS

LA Distributors, New York City, importer and distributor of Lames and Erbi shotguns, also stocks the Cattleman line of single action revolvers. Pictured here (from left to right) are the Cattleman Buntline Magnum with 18″ barrel and removable shoulder stock, the Cattleman Magnum, and the Cattleman Buckhorn Magnum.

Ithacagun, long famous for fine quality firearms, displays its form with the three shotguns shown here. From the left are: the Model 51 Deluxe Trap auto-loader, the Model 280 English Double, and the Competition Single Barrel Trap.

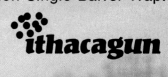

ithacagun

Pigeon Grade Superposed Shotgun

New Grade V Browning Automatic Rifle

Olympian Grade High-Power Rifle

Browning craftsmanship shows inside and out

Beauty and function are two sides of the same coin with Browning. One flows naturally from the other. The silky movement of the action, the close interaction of all working parts is achieved with the same painstaking care as the outside embellishments. The result is a sporting arm that performs as good as it looks. Rugged good looks and reliable, accurate performance are inseparable partners, vital qualities in every Browning. Put there by our love for fine sporting arms...

Doesn't that tell you a lot about our new center fire ammunition!

BROWNING

Two examples of the distinguished line of imports from Garcia Sporting Arms Corporation are the Rossi double-barrel hammer shotgun, a recreation of an old favorite, and the Astra Constable auto pistol.

Most HUNTERS prefer to set their sights once and then leave them alone, except to re-establish the originally selected zero setting. The choice of this setting is no problem if one shoots only at short-to-medium ranges, always using the same load. On the other hand, a bit of calculation is required to choose and make use of a "best" setting if one uses several different loads with potentially wide variations in shooting ranges. A typical instance of this problem might be the use of a 300 Weatherby Magnum with 200-gr. loads for large game at close-to-medium ranges, and 150-gr. loads for medium game at long ranges.

This article describes a simple step-by-step procedure by which anyone can figure out his own best sight setting, and then construct a trajectory chart that will help him put the shots where he wants them. Before getting into this procedure, however, let's make sure we have a clear picture of the basic relationships between bore axis, line of sight, and the bullet trajectory.

In order to show the relationships between bore axis, line of sight, and trajectory as we have done in fig. 1, the vertical dimensions of the sketch have been greatly exaggerated with respect to the horizontal. The reason for this is fairly obvious, since the sketch would be about 1800 inches long if we used the same scale for the horizontal dimensions as for the vertical. Conversely, if we matched the vertical scale to the horizontal, the diagram would be about two hundreths (.02″) of an inch high. This distortion is potentially significant for a reason to be mentioned later, but need not trouble us if we use the sketch simply to *identify* the relationships—not to *measure* them. So, with this comment on distortion filed away for future reference, let's see what the sketch tells us. Basically we're dealing with a rather simple picture.

The problem involves three physical objects: the SIGHT, the RIFLE and the BULLET; and three lines, each of which has a definite relationship to one of these objects. The SIGHT gives us the "line of sight," which is a straight line. The "bore axis" is also a straight line extending from the center line of the bore, and is the path that the bullet would follow if gravitational effects did not cause it to drop away at a continually increasing rate. The "trajectory" is, of course, the actual path followed by the bullet. Now, since the sight is normally located above the bore of the rifle, and since the bore must be inclined upward in order to have the bullet strike a point on the line of sight, there will always be a point of intersection (i), where the bore axis crosses the line of sight. The location of this point is useful for preliminary zeroing adjustments in a manner that we'll describe later. Generally, the bore axis and line of sight will intersect somewhere between 10 and 40 yards from the muzzle.

To complete our picture of the problem we need to add some dimensioning lines to our sketch as shown in fig. 2. Beginning at

SIGHTING THE LONG RANGE MAGNUM

An easy, step-by-step method for constructing and using a trajectory chart tailored to the individual's ideas and requirements.

Harold O. Davidson

Fig. 1

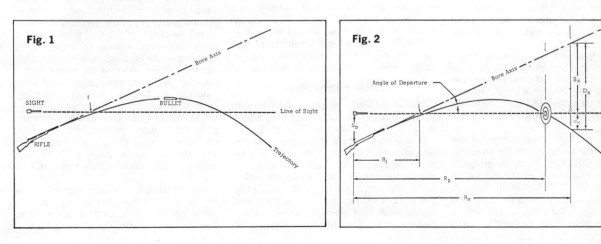

Fig. 2

the left-hand side of the diagram, the first relationship shown is S_o, the vertical distance between the line of sight and the bore axis measured at some convenient point near the breech of the rifle. An easy method for a scope-sighted bolt action rifle is to open the bolt and measure the distance from the center of the scope eyepiece to the center line of the bolt. This can be done with sufficient accuracy by estimating the centers, although one can do it more precisely by calipering the top edge of eyepiece to bottom of bolt distance, and then subtracting from this one-half the sum of the eyepiece and bolt diameters. The distance S_o typically ranges from about 1.5″ for low-mounted scopes to about 2.0″. For my own 7x61mm with a 6x scope in Bausch & Lomb mounts S_o is 1.56″. S_o is one of the basic pieces of information we'll need for our sight-setting and trajectory-chart calculations.

Moving to the next relationship in our sketch, we find the quantity R_i, which is the range to the intersection point i, where the line of sight crosses under the bore axis, as previously mentioned. This is a quantity that we calculate rather than measure, and the method for doing this is part of our procedure.

Angle of Departure

Moving again to the right, fig. 2 shows the "angle of departure" as the angle between the bore axis (along which the bullet initially "departs" from the rifle—hence, "angle of *departure*"), and the line of sight. The angle of departure is, of course, greatly exaggerated in this sketch since the actual angle will normally be less than a sixth of a degree, or 10 minutes. Although we shall have no need to measure, or even to calculate the angle of departure, there are two useful facts concerning this angle that should be noted and remembered:

1. What we actually do in "setting the sights" of a rifle is to set the angle of departure.
2. For a *given angle of departure*, the *flattest* shooting load will have the *highest* mid-range trajectory.

Let's emphasize the first part of the second statement—for a *given angle of departure*—since most of the mid-range trajectory data we see are computed for a *given zero range*. In the latter case, the flattest shooting load does, of course, have the lowest mid-range trajectory. The situation is reversed, however, when we consider a fixed angle of departure, and we will make use of this fact in our sight-setting procedure.

The next quantity, R_z, is of major interest since it is the "zero range," the distance to the point at which the trajectory crosses and drops below the line of sight. We will, therefore, have a good deal more to do with this relationship, but for the moment let's go on to R_x.

Recalling our high school algebra, x was always the unknown or variable quantity, so we've used R_x to indicate the range to any point in which we might be interested; for example, 100, 200, 300 or 400 yards. In this sketch x is shown as a point beyond the zero range. There are, in addition to range, three other quantities pertaining to

the point x that we need to consider. Studying the sketch we see that D_x is simply the distance that the bullet has dropped below the bore-axis line, while S_x is the distance between the bore axis and the line of sight at point x. The third quantity, d_x, is, of course, the distance between the line of sight and the bullet trajectory— or the difference between the line of sight and the actual bullet impact point at range R_x.

Now, our ability to find out what d_x is for any particular range depends upon a simple basic relationship between the three quantities we've just mentioned:

$$d_x = S_x - D_x$$

Let's go through it once again, in English. What we've just said is that we can tell how much above or below the line of sight the center of impact will be at any particular range, x, if we have just two pieces of information. One is the drop of the bullet below the bore axis (determined by the laws of gravity and ballistics); the other is the distance between the bore axis and the line of sight (determined by our sight setting and the laws of geometry).

This sounds relatively simple, and indeed it is. Suppose, for example, that we want to know where the 150-gr. 300 Weatherby bullet will impact at 450 yards, if the rifle has been zeroed in for 350? Jumping ahead in our story, we find from Table 1 that the drop from bore axis (D_x) is 38″ at 450 yards, and from the simple computational procedure outlined in fig. 5 and described later in detail, we find that the distance between bore axis and the line of sight is 27.7″ (for a 350-yard zero sight setting). Subtracting the drop of 38″ from this latter value gives us 27.7 −38 = −10.3″. The minus sign indicates that the impact will be 10.3″ *below* the point of aim. (A plus sign would indicate that the trajectory lies *above* the line of sight.)

Now that we've seen how simple the basic procedure is we can turn to the three questions we have to answer in order to apply it:

1. What should the zero range be?
2. How do we find the bullet drop (D_x) from the bore axis at the zero and other ranges?
3. How do we figure out the distance (S_x) between the bore axis and the line of sight?

After showing how answers to each of these questions can be obtained, we will describe a simple worksheet that will enable anyone to get the results he wants in less time than it takes to read about it— and with no knowledge whatever of the "new math" that high school students are baffling their parents with these days.

Selecting Zero Range

One of the first things one discovers in looking into the question of choosing a zero range is the relative scarcity of guidance. The published data of the major ammunition makers is of very little use since, in many instances, they are based on assumed zero ranges that are quite unrealistic for the cartridges in question, and the probable conditions of their employment in the field. (For example, a Remington-Peters brochure bearing the recent data of

1968 gives trajectory data based on an assumed 100-yard zero for the 250-3000 Savage, and a 200-yard zero for the 7mm Remington Magnum.) In the end one finds that there are no absolute answers to the question of the range at which a hunting rifle should be zeroed. However, there are some pretty good guidelines; namely:

1. Select the *flattest* shooting load from among the various loads to be used in the field; then . . .
2. For this selected load determine the range which gives the *maximum* mid-range trajectory that *you* can tolerate, for the kind of shooting *you* expect to do, without changing your aiming point (that is, without deliberately holding low on mid-range targets to compensate for an excessive rise of the bullet over the line of sight).

These are the principles I've found useful, and there is a simple logic for them. In the first place, it is clearly desirable for the rifle to be sighted essentially "point blank" out to the zero range, so that although one might fudge the aiming point just a little at mid-range, there's no need to memorize trajectory data. The reason for this is that we should expect to take all our running shots within the zero range, and we don't want to be figuring out vertical adjustments in the aiming point at the same time we're trying to judge the correct lead. On the other hand, long shots beyond zero range will be taken more deliberately, and here we'll be in a better position to recall trajectory data and figure out how much to hold over to put the center of impact on target.

The reason for starting with the flattest shooting load for working out the zero range, and the corresponding sight setting, is the previously stated fact that for a given angle of departure the flattest shooting load will give us the *highest* mid-range trajectory. Hence, if we sight the flattest shooting load to give the maximum mid-range trajectory we can accept, all other loads will generally shoot under this limit out to their zero ranges. Of course, the zero ranges for these loads will also be less than for the flattest shooting load.

As we have said, the selection of a maximum mid-range trajectory, and hence the zero range, is partly a matter of judgment and purpose. My inclination is to stretch the point blank range of the long range load as far as possible, accepting a mid-range trajectory for this load in excess of what experts generally recommend. This is not as much of a penalty as it might seem, however, because in areas where running shots at close to medium range are most likely, one may use a load with a heavier bullet at lower muzzle velocity, which gives a smaller mid-range trajectory as we've just noted. Applying this approach to my 7mm Magnum, for example, gives a 350-yard zero range with the 140-gr. bullet, and a mid-range of about 5″. With this same sight setting a 175-gr. load zeroes at 225 yards with a mid-range of barely 3″.

Having discussed the guidelines for selecting a zero range, let's get on with the procedure for calculating its value. To do this we take advantage of a well-estab-

Table 1

Bullet Drop of Commercial Magnum Cartridges from 257 to 308 caliber, to 600 yards range

$(D_x = \text{drop in inches at indicated yards})$

Cartridge	Bullet/grs.	MV*	100	200	250	300	350	400	450	500	550	600
257 Weatherby Magnum	87	3825	1.3	5.6	9.3	14.3	21.3	30	40	51	69	87
	100	3555	1.5	6.4	10.1	15.8	22.3	31	41	54	68	85
	117	3300	1.7	7.5	12.2	18.5	26.5	37	50	63	80	102
264 Winchester Magnum	100	3700	1.3	5.8	9.4	14.1	19.9	28	37	49	61	76
	140	3200	1.8	7.5	12.0	17.7	25.3	34	44	57	70	88
270 Weatherby Magnum	100	3760	1.3	5.9	9.7	15.0	22.0	30	40	52	67	85
	130	3375	1.7	6.9	11.1	16.8	23.9	32	43	55	69	87
	150	3245	1.8	7.3	12.1	18.0	25.3	34	45	58	74	91
7mm Weatherby Magnum	139	3300	1.8	7.3	12.1	18.0	25.3	34	45	58	74	91
	154	3160	1.9	7.8	12.6	18.5	26.5	35	46	60	76	93
7mm Remington Magnum	150	3260	1.8	7.4	12.0	17.8	25.3	34	46	58	75	92
	175	3070	2.0	8.5	14.0	21.3	30.6	42	55	71	91	114
7x61 S&H (Norma)	160	3100	2.0	7.9	12.0	17.0	26.0	37	49	64	78	96
300 Winchester Magnum	150	3400	1.7	6.8	11.1	17.0	24.0	33	44	58	71	89
	180	3070	1.9	8.1	14.1	19.4	26.8	36	47	61	76	94
300 Weatherby Magnum	150	3545	1.5	6.2	10.1	15.3	21.3	29	38	50	64	79
	180	3245	1.8	7.4	11.7	17.6	25.5	34	44	57	72	89
	220	2905	2.2	9.4	15.2	22.7	32.0	44	58	74	94	117
308 Norma Magnum†	180	3100	1.9	8.1	14.0	19.2	26.5	36	46	60	75	92

* Manufacturer's data based on 26" barrel
† Manufacturer's data based on 24" barrel

lished rule-of-thumb; namely, that the *bullet drop at the zero range is just about four times the mid-range trajectory.* Let's assume, for example, that we're selecting the zero range for the factory 100-gr. load in a 264 Winchester Magnum and have decided on a maximum midrange trajectory of 4", give or take a few tenths. Using the rule of four, we multiply 4" by 4, which gives a bullet drop of 16" at the zero range.

The final step in determining the zero range involves nothing more than examination of a drop table in order to pick out the range which corresponds to the previously calculated zero range drop. Thus, we find in Table 1 that the 100-gr. 264 Magnum bullet (in factory loading) will drop 16" below the bore axis in just a bit over 300 yards. (The table shows 14.1"). We can also see from Table 1 that if we chose 350 yards as the zero range, the mid-range would be about 5".

Bullet Drop Data - Where to Find it

Until recently, the shooter in search of drop data had almost no alternative except to calculate them himself by means of the *Speer Ballistics Calculator*[1], or by means of the Ingalls tables using a procedure described in *Hatcher's Notebook.*[2] Data such as shown in Table 1 were and are available from manufacturers' standard loads to a range of 300 yards in most cases, and 500 yards for the small-to-medium-bore magnums. However, these tables are only applicable for the factory bullet and for muzzle velocities close to the listed MV. Because of differences in barrel length, and for other reasons, one may find that he actually gets muzzle velocities quite different from those listed by the factory, in which case the "standard" drop data are not applicable. Hence there has been a need for a universal set of tables from which drop data could be readily obtained for any reasonable combination of ballistic coefficient and muzzle velocity.

The Hornady tables[3] go half-way toward the desired objective since they provide for many different muzzle velocities. However, they were designed only for use with Hornady bullets, thus application of the tables for other bullets, while possible, is inconvenient. Shooters using these tables should check to be sure that they are printed in *brown ink*. The initial printing in green ink contained appreciable errors which have been corrected in the new printing. Hornady will replace the old green tables with the corrected versions if the owner will mail in his copy of the *Handbook* together with name and address.

The Winchester-Western tables[4] compiled under the direction of E.D. Lowry are by all odds the most comprehensive, publicly available tabulation of small arms exterior ballistic data. However, the price tag of $50 per copy is apt to dampen the enthusiasm of many shooters.

The Gun Digest tables* (compiled by the author, but not needed in this issue) were designed to meet the need for a con-

*Shown first in the Handloader's Digest. 5th ed., Northfield, Ill. 1970.

venient, economical source of bullet drop and remaining velocity data for a wide range of bullet (ballistic coefficient) and muzzle velocity combinations. Although they lack several types of information provided by the Lowry tables, they are more extensive than the latter with respect to the upper limit of range for the higher ballistic coefficients.

It should be clear by now that any set of ballistic data one gets has got to be based on some specified or assumed muzzle velocity. Thus, to get *accurate results*, one must somehow make sure that the ballistic data he uses are based on a muzzle velocity about the same as the velocity he actually gets from his particular loads in his individual rifle. The best way to do this is by chronograph testing. This used to be expensive and troublesome, but excellent chronographs (such as the Oehler) are now available at about the price of a good spotting scope—under $100.

Distance (S_x) Between Line of Sight and Bore Axis

As it happens, this final item of information that we need for computing trajectories can be calculated from data that we already have: namely, the zero range (R_z), drop at the selected zero range (D_z) and the vertical distance (S_o) between the line of sight and the bore axis at the breech. The formula [5] for finding S_x from this information is:

$$S_x = R_x \left(\frac{D_x + S_o}{R_z} \right) - S_o$$

To see how the formula works, let's take a practical example such as figuring out the trajectory for the 150-gr. 300 Weatherby in a rifle with scope mounted 1.5" above the bore axis, and zeroed at 350 yards. From Table 1 we find that the drop at 350 yards is 21.3" (assuming we get the advertised muzzle velocity). Plugging these numbers into the formula gives us:

$$S_x = R_x \left(\frac{21.3 + 1.5}{350} \right) - 1.5$$

$$= R_x (.065) - 1.5$$

Thus, when $R_x = 100$, we have $S_x = 100$ x .065 − 1.5 = 6.5 − 1.5 = 5". From here on it's easy to figure out that S_x is 10.5" when R_x is 200 yards, and so forth. Going back to an earlier point in the discussion, we noted that there is always a point where the bore axis crosses the line of sight, and S_x, therefore, is zero. Knowing the range to this point comes in handy for preliminary adjustment of sights through the bore sighting technique.

Bore Sighting Formula

The formula for finding the range to the point where the line of sight and bore axis intersect is:

$$R_i = R_z \left(\frac{S_o}{D_z + S_o} \right)$$

For the example we just used:

$$R_i = 350 \left(\frac{1.5}{21.3 + 1.5} \right)$$

$$= 350 \times .658$$

$$= 23 \text{ yards}$$

This tells us that by bore sighting on a target at the convenient backyard range of about 70 feet, and setting the scope crosshairs or dot on the same point we should require very little time on the firing range to make the final zeroing-in adjustments.

Worksheet for Trajectory Calculations

The whole process of trajectory calculation will be made as simple as possible, and the likelihood of error will be minimized, by making a copy of the worksheet shown in fig. 3. Fig. 4 shows a slightly different version of the same form, with sample calculations for the 300 Weatherby trajectory example that we used previously.

In using the worksheet method for trajectory calculation we start out, as before, by determining what the zero range (R_z) will be; and noting the drop D_z at the zero range. Then we calculate the value of

$$\frac{D_z + S_o}{R_z}$$

which is

$$\frac{21.3 + 1.5}{350} = .065,$$

as we previously found. Enter this number in the blanks in Line 1a as shown. Now, multiply this value in Line 1a (.065) by the range value immediately above it in Line 0, and place the result in the space just below in Line 1b. For the example in fig. 4, these results are 6.5, 13.0, 16.2, etc. The last two spaces of Line 1b have been left blank so that the reader may complete the example himself for practice.

Next, take the previously measured value of the vertical distance at the breech between the line of sight and bore axis (S_0) and write it in the blanks of Line 2a (1.5" for this example). Then, simply subtract this value from the number above it in Line 1b, and put the result in the space below in Line 2b. This result is S_x the distance between line of sight and bore axis, at each of the ranges that we'll use in drawing a trajectory chart.

Notice at this point that the procedure in using fig. 3 would be the same as we've outlined in the example using fig. 4, except that in the example we've used two extra lines (1a and 2a) to give a clearer picture of the arithmetic. Once this is understood, the shorter form shown in fig. 3 is apt to be more convenient.

The remainder of the procedure is elementary. In Line 3 of fig. 4 copy bullet drop data from whatever source is being used (Table 1 in this example). Next, subtract this value from the number above it and put down the answers in the space below in Line 4. And that's all there is to it. The results in Line 4 give the location of the

Fig. 3   Layout for Simplified Trajectory Calculations

Line No.	Instruction	100	200	250	300	350	400	450	500	550	600
0											
1	(Line 0) x ( )^a										
2	(Line 1) − ( )^b = S_x										
3	Enter D_x for ___ load^c										
4	(Line 2) − (Line 3)										
5	Enter D_x for ___ load^c										
6	(Line 2) − (Line 5)										
7	Enter correction factor, if any										
8	(Line 6) + (Line 7)										
9	Enter D_x for ___ load^c										
10	(Line 2) − (Line 9)										
11	Enter correction factor, if any^d										
12	(Line 10) + (Line 11)										

Range (R_x) Yds

Notes:

a. Compute numerical value of $\dfrac{D_z + S_o}{R_z}$ and enter result in blank space; to be multiplied by R_x.

R_z = range to which rifle will be zeroed.

D_z = drop at the zero range, R_z.

S_o = vertical distance at breech between line of sight and bore axis.

b. Enter value of S_o in this blank.

c. Enter designation of load in this blank and fill in blanks in columns with appropriate bullet drop data for 100 yds, 200 yds, etc.

d. See text of article for explanation of corrections and method of calculation.

Fig. 4 Sample Trajectory Calculations for 300 Weatherby Magnum (150-, 180- and 220-gr. factory loads)

Line No.	Instruction	Range (R_x), yds.									
		100	200	250	300	350	400	450	500	550	600
0											
1a	$(D_z + S_o) \div R_z$	.065	.065	.065	.065	.065	.065	.065	.065	.065	.065
1b	(Line 0) x (Line 1a)[a]	6.5	13.0	16.2	19.5	22.8	26.0	29.2	32.5		
2a	S_o =	1.5	1.5	1.5	1.5	1.5	1.5	1.5	1.5		
2b	(Line 1b) - (Line 2a)	5.0	11.2	14.7	18.0	21.3	24.5	27.7	31.0		
3	Enter D_x for 150 gr. load	1.5	6.2	10.1	15.3	21.3	29	38	50	64	79
4	(Line 2) - (Line 3)	+3.5	+5.3	+4.6	+2.7	(.1)	-4.5	-10.3			
5	Enter D_x for 180 gr. load	1.8	7.4	11.7	17.6	25.5	34	44	57	72	89
6	(Line 2) - (Line 5)	+3.2	+4.1	+3.0	+0.4	-4.3					
7	Enter correction factor, if any	NONE									
8	(Line 6) + (Line 7)										
9	Enter D_x for 220 gr. load	2.2	9.4	15.2	22.7	32.0	44				
10	(Line 2) - (Line 9)	+2.7	+2.1	-0.5	-4.7	-10.8					
11	Enter correction factor, if any	+1.9	+3.7	+4.6	+5.6	+6.5					
12	(Line 10) + (Line 11)	+4.6	+5.8	+4.1	+0.9	-4.3					

Notes:

a. R_z = 350 yds; zero range for 150 gr. load.

D_z = 21.2"; drop at 350 yards.

S_o = 1.5"; vertical distance at breech between line of sight and bore axis.

trajectory above and below the line of sight at the ranges used in the calculations. Note again that a positive value in Line 4 means that the bullet is above the line of sight by the indicated distance, whereas a negative value indicates that the trajectory is below the line of sight.

Calculations for Other Loads

The calculation of trajectories for other loads to be used with the same sight setting is even simpler. For additional loads we simply enter the bullet drop data in a new line on the form, subtract from Line 2 as before, and record the results (as shown in Lines 5 and 6 of fig. 4 for the 300 Weatherby 180-gr. load, and in Lines 9 and 10 for the 220-gr. load).

Once these results are in hand it is a simple matter to determine what the zero range should be for the additional loads. By scanning the results we can find the 50-yard segment of range in which the trajectory crosses the line of sight. Thus, it can be determined from Line 6 of fig. 4 that the zero range for the 180-gr. load should be between 300 and 350 yards when the rifle is zeroed for 350 with the 150-gr. load and by comparing the relative magnitude of d_x at 300 and 350 yards (i.e., + 0.4 versus − 4.3) we can make a pretty fair guess that the zero range is close to 300 yards.

Determining Correction Factors— Range Firing Essential

In the preceding paragraphs we have explained the calculation of what zero ranges

"should" be for other loads, implying that they could actually be a bit different. One reason for this is that no rifle barrel is absolutely rigid. During the millisecond or so that it takes for the bullet to accelerate out of the barrel, vibrations are set up in the barrel such that the true angle of departure may not be exactly the same as we would find by measuring the angle between the line of sight and the bore axis with the rifle at rest. This is of no concern in regard to the zero setting for our "basic" load since we adjust this to our selected zero range by firing. The "expected" zero ranges for our other loads were then computed on the basis of difference in bullet drop, assuming the *same* effective angle of departure. But the barrel *may not behave* in exactly the same way with different loads and we may thus have slight differences in the angle of departure even though the sight adjustments remain fixed.

For these reasons we should also do some range firing of our other loads to see whether the center of impact of the groups is actually at the predicted position with reference to the line of sight. Our normal inclination is to do this firing at a convenient range, which is often no more than 100 yards for those of us living in highly urbanized sections of the country. A glance back at fig. 4, however, reminds us that at 100 yards the predicted distance between impact points for the 150-gr. and 180-gr. loads is only three-tenths of an inch (.30″). Such small differences are, of course, almost impossible to verify. Thus, if we're

really serious about long range shooting, we'll be well advised to do our range firing for sighting and trajectory checking at reasonably long ranges. If it's impossible to do this before getting out on a hunting trip, it's worth taking a couple of hours the first day to set up a target at, say, 350 yards and let off 15 or 20 rounds.

As a matter of fact, there's much to be said for the idea that this ought to be a regular ritual for those of us who can spend but little time in the field during most of the year. For one thing, it helps to get back the feel of one's rifle. And for another, it's surprising how quickly one forgets in Washington, D.C., or Peoria, what 350 yards looks like in Wyoming. Pacing it off and then walking it several more times to check the target helps to restore one's sense of distance, and pays off when it comes time to decide where to put the cross hairs on a trophy buck. The last time I failed to follow this first-day warm-up routine I overshot three standing bucks the first afternoon, because my city-calibrated vision put the ranges at 425 to 450 yards. As it turned out they were all at about 300.

So much for the additional virtues of range firing. Our immediate interest in firing is simply to adjust the sights so that the "basic" load impacts on the point of aim at our desired zero range—in this example 350 yards—and then to determine whether the additional loads we want to use with the same sight setting will actually behave in accord with the calculated trajectories. For this purpose we might as

Fig. 5   Zero to 600-yard Trajectory Chart (300 Weatherby Magnum)

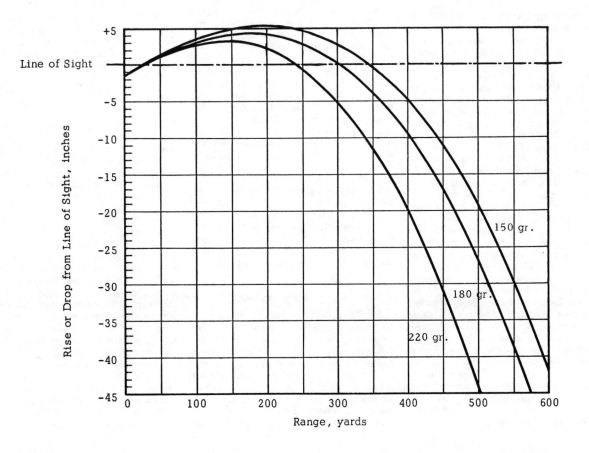

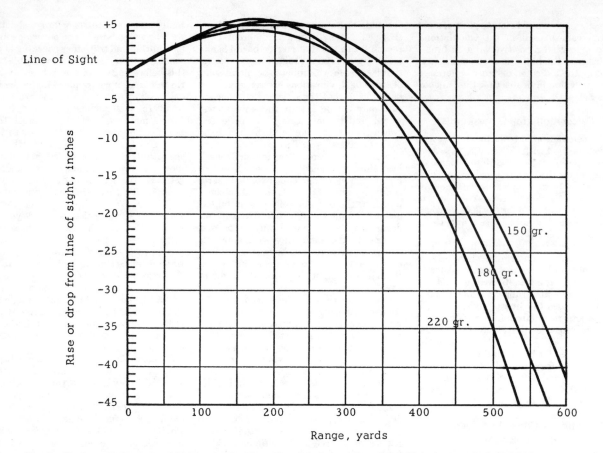

Fig. 6   Trajectory Chart for 300 Weatherby Magnum with Corrections for shift in Impact Point of 200-gr. Load

well stick to the same range we used for sighting, 350 yards, in which case we expect the 180-gr. load to group around a center of impact some 4.3″ below the aiming point, while the 220-gr. load should group some 10.8 inches low.

Now let's see what we have to do if the loads do not perform as predicted. To make the problem as tricky as possible let's assume that the 180-gr. load comes through as expected, but the 220 load impacts right on top of the 180—in other words, about 6.5″ higher than predicted by our calculations. Does this mean that we can discard the 220-gr. trajectory data and use the 180-gr. data in place of it? Not at all, since we know from the bullet drop information that the trajectories must be different. And since we know that the trajectories are different, we may conclude that the coincidence of impact points was due to change in the effective angle of departure for the 220-gr. load. Corrections must therefore be added to our calculated data for the 220-gr. bullet trajectory. This turns out to be the simplest task of all in view of the fact that *a deviation of the effective angle of departure is equivalent to a change in sight adjustment.* Hence we have merely to imagine that we've adjusted the sights to raise the impact point 6.5″ at 350 yards, and then ask ourselves what the change will be at 100 yards, 200 yards, etc. As anyone reading this article doubtless knows, we simple divide the 6.5″ by 350 yards to get inches per yard (.0186) and then multiply the result successively by 100 yards, 200 yards, and so on to get the corrections shown in Line 11 of fig. 4.

Trajectory Charts

The addition of these corrections to Line 10 gives the results in Line 12, and together with Lines 4 and 6, gives the final trajectory table which is now tailored to the performance of *your* selected loads, in *your* particular rifle, with *your* "best" sight setting. Or, instead of a trajectory table it may be handier to plot the results in chart form and draw in the trajectory curves, as shown in fig. 5 and 6. These charts show the results of our calculations for the 300 Weatherby example without corrections (fig. 5), and with corrections included (fig. 6). A comparison of the two charts emphasizes the desirability of range firing each load to verify correspondence between calculated and actual impact points.

Because the trajectory chart gives us the complete picture of how our rifle shoots, it's a handy item to have in the field. For this purpose the chart may first be drawn to some conveniently large scale, and then reduced by photostatic reproduction to a pocket-sized card and sealed in plastic.

Range Zone System

Another scheme for using trajectory information to adjust the aiming point for long range shots involves dividing the range into zones, so selected that each zone represents the same change in d_x as every other zone. The advantage of this scheme is that it condenses the trajectory curve to a handful of range intervals that are more easily remembered than the whole trajectory curve. A typical "range zone" trajectory table, based on a 5″ elevation increment, is shown in Table 2.

In using the range zone system we don't attempt to guess the exact range to the target, but simply estimate the range zone. Thus, a target which appears to be about 450 yards away would be in range zone 2. Since the aiming point adjustment is simply the range zone number multiplied by the elevation increment, we would know immediately that to hit this target we should hold high by 2 x 5 = 10 inches.

Note that in this example our problem is further simplified by the fact that the range zone interval is constant from 500 to 600 yards. (Strictly speaking, the interval does decrease slightly, but for practical purposes we can neglect this). Hence we have only to remember the three range zones from 380 to 500 yards, plus the fact that each additional 20 yards of range between 500 and 600 yards increases the zone number by one.

It is true that with this system the aiming point adjustment can be in error by as much as half the elevation increment even when we have selected the correct range zone. This is not nearly the limitation it might seem, however, since the average error we can expect on this account is probably a good deal less than the errors involved on direct range estimations. It is our considered judgment, therefore, that the over-all results obtained by this method will be just as good[6] as those obtained by attempting to estimate the exact range, and then selecting an aiming point adjustment from the full trajectory curve.

Other things being equal, or nearly so,

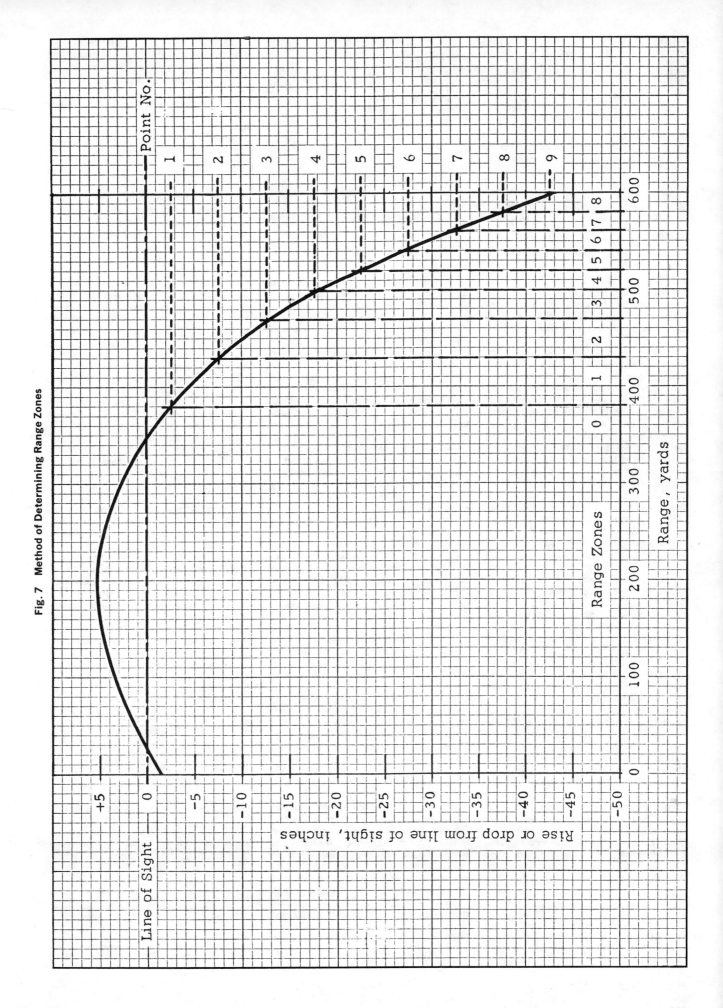

Fig. 7 Method of Determining Range Zones

Table 2
Range Zone Trajectory 150=gr.
300 Weatherby
(5" Elevation Increments)

Range Zone number	Range Zone, yards	Zone Interval, yards	Hold High by inches
0	0-380	350	0
1	380-430	50	5
2	430-470	40	10
3	470-500	30	15
4	500-520	20	20
5	520-540	20	25
6	540-560	20	30
7	560-580	20	35
8	580-600	20	40

the simplest scheme is generally the best. So, let's take a look at the procedure for working out a range zone table. The easiest way to do this is to begin with trajectory curves as we have already plotted in fig. 5 and 6. For purposes of illustration we'll confine ourselves to the 150-gr. trajectory.

To minimize drafting labor we'll draw our trajectory on 10 lines to the inch cross-section paper, choosing a range scale of 1 inch to 100 yards and an elevation scale of 1 inch to 10 inches. With our basic information in hand we now have to decide on the elevation interval. This decision will be a compromise, since the smaller the interval the larger the number of zones we get. If we get too many range zones the advantage of simplicity is lost. On the other hand, if we make the interval too large we begin to sacrifice accuracy. It appears that the best compromise is around five or six inches for the elevation interval.

Having decided on the elevation interval we take the trajectory chart and mark off a number of points, using the vertical (elevation) scale. Starting with the line-of-sight, we come down a distance equal to *half* the elevation interval and mark off point number "1" as shown on the right-hand side of fig. 7. The second point is marked off *one and a half* intervals below the line-of-sight. Similarly, for each successive point the distance is increased by *one full interval*. When a sufficient number of points have been marked off we then draw through each point a line, parallel to the line-of-sight, to an intersection with the trajectory curve. Now, from each of these intersection points we drop a *vertical* line to the range scale along the bottom of the figure. It can be seen that these lines divide the range scale into segments which are the range zones we're looking for. In selecting the zones, it will make no practical difference if we shift the lines slightly, such as from 378 yards to 380 yards, in order to get zone intervals that are easy to remember. Thus, Zone No. 0 extends from zero yards to the first line, which is at 380 yards. Zone No. 1 covers 380 to 430 yards, and so on. And that's all there is to it.

Short-Cut Methods

The procedures outlined here, do, we think, bear out the claims of inherent simplicity that we've made for them. However, it does require time to make the calculations and to conduct the required range firings to establish the basic sight setting, and to determine what, if any, corrections are needed to the calculated trajectories of additional loads to be used with the basic sight setting. In our opinion this is a minimum recipe for constructing reliable trajectory charts, and we would have no quarrels with a suggestion that additional firing at several different ranges is desirable. On the other hand, we do not subscribe to "short-cut" graphical methods of trajectory calculations that have sometimes been proposed in the shooting literature.

All of the graphic methods that we've seen are based on the use of an underlay sheet carrying an elevation scale, the sight line, and an index point. The trajectory, range ordinates, and a second index point are plotted on a transparent overlay. To use the device, the two index points are aligned and the overlay is rotated with respect to the lower chart to give the desired point of coincidence between trajectory and line of sight. In one quick and easy maneuver one seems to get the same result that we finally obtained in fig. 6. Unfortunately, however, it's not the same result. As we noted early in the discussion, the only way we can construct a useful trajectory chart is by greatly exaggerating the vertical scale relative to the horizontal. In fig. 6. for example, the distortion factor is 360-to-1, which is to say that the vertical dimensions of the chart are 360 times greater than they should be for true proportion to the horizontal. For any particular angle of departure we can construct an accurate trajectory curve as we did in figs. 5 and 6, but because we have plotted this curve in distorted scale any appreciable rotation of it (i.e., change in the angle of departure) against our fixed elevation scale will lead to errors.

We can demonstrate this fact to ourselves by tracing the 220-gr. trajectory from fig. 5 and then superimposing it on the 220-gr. trajectory of fig. 6 so that the two curves are coincident at, say, 0 and 300 yards. When we do this we find that the errors are comparatively small at mid-range, so that we could use the graphic short cuts in place of the rule of thumb mentioned earlier for estimating the mid-range trajectory. The errors become progressively larger, however, as we move out beyond the zero range and thus the graphic short cuts are unreliable for the construction of long-range trajectory charts. We might also note that the graphic methods require the same basic information that we need for the method described in this article. Once we have this information, the time required to carry out our procedure (except for range firing) is just about right to provide pleasant occupation for a winter's evening. So, in the final analysis, there is little real advantage in the graphic short cut methods.

Closing Remarks

The stated purpose of the article was to describe a procedure that any sportsman with some patience and a little arithmetic can apply to determine a single "best" sight setting, and use it effectively. Hence we have kept personal inclinations pretty much out of the discussion. The cartridge used in the example was selected as being more or less representative of a class of modern, high-velocity magnums; and also because of the fact that three different commercial loads are available for it. Personally, I have a slight preference for the 7mm Magnums for long range work.

The zero range used in the example gives a mid-range trajectory that may seem rather high to some hunters for "point blank" sighting. This does happen to represent a personal bias, and it is deliberately high based on the fact that I don't expect to use the maximum velocity/light bullet loads for mid-range shots. My choice for this shooting is a heavier bullet that "tops off" at about 3" with the same sight setting on my rifle that gives a 350-yard zero range with the flattest shooting load.

The reasons for these choices are several. First of all, in order to expand reliably at reduced velocities associated with the long ranges the bullet must not be too heavily constructed. It tends therefore to be overly sensitive at the higher mid-range velocities. Moreover, mid-range shots are more likely to be taken at running targets, and from adverse angles, so that the capability for maximum penetration with a good exit wound is comparatively more important. Finally, the closer range shots are more frequently accompanied by the problem of intervening brush—which again indicates the use of a bullet with high sectional density.

References

1. Speer Products Co., Lewiston, Idaho.
2. The Stackpole Co., Harrisburg, Pa.
3. *Hornady Handbook of Cartridge Reloading.*
4. *Exterior Ballistics of Small Arms Projectiles* by E.D. Lowry, Research Department, Winchester-Western Division, Olin Mathieson Chemical Corporation, 1965, New Haven, Conn.
5. Readers interested in the derivation of this formula can obtain it from the relationships diagrammed in fig. 2, by applying the principle of similar triangles and using the fact that $S_z=D_z$.
6. Perhaps we should say "Just as bad." In this discussion we've used as an example one of the flattest shooting commercial Magnum cartridges ever offered. Nevertheless, we find that as our range goes beyond 500 yards, a 20-yard change in the range involves a 5" change in the point of impact. Estimating range to within 20 yards at 500 yards requires that errors cannot exceed 4%. Tests by the Army indicate that an average GI has about a fifty-fifty chance of estimating range to within 5% using a coincidence range-finder. Using a stadia-type range-finder he'll come within only 10%, about half the time. With plain old "eyeball" range estimating errors will exceed 20% of range more than half the time. To be sure, an experienced rifleman will do better than this. Even so, there's an upper limit beyond which the chances of maiming as against clean killing of game say that we should refrain from shooting.

A thousand years have elapsed between the Chinese "arrows of fire" and today's incredible guided missiles, yet in a sense both are versions of the same weapon — rockets. In this millennium, as this historian shows, many battles have been decided in . . .

THE ROCKETS RED GLARE

by Fairfax Downey

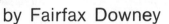

At the Battle of New Orleans in January, 1815, American troops under Gen. Andrew Jackson were bombarded by rockets which did extensive damage. In this case, however, the rockets' success was temporary and the victory fell to American musketry and artillery fire.

AMONG ARTILLERY weapons, the rocket owns one of the longest and most curious histories. Its lineage stretches straight back to the arrow. Indeed, the first war rockets were shafts with incendiary or explosive tips shot from bows — the Chinese "arrows of flying fire." Despite the rocket's proven potency, it disappears from warfare for long periods, then reappears and vanishes again, finally to be developed in modern times as the mighty guided missile. In a number of actions it was as decisive as cannon, and to it belongs the distinction of supplying a line for the United States' national anthem.

Fire arrows containing gunpowder, some of them propelled like rockets, were in military use in China as early as the year 1000.[1] Both in the Orient and in Europe they were sporadically employed in the 14th and 15th centuries, along with the Roman candle, ancestor of the flame-thrower, which originated in the East as a gunpowder-filled bamboo tube.[2] A single rocket hit is said to have turned the tide in the siege of the island of Chiozza in

1379 by setting afire a tower, the center of resistance. Four and a half centuries later victory was lost in a battle of the War of 1812 when one struck a general.

Rockets, it was early learned, were particularly effective against cavalry because of the terror they caused horses. It was that factor which, after a hiatus, brought them to the fore again toward the end of the 18th century. Arsenals of Indian potentates were filled with large ones in iron tubes weighing from 6 to 12 pounds, launched through 10-foot bamboo poles. Hydar Ali and his son, Tipoo Sahib, who increased his rocket corps from 1200 to 5000 men, employed mass flights to rout British cavalry.[3]

So convincing a demonstration of rocket power aroused European interest, and naturally the British, its target, were most concerned. A gunnery specialist, Col. William Congreve, reading reports of the Indian campaign, began experiments about 1801 with the largest fireworks rockets on the market, bought out of his own pocket, to develop them as weapons.

He increased the 500-yard range of the Indian missiles to 2000, obtained the backing of the authorities, and was ready in 1805 to try them out in action.[4]

British warships twice bombarded Boulogne with rockets, and in 1807 deluged Copenhagen with flights of 25,000, burning most of the city to the ground. Three rocket attacks on Danzig forced its surrender in 1813. That same year the British Rocket Brigade, operating with the Royal Horse Artillery whose 6-pounder guns were far outranged by the missiles, played a dashing part in the Battle of Leipzig. Charging, the mounted rocketeers went into action at close range to storm a key village, then broke a French rally attempting to retake it. The feat won the Brigade the right to inscribe "Leipzig" on its appointments. Rockets also were used at Waterloo.

As father of the war rocket in the West, Congreve exerted enormous influence on military establishments. "Denmark, Egypt, France, Italy, the Netherlands, Poland, Prussia, Sardinia, Spain, and Sweden attached rocket batteries to their artillery. Austria, England, Greece, and Russia had rocket corps which were independent units . . . The United States formed rocket units."[5] The colonel, knighted for his services, had by 1817 raised rocket ranges to 3000 yards. Their warheads duplicated all types of artillery ammunition then in use except for solid roundshot. They comprised incendiaries, bombs, and a shrapnel type with a load of carbine balls, as well as parachute-borne flares. Not far below cannon of the period in accuracy, they were of course considerably cheaper to produce. Recoil was converted into propelling force. Another notable advantage was the far

combustion engine which would minimize the problem of the weight of cannon. Yet his prevision of the effect of rockets on warfare would hold good for modern guided missiles.

War Use in the U.S.

A rocket brigade, Royal Marine Artillery, accompanied the British army invading the United States in the War of 1812 and saw action on both the northern and southern fronts. After the American victory at Chippewa in the former campaign, the adversaries engaged again at Lundy's Lane, close to Niagara Falls. An American charge carried enemy batteries, which had been inflicting heavy casualties, and the field was in a fair way to be won when Gen. Jacob Brown and his second in command, Winfield Scott, were both twice wounded. Brown's first in-

Model of Congreve rocket launcher, as made by Val Forgett, Jr. William Congreve, a British colonel, did extensive experimentation with rockets at the beginning of 19th century. "The rocket," he said, "is, in truth, an arm by which the whole system of military tactics is destined to be changed."

lighter weight of the missiles and their launchers compared to guns and their equipment. Thin-walled copper tubes served to guide single rockets, collapsible wooden frames for mass bombardments. The Congreve rocket transport wagon was compact and efficient.

Soul of Artillery

"The soul of artillery without the body," Congreve called his rockets. On his death in 1826, plans were found among his papers for an 8"-diameter rocket and notes on missiles to weigh as much as 1000 pounds.[6] He had uttered a prophecy which the future bid fair to see fulfilled:

"The rocket is, in truth, an arm by which the whole system of military tactics is destined to be changed."[7]

He could not foresee that soon forthcoming improvements in conventional artillery would relegate rockets to supplementary weapons, nor, far less, the appearance of the internal

jury, a musket ball through a thigh, was not as severe as his second: a heavy blow from the stick of a Congreve rocket. Although still conscious, the general was suffering from shock to such a degree that he ordered a withdrawal instead of the advance that would have gained the day. The British reoccupied lost ground and held the battlefield. More hard fighting was required before U.S. forces ended the threat from the north, and hostilities shifted southward.

A British army of 4500 was landed from a fleet sailing up Chesapeake Bay on the Maryland shore near the village of Bladensburg to drive for Washington, the American capital, a few miles away. The invader's veteran troops, while weak in field guns, were supported by a strong rocket battery, and it was the novel weapon, together with inept American command, that swayed the issue.

When the battle opened August 24, 1814, defenders beating back the British assault saw a bright flash across the river behind the scarlet col-

The drawings with this article are from *Volkommene Geschütz Feuer-Werke* by Casimir Simienowicz (Frankfurt, Germany, 1676).

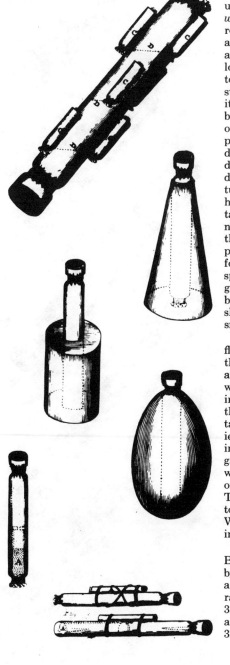

umns and heard a strange, roaring *whoosh*. To gaping ranks this first rocket in their experience, a soaring apparition spitting sparks and trailing a blazing trail, looked like "a comet low in the sky." "It cleared the tree-tops, seemed to hang there for an instant before it plunged downward in its fiery arc. A man couldn't see a bullet coming; if his number wasn't on it, he heard only the humm of its passing. But this swooping thing was dreadfully personal. It appeared to be darting directly at each watching soldier, making him shake in his boots, turning his knees to water. Only when he saw it strike the ground some distance in front could he believe it was not headed straight for him. Even then the menace of the thing with a pointed iron head and a scorched 8-foot stick was not ended. Smoking and sputtering, it writhed through the grass like a serpent. Then a time fuse burst its black powder charge with a sharp report and a spurt of acrid smoke."[8]

Rocketeers now jerked lanyards to flintlock mechanisms for long lines of their missiles, ready in their troughs, and volleys flamed. The first flight was high, but the second grazed heads in the trenches. It did not matter that they caused no heavy casualties. Their targets were "more minds than bodies." Three American regiments broke in panic and raced for the rear. A gallant stand by a naval contingent with ships' guns, along with batteries of field artillery, could not hold long. The British swept over them and on to capture Washington and burn the White House and other public buildings.

The harbor of Baltimore, the next British objective, was strongly guarded by Fort McHenry whose formidable armament of guns and howitzers ranged through 18-pounders, 24s, and 32s on to fifteen 42s. First the city's approaches, defended by a brigade of 3200, were attacked, As the initial as-

sault was stalled by spirited resistance, a mounted rocket troop trotted forward. Pack artillery in effect, it carried missiles and launchers in leather buckets slung to saddles, with spare ammunition on led horses and in tumbrils. Rocketeers dismounted and opened fire within 30 seconds. Attaining a rate of fire of 4 rounds per minute, they poured a deluge of 480 6-pound rockets on the foe in 5 minutes. Field guns chimed in with volleys of shrapnel, the shell invented in 1784 by a Briton whose name it bore. New to Americans, the projectiles, burst in flight by a time fuse to spray out widening cones of balls, wrought havoc on their ranks and flung them back in retreat. However, the triumphant British advance halted short of the city to let the navy deal with Fort McHenry.

On the morning of September 13, 1814, the fleet commenced a bombardment that would continue through the night. Francis Scott Key, one-time American artillery officer held as hostage aboard the flagship, watched the big mortars of the bomb ships spew out their 200-pound loads to soar up in lofty arcs and swoop down on the fort and the flag of red, white, and blue fluttering from its staff. He saw the rocket ship *Erebus* spout broadsides of 32-pound incendiaries, "reaching out with fiery fingers for the houses in the fort, the ready ammunition in the batteries and bastions, the plank platforms and revetments, and the gunboats moored in the channel."[9] He thrilled to the valiant reply by McHenry's gunners, fire that held the fleet at bay and beat off an attack by a landing party in barges. At the end of the night bombardment's awful grandeur—"the rocket's red glare, the bombs bursting in air"—he beheld by the dawn's early light that the flag was still there, that the Star-Spangled Banner yet waved. Then he wrote down those immortal words of his, and a national anthem was born.

Once more rockets played a part in the war. At the Battle of New Orleans they sped down on the cotton-bale-barricaded American position January 1, 1815. Swishing through cannonading, they spread dismay as before. Gen. Andrew Jackson strode along the trenches shouting, "Don't mind these rockets. They are mere toys to amuse children." Such reassurance fell flat when the missiles exploded two caissons, dismounted three guns, and set cotton bales afire. But the rockets' success, isolated and temporary, was of small account. It was to American musketry and artillery fire that final victory was due.

American Improvements

America, having like the British in India and the Danes been rocket targets, adopted them and proceeded to improve them. William Hale replaced the stablizing stick by adding 3 metal vanes to the exhaust nozzle, thus increasing accuracy and range by giving the missile a rotary twist as rifling does a bullet or shell. Some, though slight, use of rockets was made in the War with Mexico, also in the Civil War when the Confederates manufactured about 4000 in the Richmond arsenal. Jeb Stuart once launched a flight on Federal troops, though with little beyond morale effect. "Stuart opened on them with a Congreve rocket battery, the first and last time the latter ever appeared in action with us," his engineer officer, Lt. Col. Blackford, recorded. "It had been gotten up by some foreign chap who managed it on this occasion. They were huge rockets, fired from a sort of gun carriage, with a shell at the end which exploded in due time, scattering 'liquid damnation,' as the men called it. Their course was very erratic; they went straight enough in their first flight, but after striking, the flight might be continued in any other course, even directly back towards where it came from. Great consternation was occasioned in the camps of the enemy as these unearthly serpents went zig-zagging about among them. . . . A few tents were fired, but the rockets proved to be of little practical value."[10]

Rockets, gradually dropped by military services, survived only for signaling, to carry lifelines to ships in distress, and as propellants for whaling harpoons. They did not emerge from eclipse until a period before World War II when Dr. Robert H. Goddard, an American, and foreign scientists, notably the Germans, began developing them both as weaponry and as power for passenger-carrying spaceships. In the former category were produced the American anti-tank bazooka, forerunner of recoilless guns, various types of multiple rocket-throwers employed by all belligerents, and finally the formidable German V-2.* Despite them and the mighty legion of their post-war successors, it may still be declared, as it was in 1944, that, "The modern war rockets do not replace artillery in any way; they merely augment it."[11] It might also be added, more deeply than ever they merge with it. Whereof the new U.S. artillery insignia—a missile superimposed on the traditional crossed cannon—serves as a token. •

Bibliography

1. *Artillery and Warfare During the 13th and 14th Centuries*, John N. Patrick (Logan, Utah, 1961).
2. *The Ancient Engineers*, L. Sprague De-Camp (Garden City, N. Y., 1963).
3. *A Narrative of the Military Operations . . . against Hyder Ally*, Inness Munroe (London, 1789).
4. *Rockets*, Willy Ley (New York City, 1944).
5. *Ibid.*
6. *Ibid.*
7. *Thunderbolts*, Maj. Gen. J. F. C. Fuller (London, 1946).
8. *Sound of the Guns*, Fairfax Downey (New York City, 1955).
9. *The Perilous Fight*, Neil Swanson (New York City, 1945).
10. *War Years with Jeb Stuart*, Lt. Col. W. W. Blackford (New York City, 1945).
11. Ley, op. cit.

*The German V-1, propelled by jet engines, was not a true rocket.

"GUN FEVER"

Swap Shop

Honest John is a mighty smart old hosstrader, that's for sure, but you can beat him on this swap, huh? Or will you?

by Guy L. Aurand

THERE IS A vile malady that relentlessly stalks the sportsman . . . a disease so terrible that booze, drugs and gambling are miniscule in comparison. This dread affliction strikes unerringly at the gunners of our great land. It reduces the brain to a febrile organ, the hands tremble, eyes burn feverishly, the lips parch and the salivary glands cease functioning, thus causing the tongue to swell and make speech labored and difficult. Medical science has found no miracle drug to combat this evil affliction; in fact, there isn't even a name for it. Until the profession comes up with a better term, it will continue being awesomely referred to as *swapitis!*

My latest bout with this destroyer of souls was a doozy. When it struck me down I owned a sweet little 5 lb.

10 oz. 20-bore Darne; but when the fever left my bowed frame I found that I was the owner of an elderly 16-ga. Winchester Model 12 with assorted aches and pains. This is even more remarkable when it is considered that I am strictly a double man, with no affection for pumps or self-feeders. Well, perhaps my tale may help some other unwary gunner avoid this plague . . .

I walked into my friendly gun dealer's one morning to purchase a tin of gun oil and spotted a trim-looking Spanish 20 bore in his racks. It had some scratching on the action, top lever and guard and at the breech of the barrels, but this didn't keep it from handling like a dream. That straight stock snuggled under my cheek bone and it swung like a feath-

er. The stock was also a much handsomer piece of walnut than my Darne's, and the gun tipped the scales at just 5½ lb.

It was at this point that my brain cells first showed signs of idiocy. Testing the pulls I found that the right lock let down crisply, but the left one sounded soft and the firing pin just lazily poked through the standing breech.

Nothing to worry about, Happy Boy assured me; just needed a bit of wood relieved in the stock mortise to free up the hammer. He would have it ready in the morning and, he whispered in an aside, that little Spanish dilly could be mine for just a double sawbuck and my Darne.

I managed to survive the long, long night time hours and was parked at his emporium the next morning a full hour before he opened. Away went my picture of Andy Jackson and the Darne and I rodded for home with my new birding piece.

To check shot placement I stapled a paper to my pattern board and let fly at 10 yards. The cluster of pellets struck 6 inches low . . . with either barrel. As I cogitated on this revolting circumstance my mind was beginning to register some disturbing data. For the first time I noted that the stamp used to strike the maker's name had not been held in good register with the barrels, as only the top half of the letters was visible. (Incidentally, I never did puzzle out who made the gun). I removed the fore-end and unhooked the barrels. The proof marks on the flats were as shoddily impressed as was the inscription on the barrels.

The gun had the lockup typical of most A&D-type Spanish doubles—twin underbolts and the Purdey-type concealed extension that locked atop the extractor guide. It is an excellent bolting system and quite reliable in a well-crafted gun. Let me go on record now and state that many fine guns by AYA, Sarasqueta and other makers come out of Spain, and are finely fitted and superlatively built to give a lifetime of service, but this piece of mine must have been fabricated with a hammer and cold chisel in a dark cellar by the light of a flickering torch.

The automatic safety would at times struggle back to its position when the gun was opened, but at other times it had to be nudged back with the thumb. When the barrels were opened they didn't drop far enough to remove or insert a shell, so extra force had to be exerted to force the tubes downward, against the pressure of the mainsprings. This was great for developing strong wrists, but it made for damned slow loading. Also this paragon of the gunmaker's art had a cute trick with the top lever. At times it would lie well over to the right of the tang, like the old American rotary bolt lockup; at other times as the gun was closed the lever might position itself centered on the tang, or it might flop way over to the left. I began to regard my new smoothbore with suspicion.

Swapitis—Phase Two

The second phase of swapitis is usually recognizable by profuse sweating . . . occurring at just about the time the Nimrod has a gnawing suspicion that he has goofed rather badly. Strong black coffee is highly recommended at this stage, and six cups and a pack of butts later I had formulated my plan of action. I had convinced myself that the gun was not the clunker it appeared to be and all would be well.

Beware of false heights of confidence, for swapitis will raise one's hopes on high, only to dash them to the lowest depths without fail. It is a roller coaster of emotional instability!

However, my confidence was on the upswing. Raising the pattern was no problem. I took the barrels out back to a small elm tree. Holding the muzzle in one hand and the middle of the barrels in the other, I swung the gun against the tree, striking against the top rib midway between my hands so the upward bend would be toward the muzzle and not back where the fore-end fitted. A couple of raps and I put the gun together and headed for the pattern board again. At 10 yards the charge obliterated the aiming spot. I tacked up a fresh paper and moved back to the 35-yard marker. I should have quit at 10; at 35 those tubes didn't pattern shot, they sprayed it. I knew there was shot in the shells for there were scattered holes in the paper. Like I said, black despair and more sweat, only this time java and smokes were no help at all.

That night I tossed and slept fitfully with that accursed double prying at my sanity. I awoke hollow-eyed with the dawn, spurred to action with a devilish plan my tortured mind had evolved—a devilish plan perhaps, but so simple. I put the barrels across two padded blocks and by rhythmically pushing down on them I straightened the barrels to their original shape.

Adios to the Spanish

Back to the Friendly Dealer I hied myself, with the explanation that the Spanish featherweight was kicking me silly. Smiling Sam gravely informed me that the Spanish was now a used gun with a corresponding depreciation. However, as we were such old

friends I could trade it back to him for anything in his racks that didn't cost over seventy bucks. Hell's fire, the Darne had cost me over two hundred!

Well, I knew I positively didn't want the Spanish, and in my ravaged condition I accepted his generous offer meekly. I have often wondered, though, if the cards were stacked against me, for the only thing in his lineup in the seventy-dollar class was an old 16-ga. Winchester Model 12 pump, with a Poly-Choke topping off a 25″ barrel. A jab at the action release and the slide moved back and forth, the breech-block dutifully wagging to and fro. The finish wasn't too hot, but I figured it was way ahead of the foreigner.

Suffice it to say that I tottered out with the pump.

You would assume that by this time I was entitled to a wee bit of Irish luck for a change but, alas, such was not to be.

Back at the pattern board I found that the Winchester printed low and to the left at 10 yards. Anyone knows that the proper way to bend a single tube is to put the barrel into a vise with the jaws well padded, clamping the barrel just back of the muzzle, and then to gently force the rear of the barrel over enough to spring it slightly in the direction one wants the pattern to move. It's no great job and can be done quicker than telling.

But in my agitated state did I do that? You just know I didn't! I padded the jaws, clamped the barrel just back of the barrel band, put a pipe wrench on the barrel and proceeded to cave two huge dents into the tube.

Over the telephone I found that I

could have the dents removed for six bucks. That did it. I figured Chuckling Charlie could make his groceries from somebody else with no further help from me.

Anyone Can Remove Dents

I didn't have a lathe, so I couldn't turn up a mandrel to remove the dents. I did have a cut-off section of 22-cal. rifle barrel that miked up at .680". A 16 bore mikes out at about .662", so a few passes with a fine mill file and I had a makeshift plug that I could just tap down into the tube with a rod. I tapped it up to the dents and applied a brass hammer to the outside of the barrel and eventually finished a fair job of ironing out the wrinkles. Then I clamped the barrel in the vise and sprung it by hand. It took about two more tries to get the pattern dead on.

Were my troubles over now? Not by a long shot!

While patterning the gun I had one misfire and the arm balked at feeding from the magazine to the chamber. By this time I was fit for a straight jacket and a one-way ticket to the funny farm.

I removed the trigger plate screw and pried the plate and its mechanism free of the frame. Corruption fell out in chunks. I removed the ejector and breechblock and dunked everything in a pan of solvent. From the dirt and caked accumulation of residue that covered the action walls and recesses, I don't think they had ever been cleaned. When I wiped off the breechblock I noticed that though the firing pin was locked in a retracted position, the front end of the pin waggled back and forth through the hole in the nose.

That explained the misfire—a broken firing pin. I hopped into the Falcon and toted the breechblock back to the Purveyor of Muskets. He opined that inasmuch as I had just got the gun that morning, he felt morally obligated to install a new firing pin, and disappeared into his workshop.

Anyone can Replace Pin

It usually takes a couple of minutes to wind out the firing pin retaining screw, which also holds the firing pin retractor in place, and slip in a new pin. Ordinarily, that is. I happened to have the only Winchester I ever heard of that had a broken retaining screw. This screw is inserted from the left side of the block, and threads into a blind hole. It took an hour and a half to remove the busted screw! Well, to shorten a sad tale, at the finish of the operation Daring Dan tossed me the breechblock, complete with a new firing pin but having a mismated screw forced into place to hold the works together. That bugged me. What the hell good was it if I had to replace another pin? Back home I tried to get

that bastard screw out. No dice; it would turn, but couldn't be removed.

The Model 12 is a pretty rugged firearm but it is noted for occasionally breaking firing pins. I had a small hand grinder and I managed to grind out the hardened screw. I had no small taps so I couldn't tap out the hole for a larger screw. The only solution that occurred to me was to drill completely through the block and insert a pin to hold the assembly in place. The only drawback here was that I had no drill press, only a quarter-inch electric hand drill, but that was no obstacle to a man with determination . . . or is desperation a better word!

I clamped the block in the vise, selected a drill bit just small enough to enter the hole and had at it. I don't know what the specs are for the steel Winchester uses for breechblocks, but take it from me, it is tough. Using lots of oil and breaking a handful of bits, I finally chewed a hole through. Mind you, this was free hand work. I dropped in the firing pin, inserted the firing pin retainer, and used a broken drill shank for a pin. Went together like a charm. The only hitch was that the firing pin retainer now positioned too low and the firing pin was immovable. My "precision" drilling was off. I filed the angles on the retainer until it freed up and then had to grind the notch in the firing pin a hair deeper, but I was in business, I hoped.

I shook the solvent off the rest of

the parts and liberally oiled them, put the gun together again, and the feeding problems cleared up. She pumped and worked slick as buttered glass. Things were looking better, at least they were until I decided to make one more pass with my 22 barrel plug. I tinned one side of the plug to make a snug fit and drove it into the barrel. It was snug! I was pounding it through the barrel when something plunked onto the floor. My Poly-Choke had popped off the barrel!

Anyone Can Install Poly

I picked it up and swore. In attaching a Poly, the barrel normally is threaded and the choke body screws onto the barrel—a good solid attachment. This particular Poly had just been stuck on the barrel. Someone had filed the threads away inside the choke body, tapering to the front; the barrel had been filed to a taper at the muzzle and the choke driven on.

I think I must have started to really come unglued then, because I collapsed in laughter—it just struck me so funny that anyone would attach a Poly in such a slipshod fashion. That choke should have shot off the barrel the first time a cartridge was triggered.

What to do? I didn't want to try silver soldering the choke into place because the high temp of 1200 degrees seemed likely to untemper the spring fingers attached to the choke body. The only thing left was to try soft soldering the choke in place. I tinned the barrel at the muzzle. I stuffed the spring collet with rags and wrapped the fingers with cloth, and while my son kept the rags wet with water I took the torch and tinned the body inside. Setting the choke on the barrel I heated the assembly and pushed it into place with a flat iron bar, tapping it the last bit with a brass hammer.

When it cooled, I trudged wearily back to the pattern board. Now it shot high and to the right. Another bending session at the vise soon had it centered again. I cold-blued the metal, cut off the pistol grip to make a straight stock of it, and refinished the wood. A section of old wooden cleaning rod made a plug for the magazine. She's now digested several cases of shells and the choke has stayed put.

I'm pretty well recuperated from my attack of swapitis by this time, but I miss the little Darne, I can't even look at a Spanish onion, and I force myself to ignore the financial shortcomings of this debacle.

Believe me, my friends, if you have the slightest suspicion that swapitis is about to attack you, ask your best friend to tie you to your bed until the symptoms pass; you'll bless him for it later.

By the way, do you know anyone who's interested in a hand-finished, 16-ga. Model 12 Winchester?   ●

HANDGUNS
U.S. & FOREIGN 1971-72

by GEORGE C. NONTE
and the editors

THE WORLD never stands still. Those handgun fanciers who thought that it might—as far as their pet interests were involved after GCA '68—should by now admit that they were mistaken. The ban on interstate sales and the severe sales-recording requirements of that law were strongly expected to produce less handgun activity—that is, fewer sales, fewer new models, perhaps fewer producers, etc.

But, after all was said and done, it just didn't work out that way. After the initial drop-off in sales—perhaps because of a poor understanding of the law rather than to its restrictions—handgun sales seem to be doing as well as ever. I know for a fact that in my own area, none of our gunshops can keep good handguns in stock for any length of time. Nor are any of our major handgun manufacturers finding any trouble whatever in selling all the guns they can make; and they're making more now than ever before. More in simple numbers and more in numbers of models and variations thereof. Anyone who doubts the last part of that statement need only take a quick count of the makes and models listed in this issue of the GUN DIGEST.

Maybe we should take a look at this phenomenon. The proponents of GCA '68 made no bones about the fact that they hoped—intended—that it should reduce the numbers of handguns in private ownership, and that it would also reduce the total numbers of guns at large throughout the country. We, too, believed that. We fully expected that the restrictions would make buying a new gun so inconvenient that would-be handgunners by the thousands would simply forget the whole thing and turn to tennis, whiskey or girl watching.

This seems not to have happened, for which we give thanks. Our handgunners have given notice, through their buying, that they don't intend to be intimidated by regulations. Sort of a "rebellion by compliance," if there is any such thing. They're saying, in effect, "You can make it hard for us to obtain the guns we want, but you can't force us to give them up. We'll follow your silly damn rules to the letter." We have lived with those restrictions for over 30 months now (as this is written), and I'm proud of our law-abiding, legitimate handgunners who have put up with all manner of useless, disagreeable harassment and restrictions to keep the shooting game going.

Far from being dead, civilian handgun shooting and ownership is holding its own quite well. Neither is it being legislated out of existence—in fact, participation appears greater now than ever before.

• • •

This marks the year that several previously-announced new models have actually begun to show up on dealers' shelves—particularly the Ruger Security-Six, the Wesson M-12 and American Firearms' stainless steel pocket auto. These makers had promised and advertised delivery at least a full year before guns were available. Sure, there were "extenuating circumstances," unforseen problems, and the like, but there ought to be an end to this practice. In our considered opinion, such gambits don't sell more guns—they may sell even fewer. We want to commend Smith & Wesson for the manner in which it handled its new M-61 pocket auto. There were no ads, no ballyhoo, until the guns were in the warehouse, ready for shipment.

It seems to me I've heard fewer complaints about defective *new* handguns this year than last. That doesn't mean there haven't been complaints—there have. Apparently those efforts the makers have been telling us about are the functional quality, at least, of new guns. Still, it will pay you to check any new handgun as thoroughly as possible immediately after purchase. This is especially true if a gun is being bought for police service, for personal or home defense. The cop who buys a new gun and never fires it until his first gunfight is becoming scarcer, but he still does exist. As Bill Jordan says in his book on the subject, "there's no such thing as second place in a gunfight." Second place is where you'll be, too, if you don't check that new gun out seven ways from Sunday as soon as it is in your hands.

This is also the year that has brought quite a few of the old guns back. After being barred from importation by ATFD regulations stemming from GCA '68, they have now been revised and dressed up to qualify for importation. More about them as we go along.

There are, though, quite a few new or considerably improved and/or changed models, so let's take a look at them.

Ammunition

The past year has seen the announcement and actual sale of more high-performance handgun ammunition than any similar period. The genuine high-performance load is here to stay, particularly in 38 Special, though 9mm P, 38 Super, and 45 ACP came in for their share of attention. These developments followed on the success of the 110-gr. HP and SP loads by Super Vel.

To date ten 38 loads alone have been introduced (see table). No such loads were actually available a mere 5 years back. Now, though, both police and sportsmen demand them for their vastly improved effect on live targets. With over a dozen loads already offered, there are still more in the offing, so the field will soon be loaded. Just to prove load development isn't all that easy, and that even the big outfits do goof—Remington *recalled* all the early lots of their 125- and 158-gr. JHP loads sold to law enforcement agencies last October. Why? Well, they discovered that the powder/primer combination produced erratic ignition—even misfires—at sub-zero temperatures. Naturally, no cop can afford that. We assume the problem has been licked by now.

In 9mm Parabellum (Luger) ammo we now have the Norma 110-gr. HP and SP, the Remington 115-gr. HP, the S&W-Fiocchi 100- and 115-gr. JHP and the Super Vel 90-gr. JHP and 112-gr. JSP. The Norma loads expand very poorly and the Remington not at all. Both Super Vel loads expand very well, often to over 60 caliber. Comparable to the 9mm is the 38 Super Auto with 105-gr. JHP and 112-gr. JSP by Super Vel, both of which expand very well.

Our old standby, the 45 Auto, is now served by 2 high-performance loads. Oldest is the 230-gr. H/SP by Norma, which expanded little in our tests; second is the new 190-gr. JHP Super Vel load, which produces expansion of 80 to 90 caliber in boars, bears, and the like at short ranges. It is the first truly successful expanding-bullet load to be offered in this caliber.

Of course, similar loads have been introduced by the same firms for the 357, 41 and 44 Magnums—but we needn't detail these because they began life as high-performance cartridges.

Component makers are no less interested in high-performance ammunition. *All* major bullet makers now offer an overwhelming array of jacketed hollow- and soft point bullets designed to duplicate factory-load performance. Most—not all—are very close copies of the original highly successful Super Vel designs.

The name "S&W-Fiocchi" appearing above may cause a bit of confusion. What happened is this: Fiocchi of Italy bought the Alcan Co., then sold a half-interest in it to Smith & Wesson (which is owned by Bangor Punta). S&W desired its own brand of handgun ammunition to sell with its guns, so tooled the old Alcan plant to load 38 Spl., 9mm P, and 357 Magnum cartridges. The headstamp agreed upon by all was (is) "S&W/F," standing for Smith & Wesson/Fiocchi. The resulting ammunition is sold in blue and silver S&W/F boxes by S&W, but also with the same headstamp in red, white, and blue Alcan boxes by S&W/F under the old Alcan name, which continues in existence only as a product label and logo. Everything clear now? Sorry about that.

The 44 Auto Mag has a completely shrouded rotary bolt with 6 locking lugs. Barrel/receiver assembly is slightly rearward, bolt open.

American Firearms

American Firearms has finally got its stainless steel 25-caliber auto pistol into production. A very simple gun, as most of the type are, its major claim to fame is that virtually all of its parts are made from stainless steel, brightly polished on the outside. It is a bit hefty for its type, weighing a full pound, and it's substantially larger than some otherwise comparable guns —probably because the makers intend to offer it later in larger calibers. The larger dimensions will be required for 32 and 380 ACP calibers.

Striker-fired, the gun combines features of the Clement, Bayard and Liliput designs of half a century or more back. The recoil spring is below the barrel, the latter an integral part of the receiver casting. The sear also serves as an ejector. Sights are rudimentary, and the thumb safety is hard to operate. Disassembly is quick and easy, but the likelihood of losing the firing pin and recoil spring is high, since two hands aren't quite enough to keep them under control as the slide and receiver are separated. Re-assembly is very difficult in regard to replacing the recoil spring. We solved this by drilling a hole in the spring guide and using a pin through it to hold the spring in a pre-compressed state until it is covered by the slide. Maybe the makers will consider such a change. The gun functions well and delivers the degree of accuracy generally expected of the type. Our sample gun placed its shots about 8" high and 6" right of the aiming point at 20 feet.

44 Auto Mag

Contrary to what you might have heard or read, there is a 44 Auto Mag pistol— hundreds of them are being assembled and delivered from Harry Sanford's Pasadena plant, and by the time you read this there'll be thousands, even hundreds, of happy 44 Auto Mag owners around the world. The acceptance of this (stainless steel) pistol has been remarkable, by all accounts, with over 8000 orders on hand before the first gun was shipped.

The 44 Auto Mag, of excellent workmanship, shows fully modern design-engineering and years of hard work on the part of Harry Sanford.

Although massive, the pistol is well-balanced, and can be comfortably fired with one hand, using 18 grains of Norma 1020 powder pushing a 240-gr. bullet at 1475 fps. The action itself is in two basic parts— the barrel/receiver assembly and the bolt/ frame assembly.

The barrel/receiver assembly sports a full length integral vent rib, the unit electronically welded together. There's a fully adjustable serrated square blade rear sight and a ramp front.

The test gun had stippled front and back straps but later models will be grooved, similar to other popular pistols. The black polyurethane grips show sharp checkering, and conform closely to the 45 auto grips, but the web section is a little uncomfortable for me. Those with larger hands would have no problem.

The action, basically a short-recoil, rotary bolt system, appears like that of the M16 rifle. On firing an accelerator and recoil unlocks the bolt. This compresses the recoil springs, located on each side of the frame, ejects the fired case and, on the bolt's return picks up a fresh round, engages the locking splines and puts the gun in battery. The rising magazine follower locks the bolt open on the last shot. The test gun worked smoothly and reliably, with minimum recoil; the same load fired in a revolver would give much more recoil.

Unlike revolvers, there's no gas leakage in the 44 Auto Mag, so greater velocity from the 6½" barrel results.

When the barrel assembly is removed, the complete bolt unit is exposed for cleaning and lubrication. This is quickly done by locking the bolt to the rear, then releasing the catch on the left front of the frame and sliding the barrel assembly forward. The bolt has 6 locking lugs, operating within the frame by means of a large pin inserted through a cam slot in the bolt body to provide rotation and retention. The trigger linkage is similar to that of popular contemporary target arms of the 22 rimfire variety. All screws are Allen-head type, flush seated for a clean, neat look.

The Auto Mag handled loads ranging from 8 grains of Unique to 18 grains of Norma's 1020, the last pushing a 240-gr. bullet at 1450 fps. Consistent 10-ring accuracy at 50 yards is commonplace, the gun hand held and the shooting witnessed by me. At this time the big boomer is being tested on big game by Auto Mag's Gerry Ogniebene, Executive Vice President (and professional hunters). One-shot clean kills have been reported at ranges up to 100 yards.

The ammo this new pistol uses is called, unsurprisingly, the 44 Auto Mag, the rimless cases made from 308 rifle brass cut to 1.30" long and reamed to a wall thickness of .015". Dies and reamers are or will be available for making and tooling your own, but factory ammo is supposed to be available from Norma Precision, as well as primed brass and components. W. Rickell

---

44 Auto Mag Specifications

Barrel: 6½"
Rifling: 1 turn in 18", 8 grooves
Sights: Adj. rear, white outlined, non-glare ramp front, on full-length vent rib
Action: Short recoil, 6-lug rotary bolt
Magazine cap.: 7 rounds
Stocks: Polyurethane, checkered
Trigger: Fully adj., grooved
Hammer: Exposed, deeply knurled
Finish: Satin stainless steel
Over-all: 11½"
Price: $247.50
Special Features:
All stainless construction, quick take down, won't fire unless completely in battery. Quick action safety, grooved straps for non-slip grip, inertial firing pin. Functions with light or heavy loads without changing recoil springs, bolt locks open after last shot.

Charter Arms latest offering—the Undercoverette in 32 S&W Long caliber.

Bernardelli Model 69 target autoloader in 22 Long Rifle.

Benet Arms/Gold Rush

Bill Edwards continues to handle the full line of full-scale, metal non-guns made in Japan. Most parts function the same as the original arm, and they come complete with cartridges which can be loaded with paper caps and fired. No permits are necessary and 18 types offered are mailable, from $12.95 for a Walther PPK to $49.95 for a full size Schmeisser MP40. For UNCLE fans there is even a Walther P-38 set complete with eight accessories for $49.50.

Edwards also handles a full line of sporting and target arms, including the 9mm MAB P.15S and P.15 "Competition" pistols, and the 9mm or 7.65mm SIG P210 pistols in 4 models, these priced from $197 to $249, plus the 22 LR conversion kit at $119. The P.15 has a 16-round capacity, a nice solid feel, and accuracy equal to or better than most handguns in its price range. The SIG P210 is without a doubt the ultimate autoloading pistol in 9mm caliber; the quality of workmanship is what one would expect from a country known for watchmaking—excellent, with precision fitting, as is the conversion kit. Of 7 rimfire conversion units tested by this writer for various pistols and one revolver, the SIG model proved to be the most accurate and fastest to assemble on the basic handgun.

The Bernardelli 69 is a dressed-up target version of the M60 autoloader. Chambered for the 22 LR, the M69 has large wraparound walnut stocks, with thumbrest and checkering; the checkering is deep and even, but the diamond tops are flat. The front strap of the grip is grooved and the 10-round magazine has a finger-rest floorplate. The barrel is 5.9", and fastened to it via a crossbolt is a ribbed balance weight. The weight appears to be a part of the slide, but is actually slung below the barrel so the front of the slide fits into its countersunk rear surface. The top of the weight is fitted with a grooved sight rib, housing a fully adjustable rear sight and replaceable front sight; sight radius is 7".

Accuracy of the M69 at 25 yards, fired from the bench with sandbag wrist rests, ranged between 2$\frac{1}{16}$" and 3$\frac{1}{16}$" for 5-shot groups, using 5 brands of ammunition. No difficulty with feeding or ejection was experienced during the firing of 300 rounds.

Priced at $99.50, the M69 comes with a spare magazine, hex wrench for balance-weight removal, small screwdriver, cleaning rod, small plastic oil container, and 2 spare front sight blades of different widths.

Browning's new 380 auto pistol has adjustable sights, magazine with shelf, longer barrel.

Charter Arms

Two new items have appeared since the 25th GD—the Dual Pathfinder and the Undercoverette—and there may be another by the time you read this. The first lists at $110 and consists of the Pathfinder 22 with 3-inch barrel, and an extra cylinder chambered for the 22 WRM cartridge. Hand-checkered walnut Bulldog stocks are standard and both cylinders are 6-shot. Sights consist of a serrated ramp front blade and a snag-free, fully adjustable square notch rear. The $80 Undercoverette is chambered for the 32 S&W long cartridge, is identical to the UndercoverR except for the caliber, weighs ½-ounce more and has a 6-shot cylinder instead of a 5-shot one. Sights are the serrated ramp front and a fixed square notch rear; barrel length is 2 inches. Both the Dual Pathfinder and the Undercoverette feature the exclusive lifetime unbreakable firing pin.

The third new item is a 5-shot heavy-caliber model similar to the UndercoverR. It would have been available several months earlier but Doug McClenahan—the man behind the UndercoverR basic design—was in a serious accident. Doug is a very talented gent and his loss would have been felt by the entire shooting world. Doug is recovering slowly, and in due time the new model will be ready. The drawings this writer has examined call for a slightly larger model chambered for the 44 special cartridge and possibly for the 357 Magnum. Which caliber will be first hasn't been decided definitely as this is written (late December '70). Regardless, the new model will have a 5-shot cylinder and 3-inch barrel.   LS

Browning

Browning was understandably miffed when GCA '68 forbade importation of their fine 60-year-old-design 380 Pocket Model autoloader. Beautifully finished and quite reliable, it was the favorite of many, those who carried a small auto as a hideout or spare gun. It is back now, revised to comply with the regulations, but hardly recognizable as the get of its trim father. Barrel and slide have been lengthened about ¾", and it has adjustable target-type sights, these appearing to be the same as those on the Browning Nomad 22 RF autoloader. In addition, the extractor has been changed so as to protrude and function as a cartridge indicator when there is a round in the chamber, and a very shallow thumb rest has been added to the left stock plate. The excellence is still all there, but the added length and frills make it far less desirable than its daddy as a pocket defense gun. As John Amber and I looked it over closely at the NSGA show, we were both convinced that it is now too good for the 380 cartridge, and should be adapted to the 22 LR, thus making a very fine all-purpose gun. In fact, if time permits, we just might gather round John's basement lathe and do a little converting on our own.

This matched pair of Lee/Grant commemoratives, in 1851 Navy Model styles marks the first production of percussion revolvers by Colt's in 75 years. These commemorative issues are also available separately in walnut cases with authentic accessories.

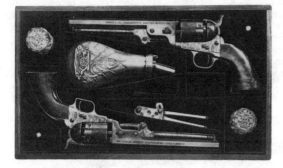

Colt's NRA Commemoratives. There are 6 variations of the Single Action Army plus the Gold Cup National Match 45.

New Colt's Trooper Model

All of the former options on Colt's Trooper MK II revolver are now standard, but the price tag is below comparable competitive models. Target hammers, triggers and stocks are now standard features on the new Trooper MK III 357 Magnum/38 Spl. double action revolver.

The Trooper MK III is also available in highly polished nickel finish with blued steel trigger and sights. The hammer is color case-hardened, and the top is glare-proof plated for easier sighting.

The blued MK III is $142, the nickeled version $149.95.

New All-Steel Colt Auto

The Combat-Commander has an all-steel frame, and a straight mainspring housing with a lanyard loop rather than an arched housing.

The all-steel frame has increased the alloy Commander's total weight by about 9 ounces, and provides a better-holding gun for competitive shooting. In addition the new Combat Commander—offered in 45 ACP, 38 Super and 9mm—will have wood stocks, not the plastic ones formerly used.

Available with blue or satin-nickel finish, the Colt C.C. sells for $125.00.

Colt's NRA Centennial Models

Colt is honoring the 100th anniversary of the National Rifle Association with a Seven Gun Salute!

The new Colt Commemoratives consist of six variations of the famous Single Action Army "Peacemaker" and the 45-caliber Gold Cup National Match automatic pistol, both a tribute to the NRA and the American shooter.

The Colt SAA will have three traditional barrel lengths—4¾", 5½" and 7½", and two calibers, 45 Colt and 357 Magnum. This is the first commemorative gun to be issued in 357 Magnum caliber. The Gold Cup National Match, made in 45 caliber only, is the first Gold Cup commemorative. Blued finish only. The Single Action Army variations have Colt's color case-hardened frames.

The left side of the Gold Cup receiver is inscribed in two lines, "1871 - NRA Centennial - 1971 / The First 100 Years of Service." The right side of the receiver reads "Gold Cup National Match," with a symbol of a gold loving cup. "1871 - NRA Centennial - 1971" appears on the Single Action Armys. All inscriptions are etched in gold, and all 7 guns have NRA medallions imbedded in the grips.

All of the Colt NRA guns are presented in genuine walnut cases, the lids fitted with an official NRA Centennial medallion embedded in Lucite, and it is visible on the inside of the lid as well. The box also carries the Serpentine Colt Medallion in antique gold and an old gold velvet lining.

For the first time in some 75 years, percussion revolvers are being made under Colt's blue dome in Hartford, Conn.

The Colt 1851 Navy revolver, easily the most popular of all Colt percussion guns, is now in production—and made as well to the most authentic specifications and quality standards.

The guns will be available initially as commemorative issues—one as the Robert E. Lee Commemorative, the other the Ulysses S. Grant Commemorative. They will be sold separately, and as a matched pair.

The guns will match 1851 Navy Model specifications in all particulars—36 caliber, with 7½" octagon barrel and right hand, 7-groove twist. The unfluted cylinder carries the Naval scene honoring the successful engagement of the Texas Navy with Mexican ships. COLT'S PATENT and the serial number is on one line, under which is "Engraved by W. L. Ormsby, New York." Encircling the front outer edge of the cylinder is the inscription, "Engaged 16 May 1843."

The frames combine color case-hardening and Royal blue; back straps and trigger guards are silver-plated, and the grips are one piece. The Lee model has a round trigger guard, the Grant model a square-back guard. Serial numbers will start at 251 REL and run to 5000 REL for the Lee and 251 USG to 5000 USG on the Grant. Only 250 matched pairs will be issued, serial numbers from 1 GLP to 250 GLP.

Presentation cases, of American walnut for all three styles, carry a Colt serpentine medallion embedded in the lower right corner of the lid, and a two line inscription, branded in the lid center, reads, "Robert E. Lee Commemorative/Nineteen Hundred Seventy One." A similar inscription is branded on the Grant case. For the matched pair, the 3-line center-lid inscription reads "Ulysses S. Grant/Robert E. Lee/Nineteen Hundred Seventy One." In the bottom left corner of the lid is the inscription, "Matched Pair." The case is grey-velvet lined, while the Grant has a blue-velvet lining. The matched-pair case shows a burgundy colored lining.

Each case, compartmented in keeping with its 1851 predecessor, contains a powder flask, bullet mould, nipple wrench, cap box and balls. The flask is made by Dixon in England, where the original 1851 Navy flasks were manufactured.

New Colt Single Action 22s

Two newly-designed single action 22 revolvers, the Peacemaker and the New Frontier, are now available—or soon should be.

Both are ⅞-scale models of the big 45 SAA counterparts, and have many feature of the latter, including frame.

Both guns offer a new and patented bolt-lockup system, the most durable and simplest of its kind ever produced by Colt's. The new guns are also of all-steel construction, no alloy parts. Outside, the new Colt 22s show Colt's quality blue finish and a color case-hardened frame. The New Frontier 22 has the adjustable Colt Accro sight at the back, and a ramp-style serrated front. The frame-design protects the rear sight.

Barrel lengths for both guns are 4¾", 6" and 7½". The ejector rod housing has been redesigned so that the ejector rod head fits snugly against the barrel, preventing any catching or snagging.

Both handle 22 Shorts, Long, and Long Rifle cartridges, and a 22 Magnum (WMR) dual cylinder is available. Grips are regular SAA hard rubber design with an embossed eagle.

Day Arms

Day Arms Corp. (7515 Stagecoach Lane, San Antonio, Texas 78227) makers of the "30-X Conversion" for 45 Colt autos, does 45 accuracy jobs also. A new service is installation of a "Gold Cup" adjustable rear sight and a low ramp front sight on Gov't Model guns or slides. The ramp front is silver soldered on, while the rear dovetail is filled in, then slots are milled for the GC rear sight. $28.50 is the tab, but that covers the necessary rebluing, too. This job puts the sights lower on the standard "Gold Cup," and a rounded rear sight blade is available, one that won't catch or snag on clothing. Only the slide is needed, so shipping is no problem: Prices will be quoted on other custom work.

Day 30X Test

Our own test sample of the Day 30X 22 LR Conversion unit arrived too late to give it an extended test. Attaching the unit to a GI 45 was quick and simple, just as the makers said it would be. In fact, it took considerably longer to disassemble the tuned 45, a special tool having to be used to remove the oversized barrel bushing. It was an equally fast job to convert the 45 magazines—the 5-shot adaptors snapped in on top of the regular follower without a hitch of any kind.

Fifty rounds of CCI High Speed cartridges were shot from 25 yards in 5-shot strings. I sat down, used a 2-hand hold with my elbows on my knees—no gun rest as such. The largest groups ran about 2", the smallest just over an inch. The over-all average ran 1⅝", the shots printing into fairly round groups. Functioning was perfect, no bobbles, no failures to feed or eject.

I regret I couldn't try the Day outfit on a Gold Cup or NM Colt. My old (WW I) 1911 auto allowed sideways movement between the frame and the Day slide, hardly conducive to best accuracy.

The Day 30X appears to be a fully reliable, accurate shooting accessory for the 45 ACP shooter, made to order for those who want 22 LR practice with it.   JTA

The Electroarm

Independent Research and Development, Inc. (6304 Locker Lane, San Antonio, Tex. 78238) has started production on the electric trigger free pistol designed and pioneered by Major Franklin Greene of USAF Pistol Team fame. Introduced during the 1964 Olympics held in Tokyo, his first effort was a Hammerli converted to an electric trigger. Later, 5 prototypes, built by Major Greene, were used in all American and Olympic free pistol competition, and they hold all American records.

The latest Greene pistol, while essentially the original design, differs in the grip configuration and the total encasement of the external wiring. Although the orthopedic-type grip pictured will be available, a newly-designed grip assembly, like that of the 45 Gov't. auto, will then be on production models. This will, then, permit a greater variety of shapes and styles.

The new pistol is a single shot, bolt action type, chambered for the 22 Long Rifle cartridge. Over-all length is 15 inches with a 9½ inch barrel, weight with the orthopedic grips is about 52 ounces. Deluxe Bo-Mar sights are standard. Steel parts are a dull, matte blue, the aluminum parts red anodized. The power supply is a 15-volt battery, housed in the grip, reportedly good for some 2500 rounds. The trigger is simply an electric switch, so there's no trigger travel; merely touching the switch activates the sear, releasing the firing pin. This takes a total of .004 seconds (4 milliseconds) from trigger to ignition. Total firing pin travel is .150 (150-thousandths) inch.

The Electroarm consists of three major parts, each independent of the other. These are the barrel/receiver assembly, grip assembly (housing the electrical components and battery) and the switch/trigger guard assembly. Each can be adjusted independently of each other to give the shooter the fit and feel that's right for him. The barrel assembly has a long bottom dovetail on which the grip travels fore and aft to give the desired balance, which is achieved without changing weight, sight picture or point of impact. The trigger guard can also be independently moved to attain the proper feel and fit. The internal parts and the bolt mechanism are completely sealed, so very little cleaning is required. The bolt assembly is permanently lubricated as well.

Electroarm grip recess houses battery and other electric components.

Each unit is functionally connected by electrical wiring only. Trigger letoff is adjustable from 2 grams to 4 ounces, but no matter what the pull is the electrical components always work the same.

There are two major safeties on the pistol: A) the gun cannot be fired until the bolt is at least 90% closed; B) the firing mechanism cannot be activated until the microswitch in the base of the grip is depressed.

Initial production of the Electroarm will total only 200 units, these cased with proper accessories and selling for about $550 each. A deposit of $100 is required, with serial number allocation on a first-come, first-served basis. Deliveries will begin in the spring of 1972.

Following this limited production a standard model will be offered at a much lower—but not yet set—price, and there will also be a rifle built on the same principle.   Walter L. Rickell

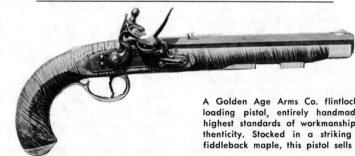

A Golden Age Arms Co. flintlock muzzle-loading pistol, entirely handmade to the highest standards of workmanship and authenticity. Stocked in a striking piece of fiddleback maple, this pistol sells for $195.

Golden Age Arms Co.

I saw and handled many of the numerous products this specialty firm makes or distributes during my visit to the 1971 NRA meetings. I can therefore assure you that quality, genuine usefulness and good-value-for-money are guiding principles with Jim Johnston, the new proprietor. Their big catalog—154 pages, plus index— is filled with hundreds of items for the muzzle-loading shooter, plus an extensive listing of books on black powder shooting and kindred subjects.

Barrels are a major product at Golden Age, these 44" long octagonal, rifled with 7 grooves making 1 turn in 48", and special-ly cut for round ball use. Pistol barrels of ML type are also offered, while complete rifles in the Pennsylvania-Kentucky style (see illustration) are another main specialty, these offered as kits or completed arms at various prices. In addition, Jim offers the widest range I've seen of locks—flint or caplock—triggers, rifle and pistol furniture of every kind, including at least 10 different patchboxes, knives and tomahawks, ad infinitum. I doubt if there's anything having to do with ML firearms that can't be found in the Golden Age catalog— there's even a good range of ML cannon! Send $1 to Box 82, Worthington, O. 43085.   JTA

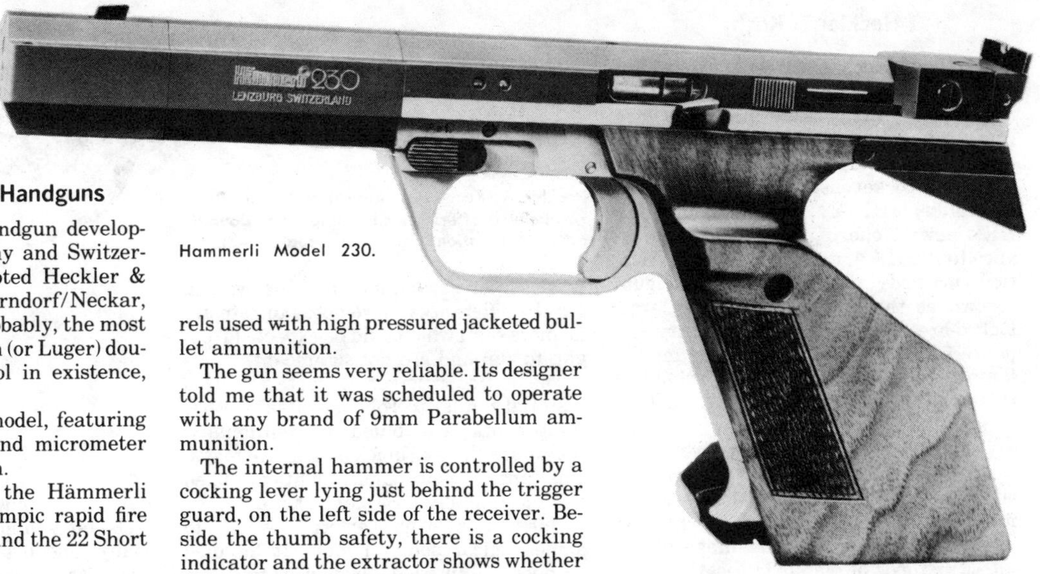

Hammerli Model 230.

Two New European Handguns

The latest European handgun developments come from Germany and Switzerland. In Germany, the noted Heckler & Koch company, from Oberndorf/Neckar, has introduced what is, probably, the most advanced 9mm Parabellum (or Luger) double action automatic pistol in existence, the Model P9S.

A single action target model, featuring interchangeable barrels and micrometer rear sight, will follow soon.

The Swiss handgun is the Hämmerli 230, a very advanced Olympic rapid fire pistol expressely built around the 22 Short cartridge.

The H&K pistol, which I checked out in Oberndorf, had an excellent 3-lb. single action pull and an 8-lb. DA pull, outstanding on a service type automatic pistol. There is some take-up before the single action pull, as in most automatic pistols, but the DA pull is smooth and quite long, without the final hard point of the Mauser HSC or Le Francais models, for instance. Trigger finger position is good for small to medium hands in single action, but is quite extended in double action because of the long pull required to obtain a smooth cocking stroke.

The H&K P9S has several other unusual characteristics: Operated on the delayed blow-back principle of the H&K German G3 service rifle, the new auto features a 2-piece bolt operated by rollers located inside a stamped sheet-metal slide. The non-recoiling barrel, easily removable by hand, is of revolutionary construction; instead of being normally rifled, its bore is polygonal! The accuracy of the specimen tested was of the highest level. Wear resistance is most unusual, for I was shown two sample guns which had fired 20,000 and 23,000 rounds of mixed European ammunition during endurance tests performed in Germany. These figures are extremely high for bar-rels used with high pressured jacketed bullet ammunition.

The gun seems very reliable. Its designer told me that it was scheduled to operate with any brand of 9mm Parabellum ammunition.

The internal hammer is controlled by a cocking lever lying just behind the trigger guard, on the left side of the receiver. Beside the thumb safety, there is a cocking indicator and the extractor shows whether there is a round in the chamber. The receiver and most of the lockwork components consist of steel stampings.

The P9S was test shot off-hand, using GECO (German) ammunition. Most rounds went into a 4" circle at 25 meters (27 yards), which is excellent. The production grip is a bit too straight and too big for my smallish hand. In double action, an 8" circle was consistently hit at the same range, again very good for DA shooting.

This gun seems quite intricate for a service model in view of its bolt system and of the leverage required to get a smooth double-action pull, but field stripping is very easy. In spite of its unusual appearance, the H&K P9S has so many appealing features that it will certainly enjoy a big commercial success in its class.

The Hammerli Model 230 is full of gadgets for the Olympic rapid fire shooter. The light steel bolt slides into a precision machined steel receiver, which carries the barrel and the balance weights. The trigger pull is adjustable down to 150 grams (about 5 oz.). Adjustment screws are also provided for trigger slack, backlash, sear and hammer engagement. Three trigger lengths are available, providing the best finger position for virtually every shooter.

The wrap-around walnut stocks are made with a fixed thumb rest, an adjustable palm rest and a spring-operated rubber tang pressing against the shooter's hand on firing. The stainless steel magazine's sturdy lips can be checked for proper spacing with a very clever composite tool.

Beside the usual balance weights sliding over the barrel, a highly sophisticated recoil compensator is provided; gas is taken off through two pair of ports, located on both sides of the barrel (at 1.26" and 1.52" from the breech) the gas driven through two stainless steel tubes, acting also as balance weight guides, into the front balance weight, which has two upper vent holes acting as a muzzle brake. This very efficient device does not impair accuracy.

The pre-production sample, testfired in the Lenzburg factory, operated perfectly with the German RWS and Swiss 22 Short ammunition available. Slide operation is very fast, trigger pull excellent and muzzle climb is minimal. Workmanship, of course, is beautiful. Raymond Caranta.

Hämmerli M230 Olympic Pistol

Technical Data

Caliber:	22 Short
Over-all:	11.38" (295mm)
Barrel:	6.3" (160mm)
Height:	5.7" (145mm)
Width:	1.9" (49mm)
Mag. cap.:	6 rounds
Slide stop:	Optional
Weight empty:	44 oz. (1240 grammes)
Trigger pull:	Adj. 5 to 11 oz. (150-300 grammes) Trigger slack, sear engagement and backlash adj. screws.
Sight radius:	10.0" (253mm)
Sights:	⅛" U-notch rear in removable leaf, click adj. for windage and elevation. (1 click = 10mm (.4") at 25 meters (27 yards); ⅛" wide, square, undercut front.
Features:	Balance weights: special muzzle brake; 3 trigger lengths; 2 standard stock options plus custom stocks.

H&K P9S Auto Pistol

Technical Data

Caliber:	9mm Parabellum (Luger)
Over-all:	7.6"
Barrel:	4.0"
Height:	5.4"
Width:	1.3"
Mag. release:	Under butt.
Mag. cap.:	9 rounds
Mag. Ident.:	Single row box type with 7 counting holes and sliding floorplate. Marked "P9" at bottom front end of left side.
Slide stop:	Cocking lever controls slide release when magazine is empty.
Wt., empty:	32½ oz. approx.
Trigger pull:	SA, 3 lb., DA, 8 lb.
Sight radius:	5.8"
Sights:	⅛" square notch rear; ⅛" serrated square blade front, both dovetailed in slide.
Finish:	Blued metal. Wrap-around plastic stock. Front strap, trigger guard and lower surface of receiver plastic coated.
Features:	Thumb type safety; loading/cocking indicators. Selective double action.
Thumb Safety:	Left side of slide in serrated area.
Receiver:	Steel stamping.
Construction:	Internal hammer. Cocking lever on left side of receiver, behind trigger guard. Roller hesitation lock. Removable non-recoiling barrel.

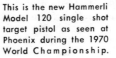

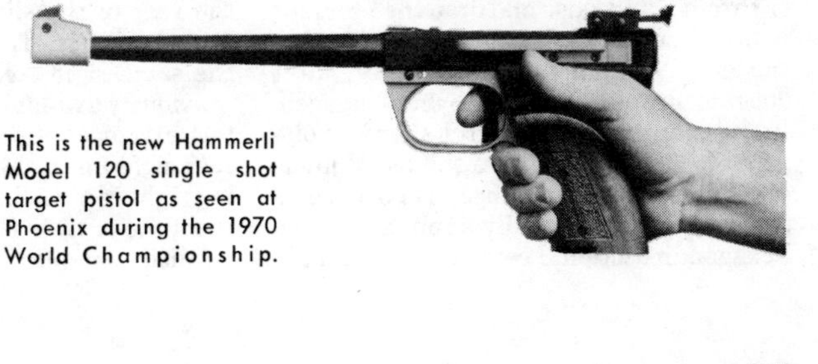

This is the new Hammerli Model 120 single shot target pistol as seen at Phoenix during the 1970 World Championship.

Heckler & Koch

Heckler & Koch is a West German firm mainly devoted to the production of German military weapons. Several years back it generated considerable comment by introducing the multi-calibered HK-4 double-action pocket pistol. (H&R now offer a two-caliber HK—22 LR and 380 ACP.) HK's newest offering, similar in appearance to the HK-4, uses some basic fabrication methods pioneered in that gun. Known as the P-9, it is a rather large, locked-breech, double-action, military and police type autoloader chambered for the 9mm Parabellum round. HK says that late this year initial production of a 45 ACP version will begin.

The P-9 uses steel stampings welded to castings and machined parts to form the slide and receiver. Other parts are also formed by stamping, casting, and sintering where possible to take advantage of the latest methods of metals fabrication.

The barrel is fixed rigidly to the receiver; in full battery the slide is locked to a barrel extension by two vertical steel rollers riding in a separate breechblock inside the slide. The rollers are cammed out into seats in the barrel extension by a wedge-shaped finger extending forward between them. When a cartridge is fired, the cartridge case thrusts rearward against the breech face, and this thrust is diverted through the rollers and angled cam surfaces into rearward movement of the slide body; this withdraws the finger from between the rollers, unlocking the breechblock from the barrel extension so that the slide may carry it back also. While this system does not provide positive mechanical locking of the breech, the breechblock is forced to remain in full contact with the barrel for a short time while the slide starts moving, during which time the bullet does leave the barrel and pressure drops to an acceptable level. This same system is satisfactory with other HK weapons handling all manner of cartridges up through the 50 caliber Browning. Thus it is more than adequate for the 33,000 psi maximum chamber pressure of the 9mm Parabellum load.

Externally the P-9 looks very much like an overgrown Walther PP with its hammer spur hidden. The fully enclosed hammer is incorporated into an unusual double/single-action lockwork design with quite a long trigger travel. An indicator pin protrudes through the back of the receiver when the hammer is cocked, and a button on the extractor rises to be seen or felt when a round is chambered. The cocked hammer may be safely lowered on a chambered round by means of a cocking lever protruding forward from under the left stock; this same lever may later be used to re-cock the hammer for deliberate fire. Alternatively, simply pulling the trigger through will raise and drop the hammer to fire. A separate thumb safety is fitted to the left side of the slide ala Walther, but it does *not* drop the hammer when engaged.

The stainless steel barrel shows "polygonal" rifling rather than the usual lands and grooves. At first glance the bore seems smooth, but it is actually a much-rounded hexagon in section. Less friction and high-

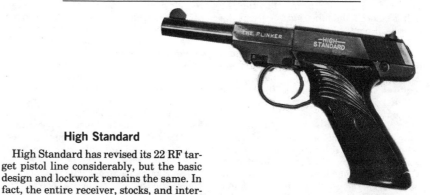

Heckler & Koch P9S Auto Pistol, cal. 9mm Parabellum, offers selective single- or double-action operation, other unusual features.

er velocities are claimed for this system, but the differences we've noted to date are no more than what could be expected from gun to gun and are not significant.

The entire receiver is coated with a material similar to Teflon, while the other components are blued conventionally. Stocks are checked black plastic and magazine capacity is 9 rounds. Sights are fixed and open, amply large for quick use.

Our sample P-9 has performed well from a mechanical point of view. It handled without malfunction a wide variety of factory and handloaded ammunition, and delivered satisfactory accuracy. The stock profile, plus trigger reach and travel, make double-action firing hard for anyone with-

out large hands or long fingers. The grip feels boxy and a bit uncomfortable to many, and over-all appearance leaves a good bit to be desired aesthetically. However, it's an advanced, efficient handgun.

A few P-9s were imported by Centennial Arms, but those may be all for a while. The $200 price rather limits the P-9's appeal.

High Standard

High Standard has revised its 22 RF target pistol line considerably, but the basic design and lockwork remains the same. In fact, the entire receiver, stocks, and internal parts are simply those of the Citation Military Model in existence for several years. The changes are elsewhere.

The new HS model, called the Victor, carries a slab-sided barrel (virtually rectangular in section but quite deep) that matches the receiver width. Atop this new barrel is a full-length ventilated sighting rib. It extends back over the slide, which has been reduced in height for that purpose. The slide now reciprocates in a tunnel formed between receiver and rib. The micrometer rear sight is installed at the

High Standard's newest auto, the Plinker.

In the revolver line High Standard has revised its old Sentinel design to produce what is now called the "22 Kit Gun." It is a 9-shot, double-action, solid-frame, swing-out cylinder revolver with a fairly small frame and adjustable sights. It is intended as a plinking and fun gun, something to take along on fishing and hunting trips, not as a serious target arm. As such, it does the job nicely at a price substantially less than the classic S&W Kit Gun.

rear of the rib extension, placing it over the rear of the slide in the generally accepted position. This places both sights on the same rigid steel base, something not previously available on High Standard pistols except at the expense of putting the rear sight up on the barrel and thus reducing sight radius. Barrel length is 5½", and the time-proven HS barrel quick-change method remains.

9-shot Kit Gun from High Standard.

Cattleman single action revolver from LA Distr.

Western Valley Arms Co. offers the K25 automatic.

Llama Model IXA in 45 ACP with grip safety from Stoeger.

Intercontinental Arms

Dakota single-action revolvers, made by Hammerli in Switzerland, have been imported by Intercontinental Arms for some time. These were basically good, serviceable copies of the venerable Single Action Colt, and as such were well-known and liked for some time. Now, though, they're being made with a manual hammer safety, which takes much of the accidental-firing onus off the design. This good design consists of a simple knurled sleeve, rotating around a pin in the hammer. When rolled forward, the sleeve strikes the receiver and stops the hammer short of striking the primer of a chambered cartridge; rolled backward, the sleeve presents a flat which does *not* strike the reciever, and so allows the firing pin to strike the primer. Simple and effective.

LA Distributors

Cattleman SAA Colt copies marketed by LA Distributors also have a safety added—this is an automatic one, enclosed by the frame, and functioning so that the hammer can not fall far enough to strike a primer unless the trigger is held fully rearward. This is also an excellent addition to the basic design. It will make for safer handling, particularly among those less-knowledgeable enthusiasts who buy the Frontier Colt or its copies for romantic appeal rather then mechanical excellence.

Sterling Arms

Sterling Arms is another one of the new firms to rise up over the past few years in spite of handgun controls. Last year it introduced a line of conventional blowback 22 rimfire autoloading pistols reminiscent of the old High-Standard Model HDM—not that many, if any, of them were seen about. This year they've got a 380 ACP pocket pistol. It looks for all the world as if someone had taken a hacksaw to the ex-

isting Sterling 22 auto, lopped off the barrel flush with the front of the receiver, then amputated about an inch from the bottom of the butt. Between the two saw-cuts, the gun is identical to the 22. The external hammer remains, and rudimentary fixed sights are fitted.

The resulting gun looks a bit odd, perhaps as if it had been designed 40 or more years ago, but it does function well with standard round-nose full-jacket 380 cartridges—though with less energy and velocity than more conventional 380s. It is a bit muzzle-light compared to such pistols as Llama, Walther, Mauser, et al. Still, it is the only pistol of this caliber in U.S. production at this time—not to mention that most of the more advanced foreign designs command $30-odd dollars more over the counter.

Stoeger

The Llama Model XIV (in caliber 380) also got the heave-ho in 1968 from the Alcohol & Tobacco people in its original form, but it's now back in new guise, imported by Stoeger as before. This locked-breech, miniature copy of the Colt Gov't. Model 45 now carries a cartridge indicator in the top of the slide, thumb-rest stocks, and an adjustable rear sight in order to qualify for importation under the new rules.

In this instance, over-all characteristics, size and handling have not suffered from the changes, so it is as useful as ever as a second or hideout gun—for which purpose scores of police officers known to me use it.

After an absence of over 15 years, another Llama auto pistol has returned to the U.S. market as an apparent result of the GCA '68. This is the Model XI "Especial" in 9mm Parabellum (Luger) caliber. Where other Llamas are line-for-line Colt Gov't. Model copies, the M-XI has a solid back strap, a pivoted trigger and single sear bar/disconnector, external hook-type extractor, and it's substantially smaller

than the 45/38 Llama. In fact, it resembles nothing so much as the competitive 9mm Star Model B. In function and design the lockwork is identical to the Star. Being smaller and lighter than the big Llamas, the M-XI is a much more comfortable-carrying gun, and it will safely and reliably handle all the current crop of high-performance 9mm ammunition. Years ago I carried a Model XI in some interesting parts of the world. It never let me down, and I grew quite fond of the design.

Western Valley Arms Co.

Western Valley Arms Co. is another new firm caused by GCA '68 to get into pistol making. Recognizing the dearth of domestic very small pistols, WVA has developed a true pocket/purse size, 25 ACP selfloader, a mere 4" over-all.

Called the K25, it presents nothing new from mechanical, design, or technological viewpoints. It is best described as an approximate copy of the Colt/Browning 25 once so popular. In the interest of simplicity, it eliminates the grip safety and uses a push-through rather than a pivoted manual safety. Construction is of steel throughout, with smooth wood stocks. Takedown is traditional Browning, finish is blue. This is a simple, sound, utilitarian pistol for those who like tiny guns and cartridges. Price is good, for these days, about $55.

The K-25 is a new American-made 25 ACP caliber autoloader that's light and compact—4 inches over-all, weight is only 8 ounces, yet the frame and slide are of steel. The magazine holds 6 rounds, there's a push-button safety and a cocking indicator. No sights as such—the top of the slide has a matt finish channel for sighting. The metal carries a high-luster blue, while the smooth grips are made of Cycolac.

We've had no sample so far, but the exclusive distributor—Western Valley Arms Co., 524 W. Main St., Alhambra, Ca. 91801—say that the K-25 has passed rigid safety and performance tests. Retail, $54.50.

Accessories

Time was when handgun accessories were few indeed—new sights, trigger shoes and custom stocks. Today, though, there are more than you can count. We'll list as many as space permits.

Caraville Arms has introduced a squeeze-cocking device called the Double-Ace for Colt GI 45 (also 38 Super and 9mm) in all its variations, and for the *exact* foreign copies. It is assembled to a stainless steel housing which replaces *both* the grip safety and mainspring housing. With the hammer at rest, the bottom of the housing is held rearward; squeezing depresses the housing and compresses the mainspring to cock the hammer; whereupon trigger pressure fires the gun. Or, with the trigger depressed and the hammer at forward, squeezing the housing raises and drops the hammer to fire. An unusual system, and a practical one for those who can handle the greater fore-and-aft dimensions given the gun by the Double-Ace. About $40, reasonable enough.

Dan Dwyer produces unusual Colt GM barrels in 45 only (though I suppose he would not object to making one in 38 Super). In addition to matched barrel/bushing sets for serious competition, he offers the same quality barrels in 6" and 7¼" length with a proper target front sight installed on the barrel muzzle. This allows maximum sight radius with the longer barrels without excessive slide modification. Dwyer prefers to fit all barrels and bushings to the slide in his own shop for best results. Dwyer is also designer and maker of the Group Gripper, which generally produces noticeably improved accuracy in any GI 45, 38, or 9mm (won't fit Commander). It consists of a special toothed barrel link and modified recoil-spring guide containing a powerful flat spring which places the link under load. This is a drop-in unit anyone can install. Another Dwyer product is a *semi-arched* mainspring housing which suits many people better than either the flat or arched originals.

Colt Commander cutaway shows functioning of Caraville Arms squeeze-cocking device.

Armand Swensen offers a boon to the southpaw shooter of the big autos. It is his ambidexterous safety which places a well-shaped thumb safety lever on the right side of the gun as well as the left. Swensen is probably better known for his superb custom-conversions of the 45 Colt Auto and Browning H-P for combat shooting.

Seventrees Ltd. offers a unique conversion kit for the double-action S&W M39 9mm auto to improve its combat utility. This comprises a shortened and lightened slide and barrel (3¼") mounting the special, patented Seventrees combat sight. This entire unit slips right into place on the standard M39, shortening it ¾" and reducing weight noticeably. Seventrees will also further modify the entire gun extensively, reducing weight to 20 ounces, height by ½", and length by another ½", and calls the end products the ASP. The unique Seventrees combat sight is a single block broken by a tapered groove lined with reflective or flourescent material. One simply aligns the target in or over the groove (notch) so that equal amounts of reflective material are visible around the notch at both sides and bottom. Very fast and effective, especially in poor light. It is not a long range sight.

Scopes for handguns, once seen destined for very limited use, seem to be coming back slightly. Hutson Corp. is now delivering a very compact and effective model and, of course, the original Bushnell Phantom is still available. The Hutson Handgunner, now offered only in 1x or unit power, will soon have a companion of close to 2x.

Many owners of obsolete autoloading pistols have often bemoaned the fact that replacement magazines were a great problem. The magazine is not only the most perishable part, but is easily lost or mislaid. Triple K Mfg. Co. now offers replacement magazines for just about any pistol you can name. As this is written, new-production magazines can be supplied for over 800 models and calibers. Moreover, if you do come up with something they can't fit from stock, they'll build you a custom magazine very reasonably.

Probably the most significant parts/accessory offers have been the *new* aluminum alloy and steel M1911A1 45 Auto frames from A&R Sales and Potomac Arms respectively. Both frames, basically investment castings, are machined in critical areas. We've built guns on both and they work quite well. Both were brought out so those with a stock of cheap ("liberated," often) 45 parts could build a gun. Properly done, this produces a serviceable gun, *assuming* all those surplus small parts are correct to begin with. That isn't always a safe assumption, however, for some of that stuff is junk. If you elect to make up a gun this way, better pay a competent gunsmith to put it together and check everything thoroughly.

Aside from all that, dozens of small firms now offer a wide variety of handgun accessories and replacement parts. Even the major makers now offer more options than ever before.

S&W M39 conversion by Seventrees, Ltd. is shorter and lighter in weight and more easily concealable.

Walnut stock for Colt cap and ball revolver from Navy Arms.

Numrich

Numrich Arms is now making new replacement barrels for Luger pistols. Carefully manufactured from ordnance steel to the original military specifications, the new barrels are blued, carry a front sight and are unmarked. Price, $12.95.

Numrich Arms makes new 45 caliber barrels that will fit most military (1911, 1911A) or commercial automatic pistols manufactured by Colt. Precision rifled and manufactured from ordnance steel to rigid military specs, they're furnished completely blued, ready for installation. Price, $13.95.

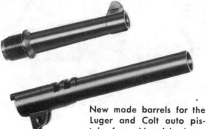

New made barrels for the Luger and Colt auto pistols from Numrich Arms.

Hogue Custom Grips

Hogue Custom Grips (Box 1001, Cambria, Ca. 93428) offers a new line of custom made handgun stocks. Guy Hogue, a retired Los Angeles police officer, hand makes these grips in various combat styles and of four South American hardwoods—Goncalo Alves, Pau Ferro, Shedua and Brazilian Rosewood. All of Hogue's grips are custom made to the customer's hand measurements, and they can be had checkered or smooth. Prices range from $5 for unfinished blocks to fully finished and checkered grips for $19.

Finger groove grips of this kind should prove a big help in double-action combat type shooting, helping to position the hand the same way each time the gun is gripped. A brochure, free, is available on request.

Navy Arms Stocks

Navy Arms is again offering genuine walnut shoulder stocks for their own—and other—replica revolvers. These brass-trimmed, lustrous stocks appear to be well made. They're said to fit all Colt-type or other similar-framed replicas, but specify the make and model for which you're ordering. $35 for standard-size stocks, $45 for Dragoon-type caplock revolvers.

Cloyce custom grip.

Hogue custom grip.

Cloyce's Gun Stocks

Stocks for revolvers and autoloaders, that is, and a look through Cloyce's latest catalog reveals an extensive line indeed. Target type stocks are a specialty—with and without thumb rests, palm shelves and finger grooves—but holster and combat style grips are also offered as well, and in good variety. The stock pictured is Cloyce's D-10-FG, made for all Colt and S&W hide-out revolvers, and without the finger grooves if so desired. $16.50 as shown, in genuine walnut.

A near dozen different stock woods are offered, which may be had plain, checkered or carved. Cloyce's stocks are handmade, to the customer's hand dimensions, so their catalog and ordering instructions are needed first. Prices start at $4.50 (for the 45 ACP, hardball style) and run to $35 for an elaborate Target Stock in laminated wood.　　　　　JTA

45 Auto Aluminum Frame

AR Sales (9916¾ Rush St., South El Monte, CA. 91733) is a new company offering aluminum alloy 45 Auto frames at $34.50, complete with grip-screw bushings, plunger tube and ejector. They're all ready to assemble into a 45 ACP, 38 Super, 9mm or 22 rimfire handgun, using surplus government parts or new commercial Colt parts.

AR Sales also manufactures 45 Auto

New aluminum frames for the auto enthusiast made by AR Sales.

parts and accessories—a barrel bushing wrench is $1.75, oversized barrel bushings are $4.95 (made for standard 45 ACP or Commander models), a "Commando" hammer at $5.95. This hammer, styled after the popular Commander version, will function with the long grip safety. Last, a complete line of triggers, long and short, these at $5.95 and $6.95, including a built-in and adjustable trigger stop. They're made in aluminum or steel.

Later on, maybe this year, ARS will offer slides for the 1911 45, et al. They'll be made in all lengths, Bob Cat to Long Slide, with or without sight dovetails, or milled for such popular sights as the K-38 S&W rear.

IRS classifies the new frames as complete pistols, so they have to be shipped to an FFL holder. For $5 extra these frames are available with personalized serial numbers, which can be any 3 letters and 5 numbers, such as ABC 00001. All other handgun parts can be shipped via regular post office traffic. ARS offers a complete list of parts for the 45 Auto, M1 Carbine, M1 and AR-15.　　　　W. L. Rickell

New French Handgun Collector's Guide

The *Guide des Collectionneurs d'Armes de Poing* (Handgun Collector's Guide), by Raymond Caranta and Ives Cadiou, published by Mssrs. Crepin-LeBlond in Paris (France), is a basic manual for French collectors.

This large clothbound book, comprising some 400 8¼"x10½" pages, has more than 300 illustrations (200 scale line drawings by a French master, Jean Jordanoglou, plus many color and black-and-white plates).

The new book, which gives average values for the antique market in France, describes accurately, in several hundred in-

dividual data sheets, the French, Belgian and Swiss service handguns up to the latest models; the most popular American revolvers designed before 1885 available in France, and a large number of miscellaneous European flintlock, percussion and cartridge handguns of the 18th and 19th centuries.

While the text is in French, the invaluable data offered for each gun described and the values—put down in accordance with American standard conditions—may be easily converted. The excellent illustrations, of course, need no translation.

Mr. Caranta was the winner of our Townsend Whelen Award for his "A History of French Handguns," published in the 23d edition of Gun Digest.　　　　JTA

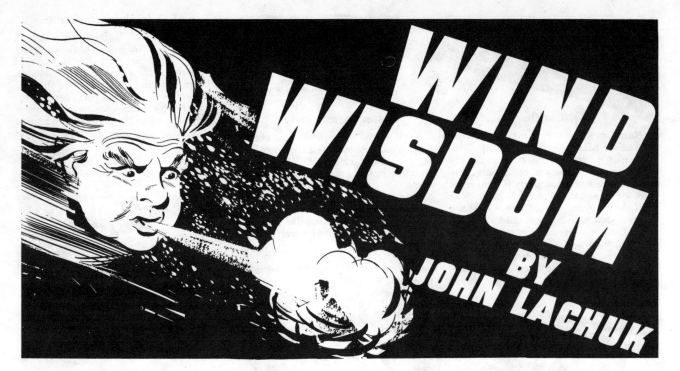

WIND WISDOM

BY JOHN LACHUK

Doping the wind correctly, whether at game or targets, can make the difference between collecting or losing. Here's a short, painless course in how to do it.

THE OCEAN of atmosphere that surrounds us is in a constant state of agitation and motion. The over-all pattern of air movements is fairly consistent and predictable, but at any given time and place, winds can blow from any point of the compass, at any random velocity. Often within the space of minutes, the whimsical wind changes directions and speed a dozen times.

One of the neophyte nimrod's most important lessons begins when his marksmanship wilts before the wind. Every textbook on shooting stresses allowance for trajectory, but few mention that wind deflection can affect a bullet's path as much as gravity. For example, a 220 Swift, sighted for 100 yards, drops 11.3 inches at 300 yards. A 10 mph crosswind, which could hardly be classified as a howling hurricane, will move this same bullet horizontally 11.6 inches at 300 yards. The effect is rather like crossing a river in a small boat. If you set out straight across, you must inevitably dock downstream on the other side. The hunter's failure to allow for the effect of wind, has left many a deer, bear, coyote, squirrel *et al* scared but alive and wiser. Hopefully the hunter was wiser for the experience, also!

Ballisticians don't agree on all aspects of wind deflection, but most believe that it is directly related to the *delay* factor of any given bullet at a given velocity. *Delay* is the difference between the actual time of flight of a bullet, and the theoretical or calculated time and flight for the same

bullet at the same muzzle velocity, fired in a vacuum.

Theoretically, in a vacuum, a G.I. 150-gr. M-2 bullet launched at 2700 fps from a 30-06 should travel 900 yards in one second. Actually, it takes 1.6 seconds to cover that distance. Knowing the delay time of .6 seconds you can calculate the approximate wind drift. Given a crosswind of 10 mph (15 feet per second), the bullet would drift 15 x .6, or about 9 feet.

The Delay Factor

The delay factor is tied to a bullet's ability to overcome air resistance, as indicated by its *ballistic coefficient*, which is arrived at by combining the *sectional density* (bullets weight related to its cross section), with the bullet's *coefficient of form*. Superior sectional density results when a bullet is comparatively long, in relation to its weight. Given the same sectional density, a sharp pointed bullet will have a higher ballistic coefficient than a blunt or round-nosed. For instance, both Speer's 180-gr. Round Nose and 180-gr. Spitzer point have a sectional density of .270. However, the Round Nose has a ballistic coefficient of .288, compared to .435 for the Spitzer. The higher the ballistic coefficient, the less air resistance *and* wind drift.

This explains why high velocity 22 centerfire cartridges are more susceptible to the lure of the siren wind than larger bores. Bullets normally used in a centerfire small bore possess low ballistic coefficients. A 22

cal. 55-gr. Speer Spitzer has a ballistic coefficient of .209, as opposed to .271 for a 6mm 80-gr. Spitzer, .354 for a 100-gr. 25 cal. Spitzer, or .395 for the 270 130-gr. Spitzer.

In their exceptionally complete *Manual For Reloading Ammunition No. 7*, Speer gives the sectional density and ballistic coefficient for each bullet they manufacture, making for easy comparisons of their wind-bucking qualities.

Another excellent loading manual, the *Hornady Handbook of Cartridge Reloading*, contains not only the sectional density and ballistic coefficient of every Hornady bullet, but also lists remaining velocity, energy, etc., out to 500 yards, allowing informed comparisons of drop and wind drift.

A lot of wind drift problems can be left at the reloading bench or dealer's counter simply by choosing the right bullet. Generally, this is the longest, sharpest-pointed bullet available, for your chosen caliber, that will do the required job. If your target is elk or moose this presents no difficulty, but if you're after squirrels or prairie dogs, a compromise is necessary in order to get the heaviest bullet that will still provide explosive killing power and freedom from ricochets.

I've gotten the best results on long range varmint shooting using a 257 Weatherby, with 100-gr. bullets, and the 240 Weatherby or 6mm Remington, using 85-gr. Sierra, 87-gr. Hornady or 90-gr. Speer bullets. Those calibers and bullet weights offer superior wind-bucking ability coupled with megaton destruction.

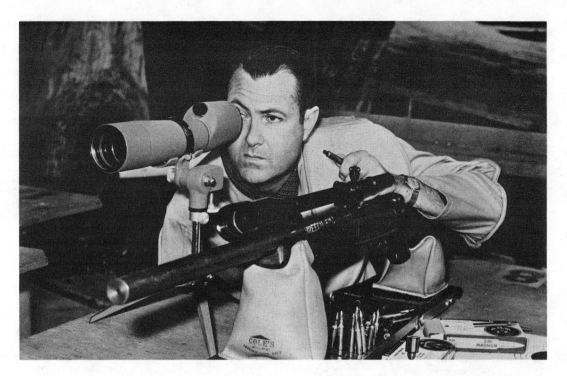

Target shooters often focus their spotting scope about half to two-thirds of the way out to the targets, dope the wind by watching the slant and speed of the heat waves or "schlieren" of the mirage, as it follows the wind across the range. Winds of 14 to 15 mph blow the mirage away completely, making it useless as a wind gauge. Looks like Lachuk threw that last one!

Prairie Dog Practice

Because of the number and variety of targets offered, more can be learned about wind deflection in a few afternoons of shooting prairie dogs or chucks than during a lifetime of deer hunting, if you but make the effort to see and remember. Use a rifle of mild recoil, say one of the currently popular 6mm bores, with a 10 to 12 power scope, to spot those all too common puffs of dust. Or have a companion with binoculars spotting for you. As you correct for your misses and get on target, note the direction and apparent strength of the wind. File this data in your memory bank for future referral. Your percentage of hits will begin to climb like the price of gold.

A little experience will lead to surprisingly effective shooting in brisk winds, even if all your shots are not perfect. On a recent rock chuck foray in Wyoming, the wind blew so hard that it took two hands and a foot to push the car door open. I sighted a chuck broadside to me, clinging to a rock about 125 yards distant. The wind ruffled its fur from the south end, as I held my crosshairs well astern, hoping to drill the marmot through the shoulders. An 80-gr. Sierra from my 6mm Remington removed its head as neatly as by a guillotine.

Big game offers larger targets than varmints, but they are often found at extreme ranges, where correct wind doping becomes crucial. I can remember a deer or two and an antelope that avoided my trophy collection, courtesy of the wayward wind.

While hunting, never compensate for the wind by cranking away at your micrometer receiver sight or scope dials. About the time you think you have the wind cannily doped, it changes! Taking "Kentucky windage" hasn't been improved upon in over a hundred years.

Another way—sometimes—to decrease wind drift is to increase velocity, although the correlation between higher velocity and reduced wind drift is not as absolute as that existing between higher ballistic coefficient and reduced wind drift. Increasing velocity with a given bullet doesn't *necessarily* result in a corresponding reduction in wind drift, because higher muzzle velocity also steps up air resistance. While the high velocity bullet may arrive at the target sooner, its delay time may be greater than the same bullet starting at a lower muzzle velocity. An example of this phenomenon is found in the 22 Long Rifle regular speed, which leaves the muzzle at 1145 fps, and requires *less* correction for crosswind than does the 22 LR high speed, with a muzzle velocity of 1335 fps.

Velocity Brackets

On the other hand, a Sierra 180-gr. Matchking, loaded with 57 grains of 4350, for 2850 fps in a 30-06, requires 8 minutes windage correction at 1000 yards for a 10 mph crosswind versus 7 minutes correction for the same bullet loaded in a 300 H & H Magnum ahead of 67 grains of 4350, for 3150 fps. That's about 10 inches difference on the target.

Homer S. Powley, famed ballistics expert and designer of the *Powley Computer for Handloaders*, attributes this anomaly to ". . . a peculiarity of the muzzle velocity and ballistic coefficient combination that (causes) muzzle velocities higher or lower than the standard 1145 fps (to) require more wind allowance."

The late Townsend Whelen surmised that ". . . there are certain zones of velocity for various bullets within which the deflection may be considerably more or less than in other zones, and a zone of higher velocity may actually result in more deflection than a lower one."

Boat-tailed bullets enjoy a certain advantage over flat based in the matter of wind deflection. A case in point: the Sierra Matchking 180-gr. Spitzer pointed boat-tail is deflected 30 inches less at 1000 yards than a 180-gr. Spitzer pointed flat base. This advantage may be less apparent at normal hunting ranges.

On sunny days, air in contact with the warm ground rises in visible wavy streaks called *mirage*. In still air, the schlieren from the mirage rise straight up, but the wavy streaks slant noticeably to follow any wind. Mirage is best seen against a light background, such as a hillside of browning grass, or against the sky, preferably through a 10X or higher magnification scope. Target shooters often focus their spotting scopes about two-thirds of the way out to the targets, and "dope" the mirage

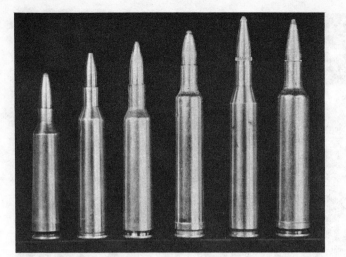

From left—22-250; 220 Swift; 6mm Remington; 240 Weatherby; 25-06 and 257 Weatherby. 22-250 and 220 Swift are hot 22 centerfire rounds, but they fall short when it comes to bucking wind. Bullets of relatively low ballistic coefficient lose all that velocity all too soon, tend to bow to the will of any vagrant wind. Good wind buckers are 6mm Remington and 240 Weatherby, when using bullets of 80- to 100-gr. weight. Best wind buckers of all are hot 25s, the 25-06 and 257 Weatherby. Long bullets with high ballistic coefficient and good "pointy" ogives, coupled with high sustained velocity, make these cartridges resist the push of strong breezes.

before each shot. Studied observation of this phenomenon can make it your most valuable gauge of wind speed and direction.

Winds of 14 to 15 mph literally blow the mirage away, making it useless as a wind indicator. But then, who needs mirage to tell him when the wind is blowing 15 mph? A pith ball hung on a string offers a rough indication of wind speed and direction at your position, but bear in mind that you may be shooting from a fairly sheltered location, with little wind, while your quarry stands upon a windswept hillock, confident that nature's invisible barrier will protect him.

Perhaps it's better to observe nature's landscaping near your target. Tall grass is a pretty good wind gauge. Gently swaying, it whispers, "The wind is about 10 mph." Rippling and dancing, it warns, "The wind is approaching 15 mph."

Wind Signals

At fifteen mph the wind begins

to raise dust and loose paper, and small branches are moved. Wind at this speed could be termed "strong." A "very strong" 20 mph wind sets small leafy trees to swaying, and makes you pull your hat tighter. A "gentle breeze" of 5 mph merely rustles the leaves and can be lightly felt on the face. A 10 mph wind keeps leaves and small twigs in constant motion, and might be called "fresh."

Watch high trees as well as low grass. Wind speed increases slightly with distance above the ground, because the earth's surface creates friction with moving air, slowing its movement near the ground. Uneven terrain is likely to impede the air more, causing increased turbulence and unpredictable gusts that compound your problem.

If we picture the shooter at 6 o'clock and the target at 12, sidewinds from 3 or 9 o'clock have the greatest effect upon the point of impact. Quartering winds, from 10:30, 1:30, 4:30 or 7:30, can be assumed to have roughly half as much disruptive

effect. Winds from 12 or 6 o'clock slow or accelerate the bullet slightly causing a higher or lower impact point, but the effect over normal hunting ranges is negligible with winds under 25 mph.

The effect of a crosswind upon the bullet's path is directly proportional to the wind velocity. Thus a 5 mph wind has half the effect of a 10 mph wind. A 20 mph wind has twice the effect of a 10 mph wind, etc.

Wind affects the bullet's path more in the last half to one-third of the distance to the target. Thus doubling the range increases the wind deflection four-fold. Cutting the range in half reduces wind deflection to one-fourth.

Wind Doping

On a normal, average day (no storm), the air tends to be more or less calm at sunrise, with winds rising to a median for the day about 10: A.M., increasing steadily in velocity until 2:00 or 3:00 P.M., then delining toward a comparative calm at sunset. Moral: hunt early and late, siesta at mid-day. Continuous anemometer readings, taken over a long period of time, indicate that winds tend to rise and fall in more or less rhythmic

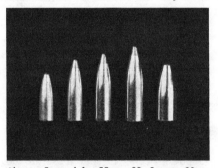

Above: From left—55-gr. 22 Speer; 80-gr. 6mm Speer; 100-gr. 25 Speer; Speer 130-gr. 270 and Sierra 110-gr. hollow point 30. Speer 55-gr. 22 has a ballistic coefficient of only .209, compared to .271 for the 2nd bullet, .354 for No. 3 or .395 for the 130-gr. 270. As the BC improves, wind-bucking ability picks up apace The Sierra 110-gr. 30-cal. HP (right) is an ugly little brute, but makes a pretty fair varmint slug, with its BC of .254. Still it's not the best bullet in a high wind! ● Below: From left—Sierra 180-gr. Matchking Spitzer boat-tail; 180-gr. Sierra Spitzer flat base; 180-gr. Speer round nose and 180-gr. Speer Spitzer. Sierra 180/Matchking is deflected 30" less at 100 yards by a 10 mph cross wind than a 180-gr. Sierra (2nd bullet) because the former's boat-tail reduces drag. Speer 180-gr. RN has same sectional density as its spitzer-pointed cousin, but blunt shape results in a low ballistic coefficient, making the round nose a poor wind bucker.

Wind Displacement Chart:
Assuming a 10 mph wind at 3 o'clock or 9 o'clock
(Drift is proportional to wind velocity. Double for 20 mph, cut in half for 5 mph, etc.)

Cartridge	Bullet/grs.	V/approx.	Deflection in inches (approximate)			
			100 yds.	200 yds.	300 yds.	400 yds.
22-250						
225 Win.						
224 Weath.	55	3700 fps	0.9	3.6	8.3	15.1
6mm Rem.	85	3250 fps	0.9	3.5	7.9	14.4
243 Win.	100	3100 fps	0.8	2.9	6.7	12.2
264 Win.						
7mm Rem.	140	3100 fps	0.5	1.9	4.6	8.6
7mm Weath.	160	3250 fps	0.5	2.1	4.9	9.0
270 Win.	130	3150 fps	0.7	2.6	6.0	11.1
30-06	150	3000 fps	0.8	3.2	7.2	13.2
30-06	180	2700 fps	0.8	3.1	7.0	12.7
300 Weath.	180	3150 fps	0.6	2.5	5.6	10.4

cycles of 6 to 8 minutes. If you have the time, and don't want to dope the shot, just wait for a lull in the breeze.

Various rules of thumb provide handy guides to wind compensation. An Army marksmanship manual suggests a formula for 30-06 M-2 ball ammo. "The range in hundreds of yards (expressed as a single figure) times the velocity of the wind in miles per hour, divided by ten is the number of quarter points (minutes) of wind correction to allow for a 3 or 9 o'clock wind. Winds one hour from 3 or 9 o'clock (2, 4, 8 and 10 o'clock) require about the same windage; 1, 5, 7 and 11 o'clock winds require half as much allowance as those from 3 or 9 o'clock."

Parker O. Ackley's highly informative *Handbook for Shooters and Reloaders*, volume 1, contains a number of complex equations for mathematically computing the exact deflection of a given bullet at a given velocity, assuming a consistent wind direction and speed over the bullet's path. However, the only thing consistent about wind is its inconsistency. An educated guess is likely to be as accurate as a scientific computation.

Doping wind has about it the essence of black magic, combined with pure instinct. Competition rifle shooters watch all of the usual wind indicators, mirage, blowing grass, trees, flags, etc. meticulously calculate the required number of clicks on their scope or micrometer rear sight—then utter a fervent prayer as they squeeze off the shot!

Just remember that hunters don't get many sighter shots so it pays to know the game. Experience is still the best teacher providing only that you are aware enough to profit by it, and remember what you learned. ●

Windage & Elevation For 22 Rimfires

BECAUSE rifle shooters all over the country are becoming more and more "ballistic-minded," angles of elevation for various ranges and the effect of wind on the bullet's point of impact are subjects of particular interest to the rimfire rifle shooter.

The shooter who can properly "dope" the wind is the lad who generally walks away with the trophies or brings back the game. Figuring out probable bullet deflection in various winds always presents an interestingly difficult problem, for some curious things can happen.

Remington has now brought these figures up to date on the basis of the latest available ballistic measurements.

Examination of the windage tables for the Standard Velocity cartridge and the Hi-Speed cartridge reveals that *apparently*, in the same wind, the higher speed bullet is deflected more than the other! This, however, is not as surprising as it might seem; it must be remembered that wind deflection is computed by multiplying the difference between the actual time of flight in air, and the time of flight in vacuum, by the cross-range wind velocity.

Expressed as a formula this can be written as:

$$D = 12W (T_a - T_v)$$

D = Deflection in inches
W = Cross-range component of wind velocity in fps
T_a = Time of flight of bullet in air
T_v = Time of flight of bullet in vacuum

For example, consider 22 LR Standard Velocity and 22 LR Hi-Speed bullets at 100 yards. The respective times of flight in air are approximately .287 seconds for the Standard 22 LR and .259 seconds for the Hi-Speed. The respective times of flight in vacuum, however, are .262 and .225 seconds respectively. Hence, the difference in times of flight under the two conditions are (.287−.262) = .025 seconds for the Standard Velocity and (.259−.225) = .035 seconds for the Hi-Speed. Multiplying these figures by the effective cross-range wind velocity will give a larger deflection to the Hi-Speed bullet. The tables follow:

TABLE OF WIND ALLOWANCE
22 LR—Standard Velocity 40-gr. Bullet, MV=1145 fps

Inches and Minutes Bullet is Deflected

Distance	Wind, miles per hour	by 1, 5, 7, 11 o'clock wind In.	Min.	by 2, 4, 8, 10 o'clock wind In.	Min.	by 3 and 9 o'clock wind In.	Min.
50 yards 1 min.- ½-inch	5	0.3	0.7	0.6	1.2	0.7	1.4
	10	0.7	1.4	1.1	2.2	1.3	2.6
	15	1.0	2.0	1.7	3.4	1.9	3.8
	20	1.3	2.6	2.3	4.6	2.6	5.2
100 yards 1 min.- 1 inch	5	1.1	1.1	1.9	1.9	2.2	2.2
	10	2.2	2.2	3.8	3.8	4.4	4.4
	15	3.3	3.3	5.7	5.7	6.6	6.6
	20	4.4	4.4	7.6	7.6	8.8	8.8
200 yards 1 min.- 2 inches	5	4.1	2.1	7.0	3.5	8.2	4.1
	10	8.2	4.1	14.0	7.0	16.4	8.2
	15	12.3	6.2	21.0	10.5	24.6	12.3
	20	16.4	8.2	28.0	14.0	32.8	16.4

22 LR Hi-Speed 40-gr. Bullet, MV=1335 fps

Inches and Minutes Bullet is Deflected

Distance	Wind, miles per hour	by 1, 5, 7, 11 o'clock wind In.	Min.	by 2, 4, 8, 10 o'clock wind In.	Min.	by 3 and 9 o'clock wind In.	Min.
50 yards 1 min.- ½-inch	5	0.4	0.8	0.7	1.4	0.8	1.6
	10	0.8	1.6	1.4	2.8	1.6	3.2
	15	1.2	2.4	2.1	4.2	2.4	4.8
	20	1.6	3.2	2.8	5.6	3.2	6.4
100 yards 1 min.- 1 inch	5	1.5	1.5	2.6	2.6	3.0	3.0
	10	3.0	3.0	5.2	5.2	6.0	6.0
	15	4.5	4.5	7.8	7.8	9.0	9.0
	20	6.0	6.0	10.4	10.4	12.0	12.0
200 yards 1 min.- 2 inches	5	5.1	2.6	4.4	4.4	10.2	5.1
	10	10.2	5.1	8.8	8.8	20.4	10.2
	15	15.3	7.7	13.2	13.2	30.6	15.3
	20	20.4	10.2	17.6	17.6	40.8	20.4

ANGLES OF DEPARTURE—MINUTES
22 LR Cartridges

Range, Yards	22 LR Std. Vel. MV=1145 fps	22 LR Hi-Speed MV=1335 fps
25	3.3	2.5
50	6.8	5.2
75	10.6	8.2
100	14.4	11.4
125	18.5	14.8
150	22.6	18.4
175	27.2	22.2
200	31.7	26.0

Screw Barrel Pistols...◆◆◆an extensive detailed survey

There were times, on London's dark, foggy streets of 300 years ago, when a dependable gun which could be tucked into a pocket was desperately needed. The screw barrel pistol answered this need—and continued to do so for two centuries. This is its story

by Louis W. Steinwedel

Top—An exceptionally fine specimen of the Queen Anne screw barrel gun by H. Delany of London, ca. 1710. When rifled, such pistols were quite accurate. Above—the bizarre and much sought Segallas pistol, ca. 1720-1780. After the top barrels were fired the barrel cluster could be turned over to align and fire the two fresh barrels. Middle—Wrench for unscrewing barrel (squared handle) plus bullet mould.

Barrel is detached from one of this pair of screw barrel pistols and stands near threaded breech. Four notches in muzzle are not rifling, as casual observation might suggest, but the indents which accept the square end of wrench-mould, right, used to remove barrel for loading and to replace it.

As AN OBSTINATE fog rolled off the Thames, John Baker bid good night to the pleasures of a pewter mug of English ale and the challenge of a backgammon board and stepped out into the night, bundling his great-coat about him against the damp chill of the darkness. Lighting in the London streets of the 1760s was largely limited to heavenly sources and so he picked his way cautiously.

In the middle of the next block a chill not of climatic origin gripped Baker as the fog-muffled but unmistakable clack of boot leather on cobblestones came up from behind. His hand instinctively went to his pocket and emerged with a fully cocked flintlock pistol. As a pair of menacing figures loomed out of the night, Baker's finger jerked. There was a dull *boom,* and an orange flame weakly illuminated the scene. The pistol ball whizzed harmlessly past its targets.

The two unwashed figures flashed evil smiles and closed in with knives drawn. Suddenly, a second shot blazed through the fog and the first figure stumbled back with a groan; the second faltered and then pressed the attack. A third shot sent him to the slimy cobblestones, a dumfounded look on his face.

"Scoundrels!," Baker exclaimed. "But for the talented fingers of Mr. Segallas, what a fix I'd been in." Lovingly hefting his bizarre-looking but exceedingly practical little gun, John Baker was comforted by the thought that it still contained another charge for the remainder of his walk home.

* * *

This little episode illustrates the need for defensive pocket guns that existed in years past and which has continued to the present. Man in his inventive genius has answered this need in a hundred clever, formidable, and fascinating ways, since he first learned how to make a gun diminutive enough to be called a true pocket pistol. Baker's 4-barrel pistol was an advanced type.

The small pistol that, tucked in the sash of power politicians of long ago, sometimes did more to change history than the might of 10,000 muskets, took its first great step forward in mid-17th century England. At that time a small handful of master gunsmiths there began to show their brocade-cloaked customers a little breechloading pistol that instantly captured the imagination. The design was patently simple,

but astonishingly effective. This was the screw barrel or "turn off" pistol, so called because the barrel could be twisted off with a few turns to reveal a small, elongated powder chamber topped by a concavity in which a round ball was placed after the powder chamber had been filled. To load, the shooter simply screwed off the barrel, poured in some powder (no measure was necessary as it was impossible to overload), topped it with a ball, and screwed the barrel back into place.

Loading a screw barrel gun, if less confusing, was not measurably less incommodious than ordinary muzzle loading, but the results were frighteningly superior. Since the bullet was breech loaded rather than shoved through the barrel in the usual fashion, a ball the exact size of the bore could be used. Not only did this give greater accuracy than the loose fitting projectile of the muzzle-loader, but also the tight fit and greater resistance allowed the slow igniting powder charge to burn completely before the ball was forced out the muzzle. Maximum pressure and velocity were thereby produced and in the screw barrel system a short barrel gave ballistics equal to or surpassing those delivered by the cumbersome muzzle-loaders which needed long barrels to ensure the full burning of the low grade black powder of the day.

It was obviously impossible to double-load a screw barrel pistol, as was occasionally done with an ordinary muzzle-loader. Multiple loading of muzzle-loading weapons happened often. After the battle of Gettysburg

one musket was found with 20 charges jammed in, one atop the other.

Rifled or Not

When screw barrel pistol bores were rifled, the resulting accuracy was phenomenal. With the exception of a few other breech-loading flintlocks, such as Maj. Patrick Ferguson's famous gun, it was not equaled until some two centuries later with the advent of Christian Sharps' guns and then the metallic cartridge. Oddly enough, the guns built early in the 17th century seem to have been rifled more frequently than later specimens, probably because most of the later guns were pocket pistols intended for use at limited range where even smoothbore accuracy was deadly enough.

Some screw barrel guns will appear to be rifled when they are not. The muzzles reveal cuts—usually four in number—that look like rifling, but a look behind the muzzle proper will reveal the smooth interior. The squarish form of the muzzle was made so to accept a square-ended tool, often needed to unscrew the barrel. Other barrels carried a boss or small projection behind the barrel, usually near the breech end, that allowed the use of a spanner or wrench of open, semi-round form to encircle the barrel at the stud position, thus adding leverage for removal or tightening.

An example of the screw barrel's superiority occurred in 1643, while England was racked by civil war. When the Royalist army stopped one afternoon, young Prince Rupert demonstrated his marksmanship on the

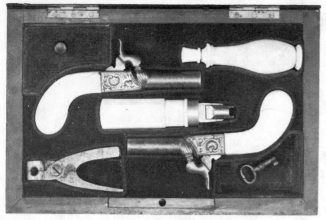

An elegant and petite pair of percussion screw barrel pocket pistols with ivory stocks, ivory handled wrench and flask.

head of an iron chanticleer weathervane perched about 30 yards distant on the steeple of St. Mary's Church at Stafford. The marksman's uncle, King Charles, congratulated him on such a precise shot, but hinted that it might have been a piece of sharp luck rather than a sharp eye. Piqued at the oblique affront to him and his armament, the prince flashed forth his pistol's mate and proceeded to puncture the iron tailfeathers of the weathercock.*

The screw barrel principle was adapted to larger pistols, martial pistols (often with small chains to fasten the barrel to the breech section), and occasionally even to military carbines, but the system was best suited to compact arms for personal defense. Because of the high compression offered by the gas-tight sealing of the powder chamber and the tight-fitting ball, even the most diminutive pocket pistol of 40 or 45 caliber was more devastating than a hefty conventional piece of 50 or 60 caliber. The screw barrel breechloader was even a pretty good weapon against an adversary protected by a typical steel breastplate of the day. These primeval "bullet proof vests" were hangovers from the days of knights in full armor and were generally only "proofed" with a shot from an ordinary muzzle-loading pistol. The higher velocity of a breechloader would "likely blow a neat round hole through the average pistol proof breastplate," as John Nigel George phrased it in his comprehensive work, *English Pistols and Revolvers* (Onslow County, N.C., 1938).

Though generally unsuitable for military use, the screw barrel pistol's refinement into a reliable pocket piece made it very much at home in the dark streets of London where gangs of cutthroats waited for the careless stroller. Protection of life and limb largely remained a do-it-yourself af-

*An apocryphal tale, in our opinion, and a story that, like so many others, has lost nothing in the telling. Robert Held also relates this yarn in his *The Age of Firearms* (New York, 1957). It is doubtful that one in 1000 screw barrel pistols was in fact rifled; the rifled appearance of the muzzles of such pieces has led both writers and collectors astray. There is some excuse for the former, almost none for the latter.

fair in London until Sir Robert Peel created the London police in 1829. Even then, street bandits met this interference defiantly, and for a time a London policeman had as much chance as a hungry Turk in a Greek restaurant. Then the early day equivalent of "Q Section" came to the rescue with a specially designed screw barrel hideout pistol which could be brought into play at the crucial moment, and the situation changed.

The design of the London Police Model was rather distinctive. Unlike most pistols of its type, it was made with a flat rather than a rounded butt, nicely checkered. The breech was brass and the barrel and fittings were blued steel. Each gun was marked with the name of the maker and the police district from which it was issued. Surviving specimens are scarce collector's items.

Screw Barrel History

The screw barrel gun changed little in basic form during its reign of popularity which spanned three centuries. It appeared in the mid-1600s as a long, slim weapon with a flared muzzle that resembled a miniature cannon. From that came the nickname "cannon barreled pistol." It was also

sometimes called the "Queen Anne's pistol," for the sovereign, just as a certain style of simple English furniture still bears her name.

Actually, the cannon muzzle characteristic had mostly vanished from English-built pieces by the early part of the 18th century but it continued in favor on foreign-made specimens, notably Belgian, even into the 1840s. By that time the gun had advanced to percussion ignition and grown slightly smaller and generally less well made. Barrels were either of steel or brass, although I have recently examined two specimens with barrels of German silver.

The attention, interest and genius which was spent upon the little screw barrel guns is obvious from their many refinements and innovations. One of the most practical was the sliding safety bolt which rode along the top or backstrap. This locked the cover over the pan of priming powder—important in a defense arm because in drawing a small flintlock you can easily catch the awkward, upright frizzen in the pocket, uncovering the flashpan and spilling the priming charge. Secondly, the safety permitted carrying the gun at full cock, loaded and ready for action. This sliding safety is found only on the boxlock design of pistol, not on the Queen Anne sidelock pistols.

The operation was simple; when the hammer was cocked the bolt could be shoved forward with the thumb to engage a notch in the rear of the hammer. This movement simultaneously locked the trigger mechanism and positively kept the hammer from falling even if the trigger were pulled accidentally. When the sliding bolt was pushed into safety position, a small pin in the forward part entered a hole in the base of the frizzen, locking it and the pan cover and giving double protection against accidental discharge. A raised nub at the rear

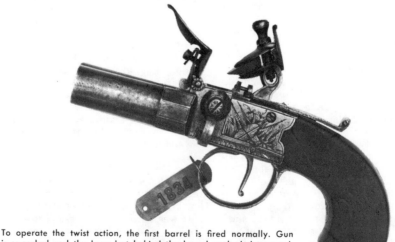

To operate the twist action, the first barrel is fired normally. Gun is re-cocked and the lever just behind the barrel pushed downward. This rotates a horizontal steel cylinder which is notched to contain a priming charge. This second inner flash pan is connected to the second barrel by a flash channel in the cylinder.

allowed the "safety" to be flicked off with one easy movement. This 18th century safety is actually easier to operate than the safety on a modern automatic because of its natural, accessible position.

Another hallmark of many screw barrel guns of the 1700s and early 1800s was a miniature bayonet which folded back under the barrels. This ace-in-the-hole touch is generally credited to English gunmaker John Waters, who practiced in Birmingham from the middle to the later 1700s. This spring-loaded bayonet hinged at the muzzle end of the barrel and could be folded back under tension. Its tip was held in place in a slot at the forward end of the sliding trigger guard. A slight rearward pressure against the inside rear surface of the trigger guard allowed the spring-loaded bayonet to thrust forward, switch-blade fashion, ready for business. On a pocket sized pistol the bayonet was limited to about 2" in length but, sharply pointed and keenly honed, it lent an air of authority to even an empty gun.

The baby bayonet also served another purpose; when bent back at a 90° angle, it made a very convenient handle or lever with which to unscrew the barrel for reloading. A rare type of screw barrel gun had a genuine lever for unscrewing the barrel. It was constructed in the same under-barrel fashion as the spring bayonet.

Screw Barrel Bayonets

This marriage of blade and pistol was carried from the merely cute to the sublime, as illustrated by an especially unusual piece discussed by John Nigel George in his book. Around 1720 an imaginative English gunsmith concealed a screw barrel pistol in the hilt of a naval officer's sword. The existence of this rather unholy alliance was revealed only by a small flintlock hammer protruding from the pommel —easily overlooked in the heat of a hand-to-hand encounter. Such a weapon was diabolical; even if a well-aimed thrust were fought off, the opponent could still find himself looking down the barrel of a pistol. Not very sporting, old chap, but eminently practical for the unaccomplished swordsman.

Those willing to forego the extra insurance of the spring bayonet could get an even more compact pistol using the so-called "folding trigger." Introduced in the very late 1700s this gained widespread popularity which has not yet completely fallen from favor on certain types of European pocket guns.

The folding trigger consisted of a flat bar which folded into a small recess on the underside of the frame when the hammer was down. When the hammer was cocked, the spring-loaded trigger would snap into normal firing position. Colt collectors will be familiar with the design because it was so popular by the 1830s that Samuel Colt adapted it to his Paterson pistols.

The folding trigger helped the trend toward "miniaturizing" pocket weapons. I have examined a number of these gems of the English gunsmith's art which measure barely 4" over-all. The elegant workmanship on some make them resemble jewelry more than armament and belie their deadly effectiveness.

A typical example of the flintlock screw barrel pistol from its classic period of 1800 to 1820 is a piece in my own collection which combines most of the above features. Of average quality, it was made in Ipswich, England, by a gunsmith named Harcourt who worked from about 1780 to 1820. The piece is typical of the "suburban" or provincial makers who by the mid-1700s had learned to make guns as good as the average quality turned out by London artisans—and at considerably lower prices.

In this 6½" 40-cal. pocket gun Harcourt produced a sound, honestly made pistol which likely served its original owner for many a year. After nearly a century and a half the sliding safety bolt and spring bayonet still operate smartly, and the gun could still provide a measure of security in a dark and dangerous city. The Harcourt gun is obviously not "jewelry;" in fact, it has a functionalistic plainness about it. Its only decoration consists of some neat line engraving around the frame, hammer, and backstrap, a die-stamped flag and drum motif on the right side and a similar pattern on the left containing an oval with the maker's name.

Another, not so typical, example is a 45-cal. folding trigger model built *circa* 1810 and marked "Spencer Northallerton" which I found nestled among some bronze statues at an antique show. The gun had been converted to percussion, and the converter made most curious use of the hinge left by the discarded frizzen and pan cover, fitting a spring-loaded cap retainer through it which served to hold the early top-hat cap firmly in place. The apparent uncertainty in that transition period of the 1830s about losing the cap is fascinating, particularly since George calls such retaining mechanisms not at all common. The rest of the 5¾" gun shows better than average engraving and attention to detail, with an elegant silver lion's head buttcap.

Multi-Shot Types

Most surviving specimens of the screw barrel pistol are simple single shot affairs, but the compact simplicity of the design lent itself well to multi-shot weapons and gunsmiths went after firepower on a grandiose scale. Double barrel models are not rare and some specimens contain up to a half-dozen screw barrels clustered together.

While some doubles were simply a pair of pistols blended into one with twin locks, etc., others were credits to the creativity of the 18th century mind. The "turnover" technique was a clever but somewhat clumsy approach in which the pistol was built with a pair of over-under barrels. After the top barrel was fired the

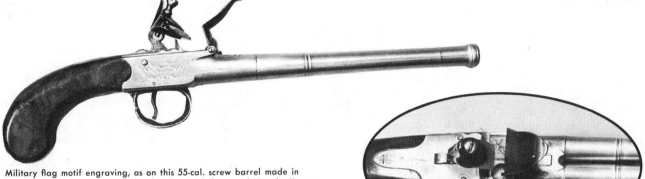

Military flag motif engraving, as on this 55-cal. screw barrel made in London ca. 1780, was popular in that era, and the proud "London" stamp assured quality. Right—Top view of a side-by-side screw barrel double pistol shows the simple slide-action principle. After right barrel is fired, the plate is pulled back to expose the primed pan of the second barrel. The extra-wide frizzen serves both pans.

Left—An unusual London-built rotating-action screw barrel composed of a side-by-side double with another underslung barrel of smaller caliber. The turning cylinder has two flashpan notches. Right —A superb pair of classic twist-action screw barrel doubles with folding spring bayonets, by the famous London gunsmith T. Twigg. Ca. 1820. Twigg also built an ingenious 6-shot screw barrel pepperbox.

shooter released a small catch and the barrels could be pivoted through a 180° turn to align the fresh barrel—complete with its own frizzen and flash pan—with the single, center-mounted flintlock hammer. A brace of pistols which Napoleon carried on his ill-fated flirtation with Russia was of this type. Now preserved at the Harold's Club Museum in Reno, Nev., the pistols are plain almost to the point of sterility and seem to betray the usual French flair for elegance.

The same turnover principle with a separate frizzen and pan for each barrel had been applied earlier by a London firm which operated from about 1720 to 1779 and whose products were identified with the name "Segallas." This surprisingly tiny 4-shot effort represented the screw barrel pocket pistol raised to its nearly ultimate form. With the spiny frizzens sticking out from top and bottom, the Segallas repeater was no paragon of compactness despite its small size, but the security of its 4 shots endeared it to Englishmen in spite of its unorthodox shape. Weighty all-steel construction rather than the usual walnut grips added even more to the little weapon's utility in a hostile encounter. If one had to be out after dark in London of the mid-1700s a Segallas was a handy companion.

A Segallas type pistol is virtually the pot of gold at the end of the rainbow for a collector of flintlocks generally or pocket pistols in particular. For a long time collectors have accepted the Segallas as an English product, basing this assumption on the London address occasionally found on specimens. The belief is reinforced by the advanced design and fine finish generally associated with the respected English gunsmith. However, it is doubtful if the Segallas can be held out any longer as an English gun. Few Segallas pistols bear English proof marks, as required by law, even though their markings indicate they were made in London. A peculiar set of circumstances to say the least.

Segallas Unmasked

Close examination of a number of Segallas pistols reveals that despite their clever design and fine finish they cannot boast the excellence of the English craftsman, particularly in the lockwork where skill really mattered the most. They are almost surely Continental in origin, probably imported into England, or perhaps assembled there, for the benefit of affluent Englishmen.

The obvious supposition for masquerading the Segallas, and many other pocket guns that followed it, as an English product was the enviable reputation for fine guns which the tight little isle had attained as early as Queen Anne's time. By the first part of the 18th century it was a foregone conclusion that if you wanted the best gun that a heavy purse could buy you naturally bought a piece with the magic word that guaranteed quality—"London."

Imitation being the sincerest form of flattery and sometimes the quickest road to profit, many guns made in various European countries began to invade not only England but the entire world bearing British sounding names and fashionable but often fictitious London addresses. The practice continued for a long time, and did not escape the attention even of American makers. The Manhattan Firearms Co. of New Jersey was prone to market some of its second-quality Civil War era percussion revolvers under the pretentious name of "The London Pistol Co." As with the Segallas guns of a hundred years earlier, products of the London Pistol Co. lacked government proof markings, yet many collectors still think of these percussion revolvers made in New Jersey as English copies of American design.

English innovation was not to be outdone by the alien exotica of the Segallas. Although Englishmen seem to have a penchant for taking a proven mechanism—be it flintlock of the 18th century or internal combustion engine of the 20th—and pushing it to the pinnacle of perfection, a canny ingenuity was equally the hallmark of the English gunmaker. For instance, the firm of Brasher which operated in London from about 1780 to 1800 offered a formidable yet neat looking screw barrel pocket pistol with 6 barrels arranged in three layers of doubles. A selector mounted in the frame was twisted in sequence to connect each barrel with the flashpan, which had to be primed separately for each shot. T. Twigg, another London maker of the 1700s, combined the screw barrel and the pepperbox in his attempt at a repeater. Six barrels screwed into a revolving cylinder breech which contained a powder chamber and bullet receptacle for each. This "screw barrel pepperbox" had the drawback of requiring separate priming for each shot and the barrels had to be turned by hand. Nevertheless, it was a step in the right direction and a harbinger of things to come in the form of the famous Collier flintlock revolver and finally Colt's own revolver.

Twigg's pepperbox, Brasher's six-shooter, the unlikely looking Segallas pistols, and other early attempts at repeating firepower were the rare exception rather than the rule. Such experiments were too expensive and too complicated for most people.

Twist Actions

The only really practical screw barrel repeater was the over-under double which enjoyed great popularity from about 1800 to 1825. The "twist action" used on these little doubles was ingenious and deserves description. Twist action vertical doubles were built with a center-hung boxlock hammer bearing upon a single small frizzen and pan. A small steel cylinder having a lever on one end extends

Left—Magnificently preserved four barrel twist action pistol. This type was handy in the crime-infested streets of old London, which had little protection until Sir Robert Peel founded the London police in 1829.

Right—a battered screw barrel from the collection of President Rutherford B. Hayes. It has a sliding safety and folding trigger. Many guns like this were converted to percussion in the 1830s and 1840s.

through the frame. Opening the pan cover and revolving the lever about a quarter-turn exposes a small second pan formed by a notch cut into the cylinder.

To load the twist action, the shooter first turned off both barrels and inserted the powder and projectiles in the ordinary way. Then, the lever was turned to roll the bottom flashpan forward to receive its priming charge. The lever was then returned to its original position, causing the bottom pan to disappear into the frame and exposing the normal or top pan. This was primed as usual and the pan cover closed. The top flashpan was connected to the the top barrel and the lower pan cut into the rotating cylinder connected to the bottom barrel.

Over-under screw barrel doubles were the perfect choice as a personal defense weapon of the early 1800s. The twist action rotating cylinder, for all its ingenuity, was a simple device and did not make a double barreled pistol prohibitively more expensive than a single shot. The double retained all of the desirable characteristics of the single shot and was not appreciably bulkier and only slightly heavier than a single barrel with a folding bayonet. Of numerous examples that I have examined, not one suffered in balance or feel.

The twist action's repriming system gave it a great advantage over most of the more exotic multi-shot guns, since it didn't require manual repriming before the second shot. For the second shot all you had to do was recock, snap the frizzen back in place and twist the lever on the left side of the frame. The whole operation could be accomplished very quickly.

A less sophisticated and probably older system of igniting twin barrels in a flintlock pistol was the so-called "slide action" as found on the less popular side by side doubles. In profile, a slide action pistol looks like a single shot, but from above it is seen that the frizzen and pan cover are extra wide, extending almost the full width of the barrels. Under this wide cover were twin pans, side by side, one directly over each barrel. A sliding lever on the left operated a piece of flat sliding steel which moved forward to cover the left pan and keep it from igniting when the right side was fired. Doubles of this type were built in London by J. Rea from about 1780 to 1826, by Knubley, who worked from about 1750 to 1800, and probably by others.

In the early decades of the 1800s the flintlock mechanism was elevated to its ultimate perfection by the almost legendary Joseph Manton (1795 to 1835), Joseph Gulley (1800 to 1832), and a small handful of contemporaries to whom absolute perfection rather than mere financial success was a goal. This striving to perfect the flintlock became doomed in 1807 when the Scottish minister of Belhelvie in Aberdeenshire, Alexander Forsyth, was granted a patent for his detonating system which evolved into the simple copper percussion cap. The acceptance of the percussion system came in the mid-1820s and '30s and it had two effects on screw barrel pistols, which continued in equal or even greater favor than before. First, since a percussion hammer is smaller and less complicated than the jawed flintlock cock, the new "detonating" pocket pistols gained a little in compactness. They also gained a little in speed since the smooth, solid surface of the percussion hammer was easier and quicker to use. Secondly, because the percussion cap system offered a better gas seal at the breech than a flintlock it developed a bit higher pressure and velocity.

Conversions

When the percussion system gained widespread acceptance, vast quantities of guns underwent conversion from flint to cap ignition, with conversions varying from the workmanlike professional to the makeshift. One of the problems encountered with ordinary sidelock guns was that a screw plug had to be fitted into an enlargement of the old vent hole in order to hold the nipple. Unless this new plug were fitted with a clean out screw it was all but impossible to clean the inside and it soon corroded to block the channel from cap to charge. However, since most screw barrel pocket pistols were built with center-mounted boxlock actions they were exceedingly simple to convert. It was simply a matter of removing the frizzen and pan cover—about 30 seconds work with a screw driver—replacing the flint cock with a percussion hammer, enlarging the vent hole and tapping it, and finally screwing a nipple into place.

The screw barrel pistol never gained the wide popularity in America that it did in England and Europe, although it is interesting to recall that Lewis and Clark carried a small pair of screw barrel pocket pistols with them (listed in their records at $10 value) on their 1804 expedition. For the most part, there was little need for such a specialized weapon in pioneer America. While urban Londoners required discreet pocket armament that could sometimes double as an ornamented status symbol, frontier Americans were more interested in heavy lead throwers that could supplement a rifle or musket in stopping a charging Indian or grizzly.

The screw barrel pistol was a favorite pocket protector for over two centuries, well into the era of the metallic cartridge, which was the only innovation which could top it for efficiency. Dr. Carl P. Russell in his work *Guns on the Early Frontiers* (Berkeley, Calif., 1957), notes that "not until the 1870s did the screw barrel pistol go entirely out of use. Today, screw barrel pistols as a class are a fascinating area for collectors that has been explored mostly only in bits and pieces. A collection of 'turn off' pistols is a highly rewarding endeavour. In fact, nothing I can think of brings home the fact more clearly that enlightened 20th century man with all his space age technology has little on the Old Masters of the gunsmith's art who had so very little to work with other than two willing hands and a fertile brain." ●

Art of the Engraver

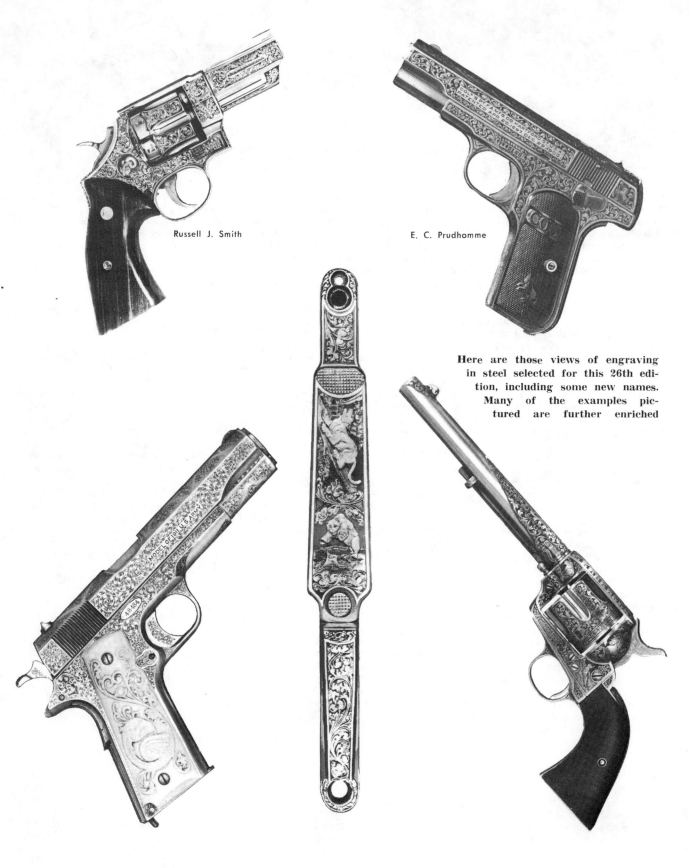

Russell J. Smith

E. C. Prudhomme

Here are those views of engraving in steel selected for this 26th edition, including some new names. Many of the examples pictured are further enriched

John Rohner

Russell J. Smith

E. C. Prudhomme

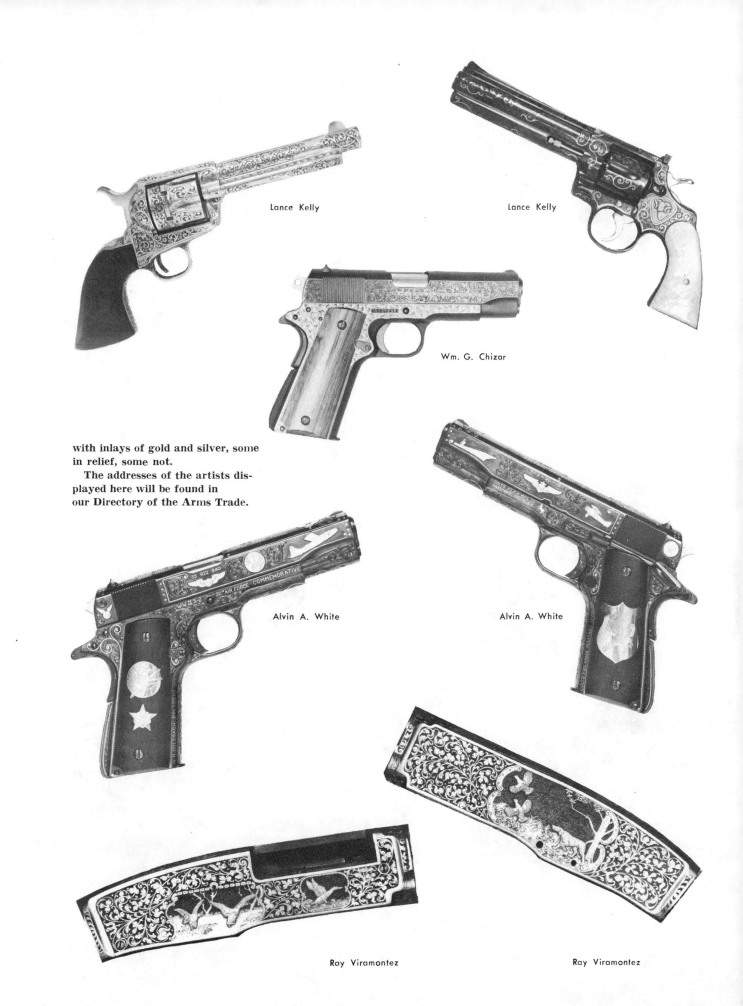

Lance Kelly

Lance Kelly

Wm. G. Chizar

with inlays of gold and silver, some
in relief, some not.

The addresses of the artists displayed here will be found in
our Directory of the Arms Trade.

Alvin A. White

Alvin A. White

Ray Viramontez

Ray Viramontez

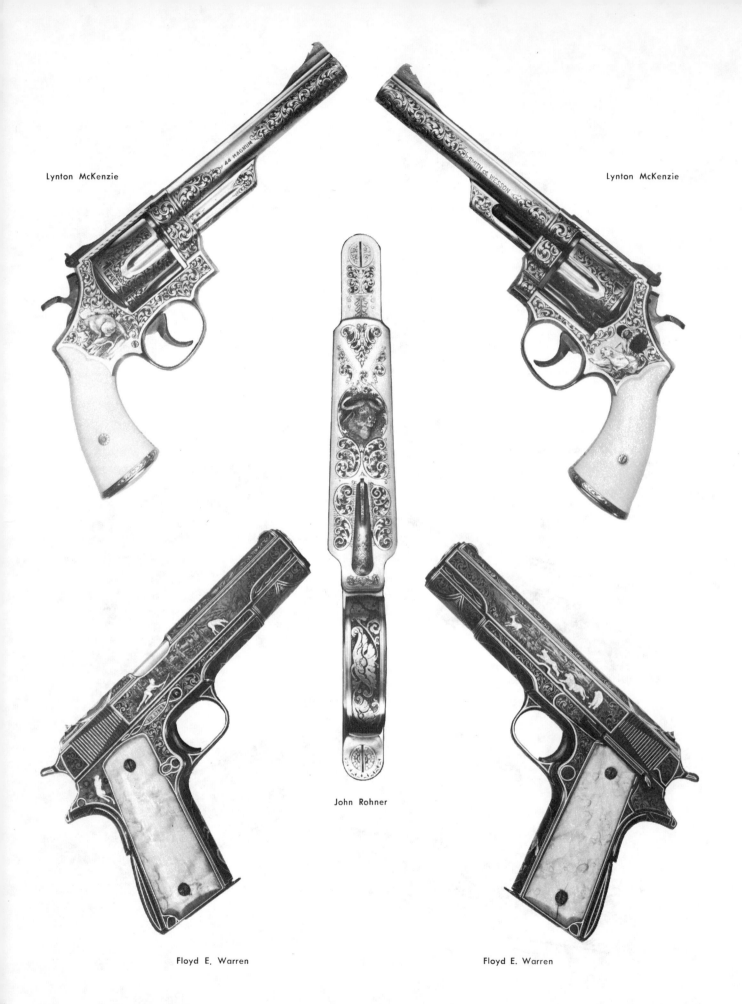

Lynton McKenzie

Lynton McKenzie

John Rohner

Floyd E. Warren

Floyd E. Warren

John Warren

John Warren

F. R. Gurney

Ray Bossi

Paul Jaeger

Albin Obiltschnig

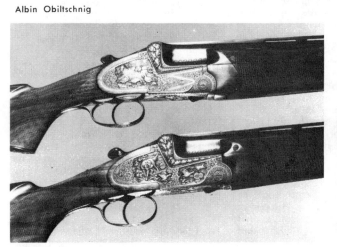

Neil Hartliep

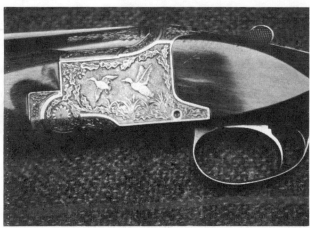

My wife Bobbie uses her 257 Roberts, carrying a Weaver V9 scope, for all her big game and varmint hunting. This 25-lb. bobcat is one that many men, including her husband, have yet to collect!

THE 25 IS STILL ALIVE AND WELL, AND LIVING IN FORT COLLINS, COLORADO!

THIS IS AN age that sees new cartridges coming into existence almost as fast as they can be dreamed up, most of them filling a gap in the lineup of modern cartridges. Many, however, are simply modern versions of older "outdated" cartridges.

Unfortunately, in this process, room has to be made on an already saturated market. To do that, some cartridges have to be discontinued as factory chamberings in new rifles.

There are those of us who bemoan the passing of some of the older, tried and proven cartridges. Usually, our wails are caused by the discontinuation of a specific cartridge, not a full lineup of cartridges in a certain bore diameter. Yet that is just what has happened to the 25 calibers.

Those who know me are convinced I'm some kind of a nut. As long as the reference is to the 25 calibers, I'll concede the point because, to my way of thinking, there isn't a better, more versatile *bore diameter* (not caliber, mind you) than the quarter-incher. To illustrate my point, my family has a total of 17 centerfire rifles in our gun cabinet, and 10 of those are 25s. Sentiment alone isn't the reason we hang onto these rifles. In most cases, we feel nothing else does the job quite as well.

However, the new and different is what sells and gun manufacturers are in business to sell new firearms. This means that the old, no matter how

much better than a new one it might be, must be replaced. There are exceptions, of course. The shooting public might be eager for new products, but it is also stubborn when a favorite cartridge is involved. That is one reason the venerable 30-30 is still one of the most common cartridges used by deer hunters. It has been around for some 75 years, but still shows no sign of passing out of the picture. The 30-06 is almost as old and, in spite of the ballyhoo of some who declare it obsolete, will be around for a good many years yet. Although a youngster in comparison to the 30-30 and 30-06, the 270 continues to grow in popularity after 44 years of existence.

In general, however, yesteryear's cartridges have faded out of the picture. The 25s are good examples of this. Not so long ago the prospective shooter had no less than 6 factory 25s to choose from. Today there are only two—the brand new 25-06 and the 257 Weatherby Magnum, the latter a relative newcomer also.

As a result, a man looking for a 250-3000 Savage or 257 Roberts will pay almost as much for a good used one today as he would have when they were brand new. These two excellent cartridges, replaced by the 243 Winchester and 6mm Remington, are more versatile than their successors. I'll support that statement a little later. First, though, let's look at some of these "obsolete" 25s and see what

their advantages were—and are.

Early 25s

The forerunner of modern centerfire 25s was the 25-20 Single Shot. This gently tapered case was brought out in 1882 by J. Francis Rabbeth, a well-known rifleman and writer of that era. He designed it for use with 67- and 77-gr. bullets, but when the factory brought it out in 1886 an 86-gr. bullet was used. Remington, Stevens and Winchester 25-20 barrels have slow twists, about 1 turn in 12 to 14 inches, to stabilize the lighter bullets as well as factory loads.

The more modern, and much more popular, 25-20 Repeater (WCF) is a direct descendant of the 25-20 SS, having a sharper shoulder and shorter over-all length. It was brought out around 1893 for use in the short Model 92 Winchester and Marlin lever actions. Winchester and Savage both chambered lightweight bolt actions for this cartridge and these were more accurate, but not more popular, than the lever actions. Several single shots also chambered this round.

The 25-20 Repeater was the first centerfire varmint caliber to catch the fancy of the general shooting public. Its short length, abrupt (for its time) shoulder and inherent accuracy, plus a variety of cast and jacketed bullets, adapted it for use on edible game as well as on varmints. It reigned as varmint king for over 35 years. I know

There are those who clamor for a factory 25, the author one of the most vociferous. He's sold his family on the two-bit bore, certainly, and as recent events show, he's convinced Remington!

by RON TERRELL

The author bagged this red-furred coyote with his wife's 257 while on a deer hunting trip.

an old-timer in Northern California who still uses the 25-20 Model 92 he was given as a boy, and he's never failed to bring home his game—up to and including deer.

Factory-loaded 25-20 ammo is a mild 2250 fps, with the 60-gr. Hollow Point bullet, and a tortoise-paced 1460 for the 86-gr. load. This isn't quite up to the potential of this cartridge but it's pretty close—particularly in the 60-gr. for varmints. My 12-year-old boy's first centerfire rifle was a 23B Savage, and we have handloaded his ammo to just over 2300 fps. 10.5 grains of 2400 powder gives the best accuracy/velocity/pressure combination with Remington or Winchester's 60-gr. hollow point bullet. That's our standard load. On those days when Jim can't stay out of school for a trip to the hills, that slimmed down Savage sometimes finds its way into my hands—just for the fun of it.

Two other 25s, the 25-25 and 25-21, quickly followed the 25-20 but didn't last long. 25-20 WCF rifles lost out commercially in the early '30s, the only strictly varmint 25 available to the rifleman. The introduction of the 22 Hornet sounded the death knell of the 25-20 but, you know something? Find a man with an ancient Model 92 in 25-20 and just see if he'll part with it. My guess is he won't —not for less than what you would pay for a gilt-edged sporter, anyway.

By the time the 25-20 was discon-

tinued, other 25s had been brought out as commercial loadings. The best of these were two like-powered competitors: the 25-35 and 25 Remington. Both were chambered in some fast-handling rifles, but weren't greatly mourned in passing.

It was in 1895 that Winchester brought out their 25-35 cartridge and Marlin introduced their version — called the 25-36—shortly thereafter. The 25-35 is still in limited use but the 25-36 has long since passed away. The 25-35, a rimmed small brother to the 30-30, was chambered in many of the same rifles. Most popular was the 94 Winchester but Savage also chambered their 99 lever action for the 25-35. Various single shot rifles were also made in this caliber.

The 94 and the 99, in 25-35 improved form, have accounted for numerous fox, coyote and other varmints in the hands of my family. My Dad, Grady Terrell, uses the 94 on predators that cross his Oklahoma farm, and I use the 99 on Colorado coyote and bobcat. Both rifles were rechambered by Claude Simmons, LaPorte, Colo., gunsmith, to the 25-35 Ackley's Improved. For this cartridge, modern 30-30 or 32 Special brass has to be used since older 25-35s rupture at the shoulder when fired in the Improved chamber. The stronger 30-30 brass is sized down in my RCBS dies, then fire-formed with standard loads.

The 94 Winchester requires round-

nosed bullets because of its tubular magazine, so my Dad's loading is limited. He's done pretty well with Remington's 117-gr. round nose, however. The 99's rotary magazine permits the use of lightweight, pointed bullets for increased versatility.

Ackley rates the 25-35 Improved as one of the better wildcats, giving a surprising increase of velocity over the standard cartridge. With Speer's 87-gr. spitzer ahead of 41 grains of 4895 and CCI primers, my 20″ barreled Savage gives a chronographed velocity of 3240 fps—better than the standard 250 Savage loading, and almost as good as handloads in my 257 Roberts. My 14-year-old daughter Susan is partial to lever actions, and claims this short-barreled Savage for her own.

The 25 Remington is basically a rimless 25-35. Case capacity of the two is almost identical, and their ballistics are so nearly the same that identical loads can be used. The 25 Remington has a slight legal edge over the standard 25-35, in that the 25 Remington is permitted for big game in Colorado, the 25-35 is not. Colorado law requires that a cartridge must produce 1000 foot pounds of energy at 100 yards to be legal for use on any big game animal. Factory-loaded 25-35s fall 5 ft. lbs. shy of that mark while the 25 Remington is the same amount over.

Only Remington got very enthusi-

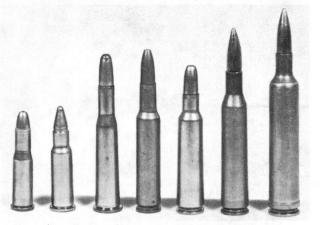

Many 25s were once factory made. Here are some, from left: 25-20, 256 Win. Mag., 25-35, 25 Rem., 250-3000 Savage, 257 Roberts and 257 Wea. Mag.

Among this group of 25-caliber wildcats the one at the far right was chosen for new factory production. From left: 25-35 Imp., 250-3000 Imp., 25 Souper, 25 Krag, 257 Roberts Imp., 25-284 and 25-06.

astic about this medium-powered cartridge. Their slide-, auto- and bolt action rifles were the only ones made for it in quantity. This is unfortunate because handloaded 75- and 87-gr. bullets made this a fine varmint cartridge. Remington's pump-action Models 14 (discontinued in 1935) and 141 had spiraled magazine tubes that prevented pointed bullets from resting against the primer of the cartridge in front of them. This minimized the danger of an accidental discharge during recoil and adapted this pump action for a variety of bullets.

My M14 in 25 caliber bears serial number 52380 and, according to Remington records, was made in 1916. Still in excellent condition, it's used regularly. Jim wants it for his deer rifle; in a couple of years, when he turns 14, he can get his first big game license.

The greatest loss to the shooting public—I think—was the discontinuance of the 250 Savage and 257 Roberts as factory chamberings. Both were excellent cartridges for all-purpose hunting use, as well as target competition, and they've earned perpetual places of honor in shooting history.

Newton Designs

Charles Newton was ahead of the commercial ammunition designers by about 20 years. His line of sharp-shouldered cartridges was considered radical when he first introduced them. Credited with designing the 250-3000, Harvey O. Donaldson actually made the final suggestion to the Savage people about using a shortened 30-06 case instead of the rimmed Krag case submitted by Newton. Savage introduced the 250-3000 in 1915. Velocity sold rifles then as it does now, however, so instead of bringing out this cartridge with the 100-gr. bullet suggested by Newton, Savage reduced the weight to 87 grains in order to achieve a 3000 fps. Newton kept pushing for a 100-gr. loading and Peters finally brought it out in 1933 — several months after Newton's death. This loading lived up to Newton's prediction of giving the finest accuracy and game-killing potential, and current sales indicate that more ammunition in this weight is sold across the counter today than the lighter bullet weight.

Savage carried the 250-3000 in their 99 lever action rifles until 1960. During its 45-year lifespan, the 250 gained honor as a target champion and top game getter. The low recoil and mild muzzle blast made it a favorite of young and old, men and women alike. It was used on game of all sizes and, although not considered an elk cartridge, many hunters never felt need for anything more powerful.

In the earlier days of the 250's existence, factory ammunition was loaded to a certain pressure level and then standardized. It almost took an Act of Congress to change it once it was set. World War I brought about some tremendous developments in firearms manufacture and ammunition-loading procedures, and the following years saw great progress in powder and component development. This has resulted in higher velocities at the same pressure levels established for some cartridges over 25 years ago. By way of comparison, the 243 WCF is the cartridge modern riflemen tout as being better than the 250-3000. When factory loadings are compared, their argument is sound. Let's look at it this way, however. A handloader with a choice of 4350, 4320 or 4895 powders loads his ancient 250 to the original pressure level of 50,000 psi and, lo and behold, the 100-gr. 25 caliber bullet exits the muzzle *faster* than the 105-gr. 243 slug does—and from a shorter barrel at that. Remember that most published velocities (unless specifically stated otherwise) are taken from a 26″ barrel. Firing these hotrock 243s in the shorter barrels usually attached to across-the-counter rifles drops the MV considerably. Remember, too, not one reloading manual lists or recommends a load that duplicates the factory published ballistics. A velocity of 3200 fps is available in a handload-

A wide assortment of 25 bullets are made. From left, this partial line-up includes: Remington 60-gr. H.P., Hornady 60-gr. Sp.P., Hornady 75-gr. H.P., Sierra 75-gr. H.P., Sierra 87-gr. S.P., Speer 100-gr. S.P., Hornady 100-gr. Sp.P., Sierra 100-gr. S.P., Arizona Bullet Co. 100-gr. S.P., Nosler 100-gr. S.P., Nosler 100-gr. Semi-Blunt, Norma 100-gr. S.P., Western Tool & Copper 100-gr. H.P., W.T.&C. S.P., Remington 100-gr. S.P. Core-Lokt, Nosler 117-gr. S.B., Remington 117-gr. R.N., A.B.C. 120-gr. S.P., Speer 120-gr. S.P., and Barnes 125-gr. S.P.

ed 250 with an 87-gr. bullet and the 100 grainer can be pushed along at 3090. This comparison, not meant to take anything from the 243, simply shows that the 250 is very much alive and even better than its successor as an all-round cartridge.

One of the all-time great cartridges earned its reputation in spite of pretty severe handicaps. The story of the 257 Roberts is as familiar to gun enthusiasts as the problems on "Peyton Place" are to the fans of that television show. This cartridge was developed by Major Ned H. Roberts. He had started experimenting with various 25s in the early 1900s, having several rifles made up to chamber cartridges he designed or co-designed with A. O. Niedner. He ended up with a necked-down 7mm case with a long sloping shoulder, and had Griffin & Howe make him a rifle for it. Performance was excellent and a number of friends and acquaintances had similar rifles made up on various actions. By the time Remington got around to bringing out their version of this cartridge in 1932, approximately 600 custom 25 Niedner-Roberts rifles had been made up.

257 Roberts

Remington sharpened the shoulder on their version to ease brass production, and called it the 257 Roberts to avoid confusion with the earlier-designed case. Before their brainchild was off the drawing board, however, they smacked it in the chops by standardizing production with blunt-nosed bullets seated deeply, giving a short over-all length. Accuracy was quite acceptable with these bullets but velocity dropped off so quickly that it wasn't any better than the 250-3000. To make matters even worse, they built their rifles with such a short magazine that this error couldn't be corrected by the handloader.

In spite of all of these manufacturing hang-ups, the 257 gained in popularity rapidly. Knowledgeable gun enthusiasts either chose the great Model 70 Winchester in this chambering (which had a longer action and magazine) or procured a custom rifle. Multitudes of military Enfields, Mausers and Springfields were rebarreled and chambered for the 257, bullets were

seated farther out in the case neck, and the day of the 257 had arrived!

Factory-loaded 257 ballistics are far from impressive. The heaviest loading available sends a round-nosed 117-gr. bullet down range at only 2600 fps. The best bullet weight for the 257, the 100 grainer, is loaded to a modest 2900. Winchester made a noble attempt to rectify many of the earlier mistakes by bringing out an 87-gr. loading in 1954. This moved along at 3220 fps but too much damage had already been done. There are recent indications that the arms companies are planning to bring out loaded 257 Roberts ammo that equals what handloaders have been doing for 35 years. If this does come about, it will help the 257 image tremendously.

The handloader is again the one who brings out the full potential of a mistreated cartridge. Ned Roberts and other early experimenters were limited to very few suitable slow-burning powders. The progressive development of powders with slower-burning rates continually broadened the capabilities of the 257 and other similar cartridges. Col. Townsend Whelen, a 257 admirer, did extensive experimenting with various bullets and powders for it. When 4350 powder was developed, he considered it the ultimate powder for use in the 257, one that finally made it possible to realize the full potential of this quarter-incher.

The modern handloader, using 4831, 4350 or other similar slow-burning powders, can choose from a wide variety of 25-cal. bullets. There are more 25s than any of its competitors offer. Weights range from 60 grains to a high of 125 grains. Between these extremes, the 25 user can choose from over a score of different manufacturer's offerings.

Speer offers the widest range of bullet weights (60, 87, 100 and 120 grains) but several others are close competitors. Hornady and Remington have 60 grainers but stop at the 117-gr. mark. Hornady added a 75-gr. hollow point to his line (which also includes the standard 87- and 100-gr. selections) that is a top varmint slug in the small- and medium-capacity 25s. All other bullet makers include several weights of 25-cal. soft points

in their listings.

I found out by personal experience that one 257 in a family isn't enough. After coming home from several family trips afield and realizing that my wife and kids had done all the shooting, I felt it was time to give my better half a rifle fitted just to her 5'2" frame. An attempt at finding a more suitable cartridge to use in making this new rifle was fruitless so I sashayed out to Claude's gunshop with another '03A3 action to be barreled to 257 Roberts. Now, Bobbie and I both use 257s on our trips afield.

The only commercial 25-cal. rifle until recently was Weatherby's 257 Magnum. Roy has earned an enviable reputation with his rifles and calibers, and the 257 Magnum is one of his better efforts, in my opinion. The Weatherby Mark V action is rated as the world's strongest and the line-up of Weatherby Magnums ranges from the 224 Varmintmaster up through the monstrous 460 Magnum. All WM cases are belted for greater strength and more accurate headspacing.

The 257 Weatherby is overbore capacity compared with the standard 257 Roberts and 250-3000, but not to the point of stripping a barrel too quickly. Velocities from this 257 WM make it quite clear that there is plenty of life left in this number. When a 100-gr. bullet exits the muzzle at a velocity of 3600 fps there can be no doubt about something taking place when it hits game.

Other 25s

There were and are numerous other 25 calibers in the field, all of them wildcats except for one. That was the only new 25 in recent years, the ill-fated 256 Winchester Magnum. It seems ridiculous to compare this cartridge with the 257 WM, nevertheless this midget magnum is of the same bore diameter and bears the magic "Magnum" headstamp.

Winchester announced the 256 in 1961 but it was over a year before a firearm chambering this necked-down 357 Magnum appeared on the market. It was beset by problems from the beginning. Intended for use in rifles and revolvers, the problems of chambering it in a revolver are apparently too great to overcome. Smith & Wes-

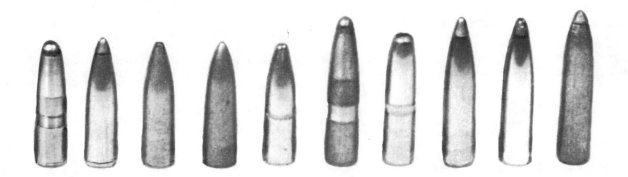

son and Ruger both tried to iron out the problem of cases backing out against the recoil plate and locking up the cylinder, but neither was able to do so. Ruger finally came up with the "Hawkeye," an 8½" barreled single shot pistol, and handgunners had a fine single shot for use on varmint.

Only Marlin brought out a rifle for this round. They beefed up their short-throw "Levermatic" series and called it the Model 62. It was supposed to have been chambered for the 357 Magnum, 256 Winchester Magnum and 22 Jet cartridges, but the first and last never made it. I picked up one of the early Marlins in this newest 25 and modified it for my oldest girl, Susan. Even today, when she's older and uses a more powerful centerfire on big game, Susan still prefers taking along her "first" rifle for plinking and coyote-calling trips.

The author's family, 25 shooters all. From left: Jimmy with an altered M23 Savage in 25-20 with Weaver K-3 scope; Susan with Marlin M62 in 256 Win. Mag. and Weaver V4.5 scope; Bobbie with her custom Springfield 03A3 in 257 Roberts with Leupold 2x-7x variable, and Ron with a Springfield 03A3 in 257 Roberts and B&L's BalVar 8.

This one short-lived attempt to bring out a new factory 25 missed the boat for the arms industry as well as for the shooter. The shooting public wants an all-round cartridge, while the manufacturers want a cartridge that will sell rifles and ammunition. To meet both requirements, the manufacturers are going to have to look back to the 250-3000, 257 Roberts or one of the wildcat 25s for their new offering—and that's exactly what happened!

It was not in the cards, though, that the 250 or the 257 Roberts would become the new factory 25. While still very much alive in the varmint and game fields, and gunsmiths across the country do a good business building custom rifles in both calibers, for an arms company to bring out a new cartridge identical to one they discontinued is an almost unheard of action.

The new factory 25, as we know, is based on a currently available wildcat—which isn't a bad idea. This has

been done, the 22-250 being a good example.

New 25s?

There are several likely wildcat 25 candidates. The 25-35 Improved, because of its rim, is suitable for use in single-shot actions or in the 99 Savage. The 25 Krag is another good rimmed wildcat, but neither is very well suited for use in bolt actions. They probably did not get much enthusiasm as a new-cartridge candidate.

P. O. Ackley has probably done as much wildcatting development as anyone, and two of his brainchildren deserve serious consideration. The 250-3000 Ackley Improved increases the potential of this medium-capacity case to the point that it equals and even exceeds the standard 257 Roberts in some loadings. Ackley rates this as one of the very best of the so-called Improved cartridges; he says it has a better velocity increase with a lower percentage of increased powder charges than any of the others in this bore diameter. He rates it of almost ideal case capacity in relation to bore diameter.

Another wildcat 25 that might have got strong consideration as a factory 25 is the 257 Ackley Improved Roberts. According to Ackley's *Reloading Manual*, this "is a relatively efficient cartridge, flexible and comes close to the mythical 'all-round cartridge'." Just about maximum capacity for the 25 bore, it still retains a good balance between performance and barrel life.

Dave Andrews, ballistician for Speer Bullet Company, has a 257 Improved on an F.N. action that he says gives exceptional accuracy and consistent velocity. With Speer's 87-gr. bullet, Dave uses 53 grains of 4350 and CCI 200 primers for a chronographed velocity of 3570 fps. The

100 grainer is pushed at 3380, using a maximum loading of 52/4350. Using Barnes' 125-gr. bullet puts the 257 Improved up close to the popular 270/130-gr. loading.

When a new factory cartridge appears, wildcatters rush in with all kinds of variations, necking it up and down to both extremes. This was the case with the new 284 Winchester, introduced in 1963. One of the fastest with the mostest was Bob Hutton of Hutton's Rifle Ranch, Topanga, Calif. He used the 284 case to come up with several useful wildcats, one of the best being the 25-284.

The 284 was developed specifically to give 270 velocities in a case that would be short enough to work through the shorter lever- and auto actions of the Winchester 88 and 100 and Savage's 99. The 25-284 case capacity and velocity is so nearly identical to that of the 25-06 that it should fill the requirements of the arms companies for a new case with more or less magnum qualifications and, at the same time, satisfy the demands of us 25-cal. enthusiasts for a new worthwhile and all-round 25.

Most popular of the 25 wildcats is the 25-06 or 25-06 Niedner as it is often called. In existence since about 1910, the 25-06 was the one selected to follow the 22-250 up from the ranks of wildcat to commercial cartridge. Ackley rates this as an over-bore capacity cartridge but nevertheless an excellent one. With the development of slow-burning powders like 4350 and 4831, this cartridge came into its own, is not now of over-bore capacity, and barrel life is good. This is one of the best of the 25 wildcats and an extremely popular one. One of the projects that keep gunsmiths busy is building custom rifles chambered for this old-timer. A number of commercial outfits offer barrels, barreled actions and complete rifles chambered for this wildcat. For example, Herter's, Inc., of Waseca, Minn., fit a Douglas barrel to their U9 action and sell the completed rifle for less than a "C" note. I can testify to the quality of workmanship of this latest addition to my family's 25 collection. My U9, topped off by Redfield's mounts and 4X-12X variable scope, consistently delivers minute of angle 5-shot groups with a variety of bullets and powders.

The 25-06 is of special interest to the midwest and western hunter who takes his game at long range; loaded with 100- to 120-gr. bullets it's a top game getter. Loaded with good quality 87-gr. bullets to about 3450 fps, it is a destructive long-range varmint cartridge. It is at its best with bullets weighing 100 grains or better, however.

Well, the many rumors have now been confirmed, and the new factory quarter-incher is the 25-06 just as Adolph Niedner planned it so many years ago. The 25 is still alive! ●

BIG BULLETS FOR LITTLE GUNS

BY WILLIAM R. WEIR

Are you trying for that last foot second of velocity from your short-barreled revolver? Do an about face, says the author, who tells how and why they'll give better stop-power, greater shock-power.

IF YOU SAW A friend trying to turn a farm tractor into a drag racer, you'd probably wonder what happened to poor old Charlie to drive him over the brink—and you'd have reason. The tractor is designed to exert maximum power over any kind of reasonably firm surface; the drag racer, to reach maximum speed over a quarter-mile of billiard-table-smooth track.

The current trend toward hotter cartridges in lighter guns, however, is leading many shooters to a similar folly. They're trying to develop magnum-type loads for their snub-nose, ultra light 38 specials. This is about as reasonable as expecting to break 200 m.p.h. in a corn picker. Such experimental loads usually turn out to be full of sound and fury, signifying little increase in power on target, however shocking they may be to the shooter.

What's really unfortunate about this feverish pursuit of high velocity is that shooters engaged in it are missing a chance to turn their little 13 to 15 ounce 38s into really deadly instruments. One reason for their trouble is that they seem a bit confused about just what the snub-nose 38 is supposed to do.

These revolvers were designed for the detective or off-duty policeman who has to carry a gun chambering the service cartridge but wants a minimum of weight and bulk. Such a gun, being an arm the officer uses primarily for self-defense, would almost always be used at short range. Unlike the uniformed highway patrolman's sidearm, it would seldom be called upon to penetrate auto bodies or engage in long (pistol) range gunfights.

After the 357 Magnum was developed for handgun hunters, it was adopted by a number of police agencies for their uniformed men. The cartridge combined great accuracy, penetration and stopping power in any revolver with a moderate to long barrel, so it was an excellent choice. Those fascinating figures in the ballistics tables, however, are achieved in an 8⅜-inch barrel. Velocity and energy figures drop like a gambler's bank account when you shorten the barrel. A Magnum with a 2-inch barrel would toss its 158-gr. slug no faster than 1060 feet per second (fps.). That's about 30 fps less than you'd get with 38 Special high speeds in a 6-inch barrel and some 200 fps less than some handloaded 38 Specials will give you in a 5-inch barrel.

MV Versus Barrel Length

But if magnum velocities plummet when you shorten the barrel, Magnum pressures drop hardly at all. So the 2½-inch barrel "under cover" magnums now on sale weigh between 33 and 39 ounces. For that kind of weight, you could shorten the barrel of a 45 ACP revolver and get an arm with equal accuracy, superior stopping power and a lot less noise and muzzle blast. Not many plainclothesmen, though, want to tote around 35 or so ounces of steel.

All of which brings us back to the ultra light 38. These little guns are barely adequate to handle factory high speed loads, and only a certified lunatic would use them with some of the handloads a heavy frame 38 will digest. The usual procedure for hopping up the little guns is to use an unusually light bullet with a heavy powder charge. Some of these loads are quite impressive—in a 6-inch barrel.

Here's a rule of thumb: The higher a cartridge's maximum velocity, the more sharply velocity drops when you shorten the barrel. When you go from a 6-inch to a 2-inch barrel, the 357 Magnum loses 270 foot-seconds; the 38 Special high speed loses about 95,

Cast bullet loads in 38 Special. Left pair—200-gr. blunt nose; center pair—150-gr. semi-WC; right two—160-gr. HP.

and the regular 158-gr. 38 Special service load loses about 80.

Another rule: All other things being equal (e.g., maximum velocity), the heavier the bullet in a particular caliber, the less sharp the velocity drop as you shorten the barrel. The late Maj. Gen. Julian S. Hatcher, onetime chief of Army Ordnance, conducted extensive tests with the 38 special Super Police (200-gr. bullet) load.* In a 7½-inch barrel, he got an instrumental velocity of 656 fps; in a 6-inch barrel, 671 fps; in a 2-inch barrel, 623. The velocity loss for those 4 inches was only 48 fps. While these are instrumental velocities and are somewhat lower than the true muzzle veloc-

*Textbook of Pistols & Revolvers. (Plantersville, S.C., 1935).

ity, they accurately show the relationship between velocity and barrel length.

Current loadings give the 200-gr. bullet in the 38 Special a muzzle velocity of 730 fps from the 6-inch barrel. Allowing a velocity loss of 50 fps, you still get 680 foot-seconds from the 2-inch barrel. Obviously, the short barrel handles this 38 Special load much more efficiently than it handles the others.

So what good is a bullet with less than 700 fps velocity?

In the early 1930's, the British armed forces decided to replace their ponderous 455 revolver with a smaller and lighter arm firing what they referred to as the 380-200 cartridge. This was simply the old American 38

S&W Super Police load—a less powerful cartridge than the one we've been discussing, developing about 600 footseconds in a 5-inch barrel.

The British had already tried a number of 38 and 9mm cartridges but rejected them all as having insufficient stopping power. (At this time, the submachine gun was little used by John Bull's boys, and there was no need to have the handgun cartridge fit an SMG.) Tests and experience, however, convinced them that the 380-200 would stop as well as the 455. The reason they gave was rather quaint.

"The quality of efficiency depends to some extent on the massive soft lead bullet and the relatively low velocity rather than on any inherent magic in the caliber."

Smith and Wesson 38-44 Heavy Duty model (above) can take heavy loads like the 155-gr. hollow point ahead of 12.5 grains of 2400. Such a cartridge would be most unpleasant—and possibly dangerous —to shoot in the lightweight S&W Bodyguard, below.

This 200-gr. bullet keyholed through one thick telephone book, hence penetrated only halfway into second book.

In other words, British Ordnance contended that low velocity improved stopping power. Now, as any apprentice ballistician can prove, this is utter nonsense. However, the 380-200 had no trouble knocking down fanatical Pathans in the Khyber Pass, and there's no reason to believe that the Pathans were any less tough than the Moros of the Philippines.

The big, slow 200-gr. slug worked, but why? It certainly wasn't muzzle energy. The 380-200 developed some 170 foot-pounds of energy, which put it in a class with the pipsqueak 38 Short Colt. By way of comparison, the 38 Special 158-gr. service load develops 256 foot-pounds from a 6-inch barrel and 207 from a 2-inch tube. Figures for the 38 Special Super Police are 236 and 206, which also shows how the gap between the 158- and 200-gr. loads narrows as you shorten the barrel.

Stopping Power

Muzzle energy, of course, is not stopping power. If it were, the 7.63mm Mauser pistol would be one of the best, instead of one of the poorest (by U.S. Army tests) manstoppers around.

General Hatcher worked out what is probably the best system of calculating pistol cartridge stopping power. It's based on the momentum of the bullet, multiplied by its squared diameter and a factor for material of the bullet and the shape of its point.*

Momentum is mass multiplied by velocity. To determine a bullet's mass, find its weight in pounds, which involves dividing its weight in grains by 7000, then divide the result by 32.16, the acceleration of gravity. The squared diameter of a 38 Caliber bullet is .102. Hatcher assigned a factor of 1000 for the round-nose, lead, 158-gr. 38 Special slug. The blunter 200-gr. slug got a factor of 1050. What you get with the Hatcher formula is a number that stands for nothing by itself,

*Op. cit.

but when compared with similar figures for other cartridges, usually gives you a pretty good idea of how a particular load compares as a stopper.

With the Hatcher formula, the 200-gr. 38 Special gets a relative stopping-power rating of 69.5; the 158-gr. service load, 61.8. Both figures are based on 6-inch barrel velocities. With a 2-inch barrel, the 200-gr. load's advantage would increase, giving an RSP score of 63.6 for the heavier bullet and a score of 55.1 for the lighter.

Note that the 200-gr. 38 Special has more theoretical stopping ability when used in a revolver with a 2-inch barrel than the 158-gr. service load has in a gun with a 6-inch barrel, much more than the service load in a snub-nose gun. The Super Police load's theoretical stopping power in short-barrel guns isn't as good as that of the factory high speed load. But these high speed loads are so disturbing to the shooter of ultra light revolvers that all but the most highly trained men find it extremely hard to fire fast and accurate successive shots.

Penetration

Hatcher's relative stopping power formula indicates that the 38 Special with the 200-gr. bullet is a good load, but it doesn't tell the whole story. For that, we have to look at another Hatcher formula—this time one for calculating penetration. The formula itself—striking energy multiplied by the product of the bullet's squared diameter and a factor for the resistance of the material—needn't concern us. What's important is how well it was able to predict penetration. When Hatcher compared his calculations with actual test results, he found that he had been able to predict the penetration in 7/8-inch pine boards of almost every load tested. One glaring exception was the 200-gr. load for the 38 Special. Calculated penetration was 6.9 boards. Actual penetration was only 4 boards.

The reason? The 200-gr. 38 bullet has too much weight for its diameter to be stabilized with the twist provided by Colt or Smith and Wesson rifling. So it tumbled end-over-end as it ploughed through the boards.

Tests by the author confirmed this result. The 200-gr. bullet grouped well at 25 and 50 yards when fired from a Smith and Wesson revolver (twist rate: 1 turn in 18⅔ inches). When fired at two large telephone books at 25 feet, however, the bullet invariably tumbled, usually entering the cover of the second book broadside, and never penetrated completely through both books. On the other hand 158-gr. loads—the round-nose service load and a semi-wadcutter loaded to service load velocity—always passed through both books without any keyholing at all.

Tumbling by a long bullet like the 200-gr. 38 slug multiplies stopping power many times, putting it, as the British found, in the 45 caliber class.

It seems too bad then, that so many police officers are neglecting this perfect "snub gun" load (handloaders can duplicate it with Lyman's 195-gr. 358430 bullet and 3.8 grains of Unique) while they dream the impossible dream of a 14-ounce, 2-inch barrel Magnum. ●

38 Special loads: 200-gr. blunt-nosed bullet (left) and standard 158-gr. service bullet.

The National Shooting Sports Foundation

Several valuable booklets—notably *Model Firearms Legislation* and *A Compilation of the Federal Gun Control Act of 1968*—are now available in revised, up-to-date editions. These publications help you and your political representatives understand better the many problems of firearms ownership, the urgent need for positive, protective legislation.

THE NATIONAL Shooting Sports Foundation offers the best studies in the U.S. on the ownership and use of firearms. Alan S. Krug, director of research, has published a series of studies on the problems of firearms ownership in today's society.

Made to assist sportsmen, conservation and law enforcement agencies and lawmakers, the sources of all information, including statistical data, are documented. Because of their objectivity and authenticity, the NSSF has received numerous requests for copies from state attorneys general, governors and legislators.

Now available is the 3rd edition of *Model Firearms Legislation,* a 44-page book which shows model starter bills for sportsmen to consider on pre-emption, lawful transport, hunter safety, etc.

More than 3 years ago the NSSF began a long-range program of positive and protective legislation to insure the welfare of the shooting sports. For instance, the NSSF's model pre-emption bill states, "The legislature hereby declares that it is occupying the whole field of regulation of the transfer, ownership, possession and transportation of firearms to the exclusion of all existing and future county, city, town or municipal ordinances or regulations relating thereto. Any such ordinances are hereby declared null and void."

A state pre-emption bill insures that cities and counties cannot pass different and conflicting laws. Such laws only confuse sportsmen, so much so that they rarely know when they're acting legally or are violating some vague clause in a poorly drafted law.

A special feature of the NSSF book is that the wording of model bills is in the 2 left columns on each page, while the third column gives a step-by-step explanation of why the bill was drafted and what it does. The reasoning behind each phrase or paragraph is clear and easily understood.

The book also has a section on definitions, always a problem in drafting any bill. This section not only helps the law-maker, but it also will help standardize definitions across the nation, avoiding the hodgepodge of unclear definitions written by many anti-gun legislatures.

One of the model bills would prohibit a tax on firearms ownership. The bill states, in part: "No license or registration fee or tax shall ever be imposed on firearms transferred, owned, possessed or transported for the above (lawful) purposes."

Krug says, "Sportsmen in every state should support a bill prohibiting taxes on firearms ownership. The time to do it is now, especially in low population states where there has been little problem with anti-gun bills. Once the bill is passed, it becomes a long-range protection for sportsmen. It is always difficult to repeal a bill. It is not easy to get sportsmen to be for a bill and support it. However, once a bill becomes law and the sportsmen believe in and depend on the rights established by the bill, if anyone ever tries to repeal it, the sportsmen immediately rally to defend it. It would be even better if the principle was incorporated into the state constitution."

"The most important shooter's program in America today," Krug went on, "is the passage of long-range bills protecting the welfare of hunting and shooting."

To help cover printing and distribution costs, the 3rd ed. of *Model Firearms Legislation* sells for $1.

A Compilation of the Federal Gun Control Act of 1968, also called Gun Comp, is a valuable reference for hunters and shooters. It presents the act itself, regulations under the act up to January, 1971, forms required by the act, questions and answers and sources of other information on federal firearms laws.

This 60-page book, also $1, is an excellent publication to show to legislators. Krug says, "Few lawmakers, and especially the general public, realize how comprehensive the Gun Control Act of 1968 is. Newspaper editorials frequently demand legislation which is already a part of the act. Many state bills are introduced each year which would duplicate the act's provisions."

Gun Comp is the best means of showing a newspaper editor or lawmaker the scope of the act. The sheer volume of complicated regulations and forms makes them realize, usually with a quick glance, the wide coverage of the act.

Fact Pack II covers the ownership and use of firearms based on documented statistics. A valuable book for sportsmen and lawmakers, it is especially useful as a reference in writing articles on firearms legislation and preparing statements for hearings.

As a service to sportsmen, William E. Talley, president of the NSSF, recently announced a new program of selling publications in bulk to clubs at cost. Now any organized club, local or state, can order NSSF publications in carton lots at cost. A special cost list will be sent to any club official.

A booklet which sportsmen should order for club distribution to neighbors, schools and libraries is *The Hunter and Conservation.* The 24-page booklet, with an easy-to-read style, lists the many conservation accomplishments of hunters over the past 75 years. It is the best booklet ever written on how the hunter spends his time and money for wildlife.

There is an increasing anti-hunting sentiment in America in some of the urban press. One way sportsmen can help counteract it is by starting a pro-hunting program to inform their friends and neighbors of the many plus factors in the shooting sports. Almost any club can afford a carton (600 for $35) of *The Hunter and Conservation* for distribution in its community.

The NSSF has a variety of literature on shooting promotion, including kits with patches—and new pieces are added annually to help sportsmen. For a catalog, free, write: National Shooting Sports Foundation, 1075 Post Road, Riverside, Conn. 06878.

by B. W. Brian

WANTED!
A New Pistol Cartridge

Many new handgun loads have appeared in recent years, but all have been
for revolvers or single shots. Why none for automatics?
Here's a plea — and suggestions — for this too-long neglected field

THE LAST DECADE has seen a number of handgun cartridges introduced in the U.S., among them the 41 and 44 Magnums, 22 Jet and 221 Fireball, all by Remington, and the 256 Magnum by Winchester. These cartridges were either for revolvers or single shot handguns; none was designed for use in automatic pistols. In fact, the last new automatic pistol cartridge in the U.S.—the 38 Super—appeared in 1929, and it wasn't really new; it was simply the old 1900 38 ACP loaded to equal the 9mm Mauser of 1912, and given a new name for use in a different pistol.

A quick check of the more common pistol cartridges (see accompanying table) indicates that nearly all were developed over a half-century ago. Since that time we've had several new foreign and U.S. automatic pistols designed for existing cartridges—usually the 9mm Parabellum (Luger). It's about time we had a new pistol cartridge.

In the mid 1930s France adopted a 7.65mm cartridge—nearly identical to the 30 Pedersen of World War I—with ballistics slightly better than those of the 32 ACP. (They have since adopted the 9mm Parabellum.) In the early 1940s Germany developed a new cartridge which was ballistically somewhere between the 380 ACP and the 9mm Parabellum and known as the 9mm Ultra. World War II ended before the cartridge was adopted. A few years later, in the late 1940s, a new 9.2mm Russian cartridge, slightly larger but very similar to the 9mm Ultra, appeared along with two new automatic pistols. This is the way things stand in 1965. Our own 45 ACP is now 60 years ancient, and some of the other automatic pistol cartridges, including the 9mm Parabellum, are even older.

Popular Military Cartridges

Automatic pistol cartridges are generally designed with a hope of military adoption, since the commercial sale in many countries would hardly pay for the development work. Today the two most popular military pistol cartridges are the 9mm Parabellum and the 45 ACP, with the former being the more widely used. (Until recently the 7.62mm Russian—practically identical with the 7.63mm Mauser—cartridge ranked a close third and possibly even second, because of its use by many Soviet satellites.)

Promoters of the 9mm say it is easier to learn to shoot than the 45 because it has less recoil. They also point out that its ammunition weighs less per round, permitting more to be carried, and claim it has satisfactory stopping power as a result of its velocity, which is considerably higher than the 45's. This velocity also makes hits at longer than ordinary ranges easier than with the 45.

On the other side of the fence, fans of the 45 insist that although this caliber might take more practice to handle properly, its bullet, being approximately twice as heavy as the 9mm and having much greater cross-sectional area, provides stopping power which cannot be readily calculated on paper. As to long-range shooting, they take the stand that few individuals can shoot any handgun well enough to make this aspect important.

Recent years have seen an increase in the use of the handgun for game hunting. Except for some small caliber singleshots, such as the Remington XP-100, for use on varmints, these handguns have been revolvers chambered for the larger calibers such as the 41 and 44 Magnums. These handguns were not produced with the military in mind, and even the various police departments shy away from the magnums. Therefore, they were manufactured for the handgun hunter and shooter.

Left to right: (1) 41 Rem. Magnum, 210-gr. SP; (2) 357 Norma Magnum, 158-gr. HJ; (3) 44 Rimless Auto Magnum, 200-gr. SP; (4) 9mm Luger, 116-gr. Norma; (5) 44 Auto Short, 200-gr. SP; (6) 400 Gamestopper, 180-gr. SP; (7) 45 ACP Federal Match; (8) 400 Gamestopper Short, 180-gr. SP; (9) 355 H-V, 115-gr. FJ; (10) 7.63mm Mauser, 86-gr. FJ; (11) 44 Auto-Mag, 200-gr. SP; (12) 355 H-V Auto-Mag, 115-gr. FJ.

Except for the revolver cartridges and the 44 Rimless Auto Magnum, all these will fit magazines of available autoloading pistols. The 44s might not greatly surpass the 45 ACP, but the 400s and the 355 H-V could well outshine anything now offered automatic pistol shooters.

Update the Colt M1911?

Now, about that new automatic pistol cartridge. We already have an automatic pistol of modern design which could be modified to handle it— the S&W Model 39. Or the Colt M1911 could be brought up to date. It's time. (Even its inventor, John Browning, didn't think the M1911 was the last word, as indicated by his improvement in the early 1920's which eventually became the Belgium-produced M1935.) Other countries have improved versions—takedown latches, reduction of parts, etc.—of the M1911. If we bring out a new pistol cartridge you can bet that some of these foreign automatics will be chambered for it.

Actual size of a new cartridge will be limited in both diameter and length by the size of the magazine which can be placed in the conventional automatic pistol grip. In plain words, any new automatic pistol cartridge cannot be much larger in diameter than the 45 ACP (.476"), nor longer than the 7.63mm Mauser (1.36"). Caliber? Why not a 44 with a 200-gr. bullet, or better yet why not a 400 with a 180-gr. bullet? Using a straight-sided rimless case with a length exceeding that of the 45 ACP, it should be possible to push the 180-gr. bullet along at a muzzle velocity of 1300-1400 feet per second to give it a muzzle energy of approximately 700-800 foot pounds, nearly double that of present automatic pistol cartridges and comparable to the 357 Magnum revolver load or the 32-40 rifle cartridge.

Pictured here are a number of wildcats which might prove suitable. The 44 Rimless Auto Magnum and 44 Auto Short are based on the 7x57mm rifle case, shortened and blown out. The longer case has the same external dimensions as the regular 44 Magnum, except it is rimless; the Short case is 27mm long.

The 400 Gamestopper and the 355 H-V are based on the 7.65mm Swiss M.P. case, shortened and blown out to minimum body taper. The 400 has a case length of 26½mm, with a Short version being 25mm long. Both Gamestoppers headspace on the mouth. The 355 H-V is blown out and necked down to take 9mm (.355") bullets. Its case is 27½mm long and it headspaces on the shoulder.

The 44 Auto Magnum is the same as the 44 Auto Short, except that it is made from 30-06 brass which has a different head thickness and extractor groove, and case length is 25mm.

The 355 H-V Auto Magnum is made from 7x57mm brass, shortened to 25mm and necked down to hold 9mm bullets. Body taper is unchanged. It headspaces on the shoulder. Indications are this could be the real barn-burner of the lot.

Is one of these in the future? It could be. It's a long time overdue. ●

Common U.S. & Foreign Automatic Pistol Cartridges

Cartridge	Bullet (grs.)	Velocity (fps)	Energy (fp)	Introduced
25 ACP (6.35mm)	50	820	75	1906
7.63mm Mauser	85	1420	380	1893
7.65mm Luger	93	1200	325	1900
32 ACP (7.65mm)	71	980	152	1899
9mm Browning Long	110	1100	300	1903
9mm Luger	124	1150	365	1902
9mm Bayard	126	1148	365	1903
9mm Steyr	116	1200	370	1911
380 ACP (9mm Short)	95	970	199	1908
38 ACP	130	1070	300	1900
38 Super	130	1300	488	1929
45 ACP	230	800	330	1905

Note: This table does not include all currently manufactured automatic pistol cartridges; however, a fair representation has been listed. All ballistics quoted are approximate only, as bullet weight, velocity, and energy figures vary among different loadings. The 9mm Luger (Parabellum) and 7.62mm Russian (nearly identical with the 7.63mm Mauser) are generally loaded to a higher velocity for military use. The year of introduction will vary according to where the pistol first was manufactured: some of the Browning designs were manufactured in Belgium before being introduced into the US.

POWDER FLASKS

by DON SHINER

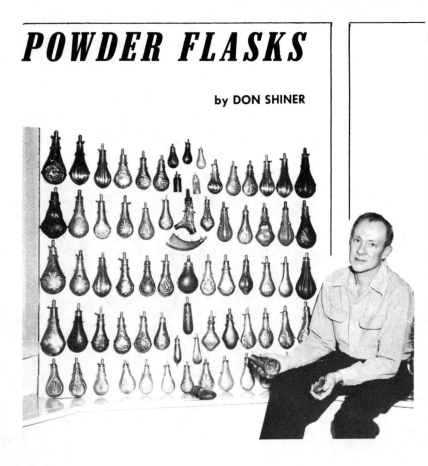

ONE OF THE largest collections of old powder flasks in the country has been gathered together by Justin V. Anslinger of Richmond, Virginia, with well over 100 in his collection. Some are made of copper, some of zinc or brass; many are beautifully engraved with shells, pheasants, deer and other scenes.

Following the invention of early firearms, gunpowder was carried in simple hollow steer horns, but as guns developed, more elaborate ivory, bone and metal powder flasks were created as companions for firearms. Those that were made between 1825 and 1900 — the span of years represented in Anslinger's collection — were highly decorated and incorporated devices which even measured the charge of powder.

One rare item Anslinger likes to display is an oval-shaped horn flask of the type carried by Napoleon's army. Another is made of stag horn, of German manufacture, which carries a biblical scene. Others were made in France and shipped to this country, according to still legible stampings, and still others were made in this country when the West was being pioneered. Anslinger has searched the U.S. to augment his unique collection. ⊕

The Shooter's Showcase

Sid Bell Originals

If you like exquisitely carved miniature animals, executed in sterling silver (gold, too, in some models) as tie tacks, lapel pins, etc., write to Box 188, Tully, N.Y. 13059, for his illustrated brochure. New numbers include bighorn and Dall sheep in full three dimensions, plus a like buffalo he's recently completed for the Colt Mfg. Co. to celebrate their new Sharps Sporting Rifle.

10X Jacket

I've been wearing a new version of the 10X Perry Pistol Jacket, this one in olive-drab (No. 405, price $17.95), that I've found quite generally useful, never mind handgun shooting. I like the 4 pockets—2 big breast pockets and 2 large bellows-type below, room for almost anything! It's a comfortable coat, too—bi-swing shoulder, sleeves that can be rolled up, and it's virtually windproof.

10X has a tremendous array of outdoor clothing this year, a variety too great to detail here, but among the brand new items I was taken with the Sporter Hunting Coat (No. 457 at $34.95), which has a nylon outer shell with a rubberized interior, a back game bag that's blood proof and can be reached through 2 front zippered openings. Matching this clover-green jacket are their Brush Hunter pants, covered in nylon from the crotch to the bottoms in front, and at the back to the bend of the knees. Cuff-to-knee zippers let them be put on or off over boots, too, and they're made with a double seat for dryness. No. 557, $26.95 a pair.

Other brush pants run from $15.95 to $23.95, and there's much more to see in the big 1971 10X catalog, including many products for women, for warm and cold weather use by shooters and hunters. Ask 10X Mfg. Co. (100 S.W. Third St., Des Moines, Iowa 50309) for a copy.

GCA-1968

A Compilation of the Federal Gun Control Act of 1968, brought up to date as of January, 1971, by the National Shooting Sports Foundation, is now available at $1 a copy, retail. Prepared by Scott Krug of the NSSF, this 64-page large format booklet is a well-prepared, excellent publication that should be in the hands of lawmakers, police officials, attorneys general and newspaper editors.

Few people—including a fair number of those in the positions mentioned—have any clear idea of just how inclusive the GCA-1968 is, how vast its scope. Right now there are bills before many state and local legislatures that would duplicate—or worse, nearly duplicate—the GCA-1968.

We urge our readers to obtain copies of this new publication from their local dealers, and to distribute them where they'll do the most good. Dealers—and others—may order in bulk at $40 per 100 copies.

Write to NSSF, 1075 Post Rd., Riverside, Conn. 06878.

T/C Hawken Parts

The new Thompson/Center Hawken rifle, described elsewhere in this issue, is now available in its component parts—the heat-treated, color-hardened and scroll-decorated percussion lock sells for $26.50; breech plug and tang (the two units making a hooked-breech setup) are $10, supplied in the white; the adjustable double-set triggers, blued and ready to install, are $12.50 and the scrolled guard, color-hardened steel and in fully finished condition, is $4.50. A descriptive leaflet is available, no cost.

Clymer Mfg. Co.

Longtime makers of tools for the gunsmith—chambering reamers, headspace gauges and the like—Clymer now offers Bullet Swaging Dies for use in ⅞-14 thread presses, made in 30, 38, 44 and 45 caliber, with nose punches in most popular styles. Heat treated to 52-55 Rockwell, the dies are then honed to 4-6 micro inches—and that's smooth! Fully adjustable for bullet weight, the complete die costs $18.95.

Extra nose punches are $4.75 each, and a lead wire cutter, for 3 sizes of wire, is $14.95.

Ellwood Epps

This old-established Canadian gunshop and sports store (Box 338, Clinton, Ontario) was sold recently to W. E. Collins and P. B. Gemeinhardt. The gunsmithing/custom gun divisions have been fully reorganized for faster service, the new owners have told us, and that multi-die case forming set we reported on last year is now in production, cost $19.95. They'll gladly send full details on the new setup, and their new big catalog, showing 8000-plus items ($1) should be ready as you read this.

Ellwood Epps, an old friend, opened his Clinton shop in 1937, a long time ago. We're sorry to see him go, but he's got a good rest coming.

Lead Poisoned Waterfowl

The death of wildfowl, particularly mallards, through the eating of lead pellets lying on the bottom of ponds and other waters, was documented nearly a century ago. Further reports to the same effect were made in the 1900s and the 1930s, and in the 1950s, following a joint study, it was estimated that 2% to 3% of all North American waterfowl were being killed annually by lead poisoning.

Since those years, numerous reports have indicated that such poisoning was becoming worse, if only because of greater numbers of duck hunters afield.

The use of soft iron shot in place of lead shot has been explored since 1966 by the Sporting Arms and Ammunition Manufacturers Institute (SAAMI), but without any real success so far, but it has been recently said that U.S. Steel was producing soft iron shot that would not age-harden (that has been a problem). SAAMI purportedly commented that the USS iron shot appeared to be satisfactory, and that its testing would continue.

Will soft iron shot be generally available a year or two hence? Maybe, perhaps not. Five ammunition firms are at work now to make soft iron shot, other companies are trying to perfect—and make ballistically acceptable—such shot. Much testing will be required, and soft iron shot will need to be made at an acceptable economical level. It will have to be determined whether otherwise acceptable soft iron shot does, in fact, harden with age or not.

Woods Sport-Toters

That's what Woods calls a new duffel bag being offered to the traveling sportsman. Lightweight and roomy, the Woods carryall is made of 10-oz., pearl grey Permasol canvas. It's reinforced at all strain points with leather and nylon webbing, the comfortable handles are made of soft black padded leather.

A full-length heavy-duty zipper opens the main compartment, a zippered side pocket is handy for small items, and "D" rings on the straps will carry a rifle, shotgun, etc. The large one is 30" x 14", sells for about $19, the 21" x 9" size is $15.

17 Caliber O'Brien

Much—if not most—of the current popularity of 17 caliber rifles lies with Vern O'Brien (224 Tropicana 128, Las Vegas, Nev. 89109), an enthusiast for the mini-bore for many years. Vern at one time made 17s in great variety, hunted with them—successfully if maybe foolishly—for big brown bears, was instrumental in getting H&R to bring out the first production version.

O'Brien now stocks everything connected with the 17s—bullets in several weights, a variety of cleaning rods, brushes, tips, etc., RCBS dies for most chamberings, funnels, formed cases, load data—you call it.

Creed Ammo Pouch

Creed Enterprises, (13167 East Garvey Ave., Baldwin Park, Ca. 91706) has developed an unusual ammo carrier. It attaches to the belt lying flat to the body, and is opened by simply pulling a tab; it closes at a touch via spring tension. Made of top quality cowhide, with a waterproof plastic lining, its ingenious metal closing device is like that used in tobacco pouches. Capacity is good—250 22 rimfires or about 50 rounds of 44 Magnum, a score of 30-06s, etc. A useful item, it sells for $6.95 in black or brown.

Hunting License Sales Rise Again

Hunting license holders rose to 15,370,-481, an increase of 101,000 over 1969. Expenditures by hunters for licenses and permits exceeded the 1969 total by nearly $6 million for a new high of $101,607,879.

License monies enable States to carry out fish and wildlife conservation and management activities. Additional funds come from Federal Aid in Fish and Wildlife Restoration programs, under which States are reimbursed up to 75% of the cost of approved projects. For the current fiscal year, which ends June 30, 1971, $43,905,000 was apportioned.

Cumberland Arms

Based in Manchester, Tenn. 37355, at 1222 Oak Dr., this firm tells us they'll be marketing Martini-actioned barrels soon in 218 Bee, 22 Hornet, 225 Winchester, 30-40 Krag and other rimmed cartridges. Barrels will be medium-heavy, standard length 28″, and actions offered blued or case-colored. Price will be about $100 standard, $10 more for the colored (and engraved) set.

Cumberland also offers loaded handgun cartridges; bullets also, and formed 25-06 cases.

Off-Road RV Use

Secretary of the Interior Rogers C.B. Morton today announced in mid-April the formation of a Departmental team to investigate the use of snowmobiles, dune buggies, motorbikes, motorcycles, and other types of motorized off-road recreational vehicles on public lands.

Secretary Morton said he was deeply concerned that unregulated use of some desert lands, dune areas, elk and deer wintering yards and other Federal lands could be causing irreparable damage. Such abuse, he added, of fragile public refuges and wild areas must be stopped.

The guidelines and recommendations formed by the study group will serve as a basis upon which a Departmental policy can be developed, Morton said.

Admittedly, off-road RV use is "... one of many legitimate uses of Federally-owned lands. At the same time there are areas which are being adversely affected by vehicular use of this type," the Secretary said, adding:

"I am directing this Department, in cooperation with States and other Federal agencies, conservation interests, and the industry to develop a management plan which will assure an optimum of recreational use with a minimum of environmental conflict."

New Blue Book

The new 1971-72 issue of Williams' *Blue Book of Gun Dealing* has just been released, price $2.95. It lists nearly 2000 firearms and scopes, giving their current retail price, description and also their worth in poor, good and excellent condition. Anyone who trades or deals in firearms will find this new 84-page booklet a good investment. Included are tips on what guns not to buy, making a used gun saleable, fitting the gun and other articles of interest. Williams Gun Sight, 7300 Lapeer Rd., Davison, Mich. 48423.

Razor Edge

The gadget shown here, attached to a knife—*any* knife—maintains the exact honing angle needed to develop a razor edge—an edge that will shave hair is guaranteed!

The complete kit contains the Razor Edge device (for knife or arrowheads, so specify), one Coarse and one Ultra Fine hone, cost $11.95. For $3 more, both Razor Edge clamps are furnished, and a zippered pouch to hold the lot is $4.95 extra. Full instructions are furnished.

A good tool—we've seen the maker (John Juranitch) use it, we've used it, and it does produce an edge that shaves your whiskers. Write to Razor Edge, Box 203, Butler, Wis. 53007.

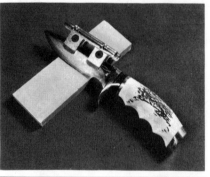

The New Ecology

Concern with ecological balances and the environment as a whole is not new. Only a broad public awareness of these factors is recent. For too many years the general public ignored the early warnings of fishermen, hunters, bird watchers, wilderness clubs, wildlife biologists and other outdoors-oriented groups with practical or professional understanding of the ecological destruction they were witnessing.

The motives of such groups were suspect, unfortunately—fewer fish in the creel, less game in the bag, loss of a favorite wilderness trail, or places to seek new bird sightings to lengthen a life list—and were of little concern to the rest of the public. Now everyone is becoming aware that lakes and streams no longer fit for fish may also be unfit for drinking water or swimming; that the filling of still another marsh not only robs the waterfowler and the bird watcher, but threatens a wide variety of aquatic life as well, to the detriment of both commercial and sport fishermen; that polluted air not only makes buildings dirty on the outside, but people dirty on the inside.

Consequently, many new organizations

and groups are forming to attack environmental problems. Some of these are already providing valuable public service in testing new environmental laws, providing the public with a forum for their views and informing them of proposed governmental action. The limited experience of some of these new groups, however, often leads them to take an oversimplified approach to environmental problems, many of which are extremely complex and require the evaluation of environmental and ecological experts.

Similarly, the time has come for those groups with established credentials to develop a broader viewpoint of the environmental-ecological situation that goes beyond their own immediate area of interest.

It's time for all of us to realize that, while some areas should be left forever wild, others may benefit from a degree of commercial utilization and multiple use; that there are areas where trees should not be cut and areas where they should; that while total recreation, power needs, flood control and the like may dictate

man's modification of some waterways, we must not sacrifice the values offered by many streams, rivers and lakes as nature created them; that some wildlife species (few of which, incidentally, are in the game category), need special protection for their very survival, while the well-being of others is best served by both management and controlled harvest.

Above all we must recognize that, in the absence of co-ordinated nationwide planning, factors such as population expansion and commercial land development constitute the greatest threat to our American outdoors.

We need very badly today a more common meeting of the minds of all groups concerned with the outdoors. It is wasteful and tragic for any one group to spend its energy in opposing another. It has become critical that all these energies be combined and directed against the truly serious environmental problems that threaten our entire society. As some have already suggested, the most endangered species today may well be man. But only man, through mutual effort and understanding, can take himself off the endangered list.

H&B Forge Co.

The tomahawks pictured here are hand-forged for H&B (Route 2, Greenwich, Ohio 44837) by Amish blacksmiths in the old traditional style—a cold-rolled eye of mild steel carries a bit formed of "plow share" steel, a tough 10-80 alloy that H&B holds to about 48 Rockwell. This degree of hardness allows file sharpening instead of grinding. Made essentially for throwing in tomahawk matches, H&B 'hawks are made with a 1° tapered eye for easy tightening or replacement of the select, straight-grained hickory handles furnished on all H&B Tomahawks. Made in several styles and types, the 'hawks shown are, from left: the Shawnee standard, showing hammer marks, at $12; the Squaw, with a 15" handle and lighter head, at $11.50, and H&B best, the fully-polished Iriquois—with "weeping heart" cutout filled with brass and 44 solid brass tacks in the handle—at $30. Spare handles are $1.75-$2. H&B have other hand-crafted items of interest—flint strikers, belt buckles, candle holders, etc. Ask for a folder/catalog.

Rust Removers-Inhibitors

Surcon, Inc. (Zieglerville, Pa. 19492) has several products that will interest gun owners—and owner/users of other ferric items. Oxtrol removes rust, down to the bare metal, then deposits a coating that prevents re-rusting or corrosion *for a time.* Oxtrol does not attack the metal itself, therefore is useful on fine tools, engraving, etc. It is *not* flammable, is faster working when heated to 150° F., but *must not be used on blued surfaces!*

Service Saver prevents rust via water displacement, is recommended for use on metal treated with Oxtrol as a further corrosion preventive.

Kit-in-a-Kan is Surcon's new rust inhibitor for black powder shooters. To use, spray or pour KIAK into the muzzle, let set for 10 minutes, then clean bore easily. The fouling, carbon, whatever, has been effectively softened. Can't clean right away? Use KIAK as before, let the gun alone for as long as 10 days. It won't rust or corrode, say the makers. Surcon also suggests wetting patches with KIAK for extended, no-cleaning shooting. Write for full instructions, quantity packaging and prices.

1971 Shooters Calendar

Want to know where and when the major shooting events will take place in the U.S., in Canada and elsewhere in the world? Ask your gun-sports shop dealer for a copy of the above title. The pamphlet, published by the National Shooting Sports Foundation, is free.

● *George W. Blakeslee* is a recent listee in our Directory of the Arms Trade (page 472). His speciality is Collectors Cartridges, which he buys, sells and trades for, but he also makes and offers top quality powder horns, priced from $15 to $75.

● *We have received* a number of complaints about the Alaska Sleeping Bag Co., of Beaverton, Ore. These letters to us cited: Failure to answer repeated inquiries about long-delayed delivery—or non-delivery—of goods ordered, despite checks having been sent and cashed.

● *W. Kleinendorst* (Taylortown Rd., Montville, N.Y. 07045) has sent us samples of his well-made Rifle Cleaning Cables. Nylon covered steel cables guard against bore damage, with all other parts solid brass. Each has a swiveling finger ring, for pulling through, and at the other end a loop or a thread for brushes. No. 1, 30" long, with fixed loop tip, handles 17 to 30 caliber or larger depending on patch size used, is $3.50 postpaid, and seems the most useful of the 4 styles offered, if a simple emergency pull-through is wanted. The other types, usable with brass or bristle brushes, also include loop tips, sell for $5 each PP, mailed in a handy pocket container.

● *Ted Fellowes* (9245 - 16th Ave. S.W., Seattle, WA 98106), muzzle-loading rifle-maker on a custom, made-to-order basis only, wrote to say that he now has on hand the best stock of muzzle-loading supplies of anyone in the northwest. Does "best" mean "biggest" or . . . ?

● *The quail hunter* growls at the rabbit hunter and his beagles. The trophy hunter growls at the meat hunter. The backpacker may growl at them all. Thus millions of American outdoorsmen, with hundreds of varied interests that too often divide us and dilute our strength. Yet, all American outdoorsmen have common enemies. The same social, economic and political threats to birdhunting also threaten birdwatching.

One way to slow these enemies is to pour muscle, money and brains into effective organizations. For hunter and non-hunter alike, there's the National Wildlife Federation, The Izaak Walton League of America, The Sierra Club, the National Audubon Society and The Wilderness Society. They're all regiments of the same army, and they badly need recruits during 1971.

What can you do for the American outdoors? Take a lesson from the spoilers: study, learn, organize, make yourselves heard and felt, and put on some real political weight. John Madson

Euroarms of Italy

The fancy, engraved 50-caliber flintlock pistol pictured nearby—made in the 1768 Brescian style—is the Zanotti, distributed exclusively by Euroarms (Via Solferino 13A, Brescia 25100, Italy), who are also the makers of various Colt, Remington and other replica arms sold in the U.S. For example, see the Winchester 1873 replica carbine mentioned in our comments on Gold Rush Gunshop firearms, elsewhere in this edition. The elaborately chiseled Zanotti pistols, furnished cased, sell for $100 at retail.

RTVs in Wildlife Refuges

The Bureau of Sport Fisheries and Wildlife announced recently that the environmental effects of motorized rough terrain vehicles (RTV), including snowmobiles and dune buggies, will be considered before any national wildlife refuge area is opened for these uses.

Possible effects of such use on wildlife, habitat, recreational values, and physical resources will be determined by on-site investigations conducted by the refuge staffs. When permitted, motorized vehicles may be operated only in designated areas or on clearly marked routes.

Refuge managers may close any area to this type of use if it becomes necessary to protect resources, and if off-road activities conflict with the primary purposes for which the national wildlife refuges were established. (Editor's note: Hooray!)

Harry Owen

Walther adapters for many rifles and Krieghoff insert barrels for shotguns are now available from Harry Owen (Box 774, Sunnyvale, CA. 94088).

Walther adapters fire 22 LR and 22 RF Magnums in 221 Fireball, 222, 222 Mag., and others; also 308, 300 Win. Mag., etc. Pistol adapters, $32 each, fire 22 LR and 22 Mag. in 45 ACP pistols and 22 LR only in 9mm pistols.

Krieghoff insert barrels convert any 12, 16 or 20 bore break-open shotgun to fire 22 LR or 22 Mag. They're particularly useful in combination guns with rifle sights and/or scope mounts, such as Savage M24V, Tikka, and many others. They can be removed or reinserted in the hunting field without loss of zero in about 30 seconds. The insert barrels shoot as accurately as many 22 and 22 Magnum rifles.

Owen also carries such unusual items as factory-made mounts for combination guns. Write for details and prices.

Let's Shoot Sharptails!

Here's detailed advice from a Canadian expert on how, when and where
to find these good-sized, succulent-eating game birds, plus notes on the top
dogs for hunting them and the best guns and loads for bagging them

by Jerome J. Knap

A good retriever, such as this Labrador, can double-up as a flushing dog,
but pointers are best for general use, Knap feels.

IT WAS A FINE, clear October morning with a mild wind blowing from the west. The willows along the creeks and the plum and rose thickets on the ridges were already bare.

Through the grass not far ahead of us, my German shorthair May was methodically cutting back and forth. She angled up to the right and struck a sudden point near a clump of willows by the creek. We walked in slowly, shotguns ready.

Suddenly came the roar of powerful wings and the loud, indescribable cackling of a large covey of sharptails. The air seemed full of birds. My shotgun made an arc and I pressed the trigger. A miss — which

I quickly corrected with my second shot. I heard my partner shoot twice, but somehow the shots seemed far away.

The dog was standing rock steady, waiting for my command to fetch. When I gave the order, she leaped forward with the eagerness so characteristic of all good hunting dogs.

"It was beautiful the way May locked up that covey," my companion said as he walked toward me. Then, nonchalantly, "I knocked down a couple of birds. How did you make out?"

"One," I answered. "I missed my first shot. I must have stopped my swing."

By this time May had retrieved my bird. I examined it carefully — a juvenile cock of about 20 ounces. It had been several years since I last hunted prairie sharptails and I was looking forward to it.

Three Kinds of Sharptails

Most upland game hunters believe that the sharptail grouse, like its cousin the prairie chicken, is a bird of the prairies. This belief is only partially correct. The error lies in the fact that there are three sub-species of sharptails. The Columbian sharptail ranges from British Columbia through the Rocky Mountain states to Colorado. The prairie sharptail ranges from the plains of the Canadian "prairie provinces" south through the midwestern states to New Mexico and as far east as Illinois. The northern sharptail ranges from Alaska eastward to Ungava of Quebec and south through upper Ontario to Michigan.

As a result of this wide distribution, the habitat requirements for the three sub-species are different. The Columbian and prairie sharptails are birds of the short grass prairie and of foothills interspersed with brush and thickets. The northern sharptail is a bird of the northern park-lands, cut-overs and muskeg. The habitat re-

cannot be turned into wheat or corn fields. Even more important, with time the sharptails learned to take some advantage of the table spread for them by the corn growers and the wheat farmers. Consequently, the birds have made a surprisingly good comeback in many western states and provinces. Today, sharptails are beginning to rank as one of our more important game birds.

In order to hunt any game successfully, you must know its habits and habitat requirements. In farming country, the best places to hunt sharptails are the areas where not all the sod has been broken by the

of the cooler weather, but also because the stubble fields will have weathered and thus cannot provide a bountiful fare. Some may even have been plowed. The birds will now be feeding mostly on native foods such as weed seeds, dry berries, and even green shoots of grass and clover. As a result, the feeding range of a local sharptail population will be more variable, and thus harder to predict. This means that hunting plans must be adjusted according to the time of day, weather, and season, for maximum success.

In grazing country, the rolling prairie and foothills interspersed with yucca patches, plum and rose thickets along creeks are the places to hunt. Since corn and grain stubbles are rare, the birds must rely on native foods. During the early season, wild cherries, various soft berries and wild plums are preferred foods. Later on, the hard berries, rose hips and weed seeds are eaten. Green grass shoots and clover are also eaten, but mainly for their moisture content. With the coming of snow, the birds "bud" in trees and bushes.

The early fall pattern of feeding during the cooler hours of the morning and late afternoon and dusting and loafing in some shady nook during the midday heat is repeated. With the approach of cooler weather in late fall, this pattern is again disrupted to a high degree.

Where sharptails rely predominantly on native foods, the hunter must learn what they are feeding on. The crop contents of several bagged birds should make this clear. Food preferences change as the season progresses, because certain fruits and berries are palatable only after the first frost, while others will long since have withered. They will also vary from area to area, because certain shrubs may not even grow in a specific place, or the fruit may have had a poor season for peak abundance.

Best Hunting Time

Early season hunting is the most productive. The young birds hold well for a dog — they have not become experienced in evading man with a gun — and at this time the cocks, both mature birds and juveniles, gather into large coveys on the dancing grounds for the fall dance. The dancing continues until the first deep snow or excessively cold weather. These coveys may contain 40 or 50 birds, thus sharptails shot from large coveys during the early fall will invariably be males, while small coveys, up to 6 or 7 birds, usually consist of an old hen with her juvenile daughters.

With cold weather, the whole sharptail population of a normal two- or three-mile range gathers into large coveys. These may number well over 100 birds. Such coveys are very hard

A cooked lunch at midday gives this group of sharptail hunters a chance to relax before hitting the wide fields again.

quirement can be interpreted as being two-branched. The habits of the birds, and hence hunting methods, will also differ. All this makes generalized thinking and writing about sharptails difficult.

The chosen range of the prairie sharptail, and to a lesser extent of the Columbian, overlaps that of the prairie chicken in many areas. The plowing of the best grasslands to wheat and corn fields sounded the death knell for countless prairie chickens and sharptails, but almost from the start the sharptails fared better than the prairie chickens. The sharptail can do with less short grass and even shows preference for rough, brushy country which in many cases

plow. Such areas will not only have the grain stubbles which have become important feeding areas for the birds in early fall, but will also have the needed roosting and loafing covers of grass, which may be even further enhanced by clumps of brush. This usually means that poor or marginal farms produce more sharptails than good farms.

In the hot days of early fall, the birds will feed in the stubble fields during the cooler hours of the morning and late afternoon. During midday, they will loaf in the shady clumps of brush, grass or willows along watercourses. Later on in the fall, this particular feeding pattern will be somewhat disrupted. This is a result mostly

for dogs to handle, and even more difficult for the hunter to approach. The birds will frequently flush wildly, far beyond effective shotgun range.

Something the hunter should consider are the sharptail migrations. A fairly good range may be completely abandoned for reasons not yet fully understood. Another area, which has only a small population one month, may be crawling with sharptails the next. Needless to say, these migrations have a very obvious effect on hunting success. Large migrations have not taken place in recent years, but the late Ernest Thompson Seton reported sharptail migrations totaling tens of thousands of birds.

Weather is a very important factor in sharptail shooting. On windy days, when the rustling of grass and bushes is almost continuous, the birds will be nervous and wild. On such days, they will usually be found in thick cover, on the lee sides of hills and ridges. Shooting will be difficult because the birds will flush very wildly. However, on calm or, even better, drizzly days, they fly and run reluctantly. Sitting tight, they become easy for dogs to handle and hunters to approach.

The two cardinal mistakes of most sharptail hunters are talking and exposure. If you want the maximum possibility for success, stay below and walk around the hill tops. Doing this, the birds won't detect you, particularly important in sparse cover, where they can see a great distance.

All grouse react strongly to the sound of a human voice, but it seems to me that sharptails do so to the highest degree. Talking should not often be necessary during the actual hunt, but when it is, the conversation should be in low tones. Strategy should be decided upon and instructions given beforehand. During the hunt, attention can be drawn by a soft whistle. There should definitely be no shouting at dogs. They should be controlled entirely by the whistle and hand signals.

Talking during a hunt may mean that the sharptails will flush a few yards farther from the shooter, and these few yards may make all the difference between having one shot or two. Even more important, they may mean the difference between a cleanly killed or a crippled bird.

Pointers Best Dogs

A good pointing dog that also retrieves is invaluable in sharptail hunting. The smaller coveys of early fall have a strong tendency to run. This requires bold tactics on the part of the dog in order to "lock" the birds tightly. In the late fall, coveys flush easily, thus the dog has to learn to approach the birds slowly and gently, and to point from a distance longer than normal. It takes a good deal of experience before a dog learns to handle sharptails well. One thing is certain: a wild, uncontrollable dog is best left at home. He will flush more birds than he will hold.

In my opinion a fast, wide-ranging dog is preferable. Such a dog will cover more ground, and thus will find more birds, than a narrow-ranging one. The dog, of course, must be thorough. The pointer is, without a doubt, the best bet. However, setters and European pointing dogs can put up very creditable performances. My German shorthair certainly became a reasonably efficient sharptail dog. Even the large spaniels and those retrievers trained to range close and flush game can be of value. Some of the most outstanding sharptail dogs that I have seen in action were veterans of the U.S. Chicken Championship held annually in the Pine Barrens of Wisconsin.

The Columbian and prairie sharptails are shotgunners' birds. When they flush on the edge of effective shotgun range, they are very difficult to bag. However, under normal conditions I would rate their sporting potential slightly lower than that of Hungarian partridge. The sharptail is a bigger target and does not seem as fast on the wing as the Hun. The sharptails have one unnerving habit, though, the loud cackling sound they make when flushed unnerving many hunters.

Guns for Sharptails

Choosing a shotgun for sharptails is not particularly difficult. Any light field gun capable of shooting 1⅛-oz. loads will do. I use two, both 12 gauges—a Fox double bored modified and full and a Remington 11-48 auto fitted with a Poly-Choke to an over-all barrel length of 25″. Several friends use M37 Ithaca Featherlight pumps, also with Poly-Chokes (we like the easy adaptability for range which this device allows), and another friend uses a Winchester M12 having modified choke. A very good friend who is an outstanding wing shot uses a

Shotguns used by author and friends include, from top, Browning Superposed, Fox Model B side-by-side, Remington 11-48 auto and Ithaca Featherlight pump. The 12 gauge is favored, with #6 or #7½ shot, 1¼ oz. of the larger size being the best all-round load.

Holland & Holland double. He has two sets of barrels, one bored one-quarter and one-half choke, the other one-half and full. My frequent hunting companion uses a Browning Superposed Lightning with improved cylinder and modified barrels. All these guns are 12 gauge—the bore I would suggest.

During the early season, most birds will be killed within 30 or 40 yards. For this shooting I use 1⅛-oz. loads of #7½ shot with excellent results. Later on, when the birds gather into large coveys, ranges increase up to the maximum killing range of the shotgun. I then switch to 1¼-oz. loads of #6 shot. This is definitely the best all-round sharptail load, and seems preferred by the majority of sharptail hunters.

For early season shooting, a choke delivering an evenly distributed 50% pattern is ideal. This type of choke is frequently called a ¼ choke in Canada or improved cylinder in the U.S. It will kill birds cleanly to about 40 yards, but will not mutilate them at 30.

The whole aspect of patterns can be put to a mathematical test. Using Sir Gerald Burrard's formula to arrive at a target area (88% of a bird's weight in ounces represents the square-inch area of a passing bird),* we see that a sharptail weighing 26 ounces will present about a 23 square-inch target.* On the average it will take 4 pellets of #6 shot and 5 or 6 #7½s to kill a grouse. A 1⅛-oz. load of #7½ shot has some 394 pellets, while a 1¼-oz. load of #6 has about 280 pellets. With 50% patterns, these loads will deliver about 197 and 140 pellets, respectively, into a 30″ circle at 40 yards. The area of the sharptail is roughly that of a 5″ circle. Since areas of circles are proportionate to the squares of their diameters, the ratio between the 30″ pattern and the bird is as 900 : 25, or 36 : 1. Dividing 36 into 197 gives some five #7½ shot in the bird, on the average, or about four #6s.

From this it's obvious that 40 yards is the outside limit with these loads in this choke, with better results to be expected at 30-35 yards. To kill sharptails past 40 yards, a tighter choke will be needed. Jack O'Connor, Francis Sell and others have said that beyond 40 yards there is at least an 8-9% pattern loss for every 5 yards of additional range. Thus, to kill a sharptail at 60 yards, a shotgun has to be capable of shooting an 82-86% pattern at 40 yards. This type of performance is difficult to achieve. It might be done with carefully assembled handloads and a tightly bored barrel. However, even if we possess a shotgun capable of such long-range kills, we are still faced with the problem of hitting at that range. Only the finest wingshots can do this regularly. Hence, we can see that for success here it would take a shooter, gun and ammunition of exceptional merit. Since most of us do not have the skill to regularly hit any game bird at 60 yards, we do not need as tightly patterning a shotgun. Most full choke barrels pattern around 70%. This density will kill sharptails up to 50 yards, and this range more closely approaches the shooting ability of many shotgunners.

From the above information we can deduce that a modified choke would have the advantage when the birds are holding well during the early part of

*Maj. Sir Gerald Burrard was the author of *The Modern Shotgun,* first published in London in about 1930. This monumental work, in which the formula mentioned is covered, appeared in several editions and is an outstanding source for information on all aspects of shotguns. See book section.

Columbian and prairie sharptails have learned to live in a habitat altered by the wheat farmer, and they can often be found in grain stubble, as shown above.

the season, but when they are flushing more wildly, a full choke would get the nod. A variable choke device will add versatility to any single barreled shotgun used for sharptails, but for my money, the ideal choice is a light double, side-by-side or over-under, bored full and modified.

Northern Sharptails

The northern sharptail is a bird of the big burns, park-lands, cut-overs and muskeg, but in winter it will inhabit scrub land and even seek the protection of timber edges. In the fall, these birds feed on a large variety of wild fruits and berries. In winter, they feed on any dry fruit that may still be hanging on the trees, but their main diet is buds from such trees as cherry, willow, birch, and poplar. Again, they must be hunted near their source of food and cover. Northern sharptails also migrate to some extent. As winter approaches, their feet, like the feet of all grouse, become covered with fine feathers, and projections, which act like snowshoes, appear on their toes. In temperatures that frequently fall to 50 or 60 degrees below zero, sharptails, like their cousins the ruffed grouse, will at times burrow themselves into the loose snow for protection.

The northern sharptail is less wild than the other sub-species of sharptails, primarily because of its infrequent contact with man. The human population throughout much of its range is very sparse. Only Indians and a rare lumberman, big game hunter or trapper hunt the birds. Consequently, seasons and bag limits are generous, but even so the birds are underharvested. Because of their tameness, northern sharptails are pri-

marily a target for riflemen and handgunners.

The 22 rimfire is the favorite caliber with many visiting hunters, but it is not always the best choice. Head or neck shots are almost mandatory with the 22 because a body-shot bird has, at times, the strength to fly 40 or 50 yards before dying. Recovery of such birds in the thick ground cover of slash, muskeg or brush is usually impossible without a dog. Small game loads in a big game rifle insure clean kills even with body-shot birds. A good grouse load for my 30-06 is a size #1 buckshot ahead of 3.3 grains of Bullseye. Every big game hunter planning a hunt in the northern big game country should assemble some small game loads for his rifle, adjusting the powder charge so the buckshot strikes near point of aim at about 25 yards when the scope is zeroed as desired with the full-charge load.

Most northern inhabitants are primarily meat hunters. For this reason many prefer to use a small-bore shotgun, usually the 410, for their sharptail shooting. There is no doubt that head shots are easier to make on sitting sharptails with a shotgun, and thus a high percentage of clean kills is insured. There is, of course, little or no sport in this type of shooting. However, in sections of its range, the bird becomes a fine shotgun target. The northern sharptail does not need to learn how to fly, just to fear man.

The sharptail grouse is a fine table bird. Seton claimed that a sharptail split in two, rubbed and doused with bacon drippings and then broiled slowly over a bed of hardwood coals exceeds in flavor that of any other game bird. Most sharptail hunters, I think, will agree. ●

AMERICAN
BULLETED
CARTRIDGES

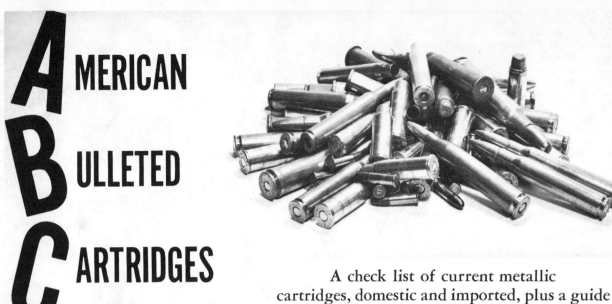

by KENNETH L. WATERS

A check list of current metallic cartridges, domestic and imported, plus a guide to performance and selection.

LATEST DEVELOPMENTS IN METALLIC CARTRIDGES

1971 may have been the Year of the Suckling Pig in the Chinese calendar, but to American shooters and reloaders it will almost surely be thought of as the Year of the Bullet; this because so many new bullets have been introduced during the past 12 months.

Just about all major bulletmakers have been busy plugging the gaps in their caliber line-up, offering new bullets specifically designed for some of the newer cartridges, in a few cases even working to replace an entire line with slugs having different construction and point conformation.

This is good news, especially for the handloader, who is thereby given greater flexibility in preparing top grade ammunition for specific purposes.

Particularly gratifying has been a continuation of the trend towards round-nose bullets for handguns, either with solid expanding or hollow-points, and away from semi-wadcutters.

The new soft-noses—particularly those with big hollow points—have already established their ability to expand well when given enough velocity. Too, their better ballistic form helps retain initial velocities over longer ranges.

Turn to our Reloading Review pages for Mr. Waters' further comments on the new bullets.

NEW CARTRIDGES
The 17 Remington

Since 1950, the old but highly progressive Remington Arms has introduced 15 new cartridges! 1971 witnessed the birth of a sixteenth—the 17 Remington. The ultra smallbore clan have been clamoring for just such a cartridge, and the boys at Ilion must have decided that where there was so much sound, there must be some fury (or at least a passel of shooters' dollars).

Anyway, the new round is now a fact, made up on the 223 Remington case necked down and with a shoulder moved back .087" to provide a

longer neck. Over-all case length, diameter and shoulder angle of the 223 have been retained. The bullet is a 25-gr. HP of "Power-Lokt" design measuring .1725" in diameter, making this (according to Remington) the smallest diameter bullet ever produced for a commercially made centerfire cartridge.

From a 24" barrel with 1-in-9" rifling twist, this little bullet shows the following ballistics:

Range (yds.)	Muzzle	100	200	300	400	500
Velocity (fps)	4020	3290	2630	2060	1590	1240
Energy (ft/lbs.)	900	600	380	230	140	90
Trajectory (in.)* Sighted @ 200 yds.	—	+1.2	0	−6.3	−21.2	−50.4

*Trajectory based on an iron sight height of 0.9" above the bore.

It will be seen from the above that the trajectory of the 17 Remington closely parallels those of the 243 Winchester and 6mm Remington out to 300 yards. Beyond that point, however, the 17 drops off more steeply. It is not appreciably flatter than the 223 or 222 Magnum cartridges though, and doesn't come up to the great 22-250.

(Remington's claim that the new 17 is "the fastest factory-loaded round now in existence" is quite true, the operative word being "now." The discontinued 220 Swift had almost 100 fps more velocity at the muzzle [factory ballistics in both instances]. By the way, at the 1971 NRA meeting Colt said that their Colt-Sharps single shot rifle will be chambered for the 220S, so it would seem that W-W or R-P will have to renew production of the cartridge. Or does it? Norma has had the 220S in the list for some time.

REMINGTON CALIBERS INTRODUCED SINCE 1950—From 1. to r. 5mm Rem. R.F. Mag., 44 Rem. Mag., 22 Rem. "Jet" Mag., 221 Rem. "Fire Ball," 17 Rem., 222 Rem., 223 Rem., 222 Rem. Mag., 22-250 Rem., 244 Rem., 6mm Rem., 25-06 Rem., 6.5mm Rem. Mag., 230 Rem., 7mm Rem. Mag., 350 Rem. Mag.

For some reason [probably because of the exsistence of earlier 17 wildcats, many with less than smooth, well-polished bores] the word has got around that the 17s are hard to clean. Not true, says Remington, nor does their 17 call for *highly* frequent cleaning. The benchresters have demonstrated that cleaning every 20-25 rounds is required if best accuracy is to be retained, and that is equally as true for the 17 as it is for the 222, et al. I agree, of several 17s I've had, two fouled quickly and were hard to clean, but a couple of others—an A&M 17 Javelina and H&R's 17/223—offered no problems at all.

Cleaning gear for the 17 may be scarce for a while, but only because there's been little call. Outers Labs has been making an excellent stainless steel, one-piece rod for a year or so, plus assorted brushes, etc., as well as a 3-piece job.)   ED.

Remington must have worked hard to produce this round and the rifle for it, so credit must be given where credit is due, but I wish that same effort had been put into work developing a rimmed deer cartridge with modern ballistics to replace the old 30-30.

New 25-06 Load

The earlier 25-06 Remington 87-gr. varmint load has now been augmented by a 120-gr. PSP load with Core-Lokt bullet for deer and big game. Leaving the muzzle of a 26" barrel at 3120 fps, remaining velocity is still an astonishing 2130 out at 400 yards, 1910 at 500. This means a remaining energy at 400 of 1210 f.p. almost half of the 2590 it started out with. A truly great round with flat trajectory—only 19.9" drop at 400 yards from 200-yard zero.

New Remington Handgun Ammo

First, there is a 9mm Luger cartridge with a 115-gr. serrated HP loaded to a muzzle velocity of 1160 fps (4" test barrel). Next, in 357 Magnum, there's a 158-gr. loading with scalloped SP bullet that proved so successful in the 38 Specials. 1550 fps out of an 8¾" barrel is claimed for this one, and the combination of bullet construction and speed makes for a highly potent handgun round indeed!

The third cartridge, and the muscle-man of the group, is a 44 Magnum 240-gr. loading, its scalloped-jacket HP bullet starting out at 1470 fps from a 6½" barrel. At 50 yards its energy equals that of the heavy 357 load at the muzzle, while at 100 yards it still has 1150 fps and 705 f.p. of energy left. Quite a handgun round for those who can handle it! After witnessing the way in which the new 38 Specials can kill, these 357s and 44s are a foregone conclusion.

Norma

Norma Precision of South Lansing, N.Y., has announced a new cartridge —new to this country, that is—the 7.5 Swiss (full name, 7.5 x55 Schmidt-Rubin).

Loaded in cases pocketed for American primers, and thus easily reloadable, this rimless bottleneck cartridge has a 180-gr. semi-pointed SPBT bullet (with steel jacket clad in gilding metal) rated at 2650 fps muzzle velocity. This new round, as well as empty cases available to reloaders, should be a real boon to the many owners of Swiss Model 1911 military rifles.

Federal

Federal had 6 new loadings during 1970. These were the 25 Automatic with 50-gr. bullet, the 32 Auto with 71-gr., a 110-gr. 30 Carbine, 95-gr. 380 Auto, 123-gr. 9mm Luger, and a 357 Magnum with 158-gr. JSP bullet. Federal's listing now totals 7 handgun and 16 rifle calibers, with more of the newer cartridges to come. This is quality ammunition, fully dependable.

S&W-Fiocchi-Alcan

The merged firms of Smith & Wesson, Fiocchi and Alcan have started to make centerfire ammunition for handguns.

Early in 1971, they had three 38 Special loads ready—a 110-gr. JHP, a 148-gr. lead full wadcutter target load, and a standard 158-gr. RN lead bullet cartridge. MVs for these are 1390, 800 and 910 fps respectively (barrel length not specified). Brass cases are nickel or chrome plated, and bear the S&W-F headstamp.

Coming soon will be another three in 38 Special—jacketed bullets of 125-to 158 grains, 4 loadings for the 357 Magnum featuring jacketed bullets of 110- to 158 grains, and a foursome of 9mm Parabellums in 100- to 115-gr. weights, including HPs, SPs, and a full-metal-jacketed number. Knowledge of these new cartridges came too late to permit testing them.

Federal Cartridge has introduced its "Cartridge Carrier" pack in 11 popular calibers. The polyethylene pack fits any belt.

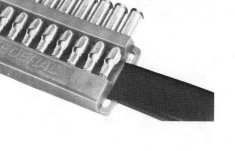

Part 1. RIFLE CARTRIDGES

The Centerfires

22 HORNET One of the most useful smallbore cartridges, and the first standard 22 specifically for varmint hunting. Since its appearance in 1930 it has earned a reputation for fine accuracy, flat trajectory, and quick bullet expansion. Effective to 175 yards on foxes, woodchucks, and jack rabbits, excellent for wild turkeys, it should definitely not be used on deer.

218 BEE Introduced in 1938 for the lever action Model 65 Winchester, its use was extended to bolt actions where its greater powder capacity, higher velocity and flatter trajectory from a stronger case made it a better choice than the Hornet. Effective on the same game species as the Hornet. Not available in any rifle today.

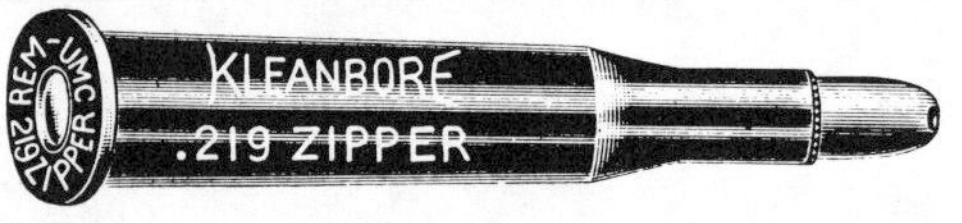

22 REMINGTON JET See Part II — Handgun Cartridges.

220 SWIFT Highest velocity standard sporting rifle cartridge ever produced commercially in the U.S. Its 48-gr. bullet, leaving the muzzle at 4140 fps, is virtually a bomb, unfit for use on large game animals. As a long range varmint cartridge it is one of the finest, needing only a longer, heavier bullet less sensitive to wind. Popularity of the Swift has declined to the point where Winchester has discontinued production of both rifles and cartridges for it. However, empty Swift cases are available, as well as ammo, from Norma Precision.

222 REMINGTON First of the post-WW II cartridges, the 222 has climbed rapidly to fame as a benchrest target and varmint round. Its better-designed bullets and finer accuracy have extended practical small varmint range to about 225 yards. This, together with its availability in numerous strong bolt action rifles, has made the older Bee and Zipper obsolete.

222 REMINGTON MAGNUM Big Brother to the standard 222, this later and longer cartridge combines increased power and velocity with the fine accuracy of its forerunner to give varmint shooters one of the best balanced, most practical 'chuck cartridges ever developed. 55- and 60-gr. spitzer bullets buck the wind better than the 50-gr. standard 222 bullet, and arrive at a 200-yard target with some 25% more energy to boot. Rifles for the 222 Magnum have been dropped because of its close similarity to the 223 Remington (or 5.56mm) in use by our military. Factory ammunition is still made by Remington in HP and PSP style, but not by Winchester.

222 SUPER RIMMED Developed in Australia, this rimmed version of our 222 Remington emigrated first to Canada and thence to the U.S. An ideal choice for chambering in single shot rifles, case dimensions (except for the rim), ballistics and loading data all duplicate those of the standard 222. Velocities may be somewhat higher however, in the longer barrels common to single shot rifles.

223 REMINGTON Adopted by the U.S. military forces as the 5.56mm with full metal jacketed 55-gr. bullets, its civilian name is 223 Remington, under which headstamp a soft point bullet is loaded. Identical ballistically to the 222 Magnum, the 223's case dimensions differ enough so that they should never be fired in a 222 Magnum chamber; they'll go in, but hazardous excess headspace will be present with a probability of case separations. Rifles for the 223 have a twist rate of 1-in-12″ rather than the 1-in-14″ of most 22 centerfires, this to insure bullet stability all the way out to 600-yards. Case capacity is about a grain less than the 222 Magnum and its neck is about 1/16″ shorter, making the 222 Magnum a better choice for handloaders. Future government surplus ammunition will probably be available for the 223, however.

225 WINCHESTER Intended as a successor to the 220 Swift (in Winchester rifles), this new high performance cartridge has done more than that; it has also superseded the discontinued 219 Zipper in its role as the most powerful rimmed 22 centerfire. Although officially classified as "semi-rimless," the 225 does have a rim, easily sufficient to permit its use in single shot rifles while still fitting the bolt heads and extractors (of 270, 30-06 dimensions) of modern standard rimless cartridge repeaters. Closely similar in design to the 219 Improved Zipper (but differing in certain vital dimensions), the 225 Winchester is loaded to higher pressures than the old standard 219 Zipper, developing 540 fps greater muzzle velocity for a trajectory that is almost twice as flat. Factory cartridges in this new caliber are loaded with outstanding uniformity and provide excellent accuracy.

22/250 REMINGTON A long time favorite wildcat with both varminters and benchrest shooters, the 22/250 was standardized by Remington in 1965 and shows signs of rapidly growing popularity. Generally considered to be better designed than the Swift, it will give nearly as high velocities with bullets of the same weight. Because it is slower, case and barrel life are longer. Case capacity to bore ratio in the 22/250 is most favorable, and its short over-all loaded cartridge length of 2.35″ makes it readily adaptable to short-action box magazine repeaters. Either new 22/250 Remington or Norma cases, or reformed 250 Savage brass may be used for reloading.

243 WINCHESTER One of the new 6mm or 24 caliber compromises between 22 and 25 calibers, having in large measure the best features of both. A 100-gr. bullet with high sectional density at 3,070 fs for deer and antelope, and an 80-gr. at 3,500 for long range varmints, provide accuracy equal to the Swift and far better wind-bucking and killing power. Excellent for the one-gun hunter of game not larger than deer.

244 REMINGTON Remington's first 6mm or 24-cal. rifle, never very popular because of its 1-in-12″ rifling twist which kept bullet weight to 90 grains in spitzer form. Heavier bullets **can** be stabilized if made with a blunt round nose. Shooters wanted a dual-purpose rifle, however, one in which they could use 100-gr. spitzers for big game, so many picked the lesser-capacity 243. Despite the fact that neither shooters nor game could tell the difference between 90- and 100-gr. bullets, the 244 slipped and Remington ceased production of rifles in this caliber. A single factory load with 90-gr. bullet is still made for it, however.

6mm REMINGTON Identical in case dimensions to the older 244 Remington, this newer cartridge is loaded with the 100-gr. bullet demanded by deer hunters. Remington lists MV as 3190 fps, and barrels have a rifling twist of 1-in-9″ to stabilize the longer bullet. Despite the fact that 75- and 90-gr. 244 cartridges can also be used in 6mm rifles, shooters wanted a varmint round bearing the 6mm headstamp. Hence, in 1965 Remington announced an additional load using their new 80-gr. Power-Lokt bullet, which has proven exceptionally accurate and flat shooting. The 6mm is therefore an even better dual purpose cartridge than the 243.

25-20 WCF Prior to the coming of the Hornet and Bee, this 1893-born round was the top small-game/varmint cartridge. Today we have better pest loads, but there is still a useful place for the 25-20 among those who hunt for stew or seek the lordly wild turkey. W-W and R-P have dropped the 60-gr. open-point varmint loading—at 2250 fps such a good little 'chuck load — and henceforth will offer only a pair of 86-gr. loads at 1460 fps. It would have been better if they had dropped the old round with plain lead bullet instead of the more accurate and faster hollow point.

25-35 WINCHESTER Another cartridge from the 1890's, this one **can** be used for deer. Currently obtainable only as a 117-gr. soft point at 2,300 fs, the 25-35's chief claim to fame lies in its reputation as one of the most accurate cartridges ever developed for lever action rifles, and one of the lightest recoiling.

250 SAVAGE Popularly known as the "250-3000" because of its velocity with an 87-gr. bullet, this fine cartridge appeared in 1915 as one of our earliest really high speed loads. 100-gr. bullets are loaded to 2,820 fs. Quick killing power, flat trajectory, and light recoil have kept this cartridge popular for over 40 years. Use 100-gr. bullets for deer and 87's for varmints. In wind-swept areas, the 100 grain is preferred, even for varmints.

256 WINCHESTER MAGNUM See Part II—Handgun Cartridges.

257 ROBERTS Named for its famous originator, Major Ned Roberts, this was to have been an extra long range varmint cartridge, but with factory production came additional bullet weights, making it one of our more versatile rounds. Although no rifles of standard make are now being chambered for the 257, W-W still offers an 87-gr. load at 3200 fps for varmints, a 100-gr. Silvertip at 2900 fps for deer/antelope, and a 117-gr. Power-Point at 2650 fps for the woods hunter. Remington lists only a single loading—the least useful 117-gr. RN—but it can be efficiently reloaded with the newer 120-gr. spitzer bullets to equal or better 243/6mm performance.

25-06 REMINGTON Wisely, Remington decided to adopt and standardize this old wildcat based as much upon popular demand as upon its proven excellence ballistically. It is without doubt one of our very finest "all-round" cartridges for American game in the contiguous 48 states (that is, not including the great bears of Alaska). Ideally, it is not an elk or moose cartridge, but as a long range load for all medium game as well as varmints, it is superb with its 87-gr. HP at 3500 fps and 120-gr. PSP at 3120 fps. Sighted for 200 yards, either bullet drops only some 19″ at 400, and the heavier bullet has 1210 f.p. of energy left at that far-out range, or just slightly less than a 30-30 at only 100-yards. For all practical purposes, the 25-06 with 120-gr. bullet is the equal of the 6.5 Magnum, and treads close on the heels of the 270.

*As independently chronographed, actually about 3350. Ed.

6.5 REMINGTON MAGNUM One of a pair of short-short belted magnums developed by Remington for short-receiver bolt action rifles, powder capacity is very close to that of the 270, hence its ballistics are also much the same when using bullets of similar sectional density in equal length barrels. With its 100-gr. bullet at 3450 fps for varmints and 120-gr. game load at 3220 fps, it is even closer in performance to the 25-06, standing mid-way between the 6mm and the larger 7mm Remington Magnum. The only real advantage of the 6.5 over the 25-06 is in its ability to handle still heavier bullets, and for this purpose the 270 and 280 are even better.

264 WINCHESTER MAGNUM The third cartridge produced in Winchester's series of medium-short belted cases, the 264 offers magnum velocities and power from standard-length bolt actions. This is a cartridge with a specific purpose—the delivery of a controlled expansion bullet with flat trajectory and high residual energy at ultra long ranges. This it does. Accuracy with the 264 sometimes is less than it might be, chiefly because of a mis-matching of bore-groove diameters and the bullets available. However, given the right combination, the 264 shoots very well; Sierra bullets are a good choice. With the 264 or the 6.5 Magnum, select those bullets which will stand the high rotational forces of their quick-twist rifling.

270 WINCHESTER Superior to the 257 and 6mms for western use and for game larger than deer, the 270 has earned a good reputation among open country hunters. Its flat trajectory and high velocity with 130-gr. bullet at 3140 fps makes hitting easier over long, difficult-to-estimate ranges. Thus, as a mule deer, sheep and goat cartridge it is all anyone could ask for. For larger and heavier game of the caribou, elk and moose species, Winchester loads a 150-gr. Power-Point bullet to an increased muzzle velocity of 2900 fps, while Remington offers a 150-gr. round nose Core-Lokt at 2800 for woods hunting. The 100-gr. load is excellent for varmints, and is a good choice on antelope, too.

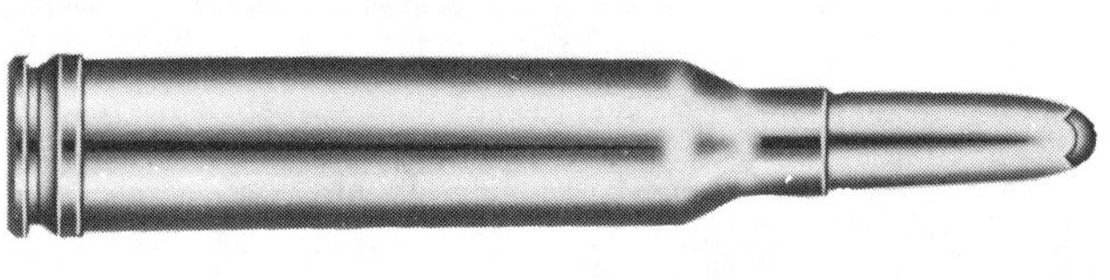

7mm REMINGTON MAGNUM Rifle cartridge of 1962, this short-case belted magnum mates the striking power of a 180-gr. 30-06 with the velocity and flat trajectory of a 130-gr. 270. The 175-gr. load has 21½% greater muzzle energy than the 180-gr. 30-06, and the 150-gr. is traveling 12% faster than the 130-gr. 270 bullet out at 300 yards. Various "wildcat" 7mm Magnum cartridges have evidenced their game killing ability in all corners of the globe, and now we have a factory standard cartridge capable of doing the same. In 1965, Remington added a 175-gr. factory loading having a pointed Core-Lokt bullet designed to retain high velocity over longer ranges. Starting out at the muzzle with the same 3070 fps as the round-nose bullet, remaining velocity of the new spitzer slug is 340 fs higher at 300 yards and 460 fs faster at 500 yards, even equaling the 150-gr. bullet by the time 300 yards is reached. In 1967, Remington added still another loading, this time a 125-gr. PSP at 3430 MV, thus making available a lightweight, high speed bullet with correspondingly flat trajectory for use on the smaller species of big game under long range conditions. This load should **not** be used in taking really large game, especially at short to medium ranges where velocity is still high.

280 REMINGTON One of our very best—if not **the** best—"all-round" cartridges, the 280 has been sadly overlooked, bucking, as it does, the popularity and head start of the closely similar 270, and over-shadowed by the newer 7mm Remington Magnum. Originally, its attraction lay in the splendid selection of factory loads available. Four bullet weights—100-, 125-, 150- and 165-gr.—gave the 280 a flexibility unequaled by the 270 unless the latter were handloaded, and with lower chamber pressures to boot. However, shooters have shown a preference for the 7mm Magnum, with the result that Remington has discontinued the 100- and 125-gr. 280 loads, and only their M742 autoloader is still being chambered for it—most regrettable.

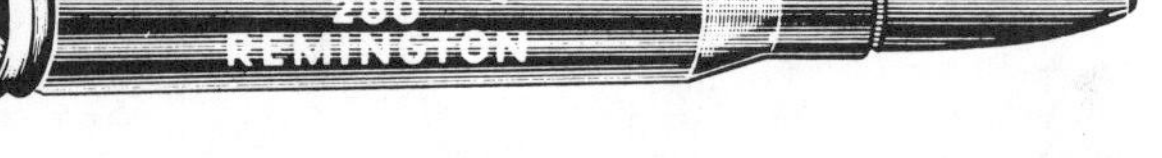

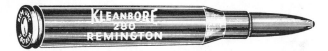

284 WINCHESTER Unusual for American cartridges, this short-cased round has a body diameter larger than its rim, giving it a powder capacity only about 1 grain less than the 280 Remington, even though ½-inch shorter, while retaining a "standard" size rim (common to such calibers as the 270, 280, 308 and 30-06), in order to permit use of the 284 cartridge with existing bolt face dimensions. Designed to give short action rifles (specifically the Winchester M88 lever action and M100 autoloader) ballistics equaling the longer 270 Winchester and 280 Remington cartridges, there is no reason why bolt action rifles shouldn't be chambered for it.

7mm MAUSER Originating as the Spanish military cartridge of 1893, the 7x57mm became popular the world over and today's factory loadings are better than ever. It will handle any game that the 270 will, but if used for antelope or other plains game at long range, either Federal's or Dominion's 139-gr. at 2900 fps, or Norma's 150-gr. load at 2756 fps should be specified. For varmints, Norma offers a 110-gr. bullet loading at 3068 fps MV. These modern high velocity versions have given the 7x57 new appeal. However, the standard U.S. cartridge with 175-gr. round-nose bullet of high sectional density is still the best choice for big game, especially when hunting in brush or woods.

30 CARBINE Commercial jacketed SP cartridges are loaded by W-W, R-P, Federal and Norma for use in the 30 M-1 Carbine and Ruger revolver. Winchester's 110-gr. is a hollow point; the other 3 are all RNSPs. All have a rated MV of 1970-1980 fps from an 18" barrel; at only 100-yards, velocity is down to 1540 fps with 575 f.p. energy. From this it should be obvious that the 30 Carbine is not an adequate deer load. If used on varmints, it may ricochet badly.

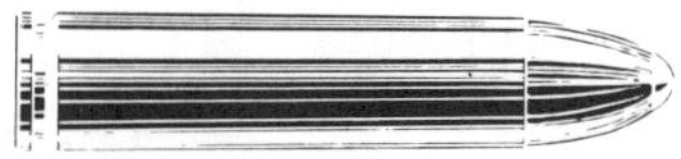

30-30 WCF & 32 WINCHESTER SPECIAL Old favorites of the deer hunter and rancher, these cartridges continue to be popular more because of the light, handy carbines which use them than because of any attribute of the cartridges themselves. For the indifferent marksman they are wonders, having neither great bullet weight nor high velocity. These are deer cartridges and should not be "stretched." They're neither flat shooting nor accurate enough for varmints, nor do they have the power to be good moose killers.

30 & 32 REMINGTON Rimless versions of the 30-30 and 32 Special for the Remington line of autoloaders and slide action rifles (Models 8, 81, 14 and 141), bullet weights and velocities are the same (except no 150-gr. bullets), and there is no difference in killing power. Depends solely on which rifle action the shooter chooses as to which cartridge he uses.

300 SAVAGE Developed by Savage to approximate early 30-06 ballistics in their Model 99 lever action, this cartridge had a phenomenal acceptance for a time. It has an extremely short case neck, making it difficult to reload, but with 150- and 180-gr. factory loads it is a quick killer on deer. The lighter bullet should be chosen where flat trajectory and rapid expansion counts, but for wooded country, or for bear, moose and caribou, use the 180-gr. bullet.

30-40 KRAG Generally called the "Krag," this old military cartridge looks good in "civies." Rifles are no longer made for it, but the Krag bolt actions and Winchester Model 95 lever actions just don't seem to wear out. 180- and 220-gr. bullet loadings are available, with the former as best choice for deer, or mountain hunting requiring the flattest possible trajectory, while the latter is a long brush-cutter slow to open up and offering deeper penetration on heavy game than the faster 30-06, assuming like bullets.

308 WINCHESTER Commercial version of the 7.62mm NATO cartridge, the 308 is a big stick in a small bundle. A stubby cartridge, resembling the 300 Savage with a longer neck but still half-an-inch shorter than the 30-06, this hot little number comes within 100 fs of equaling 30-06 velocities. When first brought out, only 150- and 180-gr. bullets were available in factory loads, but now there is a 110-gr. varmint load and a dandy 200-gr. for the heavier stuff. As the new service cartridge, it will prove increasingly popular for target work as well as hunting.

30-06 SPRINGFIELD American military cartridge since 1906, this has been the standard by which all other big game cartridges were compared. Many have called it our most versatile all-round cartridge, for there are many bullets available, from the 110-gr. for varmints, through the flat-shooting 150-gr. to the 180-gr. "all-purpose," and finally up to a 220-gr. for big game and timber hunting. Except for Alaskan brown bear, buffalo, and rear-angling shots on elk, it is probably adequate for any North American game.

300 H&H MAGNUM Introduced in 1925 as the "Super-Thirty," this was the first factory cartridge giving a velocity in excess of 3000 fps with a 150-gr. bullet. Re-named "300 H&H Magnum" by Americans, it soon demonstrated its superiority as a big game cartridge and, starting in 1935, as a long range target load in the Wimbledon Cup Match at Camp Perry. By virtue of its larger belted case and heavier powder charge, the 300 H&H moves 180-gr. bullets 220 fps faster than the 30-06 with an additional quarter-ton of energy. This gives the shooter who is able to handle the increased recoil flatter trajectory with less wind deflection and more remaining knock-down power.

300 WINCHESTER MAGNUM Recognizing the average American hunter's predilection for 30-cal. rifles as the favorite all-round bore size, Winchester in 1963 introduced this modern 300 Magnum, thereby spelling the doom of the fine old 300 H&H after 38 years. MV of the new round runs 150 to 200 fps higher than the 300 H&H with equal bullet weights, delivering almost 24% greater remaining energy at 400 yards (180-gr. bullet), and 13% flatter trajectory at the same range. Ballistics also exceed by a considerable margin those of smaller bore magnums. The 300 Winchester Magnum with proper bullet weights is adequate for all our big game from deer and antelope to elk, caribou, moose and even the great bears, plus African game of similar weight.

303 BRITISH British service cartridge for over half a century, the 303 has long been popular in Canada, and now with thousands of surplus military rifles in the hands of U.S. shooters its use on this side of the border has increased enormously. Consequently, a wide variety of factory loads have been made available including the old standard 215-gr. round-nose from Remington, Norma and Dominion at 2180-2200 fps; a 180-gr. from Remington, Winchester, Federal, Dominion and Norma averaging 2540 fps (Dominion, 2610); 150-gr. Dominion and Norma at 2720 fps. and even a 130-gr. Norma load traveling 2790 fps. The 303 has thus become a quite effective multi-purpose cartridge for North American game.

303 SAVAGE Another light deer cartridge of the 30-30 class, but in this one some velocity was traded for more bullet weight, 180- and 190-gr. bullets being given 100 to 200 fs less speed. 30-30 killing power, with penetration slightly increased at the expense of a more arched trajectory.

32-20 WFC An almost obsolete little cartridge that refuses to die, it should have been named the 30-20 for it uses a 30-cal. bullet. Too light and under-powered for deer, and with the former 80-gr. high speed HP now gone, this old round with its 100-gr. bullet at 1290 fps is best used for turkeys and edible small game.

32-40 WINCHESTER Another old timer for which rifles are no longer made, this one began life as a single shot target cartridge, but was soon adapted to repeating hunting rifles. Its 165-gr. bullet lacks the velocity and punch of a 30-30, especially since the high velocity loading was discontinued, but it is still sometimes seen in the deer woods. Now only Winchester and Dominion produce 32-40 factory loads.

8mm MAUSER Underloaded by American ammunition makers because of the wide variations in quality and bore diameter of foreign rifles chambering it, this cartridge has ballistics about like the 30-40 Krag and is a good deer slayer. As loaded by Norma and imported into this country it is quite different, acquiring 30-06 powers. Caution here is to make sure of your rifle. Strength and accuracy vary widely with the individual rifle. Given a good one, this can be a fine big game cartridge using the stepped-up loadings. Do NOT mix with 30-06 rounds!

338 WINCHESTER MAGNUM Long awaited by many big game hunters, the 338 has shown itself to be a leading contender for the all-round rifle crown, killing large game such as brown bear and bison with the aplomb of a 375 H&H, or whitetail deer with less meat destruction than a quick-expanding 270 bullet. This is a modern, high-efficiency cartridge with flat trajectory slightly bettering the 30-06-180 gr. and 270-150 gr. loads, while delivering about 25% more striking energy at 200 and 300 yards than the 30-06. The great sectional density of the heavier bullets insures penetration and resistance to deflection by wind or brush, especially when the 275-grain Speer bullets are handloaded. Recoil is greater than with lesser cartridges, but not excessive for the shooter used to firing heavy 30-06 loads in light sporting rifles. The 338 will become increasingly popular with hunters who mix elk and moose with their regular deer menu.

348 WINCHESTER Lever action cartridge for really big game as well as deer, this is one of our most powerful rimmed cases. It appeared in 1936 for the Winchester Model 71—the only rifle ever commercially chambered for it—and originally offered considerable versatility with factory loads in 150-, 200- and 250-gr. bullet weights. Today, only a single loading with 200-gr. bullet is available, no rifles are made for it, and the cartridge is making a last stand in Alaska where its power, combined with a handy, smooth-working rifle keep it in use. The old 150-gr. load isn't missed much, but at least one ammo maker should produce the hard-hitting 250-gr. load.

35 REMINGTON With 200-gr. bullet, the 35 has been found to have considerably more anchoring power than the smaller 30's and 32's. Then too, it's good for getting through brush without deflection, and leaves a better blood trail. To 200 yards there's little difference in trajectory from the 30-30 and it has the advantage of being effective on larger game such as moose at moderate ranges, without excessive recoil. Highly recommended for Eastern deer and black bear, this praise does **not** include the pointed 150-gr. load. Stick to the 200-gr. for best results.

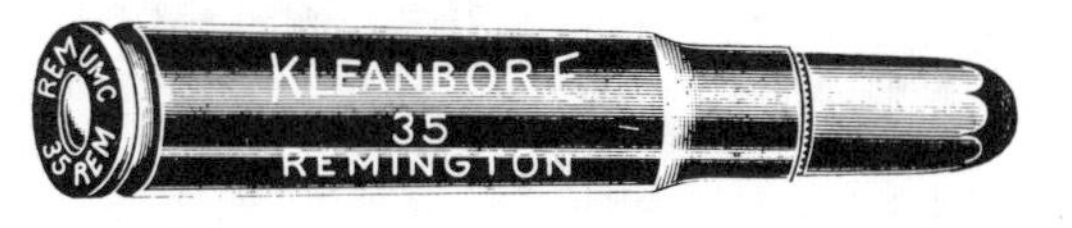

351 WINCHESTER SELF-LOADER Chambered only in the now-obsolete Winchester '07 autoloading rifle, the 351 hangs on because of its widespread use by police departments. For close wood ranges it can be used for deer and will kill with a proper hit.

358 WINCHESTER Larger caliber version of the 308 Winchester, the 358 drives 200-gr. bullets at 2530 fps, and 250-gr. at 2250. Each gives better than 2800 f.p. energy at the muzzle, and some 2200 f.p. at 100 yards. Trajectory of the 200-gr. matches that of the 180-gr. 300 Savage to 300 yards, hence it is not restricted to short ranges only. A splendid woods cartridge for moose, elk and deer, it has, unfortunately, been overlooked by many hunters.

350 REMINGTON MAGNUM First commercial cartridge to deserve the term Short Magnum, and one of the most practical big game rounds to appear in recent years, the 350 Magnum is especially notable for the restraint built into its design. Either standard length or short actions will accommodate its squat hull and deep-seated bullets, and its power is an almost perfect compromise, for American big game, between too much and not enough. This stems directly from its powder capacity, about 7% more than that of a 30-06 when both cases are filled to the base of their necks. 200-gr. bullets have a MV of 2710 fps, while 250-grainers reach 2410 fps, both from only a 20" carbine barrel. The old 35 Remington is thus hopelessly outclassed and the 35 Whelen challenged by a cartridge that is still within the recoil limitations of once-a-year hunters. Deer hunters and those who are recoil-shy should use the 200-gr. load, which delivers noticeably less kick.

375 H&H MAGNUM World-wide big game cartridge and champion of the "mediums," the 375 H&H dates back to 1912 but can still boast no peer as an all-round load for big and dangerous game. It will dispatch the largest American game as well as most African species. If necessary, it will kill an elephant, and yet its big 270-gr. slug will travel over long ranges as flat as a 180-gr. 30-06 to kill mountain game without excessive meat destruction. There is also a 300-gr. bullet turning up over 2 tons of muzzle energy. Cartridges may be purchased in almost all of the big game regions of the world. Its one disadvantage is its quite heavy recoil.

38-40 WINCHESTER This "38" actually measures 40 caliber and should have been named "40-40." Many deer are still killed yearly by its 180-gr. bullet, loafing along at 1,330 fs, mostly because it punches a big enough hole to let out a lot of blood. It's obsolete and there are a lot of better cartridges, but for short ranges (under 100 yards), it will still do the trick.

38-55 WINCHESTER Like the 32-40, this cartridge started out as a target load for single shot rifles, in which it quickly established a reputation for fine accuracy. Its use spread to repeating hunting rifles where the 255-gr. bullet proved to be a more sure stopper than the 30-30. It tends to ignore brush, but its low velocity means a rainbow-trajectory and so it lost the popularity race. No rifles are made for it.

44-40 WINCHESTER Big brother of the 38-40, this is the same type of short, low-velocity cartridge, varying only by being slightly larger in bullet diameter and weight (200 grains). Under 100 yards it will kill as well as a 30-30.

44 REMINGTON MAGNUM Originally developed as a super-powered revolver cartridge, the 44 Magnum gradually evolved into a carbine deer load. Remington and Norma load a 240-gr. Jacketed SP, and Winchester a hollow point of the same weight—all at some 1750 fps from 18½" barrels. Handy little rifles by Ruger, Winchester and Marlin, plus a bolt action from Remington, have helped popularize this round, but it should be restricted to woods ranges not exceeding 150 yards.

444 MARLIN In essence a "super" 44 Magnum since it uses the same 240-gr. .429" jacketed SP bullet but in a long, straight 2.22" case, the 444 Marlin provides 30% higher MV with 88% greater ME! At the muzzle its energy is greater even than that of the 30-06, at least on paper, but the blunt, relatively short bullet sheds velocity so fast that at only 100 yards it is down to the power level of the 7mm Mauser and 300 Savage. However, the 444 will be hitting as hard at 200 yards as the 35 Remington at 150, making it a fine deer and black bear cartridge to this range, while at 100 yards or less it is capable of handling just about any North American big game. Its biggest need is for a heavier constructed bullet that will not break up on the tough muscles and bone structure of such game or any intervening brush. Such bullets are already available to handloaders.

45-70 Still potent after 85 years, some of which was on the battlefield, but even more in the hunting fields, this old timer asks only to be used within ranges where its trajectory isn't too steep. Other than that, its user can count on a kill (if he does his part) whether the game be a small deer or a big moose. Excessive drop makes hitting tough beyond 150 yards, despite its ability to kill well-beyond that distance.

458 WINCHESTER Second most powerful American cartridge, the 458 has already won its spurs in Africa; the special Model 70 rifle chambered for it is known as the "African" Model. It is well named, for the massive 500-gr. full-steel-jacketed and 510-gr. soft-points are an "over-dose" for practically all other game with the exceptions of Indian tiger, Asian gaur, and Alaskan brown bear. Heavy bullet weight and high speed for its caliber combine to make this more than just a good killing cartridge—it is a "stopping load," designed to break down the most ponderous and dangerous beasts, and this it will do. For an American going to Africa for elephant, buffalo and rhino it is top choice. The soft point should be used on even the largest soft-skinned game, for the solid bullet is a specialized number for elephants. Has greatest recoil of all American cartridges except the 460 Weatherby.

THE WEATHERBY CARTRIDGES

Weatherby Magnum cartridges have been factory produced for many years now, and are sold at sporting goods stores all over America and in many foreign countries. The brass cases are produced in Sweden, but all other components are American-made and assembled. They therefore qualify as American ammunition and merit inclusion in this analysis of cartridges on the U.S. market.

224 WEATHERBY VARMINTMASTER Smallest of the Weatherby's, the 224 also has the smallest capacity of any belted case. Despite its modest size, however, velocities over 3700 fps with 50-gr. bullets and 3600 fps with 55-gr. have been chronographed, making it a close competitor of the 22-250. It is thus an efficient case which, in combination with the added safety features of good base thickness and positive headspacing provided by the belt, rates as an impressive performer. For those varminters who feel a need for more velocity than the 222 or 222 Magnum, but are willing to settle for less than the 220 Swift, the 224 Weatherby is an outstanding choice.

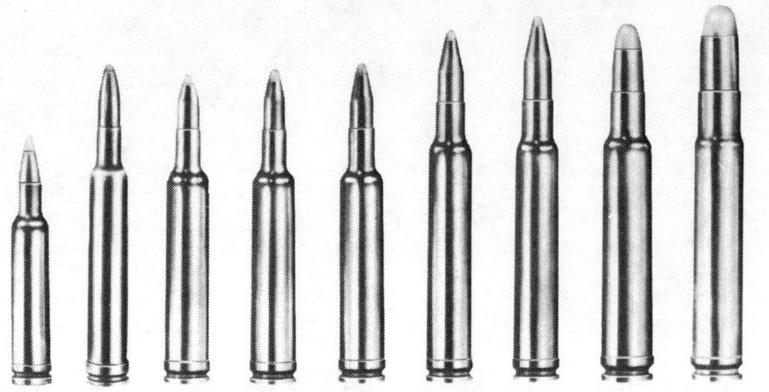

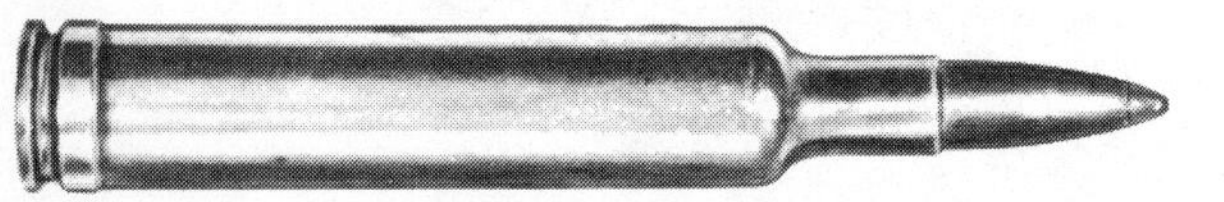

240 WEATHERBY MAGNUM Highest velocity of all factory-loaded 24 calibers, with the single exception of Holland & Holland's 244 Magnum, this medium capacity Weatherby features an entirely new belted case of reduced dimensions, capable of driving 70-gr. 6mm bullets to 3850 fps, 90-gr. to 3500, and 100-gr. to 3395 fps. It is thus some 200-300 fs faster than the 6mm Remington, and 300-400 fs ahead of the 243 Winchester. With loads giving sufficiently fine accuracy, this should prove to be an outstanding cartridge for open country deer and antelope shooting in combination with summer use as a long range varmint round.

257 WEATHERBY MAGNUM For varmint shooting at extremely long range or for the lighter species of big game in open country, where a premium is placed on flat trajectory and rapid bullet expansion, this cartridge is outstanding. Offering the flattest trajectory of any known 25-caliber cartridge, it utilizes the maximum loads of present-day powders that can be efficiently burned in this caliber to provide the highest striking energy for its bore size. In these combined respects, it is exceeded only by the 264 Winchester Magnum in cartridges under 270 caliber, and even there the difference is negligible.

270 WEATHERBY MAGNUM Next step up in the Weatherby line, the 270 WM is also a better choice for those who place more emphasis on big game hunting, but would still like to use the same rifle for off-season varminting. Bullets of 100, 130 and 150 grains are available with energies and trajectories close to Winchester's 264 Magnum with, however, a somewhat better bullet selection for greater flexibility. While 270 WM muzzle velocities are around 300 fps faster than the standard 270, at 300 yards the speed differential is little more than 100 fs with the lighter bullets but some 270 fs ahead in 150-gr. loadings.

7mm WEATHERBY MAGNUM This cartridge so closely parallels the 270 WM in almost all respects that little more need be said about it, except to note that there's a .007" bigger bullet and heavier bullet selection (to 175 grains) in the 7mm. In any event, there is little to choose between the 7mm WM and the newer 7mm Remington Magnum.

300 WEATHERBY MAGNUM Weatherby says this is his most popular and versatile caliber, and it's not hard to see why. With equal bullet weights, the 300 Weatherby develops from 285 to 355 fps more muzzle velocity than the 300 H&H Magnum for a noticeable increase in power. This cartridge is also liked for the nice balance it strikes between the large and small bores. For example, the 180-gr. 300 WM load offers some 500 fs velocity advantage over the 270-gr. 375 H&H Magnum with a consequent flattening of trajectory by 27%, and yet when loaded with a 150-gr. spitzer bullet it is both faster and flatter shooting than either the 270 or 7mm Weatherby Magnums. Despite some rather extreme claims for it the 300 Weatherby Magnum is doubtless one of the finest all-round big game cartridges.

340 WEATHERBY MAGNUM This is Weatherby's newest big game cartridge, produced to satisfy those hunters who want still more bullet weight than the 300's 220 grains, but at the same time wish to retain the 300's velocity and trajectory characteristics. This it does, giving a 250-gr. bullet only 55 fs less muzzle velocity than the 220-gr. 300 WM. Recoil is up, however, and the man who selects the 340 in preference to a 300 should be reasonably sure he needs its extra punch. For the great Alaskan bear it would appear to be a better choice, but for an all-round rifle involving mostly smaller game, the 300 would get the nod. The 340 WM uses the same bullets as the 338 Winchester Magnum, but boosts bullet speeds by 150 to 210 fps. An excellent moose, elk and bear cartridge.

378 WEATHERBY MAGNUM With this truly "magnum-size" cartridge we enter the field of specialized big game calibers. The latest Weatherby catalog states that it was "designed for the purpose of killing thick-skinned animals where extremely deep penetration is needed." With bullet weights of 270- and 300-gr. at velocities of 2900 to 3180 fps, it should be obvious that while striking power is unquestionably great, so is its recoil; entirely too much, in fact, for the average hunter not used to handling such heavy comeback. Experienced African and Arctic hunters, however, accustomed to the slam of the 375 H&H and larger rifles, report the 378 WM to be a most effective cartridge for the big stuff. With the adoption of the 378, Weatherby has discontinued production of the 375 WM, although ammunition for the older caliber is still being made. Despite its designation, the 378 uses the same bullets as the 375 Weatherby and the 375 H&H Magnum.

460 WEATHERBY MAGNUM Comments made on the 378 WM apply with even greater force to this largest and most powerful of all American cartridges. Using the same oversize belted case as the 378 Weatherby, its energy of 8000 fp with 500-gr. bullet is so great that it would normally be selected for only the very largest and dangerous game including elephant, rhino and buffalo. Some authorities feel that the 378 Weatherby would be adequate for such animals were it not for African game laws requiring rifles of 40 caliber or over for those species. Here again the name may be misleading, since the 460 WM uses the same size bullets as the 458 Winchester, only at a phenomenal increase of 570 fps muzzle velocity and nearly 3000 foot pounds of ME.

AMERICANIZED IMPORTED CARTRIDGES

We include here summaries on some of the popular and significant cartridges produced in Europe for the U.S. market. Some were actually designed in this country, others of overseas origin were specifically intended for export to the States; since most of them are encountered with increasing frequency, it is reasonable to think of them as "American" by use if not by manufacture. Only those loaded with American-type "Boxer" primers are included.

6.5x54 MS An old but still liked cartridge for the Mannlicher-Schoenauer carbines, Norma offers five different versions with bullet weights of 77, 139 and 156 grains at muzzle speeds of 3117, 2580 and 2461 fps. A modest capacity round, the 6.5 MS built its reputation as a game cartridge **not** on velocity, but rather on the deep penetration of its long pencil-like round nose bullets. In its heaviest bullet weight, it has been well-liked in Maine as an effective black bear load.

6.5x55 SWEDISH Long the military cartridge of Sweden and Norway, the 6.5x55 has become quite common in the U.S., partly because of thousands of imported surplus military rifles and the fine Schultz & Larsen target rifles. With its light recoil, resistance to wind deflection and excellent accuracy, it has justified its Scandinavian reputation and is seen increasingly on our target ranges. Norma offers 6 different loadings with bullet weights of 77, 93, 139 and 156 grains at velocities somewhat above those of the smaller Mannlicher cartridge. The 139-gr. load is probably the most popular here.

7x61 S&H A modern high velocity big game round with Norma short belted case, the brain-child of Americans Phil Sharpe and Dick Hart, this shell is only 4mm longer than the old 7x57 Mauser case but velocity with 160-gr. boat-tails is 3100 fps at muzzle of a 26" barrel, according to the Norma table. In 1968, Norma improved the 7x61 case by changing its interior dimensions to provide thinner but stronger case walls, Known as the Super 7x61, exterior dimensions remain exactly the same as formerly, hence the new version will fit all rifles chambered for the older 7x61 S&H, but due to a slightly increased powder capacity, velocity is rated 50 fs higher; (3150 with 160-gr. bullet from 26" barrels).

30 U.S. CARBINE To satisfy the demand for 30 Carbine ammo, Norma produces one with full metal jacket, the other in soft point, both 110 grain. This last, the one hunter-owners most sought, is at best little more than a small game cartridge, since velocity and energy are down to 1595 fs and 622 fp respectively at only 100 yards. Fast repeat shots should not be counted on to make up for inadequate power; this cartridge should not be selected for deer or other big game hunting.

308 NORMA MAGNUM A short magnum tailored to American big game fields. Its 180-gr. bullet steps out at a velocity 400 fs faster than the 180-gr. 30-06, is 180 fs ahead of the great 300 H&H, equals the new 300 Winchester Magnum and even approaches the much larger 300 Weatherby. Advantage of the Norma cartridge (true also of the 300 Win. Mag.) is that it has the same over-all length as a 30-06, hence will fit in '06 magazines and only requires re-chambering the barrel and opening up the bolt face, plus an extractor alteration, to convert an '06 to 308 Magnum. Pressures run pretty high in this case, so only rifles with strong actions should be converted to the new cartridge. Only factory load is with 180-gr. "Dual-Core" bullets, but the cases may be reloaded with American primers and any 30-cal. bullets from 110- to 220-gr. weight. It is thus a versatile as well as powerful high performance cartridge.

NORMA 7.62mm RUSSIAN Imported by Norma-Precision for American owners of Winchester Model 1895 and surplus military rifles in this caliber, the 7.62mm is furnished with the Tri-Clad soft point 180-gr. bullet developing 2625 fps muzzle velocity and more than 2750 fp energy. This is a rimmed bottle-necked case, ballistically almost identical to our 308, thus only slightly inferior to the 30-06. Formerly loaded in this country with either 145-gr. or 150-gr. bullets at 2820 fps, those ballistics may be reproduced in these new cases by handloaders desiring a lighter, faster bullet loading.

303 BRITISH HV Another modernized old cartridge is Norma's high velocity loadings of the 303 British. As loaded by Remington with a 215-gr. bullet and by Winchester with a 180-gr., pressure limitations of the Lee-Enfield action have held velocities to a sedate 2180-2540 fps, and owners of surplus 303's have wondered how they could obtain higher speeds. The safest way is to decrease bullet weight, and this is just what Norma has done. Two Norma factory loads include a 150-gr. bullet at 2720 fps and a 130-gr. at 2789, either of which will shoot flatter and open quicker on impact than the heavier bullets. If you use a 303 for open country hunting of deer or antelope, give these new loads a try.

7.65 ARGENTINE Originally known as the 7.65mm Belgian Mauser, this cartridge was once loaded in the U.S. and chambered in such popular rifles as the Remington 30-S and Winchester 54 and 70, but was discontinued about the time of WW 2 for lack of demand. Importation of surplus Argentine military Mausers has reversed the picture and there is once again a need for this surprisingly efficient round. Norma offers a single 150-gr. soft point with 2920 fs muzzle velocity and 2105 fs at **300** yards for a midrange trajectory height of only 5.8". Regardless of the fact that this cartridge was designed over 70 years ago, in its modern version it is still an excellent deer cartridge. Bullet (not cartridge) size is the same as a 303 British—.311"-.312".

8x57-JR and 8x57-JRS Rimmed versions of the famous 8x57 Mauser cartridge, the 8x57-JR is loaded by Norma with a 196-gr. .318" bullet, while the 8x57-JRS has the same weight but in .323" diameter. Post-war rifles generally have the larger bore size, while pre-war rifles usually (but not necessarily) have the .318" bore. In any event, the proof markings on the barrel should be carefully examined and only those cartridges with the proper size bullets used. Both of the 8x57 rimmed rounds are good deer and black bear cartridges.

358 NORMA MAGNUM First of the new line of Norma Magnums, this 35-caliber number was offered to the market in 1959 and since then has steadily gained favor among big game hunters here and abroad. In the Scandinavian countries, the 358 Norma has become a favorite of moose hunters, a use for which it is well-fitted almost anywhere. A 250-gr. bullet at 2790 fps from a 23" barrel gives 4322 fp energy—some 1500 more than a 220-gr. 30-06—and energy close to the 4500 fp of a 375 Magnum. With a 200-gr. bullet, 3100 fps can be reached with permissible pressures, so that the 358 Norma may be thought of as a direct competitor of the 338 Winchester, both ballistically and as concerns adaptability to game species. It should fill the bill as a powerful "medium" bore for African hunting, and of course is a natural for Canadian and Alaskan large game.

RIMFIRE CARTRIDGES

5mm REMINGTON RIMFIRE MAGNUM Although originally announced in the fall of 1967, this 20-cal. bottle-necked high velocity rimfire was not offered on sale until 1970, for various problems arose in providing adequate breech support for case rims. These were finally overcome and this cartridge now ranks as our most powerful rimfire. It has a 38-gr. Power-Lokt HP bullet of .2045" diameter with muzzle velocity of 2100 fps and 372 f.p. Remaining speeds are 1605 fps at 100 yards, and 1400 at 150, which is about its limit on varmints. You'll need a special cleaning rod for this one, as 22-cal. rods are too large.

22 SHORT The economical shooting gallery cartridge. Accurate to 50 yards, this old load is still a popular number. Three loadings—Standard, High Speed and Gallery—give it a usefulness second only to the indispensable 22 Long Rifle. It is **not** a game cartridge, however, and its use on live targets should be restricted to rats, snakes, starlings and the like, since even in the high speed load its light bullet gives but half the energy of the Long Rifle.

22 LONG Only the High Speed loading of this little "betwixt and between" cartridge survives. Having neither the accuracy of the Short nor the power of the Long Rifle it is not recommended except for those few old repeating rifles chambered especially for it.

22 LONG RIFLE Finest and most versatile rimfire cartridge ever developed, it is today better than ever. Four loadings fit it for just about everything except big game hunting. This is everybody's cartridge, with the gilt-edged accuracy of the special Match loads for serious competition, the Standard rounds for economical practice, the High Speeds for small game hunting (with hollow-point bullets), and the Shot cartridges for pest destruction. The High Speed with plain bullet is not recommended for **any** of these uses. For hunting, better use the hollow-point for humane kills, and even try for a head shot. Pass up shots beyond 75 yards and be content with squirrels, rabbits and birds.

22 WINCHESTER AUTOMATIC Useful only to owners of the old Winchester Model 1903 autoloader, it is less powerful than the Long Rifle.

22 WRF (or REMINGTON SPECIAL) More powerful than any Long Rifle load and a far better hunting cartridge, it deserves to be more popular. Its flat-nose bullet, of slightly greater diameter and 5 grains more weight than a Long Rifle, is faster, and turns up a third more energy. For squirrel hunters it is hard to beat, and rifles for it should again be made.

22 WINCHESTER MAGNUM RIMFIRE Now in second place to the 5mm Remington Rimfire Magnum as far as velocity and energy are concerned, the 22 WMR remains an excellent choice for the rimfire rifleman who wants greater shock power than the 22 LR offers—and wants it in other than a Remington or Winchester rifle. Chambering for the 22 WMR is offered by numerous other rifle makers, and by a few handgun manufacturers as well. It appears unlikely that the 5mm RRM will appear as a handgun round.

Part II. HANDGUN CARTRIDGES
(Rimfire & Centerfire)

22 SHORT RF This little cartridge is currently experiencing a revival of popularity because of its adaptability to rapid-fire international-type shooting in the autoloading pistols made especially for it.

22 LONG RF See Rifle Cartridge Section.

22 LONG RIFLE RF Just as with rifles, this cartridge has done more than any other to popularize shooting and training with the handgun. In either revolver or "automatic" it is highly accurate and makes a fine companion for hunter and trapper. Ammo is easily carried, yet will kill small game better than some larger centerfires. Use high speeds for hunting and standards for target work.

22 REMINGTON JET First of the CF handgun cartridges to appear, this little bottleneck was introduced in March of 1961 when Smith & Wesson announced their Magnum M53 revolver. Besides the 22 Jet this gun handles (via cylinder inserts) 22 Shorts, Longs and Long Rifles. The factory-announced muzzle velocity of 2460 fps (obtained in closed-breech test barrels) has not been achieved in revolvers with their open gap between cylinder and barrel. However, the 1870 fps reached with 6" barrels (2100 with 8⅜") makes this a respectable handgun varmint cartridge in any man's language.

221 REMINGTON FIREBALL The second 22-cal. CF cartridge to be introduced by Remington, it established a precedent in 1963 by being chambered in the first American commercial bolt action pistol. 2650 fps has been reached with a 50-gr. bullet from its 10½" barrel, equal to a factory 22 Hornet with 45-gr. bullet fired in a full-length rifle barrel.

256 WINCHESTER MAGNUM Winchester's entry in the high speed, flat trajectory handgun cartridge field had trouble getting off the ground after it was announced in April, 1961, but it has finally developed as **both** a handgun and rifle cartridge. Early published factory velocities were **lower** than those actually attained, first tables saying 2000 fps for the 60-gr. SP bullet, whereas independent chronographs registered 2350 fps from the 8½" barrel of a Ruger Hawkeye.

25 AUTO Smallest of production centerfires, this is strictly for use in defensive weapons —tiny automatics lacking both power and accuracy, firing 50-gr. metal case bullets with less energy than even the standard velocity 22 LR.

30 CARBINE In producing his Blackhawk revolver chambered for the 30 Carbine cartridge, Bill Ruger has made this round properly classifiable as a handgun load. For the considerable number of today's pistol shooters seeking a high speed, flat-shooting revolver cartridge without the heavy recoil of a 44 or 41 Magnum, but with more bullet weight and diameter than a 22 caliber, the 30 Carbine may provide the answer. Factory and GI loads produce velocities varying from 1400 to 1530 fps from our 7½" barrel test revolver, giving them some 40% more muzzle energy than the 22 Jet. As a revolver load it will be liked particularly by owners of carbines in the same caliber as a companion piece.

30 LUGER A bottle-necked cartridge for automatic pistols firing a 93-gr. metal case bullet at 1,220 fs. Flat shooting with high paper energy, expansion is lacking due to bullet construction, severely limiting its game-killing or man-stopping capabilities. However, it far out-classes the 32 ACP.

32 AUTO Next step up in the caliber scale for automatics, this is a very popular cartridge here and abroad for pocket pistols. Many are used by foreign police where it is known as the 7.65mm, but again a small (71-gr.) round nose metal case bullet gives energy only in the high speed 22 Long Rifle class and no bullet expansion. Not recommended for hunting or defense use.

32 S&W & 32 S&W LONG These are the most popular of the 32's for revolvers, the shorter load used in innumerable old "bureau-drawer specials," the accurate Long in target and light police revolvers. The Long should always be chosen if the gun will handle it. A good small game cartridge but lacks power for police work.

32 COLT SHORT & LONG A pair of "obsolete" cartridges used in old-model Colt pocket revolvers, they are less accurate and less powerful than the 32 S&W Long, and will not chamber in modern 32-caliber revolvers.

32-20 WINCHESTER Best of all the 32's for revolvers, using 100-gr. bullets in both lead and soft point types with flat nose, this is the smallest caliber practical for serious police and defensive use. Trajectory is also flatter due to higher velocity, making this a good hunting cartridge for varmints and small game. Do NOT use the "High Velocity" rifle loads in revolvers.

38 AUTO and 38 SUPER AUTOMATIC The 38 Automatic cartridge is intended to be used in the original Colt 38 Automatic pistols, Models of 1900 and 1902. When the Colt Super 38 appeared about 1925, a new, more powerful loading was offered under the name of Super 38 for this stronger pistol. These Super 38 Automatic cartridges should not be fired in the early model Colt pistols in view of their system of slide attachment and the higher pressures of the Super cartridge. Even the regular 38 Automatic is closely comparable to the 9mm Luger in power, and the 38 Super will give the 357 Magnum a run for its money in barrels of equal length. If loaded with soft point bullets, both of these 38 Auto cartridges would make good game killing loads. Either cartridge will function properly in the Super automatic pistol.

380 AUTO Designed to give more power in a straight blow-back automatic pistol than is provided by the 32 ACP cartridge, and yet keep down chamber pressure and recoil to stay within the limitations of small pocket pistols, it is the smallest auto pistol cartridge which can be recommended for defense. Super Vel's modern loading of an 80-gr. JHP bullet at 1026 fps considerably increases the effectiveness of this cartridge.

9mm LUGER Improved bullet designs and modern high speed loadings have greatly upped the stopping power and all-round utility of the well-known 9mm Parabellum or Luger. To the old 124-gr. metal cased loading at 1120 fps have been added a 115-gr. JHP at 1160 fps (Rem.), a 100-gr. Power Point at 1325 fps (Win.), and either a 110-gr. SP at 1325 or 90-gr. JHP at 1422 fps by Super Vel. Long a European military pistol cartridge, the 9mm has now become an International cartridge with wide spread civilian and growing police use as well.

38 S&W A favorite cartridge for pocket revolvers, with 146-gr bullet, and adopted by the British military during World War II, when it was known as the 38-200 (as it was loaded with a 200-gr. bullet). Nothing smaller is recommended for defensive use.

38 COLT SHORT & LONG The 38 Short was used in early Colt house defense guns and the Long was the cartridge which failed to stop fanatical Moros during the Philippine Insurrection. Either may be used in a 38 Special revolver, but both are out-classed by that cartridge for any purpose, hence seldom used.

38 SPECIAL As with the 9mm, this cartridge—once considered marginal for police, defensive and combat use—has become, with the introduction of new bullets and high speed loadings, a far more effective "stopper" than was formerly thought possible. Hollow point and expanding soft points ranging from 110-gr. and 125-gr. at 1370 fps, to 158-gr. bullets at 1150 fps (from 6" barrels) have given this old cartridge a new lease on life. In its milder loadings, it continues to be our most accurate centerfire target cartridge for handguns.

357 MAGNUM A high velocity revolver cartridge ideally suited to the needs of police officers and field shooters, its 158-gr. bullet travels at a far higher velocity and delivers an even greater increase in striking energy than the same weight bullet from a 38 Special of equal barrel length. With metal piercing bullet it will penetrate an automobile body, and with the flat-point lead bullet it will kill game of considerable size. An even better choice of bullet for field use is the soft point Remington or Norma half-jacket which will not lead up barrels as do the ordinary lead bullets at high velocity. One of our three best long range revolver cartridges, a gun in this caliber has the added advantage of chambering all 38 Special cartridges for target work.

38-40 WINCHESTER See Part I—CF Rifle Cartridges.

41 MAGNUM Produced by Remington for Smith & Wesson revolvers in response to demands for a more potent police cartridge, this new 41 Magnum fills the gap between the 357 and 44 Magnums. Two loads are offered, one a 210-gr. SP at 1500 fps, the other a 210-gr. lead bullet at 1050 fps, both MV figures from 8¾" bbls. In the more common 6" bbl., velocities run 1342 and 986. A potent and accurate cartridge in SP version, trajectory is practically as flat as the 44 Magnum is; it penetrates even deeper, though bullet energy is less. Recoil, only 75% of a 44 Magnum's, makes it a much more pleasant load to shoot. It may well find more use in the game fields than on the policeman's beat. Recoil and gun weight are both heavy for police use, and so far the lead bullet loads have shown only mediocre accuracy. Bullet diameter is .410" and will not interchange with the old 41 Long Colt.

44-40 WINCHESTER See Part I—CF Rifle Cartridges.

44 S&W SPECIAL Developed as a target cartridge from the earlier 44 S&W Russian, the 44 Special has never been loaded by the factories to its velocity potential. The 246-gr. lead bullets travel slowly (755 fs), which is of no matter on target ranges where their high accuracy is paramount. Only when properly handloaded is its true power capacity realized.

44 REMINGTON MAGNUM Quite in a class by itself, this extremely powerful revolver cartridge with standard factory loadings of 240-gr. lead or jacketed SP and HP bullets at 1470 fps (from 6½" barrels) ranks high in stopping power and recoil. Muzzle energy of 1150 f.p. is more than twice that of the hottest 38 Specials, but so is recoil, and gun weight too must be higher, making this a cartridge for specialized use by veteran handgunners. It most definitely cannot be recommended for beginning handgunners! Those shooters seeking a lighter load for target practice may use the mild old 44 S&W Special.

45 COLT Most famous of all American revolver cartridges and still one of the best, whether the target be criminal or beast. For close range work we would prefer its big 250-gr. bullet to the 357 Magnum. Now that new guns are again being made for the old 45, its historical background as well as its effective power should ensure a continued popularity and long life.

45 AUTO Official U.S. Army sidearm cartridge since 1911 and spanning 4 wars, this largest American round for automatic pistols has thoroughly proven itself, both in combat and on the target range. Difficult to control until mastered, but inherently accurate in accurized pistols, its already wide popularity has been given assists in the form of special target loads with 185- and 210-gr. match bullets at very low velocity, plus some stepped up prescriptions, typical of which is Super Vel's 190-gr. JHP at 1060 fps. Probably more shooters than ever before are using this cartridge for a wide range of activities from police sidearm to hunting. On competitive target ranges it often supplants the 38 Special in the centerfire matches. It is a good all-round choice for big bore pistol shooters.

45 AUTO RIM Companion of the 45 ACP, this thick-rimmed cartridge was developed for use in revolvers chambered for the 45 Auto round, without the necessity of using half-moon clips. Its 230-gr. lead bullets at 810 fps MV (from 5½" barrel) makes it suitable for either police or field use. Shallow rifling in these revolvers requires that bullets be cast hard or jacketed.

CENTERFIRE RIFLE CARTRIDGES — BALLISTICS AND PRICES

Winchester-Western, Remington-Peters, Federal and Speer-DWM

Most of these centerfire loads are available from Winchester-Western and Remington-Peters. Loads available from only one source are marked by a letter, thus: Winchester (a); Western (b); Remington (c); Peters (d); Speer-DWM (f). Those fewer cartridges also available from Federal are marked (e). Contrary to previous practice, W-W and R-P prices are not necessarily uniform, hence prices are approximate.

Cartridge	Bullet		Velocity (fps)				Energy (ft. lbs.)				Mid-Range Trajectory			Price
	Wt. Grs.	Type	Muzzle	100 yds.	200 yds.	300 yds.	Muzzle	100 yds.	200 yds.	300 yds.	100 yds.	200 yds.	300 yds.	for 20*
17 Remington	25	HP, PL	4020	3290	2630	2060	900	600	380	230	Not Available			$4.85
218 Bee*	46	HP	2860	2160	1610	1200	835	475	265	145	0.7	3.8	11.5	10.50
22 Hornet*	45	SP	2690	2030	1510	1150	720	410	230	130	0.8	4.3	13.0	10.10
22 Hornet* (c, d)	45	HP	2690	2030	1510	1150	720	410	230	130	0.8	4.3	13.0	10.10
22 Hornet*	46	HP	2690	2030	1510	1150	740	420	235	135	0.8	4.3	13.0	10.10
222 Remington (e)	50	PSP, MC, PL†	3200	2660	2170	1750	1140	785	520	340	0.5	2.5	7.0	4.10
222 Remington Magnum (c, d)	55	SP, PL†	3300	2800	2340	1930	1330	955	670	455	0.5	2.3	6.1	4.50
222 Remington Magnum (c, d)	55	HP, PL	3300	2830	2400	2010	1330	975	700	490	Not Available			4.85
223 Remington (c, d, e)	55	SP, PL†	3300	2800	2340	1930	1330	955	670	455	0.5	2.1	5.4	4.50
22-250 Remington	55	PSP	3810	3270	2770	2320	1770	1300	935	655	0.3	1.6	4.4	4.50
22-250 Remington (c, d)	55	HP, PL	3810	3330	2890	2490	1770	1360	1020	760	Not Available			4.85
225 Winchester (a, b)	55	PSP	3650	3140	2680	2270	1630	1200	875	630	0.4	1.8	4.8	4.50
243 Winchester (e)	80	PSP, PL†	3500	3080	2720	2410	2180	1690	1320	1030	0.4	1.8	4.7	5.70
243 Winchester (c, d)	80	HP, PL	3450	3050	2675	2330	2115	1650	1270	965	Not Available			6.10
243 Winchester (e)	100	PP, CL, PSP	3070	2790	2540	2320	2090	1730	1430	1190	0.5	2.2	5.5	5.70
6mm Remington (c, d)	80	PSP, HP, PL†	3450	3130	2750	2400	2220	1740	1340	1018	0.4	1.8	4.7	5.70
6mm Remington (c, d)	100	PCL	3190	2920	2660	2420	2260	1890	1570	1300	0.5	2.1	5.1	5.70
244 Remington (c, d)	90	PSP	3200	2850	2530	2230	2050	1630	1280	995	0.5	2.1	5.5	5.70
25-06 Remington (c, d)	87	HP	3500	3070	2680	2310	2370	1820	1390	1030	Not Available			6.20
25-06 Remington (c, d)	120	PSP, CL	3120	2850	2600	2360	2590	2160	1800	1480	Not Available			6.20
25-20 Winchester*	86	L, Lu	1460	1180	1030	940	405	265	200	170	2.6	12.5	32.0	8.00
25-20 Winchester*	86	SP	1460	1180	1030	940	405	265	200	170	2.6	12.5	32.0	8.95
25-35 Winchester	117	SP, CL	2300	1910	1600	1340	1370	945	665	465	1.0	4.6	12.5	5.60
250 Savage (a, b)	87	PSP, SP	3030	2660	2330	2060	1770	1370	1050	820	0.6	2.5	6.4	5.35
250 Savage	100	ST, CL, PSP	2820	2460	2140	1870	1760	1340	1020	775	0.6	2.9	7.4	5.35
256 Winchester Magnum* (b)	60	OPE	2800	2070	1570	1220	1040	570	330	200	0.8	4.0	12.0	9.85
257 Roberts (a, b)	87	PSP	3200	2840	2500	2190	1980	1560	1210	925	0.5	2.2	5.7	5.85
257 Roberts (a, b)	100	ST, CL	2900	2540	2210	1920	1870	1430	1080	820	0.6	2.7	7.0	5.85
257 Roberts	117	PP, CL	2650	2280	1950	1690	1820	1350	985	740	0.7	3.4	8.8	5.85
6.5 Remington Magnum (c)	100	PSPCL	3450	3070	2690	2320	2640	2090	1610	1190	Not Available			7.70
6.5mm Remington Magnum (c)	120	PSPCL	3030	2750	2480	2230	2450	2010	1640	1330	0.5	2.3	5.7	7.70
264 Winchester Magnum	100	PSP, CL	3700	3260	2880	2550	3040	2360	1840	1440	0.4	1.6	4.2	7.70
264 Winchester Magnum	140	PP, CL	3200	2490	2700	2480	3180	2690	2270	1910	0.5	2.0	4.9	7.70
270 Winchester	100	PSP	3480	3070	2690	2340	2690	2090	1600	1215	0.4	1.8	4.8	6.20
270 Winchester (e)	130	PP, PSP	3140	2880	2630	2400	2850	2390	2000	1660	0.5	2.1	5.3	6.20
270 Winchester	130	ST, CL, BP, PP	3140	2850	2580	2320	2840	2340	1920	1550	0.5	2.1	5.3	6.20
270 Winchester (c, d)	150	CL	2800	2440	2140	1870	2610	1980	1520	1160	0.6	2.9	7.6	6.20
270 Winchester (a, b, e)	150	PP	2900	2620	2380	2160	2800	2290	1890	1550	0.6	2.5	6.3	6.20
280 Remington (c, d)	150	PCL	2900	2670	2450	2220	2800	2370	2000	1640	0.6	2.5	6.1	6.20
280 Remington (c, d)	165	CL	2820	2510	2220	1970	2910	2310	1810	1420	0.6	2.8	7.2	6.20
284 Winchester (a, b)	125	PP	3200	2880	2590	2310	2840	2300	1860	1480	0.5	2.1	5.3	6.20
284 Winchester (a, b)	150	PP	2900	2630	2380	2160	2800	2300	1890	1550	0.6	2.5	6.3	6.20
7mm Mauser (e)	139	SP	2710	2440	2190	1960	2280	1850	1490	1190	0.7	3.0	7.8	5.65
7mm Mauser (e)	175	SP	2490	2170	1900	1680	2410	1830	1400	1100	0.8	3.7	9.5	6.20
7mm Remington Magnum	125	CL	3430	3080	2750	2450	3260	2630	2100	1660	0.6	1.8	4.7	7.70
7mm Remington Magnum (e)	150	PP, CL	3260	2970	2700	2450	3540	2940	2430	1990	0.4	2.0	4.9	7.70
7mm Remington Magnum (e)	175	PP	3070	2720	2400	2120	3660	2870	2240	1750	0.5	2.4	6.1	7.70
7mm Remington Magnum (c, d)	175	PCL	3070	2860	2660	2460	3660	3170	2740	2350	0.5	2.1	5.2	7.70
30 Carbine* (e)	110	HSP, SP	1980	1540	1230	1040	950	575	370	260	1.4	7.5	21.7	9.75
30-30 Winchester (c, d)	150	CL	2410	1960	1620	1360	1930	1280	875	616	0.9	4.5	12.5	4.85
30-30 Winchester (e)	150	HP	2410	2020	1700	1430	1930	1360	960	680	0.9	4.2	11.0	4.85
30-30 Winchester (a, b)	150	PP, ST, OPE	2410	2020	1700	1430	1930	1360	960	680	0.9	4.2	11.0	4.85
30-30 Winchester (e)	170	PP, HP, CL, ST, MC	2220	1890	1630	1410	1860	1350	1000	750	1.2	4.6	12.5	4.85
30 Remington	170	ST, CL	2120	1820	1560	1350	1700	1250	920	690	1.1	5.3	14.0	5.70
30-06 Springfield (a, b)	110	PSP	3370	2830	2350	1920	2770	1960	1350	900	0.5	2.2	6.0	6.20
30-06 Springfield	125	PSP	3200	2810	2480	2200	2840	2190	1710	1340	0.5	2.2	5.6	6.20
30-06 Springfield (c, d)	150	BP	2970	2710	2470	2240	2930	2440	2030	1670	0.5	2.4	6.0	6.20
30-06 Springfield (e)	150	PP	2970	2620	2300	2010	2930	2280	1760	1340	0.6	2.5	6.5	6.20
30-06 Springfield	150	ST, PCL, PSP	2970	2670	2400	2130	2930	2370	1920	1510	0.6	2.4	6.1	6.20
30-06 Springfield	180	PP, CL, PSP	2700	2330	2010	1740	2910	2170	1610	1210	0.7	3.1	8.3	6.20
30-06 Springfield (e)	180	ST, BP, PCL	2700	2470	2250	2040	2910	2440	2020	1660	0.7	2.9	7.0	6.20
30-06 Springfield	180	MCBT, MAT	2700	2520	2350	2190	2910	2540	2200	1900	0.6	2.8	6.7	9.20
30-06 Springfield	220	PP, CL	2410	2120	1870	1670	2830	2190	1710	1360	0.8	3.9	9.8	6.20
30-06 Springfield (a, b)	220	ST	2410	2180	1980	1790	2830	2320	1910	1560	0.8	3.7	9.2	6.20
30-40 Krag	180	PP, CL	2470	2120	1830	1590	2440	1790	1340	1010	0.8	3.8	9.9	6.30
30-40 Krag	180	ST, PCL	2470	2250	2040	1850	2440	2020	1660	1370	0.8	3.5	8.5	6.30
30-40 Krag (a, b)	220	ST	2200	1990	1800	1630	2360	1930	1580	1300	1.0	4.4	11.0	6.30
300 Winchester Magnum (e)	150	PP, PCL	3400	3050	2730	2430	3850	3100	2480	1970	0.4	1.9	4.8	9.10
300 Winchester Magnum (e)	180	PP, PCL	3070	2850	2640	2440	3770	3250	2790	2380	0.5	2.1	5.3	9.10
300 Winchester Mag (a, b)	220	ST	2720	2490	2270	2060	3620	3030	2520	2070	0.6	2.9	6.9	9.10
300 H&H Magnum (a, b)	150	ST	3190	2870	2580	2300	3390	2740	2220	1760	0.5	2.1	5.2	9.10
300 H&H Magnum	180	ST, PCL	2920	2670	2440	2220	3400	2850	2380	1970	0.6	2.4	5.8	9.10
300 H&H Magnum (a, b)	220	ST, CL	2620	2370	2150	1940	3350	2740	2260	1840	0.7	3.1	7.7	9.10
300 Savage (e)	150	PP	2670	2350	2060	1800	2370	1840	1410	1080	0.7	3.2	8.0	6.05
300 Savage	150	ST, PCL	2670	2390	2130	1890	2370	1900	1510	1190	0.7	3.0	7.6	6.05
300 Savage (c, d)	150	CL	2670	2270	1930	1660	2370	1710	1240	916	0.7	3.3	9.3	6.05
300 Savage (e)	180	PP, CL	2370	2040	1760	1520	2240	1660	1240	920	0.9	4.1	10.5	6.05
300 Savage	180	ST, PCL	2370	2160	1960	1770	2240	1860	1530	1250	0.9	3.7	9.2	6.05
303 Savage (c, d)	180	CL	2140	1810	1550	1340	1830	1310	960	715	1.1	5.4	14.0	6.25
303 Savage (a, b)	190	ST	1980	1680	1440	1250	1650	1190	875	660	1.3	6.2	15.5	6.25
303 British (e)	180	PP, CL	2540	2300	2090	1900	2580	2120	1750	1440	0.7	3.3	8.2	6.25
303 British (c, d)	215	SP	2180	1900	1660	1460	2270	1720	1310	1020	1.1	4.9	12.5	6.25
308 Winchester (a, b)	110	PSP	3340	2810	2340	1920	2730	1930	1340	900	0.5	2.2	6.0	6.20
308 Winchester (a, b)	125	PSP	3100	2740	2430	2160	2670	2080	1640	1300	0.5	2.3	5.9	6.20
308 Winchester (e)	150	PP	2860	2520	2210	1930	2730	2120	1630	1240	0.6	2.7	7.0	6.20
308 Winchester	150	ST, PCL	2860	2570	2300	2050	2730	2200	1760	1400	0.6	2.6	6.5	6.20
308 Winchester (e)	180	PP, CL	2610	2250	1940	1680	2720	2020	1500	1130	0.7	3.4	8.9	6.20
308 Winchester	180	ST, PCL	2610	2390	2170	1970	2720	2280	1870	1540	0.8	3.1	7.4	6.20
308 Winchester (a, b)	200	ST	2450	2210	1980	1770	2670	2170	1750	1400	0.8	3.6	9.0	6.20
32 Winchester Special (c, d, e)	170	HP, CL	2280	1920	1630	1410	1960	1390	1000	750	1.0	4.8	12.5	5.00
32 Winchester Special	170	PP, ST	2280	1870	1560	1330	1960	1320	920	665	1.0	4.8	13.0	5.00
32 Remington (c, d)	170	CL	2120	1800	1540	1340	1700	1220	895	680	1.0	4.9	13.0	5.90
32 Remington (a, b)	170	ST	2120	1760	1460	1220	1700	1170	805	560	1.1	5.3	14.5	5.90
32-20 Winchester*	100	SP	1290	1060	940	840	370	250	195	155	3.3	15.5	38.0	8.70
32-20 Winchester*	100	SP, L, Lu	1290	1060	940	840	370	250	195	155	3.3	15.5	38.0	7.00

CENTERFIRE RIFLE CARTRIDGES — BALLISTICS AND PRICES (continued)

Cartridge	Bullet Wt. Grs.	Bullet Type	Velocity (fps) Muzzle	100 yds.	200 yds.	300 yds.	Energy (ft. lbs.) Muzzle	100 yds.	200 yds.	300 yds.	Mid-Range Trajectory 100 yds.	200 yds.	300 yds.	Price for 20*
8mm Mauser (e)	170	PP, CL	2570	2140	1790	1520	2490	1730	1210	870	0.8	3.9	10.5	$6.20
338 Winchester Magnum (a, b)	200	PP	3000	2690	2410	2170	4000	3210	2580	2090	0.5	2.4	6.0	8.35
338 Winchester Magnum (a, b)	250	ST	2700	2430	2180	1940	4050	3280	2640	2090	0.7	3.0	7.4	8.35
338 Winchester Magnum (a, b)	300	PP	2450	2160	1910	1690	4000	3110	2430	1900	0.8	3.7	9.5	8.35
348 Winchester (a)	200	ST	2530	2220	1940	1680	2840	2190	765	509	0.4	1.7	4.7	8.65
348 Winchester (c, d)	200	CL	2530	2140	1820	1570	2840	2030	1470	1090	0.8	3.8	10.0	8.65
35 Remington (c, d)	150	CL	2400	1960	1580	1280	1920	1280	835	545	0.9	4.6	13.0	5.65
35 Remington (e)	200	PP, ST, CL	2100	1710	1390	1160	1950	1300	860	605	1.2	6.0	16.5	5.65
350 Remington Magnum (c, d)	200	PCL	2710	2410	2130	1870	3260	2570	2000	1550	Not Available			7.70
350 Remington Magnum (c, d)	250	PCL	2410	2190	1980	1790	3220	2660	2180	1780	Not Available			7.70
351 Winchester Self-Loading°	180	SP	1850	1560	1310	1140	1370	975	685	520	1.5	7.8	21.5	12.30
358 Winchester (a, b)	200	ST	2530	2210	1910	1640	2840	2160	1610	1190	0.8	3.6	9.4	7.55
358 Winchester (a, b)	250	ST	2250	2010	1780	1570	2810	2230	1760	1370	1.0	4.4	11.0	7.55
375 H&H Magnum	270	PP, SP	2740	2460	2210	1990	4500	3620	2920	2370	0.7	2.9	7.1	9.90
375 H&H Magnum	300	ST	2550	2280	2040	1830	4330	3460	2770	2230	0.7	3.3	8.3	9.90
375 H&H Magnum	300	MC	2550	2180	1860	1590	4330	3160	2300	1680	0.7	3.6	9.3	9.90
38-40 Winchester°	180	SP	1330	1070	960	850	705	455	370	290	3.2	15.0	36.5	10.40
44 Magnum° (c, d)	240	SP	1750	1360	1110	980	1630	985	655	510	1.6	8.4	—	10.65
44 Magnum (b)	240	HSP	1750	1350	1090	950	1630	970	635	480	1.8	9.4	26.0	4.40
444 Marlin (c)	240	SP	2400	1845	1410	1125	3070	1815	1060	675	Not Available			6.15
44-40 Winchester°	200	SP	1310	1050	940	830	760	490	390	305	3.3	15.0	36.5	12.50
45-70 Government	405	SP	1320	1160	1050	990	1570	1210	990	880	2.9	13.0	32.5	7.65
458 Winchester Magnum	500	MC	2130	1910	1700	1520	5040	4050	3210	2570	1.1	4.8	12.0	18.40
458 Winchester Magnum	510	SP	2130	1840	1600	1400	5140	3830	2900	2220	1.1	5.1	13.5	12.10

° Price for 50   HP—Hollow Point   SP—Soft Point   PSP—Pointed Soft Point   PP—Power Point   L—Lead   Lu—Lubaloy   ST—Silvertip
HSP—Hollow Soft Point   MC—Metal Case   BT—Boat Tail   MAT—Match   BP—Bronze Point   CL—Core Lokt   PCL—Pointed Core Lokt
OPE—Open Point Expanding   †PL—Power-Lokt (slightly higher price)   (1) Not safe in handguns or Win. M73.

WEATHERBY MAGNUM CARTRIDGES — BALLISTICS AND PRICES

Cartridge	Bullet Wt. Grs.	Bullet Type	Velocity (fps) Muzzle	100 yds.	200 yds.	300 yds.	Energy (ft. lbs.) Muzzle	100 yds.	200 yds.	300 yds.	Mid-Range Trajectory 100 yds.	200 yds.	300 yds.	Price for 20
224 Weatherby Varmintmaster	50	PE	3750	3160	2625	2140	1562	1109	1670	1250	0.7	3.6	9.0	$5.95
224 Weatherby Varmintmaster	55	PE	3650	3150	2685	2270	1627	1212	881	629	0.4	1.7	4.5	5.95
240 Weatherby	70	PE	3850	3395	2975	2585	2304	1788	1376	1038	0.3	1.5	3.9	6.95
240 Weatherby	90	PE	3500	3135	2795	2475	2444	1960	1559	1222	0.4	1.8	4.5	6.95
240 Weatherby	100	PE	3395	3115	2850	2595	2554	2150	1804	1495	0.4	1.8	4.4	6.95
257 Weatherby	87	PE	3825	3290	2835	2450	2828	2087	1553	1160	0.3	1.6	4.4	7.75
257 Weatherby	100	PE	3555	3150	2815	2500	2802	2199	1760	1338	0.4	1.7	4.4	7.75
257 Weatherby	117	SPE	3300	2900	2550	2250	2824	2184	1689	1315	0.4	2.4	6.8	7.75
270 Weatherby	100	PE	3760	3625	2825	2435	3140	2363	1773	1317	0.4	1.6	4.3	7.75
270 Weatherby	130	PE	3375	3050	2750	2480	3283	2685	2183	1775	0.4	1.8	4.5	7.75
270 Weatherby	150	PE	3245	2955	2675	2430	3501	2909	2385	1967	0.5	2.0	5.0	7.75
7mm Weatherby	139	PE	3300	2995	2715	2465	3355	2770	2275	1877	0.4	1.9	4.9	7.75
7mm Weatherby	154	PE	3160	2885	2640	2415	3406	2874	2384	1994	0.5	2.0	5.0	7.75
300 Weatherby	150	PE	3545	3195	2890	2615	4179	3393	2783	2279	0.4	1.5	3.9	8.95
300 Weatherby	180	PE	3245	2960	2705	2475	4201	3501	2925	2448	0.4	1.9	5.2	8.95
300 Weatherby	220	SPE	2905	2610	2385	2150	4123	3329	2757	2257	0.6	2.5	6.7	8.95
340 Weatherby	200	PE	3210	2905	2615	2345	4566	3748	3038	2442	0.5	2.1	5.3	8.95
340 Weatherby	210	Nosler	3165	2910	2665	2435	4660	3948	3312	2766	0.5	2.1	5.0	10.95
340 Weatherby	250	SPE	2850	2580	2325	2090	4510	3695	3000	2425	0.6	2.7	6.7	8.95
378 Weatherby	270	SPE	3180	2850	2600	2315	6051	4871	4053	3210	0.5	2.0	5.2	17.50
378 Weatherby	300	SPE, FMJ	2925	2610	2380	2125	5700	4539	3774	3009	0.6	2.5	6.2	17.50
460 Weatherby	500	RN, FMJ	2700	2330	2005	1730	8095	6025	4465	3320	0.7	3.3	10.0	17.50

Trajectory is given from scope height. Velocities chronographed using 26″ bbls. Available with Nosler bullets; add $2.00 per box.
SPE—Semi-Pointed Expanding   RN—Round Nose   PE—Pointed Expanding   FMJ—Full Metal Jacket

RIMFIRE CARTRIDGES — BALLISTICS AND PRICES

Remington-Peters, Winchester-Western, Federal & Cascade Cartridge, Inc.

All loads available from all manufacturers except as indicated: R-P (a); W-W (b); Fed. (c); CCI (d). All prices are approximate.

CARTRIDGE	BULLET WT. GRS.	BULLET TYPE	VELOCITY FT. PER SEC. MUZZLE	100 YDS.	ENERGY FT. LBS. MUZZLE	100 YDS.	MID-RANGE TRAJECTORY 100 YDS.	HANDGUN BARREL LENGTH	BALLISTICS M.V. F.P.S.	M.E. F.P.	PRICE FOR 50
22 Short T22 (a, b)	29	C, L°	1045	810	70	42	5.6	6″	865	48	$ .88
22 Short Hi-Vel.	29	C, L	1125	920	81	54	4.3	6″	1035	69	.88
22 Short HP Hi-Vel. (a, b, c)	27	C, L	1155	920	80	51	4.2	—	—	—	.99
22 Short (a, b)	29	D	1045	—	70	—	—	—	—	(per 500)	7.93
22 Short (a, b)	15	D	1710	—	97	—	—	—	—	(per 500)	7.93
22 Long Hi-Vel.	29	C, L	1240	965	99	60	3.8	6″	1095	77	.99
22 Long Rifle T22 (a, b)†¹	40	L°	1145	975	116	84	4.0	6″	950	80	1.04
22 Long Rifle (b)†²	40	L°	1120	950	111	80	4.2	—	—	—	1.65
22 Long Rifle (b)†³	40	L°	—	—	—	—	—	6¾″	1060	100	1.65
22 Long Rifle (d)†⁴	40	C	1165	980	121	84	4.0	—	—	—	.99
22 Long Rifle Hi-Vel.	40	C, L	1285	1025	147	93	3.4	6″	1125	112	1.04
22 Long Rifle HP Hi-Vel. (b, d)	37	C, L	1315	1020	142	85	3.4	—	—	—	1.15
22 Long Rifle HP Hi-Vel. (a, c)	36	C	1365	1040	149	86	3.4	—	—	—	1.15
22 Long Rifle (b, c)	No.	12 Shot	—	—	—	—	—	—	—	—	2.11
22 WRF [Rem. Spl.] (a, b)	45	C, L	1450	1110	210	123	2.7	—	—	—	2.86
22 WRF Mag. (b)	40	JHP	2000	1390	355	170	1.6	6½″	1550	213	3.68
22 WRF Mag. (b)	40	MC	2000	1390	355	170	1.6	6½″	1550	213	3.68
22 Win. Auto Inside lub. (a, b)	45	C, L	1055	930	111	86	4.6	—	—	—	2.86
5mm Rem. RFM (a)	38	PLHP	2100	1605	372	217	Not Available				4.00

†—Target loads of these ballistics available in: (1) Rem. Match; (2) W-W LV EZXS, Super Match Mark III; (3) Super Match Mark IV and
EZXS Pistol Match; (4) CCI Mini-Group.   C—Copper plated   L—Lead (Wax Coated)   L°—Lead, lubricated   D—Disintegrating
MC—Metal Case   HP—Hollow Point   JHP—Jacket Hollow Point   PLHP—Power-Lokt Hollow Point

NORMA C.F. RIFLE CARTRIDGES — BALLISTICS AND PRICES

Norma ammunition loaded to standard velocity and pressure is now available with Nosler bullets in the following loads: 270 Win., 130-, 150-gr.; Super 7x61 (S&H), 160-gr.; 308 Win., 180-gr.; 30-06, 150-, 180-gr., all at slightly higher prices. All ballistic figures are computed from a line of sight one inch above center of bore at muzzle.

Cartridge	Bullet Wt. Grs.	Type	V Muzzle	V 100 yds.	V 200 yds.	V 300 yds.	E Muzzle	E 100 yds.	E 200 yds.	E 300 yds.	Tr. 100 yds.	Tr. 200 yds.	Tr. 300 yds.	Price for 20
220 Swift	50	PSP	4111	3611	3133	2681	1877	1448	1090	799	.2	.9	3.0	$5.35
222 Remington	50	PSP	3200	2660	2170	1750	1137	786	523	340	.0	2.0	6.2	4.10
223	55	SPP	3300	2900	2520	2160	1330	1027	776	570	.4	2.4	6.8	4.50
22-250	50	SPS	3800	3300	2810	2350	1600	1209	885	613	Not Available			4.50
	55	SPS	3650	3200	2780	2400	1637	1251	944	704	Not Available			4.50
243 Winchester	80	SP	3500	3070	2660	2290	2041	1570	1179	873	.0	1.4	4.1	5.70
	100	PSP	3070	2790	2540	2320	2093	1729	1433	1195	.1	1.8	5.0	5.70
6mm Remington	100	SPS	3190	2920	2660	2420	2260	1890	1570	1300	.4	2.1	5.3	5.70
250 Savage	87	PSP	3032	2685	2357	2054	1776	1393	1074	815	.0	1.9	5.8	5.35
	100	PSP	2822	2514	2223	1956	1769	1404	1098	850	.1	2.2	6.6	5.35
6.5 Carcano	156	SPRN	2000	1810	1640	1485	1386	1135	932	764	Not Available			7.00
6.5 Japanese	139	PSPBT	2428	2280	2130	1990	1820	1605	1401	1223	.3	2.8	7.7	7.00
	156	SPRN	2067	1871	1692	1529	1481	1213	992	810	.6	4.4	11.9	7.00
6.5 x 54 MS	139	PSPBT	2580	2420	2270	2120	2056	1808	1591	1388	.2	2.4	6.5	7.00
	156	SPRN	2461	2240	2033	1840	2098	1738	1432	1173	.3	3.0	8.2	7.00
6.5 x 55	139	PSPBT	2789	2630	2470	2320	2402	2136	1883	1662	.1	2.0	5.6	7.00
	156	SPRN	2493	2271	2062	1867	2153	1787	1473	1208	.3	2.9	7.9	7.00
270 Winchester	110	PSP	3248	2966	2694	2435	2578	2150	1773	1448	.1	1.4	4.3	6.20
	130	PSPBT	3140	2884	2639	2404	2847	2401	2011	1669	.0	1.6	4.7	6.20
	150	PSPBT	2802	2616	2436	2262	2616	2280	1977	1705	.1	2.0	5.7	6.20
7 x 57	110	PSP	3068	2792	2528	2277	2300	1904	1561	1267	.0	1.6	5.0	6.20
	150	PSPBT	2756	2539	2331	2133	2530	2148	1810	1516	.1	2.2	6.2	6.20
	175	SPRN	2490	2170	1900	1680	2410	1830	1403	1097	.4	3.3	9.0	6.20
7mm Remington Magnum	150	SPSBT	3260	2970	2700	2450	3540	2945	2435	1990	.4	2.0	4.9	7.70
	175	SPRN	3070	2720	2400	2120	3660	2870	2240	1590	.5	2.4	6.1	7.70
7 x 61 S & H (26 in.)	160	PSPBT	3100	2927	2757	2595	3415	3045	2701	2393	.0	1.5	4.3	8.20
30 U.S. Carbine	110	SPRN	1970	1595	1300	1090	948	622	413	290	.8	6.4	19.0	3.95
30-30 Winchester	150	SPFP	2410	2075	1790	1550	1934	1433	1066	799	.9	4.2	11	4.85
	170	SPFP	2220	1890	1630	1410	1861	1349	1003	750	.7	4.1	11.9	4.85
308 Winchester	130	PSPBT	2900	2590	2300	2030	2428	1937	1527	1190	.1	2.1	6.2	6.20
	150	PSPBT	2860	2570	2300	2050	2725	2200	1762	1400	.1	2.0	5.9	6.20
	180	PSPBT	2610	2400	2210	2020	2725	2303	1952	1631	.2	2.5	6.6	6.20
	180	SPDC	2610	2400	2210	2020	2725	2303	1952	1631	.7	3.4	8.9	6.70
7.62 Russian	180	PSPBT	2624	2415	2222	2030	2749	2326	1970	1644	.2	2.5	6.6	7.00
308 Norma Magnum	180	DC	3100	2881	2668	2464	3842	3318	2846	2427	.0	1.6	4.6	9.30
30-06	130	PSPBT	3281	2951	2636	2338	3108	2514	2006	1578	.1	1.5	4.6	6.20
	150	PS	2972	2680	2402	2141	2943	2393	1922	1527	.0	1.9	5.7	6.20
	180	PSPBT, SPDC	2700	2494	2296	2109	2914	2487	2107	1778	.1	2.3	6.4	6.20
	220	SPRN	2411	2197	1996	1809	2840	2358	1947	1599	.3	3.1	8.5	6.20
7.65 Argentine	150	PSP	2920	2630	2355	2105	2841	2304	1848	1476	.1	2.0	5.8	7.00
303 British	130	PSP	2789	2483	2195	1929	2246	1780	1391	1075	.1	2.3	6.7	6.25
	150	PSP	2720	2440	2170	1930	2465	1983	1569	1241	.1	2.2	6.5	6.25
	180	PSPBT	2540	2340	2147	1965	2579	2189	1843	1544	.2	2.7	7.3	6.25
7.7 Japanese	130	PSP	2950	2635	2340	2065	2513	2004	1581	1231	.1	2.0	5.9	7.00
	180	PSPBT	2493	2292	2101	1922	2484	2100	1765	1477	.3	2.8	7.7	7.00
8 x 57 JS	123	PSP	2887	2515	2170	1857	2277	1728	1286	942	.1	2.3	6.8	6.20
	159	SPRN	2723	2362	2030	1734	2618	1970	1455	1062	.2	2.6	7.9	6.20
	196	SPRN	2526	2195	1894	1627	2778	2097	1562	1152	.3	3.1	9.1	6.20
358 Norma Magnum	250	SPS	2790	2493	2231	2001	4322	3451	2764	2223	.2	2.4	6.6	8.90
44 Magnum°	240	SPFP	1750				1640				Not Available			4.45

P—Pointed SP—Soft Point HP—Hollow Point FP—Flat Point RN—Round Nose BT—Boat Tail MC—Metal Case
DC—Dual Core SPS—Soft Point Semi-Pointed NA—Not announced °Price for 50

CENTERFIRE HANDGUN CARTRIDGES — BALLISTICS AND PRICES

Winchester-Western, Remington-Peters, Norma and Federal

Most loads are available from W-W and R-P. All available Norma loads are listed. Federal cartridges are marked with an asterisk. Other loads supplied by only one source are indicated by a letter, thus: Norma (a); R-P (b); W-W (c). Prices are approximate.

Cartridge	Bullet Gr.	Style	Muzzle Velocity	Muzzle Energy	Barrel Inches	Price Per 50
22 Jet (b)	40	SP	2100	390	8⅜	$9.85
221 Fireball (b)	50	SP	2650	780	10½	4.55
25 (6.35mm) Auto*	50	MC	810	73	2	5.55
256 Winchester Magnum (c)	60	HP	2350	735	8½	9.85
30 (7.65mm) Luger Auto	93	MC	1220	307	4½	8.80
32 S&W Blank (b, c)	No bullet		—	—	—	4.20
32 S&W Blank, BP (c)	No bullet		—	—	—	4.20
32 Short Colt	80	Lead	745	100	4	4.85
32 Long Colt, IL (c)	82	Lub.	755	104	4	5.05
32 Colt New Police	100	Lead	680	100	4	5.90
32 (7.65mm) Auto*	71	MC	960	145	4	6.35
32 (7.65mm) Auto Pistol (a)	77	MC	900	162	4	6.35
32 S&W	88	Lead	680	90	3	4.85
32 S&W Long	98	Lead	705	115	4	5.05
32-20 Winchester	100	Lead	1030	271	6	7.00
32-20 Winchester	100	SP	1030	271	6	8.70
357 Magnum (b)*	158	SP	1550	845	8⅜	8.30
357 Magnum	158	MP	1410	695	8⅜	8.05
357 Magnum	158	Lead	1410	696	8⅜	7.05
357 Magnum (a)	158	JHP	1450	735	8⅜	8.45
9mm Luger (a)	116	MC	1165	349	4	7.90
9mm Luger Auto*	124	MC	1120	345	4	7.90
38 S&W Blank	No bullet		—	—	—	4.35
38 Smith & Wesson	146	Lead	685	150	4	5.95
38 S&W (a)	146	Lead	730	172	4	5.95
38 Special Blank	No bullet		—	—	—	6.80
38 Special, IL (c)	150	Lub.	1060	375	6	6.50
38 Special, IL (c)	150	MP	1060	375	6	7.75
38 Special	158	Lead	855	256	6	6.00
38 Special	200	Lead	730	236	6	6.25
38 Special	158	MP	855	256	6	7.45
38 Special (b)	125	SJHP	Not available			7.45
38 Special (b)	158	SJHP	Not available			7.45
38 Special WC (b)	148	Lead	770	195	6	6.25
38 Special Match, IL (c)	148	Lead	770	195	6	6.25
38 Special Match, IL (b, c)	158	Lead	855	256	6	6.15
38 Special Hi-Speed*	158	Lead	1090	425	6	6.65
38 Special (a)	158	RN	900	320	6	6.15
38 Short Colt	125	Lead	730	150	6	5.45
38 Short Colt, Greased (c)	130	Lub.	730	155	6	5.45
38 Long Colt	150	Lead	730	175	6	6.00
38 Super Auto (b)	130	MC	1280	475	5	6.70
38 Auto, for Colt 38 Super (c)	130	MC	1280	475	5	6.70
38 Auto	130	MC	1040	312	4½	6.70
380 Auto*	95	MC	955	192	3¾	6.50
38-40 Winchester	180	SP	975	380	5	10.40
41 Remington Magnum (b)	210	Lead	1050	515	8¾	9.25
41 Remington Magnum (b)	210	SP	1500	1050	8¾	10.60
44 S&W Special	246	Lead	755	311	6½	8.15
44 Remington Magnum	240	SP	1470	1150	6½	11.00
44 Remington Magnum	240	Lead	1470	1150	6½	10.65
44-40 Winchester	200	SP	975	420	7½	12.50
45 Colt	250	Lead	860	410	5½	8.15
45 Colt, IL (c)	255	Lub., L	860	410	5½	8.15
45 Auto	230	MC	850	369	5	8.50
45 ACP (a)	230	JHP	850	370	5	9.05
45 Auto WC*	185	MC	775	245	5	8.95
45 Auto MC (a, b)	230	MC	850	369	5	9.05
45 Auto Match (c)	185	MC	775	247	5	8.95
45 Auto Match, IL (c)	210	Lead	710	235	5	9.05
45 Auto Match*	230	MC	850	370	5	9.05
45 Auto Rim (b)	230	Lead	810	335	5½	8.70

IL—Inside Lub. JSP—Jacketed Soft Point WC—Wad Cutter
RN—Round Nose HP—Hollow Point Lub—Lubricated
MC—Metal Case SP—Soft Point MP—Metal Point
LGC—Lead, Gas Check JHP—Jacketed Hollow Point

SUPER VEL HANDGUN CARTRIDGES — BALLISTICS AND PRICES

The cartridges listed below are perhaps the most powerful and destructive of these calibers commercially manufactured. Bullets listed can be had as components — other weights (not loaded by Super Vel) are also available.

Cartridge	Bullet Gr.	Style	Muzzle Velocity	Muzzle Energy	Barrel Inches	Price Per 50
380 ACP	80	JHP	1026	188	5	$7.45
9mm Luger	90	JHP	1422	402	5	7.90
9mm Luger	110	SP	1325	428	5	7.90
38 Special	110	JHP/SP	1370	458	6	7.45
38 Special Match	147	HBWC	775	196	6	6.25
38 Special Int.	158	Lead	1110	439	6	6.15
357 Magnum	110	JHP/SP	1690	697	6	8.35
357 Magnum	137	JHP/SP	1620	796	6	8.35
44 Magnum	180	JHP/SP	2005	1607	6	†4.85
45 Auto	190	JHP	1060	473	5	9.45

JHP—Jacketed Hollow Point SP—Jacketed Soft Point
HBWC—Hollow Base Wad Cutter †Price per 20

SHOTSHELL LOADS AND PRICES

Winchester-Western, Remington-Peters, Federal & Eley

In certain loadings one manufacturer may offer fewer or more shot sizes than another, but in general all makers offer equivalent loadings. Sources are indicated by letters, thus: W-W (a); R-P (b); Fed. (c); Eley (d). Prices are approximate.

GAUGE	Length Shell Ins.	Powder Equiv. Drams	Shot Ozs.	Shot Size	PRICE FOR 25
MAGNUM LOADS					
10 (a[1], b)	3½	5	2	2	$10.05
12 (a, b, c)	3	4½	1⅞	BB, 2, 4	6.60
12 (a[1], b)	3	4¼	1⅝	2, 4, 6	6.10
12 (a)	3	Max	1⅜	2, 4, 6	5.65
12 (a[1], b, c, d)	2¾	4	1½	2, 4, 5, 6	5.65
16 (a, b, c, d)	2¾	3½	1¼	2, 4, 6	4.85
20 (a, b, c)	3	3¼	1¼	4, 6, 7½	4.95
20 (a[1])	3	Max	1 3/16	4	7.00
20 (a[1], b, c, d)	2¾	3	1⅛	2, 4, 6, 7½	4.40
LONG RANGE LOADS					
10 (a, b)	2⅞	4¾	1⅝	4	5.95
12 (a[1], b, c, d)	2¾	3¾	1¼	BB, 2, 4, 5, 6, 7½, 9	4.40
16 (a, b, c, d)	2¾	3¼	1⅛	4, 5, 6, 7½, 9	4.05
20 (a[1], b, c, d)	2¾	2¾	1	4, 5, 6, 7½, 9	3.85
28 (a, b)	2¾	2¼	¾	6, 7½, 9	3.85
28 (c)	2¾	2¼	⅞	4, 6, 7½, 9	3.85
FIELD LOADS					
12 (a, b, c)	2¾	3¼	1¼	7½, 8	3.95
12 (a, b, c, d)	2¾	3¼	1⅛	4, 5, 6, 7½, 8, 9	3.75
12 (a, b, c, d)	2¾	3	1	4, 5, 6, 8	3.50
16 (a, b, c, d)	2¾	2¾	1⅛	4, 5, 6, 7½, 8, 9	3.50
16 (a, b, c)	2¾	2½	1	6, 8	3.35
20 (a, b, c, d)	2¾	2½	1	4, 5, 6, 7½, 8, 9	3.40
20 (a, b, c)	2¾	2¼	⅞	6, 8	3.10
SCATTER LOADS					
12 (a, b)	2¾	3	1⅛	8	3.90
TARGET LOADS					
12 (a, b, c)	2¾	3	1⅛	7½, 8	3.65
12 (a, b, c)	2¾	2¾	1⅛	7½, 8	3.65
16 (a, b, c)	2¾	2½	1	9	3.35
20 (a, b, c)	2¾	2¼	⅞	9	3.10
28 (a, c)	2¾	2¼	¾	9	3.85
410 (a, b, c, d)	3	Max	¾	9	3.50
410 (a, b, c)	2½	Max	½	9	2.95
SKEET & TRAP					
12 (a, b, c, d)	2¾	3	1⅛	7½, 8, 9	3.65
12 (a, b, c, d)	2¾	2¾	1⅛	7½, 8, 9	3.65
16 (a, b, c, d)	2¾	2½	1	9	3.35
16 (c)	2¾	1⅛	1⅛	8, 9	3.35
20 (a, b, c)	2¾	2¼	⅞	9	3.10
BUCKSHOT					
12 (a, b, c)	3 Mag.	4½	—	00 Buck—15 pellets	7.60
12 (a, b, c)	3 Mag.	4½	—	4 Buck—41 pellets	7.60
12 (b)	2¾ Mag.	4	—	1 Buck—20 pellets	6.60
12 (a, b, c)	2¾ Mag.	4	—	00 Buck—12 pellets	6.60
12 (a, b, c)	2¾	3¾	—	00 Buck— 9 pellets	5.85
12 (a, b, c)	2¾	3¾	—	0 Buck—12 pellets	5.85
12 (a, b, c)	2¾	3¾	—	1 Buck—16 pellets	5.85
12 (a, b, c)	2¾	3¾	—	4 Buck—27 pellets	5.85
16 (a, b, c)	2¾	3	—	1 Buck—12 pellets	5.85
20 (a, b, c)	2¾	2¾	—	3 Buck—20 pellets	5.85
RIFLED SLUGS					
12 (a, b, c, d)	2¾	3¾	1	Slug	6.90
16 (a, b, c)	2¾	3	⅞	Slug	6.55
20 (a, b, c)	2¾	2¾	⅝	Slug	6.30
410 (a, b, c)	2½	Max	⅕	Slug	5.95

W-W 410, 28- and 10-ga. Magnum shells available in paper cases only, as are their scatter and target loads; their skeet and trap loads come in both plastic and paper.

RP shells are all of plastic with Power Piston wads except: 12 ga. scatter loads have Post Wad: all 10 ga., 410-3" and rifled slug loads have standard wad columns.

Federal magnum, long range, buckshot, slug and all 410 loads are made in plastic only. Field loads are available in both paper and plastic.

Eley shotshells are of plastic-coated paper.

[1]—These loads available from W-W with Lubaloy shot at higher price.

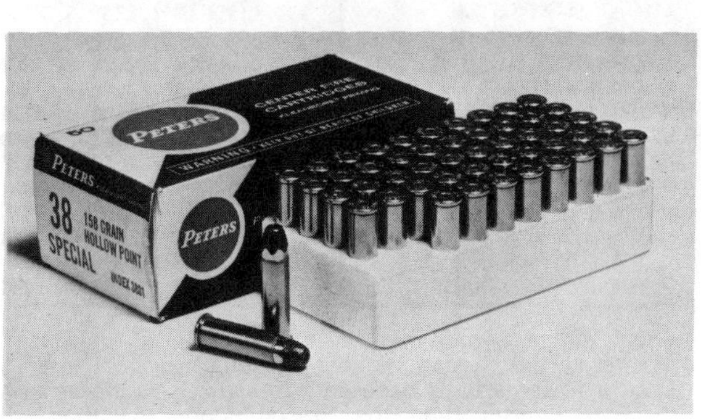

BALLISTICS

KKSP—'Kling-Kor' Soft Point
PSP—Pointed Soft Point
SP—Soft Point
CPE—Copper Point Expanding

MC—Metal Cased (Hard Point)
PNEU—Pneumatic
HP—Hollow Point
ST—'Sabretip'

DESCRIPTION	Bullet Wt. Grains	Bullet Type	Velocity in Feet per Second Muzzle	100 Yds.	200 Yds.	300 Yds.	400 Yds.	500 Yds.	Energy in Foot Pounds Muzzle	100 Yds.	200 Yds.	300 Yds.	400 Yds.	500 Yds.
22 HORNET	45	PSP	2690	2030	1510	1150	—	—	720	410	230	130	—	—
22 SAVAGE	70	PSP	2800	2440	2110	1840	—	—	1220	925	690	525	—	—
222 REMINGTON	50	PSP	3200	2600	2170	1750	—	—	1140	785	520	340	—	—
243 WINCHESTER	75	PSP	3500	3070	2660	2290	1960	1670	2040	1570	1180	875	640	465
243 WINCHESTER	100	PSP	3070	2790	2540	2320	2120	1940	2090	1730	1430	1190	995	835
244 REMINGTON	75	PSP	3500	3070	2660	2290	1960	1670	2040	1570	1180	875	640	465
6.5 x 53 MM MAN.-SCH.	160	SP	2160	1950	1750	1570	—	—	1660	1350	1090	875	—	—
6.5 x 55 MM	160	SP	2420	2190	1960	1760	1580	1420	2080	1700	1360	1110	885	715
25-20 WINCHESTER	86	SP	1460	1180	1030	940	—	—	405	265	200	170	—	—
25-35 WINCHESTER	117	SP	2300	1910	1600	1340	—	—	1370	945	665	465	—	—
250 SAVAGE	100	PSP	2820	2460	2140	1870	—	—	1760	1340	1020	775	—	—
257 ROBERTS	117	PSP	2650	2280	1950	1690	—	—	1820	1350	985	740	—	—
270 WINCHESTER	100	PSP	3480	3070	2690	2340	2010	1700	2690	2090	1600	1215	890	640
270 WINCHESTER	130	PSP	3140	2850	2580	2320	2090	1860	2840	2340	1920	1550	1260	1000
270 WINCHESTER	160	KKSP	2800	2530	2280	2050	1840	1580	2790	2270	1850	1490	1200	—
7 x 57 MM MAUSER	139	PSP	2800	2500	2240	1990	1770	1580	2420	1930	1550	1220	965	770
7 x 57 MM MAUSER	160	KKSP	2650	2330	2040	1780	1550	1350	2500	1930	1480	1130	855	645
7 MM REMINGTON MAGNUM	175	SP	3070	2720	2400	2120	1870	1640	3660	2870	2240	1750	1360	1040
30-30 WINCHESTER	150	PNEU	2410	2020	1700	1430	—	—	1930	1360	960	680	—	—
30-30 WINCHESTER	170	KKSP	2220	1890	1630	1410	—	—	1860	1350	1000	750	—	—
30-30 WINCHESTER	170	ST	2220	1890	1630	1410	—	—	1860	1350	1000	750	—	—
30-30 WINCHESTER	170	MC	2220	1890	1630	1410	—	—	1860	1350	1000	750	—	—
30-30 WINCHESTER	150	ST	2410	2020	1700	1430	—	—	1930	1360	960	680	—	—
30 REMINGTON	170	KKSP	2120	1820	1560	1350	—	—	1700	1250	920	690	—	—
30-40 KRAG	180	KKSP	2470	2120	1830	1590	1400	—	2440	1790	1340	1010	785	—
30-06 SPRINGFIELD	130	HP	3150	2730	2470	2170	1920	1690	2870	2160	1770	1360	1060	820
30-06 SPRINGFIELD	150	PSP	2970	2670	2400	2130	1890	1670	2930	2370	1920	1510	1190	930
30-06 SPRINGFIELD	150	ST	2970	2670	2400	2130	1890	1670	2930	2370	1920	1510	1190	930
30-06 SPRINGFIELD	180	KKSP	2700	2330	2010	1740	1520	—	2910	2170	1610	1210	920	—
30-06 SPRINGFIELD	180	CPE	2700	2480	2280	2080	1900	1730	2910	2460	2080	1730	1440	1190
30-06 SPRINGFIELD	180	ST	2700	2470	2250	2040	1850	1670	2910	2440	2020	1660	1370	1110
30-06 SPRINGFIELD	220	KKSP	2410	2120	1870	1670	1480	—	2830	2190	1710	1360	1070	—
300 WINCHESTER-MAGNUM	180	ST	3070	2850	2640	2440	2250	2060	3770	3250	2790	2380	2020	1700
300 HOLLAND & HOLLAND MAGNUM	180	PSP	2920	2670	2440	2220	2020	1830	3400	2850	2380	1970	1630	1340
300 SAVAGE	150	PSP	2670	2390	2130	1890	1660	—	2370	1900	1510	1190	915	—
3C0 SAVAGE	150	ST	2670	2390	2130	1890	1660	—	2370	1900	1510	1190	915	—
300 SAVAGE	180	KKSP	2370	2040	1760	1520	1340	—	2240	1660	1240	920	715	—
300 SAVAGE	180	ST	2370	2160	1960	1770	1600	—	2240	1860	1530	1250	1020	—
303 SAVAGE	190	KKSP	1980	1680	1440	1250	—	—	1650	1190	875	660	—	—
303 BRITISH	150	PSP	2720	2420	2150	1900	1670	1470	2460	1950	1540	1200	930	720
303 BRITISH	150	ST	2720	2420	2150	1900	1670	1470	2460	1950	1540	1200	930	720
303 BRITISH	180	KKSP	2540	2180	1860	1590	1360	—	2580	1900	1380	1010	740	—
303 BRITISH	180	CPE	2540	2330	2130	1940	1760	1600	2580	2170	1810	1500	1240	1020
303 BRITISH	180	ST	2540	2300	2090	1900	1730	1580	2580	2120	1750	1440	1200	1000
303 BRITISH	215	KKSP	2180	1900	1660	1460	1250	—	2270	1720	1310	1020	750	—
308 WINCHESTER	130	HP	2930	2590	2290	2010	1770	1560	2480	1940	1520	1170	905	700
308 WINCHESTER	150	PSP	2860	2570	2300	2050	1810	1590	2730	2200	1760	1400	1090	840
308 WINCHESTER	150	ST	2860	2570	2300	2050	1810	1590	2730	2200	1760	1400	1090	840
308 WINCHESTER	180	KKSP	2610	2240	1920	1640	1400	—	2720	2010	1470	1070	785	—
308 WINCHESTER	180	ST	2610	2390	2170	1970	1780	1600	2720	2280	1870	1540	1260	1010
308 WINCHESTER	200	KKSP	2450	2210	1980	1770	1580	1410	2670	2170	1750	1400	1110	875
8 MM MAUSER	170	PSP	2570	2300	2040	1810	1600	—	2490	2000	1570	1240	965	—
32-20 WINCHESTER	115	SP	1480	1220	1050	940	—	—	560	380	280	225	—	—
32 WINCHESTER SPECIAL	170	KKSP	2280	1920	1630	1410	—	—	1960	1390	1000	750	—	—
32 WINCHESTER SPECIAL	170	ST	2280	1920	1630	1410	—	—	1960	1390	1000	750	—	—
32 REMINGTON	170	KKSP	2120	1800	1540	1340	—	—	1700	1220	895	680	—	—
32-40 WINCHESTER	170	KKSP	1540	1340	1170	1050	—	—	895	680	515	415	—	—
35 REMINGTON	200	SP	2100	1710	1390	1160	—	—	1950	1300	865	605	—	—
351 WINCHESTER SELF-LOADING	180	SP	1850	1560	1310	1140	—	—	1370	975	685	520	—	—
358 (8.8 MM) WINCHESTER	200	KKSP	2530	2210	1910	1640	1400	—	2840	2160	1610	1190	870	—
38-40 WINCHESTER	180	SP	1330	1070	960	850	—	—	705	455	370	290	—	—
38-55 WINCHESTER	255	SP	1600	1410	1240	1110	—	—	1450	1130	880	700	—	—
43 (11 MM) MAUSER	385	LEAD	1360	1150	1030	940	—	—	1580	1130	910	750	—	—
44-40 WINCHESTER	200	SP	1310	1050	940	830	—	—	760	490	390	305	—	—
44 REMINGTON MAGNUM	240	SP	1850	1450	1150	980	—	—	1820	1120	710	510	—	—

Short Range Sighting-in—It is preferable to sight-in a rifle at the "recommended sighting" range. However, it is sometimes necessary to sight-in a rifle at a distance shorter than the "recommended sighting" range because you don't have the necessary yardage available. To do this, find from the range table at what distance the bullet will first cross the line of sight. Put up a target at this distance and from a firm rest fire

and Range Table

RANGE TABLE—Values shown in this table are based on a sight height 1½" above line of bore. RECOMMENDED SIGHTING: ⊕ Indicates the most favourable sighting range in order to minimize the sighting problem at shorter and longer ranges. + Indicates inches high; − Indicates inches low.

RANGE

First Crosses Line of Sight App. Yds.	50 Yds.	75 Yds.	100 Yds.	125 Yds.	150 Yds.	200 Yds.	250 Yds.	300 Yds.	400 Yds.	500 Yds.	Bullet Wt. Grains	Type	DESCRIPTION
29.0	—	+1.5	—	—	⊕	-4.0	—	—	—	—	45	PSP	22 HORNET
25.0	—	—	+2.0	—	—	⊕	-4.5	—	—	—	70	PSP	22 SAVAGE
30.0	—	—	+2.0	—	—	⊕	-3.5	—	—	—	50	PSP	222 REMINGTON
30.0	—	—	—	+2.5	—	—	⊕	-3.0	-15.5	-36.5	75	PSP	243 WINCHESTER
27.5	—	—	—	+3.0	—	—	⊕	-3.5	-16.5	-35.5	100	PSP	243 WINCHESTER
30.0	—	—	—	+2.5	—	—	⊕	-3.0	-15.5	-36.5	75	PSP	244 REMINGTON
25.5	—	+1.5	—	—	⊕	-4.0	—	—	—	—	160	SP	6.5 x 53 MM MAN.-SCH.
21.0	—	—	+3.5	—	—	⊕	-5.0	-13.0	-39.0	—	160	SP	6.5 x 55 MM
16.0	+2.0	—	⊕	-4.0	—	—	—	—	—	—	86	SP	25-20 WINCHESTER
23.0	—	+1.5	—	—	⊕	-4.5	—	—	—	—	117	SP	25-35 WINCHESTER
27.5	—	—	+2.0	—	—	⊕	-3.5	—	—	—	100	PSP	250 SAVAGE
24.0	—	—	+2.5	—	—	⊕	-4.5	—	—	—	117	PSP	257 ROBERTS
31.5	—	—	—	+2.5	—	—	⊕	-3.5	-14.5	-33.5	100	PSP	270 WINCHESTER
27.5	—	—	—	+3.0	—	—	⊕	-4.0	-16.0	-35.5	130	PSP	270 WINCHESTER
28.5	—	—	+2.0	—	—	⊕	-4.0	—	-25.0	—	160	KKSP	270 WINCHESTER
27.0	—	—	—	+4.0	—	—	⊕	-4.5	-18.5	-41.0	139	PSP	7 x 57 MM MAUSER
29.0	—	—	+2.5	—	—	⊕	-4.0	—	-28.5	—	160	KKSP	7 x 57 MM MAUSER
25.0	—	—	—	+3.5	—	—	⊕	-4.0	-18.0	-43.0	175	SP	7 MM REMINGTON MAGNUM
27.0	—	+1.5	—	—	⊕	-4.0	—	—	—	—	150	PNEU	30-30 WINCHESTER
23.0	—	+1.5	—	—	⊕	-4.5	—	—	—	—	170	KKSP	30-30 WINCHESTER
23.0	—	+1.5	—	—	⊕	-4.5	—	—	—	—	170	ST	30-30 WINCHESTER
23.0	—	+1.5	—	—	⊕	-4.5	—	—	—	—	170	MC	30-30 WINCHESTER
27.0	—	+1.5	—	—	⊕	-4.0	—	—	—	—	150	ST	30-30 WINCHESTER
20.0	—	+2.0	—	—	⊕	-5.0	—	—	—	—	170	KKSP	30 REMINGTON
21.0	—	—	+3.0	—	—	⊕	-5.5	—	-41.0	—	180	KKSP	30-30 KRAG
27.0	—	—	—	+3.0	—	—	⊕	-4.0	-19.5	-47.0	130	HP	30-06 SPRINGFIELD
25.0	—	—	—	+3.5	—	—	⊕	-4.0	-17.5	-41.0	150	PSP	30-06 SPRINGFIELD
25.0	—	—	—	+3.5	—	—	⊕	-4.0	-17.5	-41.0	150	ST	30-06 SPRINGFIELD
24.0	—	—	+2.5	—	—	⊕	-4.0	—	-32.5	—	180	KKSP	30-06 SPRINGFIELD
21.0	—	—	—	+4.0	—	—	⊕	-4.5	-20.5	-46.0	180	CPE	30-06 SPRINGFIELD
20.0	—	—	—	+4.0	—	—	⊕	-4.5	-21.0	-48.5	180	ST	30-06 SPRINGFIELD
21.0	—	—	+3.0	—	—	⊕	-5.5	—	-41.0	—	220	KKSP	30-06 SPRINGFIELD
27.5	—	—	—	+3.0	—	—	⊕	-3.5	-14.5	-32.5	180	ST	300 WINCHESTER-MAGNUM
25.0	—	—	—	+3.5	—	—	⊕	-4.0	-17.5	-39.0	180	PSP	300 HOLLAND & HOLLAND MAGNUM
26.0	—	—	+2.5	—	—	⊕	-3.5	—	-29.0	—	150	PSP	300 SAVAGE
26.0	—	—	+2.5	—	—	⊕	-3.5	—	-29.0	—	150	ST	300 SAVAGE
20.0	—	—	+3.5	—	—	⊕	-5.5	—	-43.0	—	180	KKSP	300 SAVAGE
21.5	—	—	+3.0	—	—	⊕	-5.5	—	-35.0	—	180	ST	300 SAVAGE
17.5	—	—	+3.0	—	—	⊕	-5.5	—	—	—	190	KKSP	303 SAVAGE
22.0	—	—	—	+4.5	—	—	⊕	-5.0	-23.0	-53.5	150	PSP	303 BRITISH
22.0	—	—	—	+4.5	—	—	⊕	-5.0	-23.0	-53.5	150	ST	303 BRITISH
23.0	—	—	+3.0	—	—	⊕	-5.0	—	-41.0	—	180	KKSP	303 BRITISH
19.0	—	—	—	+4.5	—	—	⊕	-5.0	-23.0	-52.5	180	CPE	303 BRITISH
17.5	—	—	—	+5.0	—	—	⊕	-5.5	-26.5	-71.0	180	ST	303 BRITISH
16.0	—	—	+4.5	—	—	⊕	-7.0	—	-54.0	—	215	KKSP	303 BRITISH
23.5	—	—	—	+3.5	—	—	⊕	-4.5	-23.5	-59.0	130	HP	308 WINCHESTER
25.0	—	—	—	+3.5	—	—	⊕	-4.5	-20.0	-47.5	150	PSP	308 WINCHESTER
25.0	—	—	—	+3.5	—	—	⊕	-4.5	-20.0	-47.5	150	ST	308 WINCHESTER
23.0	—	—	+3.0	—	—	⊕	-5.5	—	-38.0	—	180	KKSP	308 WINCHESTER
22.0	—	—	—	+4.5	—	—	⊕	-5.0	-21.5	-51.5	180	ST	308 WINCHESTER
22.0	—	—	+3.0	—	—	⊕	-5.0	-12.0	-35.0	-48.5	200	KKSP	308 WINCHESTER
22.5	—	—	+3.5	—	—	⊕	-5.5	—	-33.5	—	170	PSP	8 MM MAUSER
16.5	+2.0	—	⊕	-3.5	—	—	—	—	—	—	115	SP	32-20 WINCHESTER
23.0	—	+2.0	—	—	⊕	-4.5	—	—	—	—	170	KKSP	32 WINCHESTER SPECIAL
23.0	—	+2.0	—	—	⊕	-4.5	—	—	—	—	170	ST	32 WINCHESTER SPECIAL
20.0	—	+2.0	—	—	⊕	-5.0	—	—	—	—	170	KKSP	32 REMINGTON
21.0	+1.0	—	⊕	-2.5	—	—	—	—	—	—	170	KKSP	32-40 WINCHESTER
19.5	—	+2.5	—	—	⊕	-6.0	—	—	—	—	200	SP	35 REMINGTON
16.0	—	+3.0	—	—	⊕	-7.5	—	—	—	—	180	SP	351 WINCHESTER SELF-LOADING
20.5	—	—	+3.0	—	—	⊕	-5.0	—	-38.5	—	200	KKSP	358 (8.8 MM) WINCHESTER
14.5	+2.5	—	⊕	-4.0	—	—	—	—	—	—	180	SP	38-40 WINCHESTER
13.5	—	+4.0	—	—	⊕	-8.5	—	—	—	—	255	SP	38-55 WINCHESTER
16.0	+2.0	—	⊕	-3.5	—	—	—	—	—	—	385	LEAD	43 (11 MM) MAUSER
12.5	+3.0	—	⊕	-4.5	—	—	—	—	—	—	200	SP	44-40 WINCHESTER
13.0	—	+4.5	—	—	⊕	-8.0	—	—	—	—	240	SP	44 REMINGTON MAGNUM

a three-shot group. The centre point of the group is the "centre of impact"—the average spot where the bullets strike. Adjust sights to bring the centre of impact to the centre of the target then fire another group. If the centre of impact is on target the rifle will be sighted in at the range recommended in the range table. It is, however, desirable to fire a target at that range as soon as possible as a double check.

SPEER-DWM C.F. RIFLE CARTRIDGES—BALLISTICS AND PRICES

These DWM metric calibers are imported by Speer, Inc. The Starkmantel (strong-jacket, soft-point) bullets have apparently been discontinued. Metric cases and bullets for calibers listed may be special-ordered from Speer. U.S. calibers offered by Speer-DWM will be found elsewhere in this section.

Caliber	Bullet Wt. Grs.	Bullet Type	Velocity Muzzle	100 yds.	200 yds.	300 yds.	Energy Muzzle	100 yds.	200 yds.	300 yds.	Mid-Range Trajectory 100 yds.	200 yds.	300 yds.	Price for 10
5.6 x 35R Vierling*	46	SP	2030	1500	1140		418	224	130		1.2	7.5		$6.65
5.6 x 50R (Rimmed) Mag.*	50	PSP			Not Available									6.65†
5.6 x 52R (Savage H.P.)	71	PSP	2850	2460	2320	2200	1280	947	846	766	.3	2.3	6.5	4.70
5.6 x 61 SE	77	PSP	3700	3360	3060	2790	2350	1920	1605	1345	.1	1.1	3.4	11.85
5.6 x 61R	77	PSP	3480	3140	2840	2560	2070	1690	1370	1120	.1	1.3	4.0	11.85
6.5 x 54 MS	159	SP	2170	1925	1705	1485	1660	1300	1025	810	.5	4.1	11.5	4.05
6.5 x 57 Mauser	93	PSP	3350	2930	2570	2260	2300	1760	1350	1040	.1	1.7	4.8	4.35
6.5 x 57 R	93	PSP	3350	2930	2570	2260	2300	1760	1350	1040	.1	1.7	4.8	4.70
7 x 57 Mauser	103	PSP	3330	2865	2450	2060	2550	1890	1380	977	.1	1.7	5.2	4.05
	162	TIG	2785	2480	2250	2060	2780	2200	1820	1520	.3	2.4	6.7	4.70
7 x 57 R	103	PSP	3260	2810	2390	2000	2430	1820	1320	920	.1	1.8	5.3	4.25
	139	SP	2550	2240	1960	1720	2000	1540	1190	910	.3	2.9	8.6	4.25
	162	TIG	2710	2420	2210	2020	2640	2120	1750	1460	.3	2.4	6.9	5.25
7 x 64	103	PSP	3572	3110	2685	2283	2930	2230	1670	1190	.1	1.4	4.4	4.35
	139	SP	3000	2570	2260	1980	2780	2040	1570	1200	.2	2.2	6.4	4.35
	162	TIG	2960	2603	2375	2200	3150	2440	2030	1740	.2	2.0	6.0	6.10
	177	TIG	2880	2665	2490	2325	3270	2820	2440	2130	.2	2.0	5.6	6.80
7 x 65 R	103	PSP	3480	3010	2590	2200	2770	2100	1540	1120	.1	1.5	4.7	4.90†
	139	SP	3000	2570	2260	1980	2780	2040	1570	1200	.2	2.2	6.4	4.90†
	162	TIG	2887	2540	2320	2140	3000	2320	1930	1650	.2	2.2	6.3	6.95†
	177	TIG	2820	2600	2420	2255	3120	2660	2300	2000	.2	2.1	5.9	7.60†
7mm SE	169	ToSto	3300	3045	2825	2620	4090	3480	3010	2600	.1	1.4	3.9	11.85
7 x 75 R SE	169	ToSto	3070	2840	2630	2430	3550	3050	2620	2240	.1	1.6	4.5	11.85
30-06	180	TUG	2854	2562	2306	2077	3261	2632	2133	1726	.2	2.2	6.3	5.20†
8 x 57 JS	123	SP	2968	2339	1805	1318	2415	1497	897	477	.2	2.7	8.8	3.85
	198	TIG	2732	2415	2181	1985	3276	2560	2083	1736	.3	2.5	7.1	4.55
8 x 57 JR	196	SP	2391	1991	1742	1565	2488	1736	1316	1056	.5	3.9	11.2	3.70
8 x 57 JRS	123	SP	2970	2340	1805	1318	2415	1497	897	477	.2	2.7	8.8	4.05
	196	SP	2480	2140	1870	1640	2680	2000	1510	1165	.4	3.3	9.4	4.05
	198	TIG	2600	2320	2105	1930	2970	2350	1950	1620	.3	2.7	7.6	4.90
8 x 60 S	196	SP	2585	2162	1890	1690	2905	2030	1560	1245	.4	3.2	9.2	4.55
	198	TIG	2780	2450	2205	2010	3390	2625	2130	1770	.3	2.4	6.9	5.75
9.3 x 62	293	TUG	2515	2310	2120	2020	4110	3480	3010	2634	.3	2.8	7.5	5.90†
9.3 x 64	293	TUG	2640	2450	2290	2145	4550	3900	3410	3000	.3	2.4	6.6	8.75†
9.3 x 72 R	193	FP	1925	1600	1400	1245	1590	1090	835	666	.5	5.7	16.6	6.05†
9.3 x 74 R	293	TUG	2360	2160	1998	1870	3580	3000	2560	2250	.3	3.1	8.7	8.00

*Price for 20   †Boxer Primed   FP—Flat Point   SP—Soft Point   PSP—Pointed Soft Point   TIG—Brenneke Torpedo Ideal
TUG—Brenneke Torpedo Universal   ToSto—vom Hofe Torpedo Stopring

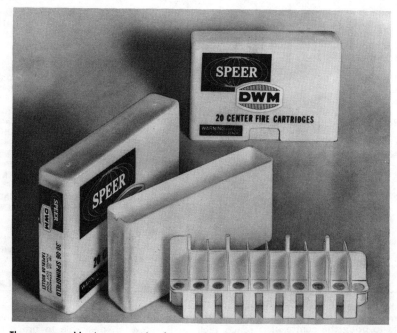

The new reusable 4-way cartridge box in which all Speer-DWM ammo will be packed.

BROWNING 22 AUTO CHALLENGER PISTOL

Caliber: 22 LR, 10-shot magazine.
Barrel: 4½ inches or 6¾ inches.
Length: 8⅞" over-all (4½" bbl.). **Weight:** 35 oz. (4½" bbl.).
Stocks: Select walnut, hand checkered, wrap-around.
Features: Steel frame, manual stop-open latch (automatic after last shot); gold plated grooved trigger; trigger pull adjustment screw on rear face of frame.
Sights: ⅛" non-glare blade front; frame-mtd. rear, screw adj. for w. & e.
Price: Blue, either bbl. **$86.50**   Engraved and gold inlaid . **$254.50**
Price: Renaissance Grade, engraved and chrome plated **$255.00**

BROWNING 22 AUTO MEDALIST PISTOL

Caliber: 22 LR, 10-shot magazine.
Barrel: 6¾", med.-heavy vent. rib.
Length: 11⅛" over-all. **Weight:** 46 oz. less weights.
Stocks: Full wrap-around thumbrest of select checkered walnut; matching fore-end. Left hand grips available.
Features: Dry-fire mechanism permits practice without mechanical harm. Fore-end holds variable weights. Trigger adj. for weight of pull and backlash.
Sights: ⅛" undercut removable blade front; rear frame-mtd., has micrometer clicks adj. for w. and e. Sight radius, 9½".
Price: Blued . . . . **$138.50**   Engraved and gold inlaid **$334.50**
Price: Renaissance Grade, chrome plated **$325.00**

BROWNING INTERNATIONAL MEDALIST PISTOL

Caliber: 22LR, 10-shot magazine.
Barrel: 5.9", med.-heavy vent. rib.
Length: 10¹⁵⁄₁₆" over-all. **Weight:** 42 oz.
Stocks: Select walnut, full wraparound with thumb rest, I.8" max. width.
Features: The International Medalist pistol meets all International Shooting Union regulations. The regular Medalist qualifies under N.R.A. pistol regulations.
Sights: Identical to those of standard Medalist, sight radius is 8.6".
Price: Blued **$132.50**

COLT WOODSMAN MATCH TARGET AUTO PISTOL

Caliber: 22LR, 10-shot magazine.
Barrel: 4½ inches, 6 inches.
Length: 9 inches (4½" bbl.). **Weight:** 40 oz. (6" bbl.), 36 oz. (4½" bbl.).
Stocks: Walnut with thumbrest; checkered.
Features: Wide trigger, automatic slide stop.
Sights: Ramp front with removable undercut blade; ⅛" standard, ¹⁄₁₀" on special order; Colt-Elliason adjustable rear.
Price: Colt Blue only **$115.50**

COLT WOODSMAN SPORT AND TARGET MODEL

Caliber: 22LR, 10-shot magazine.
Barrel: 4½ inches, 6 inches.
Length: 9 inches (4½" bbl.). **Weight:** 30 oz. (4½" bbl.). 32 oz. (6" bbl.).
Stocks: Walnut with thumbrest; checkered.
Features: Wide trigger, automatic slide stop.
Sights: Ramp front with removable blade, adjustable rear.
Price: Colt Blue only **$100.00**

COLT TARGETSMAN

Same as Woodsman S&T model except: 6" bbl. only; fixed blade front sight, economy adj. rear; without auto. slide stop **$82.50**

COLT GOLD CUP NAT'L MATCH AUTO

Caliber: 45 ACP or Wad Cutter; 38 Spec. W.C. 7-shot magazine.
Barrel: 5", with new design bushing.
Length: 8½ inches. **Weight:** 37 oz.
Stocks: Checkered walnut, gold plated medallion.
Features: Arched or flat housing; wide, grooved trigger with adj. stop; ribbed-top slide, hand fitted, with improved ejection port.
Sights: Patridge front, Colt-Elliason rear adj. for w. and e.
Price: Colt Royal Blue **$190.00**

COLT GOLD CUP NAT'L MATCH Mk IV SERIES 70 AUTO

Identical to the Gold Cup except fitted with a split-finger, collet-type barrel bushing and reverse-taper barrel to match for improved accuracy.
Price: **$190.00**

HI-STANDARD SUPERMATIC STANDARD CITATION
Caliber: 22 LR, 10-shot magazine.
Barrel: 5½" bull weight.
Length: 10 inches (5½" bbl.). **Weight:** 42 oz. (5½" bbl.).
Stocks: Checkered walnut with or w/o thumbrest, right or left.
Features: Adjustable trigger pull; anti-backlash trigger adjustment; double acting safety; rebounding firing pin. Back & front straps stippled.
Sights: Undercut ramp front; click adjustable square notch rear.
Price: 5½" bull barrel $120.00

HI-STANDARD SUPERMATIC CITATION MILITARY
Caliber: 22 LR, 10-shot magazine.
Barrel: 5½" bull, 7¼" fluted.
Length: 9¾ inches (5½" bbl.). **Weight:** 44½ oz.
Stocks: Checkered walnut with or w/o thumbrest, right or left.
Features: Same as regular Citation plus military style grip, stippled front- and backstraps, positive magazine latch.
Sights: Undercut ramp front; frame mounted rear, click adj.
Price: Either bbl. length $120.00

HI-STANDARD S'MATIC TOURNAMENT MILITARY
Caliber: 22 LR, 10-shot.
Barrel: 5½" bull, 6¾" tapered.
Length: 9¾" (5½" bbl.). **Weight:** 45 oz.
Stocks: Checkered walnut, thumbrest for either hand.
Features: Military type grip; 5½" bbl. notched for stabilizer; non-adj. trigger; positive magazine safety; otherwise like regular Citations.
Sights: Ramp-mounted undercut front blade, adj. rear on slide.
Price: Either bbl. length $100.00

HI-STANDARD (*ISU) OLYMPIC AUTO PISTOL
Caliber: 22 Short, 10-shot magazine.
Barrel: 6¾" round tapered, with stabilizer.
Length: 11¼". **Weight:** 40 oz.
Stocks: Checkered walnut w or w/0 thumbrest, right or left.
Features: Integral stabilizer with two removable weights. Trigger adj. for pull and anti-backlash; Citation grade finish.
Sights: Undercut ramp front; click adj., square notch rear.
Price: Blued $132.50
*Complies with all International Shooting Union regulations.

HI-STANDARD (*ISU) OLYMPIC MILITARY AUTO
Caliber: 22 Short, 10-shot magazine.
Barrel: 6¾" round tapered, with stabilizer.
Length: 11 inches. **Weight:** 40½ oz.
Stocks: Checkered walnut w or w/o thumbrest, right or left.
Features: Integral stabilizer with two removable weights; adj. trigger with anti-backlash screw. Grip as on military 45.
Sights: Undercut ramp front; frame mounted rear, click adj.
Price: Blued $137.50

HI-STANDARD SUPERMATIC TROPHY MILITARY
Caliber: 22 LR, 10-shot magazine.
Barrel: 5½" heavy, 7¼" fluted.
Length: 9¾ inches (5½" bbl.). **Weight:** 44½ oz.
Stocks: Checkered walnut with or w/o thumbrest, right or left.
Features: Grip duplicates feel of military 45; positive action mag. latch; front- and backstraps stippled. Adj. trigger, anti-backlash screw.
Sights: Undercut ramp front; frame mounted rear, click adj.
Price: Either bbl. length $132.50
Accessories for Hi-Standard Supermatics
   Stabilizers (furnished on Olympics) $6.00
   2 oz. wgt., **$2.25**. 3 oz. wgt., **$2.75**. Extra magazines **$5.50 to $7.00**

RUGER Mark 1 TARGET MODEL AUTO PISTOL
Caliber: 22 LR only, 9-shot magazine.
Barrel: 6⅞" or 5½" bull barrel (6-groove, 14" twist).
Length: 10⅞ inches (6⅞" bbl.). **Weight:** 42 oz. with 6⅞" bbl.
Stocks: Checkered hard rubber.
Features: Rear sight mounted on receiver, does not move with slide; wide, grooved trigger.
Sights: ⅛" blade front, micro click rear, adjustable for w. and e. Sight radius 9⅜" (with 6⅞" bbl.).
Price: Blued, either barrel length $67.50
Price: Checkered walnut panels with left thumbrest $71.50

SMITH & WESSON 22 AUTO PISTOL Model 41
Caliber: 22 LR or 22 S, 10-shot clip.
Barrel: 5" or 7⅜", sight radius 9⁵/₁₆" (7⅜" bbl.).
Length: 12", incl. detachable muzzle brake, (7⅜" bbl. only).
Weight: 43½ oz. (7⅜" bbl.).
Stocks: Checkered walnut with thumbrest, usable with either hand.
Features: ⅜" wide, grooved trigger with adj. stop; wgts. available to make pistol up to 59 oz.
Sights: Front, ⅛" Patridge undercut; micro click rear adj. for w. and e.
Price: S&W Bright Blue, satin matted bbl., either caliber $131.50

SMITH & WESSON 22 MATCH HEAVY BARREL M-41
Caliber: 22 LR, 10-shot clip.
Barrel: 5½" heavy, without muzzle brake. Sight radius, 8".
Length: 9". **Weight:** 44½ oz.
Stocks: Checkered walnut with modified thumbrest, usable with either hand.
Features: ⅜" wide, grooved trigger; adj. trigger stop.
Sights: ⅛" Patridge on ramp base. S&W micro click rear, adj. for w. and e.
Price: S&W Bright Blue, satin matted top area $131.50

S & W 22 AUTO HEAVY BARREL EFS Model 41
Same as Model 41 Heavy Barrel but with extendible ⅛" front sight.
Without muzzle brake or weights. Blued $144.50

SMITH & WESSON CONVERSION KIT
Converts Models 41 and 46 from 22 Short to 22 LR and vice versa. Consists of barrel, slide, magazine, slide stop and recoil spring.
Price, parts only $61.70
Price, factory installed and tested $70.60
Price, 5½ heavy bbl. only with sights for M41 or M46 .... $35.30

SMITH & WESSON 38 MASTER Model 52 AUTO
Caliber: 38 Special (for Mid-range W.C. with flush-seated bullet only). 5-shot magazine.
Barrel: 5".
Length: 8⅝". **Weight:** 41 oz. with empty magazine.
Features: Top sighting surfaces matte finished. Locked breech, moving barrel system; checked for 10-ring groups at 50 yards. Coin-adj. sight screws. Dry firing permissible if manual safety on.
Stocks: Checkered walnut.
Sights: ⅛" Patridge front, S&W micro click rear adj. for w. and e.
Price: S&W Bright Blue $197.00

STERLING TARGET "CUP" SERIES AUTO PISTOL
Caliber: 22 LR, 10-shot magazine.
Barrel: 4½", 6", and 8".
Length: 9" (4½" bbl.). **Weight:** 36 oz. (4½" bbl.).
Stocks: Checkered plastic.
Features: Adjustable trigger and balance weights; sear lock safety.
Sights: ⅛" blade front; Click adj. square notch rear.
Price: Blued (M283) $117.00
Price: Blued with 6" tapered barrel (M284) $112.00

COLT DIAMONDBACK REVOLVER

Caliber: 22 S, L or LR, or 38 Special, 6 shot.
Barrel: 2½" or 4", with ventilated rib.
Length: 9" (4" bbl.). **Weight:** 25 oz. (2½" bbl.), 28½ oz. (4" bbl.).
Stocks: Checkered walnut, target type, square butt.
Features: Ventilated rib; grooved, crisp trigger; swing-out cylinder; wide hammer spur.
Sights: Ramp front, adj. notch rear.
Price: Colt Blue **$135.00**

COLT OFFICERS MODEL MATCH REVOLVER

Caliber: 22 LR or 38 Special, 6 shot.
Barrel: 6 inches.
Length: 11¼". **Weight:** 43 oz. (22 cal.), 39 oz. (38 cal.).
Stocks: Checkered walnut, square butt.
Features: Grooved trigger, wide hammer spur, hand fitted swing-out cyl. action.
Sights: Undercut ⅛" removable blade front, adjustable rear.
Price: Blued **$143.00**

COLT NEW POLICE PYTHON REVOLVER

Caliber: 357 Magnum (handles all 38 Spec.), 6 shot.
Barrel: 2½", 4" or 6", with ventilated rib.
Length: 9¼" (4" bbl.). **Weight:** 41 oz. (4" bbl.).
Stocks: Checkered walnut, target type, square butt.
Features: Ventilated rib; grooved, crisp trigger; swing-out cylinder; wide hammer spur.
Sights: ⅛" ramp front, adj. notch rear.
Price: Colt Royal Blue ...... **$190.00** Nickeled **$218.50**

SMITH & WESSON 1953 Model 35, 22/32 TARGET

Caliber: 22 S, L or LR, 6 shot.
Barrel: 6 inches.
Length: 10½ inches. **Weight:** 25 oz.
Stocks: Checkered walnut, Magna.
Sights: Front, ¹/₁₀" Patridge, micro click rear, adjustable for w. and e.
Price: Blued **$106.00**

SMITH & WESSON 22 CENTER FIRE MAGNUM M-53

Caliber: Rem. 22 Jet and 22 S, L, LR with inserts. 6 shot.
Barrel: 4", 6" or 8⅜".
Length: 11½" (6" bbl.). **Weight:** 40 oz.
Stocks: Checkered walnut, target.
Features: Grooved tangs and trigger, swing-out cylinder revolver.
Sights: ⅛" Baughman Quick Draw front, micro click rear, adjustable for w. and e.
Price: Blued **$144.50**
Price: Extra cylinder for 22 RF. (fitted) **$35.30**

SMITH & WESSON MASTERPIECE TARGET MODELS

Model: K-22 (M17).	K-22 (M48).
Caliber: 22 LR, 6 shot.	22 RF Magnum, 6 shot.
Barrel: 6", 8⅜".	4", 6" or 8⅜".
Length: 11⅛" (6" bbl.).	11⅛" (6" bbl.).
Weight: 38½ oz. (6" bbl.).	39 oz.(6" bbl.).
Model: K-32 (M16). (Illus.)	K-38 (M14).
Caliber: 32 S&W Long, 6 shot.	38 S&W Special, 6 shot.
Barrel: 6 inches.	6", 8⅜".
Length: 11⅛ inches.	11⅛ inches. (6" bbl.)
Weight: 38½ oz. (Loaded).	38½ oz. (6", loaded).

Features: All Masterpiece models have: checkered walnut, Magna stocks; grooved tang and trigger; ⅛" Patridge front sight, micro. adj. rear sights. Swing out cylinder revolver.
Price: Blued, all calibers **$107.50**

U.S. HANDGUNS—TARGET REVOLVERS

SMITH & WESSON K-38 MASTERPIECE Single Action

Same as the M14 K-38 Masterpiece except single action only, and is supplied with target type hammer and trigger.

Price: Blued **$119.50**

SMITH & WESSON COMBAT MASTERPIECE REVOLVER

Caliber: 38 Special (M15) or 22 LR (M18), 6 shot.
Barrel: 2″ (M15) 4″ (M18)
Length: 9⅛″ (4″ bbl.). **Weight:** Loaded, 22 36½ oz, 38 30oz.
Stocks: Checkered walnut, Magna. Grooved tangs and trigger.
Sights: Front, ⅛″ Baughman Quick Draw on ramp, micro click rear, adjustable for w. and e.

Price: Blued **$97.50**

SMITH & WESSON 1955 Model 25, 45 TARGET

Caliber: 45 ACP and 45 AR, 6 shot.
Barrel: 6½″ (heavy target type).
Length: 11⅞ inches. **Weight:** 45 oz.
Stocks: Checkered walnut target.
Features: Tangs and trigger grooved; target trigger and hammer standard, checkered target hammer. Swing-out cylinder revolver.
Sights: ⅛″ Patridge front, micro click rear, adjustable for w. and e.

Price: Blued **$138.50**

SMITH & WESSON ACCESSORIES

Target hammers with low, broad, deeply-checkered spur, and wide-swaged, grooved target trigger. For all frame sizes, $4.65 (target hammers not available for small frames). Target stocks: for large-frame guns, $9.95 to $11.45; for med.-frame guns, $7.85-$9.95; for small-frame guns, $6.60. These prices applicable only when specified on original order.
As separately-ordered parts: target hammers and triggers, $7.65; stocks, $8.85-$11.65.

U.S. HANDGUNS—SERVICE & SPORT

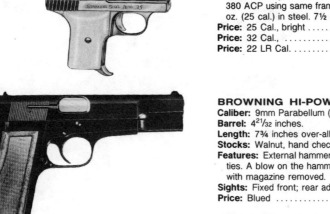

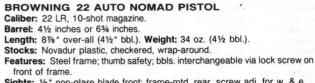

AMERICAN FIREARMS STAINLESS PISTOL

Made entirely of stainless steel, finished bright. Calibers 22 LR, 25, 32 and 380 ACP using same frame and slide. 4.4″ long, 3.52″ high, .90″ wide, 14 oz. (25 cal.) in steel. 7½ oz. with alloy frame. 7-shot magazine (25 cal.).

Price: 25 Cal., bright **$58.50**	Blued **$44.50**
Price: 32 Cal., ... **$67.50**	380 Cal. **$74.50**
Price: 22 LR Cal. **$69.95**	25 Cal. lightweight **$47.50**

BROWNING HI-POWER 9mm AUTOMATIC PISTOL

Caliber: 9mm Parabellum (Luger), 13-shot magazine.
Barrel: 4²¹⁄₃₂ inches.
Length: 7¾ inches over-all. **Weight:** 32 oz.
Stocks: Walnut, hand checkered.
Features: External hammer with half-cock safety, thumb and magazine safeties. A blow on the hammer cannot discharge a cartridge; cannot be fired with magazine removed.
Sights: Fixed front; rear adj. for w.

Price: Blued **$112.50**

BROWNING RENAISSANCE HI-POWER 9mm AUTO

Same as Browning Hi-Power 9mm Auto except: fully engraved, chrome plated, polyester pearl grips **$284.50**

BROWNING 22 AUTO NOMAD PISTOL

Caliber: 22 LR, 10-shot magazine.
Barrel: 4½ inches or 6¾ inches.
Length: 8⅞″ over-all (4½″ bbl.). **Weight:** 34 oz. (4½″ bbl.).
Stocks: Novadur plastic, checkered, wrap-around.
Features: Steel frame; thumb safety; bbls. interchangeable via lock screw on front of frame.
Sights: ⅛″ non-glare blade front; frame-mtd. rear, screw adj. for w. & e.

Price: Blued, either bbl. **$71.50**

COLT GOVT. SUPER 38 AUTO PISTOL
Caliber: 38 Super Auto, 9 shot.
Barrel: 5 inches.
Length: 8½ inches. **Weight:** 39 oz.
Stocks: Checkered Coltwood. Grooved trigger.
Features: Grip and thumb safeties; grooved trigger and hammer; arched mainspring housing.
Sights: Fixed, glare-proofed ramp front, square notch rear.
Price: Blued .... $125.00   Nickeled $143.75

COLT MK IV/SERIES 70 45 GOV'T MODEL AUTO PISTOL
Identical to 38 Super and previous 45 Government Model except for addition of a split-finger, collet-type barrel bushing and reverse-taper barrel to match for improved accuracy.
Price: Blued .... $125.00   Nickeled $143.75

COLT CONVERSION UNIT
Permits the 45 and 38 Super Automatic pistols to use the economical 22 LR cartridge. No tools needed. Adjustable rear sight; 10-shot magazine. Designed to give recoil effect of the larger calibers. Not adaptable to Commander models. Blue finish $70.00

COLT COMMANDER AUTO PISTOL
Caliber: 45 ACP, 7 shot; 38 Super Auto, 9 shot; 9mm Luger, 9 shot.
Barrel: 4¼ inches.
Length: 8 inches. **Weight:** 26½ oz.
Stocks: Checkered Coltwood.
Features: Grooved trigger and hammer spur; arched housing; grip and thumb safeties.
Sights: Fixed, glare-proofed ramp front, square notch rear.
Price: Blued $125.00

COLT HUNTSMAN AUTO PISTOL
Caliber: 22 LR, 10-shot magazine.
Barrel: 4½ inches, 6 inches.
Length: 9" (4½" bbl.). **Weight:** 30 oz. (4½" bbl.), 31½ oz. (6" bbl.).
Stocks: Checkered walnut. Wide trigger.
Sights: Fixed ramp front, square notch rear, non-adjustable.
Price: Colt Blue $71.50

COLT POCKET AUTOMATIC
Caliber: 25 ACP, 6-shot magazine.
Barrel: 2½ inch.
Length: 4⅜" over-all. **Weight:** 12 oz.
Stocks: Fully checkered walnut.
Sights: Fixed on full-length serrated rib.
Features: Thumb and magazine safeties; round-top grooved visible hammer
Price: Colt blue $62.00

COLT DERINGERS
Caliber: 22 Short, single-shot.
Barrel: 2½", side swing, blued.
Length: 4¹⁵/₁₆" overall. **Weight:** 7¾ oz.
Stocks: Brown plastic, smooth.
Features: Fixed open sights, stud trigger, auto. ejection, single action, presentation case.
Price: Gold frame (cased pair) $57.50
Price: 14K Gold frame, pearlite grips (cased pair) $63.00

F.I.E. E27 TITAN PISTOL
Caliber: 25, 6-shot magazine
Barrel: 2-1/2 inches.
Length: 4-3/4 inches over-all. **Weight:** 11-3/4 oz.
Stocks: Checkered plastic.
Features: Visible hammer; fast simple takedown.
Sights: Fixed.
Price: Blued .... $34.50   Chromed: $37.50

HI-STANDARD PLINKER AUTO PISTOL
Caliber: 22 LR, 10-shot magazine.
Barrel: 4½ or 6½ inches.
Length: 9 inches (4½" bbl.). **Weight:** 32 oz. (4½" bbl.).
Stocks: Checkered plastic grips. Grooved trigger.
Features: Non slip trigger, interchangeable bbls., moulded target grips.
Sights: Fixed, ramp front, square notch rear.
Price: Blued $59.95

HI-STANDARD MODEL D-100 and DM-101 DERRINGER
Caliber: 22 S, L or LR: 22 Rimfire Magnum. 2 shot.
Barrel: 3½", over and under, rifled.
Length: 5 inches. **Weight.** 11 oz.
Stocks: Smooth plastic.
Features: Hammerless, integral safety hammerblock, all steel unit is encased in a black, anodized alloy housing. Recessed chamber. Dual extraction. Top break, double action.
Sights: Fixed, open.
Price: Blued .... $44.95   Nickel $54.95
Price: 22 WMR, Blue ..... $46.95   Nickel $56.95

HI-STANDARD SHARPSHOOTER AUTO PISTOL
Caliber: 22 LR, 10-shot magazine.
Barrel: 5½ inches.
Length: 9" over-all. **Weight:** 42 oz.
Stocks: Checkered laminated plastic.
Features: Wide, scored trigger; new hammer-sear design; new "jam-free" ejection. Slide lock, push-button take down.
Sights: Fixed, ramp front, square notch rear adj. for w. & e.
Price: Blued $79.50

RUGER STANDARD MODEL AUTO PISTOL
Caliber: 22 LR, 9-shot magazine.
Barrel: 4¾ or 6 inches.
Length: 8¾" (4¾" bbl.). **Weight:** 36 oz. (4¾" bbl.).
Stocks: Checkered hard rubber.
Sights: Fixed, wide blade front, square notch rear.
Price: Blued $47.50
Price: With checkered walnut grips $53.50

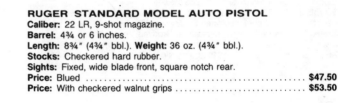

STERLING "TRAPPER" SERIES AUTO PISTOL
Caliber: 22 LR, 10-shot magazine.
Barrel: 4½" or 6".
Length: 9" (4½" bbl.). **Weight:** 36 oz. (4½" bbl.).
Stocks: Checkered plastic.
Sights: Fixed ramp (6" bbl.) or blade (4½" bbl.) front. Square notch rear.
Features: Interchangeable safety (4½" bbl.).
Price: Blued (M286) 4½" or 6" tapered $74.50
Price: Blued (M285) 4½" heavy bbl. $69.50

SMITH & WESSON 9mm MODEL 39 AUTO PISTOL
Caliber: 9mm Luger, 8-shot clip.
Barrel: 4 inches.
Length: 7⁷⁄₁₆". **Weight:** 26½ oz., without magazine.
Stocks: Checkered walnut.
Features: Magazine disconnector, positive firing pin lock and hammer-release safety; alloy frame with lanyard loop; locked-breech, short-recoil double action; slide locks open on last shot.
Sights: ⅛" serrated ramp front, adjustable rear.
Price: Blued .... $110.00   Nickeled $118.00

SMITH & WESSON M61 PISTOL
Caliber: 22 LR, 5-shot.
Barrel: 2⅛"
Length: 4¹³⁄₁₆". **Weight:** 14 oz.
Stocks: Checkered with cocking indicator pin protruding through left grip.
Features: Elementary blow-back pocket pistol with alloy frame.
Sights: Fixed square notch.
Price: Blued .... $46.50   Nickeled $55.50

U.S. HANDGUNS—SERVICE & SPORT

STOEGER LUGER 22 AUTO PISTOL
Caliber: 22 LR, 12-shot (11 in magazine, 1 in chamber).
Barrel: 4½" or 5½".
Weight: 30 oz.
Stocks: Smooth wood, identical to P-08.
Features: Action remains open after last shot and as magazine is removed. Grip and balance identical to P-08.
Price: 4½" Barrel $69.95
Price: 5½" Barrel $72.95

U.S. HANDGUNS—REVOLVERS OVER $90

COLT DETECTIVE SPECIAL
Caliber: 32 New Police or 38 Special, 6 shot.
Barrel: 2", 3" (32 NP available in 2" only).
Length: 6¾" (2" bbl.). **Weight:** 21 oz. (2" bbl.).
Stocks: Checkered walnut, round butt. Grooved trigger.
Sights: Fixed, glare-proofed ramp front, square notch rear.
Price: Blued .... **$96.50**   Nickeled **$111.00**
Price: Blued, 38 Spec., 2", with hammer shroud installed **$102.50**

COLT COBRA REVOLVER
Caliber: 32 New Police or 38 Special, 6 shot.
Barrel: 2", 3" (22 LR available in 3" only. 4" available in 38 Spec. only).
Length: 6¾" (2" bbl.). **Weight:** 15 oz. (2" bbl.), 17 oz. (4" bbl.).
Stocks: Checkered walnut, round butt. Grooved trigger.
Sights: Fixed, glare-proofed ramp front, square notch rear.
Price: Blued .... **$101.00**   Nickeled **$116.15**
Price: Blued, 38 Spec. With hammer shroud installed **$107.00**

COLT AGENT REVOLVER
Caliber: 38 Special, 6 shot.
Barrel: 2" (Twist, 1-16).
Length: 6¾". **Weight:** 14 oz.
Stocks: Checkered walnut, round butt. Grooved trigger.
Sights: Fixed, glare-proofed ramp front, square notch rear.
Price: Blued .... **$101.00**   With a hammer shroud installed   **$107.00**

COLT OFFICIAL POLICE Mk III REVOLVER
Caliber: 38 Special, 6 shot.
Barrel: 4", 5" and 6".
Length: 9¼" (4" bbl.).
Weight: 36 oz. (38 cal., 6" bbl.).
Stocks: Checkered walnut, square butt.
Sights: Fixed, glare-proofed ramp front, square notch rear.
Price: Blued **$115.00**

COLT HAMMER SHROUD
Facilitates quick draw from holster or pocket. Hammer spur projects just enough to allow for cocking for single action firing. Fits only Colt Detective Special, Cobra and Agent revolvers. Factory installed on new guns, **$5**, or as a kit for installation. Blued only **$6.00**
Factory installed on your gun (listed above). Blued only **$7.50**

COLT LAWMAN Mk III Revolver
Same as Official Police Mk III but with 4" heavy barrel. Weight 36 oz. 38 Special only. Also as Metropolitan Mk III in 357 Magnum caliber.
Price: **$115.00**

COLT POLICE POSITIVE REVOLVER
Caliber: 32 New Police or 38 Special, 6 shot.
Barrel: 4", 5". (32 NP available in 4" only).
Length: 8¾" (4" bbl.). **Weight:** 23 oz. (38 cal.).
Stocks: Checkered walnut, round butt. Grooved trigger.
Sights: Fixed, glare-proofed ramp front, square notch rear.
Price: Blued .... **$96.50**   Nickeled, 4" bbl. only **$107.50**

COLT TROOPER MK III REVOLVER
Caliber: 38 Special or 357 Magnum, 6-shot.
Barrel: 4″ 6″ (357 only).
Length: 9¼″ (4″ bbl.). **Weight:** 40 oz. (4″ bbl.), 39 oz. (6″ bbl.).
Stock: Checkered walnut, square butt. Grooved trigger.
Sights: Fixed ramp front with ⅛″ blade, adj. notch rear.
Price: Blued **$135.00**. With wide spur hammer and target stocks   **$142.00**

RUGER SECURITY SIX REVOLVER
Caliber: 357 Magnum and 38 Special, 6 shot.
Barrel: 2¾″, 4″ or 6″.
Length: 9¼″ (4″ bbl.). **Weight:** 33½ oz. (4″ bbl.).
Stocks: Checkered walnut, semi-target style.
Features: Solid frame with barrel, sighting rib and ejector rod housing combined in one integral unit. Can be "taken-down" using only a coin.
Sights: Fixed, or w. and e. adjustable rear.
Price: With fixed sights **$89.00**
Price: With adjustable rear sight **$97.50**

SMITH & WESSON M&P Model 10 REVOLVER
Caliber: 38 Special, 6 shot.
Barrel: 2″, 4″, 5″ or 6″
Length: 9″ (4″ bbl.). **Weigth:** 30½ oz. (4″ bbl.).
Stocks: Checkered walnut, Magna. Round or square butt.
Sights: Fixed, ⅛″ ramp front, square notch rear.
Price: Blued .... **$84.00**   Nickeled **$92.00**

SMITH & WESSON 38 M&P Heavy Barrel Model 10
Same as regular M&P except: 4″ ribbed bbl. with ⅛″ ramp front sight, square rear, square butt, wgt. 34 oz.
Price: Blued .... **$84.00**   Nickeled **$92.00**

SMITH & WESSON 38 M&P AIRWEIGHT Model 12
Caliber: 38 Special, 6 shot.
Barrel: 2 or 4 inches.
Length: 6⅞″. **Weight:** 18 oz. (2″ bbl.)
Stocks: Checkered walnut, Magna. Round or square butt.
Sights: Fixed, ⅛″ serrated ramp front, square notch rear.
Price: Blued .... **$86.50**   Nickeled **$94.50**

SMITH & WESSON 1953 Model 34, 22/32 KIT GUN
Caliber: 22 LR, 6 shot.
Barrel: 2 inches, 4 inches.
Length: 8 inches (4″ bbl. and round butt). **Weight:** 22½ oz. (4″ bbl.).
Stocks: Checkered walnut, round or square butt.
Sights: Front, ¹/₁₀″ serrated ramp, micro. click rear, adjustable for w. & e.
Price: Blued .... **$98.50**   Nickeled **$106.50**

SMITH & WESSON Model 51 22/32 KIT GUN
Same as Model 34 except chambered for 22 WRF Magnum; 3½″ barrel; weight, 24 oz. Choice of round or square butt.
Price: Blued .... **$105.50**   Nickeled **$113.50**

SMITH & WESSON KIT GUN AIRWEIGHT (Model 43, not illus.)
Same as M34 except 3½″ barrel, square butt; weight 14¼ oz. 22LR.
Price: Blued .... **$105.50**   Nickeled **$113.50**

SMITH & WESSON 32 HAND EJECTOR Model 30
Caliber: 32 S&W Long, 6 shot.
Barrel: 2″, 3″, 4″.
Length: 8 inches (4″ bbl.). **Weight:** 18 oz. (4″ bbl.).
Stocks: Checkered walnut, Magna.
Sights: Fixed, 1/10″ serrated ramp front, square notch rear.
Price: Blued .... **$84.00**　　Nickeled **$92.00**

SMITH & WESSON TERRIER Model 32 REVOLVER
Same as 32 Hand Ejector except: 38 S&W cal.; 2″ bbl. only; 5 shots.
6¼ inches over-all.
Price: Blued .... **$84.00**　　Nickeled **$92.00**

SMITH & WESSON 41 M&P Model 58 REVOLVER
Caliber: 41 Magnum, 6 shot.
Barrel: 4 inches.
Length: 9¼ inches. **Weight:** 41 oz.
Stocks: Checkered walnut, Magna.
Sights: Fixed, 1/8″ serrated ramp front, square notch rear.
Price: Blued .... **$105.50**　　Nickeled **$113.50**

SMITH & WESSON 41 MAGNUM Model 57 REVOLVER
Caliber: 41 Magnum, 6 shot.
Barrel: 4″, 6″ or 8⅜″.
Length: 11⅜ inches (6″ bbl.). **Weight:** 48 oz. (6″ bbl.).
Stocks: Oversize target type checkered Goncala Alves wood and target
　hammer. Tang and target trigger grooved.
Sights: 1/8″ red ramp front, micro. click rear, adj. for w. and e.
Price S&W Bright Blue or Nickel **$181.00**

SMITH & WESSON 44 MAGNUM Model 29 REVOLVER
Caliber: 44 Magnum, 44 Special or 44 Russian, 6 shot.
Barrel: 4″, 6½″, 8⅜″.
Length: 11⅞″ (6½″ bbl.). **Weight:** 47 oz. (6½i bbl.), 43 oz. (4″ bbl.).
Stocks: Oversize target type, checkered Goncala Alves. Tangs and target
　trigger grooved, checkered target hammer.
Sights: 1/8″ red ramp-front, micro. click rear, adjustable for w. and e.
Price: S&W Bright Blue or Nickel **$181.00**

SMITH & WESSON HIGHWAY PATROLMAN Model 28
Caliber: 357 Magnum and 38 Special, 6 shot.
Barrel: 4 inches, 6 inches.
Length: 11¼ inches (6″ bbl.). **Weight:** 44 oz. (6″ bbl.).
Stocks: Checkered walnut, Magna. Grooved tangs and trigger.
Sights: Front, 1/8″ Baughman Quick Draw, on plain ramp. micro click rear,
　adjustable for w. and e.
Price: S&W Satin Blue, sandblasted frame edging and barrel top . **$107.50**
Price: With target stocks **$115.00**

SMITH & WESSON 38 CHIEFS SPECIAL & AIRWEIGHT
Caliber: 38 Special, 5 shot.
Barrel: 2 inches, 3 inches.
Length: 6½ inches. (2″ bbl. and round butt). **Weight:** 19 oz. (2″ bbl.; 14 oz.
　AIRWEIGHT).
Stocks: Checkered walnut, Magna. Round or square butt.
Sights: Fixed, 1/10″ serrated ramp front, square notch rear.
Price: Blued std. M-36 .... **$84.00**　　Standard weight **$92.00**
Price: Blued AIR'W M-37 .. **$86.50**　　AIRWEIGHT **$94.50**

SMITH & WESSON CHIEFS SPECIAL STAINLESS
Model 60
Same as Model 36 except: 2″ bbl. and round butt only.
Price: Stainless steel **$110.00**

SMITH & WESSON BODYGUARD Model 38 REVOLVER
Caliber: 38 Special; 5 shot, double action revolver.
Barrel: 2 inches.
Length: 6⅜ inches. **Weight:** 14½ oz.
Features: Alloy frame; integral hammer shroud.
Stocks: Checkered walnut, Magna.
Sights: Fixed ¹/₁₀″ serrated ramp front, square notch rear.
Price: Blued .... **$86.50**   Nickeled **$94.50**

SMITH & WESSON BODYGUARD Model 49 REVOLVER
Same as Model 38 except steel construction. Weight 20½ oz.
Price: Blued .... **$86.00**   Nickeled **$94.00**

SMITH & WESSON CENTENNIAL Model 40
& AIRWEIGHT Model 42 REVOLVERS
Caliber: 38 Special, 5 shot.
Barrel: 2 inches.
Length: 6½″. **Weight:** 19 oz. (Standard weight), 13 oz. (AIRWEIGHT).
Stocks: Smooth walnut, Magna.
Sights: Fixed ¹/₁₀″ serrated ramp front, square notch rear.
Price: Blued, standard wgt. **$90.50**   Nickeled, standard wgt. ... **$98.50**
Price: Blued AIRWEIGHT .. **$96.50**   Nickeled, AIRWEIGHT **$104.50**

SMITH & WESSON 32 & 38 REGULATION POLICE
Caliber: 32 S&W Long (M31), 6 shot. 38 S&W (M33) (Illus.), 5 shot.
Barrel: 2″, 3″, 4″. (4″ only in 38 S&W).
Length: 8½ inches (4″ bbl.).
Weight: 18¾ oz. (4″ bbl., in 32 cal.), 18 oz. (38 cal.).
Stocks: Checkered walnut, Magna.
Sights: Fixed, ¹/₁₀″ serrated ramp front, square notch rear.
Price: Blued .... **$84.00**   Nickeled **$92.00**

SMITH & WESSON 357 COMBAT MAGNUM Model 19
Caliber: 357 Magnum and 38 Special, 6 shot.
Barrel: 2½″, 4″, 6″.
Length: 9½ inches (4″ bbl.). **Weight:** 35 oz.
Stocks: Checkered Goncala Alves, target. Grooved tangs and trigger.
Sights: Front, ⅛″ Baughman Quick Draw on 2½″ or 4″ bbl., Patridge on 6
  bbl., micro click rear adjustable for w. and e.
Price: S&W Bright Blue or Nickel **$135.00**

SMITH & WESSON 357 MAGNUM M-27 REVOLVER
Caliber: 357 Magnum and 38 Special, 6 shot.
Barrel: 3½″, 5″, 6″, 8⅜″.
Length: 11¼″ (6″ bbl.). **Weight:** 44 oz. (6″ bbl.).
Stocks: Checkered walnut, Magna. Grooved tangs and trigger.
Sights: Any S&W target front, micro click rear, adjustable for w. and e.
Price: S&W Bright Blue or Nickel **$156.50**

DAN WESSON MODEL 12 REVOLVER
Caliber: 357 Magnum, 6-shot.
Barrel: 2½″, 4″ or 6″ interchangeable.
Length: 9″ (4″ bbl.). **Weight:** 38 oz. (4″ bbl.).
Stock: Three sets of stocks supplied in varying size, angle and style.
Sights: Two adj. rear sights (target or combat) supplied. ⅛″ front sight adj.
  for E.
Features: Wide spur (⅜″) hammer; barrel shroud offered in aluminum or
  steel for weight and balance preference. Tools supplied for barrel and grip
  changing.
Price: Blue (approx.) **$110.00**
Price: With fixed sights **$95.00**

CHARTER ARMS "UNDERCOVER 2" REVOLVER
Caliber: 38 Special, 5 shot.
Barrel: 2″ or 3.
Length: 6¼″ (round butt). **Weight:** 16 oz.
Features: Wide trigger and hammer spur
Stocks: Smooth walnut, round or square butt available.
Sights: Fixed; matted ramp front, ⅛″ wide blade.
Price: Polished Blue ...... **$80.00**   Nickel.................... **$85.23**
Price: With checkered, finger-rest bulldog grips (blue) 86.50

CHARTER ARMS UNDERCOVERETTE
Like the Undercover, but a 6-shot 32 S&W Long revolver available with 2″ barrel only, and weighing 16½ oz.
Price: Polished blue **$80.00**

CHARTER ARMS PATHFINDER
Same as Undercover but in 22 LR caliber, and has 3″ bbl. Fitted with adjustable rear sight, ramp front. Weight 18½ oz.
Price: Blued **$87.50**
Price: With checkered, finger-rest bulldog grips 94.00

CHARTER ARMS DUAL PATHFINDER
Like the Pathfinder but with an extra cylinder chambering 22 WRM cartridges. Hand checkered walnut grips are standard on this model.
Price: Blued **$110.00**

F.I.E. G32 GUARDIAN REVOLVER
Caliber: 32 S&W Long, 7-shot.
Barrel: 2-¼ inches.
Length: 6-¾ inches over-all. **Weight:** 24 oz.
Features: Swing-out cylinder.
Stocks: Plastic.
Sights: Fixed.
Price: Blued .... **$44.95**   Chromed **$49.50**

F.I.E. "38" Model F38 REVOLVER
Caliber: 38 Special.
Barrel: 2 inches.
Length: 6-¼ inches over-all. **Weight:** 27 oz.
Features: Swing-out cylinder.
Stocks: Plastic Bulldog.
Sights: Fixed.
Price: Blued .... **$49.95**   Chromed **$55.95**

F.I.E. T18 TITAN REVOLVER
Caliber: 22 LR, 6-shot.
Barrel: 1-¾ inches.
Length: 5-¾ inches over-all. **Weight:** 16 oz.
Features: Swing-out cylinder with quick release.
Stocks: Checkered plastic.
Sights: Fixed.
Price: Blued .... **$20.25**   Chromed **$21.80**

F.I.E. E14 TITANIC REVOLVER
Caliber: 32 S&W Long, 5-shot.
Barrel: 1-¾ inches.
Length: 6 inches over-all. **Weight:** 18 oz.
Features: Solid frame, easily removable cylinder.
Stocks: Black plastic.
Sights: Fixed.
Price: Blued **$34.50**

FIREARMS INTERNATIONAL REGENT
Caliber: 22 LR, 8-shot or 32 S&W Long, 6-shot.
Barrel: 37″, 4″ or 6″ round (2½″ or 4″ in 32 S&W Long).
Weight: 28 oz. (4″ bbl.).
Features: Swing-out cylinder, recessed for cartridge rims.
Stocks: Checkered composition.
Sights: Fixed; ramp front.
Price: Blued, 22 LR **$34.95**
Price: Blued, 32 S&W Long 39.95

H&R Model 940 Ultra "Side-Kick" REVOLVER
Caliber: 22 S, L or LR, 9 shot.
Barrel: 6″ target weight with ventilated rib.
Weight: 33 oz.
Features: Swing-out, safety rim cylinder; safety lock and key.
Stocks: Checkered walnut with thumbrest.
Sights: Ramp front; rear adjustable for w. and e.
Price: H&R Crown-Luster Blue **$62.95**

H&R Model 939 Ultra "Side-Kick" REVOLVER
Like the Model 940 but with a flat-sided barrel.
Price: H&R Crown-Luster Blue **$64.95**

HARRINGTON & RICHARDSON Model 732 Guardsman
Caliber: 32 S&W or 32 S&W Long, 6 shot.
Barrel: 2½″ or 4″ round barrel.
Weight: 23½ oz. (2½″ bbl.), 26 oz. (4″ bbl.).
Features: Swing-out cylinder with auto. extractor return. Pat. safety rim cylin-
der. Grooved trigger.
Stocks: Checkered, black Cycolac.
Sights: Blade front; adjustable rear on 4″ model.
Price: Blued **$49.95**
Chromed (Model 733) 2½″ bbl. only **$54.95**

HARRINGTON & RICHARDSON Model 900 REVOLVER
Caliber: 22 S, L or LR, 9 shot.
Barrel: 2½″, 4″, or 6″ round bbl.
Weight: 20 oz. (2½″ bbl.), 26 oz. (6″ bbl.).
Features: Snap-out cylinder; simultaneous push-pin extraction; coil springs;
safety rim cylinder; Round-grip frame with 2½″ bbl.
Stocks: Checkered, black Cycolac.
Sights: Fixed, blade front, square notch rear.
Price: Blued **$43.95**

HARRINGTON & RICHARDSON Model 622 REVOLVER
Caliber: 22 S, L or LR, 6 shot.
Barrel: 2½″, 4″, or 6″ round bbl.
Weight: 22 oz. (2½″ bbl.).
Features: Solid steel, square-built frame; snap-out safety rim cylinder; non-
glare finish on frame; coil springs.
Stocks: Checkered black Cycolac.
Sights: Fixed, blade front, square notch rear.
Price: Blued, 2½″, 4″, or 6″ bbl. **$37.95**

HARRINGTON & RICHARDSON Model 926 REVOLVER
Caliber: 22 S, L, or LR, 9-shot, 38 S&W 5-shot.
Barrel: 4″. **Weight:** 31 oz.
Features: Top-break, double or single action
Stocks: Checkered walnut.
Sights: Fixed front, read adj. for w.
Price: Blued **$64.95**

HARRINGTON & RICHARDSON SPORTSMAN Model 999 REVOLVER
Caliber: 22 S, L or LR, 9 shot.
Barrel: 6″ top-break (16″ twist), integral vent,-rib.
Length: 10½″. **Weight:** 30 oz.
Features: Wide hammer spur; rest for second finger.
Stocks: Checkered walnut, semi-thumbrest.
Sights: Front adjustable for elevation, rear for windage.
Price: Blued **$69.95**

HARRINGTON & RICHARDSON Model 925 "Defender"
Caliber: 38 S&W 5 shot.
Barrel: 2½".
Weight: 22 oz. **Length:** 7½" over-all.
Features: Top-break double action, push pin extractor.
Stocks: Smooth walnut, birshead style.
Sights: Rear with windage adj.
Price: H&R Crown Luster Blue $59.95

HARRINGTON & RICHARDSON Model 929 "Side-Kick"
Caliber: 22 S, L or LR, 9 shot.
Barrel: 2½", 4" or 6".
Weight: 26 oz. (4" bbl.).
Features: Swing-out cylinder with auto. extractor return. Pat. safety rim cylinder. Grooved trigger. Round-grip frame.
Stocks: Checkered, black Cycolac.
Sights: Blade front; adjustable rear on 4" and 6" models.
Price: Blued, 2½", 4" or 6" bbl. $49.95
Price: Nickel (Model 930), 4" bbl. 54.95

HARRINGTON & RICHARDSON M-949 FORTY-NINER
Caliber: 22 S, L or LR, 9 shot.
Barrel: 5½" round with ejector rod.
Weight: 31 oz.
Features: Contoured loading gate; wide hammer spur; single and double action. Western type ejector-housing.
Stocks: One-piece smooth walnut frontier style.
Sights: Round blade front, adj. rear.
Price: H&R Crown-Luster Blue $44.95

STANDARD DOUBLE-NINE CONVERTIBLE REVOLVER
Caliber: 22 S, L or LR, 9-shot (22 WRM with extra cylinder).
Barrel: 5½", dummy ejector rod fitted.
Length: 11 inches. **Weight:** 32 oz.
Stocks: Smooth walnut, frontier style with medallion
Features: Western styling; rebounding hammer with auto safety block; spring-loaded ejection.
Sights: Fixed blade front, notched rear.
Price: Blued . . . . $77.50   Nickeled 85.50
  As above but in 22 WRM only (no extra cylinder for other rimfire cartridges)
Price: Blue . . . . $72.50 Nickeled $79.50
  Deluxe Double-Nine with adjustable Patridge type sights available in blue only.
Price: Convertible . . . . $87.50   Magnum only $82.50

HIGH STANDARD LONG HORN CONVERTIBLE REVOLVER
Same as the Double-Nine convertible but with a 9½" bbl., fixed sights, blued only, **Weight:** 40 oz.
Price: . . . . $87.50   Magnum only $82.50

HIGH STANDARD DURANGO REVOLVER
A variation of the High Standard Double-Nine with a brass finished trigger guard and backstrap. 4½" bbl., 10" over-all, weight 26¼ oz. 22 S, L or LR only. Walnut grips.
Price: Blued $59.95
  As above but with 5½" bbl., weight 27 oz.
Price: Blued . . . . $59.95   Nickeled $64.95

HIGH STANDARD HOMBRE REVOLVER
Same as the Durango except 4½" bbl. only, no ejector rod housing or brass finish. Weight 25¼ oz.
Price: Blued . . . . $49.95   Nickeled $54.95

U.S. HANDGUNS—REVOLVERS UNDER $90

IVER JOHNSON MODEL 50A SIDEWINDER REVOLVER
Caliber: 22 S, L, LR, 8 shot.
Barrel: 6 inches.
Length: 11¼". **Weight:** 31 oz.
Features: Wide spur hammer, half-cock safety, scored trigger, Flash Control cylinder, recessed shell head, push rod ejector.
Stocks: Plastic Stag Horn.
Sights: Fixed, blade front.
Price: Blued **$44.75**

IVER JOHNSON TARGET MODEL 57A REVOLVER
Caliber: 22 S or LR, 8 shot, double action.
Barrel: 4½", 6".
Length: 10¾" (6" bbl.). **Weight:** 30½ oz. (6" bbl.).
Features: Flash Control cylinder, adj. mainspring.
Stocks: Checkered thumbrest, Tenite: (walnut, **$5.80**, checkered walnut, **$9.20** extra).
Sights: Adjustable Patridge type.
Price: Blued, in flocked case **$44.75**

IVER JOHNSON TARGET MODEL 55A REVOLVER
Same as Model 57A except without adjustable sights. Price, blued, in flocked case. **$41.50**

IVER JOHNSON CADET Model 55SA
Same as Model 55 except with 2½" barrel only, rounded tenite grips; weight 24 oz. Price, blued, in flocked case **$41.50**
Also available in 32 or 38 S&W caliber, 5 shot **41.50**

IVER JOHNSON MODEL 67 VIKING REVOLVER
Caliber: 22 S or LR, 8 shot.
Barrel: 4½" or 6" chrome-lined heavy.
Length: 9½" (4½" bbl.). **Weight:** 34 oz. (6" bbl.).
Features: Cyl. front recessed for Flash Control, chambers also recessed for cartridge rims. Matted top, wide trigger. "Hammer-the-Hammer" action.
Stocks: Checkered, thumbrest plastic.
Sights: Adjustable Patridge type.
Price: Blued **$57.50**

IVER JOHNSON VIKING 67S SNUB REVOLVER
Same as M67 Viking except has 2¾" barrel, smooth rounded stocks, 7" over all, weighs 25 oz. (target stocks available) **$57.50**
Also available in 32 and 38 S&W calibers or Colt N.P., 5 shot **57.50**

IVER JOHNSON TRAILSMAN 66 REVOLVER
Same as M67 Viking but with rebounding hammer. 6" bbl. only.
Price: **$53.75**

U.S. HANDGUNS—SINGLE ACTION REVOLVERS

COLT SINGLE ACTION ARMY REVOLVER
Caliber: 357 Magnum or 45 Colt, 6 shot.
Barrel: 4¾", 5½" or 7½".
Length: 11½" (5½" bbl.). **Weight:** 37 oz. (5½" bbl.).
Stocks: Checkered hard rubber. (Walnut stocks **$5.00** extra).
Sights: Fixed. Grooved top strap, blade front.
Price: Blued and case hardened in color **$190.00**
Price: Nickel with walnut stocks **225.00**
Price: Buntline Spec., cal. 45 only. 12 bbl., st'd. stocks **215.00**

COLT SINGLE ACTION ARMY—NEW FRONTIER
Same specifications as standard Single Action Army except: flat-top frame; high polished finish, blue and case colored; ramp front sight and target rear adj. for windage and elevation; smooth walnut stocks with silver medallion.
Price: **$225.00**

COLT SINGLE ACTION FRONTIER SCOUT REVOLVER
Caliber: 22 S, L, LR, 6 shot.
Barrel: 4¾" or 9½" (Buntline), steel.
Length: 9⁵⁄₁₆" (4¾" bbl.); 14¾" (9½" bbl.).
Weight: 24 oz. (4¾" bbl.); 34 oz. (9½" bbl.).
Stocks: Black checkered composition, Staglite on Buntline.
Sights: Blade front, fixed notch rear.
Features: Alloy frame; blued finish. Walnut stocks **$5.00** extra.
Price: 4¾" bbl. .... **$71.50**   Blued, 9½" Buntline **$82.50**

U.S. HANDGUNS—SINGLE ACTION REVOLVERS

COLT FRONTIER SCOUT '62 REVOLVER
Same as "K" Scout except "Midnight Blue" only, "Staglite" stocks, wgt. 30 oz., Price, 4¾" bbl. .... **$82.50**   9½" Buntline **$93.50**

COLT FRONTIER SCOUT NICKEL REVOLVER
Same as Standard Frontier Scout except: heavier frame, walnut stocks.
Weight: 30 oz.
Price: 4¾" bbl. **$93.50**
Price: 9½" Buntline **$105.50**

COLT FRONTIER SCOUTS with Dual Cylinders
Same as regular Frontier Scouts except: furnished with two interchangeable cylinders; one chambered for 22 LR; the other for 22 RF Magnum.
Frontier Scout **$83.50** Nickel Scout **$105.50** "62" Scout **$94.50**
Frontier Buntline **94.50** Nickel Buntline **116.50** "62" Buntline **105.50**

F.I.E. E15 BUFFALO SCOUT REVOLVER
Caliber: 22 LR, 6-shot.
Barrel: 4¾".
Length: 10" over-all. **Weight:** 30 oz.
Stocks: Black plastic.
Features: Slide spring ejector.
Sights: Fixed.
Price: Blued **$28.50**
Price: Model E15M with extra interchangeable 22 WMR Mag. cylinder, blued **$34.50**

RUGER BEARCAT REVOLVER
Caliber: 22 S, L, or LR, 6 shot.
Barrel: 4" round, with ejector rod.
Length: 8⅞ inches. **Weight:** 17 oz.
Stocks: Genuine walnut with medallion.
Sights: Fixed; Patridge front, square notch rear.
Features: Alloy solid frame, patented Ruger coil-spring action; non-fluted, engraved cylinder.
Price: Blued **$44.00**

RUGER SINGLE SIX REVOLVER
Caliber: 22 S, L or LR; 6 shots.
Barrel: 5½" (6 groove, 14" twist).
Length: 11⅞". **Weight:** 36 oz.
Stocks: Smooth walnut.
Sights: Fixed; blade front, square notch rear.
Features: Independent firing pin in frame; coil springs throughout; recessed chambers.
Price: Blued **$64.25**

RUGER SINGLE SIX CONVERTIBLE REVOLVER
Same as regular Single Six except furnished with two interchangeable cylinders: one-chambered for 22 S, L or LR; the other for 22 RF Magnum. Choice of 5½", 6½" or 9½" barrel.
Price: with 5½" or 6½" barrel **$69.50**
9½" barrel **$78.00**

RUGER SUPER SINGLE SIX CONVERTIBLE REVOLVER
Same as the Single Six except: frame with intergral ribs, which protect the adj. rear sight, similar to the Blackhawk; blade front sight on ramp base. 5½" or 6½" bbl.
With extra 22 Magnum cylinder in cloth pouch **$78.00**

RUGER 357 or 41 MAGNUM BLACKHAWK REVOLVER
Caliber: 41 or 357 Magnum, 6 shot.
Barrel: 4⅝" or 6½" (6-groove, 20", 41; 8-groove, 16" twist 357 twist).
Length: 12⅛" (6½" bbl.). **Weight:** 40 oz. (6½" bbl.).
Stocks: Smooth genuine walnut.
Sights: Ramp front ⅛", micro click rear adj. for w. and e.
Features: Coil springs throughout, flat-top frame, long sight radius, floating alloy firing pin in frame. Solid frame.
Price: Blued **$98.50**

RUGER 357 MAGNUM—9MM CONVERTIBLE BLACKHAWK
Same as the 357 Magnum except furnished with interchangeable cylinders for 9mm Parabellum and 357 Magnum cartridges **110.00**
9mm cylinder, fitted to your 357 Blackhawk **16.00**

U.S. HANDGUNS—SINGLE ACTION REVOLVERS

RUGER SUPER BLACKHAWK 44 MAGNUM REVOLVER
Caliber: 44 Magnum, 6 shot. Also fires 44 Spec.
Barrel: 7½" inches (6-groove 20" twist).
Length: 13⅜ inches. **Weight:** 48 oz.
Stocks: Smooth genuine walnut.
Features: Large grip solid frame of steel; square-back guard; flat top-strap; non-fluted cylinder; wide, serrated trigger; wide-spur hammer.
Price: **$125.00**

RUGER 30 CARBINE BLACKHAWK REVOLVER
Same as the 44 Magnum except fluted cylinder, round back trigger guard, weight 44 oz., 13⅛" over-all. Blued only **$98.50**

U.S. HANDGUNS—MISCELLANEOUS

CHALLANGER HOPKINS & ALLEN M-L BOOT PISTOL
Caliber: 36 or 45, single shot percussion.
Barrel: 6 inch octagonal, regular or gain twist.
Length: 13 inches. **Weight:** 34 oz.
Stocks: Smooth walnut, birdshead style.
Features: Underhammer lockwork, match trigger.
Sights: Fixed blade front, adj. rear.
Price: **$39.95**

MERRILL SPORTSMAN'S SINGLE SHOT
Caliber: 22 S, L, LR, 22WMR, 22WRF, 22 Rem. Jet, 22 Hornet, 117 K-Hornet, 357, 38 Spl., 256 Win. Mag., 45 Colt/410 (3").
Barrel: 9" hinged type break-open. Semi-octagon.
Length: 10½". **Weight:** 54 oz.
Stocks: Smooth walnut with thumb & heel rest.
Sights: Front 125" blade, square notch rear adj. for w. & e.
Features: .355" rib on top, grooved for scope mounts, auto. safety, cocking indicator, hammerless.
Price: **$129.50**
Price: Extra bbls. . . . . **$35.00**   Wrist rest attachment **7.95**

REMINGTON MODEL XP-100 Bolt Action Pistol
Caliber: 221 Fireball, single shot.
Barrel: 10½ inches, ventilated rib.
Length: 16¾ inches. **Weight:** 60 oz.
Stocks: Brown nylon one-piece, checkered grip with white spacers.
Features: Fits left or right hand, is shaped to fit fingers and heel of hand. Grooved trigger. Rotating thumb safety, cavity in fore-end permits insertion of up to five 38 cal., 130-gr. metal jacketed bullets to adjust weight and balance. Included is a black vinyl, zippered case.
Sights: Fixed front, rear adj. for w. and e. Tapped for scope mount.
Price: Including case **$109.95**

THOMPSON-CENTER ARMS CONTENDER
Caliber: 22 S, L, LR, 22 WMR, 22 Rem. Jet, 22 Hornet, 22 K Hornet, 256 Win., 9mm Parabellum, 38 Super, 357/44 B & D, 38 Spl., 357 Mag., also 222 Rem. 30 M1, 45 ACP, 44 Mag. 5mm Rem., 45 Long Colt.
Barrel: 8¾", 10", tapered octagon. Single shot.
Length: 13¼" (10" bbl.). **Weight:** 43 oz. (10" bbl.).
Stocks: Select checkered walnut grip and fore-end, with thumb rest. Right or left hand.
Sights: Under cut blade ramp front, rear adj. for w. & e.
Features: Break open action with auto-safety. Single action only. Interchangeable bbls., both caliber (rim & center fire), and length. Grooved for scope. Engraved frame.
Price: Blued (rimfire Cals.) **$135.00**
Price: Blued (centerfire Cals.) **$144.00**
Price: Extra bbls. (Rimfire) **$36.00**   Extra bbls. (centerfire) **$45.00**
Price: Bushnell Phantom scope base **$5.00**
Fitted walnut case **29.50**

TINGLE BLACK POWDER M1960 PISTOL
Caliber: 40, single shot, percussion.
Barrel: 8", 9", 10", or 12" octagon.
Length: 11¾ inches. **Weight:** 33 oz. (8" bbl.).
Stocks: Walnut, one piece.
Features: 6-groove bbl., easily removable for cleaning; 1-in-30 twist.
Sights: Fixed blade front, w. adj. rear.
Price: **$64.95**
Price: With detachable shoulder stock, **$19.50** extra.

UNIVERSAL ENFORCER AUTO CARBINE
Caliber: 30 M1 Carbine, 30-shot magazine.
Barrel: 10¼" with 12-groove rifling.
Length: 17¾". **Weight:** 4½ lbs.
Stocks: American walnut with handguard.
Features: Uses surplus 5- or 15-shot magazine. 4½-6 lb. trigger pull.
Sights: Gold bead ramp front. Peep rear adj. for w. and e. 14" sight radius.
Price: Blue finish **$129.95**
Price: Nickel plated finish **$149.95**
Price: Gold plated finish **$175.00**

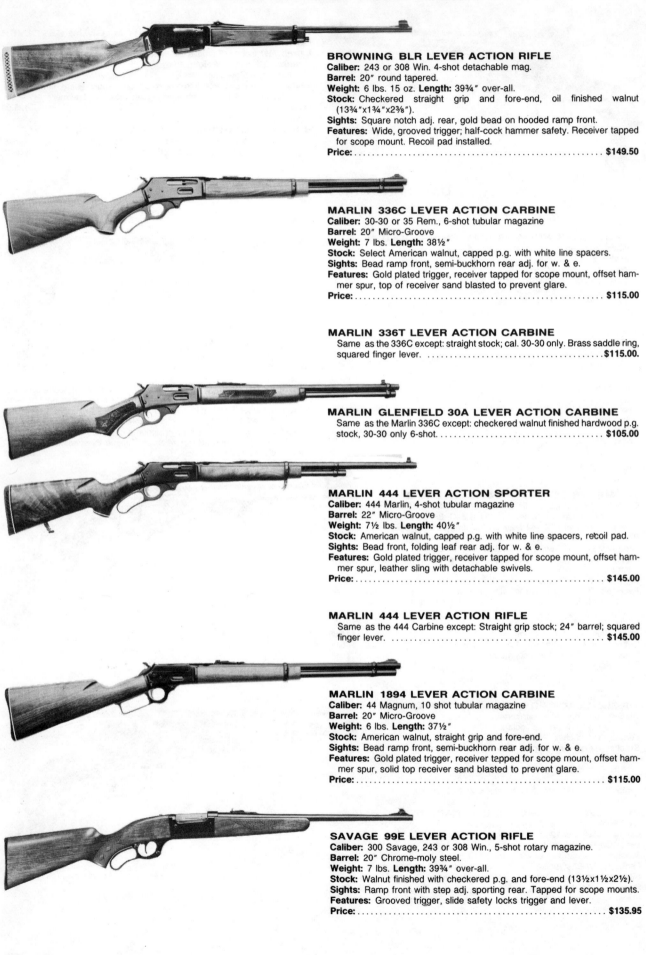

BROWNING BLR LEVER ACTION RIFLE
Caliber: 243 or 308 Win. 4-shot detachable mag.
Barrel: 20″ round tapered.
Weight: 6 lbs. 15 oz. **Length:** 39¾″ over-all.
Stock: Checkered straight grip and fore-end, oil finished walnut (13¾″x1¾″x2⅜″).
Sights: Square notch adj. rear, gold bead on hooded ramp front.
Features: Wide, grooved trigger; half-cock hammer safety. Receiver tapped for scope mount. Recoil pad installed.
Price: $149.50

MARLIN 336C LEVER ACTION CARBINE
Caliber: 30-30 or 35 Rem., 6-shot tubular magazine
Barrel: 20″ Micro-Groove
Weight: 7 lbs. **Length:** 38½″
Stock: Select American walnut, capped p.g. with white line spacers.
Sights: Bead ramp front, semi-buckhorn rear adj. for w. & e.
Features: Gold plated trigger, receiver tapped for scope mount, offset hammer spur, top of receiver sand blasted to prevent glare.
Price: $115.00

MARLIN 336T LEVER ACTION CARBINE
Same as the 336C except: straight stock; cal. 30-30 only. Brass saddle ring, squared finger lever. .... $115.00.

MARLIN GLENFIELD 30A LEVER ACTION CARBINE
Same as the Marlin 336C except: checkered walnut finished hardwood p.g. stock, 30-30 only 6-shot. $105.00

MARLIN 444 LEVER ACTION SPORTER
Caliber: 444 Marlin, 4-shot tubular magazine
Barrel: 22″ Micro-Groove
Weight: 7½ lbs. **Length:** 40½″
Stock: American walnut, capped p.g. with white line spacers, recoil pad.
Sights: Bead front, folding leaf rear adj. for w. & e.
Features: Gold plated trigger, receiver tapped for scope mount, offset hammer spur, leather sling with detachable swivels.
Price: $145.00

MARLIN 444 LEVER ACTION RIFLE
Same as the 444 Carbine except: Straight grip stock; 24″ barrel; squared finger lever. $145.00

MARLIN 1894 LEVER ACTION CARBINE
Caliber: 44 Magnum, 10 shot tubular magazine
Barrel: 20″ Micro-Groove
Weight: 6 lbs. **Length:** 37½″
Stock: American walnut, straight grip and fore-end.
Sights: Bead ramp front, semi-buckhorn rear adj. for w. & e.
Features: Gold plated trigger, receiver tapped for scope mount, offset hammer spur, solid top receiver sand blasted to prevent glare.
Price: $115.00

SAVAGE 99E LEVER ACTION RIFLE
Caliber: 300 Savage, 243 or 308 Win., 5-shot rotary magazine.
Barrel: 20″ Chrome-moly steel.
Weight: 7 lbs. **Length:** 39¾″ over-all.
Stock: Walnut finished with checkered p.g. and fore-end (13½x1½x2½).
Sights: Ramp front with step adj. sporting rear. Tapped for scope mounts.
Features: Grooved trigger, slide safety locks trigger and lever.
Price: $135.95

SAVAGE 99A LEVER ACTION RIFLE

Same as the 99E except: straight-grip walnut stock with schnabel fore-end, top tang safety. Folding leaf rear sight. Available in 250-300 (250 Savage) 300 Savage, 243 or 308 Win. **$154.95**

SAVAGE 99F LIGHTWEIGHT CARBINE

Same as 99E except: 22" lightweight bbl. Mag. indicator on left side. Select walnut stock with checkered p.g. and fore-end, aluminum buttplate. Wgt. 6½ lbs., 41¾" over-all. Cals. 300 Sav., 243 and 308 Win. **$159.95**

SAVAGE 99C LEVER ACTION CLIP RIFLE

Similar to M99F except: Detachable staggered clip magazine with push-button ejection (4-shot capacity: 3 in 284). Wgt. about 6¾ lbs., 41¾" over-all with 22" bbl. Cals. 243, 284, 308 .... **$159.95**

SAVAGE 99DL CARBINE

Same as 99F except: High comb Monte Carlo stock; anodized aluminum buttplate; slim fore-end; sling swivels. Wgt. 6¾ lbs., 41¾" over-all. Cals: 243 and 308 Win. **$164.95**

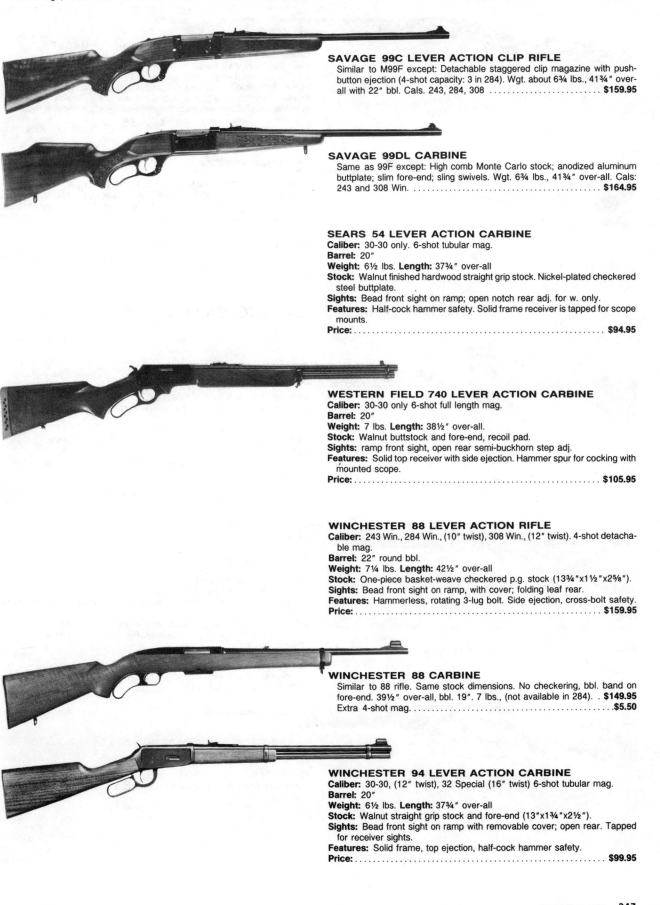

SEARS 54 LEVER ACTION CARBINE

Caliber: 30-30 only. 6-shot tubular mag.
Barrel: 20"
Weight: 6½ lbs. **Length:** 37¾" over-all
Stock: Walnut finished hardwood straight grip stock. Nickel-plated checkered steel buttplate.
Sights: Bead front sight on ramp; open notch rear adj. for w. only.
Features: Half-cock hammer safety. Solid frame receiver is tapped for scope mounts.
Price: **$94.95**

WESTERN FIELD 740 LEVER ACTION CARBINE

Caliber: 30-30 only 6-shot full length mag.
Barrel: 20"
Weight: 7 lbs. **Length:** 38½" over-all.
Stock: Walnut buttstock and fore-end, recoil pad.
Sights: ramp front sight, open rear semi-buckhorn step adj.
Features: Solid top receiver with side ejection. Hammer spur for cocking with mounted scope.
Price: **$105.95**

WINCHESTER 88 LEVER ACTION RIFLE

Caliber: 243 Win., 284 Win., (10" twist), 308 Win., (12" twist). 4-shot detachable mag.
Barrel: 22" round bbl.
Weight: 7¼ lbs. **Length:** 42½" over-all.
Stock: One-piece basket-weave checkered p.g. stock (13¾"x1½"x2⅝").
Sights: Bead front sight on ramp, with cover; folding leaf rear.
Features: Hammerless, rotating 3-lug bolt. Side ejection, cross-bolt safety.
Price: **$159.95**

WINCHESTER 88 CARBINE

Similar to 88 rifle. Same stock dimensions. No checkering, bbl. band on fore-end. 39½" over-all, bbl. 19". 7 lbs., (not available in 284). . **$149.95**
Extra 4-shot mag. **$5.50**

WINCHESTER 94 LEVER ACTION CARBINE

Caliber: 30-30, (12" twist), 32 Special (16" twist) 6-shot tubular mag.
Barrel: 20"
Weight: 6½ lbs. **Length:** 37¾" over-all
Stock: Walnut straight grip stock and fore-end (13"x1¾"x2½").
Sights: Bead front sight on ramp with removable cover; open rear. Tapped for receiver sights.
Features: Solid frame, top ejection, half-cock hammer safety.
Price: **$99.95**

U.S. CENTERFIRE RIFLES—LEVER ACTION

WINCHESTER 94 44 MAGNUM CARBINE
Similar to 94 lever action except: 44 Magnum only, 10-shot magazine, wgt 6½ lbs. and 38″ twist **$109.95**

WINCHESTER 94 ANTIQUE CARBINE
Same as M94 except: color case-hardened and scroll-engraved receiver, brass-plated loading gate and saddle ring. 30-30 only **$109.95**

WINCHESTER 94 NRA CENTENNIAL MUSKET
Caliber: 30-30 only (12″ twist), 7-shot tubular magazine.
Barrel: 26″ round tapered.
Weight: 7⅛ lbs. **Length:** 44″ over-all
Stock: Semi-fancy square comb walnut with capped full-length fore-end.
Sights: Blade front, calibrated folding leaf rear.
Features: NRA Centennial medallion embedded in stock, receiver decorated, detachable sling swivels black chrome finish.
Price: **$149.95**

WINCHESTER 94 NRA CENTENNIAL RIFLE
Similar to the NRA Musket except: 5-shot capacity, 24″ bbl., 42″ over-all, 6⅝ lbs. Half-magazine and semi-pistol grip stock. Hooded ramp front, adj. semi-buckhorn rear sights **$149.95**

WINCHESTER 94 NRA CENTENNIAL SET
A matched set of one rifle and one musket as described above **$324.95**

U.S. CENTERFIRE RIFLES—AUTOLOADING

ARMALITE AR-180 SPORTER CARBINE
Caliber: 233 semi-automatic, gas operated carbine.
Barrel: 18¼″ (12″ twist).
Weight: 6½ lbs. **Length:** 38″ over-all
Stock: Nylon folding stock, phenolic fiber-glass heat dissipating, fore-end.
Sight: Flip-up "L" type sight adj. for w., post front adj. for e.
Features: Safety lever accessible from both sides. Flash hider slotted to prevent muzzle climb.
Price: **$237.00**
3x (2.75 x 20mm) scope with detachable side-mount **$79.70**
Extra 5-round magazine **$14.95**

BROWNING HIGH-POWER AUTO RIFLE
Caliber: 270, 308, 243 Win., and 30-06.
Barrel: 22″ round tapered.
Weight: 7⅜ lbs. **Length:** 43½″ over-all.
Stock: French walnut p.g. stock (13⅝″x2″x1⅝″) and fore-end, hand checkered.
Sights: Adj. folding-leaf rear, gold bead on hooded ramp front.
Features: Detachable 4-round magazine. Receiver tapped for scope mounts. Trigger pull 4 lbs.
Price: Grade I **$199.50**
Grade II. Same as Grade I except hand-rubbed selected French walnut stock, hand engraved receiver **$217.50**
Other Grades and prices to **880.00**

BROWNING MAGNUM AUTO RIFLE
Same as the standard caliber model, except weighs 8½ lbs., 45¼″ over-all 24″ bbl., 3-round mag., Cals. 7mm Mag., 300 Win. Mag. and 338 Mag.
Grade I .... **$216.50**   Grade II **$234.50**
Other Grades and prices to **880.00**

HARRINGTON & RICHARDSON 360 ULTRA AUTO
Caliber: 243, 308 Winchester. 3 round mag.
Barrel: 22″ round, tapered.
Weight: 7½ lbs. **Length:** 43½″ over-all.
Stock: One-piece American walnut Monte Carlo p.g. stock, roll-over cheekpiece.
Sights: Open adj. rear sight, gold bead ramp front.
Features: Sliding trigger guard safety. Manually operated bolt stop. Receiver tapped for scope mount.
Price: **$189.00**
Also available with full roll-over cheekpiece for left or right hand shooters as Model 361 .... **$199.95**

PLAINFIELD MACHINE CO. CARBINE

Caliber: 30 U.S. Carbine or 223 (5.7mm)
Barrel: 18″ six-groove.
Weight: 5½ lbs. **Length:** 35½″ over-all
Stock: Glossy finished hard wood.
Sights: Click adj. open rear, gold bead ramp front.
Features: Gas operated semi-auto carbine. 15-shot detachable magazine.
Price: $105.00
Paratrooper. With telescoping wire stock, front vertical hand grip $125.00
Plainfielder. With walnut Monte Carlo sporting p.g. stock $125.00

REMINGTON 742 WOODMASTER AUTO RIFLE

Caliber: 243 Win., 6mm Rem., 280 Rem., 308 Win. and 30-06.
Barrel: 22″ round tapered.
Weight: 7½ lbs. **Length:** 42″ over-all
Stock: Walnut (13¼″x1⅝″x2¼″) deluxe checkered p.g. and fore-end.
Sights: Gold bead front sight on ramp; step rear sight with windage adj.
Features: Positive cross-bolt safety. Receiver tapped for scope mount. 4-shot clip mag.
Price: $169.95
Extra 4-shot clip magazine $5.25
Sling strap and swivels (installed) 9.10
Peerless (D) and Premier (F) grades .... $595.00 and 1295.00
Premier with gold inlays 2000.00

REMINGTON 742 BDL WOODSMASTER

Same as 742 except: "stepped" receiver, Monte Carlo with cheekpiece (right or left), whiteline spacers, basket-weave checkering on p.g. and fore-end, black fore-end tip, RKW finish (13⁵/₁₆″x1⅝″x1¹³/₁₆″x2½″). Cals. 30-06, 308 .... $189.95

REMINGTON 742 CARBINE

Same as M742 except: 18½″ bbl., 38½″ over-all, wgt. 6¾ lbs. Cals: 30-06, 308 Win. $169.95

RUGER 44 AUTOLOADING CARBINE

Caliber: 44 Magnum, 4-shot tubular magazine.
Barrel: 18½″ round tapered.
Weight: 5¾ lbs. **Length:** 36¾″ over-all
Stock: One-piece walnut p.g. stock (13⅜″x1⅝″x2¼″)
Sights: Sourdough front, folding leaf rear sights.
Features: Wide, curved trigger. Sliding cross-bolt safety. Receiver tapped for scope mount.
Price: $117.00
Model 44-RS Deluxe with built-in receiver sight, carbine stock and swivels $122.00

RUGER 44 SPORTER CARBINE

Same as Ruger autoloader except: sporter stock with Monte Carlo comb, flat buttplate; full pistol grip with cap; longer streamlined fore-end, relieved for fingertips; sling swivels. Cal. 44 Magnum $125.00

UNIVERSAL 1000 AUTOLOADING CARBINE

Caliber: 30 M1, 5-shot magazine.
Barrel: 18″
Weight: 5½ lbs. **Length:** 35½″ over-all
Stock: Walnut stock inletted for "issue" sling and oiler;
Sights: Blade front aperture rear. With protective wings, adj.
Features: Gas operated, hammerless. Cross lock safety. Receiver tapped for scope mounts.
Price: $116.95
Universal also offers other versions of their basic M1000 Carbine, including two models handling the 256 cartridge, at prices ranging from $129.95 to $175.00

UNIVERSAL 1020 TEFLON CARBINE

Same as the 1000 Carbine but has soft, dull Teflon finish said to be self-lubricating, water and scuff resistant. Available in black, tan, blue, green and olive colored finishes, with a high finish American walnut Monte Carlo stock.
Price: $149.95

WINCHESTER 100 AUTOLOADING RIFLE

Caliber: 243, 284 (10″ twist), and 308 (12″ twist).
Barrel: 22″ round, tapered.
Weight: 7¼ lbs. **Length:** 42½″ over-all
Stock: One piece walnut p.g. stock (13¾″x1½″x2⅝″), semi-beavertail fore-end, basketweave checkered.
Sights: Bead front and folding-leaf rear sights.
Features: Detachable box magazine. Sling swivels installed.
Price: $169.95

WINCHESTER 100 AUTOLOADING CARBINE

Similar to 100 Autoloading rifle, with same stock dimensions. No checkering. Bbl. band on fore-end 39½″ over-all. Bbl. 19″. Wgt. 7 lbs. Cals. 243 (10″ twist) and 308 (12″ twist) $159.95
Extra magazine 5.50

U.S. CENTERFIRE RIFLES—SLIDE ACTION

REMINGTON 760 GAMEMASTER SLIDE ACTION
Caliber: 6mm Rem., 243, 270, 308 Win., 30-06.
Barrel: 22″ round tapered.
Weight: 7½ lbs. **Length:** 42″ over-all.
Stock: Checkered walnut p.g. and fore-end (13¼″x1⅝″x2⅛″) RKW finish
Sights: Gold bead front sight on matted ramp, open step adj. sporting rear.
Features: Detachable 4-shot clip. Cross-bolt safety. Receiver tapped for scope mount.
Price: **$149.95**
   Sling strap and swivels (installed) **$9.10**
   Extra 4-shot clip **4.50**

REMINGTON 760 BDL GAMEMASTER
Same as 760 except: "stepped receiver," Monte Carlo stock with cheek-piece (right or left), whiteline spacer, basket-weave checkering on p.g. and fore-end, black fore-end tip, RKW finish. (13⁵⁄₁₆″x1⅝″x1¹³⁄₁₆″x2½″). Cals. 270, 30.06, 308 . . . . **$169.95**

REMINGTON 760 GAMEMASTER CARBINE
Same as M760 except has 18½″ barrel. Wgt. 7¼ lbs., 38½″ over-all. Cals: 308 Win. and 30.06 . . . . **$149.95**
Also in Peerless (D) and Premier (F) grades . . . . . **$595.00** and **$1295.00**
(F), with gold inlay **$2000.00**

SAVAGE MODEL 170 SLIDE ACTION
Caliber: 30-30 only. 3-shot mag.
Barrel: 22″ round tapered.
Weight: 6¾ lbs. **Length:** 41½″ over-all.
Stock: Walnut (14″x1½″x2½″), with checkered p.g. Hard rubber buttplate.
Sights: Gold bead ramp front, folding-leaf rear.
Features: Hammerless, solid frame tapped for scope mount. Top tang safety.
Price: **$99.95**

SAVAGE SCOPEGUN MODEL 170
Standard Model 170 equipped by factory with mounts and 1½-4x. variable scope **$137.95**

U.S. CENTERFIRE RIFLES—BOLT ACTION

BROWNING HIGH POWER RIFLE
Caliber: 222, 222 Mag., 22-250, 243, 308, 270, 30-06, 7mm Rem. Mag., 300 Win. Mag., 308 Norma, 338 Win. Mag. 375 H&H, 458 Win. Mag.
Barrel: 22″ standard, 24″ Magnum.
Weight: 6⅛ to 8¼ lbs. **Length:** 43″
Stock: Checkered walnut p.g. with Monte Carlo (13⅝″x1⅝″x2⅜″).
Sights: Hooded ramp front, removable adj. folding-leaf rear; except none on 458.
Features: 3-position side safety, hinged floorplate, receiver tapped for scope mount.
Price: Safari Grade . . . . **$237.50** to **$267.50**
   Medallion Grade . . . . **$400.00** to **$415.00**
   Olympian Grade . . . . **$670.00** to **$685.00**

U.S. CENTERFIRE RIFLES—BOLT ACTION

CHAMPLIN PREMIER RIFLE
Caliber: 270, 30-06, 7mm Rem. and 300 Win. Mag.
Barrel: 24″ either round or octagon.
Weight: About 8 lbs. **Length:** 50-52″
Stock: Hand inletted oil finished select Claro walnut with Monte Carlo, ebony fore-end tip, steel p.g. cap.
Sights: 3-leaf folding rear, bead on ramp front.
Features: Available in most standard chamberings, many options to customer specifications at additional cost.
Price: **$890.00**

HARRINGTON & RICHARDSON 300 BOLT ACTION
Caliber: 22-250, 243, 270, 308, 30-06 (5-shot), 7mm Rem. Mag., 300 Win. Mag. (3-shot)
Barrel: 22″ round, tapered.
Weight: 7¾ lbs. **Length:** 42½″ over-all.
Stock: American walnut, hand checkered p.g. and fore-end, Monte Carlo, roll-over cheekpiece.
Sights: Adjustable rear, gold bead ramp front.
Features: Hinged floorplate; sliding side safety; sling swivels, recoil pad. Receiver tapped for scope mount.
Price: **$225.00**

HARRINGTON & RICHARDSON 301 ULTRA CARBINE
Similar to M300, except: Mannlicher style stock (no roll-over cheek-piece) metal fore-end tip. 18″ bbl., 39″ over all, wgt. 7¼ lbs., not available in 22-250. . . . . **$239.00**

HARRINGTON & RICHARDSON 317 ULTRA WILDCAT
Caliber: 17 Rem., 222, 223 or 17/223 (handload) 6-shot magazine.
Barrel: 20″ round, tapered.
Weight: 5¼ lbs. **Length:** 38½″ over-all.
Stock: Walnut, hand polished, hand checkered capped p.g. and fore-end, with Monte Carlo.
Sights: None. Receiver dovetailed for integral scope mounts.
Features: 3-section brass cleaning rod, brush and tip included. Sliding side safety, adj. trigger.
Price: **$249.00**
Model 317P has better wood, basketweave checkering **$450.00**

HARRINGTON & RICHARDSON 330 HUNTER'S RIFLE
Caliber: 243, 270, 30-06, 308, 7mm Rem. or 300 Win.
Barrel: 22″ round tapered.
Weight: 7⅛ lbs. **Length:** 42½″ over-all
Stock: Walnut with Monte Carlo and hand checkered p.g.
Sights: Gold bead on ramp front, rear adj. for w. & e.
Features: Hinged floorplate, adj. trigger, sliding side safety. Receiver tapped for scope mounts.
Price: **$140.00**

HARRINGTON & RICHARDSON 370 ULTRA MEDALIST
Caliber: 22-250, 6mm Rem. and 243. 5-shot magazine.
Barrel: 24″ heavy varmint-target weight.
Weight: 9½ lbs. **Length:** 44¾″ over-all.
Stock: Oil finished walnut, full p.g. and roll-over comb; recoil pad installed.
Sights: None. Bbl. and receiver tapped for open sights and/or scope mounts.
Features: Sliding side safety, adj. trigger, sling swivels installed.
Price: **$245.00**

ITHACA LSA-55 BOLT ACTION RIFLE
Caliber: 243, 308, 22-250, 6mm Rem. 270 and 30-06.
Barrel: 23″ round tapered, full-floating.
Weight: About 6½ lbs. **Length:** 41½″ over-all
Stock: Hand checkered walnut, Monte Carlo with built-in swell on p.g.
Sights: Removable rear adj. for w. & e. ramp front.
Features: Detachable 3-shot magazine (5-shot available), adj. trigger, top tang safety. Receiver tapped for scope mounts.
Price: 243, 308, 22-250 & 6mm **$159.95**
Price: 270 & 30-06 . . . . **$174.95**

ITHACA LSA-55 DELUXE BOLT ACTION
Same as the std. except rollover cheekpiece, fore-end tip and pistol grip cap of rosewood with white spacers. Scope mount rings supplied. Sling swivels installed.
Price: 243, 308, 22-250 & 6mm **$199.95**
Price: 270 & 30-06 .... **$214.95**

ITHACA LSA-65 BOLT ACTION RIFLE
Same as the LSA-55 except in 270 or 30-06 caliber (5-shot clip unavailable).
Price: **$174.95**
LSA-65 Deluxe **$214.95**

MOSSBERG 800 BOLT ACTION RIFLE
Caliber: 22-250, 243 and 308. 4-shot magazine.
Barrel: 22″ AC-KRO-GRUV round tapered.
Weight: 6½ lbs. **Length:** 42″ over-all.
Stock: Walnut, Monte Carlo, checkered p.g. and fore-end.
Sights: Gold bead ramp front, adj. folding-leaf rear.
Features: Top tang safety, hinged floorplate, 1″ sling swivels installed. Receiver tapped for scope mounts.
Price: **$112.45**

MOSSBERG 800V TARGET-VARMINT RIFLE
Model 800 with heavy 24″ bbl, target scope bases, no iron sights. Cals. 243 and 22-250 only. 44″ overall, wgt. about 9½ lbs. **$124.95**

MOSSBERG 800SM SCOPED RIFLE
Same as M800 except has Mossberg M84 4x scope, but no iron sights. Wgt. 7½ lbs. **$129.95**

MOSSBERG 800M MANNLICHER RIFLE
Same as M800 except has one piece Mannlicher style stock, flat bolt handle, 20″ bbl., 40″ over-all, weight 6½ lbs. **$139.95**

MOSSBERG 800D DELUXE RIFLE
Super grade M800 with special finish and Monte Carlo rollover-comb stock with wgt. 6¾ lbs. **$170.00**

MOSSBERG 810 BOLT ACTION RIFLE
Caliber: 30-06 only, 4-shot magazine.
Barrel: 22″ AC-KRO-GRUV, straight taper.
Weight: 7½ to 8 lbs. **Length:** 42″ over-all.
Stock: Walnut Monte Carlo with checkered fore-end and capped p.g. recoil pad and sling swivels installed.
Sights: Gold bead on ramp front, folding-leaf rear.
Features: Receiver tapped for metallic sight or scope mounts. Top tang safety. Detachable box magazine.
Price: **$124.95**

RANGER ARMS TEXAS MAVERICK RIFLE
Caliber: 22-250, 243, 6mm Rem., 308 Win., 6.5 and 350 Rem. Mag.
Barrel: 22″ or 24″ round tapered.
Weight: 7¾ lbs. **Length:** 44″ over-all.
Stock: English or Claro walnut, Monte Carlo w/cheekpiece. Skip-line checkering/rosewood p.g. and fore-end cap, recoil pad installed.
Sights: None. Receiver tapped for scope mounts.
Features: Push-button safety, adj. trigger, available in left or right hand models at same price.
Price: Statesman Grade **$325.00**
Other grades and models (including thumb hole and Mannlicher types). Prices to **$475.00**

RANGER ARMS TEXAS MAGNUM RIFLE
Same as the Maverick except 25-06 in 270, 30-06, 7mm Rem., 300 or 338 Win. Mag., Norma Magnum Calibers. Optional 24″ or 25½″ bbls. Wgt. 8¼ lbs. .... **$325.00** to **$475.00**

REMINGTON 700 BDL BOLT ACTION RIFLE
Same as 700-ADL except: fleur-de-lis checkering; black fore-end tip and p.g. cap, white line spacers. Matted receiver top, quick release floorplate. Hooded ramp front sight. Q.D. swivels and l″ sling **$169.95**
Available in 6.5 Rem. Mag., 350 Rem. Mag., 7mm Rem. Mag., 264 and 300 Win. Mag., (all with recoil pad installed) or 17 Rem. caliber. 44½″ over-all, weight 7½ lbs. **$184.95**
Peerless Grade .... **$595.00**   Premier Grade **$1295.00**

REMINGTON 700 BDL VARMINT
Same as 700 BDL, except: 24″ heavy bbl., 43½″ over-all, wgt. 9 lbs. Cals. 222, 223, 22-250, 6mm Rem., 243 and 25-06. No sights. **$184.95**

REMINGTON 700 ADL BOLT ACTION RIFLE
Caliber: 222, 22-250, 6mm Rem., 243, 25-06, 270, 7mm Rem. Mag., 308 and 30-06.
Barrel: 22″ or 24″ round tapered.
Weight: 7 lbs. **Length:** 41½″ to 43½″
Stock: Walnut, RKW finished p.g. stock with impressed checkering, Monte Carlo (13⅜″x1⅝″x2⅜″).
Sights: Gold bead ramp front; removable, step-adj. rear with windage screw.
Features: Side safety, adj. trigger, blind magazine, receiver tapped for scope mounts.
Price: (except 7mm Rem. Mag.) **$149.95**
7mm Rem. Mag. **$164.95**

REMINGTON 700 SAFARI
Same as the 700 BDL except: 375 H&H or 458 Win. Magnum calibers only. Hand checkered, oil finished stock with recoil pad installed. Delivery time is about five months. **$344.95**

REMINGTON 700 C CUSTOM RIFLE
Same as the 700 BDL except choice of 20″, 22″ or 24″ bbl. with or without sights. Jewelled bolt, with or without hinged floor plate. Select American walnut stock is hand checkered, rosewood fore-end & grip cap. Hand lapped barrel. 16 weeks for delivery after placing order **$345.00**
M700 C Custom Magnum **$357.00**
Optional extras: recoil pad **$12.00**, oil finish **$13.75**, left hand cheekpiece **$25.00**.

U.S. CENTERFIRE RIFLES—BOLT ACTION

REMINGTON 788 BOLT ACTION RIFLE
Caliber: 222 (5-shot), 22-250, 6mm Rem., 243, 30-30 and 308 (4-shot).
Barrel: 22" round tapered (24" in 222 and 22-250).
Weight: 7-7½ lbs. **Length:** 41" over-all.
Stock: Walnut finished hardwood with Monte Carlo and p.g. (13⅝"x1⅞"x2⅝").
Sights: Blade ramp front, open rear adj. for w. & e.
Features: Detachable box magazine, thumb safety, receiver tapped for scope mounts.
Price: **$99.95**
   Sling strap and swivels, installed **$5.40**

REMINGTON 788 LEFT HAND BOLT ACTION
Same as 788 except cals. 6mm & 308 only and left hand stock and action.
.... **$104.95**

RUGER 77 BOLT ACTION RIFLE
Caliber: 22-250, 6mm. Rem., 243 and 308 (5-shot), 284, 6.5 and 350 Rem. Mag. (3-shot)
Barrel: 22" round tapered.
Weight: About 7 lbs. **Length:** 42" over-all.
Stock: Checkered American walnut (13¾"x1⅝"x2⅛") p.g. cap; sling swivel studs and recoil pad.
Sights: Optional gold bead ramp front and folding-leaf adj. rear or scope rings.
Features: Integral scope mount bases, hinged floorplate; fully adj. trigger, top tang safety.
Price: **$165.00**
   With scope rings and metallic sights **$179.00**
   Also available in 22-250 with heavy 24" bbl., drilled and tapped for target scope blocks **$165.00**

RUGER MODEL 77 MAGNUM RIFLE
Same as the M77 except: caliber 270 or 30-06 (5-shot) with 22" bbl. and 25-06 or 7mm Rem. Mag. (3-shot) with 24" bbl. With either metallic sights or scope rings. **$165.00**
With both, metallic sights and scope rings. **$179.00**
Also available in 25-06 with heavy 24" bbl., drilled and tapped for target scope blocks. **$165.00**

SAVAGE 110E BOLT ACTION RIFLE
Caliber: 30-06 and 243, 4-shot. Also 7mm Rem. Mag., 3-shot at $15 extra.
Barrel: 20" round tapered (7mm 24" stainless).
Weight: 6¾ lbs. (7mm-7¾ lbs.) **Length:** 40½" (20" bbl.)
Stock: Walnut finished hardwood with Monte Carlo, checkered p.g. and fore-end, hard rubber buttplate.
Sights: Gold bead removable ramp front, step adj. rear.
Features: Top tang safety, receiver tapped for peep or scope sights. Right or left hand models available.
Price: Right hand .... **$121.95**   Left hand **$127.95**

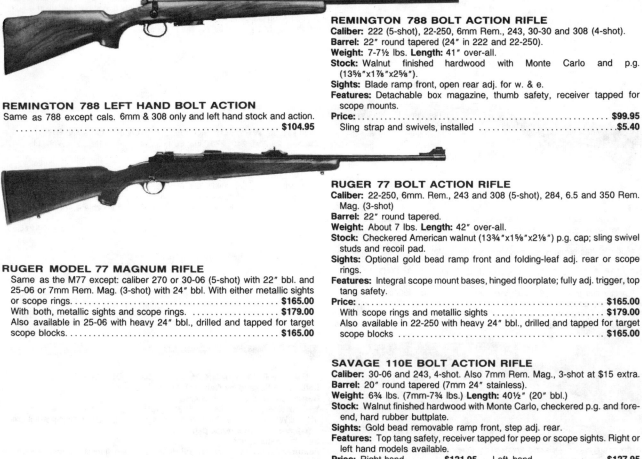

SAVAGE 110D BOLT ACTION RIFLE
Same as 110E except: 22" bbl. (24" on Mag. and 22-250 cals.); walnut stock; aluminum buttplate (recoil pad on mag.); folding-leaf rear sight (none on 22-250); weight 6¾-8 lbs. Cals. 22-250, 243, 270 and 30-06. Also available in 7mm Rem. or 300 Win. Mag. at $15 extra.
Price: Right hand .... **$144.95**   Left hand **$149.95**

SAVAGE 110C BOLT ACTION RIFLE
Same as the 110D except: Detachable box magazine. Cals. 243, 25-06, 270 and 30-06 (4-shot). Also in 7mm Rem. or 300 Win. Mag. (3-shot) at $15 extra.
Price: Right hand. .... **$146.95**   Left hand **$152.95**

SAVAGE 110 Barreled Actions
Same as used on the 110D rifles. No stock or sights. Cals. 22-250, 243, 270 and 30-06. Also in 7mm Rem. and 300 Win. Mag. at $10 extra.
Price: Right hand .... **$94.00**   Left hand **$98.00**
Actions only. Write to Savage for prices.

SAVAGE 340 CLIP REPEATER
Caliber: 222 Rem. (4-shot) and 30-30 (3-shot).
Barrel: 24" and 22" respectively.
Weight: About 6½ lbs. **Length:** 40"-42"
Stock: Walnut, Monte Carlo, checkered p.g. and fore-end white line spacers.
Sights: Gold bead ramp front, folding-leaf rear.
Features: Detachable clip magazine, sliding thumb safety, receiver tapped for scope mounts.
Price: **$89.95**

SEARS MODEL 53 BOLT ACTION RIFLE
Caliber: 243 or 30-06. 5-shot mag.
Barrel: 22" round tapered (10" twist).
Weight: 6¾ lbs. **Length:** 42⅜" over-all.
Stock: Walnut finished hardwood, Monte Carlo comb, checkered p.g. and fore-end.
Sights: Bead ramp front, semi-buckhorn folding rear.
Features: Wide serrated trigger, 3-position bolt head safety, receiver tapped for sights and scope mounts.
Price: **$129.95**

SEARS TED WILLIAMS MODEL 53 RIFLE
Same as Sears M53 except: 30-06 only, American walnut stock, recoil pad, black fore-end tip, 1" detachable sling swivels and sling, medallion on p.g. engine turned bolt, scrolled floorplate.
Price: **$167.50**

SMITH & WESSON MODEL A BOLT ACTION RIFLE
Caliber: 22-250, 243, 270, 308, 30-06, 7mm Rem. Mag., 300 Win. Mag.
Barrel: 23¾" round tapered.
Weight: About 7 lbs. **Length:** 44¼" over-all
Stock: European walnut, skip-line checkered p.g. & fore-end (rosewood tipped), Monte Carlo with cheekpiece.
Sights: Silver bead hooded ramp front, folding-leaf rear.
Features: Sliding side safety, adj. trigger, hinged floorplate, receiver tapped for scope mounts.
Price: **$215.50**

SMITH & WESSON MODEL B & C BOLT ACTION RIFLES
Same as Model A except: 20¾" bbl. Cals. 243, 270, 308 and 30-06. Monte Carlo p.g. stock with schnabel fore-end. Weight 6.6 lbs. 41¼" over-all. **$202.50**
Model C has straight p.g. stock (no Monte Carlo) **$192.50**

SMITH & WESSON MODEL D & E BOLT ACTION RIFLES
Exactly like the Models C & B respectively, except: full-length fore-end Mannlicher stock.
Model D (no Monte Carlo) **$221.00**
Model E (Monte Carlo) **$225.00**

WEATHERBY MARK V RIFLE Left Hand
Available in all Weatherby calibers except 224 and 22-250 (and 26" ¼ contour 300WM). Complete left handed action; stock with cheekpiece on right side. Prices are $10 higher than right hand models except the 378 and 460WM are unchanged.

WEATHERBY MARK V BOLT ACTION RIFLE
Caiber: All Weatherby Cals., 22-250 and 30-06.
Barrel: 24" or 26" round tapered.
Weight: 6½-10½ lbs. **Length:** 43¼"-46½"
Stock: Walnut, Monte Carlo with cheekpiece, high luster finish, checkered p.g. and fore-end, recoil pad.
Sights: Optional (extra).
Features: Cocking indicator, adj. trigger, hinged floorplate, thumb safety, quick detachable sling swivels.
Price: Cals. 224 and 22-250, std. bbl. **$299.50**
 With 26" semi-target bbl. **309.50**
 Cals. 240, 257, 270, 7mm, 30-06 and 300 (24" bbl.) **339.50**
 With 26"¼ contour bbl. **349.50**
 Cal. 340 (26" bbl.) **349.50**
 Cal. 378 (26" bbl.) **455.00**
 Cal. 460 (26" bbl.) **525.00**

WEATHERBY VANGUARD BOLT ACTION RIFLE
Caliber: 243, 30-06 and 308 (5-shot), 264, 7mm Rem. and 300 Win. Mag. (3-shot).
Barrel: 24" hammer forged.
Weight: 7⅞ lbs. **Length:** 44½" over-all.
Stock: American walnut, p.g. cap and fore-end tip, hand inletted and checkered, 13½" pull.
Sights: Optional, available at extra cost.
Features: Side safety, adj. trigger, hinged floorplate, receiver tapped for scope mounts.
Price: **$199.50**

WESTERN FIELD 730 BOLT ACTION RIFLE
Caliber: 30-06 only.
Barrel: 22" round tapered.
Weight: 8 lbs. 8 oz.
Stock: Walnut with Monte Carlo comb, checkered p.g. and fore-end, recoil pad, sling swivels.
Sights: Bead ramp front, folding rear.
Features: Light weight sporter with removable magazine; top receiver safety.
Price: **$122.95**

WESTERN FIELD 775-776 BOLT ACTION RIFLES
Caliber: 308 (M-775), 243 (M-776). 5-shot mag.
Barrel: 22" round tapered.
Weight: 9 lbs. **Length:** 42" over-all.
Stock: Handrubbed American Walnut with roll-over cheekpiece, recoil pad.
Sights: Bead ramp front, folding rear.
Features: Hinged floor plate; short throw bolt action with 6 locking lugs and recessed bolt head; receiver tapped for sights and scope.
Price: **$139.00**

WESTERN FIELD 780 BOLT ACTION RIFLE
Same as 775-776 except: Monte Carlo stock without recoil pad or p.g. Calibers: 308 and 243.
Price: **$110.95**

WINCHESTER 70 STANDARD RIFLE

Caliber: 222, 22-250, 225, 243, 270, 308 and 30-06, 5-shot
Barrel: 22" swaged, floating. 10" twist (225, 222 & 22-250 have 14" twist, 308 is 12").
Weight: 7½ lbs. **Length:** 42½" over-all.
Stock: Walnut, Monte Carlo, (13½"x1¾"x1½"x2⅛") checkered p.g. and fore-end.
Sights: Removable hooded bead ramp front, adj. open rear.
Features: Sling swivels installed, steel p.g. cap, hinged floorplate, receiver tapped for scope mounts.
Price: **$174.95**

WINCHESTER 70 MAGNUM RIFLE

Same as M70 Standard except with recoil pad and in these magnum cals.: 7 Rem., 264, 300, 338 Win., 375 H&H, 3-round mag. capacity. Wgt. 7¾ lbs. (8½ lbs. in 375), 24" bbl., 44½" over-all. R.H. twist: 9" in 264, 9½" in 7mm, 10" in 300, 338. .... **$189.95**
Cal. 375 H&H **$249.95**

WINCHESTER 70 AFRICAN

Same as M70 Standard except: 458 Win. Mag. only, 4-shot. 22" non-floating heavy bbl. 14" twist. Stock measures 13½"x1⅜"x1¾"x2⅜", has ebony fore-end tip and grip cap; wgt. 8½ lbs., recoil pad and special rear sight. **$359.95**

WINCHESTER 70 VARMINT RIFLE

Same as M70 Standard except: 222, 22-250, and 243 only, target scope blocks, no sights, 24" heavy bbl., 14" twist in 22-250, 10" twist in 243. 44½" over-all, 9¾ lbs. Stock measures 13½"x9⁄16"x15⁄16"x⅜" from bore line.
.... **$189.95**

WINCHESTER 70 TARGET RIFLE

Same as M70 except: heavy 24" barrel, contoured aluminum handstop that fits left and right hand shooter, high comb target stock. Tapped for micrometer sights, clip slot in receiver, cals. 308 and 30-06. .... **$239.95**

WINCHESTER 70 MANNLICHER

Same as M70 Standard except: 19" barrel bedded full length in Mannlicher-style stock of American walnut with Monte Carlo profile and raised cheekpiece. Length 39½" over-all, weight about 7 lbs. Available in 243, 270, 308 Win. or 30-06. .... **$259.95**

WINCHESTER 70 DELUXE RIFLE

Same as M70 Standard except: presentation-checkered semi-fancy walnut stock, ebony p.g. cap and fore-end tip with white spacers, knurled bolt knob, non-slip rubber buttplate. Cals. 243, 270, 30-06, 300 Win. Mag. (recoil pad).
.... **$349.95**

WINCHESTER 70 BARRELED ACTIONS

No stock, sights or scope blocks. Receivers are tapped for sights and scope mounts. Standard cals. 222, 22-250, 243, 270, 308 and 30-06. . **$128.95**
Magnum cals. 264, 300 and 338 Win., 7mm Re. **143.95**
Varmint cals. 222, 22-250 and 243 .... **143.95**
Target cals. 308 and 30-06 .... **173.95**

WINCHESTER 770 BOLT ACTION RIFLE

Caliber: 222, 22-250, 243, 270, 30-06 & 308 (4-shot)
Barrel: 22" round tapered.
Weight: 7⅛ lbs. **Length:** 42½" over-all.
Stock: Walnut, Monte Carlo (13½"x1¾"x2⅛"x1½") checkered p.g. and fore-end with caps.
Sights: Hooded ramp front, adj. open rear (both are detachable).
Features: Three position safety, engine turned bolt, sling swivels installed.
Price: **$139.95**

WINCHESTER 770 MAGNUM BOLT ACTION
Same as the 770 except: cals. 264, 7mm Rem. and 300 Win. Magnum (3-shot). Rubber recoil pad, 24" bbl., 44½" over-all; wgt. 7¼ lbs. 9" (264), 9½" (7mm) & 10" (300) twist **$154.95**

WINCHESTER 670 BOLT ACTION RIFLE
Caliber: 243 and 30-06, 4-shot
Barrel: 22" full floating.
Weight: 7 lbs. **Length:** 42½" over-all.
Stock: Monte Carlo stock (13½"x1¾"x1½"x2⅛"), checkered p.g. and fore-end.
Sights: Ramp front sight and adj. open rear (both easily detachable for scope-only use).
Features: Wide serrated trigger, two position safety, red cocking indicator.
Price: **$129.95**

WINSLOW BOLT ACTION RIFLE
Caliber: All standard cartridges (magnum add $10).
Barrel: 24" Douglas premium. (Magnums 26")
Weight: 7-7½ lbs. **Length:** 43" over-all.
Stock: Hand rubbed black walnut, choice of 3 styles
Sights: None. Metallics available at extra cost.
Features: Receiver tapped for scope mounts, QD swivels and recoil pad installed. 4-shot blind mag.
Price: Regal Grade **$390.00**
Regent, Regimental, Crown, Emperor and Imperial grades in ascending order of carving, engraving and inlaying, to **$3500.00**
Regal grade Varmint in 17/222 (std or Mag.) or 17/223. Priced from **430.00**
Left hand models at $60 extra.

U.S. CENTERFIRE RIFLES—SINGLE SHOT & MUZZLE LOADING

CHALLANGER GOLDEN EAGLE PERCUSSION RIFLE
Caliber: 36, 45 or 58.
Barrel: 32" octagonal (also 20" carbine 45-cal.)
Weight: 9 lbs. **Length:** 49" over-all.
Stock: Oil finished walnut, half-stock fore-end.
Sights: Brass blade front, both notch open and aperture rear sights.
Features: Under hammer design, solid brass furniture, (buttplate, engraved patch box, fore-end tip, etc.)
Price: **$109.95**

CHALLANGER HOPKINS & ALLEN HERITAGE
Caliber: 36 or 45
Barrel: 32" octagonal (¹⁵/₁₆" across the flats) uniform rifling.
Weight: 8½ lbs. **Length:** 49" over-all.
Stock: Walnut, straight grip and fore-end.
Sights: Hooded ring aperture front, both open step adj. and tang peep sights.
Features: Brass patch box, crescent buttplate and trigger guard extension. Under hammer, muzzle loading percussion rifle.
Price: **$99.95**
Offhand Deluxe. Plain version of the Heritage **$87.95**

CHALLANGER HOPKINS & ALLEN BUGGY CARBINE
Caliber: 36 or 45
Barrel: 20" octagonal (¹⁵/₁₆" across the flats).
Weight: 5½ lbs. **Length:** 37" over-all.
Stock: Walnut straight grip stock and fore-end, flat buttplate.
Sights: Hooded blade front sight, open adj. rear.
Features: Underhammer, percussion single shot muzzle-loading rifle. Short, light and fast handling.
Price: **$84.95**

CHALLANGER HOPKINS & ALLEN 45 TARGET
Caliber: 45
Barrel: Heavy 32" octagonal (1⅛" across the flats).
Weight: 11 lbs. **Length:** 49" over-all.
Stock: Straight grip walnut stock.
Sights: Hooded blade front, open step adj. rear.
Features: No fore-end or ramrod ferrules. Made for bench shooting. Under hammer, percussion muzzle loading rifle.
Price: **$84.95**

CHALLANGER HOPKINS & ALLEN OVER/UNDER RIFLE
Caliber: 45
Barrel: 28" blued octagonal
Weight: 8½ lbs. **Length:** 43" over-all.
Stock: Walnut stock and crescent buttplate.
Sights: Each barrel has its own set of sights targeted to the same point of impact.
Features: Brass furniture. Rotating barrels permit firing 2 shots before reloading.
Price: **$139.95**

CHALLANGER HOPKINS & ALLEN DEER STALKER
Caliber: 58
Barrel: 32" octagonal
Weight: 9½ lbs. **Length:** 49" over-all.
Stock: Walnut straight grip stock and fore-end.
Sights: Hooded blade front, step adj. rear.
Features: Single shot percussion muzzle-loader of large bore designed for hunting.
Price: **$87.95**

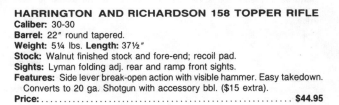

CHALLANGER HOPKINS & ALLEN MINUTEMAN
Caliber: 36 or 45
Barrel: 39" octagon ($^{15}/_{16}$" across the flats)
Weight: 9½ lbs. **Length:** 55" over-all.
Stock: Traditional full length maple, Kentucky style.
Sights: Fixed, silver blade front notched rear.
Features: Brass crescent buttplate, trigger guard and patch box. Available in flint or percussion.
Price: **$179.95**

HARRINGTON & RICHARDSON OFFICERS MODEL 1873
Caliber: 45-70, single shot.
Barrel: 26" round.
Weight: About 8 lbs. **Length:** 44" over-all
Stock: Oil finished walnut, checkered at wrist and fore-end white metal tipped.
Sights: Blade front, vernier tang rear adj. for w. & e.
Features: Replica of the 1873 Springfield has engraved breech block, side lock and hammer. Each comes with commemorative plaque.
Price: **$250.00**
Rifles with serial no. under 3000 .... **$275.00**
Those numbered less than 1500 .... **$300.00**

CHALLANGER PENNSYLVANIA LONG RIFLE
Caliber: 36 or 45
Barrel: 39" octagonal.
Weight: 10½ lbs. **Length:** 55" over-all.
Stock: Full-length tiger striped maple, traditional Pennsylvania form.
Sights: Brass blade front, open notch rear.
Features: Solid brass engraved furniture (crescent buttplate, patch box, fore-end cap, etc.)
Price: Flint or percussion form **$179.95**

HARRINGTON AND RICHARDSON 158 TOPPER RIFLE
Caliber: 30-30
Barrel: 22" round tapered.
Weight: 5¼ lbs. **Length:** 37½"
Stock: Walnut finished stock and fore-end; recoil pad.
Sights: Lyman folding adj. rear and ramp front sights.
Features: Side lever break-open action with visible hammer. Easy takedown. Converts to 20 ga. Shotgun with accessory bbl. ($15 extra).
Price: **$44.95**

RUGER NUMBER ONE SINGLE SHOT
Caliber: 22-250, 243, 6mm Rem., 25-06, 270, 7mm Rem. Mag., 300 Win.
Barrel: 26" round tapered with quarter-rib.
Weight: 8 lbs. **Length:** 42" over-all.
Stock: Walnut, two-piece, checkered p.g. and fore-end (either semi-beavertail or Henry style).
Sights: None, 1" scope rings supplied for integral mounts.
Features: Under lever, hammerless falling block design has auto ejector, top tang safety.
Price: **$265.00**

SHARPS MODEL 78 SINGLE SHOT RIFLE
Caliber: 17 through 50 (specify).
Barrel: 26" to 36" choice of weight and contour.
Weight: 6¾ to 16 lbs. **Length:** Varies with bbl.
Stock: Two-piece walnut, rubber buttplate, choice of woods, cheekpiece, buttplate and checkering.
Features: Falling block underlever action, internal hammer, selective breech-block safety, combination single-set trigger, receiver tapped for scope mounts.
Price: Grade I ...... **$295.00**   Grade II **$399.50**
Custom grades to **$5000.00**

TINGLE M1962 MUZZLE LOADING RIFLE
Caliber: 36 or 44
Barrel: 32" octagon, hook breech, 52" twist.
Weight: 10 lbs. **Length:** 48" over-all.
Stock: One-piece walnut with concave cheekpiece.
Sights: Blade front, step adj. V-notch rear.
Features: Solid brass furniture, double-set trigger with adj. pull, percussion lock.
Price: **$139.95**

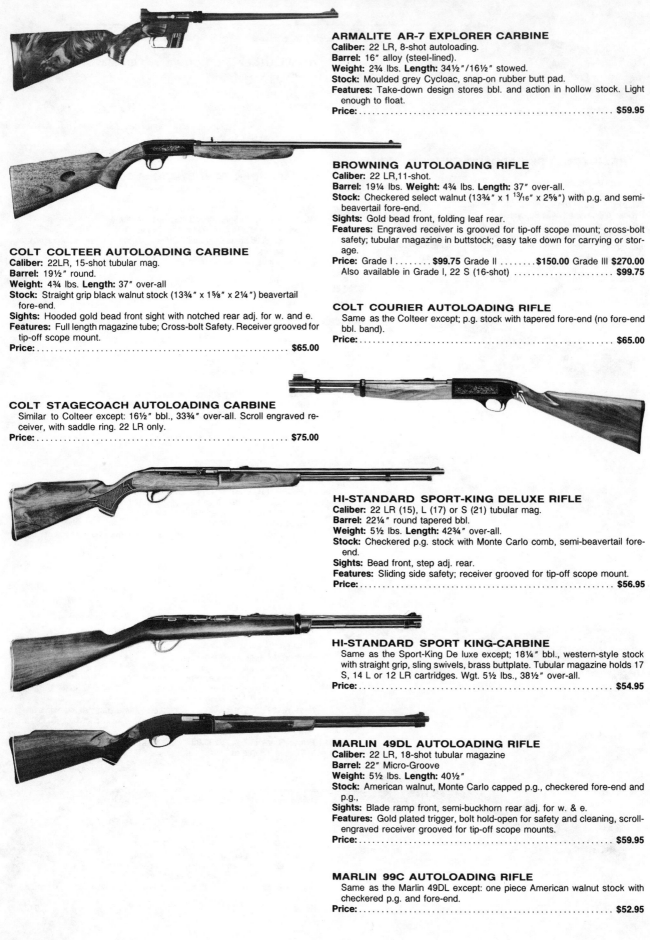

ARMALITE AR-7 EXPLORER CARBINE
Caliber: 22 LR, 8-shot autoloading.
Barrel: 16" alloy (steel-lined).
Weight: 2¾ lbs. **Length:** 34½"/16½" stowed.
Stock: Moulded grey Cycloac, snap-on rubber butt pad.
Features: Take-down design stores bbl. and action in hollow stock. Light enough to float.
Price: **$59.95**

BROWNING AUTOLOADING RIFLE
Caliber: 22 LR,11-shot.
Barrel: 19¼ lbs. **Weight:** 4¾ lbs. **Length:** 37" over-all.
Stock: Checkered select walnut (13¾" x 1 ¹³/₁₆" x 2⅝") with p.g. and semi-beavertail fore-end.
Sights: Gold bead front, folding leaf rear.
Features: Engraved receiver is grooved for tip-off scope mount; cross-bolt safety; tubular magazine in buttstock; easy take down for carrying or storage.
Price: Grade I . . . . **$99.75** Grade II . . . . **$150.00** Grade III **$270.00**
Also available in Grade I, 22 S (16-shot) **$99.75**

COLT COLTEER AUTOLOADING CARBINE
Caliber: 22LR, 15-shot tubular mag.
Barrel: 19½" round.
Weight: 4¾ lbs. **Length:** 37" over-all
Stock: Straight grip black walnut stock (13¾" x 1⅝" x 2¼") beavertail fore-end.
Sights: Hooded gold bead front sight with notched rear adj. for w. and e.
Features: Full length magazine tube; Cross-bolt Safety. Receiver grooved for tip-off scope mount.
Price: **$65.00**

COLT COURIER AUTOLOADING RIFLE
Same as the Colteer except; p.g. stock with tapered fore-end (no fore-end bbl. band).
Price: **$65.00**

COLT STAGECOACH AUTOLOADING CARBINE
Similar to Colteer except: 16½" bbl., 33¾" over-all. Scroll engraved receiver, with saddle ring. 22 LR only.
Price: **$75.00**

HI-STANDARD SPORT-KING DELUXE RIFLE
Caliber: 22 LR (15), L (17) or S (21) tubular mag.
Barrel: 22¼" round tapered bbl.
Weight: 5½ lbs. **Length:** 42¾" over-all.
Stock: Checkered p.g. stock with Monte Carlo comb, semi-beavertail fore-end.
Sights: Bead front, step adj. rear.
Features: Sliding side safety; receiver grooved for tip-off scope mount.
Price: **$56.95**

HI-STANDARD SPORT KING-CARBINE
Same as the Sport-King De luxe except; 18¼" bbl., western-style stock with straight grip, sling swivels, brass buttplate. Tubular magazine holds 17 S, 14 L or 12 LR cartridges. Wgt. 5½ lbs. 38½" over-all.
Price: **$54.95**

MARLIN 49DL AUTOLOADING RIFLE
Caliber: 22 LR, 18-shot tubular magazine
Barrel: 22" Micro-Groove
Weight: 5½ lbs. **Length:** 40½"
Stock: American walnut, Monte Carlo capped p.g., checkered fore-end and p.g.,
Sights: Blade ramp front, semi-buckhorn rear adj. for w. & e.
Features: Gold plated trigger, bolt hold-open for safety and cleaning, scroll-engraved receiver grooved for tip-off scope mounts.
Price: **$59.95**

MARLIN 99C AUTOLOADING RIFLE
Same as the Marlin 49DL except: one piece American walnut stock with checkered p.g. and fore-end.
Price: **$52.95**

MARLIN 99 M1 AUTOLOADING CARBINE
Caliber: 22 LR, 9-shot tubular magazine
Barrel: 18" Micro-Groove
Weight: 4½ lbs. **Length:** 37"
Stock: Monte Carlo American walnut with p.g. and handguard. White butt-plate spacer.
Sights: Blade on band type ramp front, removable flat-top mid-sight adj. for w. & e.
Features: Gold plated trigger, bolt hold-open, serrated receiver top is grooved for tip-off scope mount, sling swivels attached.
Price: $52.95

MARLIN 989 M2 AUTOLOADING CARBINE
Same as the Marlin 99 M1 carbine except 7-shot detachable clip magazine.
Price: $52.95

MARLIN GLENFIELD 60 AUTOLOADER
Caliber: 22 LR, 18-shot tubular mag.
Barrel: 22" round tapered.
Weight: About 5½ lbs. **Length:** 41" Over-all.
Stock: Walnut finished Monte Carlo, checkered p.g. and fore-end.
Sights: Blade ramp front, step adj. rear.
Features: Chrome plated trigger, matted receiver is grooved for tip-off mounts.
Price: $44.95

MOSSBERG MODEL 350K RIFLE
Caliber: 22 LR, 7-shot clip.
Barrel: 23½" AC-KRO-GROV
Weight: about 6 lbs. **Length:** 43½" over-all.
Stock: Walnut finish p.g. stock with cheekpiece and Monte Carlo comb.
Sights: Open step adj. rear sight, bead front
Features: Sliding side safety, sling swivels receiver grooved for tip-off scope mount.
Price: $48.95

MOSSBERG MODEL 351K RIFLE
Caliber: 22 LR only, 15-shot mag.
Barrel: 24" "AC-KRO-GRUV"
Weight: 6 lbs. **Length:** 43" over-all.
Stock: One-piece walnut finish, Monte Carlo comb. and cheekpiece.
Sights: Open step adj. rear and bead front sights.
Features: Tubular magazine loads through port in buttstock, sliding side safety, receiver grooved for tip-off scope mount.
Price: $49.95

MOSSBERG MODEL 351C CARBINE
Same as Mossberg 351K except: 18½" bbl., bbl. band, sling swivels; wgt. 5½ lbs., 38½" over-all.
Price: $51.95

MOSSBERG MODEL 352K RIFLE
Same as the Model 350K except: Two position extension fore-end of black Tenite for steady firing from the prone position. Sling swivels and web strap on left of stock.
Price: $49.95

MOSSBERG MODEL 430 RIFLE
Caliber: 22 LR, 18-shot tubular mag.
Barrel: 24" round.
Weight: 6¼ lbs. **Length:** 43½" over-all.
Stock: Two-piece walnut, checkered p.g. and fore-end, buttplate and p.g. cap w/white liners.
Sights: Open step adj. U-notch rear, gold bead front.
Features: Top tang safety, bolt locks open after last shot. Receiver grooved for tip-off mount.
Price: $62.95

MOSSBERG MODEL 432 WESTERN CARBINE
Same as the Model 430 except: 20" bbl., straight grip stock (no checkering). 15-shot tubular magazine (22 LR only). Wgt 6 lbs., 39½" over-all.
Price: $54.95

NOBLE 885 AUTOLOADING RIFLE
Caliber: 22 LR, 15-shot tubular mag.
Barrel: 22" round tapered.
Weight: 5½ lbs. **Length:** 42" over-all.
Stock: One-piece, walnut finished with p.g.
Sights: Blade ramp front, step adj. open rear.
Features: Top tang safety, hard rubber buttplate, receiver grooved for tip-off scope mount.
Price: **$49.95**

REMINGTON 552A AUTOLOADING RIFLE
Caliber: 22 S (20), L (17) or LR (15) tubular mag.
Barrel: 23" round tapered.
Weight: about 5¾ lbs. **Length:** 42" over-all.
Stock: Full-size, walnut with p.g.
Sights: Bead front, step adj. open rear.
Features: Positive cross-bolt safety, receiver grooved for tip-off mount.
Price: **$69.95**
Price: M552GS (22 Short only) **$81.95**

REMINGTON MODEL 552BDL AUTO RIFLE
Same as Model 552A except: Du Pont RKW finished checkered fore-end and capped p.g. stock. Blade ramp front and fully adj. rear sights.
Price: **$79.95**

REMINGTON 552C AUTOLOADING CARBINE
Same as the Model 552A rifle except: 21" bbl., weight 5½ lbs., 40" over-all.
Price: **$69.95**

REMINGTON NYLON 66MB AUTO RIFLE
Caliber: 22 LR, 14-shot tubular mag.
Barrel: 19⅝" round tapered.
Weight: 4 lbs. **Length:** 38½" over-all.
Stock: Moulded Mohawk Brown Nylon, checkered p.g. and fore-end.
Sights: Blade ramp front, adj. open rear.
Features: Top tang safety, double extractors, receiver grooved for tip-off mounts.
Price: **$59.95**

REMINGTON NYLON 66AB AUTO RIFLE
Same as the Model 66MB except: Apache Black Nylon stock, chrome plated receiver.
Price: **$64.95**

REMINGTON NYLON 77 AUTO RIFLE
Same as Nylon 66 rifle except: removable 5-shot 22 LR clip magazine.
Price: **$54.95**
Extra 5-shot clip .... **$2.75**   Extra 10-shot clip **$3.50**

RUGER 10/22 AUTOLOADING CARBINE
Caliber: 22 LR, 10-shot rotary mag.
Barrel: 18½" round tapered.
Weight: 5 lbs. **Length:** 37" over-all.
Stock: American walnut with p.g. and bbl. band.
Sights: Gold bead front, fully adj. folding leaf rear.
Features: Detachable rotary magazine fits flush into stock, cross-bolt safety, receiver tapped and grooved for scope blocks or tip-off mount.
Price: **$56.50**

RUGER 10/22 AUTO SPORTER
Same as 10/22 Carbine except: Sporter style Monte Carlo stock with straight buttplate, p.g. cap, fluted fore-end and sling swivels.
Price: **$64.50**

SAVAGE 60 AUTOLOADING RIFLE
Caliber: 22 LR, 15-shot tubular mag.
Barrel: 20" round tapered.
Weight: About 6 lbs. **Length:** 40½" over-all.
Stock: Walnut, Monte Carlo, checkered p.g. and semi-beavertail fore-end.
Sights: Gold bead ramp front, Step adj. open rear.
Features: White line buttplate, top tang safety, receiver grooved for tip-off mount.
Price: **$57.95**

U.S. RIMFIRE RIFLES—AUTOLOADING

SAVAGE 90 AUTOLOADING CARBINE
Same as the 60 rifle except: 10-shot tubular magazine (22 LR only), 16½" bbl., 37½" over-all. Gold bead blade front and folding leaf rear sights. Sling swivels installed on Monte Carlo stock, no checkering.
Price: **$54.95**

SAVAGE STEVENS 88 AUTOLOADING RIFLE
Same as the 66 rifle except: Checkered walnut finished stock. Blade front sight. Wgt. 5¾ lbs.
Price: **$49.95**

SEARS MODEL 3T AUTOLOADING RIFLE
Caliber: 22 S(21), L(17) or LR(15). Tubular Mag.
Barrel: 20½" round (16" twist).
Weight: 5 lbs. **Length:** 39" over-all.
Stock: Walnut finished hardwood, with p.g.
Sights: Blade front, step adj. open rear.
Features: Cross-bolt safety; burnished bolt handle, trigger and mag. cap; receiver grooved for tip-off scope mount.
Price: **$46.99**

SEARS TED WILLIAMS 3T AUTO
Same as 3T except: magazine cap, bolt handle and trigger are nickel plated; fluted walnut stock, checkered p.g. and fore-end, p.g. cap; white line buttplate spacer.
Price: **$75.00**

WEATHERBY MARK XXII AUTOLOADING RIFLE
Caliber: 22 LR only, 5- or 10-shot clip loaded.
Barrel: 24" round contoured.
Weight: 6 lbs. **Length:** 42½" over-all.
Stock: Walnut, Monte Carlo comb and cheekpiece, rosewood p.g. cap and fore-end tip. Skip-line checkering.
Sights: Gold bead rampfront, 3-leaf folding rear.
Features: Thumb operated side safety also acts as single shot selector. Receiver grooved for tip-off scope mount. Single pin release for quick takedown.
Price: **$119.50**
Extra 5-shot clip . . . .**$3.95**   Extra 10-shot clip **$4.50**

WESTERN FIELD 892 AUTO RIFLE
Caliber: 22LR only, 18-shot tubular mag.
Barrel: 24" round.
Weight: 6¾ lbs. **Length:** 44½" over-all.
Stock: Checkered walnut with p.g.
Sights: Gold bead front, U-notched open rear.
Features: Gold plated, grooved trigger; damascened bolt.
Price: **$59.95**

WESTERN FIELD 846 AUTO RIFLE
Caliber: 22 LR only, 15-shot tubular mag.
Barrel: 18½" round.
Weight: 5¼ lbs. **Length:** 38½" over-all.
Stock: Walnut finish p.g. stock and fore-end.
Sights: Gold-tone bead front, step adj. rear.
Features: Crossbolt safety.
Price: **$47.99**

WESTERN FIELD 850 AUTO RIFLE
Caliber: 22S, L, LR, 7-shot clip.
Barrel: 18½" round.
Weight: 5½ lbs. **Length:** 39" over-all.
Stock: Walnut finish with p.g.
Sights: Bead front, step adj. rear.
Features: Thumb operated safety; 3-way magazine.
Price: **$36.99**

U.S. RIMFIRE RIFLES—AUTOLOADING

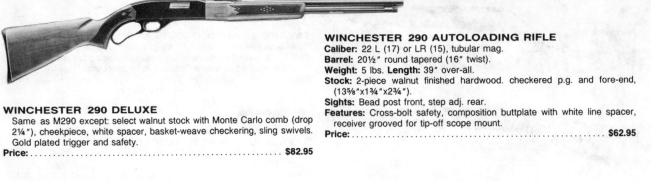

WINCHESTER 290 AUTOLOADING RIFLE
Caliber: 22 L (17) or LR (15), tubular mag.
Barrel: 20½″ round tapered (16″ twist).
Weight: 5 lbs. **Length:** 39″ over-all.
Stock: 2-piece walnut finished hardwood. checkered p.g. and fore-end, (13⅝″x1¾″x2¾″).
Sights: Bead post front, step adj. rear.
Features: Cross-bolt safety, composition buttplate with white line spacer, receiver grooved for tip-off scope mount.
Price: **$62.95**

WINCHESTER 290 DELUXE
Same as M290 except: select walnut stock with Monte Carlo comb (drop 2¼″), cheekpiece, white spacer, basket-weave checkering, sling swivels. Gold plated trigger and safety.
Price: **$82.95**

WINCHESTER 190 AUTO RIFLE
Same as M290 except: No checkering, pistol grip cap or buttplate spacer.
Price: **$52.95**

WINCHESTER 190 AUTO CARBINE
Same as 190 rifle except: Carbine has barrel band and sling swivels.
Price: **$54.95**

U.S. RIMFIRE RIFLES—BOLT ACTION

BROWNING T-BOLT T-1 REPEATING RIFLE
Caliber: 22 LR (S and L also, with single-shot adapter)
Barrel: 22″ round, straight taper.
Weight: 5½ lbs. **Length:** 39¼″ over-all
Stock: One-piece walnut with p.g. (13½″x1⁵/₁₆″x3″). Lacquer finish, no checkering.
Sights: Blade ramp front, aperture rear adj. for w. & e.
Features: 5-shot clip loading, straight-pull-back breech bolt, double extractors, side ejection. Available with left or right hand action.
Price: **$65.50**

BROWNING T-BOLT T-2 REPEATING RIFLE
Same as T-1 except: 24″ bbl.; stock of figured walnut with checkered p.g. and fore-end; wgt. 6 lbs.; 41¼″ over-all. Left or right hand action.
Price: **$88.50**

HARRINGTON & RICHARDSON 865 PLAINSMAN RIFLE
Caliber: 22 S, L or LR. 5-shot clip mag.
Barrel: 22″ round tapered.
Weight: 5 lbs. **Length:** 39″ over-all.
Stock: Walnut finished hardwood with Monte Carlo and p.g.
Sights: Blade front, step adj. open rear.
Features: Cocking indicator, sliding side safety, receiver grooved for tip-off scope mounts.
Price: **$44.95**
Price: M866 with Mannlicher stock **$49.95**

MARLIN 780 BOLT ACTION RIFLE
Caliber: 22 S, L, or LR; 7-shot clip magazine.
Barrel: 22″ Micro-Groove
Weight: 5½ lbs. **Length:** 41″
Stock: Monte Carlo American walnut with checkered p.g. White line spacer at buttplate.
Sights: Blade on band ramp front sight, semibuckhorn rear adj. for w. & e.
Features: Gold plated trigger, receiver anti-glare serrated and grooved for tip-off scope mount.
Price: **$48.95**

MARLIN 781 BOLT ACTION RIFLE
Same as the Marlin 780 except: tubular magazine holds 25 Shorts, 19 Longs or 17 Long Rifle cartridges. Weight 6 lbs. **$49.95**

MARLIN 782 BOLT ACTION RIFLE
Same as the Marlin 780 except: 22 Rimfire Magnum cal. only, weight about 6 lbs. Sling and swivels attached. **$53.95**

MARLIN 783 BOLT ACTION RIFLE
Same as Marlin 782 except: Tubular magazine holds 13 rounds of 22 Rimfire Magnum ammunition. **$54.95**

U.S. RIMFIRE RIFLES—BOLT ACTION

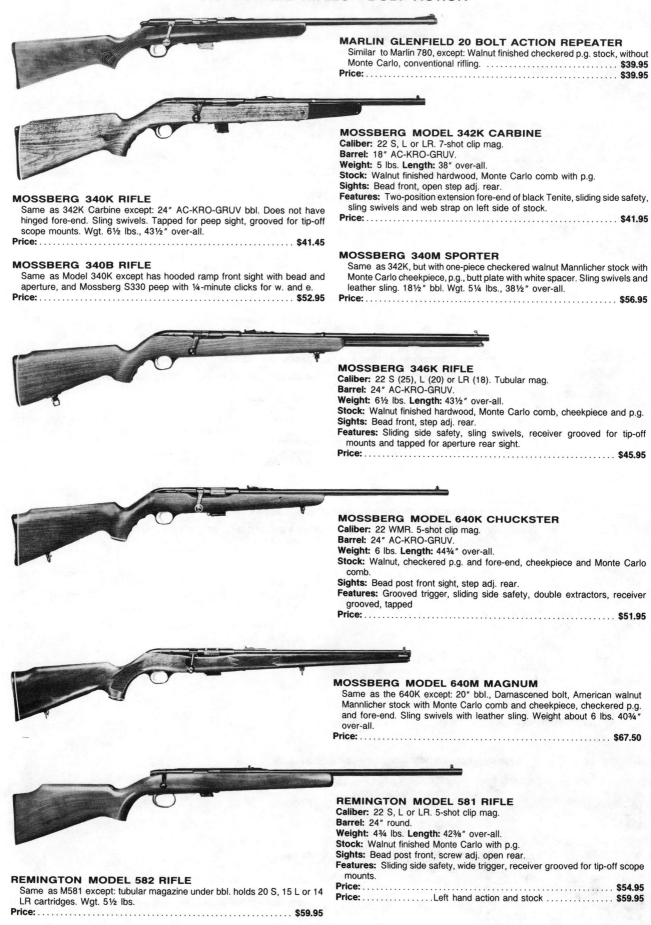

MARLIN GLENFIELD 20 BOLT ACTION REPEATER
Similar to Marlin 780, except: Walnut finished checkered p.g. stock, without Monte Carlo, conventional rifling. $39.95
Price: $39.95

MOSSBERG 340K RIFLE
Same as 342K Carbine except: 24" AC-KRO-GRUV bbl. Does not have hinged fore-end. Sling swivels. Tapped for peep sight, grooved for tip-off scope mounts. Wgt. 6½ lbs., 43½" over-all.
Price: $41.45

MOSSBERG 340B RIFLE
Same as Model 340K except has hooded ramp front sight with bead and aperture, and Mossberg S330 peep with ¼-minute clicks for w. and e.
Price: $52.95

MOSSBERG MODEL 342K CARBINE
Caliber: 22 S, L or LR. 7-shot clip mag.
Barrel: 18" AC-KRO-GRUV.
Weight: 5 lbs. **Length:** 38" over-all.
Stock: Walnut finished hardwood, Monte Carlo comb with p.g.
Sights: Bead front, open step adj. rear.
Features: Two-position extension fore-end of black Tenite, sliding side safety, sling swivels and web strap on left side of stock.
Price: $41.95

MOSSBERG 340M SPORTER
Same as 342K, but with one-piece checkered walnut Mannlicher stock with Monte Carlo cheekpiece, p.g., butt plate with white spacer. Sling swivels and leather sling. 18½" bbl. Wgt. 5¼ lbs., 38½" over-all.
Price: $56.95

MOSSBERG 346K RIFLE
Caliber: 22 S (25), L (20) or LR (18). Tubular mag.
Barrel: 24" AC-KRO-GRUV.
Weight: 6½ lbs. **Length:** 43½" over-all.
Stock: Walnut finished hardwood, Monte Carlo comb, cheekpiece and p.g.
Sights: Bead front, step adj. rear.
Features: Sliding side safety, sling swivels, receiver grooved for tip-off mounts and tapped for aperture rear sight.
Price: $45.95

MOSSBERG MODEL 640K CHUCKSTER
Caliber: 22 WMR. 5-shot clip mag.
Barrel: 24" AC-KRO-GRUV.
Weight: 6 lbs. **Length:** 44¾" over-all.
Stock: Walnut, checkered p.g. and fore-end, cheekpiece and Monte Carlo comb.
Sights: Bead post front sight, step adj. rear.
Features: Grooved trigger, sliding side safety, double extractors, receiver grooved, tapped
Price: $51.95

MOSSBERG MODEL 640M MAGNUM
Same as the 640K except: 20" bbl., Damascened bolt, American walnut Mannlicher stock with Monte Carlo comb and cheekpiece, checkered p.g. and fore-end. Sling swivels with leather sling. Weight about 6 lbs. 40¾" over-all.
Price: $67.50

REMINGTON MODEL 581 RIFLE
Caliber: 22 S, L or LR. 5-shot clip mag.
Barrel: 24" round.
Weight: 4¾ lbs. **Length:** 42⅜" over-all.
Stock: Walnut finished Monte Carlo with p.g.
Sights: Bead post front, screw adj. open rear.
Features: Sliding side safety, wide trigger, receiver grooved for tip-off scope mounts.
Price: $54.95
Price: ....Left hand action and stock $59.95

REMINGTON MODEL 582 RIFLE
Same as M581 except: tubular magazine under bbl. holds 20 S, 15 L or 14 LR cartridges. Wgt. 5½ lbs.
Price: $59.95

REMINGTON MODEL 592 RIFLE
Same as the M591 except: tubular magazine under bbl. holds ten 5mm Remington RFM cartridges.
Price: **$74.95**

REMINGTON MODEL 591 RIFLE
Caliber: 5mm Remington RFM. 4-shot clip mag.
Barrel: 24" round.
Weight: 5 lbs. **Length:** 42⅜" over-all.
Stock: Walnut finished hardwood, Monte Carlo comb, black p.g. cap and buttplate.
Sights: Bead post front, screw adj. open rear.
Features: Sliding thumb safety, detachable sights, receiver grooved for tip-off scope mounts.
Price: **$69.95**

SAVAGE/ANSCHUTZ 164 BOLT ACTION RIFLE
Caliber: 22 LR. 5-shot clip mag.
Barrel: 24" round tapered.
Weight: 6 lbs. **Length:** 40¾" over-all
Stock: Walnut, hand checkered p.g. and fore-end, Monte Carlo comb and cheekpiece, schnabel fore-end.
Sights: Hooded ramp gold bead front, folding-leaf rear.
Features: Fully adj. single stage trigger, sliding side safety, receiver grooved for tip-off mount.
Price: **$89.50**
Price: Model 164M in 22 WRM (4-shot) **$105.50**

SAVAGE/ANSCHUTZ MODEL 54 SPORTER
Caliber: 22 LR. 5-shot clip mag.
Barrel: 23" round tapered.
Weight: 6¾ lbs. **Length:** 42" over-all.
Stock: French walnut, checkered p.g. and fore-end. Monte Carlo roll-over comb, schnabel fore-end tip.
Sights: Hooded ramp gold bead front, folding-leaf rear.
Features: Adj. single stage trigger, wing safety, receiver grooved for tip-off mount, tapped for scope blocks.
Price: **$157.50**

SAVAGE MODEL 65 RIFLE
Caliber: 22 S, L or LR. 5-shot clip mag.
Barrel: 20" lightweight, free floating.
Weight: 5 lbs. **Length:** 39" over-all.
Stock: Walnut, Monte Carlo comb. checkered p.g. and fore-end.
Sights: Gold bead ramp front, step adj. open rear.
Features: Sliding side safety, double extractors, receiver grooved for tip-off scope mount.
Price: **$46.95**
Price: Model 65M in 22 WMR (5-shot) **$49.95**

SEARS MODEL 2 BOLT ACTION RIFLE
Caliber: 22 S, L or LR. 6-shot clip mag.
Barrel: 20¾" round tapered.
Weight: 5 lbs. **Length:** 40" over-all.
Stock: Walnut finished hardwood, Monte Carlo comb, p.g.
Sights: Gold bead ramp front, step adj. open rear
Features: Sliding side safety, sling swivels attached, receiver grooved for tip-off scope mount.
Price: **$36.99**
Price: Model 2M (22 WMR only) **$40.97**
Price: Model 27 (tubular mag. 19S, 15L or 13LR) **$39.99**

SAVAGE/STEVENS MODEL 34 RIFLE
Same as the Model 65 except: walnut finished hard wood stock, bead post front sight.
Price: **$39.95**
Price: .... Model 34M in 22 WMR (5-shot) **$44.95**

SAVAGE/STEVENS MODEL 46 RIFLE
Same as the Model 34 except: tubular magazine holds 22 S, 17 L or 15 LR cartridges. Available in 22 rimfire only (not magnum).
Price: **$44.95**

U.S. RIMFIRE RIFLES—BOLT ACTION

WESTERN FIELD 830 BOLT ACTION RIFLE
Caliber: 22 S, L, LR, 7-shot clip mag.
Barrel: 24″ round.
Weight: 6 lbs. **Length:** 44¾″ over-all.
Stock: Walnut finish.
Sights: Bead front, step adj. rear.
Price: **$38.99**

WESTERN FIELD 822 BOLT ACTION RIFLE
Same as MM830 except chambered for 22 WMR Magnum; 6-shot clip mag.;
sling swivels; cheekpiece stock.
Price: **$49.95**

WINCHESTER MODEL 141 BOLT ACTION RIFLE
Caliber: 22 S(15), L(15) or LR(13). Tubular mag.
Barrel: 20¾″ round tapered.
Weight: 5 lbs. **Length:** 40″ over-all.
Stock: Walnut finished hardwood with p.g. (13½″ x 1½″ x 2½″).
Sights: Bead ramp front, step adj. open rear.
Features: Twin extractors, cocking indicator, tubular magazine in buttstock.
Price: **$48.95**

WESTERN FIELD 842 BOLT ACTION RIFLE
Caliber: 22 S (25), L (20), LR (18), tubular mag.
Barrel: 24″ round.
Weight: 6¼ lbs. **Length:** 43½″ over-all.
Stock: Walnut Monte Carlo comb.
Sights: Bead front, step adj. rear.
Features: Thumb safety; grooved for tip-off mount.
Price: **$43.99**

WINCHESTER 320 BOLT ACTION REPEATER
Caliber: 22 Short, Long or Long Rifle (5-shot).
Barrel: 22″ round tapered.
Weight: 5⅝ lbs. **Length:** 39½″ over-all.
Stock: Walnut, Monte Carlo, checkered p.g. and fore-end. 13½″ pull.
Sights: Bead on ramp front, step adj. rear.
Features: Wide serrated trigger, positive safety, matted receiver is tapped for scope and micrometer sights. Sling swivels installed.
Price: **$57.50**
Extra 5-shot clip **$2.75**

WINCHESTER 325 BOLT ACTION REPEATER
Same as the Winchester Model 320 except; chambered for the 22 WMR cartridge only.
Price: **$62.50**

U.S. RIMFIRE RIFLES—LEVER ACTION

BROWNING BL-22 LEVER ACTION RIFLE
Caliber: 22 S(22), L(17) or LR(15). Tubular mag.
Barrel: 20″ round tapered.
Weight: 5 lbs. **Length:** 36¾″ over-all.
Stock: Walnut, 2-piece straight grip western style.
Sights: Bead post front, folding-leaf rear.
Features: ½-cock safety, receiver grooved for tip-off scope mounts.
Price: Grade I **$74.50**
Price: Grade II, engraved receiver, checkered grip and fore-end . . . **$94.50**
Weight: 5½ lbs. **Length:** 37½″ over-all.

MARLIN 39D LEVER ACTION CARBINE
Caliber: 22 S (21), L (16) or LR (15), tubular magazine.
Barrel: 20½″ Micro-Groove
Weight: 5¾ lbs. **Length:** 36½″
Stock: American walnut with white line spacers at p.g. cap and buttplate.
Sights: Blade front, semi-buckhorn rear adj. for w. & e.
Features: Receiver tapped for aperture sights and scope mount (adapter base incl.) offset hammer spur.
Price: **$99.95**

MARLIN 39 ARTICLE II LEVER ACTION RIFLE
Caliber: 22 S (26), L (21) or LR (19); tubular magazine.
Barrel: 24″ Micro-Groove, full-length tapered octagon.
Weight: 6¾ lbs. **Length:** 40″
Stock: American walnut with full p.g.,
Sights: Bead front, semi-buckhorn rear adj. for w. & e.
Features: Made in limited numbers to commemorate 100th NRA anniversary. Medallion fixed to right side of action, solid brass buttplate and fore-end cap.
Price: **$135.00**

MARLIN 39 ARTICLE II LEVER ACTION CARBINE
Same as the Article II rifle except: straight grip stock, squared finger lever, 20″ bbl., weight 6 lbs. 36″ over-all, mag. capacity 21 Shorts, 16 Longs or 15 Long Rifle cartridges. **$135.00**

U.S. RIMFIRE RIFLES—LEVER ACTION

MOSSBERG 402 PALOMINO CARBINE
Caliber: 22 S(18), L(15) or LR(13). Tubular mag.
Barrel: 20" round.
Weight: 4¾ lbs. **Length:** 36½" over-all.
Stock: Walnut, Monte Carlo, checkered beavertail fore-end and p.g.
Sights: Bead post front, step adj. rear.
Features: Gold plated grooved trigger, double extractors, cross-bolt safety, sling swivels, receiver grooved for tip-off scope mount.
Price: $64.95

NOBLE MODEL 875 LEVER ACTION RIFLE
Caliber: 22 S(21), L(17) or LR(15). Tubular mag.
Barrel: 24" round tapered.
Weight: 5½ lbs. **Length:** 42" over-all.
Stock: One-piece semi-p.g. walnut finished hardwood (13½" x 1¾" x 2¾").
Sights: Patridge type ramp front, step adj. open rear.
Features: Sliding side safety, hard rubber buttplate, receiver grooved for tip-off scope mount.
Price: $54.85

SEARS MODEL 5 LEVER ACTION RIFLE
Caliber: 22 S(21), L(17) or LR(15). Tubular Mag.
Barrel: 20½" round tapered (16" twist).
Weight: 5 lbs. **Length:** 39" over-all.
Stock: Walnut finished hardwood with p.g.
Sights: Tapered post ramp front, step adj. open rear.
Features: Cross-bolt safety, nickel plated trigger, receiver grooved for tip-off scope mount.
Price: $55.99

WESTERN FIELD 865 LEVER ACTION CARBINE
Caliber: 22 S (20), L (15), LR (13), tubular mag.
Barrel: 20" round tapered.
Weight: 7 lbs. **Length:** 36½" over-all.
Stock: Walnut finish pistol grip stock with Monte Carlo comb, beavertail fore-end.
Sights: Bead front, step adj. front.
Price: $58.95

WINCHESTER MODEL 250 LEVER ACTION RIFLE
Caliber: 22 S(21), L(17) or LR(15). Tubular mag.
Barrel: 20½" round (16" twist).
Weight: 5 lbs. **Length:** 39" over-all.
Stock: Two-piece walnut finished hardwood, checkered p.g. and fore-end (13⅝" x 1¾" x 2¾").
Sights: Bead post ramp front, step adj. open rear.
Features: Cross-bolt safety, composition buttplate with white line spacer, receiver grooved for tip-off scope mount.
Price: $64.95

WINCHESTER MODEL 250 DELUXE
Same as the M250 except: select walnut stock with Monte Carlo comb (2¼" drop), cheekpiece, basketweave checkering, sling swivels, gold plated trigger and safety.
Price: $84.95

WINCHESTER 150 LEVER ACTION CARBINE
Same as M250 except straight stock (no p.g.), no checkering or spacers. With barrel band and swivels.
Price: $57.95

U.S. RIMFIRE RIFLES—SLIDE ACTION

HIGH STANDARD SPORT KING PUMP RIFLE
Caliber: 22 S(24), L(19) or LR(17). Tubular mag.
Barrel: 24" round tapered.
Weight: 5½ lbs. **Length:** 41¾" over-all.
Stock: Walnut finished hardwood, Monte Carlo comb, p.g. and grooved semi-beavertail fore-end.
Sights: Bead post front, step adj. open rear.
Features: Side loading port, steel-to-steel breech lock-up, cross-bolt safety, receiver grooved for tip-off scope mount.
Price: $59.95

NOBLE MODEL 835 PUMP RIFLE
Caliber: 22 S(21), L(17) or LR(15). Tubular mag.
Barrel: 24" round tapered.
Weight: 5½ lbs. **Length:** 42" over-all.
Stock: Walnut finished hardwood, semi-p.g. and grooved fore-end. (13½" x 1¾" x 2¾").
Sights: Bead ramp front, step adj. open rear.
Features: Sliding side safety, hard rubber buttplate, receiver grooved for tip-off scope mount.
Price: $52.10

REMINGTON 572 FIELDMASTER PUMP RIFLE
Caliber: 22 S(20), L(17) or LR(14). Tubular mag.
Barrel: 24" round tapered.
Weight: 5½ lbs. **Length:** 42" over-all.
Stock: Genuine walnut with p.g. and grooved slide handle.
Sights: Bead post front, step adj. open rear.
Features: Cross-bolt safety, removing inner mag. tube converts rifle to single shot, receiver grooved for tip-off scope mount.
Price: **$69.95**

REMINGTON MODEL 572 SB
Similar to the 572, but has smoothbore bbl. choked for 22 LR shot cartridges.
Sling and swivels installed. **$7.50**
Price: **$79.95**

REMINGTON MODEL 572 BDL DELUXE
Same as the 572 except: p.g. cap, RKW finish, checkered grip and fore-end, ramp front and fully adj. rear sights.
Price: **$79.95**

WINCHESTER MODEL 270 PUMP RIFLE
Caliber: 22 S(21), L(17) or LR(15). Tubular mag.
Barrel: 20½" round (16" twist).
Weight: 5 lbs. **Length:** 39" over-all.
Stock: Walnut finished hardwood, checkered p.g. and fore-end (13⅝" x 1¾" x 2¾").
Sights: Square post ramp front, adj. open rear.
Features: Cross-bolt safety, composition buttplate with white line spacer, receiver grooved for tip-off scope mount.
Price: **$66.95**

WINCHESTER 270 DELUXE PUMP RIFLE
Same as M270 except: Select walnut stock with Monte Carlo comb (drop 2¼"), cheekpiece, white spacer, basketweave checkering, swivels; gold plated trigger and safety.
Price: **$86.95**

U.S. RIMFIRE RIFLES—SINGLE SHOT

CHALLANGER FRONTIERSMAN RIFLE
Caliber: 22 S. L or LR. Single-shot.
Barrel: 18" round.
Weight: 5½ lbs. **Length:** 34" over-all.
Stock: Two-piece walnut finished hardwood, straight grip, fore-end with bbl. band.
Sights: Blade front, step adj. open rear.
Features: Martini-type lever action, auto ejector, ¼-cock dry firing capability.
Price: **$29.95**
Price: Chambered for 22 WRM only **$34.95**
Price: Deluxe, gold plated hammer and trigger **$34.95**
Price: Deluxe 22 WRM **$39.95**

GARCIA BRONCO 22 RIFLE
Caliber: 22 S, L or LR. Single-shot.
Barrel: 15" round.
Weight: 3 lbs. **Length:** 32" over-all.
Stock: Skeletonized crackle finished alloy casting.
Sights: Protected blade front, adj. rear.
Features: Cross-bolt safety, swing-out chamber, ultra lightweight for easy portability.
Price: **$19.95**
Price: Chambered for 22 WRM only **$21.50**

HARRINGTON & RICHARDSON MODEL 750 PIONEER
Caliber: 22 S, L or LR. Single-shot.
Barrel: 22" round tapered.
Weight: 5 lbs. **Length:** 39" over-all.
Stock: Walnut finished hardwood with Monte Carlo comb and p.g.
Sights: Blade front, step adj. open rear.
Features: Double extractors, feed platform, cocking indicator. sliding side safety, receiver grooved for tip-off scope mount, tapped for aperture sight.
Price: **$33.95**
Price: M751 with Mannlicher stock **$38.95**

ITHACA MODEL 49 SADDLEGUN
Caliber: 22 S, L or LR. Single-shot.
Barrel: 18" round.
Weight: About 5½ lbs. **Length:** 34½" over-all
Stock: Two-piece walnut, checkered straight grip, fore-end has bbl. band.
Sights: Bead post front, step adj. open rear.
Features: Rebounding hammer safety, Martini-type lever action, rifle can be ordered with shorter (youth) stock at no extra cost.
Price: **$29.95**
Price: Chambered for 22 WRM only **$37.95**

ITHACA MODEL 49 DELUXE
Same as the M49 except: figured walnut stock, better finish, gold plated trigger and hammer, Sling and swivels installed.
Price: **$39.95**
Price: Presentation Model (engraved) **$150.00**

MARLIN 101 SINGLE SHOT RIFLE
Caliber: 22 S, L or LR; Single shot.
Barrel: 22" Micro-Groove
Weight: 4½ lbs. **Length:** 40"
Stock: Monte Carlo American walnut with p.g. and white line spacer at butt-plate.
Sights: Blade band ramp front, semi-buckhorn rear adj. for w. & e.
Features: Gold plated trigger, T-shaped cocking knob, non-jamming feed throat, receiver grooved for tip-off scope mount.
Price: **$34.95**

MARLIN GLENFIELD MODEL 10 RIFLE
Same as the Marlin 101 except: checkered walnut finished hardwood stock.
Price: **$27.95**

MOSSBERG MODEL 320B RIFLE
Caliber: 22 S, L or LR. Single-shot.
Barrel: 24" round tapered.
Weight: About 6½ lbs. **Length:** 43½" over-all.
Stock: Walnut finished hardwood, Monte Carlo comb, cheekpiece and p.g.
Sights: Hooded ramp front, adj. aperture rear.
Features: Drop-in loading platform, automatic sliding side safety, sling swivels attached.
Price: **$42.50**

NOBLE MODEL 822 RIFLE
Caliber: 22 S, L or LR. Single-shot.
Barrel: 22" round tapered.
Weight: About 5 lbs. **Length:** 38" over-all.
Stock: Walnut finished hardwood, p.g. and hard rubber buttplate (13¾" x 1½" x 2⅝").
Sights: Patridge-type ramp front, step adj. open rear.
Features: Bolt action, independent hand cocking, one-piece steel receiver and barrel.
Price: **$24.95**

REMINGTON MODEL 580 SINGLE SHOT RIFLE
Caliber: 22 S, L or LR. Single-shot.
Barrel: 24" round tapered.
Weight: 4¾ lbs. **Length:** 42⅜" over-all.
Stock: Walnut finished hardwood, Monte Carlo comb and p.g., black composition buttplate.
Sights: Bead post front, screw-lock adj. rear.
Features: Single screw take-down, integral loading platform, sliding side safety, receiver grooved for tip-off mount, can be had with 1" shorter (youth) stock.
Price: **$44.95**
Price: M580 SB (smooth bore) **$49.95**

SAVAGE MODEL 63K SINGLE SHOT RIFLE
Caliber: 22 S, L or LR. Single-shot.
Barrel: 18″ round tapered.
Weight; 4 lbs. **Length:** 36″ over-all.
Stock: Walnut finished hardwood, checkered p.g. and fore-end, Monte Carlo comb.
Sights: Hooded bead ramp front, step adj. open rear.
Features: Cocks on opening, automatic safety, key locks trigger to prevent unauthorized use.
Price: **$33.95**
Price: 63 KM (22 WMR) **$36.95**

SAVAGE STEVENS MODEL 73 SINGLE SHOT RIFLE
Caliber: 22 S, L or LR. Single-shot.
Barrel: 20″ round tapered.
Weight: 4¾ lbs. **Length:** 38½″ over-all.
Stock: Walnut finished hardwood, checkered p.g. and fore-end, Monte Carlo comb.
Sights: Bead post front, step adj. open rear.
Features: Cocks on opening, automatic safety, key locks trigger against unauthorized use, may be had with 12″ pull stock (youth model) at same cost.
Price: **$26.95**

SAVAGE STEVENS FAVORITE RIFLE
Caliber: 22 S, L or LR. Single-shot.
Barrel: 22″ full octagon.
Weight: 4½ lbs. **Length:** 37″ over-all.
Stock: two-piece, straight grip American walnut with schnabel fore-end (13¼″ x 1½″ x 2½″).
Sights: Brass blade front, step adj. open rear.
Features: Color case hardened receiver, gold plated hammer and trigger, solid brass crescent buttplate and medallion inlaid in buttstock. Available only during 1971.
Price: **$75.00**

WESTERN FIELD 815 SINGLE SHOT RIFLE
Caliber: 22
Barrel: 24″ round tapered, 8-groove rifling.
Weight: 7¾ lbs. **Length:** 43½″ over-all.
Stock: Walnut finish with p.g. and Monte Carlo comb.
Sights: Bead front, step adj. rear.
Features: Automatic safety; receiver grooved for mount.
Price: **$26.99**

SEARS MODEL 1 SINGLE SHOT RIFLE
Caliber: 22 S, L or LR.
Barrel: 20¾″ round tapered.
Weight: 5 lbs. **Length:** 40″ over-all.
Stock: Walnut finished birch with p.g.
Sights: Bead post front, step adj. open rear.
Features: Automatic safety, cocking indicator, self-cocking bolt action.
Price: **$24.99**

WINCHESTER MODEL 121 RIFLE
Caliber: 22 S, L or LR. Single-shot.
Barrel: 20¾″ round tapered (16″ twist).
Weight: 5 lbs. **Length:** 40″ over-all.
Stock: Walnut finished hardwood, Monte Carlo comb, p.g. (13½″ x 1½″ x 2½″).
Sights: Bead post front, step adj. open rear.
Features: Twin extractors, sliding side safety, red cocking indicator, receiver grooved for tip-off mount.
Price: **$26.95**

WINCHESTER MODEL 310 RIFLE
Caliber: 22 S, L or LR. Single-shot.
Barrel: 22″ round tapered (16″ twist).
Weight: 5⅝ lbs. **Length:** 39½″ over-all.
Stock: Walnut, fluted Monte Carlo comb, checkered p.g. and fore-end (13½″ x 1⅝″ x 2⁷⁄₁₆″).
Sights: Bead post ramp front, step adj. open rear.
Features: Twin extractors, sliding side safety, wide serrated trigger, receiver grooved for tip-off scope mounts tapped for aperture rear sight.
Price: **$44.95**

ANSCHUTZ 1411 MATCH 54 RIFLE

Caliber: 22 LR. Single shot.
Barrel: 27½ round ($^{15}/_{16}$" dia.)
Weight: 11 lbs. **Length:** 46" over-all.
Stock: French walnut, American prone style with Monte Carlo, cast-off cheekpiece, checkered p.g., beavertail fore-end with swivel rail and adj. swivel, adj. rubber buttplate.
Sights: None. Receiver grooved for Anshutz sights (extra). Scope blocks.
Features: Single stage adj. trigger, wing safety, short firing pin travel. Available from Savage Arms.
Price: **$179.50**
Price: Left hand stocked rifle, no sights **192.00**

ANSCHUTZ 1413 SUPER MATCH RIFLE

Same as the model 1411 except: International type stock with cheekpiece, adj. aluminum hook buttplate, weight 15½ lbs., 50" over-all. Available from Savage Arms.
Price **$350.00**
Price: Left hand stocked rifle, no sights **365.00**

ANSCHUTZ 1407 MATCH 54 RIFLE

Same as the model 1411 except: 26" bbl. (⅞" dia.), weight 10 lbs., 44½" over-all to conform to ISU requirements and also suitable for NRA matches. Available from Savage Arms.
Price: **$179.50**
Price: Left hand stocked rifle, no sights **192.00**

SAVAGE/ANSCHUTZ 64 MATCH RIFLE

Caliber: 22 LR only. Single shot.
Barrel: 26" round ($^{11}/_{16}$" dia.)
Weight: 7¼ lbs. **Length:** 44" over-all.
Stock: Walnut finished hardwood, cheekpiece, checkered p.g., beavertail fore-end, adj. buttplate.
Sights: None (extra). Scope blocks.
Features: Sliding side safety, adj. single stage trigger, receiver grooved for Anschutz sights.
Price: . . . . **$79.95** 64L (Left hand) **$89.95**
As above but with Anschutz 6723 Match Sight Set.
Price: Model 64S (Right hand) . **$105.00** 64SL (Left hand) **$115.00**

MOSSBERG MODEL 144LS TARGET RIFLE

Caliber: 22 LR only. 7-shot clip.
Barrel: 26" round ($^{15}/_{16}$" dia.)
Weight: About 8 lbs. **Length:** 43" over-all.
Stock: Walnut with high thick comb, cheekpiece, p.g., beavertail fore-end, adj. handstop and sling swivels.
Sights: Lyman 17A globe front, micrometer adj. rear.
Features: Wide grooved trigger adj. for wgt. of pull, thumb safety, receiver grooved for scope mounting.
Price: **$69.95**

REMINGTON INTERNATIONAL FREE RIFLE

Caliber: 222 Rem., 222 Rem. Mag., 223 Rem., 7.62 NATO (308 Win.), 30-06 only. Single shot.
Barrel: 27¼" heavy.
Weight: 15 lbs. **Length:** 47"
Stock: Semi-finished laminated walnut. Adj. hook buttplate, palm rest, and frontsling swivel.
Sights: None. Scope blocks installed.
Features: Action is 40-XB type. 2 oz. trigger.
Price: Special order **$395.00**

REMINGTON 40-XB RANGEMASTER TARGET Rimfire
Caliber: 22 LR only. Single shot.
Barrel: 28″ standard or heavy.
Weight: 10 lbs. (std.), 11¼ lbs. (hvy.). **Length:** 47″ over-all.
Stock: American walnut, p.g. guide rail with adj. swivel block and handstop, beavertail fore-end.
Sights: None. Receiver tapped for sights and scope blocks. (Redfield Olympic sight set optional at $35 extra.)
Features: Positive thumb safety, adj. trigger, loading platform, double extractors.
Price: $199.95

REMINGTON 40-XB RANGEMASTER TARGET Centerfire
Caliber: 222 Rem., 222 Rem. Mag., 223 Rem., 7.62 NATO (308 Win.), 30-06 only. Single shot.
Barrel: 27¼″ round (Stand. dia.-¾″, Hvy. dia.-⅞″)
Weight: SH2-9¼ lbs., Hvy.—11¼ **Length:** 47″
Stock: American walnut with high comb and beavertail fore-end stop. Rubber non-slip buttplate.
Sights: None. Scope blocks installed.
Features: Adjustable trigger pull. Receiver drilled and tapped for sights.
Price: Standard single-shot, ordance steel $249.95
Standard ss., stainless steel 269.95
Repeating model 269.95
Extra for 2 oz. trigger 20.00

REMINGTON 540X MATCH TARGET RIFLE
Caliber: 22 LR. Single shot.
Barrel: 26″ heavy.
Weight: 8 lbs. **Length:** 43½″ to 47″
Stock: Target style with Monte Carlo, cheekpiece and thumbrest groove. Adj. buttplate and full length guide rail.
Sights: Redfield #75 rear sight with ¼ min. clicks. #63 Globe front sight with 7 inserts. Optional.
Features: Adjustable trigger pull. Rear locking bolt with 6 lugs, double extractors.
Price: Without sights ...... **$99.95.** With sights **$119.95**
For sling with front swivel block assembly installed add **$6.95.**

WINCHESTER 52D BARRELED ACTIONS
No stock or sights. Receiver and bbl. drilled and tapped for metallic sights or scope blocks **$134.95**

WINCHESTER 52D BOLT ACTION TARGET RIFLE
Caliber: 22 LR only. Single shot.
Barrel: 28″, standard or heavy weight.
Weight: 9¾ lbs. Std. 11 lbs. Hvy. **Length:** 46″
Stock: Marksman stock of choice walnut with full length accessory channel and adj. bedding device and non-slip butt pad.
Sights: None. Barrel tapped for front sight bases.
Features: Adjustable trigger.
Price: **$172.95**

WINCHESTER 70 INT'L ARMY MATCH RIFLE
Caliber: 308 (7.62mm NATO) 5-shot.
Barrel: 24″ heavy-contour.
Weight: 11 lbs. **Length:** 43¼″ over-all.
Stock: Oil finished walnut, (12″ x 1¼″ x 1¼″) meets ISU requirements.
Sights: None. Receiver tapped for M70 sights (available at extra cost).
Features: Fore-end rail takes most std. accessories, vertically adj. buttplate, externally adj. trigger, glass bedded action.
Price: **$399.95**

WINCHESTER 52 INTERNATIONAL MATCH RIFLE
Caliber: 22 LR. Single shot.
Barrel: 28″ heavy bbl.
Weight: 13½ lbs. **Length:** 44½″
Stock: Laminated International-style, aluminum fore-end assembly, adj. palm rest.
Sights: Receiver tapped for sights and scope bases; scope blocks are included.
Features: Non-drag trigger. Lead-lapped barrel with Winchester muzzle counterbore.
Price: **$360.00**
With Kenyon trigger 395.00
With ISU trigger 400.00

Browning Auto-5 Light 12, 20 and Sweet 16
Same as Std. Auto-5 except: 26″ bbls. (Skeet boring in 12 & 20 ga., Cyl., Imp. Cyl., Mod. in 16 and 20 ga.); 28″ bbls. (Skeet in 12 ga., Full in 16 ga., Mod., Full); 30″ (Full in 12 ga). Gold plated trigger. Wgt. 12 ga. 7¼ lbs., 16 ga. 6¾ lbs., 20 ga. 6⅜ lbs. **$204.50**
Price: With vent. rib. Wgt. 12 ga. 7½ lbs., 16 ga. 6⅞ lbs., 20 ga. 6½ lbs. **$219.50**

Browning Auto-5 Magnum 12
Same as Std. Auto-5 except: chambered for 3″ magnum shells (also handles 2¾″ magnum and 2¾″ HV loads). 28″ Mod., Full; 30″ and 32″ (Full) bbls. 14″x1⅝″x2½″ stock. Recoil pad. Wgt. 8¾ lbs.
Price: .... **$207.50**   With vent. rib. Wgt. 9 lbs. **$222.50**

BROWNING AUTO-5 Standard
Gauge: 12 only (5-shot; 3-shot plug furnished). 2¾″ chambers.
Action: Recoil operated autoloader; takedown; extra bbls. interchange without factory fitting; mag. cut-off; cross-bolt safety (left-hand available).
Barrel: 26″ (Cyl., Imp. Cyl.); 28″ (Mod., Full); 30″, 32″. (Full). Matted top, medium bead sight.
Stock: 14¼″x1⅝″x2½″. French walnut, hand checkered half-pistol grip and fore-end.
Weight: 7¾ to 8¼ lbs., depending on barrel.
Features: Receiver hand engraved with scroll designs and border; double extractors; bbl. and guide ring forged together.
Price: .... **$194.50**   With vent. rib **$209.50**

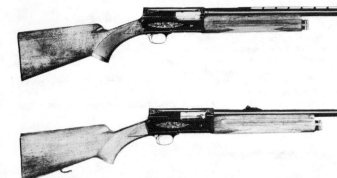

Browning Auto-5 Magnum 20
Same as Magnum 12 except barrels 28″ Full or Mod., or 26″ Full, Mod. or Imp. Cyl. 7 lbs. **$207.50**
With ventilated rib, 7½ lbs. **222.50**

Browning Auto-5 Standard Trap
Same as the Auto-5 Standard except: Stock(14⅜″x1⅜″x1¾″), 30″ vent. rib bbl. (Full). Wgt. 8¼ lbs. **$209.50**

Browning Auto-5 Light Trap
Same as Standard Trap except: Wgt. 7¾ lbs. **$219.50**

Browning Auto-5 Light Skeet
Same as Light Standard except: 12 and 20 ga. only, 26″ or 28″ bbl. (Skeet). Wgt. 6¼-7¼ lbs. **$204.50**
With vent. rib. Wgt. 6⅜-7½ lbs. **219.50**

Browning Auto-5 Buck Special
Same as Std. A-5 except: 24″ bbl. choked for slugs, gold bead front sight on contoured ramp, rear sight adj. for w.&e. Wgt. (12 ga.) 7⅝ lbs.
Price: **$207.50**

BROWNING AUTO-5 Light 12, 16, 20, or 12 Buck Special
Same as Std. Buck Special except: with gold trigger and of less weight. Wgt. 12 ga., 7 lbs.; 16 ga., 6⅜ lbs.; 20 ga., 6 lbs. 2 oz.; 3″ Magnum 12, 8¼ lbs.
Price: **$217.50**
All Buck Specials are available with carrying sling, detachable swivels and swivel attachments for $7.00 extra.

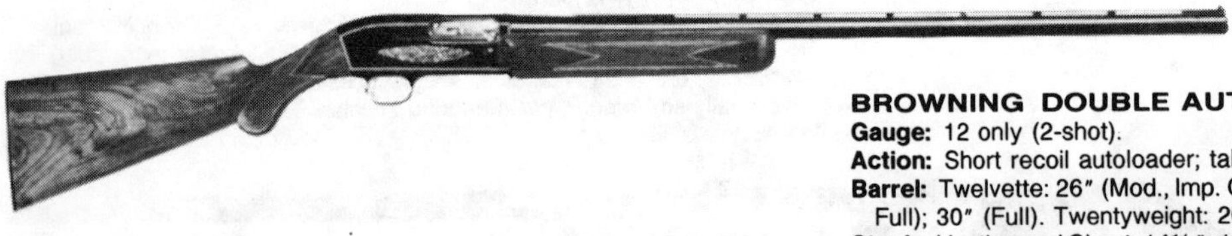

BROWNING DOUBLE AUTOMATIC
Gauge: 12 only (2-shot).
Action: Short recoil autoloader; takedown. Trigger guard safety.
Barrel: Twelvette: 26″ (Mod., Imp. Cyl., Cyl., or Skeet); 28″ (Mod., Skeet and Full); 30″ (Full). Twentyweight: 26½″ (all chokes).
Stock: Hunting and Skeet, 14¼″x1⅝″x2½″. Trap, 14⅜″x1⅜″x1¾″. French walnut, hand checkered, full p.g.
Weight: Twelvette, 6⅞ lbs.; Twentyweight, 6 lbs.
Features: Soft recoil; visible side loading; shoots all 2¾″ loads without adjustment; hand engraved receiver, black and gold finish; crisp, gold plated trigger. Safety in rear of trigger guard, convenient to either hand. Low, ¼″ wide vent. rib optional.
Price: Twelvette, matted bbl. .. **$239.50**   Vent. rib bbl. **$254.50**
Price: Twentyweight, matted bbl. **254.50**   Vent. rib bbl. **269.50**
Price: Extra Twentyweight bbls., matted rib **88.50**
Vent. rib **103.50**
Price: Extra Twelvette bbls., matted bbl. **78.50**
Vent. rib **93.50**
Price: Twelvette Trap with 30″ vent. rib bbl. **254.50**
Price: Twelvette Skeet, matted bbl. **239.50**
Vent. rib bbl. **254.50**
Price: Twentyweight Skeet, matted bbl. **254.50**
Vent. rib bbl. **269.50**

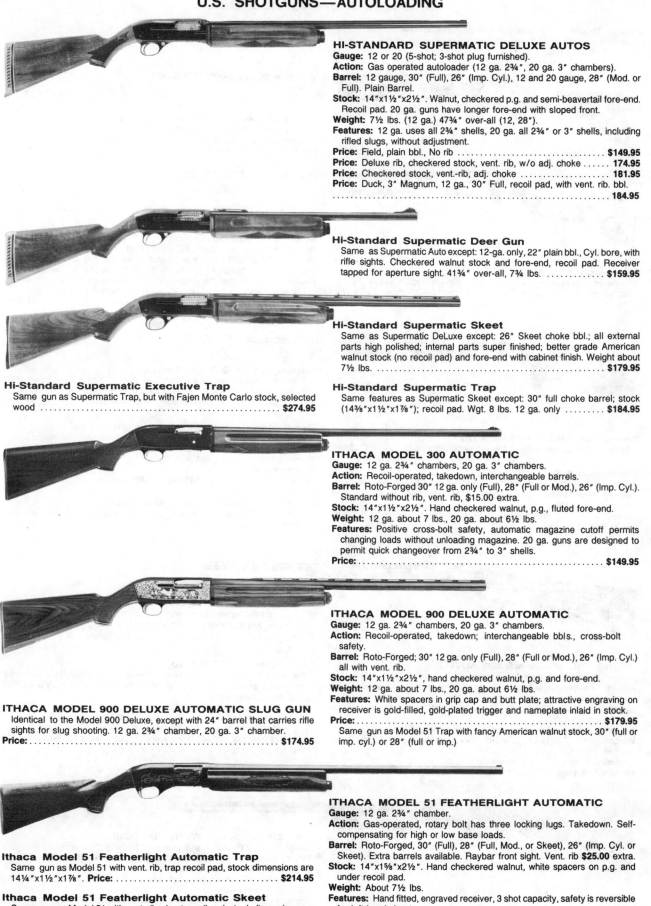

HI-STANDARD SUPERMATIC DELUXE AUTOS
Gauge: 12 or 20 (5-shot; 3-shot plug furnished).
Action: Gas operated autoloader (12 ga. 2¾", 20 ga. 3" chambers).
Barrel: 12 gauge, 30" (Full), 26" (Imp. Cyl.), 12 and 20 gauge, 28" (Mod. or Full). Plain Barrel.
Stock: 14"x1½"x2½". Walnut, checkered p.g. and semi-beavertail fore-end. Recoil pad. 20 ga. guns have longer fore-end with sloped front.
Weight: 7½ lbs. (12 ga.) 47¾" over-all (12, 28").
Features: 12 ga. uses all 2¾" shells, 20 ga. all 2¾" or 3" shells, including rifled slugs, without adjustment.
Price: Field, plain bbl., No rib **$149.95**
Price: Deluxe rib, checkered stock, vent. rib, w/o adj. choke **174.95**
Price: Checkered stock, vent.-rib, adj. choke **181.95**
Price: Duck, 3" Magnum, 12 ga., 30" Full, recoil pad, with vent. rib. bbl.
.... **184.95**

Hi-Standard Supermatic Deer Gun
Same as Supermatic Auto except: 12-ga. only, 22" plain bbl., Cyl. bore, with rifle sights. Checkered walnut stock and fore-end, recoil pad. Receiver tapped for aperture sight. 41¾" over-all, 7¾ lbs. **$159.95**

Hi-Standard Supermatic Skeet
Same as Supermatic DeLuxe except: 26" Skeet choke bbl.; all external parts high polished; internal parts super finished; better grade American walnut stock (no recoil pad) and fore-end with cabinet finish. Weight about 7½ lbs. **$179.95**

Hi-Standard Supermatic Executive Trap
Same gun as Supermatic Trap, but with Fajen Monte Carlo stock, selected wood **$274.95**

Hi-Standard Supermatic Trap
Same features as Supermatic Skeet except: 30" full choke barrel; stock (14⅜"x1½"x1⅞"); recoil pad. Wgt. 8 lbs. 12 ga. only **$184.95**

ITHACA MODEL 300 AUTOMATIC
Gauge: 12 ga. 2¾" chambers, 20 ga. 3" chambers.
Action: Recoil-operated, takedown, interchangeable barrels.
Barrel: Roto-Forged 30" 12 ga. only (Full), 28" (Full or Mod.), 26" (Imp. Cyl.). Standard without rib, vent. rib, $15.00 extra.
Stock: 14"x1½"x2½". Hand checkered walnut, p.g., fluted fore-end.
Weight: 12 ga. about 7 lbs., 20 ga. about 6½ lbs.
Features: Positive cross-bolt safety, automatic magazine cutoff permits changing loads without unloading magazine. 20 ga. guns are designed to permit quick changeover from 2¾" to 3" shells.
Price: **$149.95**

ITHACA MODEL 900 DELUXE AUTOMATIC
Gauge: 12 ga. 2¾" chambers, 20 ga. 3" chambers.
Action: Recoil-operated, takedown; interchangeable bbls., cross-bolt safety.
Barrel: Roto-Forged; 30" 12 ga. only (Full), 28" (Full or Mod.), 26" (Imp. Cyl.) all with vent. rib.
Stock: 14"x1½"x2½", hand checkered walnut, p.g. and fore-end.
Weight: 12 ga. about 7 lbs., 20 ga. about 6½ lbs.
Features: White spacers in grip cap and butt plate; attractive engraving on receiver is gold-filled, gold-plated trigger and nameplate inlaid in stock.
Price: **$179.95**
Same gun as Model 51 Trap with fancy American walnut stock, 30" (full or imp. cyl.) or 28" (full or imp.)

ITHACA MODEL 900 DELUXE AUTOMATIC SLUG GUN
Identical to the Model 900 Deluxe, except with 24" barrel that carries rifle sights for slug shooting. 12 ga. 2¾" chamber, 20 ga. 3" chamber.
Price: **$174.95**

ITHACA MODEL 51 FEATHERLIGHT AUTOMATIC
Gauge: 12 ga. 2¾" chamber.
Action: Gas-operated, rotary bolt has three locking lugs. Takedown. Self-compensating for high or low base loads.
Barrel: Roto-Forged, 30" (Full), 28" (Full, Mod., or Skeet), 26" (Imp. Cyl. or Skeet). Extra barrels available. Raybar front sight. Vent. rib **$25.00** extra.
Stock: 14"x1⅝"x2½". Hand checkered walnut, white spacers on p.g. and under recoil pad.
Weight: About 7½ lbs.
Features: Hand fitted, engraved receiver, 3 shot capacity, safety is reversible for left hand shooter.
Price: Standard **$179.95**

Ithaca Model 51 Featherlight Automatic Trap
Same gun as Model 51 with vent. rib, trap recoil pad, stock dimensions are 14¼"x1½"x1⅞". **Price:** **$214.95**

Ithaca Model 51 Featherlight Automatic Skeet
Same gun as Model 51 with vent. rib, skeet recoil pad, stock dimensions are 14"x1⅝"x2½". **Price:** **$209.95**

Ithaca Model 51 Featherlight Deluxe Skeet
Same gun as Model 51 Skeet with fancy American walnut stock, 28" or 26" (Skeet) barrel. **Price:** **$234.95**

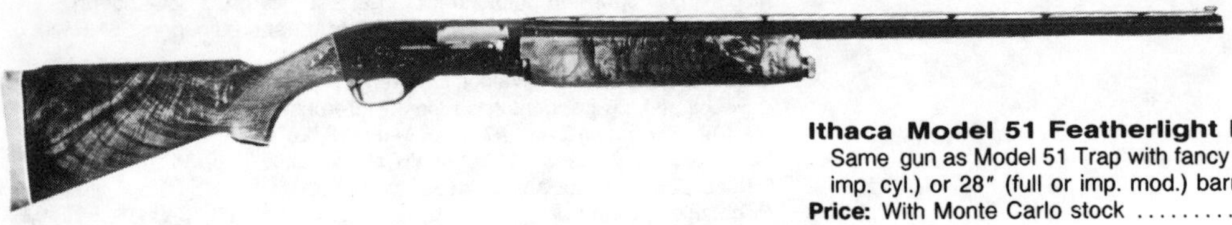

Ithaca Model 51 Featherlight Deluxe Trap
Same gun as Model 51 Trap with fancy American walnut stock, 30" (full or imp. cyl.) or 28" (full or imp. mod.) barrel. **Price:** **$244.95**
Price: With Monte Carlo stock **$254.95**

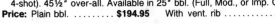

REMINGTON MODEL 1100 AUTO
Gauge: 12, 16, 20 (5-shot); 3-shot plug furnished.
Action: Gas-o-erated autoloader.
Barrel: 26" (Imp. Cyl., Mod.), 28" (Mod., Full), 30" Full in 12 ga. only.
Stock: 14"x1½"x2½" American Walnut, checkered p.g. and fore-end.
Weight: 12 ga. 7½ lbs., 16 ga. 7⅜ lbs., 20 ga. 7¼ lbs.; 48" over-all (28" bbl.).
Features: Quickly interchangeable barrels within gauge. Matted receiver top with scroll work on both sides of receiver. Crossbolt safety.
Price: .... **$184.95**   With vent. rib **$209.95**

Remington 1100 Magnum
Same as 1100 except: chambered for 3" magnum loads. Available in 12 ga. (30") or 20 ga. (28") Mod. or Full, 14"x1½"x2½" stock with recoil pad, Wgt. 7¾ lbs. **$204.95**

Remington 1100 Small Gauge
Same as 1100 except: 28 ga. 2¾" (5-shot) or 410, 3" (except Skeet, 2½" 4-shot). 45½" over-all. Available in 25" bbl. (Full, Mod., or Imp. Cyl.) only.
Price: Plain bbl. .... **$194.95**   With vent. rib **$219.95**

Remington 1100 20 ga. Lightweight
Basically the same design as Model 1100, but with special weight-saving features that retain strength and dependability of the standard Model 1100.
Barrel: 28" (Full, Mod.), 26" (Imp. Cyl.).
Weight: 6½ lbs.
Price: .... **$194.95**   With vent. rib **$219.95**

Remington 1100F Premier Auto
Same as 1100D except: select wood, better engraving **$1295.00**

Remington 1100D Tournament Auto
Same as 1100 Standard except: vent. rib, better wood, more extensive engraving **$595.00**

Remington 1100SA Skeet
Same as the 1100 except: 26" bbl., special skeet boring, vent. rib, ivory bead front and metal bead middle sights. 14"x1½"x2½" stock. 20 and 12 ga. only. Wgt. 7½ lbs.
Price: .... **$214.95**   1100 SB (better grade walnut) ... **$239.95**
Fore Cutts Comp add **25.00**

Remington 1100 Deer Gun
Same as 1100 except: 12 ga. only, 22" bbl. (Imp. Cyl.), rifle sights adjustable for w. and e.; recoil pad with white spacer. Weight 7¼ lbs.
Price: **$204.95**

SEARS TED WILLIAMS 300 AUTO
Gauge: 12 and 20 (3-shot) 2¾" chamber.
Action: Gas operated autoloader with self-compensating system for light or heavy loads.
Barrel: 27", 12 and 20 ga. (with adjustable choke), 28", 12 ga. only (Mod or Full), ventilated rib.
Stock: American walnut checkered p.g. and fore-end, recoil pad.
Weight: 7 lbs. (7¼ in 12 ga. w/adj. choke); 48⅝" over-all length (47⅝" w/adj. choke).
Features: Push button action release.
Price: 12 ga. (Mod or Full) **$165.00**   With adjustable choke **$175.00**

Remington 1100 TB Trap
Same as the 1100 except: better grade wood, recoil pad. 14⅜"x1⅜"x1¾" stock. Wgt. 8¼ lbs. 12 ga. only. 30" (Mod., Full) vent. rib bbl. Ivory bead front and white metal middle sight.
Price: .... **$249.95**   With Monte Carlo stock **$259.95**
Remington 1100 Extra bbls.: Plain **$49.95** (20, 28 & 410, **$47.95**). Vent. rib **$74.95** (20, 28 & 410, **$70.95**). Vent. rib Skeet **$79.95**. Vent. rib Trap **$79.95** Deer bbl. **$60.95**, Skeet, with cutts comp. **$104.95**. Available in the same gauges and chokes as shown on guns.

UNIVERSAL AUTO WING SHOTGUN
Gauge: 12 only (5-shot; 3-shot plug furnished). 2¾" chamber.
Action: Recoil operated autoloader; takedown; extra bbls. interchange without factory fitting; cross-bolt safety.
Barrels: 26", 28" or 30" (Imp. Cyl., Mod., & Full). Vent. rib, Ivory bead front & middle sights.
Stock: 14¼"x1⅝"x2½". Walnut checkered, full p.g. and grooved fore-end.
Weight: About 7 lbs.
Price: **$159.95**

U.S. SHOTGUNS—AUTOLOADING

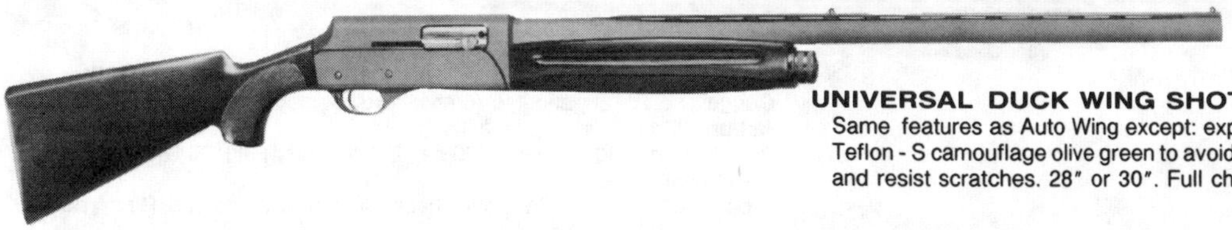

UNIVERSAL DUCK WING SHOTGUN
Same features as Auto Wing except: exposed metal parts are coated with Teflon - S camouflage olive green to avoid reflection; retard rust or corrosion and resist scratches. 28" or 30". Full choke only **$185.00**

Universal Auto Wing Deluxe
Same as the standard Auto Wing shotgun, but has photo-engraver receiver and gold plated trigger. **$175.00**

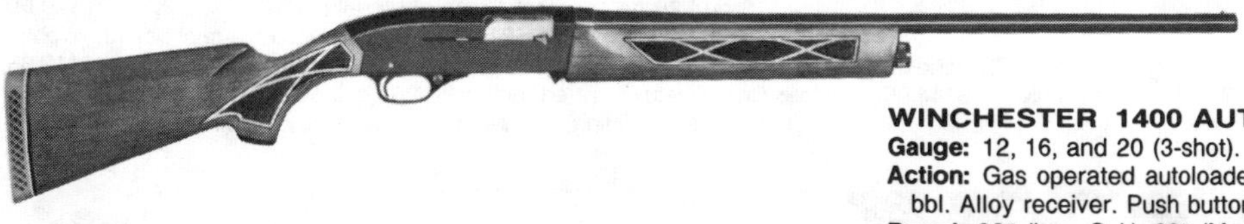

WINCHESTER 1400 AUTOMATIC MARK II
Gauge: 12, 16, and 20 (3-shot).
Action: Gas operated autoloader. Front-locking 4-lug rotating bolt locks in bbl. Alloy receiver. Push button action release.
Barrel: 26" (Imp. Cyl.), 28" (Mod., Full), 30" (Full, 12 ga. only). Metal bead front sight.
Stock: 14"x1⅜"x2⅜". American walnut, new-design checkered p.g. and fore-end; fluted comb, p.g. cap, recoil pad.
Weight: With 26" bbl., 20 ga. 6½ lbs., 16, 12 ga. 6¾ lbs.; 46⅝" over-all.
Features: Self-compensating valve adjusts for std. or magnum loads. Bbls. interchangeable without fitting. Crossbolt safety in front of trigger guard.
Price: .... **$164.95** With vent. rib **$189.95**

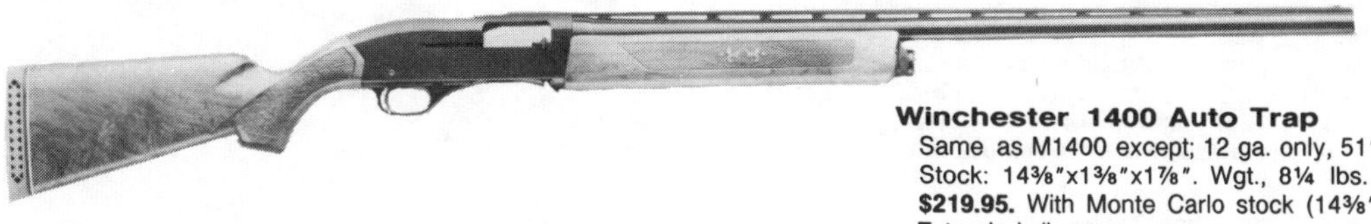

Winchester 1400 Auto Deer Gun
Same as M1400 except: 12 ga. only, 42⅝" over-all with 22" bbl. specially bored for rifled slugs. Ramp front sight, adj. open rear. Stock: 14"x1½"x2⅜". Wgt. 6½ lbs. **$179.95**

Winchester 1400 Auto Trap
Same as M1400 except; 12 ga. only, 51" over-all with 30" full choke bbl. Stock: 14⅜"x1⅜"x1⅞". Wgt., 8¼ lbs. Metal, middle, red front sights. **$219.95**. With Monte Carlo stock (14⅜"x1½"x2⅛"x1½").
Extended rib **$229.95**
With field grade M.C. walnut stock, specially tuned trigger, rib extension **$199.95**

Winchester 1400 Auto Skeet
Same as M1400 except: 12 and 20 ga. only, 26" bbl., Skeet choke, wgt. 7½ lbs. Stock: 14"x1½"x2½". Metal, middle, red front sights. 46⅝" over-all **$219.95** Field grade walnut stock and forearm **$189.95** Winchester 1400 Extra Barrels: Field, 12, 16, 20 ga. **$37.95**; with vent. rib **$68.95**; Deer Gun **$48.95**; Trap, Skeet **$79.95**

Winchester Recoil Reduction Stocks
Spring-loaded, compressible plastic stock (12-ga. only) for M12, 1200, 1400. Drop at comb increased ⅛" on Field models with vent. rib, and on Skeet model. Trap model unchanged. Weight increases ¾ lb. on Field models only.
Ordered with Skeet or trap models, additional **$5.00**
Ordered with Field models, additional **$10.00**
Not available for Deer Gun, Trap w/o Monte Carlo, or Pigeon Grade.
Winchester 1400 field model available in a left-hand version in 12 ga. 28" Mod. only **$174.95**. With vent. rib **$199.95**. Skeet **$229.95** (12 ga. only) and Trap **$239.95** (12 ga. only).
Winchester 1400 with interchangeable choke tubes which are screwed into the barrel and tightened with supplied wrench. Available in 12, 16, and 20 ga. (28") Full, Mod., and Imp. Cyl. tube.
Price: Field **$178.45**, Vent. **$203.45**. Also, L. H. in 12 ga. only plain **$188.45**. L. H. Vent. **$213.45**. Extra tubes in Full, Mod. or Imp. Cyl. **$4.95**. Wrench **$1.25**.

U.S. SHOTGUNS—SLIDE ACTION

HARRINGTON & RICHARDSON 440 PUMP
Gauge: 12, 20 (2¾" and 3" chamber), 16 (2¾"). 4-shot clip mag.
Action: Hammerless, side ejecting, slide action.
Barrel: 24", 12 and 20 ga. (Imp. Cyl.); 26", 12 and 20 ga. (Imp. Cyl. and Mod.); 28", 12 ga. (Full and Mod.), 16 ga. (Mod. only) 20 ga. (Full and Mod.); 30", 12 ga. (Full only).
Stock: Walnut p.g. stock and fore-end; recoil pad.
Weight: 6¼ lbs. 47" over-all.
Price: **$104.95**

HARRINGTON & RICHARDSON 442 PUMP
Same as the 440 except: Full length vent. rib, checkered p.g. and fore-end.
Price: **$139.95**

Hi-Standard Flite-King Skeet

Same as Flite-King DeLuxe except: No recoil pad; 26″ Skeet choke bbl.; all external parts high polished; internal parts super finished; better grade American walnut stock (14″x1½″x2½″) and fore-end with cabinet finish. Wgt. 12 ga 7½ lbs., 20, 6¼ lbs., 28 and 410 ga. 6 lbs. **$132.95**

Hi-Standard Flite-King Trap

Same features as Flite-King Skeet except: 30″ full choke; (14⅜″x1½″x1⅞″) has recoil pad. About 7¾ lbs. 12 ga. only ... **$144.95**

HI-STANDARD FLITE-KING DELUXE PUMP GUNS

Gauge: 12, 20, 28, and 410 (6 shots; 3-shot plug furnished).
Action: "Free-falling" slide action.
Barrel: 12 ga., 30″ (Full); 12, 20 ga., 28″ (Mod. or Full), 26″ (Imp. Cyl.); 410, 26″ (Full).
Stock: 14″x1½″x2½″. Walnut, checkered p.g. and fore-end. Recoil pad except: 410 & Skeet guns.
Weight: 12 ga. 7¼ lbs., 20, 410 ga. 6 lbs.
Features: Side ejection.
Price: Field **$99.95**
Price: 12 ga., with adj. choke, 27 l. bbl **109.95**
Price: De Luxe Rib, with vent. rib, w/o adj. choke **122.95**
Price: 12 and 20 ga., as above with adj. choke **129.95**
Price: Brush, 12 ga. only with 20″ cyl. bbl., grooved fore-end, adj. rifle sights. Stock: (14¼″x1½″x1⅞″) 39¾″ over-all **$112.95**
Price: Brush Deluxe, 12 ga. only with 20″ cyl. bbl., checkered p.g. and f.e., sling swivels with sling, adj. peep sight **$132.95**

Ithaca Model 37 De Luxe Featherlight

Same as Model 37 except: checkered stock with p.g. cap; beavertail fore-end; recoil pad. Wgt. 12 ga. 6¾ lbs.
Price: .... **$124.95** With vent. rib **$149.95**

Ithaca Model 37 Supreme

Same as Model 37 except: hand checkered beavertail fore-end and p.g. stock, Ithaca recoil pad and vent. rib **$199.95**
37 Supreme also with Skeet (14″x1½″x2½″) or Trap (14½″x1½″x1⅞″) stocks at no extra charge. Other options available at extra charge.

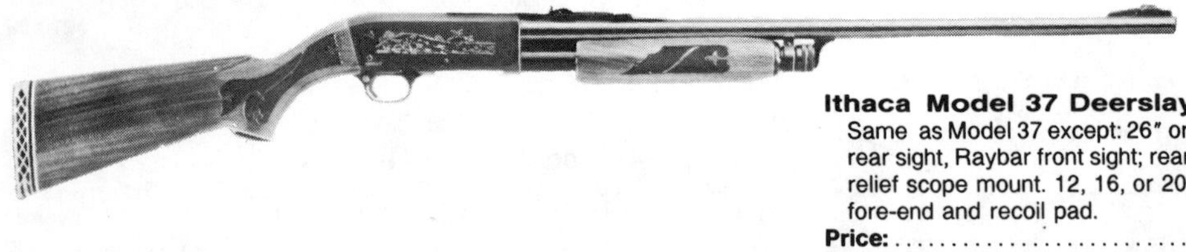

ITHACA MODEL 37 FEATHERLIGHT

Gauge: 12, 16, 20 (5-shot; 3-shot plug furnished).
Action: Slide; takedown; bottom ejection.
Barrel: 26″, 28″, 30″ in 12 ga. 26″ or 28″ in 16 or 20 ga. (Full, Mod. or Imp. Cyl.).
Stock: 14″x1⅝″x2⅝″. Checkered walnut capped p.g. stock and fore-end.
Weight: 12 ga. 6½ lbs., 16 ga. 6 lbs., 20 ga. 5¾ lbs.
Features: Ithaca Raybar front sight; decorated receiver; crossbolt safety; action release for removing shells.
Price: ...... **$119.95** With vent. rib stock (14″x1½″x2½″) **$144.95**

Ithaca Model 37 Deerslayer

Same as Model 37 except: 26″ or 20″ bbl. designed for rifled slugs; sporting rear sight, Raybar front sight; rear sight ramp grooved for Redfield long eye relief scope mount. 12, 16, or 20 gauge. With checkered stock, beavertail fore-end and recoil pad.
Price: **$139.95**
Price: As above with special select walnut stock **$159.95**

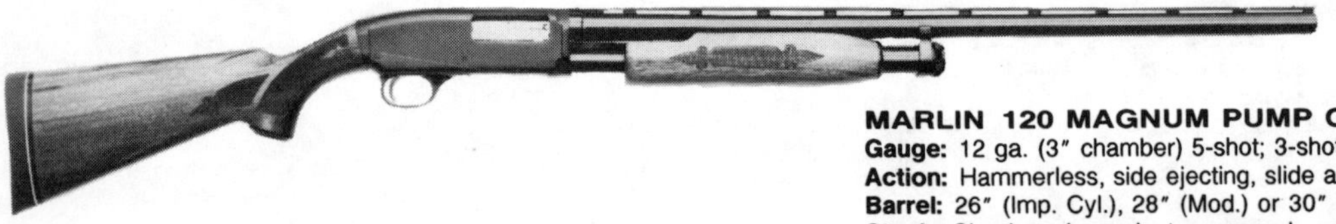

MARLIN 120 MAGNUM PUMP GUN

Gauge: 12 ga. (3″ chamber) 5-shot; 3-shot plug furnished.
Action: Hammerless, side ejecting, slide action.
Barrel: 26″ (Imp. Cyl.), 28″ (Mod.) or 30″ (Full), with vent. rib.
Stock: Checkered walnut, capped p.g., semi-beavertail fore-end (14″x1½″x2⅜″).
Weight: About 7¾ lbs. 45″ to 49″ over-all.
Features: Interchangeable bbls., slide lock release; large button cross-bolt safety.
Price: **$150.00**

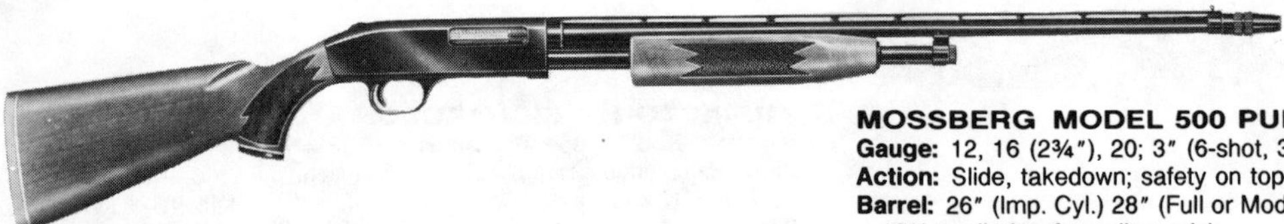

MOSSBERG MODEL 500 PUMP GUN

Gauge: 12, 16 (2¾″), 20; 3″ (6-shot, 3-shot plug furnished).
Action: Slide, takedown; safety on top of receiver.
Barrel: 26″ (Imp. Cyl.) 28″ (Full or Mod.), 30″ (Full), 12 ga. only. Also 12 ga. 18½″ cylinder, for police only).
Stock: 14″x1½″x2½″. Walnut p.g., extension fore-end. Recoil pad. 13 oz. steel plug furnished for use with Magnum barrel.
Weight: 12 ga. 6¾ lbs., 45¼″ over-all (26″ bbl.).
Features: Easy interchangeability of barrels; side ejection; disconnecting trigger makes doubles impossible; straight-line feed.
Price: Standard barrel **$95.50**
Price: With C-Lect Choke, 3″ Mag., or 24″ Slugster bbls........ **$101.50**
Price: Extra barrel, 2¾″ chamber **22.80**
Price: Extra Magnum, C-Lect Choke or Slug, bbl. **29.75**

Mossberg Model 500 Super Grade
Similar to the Model 500 except: vent. rib bbls. in 12 ga. (2¾″) or 20 ga. (3″); 26″ (Skeet), 28″ (Mod., Full), and 30″ Full (12 ga. only) 2¾″ or 3″ mag. Checkered p.g. and fore-end stock with fluted comb and recoil pad (14″x1½″x2½″).
Price: 12 or 20 ga. $114.95
Price: 12 ga. 3″ Magnun or C-Lect Choke 12 and 20 ga. 123.95

Mossberg Model 500E
Similar to Model 500 except: 410 bore only, 26″ bbl. (Full, Mod. or Imp. Cyl.); holds six 2¾″ or five 3″ shells. Walnut stock with smooth p.g. and grooved fore-end, fluted comb and recoil pad (14″x1¼″x2½″).
Weight: About 5¾ lbs., length over-all 46″.
Price: Standard barrels $95.50
Price: C-Lect Choke barrel 101.50
Price: Super Grade, 26″ Full, Mod., or Skeet bbl., vent. rib 114.95
Price: Super Grade, C-Lect Choke and vent. rib 123.95

Mossberg Model 500 APR Pigeon Grade
Similar to Model 500, but with vent. rib, rubber recoil pad, hand checkering, scroll engraving on action.
Price: $139.00
Price: 500 APKR with C-Lect-Choke $145.00
Price: 500 APTR trap gun 30″ full choke barrel, M.C. stock, 14½″x1½″x2″, additional barrels available. $145.00

NOBLE 300 SERIES PUMP GUNS
Gauge: 12 ga. (3″ chamber), 16 ga. (2¾″ chamber). 6-shot, 3-shot plug furnished.
Action: Slide, solid frame, side ejection, tang safety.
Barrel: 28″ (Mod. or Full)
Stock: Walnut p.g. (13¾″x1¾″x2¾″), with impressed checkering.
Weight: About 7½ lbs. 48″ over-all.
Features: Key Lock, protects against unauthorized use. Damascened bolt.
Price: M339 .... $95.50
With Vary-Check Choke, checkered grip recoil pad, as M336 ... 101.50
With vent. rib. checkered grip recoil pad, as M333 .... 114.95
Same as M333, with Vary-Check Choke, as M330 .... 123.95

NOBLE 390 DEERGUN
Same as Model 339 except: 24″ rifled slug bbl. guaranteed to shoot 3″ groups at 100 feet. Sling swivels and detachable carrying strap. Lyman adj. peep rear sight and post ramp front. Wgt. 7½ lbs., 48″ over-all **$106.00**

NOBLE 757 PUMP GUN
Gauge: 20 ga. only (2¾″ chamber) 5-shot, 3-shot plug furnished.
Action: Slide, solid frame; tang safety; side ejection.
Barrel: 28″ aircraft aluminum with adj. choke.
Stock: American walnut p.g. and fore-end, impressed checkering, recoil pad installed.
Weight: 4½ lbs. 48″ over-all.
Features: Receiver and barrel made of black anodized aircraft aluminum. Decorated receiver.
Price: $119.95

NOBLE 200 AND 400 SERIES PUMP GUNS
Gauge: 20 (200 Series), 410 (400 Series), 3″ chambers, 5-shot; 3-shot plug furnished.
Action: Slide, solid frame; tang safety; side ejection.
Barrel: 20 ga., 28″, 410 26″ (Mod. or Full).
Stock: Walnut, p.g. (13¾″x1½″x2⅝″), impressed checkering on fore-end. Recoil pad installed on 200 Series.
Weight: About 6½ lbs. (20 ga.), 6 lbs. (410 ga.) 48″ over-all (20 ga.).
Features: Key Lock protects against unauthorized use. Damascened bolt.
Price: M249 or M449 .... $95.50
With Vary Choke, as M246 or M446 .... $101.50
With Vent. rib, as M243 or M443 .... $114.95
With vent. rib and Vary Choke, as M240 or M440 .... $123.95

Remington 870 Magnum

Same as the M870 except 3" chamber, 12 ga. 30" bbl. (Mod. or Full), 20 ga. 28" bbl. (Mod. or Full). Recoil pad installed. Wgt., 12 ga. 8 lbs., 20 ga. 7½ lbs.

Price: Plain bbl. .... **$144.95** Vent. rib bbl. **$169.95**

Remington Model 870 Brushmaster Deluxe

Carbine version of the M870 with 20" bbl. (Imp. Cyl.) for rifled slugs. 40½" over-all, wgt. 6½ lbs. Recoil pad. Adj. rear, ramp front sights. 12 or 20 ga.
Deluxe **$144.95**

REMINGTON 870 WINGMASTER PUMP GUN

Gauge: 12, 16, 20, (5-shot; 3-shot wood plug. 12 oz. Vari-Weight steel plug furnished in 12 ga.).
Action: Takedown, slide action.
Barrel: 12, 16, 20, ga., 26" (Imp. Cyl.); 28" (Mod. or Full); 12 ga., 30" (Full).
Stock: 14"x1⅝"x2½". Checkered walnut, p.g.; fluted extension fore-end; fitted rubber recoil pad.
Weight: 7 lbs., 12 ga. (7¾ lbs. with Vari-Weight plug); 6¾ lbs., 16 ga.; 6½ lbs., 20 ga. 48½" over-all (28" bbl.).
Features: Double action bars, crossbolt safety. Receiver machined from solid steel. Hand fitted action.
  Plain bbl. .... **$124.95**   Vent. rib **$149.95**
Price: Riot gun, 18" or 20" Riot bore, (12 ga. only) **$109.95**

Remington 870 SA Skeet

Same as the M870 except: 26" bbl. Skeet bored. Vent. rib with ivory front and white metal middle beads. 14"x1⅝"x2½" stock with rubber recoil pad, 12 or 20 ga. only **$154.95**
Add **$25.00** for Cutts comp.

Remington 870D Tournament

Same as 870 except: better walnut, hand checkering, Engraved receiver & bbl. Vent.-rib. Stock dimensions to order **$595.00**

Remington 870F Premier

Same as M8700, except select walnut, better engraving **$1295.00**

Remington 870 Extra Barrels

Plain **$39.95.** Vent. rib **$64.95.** Vent. rib Skeet **$69.95.** Vent. rib Trap **$69.95.** With rifle sights **$50.95.** Available in the same gauges and chokes as shown on guns.

Remington 870 TB Trap

Same as the M870 except: 12 ga. only, 30" (Mod., Full) vent. rib. bbl., ivory front and white metal middle beads. Special sear, hammer and trigger assy. 14⅜"x1½"x1⅞" stock with recoil pad. Hand fitted action and parts. Wgt. 8 lbs. **$189.95**

Remington 870 Small Gauges

Exact copies of the large ga. Model 870, except that guns are offered in 28 and 410 ga. 25" barrel (Full, Mod., Imp. Cyl.).
Plain barrel **$134.95**
D and F grade prices same as large ga. M870 prices.

Savage Model 30-T

Same specifications as 12 ga., M30 except: 30" Full Choke bbl. with 3" chamber; Monte Carlo stock with trap dimensions (14⅝"x1½"x1½"x2¼"). Recoil pad. Over-all 50". 8 lbs. **$124.95**

Savage Model 30 Field Grade

Same as the Model 30 except plain bbl. and receiver, hard rubber buttplate **$96.95.** As M30 AC with adj. choke **$99.95**

SAVAGE MODEL 30 PUMP GUN

Gauge: 12, 20, and 410, 5-shot (410, 4-shot) 3-shot plug furnished. All gauges chambered for 3" Magnum shells.
Action: Slide, hammerless, take-down; side ejection; top tang safety.
Barrel: Vent. rib. 12, 20 ga. 26" (Imp. Cyl.); 28" (Mod. or Full); 12 ga., 30" (Full); 410, 26" (Mod. or Full).
Stock: 14"x1½"x2½". Walnut, checkered p.g., grooved extension fore-end, recoil pad.
Weight: 7 lbs. (410, 6¼ lbs.). Over-all 49½" (30" bbl.).
Features: Decorated lightweight receiver; gold plated trigger and safety; damascened bolt. Stainless steel front and middle bead sights.
Price: **$116.95**

Savage Model 30 Slug Gun

Same as the Model 30 Field Grade but with 22" bbl., 12 or 20 ga. only, with rifle sights **$99.95**

SEARS MODEL 200 PUMP GUN

Gauge: 12, and 20 (2¾" chamber) (5 shot; 3-shot plug installed).
Action: Slide, front-locking rotating bolt.
Barrel: 28" Full or Mod.
Stock: Walnut finished buttstock and fore-end; recoil pad.
Weight: About 6½" lbs.; 48⅝" over-all (28" bbl.).
Features: Alloy receiver, non-glare serrated top; cross-bolt safety. Interchangeable bbls., no special tools required, $24 extra.
Price: **$89.99**
Price: 12 ga. Magnum with 30" barrel (Full) **91.99**

Sears Ted Williams 200 Pump

Same as Standard 200 except: vent. rib bbl.; engine-turned bolt, checkered p.g. and fore-end; p.g. cap; whiteline spacers and name plate. Wgt. 7 lbs. **$125.00.** With var. choke. **$135.00.**

U.S. SHOTGUNS—SLIDE ACTION

WINCHESTER 12 SUPER PIGEON PUMP GUN
Gauge: 12 only, 6-shot (2-shot plug installed).
Action: Slide, one-piece receiver, takedown, side ejection.
Barrel: 26″, 28″, 30″, floating vent. rib, any standard choke.
Stock: Full fancy American walnut, dim. to order within mfg. limits, hand-finished, "A" checkering or carving (see Win. catalog), Monte Carlo, cheek-piece or offset avail. at extra charge.
Features: Receiver engraved, "1A," "1B," or "1C" type (see Win. catalog). Working parts hand fitted.
Weight: 7¾ lbs.
Price: **$900.00**

Winchester 1200 Skeet
Same as M1200 except: 12 and 20 ga., 26″ vent. rib bbl., b. t. fore-end, metal, middle red front sights **$199.95**

Winchester 1200 Deer Gun
Same as M1200 except: 12 ga. only, 22″ bbl. bored for rifled slugs; rifle-type sights, rear adj. for e. only **$134.95**
Winchester 1200 Extra Barrels: Field and Riot w/o sights, 12, 16, 20 ga. **$37.95.** Field with vent. rib, 12, 16, 20 ga. **$68.95.** Riot with sights and Deer Gun, 12 ga. **$48.95.** Trap, 12 ga., Full choke 30″ only, Skeet, 12, 20 ga. 26″ only **$79.95**
Winchester 1200 with interchangeable choke tubes which are screwed into the barrel and tightened with supplied wrench. Available in 12, 16 and 20 ga. (28″) Mod. tube. Price: Field **$133.45** Vent. rib **$158.45.** Extra tubes in Full, Mod. or Imp. Cyl. **$4.95.** Wrench **$1.25.**

Winchester 1200 Field 3″ Magnum
Same as 1200 except: 12 and 20 ga. only, 2¾″ or 3″ shells, 28″ and 30″ full choke bbls., 7⅝ lbs. with 28″ bbl., 48⅝″ over-all.
Price: . . . . **$139.95**   With vent. rib **$164.95**

WESTERN FIELD 550 PUMP SHOTGUN
Gauge: 12, 20 and 410.
Action: Slide action, takedown; top tang safety.
Barrel: 12 ga., 30″ (Full), 28″ (Mod.). 20 ga., 28″ (Full or Mod.). 410, 26″ (Full).
Stock: Walnut finished p.g. stock, molded buttplate, serrated fore-end.
Weight: 8½ lbs.
Features: Straight-line feed, interchangeable bbls., trigger disconnector prevents doubling.
Price: . . . . **$89.95**   410 (with rubber buttplate) **$81.95**
As above, but with variable choke in 12, 16 or 20 ga. **$99.95**
Slug gun with 24 bbl. without choke **$99.95**
Magnum 12 ga., 30″ bbl. (Full Choke) **$99.95**
Trap gun, 30″ (Full) bbl., vent. rib and trap stock, 12 ga. only . . **$139.00**
Vent. rib models available, fixed or variable choke as above . . . **$113.95**
to **$122.95**

WINCHESTER 1200 FIELD PUMP GUN
Gauge: 12, 16 and 20 (5-shot; 3-shot plug installed).
Action: Slide; front locking 4-lug rotating bolt locks into bbl. Alloy receiver, cross-bolt safety in front of trigger guard. Take-down.
Barrel: 26″ (Imp. Cyl.), 28″ (Mod., Full) and 30″ Full (12 ga. only). Metal bead front sight.
Stock: 14″x1⅜″x2⅜″. American walnut with new-design checkered p.g. and fore-end; fluted comb, recoil pad. Steel p.g. cap.
Weight: 12 ga. 6½ lbs. with 26″ bbl. 46⅝″ over-all.
Price: . . . . **$119.95**   With vent. rib **$144.95**

Winchester 1200 Trap
Same as M1200 except: 12-ga. only, 30″ Full choke vent. rib bbl., 50⅝″ over-all. 14⅜″x1⅜″x1⅞″ stock with recoil pad, b. t. fore-end. Metal, middle, red front sights **$199.95**
With Monte Carlo stock, 14⅜″x1⁷⁄₁₆″x2⅛″x1½″ **209.95**
With Monte Carlo stock and Winchoke **219.95**
Field grade walnut stock, Monte Carlo **$159.95**

Winchester Recoil Reduction Stocks
Spring-loaded, compressible plastic stock (12-ga. only) for M12, 1200, 1400. Drop at comb increased ⅛″ on Field models with vent.-rib, and on Skeet model. Trap model unchanged. Weight increases ¾ lb. on Field models only.
Ordered with trap models, additional **$50.00**

U.S. SHOTGUNS—DOUBLE BARREL

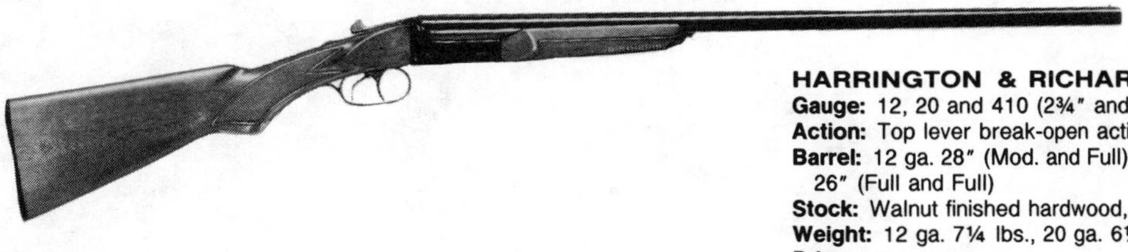

HARRINGTON & RICHARDSON MODEL 404 DOUBLE
Gauge: 12, 20 and 410 (2¾″ and 3″ shells).
Action: Top lever break-open action, top tang safety, double triggers.
Barrel: 12 ga. 28″ (Mod. and Full), 20 ga. 26″ (Imp. Cyl. and Mod.), 410 ga. 26″ (Full and Full)
Stock: Walnut finished hardwood, hand checkered p.g. and fore-end.
Weight: 12 ga. 7¼ lbs., 20 ga. 6½ lbs., 410 ga. 5½ lbs.
Price: **$99.95**
Price: With Monte Carlo stock (M404C) **$109.95**

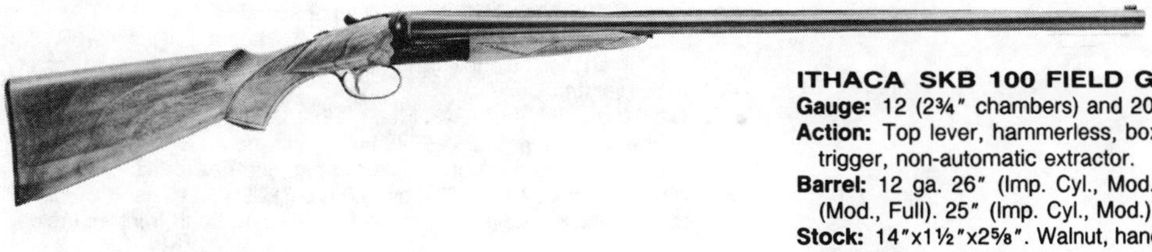

ITHACA SKB 100 FIELD GRADE DOUBLE
Gauge: 12 (2¾″ chambers) and 20 (3″).
Action: Top lever, hammerless, boxlock, automatic safety, single selective trigger, non-automatic extractor.
Barrel: 12 ga. 26″ (Imp. Cyl., Mod.). 28⅛ or 30″ (Mod., Full). 20 ga. 28″ (Mod., Full). 25″ (Imp. Cyl., Mod.).
Stock: 14″x1½″x2⅝″. Walnut, hand checkered p.g. and fore-end, p.g. cap, fluted comb.
Weight: 7 lbs. (12 ga.); 6 lbs. (20 ga.).
Features: Automatic safety. Chrome lined action and barrels, hand engraved receiver.
Price: **$189.95**

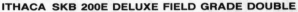

ITHACA SKB 200E DELUXE FIELD GRADE DOUBLE
Same as 100 Grade Field except: automatic selective ejectors, bead middle sight and scroll engraving on receiver, beavertail fore-end. White line spacers. Gold plated trigger and nameplate **$239.95**

Ithaca SKB 200E Skeet Grade
Same as 200E Deluxe Field Grade except: recoil pad, non-auto. safety. Bbls. 26″ 12 ga. or 25″ 20 ga. (Skeet, Skeet). Wgt. 7¼ and 6¼ lbs.
Price: **$244.95**

Ithaca SKB 280 English Double
Like the 200 Field Grade except: hand-checkered straight grip stock with wrap-around checkering; semi-beavertail fore-end. Receiver hand engraved with quail and English scroll. Durable, simulated oil-finished walnut stock.
Price: **$249.95**

NOBLE MODEL 550 DOUBLE
Gauge: 12 or 20 (2¾″ chamber).
Action: Demi-block with triple lock, with automatic selective ejectors, double triggers.
Barrels: 28″ (Mod. & Full)
Stock: Hand checkered Circassion Walnut with p.g. beavertail fore-end.
Weight: About 6⅞ lbs., 44¾″ over-all.
Features: Recoil pad, hand engraved action, gold inlay on top lever. Front and middle bead sight.
Price: **$168.00**

NOBLE MODEL 520 Double
Gauge: 12, 16, 20, 28, 410 (2¾″ chambers).
Action: Hammerless, top lever opening, double triggers, auto. safety. Hand engraved hunting scene on frame.
Barrel: 12, 16, 20 ga. 28″ (Mod., Full); 12, 16, 20, 28, ga. 26″ (Imp. Cyl., Mod.), 410 (Mod., Full). Matted rib.
Stock: 14″x1⅝″x2⅝″. Circassian walnut, hand-checkered p.g. and fore-end.
Weight: About 6-6⅞ lbs. 44¾″ over-all (28″ bbls.).
Features: Double lug locks and cross-bolt lock to bbl. extension.
Price: **$109.95**

MARLIN L. C. SMITH FIELD DOUBLE
Gauge: 12 only (2¾″ chambers).
Action: Sidelock, double trigger. Case hardened frame.
Barrel: 28″ (Mod. & Full).
Stock: Select walnut with capped p.g. checkered, (14″x1½″x2½″).
Weight: 6¾ lbs.
Features: Vent. rib, standard extractors, top auto. tang safety.
Price: **$325.00**
Price: Deluxe Model with full beavertail fore-end, better Wood and Simmons floating vent rib **$400.00**

SEARS DOUBLE BARREL GUN
Gauge: 12, 20, 410. (20 and 410, 3″ chambers).
Action: Hammerless, takedown. Double trigger, auto. safety.
Barrel: 12 ga. 30″ (Full, Mod.); 20 ga., 28″, (Full, Mod.); 12, 20 ga., 26″ (Mod., Imp., Cyl.); 410 ga. 26″ only (Full and Full).
Stock: 14″x1⅝″x2⅝″, walnut finished, p.g.
Weight: 7½ lbs. (12 ga.), 6½ lbs. (20 ga.), 6 lbs. (410).
Features: Black epoxied frame; bbl. and bbl. lug forged in one piece.
Price: **$109.99**

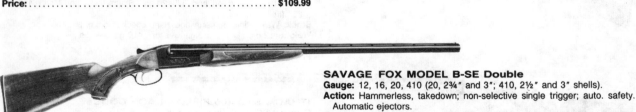

SAVAGE FOX MODEL B-SE Double
Gauge: 12, 16, 20, 410 (20, 2¾″ and 3″; 410, 2½″ and 3″ shells).
Action: Hammerless, takedown; non-selective single trigger; auto. safety. Automatic ejectors.
Barrel: 12, 20 ga. 26″ (Imp. Cyl., Mod.); 12, 16, 20 ga. 28″ (Mod., Full); 12 ga. 30″ (Mod., Full); 410, 26″ (Full, Full). Vent. rib on all.
Stock: 14″x1½″x2½″. Walnut, checkered p.g. and beavertail fore-end.
Weight: 12 ga. 7 lbs., 16 ga. 6¾ lbs., 20 ga. 6½ lbs., 410 ga. 6¼ lbs.
Features: Decorated, stain black finish frame; white bead front and middle sights.
Price: **$164.95**
Also available with double triggers, case hardened frame, without white line spacers and auto. ejectors as Model B **$139.95**

Savage Model 555 Double
Like the Fox B-SE except 12 or 20 ga. only, game scene and case hardened finish on receiver. White spacers at buttplate and capped p.g. **$172.95**

U.S. SHOTGUNS—DOUBLE BARREL

SAVAGE-STEVENS MODEL 311 DOUBLE
Gauge: 12, 16, 20, 410 (20 and 410, 3" chambers).
Action: Top lever, hammerless; double triggers, auto top tang safety.
Barrel: 12, 16, 20 ga. 26" (Imp. Cyl., Mod.); 12, 16, 20 ga. 28" (Mod., Full); 12 ga. 30" (Mod., Full); 410 ga. 26" (Full, Full).
Stock: 14"x1½"x2½". Walnut finish, p.g., fluted comb.
Weight: 6¼-7 lbs. Over-all 45¾" (30" bbl.).
Features: Box type frame, case-hardened finish.
Price: **$109.50**

UNIVERSAL DOUBLE WING DOUBLE
Gauge: 12 and 20, 3" chambers.
Action: Top break, boxlock.
Barrel: 26" (Imp. Cyl., Mod.); 28" or 30" (Mod., Full).
Stock: Walnut p.g. and fore-end, checkered.
Weight: About 7 lbs.
Features: Double triggers; Recoil pad. Beavertail style fore-end.
Price: **$116.95**
Price: 10 ga. 3½" chamber 32" Full and Full (M2030) **$139.95**

WESTERN FIELD DOUBLE Standard
Gauge: 12, 16, 20, 410 (20 and 410, 3" chambers).
Action: Hammerless, boxlock frame.
Barrel: Matted rib, white metal bead front sight. 12 ga. 30" (Mod., Full), 16 ga., 20 ga., 28" (Mod., Full), 410 ga. 26" (Full, Full).
Stock: Walnut-finished birch, full p.g., fluted comb.
Weight: 12, 16 ga. 7 lbs.; 20, 410 ga. 6½ lbs.
Features: Coil springs, auto safety, black epoxy finish action.
Price: **$109.95**

WINCHESTER 21 CUSTOM DOUBLE GUN
12, 16 or 20 ga. Almost any choke or bbl. length combination. Matted rib, 2¾" chambers, rounded frame, stock of AA-grade full fancy American walnut to customer's dimensions; straight or p.g., cheekpiece, Monte Carlo and/or offset; field. Skeet or trap fore-end.
Full fancy checkering, engine-turned receiver parts, gold plated trigger and gold oval name plate (optional) with three initials **$1,250.00**

Winchester 21 Pigeon grade
Same as Custom grade except: 3" chambers, available in 12 and 20 ga.; matted or vent. rib, leather covered pad (optional); style "A" stock carving and style "6" engraving (see Win. catalog); gold inlaid p.g. cap, gold name-plate or 3 gold initials in guard **$2,850.00**

Winchester 21 Grand American
Same as Custom and Pigeon grades except: style "B" stock carving, with style 6" engraving, all figures gold inlaid; extra pair of bbls. with beavertail fore-end, engraved and carved to match rest of gun; full leather trunk case for all, with canvas cover **$3,850.00**

U.S. SHOTGUNS—OVER-UNDER

Browning Superposed Magnum 12
Same as Browning Standard 12 ga. Superposed except 3" chambers; 30" (Full and Full or Full and Mod.) barrels, Stock, 14¼"x1⅝"x2½" with factory fitted recoil pad. Weight 8 lbs. Grade 1, **$445.00**, Pigeon **$675.00**, Diana **$895.00**, Midas **$1,255.00**.

BROWNING SUPERPOSED LIGHTNING
Same as Standard except: 7-7¼ lbs. in 12 ga. 6-6¼ lbs. in 20 ga. Grade 1 **$455.00**, Pigeon **$675.00**, Diana **$895.00**, Midas **$1,255.00**.

BROWNING SUPERPOSED LIGHTNING TRAP 12
Same as Browning Lightning Superposed except: semi-beavertail fore-end and ivory sights; stock, 14⅜"x1⁷/₁₆"x1⅝". 7¾ lbs. 30" (Full & Full, Full & Imp. Mod. or Full and Mod.). Grade 1 **$465.00**, Pigeon **$685.00**, Diana **$905.00**, Midas **$1,270.00**.

BROWNING SUPERPOSED "New Model" Skeet
Same as the Superposed Lightning except: full pistol grip stock; recoil pad; beavertail fore end and front and center ivory sights.
Price: GD-1, 12 or 20 ga. only **$450.00**

BROWNING SUPERPOSED STANDARD
Gauge: 12 & 28, 2¾" chamber; 20 & 410, 3" chamber. Any combination of Full, Imp. Mod., Mod., Imp. Cyl., Skeet, and Cyl. chokes.
Action: Takedown; single selective gold plated trigger; automatic ejectors, manual safety combined in thumb piece with bbl. selector mechanism. Actions in proportion to gauge.
Barrels: 12, 20, 28 and 410 ga., 26½" or 28", vent. rib. Solid raised rib available on special order. Steel bead front sight.
Stock: 12 ga. 14¼"x1⅝"x2½"; 20, 28 and 410 14¼"x1½"x2⅜". Select walnut, hand rubbed finish, 20-line hand checkering on semi-p.g. and fore-end. Deluxe models have fancier, finer checkering.
Weight: With 28" bbls. 12 ga. 7¾ lbs.; 20 ga. 6¾ lbs.; 28 ga. 6⅝ lbs.; 410 ga. 6⅞ lbs.
Features: Grade 1, blued steel with hand engraved scroll and rosette designs. Pigeon and Diana grades, steel in silver gray tone with hand engraved game scenes showing greater artistic design with each successive grade. Midas grade has specially blued steel with deeply hand carved background and hand engraved 18K gold-inlaid game birds.
Price: Grade 1, 12 or 20 ga . . . . . **$440.00**   28 or 410 ga **$475.00**
Price: (28 & 410 ga. only) Pigeon Grade **$675.00**, Diana **$895.00**, Midas **$1,255.00**.

SUPERPOSED BROADWAY TRAP 12

Same as Browing Lightning Superposed except: ⅝" wide vent. rib; stock, 14⅜"x1⁷/₁₆"x1⅝". 30" or 32" (Imp. Mod, Full; Mod., Full; Full, Full). 8 lbs. with 32" bbls. Grade 1 **$485.00**, Pigeon **$705.00**, Diana **$925.00**, Midas **$1,290.00**.

Browning Superposed Standard Skeet

Same as Superposed Standard except: 26½" or 28" bbls. (Skeet, Skeet). Wgt. 6½-7¾ lbs. 12 and 20 ga. Grade 1 **$450.00**; (28 and 410 ga). **$485.00**, Pigeon **$705.00**, Diana **$925.00**, Midas **$1,290.00**

Browning Superposed Combinations

Standard and Lightning models are available with these factory fitted extra barrels: 12 and 20 ga., same gauge bbls.; 12 ga., 20 ga. bbls.; 20 ga., extra sets 28 and/or 410 gauge; 28 ga., extra 410 bbls. Extra barrels may be had in Lightning weights with Standard models and vice versa. Prices range from **$750.00** (12, 20 ga., one set extra bbls. same gauge) for the Grade 1 Standard to about **$2,160.00** for the Midas grade in various combinations, all as cased sets.

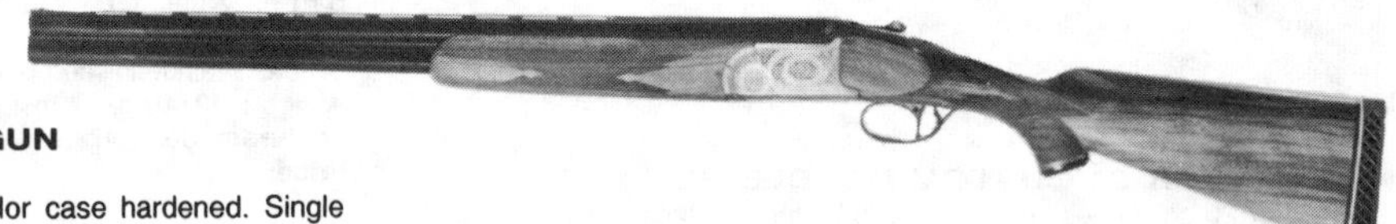

Browning Superposed Lightning Skeet

Same as Standard Skeet except: 12 and 20 ga. only. Wgt. 6½-7¾ lbs. Grade 1 **$465.00**, Pigeon **$685.00**, Diana **$905.00**, Midas **$1,270.00**.

BROWNING SUPERPOSED SUPER-LIGHT

Gauge: 12, & 20 2¾" chamber.
Action: Boxlock, top lever, single selective trigger. Bbl. selector combined with manual tang safety.
Barrels: 26½" (Mod. & Full, or Imp. Cyl. & Mod.)
Stock: Straight grip (14¼" x 1⅝" x 2½") hand checkered (fore-end and grip) select walnut.
Weight: 6⅜ lbs., average.
Features: Slender, tapered solid rib. Hand rubbed finish, engraved receiver.
Price: **$485.00**

CHAMPLIN OVER & UNDER SHOTGUN

Gauge: 12 only, 2¾" Chambers
Action: Fully engraved, choice of frosted or color case hardened. Single selective trigger.
Barrel: Any length or choke desired. Vent rib.
Stock: Custom made to customers specifications—choice of straight or p.g.
Weight: Average 7 to 8 lbs.
Price: **$695.00**
  Deluxe Grade, with finer engraving and walnut 1015.00
  Custom Grade, with engraving by one of America's foremost engravers **$1,100.00** and up.
  Trap and Skeet guns from **$745.00** to **$1065.00**

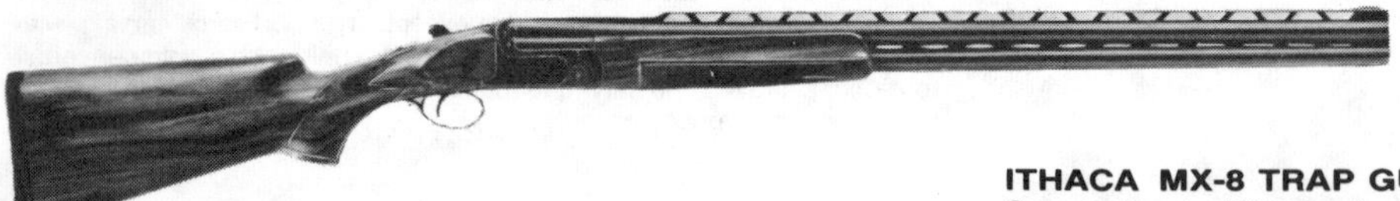

ITHACA COMPETITION I TRAP O/U

Gauge: 12 only, 2¾" chambers.
Action: Boxlock type, interchangeable hammer-trigger group. Single non-selective trigger, specify choice of firing order.
Barrel: 30" or 32", upper Full; lower, Imp.-Mod., vent rib has concave surface with deep cuts.
Stock: Interchangeable, 6 standard (1³/₁₆" to 1½" at comb x1⅜" to 1⅞" at heel) and 3 Monte Carlo (1⅜" to 1⁹/₁₆"x1⅜" to 1⁹/₁₆") of walnut; all have 14½" pull. Fore-end has slight taper and finger groove for firm grip.
Weight: About 7¾ lbs.
Features: Extra trigger-hammer groups are available to change firing sequence and/or trigger pull. Custom stocks also available.
Price: **$795.00**
  Extra trigger-hammer group 75.00

ITHACA MX-8 TRAP GUN

Gauge: 12 only, 2¾" chambers.
Action: Boxlock type, single non-selective trigger; interchangeable trigger-hammer group offers choice of firing order.
Barrel: 30" or 32", especially bored for international clay target shooting. High concave vent rib has 5" ramp.
Stock: Custom, finely checkered (oiled or lacquer finish) European walnut, interchangeable with other models, 9 available including Monte Carlo.
Weight: About 8 lbs.
Features: Ventilated middle rib has additional vent ports for maximum heat dissipation, better balance and smoother swing.
Price: **$1,295.00**
  Extra trigger-hammer group 75.00
  Extra stock 85.00

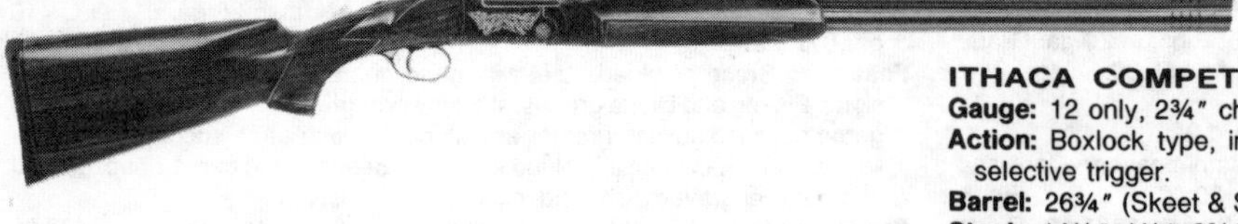

ITHACA COMPETITION I SKEET O/U

Gauge: 12 only, 2¾" chambers.
Action: Boxlock type, interchangeable hammer-trigger group. Single non-selective trigger.
Barrel: 26¾" (Skeet & Skeet). Vent rib has concave surface with deep cuts.
Stock: 14½"x1½"x2⅜", interchangeable walnut, custom stocks available.
Weight: About 7¾ lbs.
Features: Extra trigger-hammer groups to change firing order and/or weight of pull. Leather faced recoil pad has bevelled heel that will not catch. Extra stocks interchange for different style and dimension.
Price: **$875.00**
  Extra trigger-hammer group 75.00

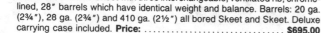

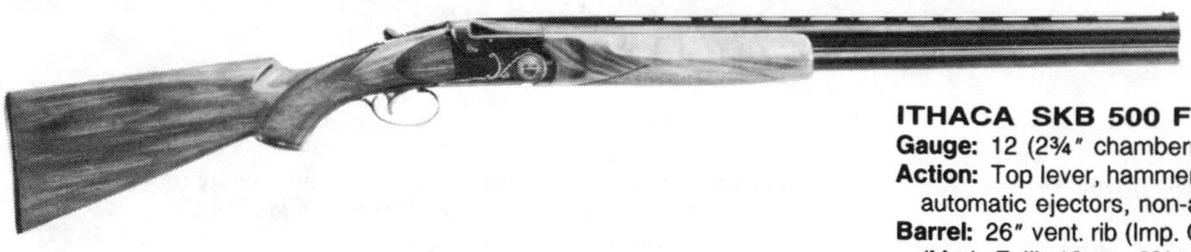

ITHACA SKB 500 FIELD GRADE O/U

Gauge: 12 (2¾" chambers), 20 (3").
Action: Top lever, hammerless, boxlock; gold-plated single selective trigger; automatic ejectors, non-auto safety.
Barrel: 26" vent. rib (Imp. Cyl., Mod.); 28" (Imp. cyl., Mod. or Mod., Full); 30" (Mod., Full); 12 ga., 2¾" chambers. 26" (Imp. Cyl., Mod.); 28" (Mod., Full); 20 ga., 3" chambers.
Stock: 14"x1½"x2⅝". Walnut, checkered p.g. and fore-end, p.g. cap, fluted comb.
Weight: 7½ lbs. (12); 6½ lbs. (20).
Features: Border scroll engraved receiver. Chrome lined bbls. and action. Raybar front sight.
Price: **$269.95**

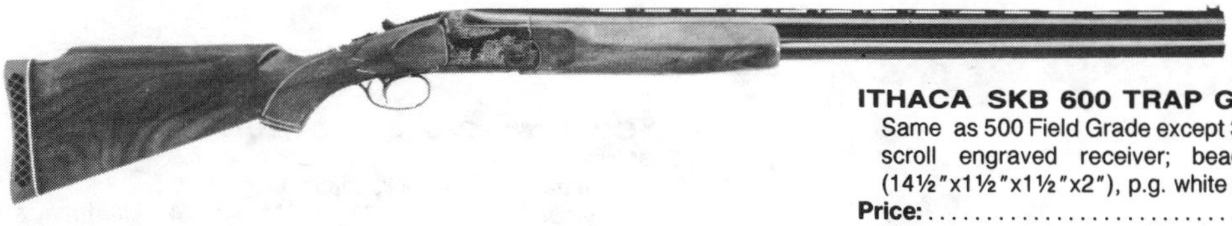

ITHACA SKB 600 TRAP GRADE O/U

Same as 500 Field Grade except 30" bbl. (Imp. Mod., Full, or Full, Full), fine scroll engraved receiver; bead middle sight; Monte Carlo stock (14½"x1½"x1½"x2"), p.g. white line spacer and recoil pad. Wgt. 7¾ lbs.
Price: **$324.95**
Field Grade 600, no recoil pad or Monte Carlo **309.95**
Field Grade 12 ga., 3" Magnum **319.95**
Trap Grade 700, select walnut oil finished stock and band engraved receiver **$399.95**

Ithaca SKB 600 Skeet Set O/U

Same as SKB 600 Skeet with three interchangeable, ventilated rib, chrome-lined, 28" barrels which have identical weight and balance. Barrels: 20 ga. (2¾"), 28 ga. (2¾") and 410 ga. (2½") all bored Skeet and Skeet. Deluxe carrying case included. **Price:** **$695.00**

Ithaca SKB 600 Skeet Grade O/U

Same as 600 Trap except: 26" or 28" bbls. (Skeet, Skeet), stock (14"x1½"x2⅝"), standard buttplate and whiteline spacer. Wgt. 7½ lbs. **$319.95**
Skeet Grade 700, select walnut oil finished stock and band engraved receiver **$399.95**

Ithaca SKB 700 Skeet Set O/U

Same as SKB 700 Skeet with above three barrels and deluxe carrying case. **Price:** **$895.00**

SAVAGE MODEL 24-S O/U

Gauge: Top bbl. 22 S, L, LR; bottom bbl. 410 or 20 ga. or 410, 3" chambers.
Action: Side lever opening; hammer has spur for bbl. selection. Separate extractors.
Barrel: 24"; top rifled; Full choke shotgun bbl. below.
Stock: 14"x1½"x2½". Walnut finish, p.g., corrugated buttplate.
Weight: 6¾ lbs. Over-all 40".
Features: Open rifle sights, rear adj. receiver grooved for scope mount.
Price: **$63.95**
With top bbl. for 22 RF Magnum **63.95**

Savage Model 24-D

Same specifications as Model 24-S except: two-way top lever opening, select walnut stock with Monte Carlo comb and beavertail fore-end, white line spacers, checkered; satin black, decorated receiver, trigger guard and lever **$77.95**
With top bbl., for 22 RF Magnum (20 ga. only) **77.95**

Savage Model 24-V

Same as Model 24-D except: 222 Rem. and 20 ga. only; satin-black frame and trigger; barrel band; folding leaf rear sight; rec. tapped for scope (scope base $2 extra) **$99.95**
With 4x scope as Model 24 V/S **130.50**

Savage Model 330 O/U Set

Identical to the Model 330 but with two sets of barrels, one in 12 ga. the other in 20 (Mod. & Full). Same fore-end fits both sets of bbls.
Price: Factory fitted **$287.95**
Price: Extra 20 ga. bbl. only (must be fitted at the factory) **$110.00**

SAVAGE MODEL 330 O/U

Gauge: 12, 2¾" chambers, 20 ga. 3" chambers.
Action: Top lever, break open. Selective single trigger, auto top tang safety locks trigger, coil springs.
Barrel: 26" (Mod. & Imp. Cyl.), 28" or 30" (Mod. & Full).
Stock: 14"x1½"x2½"). Walnut, checkered p.g. and fore-end, hard rubber plate.
Weight: About 7 lbs., 46½" (30" bbl.) over-all.
Features: Monoblock locking rails are engaged by locking shield that snaps forward as gun is closed. This shield overlaps the breech for added strength.
Price: **$199.95**

SAVAGE MODEL 440B O/U

Gauge: 12, 2¾" chambers, 20 ga. 3" chambers.
Action: Top lever, break open. Non-selective single trigger, auto. safety, all coil springs.
Barrel: 26" (Skeet & Skeet or Mod. & Imp. Cyl.), 28" (Mod. & Full), 30" 12 ga. only (Mod. & Full), all with vent rib and hard-chrome lined. **Stock:** 14"x1½"x2½". French walnut, hand checkered p.g. and fore-end, hand rubbed finish, hard rubber buttplate.
Weight: 6½ lbs., length 42½"-46½" over-all.
Features: Hand engraved steel receiver. Simple extractors. Fast hammer fall.
Price: $239.95
Trap Grade 440BT, with manual safety, extra wide trap style vent. rib, extractors, semi-beavertail fore-end, Monte Carlo stock and recoil pad. $289.95
Deluxe Grade 444B, with ejectors, single selective trigger and semi-beavertail fore-end $284.95

SEARS TED WILLIAMS O/U SHOTGUN

Gauge: 12 ga. (2¾") or 20 ga. (2¾" and 3").
Action: Boxlock, single selective trigger, selective auto-ejectors.
Barrel: 28" (Full & Mod.), 26" (Mod. & Imp. Cyl.).
Stock: Walnut, hand checkered p.g. and fore-end.
Weight: About 6¾ lbs. 45" over-all.
Features: Hand engraved steel receiver. Top Tang safety barrel selector. Full vent rib on chrome-lined barrels. Recoil pad installed.
Price: $335.00

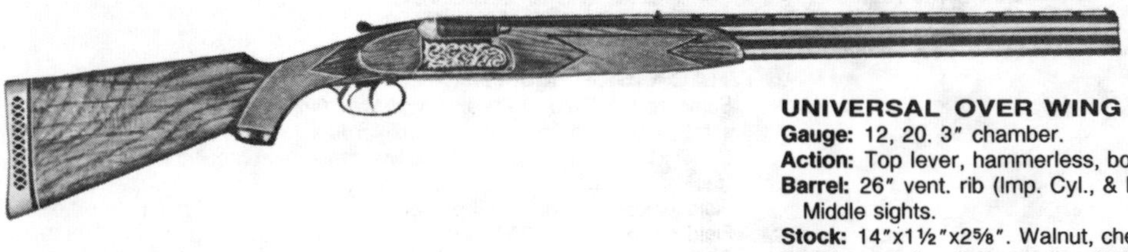

UNIVERSAL OVER WING O/U SHOTGUN

Gauge: 12, 20. 3" chamber.
Action: Top lever, hammerless, box lock, double triggers.
Barrel: 26" vent. rib (Imp. Cyl. & Mod.); 28" or 30" (Mod. & Full). Front & Middle sights.
Stock: 14"x1½"x2⅝". Walnut, checkered p.g. and fore-end. Recoil Pad.
Weight: 7½ lbs. (12); 6½ lbs. (20).
Price: $199.95
With single-trigger, engraved receiver and fancier stock 249.95

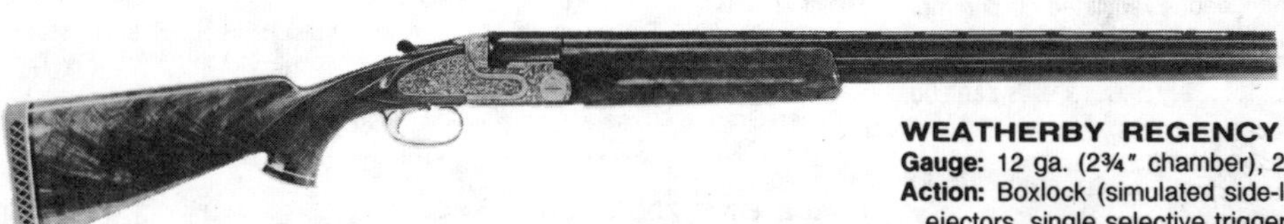

WEATHERBY REGENCY O/U SHOTGUN

Gauge: 12 ga. (2¾" chamber), 20 ga. (3" chamber).
Action: Boxlock (simulated side-lock) top lever break-open. Selective auto ejectors, single selective trigger (selector inside trigger guard).
Barrel: 28" with vent rib and bead front sight, Full & Mod., Mod. & Imp. Cyl. or Skeet & Skeet.
Stock: American walnut, checkered p.g. and fore-end (14¼"x1½"x2½").
Weight: 12 ga. 7⅜ lbs., 20 ga. 6⅞ lbs.
Features: Mechanically operated trigger. Top tang safety, Greener crossbolt, fully engraved receiver, recoil pad installed.
Price: 12 or 20 ga. $595.00

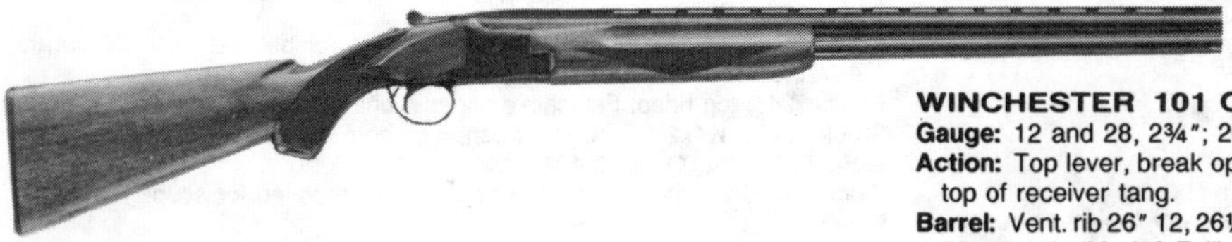

Winchester 101 Trap Gun

Same as the 101 Field gun except: Metal front and middle bead sights. 30" (Full & Full) bbl. only. 14⅜"x1⅜"x1⅞" stock with 1¼" pitch down and recoil pad. 12 ga. only $378.50
With Monte Carlo stock (14⅜"x1⅜"x1⅜"x1⅞"), 30" or 32", Full and Full or Imp. Mod. and Full $388.50

Winchester 101 Combination Trap Set

Same as M101 Trap except: Single bbl. 32" or 34" (Full) and extra over-under bbls. 30" or 32" (Imp.-Mod & Full). Includes fitted trunk case $588.00
3-bbl. set: 32" single bbl. (Full), 32" single bbl. (Imp.-Mod.), and 32" over-under bbls. (Imp.-Mod. & Full) $771.75

Winchester 101 Single Barrel Trap Gun

Same as M101 Trap except: Single bbl. 34" (Full), 32" (Full) or 32" (Imp.-Mod.) Vent.-rib. 12 ga. only. Monte Carlo stock $367.50

WINCHESTER 101 OVER/UNDER Field Gun

Gauge: 12 and 28, 2¾"; 20 and 410, 3".
Action: Top lever, break open. Manual safety combined with bbl. selector at top of receiver tang.
Barrel: Vent. rib 26" 12, 26½", 20 and 410 (Imp. Cyl., Mod.), 28" (Mod & Full), 30" 12 only (Mod. & Full). Metal bead front sight. Chrome plated chambers and bores.
Stock: 14"x1½"x2½". Checkered walnut p.g. and fore-end; fluted comb.
Weight: 12 ga. 7¾ lbs. Others 6¼ lbs.; 44¾" over-all (28" bbls.).
Features: Single selective trigger, auto ejectors. Hand engraved receiver.
Price: 12 or 20 ga. $367.50
Price: 28 or 410 ga. 388.50

Winchester 101 Magnum Field Gun

Same as 101 Field Gun except: chambers 3" Magnum shells; 12 & 20 ga. 30" (Full & Full) bbls. only; hand-engraved receiver, select French walnut stock with fluted comb, hand-checkered pistol grip and beavertail fore-end with recoil pad $367.50

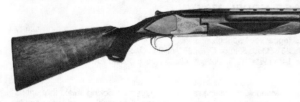

Winchester 101 Skeet

Same as M-101 except: 12 ga., 26" bbls., 20, 26½", 12, 20, 28 & 410, 28". Bored Skeet and Skeet only, 12 or 20 ga. $367.50
M101 in 28 or 410 .... 388.50

Winchester 101 Combination Skeet Set

Same as 101 20 ga. Skeet except: Includes Skeet bbls. in 410 & 28 ga. Vent. ribs match 20 ga. frame. With fitted trunk case $787.50

BROWNING BT-99 SINGLE BARREL TRAP
Gauge: 2¾" 12 gauge only.
Action: Top lever break-open hammerless, engraved.
Barrel: 32" or 34" (Mod., Imp. Mod. or Full) with ¹¹/₃₂" wide, high post floating vent rib.
Stock: French walnut, hand checkered full p.g. and beavertail fore-end, factory fitted recoil pad (14⅜"x1⁷/₁₆"x1⅝").
Weight: 8 lbs. (32" bbl.), 8⅛ lbs. (34" bbl.).
Features: Automatic ejector, gold plated trigger has about 3½ lb. pull, no safety.
Price: **$295.00**

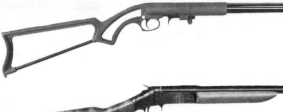

GARCIA BRONCO 410 SHOTGUN
Lightweight single shot (3" chamber), featuring swing-out chamber, skeletonized 1-pc. receiver and p.g. stock, push-button safety, 3½ lbs.
Price: **$26.95**

H & R TOPPER JR. MODEL 490
Like M158 except ideally proportioned stock for the smaller shooter. Can be cheaply changed to full size. 20 ga. (Mod.) or 410 (Full) 26" bbl. Weight 5 lbs., 40½" over-all **$41.00**

H & R TOPPER MODELS 158 and 198
Gauge: 12, 20 and 410. (2¾" or 3" chamber), 16 (2¾" only).
Action: Takedown. Side lever opening. External hammer, auto ejection. Case hardened frame.
Barrel: 12 ga., 28", 30", 32", 36"; 20 and 410 ga., 28". (Full choke). 12, 16, 20 ga. available 28" (Mod.).
Stock: Walnut finished hardwood; p.g., recoil pad. (14"x1¾"x2½").
Weight: 5 to 6½ lbs., according to gauge and bbl. length.
Features: Self-adj. bbl. lock; coil springs throughout; auto. rebound hammer.
Price: M158 .... **$39.95**
   Model 198, Topper Deluxe Chrome frame, ebony finished stock. 20 ga. and 410, 28" bbl. **$44.95**

H & R TOPPER BUCK MODEL 162
Same as M158 except 12 ga. 24" cyl. bored bbl., adj. Lyman peep rear sight, blade front, 5½ lbs.; over-all 40". Cross bolt safety: push-button action release **$42.95**

Ithaca Model 66 Supersingle Youth
Same as the 66 Standard except: 20 (26" Bbl., Mod.) and 410 ga. (26" Bbl., Full) shorter stock with recoil pad **$41.95**
With vent. rib, 20 ga. only **$51.95**

ITHACA MODEL 66 SUPERSINGLE
Gauge: 12, 20, 410 (3" chamber).
Action: Non-takedown; under lever opening.
Barrel: 12, 20 ga. 28" (Mod., Full); 12 ga., 30" (Full), 410, 26" (Full).
Stock: Straight grip walnut-finish stock and fore-end.
Weight: About 7 lbs.
Features: Rebounding hammer independent of the lever.
Price: **$36.95**
   With vent. rib, 20 ga. only **$49.95**

Ithaca Model 66 RS Supersingle Buckbuster
Same as the Model 66 Standard except: 12 and 20 ga. only, 22" bbl. with rifle sights, designed to shoot slugs **$49.95**

Ithaca 5E Grade Single Barrel Trap
Same as 4E except: Vent. rib bbl., better wood, more extensive engraving, and gold inlaid figures. Custom made: **$2,000.00**

Ithaca $4500 Grade Ejector
Same as 5E except: Special wood, better engraving, figures inlaid in green and yellow gold and platinum, gold plated trigger. **$4,500.00**
Gauge: 12 (2¾" chamber)
Weight: About 8½ lbs.

ITHACA 4E GRADE SINGLE BARREL TRAP GUN
Gauge: 12 only.
Action: Top lever break open hammerless, dual locking lugs.
Barrel: 30" or 32", rampless rib.
Stock: (14½"x1½"x1⅞"). Select walnut, checkered p.g. and beavertail fore-end, p.g. cap, recoil pad, Monte Carlo comb, cheekpiece, Cast-on, cast-off or extreme deviation from standard stock dimensions $100 extra. Reasonable deviation allowed without extra charge.
Features: Frame, top lever and trigger guard engraved. Gold name plate in stock.
Price: Custom made: **$1,500.00**

ITHACA PERAZZI SINGLE BARREL
Gauge: 12 (2¾" chamber)
Action: Top lever, break open, top tang safety.
Barrel: 32" or 34"; custom choking; ventilated rib.
Stock: Custom fitted European walnut in lacquered or oil finish.
Weight: About 8½ lbs.
Features: Hand-engraved receiver; interchangeable stocks available with some fitting.
Price: **$795.00**

SAVAGE MODEL 220L SINGLE
Gauge: 12, 16, 20, 410 (12, 20 and 410, 3" chambers).
Action: Side lever break open; automatic top tang safety; hammerless; auto ejector.
Barrel: 12 ga. 30"; 16, 20 ga. 28"; 410 ga. 26". Full choke only.
Stock: 14"x1½"x2½". Walnut, p.g. full fore-end.
Weight: About 6 lbs. Over-all 52" (30" bbl.).
Features: Unbreakable coil springs; satin black finish.
Price: **$47.95**

SAVAGE-STEVENS MODEL 94-C Single Barrel Gun
Gauge: 12, 16, 20, 410 (12, 20 and 410, 3" chambers).
Action: Top lever break open; hammer; auto. ejector.
Barrel: 12 ga. 28", 30", 36"; 16, 20 ga. 28"; 410 ga. 26". Full choke only.
Stock: 14"x1½"x2½". Walnut finish, checkered p.g. and fore-end.
Weight: About 6 lbs. Over-all 42" (26" bbl.).
Features: Color case-hardened frame, low rebounding hammer.
Price: 26" to 32" bbls. . . . . . . **$41.25** 36" bbl. **$42.50**

Stevens M94-Y Youth's Gun
Same as Model 940 except: 26" bbl., 20 ga. Mod. or 410 Full, 12½" stock with recoil pad. Wgt. about 5½ lbs. 40½" over-all. **$42.50**

SEARS SINGLE BARREL GUN
Gauge: 12, 20, 410 (All 3" chambers.)
Action: Top tang lever break-open. External hammer, auto. ejector, coil springs.
Barrel: 12 ga., 30"; 20 ga., 28"; 410, 26". Full choke only.
Stock: 14"x1½"x2½". Walnut finish hardwood, p.g.
Weight: About 7 lbs.
Features: Wide cocking lever; decorated frame.
Price: **$39.99**
Youth's Model. 12½" stock with recoil pad; 20 ga. 26" bbl., Mod. choke, or 410 ga., 26" bbl., Full choke. Wgt. about 6½ lbs.
Price: **$39.99**

UNIVERSAL SINGLE WING SHOTGUN
Gauge: 12, 20; 3" chamber.
Action: Top break, takedown, external hammer.
Barrel: 32" (Full), 30" (Full or Mod.) 12 ga. only; 28" (Mod. or Full); 26" (Mod. or Imp. Cyl.) 20 ga. only.
Stock: Walnut, p.g.
Weight: About 7 lbs.
Features: Beavertail fore-end. Automatic ojection.
Price: **$41.50**

WESTERN FIELD 100 Single Barrel Gun
Gauge: 12, 16, 20, 410 (410, 3" chamber).
Action: Hammerless; thumb slide break open.
Barrel: 12 ga., 30"; 16, 20 ga., 28"; 410 ga., 26". All Full choke.
Stock: Walnut finished, p.g., recoil pad.
Weight: 6¼ to 7 lbs.
Features: Automatic safety, auto ejector.
Price: **$48.99**
Also available as Youth's Model. 26" barrel, 20 or 410 gauge. Wgt. 6 lbs., 41" over-all **$49.99**

WINCHESTER MODEL 370 Single Barrel
Gauge: 12, 20, 410 (3" chamber); 16 and 28 (2¾").
Action: Top break, takedown, external hammer.
Barrel: 12 ga., 30", 32", 36"; 16 ga., 30", 32"; 20 and 28 ga., 28"; 410 ga., 26". Full choke only.
Stock: Hardwood p.g. (14"x1⅜"x2⅜"), full fore-end.
Weight: 5½ to 6¼ lbs. Over-all 48¼" (32" bbl.).
Features: Auto. ejection, rebounding hammer. Top snap opens left or right.
Price: . . . . **$41.95**   **Price:** 12 ga. 36" bbl. **$43.25**
Also available as Youth's Model. 12½" stock, 20 or 410 ga. Wgt. 5½ (410) or 6 lbs., 26" bbl., 40¾" overall **$43.25**

Marlin-Glenfield Model 50 Bolt Action

Same as the Marlin Goose Gun except: 12 and 20 ga., 3″. No sling or swivels. Bbls. 12 ga. 28″, 20 ga. 26″ (Full). Wgt. 7 lbs., 49″ over-all (28″ bbl.).
Price: **$49.95**

MARLIN GOOSE GUN BOLT ACTION
Gauge: 12 only, 3-shot (3″ chamber).
Action: Takedown bolt action, thumb safety, detachable clip.
Barrel: 36″, Full choke.
Stock: Walnut, p.g., recoil pad, leather strap & swivels.
Weight: 7¼ lbs., 57″ over-all.
Features: Double extractors, tapped for receiver sights. Swivels and leather carrying strap. Gold-plated trigger.
Price: **$62.95**

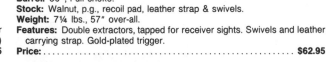

MOSSBERG MODEL 183K BOLT ACTION
Gauge: 410, 3-shot (3″ chamber).
Action: Bolt; top-loading mag.; thumb safety.
Barrel: 25″ with C-Lect-Choke.
Stock: Walnut finish, p.g., Monte Carlo comb.
Weight: 5½ lbs. 43½″ over-all.
Features: Moulded trigger guard with finger grooves.
Price: **$48.30**

MOSSBERG MODEL 395K BOLT ACTION
Gauge: 12, 3-shot (3″ chamber).
Action: Bolt; takedown; detachable clip.
Barrel: 28″ with C-Lect-Choke.
Stock: Walnut finish, p.g. Monte Carlo comb; recoil pad.
Weight: 6¾ lbs. 47½″ over-all.
Features: Streamlined action; top safety; grooved rear sight.
Price: **$59.25**
Also available in 20 ga. 3″ chamber 28″ bbl. 6¼ lbs., as M385K, **$54.55**, and in 16 ga. 28″ bbl., 6¾ lbs., as M390K **$58.20**

Mossberg Model 395S Bolt Action

Same as Model 395K except 24″ barrels with adjustable folding leaf. rear sight and ramp front, for use with slugs. Sling supplied **$61.30**

SEARS BOLT ACTION 410
Gauge: 410, single shot, 3″ chamber.
Action: Top loading, self-cocking bolt.
Barrel: 24″, Full choke.
Stock: Walnut finished hardwood, p.g., corrugated buttplate.
Weight: 4¾ lbs. 43″ over-all.
Features: Automatic thumb safety.
Price: **$34.99**
Same as above except a repeater with 2-shot detachable clip. Wgt. 5½ lbs.
. . . . **$41.99**

SEARS MODEL 140 BOLT ACTION
Gauge: 12, 20; 3-shot, (3″ chambers).
Action: Self-cocking bolt.
Barrel: 25″, with adj. choke.
Stock: Walnut finished, p.g., corrugated buttplate.
Weight: 7½ lbs. (12 ga.); 7 lbs. (20 ga.); 46″ over-all.
Features: Double extractors; thumb safety; 2 shot detachable clip.
Price: 12 or 20 ga. plain bbl. **$49.99**
Price: With adj. choke **54.99**

SAVAGE-STEVENS M51 SINGLE SHOT BOLT ACTION
Gauge: 410, 3″ chamber.
Action: Top loading, streamlined bolt action.
Barrel: 24″ Full choke.
Stock: Walnut finish, checkered fore-end and p.g.
Weight: About 4¾ lbs. Over-all 43½″.
Features: Band extractor, automatic thumb safety.
Price: **$37.95**

Savage-Stevens 59 Bolt Action

Same as Model 58 410 ga. except: tubular mag. holding five 3″ or six 2½″ shells; 3-shot plug furnished; no recoil pad. Wgt. 6 lbs. 24″ bbl., 44½″ over-all **$56.95**

SAVAGE-STEVENS 58 BOLT ACTION SHOTGUN
Gauge: 12, 16, 20 2¾″ chambers. 20 ga. also in 3″. (2-shot detachable clip).
Action: Self-cocking bolt; double extractors; thumb safety.
Barrel: 25″, Full choke.
Stock: Walnut finish, checkered fore-end and p.g., recoil pad.
Weight: 7-7½ lbs. Over-all 46″ (43½″ in 410)
Features: Crisp trigger pull.
Price: **$55.95**
Also available in 410 ga., 3″ chamber, 3-shot detachable clip, 5½ lbs. 43½″ over-all **$46.95**

WESTERN FIELD 172 BOLT ACTION SHOTGUN
Gauge: 12 (3″ chamber).
Action: Self-cocking bolt. Thumb safety, double locking lugs, detachable clip.
Barrel: 28″ adj. choke, shoots rifled slugs.
Stock: Walnut, Monte Carlo design, p.g., recoil pad.
Features: Quick removable bolt with double extractors, grooved rear sight.
Price: **$57.95**
M175 Similar to above except 20 ga., **$53.95**. Without recoil pad and adj. choke **$52.95**

FOREIGN GUNS—AUTOLOADING PISTOLS

ASTRA CONSTABLE AUTO PISTOL
A new small frame double-action auto made in Spain in calibers 22 LR, 32 ACP and 380 ACP. Capacity: 10 rounds 22, 8 rounds 32 and 7 rounds 380. Fixed sights, quick takedown without tools, non-glare rib on slide. Weight, 26 oz.; barrel length, 3½". Garcia, importer **$89.95**

BERETTA Model 90 PISTOL
A new double action pocket pistol. 3½" bbl., 6¾" over-all length, 8 round magazine; 19 oz., blue finish; checked black plastic wrap-around grips; fixed sights; sighting rib on slide. Rod extractor functions as chamber indicator. Slide stays open on last shot. In 32 ACP only. From Garcia **$129.00**

BERETTA MODEL 70S AUTO PISTOL
All-steel auto pistol in caliber 380; 7-round magazine. Fixed sights, two-piece wrap-around grips, external grooved hammer. Weight, 23¼ oz.; length over-all, 6¼"; barrel, 6". Garcia, importer **$95.00**

BERETTA MODELS 70T & 101 AUTO PISTOLS
All-purpose auto pistol with target-length barrel in 32 ACP (Model 70T) or 22 LR (Model 101). Magazine capacity: 9 rounds (32 cal.) or 10 rounds (22 cal.) Adjustable rear sight, slide remains open after last shot, checkered grips. Weight, 19 oz.; length over-all, 9½"; barrel, 6". Garcia, importer **$85.00**

BERETTA MODEL 76 AUTO PISTOL
Competition auto-loader with adjustable rear sights and 3 interchangeable front blades in caliber 22 LR; 10-round magazine. Heavy barrel, non-glare rib on slide, wrap-around checkered grips. Weight, 26 oz.; length over-all, 9½"; barrel, 6". Garcia, importer **$99.00**

BERETTA MODEL 951 AUTO PISTOL
Military and police auto-loader in caliber 9mm Parabellum; 8-round magazine. Fixed sights, crossbolt safety, external grooved hammer. Weight, 31 oz.; length over-all, 8"; barrel, 4½". Garcia, importer **$160.00**

ERMA KGP BABY
Made in 32 and 380 auto., 6-shot magazine and 2¾" barrel, this toggle-bolt pistol is reminiscent of the Luger design. Blue-black finish; checkered walnut grips; sidelock safety. Length 5¼" over-all, weight about 19 oz. R. G. Industries, Inc., importer **$89.95**

ERMA KGP 9mm AUTO PISTOL
9MM version of the P-08. 8-shot magazine. Checkered walnut grips. Toggle-bolt stays open on last shot. Fixed barrel with double action feature and falling block thumb safety lever. Open notch rear and blade front sight. Weighs 38½ oz., 4⅜" bbl., 8½" over-all. Blued. R. G. Industries, Inc., importer **$129.95**

ERMA FB1 PISTOL
Lightweight (14 oz.) 25-caliber pistol has 6-shot magazine. 5⅜" over-all with 2½" barrel, all steel frame with walnut grips and thumb safety. Blued finish. R. G. Industries, Inc., importer **$39.95**

ERMA 22 PISTOLEN

22 version of the famous Model P-08. 8-shot magazine takes 22 LR. Checkered walnut grips. Familiar toggle-bolt stays open on last shot. Open notch rear and blade front sight. 9" over-all, wgt. 36 oz. with a 4⅝" bbl. Blued. R. G. Industries, Inc., importer **$79.95**

HAWES WASP MARK I PISTOL

A basic hammerless blowback smallbore pocket pistol. 6-shot magazine, 4½" over-all, weight 12 oz., smooth white plastic grips.
25 ACP, blue . . . . **$29.95**   Chrome **$30.95**

LLAMA MODEL IXA AUTO PISTOL

45 ACP cal. Blued finish, ribbed slide, broad hammer spur and adj. square notch rear and blade front target sights. 7-shot magazine. Wgt. 2 lbs. 6 oz., 5⅜" high, 8½" over-all, 5" bbl. Thumb and grip safeties. Stoeger, importer
. . . . **$92.50**

LLAMA MODEL VIII AUTO PISTOL

Same as above except: Super 38 cal., 9-shot, 2 lbs. 6½ oz. . . . **$92.50**

MAB AUTOLOADING PISTOL

Uses a rotary unlocking system, exposed hammer. 8 or 15 shot magazine, thumb safety, fixed sights. Blued finish. Cal. 9mm, wgt. 38 oz. Mars Equipment, importers **$109.00**

MAUSER HSc AUTO PISTOL

This commercial model is made in West Germany by the original Mauser organization. In cals. 32 (8-shot) and 380 (7-shot) Auto. Pistol is 6⅜" over-all, with a 3⅜" bbl. and weighs 23 oz. Features exposed hammer spur, double action with thumb safety lever and magazine disconnect safety. Also, walnut checkered grips, blued finish and fixed sights. Interarms, importer
. . . . **$118.00**

MAUSER PARABELLUM PISTOL

Mauser is again producing Georg Luger's famous Parabellum in both 7.65 mm (6" bbl.) and 9mm (4" bbl.). Has manual and grip safeties, chamber "loaded" indicator, and hold-open to latch action open after last shot. Checkered walnut grips, blued finish, fixed sights. Interarms, importers
. . . . **$265.00**

SIG 210 AUTOMATICS

Available in 22 LR, 7.65 Luger or 9mm Luger, 8-shot 4¾" bbl., 8½" over-all, wgt. approx. 34 oz. Double pull trigger. Fixed notch rear, blade front sights. Grooved wooden grips. Thumb safety. Polished blue finish. Imported by Grieder, Benet Arms Co., & Casanova Guns **$220.00**
With checkered hard rubber grips and matte finish **197.00**
Conversion unit, available with all components necessary to convert to cal. 22 . . . . **$100.00**

SIG 210 TARGET AUTOMATICS

Same as the M210 except: 7.65mm and 9mm only. 6" bbl., adj. target trigger, micro. rear sight adj. for w. and e.; adj. front sight. Hard rubber grips and matte finish. Wgt. 38⅓ oz., 9⅔" over-all. **$249.00**
Same, but with 4¾" bbl. **225.00**

STAR MODEL A, B & P AUTOS

Based on the U. S. Pistol, M1911A1 short recoil system with half-cock and thumb safeties, exposed hammers, these pistols feature 9-shot (.38 Super Model A & 9MM Para. Model B) and 7-shot (45ACP Model P) magazines. Weigh approx. 2 lbs. 6 oz., have 5" bbl., and are 8½" over-all. They have checkered walnut grips, fixed sights and are blued. Garcia, importer
. . . . **$95.50**

ERMA 22 "NAVY" PISTOLEN

Similar to Erma 22 Luger, except with 12" barrel, walnut fore-end, adj. rear sight. 16½" over-all, 48 oz. R. G. Industries, Inc., importer **$99.95**

FOREIGN GUNS—AUTOLOADING PISTOLS

STAR MODEL FR AUTO PISTOL
All feature quick takedown, thumbrest grips, checkered backstrap, thumb- and half-cock safeties. 22 LR, 10-shot magazine; extra mag. furnished at prices shown. Garcia, importer. Standard, 5″ bbl. 26 oz. Fixed sights.
Blued . . . . . **$61.00**   Chromed . . . . . **$75.00**   Chromed, engr. **$94.95**

STAR STARLIGHT PISTOL
A recoil-operated, Browning-type design with light alloy frame. A shortened, lightened version of the Star Model B, 9mm Parabellum cal. only. 4¼″ bbl., 25 oz. blue finish, checked wood grips, fixed sights. Garcia, importer **$95.50**

WALTHER P-38 AUTOMATIC PISTOL
This commercial model is made in W. Germany of lightweight alloys, in polished blue finish. Weight 27½ oz., 8⁷/₁₆″, over-all; 4¹⁵/₁₆″ barrel. Safety locks firing pin, blocks action and drops the hammer; signal pin indicating when chamber is loaded; single or double action, external hammer. 8-shot magazine (2 furnished), checkered plastic grips and lanyard swivel are standard. Interarms, importer **$140.00**
Same but with matte finish **106.00**
Same but in 22 LR cal. with matte finish **132.00**

WALTHER MODEL PP PISTOL
A line of pocket auto pistols that feature an exposed hammer, double or single action. Indicator pin shows if chamber is loaded. Bbl. length, 3⅞″; wgt., 23 ozs., over-all, 6⁵/₁₆″, Mag. capacity, 8 shots except 380 cal. holds 7. Cals. 32 or 380. Blued. Interarms **$119.00**
In 22 LR caliber **$122.00**

WALTHER SPORT MODEL PISTOL
Basically the Walther PP in 22 LR, this pistol offers a longer barrel (6″), click rear sight, thumb rest grips, extension mag. Interarms, importer . **$122.00**

WALTHER PPKS
A shortened version of the PP, replacing the PPK which did not qualify for importation. It is the PP fitted with PPK slide and barrel. White-insert combat sights. In 22 LR, 10 shots; 32, 8; 380, 7. 3⁵/₁₆″ bbl, 6³/₁₆″ over-all, 4⁵/₁₆″ high.
32 and 380 . . . . **$119.00** 22 . . . . **$122.00**

FOREIGN GUNS—MATCH PISTOLS

HAMMERLI INTERNATIONAL AUTO PISTOLS
Adj. precision trigger set for 2 lbs. 7¹/₁₆″ bbl., high speed action, micro. rear sight adj. for w. and e. ⅛″ front sight. Muzzle brake and bbl. wgt. standard. Thumbrest, checkered grips. 22 S or LR **$215.00**
M208 has 6″ bbl., is without muzzle brake, and has a 3-lb. trigger pull. Designed for Ladies Matches, it weighs only 35 oz. Price . . . .**N.A.**
M209 offers several advanced features: 6 gas ports over chamber permit adj. of leakage for balancing to various cartridge brands or types; new combination muzzle brake and new light bolt for less jar. Cal. 22 Short only.
M209, standard walnut grips . . . .**N.A.**
M210, adj. walnut grips . . . .**N.A.**
Regular grips with thumbrest and checkering **$15.00**. Adj. grips with checkering **$40.00**. Magazine for cal. 22 S or LR **$9.00**. Additional Wgt. **$6.00**. Muzzle brake **$4.00**. Grieder, importer.

WALTHER OSP RAPID FIRE MATCH PISTOL
A newly designed pistol, complying with International Rules. 22 Short only; 5-shot magazine. Simple barrel take-down; bolt held open after last shot. Weight, about 41 oz., 11⅞″ over-all. 5¾″ bbl. Supplied with spare magazine, barrel weight, cleaning rod, brush and wrench. Interarms, importer
. . . . **$220.00**
Walther GSP variant of OSP with slabside heavy bbl., no weights.
. . . . **$240.00**

FOREIGN GUNS—REVOLVERS

ARMINIUS REVOLVERS

Solid-frame, double-action, swing-out cylinder revolvers with lock-work assembled to grip frame. Ventilated rib, 3", 4", 6" bbls., also 9½" bbl w/o vent. rib. Floating firing pin, checkered one-piece plastic grips. F.I.E. Corp., importer.

Standard model, 22 LR, 6" bbl. blued	**$39.95**
Chromed	**$45.95**
Standard model, 22 Magnum, 6" bbl., blued	**$45.95**
Combo model, 22 LR and interchangeable 22 Mag. cyl. 6" bbl., blued	**$53.55**
Combo model, same as above, chromed	**$58.95**
9½" bbl. blued	**$58.95**
Combo model with adj. sights, 6" bbl. blued	**$65.95**
9½" bbl.	**$68.95**
Target model, adj. sights, 4" bbl., 22 LR, blued	**$47.95**
Chromed	**$51.95**
Target model, adj. sights, 6" bbl., 22 LR, blued	**$47.95**
Chromed	**$51.95**
Target model, 32 S&W Long, 4" bbl., blued	**$51.95**
Chromed	**$55.95**
Target model, 38 Special, 3" or 4" bbls., blued	**$57.95**
Chromed	**$61.95**
Target model, 38 Special, 6" bbl., blued	**$61.95**

ASTRA CADIX REVOLVERS

Double action revolvers with adj. rear sight; shrouded ejector rod; one piece checkered stocks and swing out cylinder. Cals. 22 LR (9 shots) or 38 Spec. (5 shots) with 4" or 6" bbl. Wgt. 25 to 27 oz., blued, Garcia, importer **$65.50**

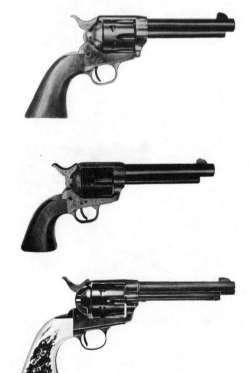

DAKOTA REVOLVERS

Single action revolvers with case hardened receivers; brass trigger guard and backstrap; fixed sights; floating firing pin and one-piece smooth walnut grips. 4⅝", 5½", or 7½" barrels ($2.25 extra for 7½") in 22 rimfire, 22 WMR, 357 Magnum or 45 Colt caliber. Intercontinental Arms **$89.75**
With extra 22 WMR cylinder **$97.20**
Also as Super Dakota in 41 and 44 Magnum calibers, 5½" and 7½" bbls. with flat-top frame, adj. sights front and rear, long magnum grip, square-back guard **$99.75**

DAKOTA ENGRAVED MODELS

Identical to $89.75 models above, and in same calibers, but heavily engraved in scroll and floral pattern on frame, cylinder and hammer. Guard and straps polished bright brass, frame finished bright, rest blue. One-piece smooth walnut grips.
4⅝" and 5½" bbls .... **$165.00**   7½" **$175.00**

HAWES WESTERN MARSHAL REVOLVERS

Single action, frontier style 6-shot revolvers made in 45 Long Colt, 357 or 44 Mag. Moulded stag grips, floating firing pin, 5½" barrel, fixed sights. All working parts of steel, blue finish over-all. Weight, 40 oz. **$89.95**
As above, but with an extra cylinder compatible with the barrel, 357 Mag./9mm, 44 Mag/44-40, 45 Colt/45ACP **$99.95**
As above but in 22 S, L or LR cal. **$54.95**   22 WMR **$57.95**
With both 22 cal. cylinders **64.95**

HAWES MONTANA MARSHAL REVOLVERS

Same as Western Marshal except: solid brass backstrap and trigger guard, hand-rubbed rosewood grips **$99.95**
As above, but in 22 cal. rimfire **64.95**

FOREIGN GUNS—REVOLVERS

HAWES CHIEF MARSHAL REVOLVER

Single action, frontier style, 6-shot revolver in 357, 44 Magnum or 45 Colt caliber. Ramp front sight, click adjustable target rear sight let into raised boss on top strap. Blue finish; smooth rosewood grips; 6″ bbl., 48 oz. 11¾″ over-all **$109.95**

HAWES TEXAS MARSHAL

Same as Western Marshal except: revolver is fully chromed with black or white Pearlite grips **$104.95**
As above, but in 22 cal. rimfire **69.95**

HAWES VIRGINIA CITY MARSHAL REVOLVER

Same as Western Marshal except frame and barrel are blue, cylinder, guard and backstrap in bright nickel plate; pearlite grips **$99.95**
As above, but in 22 cal. rimfire **$64.95**

HERTER'S GUIDE REVOLVERS

Solid-frame double-action, swing-out cylinder revolver with lockwork assembled to removable trigger guard/grip frame. Click-adjustable rear sight, ventilated rib, one-piece checked plastic grip.
22 LR, 8-shot, 4″ or 6″ bbl., blue . **$39.95**   Chromed **$44.95**
38 Spl., 6-shot, 4″ or 6″ bbl., chromed **49.95**

HERTER'S CUSTOM GRADE SUPER REVOLVER

Same as the Powermag except in 357 Mag. or 44 Mag. cal. **$59.95**

HERTER'S WESTERN SINGLE ACTION

22 rimfire, 6-shot single action revolver with 5″ bbl., plastic staghorn grip, blade front sight, rear adj. for w & e. Blued **$27.45**

I.N.A. TIGER REVOLVERS

5 shot, walnut grips, swing-out cylinder. 3″ or 4½″ barrel. Weight 13½ oz. (3″ bbl.) 38 Spl.
Blued .... **$52.95**   Nickeled **$55.95**
Same, only 32 S&W Long, 6 shot cylinder.
Blued **$50.95**

LLAMA MARTIAL 22 REVOLVER

A match revolver in 22 LR cal. with 6″ vent. rib bbl. Micro rear sight adj. for w. and e. Wide, grooved trigger and hammer. Recessed cyl. Target style, checkered walnut grips. Wgt. 26 oz. Stoeger, agents. **$74.50**

FOREIGN GUNS—REVOLVERS

LLAMA MARTIAL 38 REVOLVER
Similar to above except 38 Spl. cal., 4″ (29 oz.) or 6″ bbl. **$74.50**
Llama Martials also available in chrome or blue engraved **$112.50**
In chrome plate . . . .**.89.95**

ROSSI REVOLVERS
32 S&W Long and 38 spl. (6-shot) revolvers with swing-out cylinders, simultaneous ejection. 3″ or 4″ bbls. Wgt.: 32, 19 oz. 7″ over-all. In presentation case. Garcia, importer.
32 S & W, 4″ bbl. blue or nickel plated finish **$65.00**
38 Spl., 4″ bbl., blue or nickel plated finish . . . .**.65.00**

J. P. SAUER MEDALLION REVOLVER
6-shot swing-out cylinder double action revolver. With adj. rear sight, checkered walnut grips, wide trigger and hammer spur. Cal. 38 S&W Spl. with 3″, 4″ or 6″ bbl.; or 22 LR with 4″ or 6″ bbl. 11⅛″ over-all, wgt. about 39 oz. (6″). Blued. Hawes Firearms Co., importer. **$124.95**

J. P. SAUER TROPHY REVOLVER
Same as above except with walnut thumbrest target grips and vent. rib, 6″ bbl. only. **$139.95**

STALLION SINGLE ACTION REVOLVER
6-shot, loading and ejection through loading gate. Cals. 22 LR or 22 WMR, 5½″ or 6½″ bbl., 11⅝″ over-all (6½″), wgt. 2 lbs., 6 oz. Rear sight adj. for w.&e., ramp front. Smooth walnut grips with interior fastening. Blued. Galef, importer **$87.00**
Also in 357 Mag. or 45 Colt . . . .**.89.95**

TAURUS REVOLVER
Swing-out cylinder, checkered grips, fixed sights. Cal. 38 Spl., 4″ round bbl., 6-shot. Wgt. 32 oz. Blued or nickel. International Distributors, importer.
. . . . **$60.50**

FOREIGN GUNS—FLINTLOCKS, PERCUSSIONS, REPLICAS

DIXIE KENTUCKY PERCUSSION PISTOL
Muzzle-loading caplock single shot with 9″ octagonal rifled barrel, cal. 40. Maple stock, brass furniture, open sights. Black powder only **$62.50**
Same as above except flintlock . . . .**.69.50**
Dixie shows numerous other flintlock and percussion revolvers and pistols in their catalog 120 cost $2.00 post paid.

DIXIE FLORENTINE HOLSTER PISTOL
A flintlock with a 13″ smoothbore barrel, 21″ over-all. Walnut full stock. All furniture is ornamented in high relief and silver plated; barrel polished bright.
. . . . **$179.95**

FOREIGN GUNS—FLINTLOCKS, PERCUSSIONS, REPLICAS

DIXIE DUELING PISTOL
Muzzle-loading caplock with 9″ smooth bored barrel, caliber from 44 to 50. Rubbed maple stock, front action lock **$42.50**

DIXIE SPANISH PERCUSSION PISTOL
Caliber 40 smooth bore, checkered grip and steel fittings, with ramrod
.... **$19.95**

DIXIE PHILADELPHIA DERRINGER
Caliber 41, 3½″ barrel, blued lock and barrel checkered walnut stock
.... **$22.50**

DIXIE PERCUSSION DERRINGER
Percussion, caliber 41 with brass frame and walnut grips **$21.50**

DIXIE 1860 ARMY REVOLVER
Replica of the Colt 1860 Army with 8″ barrel, half fluted cylinder, cut for shoulder stock **$89.95**

DIXIE NAVY REVOLVER
Caliber 36 with blued steel barrel and cylinder and brass frame replica of the Colt Navy **$39.95**
Engraved model **$57.50**

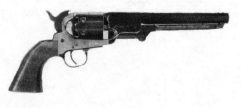

DIXIE TROPHY WINNER SINGLE SHOT PISTOL
Caliber 44 percussion with 10″ blued octagon barrel. Casehardened frame with etched western scene; fixed ramp front and adjustable rear sight. Over-all length 12¾″, weight 42 oz **$49.50**
Shotgun Pistol Barrel for above (28 ga. 10″ octagon) **$12.95**

FOREIGN GUNS—FLINTLOCKS, PERCUSSIONS, REPLICAS

F.I.E. NAVY REPLICA

A replica of the Colt 1851 Navy revolver. Caliber 36 percussion. 7½" octagon barrel; plain brass frame; one-piece wooden grips. weight 40 oz.
.... **$48.00**

Engraved version **$56.00**
Also available as the 44 Navy in 44 Cal. Similar to above but with larger diameter cylinder. Plain grade only **$50.50**

F.I.E. BABY DRAGOON REPLICA

A replica of the Colt Baby Dragoon. Caliber 31 percussion. 4" or 6" octagon barrel; engraved cylinder; plain brass frame, square back brass trigger guard **$38.15**
Presentation engraved version **$44.70**

F.I.E. SECOND MODEL DRAGOON REPLICA

A replica of the Colt 2nd Model Dragoon. Caliber 44 percussion. 7¼" round barrel; length 14" over-all; hammer, frame and rammer case hardened; barrel and cylinder blued; engraved cylinder **$90.00**

F.I.E. REMINGTON REPLICA

A replica of the New Army Remington revolver Model 1858. Caliber 44 percussion. 7¾" blued octagon barrel; plain brass frame; blued cylinder; case hardened hammer and trigger. Length 13½" over-all, weight 42 oz.
.... **$55.50**

F.I.E. TARGET PERCUSSION

Caliber 44 percussion, single shot pistol. 9" Octagon barrel; case hardened receiver; brass trim. Adjustable rear sight. Weight 43 oz. **$55.00**

F.I.E. TOWER FLINTLOCK

Caliber 69 smooth bore flintlock pistol. 9" barrel; 15½" over-all length. Solid brass trim, wood stock and ramrod. Weight 48 oz. **$28.75**
Also available with half-octagon barrel **$30.35**

F.I.E. PERCUSSION AND FLINTLOCK PISTOLS

Caliber 44 pistols in either flintlock or percussion with rifled, engraved octagon barrels, brass hardware, hardwood stocks. Barrel length 9¾", over-all length 15"; weight 40 oz. Either percussion or flintlock **$47.95**

HAWES FAVORITE PISTOL

Replica of the famous Stevens Favorite tip-up target pistol, with chrome frame and blued 8″ barrel, moulded checkered white plastic grips. Fires 22 S, L or LR single-shot. Weight, 20 oz.; length 12″ over-all **$35.95**

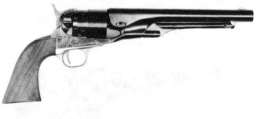

KENTUCKIAN FLINTLOCK or PERCUSSION PISTOL

A single shot pistol designed for black powder only. 9½″ octagon barrel, caliber 44, rifled. Brass front and steel rear sights are dovetailed into barrel. Case hardened, engraved lockplate. Trigger guard, barrel cap, ramrod tip and thimbles solid brass. Polished one-piece full-length stock of select walnut. Weight about 40 oz.; 15½″ over-all. Imported by Intercontinental Arms. Either form **$59.95**

MARS EQUIPMENT 44 ARMY

Exact replica of Colt's 1860 Army revolver. Caliber 44, using .451″ round ball, black powder and caps. 8″ round barrel, walnut stocks, blue finish with case hardened frame. Weight, 44 oz. **$89.95**
Similar in 36 cal. Navy, brass mounted **$49.95**

MARS EQUIPMENT BRITISH FLINTLOCK PISTOL

A replica of the British cavalry weapon of the George III period. 69 caliber, smoothbore, for BLACK POWDER ONLY. Full length walnut finished stock, steel barrel (9″) and lock, brass fittings. Lock is marked "TOWER" and GR under a crown. Weight about 3½ lbs., 15¼″ over-all **$29.95**

MARS EQUIPMENT FLINTLOCK PISTOLS

Replica of the Harpers Ferry, model 1805. 16″ over-all, 10″ bbl., 54 cal. rifled bore. Varnished wood, brass mountings. Casehardened lock-plate marked with eagle, "U.S." and "Harpers Ferry 1807" **$99.95**
Also, Virginia model similar to the M-1805 but with swivel ramrod and shorter grip. Marked "Virginia" and "Richmond 1812" **$99.95**

NAVY ARMS 1861 COLT REVOLVER

A replica of the Colt 1861 Navy, 36 caliber percussion revolver. 7½″ blued steel barrel; case hardened frame; brass back strap and trigger guard; one-piece walnut grips. Wgt. 41 oz., 13″ over-all................ **$80.00**
In presentation walnut case with powder flask, bullet mould and capper at **$125.** Engraving extra; **$60, $80, $120,** depending on style.

NAVY ARMS 1860 ARMY REVOLVER

A percussion Army revolver, a copy of the 1860 Colt, with walnut grips. Cal. 36 or 44 .... **$45.00**

FOREIGN GUNS—FLINTLOCKS, PERCUSSIONS, REPLICAS

NAVY ARMS TARGET REVOLVER
Identical to Navy 1860 Army Revolver but with full-length barrel rib extending back to form a top strap. Fitted with click-adjustable target type rear sight, hand-tuned action. In 36 or 44 percussion caliber **$125.00**

NAVY ARMS WELLS FARGO REVOLVER
A replica of the 1848 cal. 31 Colt, without rammer. Case hardened frame and hammer; 3″ of 5″ bbl., polished brass guard and straps. **$70.00**

NAVY ARMS DRAGOON REVOLVERS
Accurate copies of Colt 44 1st, 2nd and 3rd Model Dragoon revolvers. 7½″ bbls., wt. 4 lbs. 2 oz., length 14″ **$100.00**

NAVY ARMS BABY DRAGOON
Replica of the 31 cal. Colt 1848 with 3″ or 6″ barrel **$70.00**
NAVY ARMS SHOULDER STOCK of highly polished walnut, fits all Navy Arms percussion revolvers **$30.00**

NAVY ARMS "YANK" AND "SHERIFF'S" REVOLVERS
Replicas of the Colt 1851 Navy revolver. Caliber 36, percussion. 7½″ octagon barrel (Yank only); case hardened frame and loading lever; silver plated backstrap and trigger guard **$90.00**
Also available as Sheriff's model, with barrel length to customer order, with or without loading lever. Special order only **$90.00**
Engraved Yanks, **$60**, **$80**, **$120** extra, depending on style.

NAVY ARMS ROLLING BLOCK PISTOL
Exact copy of Remington Number 3 rolling block pistol. Cal 357 Magnum, with blued steel barrel, case-hardened frame, and walnut stock. Cased with accessories **$125.00**

NAVY ARMS KENTUCKY PISTOL
Flintlock, with rifled steel barrel. Case hardened, engraved lockplates. Cal. 44, 15½″ over-all. Navy Arms, importer **$80.00**
Engraved with carved stock $25.00 extra.

NAVY ARMS 1858 NEW MODEL ARMY REVOLVER
A replica of the Remington 44 caliber Civil War percussion revolver. 8″ octagon barrel; brass trigger guard; two-piece walnut grips. Weight 46 oz., 13¾″ over-all. Blued **$95.00**
Also available in 36 caliber with 7⅜″ barrel **$95.00**
Engraving extra; **$70**, **$90**, **$130**, depending on style.

POTOMAC ARMS WALKER REVOLVER
A replica of the 1847 Colt Walker, the first of the typical Colts. 9″ bbl., 15¾″ long; 4 lbs. 8 oz., case-hardened frame, hammer and rammer. Brass square-back guard, one-piece walnut grip, engraved cylinder. 44 caliber. **$110.00**

POTOMAC ARMS WELLS FARGO REVOLVER
Copy of the rammerless 1848 Colt 31 cal. revolver supplied to Wells Fargo. 3″ or 6″ bbl., case-hardened frame and hammer. Etched cylinder, square-back brass guard and straps, one-piece grip. **$75.00**

FOREIGN GUNS—FLINTLOCKS, PERCUSSIONS, REPLICAS

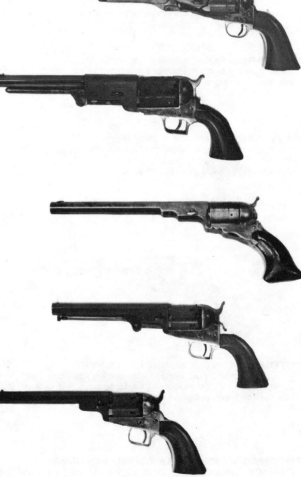

POTOMAC ARMS DRAGOON REVOLVER
Replica of the Colt 1st Model 4 Dragoon of 1848. 7½" bbl., 14" long, 4 lbs. 2 oz. Engraved cylinder, case-hardened frame, hammer and rammer; polished brass guard and straps; one-piece smooth walnut grip. . . . **$110.00**

REPLICA ARMS 44 DRAGOON
6-shot 44-cal. replica of the 2nd Dragoon Model percussion muzzle-loading revolver. 7½" bbl., blued and case-hardened. Square-back brass trigger guard. For black powder use **$104.50**
Flask **19.95**

REPLICA ARMS 1861 NAVY-1860 ARMY
36-cal., 6-shot black powder percussion Navy revolver, duplicating the Colt 1861 Navy. Frame, lever and hammer are case-hardened, rest of metal is blued. Iron or brass back strap is cut for stock **$89.95**
Same, but 44-cal. Army **89.95**
Shoulder stock, either **35.00**

REPLICA ARMS WALKER REVOLVER
A replica of the big Walker Colt, this caplock gun weighs about 4½ lbs., measures 15¾" over-all. 6-shot. Case-hardened frame, hammer and lever; brass trigger guard. Cylinder has rolled engraving scene. 44 caliber, for black powder only. 9" octagon-round barrel. Left hand twist. From Replica Arms **$115.00**
Walker powder flask **19.95**
Walker mould, single cavity **11.50**
Walker tool **3.00**
Cased, with all accessories **188.50**

REPLICA ARMS TEXAS PATERSON of 1836
Cal. 36 round ball only 6", 7½", 9" or 12" bbls. 11 groove, slow right hand twist. 17" over-all with 12" bbl. Folding trigger; smooth walnut grips. Case-hardened frame and hammer. Notch in hammer is rear sight, brass blade post front. 5-shot, blued, engraved cyl., for black powder only. From Replica Arms . . . . **$104.50.** With 12" bbl., **$109.50**
Paterson powder flask . . . . . . **$20.00** Mould **$12.50**
Capper . . . . **$12.00** Rod **$1.50**

REPLICA ARMS BABY DRAGOON of 1848
Cal. 31, 5-shot. 4", 5", 6" octagon bbl. revolver, 10⅜" (6" bbl.) over-all, wgt. 25 oz. Case-hardened frame. Square brass trigger guard and back strap. One-piece smooth walnut grips. Notched hammer rear and post front sights. Polished blue finish, etched cyl. For black powder only. From Replica Arms **$76.25**
Brass bullet mould, double cavity **11.50**
Powder flask, small **9.50**

REPLICA ARMS WELLS FARGO REVOLVER
Like the Baby Dragoon except: made with 3", 4", 5" or 6" bbl. without loading lever **$73.00**

REPLICA ARMS SINGLE SHOT PISTOL
Modern solid-frame, single-shot 44 cal. percussion pistol in frontier revolver style. 9" blued bbl., smooth one-piece wood grip, case-hardened frame and hammer. Available with interchangeable 28-gauge bbl.**$69.50.** With extra 28-gauge bbl. **$89.50**

RENEGADE PERCUSSION MODEL
Double barreled pistol, rifled, in 36 or 44 caliber, for black powder only. 8¼" blued barrels; case hardened frame. Sideplates, hammers, brass trigger guard and brass buttcap engraved. Proofed with 30% overload, certificate furnished. Weight 32 oz. Intercontinental Arms. **$39.95**

REPLICA ARMS REMINGTON 45
A modern copy of the Remington 1875 single-action revolver. In 45 Colt and 38 Spl. calibers only, blued, 6 shot. Modern automatic safety bar. **$134.95**

CENTURY SQUIBMAN AUTOLOADING RIFLE

A semiautomatic rifle with 15 round clip. Contoured 19½″ barrel with muzzle brake. Cocking indicator, grooved receiver for scope mounting, bead front sight, blade rear sight adj. for elevation. Shell deflector can be removed, hold-open bolt provision. 22LR only. Wgt. 5¾ lbs., 40½″ over-all. Century Arms, Inc., importer.
Price: **$44.50**

ERMA M22 CARBINE

A close copy of the U.S. M1 in 22 LR. 10-shot mag., 17¾″ barrel, 35⁵⁄₁₆″ over-all, original type sights. Receiver grooved for scope. 15-shot mag. also available at extra cost. 5¾ lbs. R. G. Industries, Inc., importers .. **$69.95**

F.I.E. R6 BOY'S SINGLE SHOT RIFLE

Single shot 22 LR with 18″ barrel and plastic stock. Over-all length 18″; weight 4 lbs. Key lock safety; fixed blade front and spring ramp adjustable rear sights. F.I.E. Corp., importer **$20.95**

FRANCHI CENTENNIAL AUTOLOADING RIFLE

A semi-automatic rifle with tubular magazine in the buttstock holds 11 22 L R cartridges (16 Shorts in Gallery model). Push-button crossbolt safety, receiver grooved for scope mounting. Quick takedown feature. 21″ barrel with gold bead ramp front and step adjustable open rear sights. Stock is walnut with checkered p.g. and finger-grooved semi-beavertail fore-end. Weight 5 lbs., 2 oz., 39″ over-all. Stoeger, importer **$86.95**
Deluxe model with fully engraved receiver **124.95**

GEVARM E1 AUTOLOADING RIFLE

Carbine style take down rifle. Detachable 8 shot clip, cal. 22 LR. 19½″ bbl. (6 grooves, 17½″ twist). Reversible spring guide. Striker bar on breech-block, fires from open bolt, automatic ejection. Receiver grooved for Tip-Off mounts. Blade front sight, open adj. rear. Bolt handle safety. French walnut two-piece p.g. stock and fore-end, p.g. cap. 36⅞″ over-all. Under 21″ taken down. Gevelot, Canada, importers, U.S. dists., Blumenfeld Co. .. **$73.70**

GEVARM A3 AUTOLOADING SPORTER

Same as E1 except 19½″ bbl., tunnel front sight with 5 interchangeable inserts, tangent sliding leaf rear. French walnut one-piece p.g. stock, schnabel-type fore-end tip **$92.40**

NAVY ARMS 66 RIFLE

Lever action 22 rimfire rifle built to resemble the Winchester 66. Full length tubular magazine, 14 LR capacity, brass frame and butt-plate. 19″ blued bbl. Blade front sight, open leaf rear. Straight-grip walnut-finish stock, not checkered. 39½″ over-all, wgt. 7 lbs. Navy Arms, importer **$120.00**

TRADEWINDS AUTOLOADING RIFLE

Detachable 5-shot mag., 23¾″ bbl. cal. 22 LR. Bead front sight, 3-leaf folding rear. Receiver grooved for scope mounts. Walnut p.g. stock with cheekpiece, schnabel fore-end. 41½″ over-all, 5¾ lbs. Tradewinds, importer **$89.50**

TRADEWINDS MODEL 311A RIFLE

Bolt action 22 LR repeater with detachable 5-shot clip magazine; sliding safety on receiver locks trigger and bolt handle. Open 3-leaf rear sight, hooded ramp front; receiver grooved for scope mounting. Monte Carlo walnut stock with checkered p.g. and fore-end; sling swivels. Wgt. 6 lbs., 41¼″ over-all. Tradewinds, importer **$84.50**
5-shot clip .... **$4.75** 10-shot clip **$5.75**

WALTHER KKJ—22 RF & HORNET SPORTER

Bolt action sporting rifle, cal. 22 LR, 22 WMR or 22 Hornet. 22″ barrel; 5-shot detachable clip magazine; open rear sight adjustable for w. and e. and bead front sight. Checkered Monte Carlo walnut p.g. stock (13⅞″x1⅜″x1¾″x2½″). Cross-bolt safety, receiver grooved for tip-off mounts. 41⅛″ over-all, wgt. 6 lbs. Double set triggers $10 extra. Interarms, importers **$160.00**

BSA MONARCH DELUXE VARMINT RIFLE
Same as Monarch DeLuxe except has heavy barrel, and made in 222 Rem. or 243 Win. only. About 8½ lbs. From Galef **$179.95**

CONTINENTAL ARMS RIFLE
Bolt action rifle with hinged floorplate has Siemens Martin barrel; integral half rib with express rear, hinged hooded front ramp sights; swivel holder. Stock is of French walnut, checkered fore-end and p.g. with trap in grip cap; horn or ebony tip. Available in 338, 458 Win. Mag.; 244, 375 H&H, 8x68S, 416 Rigby, 505 Gibbs or custom chambered in other calibers. Continental Arms, importer **$450.00**

HENRI DUMOULIN CUSTOM RIFLES
F.N. Mauser Supreme action, 24″ button rifled barrel, jeweled bolt, sliding side safety. Tapped for standard scope mounts. Select French walnut with beavertail fore-end, scottish hand checkering, rosewood p.g. cap and fore-

ALASKAN BOLT ACTION RIFLES
Made in Belgium, these rifles are available in three styles. Magnum rifles are chambered for 338, 300 Win. 7mm Rem. and 300 Weatherby. All have Monte Carlo stock of French walnut; p.g. and fore-end checkered and capped with rosewood; sling swivels and recoil pad attached. 24″ barrel on rifles, 20″ barrel on Magnum Carbine which has full length Mannlicher stock. No sights. Standard rifle can be had in 30-06, 243 or 7x57 but does not have recoil pad. Skinner's Sportsmans Supply, importer ..**$200.00 to $225.00**

BSA MONARCH DELUXE RIFLES
Available in 222, 243, 270, 308, 30-06 and 7mm Mag. BSA rifles feature a fully adjustable trigger, a bolt head that encloses the cartridge and is in turn enclosed by the barrel extension, a gas-proof cocking piece, hinged floorplate, silent safety with cocking indicator, integral scope dovetails, and a checkered, walnut stock with cheekpiece and recoil pad. Weight about 6¼ lbs. From Galef. **$159.95**

CETME-SPORT AUTO RIFLE
5-shot autoloader with unusual roller and cam breech-locking mechanism. Available with wood or steel (with bipod) fore-end. Flip-up aperture rear sight, protected blade front. Muzzle brake, carrying sling, spare mag., cleaning kit furnished. Cal. 308, 17¾″ 4-groove bbl. (9.4″ twist), 40″ over-all, 10½ lbs. Cannot be converted to full auto. fire. Mars Equipment, importers **$229.95**
Scope mounts with 1″ or 26mm rings **12.00**
20-shot magazine **9.00**

CONTINENTAL ARMS DOUBLE RIFLE
Boxlock action, engraved with single selective trigger and auto. ejectors. Blade front and express rear sights. Straight two-piece stock with checkered p.g. and fore-end. Chambered for 270 Win., 30-40, 8x57JRS, 303, 30-06, 375 H&H, 450 500, 450 Nitro Express, 465 or 470 Rigby. Continental Arms, importer. Write for prices.

end cap, Pachmayr recoil pad, Q.D. swivels. Calibers: Group A: 22-250, 243, 6mm, 25-06, 270, 280, 308 Win., 30-06, 358 Win.; Group B: 264, 7mm Rem., 300 Win., 308 Norma, 7x61 S&H, 338, 350 Rem.; Group C: 240, 257, 7mm, 300 and 378 Weatherby's Magnums, 300 H&H, 375 H&H; Group D: 404 Jeffrey, 416 Rigby, 425 Westley Richards, 458 Win., 505 Gibbs, 460 Weatherby.
Price: Rifle, in all four caliber groups, from **$239.50,** extra charge for group B, C, and D chamberings.
Price: Varmint rifle, same as above, but with medium heavy varmint barrel, action tapped for scope, group A calibers **$249.50,** group B calibers **$15.00** extra, group C calibers, **$29.00** extra.
Price: Carbine with 20″ bbl. Mannlicher stock, from **$253** up, in group A, B and C.
Premium wood, especially selected, from **$72.00** up, special checkering from **$36.00.** Custom engraving, silver and gold inlays, engraved name plate, etc., write for quotations to JBL Arms Co., Box 323, Dover, Pa.

FERLACH DOUBLE RIFLE
Anson & Deeley engraved, silvered action, treble lock with Greener cross bolt. 22″, 24″ or 26″ bbls., all popular calibers from 7x57mm to 300 Win. Mag. Two triggers each settable. Auto. safety and ejectors. Circassian walnut checkered p.g. stock and fore-end, with checkpiece, horn p.g. cap and buttplate; ramp front sight and express rear. Wgt. 7½-8 lbs. Flaig's, importer **$1,200.00**

FERLACH DOUBLE O-U RIFLE
Like the Ferlach side-by-side double rifle except: double Greener 4-lock action, calibers 270 to 458 Win., matted-rib bbls. Left- or right-hand cheekpiece stock. 8½-9½ lbs. Flaig's importer **$1,300.00**
Other rifles and drillings available. Write for catalog.

FOREIGN GUNS—CENTERFIRE RIFLES

FERLACH SPORTER RIFLE
98 Mauser action with all milled steel parts, Sako trigger side safety. Bolt knurled and forged for low scope mounting. Boehler steel barrel 24" long, button rifled, 6 grooves. Sights: 100 and 200 yard rear, hooded ramp front with gold bead. Tapped and drilled for scope mounting. Hand checkered Circassian walnut stock with Monte Carlo cheekpiece, rubber recoil pad, rosewood fore-end tip and p.g. cap, sling swivels. Calibers: 243, 7X57, 270, 308 Win., 30-06 **$139.00** In 25-06 **$149.00** (For test fired case in this caliber, add $10.) Flaig's, importer.

GARCIA SAKO FORESTER RIFLES
Sako L-579 medium length action and cold formed 23" barrel. Action has integral tapered dovetail scope blocks, adjustable trigger, Monte Carlo walnut stock, checkered at p.g. and fore-end. 42" over-all, wgt. 6½ lbs. Calibers: 243, 308 Win., 22-250. Garcia Sporting Arms Corp., importer.
Price: Sporter rifle **$222.00**
Price: Mannicher stocked carbine, 20" bbl., 39" over-all 250.00
Price: Heavy barrel rifle 245.00
Price: Deluxe sporter 310.00
Barreled action, lightweight, **$149.00** heavy barrel 155.00

GARCIA F.N. SUPREME RIFLES
Available in all popular calibers, incl. Magnums. 24" barrel (22" in 308), Checkered Monte Carlo p.g. stock of French walnut. Streamlined bolt sleeve; 5-shot magazine (3-Mag., 4-243, 308); sliding side safety, hinged floorplate; adjustable trigger. Hooded ramp front and Tri-Range rear sight; tapped for scope. Weight about 7¾ lbs., 44½" over-all. Garcia Sporting Arms Corp., importer. Standard calibers: **$431.00**; Magnum (264, 300 Win. Mag., 7mm Mag.) **$449.00**; Barreled action, standard: **$242.00**; Mag. calibers: **$250.00**.
Action only from $139.00 to $156.00; Benchrest actions from $142.50 to $158.00; Magnum action from $147.00 to $152.00.

GARCIA MUSKETEER RIFLE
FN Mauser Supreme bolt actions, checkered walnut, Monte Carlo stock with p.g., sling swivels. 24" barrel with Williams Guide open rear sight, hooded ramp front sight, adj. trigger, sliding thumb safety; hinged floorplate. Wgt. about 7 lbs., 44½" over-all. Garcia Sporting Arms Corp., importer. Calibers: 243 264, 270, 30-06, 308 Win., 308 Norma Mag., 7mm Rem. Mag., 300 Win. Mag.
Price: **$169.00**

GARCIA SAKO FINNBEAR RIFLE
3-lug, long L-61 action, bolt handle safety lug, cold-swaged barrel, recessed bolt face. Checkered walnut stock with Monte Carlo comb, recoil pad and sling swivels. Calibers: 264, 270, 30-06, 300 Win. Mag., 338, 7mm. Mag., 375 H&H. Garcia Sporting Arms Corp., importer.
Price: Sporter rifle **$243.00**
Price: Mannlicher stocked carbine, 20" bbl., 39" over-all 270.00
Price: Deluxe sporter 335.00

GARCIA SAKO VIXEN RIFLES
Using the L-461, shortest of Sako actions, otherwise like Garcia Sako Forrester. Four styles: standard sporter 23½" bbl., carbine with Mannlicher stock 20" bbl., Heavy Barrel 23½" bbl., and Deluxe sporter with French walnut stock, skipline checkering, engraved trigger guard and floor plate, contrasting wood p.g. and fore-end cap. Calibers: 222, 222 Mag., 223. Garcia Sporting Arms Corp., importer.
Price: Standard sporter **$208.00**
Price: Carbine 240.00
Price: Heavy Barrel 230.00
Price: Deluxe sporter 291.00
Light barreled action . . . . **$142.00**   Heavy barreled action . . . 148.00
Sako L-461 action, short and benchrest 85.00
Sako L-579 action, medium and benchrest 88.00
Sako L-61 action, long action for std. and mag. cartridges 97.00
Sako scope mount, 1" ring, low or medium 18.95
Sako scope mount, 26mm ring, low or medium 18.95
Sako adj. trigger #2 **$9.95**; #4 safety and trigger combo 15.95
Sako Dual Range Peep Sight 9.50

GARCIA SAKO FINNWOLF RIFLE
Hammerless lever action rifle with gear-operated, short lever throw. Solid frame with side ejection, detachable 4 shot box magazine, crossbolt safety behind trigger. One piece walnut stock with Monte Carlo cheekpiece, fluted comb, checkered p.g. and fore-end. Also offered with left side ejection port at no extra cost. Wgt. about 7 lbs.; 42½" over-all. Hooded ramp sight, no rear sight, mount blocks for tip-off scope mount, 243 and 308 Win. Garcia Sporting Arms Corp., importer.
Price: Standard sporter **$264.00**
Price: Deluxe Sporter 310.00

FOREIGN GUNS—CENTERFIRE RIFLES

HERTER MARK J9 RIFLES

Similar to U9 Models except: Based on improved Mauser type action (with adj. trigger), low-scope safety, integral scope mounting blocks on receiver. Cals. 22-250, 243, 6mm, 264, 270, 7mm Rem.

Mag., 308, 30-06, 300 Win. Mag. Custom Hunter Grade **$87.95**
Without sights 83.50
   Same, with Mannlicher stock ..:.. **$96.75**. With varmint stock .96.75
  Same, Presentation Grade, checkered choice walnut stock, roll-over comb, black fore-end tip and p.g. cap with white-line spacers 96.75
Without sights 91.25
   Bbld. actions, blued 62.65
    Actions, in the white (short) .... **$47.25.** Long 50.04

HERTER'S MARK U9 RIFLES

Bolt action sporters with BSA-type (British) action. Hooded, gas-diverting cocking piece, recessed bolt face encloses cartridge head, side safety, integral dovetail scope mount bases, fully adjustable trigger, hinged floor-plate. Monte Carlo p.g. stock. Q.D. swivels, ramp front sight, adj. rear. 23½″ bbl., about 6¼ lbs., all popular calibers, including Mag.

Custom Supreme Grade ... **$109.90** With Douglas bbl. **$114.95**
Same, except without sights 103.35
Same, except Presentation grade. Has selected wood stock, checkered and flared p.g. and fore-end, both capped with black plastic and white spacers .... **$122.75.** With Douglas bbl. **$138.15**
Same, except without sights ..... **$118.35.** With Douglas bbl. 131.55
Bbld. actions, polished & blued ... **$71.45.** With Douglas bbl. ..87.95
Action only, in the white specify length or cartridge 57.75
Varmint Model, with heavier stock, beavertail fore-end 109.45
Same without sights 104.45

HUSQVARNA 9000 CROWN GRADE

Mauser-type rifle in 7mm, 270, 30-06 300 Win. Mag. with 20½″ bbl. 44″ over-all. Adj. open rear, hooded ramp front sights; receiver tapped for peep and scope sights. Oiled French walnut stock with cheekpiece, checkered grip and fore-end. Hinged floorplate. Sling swivels. Wgt. about 7¼ lbs. Tradewinds. **$212.50**

HUSQVARNA 8000 IMPERIAL RIFLES

Same as 9000 Crown Grade rifles except: Select European walnut Monte Carlo stock with cheekpiece, high gloss finish, 3-leaf folding rear sight and adjustable trigger. Tradewinds, importer. **$285.00**

INTERNATIONAL BOLT ACTION RIFLE

British made Mauser-type action with jeweled bolt and hinged floorplate. Magazine holds 5 rounds, 3 in mag. cals. 24″ barrel chambered for 243, 270, 308 Win., 30-06, 22-250 or 7mm Rem. Mag. Equipped with Williams ramp front and open mid sights. Monte Carlo stock of French walnut; checkered, capped p.g. and rosewood fore-end tip; sling swivels and Pachmayr recoil pad attached. Weight, 7½ lbs., 44″ over-all. International Distributors, importer **$169.50**

KLEINGUENTHER M-V-2130 HIGH POWER RIFLE

Calibers: 243, 7mm Rem. Mag., 270, 30-06, 300 Win. Mag. and 308. Fully adjustable trigger; one-piece Mauser type trigger guard and box magazine; safety in center of bolt sleeve. 24″ barrel; weight 7⅛ lbs.; over-all length 43½″. Walnut Monte Carlo stock with cheekpiece; rosewood fore-end tip; basket weave checkering; high luster finish. Kleinguenther, importer .... **$199.00** to **$212.04**

MANNLICHER SCHOENAUER RIFLES AND CARBINES

Made in carbine style with 20″ bbl. (18¼″ in 6.5mm), wgt. about 7½ lbs. In rifle style with sporter stock and 22″ bbl., wgt. 7½-8 lbs. Carbine comes in 243, 6.5mm, 7mm, 270, 30-06, 308 and 358 Win. cals.; rifle in 243, 270 and 30-06 only. Hooded ramp front sight and folding leaf rear. Dummy sideplate aids fitting scope mount; tapped for Steyr mount. 5-shot rotary magazine. Spooned bolt handle. Walnut stock with medium high Monte Carlo comb, checkered p.g. (with cap and white spacer) and fore-end; rifle has black fore-end tip with white spacer; sling swivels. Adjustable single- or double-set trigger. From Stoeger **$348.95**

PARKER-HALE MAUSER RIFLE

Imported by JANA International, the 1200 Super series bolt action rifle has adj. trigger; hinged floorplate; hooded ramp front and folding middle sight; receiver tapped for scope mounts; sling swivels with sling and recoil pad. Monte Carlo stock with checkered p.g. and fore-end. Contrasting color fore-end tip and p.g. cap, both with white line spacers. 22″ bbl. 43″ over-all, wgt. 7½ lbs. Cal. 243, 270, 30-60, 308 Win. (5-shot) **$164.95**
7mm Rem. Mag. 300 Win. Mag. or 308 Norma Mag. 169.95

PRESENTATION RIFLE, same as the 1200 Super except with French walnut stock, fully scroll engraved action, trigger guard and magazine floor plate. Also, no sights.
Std. Cals. ....**$209.95.** Mag. Cals. ....**$219.95.**
VARMINT RIFLE, same as the 1200 Super except with a glass bedded free floating 24″, 4 lb. target bbl., target scope base blocks. Wgt. 9½ lbs. In cals. 22/250, 6mm Rem & 243 .... **$169.95**

FOREIGN GUNS—CENTERFIRE RIFLES

STEYR-MANNLICHER MODEL SL RIFLE
Receiver is machined from solid steel and has a detachable 5-shot rotary-drum magazine. Bolt has six locking lugs, cocking indicator and recessed face. Open rear, hooded ramp front sights. Safety locks bolt and sear. Choice of single- or double-set trigger. Monte Carlo stock, checkered p.g. and fore-end, epoxy finished. Available in 222 Rem., 222 Rem. Mag., or 223. Weight 6¼ lbs. Stoeger, importer **$199.95**
Carbine with full-length Mannlicher stock **210.95**
Target rifle with 28″ heavy bbl., without sights **210.95**

STEYR-MANNLICHER MODEL M RIFLE
Similar to Model L, but cals. 7x57, 250 or 30-06 . . . . **$249.95**
Carbine with full-length Mannlicher stock **259.95**

TRADEWINDS 600 VARMINT RIFLE
Short HVA action has 23¾″ medium-wgt. barrel in cals. 222 Rem., 222 Rem. Mag., 22-250, 223, 243 and 308 Win. No sights, tapped for standard scope mounts. 4 shot (3 in 22-250, 243 or 308) detachable box magazine, adjustable double set trigger. Monte Carlo European walnut stock with cheekpiece, checkered p.g. and fore-end. About 6¾ lbs. Tradewinds, importer. Test target accompanies rifle. **$162.50**
Same as above except with adj. single trigger, steel trigger guard, front sight and folding rear sight **$162.50**

SCHULTZ & LARSEN 68DL RIFLE
A 4-lug bolt action rifle with tubular receiver, 24″ bbl., adj. trigger; thumb safety; hinged floorplate. Walnut Monte Carlo stock (13½″ pull) with checkered p.g. and fore-end; white line recoil pad and grip cap; 1″ swivels. 44½″ over-all, 7½ lbs. Without sights. Cal. 264 Win., 7x61 S&H, 7mm Rem., 308 Norma 300 Win., 338 Win. Magnum; 22-250, 243 Win., 6mm Rem., 6.5x55, 270 Win., 308 Win. Fessler, importer. **$485.00**
Same except 458 Win. Mag. **588.00**

STEYR MANNLICHER MODEL L RIFLE
Similar to Model SL, but with long action for caliber 22-250 Rem., 225 or 243 Win. **$199.95**
Chambered for 308 Win. **219.95**
Target rifle with 26″ heavy bbl., without sights **210.95**
Carbine with full-length Mannlicher stock **210.95**
Carbine chambered for 308 Win. **229.95**

STEYR-MANNLICHER MODEL S RIFLE
Similar to Model M, but in cals. 7MM Rem. Mag., 257 Wby., 264 Win. Mag., 300 HH Mag., 338 Win. Mag., 375 HH Mag., & 458 Win. Mag. . . **$275.95**

TRADEWINDS "HUSKY" LIGHTWEIGHT RIFLE
HVA action. 21½″ Swedish steel barrel with hammer-forged bore. Bead front and fixed rear sights. Italian walnut stock, hand checkered, with Monte Carlo comb; cal. 22-250, 243, 270, 7mm Mag., 30-06. About 6½ lbs., 43″ over-all **$167.50**

FOREIGN GUNS—TARGET RIFLES

BSA MARTINI-INTERNATIONAL MK III 22 RIFLE
Made by Birmingham Small Arms Co., the MK III features the Martini action; new free floating barrel press-fitted into action and locked in place by two cross bolts. Available in left or right hand checkpiece models, the loading port and sight base are also reversed for southpaw shooters. 29″ barrel, 12 to 14½ lbs. Trigger adjustable from ½ to 3½ lb. pull. Dovetail base on action for tube sight mounting, regular bases on bbl. for scope mounts. Al Freeland, importer.
Without sights, light or heavy model **$210.00**
Available with Parker-Hale, Freeland or Redfield International sights at extra cost.

PARKER-HALE 1200 TX TARGET RIFLE
Cal. 7.62mm NATO (308 Win.), 5-shot magazine. 26″ free floating (1″ dia.) glass bedded bbl. Mauser '98 action (commercial) with adj. single stage trigger and triple (trigger, bolt & sear) locking sliding thumb safety. Oil finished walnut target stock (13³⁄₁₆″x1¹¹⁄₁₆″x1¹⁵⁄₁₆″) has high comb beavertail fore-end, full p.g. recoil pad and adj. hand stop. 46¾″ over-all, wgt. 10½ lbs. Jana International, importer.
Price: **$219.95**

HAMMERLI-TANNER MATCH RIFLE
Designed for 300 meter competition, this heavy (16¼ lbs.) single shot "free" rifle is available in most popular centerfire calibers. Barrel length 29½″. Micrometer click rear sight has variable aperature and is adjustable for w. and e.; globe front sight has 4 inserts. Walnut thumbhole stock has adjustable palm rest and sling swivel; buttplate adjusts to any position. Available only on special order with 6- to 10-month delivery. H. Grieder, importer **$590.00**

FOREIGN GUNS—TARGET RIFLES

SCHULTZ & LARSEN 61 MATCH RIFLE

22 LR single shot bolt action rifle meeting International Match requirements. Has a 28″ free-floating bbl., globe front sight with removable inserts. Micro. peep rear sight with removable iris discs, adj. for w. and e. 32″ sight radius. 2 adj. buttplates furnished for offhand and prone positions. Adj. palm rest. Walnut thumbhole stock with cheekpiece and adj. handrest. Full length rail under stock to adj. forward sling swivel, hand stop and plam rest. Choice of trigger systems: adj. "hair"; adj. double pull or slack trigger (4-14 oz.); or adj. double pull (3-4 lbs.). 49″ over-all; wgt. approx. 16½ lbs. Fessler, importer. **$565.00**

WALTHER KKM INTERNATIONAL 22 MATCH RIFLE

A bolt action single shot rifle with double locking lugs; wing safety on bolt; adj. trigger pull; 28″ heavy tapered bbl. (heavier bbl. without taper available). Heavy walnut stock with thumbhole; adj. hand shelf, palm rest and hook buttplate. Globe front sight with 8 inserts; aperture rear sight adj. for w. and e. Weight 15½ lbs., (with straight bbl. 17 lbs.), 46″ over-all. Cal. 22 LR. Interarms, importer **$320.00**

CARL GUSTAF MODEL 63

Swedish Mauser action match rifle. 29.1″ barrel is free-floating, has outside diameter of 0.748″. Front sight and match sling supplied, three sight inserts are furnished; GF rear sight $30.00, but any other match sight can be installed. Trigger and trigger guard are knurled for maximum control. Stock is designed for match shooting. Cheekpiece appears on both sides of stock. Calibers: 6.5x55 and 7.62 Nato. Sight radius 32.7″, 49″ over-all, wgt. 9.9 lbs. Action cocks on closing. Century Arms, Inc., importer.

Price: M63 without rear sight **$150.00**
Price: Model 63 - with GF (Swedish) rear sight **$180.00**
Price: Model 63E - w/o rear sight 160.00
Price: Model 63E - with Parker-Hale 5c rear sight 200.00
Price: Model 63E - with A.J. Parker "Twin Zero" rear sight 210.00
Price: Model 63 - Biathalon Rifle, fully equipped, on special order only, price on request.

FOREIGN GUNS—AUTOLOADING & SLIDE ACTION SHOTGUNS

BERETTA AL-2 AUTOMATIC SHOTGUN

Gas-operated in 12 or 20 ga., 2¾″ chambers. 28″ Full or Mod., 26″ Imp. Cyl. chokes, ventilated-rib interchangeable barrels. Hand-checkered p.g. walnut stock (14⅛″x1½″x2½″) and fore-end. 3-shot mag. can be emptied without working shells through action. Engraved receiver. Crossbolt safety. Wgt. 7¼ lbs. Garcia, importer **$217.00**
Also with middle bead as the AL-2 Skeet (12 ga. 26″, Skeet) and AL-2 Trap (14⅜″x1⅜″x1¾″) 12 ga. 30″ Full 227.00
Extra barrels 88.00

BERETTA AL-1 AUTOMATIC SHOT GUN

Like the AL-2, but not in Skeet or trap models, plain receiver and barrel
. . . . **$178.00**
Extra plain barrel 78.00

BREDA AUTOMATIC SHOTGUNS

Italian made in 12 or 20 ga., 2¾″ or 3″ chambers. Magazine holds four 2¾″ or three 3″ shells; extension tube (extra) for 7 shots. Nickel-chrome steel barrel with vent. rib or plain has muzzles threaded for "Quick Choke" tubes; 24½″ length. Barrel bore, breech and bolt assembly are hard chromed. Auto. magazine cut-off; push-button holds carrier latch in loading position; depressing cartridge retaining lever unloads magazine. Adjustable stock of Italian walnut has checkered p.g. and beavertail fore-end, 14″x2½″x1⅝″. Continental Arms, importer . . . . **$169.50** to **$194.50**

FOREIGN GUNS—AUTOLOADING & SLIDE ACTION SHOTGUNS

FRANCHI AUTOMATIC SHOTGUNS

Made in 12 and 20, 2¾" chamber. These Stoeger imports have alloy receivers, chrome-lined bbls., auto. cut-off, 4-shot cap., walnut checkered pistol grip and fore-end. Adj. friction piece sets recoil for standard or hi-vel. loads. 24" or 26" (Imp. Cyt.), 28" (Full or Mod.) or 30" Full (12 only). Wgt. 12, 6¼ lbs., 20, 5 lbs. Plain bbl. **$176.95**. Vent. rib bbl. **$207.95**. 3" Magnum models in 12 (32") or 20 (28") Full, with steel receivers and recoil pads. Wgt. 12, 8¼ lbs. 20, 6 lbs. Plain bbl. 12, **$185.95**. 20, **$175.95**. Vent. rib bbl. 12, **$212.95**. 20 **$202.95**

The Hunter. Same as the Standard except: vent. rib only; engraved receiver, high finish select walnut stock, chromed trigger **$239.95**
Slug Gun, 12 or 20, 22" Cyl. bbl. with blade front and rear sight adj. for w. and e.; sling swivels. 12 ga., choice of steel or allow receiver. 20 ga., alloy only **$219.95**
Dynamic 12. Same as the Standard except: 12 only, steel receiver, chromed breech bolt and lifter, **$189.95**. With vent. rib **$221.95**. Skeet Gun, **$219.95**. Slug Gun **$219.95**
Wildfowler. Same as Standard Mag. except: ventilated rib bbl. 20 has alloy receiver. 12, **$279.95**. 20 .... **$275.95**
Eldorado. Same as the Standard except: vent. rib only. Receiver scroll engraved; gold plated trigger, chromed breech bolt. Also made with 3" (magnum) chambers in 12 (32") or 20 (28") Full Choke bbls. **$345.95**
Other highly decorated Franchis, Crown **$846.95**, Diamond **$1,129.95** and Imperial **$1,359.95**.
Extra bbls. Plain **$52.95**. (Mag. **$60.00**), Vent. rib. (V.R. Mag. **$82.95**). Slug or Skeet **$74.95**.

KLEINGUENTHER SEMI-AUTOMATIC SHOTGUN

Available in left or right hand models, 12 ga. only (2¾" chamber) in 25" (Skt.), 26" (IC) 28" (Full) and 30" (Full) chrome-molybdenum barrels with vent. rib. Crossbolt safety in trigger guard; engraved hunting scene on receiver housing. Stock French walnut 14" x 1½" x 2⅜". Kleinguenther, importer **$198.34** (RH), ...**$219.80** (LH)

TRADEWINDS H-150 & H-170 AUTO SHOTGUNS

Light alloy receiver, 5-shot tubular magazine. 12 gauge only, 2¾"; 26" (Imp. Cyl.), 28" (Mod. or Full), 30" (Full). Select Italian walnut stock, p.g. and fore-end hand checkered. Wgt. 6¾ lbs. Ramp-mounted bead front sight **$159.95**
H-170, Same except vent. rib **179.95**
Deluxe 200 series, same as 170 except engraved receiver...... **227.50**
Trap model (14⅜"x1⅜"x1⅞"), 30" bbl. **227.50**

FOREIGN GUNS—SINGLE BARREL SHOTGUNS

A & F SINGLE BARREL TRAP GUN

Made in Italy, this 12 ga. gun has a vent. rib barrel, checkered walnut p.g. stock with Monte Carlo comb, and recoil pad. Abercrombie and Fitch, importer **$395.00**

ATLAS SINGLE BARREL TRAP GUN

30" or 32" vent. rib barrel of Boehler steel; chromed bore; 12 gauge only. Checkered walnut Monte Carlo stock (14½"x1⅜"x1⅞"x2¼") and beavertail fore-end; recoil pad; engraved action and auto. ejector, weighs about 8 lbs. **$365.00**
With custom engraving, gold trigger and gold lettering **425.00**

BERETTA MK II SINGLE BARREL TRAP

Receiver is Beretta BL-type with massive full-width hinge, auto ejector and hand-fitted internal parts; hand engraved. Either 32" or 34" barrel trap choked chambered for 2¾" 12 ga. shells only. Hand fitted, extra wide and extra high tapered vent rib is matted full length. Monte Carlo full p.g. stock and extra long tapered beavertail fore-end are hand checkered walnut (14⅜" x 1⅜" x 1¾"). Wgt. 8½ lbs. Garcia, importer **$395.00**

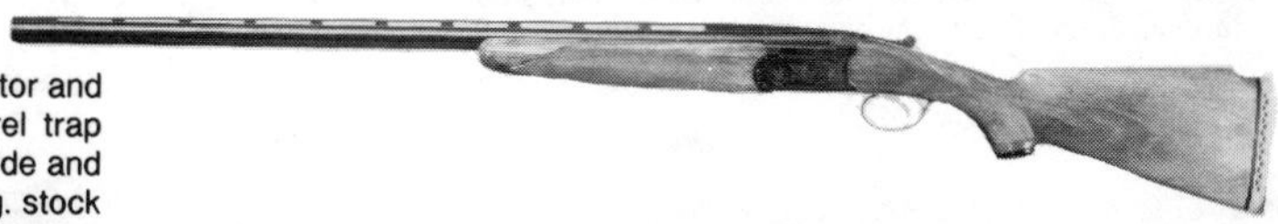

BERETTA TR-2 MONTE CARLO TRAP SHOTGUN

12 ga. only, 2¾" chambers, 32" single barrel trap-choked, with vent. rib. Crossbolt safety, auto. ejector. Monte Carlo p.g. stock of European walnut (14⅜"x1⅜"x1¾") with beavertail fore-end and trap-style recoil pad. Bbl. release in front of guard. Front and middle bead sights. Garcia, importer. Wgt. about 8¼ lbs. **$190.00**

FOREIGN GUNS—SINGLE BARREL SHOTGUNS

BERETTA FS-1 FOLDING SHOTGUN
This hammerless single is made in 12 (30″), 20 (28″), 28 or .410 ga. (26″) full choke bbl.; stock has checkered walnut grip and fore-end, the latter permanently attached. Barrel is made in Beretta mono-bloc construction. Cocks on opening; crossbolt safety in trigger guard. Wgt. from 4½ lbs. (410) to 5½ lbs. (12 ga.). Garcia, importer. **$88.00**

COMPANION FOLDING SHOTGUN
Monobloc receiver is machined from solid stock and satin chrome-plated. Available in 12, 20 and 410 ga. (3″ chambers) and 16 or 28 ga. (2¾″) with 28″ (Full) barrel (30″ Full also in 12 ga., 26″ Full only in 410). European walnut stock (14″x1½″x2⅝″) has checkered fore-end and capped p.g., plastic buttplate. Weight 4½ to 5½ lbs. Galef, importer **$49.95**
With vent. rib **55.95**

F.I.E. BRASIL SINGLE BARREL SHOTGUN
Exposed hammer gun in 12 ga. (28″ Full or Mod.), 20 ga. (28″ Full or Mod.) and 410 ga. (28″ Full). Weight 5 lbs. 10 oz., walnut stock with checkered p.g. and fore-end. F.I.E. Corp., importer **$26.95**
Also available in Boy's model (20 ga. 22″ Mod. and 410 ga. 22″ Mod.)
. . . . **$26.95**

F.I.E. SB2 SINGLE BARREL SHOTGUN
Exposed hammer gun in 12 ga. (2¾″ chamber, 28″ Full), 20 ga. (3″ chamber, 28″ Full) and 410 ga. (3″ chamber, 26″ Full). Hardwood stock and chrome plated receiver. F.I.E. Corp., importer **$28.95**
Also available in Boy's model (20 ga., 3″ chamber, 24″ Full and 410 ga. 3″ chamber, 22″ Full). 12¼″ pull on stock; plastic butt plate and chrome plated receiver **$28.95**

GARCIA-ROSSI SINGLE BARREL SHOTGUN
Available in all gauges with 29″ full-choked barrel and 2¾″ chamber, except 3″ 410. Tip-up action has exposed hammer; stock has checkered p.g. Made in Brazil. Garcia Arms Corp., importer **$34.95**

MONTE CARLO TRAP GUN
Made in Italy, this single barrel 12 ga. trap gun has a 32″ vent. rib barrel; engraved, blued receiver with automatic extractor and gold-plated trigger. Monte Carlo stock has recoil pad and hand-checkered p.g. and fore-end. Weight 8¼ lbs. Galef, importer **$149.95**

STOEGER 27 TRAP GUN
Boxlock action, single bbl., double under-locking lugs, Greener type crossbolt, ejector, has no safety. 12 ga., 30 (Imp. Mod.) or 32″ (Full) chrome lined barrels with vent. rib. Checkered Monte Carlo p.g. stock (14½″x1⅜″x2⅛″), with beavertail fore-end. 49″ over-all, wgt. 8¼ lbs. Stoeger Arms Corp., importer **$498.95**

CHARLES DALY SUPERIOR GRADE TRAP GUN
12 ga. (2¾″), 32″ (Full) Vent rib (⅜″) bbl., double beads. Scroll engraved receiver is nickel finished. Manual safety, auto ejector, recoil pad. Checkered Monte Carlo p.g. stock and beavertail forearm with Greener type lock. Chas. Daly, importer **$360.00**

DICKSON BOLT ACTION SHOTGUN
.410 (3″) Spanish made weighs 5½ lbs. 3-shot capacity. 25″ full choke bbl. Checkered p.g. and fore-end. Sliding thumb safety. American Import, importer **$34.95**

DICKSON SINGLE BARREL SHOTGUN
Exposed hammer gun with auto ejector, brass bead sight, oil finished stock. M612 12 ga. 28″ Full 2¾″; M620 20 ga. 26″ Full 3″; M6410 410 ga. 26″ Full 3″. American Import, importer **$30.75**

KRIEGHOFF SINGLE BARREL TRAP
12 ga. (2¾″) 32″ or 34″ (Full) vent. rib bbls. Internal parts are hardened heat treated steel. Mechanical trigger, short hammer fall. Monte Carlo stock with checkered p.g. and grooved beavertail fore-end. Thumb safety. Wgt. about 8½ lbs. Europa, importer. (Standard) **$750.00**
Also, San Remo grade, **$1,150.00;** Monte Carlo grade, **$2,750.00;** Crown grade, **$2,850.00** and Super Crown grade, **$3,150.00.**
Extra bbls. **$295.00**

FOREIGN GUNS—OVER-UNDER SHOTGUNS

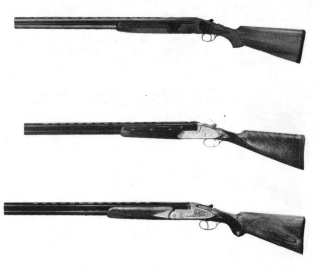

A & F PERAZZI O-U

Made in Italy, this 12 ga. features interchangeable stocks for Trap or Field, and interchangeable double or single trigger assemblies. All models have vent. ribs, hand-checkered p.g. walnut stocks with beavertail fore-ends, bright-finished actions. Abercrombie & Fitch, importer.

Trap, with 29" bbl., parallel rib, wgt. 7½ lbs. **$875.00**
Pigeon, 28" bbl., tapered rib, wgt. 7¼ lbs. 875.00
Skeet, 26" bbl., tapered rib, wgt. about 7 lbs. 950.00

ATLAS GRAND PRIX OVER-UNDER

Merkel-type sidelock action, fully engraved, 12 or 20 gauge, 26" or 28" vent. rib barrels in choice of chokes. Auto. ejectors, SST, straight or p.g. stock to order; about 7¼ lbs. Atlas, importer.

From .... **$700.00** up

ATLAS MODEL 750 OVER-UNDER

Merkel-type action, highly engraved; 12, 16 or 20 gauge, vent. rib barrels 26" or 28" in standard chokes; non-ejector, non-selective single trigger. Straight or p.g. stock, hand checkered (14½"x1½"x2½"), 6¼-7 lbs. Atlas, importer **$245.00**
Same as M750 but 3" Magnum in 12 or 20 ga. 245.00
Same as M750 but 30" bbls., and auto ejectors 265.00

ATLAS 150 SERIES OVER-UNDER SHOTGUN

12 and 20 ga. Bbls. 26" (IC & M or Skeet), 28" (M & F), 30" (F & extra F). Vent. rib. Boxlock action with crossbolt. Chromed bores, silver-plated or case-hardened engraved receiver. Single non-selective triggers. Straight or p.g. stock, checkered. wgt. 6½-7¼ lbs. Atlas Arms, importer ... **$275.00**
With ejectors **$325.00**
With better engraving, as the M160 .... 295.00
M160 with auto-ejectors, as the M180 (12 ga. only) 345.00

Beretta BL-3 DeLuxe O-U Shotgun

Same as Beretta BL-1, but with gold-plated SST, and ventilated-rib barrel. Engraved receiver. 12 ga., with 30" or 28" M&F or 26" IC&M chrome-lined barrels. Wgt. 7⅛ lbs. **$295.00**
3" Mag., 30" M&F barrels, 7⅜ lbs. **$310.00**
20 ga., (3") or 28 ga. (2¾"), 28" M&F or 26" IC&M barrels, stock 14¼"x1½"x2⅜", 2¼" pitch down, 6 lbs. **$295.00**
Trap 14⅜"x1⅜"x1¾", 1½" pitch down, with p.g. cap and contoured recoil pad. Wgt. 7¼ lbs. **$320.00**
Skeet, 12 (2¾"), 28 (2¾") or 20 (3") ga., 26" S1 & 2 barrels. Stock (12 ga.) 14¼"x1⅝"x2½" (20 ga.) 14¼"x1½"x2⅜"; both with 2" pitch down. Wgt. (12) 7 lbs.; (20) 6 lbs. **$320.00**
Extra bbls. Field **$137.00**   Trap or Skeet **$144.00**

ATLAS MODEL 87 OVER-UNDER

Similar to M750 but p.g. stock only (14"x1½"x2½"), silvered or case-hardened action. Atlas, importer **$230.00**
Same, but in 3" Magnum (as M95) 235.00
Same, but boxlock action, 26" bbls. only, double triggers, and 3" in 28 or 410 ga. only (as M65) **$195.00**
Same, but with non-selective ST (as M65-ST) 225.00

BERETTA BL-1 OVER-UNDER SHOTGUN

Low-profile Monoblock boxlock action, 12 ga., with 30" or 28" M&F or 26" IC&M chrome-moly steel barrels. Double triggers, front trigger hinged, w/o ejectors. Walnut p.g. stock (14¼"x1⅝"x2½", 2" pitch down) and fore-end hand checkered. Auto safety, 2¾" chambers. Ramp front sight, 4 fluorescent inserts. Wgt. 7 lbs. Garcia, importer **$225.00**
Extra bbls. 120.00

Beretta BL-4 DeLuxe O-U Shotgun

Similar to BL-3, with addition of selective auto. ejectors, extensive receiver engraving, deluxe hand checkering .... **$375.00 to $390.00**
Extra bbls. Field **$175.00**   Trap or Skeet **$185.00**

Beretta BL-5 Premium O-U Shotgun

Same as BL-4, except fully engraved receiver, specially selected walnut stock and fore-end, capped p.g. .... **$495.00 to $520.00**
Extra bbls. Field **$195.00**   Trap or Skeet 209.00

BERETTA S02 PRESENTATION OVER-UNDER SHOTGUN

Sidelock action, special chrome-nickel receiver, Boehler anti-rust barrels. All interior parts chromed. Receiver, tangs, screws, lever, guard, fore-end release, safety and standing breech scroll engraved, with a silver pigeon inlaid in the top lever. Trigger, safety and top lever checkered. 12 ga., ventilated rib barrels only, Skeet and trap models available. 26" Imp. Cyl. & Mod. or 28" Mod. & Full standard. Other borings to order without extra cost. Straight or p.g. stocks, perfectly matched from one-piece selected European walnut (14½"x1⅜"x2³⁄₁₆"). Double triggers standard. Wgt. from about 7¼ lbs. Garcia, importer **$1,000.00**
Same, Model S03, profusely scroll and relief engraved, fancy selected walnut **$1,200.00**
Same, Model S04, sidelocks are hand detachable, more elaborate engraving, full grain walnut stock and fore-end **$1,400.00**
Same, Model S05, gold Crown Grade symbol inlaid into top lever. Built to customer's complete specifications if desired, the whole virtually hand-made **$1,900.00**

FOREIGN GUNS—OVER-UNDER SHOTGUNS

ALLEN O-U SHOTGUNS

These Italian O-U guns are offered in a variety of grades in field and trap style. All carry vent. rib. Models are available with single non-selective, single selective, and double triggers, extractors and ejectors, extra wide trap ribs, standard and selected wood. C&M Sporting Arms Co., importer.
Price: M68 $198.95 to Model Mexico 68 at **$385.00.**

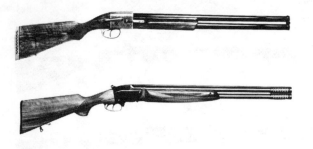

CHARLES DALY OVER-UNDER SHOTGUNS

12 ga., 2¾″ (3″ mag. in 30″ F&F), 20 (3″), 28 ga. (2¾″) or 410 (3″) chambers. Boxlock action, scroll engraved; firing pins quickly removable. Auto safety (manual on Skeet & Trap models), combined with bbl. selector; auto selective ejectors. Single selective inertia type gold-plated trigger. Checkered walnut semi-pistol grip stock and fore end (14″x1½″x2½″). Recoil pad on magnums. Vent. rib bbls. with steel bead. 20 ga. in 26″ (IC&M); 28″ (M&F). 12 ga. in 26″ (Skt., & Skt., IC&M, plus M&F in 28″ only), 30″ (M&F or F&F). Wt. 12 ga. 7 lbs.

20 ga. 6½ lbs.; in 28″ bbls. (12 or 20 ga.)	$375.00
28 or 410 gauge	400.00
12 ga., 3″ mag., F&F, 30″ bbls., 8 lbs.	375.00

Superior Grade. Same as Field Grade except: figured walnut, full p.g. stock with p.g. and grooved fore-end; special checkering **$399.00**
28 or 410 gauge 425.00
Superior Skeet. Same as Superior Grade except: 12 or 20 gauge; 26″ & 28″ bbls., manual safety. Skeet and Skeet bored **$399.00**
28 or 410 gauge 425.00
12 or 20 ga. with Slexor* 450.00

BRETTON OVER-UNDER SHOTGUN

Made in France, this 12 ga. shotgun weighs only 4½ lbs. Receiver is of heat-treated Dural; steel barrels may be unscrewed and replaced with 16 ga. or slug barrels. Continental Arms, importer **$285.00**
Deluxe engraved model **365.00**

BRNO OVER-UNDER SHOTGUNS

Made in Czechoslovakia, available in 12 or 16 ga. only. Simple design has 25 fewer parts; all parts interchange without hand fitting. Double-single trigger (rear trigger acts as selector). Skeet (illustrated), trap or field grades available. Continental Arms, importer **$210.00**

Superior Trap. Same as the Superior Skeet except: 12 ga. 30″, M&F, IM&F or F&F. Manual safety. Standard trap stock (14⅜″x1⅜″x1¾″) or Monte Carlo (14⅜″x1½″x1½″x2½″) with recoil pad **$399.00**
With Monte Carlo stock 410.00
With Selexor* (M. C. only) 450.00
With ½″ wide (Flat-Top) vent. rib. With or w/out M. C. stock 440.00
Venture Grade. Similar to Field Grade except: 12 or 20 ga. (2¾″ chambers) only, 28″ (Mod. & Full) or 26″ (Mod. & Imp. Cyl.) barrels with vent rib, single non-selective trigger and non-auto. safety. Weight, about 7 lbs.
. . . . **$335.00**

CHARLES DALY DIAMOND GRADE OVER-UNDER

Same as Daly Superior Grades except finest French walnut, more extensive checkering and a fully engraved receiver, guard, etc. **$650.00**
*Selexor: Allows either automatic selective ejection or extraction. A button on each side of the receiver provides control. RH button for lower bbl. or LH button for the upper.

CONDOR OVER-UNDER SHOTGUN

Monoblock system combined with double Purdey receiver lock and box lock action; single selective trigger is mechanically operated rather than recoil actuated. 12 ga., 28″ (Mod-Full, Mod.-IC or Skt-Skt) or 20 ga. 28″ (Mod.-Full, Mod.-IC or Skt-Skt); 2-¾″ chambers. Poldi steel barrels internally chromed; blued or case-hardened finish; vent rib; brass front and ivory center beads on skeet and trap models. Selected walnut stock 14″ x 1-½″ x 2-½″ Kleinguenther, importer **$295.00**

CONTINENTAL ARMS OVER-UNDER SHOTGUNS

The Nikko (illustrated) is a Japanese made gun available in either 12 or 20 gauge. Boxlock action is hand engraved; jeweled frame, automatic ejectors and lugs. Barrels of hard-chromed vanadium steel with vent. rib. Oil finished, checkered p.g. stock and fore-end which is completely detachable **$285.00**
Other high-grade shotguns are available from Continental. These are made in Belgium and have engraved boxlock actions; 4-way locking system; single selective trigger; selective ejectors and vent. rib. Available in all gauges for 12 through 28.
Royal Crown grade **$975.00**
Imperial Crown grade 1250.00

DICKSON GRAY EAGLE O-U

Zoli boxlock action, auto. safety, double triggers, 3″ chambers. In 12, 20 ga., 26″ bbl. (Imp. Cyl. & Mod.), 28″ (Mod. & Full). Wgt. about 7 lbs. (12 ga.), 6 lbs., 20 ga. Vent. rib. Hand checkered walnut p.g. stock and beavertail fore-end (14″x1½″x2½″). American Import Co. **$217.50**

FOREIGN GUNS—OVER-UNDER SHOTGUNS

FOREVER YOURS O-U SHOTGUNS
Ferlach-made, Anson & Deeley 4-lock type action, double Greener cross-bolt, Boehler proof steel barrels, ventilated rib, auto ejectors, double triggers, engraved action, checkered Circassian walnut pistol grip stock & split fore-end. Available with or without cheekpiece. Horn p.g. cap and buttplate. Weight 7-7½ lbs. Available in standard gauges, chokes and barrel lengths. Imported by Flaig's, **$675.00**. With single set trigger. **$750.00**

LAURONA OVER-UNDER SHOTGUN
Boxlock 12 ga. shotgun has vent. rib barrels choked Mod. and Full. Stock has checkered p.g. and fore-end. Twin-single triggers. Receiver is lightly engraved. Mars Equipment, importers **$199.00**

RICHLAND 828 OVER-UNDER
Case-hardened receiver. Rosette engraving. Walnut stock (1½"x2¼"x14¼") has skip-line hand checkering with matching quick-detachable fore-end. Ventilated rib. Non-selective single trigger. Plain extractors, non-automatic safety. Sliding crossbolt lock. In 28 ga. (2¾" chamber) with 28" (F&M) or 26" (IC&M) barrels. Weighs 5¼ lbs. (26"). . . **$268.00**

GARCIA-ROSSI OVERLAND EXPOSED HAMMER DOUBLE GUN
12 ga. (3") with 28" & 20" (F&M, IC&M) bbls; 20 ga. (3") with 26" and 20" (F&M) bbls. and 410 (3") 26" (F&F) bbls. Double triggers and hammers. Semi pistol grip stock and beavertail fore-end. Thumb lever release, bead front sight. Garcia Sporting Arms Corp. importer **$89.95**

FERLACH O-U TURKEY GUN
Boxlock action, Greener cross bolting, top snap, double triggers, Boehler steel bbls., 22" or 24". Top bbl., 12, 16 or 20 gauge; lower, 22 Hornet, 222 Rem., 243 257, 6.5x55, 270, 7x57, 30-06. Engraved action, Circassian stock, hand checkered at p.g. and fore-end. About 6½ lbs. Flaig's importer. **$650.00**
Write for catalog of drillings and combination guns.

FRANCHI FALCONET OVER & UNDER
Italian-made, this shotgun features easy-cocking action, short, fast hammer fall. Walnut stock, checkered pistol grip and fore-end; 14¼"x1⅜"x2¼", pitch down 2¾"; stocks on order within limits (¼" in comb hgt., ½" in pull). Skeet stock, 14¼"x1⅝"x2½". Trap, 14⅜"x1½"x1⅞". 12 Gauge only with vent. rib, single selective trigger and automatic ejectors. Field model has automatic safety. Field—26" (Imp. Cyl. & Mod.), 28" (Mod. & Full), or 30" (Mod. & Full). Skeet—26" (Skeet #1 & #2); Trap—30" (Mod. & Full) bbls. Chromed bores, engraved receiver. Stoeger.
Falconet Ebony (12 & 20) **$295.95**, Buckskin (12 & 20) **$305.95**, Silver (12 only) **$325.95**. Standard Skeet (12 only) **$395.95** or Std. Skeet with 12 and 20 ga. bbls. **$595.95**. Standard Trap **$395.95** or Super Trap **$495.95**. Imperial Grade **$1,099.95** or Monte Carlo Grade **$1,499.95**.

KRIEGHOFF MODEL 32 OVER-UNDER
The Europa Corp. imports this near-duplicate of the old Remington 32. A three-way safety (manual, auto or inoperative) and Boehler special steel bbls. are standard on all M32's. Made in 12 and 20 only, with selective single trigger, ejectors and ventilated rib, the M32 is available as a Skeet or field gun with 28" bbl. or as a trap gun (30" bbls.) at **$595.00**. Other bbl. lengths and chokes to order, as is a Monte Carlo stock. The San Remo grade, with fancier walnut and relief engraving, is **$995.00**. The Monte Carlo carries extra fancy wood, elaborate engraving and silver inlays, Monte Carlo stock at **$2,650.00**. The Crown Grade is like the Monte Carlo but has gold inlays, at **$2,750.00**. The Super Crown, like the Crown, has both gold and silver inlaid figurines, at **$2,950.00**.
Extra bbls. with standard borings . . . . **$275.00** to **$295.00**

LAMES OVER-UNDER SHOTGUN
Boxlock action is hand engraved, all parts are blued except single selective trigger which is gold plated. European walnut stock has hand-checkered p.g. and fore-end. Available in 12 ga. only, with 26" (Imp. Cyl. & Mod.), 28" (Imp. Cyl. & Mod. or Mod. & Full), 30" and 32" (Mod./Imp. and Full or Full and Full). LA Distributors, importer **$329.95**
Other models to **$1,599.95**. Extra bbls. **$150-$200**.

RICHLAND ARMS 844 OVER-UNDER SHOTGUN
Boxlock action of nickel-chrome steel, blued, non-selective single trigger and simple extractors. Stock (14"x1⅝"x2¼") of European walnut with checkered p.g. and fore-end. Barrels of English Vickers steel, 12 ga. only, 30" (Full & Full) 7 lbs., 3 oz., 28" (Mod. & Full) 7 lbs., or 26" (Imp. Cyl. & Mod.) 6¾ lbs. **$189.50**

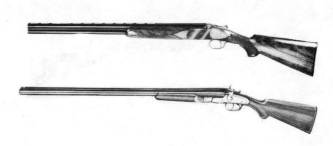

FOREIGN GUNS—OVER-UNDER SHOTGUNS

SAUER 66 OVER-UNDER
Based on the Purdey-System with Holland and Holland type removable sidelocks. Has a single selective trigger, selective automatic ejectors and the field model features an automatic slide safety. Krupp-Special steel barrels with ventilated rib, ivory front and middle bead, a selected fancy walnut stock (14¼"x1½"x2¼") with p.g., ventilated recoil pad and fine line hand checkering. Available in three grades of engraving. 12 ga. only (other gauges to be announced later). Barrel length and choke: 26" (IC&M) 28" (F&M) 30" (F&M). Wgt. 7¼ lbs. Weatherby, importer. Grade I **$685.00**, Grade II **$800.00** & Grade III **$1,285.00**.

SAUER BBF OVER-UNDER RIFLE-SHOTGUN
Stock (14½"x1⅝"x2¾") made of selected walnut, with p.g., cheekpiece and hand checkering, and is built in the classic tradition. The trigger guard is steel. 16 ga. (2¾"). Rifle barrel: 222, 243, 30-30, 30-06 and 7x65R. Barrel length: 25"; Krupp-Special gun barrel steel; Shotgun barrel full choke; rifle barrel hammer-forged; matted rib; bead front sight; folding leaf rear sight. Blitz action with Kersten lock; centrally guided firing pins; front trigger for rifle barrel designed as adjustable single-set trigger; sear safety manually operated by slide on upper tang. Wgt. 6 lbs. Weatherby, importer.

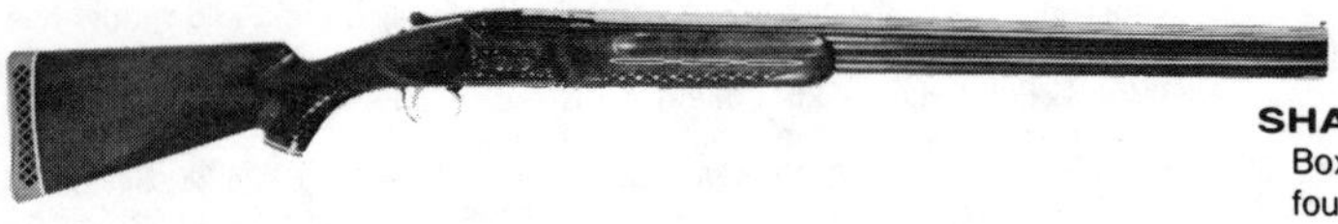

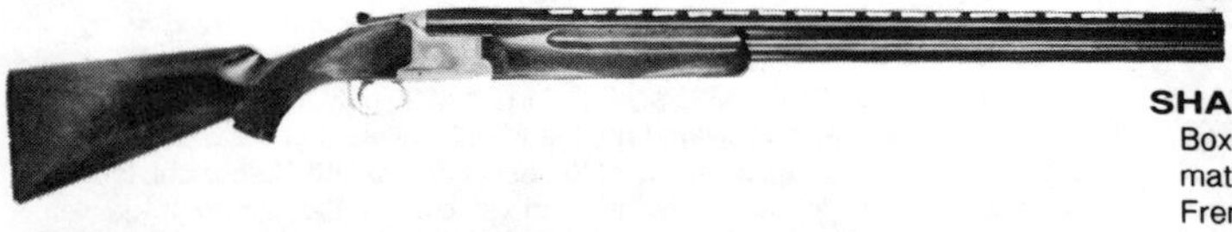

SHADOW CUSTOM GRADE OVER & UNDER
Available in 3 grades (Silver, Black and Gold). Specifications same as Shadow Indy; stock dimensions and chokes of customers choice. Delivery 6 months after acceptance of order. **$900.00, $1,200.00** & **$1,500.00**

ZOLI SILVER SNIPE OVER-UNDER
Purdey type boxlock action with crossbolt, 12 or 20 ga. (3" chambers); satin chrome-plated receiver, single selective trigger, simple extractors and auto. safety. Chrome-lined barrels with vent rib; 30" (12 ga. only, Mod. & Full), 28" (Mod. & Full), or 26" (Imp. Cyl. & Mod.). Walnut stock (12 ga., 14⅜"x1⅜"x2¹/₁₆"; 20 ga., 14⁵/₁₆"x1⅝"x2⁹/₁₆") with checkered p.g. and fore-end, plastic buttplate. Weight about 6½ lbs. Galef, importer **$234.95** Trap, Skeet models have non-auto. safety, wide non-glare vent. rib and suitable stock dimensions, 2¾" chambers **$282.95**

Trap model available with special trap stock and ventilated rib. 30" and 32" (F&F, F&M). Grade I **$755.00**, Grade II **$865.00** and Grade III, **$1,350.00**. Skeet with 26" (S&S barrels. Grade I **$755.00**, Grade II **$865.00** & Grade III **$1,350.00**.

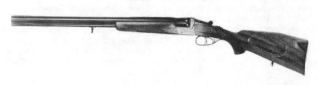

Standard Model (with arabesque engravings on action and fine hand checkering) **$735.00**
De Luxe Model (with Scotch checkering on selected walnut stock, white line spacers at p.g. and butt plate, and hunting scene engravings on action). **$845.00**

SHADOW INDY OVER & UNDER SHOTGUN
Boxlock action is hand engraved, frame with mono block construction and four lock sytem. Single selective trigger, gold plated automatic ejector, manual safety. Unique Airflow Rib of folded heat-treated four fold aluminum dissipates heat rapidly. Pearl front and silver middle sights. Stock of fancy French or Circassian walnut (14-⅜" x 1-⅜" x 1-⅞" x 1-¼" for trap; 14" x 1-½" x 2-½" x 2" for skeet). 12 ga. 2-¾" chamber only. Barrel length: Trap Model (Full - Full or IM-Full) 29-¾"; Skeet Model (Sk-Sk) 27-½". Weight: approx 7-¾ lbs. Tradewinds, importer **$475.00**

SHADOW SEVEN OVER & UNDER SHOTGUN
Boxlock action, hand engraved; solid frame; single selective trigger; automatic ejector; manual safety. Three fold aluminum Airflow Rib. Stock of French walnut (14" x 1-½" x 2-½" x 2"). 12 ga. 2-¾" chamber only. Barrel lengths 30" (Full-Mod.) and 27" (Mod. & Imp.). Field Model currently available, Trap and Skeet Models will become available soon. Weight: 7-½ lbs. approx. **$350.00**

ZOLI GOLDEN SNIPE OVER-UNDER
Same as Silver Snipe except selective auto. ejectors **$279.95**
Trap, Skeet models **$327.95**

FOREIGN GUNS—DOUBLE BARREL SHOTGUNS

A&F KNOCKABOUT DOUBLES
Made in Italy to A&F's specifications, the Mark I Knockabout is a side-by-side, in 12 (26" or 28" bbls.), 20, 28 or 410 (26"). All gauges have double triggers, plain extractors, color case-hardened action and checkered walnut p.g. stock and fore-end. About 6½ lbs. (12 ga.); 5½ lbs. (20 ga.); 5¼ lbs. (28, 410). 12 or 20 ga., **$150.** 28 and 410 **$25.00** higher. The Mark II is similar to the Mark I, but has vent. rib, ejectors and a beavertail fore-end. 12 and 20 gauge **$259.50.** The Mark III is a 12, 20 or 28 ga. over-under with single trigger, vent. rib, engraved action with antique silver finish. 26" and 28" barrels only, with choice of choke. Weight, 6¾ lbs. (12 ga.); 5½ lbs. (20 ga.). 12, 20 ga. **$289.50,** 28, 410 ga. **$297.50**

A&F ZANOTTI SHOTGUN
A custom made side-by-side double in 12 ga. (26" Mod. & Imp. Cyl. or 28" Mod. & Full); 20 and 28 ga. (26" Mod. & Imp. Cyl). 12 ga. has semi-p.g. walnut stock and beavertail fore-end; 20 and 28 ga. have straight grip and slim fore-end. All have single non-selective triggers, ejectors, gold stock inlay for initials, etc. Abercrombie & Fitch, importer.
12 or 20 gauge .... **$675.00** 28 gauge **$750.00**

FOREIGN GUNS—DOUBLE BARREL SHOTGUNS

A&F FINEST QUALITY SHOTGUNS
Abercrombie & Fitch import the famous Purdey, Holland & Holland, Boss and Westley Richards shotguns. All are custom-made and hand-finished and, while A&F carries a few models in stock, guns ordered with custom specifications usually require 1 to 2 years for delivery. All have full side locks, single or double triggers and ejectors. Westley Richards side-by-side doubles start at **$900.,** the others at **$2800.;** over-under models start at **$3400.**

ATLAS 200 SERIES DOUBLE GUNS
12, 16, 20, 28 and 410 ga., 26" (Imp. Cyl. and Mod.), or 26" and 28" (Mod. and Full), bbls. Engraved Anson & Deeley-type action. Vickers steel bbls. with chromed bores. Walnut stock with checkered semi-p.g. and beavertail fore-end. Wgt. approx. 6-7 lbs. Double trigger **$180.00**
M204 with single trigger **$210.00.** M206 with single trigger, auto ejectors **$230.00.** Note: 410, 28 ga. in M200 only.
M208 Magnum same as M200 except 12 or 20 ga., 3" chambers, **$185.00;** with single non-seleceive trigger **$195.00**

ATLAS 145 DOUBLE SHOTGUN
Similar to M200 except: Vent. rib, choice of p.g. or straight stock, full hand engraving, entire gun of nickel-chrome steel. 12 & 20 ga. only. Atlas Arms, importer **$290.00**
With two sets of bbls., 26" (Skeet 1 & 2); 28" (M & F) **395.00**

ATLAS 500 MAGNUM DOUBLE SHOTGUN
Similar to M200 Magnum except; 10 ga., 3½ chambers, 32" bbls. (F & F); 12, 20 ga., 3" chambers, 28" (M & F). Vent. rib, double triggers, recoil pad. Action especially built for magnum loads. Atlas Arms, importer . **$210.00**

ATLAS 300 DOUBLE SHOTGUN
12 and 20 ga., 26" bbls. (IC & M); 28" (M & F). Holland & Holland type sidelock action with Purdey-type lock. Hand engraved, auto ejectors. Superior walnut stock, checkered on p.g. and fore-end. Non-selective single trigger. Wgt. 7¼ lbs. (12 ga.). 6¼ lbs. (20 ga.). Atlas Arms, importer **$440.00**
Model 310, with single selective trigger **485.00**

BERNARDELLI GAMECOCK DOUBLES
Boxlock action, double underlugs, case-hardened with light engraving; plain extractors, double triggers, auto. safety. Checkered straight grip walnut stock and fore-end (14"x1½"x2¼"). 12 or 20 ga. with 25" bbls., 2¾" chambers (IC, M), 28" (M, F), wgt. 6-6½ lbs. Stoeger, importer **$230.00**
Deluxe Gamecock, like above except: sideplate action, engraved, chrome-lined bbls., selected fancy wood **$340.00**
Premier Gamecock, similar to Deluxe, except auto-ejectors, non-selective single trigger, Greener-type cross bolt, 3" chambers **$440.00**

BERETTA GR-2 DOUBLE
Greener type boxlock action, engraved receiver, coil mainsprings. Folding front trigger, auto. safety. Walnut hand-checkered stock (14"x1½"x2½", 2¼" pitch down) and semi-beavertail fore-end. 12 ga., 2¾" chambers, 30" or 28" (M&F), 26" (IC&M) barrels. 20 ga., 2¾" chambers, 28" (M&F) or 26" (IC&M) barrels. 7⅛ lbs. .... **$299.00**   Extra bbls. **145.00**

BERETTA GR-3 DOUBLE
Same as Gr-2 except single selective trigger **$325.00**
12 ga. (3" chambers), 30" M&F barrels, stock 14"x1½"x2½", (2½" pitch down), recoil pad, 8 !bs. **$325.00**
Extra bbls. **$145.00**

BERETTA GR-4 DOUBLE
Same as GR-3 except fully hand-engraved receiver, selective auto. ejectors, full p.g. stock with grip cap. 12 ga. 2¾" **$399.00**
Extra bbls. **$205.00**

BERNARDELLI ITALIA HAMMER DOUBLES
Made from modern steel, but with old-style external hammers. 12 ga. only 30" chrome-lined bbls. (M, F), 2¾" chambers. Action has Greener-type crossbolt, double triggers, engraved sideplates, double underlugs, half-cock safety. Checkered fancy walnut stock and fore-end. Stoeger, importer
.... **$264.00**
Brescia model, similar to Italia except: 12 ga., 28" or 30" bbls., 20 ga., 26" bbls. (IC, M) **$200.00**

BRESCIA SIDE-BY-SIDE SHOTGUN
Anson & Deeley lock and action with Holland-type automatic ejectors; marbeled, case-hardened finish with fine engraving. 12 ga. or 20 ga. 28" bbl. (Full, Mod. or IC) 2-¾" chambers. Weight: 6-½ lbs., over-all length 44-¼". Stock select walnut, pistol grip or straight, streamlined beavertail fore-end; ventilated recoil pad; hand checkering. Kleinguenther, importer. . **$216.20**

CENTURY FOLDING SHOTGUN
Hammer gun with side lever that opens gun, depressing button on forward part of left frame allows complete folding of this Spanish double. Chambered for the 410 3" Magnum, 27¾" barrels are choked Full and Full. Wgt. 4¾ lbs. Century Arms, Inc., importer **$54.50**

Supra De Luxe Model 5 is a better quality gun made in Belgium. Boxlock action with Greener cross-bolt and engraved game scene. Available in all gauges and barrel lengths from 26" to 32"; Skeet, trap and field models
.... **$395.00**
Model 62 is like the Model 5 but also in 12 ga. Magnum; vent. rib; Anson Deeley boxlock action, engraved; selective auto. ejectors; horn grip cap and buttplate **$495.00**
Model 40 is like the Model 5 but chambered for 10 ga. Magnum; double underlugs; 32" barrel full-choke; double triggers; weight about 10 lbs.
.... **$495.00**
The best quality sidelock gun (illustrated) is hand made in Belgium and has engraved locks, double triggers and a straight buttstock with hand checkering at the wrist and fore-end. Available singly or in matched pairs, each
.... **$2500.00**

CONTINENTAL ARMS DOUBLE GUNS
The Centaure is a hand made Belgian shotgun with triple locking lugs and side clips. French walnut stock, hand-checkered p.g. and fore-end. 12 ga., 30" barrels only **$137.50**

FOREIGN GUNS—DOUBLE BARREL SHOTGUNS

DARNE DOUBLE BARREL SHOTGUN

The unique action whose protruding double "ears," pulled rearward, slide the entire breechblock back exposing the chambers for loading. All models have raised ribs, French walnut checkered pistol grip and fore-end stocks, (14¼"x1⅝"x2½") double triggers and selective ejectors. Stoeger, importer. Bird Hunter in 12 or 20 ga., 25½" bbls. (Imp. Cyl. & Mod.). Wgt. approx 6¼ lbs.(12)—5¾ lbs. (20) **$240.00**
Pheasant Hunter De Luxe. Same as the Hunter except: 12 ga. 28" (Mod. & Full), fancy wood and engraving, **$325.00.** Quail Hunter Supreme. Same as the Deluxe but in 20 or 28 ga. only, 25½" (Imp. Cyl. & Mod.) bbls. Elaborate hand engraved action, hard-chromed bores, carrying strap and swivels **$445.00**

DAVIDSON 69SL SIDELOCK DOUBLE

12 ga. (2¾") with 30", 28" (M&F) or 26" (IC&M) bbls. Also 20 ga. (2¾") with 28" (M&F) or 26" (IC&M) bbls. Checkered walnut p.g. stock and forearm with white-line spacers. Nickel finish, engraved detachable sideplates with cocking indicators. Automatic safety, manual extractors, gold plated trigger, two brass sighting beads. Wgt. 7 lbs. (12 ga.) Davidson, importer **$129.95**

DICKSON COMPACT DOUBLE

Anson & Deeley type action, case-hardened receiver, auto-safety, single trigger. Hand-checkered walnut p.g. stock (14"x1⁹/₁₆"x2½"). 12 ga., 28" (M&F, IC&M), 3" chambers. Wgt. about 6 lbs. 12 oz. Standard Extractors, vent. rib, rubber recoil pad. American Import Co., importer. **$146.50**

DICKSON FALCON MAGNUM DOUBLE

Scroll-engraved Anson & Deeley type action, Holland type extractors, raised matted rib, auto. safety, double triggers. Checkered p.g. stock and beavertail fore-end. Recoil pad. 32" bbls., Full and Full, 3½" chambers, 10-gauge Magnum. American Import Co. **$150.00**

DICKSON FALCON DOUBLE SHOTGUN

Same as Magnum 10 except: 12 or 20 ga. in 28" M&F, or 26" IC, 3" chambers. Black plastic butt plate and p.g. cap with white spacers. American Import Co. **$121.00**

FERLACH COMPANION DOUBLE GUN

12, 16, 28 (2¾" chambers), 20, 410 (3" chambers). Choice of bbl. lengths and chokes. Anson & Deeley action, two triggers, auto. ejectors, semi-beavertail fore-end. Circassian walnut stock of standard dimensions, checkered p.g. cap, cheekpiece optional. Choice of recoil pad or horn buttplate. 6½-7 lbs. Flaig's, importer. **$500.00**

F.I.E. BRASIL SIDE BY SIDE SHOTGUN

12 ga. (26" IC-Mod., 28" Mod.-Full and 30" Full-Full), 16 ga. (26" IC-Mod. and 28" Mod.-Full), 20 ga. (26" IC-Mod. and 28" Mod.-Full) and 410 ga. (26" Mod.-Full and 26" Full-Full). Hand checkered walnut stock and fore-end, case hardened engraved receiver; blue raised matted rib; receiver proportioned to gauge. Weight: 5 lbs. 10 oz. F.I.E. Corp., importer. **$92.00**

MERCURY MAGNUM DOUBLES

10 (3½"), 12 or 20 ga. (3") magnums. 12 and 20 ga. have 28" (F&M) brazed rib bbls., 10 ga. in 32" F&F. Triple-lock Anson & Deeley type action with double triggers, front hinged; auto safety, extractors; safety gas ports; engraved frame. Walnut, checkered pistol grip stock and beavertail fore-end; (14"x1⅝"x2¼") with recoil pad. Wgt. 12 ga., 7¼ lbs., 20 ga., 6½ lbs. 45" over-all. Tradewinds, importer **$134.50**
10 ga., 10⅛ lbs., 49" over-all **159.95**

DAVIDSON 63B DOUBLE SHOTGUN

12, 16, 20, 28, 410 ga. Anson & Deeley crossbolt action (28 & 410 w/o crossbolt). Automatic tang safety. Manual extractors. Brushed nickel finish, engraved. 28 ga., 25" bbls. (IC & M); 410, 25" (F & F); 12, 16, 20 gauges; 26", 28", 30" bbls., all popular chokes. Front and middle bead sights. Spanish walnut p.g. stock hand checkered, with grip cap, white-line spacers. Davidson, importers. **$109.95**
Magnum, 12 and 20 ga., 3" chambers, 26", 28", 30" bbls. **124.95**
Magnum, 10 ga., 3½" chambers, 32" bbls. (F & F) **159.95**

DIXIE BREECH-LOADING HAMMER DOUBLES

Of modern Belgian, Italian or Spanish manufacture, proofed for heaviest smokeless powder loads, these double guns are available in 12, 16, 20 and 410 ga., regular or Magnum with 28" to 32" barrels. Case-hardened frames with modest engraving. Straight, semi-pistol or full pistol-grip halfstocks, some with checkered grip and fore-end, some smooth. Dixie Gun Works, importers .... **$125.00** to **$140.00**

KRIEGHOFF AMERICAN DRILLING

Blitz action, engraved receiver. Shotgun locks are auto-cocking with indicators. Rifle lock cocks by moving tang-mounted slide forward. Split extractors lift rifle case higher than shotshells. Wide black nylon trigger guard. Stock has checkered p.g. and beavertail fore-end, Pachmayr recoil pad. Gun comes with 22 WMR insert barrel fitted inside right shotgun tube. Available in double 12 ga. over 30-06 or 7mm Mag. 25" barrels, 41" over-all; weight, 7 lbs. Harry Owens, importer **$1,500.00**
Extra insert barrel for 22 LR .... **.24.00**

FOREIGN GUNS—DOUBLE BARREL SHOTGUNS

P.O.S. 10 GAUGE MAGNUM DOUBLE

Made in Spain, this shotgun uses Anson & Deeley top lever type action, Purdey type locks. Case hardened action, checkered Spanish walnut p.g. stock, with recoil pad, beavertail fore-end. 32" (Full) bbls., 3½" chambers. Wgt. 11 lbs. Sloan's Sporting Goods Co., importer. **$150.00**

PREMIER DOUBLE BARREL SHOTGUNS

The Continental model is an exposed hammer side-lock gun with two triggers available in 12, 16, 20 or 410. All have 26" barrels choked Mod. & Full except 410, 26". French walnut stock (14"x1⅝"x2½") checkered at p.g. and fore-end. Length 44½" over-all; weight about 7 lbs. Ed Paul's Sporting Goods, importer **$131.25**

Ambassador model is similar to above except: hammerless side-lock action with auto. safety on tang. **$144.30**
Brush King has a boxlock action and is fitted with 22" barrels choked Mod. and Imp. Cyl. available in 12 or 20 ga. only. Length 39" over-all; weight about 6 lbs. **$113.95**
Other models and grades are available. Write importer for catalog.

RICHLAND ARMS SHOTGUNS

Imports from Spain and Italy. The 200 is a demibloc side-by-side double with auto. safety, two triggers, long beavertail fore-end, walnut p.g. stock with cheekpiece and recoil pad. 12, 16, 20, 28 or 410 ga. 410 and 20 ga. with ⅜l chambers, others 2¾". 30", 28" or 22" (20-ga. only) bbls., all standard chokes **$129.50**
202 is the 200 with extra set of 12 or 20 ga. bbls. **179.50**
711 is a 10-ga., 3½" chambered long range double with 32" F&F bbls. **$149.50**

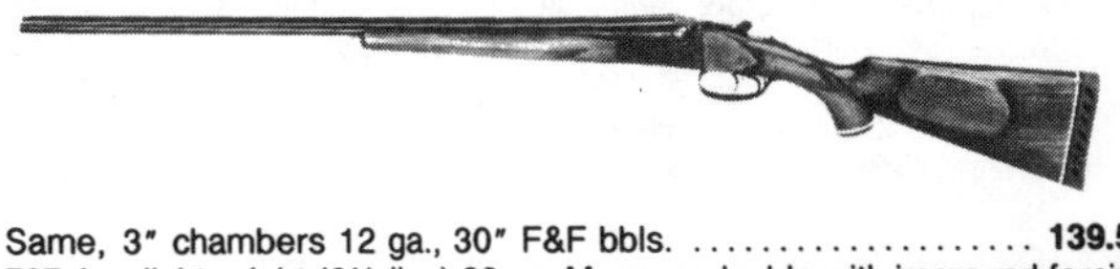

Same, 3" chambers 12 ga., 30" F&F bbls. **139.50**
707 is a lightweight (6½ lbs.) 20 ga. Magnum double with improved forcing cones, chokes and borings for 80%-85% patterns with 4's. 26" (IC&M), 28" (M&F) or 30" (F&F) bbls. Checkered walnut p.g. stock, beavertail fore-end, recoil pad **$179.50**
707-2, with two sets of barrels. 30" (M&F) & 26" (IC&M) **249.50**

SANDERSON SHOTGUNS

Illustrated is the Classic Bird Gun, M200 S-I, a lightweight double in 28 (4½ lbs.) to 12 gauge (6 lbs.); standard 2¾" or 2" chambers, with barrels from 25" up. The walnut stock has a straight grip and classic fore-end. Auto ejectors, hinged front trigger and engraved action. **$425.00** up. 2" and 2½" shells are available from Sanderson.
Belgian-made Neumann shotguns imported by Sanderson include the 10 gauge Magnum double from **$395;** 12, 20 and 410 3" doubles from **$249.50** and 20 gauge bird guns.

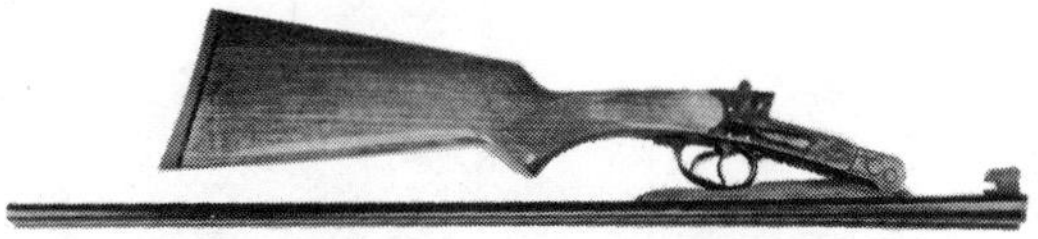

SARASQUETA DOUBLE BARREL SHOTGUN

Made in Spain with Anson & Deeley-type action and Purdey triple bolt. Receiver case hardened and engraved; hand checkered pistol grip stock and fore-end. 410 ga., 28" barrel bored Full-Full. F.I.E. Corp., importer. **$105.95**

SARASQUETA FOLDING SHOTGUN

Double barreled folding shotgun with case hardened and engraved receiver; exposed hammers. 410 ga. with 26" barrels. F.I.E. Corp., importer. **$59.95**

WEBLEY & SCOTT 700, 701, 702 DOUBLE GUNS

12 or 20 ga. Anson & Deeley action, boxlock, hammerless, top lever, no extension, solid tumbler, auto. safety. 26" bbls. (Mod. & Imp. Cyl.), 28" (F. or M. & F., M., I.P.), 30" (Full & Ful, Mod. or Imp. Cyl.). Straight or semi-pistol grip stock, hand checkered (14⅝"x1½"x2¼"). Custom fitting, recoil pad, single non-selective trigger, optional at extra cost. About 6¾ lbs. (12-28") to 5¾ lbs. in 20x28". Service Armament Co., importers.
Model 700, light scroll engraving, selected French walnut **$375.00**
Model 702, more scroll engraving, better French walnut **550.00**
Model 701, profusely scroll engraved, fancy French walnut **750.00**
Write for information on other W&S guns; from **30.00**

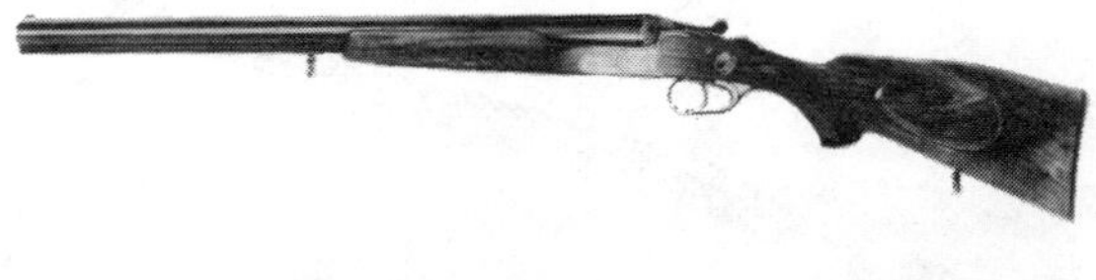

SAUER DRILLING 3000-E RIFLE-DOUBLE SHOTGUN

Finest walnut is used for the modified Monte Carlo stock (14½"x1⅝"x2¾") with p.g., cheek-piece, sling swivels, metal trigger guard and fore-end with checkering. Features a patent spring snap. 12 ga. bbls. chambered for 2¾" shells. Calibers of rifle barrels: available in 222, 243, 30-30, 30-06 and 7x65R. 25" bbl. Krupp-Special gun barrel steel; matted rib; bead front sight; automatically operated folding leaf rear sight; right barrel modified, left barrel full choke; rifle barrel hammer-forged. Blitz action with Greener cross bolt; double underlocking lugs; separate rifle cartridge extractor; front trigger acts as set trigger, adjustable for pull; vertical firing pin indicators; Greener side safety mechanism locks all 3 bbls.; sear slide safety on upper tang locks right shotgun barrel when firing rifle barrel. Wgt. 6½ to 7¼ lbs., depending on rifle caliber. Weatherby, importer.
3000-E Standard Model (with arabesque engravings on action and fine line hand checkering) **$830.00**
3000-E De Luxe Model (with Scotch checkering on selected walnut stock, white spacers at p.g. and buttplate and hunting scene engravings on action) **$945.00**

SAUER ROYAL SIDE BY SIDE

Anson & Deeley action with Greener cross bolt; double underlocking lugs; single selective trigger; automatic slide safety; side firing pin indicators. Krupp-Special steel barrel with ivory bead, matted rib. Fine arabesque engraving on grey case hardened action. Selected walnut stock (14¼"x1½"x2¼") with fine line hand checkering. White spacers at p.g. cap and ventilated recoil pad. The beavertail fore-end is furnished with a patented spring snap. 12 ga. (2¾") with 28" & 30" (F&M) bbls. 20 ga. (3") with 28" (F&M) & 26" (IC&M) bbls. Wgt. 12 ga., approx. 6½ lbs.; 20 ga. approx. 6 lbs. Weatherby, importer. **$445.00**

FOREIGN GUNS—DOUBLE BARREL SHOTGUNS

SAUER ARTEMIS SIDE BY SIDE

12 ga. (2¾") with 30" & 38" (F&M) bbls. 20 ga. (3") with 28" (F&M) & 26" (IC&M) bbls. With Holland and Holland type removable side-locks with double sear safeties and automatic selective ejectors. Stock (14¼"x1½"x2¼") and beavertail fore-end, with fine line hand checkering, are made of highly figured walnut. Krupp-Special steel barrels with ivory bead front sight, Greener cross bolt, double under locking lugs, automatic slide safety and single selective trigger. Weight about 6½ lbs. Weatherby, importer. Grade I (with fine line engraving) **$2,050.00**
Grade II (with full English arabesque engraving) **2,500.00**

ZOLI SILVER HAWK DOUBLE

Modified Anson & Deeley boxlock action with Purdey triple locks, 12 or 20 ga. (3" chambers); satin chrome-plated receiver with light engraving; double triggers, plain extractors, auto. safety, pins indicate loaded chambers. Chrome-lined barrels, 26" (Imp. Cyl. & Mod.), 28" (Mod. & Full); in 12 ga. only, 30" (Mod. & Full) and 32" (Full & Full). European walnut stock (14⅜"x1⅜"x2⁵⁄₁₆"), hand-checkered fore-end and p.g. with cap, plastic buttplate. Weight about 6¼ lbs. Galef, importer **$179.95**

FOREIGN GUNS—MUZZLE LOADERS

CENTURY MUZZLE LOADERS

Belgian made Charleville 1763 Flintlock Musket. Round barrel, 45" long smooth bore, 69 caliber. Stock walnut finished wood, brass barrel bands and trigger guard. Overall length 60". Weight 8½ lbs. Proof tested for black powder by Belgian Official Proof House. Century Arms Importers **$99.50.** Percussion action ⅔ stock, 28" blued barrel. Checkered pistol grip. Weight 3½ lbs. Ramrod, patch box. **$22.50.** Flintlock action. **$32.50.** percussion action, full length stock. 28" blued barrel. Checkered pistol grip. Weight: 4 lbs. Ramrod, patch box **$27.50.** Flintlock action **$37.50.** Also, Military flint-lock model, 50" barrel 12 ga. Ramrod **$54.50;** percussion model, 37" barrel **$49.50.** Antique rifles—Genuine antiques, made over a century ago, no two alike. **$99.00.** 28" ga. Deluxe Lightweight Percussion model, 31" part octagon barrel, walnut finished sporter stock **$27.50.** 20" ga. Double Barrel Percussion Guns, ⅔ stock **$47.50.**

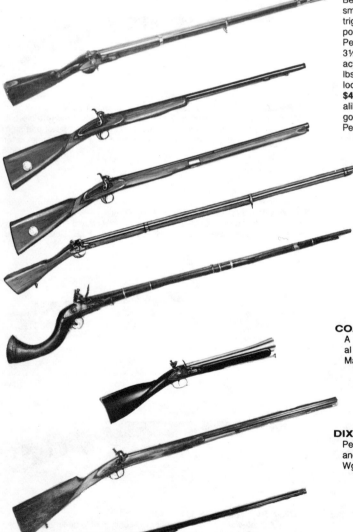

COACH GUARD BLUNDERBUSS

A close copy of the flintlock muzzleloaders used against highwaymen. Metal parts blued, wooden stock has polished, ebonized finish. Proof tested. Mars Equipment, importers **$99.95**

DIXIE HALFSTOCK RIFLE

Percussion lock 45-cal. rifle, 32" round bbl., 6 grooves. Checkered stock and fore-end, open sights, wood ramrod in two thimbles. Steel furniture. Wgt. about 7½ lbs. **$72.50**

DIXIE PERCUSSION SHOTGUNS

Newly made in Belgium from old parts. Most have cap boxes. Barrels average 32". 6 lbs., single shot, 410 to 32 ga. **$24.95**
Similar, except double barrel, about 20 ga., 8 lbs. **79.95**

FOREIGN GUNS—MUZZLE LOADERS

DIXIE SQUIRREL RIFLE
Percussion cap 45-cal. rifle with 40" bbl., 48" twist, six lands. Full length hard maple stock, stained and varnished, with patchbox. Brass furniture. Kentucky rifle sights, two, "candy-striped" cleaning rods furnished. Wgt., about 10 lbs. For black powder only. Dixie Gun Works, importer. **$139.50**
Flintlock version **149.50**
Double set triggers (installed by purchaser) **8.50**

DIXIE KENTUCKY RIFLE
A modern cal. .45 version of the Kentucky. Blued 40" octagon barrel, $^{13}/_{16}$" across the flats, 6 lands. Case-hardened, engraved lockplate, European walnut full-length stock with patchbox, brass furniture. Black powder only. 55" over-all, wgt. about 10 lbs. Percussion model **$149.50**
Flintlock model **159.50**

DIXIE DELUXE PENNSYLVANIA RIFLE
Similar to the Dixie Kentucky Rifle but with different style buttstock, fancy brass patch box and extra wide buttplate. Percussion model. . . . **$174.50**
Flintlock model. **$179.50**

DIXIE 1st MODEL BROWN BESS MUSKET
Replica of the Revolutionary War flintlock. Caliber 75 with 46" smoothbore barrel; hand engraved locks, walnut stained stock, brass furniture. Over-all length 63". . . . . **$275.00** Bayonet **$15.00**

F.I.E. KENTUCKY RIFLE
Percussion lock 45 caliber with 35" rifled octagon barrel. Hardwood stock; polished cast brass patch box, buttplate and fittings. Brass trigger guard forms a pistol grip. Plain grade . . . . **$65.00** Engraved **$70.00**

KENTUCKIAN FLINTLOCK RIFLE
Built in the image of the early Pennsylvania "Kentuckies." Fullstock, 33½" octagonal barrel, 44 caliber. Weight about 6¼ lbs., over-all 48". Engraved lockplate and brass patchbox, solid brass furniture, open sights, hardwood ramrod. Intercontinental Arms, importer **$125.00**
Also available in percussion **125.00**

KENTUCKIAN FLINTLOCK CARBINE
Same as Kentuckian rifle, but with 25½" barrel, 40" over-all. Intercontinental Arms, importer. . . . **$125.00** Also available in percussion . . . **125.00**

NAVY ARMS CARBINE
6-shot revolving carbine based on the Remington 44 Army revolver. 16" or 18" bbl., buckhorn rear sight, adjustable silver blade front. Straight grip wooden stock, curved metal buttplate, scrolled trigger guard. Navy Arms, importers **$125.00**

ZOUAVE RIFLE
A percussion muzzle-loading rifle, cal. 58, that duplicates the Civil War Remington Model 1863. Walnut ⅞-length stock with steel ramrod, sling swivels and brass patchbox in stock. Case-hardened lock, blued 33" barrel and brass furniture. Bead front and open rear sights. Wgt. 9½ lbs., 52" over-all. Navy Arms, importer **$100.00**
Zouave Carbine, 22" bbl. **100.00**
A rifle made to similar specifications is offered by Mars Equipment. **$99.95**

Guns in this section are compression powered by: A) disposable CO_2 cartridge; B) by hand pumping of air; C) by cocking a spring which compresses air. This air is released when the trigger is pulled. Calibers are 177 (BB or pellet) and 22 pellet, except for Sheridan rifles, these using a special form of 20-cal. bullet. Pellet guns are usually rifled, those for BBs only are not; 177-cal. rifles can shoot BBs also, of course.

BENJAMIN 262 SUPER CO_2 ROCKET
Caliber: 22, single shot.
Barrel: 5¾", rifled bronze liner.
Length: 9¼". **Weight:** 3 lbs.
Power: Standard CO_2 cylinder, 2-stage power.
Features: Plastic stocks. Adj. rear sight. Fingertip safety. Target outfit includes pellets, Bell target and paper targets, one CO_2 cartridge; $4.00 extra.
Price: **$27.00**

BENJAMIN 422 SEMI-AUTOMATIC PISTOL
Caliber: 22, 10-shot.
Barrel: 5⁹/₁₆", rifled bronze liner.
Length: 9". **Weight:** 2 lbs.
Power: Standard CO_2 cylinder. Muzzle velocity about 400 fps.
Features: Trigger and hammer safeties, checkered plastic thumbrest grips, adj. rear sight, blade front.
Price: Blued **$27.50**

BENJAMIN SUPER S. S. TARGET PISTOL SERIES 130
Caliber: BB, 22 and 177; single shot.
Barrel: 8 inches; BB smoothbore; 22 and 177, rifled.
Length: 11". **Weight:** 2 lbs.
Power: Hand pumped.
Features: Bolt action; fingertip safety; adj. power.
Price: M130, BB . **$32.00**   M132, 22 . . . **$32.00**   M137, 177 . **$32.00**

BSF MATCH EXPORT PISTOL
Caliber: 177 single shot
Barrel: 7" rifled
Length: 15¾ inches. **Weight:** 2 lbs. 10 oz.
Power: Spring (barrel cocking).
Features: One piece walnut grip with thumb-rest. Adjustable trigger. Bead front, rear adjustable for w. and e. Air Rifle Hdqtrs, importer.
Price: **$34.50**

CROSMAN MODEL "1300" MEDALIST II
Caliber: 22, single shot.
Barrel: 8", button rifled.
Length: 11¾". **Weight:** 32 oz.
Power: Hand pumped.
Features: Moulded plastic grip, hand size pump forearm. Cross bolt safety, self-cocking.
Price: **$30.95**

CROSMAN PEACEMAKER "44"
Caliber: 22, 6 shot.
Barrel: 4¾", button rifled.
Length: 10⅜". **Weight:** 34 oz.
Power: Crosman CO_2 Powerlet
Features: Revolving cylinder, walnut finished grips. Simulated gold hammer and trigger, positive valve design. Single-action.
Price: **$25.95**

CROSMAN FRONTIER "36"
Caliber: BB, 18-shot.
Barrel: 4¾", smoothbore.
Length: 10⅜". **Weight:** 34 oz.
Power: Crosman CO_2 Powerlet
Features: Single-action, steel barrel, revolving cylinder. Walnut finish grips.
Price: **$24.95**

PELLET GUNS—HANDGUNS

CROSMAN MARK I TARGET PISTOL
Caliber: 22, single shot.
Barrel: 7¼ inches, button rifled.
Length: 10⅝ inches. **Weight:** 43 oz.
Power: Crosman Powerlet CO^2 cylinder.
Features: New system provides same shot-to-shot velocity, adj. from 300- to 400 fps. Checkered thumbrest grips, right or left. Patridge front sight, rear adj. for w. & e. Adj. trigger.
Price: 22 or 177 .... $27.95

CROSMAN MARK II TARGET PISTOL
Same as Mark I except 177 cal. $27.95

CROSMAN 38 TARGET REVOLVER M9
Caliber: 22, 6-shot.
Barrel: 6 inches, rifled.
Length: 11 inches. **Weight:** 38 oz.
Power: CO^2 Powerlet cylinder.
Features: Double action, revolving cylinder. Adj. rear sight.
Price: $34.95

CROSMAN 38 COMBAT REVOLVER
Same as 38 Target except 3½" bbl., 38 oz. $34.95

DAISY 179 SIX GUN
Caliber: BB, 12-shot.
Barrel: Steel lined, smoothbore.
Length: 11½ inches. **Weight:** NA.
Power: Spring.
Features: Forced feed from under-barrel magazine. Single action, molded wood grained grips.
Price: $8.95

DAISY 177 BB PISTOL
Caliber: BB, 150-shot.
Barrel: Formed steel, smoothbore.
Length: 10⅜ inches. **Weight:** NA.
Power: Spring.
Features: Gravity feed, adjustable rear sight, molded plastic thumbrest grips.
Price: $8.95

DAISY CO^2 200 AUTOLOADING PISTOL
Caliber: BB, 175-shot semi-auto.
Barrel: 7½ inches, steel-lined, smoothbore.
Length: 11⁵⁄₃₂", sight radius 9". **Weight:** 24 oz.
Power: Daisy CO^2 cylinders, 8½ grams (100 shots) or 12 grams (160 shots).
Features: 175-shot magazine; constant full power; valve system eliminates gas leakage; checkered thumbrest stocks; undercut ramp front sight and adjustable rear.
Price: $23.95

DAISY/FWB 65 TARGET PISTOL
Caliber: 177, single shot.
Barrel: 7½", rifled, fixed to receiver.
Length: About 15". **Weight:** 42 oz.
Power: Spring, cocked by left-side lever.
Features: Recoiless operation, may be set to give recoil; Micro. rear sight, 14" radius. Adj. trigger; normal 17.6 oz. pull can be raised to 48 oz. for training. Checkered, thumbrest target grips. Air Rifle Hdqtrs. or Daisy, importer.
Price: $144.50

DIANA 5 TARGET PISTOL
Same as the Hy-Score 815 except: Air Rifle HQ degreases, inspects, test fires, adjusts, sights-in and repackages $36.50
Without accurizing 29.95

DIANA 6 TARGET PISTOL
Same as the Hy-Score 816 but with accurizing done as described above
Price: $59.95
Without accurizing 49.95

PELLET GUNS—HANDGUNS

HAMMERLI MASTER CO² TARGET PISTOL Model 454
Caliber: 177, single shot.
Barrel: 6.7", rifled, 12 grooves, R.H.
Length: 16". **Weight:** 38 oz.
Power: 8g. or 12g. CO² cyl., 40-60 plus shots.
Features: Easy manual loading; residual gas vented automatically; 4-way adj. trigger; ramp front sight, 7/8" blade (other widths avail.), micro-click rear; sight radius adj. 11½" to 13⅜". Bbl.- and grip weights available, $4 and $3.50.
Price: **$54.00**

HAMMERLI SINGLE TARGET PISTOL Model 452
Caliber: 177, single shot.
Barrel: 5.2 inches, rifled.
Length: 12 inches. **Weight:** 34 oz., including CO² cylinder.
Power: Standard CO² cylinder.
Features: Auto spring loader; adj. trigger; valve permits emptying CO² cylinder. Micrometer adj. rear sight. ⅛" blade front sight on ramp. H. Grieder, importer. Price incl. 10 CO² cylinders, 100 pellets.
Price: **$41.00**

HEALTHWAYS ML 175 CO² AUTOMATIC PISTOL
Caliber: BB, 100-shot repeater.
Barrel: 5¾", smooth.
Length: 9½". **Weight:** 28 oz.
Power: Standard CO² cylinder.
Features: 3 position power switch. Auto. ammunition feed. Positive safety.
Price: **$21.00**

HEALTHWAYS MA22 CO² AUTOMATIC PISTOL
Same as Healthways ML175 except rifled 22 cal. bbl., rear sight adj. for w. and e., cap. 50 lead balls. **$24.00**

HY-SCORE 816 M TARGET PISTOL
Caliber: 177, single shot.
Barrel: 7" precision rifled.
Length: 16 inches. **Weight:** 50 oz.
Power: Spring, bbl. cocking.
Features: Recoil-less firing, adj. trigger. Hooded front sight with 3 apertures, click adj. rear with 4 apertures. Plastic thumbrest target grips.
Price: In plastic case **$49.95**

HY-SCORE 815 TARGET PISTOL
Same as Hy-Score M816 except: without recoil-less system; is slightly shorter and lighter; has fixed aperture front sight. In plastic case. Also in 22 cal. **$29.95**

HY-SCORE 814 JUNIOR PISTOL
Caliber: 177 darts BBs, single shot.
Barrel: Smoothbore.
Length: About 10 inches. **Weight:** NA.
Power: Spring, compressed by screwing in breech plug.
Features: Checkered wooden grips.
Price: Blued **$5.95**

HY-SCORE 802 AUTOLOADING PISTOL
Caliber: 22, 6-shot repeater.
Barrel: 10¼ inches, rifled.
Length: 10¼ inches. **Weight:** 30½ oz.
Power: Spring.
Features: Thumbrest target grips. Recoil comparable to standard target pistols. 3-pound trigger pull. Shutter type loading.
Price: Blued $29.95. M800, same except single shot **$24.95**

PELLET GUNS—HANDGUNS

MARKSMAN REPEATER PISTOL
Caliber: 177, 20-shot repeater.
Barrel: 2½ inches, smoothbore.
Length: 8¼ inches. **Weight:** 24 oz.
Power: Spring.
Features: Thumb safety. Uses BBs, darts or pellets. Repeats with BBs only.
Price: Black finish $9.95

LUFT PISTOLE 210 TARGET
Caliber: 177, single shot.
Barrel: 4¾" rifled.
Length: 8". **Weight:** 45 oz.
Power: Spring.
Features: Same size, weight & shape as a standard auto. pistol. Simulated slide lifts, cocking the gun, as the breech is loaded. Navy Arms, importer.
Price: $17.50

SMITH & WESSON MODEL 78G
Caliber: 22, single shot.
Barrel: 8½" rifled.
Length: 11". **Weight:** 42 oz.
Power: Standard CO_2 cylinder.
Features: High-low power adjustment. Micrometer windage adjustable rear sight. Double sear, adjustable trigger. Checkered grips fit left and right hands.
Price: $35.00

WALTHER MODEL LP2
Caliber: 177, single shot.
Barrel: 9.4", rifled.
Length: 12.8". **Weight:** 20 oz.
Power: Spring-air.
Features: Recoil-less operation, cocking in grip frame. Micro-click rear sight, adj. for w. & e. 4-way adj. trigger. Plastic thumbrest grips; wood grip at extra cost. Interarms, importer.
Price: $72.00

WALTHER MODEL 53 PISTOL
Caliber: 177, single shot.
Barrel: 9⅜", rifled.
Length: 12¼". **Weight:** 42 oz.
Power: Spring.
Features: Micrometer rear sight. Interchangeable rear sight blades. Adj. trigger. Target grips. Bbl. weight available at extra cost. Interarms, Alexandria, Va, importer .
Price: $38.00

WEBLEY AIR PISTOLS

Model:	Junior	Premier
Caliber:	177	177 or 22
Barrel:	6⅛"	6½"
Weight:	24 oz.	33 oz.
Power:	Spring, barrel cocking	Same
Sights:	Adj. for elev.	Adj. for w.&e.
Trigger:	Fixed	Adj.
Price:	$19.95	$27.50

Features: Come with cardboard storage case, pellets, spare washer. Service Armament, importer.

WINCHESTER 363 TARGET PISTOL
Caliber: 177, single shot.
Barrel: 7" rifled.
Length: 16". **Weight:** 3 lbs.
Power: Spring, barrel cocking.
Features: Recoil-less firing, adj. double pull type trigger, hooded front sight with 3 apertures, click adj. rear sight. Plastic thumbrest target grips. M.V. 378 fps.
Price: $55.95

WINCHESTER 353 TARGET PISTOL
Caliber: 177 or 22, single shot.
Barrel: 7" rifled.
Length: 16". **Weight:** 2 lbs. 11 oz.
Power: Spring, barrel cocking.
Features: Plastic thumbrest target grips. Adj. double pull trigger, Micro rear sight, detachable bead front with hood. M.V. 378 fps.
Price: $34.95

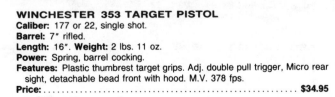

PELLET GUNS—LONG GUNS

ANSCHUTZ 250 TARGET RIFLE
Caliber: 177, single shot.
Barrel: 18½", rifled, one piece with receiver.
Length: 45". **Weight:** 11 lbs. with sights.
Power: Spring, side-lever cocking, 11 lb. pull.
Features: Recoil-less operation. Two-stage adj. trigger. Checkered walnut
  p.g. stock with Monte Carlo comb & cheekpiece; adj. buttplate; accessory
  rail. Air Rifle Hdqtrs., importer.
Price: Without sights **$158.50**
  Add **$22.75** for utility aperture sights or **$44.75** for premium aperture sights.

BAVARIA/WISCHO 55N SPORTING RIFLE
Caliber: 177 or 22, single shot.
Barrel: 16½", rifled.
Length: 40½". **Weight:** 6.4 lbs.
Power: Spring (barrel cocking).
Features: High velocity (728 fps in 177, 590 fps in 22) and accuracy combined
  with rapid loading, can be reloaded in 5 seconds. Stock is of walnut with
  checkered p.g. and buttplate. Open rear, bead front sights; receiver grooved
  for scope mounting. Trigger is adjustable. Air Rifle Headquarters, importer.
Price: **$79.95**

BSA METEOR SUPER
Caliber: 177 or 22, single-shot.
Barrel: 18½", rifled.
Length: 42". **Weight:** 6 lbs.
Power: Spring, bbl. cocking.
Features: Beechwood Monte Carlo stock, recoil pad. Adjustable single-stage
  trigger. Bead front, adjustable rear sight. Positive relocation of barrel for
  same zero shot to shot. Galef, importer.
Price: **$39.95**

BENJAMIN 3030 CO^2 REPEATER
Caliber: BB only.
Barrel: 25½", smoothbore, takedown.
Length: 36". **Weight:** 2 lbs. 13 oz.
Power: Standard CO^2 cylinder.
Features: Bolt action. 30-shot repeater with permanent-magnet, shot-holder
  ammo feed.
Price: **$25.50**

BENJAMIN SERIES 3100 SUPER 100 SHOT RIFLES
Caliber: BB, 100-shot; 22, 85-shot repeater.
Barrel: 23", rifled or smoothbore.
Length: 35". **Weight:** 6 lbs.
Power: Hand pumped.
Features: Bolt action. 100-shot, piggy back full view magazine. Bar V adj. rear
  sight. Walnut-finished p.g. stock.
Price: M3100, BB .... **$38.50**   M3120, 22 rifled **$38.50**
  Also available with custom stock at $3 extra.

BENJAMIN SERIES 362 SUPER CO^2 SINGLE SHOT
Caliber: 22 only.
Barrel: 23", rifled.
Length: 35". **Weight:** 6 lbs.
Power: Standard CO^2 cylinder. 2 power settings.
Features: Bolt action. Bronze-lined steel bbl. Adj. rear sight. Walnut-finished
  stock. Two-stage power.
Price: **$31.50**
  Also available with custom stock at $3 extra.

BENJAMIN SERIES 340 RIFLE
Caliber: 22 and 177 pellets or BB; single shot.
Barrel: 23", rifled.
Length: 35". **Weight:** 6 lbs.
Power: Hand pumped.
Features: Bolt action, walnut stock and pump handle. Adj. V sight.
Price: M340, BB . **$35.95**   M342, 22 ... **$35.95**   M347, 177 . **$35.95**
  Available with custom stock at $3 extra.

CROSMAN M-1 CARBINE
Caliber: BB, 22-shot.
Barrel: Smoothbore, steel.
Length: 35⅝". **Weight:** 4½ lbs.
Power: Spring.
Features: Patterned after U.S. M1 carbine, uses slide action cocking, military
  type adj. sights. Hardwood stock.
Price: **$20.75**

PELLET GUNS—LONG GUNS

CROSMAN MODEL 3500 SLIDEMASTER
Caliber: BB, 22 shot slide action.
Barrel: 18", smoothbore steel.
Length: 36". **Weight:** 4 lbs.
Power: High compression spring.
Features: Fast and easy cocking, hooded post front sight and fully adjustable rear sight. Scope and mount optional. High comb Monte Carlo stock.
Price: **$17.95**

CROSMAN TRAPMASTER SHOTGUN
Gauge: .380 inch, chambers Crosman CO_2 shotshells.
Action: One-stroke, side cocking single shot.
Barrel: 28" true cylinder bore, full length rib.
Stock: 14¼"x1"x2", contoured hardwood, walnut finished.
Weight: 6¼ lbs. 46" over-all.
Power: Crosman Giant CO_2 Powerlet.
Features: Pattern is about 14" dia. at 40 feet (effective range). Plastic shotshells contain about 55 No. 8 pellets. Looks and feels like other shotguns.
Price: **$49.95**

CROSMAN CO_2 SKEET SET
Includes Trapmaster shotgun, box of 25 reusable plastic break-away targets, 100 shotshells, 10 giant Powerlets and Skeet Trap with remote foot release **$89.95**

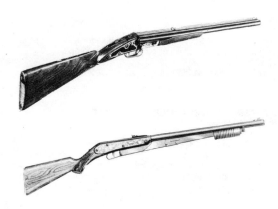

CROSMAN 1400 RIFLE
Caliber: 22, single shot.
Barrel: 19½ inches, rifled steel.
Length: 35 inches. **Weight:** About 6 lbs.
Power: Hand pumped.
Features: Bolt action. Air-Trol valve prevents air lock from over-pumping. Adj. trigger, left or right hand safety. Scope and mount optional.
Price: **$37.95**

CROSMAN POWERMATIC "500"
Caliber: BB, 50 shot semiautomatic.
Barrel: 18", smoothbore steel.
Length: 37¾". **Weight:** 4½ lbs.
Power: Crosman CO_2 Powerlet.
Features: Positive safety, over 100 shots from one Powerlet. Walnut finished stock, grooved receiver for optional scope or peep sight. Rear sight is adjustable for windage and elevation.
Price: **$23.95**

CROSMAN 622 PELL-CLIP REPEATER
Caliber: 22, 6-shot rotating, clip
Barrel: 23"
Weight: 6½ lbs. **Length:** 40"
Power: Grossman Co_2 Powerlet, pump action
Features: Removable 6-shot pell clip. Adjustable rear sight
Price: **$36.95**

CROSMAN MODEL 760 POWERMASTER
Caliber: BB, 180 shot.
Barrel: 19½", smoothbore steel.
Length: 35½". **Weight:** 4½ lbs.
Power: High compression spring.
Features: Short stroke, power determined by number of strokes. Walnut finished checkered stock and forearm. Post front sight and adjustable rear sight. Cross-bolt safety. Scope and mount optional.
Price: **$25.95**

DAISY 21 DOUBLE BARREL RIFLE
Caliber: BB, 48-shot. **Barrel:** 23½ inches, smoothbore.
Length: 37¾ inches. **Weight:** 4½ lbs.
Power: Spring, barrel cocking.
Features: Two barrels and triggers; automatic safety; beaded front ramp and open rear sights.
Price: **$23.95**

DAISY 25 PUMP GUN
Caliber: BB, 50-shot.
Barrel: 18 inches, smoothbore.
Length: 37 inches. **Weight:** NA.
Power: Pump cocking spring.
Features: Ramp front and adj. rear sights. BBs are spring-force fed.
Price: **$16.95**

DAISY 1894 SPITTIN' IMAGE CARBINE
Caliber: BB, 40-shot.
Barrel: 17½ inches, smoothbore.
Length: 35 inches.
Power: Spring.
Features: Cocks halfway on forward stroke of lever, halfway on return.
Price: $19.49
Price: With 4X Scope, as M3894 .... $26.95
Price: With fluted receiver, cocking lever, saddle ring, loading port, fore-arm
    cap and contoured butt plate, as 3030 .... $21.49

DAISY 99 TARGET SPECIAL RIFLE
Caliber: BB, 50-shot.
Barrel: 18 inches, smoothbore.
Length: 36 inches.
Power: Spring.
Features: Wood stock, beavertail fore-end; sling; hooded front sight with four
    insert apertures, adj. aperture rear.
Price: $19.95

DAISY RIFLES

Model:	95	96	102	111	1776
Caliber:	BB	BB	BB	BB	BB
Barrel:	18"	18"	13½"	18"	13½"
Length:	35⅛"	36"	30½"	35"	30½"
Power:	Spring	Spring	Spring	Spring	Spring
Capacity:	700	700	500	700	500
Price:	$12.95	$16.95	$8.95	$11.95	$9.95

Price: Model 96 with 4X scope, as M496 .... $24.45
Features: 96 has M.C. stock and oversize fore-end; 95 stock is wood, fore-
    end plastic; 111 and 1776 have plastic stocks; 102 has wood stock; 1776
    has sighting tube w/aperture and is gold finished.

DAISY HIGH POWER RIFLES

Model:	160	230	250
Caliber:	177 & BB	22	22
Barrel:	12"	15¾"	15¾"
Rifled:	No	Yes	Yes
Length:	33"	38"	38"
Weight:	3 lbs.	5 lbs.	5½ lbs.
Power:	Spring	Spring	Spring
Price:	$16.45	$27.95	$32.95

Features: All are barrel cocking with beechwood stocks. Model 160 has
    bead front and adj. rear sights. 230 and 250 have blade front and adj. rear
    target sights.

DAISY CO^2 300 REPEATER
Caliber: BB, 5-shot semi-auto.
Barrel: 22 inches, smoothbore.
Length: 37⅞ inches. **Weight:** 2 lbs. 14 oz.
Power: Daisy 8.5 or 12 gram CO^2 cylinder.
Features: Free-style stock, cross-bolt safety, 200 shot magazine capacity,
    blade front adj: open rear sights, receiver grooved for scope.
Price: $31.49
Price: With 4X scope, as CO^2 3300 .... .38.95

DAISY 572 SPITTIN' IMAGE SLIDE ACTION RIFLE
Caliber: BB, 45-shot.
Barrel: 22½ inches, smoothbore.
Length: 42¼ inches.
Power: Spring.
Features: Pump-cocking, cross-bolt safety, takedown bbl., adj. rear sight,
    under bbl. magazine, wood-grained stock and fore-end.
Price: $21.95
Price: With 4X scope, as 2572 .... 29.45

DAISY 2299 QUICK SKILL RIFLE KIT
Caliber: BB, 50-shot
Barrel: 24 inches, smoothbore.
Length: 37⅝ inches (adult stock). **Weight:** 3¼ lbs.
Power: Spring.
Features: Kit includes rifle, shooting glasses, ammo, official targets and in-
    struction manual. No sights, meant for instinct shooting instruction.
Price: $25.95

DIANA 60 TARGET RIFLE

Caliber: 177, single shot.
Barrel: 18", rifled.
Length: 43½". **Weight:** 9½ lbs. with sights and detachable bbl. sleeve.
Power: Spring (barrel cocking).
Features: Recoil-less type action, no jar. Micro. aperture rear sight, globe front with 4 inserts. Two-stage, adj. trigger, pull less than 1 lb. Checkered walnut p.g. stock with Monte Carlo comb & cheekpiece, rubber buttplate. Air Rifle Hdqtrs., importer.
Price: **$134.50**
    Add $19.00 for Tyrolean Stock.

DIANA 65 TARGET RIFLE

Same as the M60 except weighs 11 lbs., has adj. stock length; M.V. 50 fps., double trigger.
Price: **$178.95**

FEINWERKBAU 200 RIFLE

Same as F'bau 300 except: has slight recoil effect; 20" bbl., 640 fps. M.V. Available from A.R.H. or Daisy.
Price: **$144.50**

HY-SCORE RIFLES

Model:	808	806	813	801	807
Caliber:	177	177	22	22	22
Barrel:	12"	14½"	14¼"	15¾"	17⅜"
Rifled:	No	Yes	Yes	Yes	Yes
Length:	33"	36½"	36½"	38½"	41¾"
Weight:	3 lbs.	3¾ lbs.	4 lbs.	5 lbs.	5 lbs. 14 oz.
Power:	Spring	Spring	Spring	Spring	Spring
Price:	$14.95	$19.95	$25.95	$29.95	$39.95

Features: All are barrel cocking. All have adj. sights and regular triggers except 807, which has an adj. trigger. Staeble 2.2X scope and mt. available for all but 808, **$14.95.**
    M813 and scope available at a combination price of **$33.40**
    M801 available as 801M with click adj. receiver sight **$49.95**

HY-SCORE 810M OLYMPIC INTERNATIONAL RIFLE

Caliber: 177, single shot.
Barrel: 19¼" 12-groove rifled.
Length: 44". **Weight:** 9½ lbs.
Power: Spring (barrel cocking).
Features: Full cheekpiece, Monte Carlo stock, hand checkered; grooved fore-end, curved rubber buttplate. Adj. target receiver sight (includes 4 apertures), hooded front sight (includes 4 inserts).
Price: **$99.95**

DAISY VL SHOOTING SYSTEM

Caliber: 22VL caseless ctg., single shot.
Barrel: Solid steel, 6 lands and grooves 1 in 16" twist.
Length: 38 inches. **Weight:** 5 lbs.
Power: Fires 29 gr. bullet at 1,150 fps.
Features: Cartridge has no case or primer. Action has no firing pin or ejector. Cocking by recessed lever. Ignition is by air released under high pressure causing friction to ignite material at base of bullet. Also has auto. safety, plastic wood finished stock with checkered p.g. and fore-end. Rear sight adj. for w. & e.; blade front.
Price: Model 0002 .... **$39.95**

PRESENTATION VL

Same as above but with walnut stock, storage gun case with foam cushion lining, brass wall hangers and 300 rounds of ammunition Model 0003.
    $125.00

FEINWERKBAU 300 MATCH RIFLE

Caliber: 177, single shot.
Barrel: 19½" rifled steel, one piece with receiver.
Length: 42". **Weight:** 9¾ lbs.
Power: Hand cocked by side lever. Less than 10 lbs. pull required.
Features: Barrel and receiver recoil together, independent of stock, to eliminate felt recoil, are locked up when gun is cocked. Micro. rear peep sight, globe front with inserts. Trigger fully adj. Muzzle velocity 575 fps. Checkered walnut stock with Monte Carlo cheekpiece, palmswell p.g. Daisy or Air Rifle Hdqtrs., importers.
Price: 150S (9 lb. Std.) **$169.75;** 150SL (L.H.) **$188.75;** 150ST (Tyrol. stock), 150STL (L.H. Tyrol. stock) **$199.50**

HEALTHWAYS PLAINSMAN MC22 AUTO RIFLE

Caliber: 22, 75-shot.
Barrel: 20½ inches, rifled for round lead balls.
Length: 41 inches. **Weight:** 4½ lbs.
Power: CO_2 (8- or 12-gram cylinder).
Features: Up to 50 shots automatically with 12-g. cylinder; no cocking, pumping, etc. Full size p.g. wood stock.
Price: **$35.00**

    Plainsman MX175. Same as MC22 except 175" smoothbore for BBs; weighs 8 oz. less. **$30.00**

HY-SCORE 809M TARGET RIFLE

Caliber: 22, single shot.
Barrel: 19 inch rifled.
Length: 44 inches. **Weight:** 7 pounds.
Power: Spring, bbl. cocking.
Features: Adj. target receiver sight, aperture front with 4 inserts, in addition to open adj. middle sight also with 4 apertures.
Price: **$64.95**

MARKSMAN 4000 AIR RIFLE
Caliber: 177, 400-shot.
Barrel: 15-½", smoothbore.
Length: 36-½". **Weight:** 4 lbs., 2 oz.
Power: Spring, barrel cocking.
Features: Automatic safety; fixed front, adj. rear sights; shoots 177 cal. BB's pellets and darts. **Price:** **$25.00**

PIC MINUTEMAN M77 RIFLE
Caliber: 177; 22, single shot.
Barrel: 14", 6- and 10-groove rifled.
Length: 36". **Weight:** 3¼ lbs.
Power: Spring (barrel cocking).
Features: Adj. sights, grooved for scope, light wood p.g. stock., finger-grooved fore-end.
Price: 177 .... **$13.50** Price: 22 .... **$14.00**
With 4x tip-off mount scope **$5.50** extra.

SAVAGE-ANSCHUTZ 250 TARGET RIFLE
Caliber: 177, single shot.
Barrel: 18½", rifled steel fixed to receiver, movable compression cylinder.
Length: 45". **Weight:** 11 lbs. with sights.
Power: Hand cocked by side lever, about 11 lbs. cocking effort.
Features: Recoil-less shooting via oil damper and compensating piston. Two-stage trigger adj. for finger length. French walnut, Monte Carlo stock and beavertail fore-end; checkered p.g. with Wundhammer swell. Accepts Anschutz target sights.
Price: Without sights **$155.00**

SHERIDAN BLUE AND SILVER STREAK RIFLES
Caliber: 5mm (20 cal.), single shot.
Barrel: 18½", rifled.
Length: 37". **Weight:** 5 lbs.
Power: Hand pumped (swinging fore-end).
Features: Rustproof barrel and piston tube. Takedown. Thumb safety. Mannlicher type walnut stock.
Price: Blue Streak .... **$44.75** Silver Streak **$45.75**
Sheridan accessories: Intermount, a base for ⅜" Tip-Off scope mounts, **$6.75;** Sheridan-Williams 5DSH receiver sight, **$9.50;** Model 22 Targetrap, **$12.50;** Model 38 Targetrap **$30.00;** Sheridan 5mm pellets, **$2.50** for 500. Weaver of Bushnell 4 x scope and intermount installed **$20.20** extra.

SMITH & WESSON MODEL 77A
Caliber: 22, single shot.
Barrel: 22", rifled.
Length: 40". **Weight:** 6-½ lbs.
Power: Hand pumped (swinging fore-end).
Features: Adjustable notch rear sight. Monte Carlo style, walnut finish stock. Automatic safety.
Price: **$42.50**

WALTHER LG 55-M RIFLE
Caliber: 177, single shot.
Barrel: 16", rifled.
Length: 41⅜". **Weight:** 9 lbs. (9.7 lbs. with bbl. sleeve).
Power: Spring (barrel cocking).
Features: Micro. click adj. receiver sight, globe target front, 3 inserts. Walnut cheekpiece Monte Carlo, checkered p.g. stock. Tyrolean stock $10 extra. Interarms, importers.
Price: **$128.50**
Double set triggers available with any LG 55-M for $12 extra.

WALTHER LGV
Caliber: 177, single shot.
Barrel: 16", rifled.
Length: 41⅜". **Weight:** 6 lbs.
Power: Spring (barrel cocking).
Features: Micro. click adj. receiver sight; Adj. trigger. Interarms, importers.
Price: **$169.75**

PELLET GUNS—LONG GUNS

WEBLEY AIR RIFLES

Model:	Jaguar	Falcon	Mark III
Caliber:	177	177, 22	177, 22
Barrel:	NA.	17¼″	18½″
Length:	37″	41½″	43½″
Weight:	4 lbs.	6 lbs.	6 lbs.
Power:	spring	spring	spring
Sights:	open, adj.	open, adj.	globe front
Price:	**$27.50**	**$39.95**	**$75.00**

Features: Wooden p.g. stocks. Receivers grooved for scope mounts. Jaguar comes with target holder, target cards, 500 pellets, 12 darts, oil. Mk III is lever-cocking, others bbl.-cocking. Service Armament, importer.

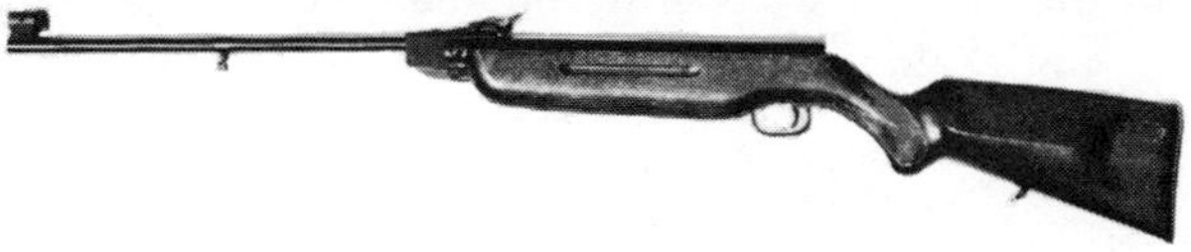

WEIHRAUCH 30 & 50 SERIES RIFLES

Model:	30 M-II	30S	50 M-II	50S	50E
Caliber:	177	177	177	177	177
Barrel:	16⅞″	16⅞″	18½″	18½″	18½″
Trigger:	fixed	fixed	fixed	adj.	adj.
Length:	40″	40″	43½″	43½″	43½″
Wgt., lbs.:	5½	5½	7	7	7¼
Price:	**$47.50**	**$52.50**	**$56.50**	**$64.50**	**$69.95**

Features: All are rifled and spring-operated by single stroke cocking. Post and ramp front sights (except 50S and 50E have globe fronts with 4 inserts). Open click rear sights, adj. for w. & e., except 30 Mk-11 has lock-screw windage. Walnut finished stocks. 50E has cheek-piece, checkering, ¾″ sling swivels. MV of all 660-67 fps. Air Rifle Hdqtrs., importer.

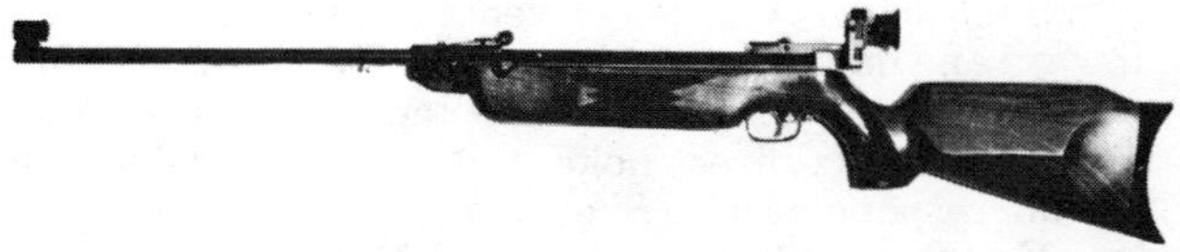

WEIHRAUCH 35 TARGET RIFLES

Model:	35/S	35L	35E
Caliber:	177	177	177
Barrel:	19½″	19½″	22″
Wgt. lbs.:	7½	7½	8
Rear sight:	open	open	open
Front sight:	All with globe and 4 interchangeable insert		
Power:	All with spring (barrel cocking).		
Price:	**$79.95**	**$89.95**	**$102.50**

Features: Trigger fully adj. and removable. Open rear sight slick adj. for w. and e. P.g. high comb stock with beavertail fore-end, walnut finish, except 35E have checkered walnut with standard cheekpiece. 35L has Tyrolean cheekpiece stock. Air Rifle Hdqtrs., importer.

WEIHRAUCH 55 TARGET RIFLES

Model:	55SF	55SM	55MM	55MM-L	55T
Caliber:	177	177	177	177	177
Barrel:	18½″	18½″	18½″	18½″	18½″
Wgt. lbs.:	7¼	8½	8½	8½	8½
Rear sight:	open	aperture	aperture	aperture	aperture
Front sight:	All with globe and 4 interchangeable insert				
Power:	All with spring (bbl. cocking) .600 fps				
Price:	**$104.50**	**$104.50**	**$128.50**	**$139.95**	**$144.50**

Features: Trigger fully adj. and removable. Micrometer rear sight adj. for w. and e., on all but 55SF and 55MM. P.g. high comb stock with beavertail fore-end, walnut finish stock on 55SF, SM. Walnut stock on 55MM, Tyrolean stock on 55T. Air Rifle Hdqtrs., importer.

WINCHESTER AIR RIFLES

Model:	416	422	423	425
Calibers:	177	177	177	22
Length:	33″	36″	36″	38″
Wgt. lbs.:	2¾	3¾	4	5
Velocity, fps:	363	480	480	543
Price:	**$17.95**	**$24.95**	**$30.50**	**$35.75**

WINCHESTER HIGH POWER AIR RIFLES

Model:	427	435	333	450
Caliber:	22	177	177	177
Length:	42″	44″	43¼″	44½″
Wgt. lbs.:	6	6½	9½	7¾
Velocity, fps:	660	693	576	693
Price:	**$42.95**	**$58.95**	**$178.95**	**$89.95**

Features: All are rifled, except 416 (smoothbore), and spring operated by single stroke cocking. **Triggers:** 416, 422 & 423—double pull type triggers. 425, 427 & 435—adjustable double pull type triggers. 333—two stage trigger adj. for wgt., pre-travel & sear-off. **Front sights:** 416 & 422—bead post front sights; 423—blade front sight with ramp. 425 & 427—hooded front sights; 450 & 333—interchangeable front sight assemblies. **Rear Sights:** 416, 422 & 423—adj. screw, 425, 427, 435 & 450—Adj. micro., 333—Adj. diopter. Also, 425, 427, 435 & 450 have dovetail bases for scope mounting. 435, 450 & 333 have rubber butt pads, cheekpieces & checkered p.g. areas. 333 has an auto. safety, when bbl. is open and red indicator when bbl. is closed.

Chokes & Brakes

Contra-Jet Muzzle Brake

The steel tube on body of the C-J device has 48 intersecting slots that dissipate energy via the mutual interference of the emerging gases. Recoil energy is reduced nearly 38% (in cal.308), accuracy is enhanced through lessened muzzle jump and flinching, yet no increase in muzzle blast occurs.   Readily fitted by a competent gunsmith, the 3" long, 3½ oz. Contra-Jet is available in 25, 28, 30, 35, 37 and 45 calibers. Cost is $24.95, installation not included.

Cutts Compensator

The Cutts Compensator is one of the oldest variable choke devices available. Manufactured by Lyman Gunsight Corporation, it is available with either a steel or aluminum body. A series of vents allows gas to escape upward and downward, reducing recoil without directing muzzle blast toward nearby shooters.   For the 12-ga. Comp body, six fixed-choke tubes are available: the Spreader—popular with Skeet shooters; Improved Cylinder; Modified; Full; Superfull, and Magnum Full. Full, Modified and Spreader tubes are available for 16, 20, 28, and .410, and an Adjustable Tube, giving Full through Improved Cylinder chokes, is offered in 12, 16, 20 and 28 gauges.   Barrel adaptors in various internal diameters are available at $1.00 to permit exact fitting of Cutts Expansion Chambers.   The Comp body with wrench and adaptor sells for $13.00; Comp Tubes are $3.75 each, the Adjustable Tube $9.75. Factory installation is $7.00, plus transportation.

Dahl Muzzle Blast Controller

Only 1½" long by ¾" in diameter, this device is claimed to reduce recoil up to 40%. An outer sleeve, threaded onto the gun muzzle, is threaded on the inside to accept a machined plug which is bored through for bullet passage. Gas behind the bullet is bled off through slots in the plug, swirled through a number of tiny passages while contained by the sleeve, and then vented upward, this final action somewhat offsetting muzzle jump. Price is $21.00, plus installation.   The 1½" collet length is fully backed-up to prevent blown patterns arising from the springiness and vibration found in unsupported collet sleeves.

Emsco Choke

E. M. Schacht of Waseca, Minn., offers the Emsco, a small diameter choke which features a precision curve rather than a taper behind the 1½" choking area. 9 settings are available in this 5 oz. attachment. Its removable recoil sleeve can be furnished in dural if desired. Choice of three sight heights. For 12, 16 or 20 gauge. Price installed, $21.95. Not installed, $16.50.

Herter's Rifle Recoil Eliminator

The Recoil Eliminator is a metal tube—1¹⁵/₁₆" long and ⅞" diam. in the standard model, same length and 1⅛" diam. in target type—which is screwed to the muzzle. Angled ports direct escaping gas upward and rearward, reducing recoil and muzzle jump. The target model has a shield to prevent muzzle blast from annoying nearby shooters. Weights are 2 oz. and 3 oz. respectively. Made for calibers 25 to 32. Price of standard, $3.00, $6.50 installed. Target, $4.50 and $7.50.

Vari-Choke

Herter's, Inc., supplies the Vari-Choke, which features a ball-bearing micro-click adjustment of the pattern sleeve, rather than the spring system used by others. This model has 8 choke settings, from Full to Improved Cylinder. With Recoil Eliminator, price is $16.75 installed; without Eliminator, $12.50.

Jet-Away Choke

Arms Ingenuity Corp., makers of the Jet-Away, say that this device controls patterns through partial venting of the powder gases which normally enlarge patterns. The Jet-Away has a series of three slots in the top of the tube and a sliding control sleeve. When the sleeve is in its rearward position, all slots are uncovered, the maximum of gas is vented and patterns are densest. To obtain more open patterns, the sleeve is moved to cover one or more slots. In 12 or 20 gauge only, the Jet-Away is made of aluminum, weighs 3 ozs. $24.95 installed.

Lyman CHOKE

The LymanCHOKE is similar to the Cutts Comp in that it comes with fixed-choke tubes or an adjustable tube, with or without recoil chamber. The adjustable tube version sells for $21.95 with recoil chamber, $19.50 without, in 12, 16 or 20 gauge.   Lyman also offers a Single-Choke Adaptor at $12.25 installed. This device may be used with or without a recoil-reduction chamber; cost of the latter is $2.45 extra.

Pendleton Dekicker

This Dekicker is unusual in that it is not a separate tube added onto a rifle muzzle but is machined into the barrel itself. Obviously, it cannot be installed by the customer. It must be sent to J. F. Mutter's Pendleton Gunshop, where a section of the bore a short distance behind the muzzle is relieved into an expansion chamber. Exit holes drilled at precise locations vent gas to lower apparent kick. Because metal is removed instead of being added, there is a small decrease in gun weight.   Installation, including barrel polishing, is $35 in calibers from the 220 Swift to 358 Magnum; $40 for 375 to 458; $40 for 460 Weatherby and large single barrel express calibers.

Poly-Choke

Poly-Choke Co., Inc., now is offering the Deluxe Signature Poly-Choke. It provides 9 choke settings (marked in 24 karat gold) to cover the complete pattern range as well as handle rifled slugs. It comes in two versions, the standard at $24.95, and the ventilated model at $27.95 installed. Fits 12, 16, 20 or 28 gauge. The Poly-Choke has been on the market for more than 30 years and is still gaining popularity.

Rex Sha-Cul Rifle Muzzle Brake

C. R. Pedersen & Son engineered the Rex Sha-Cul muzzle control tube to cut down recoil and blast. The manufacturers state that the device helps eliminate bullet wobble, thus aiding accuracy. 3" long and ¹³/₁₆" in diam., the Sha-Cul can accommodate all calibers from 22 to 458. It requires ½" of barrel thread to install. Sold on an "unconditional money-back guarantee," the price is $17.50, plus $3.50 installation.

Micrometer Receiver Sight   Receiver Sights

LYMAN No. 48
¼-min. clicks for w. & e. Any disc. Target or Stayset (hunting) knobs. Quick release slide, adjustable zero scales. Made for almost all modern big-game rifles. Price: **$17.50**   With long slide.......**$19.50**

LYMAN No. 57
¼-min. clicks. Target or Stayset knobs. Quick release slide, adjustable zero scales. Made for almost all modern rifles. Price.....**$9.50**

LYMAN No. 60
¼-min. clicks for w. and e. Extension arm permits choice of 3 positions of eye relief. Designed for use on medium-weight, small bore target rifles. Price.....................................**$9.75**

LYMAN No. 66
Fits close to the rear of flat-sided receivers, furnished with target or Stayset knobs. Quick release slide, ¼-min. adj. For most lever or slide action or flat-sided automatic rifles. Price..............**$9.50**

LYMAN No. 524 HI-LO EXTENSION RECEIVER-SIGHT
Apertures above and below for metallic and scope lines of sight. ¼-min. adj. For Win. 52 Sporter, 52 Standard (old and new), 52 Heavy Barrel (target and marksman stocks); Rem. 40X. Price.........**$19.50**

REDFIELD TROPHY
Aluminum construction. Staff detaches for scope use. Point-blank screw returns sight to same zero position. Features hunter-type knobs with coin slots, ¼-min. clicks. For most popular rifles. Price....**$10.95**

REDFIELD MICRO-STEEL
Made entirely of machined tool steel. ¼-min. micrometer click adj. with Hunter knobs. Quick detachable staff. Made for many centerfire rifles...**$14.95**

REDFIELD No. 75
For Junior Target rifles. ¼-min. clicks for w. and e. Quick detachable extension, adj. to two positions. Available in two heights, scope or standard. For 75HW—Win. 75: 75HG and SG—Sav. 19; 75HV and SV—Stev. 416, Sears Ranger; 75HM and SM—Mossberg, master actions; 75HB and SB—Ballard; 75HR and SR—Win. SS, High Wall action only; Walnut Hill and 417; 75RT—Rem. 513T; 75RS—Rem. 513S; 75RX—Rem. 521. Price **$16.95**

REDFIELD INTERNATIONAL MATCH
Spring loaded windage and elevation adjustments eliminate lost motion or backlash. Large adjusting screws. ¼-min. click values. Base and ⅞" disc. Fits same base as Olympic. Price.................**$32.95**
With base and "Sure-X" disc (see Sight Attachments). Price..**$44.85**

REDFIELD INTERNATIONAL MARK 8
⅛-min. click adj. for windage and elevation distinguishes the Mark 8 which has all of the refinements of Redfield's International Match. Equipped with standard base and ⅞" disc. Price............**$39.95**
With base and Sure-X disc (see Sight Attachments). Price..**$51.85**

REDFIELD OLYMPIC
Elevation, windage, and extension adjustments. New elevation compensation. ¼-min. click. Base and ⅞" disc. Made for practically all target rifles. Price......................................**$24.95**
Extra bases. Price....................................... 3.95
With base and Sure-X disc (see Sight Attachments). Price....**$36.85**

TRADEWIND SNAP-SHOOTER
Micrometer click elevation adjustment, sliding windage adjustment with locking screws. Designed to fit rear scope mount holes in Husqvarna HVA and FN Mauser actions. Price......................**$9.50**

WILLIAMS "FOOLPROOF"
Internal click adjustments. Positive locks. For virtually all rifles, plus Win., Rem. and Ithaca shotguns. Price.................**$12.00**
Add .50 for Twilight aperture. Extra shotgun aperture...... 2.00

B-SQUARE SPRINGFIELD
For 03A3. Windage and elevation by means of allen screws. Locks on dovetail. Wrench furnished. Price........................**$5.00**

B-SQUARE SMLE (LEE-ENFIELD)
For No. 4 and Jungle carbine. No drilling or tapping required. ³⁄₃₂" disc furnished. Price...............................**$3.95**

BUEHLER
"Little Blue Peep" auxiliary sight used with Buehler and Redfield scope mounts. Price **$3.35**
Mark IV front sight for above........................... .95

FREELAND TUBE SIGHT
Uses Unertl 1" micrometer mounts. Complete with bases for 22-cal. target rifles, inc. 52 Win., 37, 40X Rem. and BSA Martini. Price..**$42.50**

KUHARSKY AUXILIARY
Fits onto B&L or Kuharsky mounts to give emergency sighting. Includes peep rear and post front sights; extension rail slides forward for increased sight radius. Price...............................**$9.95**

LYMAN No. 40
Mounts on left side of receiver. By releasing locking lever, slide can be adjusted for elevation. Slot in aperture permits horizontal alignment. Target disc. for Sav. 40, 45, 340, 342, Stevens 58, 322, 325, Marlin 55, Moss. 185K and H&R 349. Price...................**$6.50**

LYMAN No. 53
Shotgun receiver sight, mounts compactly near rear of receiver. For most Win., Rem., Sav., Marlin, Mossberg, J. C. Higgins and Ithaca shotguns. Price **$4.40**

LYMAN No. 55
Located at rear of receiver; compact, easily adjusted. For almost all low-priced bolt action rifles. Price......................**$4.40**

REDFIELD RECORD
Aluminum construction with detachable staff for scope use. Adj. by means of locking screws. Point-blank screw returns sight to zero position. For most rifles. Price...............................**$7.95**

REDFIELD RE-22
1965 model for all dovetail-grooved 22 rifles (takes place of SS sights). Adj. for w. and e. **$7.95**

REDFIELD RE-SG
Shotgun receiver sight; mounts compactly at rear of receiver. Fits most shotguns by use of slotted base installed on receiver wall. Price **$9.95**

REDFIELD RE-24
For Savage M24's over-under rifle-shotgun.................**$9.95**

REDFIELD X-TUBE
For use with Redfield Olympic or International Match rear sights. Front telescope-type mount attaches to scope block. Price....**$24.95**

WILLIAMS 5-D SIGHT
Low cost sight for shotguns, 22's and the more popular big game rifles. Adjustment for w. and e. Fits most guns without drilling or tapping. Also for Br. SMLE. Price............................**$7.00**

WILLIAMS ACE-IN-THE-HOLE PEEP
Auxiliary sight that slips into the Williams QC scope mount. Adj. for w. and e. Price....................................**$2.50**

WILLIAMS GUIDE
Receiver sight for .30 M1 Car., M1903A3 Springfield, Savage 24's, Savage-Anschutz rifles and Wby. XXII. Utilizes military dovetail; no drilling. Double-dovetail W. adj., sliding dovetail adj. for E. Price.**$7.00**

Sporting Leaf and Tang Sights

HOPKINS & ALLEN NUMRICH MUSKET SIGHT
Three-way rear leaf sight designed for 58 cal. muzzle loading military rifles. Fixed V-notch for 50-yard range, flip-up aperture for 100 yards and V-notch for 200 yards. Particularly suited to Springfield and Zouave rifles. Price.............................**$4.95**

LYMAN No. 16
Middle sight for barrel dovetail slot mounting. Folds flat when scope or peep sight is used. Sight notch plate adjustable for e. White triangle for quick aiming. 3 heights; A—.400″ to .500″, B—.345″ to .445″, C—.500″ to .600″. Price.............................**$2.95**

MARBLE FALSE BASE
New screw-on base for most rifles replaces factory base. ⅜″ dovetail slot permits installation of any Marble rear sight. Can be had in sweat-on models also. Price **$2.00**

MARBLE FOLDING LEAF
Flat-top or semi-buckhorn style. Folds down when scope or peep sights are used. Reversible plate gives choice of "U" or "V" notch. Adjustable for elevation. Price.....................**$4.50 — $5.96**
Also available with both w. and e. adjustment.............**$4.90**

MARBLE SPORTING REAR
With white enamel diamond, gives choice of two "U" and two "V" notches of different sizes. Adjustment in height by means of double step elevator and sliding notch piece. For all rifles; screw or dovetail installation. Price ....**$4.30—$5.50**

MARBLE SPORTING REAR
Single step elevator. "U" notch with white triangle aiming aid. Lower priced version of double step model. Price.............**$2.30**

REDFIELD SEMI-BUCKHORN FOLDING LEAF
Semi-buckhorn sight for dovetail slot mounting. Sturdy spring holds sight in upright position. No. 47L .375″-.475″; No. 47H .375″-.562″ high. Price **$4.45**

REDFIELD FLAT TOP FOLDING LEAF
Same as above except flat top style. No. 46L .375″-.475″; No. 46H .375″-.562″ high. Price **$4.45**

REDFIELD SEMI-BUCKHORN SPORTING REAR
Reversible sighting plate gives choice of "U" notch or "V" notch. Five-step elevator. Fits standard dovetail slot. No. 49L for most rifles, No. 49S for 22's and carbines. Semi-buckhorn. Price...........**$4.45**

REDFIELD FLAT TOP SPORTING REAR
Same as above except flat top style. No. 48L for most rifles, No. 48S for 22's and carbines. Price.............................**$4.45**

WILLIAMS GUIDE
Open rear sight with w. and e. adjustment. Bases to fit most military and commercial barrels. Choice of square "U" or "V" notch blade, ³⁄₁₆″, ¼″, ⁵⁄₁₆″, or ⅜″ high....................................**$5.00**
Extra blades, each....................................1.25

Globe Target Front Sights

FREELAND SUPERIOR
Furnished with six 1″ plastic apertures. Available in 4½″-62½″ lengths. Made for any target rifle. Price with base............**$16.00**
Price with 6 metal insert apertures.....................19.00

FREELAND JR
Same as above except standard dovetail mounting, various heights. Price with base and 6 plastic apertures.....................**$14.00**
Price with 6 metal insert apertures.....................17.00

FREELAND TWIN SET
Two Freeland Superior or Junior Globe Front Sights, long or short, allow switching from 50 yd. to 100 yd. ranges and back again without changing rear sight adjustment. Sight adjustment compensation is built into the set; just interchange and you're "on" at either range. Set includes base and 6 plastic apertures. Twin set (long or short). **$28.00**
Price with 6 metal apertures...........................**32.00**
Price, Junior Twin Set (long or short) plastic apertures...... 26.00
Price, Junior Twin Set (long or short) metal apertures....... 30.00

FREELAND MILITARY
Short model for use with high-powered rifles where sight must not extend beyond muzzle. Screw-on base; six plastic apertures. Price **$15.00**
Price with 6 metal apertures............................18.00

LYMAN No. 17A
7 interchangeable inserts which include 4 apertures, one transparent amber and two posts .050″ and .100″ in width. Price..........**$3.75**

LYMAN No. 17A XNB
For Springfield 03 and 03A3. Replaces issue front sight and barrel band. With seven inserts. Price.............................**$6.00**

LYMAN 77
Similar to M17A, except mounts to a separate base, is quickly detachable. Base **$1.50**.   Sight...........................**$5.00**

REDFIELD Nos. 63 and 64
For rifles specially stocked for scopes where metallic sights must be same height as scopes. Instantly detachable to permit use of scope. Two styles and heights of bases. Interchangeable inserts. No. 64 is ¼″ higher. With base, Price.................................**$7.95**

REDFIELD No. 65
1″ long, ⅝″ diameter. Standard dovetail base with 7 aperture or post inserts which are not reversible. For any rifle having standard barrel slot. ¹³⁄₃₂″ height from bottom of base to center of aperture. No. 65NB same as above with narrow base for Win. 54 N.R.A., 70, and Savage 40, 45, and 99 with ramp front sight base. Price..........**$5.95**

REDFIELD No. 66
Replaces entire removable front sight stud, locked in place by screw in front of barrel band. ¾″ from bottom of base to center of aperture. For Spgfld. 1903. Price.................................**$5.95**

REDFIELD No. 68
For Win. 52, heavy barrel, Sav. 19 and 33, and other rifles requiring high front sight. ¹⁷⁄₃₂″ from bottom of base to center of aperture. Standard dovetail size only. Price.................................**$5.95**

REDFIELD OLYMPIC
Detachable. 10 inserts—5 steel, sizes .090″, .110″, .120″, .140″, .150″; one post insert, size .100″; four celluloid, sizes .090″, .110″, .120″, .140″. Celluloid inserts in clear, green, or amber, with or without cross hairs. For practically all rifles and with any type rear sight. Fits all standard Redfield, Lyman, or Fecker scope blocks. With base, Price...**$15.90**

REDFIELD INTERNATIONAL SMALLBORE FRONT
(Illustrated)
Similar to Olympic. Drop-in insertion of eared inserts. Outer sleeve prevents light leakage. Two-step base allows quick forward-backward change between 100 and 50 yards.........................**$18.90**
with standard base and inserts........................17.90

REDFIELD INTERNATIONAL MILITARY BIG BORE
Same as International Match except tube only 2¼″ long. For 30 cal. use...**$17.90**

REDFIELD 285 S RAMP
No. 285 ramp designed for 22's fits without drilling by use of dovetail filler block. Redfield Sourdough, gold tip and ivory bead front sights fit dovetail slot on ramp. Short, streamlined design. Price without front sight...**$3.25**

WOMACK DUAL RANGE
Instant change from 50 to 100 yards by rotating front knurled sleeve ½ turn. Choice of 6″ or 10″ length. Price, including 6 apertures, base and screws...**$21.00**

Ramp Sights

Williams Streamlined Ramp

JAEGER
Band type with detachable hood, gold or ivory bead. When ordering, give height and muzzle diameter. Price.......................**$7.95**

LYMAN SLIP-ON RAMP AND FRONT SIGHT
No soldering or brazing necessary, has tapered hole. Inside dia. .550" to .640". Removable hood. Price for ramp, sight and hood..**$8.20**

LYMAN SCREW-ON RAMP AND SIGHT
Used with 8-40 screws but may also be brazed on. Heights from .110" to .350". Price with sight...........................**$4.95**

MARBLE COUNTOUR RAMP
For late model Rem. 725, 740, 760, 742. ⁹⁄₁₆" between mounting screws. Price **$4.50**

MARBLE RAMPS
Available in either screw-on or sweat-on style. 5 heights; ³⁄₁₆", ⁵⁄₁₆", ³⁄₈", ⁷⁄₁₆", ⁹⁄₁₆". Standard ³⁄₈" dovetail slot. Price............**$4.25**
Hoods for above ramps...............................**1.00**

PEDERSON "REX"
Offered as the "Rex" ramp, this is a hoodless type without barrel band. Heights available are ¼" to ⁹⁄₁₆". Blued or in the white, and without sights. Price **$2.50**

REDFIELD SWEAT-ON RAMPS
Standard ³⁄₈" dovetail with screw for holding position while sweating. ⁵⁄₁₆", ³⁄₈", or ⁹⁄₁₆" high, 3³⁄₈" over all. Price, without hood..**$4.95**

REDFIELD SCREW-ON RAMPS
Same as sweat-on except has two screws for mounting. Price, without hood **$4.95**
Hoods for above ramps...............................**1.00**

WILLIAMS SHORTY RAMP
Companion to "Streamlined" ramp, about ½" shorter. Screw-on type, it is furnished in ⅛", ³⁄₁₆", ³⁄₃₂", and ³⁄₈" heights without hood only. Price **$3.50**

WILLIAMS STREAMLINED RAMP
Hooded style in screw-on or sweat-on models. Furnished in ⁹⁄₁₆", ⁷⁄₁₆", ³⁄₈", ⁵⁄₁₆", ³⁄₁₆" heights. Price with hood.................**$5.50**
Price without hood.................................**4.50**

WILLIAMS SHOTGUN RAMP
Designed to elevate the front bead for slug shooting or for guns that shoot high. Diameters to fit most 12, 16, 20 ga. guns. Fastens by screw-clamp, no drilling required. Price, with Williams gold bead.**$3.50**
Price, without bead **2.75**

Front Sights

Lyman ramp and front sight

LYMAN BLADE & DOVETAIL SIGHTS
Made with gold, silver or red beads ¹⁄₁₆" to ³⁄₃₂" wide and in varying heights for most military and commercial rifles..from **$1.70** to **$2.00**

LYMAN No. 22
Ivory bead front sight for Savage 24 series. O-U. Price......**$2.50**

MARBLE STANDARD
Ivory, red, or gold bead. For all American made rifles. ¹⁄₁₆" wide bead with semi-flat face which does not reflect light. Specify type of rifle when ordering.................................**$1.90**

MARBLE-SHEARD "GOLD"
Show up well even in darkest timber. Shows same color on different colored objects; sturdily built. Medium bead. Various models for different makes of rifles so specify type of rifle when ordering. Also made for 30 or 9 mm Lugers, Colt's Single Action Army, Bisley Model, with plain sight or any other Colt's or S & W revolver with stationary front sight. Price...**$3.20**

MARBLE COUNTOURED
Same contour and shape as Marble-Sheard but uses standard ¹⁄₁₆" or ³⁄₃₂" bead, ivory, red or gold. Specify rifle type................**$2.20**

O.S.E. ADJUSTABLE HEIGHT FRONT
Screw adjustment gives .025" change in height for each turn. 5 models give adjustments from .260" to .880". Fits ³⁄₈" dovetail barrel or ramp slots. White or gold bead. Original Sight Exchange. Price.**$2.95**

REDFIELD SOURDOUGH PATRIDGE
Gold face set at 45° angle; blackened, it serves as a target sight. Blade or dovetail styles; width .070". Square block of phosphor bronze inlaid to provide visibility in poor light. Price.................**$3.45**

REDFIELD-CARBINE BLADE TYPE
Sourdough patridge, ivory bead or gold tip, ¹⁄₁₆" only. For Win., Sav., Krag, Spgfld., Rem. Price...............................**$3.45**

REDFIELD IVORY BEAD OR GOLD TIP
¹⁄₁₆". For practically all rifles, carbines, pistols and revolvers. Price **$2.45**

REDFIELD FULL BLOCK
For Springfield 03 (not 03A3) in Sourdough, ¹⁄₁₆" gold or ivory bead. **$4.45**. Mauser Dovetail—For narrom Mauser and other European dovetail slots. Sourdough, gold or ivory bead. **$2.45**—**$3.45**. De Luxe Ramp Blades—Sourdough, ¹⁄₁₆" gold or ivory bead. Price............**$2.00**

TRADEWIND SNAP-SHOOTER
Silver inlay post. Fits ³⁄₈" dovetail; height, ³³⁄₆₄ from bottom of dovetail. Price **$1.50**

WILLIAMS BRILLIANT BEAD
Large bright bead. In .250" and .340" base widths; 7 heights from .260" to .538". Price.................................**$3.25**

WILLIAMS IVORY & GOLD BEAD
Has flat sides. Made for Williams .250" ramps. Also available in .340" width, ¹⁄₁₆" and ³⁄₃₂" bead sizes. 10-heights.............**$2.25**

WILLIAMS GUIDE BEAD SIGHT
Fits all shotguns. ⅛" ivory, red or gold bead. Screws into existing sight hole. Various thread sizes and shank lengths..........**$1.75**

Handgun Sights

Left—FDL revolver sight.
Above—Micro handgun sight.

BO-MAR DE LUXE
Gives ⅜" w. and e. adjustment at 50 yards on Colt Gov't 45, sight radius under 7". For Colt, Hi-Standard, Ruger and S&W autos. Uses existing dovetail slot. Has shield-type rear blade. $16.00

BO-MAR LOCK-UP RAMP
For Colt 38, 45 autos. Has locking barrel feature which positions and centers the barrel in relation to the slide to assure free functioning and barrel lock-up. To be installed by competent pistolsmith only. $22.50

BO-MAR HIGH STANDARD RIB
Full length, 8¾" sigh radius, for all bull barrels and military. Slide alteration required. $30.00

BO-MAR LOW PROFILE RIB
Streamlined rib with front and rear sights; 7⅛" sight radius. Brings sight line closer to the bore than standard or extended sight and ramp. Weighs 4 oz. Made for Colt Gov't 45, Super 38, and Gold Cup 45 and 38. ....$28.00
    Extended sight and ramp, 8⅛" radius, 5¾ oz. 34.00
    Rib & tuner—inserted in Low Profile Rib—accuracy tuner. Adjustable for barrel positioning. 39.95

BO-MAR FRONT SIGHTS
⅛" tapered post, made for Colt, Hi-Standard, Ruger and S&W autos. ....$3.00—$4.00

F.D.L. WONDERSIGHT
Micrometer rear sight for Colt and S&W revolvers. 1-min. clicks for windage. Sideplate screw controls elevation...................$4.95

MICRO
Click adjustable w. and e. rear with plain or undercut front sight in ¹⁄₁₀", ⅛", or ⁵⁄₃₂" widths. Standard model available for 45, Super 38 or Commander autos. Low model for above pistols plus Colt Service Ace. Also for Ruger with 4¾" or 6" barrel. Price for sets.........$15.50
    Price with ramp front sight........................18.50

MICRO
Non-adjustable sight set for 45 auto....................$7.50

Shotgun Sights

FOR DOUBLE BARREL SHOTGUNS (PRESS FIT)
Marble 214—Ivory front bead, ¹¹⁄₆₄"....$1.00; 215—same with .080" rear bead and reamers....$2.95. Marble 220—Bi-color (gold and ivory) front bead, ¹¹⁄₆₄" and .080 rear bead, with reamers....$3.95; Marble 221—front bead only....$1.90. Marble 223—Ivory rear .080....$1.00. Marble 224—Front sight reamer for 214-221 beads....$0.75; Marble 226—Rear sight reamer for 223...........................$0.75

FOR SINGLE OR DB SHOTGUNS (SCREW-ON FIT)
Marble 217—Ivory front bead ¹¹⁄₆₄"..$1.20; with tap and wrench..$2.50
Marble 218—Bi-color front, ¹¹⁄₆₄"....1.60; with tap and wrench...3.05
Marble 223T—Ivory rear .080........1.60; with tap and wrench...3.05
    Marble Bradley type sights 223BT—⅛", ⁵⁄₆₄" and ¹¹⁄₆₄" long. Gold, Ivory or Red bead $1.60

POLY-SIGHT
Luminous bead ramp front and aperture rear, connected and supported by a 12" bridge, for use on shotguns with slugs or buckshot. Adj. for windage, elevation. Not for break-open guns. Price, including installation at Poly-Choke Co., and postage $36.70

SLUG SITE
A combination V-notch rear and bead front sight made of adhesive-backed formed metal approx. 7" over-all. May be mounted, removed and re-mounted as necessary, using new adhesive from the pack supplied. $5.00

Sight Attachments

FREELAND LENS ADAPTER
Fits 1⅛" O.D. prescription ground lens to all standard tube and receiver sights for shooting without glasses. Price without lens..$10.50
    Price lens ground to prescription.....................11.50

MERIT ADAPTER FOR GLOBE FRONT SIGHTS
An Iris Shutter Disc with a special adapter for mounting in Lyman or Redfield globe front sights. Price.......................$9.00

MERIT IRIS SHUTTER DISC
Eleven clicks give 12 different apertures. No. 3 and Master, primarily target types, .022" to .125"; No. 4, ½" dia. hunting type, .025" to .155". Available for all popular sights. The Master Disc, with flexible rubber light shield, is particularly adapted to extension, scope height, and tang sights. All Merit Deluxe models have internal click spring; are hand fitted to minimum tolerance. Price..............$8.00—$11.00
Master..............$10.00   Master Deluxe.........13.00

Merit Master   Merit Hunting   Merit Deluxe
Target Disc   Disc #4   Lens Disc

MERIT LENS DISC
Similar to Merit Iris Shutter (Model 3 or Master) but incorporates provision for mounting prescription lens integrally. Lens may be obtained locally, or prescription sent to Merit. Sight disc is ⁷⁄₁₆" wide (Mod. 3), or ¾" wide (Master). Lens, ground to prescription, $7.60.
Standard tints, $9.10. Model 3 Deluxe.....................$13.00
    Master Deluxe $16.00

REDFIELD VARD (Variable Diopter)
For shooters with visual problems. By adjusting the focus ring to focus the lens system at a point between the front sight aperture and the bull and controlling the size of the iris diaphragm, a crisp sharp high-contrast sight picture can be achieved. Provision is made for a prescription lens holder for shooters whose requirements exceed the focus capability of the VARD. Comes with smoke-gray filter. Front thread is ⁹⁄₃₂—32NS and will fit International and Olympic sights now being produced. Older O/I sights with ⁷⁄₃₂ thread will be converted at the plant for $3.45 on request. Maximum magnification is 1.3X. Use of the VARD adds approximately 1.5" to the sight. Extension attaching bases listed allow the sight to move forward 1.5" to accommodate for this extra length. Prices: VARD-IRIS Combination with filter $39.95
    Iris Diaphragm only with filter........................19.95
    Prescription lens holder 1.95
    Set of 3 filters—Yellow, Sage Green and Gray............3.95

REDFIELD SURE-X SIGHTING DISC
Eight hole selective aperture. Fits any Redfield target sight. Each click changes aperture .004". Price..........................$7.95

REDFELD SIGHTING DISCS
Fit all Redfield receiver sights. .046" to .093" aperture. ⅜", ½" and ⅞" O.D. Price, each...................................$ .95

WILLIAMS APERTURES
Standard thread, fits most sights. Regular series ⅜" to ⅝" O.D., .050" to .125" hole. "Twilight" series has white reflector ring. .093" to .125" inner hole. Price, regular series..$.75. Twilight series..$1.25
    New wide open ⁵⁄₁₆" aperture for shotguns fits 5-D and Foolproof sights. Price $2.00

MERIT OPTICAL ATTACHMENT
For revolver and pistol shooters. Instantly attached by rubber suction cup to regular or shooting glasses. Any aperture .020" to .156". Price, $8.00. Deluxe (swings aside)........................$10.00

HUNTING, TARGET◆ AND VARMINT◆ SCOPES

Maker and Model	Magn.	Field at 100 Yds. (feet)	Relative Bright-ness	Eye Relief (in.)	Length (in.)	Tube Diam. (in.)	W&E Adjust-ments	Weight (ozs.)	Other Data	Price
American Import Co.										
Dickson 250	2½	43	64	3½	—	1	Int.	—	CH standard, Post available in 2½x and 4x. Aluminum tubes, centered reticles, nitrogen filled. 1" adj.	$28.95
Dickson 400	4	30	67	3½	—	1	Int.	—		30.95
Dickson 600	6	19	30	3	—	1	Int.	—		37.95
Dickson V20/154	1½-4	53-28	177-25	4-3	—	1	Int.	—		42.95
Dickson V33/257	2½-7	43-16	174-22	3	—	1	Int.	—		49.95
Dickson V40/39	3-9	30-12	196-21	3	—	1	Int.	—		55.00
Bausch & Lomb										
Custom Baltur A	2½	43	64	3¼	12¼	1	Ext.	9½	Custom models must be used with B&L or other adj. mount. Trophy models have internal ½ MOA adj. Custom variables have tapered CH. Straight powers have CH, Post $5, dot $10. Balfor B has CH; post, tapered CH, dualine, taper-dot $5, dot $10. Balvar 8B has CH; post, tapered CH, RF, dualine, taper-dot $5, dot $10.	49.95
Custom Balfor A	4	30	56	3¼	12¼	1	Ext.	9		59.95
Custom Balvar 5	2½-5	40-20	164-41	3½	12¾	1	Ext.	9½		79.95
Custom Balvar 8A	2½-8	40-12½	256-25	3½	12¾	1	Ext.	10½		99.95
Trophy Baltur B	2½	42	164	3	12⅛	1	Int.	11		49.95
Trophy Balfor B	4	30	64	3	11⅞	1	Int.	11		59.95
Trophy Balsix B	6	20	36	3	11⅞	1	Int.	10¾		69.95
Trophy Balvar 8B	2½-8	40-12½	207-20	3½	11⅞	1	Int.	12½		99.95
Browning										
22 Scope	4	24	56	2½-4	9⅜	.75	Int.	6¼	22 Scope w/mount $41.45-$42.45.	31.95
Wide Angle	5	30	58	3	11½	1	Int.	9¾	CH, Post or 4-Plex optional in big game models; dot $10 extra.	76.95
	3-9	35-12	159-19	3½	12¾	1	Int.	12½		109.95
Browning	2-7	44-16	241-20	3-4½	11¼	1	Int.	11½		99.95
Bushnell										
Scopechief IV	2¾	43	58	4	10	1	Int.	8½	Scopechief models have Command Post reticle with Magnetic Control Ring. Constantly centered reticles in Scopechiefs, Customs and Banners. Integral mounts $15 extra on Scopechiefs. Phantoms intended for handgun use.	54.50
Scopechief IV	4	32	64	3¾	11¾	1	Int.	10½		64.50
Scopechief IV	6	20	40	4	12½	1	Int.	11½		79.50
Scopechief IV	1½-4½	78-26	216-23	4¼-3¼	9¼	1	Int.	7¾		79.50
Scopechief IV	2½-8	44-15	160-16	4-3¼	11	1	Int.	11		89.50
Scopechief IV	3-9	39-13	160-18	3¾-3¼	11½	1	Int.	12¼		94.50
Scopechief 22	3-8	30-12	55-6	2½	11	⅞	Int.	7½	Mount rail. Similar 4x at $14.95.	19.95
Scopechief V	4	30	96	3½	12¼	1	Int.	10¾	Battery powered Lite-Site reticle.	69.50
Custom M	2½	49	64	4¼	10½	1	Int.	7¾		42.50
Custom M	4	27	64	3¾	11½	1	Int.	9¾		48.50
Custom M	6	19	40	3¼	13	1	Int.	10¾		51.50
Custom M	3-9	35-12½	159-18	3¾-3	12¼	1	Int.	12½	Mount rail. Similar 4x at $10.95.	69.50
Custom 22	3-7	29-13	28-5	2	10	⅞	Int.	6½		15.95
Banner	2½	45	64	4¼	10½	1	Int.	8		32.50
Banner	4	30	64	4	11¾	1	Int.	10		36.50
Banner	6	19½	29	3¾	13¼	1	Int.	10½		39.50
Banner	10	12	26	3½	14¼	1	Int.	14½	Obj. focuses for range.	56.50
Banner	1½-4	63-28	169-25	4¼-3¼	10	1	Int.	10¼		49.50
Banner	3-9	39-13	115-13	3¾-3	11¼	1	Int.	12	With 40mm obj. $57.50.	52.50
Banner	4-12	29-10	181-18	3¼	13¼	1	Int.	15½	Obj. focuses for range.	67.50
Phantom	1 1/3	24	441	6-17	7⅝	⅞	Int.	5		24.50
Phantom	2½	10	100	7-16	9¼	⅞	Int.	5½		34.50
Shotgun	1	92	337	6	9⅞	1	Int.	11½		64.50
Collins										
Bulittco	2½	40	164	3	11¼	1	Int.	9½	One-piece duralumin tube with oilproof rubber packings at lens/metal joints. Nitrogen filled.	34.95
Bulittco	4	30	64	3	11¼	1	Int.	9½		36.95
Bulittco	6	20	28	3	11¼	1	Int.	9½		38.95
Colt										
Coltmaster Jr.	4	30			12½	.75	Int.	7	Coltmaster Jr. scopes have tip-off mounts.	10.75
Coltmaster Jr.	6	20			14½	.75	Int.	8		13.75
Davis Optical										
Spot Shot 1½"	10, 12, 15, 20, 25, 30	10-4		2	25	.75	Ext.		Focus by moving non-rotating obj. lens unit. Ext. mounts included. Recoil spring $3.50 extra.	89.50
Spot Shot 1¼"	10, 12, 15, 20	10-6		2	25	.75	Ext.			69.50
Habicht										
4 S-D	4	30	64	3¼	11	1.18	Int.	13	From Del-Sports. With e. only, $62.75. With light alloy tube, (27mm), mounting rail, $69.75; same, e. only, $65.75.	63.90
Herter's										
Perfect	1	100	256	3-5	9¾	1	Int.	10¼		33.95
Mark II	2¾	44	58	3½	10¼	1	Int.	8½	A variety of reticles including dots and rangefinders available in different scopes at small price increase. Hudson Bay rimfire scopes: 4x, $17.95; 6x, 3-9x, $30.95.	31.95
Mark IV	4	30	64	3½	11½	1	Int.	9½		31.95
Mark VI	6	20	38	3½	12¾	1	Int.	10½		31.95
Mark VIII	8	15½	22	3½	12½	1	Int.	14½		38.49
Mark IA	3-9	14-41	157-18	3½	12½	1	Int.	14½		49.95
Mark XXI	4-12	11½-34	100-14	3½	13¼	1	Int.	12½		53.95
Hutson										
Handgunner	1	9	—	25	5¼	—	Ext.	3	CH. ⅞" obj. lens. Adj. in mount, $14.95.	35.00
Hy-Score										
No. 467	4	26	14	1¾	12	.75	Int.	7¼		8.95
No. 469	6	19	6	1¾	12	.75	Int.	7½	Alloy tubes. Weather and fogproof. 400 series scopes are made in Japan.	11.95
Model 461-466	2½	35	64	3	9⅞	1	Int.	8		19.95
Model 462-468	4	28	64	3	11⅝	1	Int.	10		19.95
Model 463	6	22	28.1	3	11¾	1	Int.	10		20.95
Vari-Power 464	3-9	36-16	126-12	3¼	12½	1	Int.	14		29.95
Vari-Power 471	3-9	35-14	193-18	3¼	12½	1	Int.	14		36.95

SCOPES & MOUNTS

Hunting, Target and Varmint Scopes—Continued

Maker and Model	Magn.	Field at 100 Yds. (feet)	Relative Bright-ness	Eye Relief (in.)	Length (in.)	Tube Diam. (in.)	W&E Adjust-ments	Weight (oz.)	Other Data	Price
Jason										
860	4	27¼	64	3½	12	1	Int.	9	Constantly centered reticles, ball-bearing click stops, nitrogen filled tubes, coated lenses.	19.95
864	6	17½	28	3¼	12	1	Int.	9		23.50
861	3-9	31½-12	112-12	3	13¼	1	Int.	13¾		36.95
865	3-9	31½-12	177-19	3	13½	1	Int.	15¼		39.95
Leupold										
M8	2	25	100	8-18	8.45	1	Int.	7.25	Constantly centered reticles; in addition to the crosshair reticle the post, tapered (CPC), post and duplex, and duplex reticles are optional at no extra cost. Dot reticle $10.00 extra. 2x suitable for handguns and Win. 94.	49.50
M8	3	43	45	3.85	10.13	1	Int.	8.25		59.50
M8	4	30	50	3.85	11.50	1	Int.	9.00		67.50
M8	6	18		3.85	11.7	1	Int.	10.3		79.50
M8	7½	14	32	3.60	12.60	1	Int.	12.75		84.50
M8	10	10	16	3½	13	1	Int.	13¾		97.50
M8	12	9	11	3½	14½	1	Int.	14		99.50
Vari-X II	2-7	42-18	144-17	3.7-4.12	11.00	1	Int.	10.75		89.50
Vari-X II	3-9	30.5-13	208-23	3.5-4.12	12.60	1	Int.	13.75		99.50
Lyman										
All-American	2½	43		3¼	10½	1	Int.	8¾	2, 3, or 4 minute dot reticle $10 extra. Choice of standard CH, tapered post, or tapered post and CH reticles. All-weather reticle caps. All Lyman scopes have new Perma-Center reticle which remains in optical center regardless of changes in W. & E.	49.50
All-American	3	35		3¼	11	1	Int.	9		52.95
All-American	4	30		3¼	12	1	Int.	10		62.95
All-American	6	20		3¼	13⅞	1	Int.	12¼		69.95
◆ All-American	8	14		3¼	14⅜	1	Int.	13		89.95
◆ All-American	10	12		3¼	15½	1	Int.	13½		89.95
All-American	20	5.5		2¼	17⅛	1	Int.	15¼	⅛ or ¼ MOA clicks.	109.95
◆ Super Targetspot	10, 12, 15, 20, 25, 30	12, 9.3, 8.9, 5.6, 4.3, 4	86%	2-1⅞	24-24⅜	.75	Ext.	24¼-25	Non-rotating objective lens focusing. ¼ MOA click adjustments. Sunshade, $2 extra. Steel case, $9.50 extra. 5 different dot reticles, $10.00 extra.	137.50
Marble										
A-2.5	2¾	43	164	3½	11¾	1	Int.	10¾	Duralumin tubes, nitrogen filled. Post, CH, dot or 3-post reticle. Variables have ½ MOA adj.	39.50
A-4.0	4	30	64	3½	11¾	1	Int.	10¾		39.50
VL-3.9	3-9	38½-12½	177-19	3¼	13½	1	Int.	15½		68.50
VS-3.9	3-9	37-10½	114-12	3¼	13½	1	Int.	13½		69.50
Marlin										
300	4	23	25	1½	11¾	⅞	Int.	9	Coated lenses, non-magnifying reticles. Tri-Post reticle. A 4x Glenfield M200, suitable for 22 rifles, and with ½-minute adj., is $8.00.	13.95
500	3-7	24-10	49-16	1¾	12	⅞	Int.	9½		16.95
600	3	29	144	3½	12½	1	Int.	10		32.95
700	5	20	64	3½	12½	1	Int.	11		34.95
800	1½-5	55-19	256-49	3½	11⅜	1	Int.	13½		42.95
850	2-5	50-17½	100-16	3	10¼	1	Int.	11		39.95
900	3-9	35-12	169-19	3¼	12¾	1	Int.	14		44.95
Glenfield 400	4	28	64	3½	12	1	Int.	9		20.00
Nickel										
Supra	2½	42	72	3½	11½	1.024	Int.	7½	¼ MOA click adjustments. Steel or alloy tubes. Weatherproof reticle caps. Crosshair, post and c.h. or post and crossbar reticles are standard. New "Diflex" coated lenses. Continental Arms Co.	75.00
Supralyt	4	33	30	3½	11½	1.024	Int.	8		75.00
Supra	4	32	81	3½	11¼	1.024	Int.	9		85.00
Supra	6	21	36	3½	12½	1.024	Int.	9		85.00
◆ Supra Varminter	6	24	56	3¼-5	12¼	1.024	Int.	11½		89.50
Supra Vari-Power	1-4	66.5-27.3	153-28	3½	10½	1.024	Int.	13.1		115.00
Supra Vari-Power	1½-6	60-21.6	176-36	3½	12	1.024	Int.	14.8		150.00
Supra Vari-Power	2½-6	38-21	125-36	3½	11¾	1.024	Int.	11		125.00
Supra Vari-Power	2½-9	42-15.6		3½	14½	1.024	Int.	17.3		160.00
Supra Vari-Power	4-10	30-12	100-18.5	3½	12½	.866	Int.	12½		135.00
Pacific										
2.5x Supreme	2½	36		3½	11¾	1	Int.	10	All Pacific scopes have constantly centered reticles, coated lenses and ¼ MOA adj. Nitrogen filled. Choice of crosshair or post and crosshair.	27.95
4x Supreme	4	31		3½	12½	1	Int.	12		36.95
6x Supreme	6	20		3½	11½	1	Int.	11		33.95
3-9x Supreme	3-9	34-14		3½	12½	1	Int.	13		52.95
Precise Imports										
NR-15	4	23	14	2	11	.75	Int.	6¾	Price with mount. All scopes have constanly centered reticle.	7.95
20257	3-7	23-13	43-8	3	11½	.75	Int.	7½		13.95
20265	2½	32	164	3¾	12	1	Int.	9.6		24.95
20244	4	29	64	3½	12	1	Int.	9		24.95
20249	3-9	36-13	177-19	3	13⅓	1	Int.	15		39.95
20260	10	12.2	16	3	12½	1	Int.	10½		29.95
Realist										
Apache	4	30	6	2	12½	.75	Int.	7	Scope price includes mount. Constantly centered reticles in Riflescopes. CH or P&CH standard. Dot $10 extra. Sunshades available $6.95 — $8.95. Nitrogen processed. Aluminum construction. Supplied with special mounts and range cams for most popular rifles and calibers.	9.95
Apache	6	20	4	2	13¾	.75	Int.	8		12.50
Riflescope	2½	44	66	3-5	10½	1	Int.	8		55.50
Riflescope	4	31	73	3-5	12⅜	1	Int.	9		65.50
Riflescope	6	20	38	3-5	14	1	Int.	10		75.50
Brushscope	1½-4½	65-26	225-49	3-5	11	1	Int.	11½		83.50
Riflescope	3-9	34-12	144-16	3-5	13¼	1	Int.	11		103.50
Computer	6	20	38	3-5	14⅝	1	Int.	18		119.50
Auto/Range	4	31	73	3-5	11	1	Int.	17		119.50
	1½-4½	65-26	225-49	3-5	12¼	1	Int.	17		129.50
	3-9	34-12	144-16	3-5	12¾	1	Int.	17		129.50

SCOPES & MOUNTS

Hunting, Target and Varmint Scopes—Continued

Maker and Model	Magn.	Field at 100 Yds. (feet)	Relative Bright-ness	Eye Relief (in.)	Length (in.)	Tube Diam. (in.)	W&E Adjust-ments	Weight (oz.)	Other Data	Price
Redfield										
Sportster 4X	3.9	24.5	27	3-3¾	9½	.75	Int.	6¼		31.95
Widefield 2¾	2¾	55½	49	3	10½	1	Int.	8	Constantly centered reticles; scratchproof Tuf-Coat finish; W. & E. dials adjustable to zero; weatherproof sealed. Reticle same size at all powers. Add $10 for Accu-Range, $10 for dot (not avail. in Sportster). 12X has separate parallax adj. knob, ¼" clicks.	64.95
Widefield 4	4	37½	46	3	11½	1	Int.	10		74.95
Widefield 6	6	25	44	3	13½	1	Int.	11½		84.95
Magnum 12X	12	10	13.7	3-3¾	14⅞	1	Int.	13.5		119.95
Magnum Variable	1-4	85-30	289-31	3½	9¾	1	Int.	10¼		89.95
Magnum Variable	2.3-7	44-16	182-20	3-3¾	11¾	1	Int.	11½		129.95
Widefield	2-7	49-19	121-25	3½	11¾	1	Int.	13		105.95
Widefield	3-9	39-15	144-20	3½	12½	1	Int.	14	Mounts solidly. Fine CH, Med. CH, ¼" dot.	115.95
Magnum Variable	6-18	16-5½	44.5	3½	14	1	Int.	18		139.95
3200 Target	12, 16, 20, 24,	6½, 5¼, 4, 3¾	9, 6, 3¼, 2¼	2½	23¼	1	Int.	21		169.95
Sanders										
Bisley 2½x32	2½	42	64	3	10¾	1	Int.	8¼	Alum. alloy tubes, ¼" adj., coated lenses.	32.50
Bisley 4x33	4	28	64	3	12	1	Int.	9	Two other scopes are also offered: a 3-9x at $56.50, and a 6x45 at $42. Rubber lens covers (clear plastic) are $2.50.	36.50
Bisley 6x40	6	19	45	3	12½	1	Int.	9½		38.50
Bisley 8x40	8	18	25	3¼	12½	1	Int.	9½		40.50
Bisley 10 x40	10	12½	16	2½	12½	1	Int.	10¼	Choice of reticles in CH, PCH, 3-post.	42.50
Bisley 5-13x40	5-13	29-10	64-9	3	14	1	Int.	14		60.50
Savage										
2520	2½	43		3	10¾	1	Int.	8.5		31.50
0433	4	30		3	12	1	Int.	10	Coated lenses, duralumin tubes. Reticles permanently centered.	37.50
1420	1½-4	64-25		3	10¼	1	Int.	10		47.50
3833	3-8	35-13		3	11½	1	Int.	12	For 22 rifles; price includes mounts.	59.75
2037	3-7	25-14		2	11¼	.875	Int.	8		14.95
0420	4	25½		2	11½	.75	Int.	8.5		9.75
Scope Instruments										
2650	2½	32	164	3½	11½	1	Int.	10		24.95
2652	4	29	64	3¼	11½	1	Int.	9½	Contantly centered reticles—CH or post. Nitrogen filled. Yellow haze filter.	24.95
2654	6	21	28	3	11½	1	Int.	9½		24.95
2658	3-9	29-13	113-12	3	13¼	1	Int.	14¼		37.95
2656	3-9	29-12	177-19	3½	13¼	1	Int.	16		39.95
Sears										
No. 53801	4	30		2	11½	.75	Int.	6	First three scopes for 22's only, complete with rings for grooved receivers. Crosshair or post and crosshair reticle. Big game scopes come with mount rings. Bases available to fit almost all H.P. rifles. Fixed crosshair reticle remains in center regardless of adjustment. No. 53824 for Sears M54.	12.75
No. 53802	4	28		2	11½	.75	Int.	8		8.75
No. 53803	3-6	30-16					Int.	6½		13.50
No. 53824	3	37		3-6	10⅜	1	Int.	8½		34.50
No. 53821	4	30		3¼	11¼	1	Int.	12		39.50
No. 53901	1				8	1	Int.	8½		39.50
Southern Precision										
562	2½	40	144	3½	12	1	Int.	9¼	Centered reticles, CH or post. All elements sealed.	21.95
564	4	30	64	3½	12	1	Int.	9¼		23.95
566	6	21	28	3¼	12	1	Int.	9¼		23.95
Stoeger										
4x	4	30	64	3	12	1	Int.	9		24.95
6x	6	20	28	3	12¾	1	Int.	9	CH only. ½" clicks. Obj. tube diam. 1½" in fixed powers, 1⅞" in variable.	29.95
8x	8	16	25	3	12	1	Int.	13		35.95
3x-9x	3-9	38-11	170-20	3	11½	1	Int.	12¾		46.95
Swift										
Grizzly	2½	32	159	3	11.7	1	Int.	8.5	Dot, tapered post & CH or Rangefinder reticles available on all but Zoom & Game, $2.50 extra. Rangefinder optional on Zoom & Game. All have self-centering reticles.	24.00
Stag	4	28½	64	3	11.7	1	Int.	8.5		24.50
Gamescope	4	30	64	3	11.7	1	Int.	9		36.00
Bighorn	6	18½	28	3	11.7	1	Int.	8.5		27.50
Yukon	2½-8	32½-13	164-16	3	13¼	1	Int.	11.3		38.00
Zoomscope	2½-8	41-15½	256-25	3½	12½	1	Int.	16.1		67.50
Tasco										
Zoom Utility	3-7	28-12	130-24	2¼	12	⅞	Int.	9½	Lens covers furnished. Constantly centered reticles. Write the importer, Tasco, for data on complete line.	15.95
Pistol Scope	1½	23	216	19	8⅝	⅞	Int.	7½		19.95
Sniper	2-5	36-18	150-24	3¼	11¼	1	Int.	10		39.95
Super Marksman	3-9	35-14	266-29	3.2	12⅜	1	Int.	12½		59.95
Tops										
4X	4	28½	64	3	11½	1	Int.	9½	Hard-coated lenses, nitrogen filled, shock-proof tested. Write Ed Paul, importer, for data on complete line.	23.95
8X	8	14½	16	3	13	1	Int.	10		29.95
3X-9X	3-9	33-15	175-19	3	12¾	1	Int.	14		39.95
Tradewinds										
TW-4	4	31	81	3¼	10.8	1	Int.	11	Lightweight dural tubes. Dot reticles same price, leather scope caps included. Tradewinds, Inc., importer.	54.50
TW-VARI	2.5-8	35.4-14.8	100-20.25	3¼	12¼	1	Int.	12.7		69.50
TW-Zoom	1.5-4	62-28	144-20	3¼	9.7	1	Int.	11.6	Diamond Dot reticle.	57.50

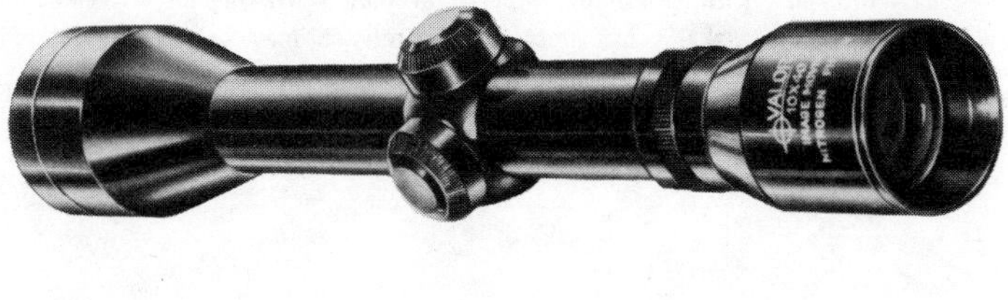

Valor 10x Super Varmint Luma-Glo Riflescope, imported by Precise Imports Corporation.

Hunting, Target and Varmint Scopes—Continued

Maker and Model	Magn.	Field at 100 Yds. (feet)	Relative Bright-ness	Eye Relief (in.)	Length (in.)	Tube Diam. (in.)	W&E Adjust-ments	Weight (oz.)	Other Data	Price
United										
Golden Hawk	4	30	64		11⅞	—	Int.	9½	Anodized tubes, nitrogen filled. Write United for data on complete line.	44.50
Golden Grizzly	6	18½	44		11⅞	1	Int.	11		55.00
Golden Falcon	4-9	29½-14	100-20		13½	1	Int.	12¼		89.50
Golden Plainsman	3-12	33-12½	169-11		13½	1	Int.	12¾		110.00
Unertl										
Falcon	2¾	40	75.5	4	11	1	Int.(1′)	10	Black dural tube in hunting models. (2 oz. more with steel tube.)	50.00
Hawk	4	34	64	4	11¾	1	Int.(1′)	10.5		54.00
Condor	6	17	40	3-4	13½	1	Int.(1′)	12		68.00
◆1″ Target	6,8,10	16-10	17.6-6.25	2	21½	.75	Ext.	21	Dural ¼ MOA click mounts. Hard coated lenses. Non-rotating objective lens focusing.	67.00
◆1¼″ Target	8,10,12,14	12-6	15.2-5	2	25	.75	Ext.	25		90.00
◆1½″ Target	8,10,12,14 16,18,20,24	11.5-3.2		2¼	25½	.75	Ext.	31		105.00
◆2″ Target	8,10,12,14 16,18,24 30,36		22.6-2.5	2¼	26¼	1	Ext.	44		145.00
◆Varmint, 1¼″	6,8,10,12	14.1-7	28-7.1	2½	19½	.875	Ext.	26	¼ MOA dehorned mounts. With target mounts.	92.00 95.00
◆Ultra Varmint, 2″	8,10, 12,15	12.6-7	39.7-11	2½	24	1	Ext.	34	With dehorned mount. With calibrated head.	115.00 132.00
◆Small Game	4,6	25-17	19.4-8.4	2¼	18	.75	Ext.	16	Same as 1″ Target but without objective lens focusing.	49.00
◆Vulture	8 10	11.2 10.9	29 18½	3-4	15⅝ 16⅛	1	E or I	15½	Price with internal adj. Price with ¼ MOA click mounts.	82.00 98.00
◆Programer 200	8,10,12,14 16,18,20,24 30,36	11.3-4	39-1.9		26½	1	Ext.	45	With new Posa mounts.	192.00
◆BV-20	20	8	4.4	—	17⅞	1	Ext.	21¼	Range focus unit near rear of tube. Price is with Posa mounts, Magnum clamp. With standard mounts and clamp ring, $131.95.	139.95
Universal										
Deluxe UC	2½	32	172	3½	12	1	Int.	9¼	Aluminum alloy tubes, centered reticles, coated lenses. Similar Standard series available at lower cost.	24.95
Deluxe UE	4	29	64	3½	12	1	Int.	9		24.95
Deluxe UG	6	17½	28	3¼	12	1	Int.	9		26.95
Deluxe UL	3-9	34-12	177-18	3	12¾	1	Int.	15¼		42.95
Weatherby										
Mark XXII	4	25	50	2½-3½	11¾	⅞	Int.	9¼	Focuses in top turret.	29.50
Imperial	2¾	47½	90	3¼-5	10½	1	Int.	9¼	¼ MOA adj. for e., 1 MOA for w. in all models. Reticles: CH, post and CH, Lee Dot or Open Dot ($12.50 extra).	79.50
Imperial 4x	4	33	81	3¼-4½	11⅛	1	Int.	10¼		89.50
Imperial 6x	6	21½	62	3¼-4½	12½	1	Int.	12⅜		99.50
Imperial Variable	2-7	48-17¾	324-27	4.3-3.1	11 3/16	1	Int.	12		109.50
Imperial Variable	2¾-10	37-14.6	296-22	4½-3½	12½	1	Int.	14⅛		119.50
Weaver										
Classic 300	3	37	—	4	10⅜	1	Int.	7	Classics have glossy anodized alloy, tubes, non-removable eyepieces, choice of all five reticles, dot $7.50 extra.	60.00
Classic 400	4	31	—	4	11¾	1	Int.	8		70.00
Classic 600	6	20	—	3¾	13⅝	1	Int.	9		80.00
Classic V700	2½-7	40-15		3¾	11¾	1	Int.	8¼		90.00
Classic V900	3-9	33-12		3¾	13	1	Int.	11		100.00
K1.5	1½	56		3-5	9¾	1	Int.	7		29.95
K2.5	2½	43		3-6	10⅜	1	Int.	8½		39.95
K3	3	37		3-6	10⅜	1	Int.	8½	Crosswires, post, rangefinder or Dual X reticle optional on all K and V scopes (except no RF in K1½, post in K8, 10, 12, or RF in V22). Dot $7.50 extra in K and V models only. Objective lens on K8, K10, K12, V9 and V12 focuses for range.	39.95
K4	4	31		3-5½	11¼	1	Int.	9½		49.95
K6	6	20		3-5	13⅝	1	Int.	11		54.95
K8	8	15		3-5	15⅜	1	Int.	12¼		59.95
K10	10	12		3-5	15½	1	Int.	12½		64.95
K12	12	10		3-5	15¾	1	Int.	12½		72.95
V4.5	1½-4½	54-21		3-5	10	1	Int.	8½		57.95
V7	2½-7	40-15		3-5	11⅝	1	Int.	10½		64.95
V9	3-9	33-12		3-5	13	1	Int.	13		72.95
V12	4-12	24-9		4	13		Int.	13		84.95
V22	3-6	30-16		2	12½	.875	Int.	4½	D model prices include N or Tip-Off mount.	15.95
D4	4	28	—	2	11⅝	.875	Int.	4		10.95
D6	6	18	—	2	12	.875	Int.	4		12.95
Williams										
Guide Line	4	29½	64	3¾	11¾	1	Int.	9½	Coated lenses, nitrogen filled tubes, ½ MOA adj. CH, dot, TNT or Guide reticle. Dot covers 3 MOA at 4x in all models.	69.00
Guide Line	1½-4½	78-26	196-22	4⅓-3¼	9½	1	Int.	7¾		99.00
Guide Line	2-6	60-20	169-18	3¼	10¼	1	Int.	10		99.00
Guide Line	3-9	39-13	161-18	3¾-3¼	12	1	Int.	14½		108.00
Zeiss										
Diatal D	4	31.5	64	3⅛	10½	1.24	Int.	11	Alloy tubes. Leather caps furnished. Turret dials not calibrated. Carl Zeiss, Inc., importer.	135.00
Diatal D	6	21	49	3⅛	12½	1.24	Int.	13½		147.00
Diavari D	1½-6	60-21	161-36	3⅛	12¼	1.18	Int.	16¼		199.00

◆Signifies target and/or varmint scope.

Hunting scopes in general are furnished with a choice of reticle—crosshairs, post with crosshairs, tapered or blunt post, or dot crosshairs, etc. The great majority of target and varmint scopes have medium or fine crosshairs but post or dot reticles may be ordered.

W—Windage E—Elevation MOA—Minute of angle or 1″ (approx.) at 100 yards, etc.

TELESCOPE MOUNTS

Maker, Model, Type	W and E Adjust.	Scopes	Suitable for	Price
Bausch & Lomb				
Custom One Piece (T)	Yes	B&L, other 1" scopes.	Most popular rifles.	38.90-52.90
Custom Two Piece (T)	Yes			26.90
Trophy (T)	No	1". With int. adj.		21.90-37.90
Browning				
One Piece (T)	W only	1" split rings	Browning FN rifles.	24.25
One Piece (T)	No	¾" split rings	Browning 22 semi-auto.	4.50
One Piece Barrel Mount Base	No	Groove mount	22 rifles with grooved receiver.	6.00
Two Piece	No	¾" ring mount.	For Browning T-bolt 22.	9.50
B-Square Co.				
Mono-Mount	No	Leupold M8-2x (mounts ahead of action)	M94 Win.	11.50
			M1 Carbine.	9.50
Buehler				
One Piece (T)	W only	¾" or 1" solid rings; ⅞", 1" or 26mm split rings. 4" or 5" spacing.	All popular models.	Solid rings—21.75 Split rings—26.75
One Piece "Micro-Dial" Universal	Yes	Same. 4" ring spacing only.	Most popular models.	Solid—28.25 Split—33.25
Two Piece (T)	W only	Same. Rings for 26.5—27 mm adjust to size by shims.	Rem. 700, 721, 722, 725; Win. 70, 52; FN; Rem. 37; Mathieu; Schultz & Larsen; Husq.	Solid—21.75 Split—26.75
Side Mount Rifle Base	W only	Offsets scope ⅝" to ¾"; takes all Buehler rings; uses adaptor plate, $4.50.	M1, 30-cal. Carbine, Mannlicher-Schoenauer, most Win. lever guns, SMLE 4 & 5 flat side.	11.25
One Piece Pistol Base	W only	Uses any Buehler rings.	S&W K, Colt, Ruger, Thompson	Base only—11.25
One Piece (T)	W only	Same.	Rem. 600 rifle and XP100 pistol.	Base only—11.25
Bushnell				
Universal (T)	W only	1" split rings	All rifles with top of action tapped for 6/48 screws. Two steel 6/48 studs are screwed into receiver holes, eliminating conventional base. Rings drop over studs, are held by opposing screws which give rough windage adj. Economy mount set.	14.95 9.75
Dual Purpose	No	Phantom	V-block bottoms lock to chrom-moly studs seated into two 6-48 holes.	5.00
Rigid	No	Phantom	Heavy loads in Colt, S&W, Ruger revolvers, Rem. XP100, Ruger Hawkeye.	5.00
94 Win.	No	Phantom	M94 Win., end of bbl. clamp or center dovetail.	5.00
Collins				
Bulittco (T)	E only	1" split rings	Rimfire rifles with grooved receivers.	4.98
Conetrol				
One Piece (T)	W only	1" solid or split rings.	Sako dovetail bases (14.95);	Huntur $20.95
Two Piece (T)	W only	Same.	for S&K bases on M1 Carb., SMLE 4 & 5, $9.90.	Gunnur $25.85 Custum $32.85
Griffin & Howe				
Standard Double Lever (S)	No	All standard models.	All popular models. (Garand $37.50; Win. 94 $30.00).	30.00
E. C. Herkner Echo (S)	No	All standard models.	All popular models. Solid or split rings.	14.50—19.75
Holden				
Ironsighter (T)	No	1" split rings	Many popular rifles. Rings have oval holes to permit use of iron sights. For 22 rimfire groover receivers, ¾, ⅞ or 1 inch tubes, $6.95. For long eye relief scopes on M94, $19.95.	14.95
International Guns Inc. handles the complete line of Parker-Hale (British) Roll-Over and other scope mounts.				
Jaeger				
QD, with windage (S)	W only	1", 26mm; 3 heights.	All popular models.	38.00
QD Railscope Mount	W only		For scopes with dovetail rib.	38.00
Jaguar				
QD Dovetail (T)	No	1", 26mm and 26½ mm rings.	For BSA Monarch rifle (Galef, importer).	16.95
Kesselring				
Standard QD (T)	W only	¾", ⅞", 1", 26mm—30mm split or solid rings.	All popular rifles, one or two piece bases.	12.50-20.00
See-Em-Under (T)	W only	Same.	Rem. 760, 740, 788, Win. 100, 88, Marlin 336	16.50
QD Dovetail (T)	W only	1", 26mm.	Steyr 22, Sako, BSA, Brno, Krico	16.50
Kwik-Site (T)	No	1" split rings	Fits Weaver type bases. Mounts scope high to permit iron sight use. Offset base for 94 Win.	14.75 19.95

Bushnell's new Scopchief IV-DM with detachable mounts for use with standard bases.

SCOPES & MOUNTS

TELESCOPE MOUNTS—Continued

Maker, Model, Type	W and E Adjust.	Scopes	Suitable for	Price
Leupold				
Detacho (T)	No	1″ only.	All popular rifles. Instantly detachable, leaving W. & E. adjustable peep sight available.	15.25
			Bases for Rem. 600 series.	9.95
			Bases for Win. M94 and Rem. XP100.	5.50—10.00
M3 (T)	Yes	1″ only.	Rem. 700, 740, Win. 70, 88, 100, Wby. Mark V, FN, others. Bases reversible to give wide latitude in mounting.	24.50
Lyman All-American				
Tru-lock (T)	No	¾″, ⅞″, 1″, 26mm, split rings.	All popular post-war rifles, plus Savage 99, 98 Mauser. One or two piece bases.	10.00
Marble				
Game Getter (T)	No	1″ only.	Many popular rifles. Has see-through base to permit use of iron sights.	14.95
Marlin				
One Piece QD (T)	No	1″ split rings	Most popular models. Glenfield model. 5.00.	6.95
Mashburn Arms				
Positive Zero (T)	With or w/o W	All standard models.	All popular models, solid or two-piece base, solid or split rings.	17.50—32.50
Numrich				
Side mount	No	1″ split rings	M1 carbine.	6.95
Pachmayr				
Lo-Swing (S)	Yes	¾″, ⅞″, 1″, 26mm solid or split loops.	All popular rifles. Scope swings aside for instant use of iron sights.	20.00
Lo-Swing (T)	Yes	¾″, ⅞″, 1″, 26mm split rings.	Adjustable base. Win. 70, 88; Rem. 721, 722, 725, 740, 760; Mar. 336; Sav. 99.	25.00
Precise Imports				
M-21 (rings only)	No	1″ tube; not over 32mm obj.	Fit Weaver bases.	3.95
M-22 (rings only)	No	1″ tube; 40mm obj. scopes		3.95
Realist				
V lock QD (T)	No	1″ split rings.	Most popular rifles.	13.00
Redfield				
JR-SR (T)	W only	¾″, 1″, 26mm.	Low, med. & high, split rings. Reversible extension front rings for 1″. 2-piece bases for Mannlicher-Schoenauer and Sako. JR-SR comes with integral folding peep sight.	29.90—43.90
Swing-Over (T) base only	No	1″. (Not for variables.)	Standard height split rings. Also for shotguns.	14.95
Ring (T)	No	¾″ and 1″.	Split rings for grooved 22's.	7.95—9.95
S&K				
Insta-Mount (T) base only	No	Takes Conetrol, Weaver, Herter or United rings.	M1903, A3, M1 Carbine, Lee Enfield #3, #4, #5, P14, M1917, M98 Mauser, FN Auto, AR-15.	6.00—27.00
			For M1 Garand, steel rings.	41.50
Conventional rings and bases	No	1″ split rings	Most popular rifles. For "see through underneath" risers, add $4.	19.00
Sako				
QD Dovetail (T)	W only	1″ or 26mm split rings.	Sako, or any rifle using Sako action. 3 heights and extension rings available. Garcia, importer.	18.95—20.65
Savage				
Detachable (T)	No	1″ split rings.	Most modern rifles. One or two piece bases.	9.75-10.25
No. 40 (S)	No	1″	For Savage 340.	3.00
Tasco				
700(T) and 800(S) series	No	1″ split rings, regular or high.	Many popular rifles. Swing mount, 9.95.	4.50—10.45
M722	No	Split rings.	For 22s with grooved receivers.	3.00
Tradewinds				
Two Piece (T)	W only	26mm or 1″ split rings.	Husqvarna, HVA rifles, actions. Scope removable w/o changing sighting. Tradewinds, imp.	14.95—18.95
Unertl				
Posa (T)	Yes	¾″, ⅞″, 1″ scopes	Unertl target or varmint scope.	25.00—26.00
¼ Click (T)	Yes	¾″, 1″ target scopes	Any with regular dovetail scope bases.	23.00—24.00
Dehorned Varmint (T)	Yes	¾″, ⅞″, 1″ scopes	Same, less base.	20.00—23.00
Weaver				
Detachable Mount (T & S)	No	¾″, ⅞″, 1″, 26mm.	Nearly all modern rifles. Extension rings, 1″ $11.00	10.50
Type N (S)	No	¾″ scopes only.	Same. High or low style mounts.	2.00
Pivot Mount (T)	No	¾″, 1″, 26mm.	Most modern big bore rifles.	13.00
Tip-Off (S)	No	⅞″.	22s with grooved receivers.	2.00, 3.00
Tip-Off (T)	No	1″, two-piece	Same. Adapter for Lee Enfield—$1.75	8.00
Williams				
Offset (S)	No	¾″, ⅞″, 1″, 26mm solid, split or extension rings.	Most rifles (with over-bore rings, $17.50). Br. S.M.L.E. (round rec.) $2.50 extra.	15.00
QC (T w/peep)	No	Same.	Same. Add $4.50 for micro. windage ring.	20.00
QC (T w/o peep)	No	Same.	Most 22 rifles, plus Mar. 36, 39, 93, 336, Sav. 23D, Win. 05, 07, 10.	17.50
Sight-Thru	No	1″, ⅞″ sleeves $1	Many modern rifles.	15.00
QC-TM-B22	No	Same.	For Browning 22 autoloader and Rem. 241.	17.50

(S)—Side Mount   (T)—Top Mount.   22mm = .866″   25.4mm = 1″   26mm = 1.024″   26.5mm = 1.045″   30mm = 1.181″

Redfield Gun Sight Company's new FRontier (FR) line of scope mounts. The front base is reversible on most rifles to provide two possible spans between rings.

SPOTTING SCOPES

BAUSCH & LOMB BALSCOPE Sr.—60mm objective, 20X. Field at 100 yds. 11.1 ft. Relative brightness, 9. Wgt., 48 oz. Length closed, 16^7/$_{16}$". Rapid prismatic focusing.. **$129.95**

 Also 15X, 30X, and 60X eyepieces, each **29.95**
 Triple eyepiece turret (without eyepiece) **19.95**
 Combination auto window/camera tripod adaptor **24.95**
 Carrying case.. **24.95**
 Tele-Master camera adapter..................................... **34.95**

BAUSCH & LOMB BALSCOPE ZOOM—15X to 60X variable power. 60mm objective. Field at 1000 yds. 150 ft. (15X) to 37½ feet (60X). Relative brightness 16 (15X) to 1 (60X). Wgt., 48 oz., 16^{11}/$_{16}$" overall. Integral tripod lug. Straight eyepiece **$159.95**

 With 45° eyepiece **169.95**

BAUSCH & LOMB BALSCOPE 20—40mm objective. 20X. Field at 100 yds., 7.5 ft. 15^3/$_8$" over-all, Wgt., 22 oz. **$29.95**

BAUSCH & LOMB BALSCOPE 10—30mm objective. 10X. Field at 100 yds. 7.5 ft. 10¼" over-all, weight, 9 oz. **$9.95**

BUSHNELL SPACEMASTER—60mm objective, 25X. Field at 100 yds., 10.5 ft. Relative brightness, 5.76. Wgt., 39 oz. Length closed, 15¼". Prism focusing, sliding sunshade **$95.00**

 15X, 20X, 25X, 40X and 60X eyepieces, each **22.50**
 20X wide angle eyepiece **27.50**

BUSHNELL SPACEMASTER 45°—Same as above except: Wgt., 43 oz., length closed 16¼". Eyepiece at 45°.. **$99.50**

BUSHNELL SPACEMASTER II—20X-45X zoom. 60mm objective. Field at 100 yards 12-7.2 ft. Relative brightness 9-1.7.Wgt.,oz.,36 length 11^5/$_8$" **$109.00**

BUSHNELL SENTRY II—20X. 50mm objective. Field at 100 yards 12 ft. Relative brightness 6.25 .... **$54.50**

 Also 32X and 48X eyepieces, each............................. **19.50**

BUSHNELL ZOOM SPOTTER—40mm objective. 9X-30X var. power **$29.50**

HUTSON CHROMATAR 60—63.4mm objective. 22.5X eyepiece at 45°. Wgt. 24 oz. 8" over-all. 10^1/$_2$" foot field at 100 yards.................. **$109.00**

 15X or 45X eyepieces, each................................... **22.00**

HY-SCORE MODEL 460—60mm objective. 15X, 20X, 25X, 40X and 60X eyepieces included. Field at 100 yds. 15.8 to 3.2 ft. Length closed 11". Wgt., 35 oz. With tripod and case.. **$182.00**

PACIFIC ZOOM—60mm objective, 15X to 50X variable. Field at 100 yds., 7½-3½ ft. Aluminum body. With adj. tripod **$94.50**

PACIFIC 15x60—60mm objective, 5 eyepieces (15X, 20X, 30X, 40X, 50X), adj. tripod. 100-yd. field, 12-3¼ ft.................................. **$89.50**

PRECISE IMPORTS, T-15—60mm objective, 15X to 30X zoom scope. About 15" long, weighs approximately 6 lbs. with adj. tripod. **$49.95**

PRECISE IMPORTS, T-19—60mm objective, interchangeable eyepieces of 15X, 20X, 30X, 40X, 60X. Sliding sunshade. Weighs about 6 lbs. with adj. tripod. **$69.95**

REDFIELD FIFTEEN-SIXTY—15X-60X zoom. 60mm objective. Field at 100 yards 15.6-3.7 ft. Relative brightness 16-1. Wgt. 48 oz., length 16¾" **$149.50**

 Tripod stand **27.50**
 Carrying case.. **29.95**

SATURN RANGER—60mm objective. 20X. Field at 100 yds., 10.4 ft. Relative brightness, 9. Eye relief, ^{9}/$_{16}$". Wgt., 33 oz. Length closed, 15^5/$_{16}$". Spiral adjustment of eyepiece. Chilford Arms **$54.50**

SATURN SCOUT—44mm objective. 20X. Field at 100 yds., 6.7 ft. Relative brightness, 4.84. Eye relief, ½". Wgt., 23 oz. Length closed, 13". Draw tube plus spiral focusing. Chilford Arms **$29.50**

SOUTHERN PRECISION MODEL 549—60mm objective and 5 eyepieces from 15X to 60X; extensible sunshade and folding tripod. Closed, 14¾", Wgt., 4¼ lbs... **$79.50**

SOUTHERN PRECISION MODEL 550—60mm objective and 4 turret-mounted eyepieces from 20X to 60X; ext. sunshade and folding tripod. Closed, 16¼", wgt., 5½ lbs. with tripod (included) **$75.00**

SOUTHERN PRECISION ZOOM MODEL 547—60mm objective, 25X to 50X; ext. sunshade folding tripod. Closed, 18", wgt. 4½ lbs. with tripod (included) **$69.50**

SOUTHERN PRECISION MODEL 546—50mm objective, 25X. Folding tripod, leather case included. Closed, 13", wgt. 3 lbs.................. **$27.00**

SWIFT TELEMASTER M841—60mm objective. 15X to 60X variable power. Field at 1000 yards 160 feet (15X) to 40 feet (60X). Wgt. 3.4 lbs. 17.6" over-all **$135.00**

 Tripod for above.. **30.50**
 Photo adapter **10.95**
 Case for above... **23.00**

SWIFT MODEL 821—60mm objective. 15X, 20X, 30X, 40X and 60X eyepieces included. Field at 100 yds., 158 to 32 ft. 18" tripod with friction clutch adj. handle. Length 13½" (without sunshade). 6 lbs........... **$96.00**

SWIFT MODEL 822—40mm objective. 20X eyepiece, tripod adapter, sunshade and dust cap. Length closed 10". Wgt. 27 oz. **$46.50**

TASCO 8TOZ—60mm objective. 20X to 60X variable power. Field at 1000 yards 158 feet (16X) to 40 feet (50X). Wgt. 4½ lbs. 18" overall ... **$79.95**

UNERTL RIGHT ANGLE—63.5mm objective. 24X. Field at 100 yds., 7 ft. Relative brightness, 6.96. Eye relief, ½". Wgt., 41 oz. Length closed, 19". Push-pull and screw-focus eyepiece. 16X and 32X eyepieces $18 each. **$110.00**

UNERTL STRAIGHT PRISMATIC—Same as Unertl Right Angle except: straight eyepiece and wgt. of 40 oz. **$92.00**

UNERTL 20X STRAIGHT PRISMATIC—54mm objective. 20X. Field at 100 yds., 8.5 ft. Relative brightness, 6.1. Eye relief, ½". Wgt., 36 oz. Length closed, 13½". Complete with lens covers **$74.00**

UNERTL TEAM SCOPE—100mm objective. 15X, 24X, 32X eyepieces. Field at 100 yds. 13 to 7.5 ft. Relative brightness, 39.06 to 9.79. Eye relief, 2" to 1½". Weight, 13 lbs. 29⅞" overall. Metal tripod, yoke and wood carrying case furnished (total weight, 80 lbs.) **$450.00**

WEATHERBY—60mm objective, 20X-45X zoom **$99.50**

 With fixed power eyepiece..................................... **85.00**
 Tripod for above.. **14.95**

SCOPE ATTACHMENTS

DAVIS TARGETEER—Objective lens/tube units that attach to front of low power scopes, increase magnification to 8X. 1¼" lens, **$25**, 1½" lens**$29.50**

HERMANN DUST CAPS—Connected leather straps, hand made, natural color. For all popular scopes..................................... **$4.00**

LEE TACKHOLE DOTS—Various size dots for all scopes. Price**$7.50—** **$15.00**

LYMAN HAZE FILTER—For morning and late afternoon hunting. Filters out blue and violet rays allowing only the best part of the spectrum to transmit through your telescope lenses. For all reflescopes **$2.75**

PGS SCOPE SHIELDS—Flexible rubber, usable at front and rear, protect scopes from snow or rain. Made for all scopes...................... **$3.95**

PREMIER RETICLES—Various size dots for all scopes, also special reticles to order. Price—**$7.00** to **$18.50. PREMIER WEATHER CAPS**— transparent, high light transmission. For all popular scopes. Price **$3.50** Special sizes**$5.00**

RING MOUNTS—Custom made for German-type claw bases. Don's Gun Shop.

STORM KING LENS CAPS—A hinged glass-and-rubber protector set (2), made in various sizes for all scopes. May be unhinged or sighted through. Anderson Gun Shop. Per pair.. **$3.45**

VISS'S SUPREME LENS COVERS—Hinged protectors for most scope models, front and rear lenses shielded. E. D. Vissing Co. Per pair, postpaid.**$4.95**

SPOTTING SCOPE STANDS

DAVIDSON MARK 245—Bipod adjustable for elevation, 9½"-14½". Side mount with two straps. Black crinkle finish. Length folded 16½". Price **$23.95**

FREELAND ALL ANGLE—Tripod adjustable for elevation. Left or right side mount with worm drive clamp. Folding legs. Clamps available for any scope tube size. Black, gray, or green crinkle finish. Price.............. **$22.75**

 Also 12" 18", 24" extensions available.................... **$3.00-5.00**

FREELAND OLYMPIC—Bipod adjustable for elevation. All angle mount with padded worm drive clamp. Folding legs. Clamps available for any scope tube size. Black, grey, or green crinkle finish. Price **$24.75**

 Also 12", 18", 24" extensions available.................... **$3.00-5.00**
 Zoom head for tripod or bipod............................... **$11.00**

FREELAND REGAL BIPOD—Choice of saddle or zoom head. All adjustment knobs are oversize for easy adjusting. Large "ball" carrying knob. Gray or green finish. **$26.75**

 Above with stability weight.................................... **34.25**
 Extensions 12"-24" **$3.00-5.00**

ARMS ASSOCIATIONS IN AMERICA AND ABROAD

Alabama Gun Collectors Assn.
Mrs. T. M. Stewart, 601 Eastwood Pl.,
Birmingham, Ala. 35216

Alamo Arms Collectors
Bill Brookshire, 410 Rector,
San Antonio, Tex. 78216

Amateur Trap Shooting Assn.
P.O. Box 246, Vandalia, O. 45377

American Military Inst.
Box 568, Washington, D.C. 20044

American Ordnance Assn.
819 Union Trust Bldg.,
Washington, D.C. 20005

American Reloaders Assn.
Dean Grennell, Box 4007, Covina, Calif. 91722

American Single Shot Rifle Assn.
G. H. Crontz, 11439 Wicker Ave.,
Cedar Lake, Ind. 46303

American Society of Arms Collectors, Inc.
Rob. F. Rubendunst, 6550 Baywood Ln.,
Cincinnati, O. 45224

Antique Arms Coll. Assn. of Conn.
A. Darling, 35 Stanley St.,
New Haven, Conn. 06511

Arapahoe Gun Collectors
Bill Rutherford, 2968 S. Broadway,
Englewood, Colo. 80110

Arizona Gun Collectors
Miles S. Vaughn, 1129 S. 6th Ave.,
Tucson, Ariz. 85701

Arkansas Gun & Cartridge Coll. Club
M. Cutrell, 2006 E. 7th, Pine Bluff, Ark. 71601

Ark-La-Tex Gun Collectors Assn.
Ray Franks, 1521 Earl St., Shreveport, La. 71108

Armor & Arms Club
J. K. Watson, 51 W. 51st St.,
New York, N.Y. 10019

Arms Collectors of the Southwest
Robert Kuban, Box 543, Yuma, Ariz. 85364

Arms and Armour Society of London
F. Wilkinson, 40 Great James St.,
Holborn, London, W.C.I.

Barberton Gun Collectors Assn.
R. N. Watters, 1108 Bevan St., Barberton, O. 44203

Bay Colony Weapons Collectors
Ronald B. Santurjian, 47 Homer Rd., Belmont, Mass.
02178

Bayou Gun Club
John West, 825 Ida, New Orleans, La.

Belton Gun Club Inc.
J. K. Phillips, P.O. Box 605, Belton S.C. 29627

Boone & Crockett Club
C/O Carnegie Museum, 4400 Forbes Ave., Pittsburgh, Pa. 15213

Calif. Hunters & Gun Owners Assoc.
V. H. Wacker, 2309 Cipriani Blvd., Belmont, Cal.
94002

Canadian Historical Arms Society
P.O. Box 901,
Edmonton, Alb., Canada

Carolina Gun Collectors Assn.
N. C. Bill Harvey, P.O. Box 464,
Wilson, N.C. 27893

Cedar Valley Gun Coll.
R. L. Harris, 1602 Wenig Rd., N.E.,
Cedar Rapids, Iowa 52402

Central Illinois Gun Collectors Assn., Inc.
Donald E. Bryan, R.R. #2,
Jacksonville, Ill. 62650

Central Indiana Gun Coll. Assn.
Paul E. Daughterty, 421 E. Washington St.,
Hartford City, Ind. 47348

Central Ohio Gun and Indian Relic Coll. Assn.
Coyt Stookey, 134 E. Ohio Ave.
Washington C.H., O. 43160

Central Penn Antique Arms Assn.
Geo. Smithgall, 549 W. Lemon St.,
Lancaster, Pa. 17603

Central States Gun Collectors Assn.
Chas. J. Versluis, 701 Broadway,
Watterloo, Ia. 50703

Chippewa Valley Weapons Collectors
J. M. Sullivan, 504 Ferry St.,
Eau Claire, Wis. 54701

Chisholm Trail Antique Gun Coll. Assn.
P.O. Box 13093, Wichita, Kans. 67213

Colorado Gun Collectors Assn.
Larry Jones, 1348 So. Yates, Denver, Colo. 80219

Crawfordsville Gun Club, Inc.
Rob. J. K. Edmonds, R.R. 2,
Crawfordsville, Ind. 47933

Cumberland Valley Arms Collectors Assn.
Mrs. S. Naylor, Rte. #2, Hagerstown, Md. 21740

Dakota Territory Gun Coll. Assn., Inc.
H. A. Jons, 1711 W. 12th St., Sioux Falls, So. Dak.
57104

Dallas Gun Collectors Assn.
D. Jackson, 8603 Angora, Dallas, Tex. 75218

Delaware Antique Arms Collectors
C. Landis, 2408 Duncan Rd.,
Wilmington, Del. 19808

Dixie Arms Collectors
Ruth Creecy, 1509 W. 7th,
Hattiesburg, Miss. 39401

Eastern Iowa Gun and Cartridge Collectors Assn.
F. Fitzpatrick, 305 N. Eliza St.,
Maquoketa, Ia. 52060

Edwardsville, Ill. Gun Collectors
A. W. Stephensmeier, 317 N. Grand Bl.,
St. Louis, Mo. 63103

Experimental Ballistics Associates
Ed Yard, 110 Kensington, Trenton, N. J. 08608

Florida Gun Collectors Assn.
Bob Marvin, P.O. Box 470, Jasper, Fla. 32052

Forks of the Delaware Weapons Assn.
John F. Scheid, 348 Bushkill St.,
Easton, Pa. 18042

Fort Dearborn Frontiersmen
Art Pardi, 434 W. Hickory, Lombard, Ill. 60148

Fort Lee Arms Collectors
W. E. Sammis, R.D. 776 Brookridge Dr.,
Valley Cottage, N. Y. 10989

Ft. Smith Dealers & Coll. Assn.
Tony Smith, 2317 No. 53, Ft. Smith, Ark. 72901

Fox Valley Arms Fellowship, Inc.
Graham Burnside, 203 Oregon Ave.,
Dundee, Ill. 60118

Four State Collectors Assn.
M. G. Wilkinson, 915 E. 10th,
Pittsburgh, Kan. 66762

Georgia Arms Collectors
James F. Watterson, 2915 Paces Lake
Ct., N.W., Atlanta, Ga. 30339

Great Lakes Weapons Coll. Assn., Inc.
E. Warnke, 7207 So. 36th St.,
Franklin, Wis. 53132

Greater Calif. Arms & Collectors Assn.
Donald L. Bullock, 8291 Carburton St.,
Long Beach, Cal. 90808

Historical Firearms Soc. of South Africa
"Minden" 11 Buchan Rd., Newlands,
Cape Town, South Africa

Houston Gun Collectors Assn.
C. McKim, 5454 Stillbrooke, Houston, Tex. 77035

Hudson-Mohawk Arms Collectors Assn., Inc.
Bennie S. Pisarz, R.D. 2, Ilion, N.Y. 13357

Illinois Gun Collectors Assn.
P. E. Pitts, P.O. Box 1524, Chicago, Ill. 60690

Illinois State Rifle Assn.
2800 N. Milwaukee Ave., Chicago, Ill. 60618

Indian Territory Gun Collectors Assn.
Joe Wanenmacher, Jr., P.O. Box 4491,
Tulsa, Okla. 74104

International Benchrest Shooters
Emory L. Tooly, 8 Cline St.,
Dolgeville, N.Y. 13329

International Cartridge Coll. Assn., Inc.
A. D. Amesbury, 4065 Montecito Ave.,
Tucson, Ariz. 85711

Iroquois Arms Collectors Assn.
Dennis Freeman, 12144 McNeeley Rd.,
Akron, N. Y. 14001

Jefferson State Arms Collectors
Art Chipman, 2251 Ross Lane,
Medford, Ore. 97501

Jersey Shore Antique Arms Collectors
Bob Holloway, 1755 McGallard Ave.,
Trenton, N. J. 08610

John Hunt Morgan Gun Coll. Assn.
P.O. Box 525, Paris, Ky. 40361

Kentuckiana Arms Coll. Assn.
Charles R. Phelps, Box 1776, Louisville, Ky. 40201

Kansas Cartridge Coll. Assn.
Bob Linder, Box 84, Plainville, Kans. 67663

Kentucky Gun Collectors Assn., Inc.
J. A. Smith, Box 64, Owensboro, Ky. 42301

Lakeshore Gun Collectors
R. N. Watters, 1108 Bevan St.,
Barberton, Ohio 44203

Lancaster Muzzle Loading Rifle Assn.
James H. Frederick, Jr., R.D. 1, Box 447,
Columbia, Pa. 17512

Les Arquebusiers de France,
Mme. Marckmann, 70 Rue des Chantiers,
78-Versailles, France

Little Fort Gun Collectors Assn.
Ernie Robinson, P.O. Box 194, Gurney, Ill. 60031

Long Island Antique Gun Coll. Assn.
Frank Davison, 8 Johnson Pl.,
Baldwin, N.Y. 11510

Los Angeles Gun & Ctg. Collectors Assn.
F. H. Ruffra, 20810 Amie Ave., Torrance, CA 90503

Lower Canada Arms Collectors Assn.
Secretary, P.O. Box 1162, St. B. Montreal 101,
Quebec, Can.

Maple Tree Gun Coll. Assn.
E. P. Hector, Meriden Rd., Lebanon, N.H. 03766

Maryland Arms Coll. Assn., Inc.
H. R. Moale, 2602 Hillcrest Ave.,
Baltimore, Md. 21234

Massachusetts Arms Collectors
John J. Callan, Jr., 15 Montague St.,
Worcester, Mass. 01603

Maumee Valley Gun Collectors Assn.
J. Jennings, 3450 Gallatin Rd., Toledo, O. 43606

Memphis Antique Weapons Assn.
F. Dauser, 3429 Jenkins, Memphis, Tenn. 38118

Memphis Gun Collectors Assn.
T. C. Lee, Jr., 166 Picardy Pl.,
Memphis, Tenn. 38111

Meramec Valley Gun Collectors
L. W. Olson, Star Route, St. Clair, Mo.

Michigan Antique Arms Coll., Inc.
W. H. Heid, 8914 Borgman Ave.,
Huntington Woods, Mich. 48070

Michigan Rifle & Pistol Assn.
John W. Novitch, 124 Moss Ave.,
Highland Park, Mich. 48203

Mid-State Arms Coll. & Shooters Club
108 W. Main St., Frankfort, N.Y. 13340

Midwest Gun Collectors Assn.
Jim VanEvery, 10924 Fisher Rd.,
Ft. Wayne, Ind. 46808

Mineral Belt Gun Coll. Assn.
G. W. Gunter, 1110 E. Cleveland Ave.,
Monett, Mo. 65708

Minnesota Weapons Coll. Assn., Inc.
W. Nemitz, 1069 S. Crestview Dr.,
Minneapolis, Minn. 55119

Mississippi Gun Collectors Assn.
Mrs. J. E. Swinney, Box 1332,
Hattiesburg, Miss. 39401

Mississippi Valley Gun & Cartridge Coll. Assn.
Mel Sims, Box 426, New Windsor, Ill. 61465

Missouri Valley Arms Collectors
Box 8204, Shawnee Mission, Kans. 66208

Montana Arms Collectors Assn.
Chris Sorensen, 175 6th Ave., W.N.
Kalispell, Mont. 59901

Muzzle Loaders' Assn. of Great Britain
M. A. Malet, 43 Sandpit Lane, St. Albans, Hertfs, England

Natl. Arms Coll. Assn., Inc.
Jim McNelley, Box 1462, Columbia, S.C. 29201

National Bench Rest Shooters Assn., Inc.
Bernice McMullen, 607 W. Line St.,
Minerva, O. 44657

National Muzzle Loading Rifle Assn.
Box 67, Friendship, Ind. 47021

National Police Officers Assn. of America
Natl. Police Hall of Fame Bldg.,
Venice, Fla. 33595

National Reloading Mfrs. Assn., Inc.
Jim Carmichel, Box 1697, Prescott, Ariz. 86301

National Rifle Assn.
1600 Rhode Island Ave., Washington, D.C. 20036

National Rifle Assn. (British)
Bisley Camp, Brookwood, Woking, Surrey, England

National Shooting Sports Fdtn., Inc.
Charles Dickey, 1075 Post Rd.,
Riverside, Conn. 06878

National Skeet Shooting Assn.
James M. Leer, Jr., 212 Linwood Bldg.,
2608 Inwood Rd., Dallas, Tex. 75235

National Sportsman's Club
P.O. Box 2003, Dallas, Tex. 75221

Nebraska Gun & Cartridge Collectors Assn.
E. M. Zalud, 710 West 6th St.,
North Platte, Neb. 69101

New Hampshire Arms Collectors Inc.
James Tillinghast, Box 5, Marlow, N. H. 03456

New Jersey Arms Collectors Club, Inc.
Joseph Rixon, 122 Bender Ave., Roselle Park, N.J.
07204

New Mexico Gun Collectors Assn.
Leroy Walton, P.O. Box 175, Tijeras, N.M. 80759

New York State Arms Collectors Assn., Inc.
Marvin Salls, R. D. 1, Ilion, N. Y. 13357

New Zealand Deerstalkers Assn.
J. M. Murphy, P.O. Box 263,
Wellington, New Zealand

Niagara Arms Collectors
Box 948, Beamsville, Ont. Canada

North Alabama Gun Coll. Assn.
Maj. Richard Keogh, P.O. Box 564,
Huntsville, Ala. 35804

North American Sportsmen's Assn.
Box 1943—2501 4th Ave. N., Billings, Mont. 59103

Northern California Historical Arms Coll. Assn.
John L. Moss, 156 Mirada Dr.,
Daly City, Ca. 94015

Northern Indiana Gun Collectors Assn.
Joe Katona, 16150 Ireland Rd.,
Mishawaka, Ind. 46544

Northern Tier Antique Gun Collectors
Cliff Breidinger, Trout Run, Pa. 17771

North-South Skirmish Assn.
John L. Rawls, P.O. Box 114,
McLean, Va. 22101

Ohio Gun Collectors, Assn., Inc.
Mrs. C. D. Rickey, 130 S. Main St.,
Prospect, O. 43342

Ontario Arms Collectors Assn.
P. Peddle, 174 Ellerslie Ave.,
Willowdale, Ont., Canada

Oregon Arms Coll. Assn. Inc.
Dan Scherlie, 2600 S.W. Roxbury, Portland, Ore.
97225

Oshawa Antique Arms Guild
Frank Folkmann, 296 Grenfell St., Apt. 38,
Oshawa, Ont., Canada

Paso Del Norte Gun Collectors Inc.
Ken Hockett, 1216 Mescalero,
El Paso, Tex. 79925

Patch & Ball Gun Collectors
J. Falerias, 1417 Raspberry Ln., Flint, Mich. 48507

Pelican Arms Collectors
B. Thompson, 9142 Cefalu Dr.,
Baton Rouge, La. 70811

U.S. Priming Device

The set of tools pictured here are contained in a brown-painted box 11"x11"x4⅛", including the hinged lid. Inside the lid, done in white chalk, is "9th N.Y." There is nothing in the screwed-on "compartment" attached to the lid; it's only a means of holding down the heavy steel unit shown. There is no identification anywhere on the outside of the box. Weight complete is 11 lbs.

The big steel piece reads, in semi-circle at top, "BUSHING FOR DRILL PRIMER OUTFIT." Below that, in 3 lines, the metal is stamped "3 C/FRANKFORD ARSENAL/G.F.J.—1911."

In the left row, at front, are 3 brass pin-holders, these taking the steel pins shown behind the charge cups seen up front, right of center. Behind the pin-holders are 3 two-diameter brass rods just under 2" long, these cross-slotted at the small ends. Next to these, at the rear, are two steel half-flute taps, very finely threaded.

In the second row, front, there's a steel 2-diameter pin, 1¹³⁄₁₆" long including the wider head. The stem diameter is about ⁵⁄₁₆". Behind this is a taper-bored steel cylinder 2³⁄₁₆" over-all, marked "DIE" on top and "F.A./3.A." on its side. In front of the big steel unit is another holed and headed steel cylinder, ⅞" long, 1" plus at its widest, and ¹¹⁄₁₆" across the smaller section.

The cylindrical hole is about ½" in diameter. Two small holes in the wide flange, and 2 others in the narrower section.

The brass charge cups mentioned have the same capacity, and the 3 small brass funnels are alike. The last items are 3 steel 5-flute reamers, of 2 diameters, and each with a slightly different size half-flute cutter at the end. These cutters, held in place by a set screw, are replaceable and adjustable.

Our best guess is that this set of tools was used by an artillery company or other unit. How many of our readers know what it is? No, no cash prizes or a free car, but we'll announce the names of the knowledgeable.

●

Shooting Publications

Write directly to the sources noted for titles listed and ask for their latest catalog. Do not order from the GUN DIGEST.

A Joint Resolution—A 4-page statement by the National Police Officers Assn. and the National Shooting Sports Foundation, outlining the role of firearms in U.S. history and voicing their stand against ill-planned restrictive gun laws. Free.[1]

Basic Pistol Marksmanship—Textbook for basic pistol courses. 25¢[2]

Basic Rifle Marksmanship—Textbook for basic rifle courses. 25¢ ea.[2]

The Elk—125-page report on the hunting and management of this game animal, more properly called *wapiti*. Extensive biblio. $1.00.[4]

Free Films—Brochure listing outdoor movies available to sportsmen's clubs. Free.[1]

The Gun Law Problem—Information about firearms legislation. Free.[2]

How to be a Crack Shot—A 14-page booklet detailing everything necessary to becoming an outstanding shot. Free.[3]

Fundamentals of Claybird Shooting—A 39-page booklet explaining the basics of Skeet and trap in non-technical terms. Many diagrams. 25¢ ea.[4]

Hunter Safety Instructor's Guide—How to conduct an NRA Hunter Safety Course. 25¢ ea.[2]

Hunting and Shooting Sportsmanship—A 4-page brochure defining the "true sportsman" and giving information on the outdoor field. Free.[1]

Junior Rifle Handbook—Information about the NRA junior program with short instruction course. (25 copies issued to each new affiliated junior club without charge.) 25¢ ea.[2]

NRA Hunter Safety Handbook—Textbook for students. 10¢ ea.[2]

National Shooting Preserve Directory—Up-to-date listing of small game preserves in the U.S. and Canada. Free.[1]

Game, Gunners and Biology—A thumbnail history of American wildlife conservation. 50¢ ea.[4]

Shooting's Fun for Everyone—The why, when, where, and how of riflery for boys and girls. 20 pp. 5¢ ea.[1]

Trap or Skeet Fundamentals—Handbooks explaining fundamentals of these two sports, complete with explicit diagrams to start beginners off right. Free.[3]

25 Foot Shooting Program—Complete information on a short range shooting program with CO_2 and pneumatic rifles and pistols. 35¢[2]

What Every Parent Should Know When a Boy or Girl Wants a Gun—Straightforward answers to the 15 questions most frequently asked by parents. 8 pp. 5¢ ea.[1]

The Cottontail Rabbit—56-page rundown on America's most popular hunting target. Where to find him, how to hunt him, how to help him. Bibliography included. $1.00 ea.[4]

For the Young Hunter—A 32-page booklet giving fundamental information on the sport. Single copies free, 15¢ each in bulk.[4]

Gray and Fox Squirrels—112-page paperbound illustrated book giving full rundown on the squirrel families named. Extensive bibliography. $1.00 ea.[4]

How to Have More Pheasant Hunting—A 16-page booklet on low cost hunting, including data on in-season stocking and how to start a small preserve. 25¢.[1]

The Mallard—80-page semi-technical report on this popular duck. Life cycle, laws and management, hunting—even politics as they affect this bird—are covered. Bibliography. $1.00 ea.[4]

NRA Booklets—Ranging from 12 to 36 pages, these are articles on specific arms or arms types. Titles available are: Sighting In; The 45 Automatic; The M1 Rifle; Telescopic Sights; Metallic Sights; Duck Hunting; U.S. Cal. 30 Carbine; Remodeling the 03A3; Remodeling the 303 Lee-Enfield; Remodeling the U.S. 1917 Rifle; M1903 Springfield Rifle; Military Rifles and Civil War Small Arms, 50¢ ea. Gun Cabinets, Racks, Cases & Pistol Boxes, 75¢. Deer Hunting, $1.00.[2]

Under the heading of "Range Plans" are 15 booklets priced from 10¢ to $1.00. All are described in an order form pamphlet available from the NRA.

NRA Digest of the Federal Gun Control Act of 1968—A 12-page booklet clearly explaining the new law and its provisions. Free to NRA members.[2]

NRA Federal Firearms Laws—A 28-page booklet digesting the several U.S. gun laws affecting the citizen today. Free to NRA members.[2]

NRA Firearms & Ammunition Fact Book—352-page book of questions and answers, ballistic charts and tables, descriptions of firearms and ammunition. NRA, Washington, D.C., 1964. $2.00 ea. ($1.75 to NRA members).

NRA Firearms Assembly Handbook, Volumes I and II—Articles describing the assembly and disassembly of various arms. Vol. I, 160 pp., covers 77 guns, Vol. II, 176 pp., 87 guns. Illustrated with exploded-view and supplementary drawings. NRA, Washington, D.C., 1960 and 1964. $3.50 ea. (2.50 to NRA members).

NRA Firearms Handling Handbook—21 major articles on the proper useage of most types of small arms available to civilians. Illus. NRA, Washington, D.C., 1962, 80 pp. $2.75 ($1.75 to NRA members).

NRA Gun Collectors Handbook—20 feature articles on all phases of gun collecting, plus a listing of all important museums. NRA, Washington, D.C., 1959. 48 pp., illus. $2.50 ($1.50 to NRA members).

NRA Handloader's Guide—Enlarged & Revised. A successor to the *NRA Illustrated Reloading Handbook*, this excellent new work covers all aspects of metallic-case and shotshell reloading. Washington, D. C., 1969, fully illus. $5.00 (NRA members, $4.00).

NRA Hunters Handbook—51 major pieces, 18 shorter ones. NRA, Washington, D.C., 1960. 72 pp., illus. $3.00 ($2.00 to NRA members).

NRA Illustrated International Shooting Handbook—18 major articles detailing shooting under ISU rules, training methods, etc. NRA, Washington, D.C., 1964. $2.50 ea. ($1.50 to NRA members).

NRA Illustrated Shotgun Handbook—50 articles covering every phase of smoothbore shooting, including exploded views of many shotguns. NRA, Washington, D.C. 1964. 128 pp. $3.00 ea. ($2.00 to NRA members).

NRA Questions and Answers Handbook—150 queries and replies on guns and shooting. NRA, Washington, D.C., 1959. 46 pp. with index, illus. $2.50 ($1.50 to NRA members).

NRA Shooters Guide—40 articles of high interest to shooters of all kinds. Over 340 illus. NRA, Washington, D.C., 1959. 72 pp., $3.00 ($2.00 to NRA members).

NRA Shooting Handbook—83 major articles plus 35 shorts on every phase of shooting. NRA, Washington, D.C., 1961. 224 pp., illus. $4.50 ($3.50 to NRA members).

Principles of Game Management—A 25-page booklet surveying in popular manner such subjects as hunting regulations, predator control, game refuges and habitat restoration. Single copies free, 15¢ each in bulk.[4]

The Ring-Necked Pheasant—Popular distillation of much of the technical literature on the "ringneck." 104-page paperbound book, appropriately illustrated. Bibliography included. $1.00 ea.[4]

Ruffed Grouse, by John Madson—108-page booklet on the life history, management and hunting of *Bonasa umbellus* in its numerous variations. Extensive biblio. $1.00.[4]

Start A Gun Club—All of the basic information needed to establish a club with clay bird shooting facilities. 24 pp. 50¢[1]

Where To Shoot Muzzle Loaders In The U.S.A.—Publ. for black powder burners, and lists more than 100 muzzle loading clubs. 10¢.[1]

The White-Tailed Deer—History, management, hunting—a complete survey in this 108-page paperbound book. Full bibliography. $1.00 ea.[4]

You and Your Lawmaker—A 22-page citizenship manual for sportsmen, showing how they can support or combat legislation affecting shooting and outdoor sports. 10¢ ea.[1]

[2]National Rifle Association of America, 1600 Rhode Island Ave., Washington, D. C. 20036

[3]Remington Arms Company, Dept. C—Bridgeport, Conn. 06602

[4]Olin Mathieson Conservation Dept., East Alton, Ill. 62024

[1]National Shooting Sports Foundation, Inc. 1075 Post Road, Riverside, Conn. 06878

Publishers: Please send review copies to John T. Amber,
20604 Collins Rd., Marengo, Ill. 60152

PERIODICAL PUBLICATIONS

Alaska Sportsman
Alaska Northwest Pub. Co., Box 4-EEE, Anchorage, Alaska 99503. $8.00 yr. Hunting and fishing articles.

American Field†
222 W. Adams St., Chicago, Ill. 60606. $9.00 yr. Field dogs and trials, occasional gun and hunting articles.

The American Rifleman (M)
National Rifle Assn., 1600 Rhode Island Ave., N.W., Wash., D.C. 20036. $7.50 yr. Firearms articles of all kinds.

The American West*
American West Publ. Co., 599 College Ave., Palo Alto, Ca. 94306. $9.00 yr.

Argosy
Popular Publ., Inc., 205 E. 42nd St., New York, N.Y. 10017. $7.00 yr.

Army (M)
Assn of the U.S. Army, 1529 18th Ave. N.W., Wash., D.C. 20036. $6.00 yr. Occasional articles on small arms

Australian Shooters' Journal
P.O. Box 90, Stafford, Qld., Brisbane 4053, Australia. Hunting and shooting articles.

Canadian Journal of Arms Collecting (Q)
Museums Restoration Service P.O. Box 2037, Sta. D, Ottawa, Ont., Canada. $4.00 yr.

Deutsches Waffen Journal
Journal-Verlag Schwend GmbH, Postfach 340, Schwabisch Hall, Germany. $10.50 yr. Antique and modern arms, their history, technical aspects, etc. German text.

Ducks Unlimited, Inc. (M)
P.O. Box 66300, Chicago, Ill. 60666.

Enforcement Journal*
Natl. Police Officers Assn., Natl. Police Academy Bldg., 1890 S. Tamiami Trail, Venice, Fla. 33595. $12.00 yr.

The Field†
The Harmsworth Press Ltd., 8 Stratton St., London W.I., England. $27.00 yr. Hunting and shooting articles.

Field & Stream
Holt, Rinehart and Winston, Inc., 383 Madison Ave., New York, N.Y. 10017. $5.00 yr. Articles on firearms plus hunting and fishing.

Fishing and Hunting Guide
Fishing and Hunting Guide Ltd., P.O. Box 48, Dolton, Ill. 60419. $3.00 yr.

Fur-Fish-Game
A. R. Harding Pub. Co., 2878 E. Main St., Columbus, Ohio 43209. $3.50 yr. "Gun Rack" column by M. H. Decker.

Gunfacts Magazine
Hazard Publications, Inc., Box 9335, Arlington, Va. 22209. $6.00 yr (8 issues, mo./bi-mo.)

The Gun Report
World Wide Gun Report, Inc., Box 111, Aledo, Ill. 61231. $6.00 yr. For the gun collector.

Gun Sport
Gun Sport Magazine Inc., Box 116, Hughesville, Md. 20637. $5.00 yr.

Gun Week†
Sidney Printing & Publishing Co., P.O. Box 150, Sidney, Ohio 45365. $5.00 yr. U.S. and possessions; $6.00 yr. Canada; $7.00 yr. foreign. Tabloid paper on guns, hunting, shooting.

Gun World
Gallant Publishing Co., 130 Olinda Pl., Brea, Calif. 92621. $5.00 yr. For the hunting, reloading and shooting enthusiast.

Guns & Ammo
Petersen Pub. Co., 8490 Sunset Blvd., Los Angeles, Calif. 90069. $5.00 yr. Guns, shooting, and technical articles.

Guns
Guns Magazine, 8150 N. Central Park Ave., Skokie, Ill. 60076. $7.50 yr. Articles for gun collectors, hunters and shooters.

Guns Plus Hunting*
M.F. Enterprises, Inc., 222 Park Ave. So., New York, N.Y. 10003. $4.50 yr.

Guns Review
Ravenhill Pub. Co. Ltd., Standard House, Bonhill St., London E.C. 2, England. $6.50 yr. For collectors and shooters.

The Handgunner (M)
U.S. Revolver Assn., 59 Alvin St., Springfield, Mass. 01104. $5.00 yr. General handgun and competition articles.

The Handloader Magazine*
Dave Wolfe Pub. Co., Box 3030, Prescott, Ariz. 86301 $7.00 yr.

Hobbies
Lightner Pub. Co., 1006 S. Michigan Ave., Chicago, Ill. 60605. $6.00 yr.; Canada $7.00; foreign $7.50. Collectors departments.

International Shooting Sport*
Union Internationale de Tir, 62 Wiesbaden-Klarenthal, Klarenthalerstr., Germany. $4.80 yr., p.p. For the International target shooter.

The Journal of the Arms & Armour Society (M)
F. Wilkinson (Secy.), 40 Great James St., Holborn, London WC1, England. $4.00 yr. Articles for the collector.

Law and Order
Law and Order Magazine, 37 W. 38th St., New York, N.Y. 10018. $4.00 yr. Articles on weapons for law enforcement.

The Luger Journal
Robt. B. Marvin, Publ., P.O. Box 12206, Plantation, Fla. 33314. $6.00 yr.

Muzzle Blasts (M)
National Muzzle Loading Rifle Assn.,P.O. Box 67, Friendship, Ind. 47021. $6.00 yr. For the black powder shooter.

National Rifle Assn. Journal (British)
Natl. Rifle Assn. (BR.), Bisley Camp, Brookwood, Woking, Surrey, England.

National Sportsman's Digest
National Sportsman's Club, Box 2003, Dallas, Tex. 75221. $8.00 yr. Subs. includes membership in the Club, etc.

National Wildlife*
Natl. Wildlife Fed. Inc., 1412-16th St. N.W., Washington, D.C. $11.00 yr. World/Assoc. membership.

New Zealand Wildlife (Q)
New Zealand Deerstalkers Assoc. Inc., P.O. Box 263, Wellington, N.Z. $2.00 U.S. and Canada, elsewhere on application. Hunting and shooting articles.

Ordnance* (M)
American Ordnance Assn., 819 Union Trust Bldg., Wash., D.C. 20005. $8.00 yr. $7.00 to members. Occasional articles on small arms and related subjects.

Outdoor Life
Popular Science Pub. Co., 355 Lexington Ave., New York, N.Y. 10017. $6.00 yr. Arms column by Jack O'Connor.

Outdoor World*
Country Beautiful Corp., 24198 W. Bluemound Rd., Waukesha, Wis. 53186. $7.95 yr. Conservation and wildlife articles.

Police
Charles C Thomas, publisher, 301-327 E. Lawrence Ave., Springfield, Ill. 62703. $11.50 yr. Articles on identification.

Police Times (M)
1100 N.E. 125th St., No. Miami, Fla. 33161.

Popular Guns*
Countrywide Publications, Inc., 222 Park Ave. So., New York, N.Y. 10003. $4.50 yr.

Popular Mechanics
Hearst Corp., 224 W. 57th St., New York, N.Y. 10019. $5.00 yr., $5.75 Canada, $7.00 foreign. Hunting and shooting articles.

Precision Shooting
Precision Shooting, Inc., 8 Cline St., Dolgeville, N.Y. 13329. $5.00 yr. Journal of the International Benchrest Shooters.

The Rifle Magazine*
Dave Wolfe Publishing Co., Box 3030, Presott, Ariz. 86301. $9.00 yr. Journal of the NBRSA.

The Rifleman (Q)
National Smallbore Rifle Assoc., 113 Southwark St., London, S. E. 1, Englnd. $7.00 (5 yrs.). Data on British Matches and International Matches, and technical shooting articles.

Rod and Gun in Canada
Rod and Gun Pub. Corp., 1219 Hotel deVille, Montreal 129, P.Q. Canada. $3.00 yr., $5.00 2 yrs., out of Canada, postage $1.00 p. yr. extra. Regular gun and shooting articles.

Saga
Gambi Public., 333 Johnson Ave., Brooklyn, N.Y. 11026. $6.00 yr. U.S., $6.50 Canada.

The Shooting Industry
Publisher's Dev. Corp., 8150 N. Central Pk., Skokie, Ill. 60076. $7.00 yr.

The Shooting Times (England)†
Cordwallis Estate, Clivemont Rd., Maidenhead, Berksh., England. $20 yr. Game shooting and firearms articles.

Shooting Times
Peoria Journal-Star, Inc., News Plaza, Peoria, Ill., 61601. $5.85 yr. Gun ads plus articles on every gun activity.

The Shotgun News‡
Snell Publishing Co., Columbus, Nebr. 68601. $3.00 yr. Sample copy 50¢. Gun ads of all kinds.

The Skeet Shooting Review
National Skeet Shooting Assn. 212 Linwood Bldg., 2608 Inwood Rd., Dallas. Tex. 75235. $9.00 yr. (Ass. membership of $10.00 includes mag.) Scores, averages, skeet articles.

Sporting Goods Business
7 E. 43rd, New York, N.Y. 10017. Trade journal.

The Sporting Goods Dealer
1212 No. Lindbergh Blvd., St. Louis, Mo. 63166. $4.00 yr. The sporting goods trade journal.

Sports Afield
The Hearst Corp., 250 W. 55th St., New York, N.Y. 10019. $5.00 yr. Pete Brown on firearms plus hunting and fishing articles.

Sports Age Magazine
Minneapolis, Minn. Trade journal.

Sports Illustrated†
Time, Inc., 540 N. Michigan Ave., Chicago, Ill. 60611. $9.00 yr. Articles on the current sporting scene.

Trap & Field
Review Pub. Co., 1100 Waterway Blvd., Indianapolis, Ind. 46202. $7.00 yr. Scores, averages, trapshooting articles.

True
Fawcett Publ., Inc., Fawcett Bldg., Greenwich, Conn. 06830. $6.00 yr. U.S. Poss., and Canada; $8.00 yr. all other countries.

Wildlife Review (Q)
Parliament Bldgs., Victoria B.C., Canada $1.00 yr.

---

* Published bi-monthly
† Published weekly
‡ Published twice per month

M Membership requirements; write for details.
Q Published Quarterly.

The Arms Library for
COLLECTOR · HUNTER · SHOOTER · OUTDOORSMAN

A selection of books—old, new and forthcoming—for everyone in the arms field, with a brief description by . . . RAY RILING

ballistics and handloading

Ballistics in the Seventeenth Century, by A. R. Hall. 1st J. & J. Harper ed. 1969 [from the Cambridge University Press ed. of 1952]. 186 pp., ilus., with tables and diagrams. $13.50.

A profound work for advanced scholars, this is a study in the relations of science and war, with reference principally to England.

The Bullet's Flight, from Powder to Target, by F. W. Mann. Ray Riling Arms Books Co., Phila., Pa. 1965. A reprint of the very scarce original work of 1909. Introduction by Homer S. Powley, 384 pp. ilus. $12.50.

One of the best known and scholarly-developed works on basic ballistics.

Cartridges of the World, by Frank C. Barnes, John T. Amber ed., Gun Digest Co., Chicago, Ill., 1969. 8½"x11", 378 pp. Profusely illus. Paperbound. $6.95.

The second edition of a comprehensive reference for hunters, collectors, handloaders and ballisticians. Covering over 1000 cartridges, loads, components, etc., from all over the world.

Centerfire American Rifle Cartridges, 1892-1963, by Ray Bearse, A. S. Barnes & Co., S. Brunswick, N.J., 1966. 198 pp., illus. $15.00.

Identification manual covering caliber, introduction date, origin, case type, etc. Self-indexed and cross-referenced. Headstamps and line drawings are included.

Centerfire Pistol and Revolver Cartridges, by H. P. White, B. D. Munhall and Ray Bearse. A. S. Barnes, N.Y., 1967. 85 pp. plus 170 pp., illus. $10.00.

A new and revised edition covering the original Volume I, Centerfire Metric Pistol and Revolver Cartridges and Volume II, Centerfire American and British Pistol and Revolver Cartridges, by White and Munhall, formerly known as Cartridge Identification.

Complete Guide to Handloading, by Phil Sharpe. Funk & Wagnalls, N.Y.C., 1953 (3rd ed., 2nd rev.) 734 pp., profusely illustrated, numerous line and halftone charts, tables, lists, etc., $10.00.

The bible of handloaders ever since its first appearance in 1937, but badly dated now.

Handloader's Digest, ed. by John T. Amber. Digest Books, Inc., Northfield, Ill., 1970. 320 pp., very well illus., stiff paper covers. $4.95.

This 5th edition contains the latest data on ballistics, maximum loads, new tools, equipment, reduced loads, etc., plus a fully illus. catalog section, current prices and specifications.

Home Guide to Cartridge Conversions, by Geo. C. Nonte, Jr., Stackpole Books, Harrisburg. Pa., 1967. 404 pp., illus. $8.95.

A new, revised and enlarged ed. of instructions, charts and tables for making ammunition no longer available, or which has become too expensive on the commercial market.

Hornady Handbook of Cartridge Reloading. Hornady Mfg. Co., Grand Island, Nebr., 1967. 360 pp., illus. $3.50.

Handloader's reference, with much detail on projectiles, ballistics, etc., on many popular U.S. and imported firearms. An excellent new work with particularly needed ballistic detail.

The Identification of Firearms and Forensic Ballistics, by G. Burrard. A. S. Barnes, New York, 1962. 217 pp., illus. $3.95.

A standard, reliable, authoritative English work in the criminal-legal field of ballistics.

Interior Ballistics, How a Gun Converts Chemical Energy to Projectile Motion, by E. D. Lowry. Doubleday and Co., N.Y., 1968. 168 pp., including index and bibliography., illus. with 4 halftones and 17 line drawings. $4.50.

An introduction to the history of small arms and weapons relative to the science of internal ballistics, especially for the layman and student.

Lyman Handbook No. 44. Lyman Gunsight Corp., Middlefield, Conn., 1967. $3.50.

Latest edition of a favorite reference for ammunition handloaders, whether novice or veteran.

Lyman Shotshell Handbook, by Jim Sheridan. Lyman Gunsight Corp., Middlefield, Conn., 1969. 160 pp., illus. $3.00

Covers reloading of all gauges, shell lengths, brands, types, etc., including reference section.

The NRA Handloader's Guide. Ashley Halsey, Jr., ed. Nat'l Rifle Assn., Washington, D.C., 1969. 312 pp., illus., paperbound. $5.00.

Revised edition of a reloading handbook, based on material published in *The American Rifleman.*

Pocket Manual for Shooters and Reloaders, by P. O. Ackley. Publ. by author, Salt Lake City, Utah, 1964. 176 pp., illus., spiral bound. $3.50.

Good coverage on standard and wildcat cartridges and related firearms in popular calibers.

Principles and Practice of Loading Ammunition, by Lt. Col. Earl Naramore. Stackpole Books, Harrisburg, Pa., 1954. 915 text pages, 240 illustrations. $14.95.

Actually two volumes in one. The first part (565 pp.) deals with ballistics and the principles of cartridge making—and the chemistry, metallurgy, and physics involved. The second part (350 pp.) is a thorough discussion of the mechanics of loading cartridges. 1967 printing.

Professional Loading of Rifle, Pistol and Shotgun Cartridges . . . , by G. L. Herter, Waseca, Minn., 1970. 830 pp., illus. $7.50.

Detailed technical loading information on small arms ammunition, with related articles on firearms and their use. A "condensed" paper-cover version of the above, 430 pp., illus. $4.50.

Shooter's Bible Black Powder Guide, by George Nonte. Shooter's Bible, Inc., S. Hackensack, N.J., 1969. 214 pp., well illus. $3.95.

Information on black powder weapons, ammunition, shooting, etc.

Shooter's Bible Reloader's Guide, 2nd ed., by R. A. Steindler. Shooter's Bible, Inc., S. Hackensack, N.J., 1968, 220 pp., fully illus. $3.95.

Comprehensive coverage of technology and methods of handloading all types of small arms ammunition. This is a useful work.

Shotshell Handbook, by Lyman Handbook Staff. Lyman Gunsight Corp., Middlefield, Conn., 1969. 160 pp., illus., stiff paper spiral-binding. $3.00.

The first book devoted exclusively to shotshell reloading. Considers: gauge, shell length, brand, case, loads, buckshot, etc., plus excellent reference section. Some color illus.

Small Arms Ammunition Identification Guide. Panther Publ., Boulder, Colo., 1968. 151 pp., illus., paperbound. $3.00.

Facsimile of a U.S. Army text on cartridge identification, which includes data on foreign ammunition used in Vietnam and elsewhere.

Small Arms Design and Ballistics, by Col. T. Whelen. 1945. Stackpole Books, Harrisburg Pa. Only Vol. II, 314 pp., illus. $6.00.

Authoritative technical data on firearms. Vol. II deals with interior and exterior ballistics.

Speer Manual for Reloading Ammunition No. 8. Speer, Inc., Lewiston, Idaho, 1970. 382 pp., illus. $3.95.

A popular manual on handloading, with authoritative articles on loading, ballistics, and related subjects. Decorated paper wrappers.

Why Not Load Your Own? by Col. T. Whelen. A. S. Barnes, New York, 1957, 4th ed., rev. 237 pp., illus, $5.95.

A basic reference on handloading, describing each step, materials and equipment. Loads for popular cartridges are given.

The Winchester-Western Ammunition Handbook. Thomas Nelson & Sons, N.Y.C., 1964. 185 pp., illus., paperbound. $.75.

Called the world's handiest handbook on ammunition for all types of shotguns, rifles and handguns. Full of facts, photographs, ballistics and statistics.

COLLECTORS

Accoutrement Plates, North and South, 1861-1865, by Wm. G. Gavin. Geo. Shumway, York, Pa., 1963. 236 pp., 220 illus. $12.00.

The 1st detailed study of Civil War belt buckles and cartridge box insignia. Dimensions, materials, details of manufacture, relative and dollar values given.

The Age of Firearms, by Robert Held. Gun Digest Publ., Northfield, Ill., 1970. New, fully rev. and corrected ed., paper covers. 192 pp., fully illus. $4.95.

A popular review of firearms since 1475 with accent on their effects on social conditions, and the craft of making functional/artistic arms.

Air Guns, by Eldon G. Wolff. Milwaukee Public Museum, Milwaukee, Wis., 1958. 198 pp., illus. Paper, $6.00.

A scholarly and comprehensive treatise, excellent for student and collectors' use, of air gun history. Every form of arm is described, and a list of 350 makers is included.

The American Bayonet, 1776-1964, by A. N. Hardin, Jr. Geo. Shumway, York, Pa., 1964. 252 pp., profusely illus. $20.00.

First comprehensive book on U.S. bayonets of all services, a standard reference for collectors. All bayonets made for long arms and described in full detail, with outstanding photographs, and historical development of principal types. Full references and bibliography.

American, British & Continental Pepperbox Firearms, by Jack Dunlap. H. J. Dunlap, Los Altos, Calif., 1964. 279 pp., 665 illus. $15.00.

Comprehensive history of production pepperpots from early 18th cent. through the cartridge pepperbox. Variations are covered, with much data of value to the collector.

American Engraved Powder Horns, by Stephen V. Grancsay. Originally published by The Metropolitan Museum of Art, at N.Y.C., 1945. 1st reprint publ. by Ray Riling Arms Books Co., Phila., Pa. 1965. 96 pp. plus 47 full-page plates. $15.00.

A study based on the J. H. Grenville Gilbert collection of historic, rare and beautiful powder horns. A scholarly work by an eminent authority. Long out of print and offered now in a limited edition of 1000 copies.

American and European Swords in the Historical Collections of the U.S. National Museum, by T. T. Belote. Benchmark Pub. Co., Glendale, N.Y., 1970. 163 pp., illus. $7.50.

A reprint of Smithsonian Institution Bulletin 163, first published in 1932.

American Knives, the First History and Collectors' Guide, by Harold L. Peterson. Scribner's, N.Y.C., 1958. 178 pp., illus. $5.95.

A timely book to whet the appetite of the ever-growing group of knife collectors.

The American Percussion Revolver, by F. M. Sellers and Sam E. Smith. Museum Restoration Service, Ottawa, Canada, 1970. 200 pp., illus. $15.00.

All inclusive from 1826 to 1870. Over 200 illus., with profuse coverage on lesser-known arms.

American Polearms, 1526-1865, by R. H. Brown. N. Flayderman Co., New Milford, Conn., 1967. 198 pp., 150 plates. $14.50.

Concise history of pikes, spears, and similar weapons used in American military forces through the Civil War.

American Socket Bayonets, 1717-1873, by D. B. Webster, Jr. Museum Rest. Service, Ottawa, Can. 1964. 48 pp., 60 illus. paperbound. $1.50.

Concise account of major types, with nomenclature, characteristics, and dimensions. Line drawings.

The American Sword 1775-1945, by H. L. Peterson. Ray Riling Arms Books Co., 1970. 286 pp. plus 60 pp. of illus. $13.50.
1970 reprint of a survey of swords worn by U.S. uniformed forces, plus the rare "American Silver Mounted Swords," (1700-1815).

Ancient Armour and Weapons in Europe, by John Hewitt. Akademische Druck- u. Verlagsanstalt, Graz, Austria, 1967. 3 vols., 1151 total pp., illus. $50.00.
Reprint of a renowned British work first published 1855-1860; covers armor, weapons, military history and tactics through the 17th century.

The Ancient Art of Warfare, by Robert Laffont. New York Grafic Society, Greenwich, Conn., 1968. (2 vols.). 1086 pp., illus. Boxed. $60.00.
A summary on warfare since 1300 B.C., covering the principal campaigns known to history, with much on weapons, equipment, and military customs of all types. Many illustrations in full color.

Antique Arms Annual, ed. by R. L. Wilson, S.P. Stevens, Texas Gun Coll. Assn., Waco, Texas. 1971. 262 pp., profusely illus. $15.00.
A magnificent work showing hundreds of fine color photographs of rare firearms. Decorated paper covers.

Antique Firearms, by Frederick Wilkinson. Guinness Signatures, London. 1st ed., 1969. 256 pp., well illus. $15.00.
Sixteen monographs on important aspects of firearms development from the 14th century to the era of the modern repeating rifle. Shows museum-quality arms, many in full color.

Antique Pistols, by S. G. Alexander, illus. by Ronald Paton. Arco Publ. Co., New York, 1963. 56 pp., 12 color plates. $15.00.
The large 8-color plates show 14 examples of the pistol-maker's art in England and U.S.A., 1690-1900. Commentary on each by a knowledgeable English collector.

Antique Weapons, A-Z, by Douglas J. Fryer. G. Bell & Sons, London, 1969. 114 pp. illus. $7.50.
A concise survey of collectors' arms, including firearms, edged weapons, polearms, etc., of European and Oriental design, classified by types.

Antique Weapons for Pleasure and Investment, by R. Akehurst. Arco Pub. Co., N.Y., 1969. 174 pp., illus. $5.95.
Reprint of an English book covering an extensive variety of arms, including Japanese and Hindu edged weapons and firearms.

Les Armes Americaines 1870-1871 de las Defense Nationale, by P. Lorain and J. Boudriot. Librarie Pierre Petitot, Paris, France, 1970. French text, 96 pp., illus. $12.50
Covers all U.S. weapons bought by the French government a century ago.

Armes a Feu Francaises Modeles Reglementaires, by J. Boudriot. Paris, 1961-1968. 4 series of booklets; 1st and 2nd series, 5 booklets; 3rd and 4th, 6 booklets. Each series, $6.75, $9.75, $10.75, $11.75, resp.
Detailed survey of all models of French military small arms, 1717-1861, with text in French and fine scale drawings. Each series covers a different period of development; the last covers percussion arms.

Armes Blanches Militaires Francaises, by Christian Aries. P. Petitot, Paris, 1968. Unpaginated, paperbound, 11 volumes. $9.50 per vol., $95.00 complete.
Pictorial survey of French military swords, in French text and line drawings in exact detail. The classifications in the various volumes are the author's own and do not follow any specific sequence. The work must be used as a complete set for maximum benefit.

Le Armi da Fuoco Portatili Italiane, dalle Origini al Risorgimento, by Gen. Agostino Gaibi. Bramante Editrice, Milan, Italy, 1962. 527 pp., 320 illus. (69 in color), in slip case. $65.00.
A magnificently produced volume covering Italian hand firearms from their beginning into the 18th cent. Italian text. Superb illus. of historic weapons, engraving, marks, related equipment. A companion book to *Armi e Armature Italiane.*

Armi E Armature Europee, by B. Thomas-O. Gamber-H. Schedelmann, Bramante Editrice, Milano, Italy, 1965. 246 pp., magnificently illus., mainly in full color. $40.00. Ed. ltd. to 1600 copies.
Italian text version of *Arms and Armor of Europe* by the same authors in German text. Text and commentary cover 50 pp., and there are 196 pp. of illus.

Armi e Armature Italiane, Fino al XVIII Secolo, by Aldo Mario Aroldi. Bramante Editrice, Milan, Italy, 1961. 544 pp., profusely illus. (much in color). In slip case, $65.00.
A luxurious work on the golden age of Italian arms and makers through the 18th cent., emphasizing body and horse armor, edged weapons, crossbows, early firearms. Italian text. Beautiful and scholarly work for the advanced collector.

Armi E Armature Orientali, by Gianni Vianello, Bramante Editrice, Milano, Italy, 1966. 423 pp. Magnificently illustrated, mainly in full-color tip-ins. $56.00 with slip case. Ed. ltd. to 1600 copies.
A new addition to a notable series of fine books in the arms and armor field. The introduction is 68 pp., 105 pp. of commentary on the 250 pp. of illus.

Arming the Troops, by Paul C. Boehret. Publ. by the author at Chalfont, Pa., 1967. 39 pp., illus. $7.50. The same in paper wrappers $5.00.
A catalog of arms makers of the early years of U.S. history, from 1775 to 1815.

The Armourer and his Craft, by Charles ffoulkes. Frederick Ungar Publ. Co., N.Y., 1967. 199 pp., illus. $9.95.
Standard British reference on body armor, 11th-16th cent.; covering notable makers, construction, decoration, and use. 1st ed. 1912, now reprinted.

Armourers Marks, by D. S. H. Gyngell. Thorsons, Ltd., England, 1959. 131 pp., illus. $7.95.
Some of the marks of armourers, swordsmiths and gunsmiths of almost every foreign country.

Arms Archives, by H. B. Lockhoven. International Small Arms Publishers, Cologne, W. Germany, 1969. Unpaginated. Illus. English and German text, loose-leaf format. Available in 3 series; "A" Handguns, "B" Automatic Weapons, "C" Longarms. Each series in 3 installments at $7.50 per installment. Binders for each series, $4.50 each.
A major breakthrough in weapons literature. Scaled photographs of arms and their cartridges, fully desc. Series "D" on Antique Firearms should be available now.

Arms and Armor, by Vesey Norman. Putnam's N.Y.C., 1964. 128 pp., 129 illus. $5.95.
Authoritative, compact coverage of European armor and weapons prior to the age of firearms. Excellent illus., many in color.

Arms & Armor from the Atelier of Ernst Schmidt, Munich, by E. Andrew Mowbray, compiler. Mowbray Co., Providence, R.I., 1967. 168 pp., well illus. $11.95.
Principally a compilation of plates from the extremely rare Schmidt catalog displaying the famous replicas of medieval armor and weapons made in his shop from about 1870 to 1930. Limited edition.

Arms and Armor in Colonial America, 1526-1783, by H. L. Peterson. Crown, New York, reprint ed., 1964. 350 pp., illus. $3.95.
Well-organized account of arms and equipment used in America's colonization and exploration, through the Revolutionary period.

Arms and Armour, by Frederick Wilkinson, A. & C. Black Ltd., London. Reprint of 1969, 63 pp., well illus. $2.95.
A concise work for young readers describing edged weapons, polearms, armor, etc., mainly of European origin.

Arms and Armour, 9th to 17th Century, by Paul Martin, C. E. Tuttle Co., Rutland, Vt., 1968. 298 pp., well illus. $15.00.
Beautiful illustrations and authoritative text on armor and accessories from the time of Charlemagne to the firearms era.

Arms and Armour of the Western World, by B. Thomas, O. Gamber & H. Schedelmann. McGraw Hill, N.Y.C., 1964. 252 pp., illus. (much in color), $27.50.
Museum quality weapons and armor shown and described in a magnificent book, which gives the association of specimen arms with the men and events of history. Superb photographs in color. Pub. 1963 in German as "Die Schonsten Waffen . . ." price $25.00.

Arms Collection of Colonel Colt, by R. L. Wilson. Herb Glass, Bullville, N.Y., 1964. 132 pp., 73 illus. Lim. deluxe ed., $16.50; trade ed., $6.50.
Samuel Colt's personal collection is well-described and photographed, plus new technical data on Colt's arms and life. 51 Colt guns and other revolving U.S. and European arms are included.

Arms Making In the Connecticut Valley, by F. J. Deyrup. George Shumway Publ., York, Pa., 1970. Reprint of the noted work originally publ. in 1948 by Smith College. 290 pp., line maps, $10.00.
A scholarly regional study of the economic development of the small arms industry 1798-1870. With statistical appendices, notes, bibliography.

The Art of the Gunmaker, by J. F. Hayward; Vol. I, 1500-1660; Vol. II, 1660-1830. St. Martin's Press, New York, 1962-64. Vol. I: 303 pp. plus 64 pp. of illus., $15.00; Vol. II: 352 pp., 220 illus., $18.50.
Comprehensive survey of firearms development and ornamentation by leading makers in Europe and the U.S. Prepared by a museum expert with excellent illus., this book offers valuable new information.

Artillery and Ammunition of the Civil War, by Warren Ripley. Van Nostrand Reinhold Co., New York, N.Y., 1st ed., 1970. 384 pp., well illus. with 662 black and white photos and line drawings. $22.50.
A fine survey covering both Union and Confederate cannon and projectiles, as well as those imported.

Arts of the Japanese Sword, by B. W. Robinson. Chas. E. Tuttle Co., Rutland, Vt., 1961. 110 pp. of descriptive text with illus., plus 100 full page plates, some in full color. $15.00.
An authoritative work, divided into 2 parts—the first on blades, tracing their history to the present day; the second on mounts and fittings. It includes forging processes; accounts of the important schools of swordsmiths; techniques employed, plus a useful appendix on care and cleaning.

Ballard Rifles in the H. J. Nunnemacher Coll., by Eldon G. Wolff. Milwaukee Public Museum, Milwaukee, Wisc., 2nd ed. 1961. Paper, 77 p. plus 4 pp. of charts and 27 plates. $2.50.
A thoroughly authoritative work on all phases of the famous rifles, their parts, patent and manufacturing history.

The Bannerman Catalogue 1903, Francis Bannerman Sons, New York, N.Y. Reprint released in 1960. 116 pp., well illus., $3.50.
A reprint in facsimile of this dealer's catalog of military goods of all descriptions, including weapons and equipment.

The Bannerman Catalog 1965, Francis Bannerman Sons, Blue Point, N.Y. The 100th anniversary ed., 1966. 264 pp., well illus. $5.00.
Latest dealer catalog of nostalgic interest on military and collector's items of all sorts.

Basic Documents on U.S. Marital Arms, commentary by Col. B. R. Lewis, reissue by Ray Riling, Phila., Pa., 1956 and 1960.
Rifle Musket Model 1855. The first issue rifle of musket caliber, a muzzle loader equipped with the Maynard primer, 32 pp. $2.00.
Rifle Musket Model 1863. The typical Union muzzle-loader of the Civil War, 26 pp. $1.50.
Breech-Loading Rifle Musket Model 1866. The first of our 50 caliber breechloading rifles, 12 pp. $1.50.
Remington Navy Rifle Model 1870. A commercial type breech-loader made at Springfield, 16 pp. $1.50.
Lee Straight Pull Navy Rifle Model 1895. A magazine cartridge arm of 6mm caliber. 23 pp. $2.75.
Breech-Loading Rifle Musket Model 1868. The first 50-70 designed as such. 20 pp. $1.50.
Peabody Breech-Loading Arms (five models)—27 pp. $2.25.
Ward-Burton Rifle Musket 1871—16 pp. $2.00.
Springfield Rifle, Carbine & Army Revolvers (cal. 45) Model 1873 including Colt and Smith & Wesson hand arms. 52 pp. $2.25.
U.S. Magazine Rifle and Carbine (cal 30) Model 1892 (the Krag Rifle) 36 pp. $2.50.

Bayonets Illustrated, by Bert Walsh. Colour Repro. Dublin, Ireland, 1970. 40 pp., illus. $5.00.
162 detailed line drawings of bayonets, from many countries and all periods.

Bayonets, an Illustrated History and Reference Guide, by F. J. Stephens. Arms and Armour Press, London, 1968. 76 pp., stiff paper wrappers, 134 photographs. $5.00.
A general historical survey of all categories of the weapon, from the U.S. and many other countries.

Bellifortis The War Hero, by Conrad Kyeser. Verlag des Vereins Deutscher Ingenieure, Dusseldorf, W. Germany. 1967. Two large facsimile volumes, 391 pp., combining Latin and German text. Superbly illus.
For the advanced collector, this is a reproduction of the oldest [A.D. 1405] German manuscript on weapons and warfare. Limited to 1,000 copies, bound in white half-vellum and boxed. $120.00.

Bilderatlas zum Grundriss der Waffenlehre, by K. T. vonSauer. Pawlas, Nurnberg, Germany, 1968. Paper folder containing 28 pp. text and 26 plates. $7.50.
Facsimile of an 1869 set of plates depicting military rifles of Germany, with explanatory pamphlet in German text.

Blunderbusses, by D. R. Baxter. Stackpole Books, Harrisburg, Pa., 1970. 80 pp., 60 illus. $4.95.
Traces blunderbuss development from the 16th century, covering basic designs, firing systems, the double blunderbuss and revolving pepperbox design.

The Book of Colt Firearms, by R. Q. Sutherland and R. L. Wilson. Privately printed, Kansas City, Mo., 1971. 600 pp. 9x12", profusely illus. $32.50
This exhaustive large work, highly informative and scholarly, contains 40 color plates showing 350 Colt firearms, plus 650 black and white photographs.

The Book of the Continental Soldier, by Harold L. Peterson. Stackpole Books, Harrisburg, Pa., 1968. 287 pp., of large format profusely illus. with halftone, line, and including art work by H. Charles McBarron, Jr., Clyde A. Risley and Peter Copeland. $12.95.
A thorough and commendable work in every pertinent aspect. Covers in satisfying detail every facet of the soldier's existence.

Book of the 22, by Richard Arnold. Barnes & Co., N.Y.C., 1962. 188 pp., illus., $2.95.
Authoritative data for the 22 rifleman and pistoleer, detailing arms of this caliber in the use throughout the world, history of the weapons and cartridges.

Bowie Knives, by R. Abels. Pub. by the author, N.Y.C., 1960. 48 pp. profusely illus. Paper covers. $2.00.
A booklet showing knives, tomahawks, related trade cards and advertisements.
Brass Spikes & Horsehair Plumes: A Study of U.S. Army Dress Helmets, 1872-1903, by Gordon Chappell, Arizona Pioneers Hist. Soc., Tucson, Ariz. 1966. 50 pp., illus. Paper covers. $2.00.
Historical monograph on military headgear of the period.
The Breech-Loader in the Service, 1816-1917, by Claud E. Fuller, N. Flayderman, New Milford, Conn., 1965. 381 pp., illus. $14.50.
Revised ed. of a 1933 historical reference on U.S. standard and experimental military shoulder arms. Much patent data, drawings, and photographs of the arms.
A voluminous work that covers handloading—and other things—in great detail. Replete with data for all cartridge forms.
British and American Infantry Weapons of World War II, by A. J. Barker. 1st ed., 1969. Arco Publishing Co., New York, N.Y. 76 pp., illus., $3.50.
A British officer's survey that includes numerous specialized weapons, all are illustrated and described.
British Military Bayonets from 1700 to 1945, by R. J. W. Latham. Arco Publ. Co., N.Y.C., 1969. 94 pp., ilus. $8.50.
History and identification catalog of British bayonets, with fine illustrations, marks, dimensions, and equipment of various British army units.
British Military Firearms 1650-1850, by H. L. Blackmore. Arco Publ. Co. Inc., New York, 1962. 296 pp. and 83 plates of photographs, line drawings, appendices and index. $10.00.
This excellent work admirably and authoritatively covers the subject in every detail. Highly recommended.
British Military Swords, From 1800 to the Present Day, by J. W. Latham, Crown Publishers, N.Y., 1967, 91 pp., illus. $3.95.
Survey of British swords used by various branches of the Army, with data on their manufacture, specifications, and procurement.
British Pistols and Guns, 1640-1940, by Ian Glendenning. Arco Publ. Co., N.Y., 1967. 194 pp., photos and drawings. $7.50.
Historical review of British firearms, with much data and illustration of furniture and decoration of fine weapons.
British Smooth-Bore Artillery, by Maj.-Gen. B. P. Hughes. Stackpole Books, Harrisburg, Pa., 1969. 144 pp., illus. $14.95.
On the muzzle-loading artillery of the 18th and 19th centuries, covering dimensions, ammunition, and application.
The British Soldier's Firearm, 1850-1864, by C. H. Roads. Herbert Jenkins, London, 1964. 332 pp., illus. $12.50.
Detailed account of development of British military arms at the acme of the muzzle-loading period. All models in use are covered, as well as ammunition.
The Canadian Gunsmiths 1608-1900, by S. James Gooding. Museum Restoration Service, Canada, 1962. 322 pp., illus. $17.50.
Comprehensive survey of the gunmakers of Canada and the products of their skill, from early settlement to the age of the breech-loader.
Cartridge Headstamp Guide, by H. P. White and B. D. Munhall. H. P. White Laboratory, Bel Air, Md., 1963. 263 pp., illus. $10.00.
An important reference on headstamping of small arms ammo, by manufacturers in many countries. Clear illus. of 1936 headstamps of every type.
Cartridges for Collectors, by Fred A. Datig. Borden Publishing Co., Alhambra, Calif., Vol. I (Centerfire), 1958; Vol. II (Rimfire and Misc.) Types, 1963; Vol. III (Additional Rimfire, Centerfire, and Plastic,) 1967. Each of the three volumes 176 pp., well illus. and each priced at $7.50.
Vol. III supplements the first two books and presents 300 additional specimens. All illus. are shown in full-scale line drawings.
Cavalry Equipment 1874. A reprint of *U.S. Ordnance Memoranda No. 18* by Francis Bannerman Sons, Blue Point, N.Y., 1969. 119 pp., 12 plates. $6.50.
An officers' report on details of equipment issued to U.S. cavalry units.
Civil War Carbines, by A. F. Lustyik. World Wide Gun Report, Inc., Aledo, Ill., 1962. 63 pp., illus. paper covers. $2.00.
Accurate, interesting summary of most carbines of the Civil War period, in booklet form, with numerous good illus.
Civil War Collector's Encyclopedia, by Francis A. Lord. Stackpole Books, Harrisburg, Pa., 1963. 384 pp., 350 illus. $17.95.
A reference work on Civil War relics, for museums, students, writers, and collectors of Union and Confederate items. Identifies arms, uniforms, accoutrements, ordnance material, currency, postage, etc. Many patent drawings. Lists of manufacturers and vendors, North and South, are given.
Civil War Guns, by Wm. B. Edwards. Stackpole Books, Harrisburg, Pa., 1962. 464 pp., over 400 illus. $5.95.
Comprehensive survey of Civil War arms, identification data, procurement procedures, and historical data. Important information on replicas, imitations, and fakes.
Classic Bowie Knives, by Robert Abels. R. Abels, Inc., N.Y., 1967. 97 pp., illus. with numerous fine examples of the subject. $7.50.
A nostalgic story of the famous blades, with trade adverts on them, and photos of users.
Collecting Duelling Pistols, by W. Keith Neal. Arms and Armour Press, London, 1968 reprint of the 1966 original. 15 pp., 23 plates, paper covers. $2.50.
A monograph on museum-quality duelling pistols. Fine photographic plates.
The Collecting of Guns, ed. by Jas. E. Serven. Stackpole Books, Harrisburg, Pa., 1964. 272 pp., illus. $24.50.
A new and massive compendium of gun lore for serious collectors by recognized experts. Separate chapters cover major categories and aspects of collecting. Over 600 firearms illus. Handsomely designed, deluxe binding in slip case. Reprint of 1966, $5.95.
Collector's Guide to American Cartridge Handguns, by DeWitt E. Sell. Stackpole Books, Harrisburg, Pa., 1963. 234 pp., illus. $3.98.
Catalogs the important U.S. makers in its field, with histories of the firms and their production models. Photos, descriptions and features of many older and current handguns are included.
Collectors' Guns, by Don Myrus. Arco Publ. Co., Inc., New York, 1962. 128 pp., illus. $3.50.
The fascinating story of firearms—from the early hand cannon to the Peacemaker—with over 200 rare photographs and illus.
Colt Firearms from 1836, by James E. Serven. Foundation Press, La Habra, Cal., 1969. 6th printing, 398 pp., very well illus. $19.95.
A dependable survey of the Colt company and its products. In addition to historical data, each Colt model is illus. and described, with production figures.
Colt Gun Book, by Lucian Cary. Arco Publ. Co. Inc., New York, 1961. 142 pp., profusely illus. $3.50.
A Colt picture book, showing the guns and the men who used them, with much data on the noted outlaws and touching on the inventor.
Colt's Variations of the Old Model Pocket Pistol, 1848 to 1872, by P. L. Shumaker. Borden Publishing Co., Alhambra, Calif., 1966 A reprint of the 1957 edition. 150 pp., illus. $6.00.
A useful tool for the Colt specialist and a welcome return of a popular source of information that had been long out-of-print.
The Complete Book of Gun Collecting, by Charles E. Chapel. Coward-McCann, Inc., N.Y.C., 1960. 222 pp., illus. $4.95.
Answers hundreds of questions for the beginner, and is a reference for the advanced collector and student of firearms. It covers hand cannon of the 14th century to arms of the present day.
Confederate Arms, by Wm. A. Albaugh III, and E. N. Simmons. Stackpole Books, Harrisburg, Pa., 1957. 278 pp., illus. $3.95.
Contains much heretofore unpublished information on the arms and associated material of the Confederacy.
Confederate Handguns, by Wm. A. Albaugh III. Hugh Benet Jr., and Edw. N. Simmons. Geo. Shumway, York, Pa., 1963. 272 pp., 125 illus. $16.00.
Every known true Confederate pistol and revolver is described and illus., with the story of its maker and procurement by the C.S.A. Much new information. Includes listing of C. W. makers and dealers, information on replicas and fakes. Indispensable to the collector and student of these arms and their period.
Cut and Thrust Weapons, by E. Wagner. Spring Books, London, 1967. 491 pp., line drawings. $17.50.
English translation of a survey of European edged weapons, their traditions, manufacture, and use.
Deanes' Manual of the History and Science of Fire-arms, by J. Deane. Standard Publications, Huntington, W. Va. 1946 facsimile reprint of the rare English original of 1858. 291 pp., three folding plates. $6.00.
A history of firearms, plus design and manufacture of military and sporting arms.
Digest of Patents Relating to Breech-Loading and Magazine Small Arms (1836-1873), by V. D. Stockbridge, Washington, 1874. Reprinted 1963 by E. N. Flayderman, Greenwich, Conn. 180 pp., 880 illus. $12.50.
An exhaustive compendium of patent documents on firearms, indexed and classified by breech mechanism types. Valuable reference for students and collectors.
Early Indian Trade Guns—1625 to 1775, by T. M. Hamilton. Museum of the Great Plains, Lawton, Okla. 1969. 34 pp., well illus., paper covers. $2.50.
Detailed descriptions of subject arms, compiled from early records and from the study of remnants found in Indian country.
Early Loading Tools and Bullet Molds, by R. H. Chamberlain. The Farm Tribune, Porterville, Ga., 1971. 75 pp., illus. Paper covers. $3.00.
An excellent aid to collectors.
Early Percussion Firearms, by Lewis Winant. Wm. Morrow & Co., Inc., N.Y.C., 1959. 292 pp., illus. $2.98.
A history of early percussion firearms ignition—from Forsyth to Winchester 44-40, from flintlocks of the 18th century to centerfires. Over 230 illus. of firearms, parts, patents, and cartridges—from some of the finest collections here and abroad.
Edged Weapons, by Fred. Wilkinson. Guinness Signatures, London, 1970. 256 pp., plus 14-page index. Excellently illus., many in full color. $12.95.
Scholarly treatment of all kinds of blades—from flint to steel, rapiers, smallswords, knives, daggers, hunting weapons, polearms, etc., plus construction and decoration.
The Encyclopedia of Military History, by R. Ernest and Trevor N. Dupuy. Harper & Row, New York, N.Y., 1970. 1st ed., 1406 pp., well illus., in line and halftone. $20.00.
This massive single volume covers the subject from 3500 B.C. to the present time. A complete reference guide to the world's military history; narration of war and combat, tactics, strategy and weaponry. Over 250 maps, illus. of weapons, fortifications, etc.
English, Irish and Scottish Firearms, by A. Merwyn Carey. Arco Publishing Co., Inc., N.Y., 1967. A reprint. 121 pp., illus. in line and halftone. $6.50.
Out-of-print since 1954, this work covers the subject from the middle of the 16th century to the end of the 19th.
English Pistols & Revolvers, by J. N. George. Arco Publ. Co., Inc., N.Y.C., 1962. 256 pp., 28 plates. $6.00.
The 2nd reprinting of a notable work first publ. in 1938. Treats of the historical development and design of English hand firearms from the 17th cent. to the present. A much better book than the former reprint, particularly as to clarity of the tipped-in plates.
English Sporting Guns and Accessories, by Macdonald Hastings. Ward Lock & Co., London. 1st ed., 1969. 96 pp., well illus. $4.00.
A delightful monograph on shotguns and accessory equipment for hunting from 1800 to the advent of the breechloader, including historic arms and ammunition.
European & American Arms, by Claude Blair. Batsford. London, and Crown Publ., N.Y.C., 1962, 192 pp., 9"x12". Profusely and magnificently illus. $6.95.
A complete visual encyclopedia on all sorts of arms of Europe and America with over 600 photographs of pieces from nearly all the major collections of Western Europe, America, and Russia, from about 1100 to 1850. A splendid text describes historical and technical developments.
European Armour in the Tower of London, by A. R. Dufty. H. M. Stationery Office, London, England, 1968. 17 pp. text, 164 plates. $12.60.
Pictorial record of almost 400 pieces of armor, helmets, and accouterments in the famous Tower of London collection.
European Arms & Armour, by Chas. H. Ashdown. Brussel & Brussel, N.Y., 1967. A reprint. 384 pp., illus. with 42 plates and 450 drawings. $5.95.
Historical survey of body armor up to the era of gunpowder, with some coverage on weapons and early firearms.
European Arms and Armour, Wallace Collection, by Sir James Mann. The Wallace Collection, London, 1962. 2 vols. 714 pp., 208 plates. $15.00.
A new edition of the catalog of an important British collection, containing historical notes and fine illus. Vol. I, on armor; Vol. II on arms of all types and accessory equipment.
European Hand Firearms of the 16th, 17th, and 18th Centuries, by H. J. Jackson and C. E. Whitlaw. Bramhall House, New York, N.Y. A reprint of the noted original. 108 pp., fine photographic plates. $5.95.
A work for scholars and collectors, including a list of arms makers. Not without error.
The Evolution of the Colt, by R. L. Wilson, R. Q. Sutherland, Kansas City, Mo., 1967. 54 pp., illus. $3.00.
Pictures the fine Colt arms of the publisher from percussion to cartridge. Includes a Colt bibliography.
Famous Guns from the Smithsonian Collection, by H. W. Bowman. Arco. Publ. Co., Inc., New York, 1967. 112 pp., illus. $3.50.
The finest of the "Famous Guns" series.
Famous Guns from the Winchester Collection, by H. W. Bowman. Arco Publ. Co., N.Y.C., 1958 and later. 144 pp., illus. $3.50.
The gems of the hand and shoulder arms in the great collection at New Haven, Conn.
Feuerwaffen von 1300 bis 1967, by Hans-Bert Lockhoven. International Small Arms Publ., Cologne, W. Germany, 1969. 96 pp., illus. $6.95.
Review of the principal developments in military smallarms from early times. German text.
'51 Colt Navies, by N. L. Swayze. Gun Hill Publ. Co., Yazoo City, Miss., 1967. 243 pp., well illus. $15.00.
The first major effort devoting its entire space to the 1851 Colt Navy revolver. There are 198 photos of models, sub-models, variations, parts, markings, documentary material, etc. Fully indexed.

Firearms Curiosa, by Lewis Winant. Ray Riling, Philadelphia, Pa. 2nd and deluxe reissue 1961, 281 pp., well illus. $8.50.

Two reissues publ. by Bonanza Books, N.Y., 1965. Same size as above, $2.98. A smaller size, 1968. $1.98.

An important work for those with an interest in odd, distinctive and unusual forms and firing.

The Firearms Dictionary, by R. A. Steindler. Stackpole Books, Harrisburg, Pa., 1970. 256 pp., nearly 200 illus. $7.95.

A super single-source reference to more than 1800 English and Foreign gun-related words, phrases and nomenclature, etc. Highly useful to all armsmen—collectors, shooters, hunters, etc.

Firearms in England in the Fourteenth Century, by T. F. Tout. Geo. Shumway, York, Pa., 1958. 58 pp., illus., paper covers. $4.00.

Reprint of a 1911 monograph on the history and manufacture of early British firearms, by a distinguished historian.

The Flintlock, Its Origin and Development, by Torsten Lenk; J. T. Hayward, Editor. Holland Press, London, 1964. 192 pp., 134 illus. $6.95.

First English-text version of the 1939 Swedish work termed "the most important book on the subject." Original illus. are reproduced, and a new index and bibliography complete this valuable book.

Flintlock Pistols, by F. Wilkinson. Stackpole Books, Harrisburg, Pa., 1968. 75 pp., illus. $4.95.

Illustrated reference guide by a British authority, covering 17th-19th century flintlock pistols.

Forsyth & Co.—Patent Gunmakers, by W. Keith Neal and D. H. L. Back. G. Bell & Sons, London, 1st ed., 1969. 280 pp., well illus. $12.95.

An excellent study of the invention and development of the percussion system by the Rev. Alexander Forsyth in the early 19th century. All Forsyth types are covered, plus a diary of events from 1768 to 1852.

The French Army in America, by E. P. Hamilton. Museum Restoration Service, Ottawa, 1967. 108 pp., illus. $3.00.

Concise historical coverage, illus. with contemporary documents and manual-of-arms plates. Text in English and French. Paper wrappers.

French Military Weapons, 1717-1938, by James E. Hicks. N. Flayderman & Co., New Milford, Conn. 1964. 281 pp., profusely illus. $9.50.

A valuable reference work, first publ. 1938 as *Notes on French Ordnance,* this rev. ed. covers hand, shoulder, and edged weapons, ammunition and artillery, with history of various systems.

The Fuller Collection of American Firearms, by H. L. Peterson. Eastern National Park & Monument Assn., 1967. 63 pp., illus. $2.50.

Illustrated catalog of principal military shoulder arms in the collection. Decorated paper wrappers.

Gamle Danske Militaervaben, by Th. Moller. Host & Sons, Denmark. 1st reprinting, 1968. 64 pp., well illus. in line. Heavy paper covers. $4.00.

Old Danish military weapons, with Danish and English text, covering weapons from 1791 to 1832, plus accoutrements.

The Gatling Gun, by Paul Wahl & D. R. Toppel. Arco Publ., N.Y.C., 1965. 168 pp., illus. $13.75.

History of the famed rapid-fire weapon used by many of the world's armies and navies from 1861.

German Mauser Rifle—Model of 1898, by J. E. Coombes and J. L. Aney. A reprint in paper covers by Francis Bannerman Sons, New York, N.Y., of their 1921 publication. 20 pp., well illus. $1.50.

Data on the subject weapon and its W. W. I development. Bayonets and ammunition are also described and illus.

German Pistols and Holsters 1934 to 1945, by R. D. Whittington III. Brownlee Books, College Station, Tex., 1969. 1st ed., limited to 2000 numbered copies. 223 pp., well illus., in halftone. $15.00.

A manual for collectors on subject items issued to the military, police and NSDAP. Covers all models of various designs, including those of foreign manufacture.

German Submachine Guns and Assault Rifles. WE, Inc., Old Greenwich, Conn., 1967. 161 pp. $5.95.

Aberdeen Proving Ground reports on over 50 models of World War II German rapid-fire weapons are reprinted.

Die Geschichtliche Entwicklung Der Handfeuerwaffen, by M. Thierbach, Akademische Druck, Graz, Austria, 1965. Vol. I, 590 pp., German text; Vol. II, 36 plates. $37.00.

The famous German work on history and development of firearms, accessories and ammunition, first published in 1886 in Dresden.

A Glossary of the Construction, Decoration and Use of Arms and Armor in all Countries and in all Times, by Geo. C. Stone, Jack Brussel, New York, 2nd reprint, 1966. 694 pp., illus. $9.95.

The outstanding work on its subject, authoritative and accurate in detail. The major portion is on oriental arms.

Great Weapons of World War I, by Com. G. Dooly. Walker & Co., N.Y., 1969. 340 pp., illus. $14.50.

Describes all the important weapons and system developments used during WWI.

The Gun and its Development, by W. W. Greener. Bonanza Books, N.Y., 1967. A reprint. 804 pp., profusely illus. $5.95.

A facsimile of the famous 9th edition of 1910. Covers history and development of arms in general with emphasis on shotguns.

The Gun Collector's Handbook of Values, by C. E. Chapel. Coward-McCann, N.Y.C., 1970. 398 pp., illus. $12.50.

The 9th rev. ed. of the best-known values reference for collectors with prices for 1971-72.

Gunmakers of Indiana, by A. W. Lindert. Publ. by the author, Homewood, Ill., 1968, 3rd ed. 284 pp., illus. Large format. $15.00.

An extensive and historical treatment, illus. with old photographs and drawings.

Guns of the Old West, by C. E. Chapel. Coward-McCann Inc., N.Y.C., 1961. 306 pp., illus. $6.95.

A definitive book on American arms that opened the frontier and won the West. Shows arms, rare pictures, advertisements, and pertinent associated material.

Guns Through the Ages, by Geoffrey Boothroyd. Sterling Publ. Co., N.Y.C., 1962. 192 pp., illus. $1.69.

A detailed illustrated history of small arms from the invention of gunpowder to today. Covers ignition methods, proof marks, fakes, ammo, etc. Bibliography.

Haandskydevaabens Bedommelse, by Johan F. Stockel. Udgivet Af Tojuhusmuseet, Copenhagen, Denmark. 2nd limited reprint, 1966. Vol. I, 397 pp., plus 6 plates, Vol. II, 1080 pp. illus. Both $35.00.

Printed in Danish but considered by scholars to be the finest and most complete source for the "makrs" and "touches" of gunmakers. Both are well illus.

Handbuch Der Waffenkunde, by Wendelin Boeheim. Akademische D. u. V., Graz, Austria, 1966. 694 pp., illus. $14.00.

One of the famous works of 1890—long out-of-print. Now in a new printing. German text. Historical weapons and armor from the Middle Ages through the 18th century.

Handfeuerwaffen, by J. Lugs. Deutscher Militarverlag, Berlin, 1956. 2 vol., 315 pp., illus. German text. $40.00.

Noted reference on small arms and their development in many nations. All types of weapons are listed described, and illustrated, with data on manufacturers.

Die Handfeuerwaffen, by Rudolf Schmidt. Vienna, Austria, 1968. Vol. I, text 225 pp., Vol. II, 76 plates. $20.00.

Reprint of an important 1875 German reference work on military small arms, much prized by knowledgeable collectors. The fine color plates in Vol. II show detailed and exploded views of many longarms and handguns.

Henry Deringer's Pocket Pistol, by John E. Parsons. Morrow, N.Y.C., 1952. Over 70 illustrations. $7.50.

An excellent and complete account of this famous maker, coupled with an extensive story on Deringer's imitators, the later cartridge derringers, etc.

Hints to Riflemen, by H. W. S. Cleveland. Distributor, Robert Halter, New Hope, Pa., 286 pp., illustrated. $6.50.

A reprint of the original 1864 edition, to which *Practical Directions for the Use of the Rifle* has been added.

A History of the Colt Revolver, by C. T. Haven and F. A. Belden. Bonanza Books, N.Y., 1967. A reprint. 711 pages large format, profusely illus. in line and halftone. $8.95.

A great and massive work, including details on other Colt arms from 1836 to 1940. A must for every Colt collector.

A History of Firearms, by W. Y. Carman. Routledge & Kegan Paul Ltd., London, England, 1955. 207 pp., illus. $4.50.

A concise coverage, from earliest times to 1914, with emphasis on artillery.

A History of Firearms, by H. L. Peterson. Chas. Scribner's Sons, N.Y.C., 1961. 57 pp., profusely illus. $3.50.

From the origin of firearms through each ignition form and improvement to the M-14. Drawings by Daniel D. Feaser.

History of Modern U.S. Military Small Arms Ammunition, by F. W. Hackley, W. H. Woodin and E. L. Scranton. Macmillan, N.Y.C., 1967. 315 pp., 8½"x11", over 500 exact-scale drawings and 100 photos. $25.00.

A superb work based on years of research by the capable authors. Covers cartridges for handguns, rifles and machine guns; miscellaneous, experimental and unidentified rounds, etc.

A History of Shooting, by Jaroslav Lugs. Spring Books, Feltham, England. 1st printing, 1968. 227 pp., well illus., with contemporary drawings and photographs. $4.98.

Historical survey dealing mainly with marksmanship, duelling and exhibition shooting in Europe and America.

A History of Spanish Firearms, by James D. Lavin. Arco Co., New York, 1965. 304 pp., illus. $9.95.

This history, beginning with the recorded appearance of gunpowder in Spain, traces the development of hand firearms through their golden age —the eighteenth century—to the death in 1825 of Isidro Soler. Copious reproductions of short and long arms, list of gun makers and their "marks" a glossary, bibliography and index are included.

A History of Weaponry, by Courtlandt Canby, Hawthorne Books, Inc., New York, 1963. 112 pp., illus. $2.98.

From the caveman's club to the M-14 rifle, from Greek fire to the ICBM.

The History of Winchester Firearms 1866-1966, ed. by T. E. Hall and P. Kuhlhoff, Winchester-Western Press, New Haven, Conn., 1966. 159 pp., illus. $10.00

Called the collector's item of the century, this 3d ed. of Geo. R. Watrous' work rises to new glory in its scope and illustrations. Beautifully produced, with a slip case showing old hunting scenes by A. B. Frost and Frederic Remington. Limited ed.

Identifying Old U.S. Muskets, Rifles & Carbines, by Col. A. Gluckman. Stackpole Books, Harrisburg, Pa., 1965. 487 pp., illus. $10.00.

Collector's guide to U.S. long arms, first publ. 1959. Numerous models of each type are described and shown, with histories of their makers.

An Introduction to British Artillery in North America, by S. J. Gooding. Museum Rest. Serv., Ottawa, 1965. 54 pp., illus., Paperbound. $1.50.

Concise account of such equipment used in America 1750-1850.

Japanese Armour, by L. J. Anderson. Stackpole Books, Harrisburg, Pa., 1968. 84 pp., illus. $4.95.

British reference on museum quality armor made by the Myochin and Saotome families between the 15th and 20th centuries.

Japanese Polearms, by R. M. Knutsen. Holland Press, London, 1963. 271 pp., well-illus. Line drawings and photos. $18.00.

Each category of Japanese spear is described and illus. in this hist. treatment, including schools of spear and sword fencing. Lists leading makers and glossary.

Japanese Sword Blades, by Alfred Dobree. George Shumway, York, Pa., 1967. 39pp., illus., in paper wrappers. $4.50.

A two-part monograph, reprinted from a notable work.

The Kentucky Rifle, by J. G. W. Dillin. Geo. Shumway, York, Pa., 1967. 5th ed. 202 pp., illus. $20.00

A respected work on the long rifles developed in colonial days and carried by pioneers and soldiers. Much information of value to collectors and historians. Limited ed.

The Leather Jacket Soldier, by O. B. Faulk. Socio-Technical Pub., Pasadena, Ca., 1971. 80 pp., illus. $10.00.

History of such Spanish military equipment of the late 18th century as lances, horse accoutrements, guns, uniforms, etc.

Longrifles of North Carolina, by John Bivins, Jr. Geo. Shumway, York, Pa., 1968. 200 pp., profusely illus. $24.00.

Historical survey of North Carolina gunmakers and their production during the 18th and 19th centuries. Over 400 gunsmiths are included. Fine photographs.

Longrifles of Note, by Geo. Shumway, Geo. Shumway, York, Pa., 1967. 90 pp., illus. Paper covers. $3.95.

A review of 35 fine American long rifles, with detailed illustrations showing their art work, plus descriptive material.

The Luger Pistol, by Fred A. Datig. Privately published, Los Angeles, Calif., 1962. 328 pp. well-illus. $8.50.

Larger, revised ed. of the story behind the most famous pistol of all time.

Manhattan Firearms, by Waldo E. Nutter, Stackpole Books, Harrisburg, Pa., 1958. 250 pp., illus., in halftone. $10.00.

Complete history of the Manhattan Firearms Mfg. Co., and its products. Excellent specialized reference.

The Mantons: Gunmakers, by W. Keith Neal and D. H. L. Back, Walker & Co., New York, 1966. 300 pp., illus. $10.95.

Well-documented account of the life and work of John and Joseph Manton, and others of the British gunmakers. A long list, with serial numbers, etc., of Manton guns, is included.

The Manufacture of Armour and Helmets in 16th Century Japan, by Sakakibara Kozan. Holland Press, London, 1963. 156 pp., 32 pp. of illus. $20.00.

Important reference on styles and steps of making Japanese armor, first publ. Tokyo, 1800. Eng. trans., revised by H. R. Robinson of Tower of London Armouries.

Mauser-Gewehre & Mauser-Patente, by R. H. Korn. Akademische Druck Graz, Austria, 1971. 440 pp. German text, most completely illustrated with copious line drawings, charts, many of them folding plates. $22.50.

Fine reprint of the extremely-rare original. Truly a must for every Mauser buff, it has never been surpassed.

Metal Uniform Insignia of the US Army in the Southwest, 1846-1902, by S. B. Brinckerhoff, Arizona Pioneers Hist. Soc., Tucson, Ariz., 1965. 28 pp., illus. Paper covers. $1.00.
Monograph on buttons, badges, buckles, and other uniform insignia.

Metallic Cartridges, T. J. Treadwell, compiler. The Armoury, N.Y.C., 1959. Unpaginated. 68 plates. Paper, $2.95. Cloth, $5.95.
A reduced-size reproduction of U.S. Ordnance Memoranda No. 14, originally publ. in 1873, on regulation and experimental cartridges manufactured and tested at Frankford Arsenal, Philadelphia, Pa.

Militaria, by Frederick Wilkinson. Hawthorn Books, New York, N.Y., 1969. 1st U.S. ed. 256 pp., well illus. in halftone. $5.95.
Introduction to military items of interest to collectors, including prints, medals, uniforms, military miniatures, weapons, badges etc.

Military Arms of Canada, by Upper Canada Hist. Arms Soc. Museum Restoration Serv., West Hill, Ont., 1963. 43 pp., illus. $1.50.
Booklet cont. 6 authoritative articles on the principal models of Canadian mil. small arms. Gives characteristics of each, makers, quantities produced.

Military Edged Weapons of the World, 1880-1965, by H. A. Maeurer Mauerer, College Pt., N.Y., 1967. 151 pp., illus. $4.50.
Various swords, blades, etc., in a private collection are dimensioned, described, and photographed. A guide for collectors. Paper wrappers.

Military Headgear in the Southwest, 1846-1890, by S. B. Brinckerhoff, Arizona Pioneers Hist. Soc., Tucson, Ariz., 1963. 16 pp., illus. Paper covers. $1.00.
Historical monograph, reprinted from the journal *Arizoniana*. With bibliography.

Military Sharps Rifles and Carbines, by R. E. Hopkins. Hopkins, Campbell, Calif., 1967. 141 pp., illus. $11.50.
A guide to the principal types, with photographs, patent data, technical details, etc.

Miniature Arms, by Merrill Lindsay. Winchester Press, New York, N.Y., 1970. 111 pp., illus. $8.95.
A concise study of small-scale replicas of firearms and other weapons of collector interest. Fine color photographs.

Monographie der K.uk. Osterr.-Ung: Blanken und Handfeuer-Waffen, by Anton Dolleczek. A Kademische Druck, Graz, Austria, 1970. 197 pp., illus. $10.00.
Facsimile reprint of a standard 1896 German work on military weapons. In German text, illus. with line drawings and color plate of regimental colors.

Montgomery Ward & Co. 1894-1895, reproduction of a 600-page catalog, ed. by Jos. J. Schroeder, Jr. Gun Digest Co., Northfield, Ill., 1970. Profusely illus. $4.95.
A nostalgic look at the past, and for the gun enthusiast a look at models and prices prevailing in the late 19th century.

Louis Napoleon on Artillery: The Development of Artillery from the 14th to the 17th Century, by W. Y. Carman, Arms and Armour Press, Middlesex, England, 1967. 24 pp., illus. Paper covers. $2.75.
A reprinting of rare original material—10 finely engraved plates, with 70 drawings, on the development of artillery, plus brief text.

The New Highland Military Discipline, by Geo. Grant. Museum Restoration Service, Ottawa, 1967. 32 pp., illus. $1.50.
Reprint of a Scottish drill manual, regimental history, with illus. contemporary and modern. Paper wrappers.

The 9-pdr. Muzzle Loading Rifle, by J. D. Chown. Museum Restoration Service, Ottawa, 1967. 32 pp., Illus. $1.50.
Reprint of an early Canadian artillery manual, with historical notes. Paper wrappers.

Notes on Canadian Shotshells, by N. Krevosheia and A. M. Provick, compilers. N. Krevosheia, Edmonton, Canada, 1967. Paper wrappers, 32 pp., illus. $2.00.
An illustrated handbook for collectors with line drawings and photos of domestic, contract, export and miscellaneous shells and their boxes, etc.

Notes on U.S. Ordnance, Vol. II, 1776-1941, by James E. Hicks. Modern Books & Crafts, Greens Farms, Conn., 1971. 252 pp., illus. $8.00.
Updated version of a standard work on development of military weapons used by U.S. forces, from handguns to coast artillery and aerial bombs. This is not to be confused with Hicks 1940 United States Ordnance, referring mainly to Ordnance correspondence as Vol. II.

One Hundred Great Guns, by Merrill Lindsay. Walker & Co., N.Y., 1967. 379 pp., fine color illus. $9.95.
Deluxe illus. history of firearms, covering all principal types of small arms and their makers. Bibliography.
A super-deLuxe edition is available at $75.00.

Ordnance Memoranda No.22. The Fabrication of Small Arms for the U.S. Service, by Lt. Col. James G. Benton. Benchmark Pub. Co., Glendale, N.Y., 1970. 229 pp., 35 plates. $9.50.
Reprint of an 1878 War Dept. pub. on U.S. production of military firearms and edged weapons.

Oriental Armour, by W. R. Robinson. Reprint by Outlet Book Co., New York, N.Y., 1970. 256 pp., well illus. $4.95.
Traces the subject material from earliest times until it was finally discarded.

The Original Mauser Magazine Sporting Rifles. Shooter's Bible, S. Hackensack, N.J. 56 pp., illus., paperbound. $1.00.
Facsimile reprint of a Mauser firearms brochure, with English text.

An Outline of the History and Development of Hand Firearms, from the Earliest Period to About the End of the Fifteenth Century, by R. C. Clephan [Original ed., 1906]. A reprint in 1946 by Standard Publications, Inc., Huntington, W.Va. 60 pp., illus. $4.00.
A worthy facsimile of a very scarce, concise and scholarly work.

The Peacemaker and Its Rivals, by John E. Parsons. Morrow, N.Y.C., 1950. 140 pp., illustrated. Appendix, bibilography, and index. $7.50
Detailed history and development of the Single Action Army Colt, with an over-all study of the six-shooter's significance in American history.

The Pennsylvania-Kentucky Rifle, by Henry J. Kauffman. Bonanza Books, N.Y., 1968. A reprint. 374 pp., illus. $3.95.
A classic work first publ. in 1960 on early long rifles. Makers descriptions, and manufacturing methods are covered.

Percussion Revolvers of the United States, by R. Thalheimer. Von Hoffman Press, St. Louis, 1970. 224 pp., illus, $15.00
Reference work on U.S. and Confederate percussion revolvers, plus a history of firearms from the hand-cannon to percussion revolvers.

Photographic Supplement of Confederate Swords, by Wm. A. Albaugh III. Wm. A Bond, Vernon, Tex., 1963. 205 pp., 300 photos. $6.95.
Over 200 specimens of C. W. edged weapons are shown, with data on their owners and makers. Useful for collectors and students.

The Powder Flask Book, by Ray Riling. Bonanza Books, N. Y. 1968. A reprint. 520 pp., large format, profusely illus. First re-issue of the 1953 original ed. $9.95. A limited number of the originals are available for inscription and autograph at $50.00.
Covers the literature on flasks, their makers, and users—hunters, shooters and the military—as well as showing the arms, cased or not, short and long. A relative price listing for collector advantage is included.

Price List of the U.S. Cartridge Company's Ammunition. A 1969 reprint of the 1891 original, publ. by J. C. Tillinghast, Marlow, N.H. 29 pp., illus., paper covers. $2.50.
Displays many of the now hard-to-find cartridges.

Quellen zur Geschichte der Feuerwaffen, by A. Essenwein [ed./compiler] Akademische Druck, Graz, Austria, 1969. One volume of text [German] plus another of fascinating plates. 178 pp., text and 197 plates. $50.00.
A fine facsimile of a rare and most interesting German source book on the "History of Firearms," taken from original drawings of 1390-1700. A treasury for the serious scholar and/or artillery buff.

The Rampant Colt, by R. L. Wilson. Thomas Haas, Spencer, Ind., 1969. 107 pp., well illus. $10.00.
Study of Samuel Colt's coat-of-arms and the rampant colt figure used on Colt firearms and in advertising.

Rapiers, by Eric Valentine. Stackpole Books, Harrisburg, Pa., 1968. 76 pp., 58 photos., 3 drawings. $4.95.
A desirable monograph, first on its subject, to be publ. in English. Covers methods of authentication, renovation, cleaning and preservation.

Red Coat and Brown Bess, by Anthony D. Darling. Museum Restoration Service, Ottawa, Ontario, Can., 1970. Paper covers, 63 pp., very well illus., in line and halftone. $3.00.
An unusually excellent treatise on the British Army in 1774-1775. Includes detailed text and illus. of various models of the "Brown Bess," plus "Records of the Battles, Sieges and Skirmishes of the American Revolution."

Remington Catalog [[price List]] of 1885,] a reprint in facsimile, by The Wyoming Armory, Inc., Cheyenne, Wyo., 1969. 48 pp., well illus., paper covers. $2.50.
All rifles, handguns, cane gun, sights, cartridges, shotguns, accessories etc. A priced catalog.

The Remington Historical Treasury of American Guns, by Harold L. Peterson. Thomas Nelson & Sons, N.Y.C., 1966. 199 pp., illus. $1.95.
A historical saga woven into first-rate Americana through the facts and details of the Remington firm and their products.

The Revolver, Its Description, Management, and Use, by P. E. Dove Arms and Armour Press, London, 1968. 57 pp., 6 engravings, stiff paper wrappers. $3.75.
A facsimile reprint of a rare classic, dealing principally with the Adams revolver compared to the qualities of the Colt.

Revolving Arms, by A. W. F. Taylerson, Walker and Co., New York, 1967. 123 pp., illus. $8.50.
A detailed history of mechanically-rotated cylinder firearms in Europe and the U.S. Primarily on handguns, but other types of revolving guns are included.

Rifled Infantry Arms, by J. Schon; trans. by Capt. J. Gorgas, USA. Dresden, 1855; facsimile reprint by W. E. Meuse, Schuylersville, N.Y., 1965. 54 pp., illus. $2.50.
Reprint of classic essay on European military small arms of the mid-19th century. Paper covers.

The Rifled Musket, by Claud E. Fuller. Stackpole Books, Harrisburg, Pa., 1958. 302 pp., illus. $4.95.
The authoritative work of the late Claud E. Fuller and basically an account of the muskets whose model dates fell within the Civil War years— 1861, 1863 and 1864. Part Two treats of the contract muskets. Some re- produced material, notably Bartlett & Gallatin's "Digest of Cartridges," is almost wholly illegibile, as is much of an 1860 Ordnance Dept. report.

G. Roth Aktiengesellschaft. Horn Co., Burlington, Vt., 1968. 28 pp., illus., paperbound. $2.50.
Reprint of a German cartridge catalog of 1913, with drawings and dimensions.

Royal Sporting Guns at Windsor, by H. L. Blackmore. H. M. Stationery Office, London, England, 1968. 60 pp. text, 52 plates. $9.54.
Catalog of the most decorative and interesting guns in the Royal Armoury collection at Windsor Castle.

Russian Military Swords, 1801-1917, by E. Mollo. Historical Research Unit, London, Eng., 1969. 56 pp., illus. $7.50.
First book in English to examine and classify the various swords used by the Russian Army from Alexander I to the Revolution. 42 photos, 27 line drawings, 10 in color.

Russian Pistols in the 17th Century, by L. Tarassuk. Geo. Shumway, York, Pa., 1968. 35 pp. plus plates. $4.00.
Monograph on museum quality Russian handguns of the 17th century. Fine, detailed photographs.

Samuel Colt Presents. R. L. Wilson, compiler. wadsworth Atheneum, Hartford, Conn., 1961. 293 pp., profusely illus. $15.00.
Showing and describing a profusion of rare and super-rare museum-quality Colt arms exhibited at the Atheneum, it is one of the most important and desirable books on rare Colt arms.

Samuel Colt's New Model Pocket Pistols, by S. G. Keogh. Priv. publ., 1964. 31 pp., 20 illus., paperbound. $3.00.
"The story of the 1855 Root model revolver," with detailed classification data and descriptions. Well-illus.

The Samurai Swords, by J. M. Yumoto. Tuttle Co., Rutland, Vt., 1958. 191 pp., illus. $4.50.
Detailed information on evaluation of specimens, including origin and development of the Japanese blade.

Savage Automatic Pistols, by James R. Carr. Publ. by the author, St. Charles, Ill., 1967. A reprint. 129 pp., illus. with numerous photos. $6.50.
Collector's guide to Savage pistols, models 1907-1922, with features, production data, and pictures of each. A reprint of the circa 1912 Savage promotional and instructive booklet titled *It Banishes Fear* is recommended to accompany the above. Paper wrappers, 32 pp. $1.50.

Schuyler, Hartley & Graham Catalog. Publ. by Norm Flavderman, Greenwich, Conn., 1961. 176 pp., illus. $9.50.
A reprint of a rare 1864 catalog of firearms, military goods, uniforms, etc. An extensive source of information for Civil War collectors.

Scottish Swords and Dirks, by John Wallace. Stackpole Books, Harrisburg, Pa., 1970. 80 pp., illus, $4.95.
An illustrated reference guide to Scottish edged weapons.

Sears, Roebuck & Co. Catalogue No. 117, J. J. Schroeder, ed. A reprint of the 1908 work. Digest Books, Inc., Northfield, Ill., 1969. 1,184 pp., profusely illus., paper covers. $3.95.
This reprint of a famous catalog brings to all arms collectors a treasured replica of the collectibles and prices of yesteryear.

The Sharps Rifle, by W. O. Smith. Morrow, N.Y.C., 1943, reprinted 1965. 138 pp., illus. $10.00.
Study of America's first successful breech-loader patented 1848, with information on its history, development, and operation.

Shosankenshu, by H. L. Joly. Holland Press, London, 1963. Unpaginated. $12.50.
List of Japanese artists' names and kakihan found on sword furniture by the late European authority. Completed in 1919, previously unpubl., this is a facsimile of Joly's MS. and line drawings. Lists nearly 3,000 names.

Shotgun Shells: Identification, Manufacturers and Checklist for Collectors, by F. H. Steward. B. and P. Associates, St. Louis, Mo., 1969. 101 pp., illus., paper covers. $4.95.
Historical data for the collector.
Single-Shot Rifles, by James J. Grant. Wm. Morrow & Co., N.Y.C., 4th printing 1964. 385 pp., illus. $8.50.
A detailed study of these rifles by a noted collector.
Small Arms, by Frederick Wilkinson, Hawthorne Books, Inc., New York, 1966. 256 pp., illus. $4.95.
A history of small firearms, techniques of the gunsmith, equipment used by combatants, sportsmen and hunters.
Small Arms and Ammunition in the United States Service, 1776-1865, by B. R. Lewis. Smithsonian Inst., Washington, D.C., 1968. 338 pp. plus 52 plates. $12.50.
2nd printing of a distinguished work for historians and collectors. A limited number of deluxe, signed and numbered copies (1st reprinting 1960) are available in full leather and gilt top at $25.
Small Arms Makers, by Robert Gardner. Bonanza Books, N.Y., 1963. 378 pp., illus, with marks and touches in line. $6.95.
A massive directory of makers of firearms, edged weapons, crossbows and polearms, with over 13,000 entries, A useful reference.
Smith and Wesson 1857-1945, by Robert J. Neal and Roy J. Jenks. A. S. Barnes and Co., Inc., N.Y.C., 1966. 500 pp., illus. with over 300 photos and 90 radiographs. $25.00.
A long-needed book, especially for knowledgeable enthusiasts and collectors. Covers an investigation of the series of handguns produced by the Smith and Wesson Company.
The Soldier's Manual, by J. H. Nesmith. (First publ. in Philadelphia in 1824.) Geo. Shumway, York, Pa., 1963. 108 pp., frontis, and 11 color plates. $4.95.
Facsimile reproduction of an important early American militia drill manual, covering exercises with musket, pistol, sword, and artillery. The color plates depict accurately the picturesque uniforms and accoutrements of elite militia corps of Phila. and vicinity. Intro. by Anne S. K. Brown traces the origin of the text matter and the early engravers.
Southern Derringers of the Mississippi Valley, by Turner Kirkland. Planeer Press, Tenn., 1971. 80 pp., illus., paper covers. $1.00.
A guide for the collector, and a much-needed study.
Sporting Guns, by Richard Akehurst. G. P. Putnam's Sons, New York, N.Y., 1968. 120 pp., excellently illus. and with 24 pp. in full color. $5.95.
One of the noted Pleasures and Treasures series. A nostalgic tracing of the history of shooting, and of the guns and rifles used by the sportsman.
Springfield Armory, Pointless Sacrifice, by C. L. Dvarecka. Prolitho Pub., Ludlow, Mass., 1968. 177 pp., illus. Paper covers. $1.00.
Story of the armory's closing; contains names, particulars and the quantities made of Springfield arms.
Springfield Muzzle-Loading Shoulder Arms, by C. E. Fuller. F. Bannerman Sons, N.Y.C., reprinted 1968. 176 pp., illus. $12.50.
Long-awaited reprint of an important 1930 reference work on weapons produced at Springfield Armory, 1795-1865, including ordnance reports, tables, etc., on flintlock and percussion models.
The Story of Allen and Wheelock Firearms, by H. H. Thomas. C. J. Krehbiel, Cincinnati, 1965. 125 pp., illus. $6.50.
Brief history of the Allen & Wheelock guns produced in mid-19th century, and their maker. Well illus. with descriptions of specimens.
The Story of Pope's Barrels, by Ray M. Smith. Stackpole Books, Harrisburg, Pa., 1964., 211 pp., illus. $10.00.
Detailed account of the achievements and life of Harry M. Pope, master rifle bbl. maker.
Superimposed Load Firearms 1360-1860, by D. R. Baxter. Privately printed for the author in Hong Kong, 1966. $22.00. Foreword by Keith Neal. Ltd. ed., 500 copies only.
Excellently illustrated with photographs, diagrams, figures and patent drawings. Covers over-under arms of all countries, and a list of gunmakers and inventors is included.
Sword, Lance and Bayonet, by Charles ffoulkes and E. C. Hopkinson. Arco Publishing Co., N.Y., 1967. 145 pp., well illus. in line and halftone. $7.50.
A facsimile reprint of the first attempt at a consecutive account of the arms, both general and official use, since the discarding of armor.
The Sword and Same, by Arai Hakuseki & Inaba Tsurio. C. E. Tuttle, Rutland, Vt., 1963. 235 pp., illus. $17.50.
Translation of classic Japanese treatise on the sword, circa 1700. Contains much curious sword-lore, with notes and illus. by the late H. L. Joly.
The 36 Calibers of the Colt Single Action Army, by David M. Brown. Publ. by the author at Albuquerque, N.M., new reprint 1971. 222 pp., well-illus. $15.00.
Edited by Bev Mann of *Guns Magazine*. This is an unusual approach to the many details of the Colt S.A. Army revolver. Halftone and line drawings of the same models make this of especial interest.
Thoughts on the Kentucky Rifle in its Golden Age, by Joe Kindig, Jr. George Shumway, York, Pa., 1970. A facsimile reprint of the 1960 original. 561 pp., replete with fine arms and data on many makers. $9.95.
Covers mainly the arms and their makers in the Lancaster area of Pennsylvania. An authoritative work.
Toxophilus, by Roger Ascham. S. R. Pub. Ltd., Yorkshire, Eng., 1968. 230 pp., illus. $7.00
A facsimile reprint of the 1788 ed. still regarded as the classic text on archery.
Treasury of the Gun, by H. L. Peterson, Crown Publishing Co.'s reprint, N.Y.C., 1965. 252 pp. profusely illus., some in color. $7.95.
A beautiful production, presenting a new high in authoritative text. Virtually every significant type of firearm of the past 650 years is shown.
Underhammer Guns, by H. C. Logan. Stackpole Books, Harrisburg, Pa., 1964. 250 pp. illus. $10.00.
A full account of an unusual form of firearm dating back to flintlock days. Both American and foreign specimens are included.
U.S. Firearms: The First Century, 1776-1875, by D. F. Butler. Winchester Press, N.Y., 1971. 320 pp., illus. $15.00.
A rich mine of carefully researched information and data on American firearms of this period. Illustrated with photos, schematics and historical documents.
U.S. Martial and Semi-Martial Single-Shot Pistols, by C. E. Chapel, Coward-McCann Inc., N.Y.C., 1962. 352 pp., over 150 illus. $7.50.
Describes in detail all single shot martial pistols used by the US. armed forces and by military units of the states. A definitive guide.
U.S. Military Firearms, 1776-1956, by Maj. Jas. E. Hicks. J. E. Hicks & Son. La Canada, Calif., 216 pp., incl. 88 pages of fine plates. $12.50.
Covering 180 years of America's hand and shoulder weapons. The most authoritative book on this subject. Packed with official data.
U.S. Military Small Arms 1816-1865, by R. M. Reilly. The Eagle Press, Inc., Baton Rouge, La., 1970. 275 pp., illus. $22.50.
Describes and superbly illustrates every known type of primary and secondary martial firearm of the period 1816-1865. Limited, numbered ed.
U.S. Sword Bayonets, 1847-1865, by R. V. Davis, Jr. Priv. prt., Pittsburgh, Pa., 1963. 36 pp., 17 pl., paper. $4.00
Histories, production data, and good photos of U. S. military sword bayonets of Civil War era.
U.S. Weapons Development 1920-25. An abridged reprint from official sources, this Section 1 covering rifles, pistols and some miscellaneous items. Design Publ., Inc. Hyattsville, Md. [circa 1968]. 57 pp., illus., paper covers. $5.00.
Dependable material for the collector and shooter.
A Universal Military Dictionary, by Captain George Smith. The rare original book was published at London in 1779. This facsimile reprint was released in 1869 by Museum Restoration Service, Ottawa, Ontario, Can. 336 pp., 16 fold-out plates. $27.50.
A most useful reference for men of arms interest. Offered only in a numbered, limited issue of 700 copies.
Waffen: Beitrag zur Historischen Waffenkunde, by J. H. Hefner-Alteneck. Akademische Druck, Graz, Austria, 1969. 58 pp., German text plus 100 plates. $30.00.
A descriptive text complements the fine illustrations depicting armor and weapons used in Europe from the middle ages through the 17th century.
Weapons, by E. Tunis. World Publishing Co., N.Y.C., 1954. 153 pp., a large book, well-illus. $4.95.
A pictorial history of arms with complementing narrative. Coverage: from the first tied stone thrown by pre-historic man to super bombs.
Weapons of the British Soldier, by Col. H. C. B. Rogers. Seeley Service & Co., London, 1960. 259 pp., illus. in line and halftone plus full color frontis. $6.50.
The story of weapons used by the British soldier throughout the ages and the many developments in personal arms during the course of history.
The Webley Story, by wm. C. Dowell, Skyrac Press, Leeds, Eng. 337 pp., profusely illus. $18.00.
Detailed study of Webley pistols and revolvers, covering over 250 specimens. This important reference also gives detailed listing of English small arms cartridge patents through 1880.
The Whitney Firearms, by Claude Fuller. Standard Publications, Huntington, W. Va., 1946. 334 pp., many plates and drawings. $12.50.
An authoritive history of all Whitney arms and their maker. Highly recommended. An exclusive with Ray Riling Arms Book Co.
Winchester—The Gun That Won the West, by H. F. Williamson. Combat Forces Press, Washington, D. C., 1952. Later eds. by Barnes, N.Y. 494 pp., profusely illus. $5.95.
A scholarly and essential economic history of an honored arms company, but the early and modern arms introduced will satisfy all but the exacting collector.
The Winchester Book, by Geo. Madis. Art & Reference House, Lancaster, Texas, 1971. 542 pp., illus. $20.00.
First release of 1,000 autographed deluxe copies at this special price. After these are sold only a standard ed. will be available, the price the same. $20.00.

GENERAL

The Adaptable Black Bear, by J. R. Matson. Dorrance & Co., Phila., Pa., 1967. 147 pp., illus. $4.00.
Complete picture of the black bear, its adaptation to environment, habits, disposition and behavior in the wild.
Age of Great Guns, by Frank E. Comparato. Stackpole Books, Harrisburg, Pa. 1965, 386 pp. illus. $11.95.
Of cannon kings and cannoneers who forged the fire-power of artillery. A highly acclaimed work of importance to artillery enthusiasts.
Air Gun Batteries, by E. G. Wolff. Public Museum, Milwaukee, Wisc., 1964. 28 pp., illus., paperbound. 75¢.
Study of discharge mechanisms on reservoir air guns.
Air Organizations of the Third Reich, Volume I, R. J. Bender, compiler. R. J. Bender, Mountain View, Ca, 192 pp., illus., some in color. $9.95.
Concise survey of the World War II Luftwaffe organizations. Shows uniforms, weapons, identification marks and badges.
The Album of Gunfighters, by J. Marvin Hunter and Noah H. Rose, Warren Hunter, Helotes, Texas, 1965. 4th printing. 236 pp., wonderfully illus., with spectacular oldtime photos. $15.00.
For the serious gunfighter fan there is nothing to equal this factual record of the men-behind-the-star and the human targets that they faced.
American Bird Decoys, by W. J. Mackey Jr. Dutton, N.Y.C., 1965. 256 pp., illus. $10.00.
The history and fine points of decoys for all gamebird species, with much data for collectors and hunters.
Covers every article in the 1951-1960 issues of *The American Rifleman*. A valuable tool for location of material published in those years.
Americans and their Guns, compiled by Jas. B. Trefethen, ed. by Jas. E. Serven, Stackpole Books, Harrisburg, Pa., 1967. 320 pp., illus. $9.95.
The National Rifle Association of America story through nearly a century of service to the nation. More than a history—a chronical of help to novice and expert in the safe and proper use of firearms for defense and recreation, as well as a guide for the collector of arms.
America's Camping Book, by Paul Cardwell, Jr. C. Scribner's Sons, New York, N.Y. 1st ed., 1969. 591 pp., well illus., in line and halftone. $10.00.
A fine illustrated guide to camping and woodcraft, with data on equipment, techniques, emergencies and nature study.
The Anatomy of Firearms, by R. L. Wallack, Simon & Schuster, N.Y.C., 1965. 320 pp., illus. $6.95.
Guide to guns of all types, ammunition, ballistics, repairs and adjustments, and related topics.
Animals in Africa, by Peter and Philippa Scott. Clarkson N. Potter, N.Y., 1963. Profusely, magnificently illus. Unpaginated. Large format. $7.95.
The enchanting story, in words and pictures, of a journey by the authors through the National Parks of Kenya to Murchison Falls Park in Uganda. Over 180 pictures in black-and-white, 20 in full color.
Animals of East Africa, by C. A. Spinage. Houghton Mifflin Co., Boston, Mass., 1963. 151 pp., illus. $7.50.
The life history, unusual observations and little known facts about these animals. Over 90 photographs, some in color.
Archery, by C. J. Longman and H. Walrond. Frederick Ungar Co., N.Y., 1967. 534 pp., illus. in line and halftone. $5.95.
Reproduction of a standard, important British reference work, first publ. in 1894, on the history, uses and techniques of archery.
Arco Gun Book, ed. by Larry Koller. Arco Publ. Co. Inc., N.Y.C., 1962. 397 pp., illus. $7.50.
A concise encyclopedia for arms collectors, shooters and hunters.
Armour, by Viscount Dillon. Geo. Shumway, York, Pa., 1968. 75 pp., illus., paperbound. $4.00.
Facsimile of British monographs titled *An Elizabethan Armourer's Album* and *Armour Notes.*
Armoured Fighting Vehicles, by Malcolm McGregor, Walker & Co., New York, 1967. 56 pp., illus. $15.00.
Describes 12 tanks and armored cars, representative of those used in the two World Wars. The illustrations in full-color are true scale drawn from actual models.

Armoured Forces, by R. M. Ogorkiewicz. Arco Pub. Co., N.Y., 1970. 475 pp., illus. $7.95.
A history of the armored forces and their vehicles.

The Art of Archerie, by Gervase Markham. A reprint of the 1634 original, publ. in London. Geo. Shumway, York, Pa., 1968. 172 pp. $12.00.
This classic treatise, written to keep alive the art of archery in warfare, treats with the making of longbows and their use. A scholarly introduction to the new issue by S. V. Grancsay adds an enlightening historical perception.

The Art and Science of Taking to the Woods, by C. B. Colby and B. Angier, Stackpole Books, Harrisburg, Pa. 1970, 288 pp. illus. $7.95. Also in paper covers. $3.95.
Illustrated camper's manual covering all types of outdoor living and transportation, for novice and expert alike.

The Art of Shooting, by C. E. Chapel. Barnes, N.Y.C., 1960. 424 pp., illus. $3.95.
A comprehensive, simplified guide to every aspect of pistol, revolver, and rifle shooting. A history of rifle development is included.

The Art of Survival, by C. Troebst. Doubleday & Co., Garden City, N.Y. 1965. 312 pp. illus. $5.95.
Narratives of devices of survival in difficult terrain or circumstances and evaluation of rescue and life-saving procedures.

The Art of the Decoy: American Bird Carvings, by Adele Earnest. Clarkson N. Potter, Inc., N.Y.C., 1966. $4.95.
The origin of a lost art explained, plus some data on the most famous carvers. Over 106 black-and-white photos, 35 line drawings and an 8-page insert in full color.

The Artillerist's Manual, by Lieut. John Gibbon. Benchmark Pub. Co., Glendale, N.Y., 1970. 568 pp., illus. $16.50.
Reprint of an 1860 textbook on U.S. artillery, covering guns, ammunition, transportation, many other facets.

Artillery and Ammunition of the Civil War, by Warren Ripley. Van Nostrand Reinhold Co., N.Y., 1970. 384 pp., illus. $22.50.
Well-illustrated survey, covering Union and Confederate cannon and projectiles, as well as imported pieces.

Artillery of the U.S. Land Service: 1848-1865, compiled by D. E. Lutz. Antique Ordnance Artificers, Jackson, Mich., 1970. 64 pp., illus. Paper wrappers. $5.00.
Known as Vol. I, **Field Artillery, 1848-1865,** and the first of a series containing drawings of the artillery used during the Civil War. Mainly taken from manuscripts in the National Archives.

Asian Fighting Arts, by D. F. Draeger and R. W. Smith. Kodansha International Ltd., Tokyo, Japan. 2nd printing, 1969. 207 pp., well illus., in line and halftone. $10.00.
A work of monumental research, interesting to all involved in the science of fighting techniques. Covers eleven Asian skills, ranging from Chinese T'ai-chi and Burmese Bando to Japanese Jujitsu and the lethal Pentjak-silak of Indonesia.

Baron von Steuben and his Regulations, by Joseph R. Riling, Ray Riling Arms Books Co., Philadelphia, Penna., 1966. 207 pp., illus. $12.50.
A documented book on this great American Major General and the creation by him of the first official "Regulations." Includes the complete facsimile of these regulations.

Better ways of Pathfinding, by R. S. Owendoff. Stackpole, Harrisburg, Pa., 1964. 96 pp., illus. $2.95.
Practical methods of finding one's way in unfamiliar areas, using maps, compass, and the sky.

Bring Your Own Wilderness Doctor, by Dr. E. Russel Kodet and Bradford Angier. Stackpole Books, Harrisburg, Pa., 1968. 127 pp., illus. in line drawings. $3.95.
Called the "outdoorsman's emergency manual" it offers security of knowing what to do best—in case of the worst.

A Bibliography of Military Books up to 1642, by Maurice J. D. Cockle. A new reprint of the Holland Press, London, 1965. 320 pp., illus. $15.00.
Describes the important military books from the invention of gunpowder to subject date. A standard reference.

Birds in Our Lives, ed. by A. Stefferud and A. L. Nelson. Gov't. Prtg. Office, Washington, D. C. 20402, 1966, 576 pp., 80 drawings, 372 photos. $9.00
61 authors have contributed to this great book, the illus. by Bob Hines. A successful effort to bring any and all readers an appreciation of—and an interest in—the part birds play in their lives.

Black Powder Guide, by Geo. Nonte, Jr. Shooter's Bible Publ., S. Hackensack, N.J., 1969. 214 pp., fully illus., $3.95.
A complete guide to muzzle-loading firearms of all types, their loading, repair and maintenance.

Black Powder Snapshots, by Herb Sherlock. Standard Publications, Huntington, W. Va. 50 pp., illus. $8.50.
Deluxe large volume containing 23 major Sherlock drawings and 95 punchy, marginal sketches.

The Book of the American West, ed. by Jay Monaghan. Julian Messner, New York, 1963. 608 pp., 200 illus. (many in color). $9.95.
A special chapter on frontier firearms is a feature of this massive work. 10 experts on Western hist. in as many fields of study contributed to the book. Illus. include works by the best contemporary artists.

The Book of the American Woodcock, by Wm. G. Sheldon, Ph.D. University of Mass. Press, Amherst, 1967. 227 pp., bibliography, appendices and index. $8.50.

Bow & Arrow Archer's Digest, ed. by Jack Lewis. Digest Books, Inc., Northfield, Ill., 1971. 320 pp., profusely illus. $5.95.
Comprehensive treatment of the art and science of archery.

The Boy's Book of Backyard Camping, by A. A. Macfarlan. Stackpole Books, Harrisburg, Pa. 1st ed. 1968. 160 pp., illus. in line. $4.50.
"How to use at-home space for the development of camping skills." Chapters on tents, equipment, cooking—all for out-of-doors enjoyment.

Boys in the Revolution, by Jack Coggins, Stackpole Books, Harrisburg, Pa., 1967. 96 pp., illus. $4.50.
Young Americans tell their part in the war for independence—what they did, what they wore, the gear they carried, the weapons they used, the ships they sailed on, the campaigns in which they fought.

British and American Tanks of WW II, by P. Chamberlain and C. Ellis. Arco Pub. Co., New York., 1969. 222 pp., illus. $9.95.
Complete, illus. history of American, British and Commonwealth tanks, 1939-1945. Photos, and precise specifications of each.

Camper's Digest, by Cecil Coffey. Digest Books, Inc., Northfield, Ill. 60093. 320 pp., paper covers, over 500 illus. $4.95.
Everything needed to be known about camping. Trails, tools, clothes, cooking, hundreds of camp grounds listed, and more.

The Camping Manual, compiled by Fred Sturges, Stackpole Books, Harrisburg, Pa., 1967. 160 pp., illus. $3.95.
An excellent refresher on the fundamentals, with a digest of the newest methods and latest advice for those who want to enjoy camping more.

Carbine Handbook, by Paul Wahl. Arco Publ. Co., N.Y.C., 1964. 80 pp., illus. Paperbound, $6.00.
A manual and guide to the U.S. Carbine, cal. .30, M1, with data on its history, operation, repair, ammunition, and shooting.

The Classic Decoy Series, Ed Zern, text; M. C. Weiller, illustrator. Winchester Press, New York, N.Y. 1969. A beautiful work picturing 24 American duck decoys in full color, printed on special paper and loose for framing. Decorated covers in slip case. Anecdotal text on each species shown. $100.00.
This deluxe collectors' work is offered in a strictly limited issue of 1000 copies, each signed by the artist and numbered.

A Colt Bibliography, by G. M. Lord. Privately produced by the author, Bothell, Wash., 1968. 32 pp., mimeographed stapled sheets. $3.00.
Lists articles, books, etc., of interest to the Colt collector, gunsmith and or historian.

Colt Commemorative Firearms, by R. L. Wilson. Chas. Kidwell, Wichita, Kans., 1969. 108 pp., $10.00.
A chronological listing and a precise description of all Colt commemoratives from 1961 through 1969.

The Complete Book of the Air Gun, by G. C. Nonte Jr. Stackpole Book, Harrisburg, Pa., 1970. 288 pp., illus. $7.95.
From plinking to Olympic competition, from BB guns to deluxe rifles, pistols, the air shotgun.

Complete Book of Rifles and Shotguns, by Jack O'Connor, Harper & Bros., N.Y.C., 1961, 477 pp., illus. $6.95.
A splendid two-part book of encyclopedic coverage on every detail of rifle and shotgun.

Complete Book of Shooting, by Jack O'Connor et al. Outdoor Life—Harper & Row, N.Y.C., 1965. 385 pp., illus. $5.95.
Fundamentals of shooting with rifle, shotgun, and handgun in the hunting field and on target ranges.

The Complete Cannoneer, compiled by M. C. Switlik. Antique Ordnance Artificers, Jackson, Mich., 1971. 106 pp., illus., paper covers. $4.50.
A must for the modern cannoneer. Compiled in two sections. Part first contains "School of the Piece" as orginally published in Artillery Drill by George S. Patton, in 1861. Part second contains current observations on the safe use of cannon.

Coping with Camp Cooking, by M. W. Stephens and G. S. Wells. Stackpole Books, Harrisburg, Pa. 1966. 94 pp., illus., decorated boards. $2.95.
Hints and recipes selected from the editors' writings appearing in *Camping Guide Magazine.*

Crusade for Wildlife, by J. B. Trefethen. Stackpole Books, Harrisburg, Pa., 1961. 377 pp., illus. $7.50.
History of the Boone and Crockett Club and its efforts to preserve wildlife in America, with accounts of the plight of threatened species.

Current American War Medals and Decorations, 1963-69, by E. E. Kerrigan. Medallic Publishing Co., Noroton Heights, Conn. 1st ed. 1969. Paper covers, 23 pp., illus. $3.00.
This supplement updates the author's *American War Medals and Decorations,* listing recently created awards and recipients.

Daggers, Bayonets & Fighting Knives of Hitler's Germany, by John R. Angolia. James Bender Pub. Co., Mountain View, CA. 1st ed. 1971. 334 pp., profusely illus. $14.95.
An exceptionally fine, useful compilation for collector, historian and student.

The Daggers and Edged Weapons of Hitler's Germany, by Maj. J. P. Atwood, Publ. privately for the author in Berlin, Germany, 1965. 240 pp. illus. New edition, 1967. $15.00.
Lavishly illus. with many plates in full color, this is an outstanding production, easily the best information (for the collector) on the subject.

Daggers and Fighting Knives of the Western World: From the Stone Age Until 1900, by Harold L. Peterson, Walker and Co., New York, 1967. 256 pp., illus. $2.98.
The only full-scale historical and analytical work on this subject, from flint knives of the stone age to British and American naval dirks.

Decoys and Decoy Carvers of Illinois, by P. W. Parmalee and F. D. Loomis. Northern Illinois University Press, DeKalb, Ill. 1st ed., 1969, 506 pp., illus. $17.50.
A comprehensive and handsome survey, replete with photographs—many in color. The work of the makers is analyzed, with comments on Illinois duck shooting over the past century.

Design and Development of Fighting Vehicles, by R. M. Ogorkiewicz. Doubleday, N.Y.C., 1968. 208 pp. plus 174 plates. $7.95.
A review of design and engineering problems of battle tanks and other armored vehicles since World War II, with evaluations of tank design.

The Details of the Rocket System, by Col. Wm. Congreve. Museum Restoration Service, Ottawa, Canada, 1970. 85 pp., illus. $10.00.
Reprint of the 1814 1st ed. with details, photos and plates of rockets and their launchers. Edition limited and numbered.

Die Handwaffen, by Werner Eckardt and Otto Morawietz. H. G. Schulz, Hamburg, 1957. 265 pp., 15 plates, 175 illus. $10.00.
An important work (in German) on German Service arms from their beginnings through World War II. A symposium on the subject—ancient, obsolete, semi-modern and modern.

Eat the Weeds, by B. C. Harris. Barre Publ., Barre, Mass., 1968. 223 pp., illus. $5.95.
Practical directions for collecting and drying herbs, for using edible plants and fruits as food and for medical purposes or as substitutes for cultivated vegetables.

Elephant, by Commander D. E. Blunt. A reprint by Neville Spearman, Ltd., London, 1971. 260 pp., illus. $10.00.
A hunter's account of the ways of the elephant in Africa and elsewhere —on hunting and conservation practices.

Encyclopedia of Firearms, ed. by H. L. Peterson. E. P. Dutton, N.Y.C., 1964. 367 pp., 100 pp. of illus. incl. color. $13.50.
Fine reference work on firearms, with articles by 45 top authorities covering classes of guns, manufacturers, ammunition, nomenclature, and related topics.

Encyclopedia of Modern Firearms, Vol. 1, compiled and publ. by Bob Brownell, Montezuma, Iowa, 1959. 1057 pp. plus index, illus. $20.00. Dist. by Bob Brownell, Montezume, Ia. 50171.
Massive accumulation of basic information on nearly all modern arms pertaining to "parts and assembly." Replete with arms photographs, exploded drawings, manufacturers' lists of parts, etc.

Explosives and Demolitions, U.S. Field Manual 5-25, Normount Armament Co., Forest Grove, Ore. 215 pp., illus., paperbound. $4.00.
A reprint of the Army FM dated 14 May 1959.

Fell's Guide to Guns and How to Use Them, by B. G. Wels. Frederick Fell, New York, N.Y. 1969. 173 pp., illus. in line and halftone. $4.95.
Aspects of the safe use of firearms for sportsmen, hunters and collectors.

Firearms, by H. L. Blackmore. E. P. Dutton, N.Y.C., 1964. 160 pp., well-illus., paperbound. $1.75.
Firearms history from its beginnings to recent times. Fine photographs of museum-quality arms.

Firearms, by Walter Buehr. Crowell Co., N.Y.C., 1967. 186 pp., illus. $5.95.
From gunpowder to guided missile, an illustrated history of firearms for military and sporting uses.

Firearms Dictionary, by R. A. "Bob" Steindler. Stackpole Books, Harrisburg, Pa., 288 pp., illus. $7.95.

Firearm Silencers, by D. B. McLean. Normount Armament Co., Forest Grove, Ore., 1968. 123 pp., illus., paperbound. $4.00.
The history, design, and development of silencers for U.S. military firearms.

Firearms, Traps & Tools of the Mountain Men, by Carl P. Russell. A. A. Knopf, N.Y., 1967. 448 pp., illus. in line drawings. $15.00.
Detailed survey of fur traders' equipment in the early days of the west.

The Fireside Book of Guns, by Larry Koller. Simon & Schuster, N.Y.C., 1959. 284 pp., illus. in artistic photography and full-color plates. $12.95.
On all counts the most beautiful and colorful production of any arms book of our time, this work adequately tells the story of firearms in America—from the first explorers to today's sportsmen.

Four Studies on the History of Arms, by Arne Hoff, et al. Tojhusmuseet, Copenhagen, 1964. 145 pp., illus., paperbound. $6.75.
A Danish museum publication containing in English text scholarly monographs on arms topics of historic interest.

Free for the Eating, by Bradford Angier, Stackpole Books, Harrisburg, Pa., 1966. 191 pp., illus. $4.95.
Discusses and illustrates 100 wild plants and 300 ways to use them.

More Free for the Eating, Wild Foods, by Bradford Angier, Stackpole Books, Harrisburg, Pa., 1969. 192 pp., illus. $4.95.
A sequel to *Free for the Eating*, being a nature-study cookbook with an additional 200 ways to prepare common wild plants.

The A. B. Frost Book, by Henry M. Reed. Charles E. Tuttle Co., Rutland, Vermont, 1967. 149 pp., of large format with over 70 plates, 44 in color, and many line drawings. $20.00.
A collection of the sketches, drawings and paintings by a famous outdoor artist (1851-1928). Includes his noted sporting and shooting masterpieces.

Fundamentals of Small Arms, U.S. TM9-2205. Normount Armament Co., Forest Grove, Ore. 236 pp., illus., paperbound. $3.50.
Reprint of the U.S. Army technical manual dated 7 May 1952.

Game Animals, by Leonard Lee Rue III. Harper & Row, N.Y., 1968. 655 pp., incl. appendix and index. Illus. with maps and photos. $6.50.
A concise guide to and field book of North American species.

Game and Fish Cookbook, by H. and J. Barnett. Grossman Publ., New York, N.Y. 1968, 162 pp., illus. $7.95.
Special culinary attention to fish and game, with interesting and different touches.

Game in the Kitchen, by B. Flood and W. C. Roux (eds.). Barre Publ., Barre, Mass. 1st ed., 1968, 234 pp., illus. $7.50.
A fish and game cookbook, with menus and information on preservation, cooking and serving.

Gas, Air and Spring Guns of the World, by W. H. B. Smith. Stackpole Books, Harrisburg, Pa., 1957. 279 pp., well illus. $10.00.
A detailed, well-documented history of the air and gas gun industry throughout the world. It includes ancient and modern arms, and it devotes a chapter to accurate velocity tests of modern arms.

German Infantry Weapons, ed. by D. B. McLean. Normount Armament Co., Forest Grove, Ore., 1966. 191 pp., illus., paperbound. $3.00.
World War II German weapons described and illustrated, from military intelligence research.

German Infantry Weapons of World War II, by A. J. Barker. Arco Publ. Co., New York, N.Y. 1969, 76 pp., illus. $3.50.
Historical and statistical data on all types of the subject weapons, ammunition, etc.

German Mauser Rifle, Model of 1898, by Coombes & Aney. F. Bannerman, N.Y.C., 1921. 20 pp., illus., paperbound. $1.50.
Reprint of a pamphlet describing a famous military rifle, its bayonets, ammunition, and accessories.

German Secret Weapons of World War II, by I. V. Hogg. Arco Pub. Co., N.Y., 1970. 80 pp., illus. $3.50.
Compact, comprehensive account of Germany's secret weapons, eccentric and brilliant. Includes plans and technical details.

German Tanks of World War II, by F. M. Von Senger und Etterlin. Stackpole Books, Harrisburg, Pa., 1969. 176 pp., nearly 300 photos and drawings. Large format. $11.95.
A fully illustrated and definitive history of German armoured fighting vehicles, 1926-1945. Written in English.

German Weapons-Uniforms-Insignia 1841-1918, by Maj. J. E. Hicks. J. E. Hicks & Son, La Canada, Calif., 1958. 158 pp., illus. $6.00.
Originally published in 1937 as *Notes on German Ordnance 1841-1918*, this new edition offers the collector a wealth of information gathered from many authentic sources.

The Golden Guide to Guns, by Larry Koller. Golden Press, N.Y.C., 1966. 160 pp., illus., paperbound, pocket-size. $1.00.
Introduction to rifles, shotguns, and handguns for all uses. Profusely illus., much in color.

Gourmet Cooking for Free, by Bradford Angier. Stackpole Books, Harrisburg, Pa. 1970. 190 pp. illus. $4.95.
Cookery of large and small game, seafood and wild plants.

Great American Guns and Frontier Fighters, by Will Bryant, Grosset & Dunlap, New York, 1961. 160 pp., illus. $3.95.
Popular account of firearms in U.S. history and of the events in which they played a part.

Great Weapons of World War II, by J. Kirk and R. Young. Bonanza Books, N.Y., 1968. 348 pp., profusely illus. The latest reprint. $4.95.
Covers, in text and picture, great and powerful weapons, planes, tanks as well as small arms, miscellaneous arms and naval attack vessels.

The Gun Digest, 1944 First Annual Edition, ed. by John T. Amber. Follett Publ. Co., Chicago, Ill., 1944, 1963. 162 pp., illus., paperbound. $2.95.
Reprint edition of the prized first edition of *The Gun Digest.* Many useful articles on small arms and their uses.

Gun Digest, 25th ed., ed. by John T. Amber. Digest Books, Inc., Northfield, Ill., 1971, 480 pp., profusely illus. $6.95.
Known as the world's greatest gun book because of its factual, informative data for shooters, hunters, collectors, reloaders and other enthusiasts. Truly of encyclopedic importance. Decorated paper wrappers.

Gun Digest Treasury, ed. by J. T. Amber, 3rd edition, 1966. Digest Books, Inc., Northfield, Ill. 416 pp., illus. Paperbound $4.95,
The best from 20 years of the GUN DIGEST, selected from the annual editions.

Gundogs, Their Care and Training, by M. Brander. A. & C Black, London, Eng., 1969. 97 pp., illus. $4.95.
A British manual on hunting dogs.

Gun Fun with Safety, by G. E. Damon. Standard Publications, Huntington, W. Va., 1947. 206 pp., well illus. $6.00.
A long out-of-print work that is still much sought. A fine general coverage of arms and ammunition, old and new, with chapters on shooting, targets, etc., with safety always upper-most.

The Gun that Made the Twenties Roar, by W. J. Helmer, Macmillan Co., N.Y. 1969. 286 pp. illus. $7.95.
Historical account of John T. Thompson and his invention, the Thompson submachine gun. Includes virtually a complete manual in detail.

Gun Trader's Guide, by Paul Wahl, Shooter's Bible, Inc., New York, 1968. 5th rev. ed. 220 pp., 8"x10", profusely illus. Paperbound. $3.95. Complete guide to the identification of modern firearms and giving their current market values.

The Gunfighter, Man or Myth? by Joseph G. Rosa, Oklahoma Press, Norman, Okla., 1969. 229 pp., illus., (including weapons). $5.95.
A well-documented work on gunfights and gunfighters of the West and elsewhere, Great treat for all gunfighter buffs.

The Gunner's Bible, by Bill Riviere. Doubleday, N.Y.C., 1965. 192 pp., illus. Paperbound. $1.95.
General Guide to modern sporting firearms and their accessories, for all shooters.

Gunology, by P. M. Doane. Winchester-Western, N.Y.C., 1968. 64 pp., illus., paperbound. $2.95.
A comprehensive course for professional sporting arms salesmen. Of great help to the arms man are the hundreds of questions on arms and hunting.

Guns, by Dudley Pope. Delacorte Press, N.Y.C., 1965. 256 pp., illus. $9.98.
Concise history of firearms, stressing early museum-quality weapons. Includes small arms as well as artillery, naval, and airborne types. Fine photographs, many in color.

Guns & Ammo 1971 Annual, Guns & Ammo magazine, Petersen Publ. Co., Los Angeles Ca., 1969. 378 pp. illus. Paper covers. $3.95.
Annual catalog of sporting firearms and accessories, with numerous articles for gun enthusiasts.

Guns Annual for 1972, edited by Jerome Rakusan, Publishers Development Corp., Skokie, Ill., 1971. 134 pp., well illus., decorated paper wrappers. $2.00.
An annual publication describing and illustrating firearms available in current markets, plus articles by experts in the field of collecting, shooting, ammunition, etc.

Guns Illustrated 1972, 4th ed., ed. by Joe J. Schroeder, Jr., Digest Books, Inc., Northfield, Ill. 1971. 288 pp., Profusely illus., paper covers. $3.95.
Revised and up-dated with latest models, prices, specifications and data on handguns, rifles, shotguns, scopes, sights, etc.

Guns and Rifles of the World, by Howard L. Blackmore, The Viking Press, New York, 1965. 290 pp. 1042 halftone and line illustrations. $30.00.
One of the finest books to come out of England. Covers firearms from the handgun to air, steam, and electric guns.

Guns and Shooting, by Maj. Sir Gerald Burrard. Barnes & Co., N.Y.C., 1962. 147 pp. $1.95.
Expanded from the author's earlier *In the Gunroom*, this contains 153 often-asked questions on shotguns and rifles, with authoritative answers covering guns, ammunition, ballistics, etc.

Guns and Shooting, a Bibliography, by R. Riling. Greenberg, N.Y.C., 1951. 434 pp., illus. $20.00.
A selected listing, with pertinent comment and anecdote, of books and printed material on arms and ammunition from 1420 to 1950.

The Guns of Harpers Ferry, by S. E. Brown Jr. Virginia Book Co., Berryville, Va., 1968. 157 pp., illus. $12.50.
Catalog of all known firearms produced at the U.S. armory at Harpers Ferry, 1798-1861, with descriptions, illustrations and a history of the operations there.

Handbook on German Military Forces, a reprint of *TM-E30-451*, originating with U.S. Military Intelligence. Publ. by the Military Press, Gaithersburg, Md. 1970. 550 pp., copious illus., many in color. $14.95.
A rare restricted handbook [many destroyed] covering military systems, doctrines, SS police, home defense, etc.

Handbook on Japanese Military Forces, a reprint of *TM-E30-480*, originating with U.S. Military Intelligence. Publ. by the Military Press, Gaithersburg, Md., 1970. 550 pp., illus., 24 pp., in color. $14.95.
A rare restricted work [many destroyed] on military systems, doctrines, police, home defense. etc.

Handbook of Self-Defense for Law Enforcement Officers, by John Martone. Arco Publ. Co., New York, N.Y., 1968. 1st ed., 4th printing, 111 pp., $3.50.
A clearly-illustrated manual on offensive and defensive techniques recommended for the use of policemen.

Hatcher's Notebook, by Maj. Gen. J. S. Hatcher. Stackpole Books, Harrisburg, Pa., 1952. 2nd ed. with four new chapters, 1957. 629 pp., illus. $11.95.
A dependable source of information for gunsmiths, ballisticians, historians, hunters, and collectors.

History of the British Army, by P. Young and J. P. Lawford. G. P. Putnam's Sons, N.Y., 1970. 304 pp., profusely illus., much in color. $15.00.
Traces history of the British Army from the early 17th century to the present.

A History of Knives, by Harold L. Peterson. Charles Scribner's Sons, N.Y.C., 1966. 64 pp., illus. $3.50.
The fine drawings of Daniel D. Feaser combine with the author's commendable text to produce an important work. From the earliest knives of prehistoric man through the evolution of the metal knife.

History of Small Arms Ammunition 1917-19. A reprint of an official U.S. Ordnance source work, *circa* 1920. Design Publ., Hyattsville, Md. Reprinted 1968. 40 pp., illus., paper covers. $5.00.
Another scarce work for the seeker of authoritative material.

A History of War and Weapons, 449 to 1660, by A. V. B. Norman and D. Pottinger. Thomas Y. Crowell Co., N.Y., 1966. 224 pp., well illus. with sketches. $6.95.
An excellent work for the scholar on the evolution of war and weapons in England. Many sketches of arms and weapons of all sorts add importance.

The History of Weapons of the American Revolution, by Geo. C. Neumann. Harper & Row, N.Y., 1967. 373 pp., fully illus. $15.00.
Collector's reference covering long arms, handguns, edged and pole weapons used in the Revolutionary War.

Home Book of Taxidermy and Tanning, by G. J. Grantz, Stackpole Books, Harrisburg, Pa., 1969, 160 pp., illus. $7.95.
Amateur's primer on mounting fish, birds, animals, and trophies.

Home in Your Pack, by Bradford Angier, Stackpole Books, Harrisburg, Pa., 1965. 192 pp., illus. $4.50.
An outdoorsman's handbook on equipment, woodcraft, and camping techniques.

Horse Equipments and Cavalry Accoutrements 1891. A reprint of U.S. Ordnance Memoranda No. 29 by Francis Bannerman Sons, Blue Point, N.Y., 1969. 23 pp., plus 20 plates. $3.50.
U.S. army cavalry equipment described and illustrated in line.

How to Build Your Home in the Woods, by Bradford Angier, Stackpole Books, Harrisburg, Pa., 1967. 310 pp., illus. $7.00.
Detailed instructions on building cabins, shelters, etc., with natural materials. How to obtain food from nature, and how to live in the wilderness in comfort.

How to Defend Yourself, your Family, and your Home, by Geo. Hunter. David McKay, N.Y.C., 1967. 307 pp., illus. $6.95.
The only book available for the public at large that advocates their ownership of firearms—including handguns. Covers laws of self-defense, setting up home protection, and much else.

How to Live in the Woods on $10.00 a Week, by Bradford Angier, Stackpole Books, Harrisburg, Pa., 1959. 269 pp., illus. $7.50.
Modern-day homesteading explained by an expert; where to go and how to achieve freedom and comfort on today's frontiers.

Indian and Oriental Armour, by Lord Egerton of Tatton. Stackpole Books, Harrisburg, Pa., 1968. 178 pp., well illus., some in color. $14.95.

New edition of a rare work which has been a key reference for students of the subject, plus a creditable source on Oriental history.

Infantry Equipment 1875. A reprint of U.S. Ordnance Memoranda No. 19 by Francis Bannerman Sons, Blue Point, N.Y., 1969. 62 pp., plus 9 plates. $6.50.

A report covering materials, supplies, etc., to outfit troops in field and garrison.

Instinct Shooting, by Mike Jennings. Dodd, Mead & Co., N.Y.C., 1959. 157 pp., 20 line drawings, illus. $3.75.

All about Lucky McDaniel and his surprisingly successful discovery of a new aerial shooting technique, one which will let almost anyone, novices *preferred*, hit flying targets with only minutes of instruction.

Introduction to Muzzle Loading, by R. O. Ackerman. Publ. by the author, Albuquerque, N.M., 1966. 20 pp., illus. with author's sketches. $1.50.

This booklet, in paper wrappers, will be Book No. 1 of a projected series. Contains a glossary of muzzle loading terms, and is aimed at the novice.

An Introduction to Tool Marks, Firearms and the Striagraph, by J. E. Davis. Chas. C. Thomas, Springfield, Ill., 1st ed., 1958. 282 pp. $8.50.

Textbook on micro-contour analysis in criminalistics, with emphasis upon the striagraph in analysis of evidence.

Ironmaker To The Confederacy, by C. B. Dew. Yale Univ. Press, New Haven, 1966. 345 pp., illus. $10.00.

History of Joseph R. Anderson's Tredegar Iron Works in Richmond, Va., which produced weapons and military equipment essential to the Confederacy's armed forces.

Japanese Infantry Weapons, ed. by D. B. McLean. Normount Armament Co., Forest Grove, Ore., 1966. 241 pp., well illus., paperbound. $3.50.

Survey of World War II Japanese weapons, based on military intelligence research.

The Japanese Sword and Its Fittings, by members of the Japanese Sword Society of New York. Cooper Union Museum, N.Y.C., 1966. Paper covers. 26 pp. of text plus many illus. $3.50.

The authoritative text in the form of a catalog describing the illus. of items in the possession of members of the society.

John Groth's World of Sport, by J. Groth. Winchester Press. N.Y., 1970. 160 pp., illus. $25.00.

Exotic and exciting sports recorded by a man whose vital drawings convey the essence of the action. 40 color paintings.

Johnson Rifles and Light Machine Guns, ed. by D. B. McLean. Normount Armament Co., Forest Grove, Ore., 1968. 55 pp., illus., paperbound. $2.00.

Manual on the only recoil-operated auto-loading rifle issued to U.S. forces.

Knife Throwing as a Modern Sport, by H. K. McEvoy and C. V. Gruzanski. Charles C. Thomas, Springfield, Ill., 1965. 57 pp., illus. $4.50.

For first time, a concise, easy-to-read and complete story on this modern sport.

A Knight and His Armour, 95 pp. $3.25.
A Knight and His Castle, 108 pp., $3.25.
A Knight and His Horse, 96 pp., $3.25.
A Knight and His Weapons, 95 pp., $3.25.

A series planned for young readers, by R. E. Oakeshott. Lutterworth Press, London, 1966. All illus. Of interest to adults as well.

Lewis Automatic Machine Gun, publ. originally by Savage Arms Co., Utica, N.Y. A reprint by L. A. Funk, Puyallup, Wash., 1969. 47 pp., illus., paper covers. $1.50.

This facsimile covers the Model 1916 gun, explaining all features of operation, action, nomenclature, stripping and assembly.

The Machine Gun, Vol. II, Part VII, by Lt. Col. G. M. Chinn. Paladin Press, Boulder, Col., n.d. 215 pp., illus. $15.00.

Reprint of a 1952 Navy publication on Soviet WW II rapid fire weapons.

Marlin Catalog of 1897. A reprint in facsimile by the Wyoming Armory, Inc., Cheyenne, Wy. 1969. 192 pp. Well illus., paper covers. $3.50.

All models are covered, cartridges, sights, engraving, accessories, reloading tools, etc.

Mexican Military Arms, The Cartridge Period, by James B. Hughes, Jr. Deep River Armory, Inc., Houston, Texas, 1967. 135 pp., photos and line drawings. $4.50.

An interesting and useful work, in imprinted wrappers, covering the period from 1866 to 1967.

Military Uniforms, 1686-1918, by Rene North. Grosset & Dunlap, N.Y., 1970. 159 pp., illus. $3.95.

Concise survey of European and U.S. military dress and its history during the principal wars. Profusely illus., with some colored drawings.

Military Uniforms of the World in Color, by Preben Kannik, translated by W. Y. Carman. MacMillan Co., N.Y., N.Y., 1968. 278 pp. incl. index, 512 illus. figures in full color. $4.95.

An excellent handbook for the collector and student. The descriptive text gives good details of equipment.

The Minute Men, by J. R. Galvin. Hawthorn Books, N.Y.C., 1967. 286 pp. $6.95.

History of the colonial militia to the beginning of the Revolutionary War, including data on the battles of Lexington and Concord.

Modern ABC's of Bow and Arrow, by G. H. Gillelan. Stackpole Books, Harrisburg, Pa., 1967. 160 pp., illus. $4.95.

Survey of techniques for beginners and experts in target archery as well as bowhunting.

Modern ABC's of Guns, by R. A. Steindler. Stackpole Books, Harrisburg, Pa. 1965. 191 pp., illus. $4.95.

Concise lexicon of today's sporting firearms, their components, ammunition, accessory equipment and use.

Modern Police Firearms, by Duke Roberts and A. P. Bristow. Glencoe Press, Beverly Hills, Ca., 1969. 170 pp., illus., in line and halftone. $5.95.

An informative work covering all pertinent details, with chapters on safety, ballistics, maintenance, marksmanship, chemical agents, the shotgun, plus legal and ethical aspects.

The New Way of the Wilderness, By Calvin Rutstrum. Macmillan Co., New York, N.Y. 1st ed., 1966 [4th printing]. 276 pp., illus. in line. $4.95.

An outdoorsman's manual on traveling and living in the open, with chapters on transportation, equipment, food, hunting and fishing for food.

L. D. Nimschke, Firearms Engraver, by R. L. Wilson. John J. Malloy, publisher, Teaneck, N.J., 1965. Quarto, 107 pp., profusely illus. $17.50.

Showing a wide variety of designs, initials and monograms and ever-so-many portions of collectors' arms. A thoroughly interesting work for the collector and an inspiration to the engraver.

No Second Place Winner, by Wm. H. Jordan, publ. by the author, Shreveport, La. (Box 4072), 1962. 114 pp., illus. $5.00.

Guns and gear of the peace officer, ably discussed by a U.S. Border Patrolman for over 30 years, and a first-class shooter with handgun, rifle, etc.

The Other Mr. Churchill, by Macdonald Hastings. Dodd Mead, N.Y.C., 1965. 336 pp., illus. $1.98.

Important biography of a great London gunmaker and forensic ballistics expert, who contributed much to the color and excellence of British firearms tradition.

Pageant of the Gun, by Harold L. Peterson. Doubleday & Co., Inc., Garden City, N.Y., 1967. 352 pp., profusely illus. $5.95.

A storehouse of stories on firearms, their romance and lore, their development and use through 10 centuries. A most satisfying history of firearms chronologically presented.

Paradise Below Zero, by Calvin Rutstrum. Macmillan Co., New York, N.Y. 1st ed., 1968. 244 pp., illus. in line and halftone. $5.95.

On the rewards and methods of camping and travel in Eskimo country, including check lists of provisions, tools, equipment, clothing and ways of getting about.

Picture Book of the Continental Soldier, by C. K. Wilbur. Stackpole Books, Harrisburg, Pa., 1969. 96 pp., well illus. $4.95.

A wealth of detailed material in text and fine drawings, depicting Revolutionary War weapons, accouterments, field equipment, and the routine of the soldier's life. Included are artillery, edged weapons, muskets, rifles, powder horns, etc.

Pocket Guide to Archery, by H. T. Sigler. Stackpole Co., Harrisburg, Pa., 1960. 96 pp., illus. $2.95.

Useful introduction to the subject, covering equipment, shooting techniques, and bow hunting of small game and deer.

Reading the Woods, by Vinson Brown. Stackpole Books, Harrisburg, Pa. 1969. 160 pp. illus. $5.95.

Clues to the past, present and future development of wooded areas by observation of signs of change, decoy, influences of water and wildlife, and the impact of man's presence.

The Records and Badges of Every Regiment and Corps in the British Army, by H. M. Chichester and Geo. Burges-Short. Fred. Muller, Ltd., London, 1970. A reprint of the 2nd ed. of 1900. 240 illus., in the text and 24 color plates $27.50.

A magnificent facsimile with gilt top giving the history, uniforms, colors and insignia in satisfying detail of much-wanted data on subject.

The Redbook of Used Gun Values 1971, publ. by Publishers Dev. Corp., Skokie, Ill., 1970. 119 pp., illus., paper covers. $2.50.

Lists many types and modifications of rifles, shotguns and handguns, arranged by makers, with prices estimated according to condition.

Riot Control—Materiel and Techniques, by Rex Applegate. Stackpole Books, Harrisburg, Pa. 1969. 320 pp., illus. $9.95.

Originally released as *Kill or Get Killed,* later as *Crowd and Riot Control.* Designed for law officer training, plus deployment of personnel, chemicals and special equipment for best results.

Round Shot and Rammers, by H. L. Peterson. Stackpole Books, Harrisburg, Pa., 1969. 128 pp., illus. $9.95.

Artillery in America Through the Civil War years, with much detail on manufacture, history, accessory equipment, and use of all types of cannon. Fine line drawings show the guns, their equipment, and the men who used them.

Second World War Combat Weapons, by Hoffschmidt & Tantum. WE, Inc., Old Greenwich, Conn., 1968. 212 pp., illus. $7.95.

German weapons, vehicles, and projectiles illustrated and described. First of a 7-vol. series.

Secret Fighting Arts of the World, by J. F. Gilbey. Tuttle, Rutland, Vt. 1963. 150 pp., illus. $3.75.

20 chapters on advanced techniques of unarmed combat, described in anecdotal form.

Shooter's Bible, No. 62, John Olson, ed. Shooter's Bible, Inc., S. Hackensack, N.J., 1970. 576 pp., illus. $4.95.

An annually-published guide to firearms, ammunition, and accessories.

Shooter's Bible Game Cook Book, by Geraldine Steindler. Follett Publ. Co., Chicago, Ill. 1965. 224 pp., illus., cloth, $6.95; paper, $4.95.

Full information on preparing game for the table, including recipes and methods of field-dressing.

Shooter's Bible Gun Trader's Guide, by Paul Wahl. Shooter's Bible, S. Hackensack, N.J., 5th edition, 1968. 220 pp., illus., paperbound. $3.95.

Revised guide to market values of modern firearms, with identification data on U.S. and imported guns.

Shooting Muzzle Loading Hand Guns, by Charles T. Haven. Guns Inc., Massachusetts, 1947. 132 pp., illus. $6.50.

A good summary of shooting methods, both contemporary and modern. Duelling with M.L. handguns is also covered.

The Shorebirds of North America, by Peter Matthiesen, ed. by Gordon Stout, with species accounts by R. S. Palmer. Viking Press, N.Y.C., 1967, 288 pp., 32 6-color plates, 10"x14", $22.50. De Luxe ltd. ed., extra bound, $50.00.

A magnificent book, probably the outstanding work on the shorebirds of the northern western world. 32 chapters cover 59 species. The illustrations are superb.

Six-guns and Saddle Leather, by Ramon F. Adams. University of Oklahoma Press, Norman, Okla., 1969. 801 pp., $19.95.

A bibliography of books and pamphlets on Western outlaws and gunmen. A brand new revised and enlarged edition.

Sketch Book 76: The American Soldier 1775-1781, by R. Klinger and R. A. Wilder, Arlington, Va., 1967. 53 pp., illus. Paper covers. $2.50.

Sketches, notes, and patterns compiled from a study of clothing and equipment used by the American foot soldier in the Revolutionary War.

Skills for Taming the Wilds, by Bradford Angier, Stackpole Books, Harrisburg, Pa., 1967. 320 pp., illus. $6.95.

A handbook of woodcraft wisdom, by a foremost authority, showing how to obtain maximum comfort from nature.

Small Arms Lexicon and Concise Encyclopedia, by Chester Mueller and John Olson. Stoeger Arms, So. Hackensack, N.J., 1968. 312 pp., 500 illus. $14.95.

Definitions, explanations, and references on antiques, optics, ballistics, etc., from A to Z. Over 3,000 entries plus appendix.

Small Arms of the World, by W. H. B. Smith and J. E. Smith. 9th ed., 1969. Stackpole Books, Harrisburg, Pa. 786 pp., profusely illus. $17.95.

A most popular firearms classic for easy reference. Covers the small arms of 42 countries, clearly showing operational principles. A timeless volume of proven worth.

Stoeger Gun Parts Catalog, compiled and published by Stoeger Arms Corporation, So. Hackensack, N.J., 1968, 416 pp., illus. $2.00.

A mail-order catalog listing over 1000 parts for pistols, rifles and shotguns domestic and foreign. Includes gunsmith tools and accessories.

Stories of the Old Duck Hunters and Other Drivel, by Gordon MacQuarrie and compiled by Zack Taylor. Stackpole Books, Harrisburg, Pa., 1967. 223 pp., illus. $5.95.

An off-beat relaxing and enjoyable group of 19 best-remembered outdoor stories, previously publ. in magazines.

Submachine Guns Caliber .45, M3 and M3A1, U.S. FM23-41 and TM 9-1217. Normount Armament Co., Forest Grove, Ore., 1967. 141 pp., illus., paperbound. $3.00.

Reprint of two U.S. Army manuals on submachine guns.

Swords & Daggers, by Frederick Wilkinson. Hawthorn Books, N.Y., 1968. 256 pp., well illus. $5.95.

Good general survey of edged weapons and polearms of collector interest, with 150 pp. of illustrations and descriptions of arms from Europe, Africa and the Orient.

Swords of Hitler's Third Reich, by Major J. R. Angolia, F. J. Stephens, Essex, England, 1969. Over 100 pp., well illus. $8.95.

A comprehensive work on the swords of the German Army, Navy, Air Force, SS, Police, Fire Dept., and many other government departments—plus belts, hangers, and accouterments—all described and illus.

Teaching Kids to Shoot, by Henry M. Stebbins. Stackpole Books, Harrisburg, Pa. 1966. 96 pp. illus. $2.95.   Designed for parents and leaders who want to develop safety conscious firearms-users.

Tear Gas Munitions, by T. F. Swearengen, Charles C. Thomas, Springfield, Ill., 1966. 569 pp., illus. $34.50.

An analysis of commercial (riot) gas guns, tear gas projectiles, grenades, small arms ammunition, and related tear gas devices.

Technical Dictionary for Weapon Enthusiasts, Shooters and Hunters, by Gustav Sybertz. Publ. by J. Neumann-Neudamm, 3508 Melsungen, W. Germany, 1969, 164 pp., semi-soft covers. $7.50.

A German-English and English-German dictionary for the sportsman. An exellent handy work.

The Thompson Gun, publ. by Numrich Arms, West Hurley, N.Y., 1967, 27 pp., illus., paper covers. $1.95.

A facsimile reprint, excellently done, of a 1923 catalog of Thompson sub-machine guns.

Thompson-Submachine Guns, compiled from original manuals by the publ. Normount Armament Co., Forest Grove, Oregon, Ill., 1968. Over 230 pp., well illus., many exploded views. Paper wrappers. $4.00.

Five reprints in one book: Basic Field Manual, Cal. 45, M1928AI (U.S. Army); Cal. 45, Model 1928, (for British); Cal. 45 (U.S. Ordnance); Model MI, Cal., 45 (U.S. Ordnance) and Ultra Modern Automatic Arms (Auto-Ordnance Corp.).

The Tournament, its Periods and Phases, by R. C. Clephan. Frederick Ungar Co., N.Y., 1967. A reprint. 195 pp., illus. with contemporary pictures plus half-tones of armor and weapons used by contestants. $9.95.

A rare and eagerly-sought work, long out-of-print. A scholarly, historical and descriptive account of jousting.

Training Your Own Bird Dog, by Henry P. Davis, G. P. Putnam's Sons, New York, N.Y. New rev. ed., 1969, 168 pp., plus 10 pp. of field trial records. Illus. with photographs. $5.95.

The reappearance of a popular and practical book for the beginner starting his first bird dog—by an internationally recognized authority.

A Treatise on Ancient Armour and Weapons, by Francis Grose. Benchmark Pub. Co., Glendale, N.Y., 1970. Irregular pagination. $12.50.

Reprint of a 1786 British monograph showing numerous items from the Tower of London and other sites.

A Treatise of Artillery, by John Muller. Museum Restoration Service, Ottawa, Canada, 1965. 216 pp., plus many plates. $17.50.

A creditable reprint of a famous and excellent original work of the third ed. of 1780, printed in London. This reprint limited to 850 numbered copies. The plates should be highly useful to the artillery buff.

Triggernometry, by Eugene Cunningham. Caxton Printers Lt., Caldwell, Id., 1970. 441 pp., illus. $7.95.

A classic study of famous outlaws and lawmen of the West—their stature as human beings, their exploits and skills in handling firearms. A reprint.

Unconventional Warfare Devices and Techniques, a reprint of Army TM 31-200-1 234 pp., illus., paper covers. $10.00.

Published primarily for U.S. Army Special Forces. Deals with destructive techniques and their applications to targets in guerrilla warfare.

Uniforms, Organization and History of the Waffen SS, by R. J. Bender and H. P. Taylor. R. J. Bender, Mountain View, Cal., 1969. 160 pp., photographs and drawings. $9.95.

The first of 4 contemplated volumes on the subject, with accompanying historical text.

Use and Maintenance of the Browning "Hi-Power" Pistol, (No. 2 Mk 1 and Commercial Models), by D. B. McLean. Normount Armament Co., Forest Grove, Ore., 1966. 48 pp., illus., paperbound. $1.50.

Covers the use, maintenance, and repair of various Browning 9mm parabellum pistols.

Warriors' Weapons, by Walter Buehr. Crowell Co., N.Y.C., 1963. 186 pp., illus. $5.95.

Illustrated history of pre-gunpowder arms, from stone ax to crossbow and catapult.

Weapons of the American Revolution, and Accoutrements, by Warren Moore. Funk & Wagnalls, N.Y., 1967. 225 pp., fine illus. $10.00.

Revolutionary era shoulder arms, pistols, edged weapons, and equipment are described and shown in fine drawings and photographs, some in color.

The Weapons Merchants, by Bernt Engelmann, Crown Publ., Inc., N.Y. 1968. 224 pp., illus. $4.95.

A true account of illegal traffic in death-dealing arms by individuals and governments.

Weapons and Tactics, Hastings to Berlin, by Jac Weller, St. Martin's Press, New York, 1966. 238 pp., illus. $6.00.

Primarily on the infantry weapons of today, with basic data on those of the past.

Weapons of War, by P. E. Cleator. Crowell Co., N.Y.C., 1968. 224 pp., illus. $6.95.

A British survey of warfare from earliest times, as influenced by the weapons available for combat.

Wild Game Cookbook, by L. E. Johnson. Benjamin Co., N.Y.C., 1968. 160 pp. $2.95.

Recipes, sauces, and cooking hints for preparation of all types of game birds and animals.

Wild Sanctuaries . . ., by Robert Murphy. E. P. Dutton & Co., Inc., New York, N.Y., 1968, 288 pp., over 250 photographs in color and monochrome, plus 32 maps, including those of the flyways. $12.95.

Concerns America's national wildlife refuges. An all-encompassing treatise on its subject with fascinating pertinent text.

The Wild Turkey, its History and Domestication, by A. W. Schorger, Univ. of Oklahoma Press, Norman, Okla., 1966. 625 pp., illus. $15.00.

Detailed coverage of habitats, characteristics, breeding, and feeding of the American wild turkey. Bibliography.

Wilderness Cookery, by Bradford Angier. Stackpole Books, Harrisburg, Pa., 1969. 256 pp., illus. $4.95.

An excellent work, one that will be of big interest to hunters, fishermen, campers, et al.

Wildwood Wisdom, by Ellsworth Jaeger. The Macmillan Company, New York, N.Y. 1964. 491 pp. well-illus. by author. $6.95.

An authoritative work, through many editions; about all there is to know about every detail for the outdoorsman.

Williams 1970-71 Blue Book of Gun Dealing. Williams Gun Sight Co., Davison, Mich., 1970. 76 pp., illus., paperbound. $2.50.

Suggested price ranges for many models of rifles, shotguns, handguns, sights, etc., with other useful information for the gun trader.

The World of the White-Tailed Deer, by L. L. Rue III. J. B. Lippincott Co., Phila., 1967. A reprint. 137 pp., fine photos. $4.95.

An eminent naturalist-writer's account of the year-round activities of the white-tailed deer.

The World's Assault Rifles (and Automatic Carbines), by D. D. Musgrave and T. B. Nelson. T. B. N. Enterprises, Alexandria, Va., 1967. 546 pp., profusely illus. $17.50.

High velocity small-bore combat rifles are shown and described in much detail, arranged by type and nationality. A companion volume to *The World's Submachine Guns,* by Nelson and Lockhoven.

The World's Submachine Guns (and Machine Pistols), by T. B. Nelson and H. B. Lockhoven. T. B. N. Enterprises, Alexandria, Va., 1962. 739 pp., profusely illus. $15.50.

The 2nd printing (1964) of the first work with descriptive data on all significant SMGs to date, arranged by national origin. A glossary in 22 languages is included. It is a companion volume to the *The World's Assault Rifles* by Musgrave and Nelson.

You and Your Retriever, by R. W. Coykendall, Jr. Doubleday & Co., Garden City, N.Y., 1963. 155 pp., illus. $4.95.

A text on early, intermediate and advanced training of retrievers, with full information for handlers.

The Young Sportsman's Guide to Camping, by J. L. Holden. Thomas Nelson & Sons, Camden, N.J., 1962. 96 pp., illus. $2.75.

A concise and dependable guide to basic techniques of camping in comfort and safety.

The Young Sportsman's Guide to Dogs, by J. R. Falk. Thomas Nelson & Sons, Camden, N.J., 1964. 96 pp., illus. $2.75.

A creditable and concise work on the history and characteristics of 29 breeds of dogs, both working and nonsporting types.

The Young Sportsman's Guide to Target Shooting, by Gene Seraphine. Thomas Nelson & Sons, Camden, N.J., 1964. 94 pp., illus. $2.95.

A basic introduction to marksmanship, including selection of firearms, sights, equipment, ammunition and range behavior.

Gunsmithing

Antique Firearms: Their Care, Repair and Restoration, by Ronald Lister. Crown Publ., New York, 1964. 220 pp., 66 plates, 24 fig. $6.50.

A workshop manual for collectors and gunsmiths, giving correct procedures for every step in preserving firearms.

Checkering and Carving of Gun Stocks, by Monte Kennedy. Stackpole Books, Harrisburg, Pa., 1962. 175 pp., illus. $10.00.

Rev., enlarged Clothbound ed. of a much sought-after, dependable work.

Complete Guide to Gunsmithing, by C. E. Chapel. Barnes & Co., N.Y.C., 1962. 479 pp., illus. $6.95.

2nd rev. edition, known earlier as *Gun Care and Repair,* of a comprehensive book on all details of gunsmithing for the hobbyist and professional.

Firearms Blueing and Browning, by R. H. Angier. Stackpole Books, Harrisburg, Pa. 151 pp., illus. $5.00.

A useful, concise text on chemical coloring methods for the gunsmith and mechanic.

Gun Engraving Review, by E. C. Prudhomme, G. E. R. Publ. Co., Shreveport, La., 1965. 150 pp., profusely illus. (some in color.) $21.95.

Excellent examples of the gun engraver's art to serve as a guide to novice or expert. Selection of tools, techniques and a directory of engravers is given.

Gunsmith Kinks, by F. R. [Bob] Brownell. F. Brownell & Son, Montezuma, Iowa. 1st ed., 1969. 496 pp., well illus. $9.95.

A widely useful accumulation of shop kinks, short cuts, techniques and pertinent comments by practicing gunsmiths from all over the world.

Gunsmithing, by Roy F. Dunlap. Stackpole Books, Harrisburg, Pa., 714 pp., illus. $10.00.

Comprehensive work on conventional techniques, incl. recent advances in the field. Valuable to rifle owners, shooters, and practicing gunsmiths.

Gunsmithing Simplified, by H. E. Macfarland. Washington, D.C., 1950, A. S. Barnes, N.Y.C., 1959. 303 pp., illus. $6.95.

A thorough dependable concise work with many helpful short-cuts.

Gunstock Finishing and Care, by A. D. Newell. Stackpole Books, Harrisburg, Pa. A new printing, 1966. 473 pp., illus. $9.50.

Amateur's and professional's handbook on the selection, use and application of protective and decorative coatings on gun stocks.

Home Gun Care & Repair, by P. O. Ackley. Stackpole Books, Harrisburg, Pa., 1969. 191 pp., illus. $5.95.

Basic reference for safe tinkering, fixing, and converting rifles, shotguns, handguns.

Home Gunsmithing Digest, by Tommy Bish. Digest Books, Inc., Northfield, Ill., 1970, 320 pp., very well illus. within stiff decorated paper covers. $4.95.

An unusually beneficial assist for gun owners doing their own repairs, maintenance, etc. 45 chapters on tools, techniques and theories.

HOW . . . by L. Cowher, W. Hunley, and L. Johnston. NMLR Assn., Indiana, 1961. 107 pp., illus. Paper covers. $2.95.

This 1961 rev. ed., enlarged by 3 chapters and additional illustrations, covers the building of a muzzle-loading rifle, target pistol, and powder horn, and tells how to make gunflints.

How to Convert Military Rifles, by Harvey Williams, *et al.* Gun Digest Publ. Co., Northfield, Ill., 1970. 88 pp., very well illus., stiff paper covers. $1.95.

The 6th and latest ed. of a popular work formerly distributed by the author's company. Gives step-by-step instructions to convert a military rifle to a good looking and easy to handle sporter.

Introduction to Modern Gunsmithing, by H. E. MacFarland. Stackpole Books, Harrisburg, Pa., 1965. 320 pp., illus. $6.95.

Up-to-date reference for all gunsmiths on care, repair, and modification of firearms, sights, and related topics.

Lock, Stock and Barrel, by R. H. McGrory. Publ. by author at Bellmore, N.Y., 1966. Paper covers, 122 pp., illus. $3.00.

A handy and useful work for the collector or the professional with many helpful procedures shown and described on antique gun repair.

Make Muzzle Loader Accessories, by Robert H. McCrory. R. H. McCrory, Bellmore, N.Y., 1967. 28 pp., paper wrappers, illus. with sketches. $1.50.

A capably executed handbook on how to make a powder horn, capper, nipple wrench, loading block and spring vise.

Master French Gunsmith's Designs of the 17th-18th Centuries, compiled by S. V. Grancsay. Winchester Press, New York, N.Y., 1970. A brand new work of 208 pp., beautifully illus. in facsimile. Numbered, limited issue of 1000 copies. $75.00.

Magnificient ornamentation of weapons taken from a superb collection of design books, gathered by a world authority. An inspiration and a must for the gunsmith-engraver.

The Modern Gunsmith, by James V. Howe. Funk & Wagnalls, N.Y.C., 1970 reprint ed. (2 vols.) 910 pp., illus. $25.00.

Guide for amateur and professional gunsmiths on firearms design, construction, repair, etc.

The Modern Kentucky Rifle, How to Build Your Own, by R. H. McCrory. McCrory, Wantagh, N.Y., 1961. 68 pp., illus., paper bound. $3.00.

A workshop manual on how to fabricate a flintlock rifle. Also some information on pistols and percussion locks.

Professional Gunsmithing, by W. J. Howe. Stackpole Books, Harrisburg, Pa., 1968 reprinting. 526 pp., illus. $10.00.
Textbook on repair and alteration of firearms, with detailed notes on equipment and commercial gunshop operation.

Recreating the Kentucky Rifle, by Wm. Buchele. Geo. Shumway, York, Pa., 1970. 189 pp., illus. $10.00.
How to build a Kentucky rifle, illustrated with line drawings and separate full-scale drawings. In paper covers, $6.50.

Restocking a Rifle, by Alvin Linden. Stackpole Books, Harrisburg, Pa., 1969. 138 combined pp., of text. Well illus. Large format. $9.95.
A re-issue in one volumne of the 3 earlier Linden instruction guides on: Stock Inletting; Shaping; Finishing of the Springfield, Enfield and Winchester M70 rifles.

handguns

Automatic Firearm Pistols, by Elmer Swanson. Wesmore Book Co., Weehawken, N.J. 1st (and only) ed. 1955. 210 pp., well illus. $15.00.
A veritable catalog exclusively on automatic handguns for collectors, with many line drawings and descriptions, plus then-market market values of each.

Automatic Pistols, by H. B. C. Pollard, WE, Old Greenwich, Conn. 1966. 110 pp., illus. $5.95.
A facsimile reprint of the scarce 1920 original. Covers historical development of military and other automatics, shooting, care, etc.

Basic Marksmanship with the Modern Handgun, by L. P. Davison, and L. A. Severson. National Police Law Enforcement Institute. n.d. 88pp. illus. $4.00. Paper covers.
A police training handbook on fundamentals of handgun selection and use, on the firing range and in combat situations.

Book of Pistols & Revolvers, by W. H. B. Smith. Stackpole Books, Harrisburg, Pa., 1968. 758 pp., profusely illus. $14.95. Buy with Book of Rifles and both are $19.95.
Rev. and enlarged, this encyclopedic reference, first publ. in 1946, continues to be the best on its subject.

Browning Hi-Power Pistols. Normount Armament Co., Forest Grove, Ore., 1968. 48 pp., illus., paperbound. $1.50.
A handbook on all models of Browning Hi-Power pistols, covering their use, maintenance and repair.

Colt Commemorative Firearms, by R. L. Wilson. Charles Kidwell, Wichita, Kans., 1969, Unpaginated, well illus. paper covers $5.95. In hard deluxe covers, limited issue of 1000 copies, each numbered. $10.00.
Description and fine color photographs of commemorative handguns issued by the Colt company, 1961-1969, all replicas of famous earlier models.

Combat Shooting for Police, by Paul B. Weston. Charles C. Thomas, Springfield, Ill., 1967. A reprint. 194 pp., illus. $8.50.
First publ. in 1960 this popular self-teaching manual gives basic concepts of defensive fire in every position.

The Encyclopedia of the Third Reich, Book 1, by R. B. Marvin. Universal Research, Inc., Fort Lauderdale, Texas, 1969, from offset typewritten copy. 37 pp., very clear and sharp illustrations, paper covers. $4.00.
This volume considers only handguns, but is a concise collector's guide to the main types of W.W. II German pistols and revolvers.

Fired In Anger, by Robt. Elman. Doubleday, Garden City, N.Y., 1968. 416 pp., illus. with 250 photos. $7.95.
Describes and illustrates the personal handguns used by famous and infamous Americans, including soldiers, outlaws and historical figures.

Gil Hebard Guns, Gil Hebard, Knoxville, Ill. Catalog No. 20, 1970, 177 pp., illus. Paperbound, $1.00.
Outstanding sales catalog of handgunner's needs, plus excellent articles by pistol experts on sport and target shooting.

The Handbook of Handgunning, by Paul B. Weston. Crown Publ., N.Y.C., 1968. 138 pp., illus. with photos. $4.95.
"New concepts in pistol and revolver shooting," by a noted firearms instructor and writer.

Handbuch der Faustfeuerwaffen, by Gerhard Bock and W. Weigel. J. Neumann-Neudamm, Melsungen, Germany, 1968. 4th and latest ed., 724 pp., including index. Profusely illus. $21.00
A truly encyclopedic work in German text on every aspect of handguns. Highly recommended for those who read German.

The Handgun, by Geoffrey Boothroyd. Crown Publishers, Inc., New York, N.Y., 1970. 564 pp., profusely illus., plus copious index. $19.95.
A massive and impressive work, excellently covering the subject from matchlocks to present-day automatics. Many anecdotes, much comment and pertinent data, including ammunition, etc.

Japanese Hand Guns, by F. E. Leithe, Borden Publ. Co., Alhambra, Calif., 1968. Unpaginated, well illus. $8.50.
Identification guide, covering models produced since the late 19th century. Brief text material gives history, descriptions, and markings.

The Luger Pistol (Pistole Parabellum), by F. A. Datig. Borden Publ. Co., Alhambra, Calif., 1962. 328 pp., well illus. $8.50.
An enlarged, rev. ed. of an important reference on the arm, its history and development from 1893 to 1945.

Lugers at Random, by Charles Kenyon, Jr. Handgun Press, Chicago, Ill. 1st ed., 1970. 416 pp., profusely illus. $15.00.
An impressive large side-opening book carrying throughout alternate facing-pages of descriptive text and clear photographs. A new boon to the Luger collector and/or shooter.

Lugers Unlimited, by F. G. Tilton, World-Wide Gun Report, Inc., Aledo, Ill., 1965. 49 pp., illus. Paper covers $2.00.
An excellent monograph about one of the most controversial pistols since the invention of hand firearms.

The Mauser Self-Loading Pistol, by Belford & Dunlap. Borden Publ. Co., Alhambra, Calif. Over 200 pp., 300 illus., large format. $12.50.
The long-awaited book on the "Broom Handles," covering their inception in 1894 to the end of production. Complete and in detail: pocket pistols, Chinese and Spanish copies, etc.

Military Pistols and Revolvers, by I. V. Hogg. Arco Pub. Co., N.Y., 1970. 80 pp., illus. $3.50.
The handguns of the two World Wars shown in halftone illus., with brief historical and descriptive text.

The Modern Handgun, by Robert Hertzberg. Arco Publ. Co., New York, N.Y., 1965. 112 pp., well illus. $3.50.
Pistols and revolvers of all types are traced from their beginnings. Data on modern marksmanship included.

Modern Pistol Shooting, by P. C. Freeman. Faber & Faber, London, England, 1968, 176 pp., illus. $4.00.
How to develop accuracy with the pistol. Fine points in technique are covered, with information on competitive target shooting.

The "Parabellum" Automatic Pistol, the English version of the official DWM handbook on Luger pistols. Normount Armament Co., Forest Grove, Oregon, Ill., 1968. 42 pp., illus. Paper wrappers. $1.00.
A user's handbook, a reference work for collectors. A reprint of the original detailed instructions on use, disassembly and maintenance. Includes three folding plates.

Pistol and Revolver Guide, by George Nonte. Stoeger Arms Corp., So. Hackensack, N.J., 1967. 192 pp., well illus. Paper wrappers. $3.95.
A history of the handgun, its selection, use and care, with a glossary and trade directory.

The Pistol Shooter's Treasury, by Gil Hebard. Gil Hebard, Knoxville, Ill., 1969. 1st ed., 112 pp. illus. in halftone and full color. Color decorated paper covers. $2.50.
A gathering of the experts, by an expert—classic articles on how to shoot a handgun and prepare for competition.

Pistolen Atlas, by Karl R. Pawlas. K. R. Pawlas, Nurenberg, Germany, 1970. Irregular pagination. 8 vol., each $8.50.
Carefully planned and impressively presented, designed for automatic arms buffs, shooters, and collectors of these handguns. Depicts auto pistols in all calibers, with descriptive data in English, French, German and Spanish. Hundreds of specimens covered in each of the 5 volumes now published. **Nos. 1,2,3,5 and 6.**. Vols. 7 and 8 expected through 1971.

Pistols, A Modern Encyclopedia, by Stebbins, Shay & Hammond. Stackpole Co., Harrisburg, Pa., 1961. 380 pp., illus. $4.98.
Comprehensive coverage of handguns for every purpose, with material on selection, ammunition, and marksmanship.

Pistols of the World, by Claude Blair. Viking Press, N.Y.C., 1968. 206 pp., plus plates, $30.00.
Authoritative review of handguns since the 16th century, with chapters on major types, manufacture, and decoration. Fine photographic illustrations.

Report of Board on Tests of Revolvers and Automatic Pistols. From The *Annual Report* of the Chief of Ordnance, 1907. Reprinted by J. C. Tillinghast, Marlow, N.H., 1969. 34 pp., 7 plates, paper covers. $3.00.
A comparison of handguns, including Luger, Savage, Colt, Webley- Fosbery and other makes.

The Revolver, 1818-1865, by Taylerson, Andrews, & Frith. Crown Publ., N.Y.C., 1968. 360 pp., illus. $7.50.
Noted British work on early revolving arms and the principal makers, giving production data and serial numbers on many models.

The Revolver, 1865-1888, by A. W. F. Taylerson. Crown Publ., N.Y.C., 1966. 292 pp., illus. $3.49.
Detailed study of 19th-century British and U.S. revolvers, by types and makers, based on study of patent records.

The Revolver 1889-1914, by A. W. F. Taylerson. Crown Pub. N.Y., 1971. 324 pp., illus. $7.50.
The concluding volume of this definitive work deals with Continental arms, American rimfire and centerfire, British centerfire, and obsolescent arms in use.

Saga of the Colt Six-Shooter, and the famous men who used it, by G. E. Virgines. Frederick Fell Co., New York, N.Y., 1969. 220 pp., well illus. $7.95.
History of the Colt Single action army revolver since 1873, with much information of interest to collectors and shooters.

Sixguns by Keith, by Elmer Keith. Stackpole Co., Harrisburg, Pa., 1968 (reprint of 1961 edition.) 335 pp., illus. $12.95.
Long a popular reference on handguns, this work covers all aspects, whether for the shooter, collector or other enthusiasts.

Smith and Wesson Catalog of 1901, a reprint facsimile by The Wyoming Armory, Inc., Cheyenne, Wyo., 1969. 72 pp., well illus., paper covers. $2.25.
All models, engraving, parts and break-down lists, etc.

System Mauser, a Pictorial History of the Model 1896 Self-Loading Pistol, by J. W. Breathed, Jr., and J. J. Schroeder, Jr. Handgun Press, Chicago, Ill., 1967. 273 pp., well illus. 1st limited ed. hardbound. $12.50.

10 Shots Quick, by Daniel K. Stern. Globe Printing Co., San Jose, Calif., 1967. 153 pp., photos. $8.50.
History of Savage-made automatic pistols, models of 1903-1917, with descriptive data for shooters and collectors.

U.S. Pistols and Revolvers Vol. 1, D. B. McLean, compiler. Normount Armament Co., Forest Grove, Ore., 1968. 2nd printing, 198 pp., well illus., paper covers. $3.50.
A useful and reliable work from authoritative sources on M1911/M1911A1 Colt pistols; M1917 S & W revolvers; M1917 and Detective Special Colt revolvers. Excellent for their use, maintenance and repair.

U.S. Test Trials 1900 Luger, by Michael Reese II. Coventry Publ. Co., Gretna, La. 1970. Illus. $7.00.
For the Luger Pistol collector.

The Webley-Fosbery Automatic Revolver. A reprint of the original undated booklet publ. by the British makers. Deep River Armory, Houston, Tex., 1968. 16 pp., illus., paper. $3.00.
An instruction manual, parts list and sales brochure on this scarce military handgun.

hunting

Advanced Hunting, by F. E. Sell. Stackpole Books, Harrisburg, Pa., 1959. 156 pp., illus. $8.50.
Postgraduate course in deer hunting, woodslore, animal habits, equipment, etc.

African Hunting, by Wm. C. Baldwin. Abercrombie & Fitch Library, N.Y., 1967. 451 pp., illus. $12.95.
Limited printing of a much-desired book giving vivid accounts of big game hunting exploits in Africa. First publ. in 1863.

After Wild Sheep in the Altai and Mongolia, by Prince Demidoff. Abercrombie & Fitch Library, N.Y., 1966. 324 pp., with photographs and drawings. $10.00.
Limited printing of a famous British work of 1900, on hunting big game in Asia. Long out-of-print.

American Partridge & Pheasant Shooting, by Frank Schley. Abercrombie & Fitch Library, N.Y.C., 1968. 238 pp., illus. $7.95.
Facsimile of an American sporting classic work, including detailed engravings of game birds.

The American Sportsman, by Elisha J. Lewis. Abercrombie & Fitch Library, N.Y., 1967. 510 pp., illus. $10.95.
Limited issue of a scarce classic American work on the hunting field, first publ. in 1851.

Animals of East Africa, by C. A. Spinage. Houghton Mifflin Co., Boston, Mass. 1963. 151 pp. illus. $7.50.
Foreword by Sir Julian Huxley, F.R.S., who calls this "The best collection of wild life photographs I have seen." Excellent for those planning a safari.

The Art of Hunting Big Game in North America, by Jack O'Connor. Alfred A. Knopf, N.Y., 1967, 404 pp., line drawings and photos. $10.00.
A complete book on the subject, from tracing the origin of game on this continent to the various techniques practised in the sport on different species. Rifles and cartridges discussed at length.
The Art of Wing Shooting, by W. B. Leffingwell. Abercrombie & Fitch Library, N.Y.C., 1968. 190 pp., illus. $7.95.
An outstanding treatise on shotgun marksmanship, first publ. 1894, with explicit drawings on techniques of leading the target.
Asian Jungle, African Bush, by Charles Askins. Stackpole Books, Harrisburg, Pa., 1959. 258 pp., illus. $10.00.
A where-to-go and how-to-do guide for game-rich Indo-China. The African section deals with game, the use of various arms and ammo on specific species.
The Australian Hunter, by Col. Allison with Ian Coombes. Cassell Australia Ltd., No. Melbourne, Australia, 1970. 212 pp., 58 photos., and 60 distribution maps and drawings. $10.00. A comprehensive guide to game, equipment, hunting and photography.
Bell of Africa, by W. D. M. Bell, with foreword and introduction by Wally Taber and Col. T. Whelen. N. Spearman and Holland Press, London, 1960. 236 pp., illus. $4.75
On elephants and the hunter extracted from Bell's own papers, it includes an appendix on rifles and rifle shooting.
Big Game Hunting in the West, by Mike Cramond. Mitchell Press, Vancouver, B.C., Can., 1965. 164 pp., illus. $5.95.
Accounts of hunting many species of big game and predators are given plus a section on rifles, equipment, and useful tips for the field.
Big Game Shooting in Africa, ed. by Major H. C. Maydon. Seeley, Service & Co., London, n.d., 445 pp. illus. $7.50.
Vol. 14 of the Lonsdale Library, with chapters by various British writers on African big game and on hunting invarious sections of Africa.
Bird Hunting Know-How, by D. M. Duffey. Van Nostrand, Princeton, N.J., 1968. 192 pp., illus. $5.95.
Game-getting techniques and sound advice on all aspects of upland bird hunting, plus data on guns and loads.
The Bobwhite Quail, its Life and Management, by Walter Rosene. Rutgers University Press, New Brunswick, N.J. 1st ed., 1969. 418 pp., photographs, maps and color plates. $20.00.
An exhaustive study of an important species which has diminished under the impact of changing agricultural and forestry practices.
Bowhunting for Deer, by H. R. Wambold. Stackpole Books, Harrisburg, Pa., 1964. 160 pp., illus. $5.95.
Useful tips on deer, their habits, anatomy, and how-when-where of hunting, plus selection and use of tackle.
A Boy and His Gun, by Edward C. Janes. A. S. Barnes & Co., New York, N.Y. 207 pp., illus., $5.00
Introduction to rifles, shooting and hunting techniques for young shooters with practical hints on game shooting with rifle or shotgun
Buckshot and Hounds, by C. J. Milling. A. S. Barnes, N.Y., 1967. 132 pp., illus. $4.95.
Deer-driving methods and traditions of the South and West, with present-day adaptations described.
Calling All Game, by Bert Popowski. Stackpole Books, Harrisburg, Pa., 1952, 306 pp. Illus. $4.95.
Practical methods of attracting game, from quail to moose, using artificial decoys and calls.
Charles Morgan on Retrievers, ed. by Ann Fowler and D. L. Walters. Abercrombie & Fitch, N.Y.C., 1968, 168 pp., illus. $12.50.
Based on years of success in schooling hunting dogs, this work gives full details of an expert's proven methods to guide experienced trainers.
Complete Book of Hunting, by Clyde Ormond. Harper & Bros., N.Y.C., 1962. 467 pp., well-illus. $6.95.
Part I is on game animals, Part II is on birds. Guns and ammunition, game, habitats, clothing, equipment, etc. hunters' tips are discussed.
The Complete Deer Hunt, by Joe DeFalco. Madison Publ. Co., New York, N.Y., 1970. 133 pp., well illus., in line and halftone. Stiff paper covers. $3.95.
A concise work covering field dressing, skinning, equipment and arms, methods of hunting, etc.
Complete Guide to Hunting Across North America, by Byron Dalrymple. Outdoor Life, Harper & Row, N.Y., 1970. 848 pp., illus. with photos and 50 maps. $10.00.
A large reference work on hunting conditions, locating game, clothing, techniques, transportation, equipment for every region, etc.
Crow Shooting, by Bert Popowski. A. S. Barnes and Co., N.Y.C., 1946. (4th printing 1957). 216 pp., illus. $5.00.
Practical and entertaining, telling how to locate roosts, build blinds and employ cover; the use of various decoys for shooting with rifle or shotgun.
Crow Shooting Secrets, by Dick Mermon. Winchester Press, New York, 1970. 149 pp., illus. $5.95.
An expert shares his secrets and touches all the bases.
The Deer Hunter's Bible, by Geo. Laycock. Doubleday, Garden City, N.Y., 1963. 154 pp., illus., paperbound. $1.95.
Handy summary of deer hunting lore, by an expert. Guns, loads, bowhunting, care of vension, field techniques are covered.
The Deer Hunter's Guide, by F. E. Sell. Stackpole Books, Harrisburg, Pa., 1964. 192 pp., illus. $5.00.
Western hunting lore for rifle- and bow-hunter, with data on woodcraft, trail signs, vension, and trophies, etc.
The Deer of North America, edit. by W. P. Taylor. Stackpole Books. Harrisburg, Pa., 1956. 668 pp., illus. incl. full-color plates. $12.50.
Leading authorities in all parts of the deer range have contributed their intimate studies of the animal.
Elephant Hunting in East Equatorial Africa, by Arthur H. Neumann. Abercrombie & Fitch Library, N.Y., 1966. 455 pp., illus. $12.50.
Limited ed. of a rare hunting book, first publ. in 1898 and difficult to locate. An account of 3 years ivory hunting under Mt. Kenia . . . the Lorogi Mountains . . . and Lake Rudolph. Over 60 illus.
The End of the Game, by P. H. Beard. Viking Press, N.Y.C., 1965. 256 pp., fine illus. $12.95.
Account of recent changes in African game country and decline of the game population.
Game Bird Hunting, by F. P. Rice & J. I. Dahl. Outdoor Life—Harper & Row, N.Y.C., 1965. 190 pp., illus. $3.95.
Survey of North American game birds of all types, written by a noted scholar and a hunter of wide experience.
Game Bird Hunting in the West, by Mike Cramond. Mitchell Press, Vancouver, B.C., Can., 1967. 246 pp., illus. $5.95.
Identification and hunting methods for each species of waterfowl and upland game birds, plus a section on shotgun types, equipment, and related subjects for the hunter.
Good Hunting, by Jas L. Clark, Univ. of Oklahoma Press, Norman, Okla., 1966. 242 pp., illus. $5.95.
Fifty years of collecting and preparing habitat groups for the American Museum.
The Great Arc of the Wild Sheep, by J. L. Clark, Univ. of Oklahoma Press, Norman, Okla., 1964. 247 pp., illus. $8.95.
Every classified variety of wild sheep is discussed, as found in North America, Asia & Europe. Numerous hunting stories by experts are included.
Great Game Animals of the World, by Russell B. Aitken. Winchester Press, N.Y., 1969. 192 pp. profusely illus. in monochrome and color. $22.50.
Accounts of man's pursuit of big game in all parts of the world, told in many fine pictures.
Great True Hunts, ed. by Peter Barrett. Prentice-Hall, Englewood Cliffs, N.J., 1967. 278 pp., illus. $4.95.
Big game hunting stories from *True* magazine, telling of hunting exploits of famous men around the world.
Green Hills of Africa, by Ernest Hemingway. Charles Scribner's Sons, N.Y., 1963. 285 pp. illus. $6.95.
A famous narrative of African big-game hunting, first published in 1935.
The Grizzly Bear, edited by B. D. and E. Haynes, Univ. of Oklahoma Press, Norman, Okla., 1966. 386 pp., illus. $6.95.
Collected stories about various encounters with the grizzly by mountain men, settlers, naturalists, scouts and others.
Grizzly Country, by Andy Russell. A. A. Knopf, N.Y.C., 1968, 302 pp., illus. $7.95.
Many-sided view of the grizzly bear and his world, by a noted guide, hunter and naturalist.
Grouse and Grouse Hunting, by Frank Woolner. Crown Pub., Co., N.Y., 1970. 192 pp., illus. $7.50.
The history, habits, habitat and methods of hunting one of America's great game birds.
Guide to Safaris, by Burk H. Steizner. Charles Scribner's Sons, New York, N.Y., 1970. 178 pp., illus. $6.95.
Discussions of the different African regions, types of safari, minimal costs, etc. Highly informative for the would-be safari-goers seeking basic information.
Gun Dog, by Richard A. Wolters, E. P. Dutton, New York, N.Y., 1969. 1st ed., 11th printing. 150 pp., well illus. $5.95.
A popular manual for upland bird shooters who want to train their dogs to perfection in minimum time.
The Gun on Saltings and Stubble, by N. M. Sedgwick. Herbert Jenkins, Ltd., Eng., 1949. 221 pp. $3.50.
Wildfowling on Britain's coastal estuaries.
How to Hunt American Game, by R. B. Vale. Stackpole Books, Harrisburg, Pa. 5th printing, 1954. 199 pp., illus. $4.00.
Wildlife habits, conservation and the encouragement of hunting. Including the author's experiences in hunting game throughout America.
How to Hunt Small American Game, by L. A. Anderson. Funk and Wagnalls, New York, N.Y., 1969. 167 pp., well illus. $5.95.
A new basic guide for the small game hunter, similar to the author's 1959 *How to Hunt Deer and Small Game.* Written for beginner and expert, covers game, guns, equipment and game habits.
How to Hunt Whitetail Deer, L. A. Anderson. Funk & Wagnalls, N.Y.C., 1968. 116 pp., illus. $5.95.
Useful reference for deer hunters, both novice and experienced, giving basic information and valuable pointers.
A Hunter's Wanderings in Africa, by Frederick Courteney Selous. Abercrombie & Fitch Library, N.Y., 1967. 455 pp., illus. $11.95.
Limited ed. of a rare and much-sought original work of 1881. A world-famous big game hunter tells of his African exploits.
The Hunter's World, by C. F. Waterman. Random House, N.Y., 1970. 250 pp., illus. $15.00.
A book for those who welcome an expert's guidance, one who understands the terrain, feed, cover, etc., of the game they hunt. Profusely illus. in color.
Hunting in Africa, by Frank C. Hibben, Hill and Wang, New York, N.Y., 1962. 236 pp., illus. $5.00.
18 true stories about exotic and dangerous African animals and the tracking and hunting of them.
Hunting Dog Know-How, by D. M. Duffey. Van Nostrand, Princeton, N.J., 1965. 177 pp., illus. $5.95.
Covers selection, breeds, and training of hunting dogs, problems in hunting and field trials.
Hunting Our Biggest Game, by Clyde Ormond. Stackpole Books, Harrisburg, Pa., 1956. 197 pp., illus. $8.95.
Practical advice for hunters on moose, elk, bear, wild sheep, trophy data, field methods, etc.
Hunting Our Medium Size Game, by Clyde Ormond. Stackpole Books, Harrisburg, Pa., 1958. 219 pp., illus. $5.00.
Covers deer, whitetails and mules; black bear; antelope; coyotes; bobcats and cougar. Included are sections on equipment, use of rifles, and care of venison.
Hunting Pronghorn Antelope, by Bert Popowski. Stackpole Books, Harrisburg, Pa., 1959. 227 pp., illus. $6.50.
Hunting the Ruffed Grouse, by Nick Sisley. Copyright, Nick Sisley, 1970. 136 pp., illus. $3.50.
A must for hunting this great game bird. The author, a grouse expert, is vice president of the Ruffed Grouse Society of America.
Hunting with Bow and Arrow, by George Laycock and Erwin Bauer. Arco Publ. Co., Inc., N.Y.C., 1966. $3.50.
A practical guide to archery as a present-day sport. Mentions equipment needed and how to select it. Illus. instructions on how to shoot with ease and accuracy.
The Imperial Collection of Audubon Animals, original text by John James Audubon and Rev. John Bachman, illus. by John James and John Woodhouse Audubon. A magnificent quarto reproduction of the rare original by Hammond, Inc., Maplewood, N.J., 1967. 307 pp., 150 animals pictured in full color. $25.00.
Each illus. accompanied by engaging text, as in the 1st ed. of 1848, including accounts of Audubon's exploring trips. A most useful work for hunters who want to know their game.
Inside Safari Hunting, by D. Holman. G. P. Putnam's Sons, N.Y., 1970. 296 pp., illus. $6.95
The work of the white hunter in Africa, based on the experiences of a second-generation professional.
Jack O'Connor's Big Game Hunts, by Jack O'Connor. E. P. Dutton, N.Y.C., 1963. 415 pp., illus. $5.95.
26 detailed chronicles of successful trips for big game, selected from *Outdoor Life.*
Krider's Sporting Anecdotes, edited by Milnor H. Klapp. Abercrombie & Fitch Library, N.Y., 1966. 292 pp., illus. $8.00.
Limited issue of the much-wanted work on Philadelphia's renowned gunsmith, John Krider, publ. first in 1853. A rich fund of knowledge on upland shooting, dogs and match shooting, etc.
Living Off the Country, by B. Angier. Stackpole Books, Harrisburg, Pa., 1959. 241 pp., illus. $5.00.
In a simple and entertaining manner the author explains how to live off nature when emergency arises and how to stay alive in the woods.

Modern ABC's of Bird Hunting, by Dave Harbour, Stackpole Books, Harrisburg, Pa., 1966. 192 pp., illus. $4.95.

From city's edge to wilderness this gives the occasional hunter the quickest way on how to increase his bag. Covers all game birds of the U.S. or Canada.

Modern Hunting with Indian Secrets, by Allan A. Macfarlan. Stackpole Books, Harrisburg, Pa., 1971. 222 pp., $6.50

How to acquire the new-old skills of the Redman, how to apply them to modern hunting.

The New Hunter's Encyclopedia, edited by Leonard Miracle and James B. Trefethen, plus specialized articles by over 60 outstanding contributors. Stackpole Books, Harrisburg, Pa. 1966. 1131 pp., profusely illus. with 2047 photos, diagrams, drawings and full-color plates. $24.95.

A massive work covering every detail of every sort of hunting in the U.S., Canada and Mexico.

Nine Centuries of Hunting Weapons, by L. G. Boccia, Editrice Edam, Firenze, Italy, 1967. 181 pp., illus. with many fine photos of superb museum quality in full color. $15.00

In Italian text, a historical survey of hunting weapons of Italian origin and their makers.

On Your Own in the Wilderness, by Col. T. Whelen and B. Angier. Stackpole Books, Harrisburg, Pa., 1958. 324 pp., illus. $5.00.

Two eminent authorities give complete, accurate, and useful data on all phases of camping and travel in primitive areas.

Pocket Guide to Animal Tracks, by L. M. Henderson. Stackpole Books, Harrisburg, Pa., 1968. 57 pp., profusely illus., and bound in paper boards. $2.95.

Delightful text plus Henderson's most accurate line drawings show many signatures—paw and hoof prints, habits and characteristics, of 44 North American small and big game.

Prehistoric Animals and Their Hunters, by I. W. Cornwall. F. A. Praeger, N.Y., 1968. 214 pp., illus. $7.50.

Describes animal species and hunting methods used in this period, plus used made of the kills.

The Puma, Mysterious American Cat, by S. P. Young and E. A. Goldman, Dover Publ., N.Y., 1964. 358 pp., illus. Paper covers $2.25.

A two-part work: the first on the history, economic status and control; the second on classifications of the races of the puma.

Ranch Life and the Hunting Trail, by Theodore Roosevelt, 1894. A fine reprint by the Winchester Press, New York, N.Y., 1969, with introduction by Kermit Roosevelt. 168 pp., and includes the Frederic Remington illustrations from the original and those added from the 1908 edition. $10.00.

The far West of the 1880s, of hunting and bags, of men and manners.

Records of North American Big Game, compiled by the Records Committee of the Boone and Crockett Club, Holt, Rinehart and Winston, N.Y.C. 3d printing of the 1964 edition. 398 pp., well illus., and with color frontis. $15.00.

The 5th issue of the famous useful series, and the largest and most complete.

The Rifle and Hound in Ceylon, by Samuel White Baker. Abercrombie & Fitch Library, N.Y., 1967. 422 pp., well illus. $12.95.

Limited printing of a classic description of elephant-hunting, deer-coursing and elk-hunting in the East. First published in the 1850s.

Rowland Ward's Records of Big Game, 13th Edition, compiled by G. A. Best. Rowland Ward Publ., Ltd., London, 1969, 38 pp., illus. $40.00.

New edition of the authoritative record of big game kills in Africa, by species.

Safari, by Elmer Keith. Safari Publ., La Jolla, Calif. 1968. 166 pp., illus. $7.95.

Guide to big game hunting in Africa, with anecdote and expert advice on hunting many species of game. Information on guns, ammunition, equipment, and planning the safari is included. Fine photographs.

Safari by Jet, through Africa and Asia, by Sister Maria del Rey, Charles Scribner's Sons, New York, N.Y., 1962. 308 pp., profusely illus., with photos. and line. $5.95.

Off-beat reading about an African-Asian grand tour, with tales of the land and the people of Tanganyika, Ceylon, the Philippines, Hong Kong, Taiwan, et al.

Shots at Whitetails, by Larry Koller. A. A. Knopf, N.Y., 1970. 359 pp., illus. $7.95.

A new reprint, with all information on guns, loads, scopes, etc., brought up to date.

A Sporting chance . . . , by D. P. Mannix. E. P. Dutton & Co., N.Y., 1967. 248 pp., illus. with 50 photos. $1.98.

Unusual methods of hunting the exotic species from hounds to falcons. Inspiring reading for those desiring to get away from the commonplace.

Sporting Guns, by Richard Akehurst. G. P. Putnam's Sons, N.Y.C., 1968. 120 pp., illus. $5.95.

History of shooting and of the guns and rifles developed to meet the hunter's needs, with anecdotes of the hunting field.

The Sportsman's Companion, by Lee Wulff. Harper & Row, N.Y.C., 1968. 413 pp., illus. $11.95.

Compendium of writings by various experts on hunting and fishing for American game. A useful reference for the outdoorsman.

Sportman's Guide to Game Animals, by Leonard Lee Rue III. Harper & Row [Outdoor Life Books], New York, N.Y. 1st ed., 2nd printing, 1969. 635 pp., illus. with photographs and maps. $6.50.

Exhaustive and capable coverage of the behavior and habits of all North American game animals.

The Standard Book of Hunting and Shooting, R. B. Stringfellow, ed. 1st ed., in 1950 by the Greystone Press, New York, N.Y. 564 pp., very well illus. $10.00.

An excellent anthology on hunting in America, giving meaningful information on all major species and on all types of guns, sights, ammunition, etc. An abridgement of the larger *Hunters Encyclopedia.*

Three Years' Hunting & Trapping in America and the Great Northwest, by J. Turner-Turner Abercrombie & Fitch Library, N.Y.C., 1967. 182 pp., illus. $10.95.

Reprint of an 1888 account of a determined quest for valuable furs in one of the world's least hospitable regions.

Tracks of an Intruder, by Gordon Young. Winchester Press, N.Y., 1970. 191 pp., illus. $5.95.

Fascinating, first hand account of how an American naturalist gained recognition as a master hunter from the Montagnard Lahu tribesmen of Southeast Asia.

Travel & Adventure in Southeast Africa, by F. C. Selous. A & F Press, N.Y.C., 1967. 522 pp., illus. $11.95.

New edition of a famous African hunting book, first published in 1893.

A Treasury of African Hunting, ed. by Peter Barrett. Winchester Press, N.Y., 1970. 251 pp., illus. $25.00.

Outstanding accounts by noted writers and experts on African hunting, covering big game and small in many sections of the continent.

The Treasury of Hunting, by Larry Koller, Odyssey Press, N.Y.C., 1965. 251 pp., illus. $7.95.

Concise accounts of all types of hunting in the U.S. Excellent illustrations, many color photographs taken in various hunting fields.

The Truth About Hunting in Today's Africa and how to go on a safari for $690.00, by G. L. Herter, Herter's, Inc., Waseca, Minn., 1970. 314 pp., well illus. $3.95.

Tells how to arrange safari costs, plus new data on weights, rifles and bullets derived from actual field tests.

The Unnatural Enemy, by Vance Bourjaily. The Dial Press, 1963. 182 pp., illus. $5.00. Beautifully written episodes of bird-hunting.

The Upland Game Hunter's Bible, by Dan Holland. Doubleday, N.Y.C., 1961. 192 pp., illus. Paper covers. $1.95.

Hunter's manual on the principal species of American upland game birds and how to hunt them.

The Varmint and Crow Hunter's Bible, by Bert Popowski. Doubleday & Co., N.Y.C., 1962. 185 pp., 150 illus. Paper covers. $1.95.

Hunting and trapping techniques described by a well-known authority. Chapters on woodchucks, crows, foxes, snakes, guns, etc.

Waterfowl in the Marshes, by A. C. Becker Jr. A. S. Barnes and Co., New York, N.Y., 1969. 155 pp., photographs. $7.50.

A highly informative and practical guide to waterfowl hunting in America.

Whitetail, by George Mattis. World Publ. Co., New York, N.Y., 1969. 273 pp., including index. Illus. $6.95.

Fundamentals and fine points of compelling interest for the deer hunter.

Wild Fowl Decoys, by Joel Barber. Dover Publ., N.Y.C., 1954. 156 pp., 134 illus., paperbound. $4.00.

A fine work on making, painting, care and use of decoys in hunting, recently reprinted. Full data on design and construction.

Wildfowling, by James Andrews, et al. Seeley, Service & Co., London, n.d. 352 pp., illus. $6.00.

Articles by British sportsmen on shooting wildfowl, guns, punting, and conditions in various areas. Vol. 29 of the Lonsdale Library.

Wildfowling At A Glance, by R. W. Coykendall, Jr. Stackpole Books, Harrisburg, Pa., 1968. 94 pp., illus. $2.95.

Covers wildfowl hunting in America, including ducks, decoys, dogs, boats, and blinds.

Winchester-Western 1970-71 Hunting Guide, by E. L. Kozicky and J. B. Madson. Winchester Press, N.Y., 1970. 126 pp., illus. Paper covers. $1.95.

A compendium of hunting information, seasons, licenses, prospects and best hunting areas.

RIFLES

The Big-Game Rifle, by Jack O'Connor, Alfred A. Knopf, N.Y.C., 1951. 371 pp., plus XI pp. Well illus. $10.00.

Discusses construction, purpose and use for all types of big game as well as ammo., sights, accessories, etc.

The Book of Rifles, by W. H. B. Smith. Stackpole Books, Harrisburg, Pa., 1963 (3rd ed.). 656 pp., profusely illus. $12.50.

An encyclopedic reference work on shoulder arms, recently up-dated. Includes rifles of all types, arranged by country of origin. Buy with Book of Pistols & Revolvers and both are $19.95.

The Boy's Book of Rifles, by C. E. Chapel. Coward-McCann, N.Y.C., 1948, rev. ed., 1960. 274 pp., illus. $3.95.

For all young men of Boy Scout age at every phase of small-caliber marksmanship and safe gun handling. It tells how to qualify for NRA medals and Scout Merit Badges for Marksmanship.

Boy's Single-Shot Rifles, by Jas. J. Grant, William Morrow & Co., Inc., New York, 1967. 608 pp., illus. $10.00.

A wealth of important new material on an ever-popular subject, authoritatively presented. By the author of *Single Shot Rifles* and *More Single Shot Rifles.*

The Breech-Loading Single-Shot Match Rifle, by N. H. Roberts and K. L. Waters, D. Van Nostrand Co., Princeton, N.J., 1967. 293 pp., fine photos. $12.50.

Account of the Schuetzen rifle in America, with material on famous shooters, gunsmiths, ammunition, and related topics.

Carbines Cal. .30 M1, M1A1, M2 and M3, by D. B. McLean. Normount Armament Co., Forest Grove, Ore., 1964. 221 pp., well illus., paperbound. $3.00.

U.S. field manual reprints on these weapons, edited and reorganized.

The First Winchester, by John E. Parsons. Winchester Press, New York, N.Y., 1969. 207 pp., well illus., $8.95.

This new printing of *The Story of the 1866 Repeating Rifle* [1st publ. 1955] is revised, and additional illustrations included.

Garand Rifles MI, MIC, MID, by Donald B. McLean. Normount Armament Co., Forest Grove, Oregon, Ill., 1968. Over 160 pp., 175 illus., paper wrappers. $3.00.

Covers all facets of the arm: battlefield use, disassembly and maintenance, all details to complete lock-stock-and-barrel repair, plus variations, grenades, ammo., and accessories; plus a section on 7.62mm NATO conversions.

How to Select and Use Your Big Game Rifle, by Henry M. Stebbins. Combat Forces Press, Washington, 1952. 237 pp., illus. $6.50.

Concise valuable data on rifles, old and new—slide action, lever, semi automatic, and single shot models are covered.

The Hunting Rifle, by Jack O'Connor. Winchester Press, N.Y., 1970. 352 pp., illus. $8.95.

An analysis, with wit and wisdon, of contemporary rifles, cartridges, accessories and hunting techniques.

Johnson Semi-Automatic Rifle, Rotary Feed Model, 1941 Instruction Manual, by the Johnson Arms Co. Design Publ., Hyattsville, Md., 1969. 72 pp. illus., paper covers. $4.00.

A reprint of the original instruction manual.

The Lee-Enfield Rifle, by E. G. B. Reynolds. Arco Publ. Co., N.Y., 1968. 224 pp., drawings and photos. $9.50.

New U.S. edition of a standard reference on models and modifications of the famous British military rifle.

Maynard Catalog of 1880, a reprint in facsimile by the Wyoming Armory, Inc., Cheyenne, Wyo., 1969. 32 pp., illus., paper covers. $2.25.

All models, sights, cartridges, targets etc.

Pictorial History of the Rifle, By G. W. P. Swenson. Ian Allan Ltd., Shepperton, Surrey, England, 1971. 184 pp., illus. $7.00.

Essentially a picture book, with over 200 rifle illustrations. The text furnishes a concise history of the rifle and its development.

Practical Dope on the .22, by F. C. Ness, Stackpole Books, Harrisburg, Pa. 4th printing, 1955. 313 pp., illus. $5.50.

Considerable pertinent information on 22 cal. rifles, actions, loads, plus test firing and data on their ballistics.

Remarks on Rifle Guns; Fowling Pieces, The Percussion Lock and Firearms in General, by Ezekiel Baker, 1st issued 1800. A reprint of the 11th ed., by Standard Publications, Inc., Huntington, W.Va., 1946. 269 pp., plus tables, etc. $7.00.

An important work written by a famous British gunmaker, with much information on many nostalgic aspects on guns and shooting.

The Rifle Book, by Jack O'Connor. Random House (Knopf), N.Y.C., 1948. 3rd ed., 1964. 338 pp., illus. $10.00.

A definitive work, out-of-print until recently, which covers actions, design, ammunition, sights and accessories.

Rifles, a Modern Encyclopedia, by H. M. Stebbins. Book Sales, New York, N.Y. 1970. A reprint of the original of 1958. 376 pp., well illus. $4.98.

A comprehensive work covering subject for target and game. A limited number of original, deluxe and numbered full-leather bound copies at $25.00.

Rifles AR15, M16, and M16A1, 5.56 mm, by D. B. McLean. Normount Armament Co., Forest Grove, Ore., 1968. Unpaginated, illus., paper covers. $3.50.

Descriptions, specifications and operation of subject models are set forth in text and picture.

Sharps Firearms, V. 3, Pt. 3, Model 1874 Rifles, by Frank M. Sellers and DeWitt Bailey II. Frank M. Sellers, Denver, Colo., 1969. 20 pp., illus., paper covers. $7.50.

A separately printed section of a continuing comprehensive collector's reference. This current work shows and describes the known M1874 variations.

Shooter's Bible Gunsight Guide, by George Nonte. Shooter's Bible, Inc., So. Hackensack, N.J., 1968. 224 pp., illus. $3.95.

Catalog data, descriptions and comment, plus articles on all types of modern gun sights.

Shooting the Percussion Rifle, by R. O. Ackerman. Publ. by the author, Albuquerque, N.M., 1966. 19 pp., illus. in line by the author. Paper wrappers, $1.50.

This well prepared work is Book No. 2 of a projected series. This one gives basic information on the use of the muzzle-loading rifle.

Single Shot Rifles and Actions, by Frank de Haas. Ed. by J. T. Amber. Published by Digest Books, Inc., Northfield, Ill. 1969. 342 pp., illus. Paper bound. $7.95. A definitive book on over 60 single shot actions and rifles, their use, repair, remodelling, etc.

Sir Charles Ross and His Rifle, by Robt Phillips and J. J. Knap. Museum Restoration Service, Ottawa, Canada., 1969. 32 pp., illus. Paper covers. $2.00.

The story of the man who invented the "Ross Model 1897 Magazine Sporting Rifle," the 1900 under the name of Bennett, and many others.

Small Bou Target Shooting, by H. G. B. Fuller. Herbert Jenkins, London, 1964. 264 pp., well illus. $5.50.

Authoritative English work, covering rifle types, buying hints, ammunition, accessories, and range technique.

Sniper Rifles of Two World Wars, by W. H. Tantum IV. Museum Restoration Service, Ottawa, Can., 1967. 32 pp., illus. $1.50.

Monograph on high-accuracy rifles used by troops in World Wars I and II and in Korea. Paper wrappers.

Springfield Rifles, M1903, M1903AI, M1903A3, M1903A4, compiled by the publ. Normount Armament Co., Forest Grove, Ore., 1968. Over 115 pp., illus., paper wrappers. $2.50.

Routine disassembly and maintenance to complete ordnance inspection and repair; bore sighting, trigger adjustment, accessories, etc.

Twenty-Two Caliber Varmint Rifles, by C. S. Landis. Stackpole Books, Harrisburg, Pa., 1947. 521 pp., profusely illustrated. $7.50.

A vast amount of data on the many wildcat 22's, including numerous scale drawings of cartridges and chambers.

United States Rifle, Cal. .30, Model of 1917, a reprint of an official government booklet by Normount Publ. Co., Forest Grove, Ore., 1969. 80 pp., line illus., paper covers. $2.00.

A training manual issued by the War Department in 1918. A much-wanted and useful booklet.

United States Rifle 7.62 mm, M14 and M14E2, a reprint of an official government booklet by Normount Armament Co., Forest Grove, Ore., 1968. 50 pp., illus., paper covers. $2.00.

U.S. Army Field Manual 23-8, first published in 1965.

Westley Richards Modern Sporting Rifles and Cartridges. A reprint of an original undated catalog of the British makers. Safari Outfitters, Richfield, Conn., 1968. 60 pp. illus., paper. $4.95.

Facsimile of issue, covers big game rifles and ammunition.

Winchester '73 & '76, the First Repeating Center-Fire Rifles, by D. F. Butler. Winchester Press, New York, N.Y., 1st ed., 1970. 95 pp., well and tastefully illus. in line, halftones and photos. Color frontispiece. $7.95.

A complete history of the subject arms and their then-new ammunition, plus details of their use on America's western frontiers.

American Partridge and Pheasant Shooting, Frank Schley. Abercrombie & Fitch Library, N.Y., 1967. 222 pp., illus. with detailed engravings of game birds. $7.95.

Limited printing of the rare sporting classic of 1877, considered for years the most important book available on the use of the scattergun.

The Art of Wing Shooting, by Wm. G. Leffingwell. Abercrombie & Fitch Library, N.Y., 1967. 192 pp., illus. $7.95.

Limited issue of a practical treatise on the use of the shotgun, first publ. in 1894. Contains a wealth of period anecdotes.

Automatic and Repeating Shotguns, by R. Arnold. Barnes & Co., N.Y.C., 1960. 173 pp., illus. $2.95.

Their history and development, with expert professional advice on choosing a gun for clay target shooting, game shooting, etc.

Book of the Shotgun, by Sports Illustrated eds. J. B. Lippincott Co., Phila. Pa., 1967. 90 pp., illus. $3.50.

A beginner's book on the shotgun and its use. Basic material on guns, ammunition, selection, form, and shooting.

Book of Shotgun Sports, by Sports Illustrated eds. J. B. Lippincott Co., Phila., Pa., 1967. 88 pp., illus., $3.50.

Introduction to target shooting, game shooting, and gunmanship.

Clay Pigeon Marksmanship, by Percy Stanbury and G. L. Carlisle. Herbert Jenkins, London, 1964. 216 pp., illus. $6.00.

Handbook on learning the skills, with data on guns & equipment and competition shooting at all types of clay targets; by two eminent British writers.

Field, Skeet and Trapshooting, by C. E. Chapel. Revised ed. Barnes & Co., N.Y.C., 1962. 291 pp., illus. $6.95.

A useful work on shotgun shooting, including gun types, ammo, accessories, marksmanship, etc.

The Game Shot's Vade Mecum, by Michael Brander, A. & C. Black, London, 1st ed., 1965. 242 pp., illus., $5.00.

A British guide on the use of the shotgun in the hunting field, covers selection, marksmanship, game behavior and hunt management.

Gough Thomas's Gun Book, by G. T. Garwood. A. & C. Black, London, England, 1969. 160 pp., illus. $8.95.

Excerpts of articles on the shotgun published in *Shooting Times,* by a noted British authority. Wide-ranging survey of every aspect on the shotgun, its use, behavior, care, and lore.

How to Shoot Straight, by Macdonald Hastings. A. S. Barnes and Co., New York, N.Y., 1970. 133 pp., illus., index ed. $5.95.

A companion volume to the author's *Churchill on Game Shooting,* and designed as a standard work on the modern game gun—a "teach-yourself" book.

The Modern Shotgun, by Maj. Sir Gerald Burrard. A. S. Barnes & Co., N.Y.C. 1961. In 2 vols. 1074 pp. Cased, $8.95.

Completely reliable and authoritative on the shotgun and its ammunition in every aspect.

The New Wildfowler in the 1970's by N. M. Sedgwick, et al. Barrie & Jenkins, London, Eng., 1970. 375 pp., illus. $10.00.

A compendium of articles on wildfowling, hunting practices and conservation. An updated reprint.

Parker, America's Finest Shotgun, by P. H. Johnson. Outlet Book Co., Inc., N.Y., 1968. 260 pp., illus. $3.95.

An account of a great sporting arm—from post Civil War until 1947, when it was sold to Remington. Values, models, etc.

Pigeon Shooting, by Richard Arnold. Faber & Faber, London, Eng., 1966. 162 pp., illus. $4.75. A practical, specialized work on pigeon shooting in flight, over decoys, how to make hideouts, decoys, etc.

Rough Shooting, by G. A. Grattan & R. Willett. Faber & Faber, London, Eng., 1968. 242 pp., illus. $6.75.

The art of shooting, dogs and their training, games, rearing and their diseases, proof marks, etc.

Score Better at Trap, by Fred Missildine. Winchester Press, N.Y., 1971. 192 pp., illus. $5.95.

Step-by-step instructions, fully illustrated, on mastering the game by one of the world's leading coaches. In paper covers, $2.95.

Shooting For Beginners, by E. N. Barclay. Percival Marshall & Co., London, 1963. 74 pp., illus. $1.75.

Concise introduction to British techniques and customs in shotgunning for game birds.

Shooting Preserve Management [The Nilo System], by E. L. Kozicky and John Madson. Winchester Press, New York, N.Y., 1969. 312 pp., photos., line drawings and diagrams. $10.00.

The new look in 13 chapters, a full account of American field shooting at Nilo Farms, the show-case of the shooting-preserve concept.

The Shotgun, by T. D. S. & J. A. Purdey. A. & C. Black, London, Eng., 1969. 144 pp., illus. with photos and diagrams. $3.95.

Reprinted 4th ed. of a well-known British work by two members of the notable gunsmith family. Covers the gun and its use in the field, at traps, and for skeet.

The Shotgun Book, by Jack O'Connor. Alfred A. Knopf, N.Y., 1965. 332 pp., plus index, illus. with line and photos. $10.00.

The definitive, authoritative book with up-to-date chapters on wild-fowling, upland gunning, trap and Skeet shooting. It includes practical advice on shotgun makes, models and functions, as well as data on actions.

Shotgun Marksmanship, by P. Stanbury & G. L. Carlisle. A. S. Barnes & Co., New York, 1969. 224 pp., illus. $6.95.

A new and revised edition for beginners, veterans, skeet shooters, hunters, etc. Valuable tips on improving marksmanship, etc.

The Shotgun Stock, by Robt. Arthur. A. S. Barnes & Co., N.Y., 1971. 175 pp., illus. $12.00.

The first and only book about the shotgun stock. Its design, construction, and embellishment. A much-needed work.

The Shotgunner's Bible, by George Laycock. Doubleday & Co., Garden City, N.Y., 1969. 173 pp., illus., paper covers. $1.95.

Coverage of shotguns, ammunition, marksmanship, hunting of various types of game, care and safety, etc.

The Shotgunner's Book, by Col. Charles Askins. Stackpole Books, Harrisburg, Pa., 1958. 365 pp., illus. $2.98.

Concise coverage of everything from design and manufacture to shooting form and ammunition.

Shotguns & Cartridges, by Gough Thomas. A. & C. Black, London, Eng., 1970. 136 pp., illus. $5.00.

An excellent work on the choice and use of guns and loads, by the gun editor of **The Shooting Times** (England).

Shotguns and Shooting, by E. S. McCawley Jr. Van Nostrand, N.Y.C., 1965. 146 pp., illus. $2.98.

Lucid coverage of shotgun development, various types, ammunition, and related subjects. Covers gun care, safety, and use in hunting fields or on skeet or trap ranges.

Shotguns by Keith, by E. Keith. Stackpole Books, Harrisburg, Pa., 1967. 307 pp., illus. A new edition, $7.95.

Guns and their accessories from history to ornamentation, their ammunition, and the practical use of American, English and European arms.

Skeet Shooting with D. Lee Braun, Robt. Campbell, ed. Grosset & Dun- lap, N.Y., 1967. 160 pp., illus. $4.95.

Thorough instructions on the fine points of Skeet shooting.

Successful Shotgun Shooting, by A. A. Montague. Winchester Press, N.Y., 1970. 160 pp., illus. $5.95.

The work of a superb shot and a great teacher; even the experts can read with profit.

Sure-Hit Shotgun Ways, by F. E. Sell, Stackpole Books, Harrisburg, Pa., 1967. 160 pp., illus. $5.95.

An expert with the scatter gun uncomplicates its effective use in every field, gives quick-skill methods for the sportsman.

Trapshooting with D. Lee Braun and the Remington Pros., ed. by R. Campbell. Remington Arms Co., Bridgeport, Conn., 1969. 157 pp., well illus., $5.95. Also in paper covers. $2.50.

America's masters of the scattergun give the secrets of professional marksmanship.

IMPORTANT NOTICE TO BOOK BUYERS

GLOSSARY FOR GUNNERS

Action Breech mechanism of a gun, by which it is loaded and unloaded.

Air Space Space in a loaded cartridge case not occupied by powder or bullet base.

Anvil In a primer or cartridge case, a fixed point against which the priming mixture is compressed, and thereby detonated, by the action of the firing pin.

Ball Earlier term for "bullet," and still used in some military terminology.

Ballistics Science of projectiles in motion.

Barrel The part(s) of a gun through which passes the bullet or shot, traveling from breech to muzzle.

Base Wad Compressed paper or other material inside a shotshell, varying in size and form.

Battery Cup Type of shotshell ignition form in which the cap or primer is held.

Belted Case Cartridge case with a band or belt at base, just ahead of extractor groove, and on which case (otherwise "rimless") positions in rifle chamber. See "Headspace."

Black Powder A mixture of charcoal, sulphur and saltpeter used as a propellant. Gives off much smoke when burned. See "Smokeless Powder."

Bore The inside of the barrel of a gun.

Bore Diameter In rifled arms, the diametrical measurement between tops of lands.

Breech Bolt The part of a breech that resists the rearward force of the combustion that occurs when a cartridge is fired.

BT Boat-tail, referring to the base taper given certain bullets to give them greater efficiency at long ranges.

Bullet The projectile *only*, not to be applied to the cartridge, which see. See also "Ball."

Bullet Mould Metallic device with a cavity(s) into which molten lead (or lead alloy) can be poured and allowed to harden into the projectile.

Caliber Bore or groove diameter expressed (in English) in decimals of an inch, otherwise in the metric system. Frequently compounded to indicate powder capacity of cartridge case; to show date of adoption; to show case length or to show proprietor, etc. E.g., 30-40, 30-06, 8x57mm or 375 Holland & Holland.

Cannelure Circumferential groove(s) around a bullet or cartridge case. In the latter refers to extractor groove, in lead bullets the lubrication grooves, in jacketed bullets the expansion point and/or where case is crimped.

Caplock Used of a muzzleloading gun whose ignition system employs a percussion cap, a small thimble-like metal cup containing a detonating mixture. This cup, placed on a "nipple," transmits flame to the powder charge when struck by the gun's hammer.

Cartridge A complete round of ammunition, made up, simply, of a cartridge case, primer, bullet (or shot) and powder.

Cartridge Case Commonly, the brass or copper envelope that contains powder, primer and projectile, but applicable to shotshells, too, whether of all brass (not common), paper and metal or plastic and metal.

CF Centerfire (cartridges); those ignited by means of (generally) a separate and replaceable primer.

Chamber That part of the bore, at the breech, formed to accept the cartridge.

Choke The constriction of a shotgun bore at the muzzle to various degrees, designed to control pellet charge spread at the target.

Chronograph An instrument which measures the velocity of a projectile.

Clip See "Magazine."

Cordite A nitroglycerine smokeless powder used mainly in Great Britain.

Crimp The bending inward of the case mouth perimeter, in order to grip and hold the bullet, or to keep the shot in a paper case intact.

Cylinder In a revolver, a cartridge container that rotates (generally) around an axis parallel to and below the barrel.

Die In handloading ammunition, any of a number of tools used to size bullets or cases, seat bullets, etc.

Drams Equivalent Term used to indicate that a certain charge of smokeless powder gives ballistics equal to a stated volumetric charge of black powder.

Drift The bullet's movement to right or left, away from the line of the bore, caused by bullet rotation or spin.

Drilling A three-barrel gun, popular in Europe, which usually combines smoothbore and rifled barrels.

Ejector Correctly the device(s) at the barrel breech or within the action that forcibly expels the fired case from the gun. See "Extractor."

Energy In bullets, the amount of work done, at given ranges, expressed in foot pounds.

Erosion More or less gradual wearing away of rifling by combustion gas, heat and bullet friction.

"Everlasting" Case Brass cartridge case made from heavy stock, intended for extended reloading life.

Extractor Device that removes or partially removes the fired cartridge case from the chamber. See "Ejector."

Firing Pin A part of the action, actuated by the trigger, that hits the primer and fires the cartridge.

Flintlock Used of a muzzleloading gun fired by means of a piece of flint, held in the hammer or "cock" jaws, striking against a steel "frizzen." Incandescent particles of steel scraped from the frizzen fall into a "pan" holding powder. This ignited powder flames through the "touch-hole," thus firing the main charge.

Follower A metal platform in a clip or magazine that pushes the cartridges upward at the proper angle for feeding into the chamber.

Gas Check A cup (usually copper) used on the base of a lead bullet to protect it from hot powder gases.

Gauge Unit of bore measurement in shotguns, determined by the number of solid lead round balls, of the bore diameter, obtainable from one pound of lead. E.g., 12 gauge means a bore of such size that 12 balls of that size make a pound of lead.

Gilding Metal A copper-zinc alloy used as bullet jacket material; usually 5% to 10% zinc.

Grooves Spiral cuts in a bore which cause the bullet to spin as it travels down the barrel.

Groove Diameter In rifled arms, the diametrical measurement between bottoms of grooves.

Group Number of shots fired into a target (number and range optional), usually with one sight setting.

Hammer A part of the action (in some guns) actuated by the trigger. The hammer drives the firing pin against the primer, thus igniting the cartridge powder charge.

Hang-fires Cartridges which fire as long as several seconds after firing pin strikes primer.

H.P. Hollow point, a design feature of certain bullets. See "Mushroom."

Headspace For rimmed cartridges, the distance from the face of the breechblock to the barrel seat for the forward surface of the case rim. For a rimless bottleneck cartridge, the distance from the face of the breechblock to a predetermined point on the shoulder of the chamber. For rimless straight cartridges, the distance from the face of the breechblock to the shoulder or ledge in the chamber. Belted cases headspace on the forward edge of the belt.

Lands That portion of the bore remaining after the rifling or grooves have been cut.

Leading Lead deposited on bore by bullets passing through.

Magazine Device or reservoir to hold extra cartridges, of many types and names. "Clip," once reserved for the slender metal strip from which cartridges are stripped into a magazine well, now refers to separate, detachable magazines also, as with those for autoloading pistols, many rifles and shotguns.

Matchlock An early form of firearm in which the priming charge was ignited by a cord or "match" of slow-burning material.

M.C. Metal Case, a form of bullet completely covered forward with copper or copper alloy (usually) jacket. Generally a military bullet type, and also termed "solids," and F.M.J. (full metal jacketed).

Mid-Range Usually used in connection with trajectory, referring to a point midway between muzzle and target or game.

Misfires Cartridges which do not fire when firing pin strikes primers.

MRT Mid Range Trajectory. See above.

Mushroom The capacity of certain bullets to expand on or after impact, also the term given to some soft point or hollow point bullets. See "S.P." and "H.P."

Muzzle End of barrel opposite to breech; point from which bullet or shot leaves barrel.

Muzzle-Loader Gun loaded through the front end of the bore, using loose powder and ball (or shot) or paper cartridges.

M.E. Muzzle Energy. See "Energy."

M.V. Muzzle Velocity. See "Velocity."

Nipple On muzzle-loading guns, the small metal cone at the rear of the barrel (or cylinder) through which the flame from the percussion cap passes to ignite the powder charge.

Ogive The radius of the curve of the nose of a bullet, usually expressed in calibers.

O.P.E. Open Point Expanding, a term for bullets of hollow point form made by Western Cartridge Co.

Over-bore Capacity Condition in which the volume of a cartridge case exceeds the amount of powder which can most efficiently be burned.

Pan See "Flintlock."

Paradox Smoothbore gun in which the final few inches of barrel are rifled to increase efficiency of round ball or bullet use. Also called "Explora" and "Fauneta" guns by Westley Richards.

Patching, Cloth Used to form a gas seal around the projectile (round ball or conical bullet) of a muzzle-loading gun and engage the rifling.

Pattern Of pellets from a shotgun, usually expressed as so many pellets within a 30-inch circle at 40 yards.

Percussion Cap Small metallic cup containing fulminating material that explodes when struck by gun's hammer. See "Nipple."

Pistol Said by some to derive from Pistoia, an early gun making center in Italy. Any small, concealable, short-barreled (2"-10") hand weapon, generally *not* a revolver.

Pressure The gas pressure generated in a cartridge on its being fired, usually expressed in (greatest) pounds per square inch (p.s.i.).

Primer In a centerfire cartridge, the small cup containing a detonating mixture, which is seated in a recess in the base of the case. In a rimfire, a similar mixture inside the folded rim of the case.

Proprietary Cartridge One developed and sold exclusively by one business organization.

Ramrod Rod, of wood or metal, used to force home the projectile in a muzzle-loading gun and sometimes to hold cleaning implements.

Rebated Rim Type of cartridge case rim smaller in diameter than the case is at a point just forward of the extractor groove.

Recoil The backward thrust of a gun caused by the reaction to the powder gases pushing the bullet forward.

Revolver A multi-shot handgun, using a revolving cylinder as a cartridge container.

RF Rimfire cartridges. Those containing their primer mixture in the rim, which is where they are struck by the firing pin.

Rifling Spiral grooving cut into the bore of rifles and handguns to impart spin to their bullets, thus assuring point-on flight and accuracy.

Rim The projecting edge of the base or "head" of certain cartridges.

Rook Cartridge Low powered cartridge developed in England for shooting pest birds and animals.

Shot Lead or lead-alloy spheres used as projectiles in smoothbore guns.

Shotgun A smoothbore gun using cartridges loaded with shot.

Shoulder The sloping portion of a bottleneck cartridge case that joins the body and neck.

Sizing In handloading cartridges, sizing (or resizing) brings the fired cartridge case back to the (full or partial) dimensions of the new or unfired case. Bullets are also sized.

Smokeless Powder Gunpowder which gives off almost no smoke when burned. See "Black Powder." Usually made by nitrating and otherwise chemically treating purified cotton waste.

S.P. Soft Point, a term used for bullets with partial metal jacketing, having some lead exposed at the front.

Trajectory Curved path of bullet in flight, a parabola.

Twist Angle of the rifling relative to the axis of the bore. Usually uniform, and expressed in turns or part-turns in so many inches. Less common, "progressive" or "gain" twist, usually starting at a rate at breech that becomes gradually faster.

Velocity Projectile speed, usually measured in feet per second (f.p.s.) at the muzzle and other distances such as 100 yards, 200 yards, etc.

Vent Orifice through the nipple.

Wad A disc of paper, felt, plastic or other material used in shotshells; sometimes in metallic cases, too, but not commonly today.

  a. Filler Wad—placed between the powder and card or Nitro wad to cushion the shot from the thrust of the hot powder gases, and to bring the shot to the proper height for correct crimping.

  b. Over-powder Wad—placed between powder and filler wads, sometimes called Nitro wads.

  c. Top Wad—thin card placed on top of the shot in roll crimp shells—star crimp shells do not require a top wad.

  d. Base Wad—these are permanently built into the shell at the base to hold the paper tube to the brass and give added support to the thin brass wall.

Wheel-lock Used of a muzzleloading gun fired by means of a piece of flint or pyrites, held in the hammer jaws, which is held over a serrated steel wheel. This wheel, set in motion by a tensioned spring, protrudes through the bottom of the "pan" (wherein powder has been placed) and bears against the flint. Sparks are created, as in the flintlock, and the gun is fired by a flame passing through the touch-hole.

Wildcat Cartridge designed by a private experimenter; not available as a factory-loaded round.

WCF Winchester Center Fire.

WRF Winchester Rim Fire.

Zero That sight setting which gives bullet group desired, and from which subsequent changes in sight settings will be made.

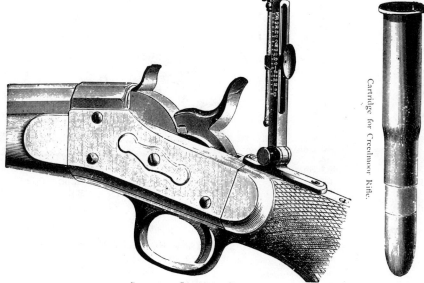

REMINGTON CREEDMOOR RIFLE.

Cartridge for Creedmoor Rifle.

FEDERAL AMMUNITION

FEDERAL CARTRIDGE CORPORATION   2700 FOSHAY TOWER   MINNEAPOLIS, MINN. 55402

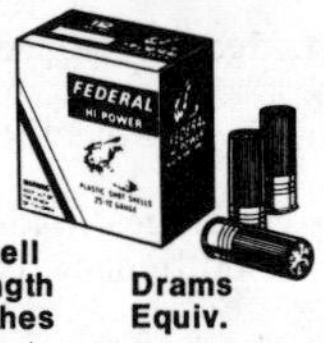

SHOT SHELL LOADS

Gauge	Shell Length Inches	Drams Equiv.	Shot Ozs.	Shot Sizes	Price Per Box
MAGNUM LOADS					
12	3	4½	1⅞	BB,2,4	6.30
12	3	4¼	1⅝	2,4,6	5.85
12	2¾	4	1½	2,4,5,6	5.35
16	2¾	3½	1¼	2,4,6	4.60
20	3	3¼	1¼	4,6,7½	4.80
20	2¾	3	1⅛	4,6,7½	4.20
HI-POWER® LOADS					
12	2¾	3¾	1¼	BB,2,4,5,6,7½,9	4.40
16	2¾	3¼	1⅛	4,5,6,7½,9	4.05
20	2¾	2¾	1	4,5,6,7½,9	3.85
28	2¾	2½	⅞	6,7½,9	3.85
410	3	Max.	¾	4,5,6,7½	3.50
410	2½	Max.	½	6,7½	2.95
FIELD LOADS					
12	2¾	3¼	1¼	7½,8,9	3.95
12	2¾	3¼	1⅛	4,5,6,7½,8,9	3.75
12	2¾	3	1	6,8	3.50
16	2¾	2¾	1⅛	4,5,6,7½,8,9	3.50
16	2¾	2½	1	6,8	3.35
20	2¾	2½	1	4,5,6,7½,8,9	3.40
20	2¾	2¼	⅞	6,8	3.10
TARGET LOADS					
12¹	2¾	2¾	1⅛	7½,8,9	3.50
12¹	2¾	3	1⅛	7½,8,9	3.50
12	2¾	2¾	1⅛	7½,8,9	3.65
12	2¾	3	1⅛	7½,8,9	3.65
12	2¾	3¼	1¼	7½,8,9	3.95
12³	2¾	3¼	1¼	7½,8	4.55
16	2¾	2¾	1⅛	7½,8,9	3.50
20²	2¾	2¼	⅞	8,9	3.10
28	2¾	2¼	¾	9	3.85
410	3	Max.	¾	9	3.50
410	2½	Max.	½	9	2.95
BUCKSHOT & RIFLED SLUG LOADS					
12	3	Sup. Mag.	—	00 Buck, 15 Pellets	1.52
12	3	Sup. Mag.	—	No. 4 Buck, 41 Pellets	1.52
12	2¾	Mag.	—	00 Buck, 12 Pellets	1.32
12	2¾	Mag.	—	No. 1 Buck, 20 Pellets	1.32
12	2¾	Max.	—	00 Buck, 9 Pellets	1.17
12	2¾	Max.	—	0 Buck, 12 Pellets	1.17
12	2¾	Max.	—	No. 1 Buck, 16 Pellets	1.17
12	2¾	Max.	—	No. 4 Buck, 27 Pellets	1.17
16	2¾	Max.	—	No. 1 Buck, 12 Pellets	1.17
20	2¾	Max.	—	No. 3 Buck, 20 Pellets	1.17
12	2¾	Max.	—	1 oz. Rifled Slug	1.38
16	2¾	Max.	—	⅞ oz. Rifled Slug	1.31
20	2¾	Max.	—	⅝ oz. Rifled Slug	1.26
410	2½	Max.	—	1/5 oz. Rifled Slug	1.19

All Plastic tubes except
¹Paper ²Offered in Plastic and Paper
³Nickel Plated Shot
Packaged 25 per box except Buckshot and slugs 5 per box.
Wad Columns: Triple-Plus in 12, 16, 20 Ga. Hi-Power and Fields.
Magnums, 28 Gauge, 410 use shot cup with conventional wads.
12 Gauge Target loads use plastic "Champion" air-chamber wad.
Buck and Rifled Slugs do not use shot cups.

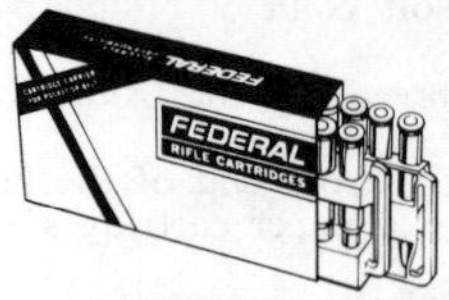

CENTERFIRE PISTOL & RIFLE

Cartridge	Gr.	Bullet Style	Muzzle Velocity	Muzzle Energy	Barrel Length Inches	Price Per Box
PISTOL						
25 (6.35mm) Auto	50	MC	810	73	2	5.55
32 Auto	71	MC	960	145	4	6.35
357 Mag.,Ni.Pl.Cs.	158	JSP	1550	845	8⅜	8.35
9 mm Luger Auto	123	MC	1120	345	4	7.90
380 Auto	95	MC	955	192	3¾	6.50
38 Special Match	148	WC	770	195	6	6.25
38 Special	158	Lead	855	256	6	6.00
38 Special, Hi-Vel.	158	Lead	1080	415	6	6.65
45 Auto Match	230	MC	850	370	5	8.50
45 Auto Match	185	WC	775	247	5	8.95
RIFLE						
222 Remington	50	SP	3200	1140	26	4.10
22250 Remington	55	SP	3810	1770	26	4.50
223 Remington	55	SP	3300	1330	26	4.50
*243 Winchester	80	SP	3500	2180	26	5.70
*243 Winchester	100	SP	3070	2090	26	5.70
*270 Winchester	130	HS	3140	2840	24	6.20
*270 Winchester	150	HS	2800	2610	24	6.20
*7 mm Mauser	175	HS	2490	2410	24	6.20
*7 mm Mauser	139	HS	2710	2280	24	6.20
7 mm Rem. Mag.	150	HS	3260	3540	26	7.70
7 mm Rem. Mag.	175	HS	3070	3660	26	7.70
30 Carbine	110	SP	1980	955	18	3.90
*3030 Winchester	150	HS	2410	1930	26	4.85
*3030 Winchester	170	HS	2220	1860	26	4.85
*3006 Springfield	150	HS	2970	2930	24	6.20
*3006 Springfield	180	HS	2700	2910	24	6.20
*3006 Springfield	125	SP	3200	2840	24	6.20
*300 Savage	150	HS	2670	2370	24	6.05
*300 Savage	180	HS	2370	2240	24	6.05
300 Win. Mag.	150	HS	3400	3850	26	9.10
300 Win. Mag	180	HS	3070	3770	26	9.10
*303 British	180	HS	2540	2580	26	6.25
*308 Winchester	150	HS	2860	2730	24	6.20
*308 Winchester	180	HS	2610	2720	24	6.20
*8mm Mauser	170	HS	2570	2490	23½	6.20
*32 Win. Special	170	HS	2280	1960	26	5.00
*35 Remington	200	HS	2100	1950	22	5.65

Pistol Cartridges Packaged 50 per box
Rifle Cartridges Packaged 20 per box
MC-Metal Case   JSP-Jacketed Soft Point   WC-Wadcutter
SP-Soft Point   HS-"Hi-Shok" Soft Point
*Caliber with "Cartridge Carrier" pack.

RIMFIRE 22'S

Cartridge	Gr.	Bullet Style	Muzzle Velocity	Barrel Length	Price Per Box
HI-POWER®					
22 Short	29	Solid	1125	24	.88
22 Short	29	Hollow Point	1155	24	.99
22 Long	29	Solid	1240	24	.93
22 Long Rifle	40	Solid	1285	24	1.04
22 Long Rifle	38	Hollow Point	1315	24	1.15
22 Long Rifle	25	No. 12 Shot	—	24	2.11
STANDARD VELOCITY					
22 Short	29	Solid	1045	24	.88
22 Long Rifle	40	Solid	1145	24	1.04

Packaged 50 per box

Directory of the Arms Trade

AMMUNITION (Commercial)

Alcan Shells, (See: Smith & Wesson-Fiocchi, Inc.)
Amron Corp., 525 Progress Ave., Waukesha, Wis. 53186
Cascade Cartridge Inc., (See Omark)
Federal Cartridge Co., 2700 Foshay Tower, Minneapolis, Minn. 55402
Frontier Cartridge Co., Inc., Box 906, Grand Island, Neb. 68801
Omark-CCI, Inc., Box 856, Lewiston, Ida. 83501
Remington Arms Co., Bridgeport, Conn. 06602
Service Armament, 689 Bergen Blvd., Ridgefield, N.J. 07657
Smith & Wesson-Fiocchi, Inc., 3640 Seminary Rd., Alton, IL 62002
Speer-DWM, Box 896, Lewiston, Ida. 83501
Super-Vel Cartridge Co., Box 40, Shelbyville, Ind. 46176
Weatherby's, 2781 E. Firestone Blvd., South Gate, Calif. 90280
Winchester-Western, East Alton, Ill. 62024

AMMUNITION (Custom)

Ammodyne, Box 1589, Los Angeles, Calif. 90053
B&K Custom Rel. Serv., Rte. 1, Lake 13, Farwell, Mich. 48622
Bill Ballard, P.O. Box 656, Billings, Mont. 59103
Jerry & Betty Bird, Box 10183, Corpus Christi, Tex. 78410
Caldwell's Loading Serv., 1314 Monroe Dr., N.E., Atlanta, Ga. 30306
Russell Campbell, 219 Leisure Dr., San Antonio, Tex. 78201
Cumberland Arms, 1222 Oak Dr., Manchester, Tenn. 37355
Custom Ammo & Gunsmithing, 390 S. Main, Moab, Utah 84532
J. Dewey Gun Co., Clinton Corners, N.Y. 12514
E. W. Ellis Sport Shop, RFD 1, Box 139, Corinth, N.Y.
Ellwood Epps, 80 King St., Clinton, Ont., Canada
Steve Filipiak, 1270 So. Raleigh, Denver, Colo. 80219
H.P.K. Co., Inc., 3750 Ridge Rd., Highland, Ind.
R. H. Keeler, 1304 S. Oak, Port Angeles, Wash. 98362
KWT Inc., 710 Cooper-Foster Pk. Rd., Lorain, O. 44053 (tungsten bullets)
Dean Lincoln, 390 S. Main, Moab, Utah 84532
Pat B. McMillan, 4908 E. Indianola, Phoenix, Ariz. 85018
Mansfield Gunshop, Box 83, New Boston, N.H. 03070
Man-Tol Shells, Box 134, Bunnell, Fla. 32010
Moody's Reloading Serv., 2108 Broadway, Helena, Mont. 59601
Numrich Arms Corp., 203 Broadway, W. Hurley, N.Y. 12491
Robert Pomeroy, Morrison Ave., East Corinth, ME 04427 (custom shells)
Sanders Cust. Gun Serv., 2358 Tyler Lane, Louisville, Ky. 40205
Shooter's Service & Dewey, Inc., Clinton Corners, N.Y. 12514
Shot Shell Components, 365 So. Moore, Lakewood, Colo. 80226
Super Vel Cartridge Corp., Shelbyville, Ind. 46176
3-D Co., Inc., Box 4411, Lincoln, Neb. 68504
James C. Tillinghast, Box 568, Marlow, N.H. 03456
True-Blue Co., 1400 E. Palmer Ave., Glendale, Calif. 91205 (blanks)
Walmax Inc. (See True-Blue)
Wanda Cartridge Co., P.O. Box 45901, Houston, Tex. 77045
Whitney Cartridge Co., Box 5872, Pasadena, CA. 91107 (shotshells)

AMMUNITION (Foreign)

Abercrombie & Fitch, Madison at 45th St., New York, N.Y. 10017
Ammodyne, Box 1859, Los Angeles, Calif. 90053 (RWS)
Canadian Ind. Ltd. (C.I.L.), Box 10, Montreal, Que., Canada
C-I-L Ammunition Inc., P.O. Box 831, Plattsburgh, N.Y. 12901
Centennial Arms Co., 3318 W. Devon Ave., Chicago, Ill. 60645 (Hirtenberg, Austrian)
Colonial Ammunition Co., Box 8511, Auckland, New Zealand
DWM, Speer Prods. Inc., Box 641, Lewiston, Ida. 83501
Gevelot of Canada, Box 1593, Saskatoon, Sask., Canada
Hy-Score Arms Co., 200 Tillary, Brooklyn, N.Y. 11201
Paul Jaeger Inc., 211 Leedom St., Jenkintown, Pa. 19046
S. E. Lazlo, 200 Tillary, Brooklyn, N.Y. 11201
NORMA-Precision, South Lansing, N.Y. 14882
Oregon Ammo Service, Box 19341, Portland, Ore. 97219
Stoeger Arms Corp., 55 Ruta Ct., So. Hackensack, N.J. 07606
James C. Tillinghast, Box 568, Marlow, N.H. 03456

ANTIQUE ARMS DEALERS

Robert Abels, 157 E. 64th St., N.Y. 10021 (Catalog $1.00)
Antique Firearms Co., 206 Wilshire Blvd., Wilson, N.C. 27893
F. Bannerman Sons, Inc., Box 126, L.I., Blue Point, N.Y. 11715

Wm. Boggs, 1783 E. Main, Columbus, Ohio 43205
Ellwood Epps Sporting Goods, 80 King St., Clinton, Ont., Canada
Farris Muzzle Guns, 1610 Gallia St., Portsmouth, Ohio 45662
A. A. Fidd, Diamond Pt. Rd., Diamond Pt., N.Y. 12824
N. Flayderman & Co., Squash Hollow, New Milford, Conn. 06776
Fulmer's Antique Firearms, Detroit Lakes, Minn. 56501
Herb Glass, Bullville, N.Y. 10915
Gold Rush Guns, Shop 1, 2211 Clement St., San Francisco, Cal. 94121
Gold Rush Guns, Shop 2, P.O. Box 33, Afton, Va. 22920
Goodman's for Guns, 1101 Olive St., St. Louis, Mo. 63101
Griffin's Guns & Antiques, R.R. 4, Peterboro, Ont., Canada
The Gun Shop, 6497 Pearl Rd., Cleveland, O. 44130
Heritage Firearms Co., 27 Danbury Rd., Rte. 7, Wilton, Conn 06897
Holbrook Arms Museum, 12953 Biscayne Blvd., N. Miami, Fla. 33161
Ed Howe, 2 Main, Coopers Mills, Me. 04341
Jackson Arms, 6209 Hillcrest Ave., Dallas, Tex. 75205
Jerry's Gun Shop, 9220 Ogden Ave., Brookfield, Ill. 60513
Lever Arms Serv. Ltd., 771 Dunsmuir St., Vancouver 1, B.C., Canada
Wm. M. Locke, 3607 Ault Pk. Rd., Cincinnati, O. 45208
John J. Malloy, Briar Ridge Rd., Danbury, Conn. 06810
Charles W. Moore, R.D. 2, Schenevus, N.Y. 12155
Museum of Historical Arms, 1038 Alton Rd., Miami Beach, Fla. 33139
National Gun Traders, Inc., Box 776, Miami, Fla. 33135
New Orleans Arms Co., Inc., 240 Chartres St., New Orleans, La. 70130
Old West Gun Room, 3509 Carlson Blvd., El Cerrito, Cal. 94530 (write for list)
Pioneer Guns, 5228 Montgomery, Norwood, O. 45212
Powell & Clements Sporting Arms, 210 E. 6th St., Cincinnati, O. 45202
Prestige Arms, 6055 W. Fond du Lac Ave., Milwaukee, WI 53218
Glode M. Requa, Box 35, Monsey, N.Y. 10952
Martin B. Retting Inc., 11029 Washington, Culver City, Calif. 90230
Ridge Guncraft, Inc., 234 N. Tulane Ave., Oak Ridge, Tenn. 37830
S.G. Intl., P.O. Box 702, Hermosa Beach, CA. 90254
Safari Outfitters Lt., Rte. 7, Ridgefield, CT 06877
San Francisco Gun Exch., 74 Fourth, San Francisco, Calif. 94103
Santa Ana Gunroom, 1638 E. 1st St., Santa Ana, Calif. 92701
Ward & Van Valkenburg, 402-30th Ave. No., Fargo, N. Dak. 58102
M. C. Wiest, 234 N. Tulane Ave., Oak Ridge, Tenn. 37830
Yeck Antique Firearms, 579 Tecumseh, Dundee, Mich. 48131

BULLET & CASE LUBRICANTS

Alpha-Molykote, Dow Corning Corp., 45 Commerce Dr., Trumbull, Ct. 06601
Birchwood-Casey Co., Inc., 7900 Fuller Rd., Eden Prairie, Minn. 55343 (Anderol)
Bullet Pouch, Box 4285, Long Beach, Calif. 90804 (Mirror-Lube)
Chopie Tool & Die Co., 531 Copeland, La Crosse, Wis. 54601 (Black-Solve)
Cooper-Woodward, Box 972, Riverside, Cal. 92502 (Perfect Lube)
Green Bay Bullets, 233 N. Ashland, Green Bay, Wis. 54303 (EZE-Size case lube)
Herter's, Inc., Waseca, Minn. 56903 (Perfect Lubricant)
Javelina Products, Box 337, San Bernardino, Cal. 92402 (Alox beeswax)
Jet-Aer Corp. 100 Sixth Ave., Paterson, N.J. 07524
Lenz Prod. Co., Box 1226, Sta. C, Canton, O. 44708 (Clenzoil)
Lyman Gun Sight Products, Middlefield, Conn. 06455 (Size-Ezy)
Micro Shooter's Supply, Box 213, Las Cruces, N. Mex. 88001 (Micro-Lube)
Nutec, Box 1187, Wilmington, Del. 19899 (Dry-Lube)
Pacific Tool Co., Box 4495, Lincoln, Neb. 68504
Phelps Rel. Inc., Box 4004, E. Orange, N.J. 07019
RCBS, Inc., Box 1919, Oroville, Calif. 95965
SAECO Rel. Inc., 726 Hopmeadow St., Simsbury, Conn. 06070
Scientific Lubricants Co., 3753 Lawrence Ave., Chicago, Ill. 60625
Shooters Accessory Supply (SAS), Box 250, N. Bend, Ore. 97459
Sports Distr. Co., Rte. 1, Rapid City, S.D. 57701 (Reloader No. 7)
Testing Systems, Inc., 2836 Mt. Carmel, Glenside, PA 19038

CHOKE DEVICES & RECOIL ABSORBERS

A & W Engineering, 6520 Rampart St., Houston, Tex. 77036 (shotgun diverter)
Arms Ingenuity Corp., Box 1, Weatogue, Conn. 06089 (Jet-Away)
Contra-Jet, 7920 49th Ave. So., Seattle, Wash. 98118
Dahl's Gun Shop, Rt. 2, Billings, Mont. 59101

THE AMERICAN IMPORT COMPANY

DICKSON FALCON GOOSE GUN

Features, Anson and Deeley engraved action. Holland type plain extractors. Hand checkered beavertail fore-end and pistol grip. Rubber recoil pad with plastic grip and white spacers. Automatic safety. Gold plated double triggers. 3½″ chambers. 10 ga. 32″ Full & Full choke, only. *Made in Spain.* $150.00

BOLT ACTION ECONOMY SHOTGUN

This little .410 does an effective job at a very low cost. Made in Spain, it weighs only 5¼ lbs. Features, three shot capacity, one in chamber, two in magazine, 25″ barrel. Checkered pistol grip and fore-end. Sliding thumb safety. Black plastic butt plate. .410 ga. 25″ Full Choke. $34.95

DICKSON MODEL RT400 RIFLESCOPE

Magnification: 4x; Objective aperture: 32mm; Exit pupil Dia. 8.1mm; Luminosity: 65.61; Field of View, 100 yds.: 29.7 ft.; Eye relief: 3.5″; Reticle: Post or Crosshair; Dia. of main tubes: 1″; Dia. of objective housing: 1.5″; Dia. of eye-piece housing: 1.375″. Other models available: 2.5x — 6x — 1.5 to 4x — 2.5 to 7x — 3 to 9x. $30.95

DICKSON GRAY EAGLE OVER AND UNDER

Barrels are chrome alloy steel with chrome plated bore. Receivers are case hardened, richly engraved with Eagle design. Automatic safety. Ventilated rib. Stock and fore-end are highly polished selected fine grain walnut. Quality hand checkering. Plastic butt and pistol grip have white spacers. Bead front sight. 3″ chambers. Available in 12 ga. 28″ Mod. & F.; 26″ Imp. Cy. & Mod. or 20 ga. 28″ Mod. & F.; 26″ Imp. Cy. & Mod. *Made in Italy by Antonio Zoli.* $219.95

SINGLE BARREL ECONOMY SHOTGUN

Single barrel economy shotgun with oil finish stock, auto ejector, brass bead sight. Available in 12 ga. 28″ F., 2¾″ chamber, in 20 ga. 26″ F. with 3″ chamber, in 410 ga. 26″ F. with 3″ chamber. $30.95

DICKSON FALCON DOUBLE

Features, case hardened Anson and Deeley action with scroll engraving. Automatic safety. Highly polished walnut stock, beavertail fore-end. Hand checkering, rubber recoil pad, plastic pistol grip with white spacers. Gold plated double triggers. 3″ chambers. Available in 12 ga. in 30″ Mod. & F., 26″ IC & Mod., 20 ga. in 28″ Mod. & F., 26″ IC & Mod., 28 ga. 26″ Mod. & F., and 410 ga. 26″ F. & F. *Made in Spain.* $123.95

AVL Ballistic Measurement Equipment

As an experienced manufacturer of high-quality electronic measuring equipment AVL also provides advanced ballistic measurement equipment for internal and external ballistics.

- Piezo-electric gas pressure measurement:
  Peak pressure — Pressure versus time — Energy;
- Measurement of ballistic velocities and cyclic rate of fire with light gates and electronic time meters;
- Single shot and continuous fire measurements (automatic weapons);
- Digital readout and printer output.

For detailed illustrated information write to:
**DEGAMO INC.
500 Ashland Av. P.O.B. 653
Chicago Heights / Ill. 60411**

or: **AVL - MESSTECHNIK
KleiststraBe 48
A-8020 GRAZ / Austria / Europe**

AVL Messtechnik

Prof. Dr. Dr.h.c. H. List
Graz/Austria

Edwards Recoil Reducer, 269 Herbert St., Alton, Ill. 62002
Emsco Chokes, 101 Second Ave., S.E., Waseca, Minn. 56093
Herter's Inc., Waseca, Minn. 56093. (Vari-Choke)
Lyman Gun Sight Products, Middlefield, Conn. 60455 (Cutts Comp.)
C. R. Pedersen & Son, Ludington, Mich. 49431 (Sha-Cul Brake)
Pendleton Dekickers, 1210 S. W. Hailey Ave., Pendleton, Ore. 97801
Poly-Choke Co., Inc., Box 296, Hartford, Conn. 06101
St. Louis Precision Products, 902 Michigan Ave., St. Louis, Mich. 48880
  (Gun-Tamer)

CHRONOGRAPHS AND PRESSURE TOOLS

A & W Eng., 6520 Rampart St., Houston, Tex. 77036 (press. tool)
Avtron, 10409 Meech Ave., Cleveland, Ohio, 44105
B-Square Co., Box 11281, Ft. Worth, Tex. 76110
Chronograph Specialists, P.O. Box 5005, Santa Ana, Calif. 92704
Herter's, Waseca, Minn. 56093
Micro-Sight Co., 242 Harbor Blvd., Belmont, Calif. 94002 (Techsonic)
Oehler Research, P.O. Box 9135, Austin, Tex. 78756
Sundtek Co., P.O. Box 744, Springfield, Ore. 97477
Telepacific Electronics Co., Inc., 3335 W. Orange Ave., Anaheim, CA
  92804
York-Cantrell, 30241 Rosebriar, St. Clair Shores, Mich. 48082 (press. tool)

CLEANING & REFINISHING SUPPLIES

ADSCO, Box 191, Ft. Kent, Me. 04743 (stock finish)
Allied Products Co., 734 N. Leavitt, Chicago, Ill. 60612 (Cor-O-Dex)
Ammodyne, Box 1589, Los Angeles, Cal. 90053 (Gun Kote)
Backus Co., 411 W. Water St., Smethport, Pa. 16749 (field gun-cleaner)
Birchwood-Casey Chem. Co., 7900 Fuller Rd., Eden Prairie, Minn. 55343
  (Anderol, etc.)
Bisonite Co., Inc., Box 84, Buffalo, N.Y. 14217
Jim Brobst, 299 Poplar St., Hamburg, Pa. 19526 (J-B Compound)
Geo. Brothers, Great Barrington, Mass. 01230 (G-B Linspeed Oil)
Browning Arms, Rt. 4, Box 624-B, Arnold, Mo. 63010
Bullet Pouch, Box 4285, Long Beach, Cal. 90804 (Mirror Lube)
Burnishine Prod. Co., 8140 N. Ridgeway, Skokie, Ill. 60076 (Stock Glaze)
C & R Distr. Corp., 449 E. 21st So., Salt Lake City, Utah 84115
Cherry Corners Gun Shop, 8010 Lafayette Rd., Rte. 1, Lodi, Ohio 44254
  (buffing compound)
Chopie Tool & Die Co., 531 Copeland, La Crosse, Wis. 54601 (Black-
  Solve)
Clenzoil Co., Box 1226, Sta., C, Canton, O. 44708
Corrosion Reaction Consultants, Inc., Dresher, Pa. 19025 (Mask)
Craftsman Wood Serv. Co., 2727 S. Mary, Chicago, Ill. 60608
Custom Industries, 18900 Detroit Ave., Lakewood, O. 44107
Dex-Kleen, Box 509 Des Moines, Ia. 50302 (gun wipers)
J. Dewey Gun Co., Clinton Corners, N.Y. 12514
Dri-Slide, Inc., Industrial Park, Fremont, Mich. 49412
Dry Film Gun Coatings, 1521—43rd St., W. Palm Beach, Fla. 33407
Electromation Comp. Corp., 11 Lincoln St., Copiague, N.Y. 11726 (ultra-
  sonic cleaning tank)
F & J Derusting Co., Inc., 247 Westcott Dr., Rahway, N.J. 07065
Forty-Five Ranch Enterpr., Box 1080, Miami, Okla. 74354
Frye Industs., 1318 N. Broadway, Santa Maria, Cal. 93454
Garcia Sptg. Arms Corp., 329 Alfred Ave., Teaneck, N.J. 07666
Gun-All Products, Box 244, Dowagiac, Mich. 49047
Percy Harms Corp., 7349 N. Hamlin, Skokie, Ill. 60076
Frank C. Hoppe Div., P.O. Box 97, Parkesburg, Pa. 19365
Hunting World, 247 E. 50th St., N.Y. 10022 (P-H Safari Kit)
J & G Rifle Ranch, Turner, MT 59542
Jet-Aer Corp., 100 Sixth Ave., Paterson, N.J. 07524 (blues & oils)
K.W. Kleinendorst, Taylortown Rd., Montville, N.J. 07045 (rifle clg. rods)
Knox Laboratories, 2335 S. Michigan Ave., Chicago, Ill. 60616
LPS Res. Labs. Inc., 2050 Cotner Ave., Los Angeles, Calif. 90025
Carl Lampert Co., 2639 So. 31st St., Milwaukee, Wis. 53215 (gun bags)
LEM Gun Spec., Box 31, College Park, Ga 30337 (Lewis Lead Remover)
Liquid Wrench, Box 10628, Charlotte, N.C. 28201 (pen. oil)
Lynx-Line Gun Products, Box 3985, Detroit, Mich. 48227
Marble Arms Co., 1120 Superior, Gladstone, Mich. 49837
Micro Sight Co., 242 Harbor Blvd., Belmont, Ca. 94002 (bedding)
Mill Run Prod., 1360 W. 9th, Cleveland, O. 44113 (Brite-Bore Kits)
Mint Luster Cleaners, 1102 N. Division, Appleton, Wis. 54911
Mistic Metal Mover, Inc., R.R. 2, P.O. Box 336, Princeton, Ill. 61356
Mitchell Chemical Co., Wampus Lane, Milford, Conn. (Gun Guard)
New Method Mfg. Co., Box 175, Bradford, Pa. 16701 (gun blue)
Numrich Arms Co., West Hurley, N.Y. 12491 (44-40 gun blue)
Nutec, Box 1187, Wilmington, Del. 19899 (Dry-Film)
Outers Laboratories, Box 37, Onalaska, Wis. 54650 (Gunslick kits)
R.E.I., 101 Wolpers, Park Forest, Ill. 60466 (whale oil lube)
Radiator Spec. Co., Charlotte, N.C. 28201 (liquid wrench)
Realist Inc., N. 93 W. 16288 Megal Dr., Menomonee Falls, Wis. 53051
Reardon Prod., 323 N. Main St., Roanoke, Ill. 61561 (Dry-Lube)
Reese Arms Co., R.R. 1, Colona, IL 61241 (Dry-film lube)
Riel & Fuller, 423 Woodrow Ave., Dunkirk, N.Y. 14048 (anti-rust oil)
Rig Products Co., Box 279, Oregon, Ill. 61061 (Rig Grease)
Rocket Chemical Co., Inc., 5390 Napa St., San Diego, Calif. 92110 (WD-
  40)
Rusteprufe Labs., 605 Wolcott St., Sparta, Wis. 54656
Service Armament, 689 Bergen Blvd., Ridgefield, N. J. 07657 (Parker-
  Hale)
Sheldon's Inc., Box 508, Antigo, Wis. 54409 (shotgun brushes)
Shooter's Serv. & Dewey (SS&D), Clinton Corners, N.Y. 12514
Silicote Corp., Box 359, Oshkosh, Wis. 54901 (Silicone cloths)
Silver Dollar Guns, 7 Balsam St., Keene, N.H. 03431 (silicone oil)
A. D. Soucy, Box 191, Ft. Kent, Me. 04743 (stock finish)
Southeastern Coatings, Ind., (SECOA), Bldg. 132, P.B.I. Airport, W. Palm
  Beach, Fla. 33406 (Teflon Coatings)
Sportsmen's Labs., Inc., Box 732, Anoka, Minn. 55303 (Gun Life lube)

Sun Ray Chemicals, 371-30th Ave., San Francisco, Calif. 94121
Surcon, Inc., P.O. Box 277, Zieglerville, Pa. 19492
Taylor & Robbins, Box 164, Rixford, Pa. 16745 (Throat Saver)
Testing Systems, Inc., 2836 Mt. Carmel, Glenside, PA 19038 (gun lube)
L.B. Thompson, 568 E. School Ave., Salem, O. 44460 (Rust bluing/
  browning)
C. S. Van Gorden, 120 Tenth Ave., Eau Claire, Wis. 54701 (Instant Blue)
WD-40 Co., 5390 Napa St., San Diego, Ca 92110
W&W Mfg. Co., Box 365, Belton, Mo. 64012 (shotgun cleaner)
Webber Gage Division, 12900 Triskett Rd., Cleveland, O. 44111 (Luger oil)
West Coast Secoa, Inc., 3915 U.S. Hwy. 98 So., Lakeland, Fla. 33803
Williams Gun Sight, 7389 Lapeer Rd., Davison, Mich. 48423 (finish kit)
Winslow Arms Co., P.O. Box 578, Osprey, Fla. 33595 (refinishing kit)
Wisconsin Platers Supply Co., 3256-A Milwaukee St., Madison, WI 53714
  (plating kit)
Woodstream Corp., P.O. Box 327, Lititz, Pa. 17543 (Mask)

COMPONENTS—BULLETS, POWDER, PRIMERS

Accuracy Bullet Co., 2443 41st St., San Francisco, Calif. 94116 (Perfecast
  bullets)
Alcan, (see: Smith & Wesson-Fiocchi, Inc.)
Bahler Die Shop, Box 386, Florence, Ore. 97439 (17 cal. bull.)
Lee Baker, 4474 Yosemite Way, Los Angeles, Calif. 90065 (17 cal. bull.)
Joe J. Balickie, 409 Rose Lane, Raleigh, N.C. 27607
Ballistic Research Industries, 116 N. Main, Sebastopol, Cal. 95472 (12 ga.
  Sabot bullets)
Bitterroot Bullet Co., Box 412, Lewiston, Ida. 83501
Centrix, 2116 N. 10th Ave., Tucson, Ariz. 85705
Kenneth E. Clark, 18738 Highway 99, Madera, CA 93637 (Bullets)
Clerke Recreation Prods., Inc., 2040 Broadway, Santa Monica, Ca. 90404
  (Lapua bullets)
Curry Bullet Co., 4504 E. Washington Blvd., Los Angeles, Calif. 90022
Colorado Custom Bullets, Rt. 1, Box 507-B, Montrose, Colo. 81401
Division Lead, 7742 W. 61 Pl., Summit, Ill. 60502
DuPont, Explosives Dept., Wilmington, Del. 19898
Elk Mountain Shooters Supply, 2020 Road 44, Pasco, Wash. 99301 (Alas-
  kan bullets)
Forty Five Ranch Enterprises, Box 1080, Miami, Okla. 74354
Godfrey Reloading Supply, R.R. #1, Box 688, Brighton, Ill. 62012 (cast
  bullets)
Lynn Godfrey, (see: Elk Mtn. Shooters Supply)
G. J. Godwin, 455 Fox Lane, Orange Park, Fla. 32073 (cast bullets)
Green Bay Bullets, 233 No. Ashland, Green Bay, Wis. 54303 (lead)
H.P.K. Co., Inc., 3750 Ridge Rd., Highland, Ind. 46322 (cast bullets)
Frank A. Hemsted, Box 281, Sunland, Calif. 91040
Hercules Powder Co., 910 Market St., Wilmington, Del. 19899
Herter's Inc., Waseca, Minn. 56093
Hi-Precision Co., 109 Third Ave., N.E., Orange City, Ia. 51041
B. E. Hodgdon, Inc., 7710 W. 50th Hwy., Shawnee Mission, Kans. 66202
Hornady Mfg. Co., Box 1848, Grand Island, Neb. 68801
N. E. House Co., Middletown Rd., E. Hampton, Conn. 06424
Jurras Munition Corp., Box 140, Shelbyville, Ind. 46176
L. L. F. Die Shop, 1281 Highway 99 North, Eugene, Ore. 97402
Lee's Precision Bullets, 4474 Yosemite Way, Los Angeles, Ca. 90065 (17
  cal.)
Lyman Gun Sight Products, Middlefield, Conn. 06455
Markell, Inc., 4115 Judah St., San Francisco, Calif. 94112
Meyer Bros., Wabasha, Minn. 55981 (shotgun slugs)
Michael's Antiques, Box 233, Copiague, L.I., NY 11726 (Balle Blondeau)
Miller Trading Co., 20 S. Front St., Wilmington, N.C. 28401
Norma-Precision, So. Lansing, N.Y. 14882
Northridge Bullet Co., P.O. Box 1208, Vista, Ca. 92083
Nosler Bullets, P.O. Box 688, Beaverton, OR 97005
Oregon Ammo Service, Box 19341, Portland, Ore. 97219
Robert Pomeroy, Morrison Ave., East Corinth, ME 04427
Rainbow Prod., P.O. Box 75, Wishram, Wash. 98673 (bullets)
Remington-Peters, Bridgeport, Conn. 06602
S.·W. M. Bullet Co., 1122 S. Cherry St., Port Angeles, Wash. 98362 (17
  cal.)
Sanderson's, 724 W. Edgewater, Portage, Wis. 53901 (cork wad)
Sierra Bullets Inc., 421 No. Altadena Dr., Pasadena, Ca. 91107
Smith & Wesson-Fiocchi, Inc., 3640 Seminary Rd., Alton, IL 62002
Speedy Bullets, Box 1262, Lincoln, Neb. 68501
Speer Products Inc., Box 896, Lewiston, Ida. 83501
C. H. Stocking, Hutchinson, Minn. 55350 (17 cal. bullet jackets)
Sullivan Arms Corp., 5204 E. 25th, Indianapolis, Ind. 46218
Super-Vel Cartr. Copr., 129 E. Franklin St., Shelbyville, Ind. 46176
Taylor Bullets, 2221734, San Antonio, Tex. 78221
True-Blue Co., 1400 E. Palmer Ave., Glendale, Calif. 91205 (blanks)
James C. Tillinghast, Box 568, Marlow, N.H. 03456
Vitt & Boos, Sugarloaf Dr., Wilton, Conn. 06897
Walmax, Inc., 1400 E. Palmer Ave., Glendale, Calif. 91205 (blanks)
Williams Custom Guns, Rt. 3, Box 809, Cleveland, Tex. 77327 (17 cal.)
Winchester-Western, New Haven, Conn. 06504
F. Wood, Box 386, Florence, Ore. 97439 (17 cal.)
Xelex Ltd., Hawksbury, Ont., Canada (powder)

CUSTOM GUNSMITHS AND CUSTOM GUN WORK

Ace Sports Center, 1590 York Ave., New York, N.Y. 10028
P. O. Ackley, P.O. Box 17347, Salt Lake City, Utah 84117
Ahlman Cust. Gun Shop, R.R. 1, Box 20, Morristown, Minn. 55052
R. E. Anderson, 706 S. 23rd St., Laramie, Wyo. 82070
Andrews' Ammunition & Arms, 7114 So. Albion, Littleton, Colo. 80120
R. J. Anderson, 1016 Riehl St., Waterloo, Ia. 50703
Arms Divs., M. R. Co., 968 Radcliffe Rd., Baltimore, Md. 21204
Bacon Creek Gun Shop, Cumberland Falls Rd., Corbin, Ky.
Bain and Davis Sptg. Gds., 599 W. Las Tunas Dr., San Gabriel, Calif.
  41776

ITALGUNS
INTERNATIONAL S.A.S.

VIA LEONARDO DA VINCI, 36

20090 ZINGONE DI TREZZANO S.N. (Milano)
ITALIA

ITALGUNS MODEL 150 OVER-UNDER CONVERTIBLE SHOTGUN

A quality field gun in 12 or 20 gauge with an optional set of rifle/shotgun barrels. Extra barrels are available in either 22 Hornet or 7x57R on top and 12 gauge shotgun below. The model 150 has a full-length vent, rib, hand checkered walnut stock and a high luster blue finish. Automatic ejectors and a non-selective single trigger are available as options. The shotgun version only in 12 or 20 gauge (regular or Magnum) sells for $188.00. The combination rifle/shotgun version is $299.20 and the shotgun complete with an extra set of rifle/shotgun barrels is $387.20.

ITALGUNS MODEL 125 OVER-UNDER SHOTGUN

A 12 gauge lightweight over-under with quality chrome lined barrels and a full length vent. rib. Available with double or single non-selective trigger, and standard or automatic ejectors. High luster blue finish with silver finish receiver; stock is hand-checkered European walnut. Weight is slightly over 6 lbs. and the price in the U.S. is $195.80.

ITALGUNS MODEL 180 SINGLE BARREL TRAP

A single barrel trap gun with quality chrome-steel barrel, vent, rib; and Monte Carlo style action. Engraved and finished in non-glare blue with a trap style recoil pad and a European walnut stock the shotgun retails for $162.80.

ITALGUNS SINGLE ACTION REVOLVER

Available in calibers ranging from 22 LR to 45 this all steel single-action is available with an automatic hammer safety at $88.00 and with a manual hammer safety at $83.60.

Joe J. Balickie, 6108 Deerwool Pl., Raleigh, N.C. 27607
Barber's Southpaw Conversions, 26 N.W. 2nd, Portland, Ore. 97209
Barta's, Rte. 1, Box 129, Cato, Wis. 54206
Bayer's Gun Shop, 213 S. 2nd, Walla Walla, Wash. 99362
Bennett Gun Works, 561 Delaware Ave., Delmar, N.Y. 12054
Irvin L. Benson, Saganaga Lake, Ontario, Canada
Gordon Bess, 708 River St., Canon City, Colo. 81212
Bruce Betts, 26 Rolla Gardens Dr., Rolla, Mo. 65401
John Bivins, Jr., 446 So. Main St., Winston-Salem, N.C. 27101
Boone Mountain Trading Post, Averyville Rd., St. Marys, Pa. 15857
T. H. Boughton, 410 Stone Rd., Rochester, N.Y. 14616
Kay H. Bowles, Pinedale, Wyo. 82941
Wm. A. Boyle, Box 5-770, College, Alaska 99701
L. H. Brown, Rte. 2, Airport Rd., Kalispell, Mont. 59901
George Bunch, 7735 Garrison Rd., Hyattsville, Md. 20784
Tom Burgess, 13906 E. 4th Ave., Opportunity, Wash. 99216 (metalsmithing only)
Leo Bustani, P.O. Box 8125, W. Palm Beach, Fla. 33407
Butler's Gun Repair Shop, Poultney, Vt. 05764
Gus Butterowe, 2520 W. Mockingbird Lane, Dallas, Tex. 75235
Caldwell Gun Shop, 5056 Roseville, No. Highlands, Calif. 95660
Cameron's Guns, 16690 W. 11th Ave., Golden, Colo. 80401
Campbell Gun Shop, Inc., 2002 Craigmore Rd., Colo. Sprgs, Colo. 80909
Dick Campbell, 1445 S. Meade, Denver, Colo. 80219
Carpenter's Gun Works, Gunshop Rd., Plattekill, N.Y. 12568
Carter Gun Works, 2211 Jefferson Pk. Ave., Charlotteville, Va. 22903
Cassell's Gun Shop, 403 West Lane, Worland, Wyo. 82401
Ray Chalmers, 18 White Clay Dr., Newark, Del. 19711
Chicago Gun Center, Inc., 3109 W. Armitage, Chicago, Ill. 60647
Chuck's Custom Gun Stocks, P.O. Box 1123, Frederick, Md. 21701
Kenneth E. Clark, 18738 Highway 99, Madera, Calif. 93637
J.K. Cloward, 2045 Eastlake Ave. E., Seattle, WA 98102
Consolidated Armslube, 905 Spruce Ave., Alamagordo, N. Mex. 88310
Crest Carving Co., 14849 Dillow St., Westminster, Ca. 92683
Philip R. Crouthamel, 817 E. Baltimore, E. Lansdowne, Pa. 19050
Custom Rifle Shop, 4550 E. Colfax Ave., Denver, Colo. 80220
Jim Cuthbert, 715 S. 5th St., Coos Bay, Ore. 97420
Dahl's Gunshop, Rt. 2, Billings, Mont. 59101
Dave's Gun Shop, 343 Potters Rd. West, Ionia, Mich. 48846
Dee Davis, 5658 So. Mayfield, Chicago, Ill. 60638
Jack Dever, Box 577, Jackson, Wyo. 83001 (S. S. Work)
J. Dewey Gun Co., Clinton Corners, N.Y. 12514
Joe E. Dillen, 1206 Juanita S.W., Massillon, Ohio 44646
Don's Gun Shop, 128 Ruxton Ave., Manitou Springs, Colo. 8029,
Drumbore Gun Shop, 119 Center St., Lehigton, PA 18235
Charles Duffy, Williams Lane, W. Hurley, N.Y. 12491
Gerald D. Eisenhauer, Rte. #3, Twin Falls, Ida. 83301
Bill English, 4411 S. W. 100th, Seattle, Wash. 98146
Ellwood Epps, 80 King St., Clinton, Ont., Canada
Ermas Firearms, Steelville, Mo. 65565
Ken Eyster, Heritage Gunsmiths Inc., 41 Bishop Rd., Centerburg, O. 43011
N. B. Fashingbauer, Box 366, Lac Du Flambeau, Wis. 54538
Ted Fellowes, 9245-16th Ave., S.W., Seattle, Wa. 98106 (muzzle loaders)
Loxley Firth Firearms, R. D. 4, Baldwinsville, N.Y. 13027
Marshall F. Fish, Westport, N.Y. 12993
Jerry Fisher, 1244—4th Ave. West, Kalispell, Mont. 59901
Flagler Gun Clinic, Box 8125, West Palm Beach, Fla. 33407 (Win. 92 & 94 Conv.)
Freeland's Scope Stands, 3737—14th Ave., Rock Island, Ill. 61201
Fred's Gun Shop, Box 725, Juneau, Alaska 99801
Frederick Gun Shop, 10 Elson Drive, Riverside, R.I. 02915
Frontier Arms, Inc., Box 2593, Cheyenne, Wyo. 82001
Fuller Gunshop, Cooper Landing, Alas. 99572
Geo. M. Fullmer, 2499 Mavis St., Oakland, Cal. 94501 (metal work)
Georgia Gun & Smith, 2175 Old Orchard Rd., Smyrna, Ga. 30080
Gibbs Rifle Products, Viola, Ida. 83872
Ed Gillman, Upper High Crest Dr., R.F.D. #1, Butler, N.J. 07405
A. R. Goode, 3306 Sellman Rd., Adelphi, Md. 20783
E. M. Greashaw, S. Centerville, RR 2, Sturgis, Mich. 49041
Griffin & Howe, 589-8th Ave., New York, N.Y. 10017
Dale M. Guise, Rt. 2, Box 239, Gardners, Pa. 17324 (Rem. left-hand conversions)
H & R Custom Gun Serv., 68 Passaic Dr., Hewitt, N.J. 07421
Harkrader's Cust. Gun Shop, 111 No. Franklin St., Christiansburg, Va. 24073
Elden Harsh, Rt. 4, London, O. 43140
Rob't W. Hart & Son, 401 Montgomery St., Nescopeck, Pa. 18635 (actions, stocks)
Hal Hartley, Box 147, Blairs Fork Rd., Lenoir, N.C. 28654
Edw. O. Hefti, 300 Fairview, College Sta., Tex. 77840
Iver Henriksen, 1211 So. 2nd, Missoula, Mont. 59801
Wm. Hobaugh, Box 657, Philipsburg, Mont. 59858
Richard Hodgson, 1550 Alpine, Boulder, Colo. 80302
Geo. Hoenig, 915 Main St., Boise, Ida. 83707
Hollis Gun Shop, 917 Rex St., Carlsbad, N.M. 88220
Wm. R. Horvath, 742 S. Scott Dr., Farwell, Mich. 48622
Huckleberry Gun Shop, 10440 Kingsbury Rd., Delton, Mich. 49046 (rust blueing)
Hurst Custom Gunstocks, RFD 1, Box 1000, Exmore, Va. 23350
Ernest Hurt, Box 1033, Muskogee, Okla. 74401
Independent Machine & Gun Shop, 1416 N. Hayes, Pocatello, Ida. 83201
Jackson's, Box 416, Selman City, Tex, 75689
Paul Jaeger, 211 Leedom, Jenkintown, Pa. 19046
Jerry's Gun Shop, 9220 Ogden Ave., Brookfield, Ill. 60513
Jerry's Gun Shop, 1527 N. Graceland Ave., Appleton, Wis. 54911
Johnson Automatics Assoc., Inc., Box 306, Hope Valley, R.I. 02832
Bob Johnson, 1730 Sprague, Spokane, Wash. 99200
Johnson's Gun Shop, 1316 N. Blackstone, Fresno, Calif. 93703
Johnson's Kenai Rifles, Box 6208, Annex Br., Anchorage, Alaska 99502
Kennedy Gun Shop, Rt. 6, Clarksville, Tenn. 37040
Monte Kennedy, R. D. 2-B, Kalispell, Mont. 59901
Kennon's Custom Rifles, 5408 Biffle, Stone Mtn., Ga. 30083

Kerr Sport Shop, Inc., 9584 Wilshire Blvd., Beverly Hills, Calif. 90212
Kess Arms Co., 12315 W. Lisbon Rd., Brookfield, Wis. 53005
Kesselring Gun Shop, Box 350, Rt. 1, Burlington, Wash. 98233
Knights Gun Store, Inc., 103 So. Jennings, Ft. Worth, Tex. 76104
Ward Koozer, Box 18, Walterville, Ore. 97489
R. Krieger & Sons, 34923 Gratiot, Mt. Clemens, Mich. 48043
Lacy's Gun Service, 1518A West Blvd., Charlotte, N.C. 28208
Harry Lawson Co., 3328 N. Richey Blvd., Tucson, Ariz. 85716
John G. Lawson, 1802 E. Columbia, Tacoma, Wa. 98404
Ledel, Inc., Main and Commerce Sts., Cheswold, Del. 19936
Art LeFeuvre, 1003 Hazel Ave., Deerfield, Ill. 60015
LeFever Arms Co., R.D. 1, Lee Center, N.Y. 13363
Max J. Lindauer, R.R. 1, Box 114, Washington, Mo. 63090
Robt. L. Lindsay, Box 805, Gaithersburg, Md. 20760
Llanerch Gun Shop, 2800 Township Line, Upper Darby, Pa. 19083
McCormick's Gun Bluing Service, 4936 E. Rosecrans Ave., Compton, Calif. 90221
Harry McGowen, Momence, IL 60954
Pat B. McMillan 4908 E. Indianola, Phoenix, Ariz. 85018
R. J. Maberry, 511 So. K, Midland, Tex. 79701
Harold E. MacFarland, Star Route, Box 84, Cottonwood, Ariz. 86326
Maryland Gun Exchange, Rt. 40 W., RD 5, Frederick, Md. 21701
Mashburn Arms Co., 112 W. Sherman, Oklahoma City, Okla. 73102
Mathews & Son, 10224 S. Paramount Blvd., Downey, Calif. 90241
Maurer Arms, 2366 Frederick Dr., Cuyahoga Falls, Ohio 44221
Middaugh's Nodak, 318 2nd St., Bismarck, N.D. 58501
C.D. Miller Guns, St. Onge, SD 57779
Earl Milliron, 1249 N.E. 166th Ave., Portland, Ore. 97230
Mills (D.H.) Custom Stocks, 401 N. Ellsworth, San Mateo, Calif. 94401 (antique)
Mitchell's Gun Repair, Rt. 1, Perryville, Ark. 72126
Natl. Gun Traders, Inc., Box 776, Miami, Fla. 33135
Clayton N. Nelson, 1725 Thompson Ave., Enid, Okla. 73701
Newman Gunshop, 119 Miller Rd., Agency, Ia. 52530
Nu-Line Guns, Inc., 3727 Jennings Rd., St. Louis, Mo. 63121
Oak Lawn Gun & Sports, Inc., 9618 Southwest Hwy., Oak Lawn, Ill. 60453
O'Brien Rifle Co., 324 Tropicana No. 128, Las Vegas, Nev. 89109
Pachmayr Gun Works, 1220 S. Grand Ave., Los Angeles, Calif. 90015
Harry Pagett Gun Shop, 125 Water St., Milford, Ohio 45150
Charles J. Parkinson, 116 Wharncliffe Rd. So., London, Ont., Canada
Pendleton Gunshop, 1210 S. W. Haley Ave., Pendleton, Ore. 97801
C. R. Pedersen & Son, Ludington, Mich. 49431
Al Petersen, Box 8, Riverhurst, Sask., Canada
A. W. Peterson Gun Shop, Rt. 1, Box 1510, Mt. Dora, Fla. 32757 (ML rifles, also)
Gene Phipps, 10 Wood's Gap Rd., Floyd, Va. 24091
Purcell's Gunshop, 915 Main St., Boise, Idaho 83702
R & M Serv. (Molezzo), 9882 E. Manning, Selma, Calif. 93662
Ready Eddie's Gun Shop, 501 Van Spanje Ave., Michigan City, IN 46360
Marion Reed Gun Shop, 1522 Colorado, Bartlesville, Okla. 74003
Fred Renard, Rt. 1, Symsonia, Ky. 42082
Ridge Guncraft, Inc., 234 N. Tulane, Oak Ridge, Tenn. 37830
Rifle Shop, Box 657, Philipsburg, Mont. 59858
Carl Roth, P.O. Box 2593, Cheyenne, WY 82001
Royal Arms, Inc., 10064 Bert Acosta, Santee, Calif. 92071
Sam's Gun Shop, 25 Squam Rd., Rockport, Mass. 01966
Sanders Custom Gun Serv., 2358 Tyler Lane, Louisville, Ky. 40205
Sandy's Custom Gunshop, Rockport, Ill. 62370
Saratoga Arms Co., R.D. 3, Box 387, Pottstown, Pa. 19464
Roy V. Schaefer, 965 W. Hilliard Lane, Eugene, Ore. 97402
George Schielke, Washington Crossing, Titusville, N.J. 08560
N.H. Schiffman Cust. Gun Serv., P.O. Box 7373, Murray, UT 84107
Schuetzen Gun Works, 1226 Prairie Rd., Colorado Springs, Colo. 80909
Schumaker's Gun Shop, 208 W. 5th Ave., Colville, Wash 99114
Schwab Gun Shop, 1103 E. Bigelow, Findlay, O. 45840
Schwartz Custom Guns, 9621 Coleman Rd., Haslett, Mich. 48840
Schwarz's Gun Shop, 41-15th St., Wellsburg, W. Va. 26070
Joseph M. Sellner, 1010 Ste. Leon Rd., Piscataway, N.J. 08854
Shaw's, 1655 S. Euclid Ave., Anaheim, Calif. 92802
Shilen Rifles, Inc., 930 N. Belt Line, Suite 134B, Irving, Tex. 75060
Harold H. Shockley, Box 355, Hanna City, Ill. 65126 (hot bluing & plating)
Shooters Service & Dewey Inc., Clinton Corner, N.Y. 12514
Walter Shultz, R.D. 3, Pottstown, Pa. 19464
The Sight Shop, 1802 E. Columbia Ave., Tacoma, Wa. 98404
Silver Dollar Guns, 7 Balsam St., Keene, NH 03431
Simmons Gun Spec., 700 Rogers Rd., Olathe, Kans. 66061
Simms Hardward Co., 2801 J St., Sacramento, Calif. 95816
Skinner's Gun Shop, Box 30, Juneau, Alaska 98801
Markus Skosples, 1119-35th St., Rock Island, Ill. 61201
Jerome F. Slezak, 1290 Marlowe, Cleveland, O. 44107
John Smith, 912 Lincoln, Carpentersville, Ill. 60110
K. E. Smith, 8766 Los Choches Rd., Lakeside, Calif. 92040
Smitty's Gunshop, 308 S. Washington, Lake City, Minn. 55041
Snapp's Gunshop, 6911 E. Washington Rd., Clare, Mich. 48617
R. Southgate, Rt. 2, Franklin, Tenn. 37064 (new Kentucky rifles)
Sportsman's Den, 1010 Stelton Rd., Piscataway, N.J. 08854
Sportsmens Equip. Co., 915 W. Washington, San Diego, Calif. 92103
Jess L. Stark, 12051 Stroud, Houston, TX 77072
Ikey Starks, 1058 Grand Ave., So. San Francisco, Calif. 94080
Keith Stegall, Box 696, Gunnison, Colo. 81230
Suter's House of Guns, 401 N. Tejon, Colorado Springs, Colo. 80902
Swanson Custom Firearms, 1051 Broadway, Denver, Colo. 80203
Armand D. Swenson, 3223 W. 154th St., Gardena, Calif. 90249
T-P Shop, 212 E. Houghton, West Branch, Mich. 48661
Talmage Ent., 1309 W. 12th St., Long Beach, Calif. 90813
Taylor & Robbins, Box 164, Rixford, Pa. 16745
Daniel Titus, 119 Morlyn Ave., Bryn Mawr, PA 19010
Tom's Gunshop, 600 Albert Pike, Hot Springs, Ark. 71901
Trinko's Gun Serv., 1406 E. Main, Watertown, Wis. 53094
C. Hunt Turner, 618 S. Grove, Webster Groves, Mo. 63119 (shotguns only)
Roy Vail, R. 1, Box 8, Warwick, N.Y. 10990

J. W. Van Patten, Box 145, Foster Hill, Milford, Pa. 18337
Walker Arms Co., R. 2, Box 38, Selma, Ala. 36701
Harold Waller, 1288 Camillo Way, El Cajon, Calif. 92021
R. A. Wardrop, Box 245, Mechanicsburg, Pa. 17055
Watertown Shooting Supplies, Box 233 Thomaston Rd., Rte. 6, Watertown, Conn. 06795
Weatherby's, 2781 Firestone Blvd., South Gate, Calif. 90280
Weber Rifle Actions, Box 515, Woodbridge, Calif. 95258
Wells Sport Store, 110 N. Summit St., Prescott, Ariz. 86301
R. A. Wells, 3452 N. 1st, Racine, Wis. 53402
Robert G. West, 6626 S. Lincoln, Littleton, Colo. 80120
Western Stocks & Guns, 2206 E. 11th, Bremerton, Wash. 98310
M. C. Wiest, 234 N. Tulane Ave., Oak Ridge, Tenn. 37830
W. C. Wilber, 400 Lucerne Dr., Spartanburg, SC 29302
Williams Custom Guns, Rt. 3, Box 509, Cleveland, Tex. 77327
Williams Gun Sight Co., 7389 Lapeer Rd., Davison, Mich. 48423
Lou Williamson, 103 S. Jennings, Ft. Worth, Tex. 76104
Wilson Gun Store Inc., R.D. 1, Rte. 225, Dauphin, Pa. 17018
Charles Winczer, 1590 York Ave., N.Y., N.Y. 10028
Robert M. Winter, Box 484, Menno, SD 57045
Lester Womack, Box 17210, Tucson, Ark. 85710
W. H. Womack, 2124 Meriwether Rd., Shreveport, La. 71108
Russ, Zeeryp, 1026 W. Skyline Dr., Morristown, Tenn. 37814

DEALERS IN COLLECTORS' CARTRIDGES

Antique Arsenal, 365 So. Moore St., Lakewood, Colo. 80226
J. A. Belton, 52 Sauve Rd., Mercier, Chateauguay Cty, Quebec, Canada
Peter Bigler, 291 Crestwood Dr., Milltown, N.J. 08850
Geo. Blakeslee, 3093 W. Monmouth, Englewood, Colo. 80110
Cameron's, 16690 W. 11th Ave., Golden, Colo. 80401
Carter Gun Works, 2211 Jefferson Pk. Ave., Charlottesville, Va. 22903
Gerry Coleman, 163 Arkell St., Hamilton, Ont., Canada
Chas. E. Duffy, Williams Lane, West Hurley, N.Y. 12419
Tom M. Dunn, 1342 So. Poplar, Casper, Wyo. 82601
Ellwood Epps, 80 King St., Clinton, Ont., Canada
Ed Howe, 2 Main St., Coopers Mills, Me. 04341
Walt Ireson, 47 Chedoke Ave., Hamilton 12, Ont., Canada
Jackson Arms, 6209 Hillcrest Ave., Dallas, Tex. 75205
Miller Bros., Rapid City, Mich. 49676
Oregon Ammo Service, Box 19341, Portland, Ore. 97219 (catlg. $2.00)
Powder Horn, 3093 W. Monmouth, Englewood, CO 80110
Martin B. Retting Inc., 11029 Washington, Culver City, Calif. 90230
Perry Spangler, 519 So. Lynch, Flint, Mich. 48503 (list 35c)
Jon Taylor House of Cartridges, 12 Cascade Bay, Brandon, Manit., Can.
Ernest Tichy, 365 S. Moore St., Lakewood, Colo. 80226
James C. Tillinghast, Box 568, Marlow, N.H. 03456 (list 50c)
Wilkins Gun Shop, 1060 N. Henderson, Galesburg, Ill. 61401 (list 50c)

ENGRAVERS, ENGRAVING, TOOLS

E. Averill, Rt. 1, 60 Chestnut St., Cooperstown, N.Y. 13326
Joseph Bayer, Sunset Ave., Sunset Hill, RD 1, Princeton, N.J. 08540
Sid Bell, Box 188, Tully, N.Y. 13159
Weldon Bledsoe, 6812 Park Place Dr., Fort Worth, Tex. 76118
Henry D. Bonham, Box 656 (Main St.), Brownville, Me. 04414
Ray Bossi, 3574 University Ave., San Diego, CA 92104
Max E. Bruehl, 4956 Elston Ave., Chicago, Ill. 60630
Burgess Vibrocrafters (BVI), Rt. 83, Grayslake, Ill. 60030
Chizar Engr. Serv., 690—12th Ave., San Francisco, Cal. 94118
Carl E. Courts, 2421 E. Anaheim St., Long Beach, Cal. 90804
Creative Carvings Inc., R.D. 2, Tully, N.Y. 13159
Bill Dyer, P.O. Box 75255, Oklahoma City, Okla. 73107
J. M. Evans, 5078 Harwood Rd., San Jose, Cal. 95124
Ken Eyster, Heritage Gunsmiths Inc., 41 Bishop Rd., Centerburg, O. 43011
Ken Flood, 63 Homestead, Stratford, Conn. 06497
Jos. Fugger, c/o Griffin & Howe, 589-8th Ave., N.Y., N.Y. 10017
Donald Glaser, 1520 West St., Emporia, Kans. 66801
Griffin & Howe, 589-8th Ave., N.Y., N.Y. 10017
F. R. Gurney, 216 Birks Bldg., Jasper Ave. & 104th St., Edmonton, Alberta, Can.
Neil Hartliep, Box 733, Fairmont, Minn. 56031
Frank E. Hendricks, Rt. 2, Box 189J, San Antonio, Tex. 78228
L. C. Hoyt, 321 E. Minnesota St., Indianapolis, Ind. 46225
Bob Izenstark, 101 Wolpers Rd., Park Forest, IL 60466
Jaqua's Sporting Goods, 25 N. Main St., Findlay, O. 45840
Paul Jaeger, 211 Leedom, Jenkintown, Pa. 19046
Robert C. Kain, R.F.D. Rte. #30, Newfane, Vermont 05345
Lance Kelly, P.O. Box 1072, Pompana Beach, Fla. 33061
Kleinguenther's, P.O. Box 1261, Seguin, TX 78155
Lynton S.M. McKenzie, 240 Chartres St., New Orleans, La. 70130
Wm. H. Mains, 2895 Seneca St., Buffalo, N.Y. 14224
Rudy Marek, Rt. 1, Box 1A, Banks, Ore. 97106
S. A. Miller, Central P.O. Box 619, Naha, Okinawa
Frank Mittermeier, 3577 E. Tremont Ave., New York, N.Y. 10465
Albin Obiltschnig, Ferlach, Austria
Pachmayr Gun Works, Inc., 1220 S. Grand Ave., Los Angeles, Calif. 90015
Hans Pfeiffer, 2005 Washington, Maywood, Ill. 60153
E. C. Prudhomme, 302 Ward Bldg., Shreveport, La. 71101
R. E. I. Engravings, 101 Wolpers, Park Forest, Ill. 60466
John R. Rohner, Sunshine Canyon, Boulder, Colo. 80302
Robert P. Runge, 94 Grove St., Ilion, N.Y. 13357
Shaw-Leibowitz, Rt. 1, Box 421, New Cumberland, W.Va. 26047 (etchers)
Russell J. Smith, 231 Springdale Rd., Westfield, Mass. 01085
Robt. Swartley, 2800 Pine St., Napa, Calif. 94559
Ray Viramontez, 5258 Robinwood, Dayton, O. 45431
Floyd E. Warren, Rt. 3, Box 87, Cortland, O. 44410
John E. Warren, P.O. Box 72, Eastham, Mass. 02642
A. A. White Engr., Inc., P.O. Box 68, Manchester, Conn. 06040

GAME CALLS

Black Duck, 1737 Davis, Whiting, Ind. 46394
Burnham Bros., Box 100-C, Marble Falls, Tex. 78654
Electronic Game Calls, Inc., 210 W. Grand, Wisconsin Rapids, Wis. 54494
Faulk's, 616 18th St., Lake Charles, La. 70601
Lohman Mfg. Co., 320 E. Spring, Neosho, Mo. 64850
M. L. Lynch, 306 Edgewood Blvd., Birmingham, Ala. 35209
Mallardtone, 2901 16th St., Moline, Ill. 61265
Phil. S. Olt Co., Box 550, Pekin, Ill. 61554
Penn's Woods Products, Inc., 19 W. Pittsburgh St., Delmont, Pa. 15626
Sport-Lore, Inc., 1757 Cherry St., Denver, Colo. 80220
Johnny Stewart Wildlife Calls, Box 7954, Waco, Tex. 76710
Thomas Game Calls, P.O. Box 336, Winnsboro, TX 75494
Weems Wild Calls, Box 7261, Ft. Worth, Tex. 76111
Wightman Electronics, Box 989, Easton, Md. 21601
Wildlife Prod. Inc., Prof. Bldg., 513 East Perkins Ave., Sandusky, Ohio 44870 (Lectro Hunter)
Tex Wirtz Ent., Inc., 1925 W. Hubbard St., Chicago, Ill. 60622

GUN CASES, CABINETS AND RACKS

Alco Carrying Cases Inc., 601 W. 26th St., New York, N.Y. 10001
Amer. Safety Gun Case Co., Holland, Mich. 49424
Aremac Co., 101 N. Verity Parkway, Middletown, O. 45042
Artistic Wood Specialties, 923-29 W. Chicago Ave., Chicago, Ill. 60622
Morton Booth Co., Box 123, Joplin, Mo. 64801
Boyt Co., Box 1108, Iowa Falls, Ia. 50126
Brewster Corp., Old Lyme, Conn. 06371
Browning Arms Co., Rt. 4, Box 624-B, Arnold, Mo. 63010
Castle Sptg. Gds., Inc., 498 Nepperhan Ave., Yonkers, N.Y. 10701
Challanger Mfg. Co., 94-28 Merrick Blvd., Jamaica, N.Y. 11433
Cincinnati Ind. Inc., (Cindus), Cincinnati (Lockland), O. 45215
Coladonato Bros., Box 156, Hazleton, Pa. 18201
Dutton's, 7840 Phillips Highway, Jacksonville, Fla. 32216 (single rack)
Ellwood Epps Sporting Goods, Clinton, Ont., Canada
Farber Bros., Inc., 821 Linden Ave., Memphis, Tenn. 38101 (truck pouch)
Ferrell Co., Rte. 3, Gallatin, Tenn. 37066 (Redi-Rack)
Flambeau Plastics Corp., 801 Lynn, Baraboo, Wis. 53913
Gun-Ho Case Mfg. Co., 110 East 10th St., St. Paul, Minn. 55101
Gun Racks, Inc., P.O. Box 22675, Houston, Tex. 77027
B. E. Hodgdon, Inc., 7710 W. 50 Hiway, Shawnee-Mission, Kans. 66202
Ithaca Gun Co., Terrace Hill, Ithaca, N.Y. 14850
J-K Imports, Box 403, Novato, Cal. 94947 (leg 'o mutton case)
Jumbo Sports Prods., P.O. Box 280-Airport Rd., Frederick, MD 21701
Kolpin Bros. Co., Inc., Box 231, Berlin, Wis. 54923
Marble Arms Corp., 1120 Superior, Gladstone, Mich. 49837
National Sports Div., 19 E. McWilliams St., Fond du Lac, Wis. 54935
Nortex Co., 2821 Main St., Dallas, Tex. 75226 (automobile gun rack)
Paul-Reed, Inc., P.O. Box 227, Charlevoix, Mich. 49720
Penguin Assoc. Inc., Box 97, Parkersburg, Pa. 19365
Precise Imp. Corp., 3 Chestnut, Suffern, N.Y. 10901
Pretto Cabinet Co., 1201 E. Walnut, Oglesby, Ill. 61348
Protecto Plastics, Inc., Box 37, Wind Gap, Pa. 18091
Richland Arms Co., 321 W. Adrian, Blissfield, Mich. 49228
Saf-T-Case, Box 10592, Dallas, Tex. 75207
San Angelo Die Castings, Box 984, San Angelo, Tex. 76901
Buddy Schoellkopf, 4100 Platinum Way, Dallas, Tex. 75237
Sile Distr., 7 Centre Market Pl., New York, N.Y. 10013 (leg o'mutton case)
Stearn Mfg. Co., Div. & 30th St., St. Cloud, Minn. 56301
Sure Shoot'n, Box 195, Jacksonville, Ill. 62650 (leg o'mutton case)
Western Holder Co., Box 33, Menomonee Falls, Wis. 53051
Woodstream Corp., Box 327, Lititz, Pa. 17543
Yield House, Inc., RFD, No. Conway, N.H. 03860

GUNS & GUN PARTS, REPLICA AND ANTIQUE

Antique Gun Parts, Inc., 569 So. Braddock Ave., Pittsburgh, Pa. 15221 (ML)
Armoury Inc., Rte. 25, New Preston, Conn. 06777
Bannerman, F., Box 126, Blue Point, Long Island, N.Y. 11715
Shelley Braverman, Athens, N.Y. 12015 (obsolete guns)
Carter Gun Works, 2211 Jefferson Pk. Ave., Charlottesville, Va. 22903
R. MacDonald Champlin, Stanyan Hill, Wentworth, N.H. 03282 (replicas)
Darr's Rifle Shop, 2309 Black Rd., Joliet, Ill. 60435 (S.S. items)
Dixie Gun Works, Inc., Hwy 51, South, Union City, Tenn. 38261
Ellwood Epps Sporting Goods, 80 King St., Clinton, Ont., Canada
Kindig's Log Cabin Sport Shop, R.D. 1, P.O. Box 275, Lodi, Ohio 44254
Edw. E. Lucas, 32 Garfield Ave., Old Bridge, N.J. 08857 (45-70)
R. M. Marek, Rt. 1, Box 1-A, Banks Ore. 97106 (cannons)
Numrich Arms Co., West Hurley, N.Y. 12491
Replica Models, Inc., 610 Franklin St., Alexandria, VA 22314
S&S Firearms, 88-21 Aubrey Ave., Glendale, N.Y. 11227
Rob. Thompson, 1031-5th Ave., N., Clinton, Ia. 52732 (Win. only)
C. H. Weisz, Box 311, Arlington, Va. 22210

GUN PARTS, U. S. AND FOREIGN

American Firearms Mfg. Co., Inc., 5732 Kenwick Dr., San Antonio, Tex. 78238 (clips)
Badger Shooter's Supply, Owen, Wisc. 54460
Shelley Braverman, Athens, N.Y. 12015
Philip R. Crouthamel, 817 E. Baltimore, E. Lansdowne, Pa. 19050
Charles E. Duffy, Williams Lane, West Hurley, N.Y. 12491
Federal Ordnance Inc., P.O. Box 36032, Los Angeles, Calif. 90036
Greeley Arms Co., Inc. 223 Little Falls Rd., Fairfield, N.J. 07006
Gunner's Armory, 2 Sonoma, San Francisco, Calif. 94133
H&B Gun Corp., 1228 Fort St., Lincoln Park, Mich. 48166
Hunter's Haven, Zero Prince St., Alexandria, Va. 22314
Bob Lovell, Box 401, Elmhurst, Ill. 60126

Kleinguenther's

Complete information is available from KLEINGUENTHER'S Distinctive Firearms, Inc. P. O. Box 1261, Seguin, Texas 78155. They also offer a wide range of .22 cal. rifles, scopes, mounts, and binoculars.

HIGH POWER RIFLE, MODEL V-2130

Calibers: .243, 7 mm Remington Magnum, .270, .30-06, .300 Winchester Magnum, and .308. Steel barrels 24" long. Drilled and tapped for Kleinguenther's quick-detachable scopemount, hand bedded for accuracy. Stock of selected walnut, Monte Carlo style with cheekpiece, rosewood forearm tip and cap with white diamond and spacer. Basket weave checkering, high luster finish. $199.00 to $212.04

BRESCIA MODEL SHOTGUN, SIDE-BY-SIDE

12 or 20 gauge. Carefully bored chrome-lined Poldi steel barrels in 28" length. Full choke, modified, improved cylinder. Select walnut stock, pistol grip or straight, streamlined Beavertail forearm, ventilated recoil pad, high luster finish, hand checkering. Chambered for 2¾" shells. Anson & Deely lock and action with Holland-type automatic ejectors, fine engraving, marbled case-hardened finish. $216.20

CONDOR MODEL OVER-AND-UNDER SHOTGUN

12 or 20 gauge. Poldi steel barrels internally chromed in 28" length. Modified and full, modified and improved cylinder, skeet and skeet chokes. Blued or case-hardened color finish, ventilated rib, brass front bead with ivory center bead on skeet and trap models. Single selective trigger. Selected Walnut stock. Chambered for 2¾" shells. $295.00

SEMI-AUTOMATIC SHOTGUN

12 gauge. Skeet, improved cylinder, and full chokes. Left hand or right hand. Ventilated rib. Stock of French Walnut. Engraved hunting scene on receiver housing. Chromium-Molybdenum steel in 25", 26", 28", and 30" lengths. Chambered for 2¾" shells. $198.34 RH, $219.80 LH.

■ KLEINGUENTHER'S Warranty of Quality ■

SMITH & WESSON PELLET GUNS

New this year to the long and distinguished line of Smith & Wesson shooting products are an air-powered rifle and a CO_2-powered pistol. Both are designed to fill a demand created by the ever-increasing popularity of pellet gun shooting.

MODEL 78G CO_2 PISTOL
Caliber: 22, single shot.
Barrel: 8½″ rifled.
Length: 11″.   **Weight:** 42 oz.
Power: Standard CO_2 cylinder.
Features: High-low power adjustment. Micrometer windage adjustable rear sight. Double sear, adjustable trigger. Checkered grips fit left and right hands.
Price $35.00
(Note: the same model will be available soon in 177 caliber)

MODEL 77A AIR RIFLE
Caliber: 22, single shot.
Barrel: 22″, rifled.
Length: 40″.   **Weight:** 6½ lbs.
Power: Hand pumped (swinging fore-end).
Features: Adjustable notch rear sight. Monte Carlo style, walnut finish stock. Automatic safety.
Price $42.50

Numrich Arms Co., West Hurley, N.Y. 12491
Pacific Intl. Import Co., 2416-16th St., Sacramento, CA 95818
Potomac Arms Corp. (see Hunter's Haven)
Reed & Co., Shokan, N.Y. 12481
Martin B. Retting, Inc., 11029 Washington, Culver City, Cal. 90230
Santa Barbara of America, Ltd., 930 N. Beltline Rd., #132, Irving, TX 75060 (barrels and barreled actions)
Sarco, Inc., 192 Central, Stirling, N.J. 07980
R. A. Saunders, 3253 Hillcrest Dr., San Antonio, Tex. 78201 (clips)
Schmid & Ladd, 14733 Hwy. 19 So., Clearwater, Fla. 33516
Sherwood Distr. Inc., 7435 Greenbush Ave., No. Hollywood, CA 91605
Clifford L. Smires, R.D., Columbus, N.J. 08022 (Mauser rifles)
Sporting Arms, Inc., 9643 Alpaca St., So. El Monte, CA 91733 (M-1 carb access.)
N. F. Strebe, 4926 Marlboro Pike, S.E., Washington, D.C. 20027
Triple-K Mfg. Co., 568-6th Ave., San Diego, CA 92101

GUNS (Foreign)

Abercrombie & Fitch, Madison at 45th, New York, N.Y. 10017
Adanac Sporting Goods, 505 Bellingham Ntl. Bk. Bldg., Bellingham, Wash. 98225
Alaskan Rifles, Box 30, Juneau, Alaska 99801
American Import Co., 1167 Mission St., San Francisco, Calif. 94103
Armi Fabbri, Casella 206, Brescia, Italy
Armoury Inc., Rte. 25, New Preston, Ct. 06777
Atlas Arms, Inc., 7952 Waukegan Rd., Niles, Ill. 60648
Benet Arms Co. (main office), Box 33, Afton, Va. 22920
Benet Arms Co., 2211 Clement St., San Francisco, Calif. 94121
Blumenfeld Co., 80 W. Virginia Ave., Memphis, Tenn. 38100
Browning Arms Co., Rt. 4, Box 624-B, Arnold, Mo. 63010
C & M Sporting Arms Co., R.R. 1, Pekin, Ill. 61554
Centennial Arms Corp., 3318 W. Devon, Chicago, Ill. 60645
Century Arms Co., 3-5 Federal St., St. Albans, Vt. 05478
Continental Arms Corp., 697 Fifth Ave., New York, N.Y. 10022
W. H. Craig, Box 927, Selma, Ala. 36701
Crusader Arms Co., Box 2801, 800 S. 4th St., Louisville, Ky. 40202
Charles Daly, Inc., 90 Chambers St., New York, N.Y. 10007
Dave's House of Guns, 9130 Viscount Row, Dallas, Tex. 75247
Davidson Firearms Co., 2703 High Pt. Rd., Greensboro, N.C. 27403 (shotguns)
Dixie Gun Works, Inc., Hwy 51, South, Union City, Tenn. 38261 ("Kentucky" rifles)
Euroarms, Via Solferino 13/A, 25100 Brescia, Italy
Europa Corp., P.O. Box 48-1367, Miami, Fla. 33148
J. Fanzoj, P.O. Box 25, Ferlach, Austria 9170
R. C. Fessler & Co., 1634 Colorado Blvd., Los Angeles, Calif. 90041
Firearms Imp. & Exp. Co., P.O. Box 691 Biscayne Annex, Miami, Fla. 33152 (I.N.A., Arminius)
Firearms International, (see: Garcia)
Flaig's Lodge, Millvale, Pa. 15209
Freeland's Scope Stands, Inc., 3737 14th Ave., Rock Island, Ill. 61201
J. L. Galef & Son, Inc., 85 Chambers, New York, N.Y. 10007
Garcia Sptg. Arms Corp., 329 Alfred Ave., Teaneck, N.J. 07666
Gevarm (see Blumenfeld Co.)
Gevelot of Can. Ltd., Box 1593, Saskatoon, Sask., Canada
Gold Rush Guns, 2211 Clement St., San Francisco, Calif. 94121 (SIG)
Gold Rush Guns #2, Box 33, Afton, Va. 22920
H. F. Grieder, Box 487, Knoxville, Ill. 61448 (Hammerli)
Harden & Knight, 5959 S.W. 49th St., Miami, Fla. 33155
Harrington & Richardson Arms Co., 320 Park Ave., Worcester, Mass. 01610 (HK pistol)
Hawes Firearms Co., 8224 Sunset Blvd., Los Angeles, Calif. 90046
Healthways, Box 45055, Los Angeles, Calif. 90061
Herter's, Waseca, Minn. 56093
Interarmco, see: Interarms (Walther)
Interarms Ltd., 10 Prince St., Alexandria, Va. 22313 (Mauser)
Intercontinental Arms, 2222 Barry Ave., Los Angeles, Calif. 90064
International Firearms Co., Ltd., Montreal 1, Que., Canada
International Distr., Box 7566, Miami, Fla. 33155
Ithaca Gun Co., Terrace Hill, Ithaca, N.Y. 14850 (Perazzi)
Italguns, Via Leonardo da Vinci 36, 20090 Trezzano, Milano, Italy
JBL Arms Co., Box 323, Dover, PA 17315
J-K Imports, Box 403, Novato, Cal. 94947 (Italian)
Paul Jaeger Inc., 211 Leedom St., Jenkintown, Pa. 19046
Jana Intl. Co., Box 1107, Denver, Colo. 80201
J. J. Jenkins, 462 Stanford Pl., Santa Barbara, CA 93105
Guy T. Jones Import Co., 905 Gervais St., Columbia, S. Car. 29201
Kleinguenther's, Box 1261, Seguin, TX 78155
L. A. Distributors, 4 Centre Market Pl., New York, N.Y. 10013
Jos. G. Landmann, 2308 Preetz/Holstein, W. Germany (JGL)
S. E. Laszlo, 200 Tillary St., Brooklyn, N.Y. 11201
Lever Arms Serv. Ltd., 771 Dunsmuir, Vancouver 1, B.C., Canada
Liberty Arms Corp., Box 306, Montrose, Calif. 91020
Marketing Unlimited, Inc., 1 Ranch Rite Rd., Yakima, WN 98901
Mars Equipment Corp., 3318 W. Devon, Chicago, Ill. 60645
Mauser-Bauer Corp., 34577 Commerce Rd., Fraser, MI 48026
McKeown's Guns, R.R. 1, Pekin, Ill. 61554
Navy Arms Co., 689 Bergen Blvd., Ridgefield, N.J. 07657
Omnipol, Washingtonova 11, Praha 1, Czechoslovakia
Harry Owen, P.O. Box 774, Sunnyvale, Ca. 94088
Pachmayr Gun Works, 1220 S. Grand Ave., Los Angeles, Calif. 90015 (Fabbri)
Pacific Intl. Import Co., 2416 - 16th St., Sacramento, CA 91605
Parker-Hale, Whittall St., Birmingham 4, England
Ed Paul Sptg. Goods, 172 Flatbush Ave., Brooklyn, N.Y. 11217 (Premier)
Precise Imp. Corp. (PIC), 3 Chestnut, Suffern, N.Y. 10901
Premier Shotguns, 172 Flatbush Ave., Brooklyn N.Y. 11217
J.L. Quick & Son Co., 1301 Laurence St., Birmingham, AL 35210
RG Industries, Inc., 2485 N.W. 20th St., Miami, FL 33142 (Erma)
Replica Arms Co., Box 640, Marietta, O. 45750

Richland Arms Co., 321 W. Adrian St., Blissfield, Mich. 49228
Sanderson's, 724 W. Edgewater, Portage, Wis. 53901
Savage Arms Corp., Westfield, Mass. 01085 (Anschutz)
Service Armament, 689 Bergen Blvd., Ridgefield, N.J. 07657 (Greener Harpoon Gun)
Sherwood Dist., Inc., 9470 Santa Monica Blvd., Beverly Hills, Ca. 90210
Simmons Spec., Inc., 700 Rogers Rd., Olathe, Kans. 66061
Skinner's Gun Shop (see Alaskan Rifles)
Sloan's Sprtg. Goods, Inc., 88 Chambers St., New York, N.Y. 10001
Solingen Cutlery, Box 306, Montrose, Calif. 91020
Spesco Corp., 3540 Browns Mill Rd. S.E., Atlanta, Ga. 30315
Sportex Intl. Ltd., 4807 Van Noord Ave., Sherman Oaks, Calif.
Stoeger Arms Co., 55 Ruta Ct., S. Hackensack, N.J. 07606
Tradewinds, Inc., P.O. Box 1191, Tacoma, Wash. 98401
Universal Firearms Corp., 3746 E. 10th Ct., Hialeah, Fla. 33013
Valor Imp. Corp., 159 S.E. 10th Hialeah, Fla. 33011
Voere (see Marketing Unlimited)
Waffen-Frankonia, Box 380, 87 Wurzburg, W. Germany
Weatherby's, 2781 Firestone Blvd., So. Gate, Calif. 90280 (Sauer)
Dan Wesson Arms, 293 So. Main, Monson, Mass. 01057
Zavodi Crvena Zastava, 29 Novembra St., No. 12, Belgrade, Yugosl.

GUNS (Pellet)

Air Rifle Hq., Grantsville, W. Va. 26147
Benjamin Air Rifle Co., 1525 So. 8th St. St. Louis, Mo. 63104
Continental Arms Corp., 697 5th Ave., New York, N.Y. 10022
Crosman Arms Co., Inc., Fairport, N.Y. 14450
Daisy Mfg. Co., Rogers, Ark. 72756 (also Feinwerkbau)
Fanta Air Rifles, Box 8122, La Crescenta, Calif. 91214
J. L. Galef & Son, Inc., 85 Chambers St., New York, N.Y. 10007 (B.S.A.)
H. F. Grieder, Box 487, Knoxville, Ill. 61448 (Hammerli)
Harrington & Richardson Arms Co., 320 Park Ave., Worcester, Mass. 01610 (Webley)
Healthways, Box 45055, Los Angeles, Calif. 90061
Gil Hebard Guns, Box 1, Knoxville, Ill. 61448
Hy-Score Arms Co., 200 Tillary St., Brooklyn, N.Y. 11201
Interarms, 10 Prince, Alexandria, Va. 22313 (Walther)
International Dist., Box 7566, Miami, Fla. 33155 (Hammerli-Master)
Kerrco, Inc., Box 368, Hastings, Nebr. 68901
Marksman Products, P.O. Box 2983, Torrance, CA 90509
Precise Imports Corp. (PIC), 3 Chestnut, Suffern, N.Y. 10901
Sears, Roebuck & Co., 825 S. St. Louis, Chicago, Ill. 60607
Service Armament, 689 Bergen Blvd., Ridgefield, N.J. 07657 (Webley, Jaguar)
Sheridan Products, Inc., 3205 Sheridan, Racine, Wis. 53403
Smith & Wesson, Springfield, Mass. 01101
Solingen Cutlery, Box 306, Montrose, Calif. 91020
Stoeger Arms Corp., 55 Ruta Ct., S. Hackensack, N.J. 07606 (Peerless)
Stuart Distr. Co., 6 Riverside Dr., Baltimore, Md. 21221

GUNS, U.S.-made

Agawam Arms Co., 916 Suffield St., Agawam, Mass. 01001
American Firearms Mfg. Co., Inc., 5732 Kenwick Dr., San Antonio, Tex. 78238
ArmaLite, 118 E. 16th St., Costa Mesa, Calif. 92627
Auto Mag Corp., 2480 E. Colorado Blvd., Pasadena, CA 91107
Caraville Arms, P.O. Box 377, Thousand Oaks, CA 91360
Champlin Firearms, Inc., Box 3191, Enid, Okla. 73701
Charter Arms Corp., 265 Asylum, Bridgeport, Conn. 06610
Clerke Recreation Prod., 2040 Broadway, Santa Monica, Ca. 90404 (22 Cal. Rev.)
Colt's, 150 Huyshope Ave., Hartford, Conn. 06102
Commando Arms, Inc., Box 10214, Knoxville, Tenn. 37919
Cumberland Arms, 1222 Oak Dr., Manchester, Tenn 37355
Day Arms Corp., 7515 Stagecoach Ln., San Antonio, Tex. 78227
Firearms Development, Inc., 218 Austin St., Denton, Tex. 76201
Firearms Intl. Corp., (see: Garcia)
Gera Arms, 1535 McKinley, Azusa, CA 91702
Golden Age Arms Co., Box 82, Worthington, O. 43085
Gyrojet (see Intercontinental Arms)
Harrington & Richardson, Park Ave., Worcester, Mass. 01610
High Standard Mfg. Co., 1817 Dixwell Ave., Hamden, Conn. 06514
Independent Res. & Development, Inc. (I.R.D.), 6304 Locker Lane, San Antonio, TX 78238
Intercontinental Arms, Inc., 2222 Barry Ave., Los Angeles, Ca. 90064
Ithaca Gun Co., Ithaca, N.Y. 14850
Iver Johnson Arms & Cycle Works, Fitchburg, Mass. 01420
Jackson Hole Arms Corp., Box T, Jackson, Wyo. 83001
J & R carbine, (see: PJK Inc.)
Kent Firearms Ltd., Inc., 14 E. Woodland Ave., Springfield, Pa. 19064
MBAssociates, (see Intercontinental Arms)
Marlin Firearms Co., 100 Kenna Dr., New Haven, Conn. 06473
Merrill Co., Inc., 209 Howard St., Fonda, Ia. 50540
O. F. Mossberg & Sons, Inc., 7 Grasso St., No. Haven, Conn. 06473
Navy Arms Co., 689 Bergen Blvd., Ridgefield, N.J. 07657
Noble Mfg. Co., S. Main St., Haydenville, Mass. 01039
Numrich Arms Corp., W. Hurley, N.Y. 12491
PJK, Inc., 1527 Royal Oak Dr., Bradbury, Ca 91010 (J&R Carbine)
Plainfield Machine Co., Inc., Box 447, Dunellen, N.J. 08812
Potomac Arms Corp., P.O. Box 35, Alexandria, Va. 22313 (ML replicas)
Ranger Arms Co., Box 704, Gainesville, Tex. 76240 (Texan Mag.)
Rau Arms Corp., 220 Metcalf Rd., El Dorado, KS 67042
Remington Arms Co., Bridgeport, Conn. 06602
Savage Arms Corp., Westfield, Mass. 01085
Sears, Roebuck & Co., 825 S. St. Louis, Chicago, Ill. 60607
Seventrees Ltd., 315 W. 39th St., New York, N.Y. 10018
Smith & Wesson, Inc., Springfield, Mass. 01101
Sporting Arms, Inc., 9643 Alpaca St., So. El Monte, CA 91733 (M-1 carbine)

Charter Arms Corporation

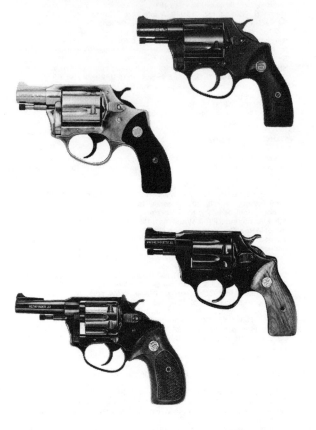

Charter Arms Corporation of Bridgeport, Connecticut, manufactures a line of small, lightweight revolvers. Their Undercover model is one of the smallest, lightest, 38 Special, steel frame revolvers made. The Undercoverette is a 32 S&W Long, 6-shot version of the Undercover, and the Pathfinder, in 22 LR, has many of the same features.

CHARTER ARMS "UNDERCOVER 2" REVOLVER
Caliber: 38 Special, 5 shot.
Barrel: 2″ or 3″.
Length: 6¼″ (round butt). **Weight:** 16 oz.
Features: Wide trigger and hammer spur.
Stocks: Smooth walnut, round or square butt available.
Sights: Fixed, matted ramp front, ⅛″ wide blade.
Price: Polished Blue ......$80.00   Nickel $85.23
Price: With checkered, finger-rest bulldog grips (blue)....... 86.50

CHARTER ARMS UNDERCOVERETTE
Like the Undercover, but a 6-shot 32 S&W Long revolver available with 2″ barrel only and weighing 16½ oz.
Price: Polished blue $80.00

CHARTER ARMS PATHFINDER
Same as Undercover but in 22 LR caliber, and has 3″ bbl. Fitted with adjustable rear sight, ramp front. weight 18½ oz.
Price: Blued $87.50
Price: With checkered, finger-rest bulldog grips 94.00

Marksman Products, Torrance, California is the manufacturer of pellet guns and accessories for pellet gun shooting. Their products include the Marksman Air Pistol, the new Marksman 4000 Air Rifle, targets for pellet gun shooting, pellets, darts, BB's, holsters and slingshots.

MARKSMAN REPEATER AIR PISTOL
Caliber: 177, 20-shot repeater.
Barrel: 2½″, smoothbore.
Length: 8¼″.   **Weight:** 24 oz.
Power: Spring.
Features: Thumb safety. Uses BB's, darts or pellets. Repeats with BB's only.
Price: ....about $12.00

MARKSMAN 4000 AIR RIFLE
Caliber: 177, 400-shot
Barrel: 15½″, smoothbore.
Length: 36½″.   **Weight:** 4 lbs. 2 oz.
Power: Spring, barrel cocking.
Features: Automatic safety; fixed front, adj. rear sights; shoots 177 cal. BB's, pellets and darts.
Price: ....about $25.00

MARKSMAN BIG GAME TARGET
Electrically operated indoor/outdoor target for use with 177 or 22 cal. pellet guns. Moving and rotating animals plus bell-ringing bulls-eye; backplate deflects spent ammo into trap. about $21.95

Sterling Arms Corp., 2206 Elmwood Ave., Buffalo, N.Y. 14216
Sturm, Ruger & Co., Southport, Conn. 06490
Thompson-Center Arms, Box 2405, Rochester, N.H. 03867 (Contender pistol)
Tingle, 1125 Smithland Pike, Shelbyville, Ind. 46176 (muzzleloader)
Universal Firearms Corp., 3746 E. 10th Ct., Hialeah, Fla. 33013
Ward's, 619 W. Chicago, Chicago, Ill. 60607 (Western Field brand)
Weatherby's, 2781 E. Firestone Blvd., South Gate, Calif. 90280
Dan Wesson Arms, 293 So. Main St., Monson, Mass. 01057
Western Valley Arms Co., 524 W. Main St., Alhambra, CA 91801
Winchester Repeating Arms Co., New Haven, Conn. 06504
Winslow Arms Co., P.O. Box 578, Osprey, Fla. 33595

GUNSMITH SCHOOLS

Colorado School of Trades, 1545 Hoyt, Denver, Colo. 80215
Lassen Junior College, 11100 Main St., Susanville, Calif. 96130
Oregon Technical Institute, Klamath Falls, Ore. 97601
Penn. Gunsmith School, 812 Ohio River Blvd., Avklon, Pittsburgh, Pa. 15202
Trinidad State Junior College, Trinidad, Colo. 81082

GUNSMITH SUPPLIES, TOOLS, SERVICES

Adams & Nelson Co., 4125 W. Fullerton, Chicago, Ill. 60639
Alamo Heat Treating Co., Box 55345, Houston, Tex. 77055
Alley Supply Co., Box 458, Sonora, Calif. 95370
American Edelstaal, Inc., 350 Broadway, New York, N.Y. 10013
American Firearms Mfg. Co., Inc., 5732 Kenwick Dr., San Antonio, Tex. 78238 (45 Conversion Kit)
Anderson & Co., 1203 Broadway, Yakima, Wash. 98902 (tang safe)
Armite Labs., 1845 Randolph St., Los Angeles, Cal. 90001 (pen oiler)
Atlas Arms Inc., 2952 Waukegan Rd., Niles, Ill. 60648
B-Square Co., Box 11281, Ft. Worth, Tex. 76110
Jim Baiar, Rt. 1-B, Box 352, Columbia Falls, Mont. 59912 (hex screws)
Benrite Co., 353 Covington, San Antonio, Tex. 78220
Bonanza Sports Mfg. Co., 412 Western Ave., Faribault, Minn. 55021
Brown & Sharpe Mfg. Co., Precision Pk., No. Kingston, R.I. 02852
Bob Brownell's, Main & Third, Montezuma, Ia. 50171
W. E. Brownell, 1852 Alessandro Trail, Vista, Calif. 92083 (checkering tools)
Maynard P. Buehler, Inc., 17 Orinda Hwy., Orinda, Calif. 94563 (Rocol lube)
Burgess Vibrocrafters, Inc. (BVI), Rte. 83, Grayslake, Ill. 60030
M. H. Canjar, 500 E. 45th, Denver, Colo. 80216 (triggers, etc.)
Centerline Prod. Box 14074, Denver, Colo. 80214
Chicago Wheel & Mfg. Co., 1101 W. Monroe St., Chicago, Ill. 60607 (Handee grinders)
Christy Gun Works, 875-57th St. Sacramento, Calif. 95819
Clymer Mfg. Co., 14241 W. 11 Mile Rd., Oak Park, Mich. 48237 (reamers)
Colbert Industries, 10107 Adella, South Gate, Calif. 90280 (Panavise)
A. Constantine & Son, Inc., 2050 Eastchester Rd., Bronx, N.Y. 10461 (wood)
Cougar & Hunter, 66398 W. Pierson Rd., Flushing, Mich. 48433 (scope jigs)
Craft Industries, 719 No. East St., Anaheim, Ca. 92800 (Gunline tools)
Dayton-Traister Co., P.O. Box 93, Oak Harbor, Wa. 98277 (triggers)
Dem-Bart Co., 3333 N. Gove St., Tacoma, Wash. 98407 (checkering tools)
Die Supply Corp., 11700 Harvard Ave., Cleveland, Ohio 44105
Ditto Industries, 527 N. Alexandria, Los Angeles, Cal. 90004 (clamp tool)
Dixie Diamond Tool Co., Inc., 6875 S.W. 81st St., Miami, Fla. 33143 (marking pencils)
Dremel Mfg. Co., P.O. Box 518, Racine, Wis. 53401 (grinders)
Chas. E. Duffy, Williams Lane, West Hurley, N.Y. 12491
Dumore Co., 1300 - 17th St., Racine, Wis. 53403
E-Z Tool Co., P.O. Box 3186, East 14th Street Sta., Des Moines, Ia. 50313 (taper lathe attachment)
Edmund Scientific Co., 101 E. Glouster Pike, Barrington, N.J. 08007
F. K. Elliott, Box 785, Ramona, Calif. 92065 (reamers)
Foredom Elec. Co., Rt. 6, Bethel, Conn. 06801 (power drills)
Forster Appelt Mfg. Co., Inc., 82 E. Lanark Ave., Lanark, Ill. 61046
Keith Francis, Box 343, Talent, Ore. 97540 (reamers)
Frantz Tools, 913 Barbara Ave., Placentia, Cal. 92670
G. R. S. Corp., Box 1157, Boulder, Colo. 80302 (Gravermeister)
Gilmore Pattern Works, 1164 N. Utica, Tulsa Okla. 74110
Gold Lode, Inc., P.O. Box 31, Addison, Ill. 60101 (gold inlay kit)
Grace Metal Prod., Box 67, Elk Rapids, Mich. 49629 (screw drivers, drifts)
Gopher Shooter's Supply, Box 246, Faribault, Minn. 55021 (screwdrivers, etc.)
The Gun Case, 11035 Maplefield SE., El Monte, Calif. 91733 (triggers)
Gunline Tools (see Craft Ind.)
H. & M. 24062 Orchard Lake Rd., Farmington, Mich. 48024 (reamers)
Hartford Reamer Co., Box 134, Lathrop Village, Mich. 48075
Hobbi-Carve (see St. Paul Mach.)
R. E. Hutchinson, Burbank Rd., Sutton, Mass. 01527 (engine turning tool)
O. Iber Co., 626 W. Randolph, Chicago, Ill. 60606
Paul Jaeger Inc., 211 Leedom St., Jenkintown, PA. 19046
Kasenite Co., Inc., 3 King St., Mahwah, N.J. 07430 (surface hrdng. comp.)
Lea Mfg. Co., 237 E. Aurora St., Waterbury, Conn. 06720
Lock's Phila. Gun Exch., 6700 Rowland Ave., Philadelphia, Pa. 19149
Marker Machine Co., Box 426, Charleston, Ill. 61920
Michaels of Oregon Co., P.O. Box 13010, Portland, Ore. 97213
Viggo Miller, P.O. Box 4181, Omaha, Neb. 68104 (trigger attachment)
Miller Single Trigger Mfg. Co., Box 69, Millersburg, Pa. 17061
Frank Mittermeier, 3577 E. Tremont, N.Y., N.Y. 10465
Moderntools Corp., Box 407, Dept. GD, Woodside, N.Y. 11377
N&J Sales, Lime Kiln Rd., Northford, Conn. 06472 (screwdrivers)
Karl A. Neise, Inc., 5602 Roosevelt Ave., Woodside, N.Y. 11377
P & S Sales, P.O. Box 45095, Tulsa, OK 74145
Palmgren, 8383 South Chicago Ave., Chicago, Ill. 60167 (vises, etc.)

C. R. Pedersen & Son, Ludington, Mich. 49431
Ponderay Lab., 210 W. Prasch, Yakima, Wash. 98902 (epoxy glass bedding)
Redford Reamer Co., Box 6604, Redford Hts. Sta, Detroit, MI 48240
Richland Arms Co., 321 W. Adrian St., Blissfield, Mich. 49228
Riley's Supply Co., Box 365, Avilla, Ind. 46710 (Niedner buttplates, caps)
Rob. A. Saunders, (see Amer. Firearms Mfg.)
Ruhr-American Corp., So. Hwy #55, Glenwood, Minn. 56334
A. G. Russell, P.O. Box 474, Fayetteville, Ark. 72701 (Arkansas stones)
Schaffner Mfg. Co., Emsworth, Pittsburgh, Pa. 15202 (polishing kits)
Schuetzen Gun Works, 1226 Prairie Rd., Colo. Springs, Colo. 80909
Shaw's, 1655 S. Euclid Ave., Anaheim, Calif. 92802
A. D. Soucy Co., Box 191, Fort Kent, Me. 04743 (ADSCO stock finish)
L. S. Starrett Co., Athol, Mass. 01331
Technological Devices, Inc., P.O. Box 3491, Stamford, Conn. 06905 (Accu-Orb circle cutters)
L.B. Thompson, 568 E. School Ave., Salem, O. 44460 (rust bluing/browning)
Timney Mfg. Co., 5624 Imperial Hwy., So. Gate, Calif. 90280 (triggers)
Stan de Treville, Box 2446, San Diego, Calif 92112 (checkering patterns)
Twin City Steel Treating Co., Inc., 1114 S. 3rd, Minneapolis, Minn. 55415
R. G. Walters Co., 3235 Hancock, San Diego, Ca. 92110
Ward Mfg. Co., 500 Ford Blvd., Hamilton, O. 45011
Will-Burt Co., P.O. Box #1, Orrville, O. 44667 (vises)
Williams Gun Sight Co., 7389 Lapeer Rd., Davison, Mich. 48423
Wilson Arms Co., Box 364, Stony Creek, Branford, Conn. 06405
Wilton Tool Corp., 9525 W. Irving Pk. Rd., Schiller Park, Ill. 60176 (vises)
Wisconsin Platers Supply Co., 3256-A Milwaukee, Madison, WI 53714 (plating kit)
Woodcraft Supply Corp., 313 Montvale, Woburn, MA 01801

HANDGUN ACCESSORIES

A & R Sales Co., 99163¾ Rush St., So. El Monte, CA 91733
Barami Corp, 6250 E. 7 Mile Rd, Detroit, Mich. 48234 (Hip-Grip)
B. L. Broadway, 1503 Jasper, Chula Vista, Calif. 92011 (machine rest)
Case Master, 4675 E. 10 Ave., Miami, Fla. 33013
Central Specialties Co., 6030 Northwest Hwy., Chicago, Ill. 60631
John Dangelzer, 3056 Frontier Pl., N.E., Albuquerque, N.M. 87106 (flasks)
Bill Dyer, 503 Midwest Bldg., Oklahoma City, Okla. 73102 (grip caps)
R. S. Frielich, 396 Broome St., New York, N.Y. 10013 (cases)
Hunt Eng., 121—17th St., Yucaipa, Calif. 92399 (Multi-Loader)
R. G. Jensen, 16153 ½ Parthenia, Sepulveda, Calif. 91343 (auxiliary chambers)
Matich Loader, Box 958, So. Pasadena, Calif. 91030 (Quick Load)
J. McArthur, 1961 Overlook Ave., Youngstown, O. 44509 (sling)
Pachmayr, 1220 S. Grand, Los Angeles, Calif. 90015 (cases)
Platt Luggage, Inc., 2301 S. Prairie, Chicago, Ill. 60616 (Cases)
Jules Reiver, 4104 Market St., Wilmington, Del. 19899 (cases)
Roger A. Smith, 19320 Heber St., Glendora, Ca. 91740 (Wrist-Loc)
Sportsmen's Equipment Co., 415 W. Washington, San Diego, Calif. 92103
M. Tyler, 1326 W. Britton, Oklahoma City, Okla. 73114 (grip adaptor)

HANDGUN GRIPS

Beckelhymer's, Hidalgo & San Bernardo, Laredo, Tex. 78040
Caray Sales Co., 2044 Hudson St., Ft. Lee, N.J. 07024
Cloyce's Gun Stocks, Box 1133, Twin Falls, Ida. 83301
Crest Carving Co., 14849 Dillow St., Westminster, CA 92683
Custom Combat Grips, 148 Shepherd Ave., Brooklyn, N.Y. 11208
Enforcer Prod. Div., Caray Sales Co., 2044 Hudson St., Fort Lee, N.J. 07024
J. M. Evans, 5078 Harwood Rd., San Jose, Cal. 95124
Fitz, Box 49797, Los Angeles, Calif. 90049
Herret's, Box 741, Twin Falls, Ida. 83301
Hogue Custom Grips, Box 1001, Cambria, CA 93428
Mershon Co., Inc., 1230 S. Grand Ave., Los Angeles, Calif. 90015
Mustang Pistol Grips, 13830 Hiway 395, Edgemont, Calif. 92508
Safety Grip Corp., Box 456, Riverside St., Miami, Fla. 33135
Sanderson Custom Pistol Stocks, 17695 Fenton, Detroit, Mich. 48219
Jay Scott, 81 Sherman Place, Garfield, N.J. 07026
Sile Dist., 7 Centre Market Pl., New York, N.Y. 10013
Sports, Inc., 5501 Broadway, Chicago, Ill. 60640 (Franzite)
John W. Womack, 3006 Bibb St., Shreveport, La 71108

HOLSTERS & LEATHER GOODS

American Sales & Mfg. Co., P.O. Box 677, Laredo, Tex. 78040
Berns-Martin, Box 335, Elberton, Ga. 30635
Bianchi Holster Co., 212 W. Foothill Blvd., Monrovia, Calif. 91016
Edward H. Bohlin, 931 N. Highland Ave., Hollywood, Calif. 90038
Boyt Co., Box 1108, Iowa Falls, Ia. 51026
E. A. Brandin Saddle Co., Rte. 2, Box 243-A, Monroe, La. 71201
Brauer Bros. Mfg. Co., 817 N. 17th, St. Louis, Mo. 63106
Browning Arms Co., Rt. 4, Box 624-B, Arnold, Mo. 63010
J. M. Bucheimer Co., Airport Rd., Frederick, Md. 21701
Cole's Acku-Rite, Box 25, Kennedy, N.Y. 14747
Colt's, 150 Huyshope Ave., Hartford, Conn. 06102
Daisy Mfg. Co., Rogers, Ark. 72756
Eugene DeMayo & Sons, Inc., 2795 Third Ave., Bronx, N.Y. 10455
Filmat Enterpr., Inc., 200 Market St., East Paterson, N.J. 07407
Flintrop Arms Co., 4034 W. National Ave., Milwaukee, Wis. 53215
Goerg Ent., 3009 S. Laurel, Port Angeles, Wash. 98362
Hoyt Holster Co., P.O. Box 1783, Costa Mesa, Cal. 92626
Don Hume, Box 351, Miami, Okla. 74354
The Hunter, 1215 12th St., Denver, Colo. 80204
Jet Sports Corp., 4 Centre Market Pl., New York, N.Y. 10013
Jumbo Sports Prods., P.O. Box 280, Airport Rd., Frederick, MD 21701

TAYRA CONCEALED WEAPON HOLSTER

Tayra Corporation of 1529 19th St. N.W., Canton, Ohio is the manufacturer of a new type concealed weapon holster that provides a good deal of comfort, concealment and speed of draw. Designed for plain clothes police, investigators and big game hunters in need of a back-up revolver, the holster is made of flexible ethylene vinyl acetate and is contour molded to fit a number of popular revolvers. The holster, which will fit scoped revolvers, is washable and remains flexible at sub-zero temperatures. A thumb released tie-down over the gun hammer and a rigid belt clip, adjustable for belts ½″ to 2″ are integral parts of the holster.

BELT CLIP

Tayra CORPORATION
CANTON, OHIO

The holster is available in sizes to fit the following revolvers: Smith & Wesson Models — 10,12,14,15,16,17,18,19 & 53; Colt—Trooper, Official Police and MK III; Hawes (J.P. Sauer) Trophy and Medallion; and Ruger Security Six. One size fits all barrel lengths. The holster in black, right-hand only, sells for $9.95.

George Lawrence Co., 306 S. W. First Ave., Portland, Ore. 97204
MMGR Corp., 5710 12th Ave., Brooklyn, N.Y. 11219
S. D. Myres Saddle Co., Box 9776, El Paso, Tex. 79988
Pony Express Sport Shop, 17460 Ventura Blvd., Encino, Calif. 91316
Red Head Brand Co., 4100 Platinum Way, Dallas, Tex. 75237
R. E. Roseberry, 810 W. 38th, Anderson, Ind. 46014
Safariland Leather Products, 1946 S. Myrtle Ave., Monrovia, Calif. 91016
Safety Speed Holster, Inc., 910 So. Vail, Montebello, Calif. 90640
San Francisco Gun Exchange, 75 Fourth St., San Francisco, Calif. 94103
Buddy Schoellkopf Products, Inc., 4100 Platinum Way, Dallas, Tex. 75237
Seventrees, Ltd., 315 W. 39 St., New York, N.Y. 10018
Sile Distr., 7 Centre Market Pl., New York, N.Y. 10013
Smith & Wesson Leather Co., 2100 Roosevelt, Springfield, Mass. 01101
Swiss-Craft Co., Inc., 33 Arctic St., Worcester, MA 01604
Tandy Leather Co., 1001 Foch, Fort Worth, Texas 76107
Tayra Corp., 1529-19th St. N.W., Canton, O. 44709
Whitco, Box 1712, Brownsville, Tex. 78520 (Hide-A-Way)
Woodland Sport and Gift Shop, Box 107, Mayfield, N.Y. 12117

HUNTING, CAMP GEAR, CLOTHING, ETC.

Abercrombie & Fitch, 45th & Madison Ave., N.Y., N.Y. 10017
Alpine Designs, Box 1081, Boulder, Colo. 80302
Alpine Hut, Box 1456, Wenatchee, Wash. 98801
Eddie Bauer, 1737 Airport Way So., Seattle, Wash. 98134
L. L. Bean, Freeport, Me. 04032
Bear Archery Co., R.R. 1, Grayling, Mich. 49738 (Himalayan backpack)
Bernzomatic Corp., 740 Driving Pk. Ave., Rochester, N.Y. 14613 (stoves & lanterns)
Big Beam, Teledyne Co., 290 E. Prairie St., Crystal Lake, Ill. 60014 (lamp)
Thos. Black & Sons, 930 Ford St., Ogdensburg, N.Y. 13669 (ctlg. 25¢)
Browning Arms Co., Rte. 1, Morgan, Utah 84050
Camouflage Mfg. Co., Box 16373, Jacksonville, Fla. 32216
Camp and Trail Outfitters, 21 Park Place, N.Y., N.Y. 10007
Camp Trails, P.O. Box 14500, Phoenix, Ariz. 85031 (packs only)
Challanger Mfg. Co., Box 550, Jamaica, N.Y. 11431 (glow safe)
Coleman Co., Inc., 250 N. St. Francis, Wichita, Kans. 67201
Colorado Outdoor Sports Co., 5450 N. Valley Hwy., Denver, Colo. 80216
Converse Rubber Co., 392 Pearl St., Malden, Mass. 02148 (boots)
Corcoran, Inc., Zero Canton Street, Stoughton, Mass, 02072
Dana Safety Heater, J. L. Galef & Son, Inc., 85 Chamber St., N.Y. N.Y. 10007
DEER-ME Prod. Co., Box 345, Anoka, Minn. 55303 (tree steps)
Dunham's Footwear, RFD 3, Brattleboro, Vt. 05301 (boots)
Edmont-Wilson, 1300 Walnut St., Coshocton, O. 43812 (gloves)
Fabrico Mfg. Corp., 1300 W. Exchange, Chicago, Ill. 60609
Filmat Enterpr., Inc., 200 Market St., East Paterson, N.J. 07407 (field dressing kit)
Freeman Ind., Inc., Tuckahoe, N.Y. 10707 (Trak-Kit)
Game-Winner, Inc., 2940 First Natl. Bk. Bldg., Atlanta, Ga. 30303
Gander Mountain, Inc., Box 248, Wilmot, Wis. 53192
George & Son 424 S.W. Washington, Portland, Ore. 97204
Gerry Mountain Sports, Inc. (see Colorado Sports)
Gokey, 94 E. 4th St., St. Paul, Minn. 55101
Greenford Products, Inc., 64 Old Orchard, Skokie, Ill. 60076 (heaters & ranges)
Gun Club Sportswear, Box 477, Des Moines, Ia. 50302
Gun-Ho Case Mfg. Co., 110 E. 10th St., St. Paul, Minn. 55101
Hawthorn Co., Div. of Kellwood Co., New Haven, Mo. 63068 (tents)
Himalayan Back Packs, Box 950, Monterey, CA 93940
Bob Hinman, 1217 W. Glen, Peoria, Ill. 61614
Holubar Mountaineering, Box 7, Boulder, Colo. 80302
Humphrey Prod., P.O. Box 2008, Kalamazoo, Mich. 49003 (camping equipment)
Hunting World, 247 E. 50th St., New York, N.Y. 10022
Kelty Pack, Inc., Box 3645, Glendale, Calif. 91201
Peter Limmer & Sons, Box 66, Intervale, N.H. 03845 (boots)
Marble Arms Corp., 1120 Superior, Gladstone, Mich. 49837
Moor & Mountain, 14 Main St., Concord Center, Mass. 01742
National Sports Div., 19 E. McWilliams St., Fond du Lac, Wis. 54935
Nimrod & Wayfarer Trailers, 500 Ford Blvd., Hamilton, O. 45011
Charles F. Orvis Co., Manchester, Vt. 05254 (fishing gear)
Paulin Infra-Red Prod. Co., 1600 S. Waterloo, Cleveland, O. 44110 (Coleman stove conv.)
Portablind, 705 Exchange Park, Dallas, TX 75235
Powerwinch Corp., 184 Garden St., Bridgeport, Conn. 06605
Primus-Sievert, 47 Larkin St., Stamford, Conn. 06906 (stoves)
Raemco, Box 882, Somerville, N.J. 08876 (stoves)
Red Head Brand Co., 4100 Platinum Way, Dallas Tex. 75237
Red Wing Shoe Co., Rte. 2, Red Wing, Minn. 55066
Refrigiwear, Inc., 71 Inip Dr., Inwood, L.I., N.Y. 11696
Reliance Prod. Ltd., 1830 Dublin Ave., Winnipeg 21, Man., Can. (tent peg)
Buddy Schoellkopf, Inc., 4100 Platinum Way, Dallas, Tex. 75237
Servus Rubber Co., 1136 2nd St., Rock Island, Ill. 61201 (footwear)
Sportsgear, Inc., 4909 Fremont Ave. So., Minneapolis, Minn. 55409 (pack sack & port. chair)
Sportsmen Prod. Inc., Box 1082, Boulder, Colo. 80302 (snowshoes)
Stearns Mfg. Co., Division & 30th St., St. Cloud, Minn. 56301
Sterno Inc., 105 Hudson St., Jersey City, N.J. 07302 (camp stoves)
Burt Stumpf, 408 Morrison Ave., Waterloo, Ill. 62298 (Easy-Way hunting vest)
10-X Mfg. Co., 100 S.W. 3rd St., Des Moines, Iowa 50309
Thermos Div., KST Co., Norwich, Conn. 06361 (Pop Tent)
Therm'x Corp., Inc., 1280 Columbus, San Francisco, Calif. 94133
Norm Thompson, 1805 N.W. Thurman St., Portland, Ore. 97209
Trailwise-The Ski Hut, 1615 University Ave., Berkeley, Calif. 94703
Travel Industries, Box 108, Oswego, Kan. 67356 (Dreamer pickup fleet)
Trigg Mfg. Co., Box 850, Danville, Ky. 40422 (clothing)
U-C-Lite Mfg. Co., 290 E. Prairie St., Crystal Lake, Ill. 60014 (Big beam car- and hand-flashlights)

Eug. Usow Mfg. Co., 1934 N. Washtenaw, Chicago, Ill. 60647 (clothing)
Ute Mountain Corp., Box 3602, Englewood, Colo. 80110 (Metal Match)
Utica Duxbak Corp., 815 Noyes St., Utica, N.Y. 13502
Visa-Therm Prod., Inc., P.O. Box 486, Bridgeport, Conn. 06601 (Astro/ Electr. vest)
Vogt. Mfg. Co., 100 Fernwood Ave., Rochester, N.Y. 14621 (fluorescent belt)
Waffen-Frankonia, Box 380, 87 Wurzburg, W. Germany
Ward Mfg. Co., 500 Ford Blvd., Hamilton, O. 45015 (trailers)
Weinbrenner Shoe Corp., Polk St., Merrill, WI 54452
Wilson Certified Foods, Inc., Box 7345, Omaha, Neb. 68107
Wisconsin Shoe Co., 1039 So. Second, Milwaukee, Wis. 53204
Woods Bag & Canvas Co., Ltd., 16 Lake St., Ogdensburg, N.Y. 13669
Woodstream Corp., Box 327, Lititz, Pa. 17543 (Hunter Seat)
Woolrich Woolen Mills, Woolrich, Pa. 17779
Yankee Mechanics, Newport, N.H. 03773 (hand winches)
Zeus Portable Generator Co., 500 Mildred, Primos, Ohio 19018

HUNTING KNIVES, AXES AND HATCHETS

Adanac Sptg. Gds., 505 Bellingham Ntl. Bk. Bldg., Bellingham, Wash. 98225
John Applebaugh, Box 68, Blackwell, Okla. 74631 (custom-knives)
Arnold Knives, Box 1427, Grand Prairie, Tex. 75050 (custom)
B.H.S. Mfg. Co., Box 24, Troy, MI 48084 (pocket axe)
L. L. Bean, Freeport, Maine 04032
Bear Archery Co., R.R. 1, Grayling, MI 49738
Lee Biggs, 3816 Via La Silva, Palo Verde, CA 92266 (custom-knives)
Ralph Bone Knife Co., 806 Avenue J, Lubbock, Tex. 79401
H. Gardner Bourne, 1252 Hope Ave., Columbus, O. 43212 (custom-knives)
D. L. Brown, 1803 Birdie Dr., Toledo, O. 43615 (custom-knives)
L. E. "Red" Brown, 301 E. Neece St., Long Beach, CA 90805 (custom-knives)
Buck Knives, Inc., P.O. Box 1267, El Cajon, CA 92022
Pete Callan, 17 Sherline Ave., New Orleans, LA 70124 (custom-knives)
W. R. Case Knives, 20 Russell Blvd., Bradford, Pa. 16701
Challanger Mfg. Co., 94-28 Merrick Blvd., Jamaica, NY 11433
Cooper Knives, P.O. Box 1423, Burbank, CA 91505 (custom, ctlg. 50¢)
Dan-D Custom Knives, Box 4479, Yuma, AZ 85364
Davis Custom Knives, 118 W. 14th, Airway Heights, WA 99001
Philip Day, Rte. 1, Box 465T, Bay Minetter, AL 36507 (custom-knives)
J. R. Dennard, 907 Greenwood Pl., Dalton, GA 30720 (custom-knives)
Chas. E. Dickey, 803 N.E. A St., Bentonville, AR 72712 (custom-knives)
T. M. Dowell, 139 St. Helen's Pl., Bend, OR 97701 (custom-knives)
Draper Knives, Box 94, Ephraim, UT 84627 (custom)
John Ek, 3214 NW 54th St., Miami, Fla. 33142 (custom-knives)
Fischer Custom Knives, Rt. 1, Box 170-M, Victoria, TX 77901
H. H. Frank, c/o Loveless, Box 837, Lawndale, CA 90260 (custom-knives)
James Furlow, 4838 Santa Fe Trail S.W., Atlanta, GA 30331 (custom-knives)
Garcia Sptg. Arms Corp., 329 Alfred Ave., Teaneck, NJ 07666
Gerber Legendary Blades, 14200 S.W. 72nd St., Portland, OR 99223
Gutman Cutlery Co., Inc., 3956 Broadway, New York, NY 10032
Gyrfalcon Inc., Kutz Bldg., 1104 Fernwood Ave., Camp Hill, PA 17011 (Skachet)
Lloyd A. Hale, 14522 Saco St., Poway, CA 92064 (custom-knives)
C. M. (Pete) Heath, 119 Grant St., Winnecone, WI 54986 (custom-knives)
D. E. Henry, Star Route, Mountain Ranch, CA 95246 (custom-knives)
G. H. Herron, 920 Murrah Ave., Aiken, SC 29801 (custom-knives)
Gil Hibben, Box 7, Manti, UT 84642 (custom-knives)
Chubby Hueske, 4808 Tamarisk Dr., Bellaire, TX 77401 (custom-knives)
Indian Ridge Traders, P.O. Box X-50, Ferndale, MI 48220
Jet-Aer Corp., 100 Sixth Ave., Paterson, NJ 07524 (G96 knives)
LaDow (Doc) Johnston, 2322 W. Country Club Parkway, Toledo, OH 43614 (custom-knives)
KA-BAR Cutlery, Inc., 5777 Grant Ave., Cleveland, OH 44105
Jon W. Kirk, 800 N. Olive, Fayetteville, AR 72701 (custom-knives)
W. Kneubuhler, P.O. Box 327, Pioneer, OH 43554 (custom-knives)
Kustom Made Knives, 418 Jolee, Richardson, TX 75080
J. I. Lane, Rte. 5, Carbondale, IL 62901 (custom-knives)
Lile Handmade Knives, Rte. 1, Box 56, Russellville, AR 72801
LocKnife, Inc., 11717 E. 23rd St., Independence, MO 64050
R. W. Loveless, Box 837, Lawndale, CA 90260 (custom-knives, ctlg. $1)
Bob Ludwig, 1028 Pecos Ave., Port Arthur, TX 77640 (custom-knives)
MAC Intl. Corp., 4848 W. Main, Skokie, IL 60076
Marble Arms Corp., 1120 Superior, Gladstone, MI 49837
Joe S. Martin, Box 6652, Lubbock, TX 79413 (custom-knives)
John T. Mims, 620 S. 28th Ave., Apt. 327, Hattiesburg, MS 39401 (custom-knives)
Mitchell Knives, 511 Ave. B, So. Houston, TX 77587 (custom)
W. F. Moran, Jr., Rt. 5, Frederick, MD 21701 (custom-knives, ctlg. 50¢)
Normark Corp., 1710 E. 78th St., Minneapolis, MN 55423
Olsen Knife Co., 7 Joy St., Howard City, MI 49329
Randall-Made Knives, Box 1988, Orlando, FL 32802 (ctlg. 25¢)
Razor Edge, Box 203, Butler, WI 53007 (knife sharpener)
Ruana Knife Works, Box 574, Bonner, MT 59823 (ctlg. 50¢)
Sanders, 2358 Tyler Lane, Louisville, KY 40205 (Bahco)
Jack D. Schmier, 16787 Mulberry Ct., Fountain Valley, CA 92708 (custom-knives)
Bob Schrimsher, Wm. Rodgers Cutlery, P.O. Box 11448, Dallas, TX 75223
John J. Schwarz, 41 Fifteenth St., Wellsburg, WV 26070 (custom-knives)
Skachet, (see: Gryfalcon Inc.)
W. J. Sonneville, 1050 Chalet Dr. W., Mobile, AL 36608 (custom-knives)
Bernard Sparks, Box 32, Dingle, ID 83233 (custom-knives)
Stone Knives, 703 Floyd Rd., Richardson, TX 75080
Thunderbird Custom Knives, 912 So. 2nd St., Blackwell, OK 74631
Tru-Balance Knife Co., 2110 Tremont Blvd., Grand Rapids, MI 49504
True-Temper, 1623 Euclid, Cleveland, OH 44100
W-K Knives, P.O. Box 327, Pioneer, OH 43554
Western Cutlery Co., 5311 Western Ave., Boulder, CO 80302

Ronnie Wilson, 145 Leech St., Weirton, WV 26062 (custom-knives)
Don Zaccagaino, 2256 Bacon Pt. Rd., Pahokee, FL 33476 (custom-knives)

LOAD TESTING & CHRONOGRAPHING

Carter Gun Works, 2211 Jefferson Pk. Ave., Charlottesville, Va. 22903
Custom Ballistics' Lab., 3354 Cumberland Dr., San Angelo, Tex. 76901
Degamo, Inc., 500 Ashland Ave., Chicago Heights, Il. 60411
J. Dewey Gun Co., Clinton Corners, N.Y. 12514
Horton Ballistics, North Waterford, Me. 04267
Hutton Rifle Ranch, 619 San Lorenzo St., Santa Monica, Ca. 90402
Jurras Co., Box 163, Shelbyville, Ind. 46176
Kennon's 5408 Biffle, Stone Mountain, Ga. 30083
Plum City Ballistics Range, RFD 1, Box 128, Plum City, Wis. 54761 '
R & M Chronograph Serv., 9882 E. Manning, Selma, Calif. 93662
Shooters Service & Dewey, Inc., Clinton Corners, N.Y. 12514 (daily fee range also)
Gene West, 137 Baylor, Pueblo, Colo. 81005
H. P. White Lab., Box 331, Bel Air, Md. 21014

METALLIC SIGHTS

B-Square Eng. Co., Box 11281, Ft. Worth, Tex. 76110
Bo-Mar Tool & Mfg. Co., Box 168, Carthage, Tex. 75633
Maynard P. Buehler, Inc., 17 Orinda Highway, Orinda, Calif. 94563
Chicago Gun Center, 3109 W. Armitage, Chicago, Ill. 60647
Christy Gun Works, 875 57th St., Sacramento, Calif. 95819
Clerke Technicorp., 2040 Broadway Ave., Santa Monica, Calif. 90404
Art Cook Supply, Rte. 2, Box 123B, Laurel, Md. 20810 (Illum. gunsight)
Firearms Dev. Lab., Box 278, Scotts Valley, Calif. 95060
Freeland's Scope Stands, Inc., 3734-14th Ave., Rock Island, Ill. 61201
P. W. Gray Co., Fairgrounds Rd., Nantucket, Mass. 02554 (shotgun)
Lyman Gun Sight Products, Middlefield, Conn. 06455
Marble Arms Corp., 1120 Superior, Gladstone, Mich. 49837
Merit Gunsight Co., P.O. Box 995, Sequim, Wash. 98382
Micro Sight Co., 242 Harbor Blvd., Belmont, Calif. 94002
Miniature Machine Co., 212 E. Spruce, Deming, N.M. 88030
Oxford Corp., 100 Benbro Dr., Buffalo, N.Y. 14225 (Illum. Sight)
C. R. Pedersen & Son, Ludington, Mich. 49431
Redfield Gun Sight Co., 1315 S. Clarkson St., Denver, Colo. 80210
Schwarz's Gun Shop, 41 - 15th St., Wellsburg, W. Va. 26070
Simmons Gun Specialties, Inc., 700 Rodgers Rd., Olathe, Kans. 66061
Slug Site Co., 3835 University, Des Moines, Ia. 50311
Williams Gun Sight Co., 7389 Lapeer Rd., Davison, Mich. 48423
W. H. Womack, 2124 Meriwether Rd., Shreveport. La. 71108

MISCELLANEOUS

Accurizing Service, Herbert G. Troester, Cayuaga, ND 58013
Adhesive Flannel, Forest City Prod., 722 Bolivar, Cleveland, O. 44115
Ammo Pouch, Creed Ent., 13167 E. Garvey Ave., Baldwin Park, CA 91706
Archery, Bear Co., R.R. 1, Grayling, Mich. 49738
Arms Books, Normount Technical Publications, Forest Grove, OR 97116
Arms Bookseller, Norm Flayderman, RFD 2, Squash Hollow, New Milford, Conn. 06776
Arms Bookseller, Rutgers, Mark Aziz, 127 Raritan Ave., Highland Park, N.J. 08904
Arms Research, American Arms Co., 1641 Maplecrest Dr., Bloomington, Ind. 47401
Barrel Band Swivels, Phil Judd, 83 E. Park St., Butte, Mont. 59701
Barrel Bedding Device, W. H. Womack, 2124 Meriwether Rd., Shreveport, La. 71108
Bedding Kit, Bisonite Co., Box 84, Buffalo, N.Y. 14217
Bedding Kit, Fenwal, Inc., 400 Main St., Ashland, Mass. 01721
Bench Rest Pedestal, Jim Brobst, 299 Poplar, Hamburg, Pa. 19526
Bench Rest Stands, Suter's, 401 Tejon, Colorado Springs, Colo. 80902
Binocular/Camera Harness, Jack Worsfold Assoc., Box 25, Forest Hill, Md. 21050
Bootdryers, Baekgaard Ltd., 1855 Janke Dr., Northbrook, Ill. 60062
Bore Collimator, Alley Supply Co., Box 458, Sonora, Calif. 95370
Bore Collimator, Collins Co., Box 40, Shepherdsville, Ky. 40165
Bore Lamp, Spacetron, Inc., Box 84, Broadview Ill. 60155
Borescope, Eder Inst. Co., 2293 N. Clybourn, Chicago, Ill. 60614
Bore Sighter, Rifleman's Bore Sighter Co., P.O. Box 1701, Saginaw, Mich. 48605
Breech Plug Wrench, Swaine Machine, 195 O'Connell, Providence, R.I. 02905
Can Thrower, Trius Prod., Box 25, Cleves, O. 45002
Capper, Muzzle-Loading, Pat Burke, 3339 Farnsworth Rd., Lapeer, Mich. 48446
Cartridge Boxes, Llanerch Gun Shop, 2800 Township Line, Upper Darby, Pa. 19083
Cartridge Boxes, Shooters Supplies, 1589 Payne Ave., St. Paul, MN 55101
Cartridge Box Labels, Milton Brynin, Box 162, Fleetwood Sta., Mt. Vernon, N.Y. 10552
Cartridge Box Labels, Jasco, Box 49751, Los Angeles, Calif. 90049
Cartridge Box Labels, Peterson Label Co., P.O. Box 186Z, Redding Ridge, CT 06876
Cartridge Carrier, N.H. Schiffman, P.O. Box 7373, Murray, UT 84107
Case Gauge, Plum City Ballistics Range, Box 128, Plum City, Wis. 54761
Chrome Brl. Lining, Marker Mach. Co., Box 426, Charleston, Ill. 61920
Color Hardening, Alamo Heat Treating Co., Box 55345, Houston, Tex. 77055
Cronoscope, Wein Prod. Inc., 115 W. 25th St., Los Angeles, Ca. 90007
Crossbows, Midwest Crossbow Co., 9043 So. Western, Chicago, Ill. 60620
Crow Caller, Wightman Elec. Inc., Box 989, Easton, Md. 21601
Custom Bluing, J. A. Wingert, 124 W. 2nd St., Waynesboro, Pa. 17268
Decoys, Carry-Lite, Inc., 3000 W. Clarke, Milwaukee, Wis. 53245

Decoys, Deeks, Inc., Box 2309, Salt Lake City, Utah 84114
Decoys, G & H Decoy Mfg. Co., P.O. Box 937, Henryetta, Okla. 74437
Decoys, Sports Haven Ltd., Box 19323, Portland, Ore. 97219
Decoys, Tex Wirtz Ent., Inc., 1925 W. Hubbard St., Chicago Ill. 60622
Decoys, Woodstream Corp., Box 327, Lititz, Pa. 17543
Distress Flares, Marsh Coulter Co., Box 333, Tecumseh, Mich. 49286
Dog House, Canine Pal Sales, 421 E. 39th St., Gary, Ind. 46409 (portable)
E-Z Loader, Del Rey Prod., P.O. Box 91561, Los Angeles, CA 90009
Ear-Valv, Sigma Eng. Co., 11320 Burbank Blvd., N. Hollywood, Cal. 91601 (Lee-Sonic)
Electric Heater, Dampp-Chaser, Inc., Box 1610, Hendersonville, N.C. 28739
Emergency Food, Tony Bolton Foods, Micro Dr., Woburn, Mass. 01801
Emergency Food, Chuck Wagon, Micro Dr., Woburn, Mass. 01801
Flares, Colt Industries, Huyshope Ave., Hartford, Conn. 06102
Flares, Goble Assoc., Box 1057, Escondido, Calif. 92025
Flares, Intercontinental Arms, 2222 Barry Ave., Los Angeles, Ca. 90064 (MBA)
Flat Springs, Alamo Heat Treating Co., Box 55345, Houston, Tex. 77055
Folding Cup, Bob Lane Co., Box 333, Branford, Conn. 06405
Game Hoist, Flanders Mfg. Co., Box 33363, Houston, Tex. 77033
Game Hoist, PIC, 3 Chestnut, Suffern, N.Y. 10901
Game Scent, Buck Stop, Inc., 3015 Grow Rd., Stanton, Mi 4888
Game Scent, Pete Rickard, Box 26, Cobleskill, N.Y. 12043 (Indian Buck lure)
Gas Pistol, Penguin Assoc., Inc., Box 97, Parkesburg, Pa. 19365
Gun Bedding Kit, Resin Div., Fenwal, Inc., 400 Main St., Ashland, Mass. 01601
Gun Jewelry, Sid Bell, Originals, Box 188, Tully, N.Y. 13159
Gun Jewelry, Al Popper, 614 Turnpike St., Stoughton, Mass. 02072
Gun Lock, Bor-Lok Prods., 4200 California St., San Francisco, CA 94118
Gun Lock, E & C Enterprises, P.O. Box 823, So. Pasadena, CA. 91030
Gun Lock Chain, Lundy Corp., 1123-24 Davenport Bk. Bldg., Davenport, Ia. 52801
Gun Lok, 4780 Old Orchard Trail, Orchard Lake, Mich. 48034
Gun Sling, Trail Guide Prods. Corp., 15407 Mc Ginty Rd., Wayzata, MN 55391
Gun Socks Covers, E & C Enterprises, P.O. Box 823, So. Pasadena, CA. 91030
Gun Socks Covers, East-Tenn Mills, Inc., Box 1030, Johnson City, Tenn. 37601
Hearing Protector, American Optical Corp., Mechanic St., Southbridge, Mass. 01550 (ear valve)
Hearing Protector, Bausch & Lomb, 635 St. Paul St., Rochester, N.Y. 14602
Hearing Protector, David Clark Co., 360 Franklin St., Worcester, Mass. 01601
Hearing Protector, Curtis Safety Prod. Co., Box 61, Webster Sq. Sta., Worcester, Mass. 01603 (ear valve)
Hearing Protector, Hodgdon, 7710 W. 50 Hiway, Shawnee Mission, Kans. 66202
Hearing Protector, Human Acoustics, Inc., 888 E. Williams St., Carson City, Nev. 89701
Hearing Protector, Sigma Eng. Co., 11320 Burbank Blvd., No. Hollywood, Ca. 91601 (Lee-Sonic ear valve)
Hearing Protector, Willson Prods., Div., P.O. Box 622, Reading, Pa. 19603
Hollow Pointer, Goerg Ent., 3009 S. Laurel St., Port Angeles, Wash. 98362
Hugger Hooks, Roman Products, Box 891, Golden, Colo. 80401
Hull Bag, D. Titus, 119 Morlyn, Bryn Mawr, Pa. 19010
Hunting Blind, Sports Haven Ltd., Box 19323, Portland, Ore. 97219
Insect Repellent, Armor, Div. of Buck Stop, Inc., 3015 Grow Rd., Stanton, Mich. 48888
Insert Barrels, (22 RF), H. Owen, P.O. Box 774, Sunnyvale, Calif. 94088
Leather Rest-Bags, B. Tuller, 29 Germania, Galeton, Pa. 16922
Lightnin-Loader, Hunter Mfg. Co., Box 2882, Van Nuys, Cal. 91404
Magazine Clip (Colyer), Great Northern Trading Post, 13001 Hwy. 65 N.E., Rte. 4, Anoka, Minn. 55303
Magazine Clips, Amer. Firearms Mfg. Co., Inc., 5732 Kenwick Dr, San Antonio, Tex. 78238
Military Museum, Lt. Col. E.H. Hoffman, 768 So. Main St., Woodstock, Va. 22664
MINI Lights, Avery Corp., Box 99, Electra, Tex. 76360
Miniature Guns, C. H. Stoppler, 1426 Walton Ave., N.Y., N.Y. 10452
Monte Carlo Pad, Frank A. Hoppe Div., P.O. Box 97, Parkesburg, Pa. 19365
Nipple Wrenches, Chopie Tool & Die Co., 531 Copeland Ave., La Crosse, Wis. 54601
Pell Remover, A. Edw. Terpening, 838 W. Darlington Rd., Tarpon Springs, Fla. 33589
Personal Firearms Record Book, Box 201, Park Ridge, Ill. 60068
Portable Gun Rest, Central Specialties Co., 630 Northwest Hwy., Chicago, Ill. 60631 (Gun-Rak)
Powder Horns, Thos. F. White, 5801 Westchester Ct., Worthington, O. 43085
Pressure Testg. Machine, York-Cantrell, Inc., 30241 Rosebriar, St. Clair Shores, Mich. 48082
Recoil Pads, etc., Mershon Co., Inc., 1230 S. Grand, Los Angeles, Cal. 90015
Recoil Pads, Pachmayr Gun Works, 1220 S. Grand Ave., Los Angeles, Cal. 90015
Recoil Reducer, J.B. Edwards, 269 Herbert St., Alton, Ill. 62002
Retriev-R-Trainer, Scientific Prod. Corp., 1108 Oronoco St., Alexandria, Va. 22314
Rifle Rests, Edw. L. Bagrosky, 13451 Philmont Ave., Philadelphia, Pa. 19116
Rifle Rests, E. L. Beecher, 2155 Demington Dr., Cleveland Hgts., O. 44106
Rifle Rests, Cole's Acku-Rite Prod., Box 25, Kennedy, N.Y. 14747
Rifle Rests, E-N Gun Prod., 1015 Van Hoy Ave., Winston-Salem, N.C. 27104
Rifle Rests, Frontier Arms, Inc., Box 2593, Cheyenne, Wyo. 82001

LEE TARGET MODEL LOADER

Lee Custom Engineering, Hartford, Wisconsin, has introduced a new loading system aimed at the benchrest shooter. The new Lee Target Model Reloader makes it possible to reload target quality ammunition without the expense of a conventional loading press.

Based on Lee's new concept of reaming the inside neck of the case perfectly concentric to the outside of the case, the system reams each case to the exact same neck thickness. The same die that resizes the case and holds it for neck reaming also aligns the case for bullet seating. During the bullet seating operation, the case is located by the neck and base and the bullet is accurately located near the point, thus insuring straight line seating with no chance for the neck to move out of dead center.

The Target Model Zero Error loader is available from Lee Custom Engineering at $24.95.

RCBS RELOADING EQUIPMENT

RCBS, Inc., of Oroville, California is the manufacturer of a full array of centerfire cartridge reloading equipment and accessories. RCBS gets its name from the "Rock Chuck Bullet Swage" Dies developed in 1943 by Fred Huntington to form jacketed bullets from fired 22 caliber copper cases. The firm's reloading tools, dies, scales, measurers and accessories are designed to provide the reloader with the means to produce safe and economical rifle and pistol ammunition.

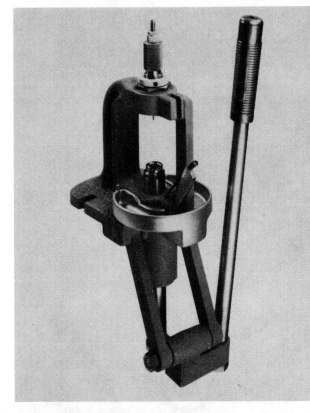

RCBS Rock Chucker Combo reloading press, designed for heavy-duty reloading, case forming and bullet making. The press, complete with dies for one caliber, sells for $64.50.

The RCBS J.R., known as the "Reloader Special" is one of the most popular reloading presses in America. It was developed with the newcomer to reloading in mind and costs $43.50 with dies for one caliber.

New to the company's line is their Priming Tool which offers accurate and uniform seating of primers in one step. It features an automatic primer feed capable of handling all large and small U.S.-made Boxer-type primers. Price (less shell holder) is $24.95.

RCBS 3-Die Sets were developed specifically to eliminate "overworking" of cases that sometimes occurs. The set consists of a sizer die, an expander die and a seater die, and costs $15.00 or $18.00 depending on caliber.

Rifle Rests, The Gun Case, 11035 Maplefield, El Monte, Cal. 91733
Rifle Rests, Harris Engr., Inc., Box 305, Fraser, Mich. 48026 (bipods)
Rifle Rests, Rob. W. Hart & Son, 401 Montgomery St., Nescopeck, Pa. 18635
Rifle Rests, Rec. Prods, Res., Inc., 158 Franklin Ave., Ridgewood, N.J. 07450 (Buttspipod)
Rifle Rests, Ten Ring Mfg. Co., Box 157, New City, N.Y. 10956 (Rifle-Mate)
Rifle Rests, Basil Tuller, 29 Germania, Galeton, PA 16922 (Protektor sandbags)
Rifle Rests, W. H. Womack, 2124 Meriwether Rd., Shreveport, La. 71108
Rifle Slings, Bianchi, 212 W. Foothill Blvd., Monrovia, Cal. 91016
RIG, NRA Scoring Plug, Rig Prod. Co., Box 279, Oregon, Ill. 60161
Rubber Cheekpiece, W. H. Lodewick, 2816 N. E. Halsey, Portland, Ore. 97232
Rust Bluing/Browning, L.B. Thompson, 568 E. School Ave., Salem, O. 44460
Safe-T-Shell, Inc., 4361 Woodhall Rd., Columbus. O. 43221 (shotgun)
Safeties, Doc Line Co., 18440 John R. St., Detroit, Mich. 48203
Safeties, Williams Gun Sight Co., 7389 Lapeer Rd., Davison, Mich. 48423
Salute Cannons, Naval Co., Rt. 611, Doylestown, Pa. 18901
Scope Safeties, W. H. Lodewick, 2816 N.E. Halsey, Portland, Ore. 97232
Sharpening Stones, Russell's Arkansas Oilstones, P.O. Box 474, Fayetteville, Ark. 72701
Shell Cracker, Stoneco, Inc., 5401 No. Federal Blvd., Denver Colo. 80200
Shell Shrinker Mfg. Co., Box 6143, Lubbock, Tex. 79413
Shooting Coats, 10-X Mfg. Co., 100 S. W. 3rd, Des Moines, Iowa 50309
Shooting/Testing Glasses, Clear View Sports Shields, P.O. Box 255, Wethersfield, Conn. 06107
Shooting Glasses, Bushnell Optical Corp., 2828 E. Foothill Blvd., Pasadena, CA 91107
Shooting Glasses, M. B. Dinsmore, Box 21, Wyomissing, Pa. 19610
Shooting Glasses, Mitchell's, Box 539, Waynesville, Mo. 65583
Shooting Ranges, Shooting Equip. Inc., 2001 N. Parkside Ave., Chicago, Ill. 60639
Shotgun Recoil Kit, CHB, 3063 Hiram, Wichita, Kan. 67217
Shotgun Sight, bi-ocular, Trius Prod., Box 25, Cleves, O. 45002
Shotshell Catcher, Old Mill Trap & Skeet, 300 Mill Ridge Rd., Secaucus, N.J. 07094 (Seymour)
Shotshell Pouches, Filmat Enterpr., Inc., 200 Market St., East Paterson, N.J. 07407
Silver Grip Caps, Bill Dyer, P.O. Box 75255, Oklahoma City, Okla. 73107
Skrimshaw Engraving, C. Milton Barringer, 18042 Murray Hill Ave., Detroit, Mich. 48235
Slide Safety (Mausers), Doc Line Co., 18440 John R., Detroit, Mich. 48203
Snap Caps, Filmat, 200 Market, East Paterson, N.J. 07407
Snowshoes, Sportsmen Prod. Inc., Box 1082, Boulder, Colo. 80302
Springfield Safety Pin, B-Square Co., P.O. Box 11281, Ft. Worth, Tex. 76110
Springs, W. Wolff Co., Box 232, Ardmore, Pa. 19003
Stock-Lo-Kater, Bill Matthews Co., 5004 Encinita Ave., Temple City, Ca. 91780
Swivels, Michaels, P.O. Box 13010, Portland, Ore. 97213
Swivels, Sile Dist., 7 Centre Market Pl., New York, N.Y. 10013
Swivels, Williams Gun Sigght Co., 7389 Lapeer Rd., Davison, Mich. 48423
Targ-Dots, Peterson Label Co., P.O. Box 186Z, Redding Ridge, CT 06876
Taxidermy, Jack Atcheson, 2309 Hancock Ave., Butte, Mont. 59701
Taxidermy, Clearfield, 603 Hanna St., Clearfield, Pa. 16830
Taxidermy, Jonas Bros., 1037 Broadway, Denver, Colo. 80203
Taxidermy, Knopp Bros., N. 6715 Division St., Spokane, Wash. 99208
Taxidermy, Mac's, 47 N. Grand Ave., Waukesha, Wis. 53186
Teenuts, Dot Product Supply Co., 10544 Lunt Ave., Rosemont, Ill. 60018
Trap, claybird, Deerback Prod., 8239 Hayle Ave., Dallas, Tex. 75227
Trap, claybird, Outers Lab., Inc., Box 37, Onalaska, Wis. 54650
Trap claybird, Trius Prod., Box 25, Cleves, O. 45002
Triggers, Canjar Rifle Acc., 500 E. 45th St., Denver, Colo. 80216
Trigger Guards, Beesley Mfg. Co., P.O. Box 17075, Salt Lake City, Utah 84117 (Bee-Safe)
Trigger Guards, Michaels, P.O. Box 13010, Portland, Ore. 97213
Trigger Pull Gauge,Ohaus, 29 Hanover Rd., Florham Park, NJ 07932
Trigger Release, Schwab Gun Shop, 1103 E. Bigelow, Findlay, O. 45840
Trigger Shoe, Flaigs, Babcock Blvd., Millvale, Pa. 15209
Trigger Shoe, Pacific Tool Co., Box 4495, Lincoln, Neb. 68504
Trigger Shoe, Melvin Tyler, 1326 W. Britton, Oklahoma City, Okla. 73114
Trophies, L. G. Balfour Co., Attleboro, Mass. 02703
Trophies, Blackinton & Co., 140 Commonwealth, Attleboro Falls, Mass. 12763
Trophies, F. H. Noble & Co., 559 W. 59th St., Chicago, Ill. 60621
Worldhunting Info., Jack Atcheson, 2309 Hancock Ave., Butte, Mont. 59701

MUZZLE LOADING BARRELS OR EQUIPMENT

Luther Adkins, Box 281, Shelbyville, Ind. 47176 (breech plugs)
Armoury, Inc., Rte. 25, New Preston, Conn. 06777
Henry S. Beverage, New Gloucester, Me. 04260 (brass bullet mould)
John Bivins, Jr., 446 So. Main, Winston-Salem, N.C. 27101
Jesse F. Booher, 2751 Ridge Ave., Dayton, Ohio 45414
G. S. Bunch, 7735 Garrison, Hyattsville, Md. 20784 (flask repair)
Pat Burke, 3339 Farnsworth Rd., Lapeer, Mich. 48446 (capper)
Challanger Mfg. Co., 94-28 Merrick Blvd., Jamaica, N.Y. 11433 (H.&A. guns)
Cherry Corners Gun Shop, Rte. 1, 8010 Lafayette Rd., Lodi, Ohio 44254
Earl T. Cureton, Rte. 6, 7017 Pine Grove Rd., Knoxville, Tenn. 37914 (powder horns)
John N. Dangelzer, 3056 Frontier Pl. N.E., Albuquerque, N. Mex. 87106 (powder flasks)
Ted Fellowes, 9245 16th Ave. S.W., Seattle, Wash. 98106
Firearms Imp. & Exp. Corp., P.O. Box 691, Biscayne Annex, Miami, Fla. 33152
Golden Age Arms Co., Box 82, Worthington, Ohio 43085

A. R. Goode, 3306 Sellman Rd., Adelphi, Md. 20783
International M. L. Parts Co., 19453 Forrer, Detroit, MI 48235
JJJJ Ranch, Wm. Large, Rte. 1, Ironton, Ohio 45638
Art LeFeuvre, 1003 Hazel Ave., Deerfield, Ill. 60015 (antique gun restoring)
Kindig's Log Cabin Sport Shop, R.D. 1, Box 275, Lodi, OH 44254
Les' Gun Shop (Les Bauska), Box 511, Kalispell, Mont. 59901
Lever Arms Serv. Ltd., 771 Dunsmuir, Vancouver 1, B.C., Canada
J. Lewis Arms Mfg., 3931 Montgomery Rd., Cincinnati, Ohio 45212 (pistol)
M.C.K.E-Z Load Co., R.R. 1, Pekin, IL 61554
Maryland Gun Exchange Inc., Rt. 40 West, RD 5, Frederick, MD 21701
Jos. W. Mellott, 334 Rockhill Rd., Pittsburgh, Pa. 15243 (barrel blanks)
Miller & Son's Replicas, Rt. 1, Box 260, Marine-on-St. Croix, MN 55047
W. L. Mowrey Gun Works, Inc., Box 711, Olney, Tex. 73674
Numrich Corp., W. Hurley, N.Y. 12491 (powder flasks)
Bob Paris, Gettysburg, Pa. 17325 (barrels)
Penna. Rifle Works, 319 E. Main St., Ligonier, Pa. 15658 (ML guns, parts)
Fred Renard, Rte. 1, Symsonia, Ky. 42082 (ML)
H. M. Schoeller, 569 So. Braddock Ave., Pittsburgh, Pa. 15221
C. E. Siler, 181 Sandhill School, Asheville, N.C., 28806 (flint locks)
Thos. F. White, 5801 Westchester Ct., Worthington, O. 43085 (powder horn)
Lou Williamson, 103 S. Jennings, Ft. Worth, Tex. 76104

PISTOLSMITHS

Alamo Heat Treating, Box 55345, Houston, Tex. 77055
Allen Assoc., 7448 Limekiln Pike, Philadelphia, Pa. 19138 (speed-cock lever for 45 ACP)
Bain and Davis Sptg. Gds., 559 W. Las Tunas Dr., San Gabriel, Cal. 91776
Behlert & Freed, Inc., 33 Herning Ave., Cranford. N.J. 07016 (short actions)
R. M. Champlin, Stanyan Hill, Wentworth, N.H. 03282
F. Bob Chow, Gun Shop, 3185 Mission, San Francisco, Calif. 94110
J.E. Clark, 7424 Broadacres Rd., Shreveport, La. 71109
Custom Gunshop, 33 Herning Ave., Cranford, N.J. 07016
Day Arms Corp., 7515 Stagecoach Lane, San Antonio, Tex. 78227
Alton S. Dinan, Jr., P.O. Box 6674, Canaan, Conn. 06018
Dan Dwyer, 915 W. Washington, San Diego, Calif. 92103
Giles' 45 Shop, Rt. 1, Box 47, Odessa, Fla. 33556
H. H. Harris, 1237 So. State, Chicago, Ill. 60605
Gil Hebard Guns, Box 1, Knoxville, Ill. 61448
Macs Accuracy Serv., 3260 Lakewood So., Seattle, Wash. 98144 (45 ACP)
Rudy Marent, 9711 Tiltree, Houston, Tex. 77034 (Hammerli)
Maryland Gun Exchange, Inc., Rte. 40 W., RD 5, Frederick, Md. 21701
Match Arms Co., 831 Mary St., Springdale, Pa. 15144
Pachmayr Gun Works, 1220 S. Grand Ave., Los Angeles, Calif. 90015
Geo. E. Sheldon, 7 Balsam St., Keene, N.H. 03431
R. L. Shockey Guns, Inc., 1614 S. Choctaw, E. Reno, Okla. 73036
Silver Dollar Guns, 7 Balsam St., Keene, N.H. 03431 (45 auto only)
Sportsmens Equipmt. Co., 915 W. Washington, San Diego, Calif. 92103
Armand D. Swenson, 3223 W. 145th St., Gardena, Calif. 90249

REBORING AND RERIFLING

P.O. Ackley, P.O. Box 17347, Salt Lake City, Utah 84117
Bain & Davis Sptg. Gds., 559 W. Las Tunas Dr., San Gabriel, Calif. 91776
Carpenter's Gun Works, Gunshop Rd., Plattekill, N.Y. 12568
Fuller Gun Shop, Cooper Landing, Alaska 99572
Ward Koozer, Box 18, Walterville, Ore. 97489
Les' Gun Shop, Box 511, Kalispell, Mont. 59901
Nu-Line Guns, 3727 Jennings Rd., St. Louis, Mo. 63121
Al Petersen, Riverhurst, Saskatchewan, Canada
Schuetzen Gun Works, 1226 Prairie Rd., Colorado Springs, Colo. 80909
Sharon Rifle Barrel Co., P.O. Box 106, Kalispell, Mont. 59901
Smith's Gun Shop, St. Lawrence Ave., Hammond, N.Y. 13647
Snapp's Gunshop, 6911 E. Washington Rd., Clare, Mich. 48617
R. Southgate, Rt. 2, Franklin, Tenn. 37064 (Muzzleloaders)
J. W. Van Patten, Box 145, Foster Hill, Milford, Pa. 18337
Robt. G. West, 6626 So. Lincoln, Littleton, Colo. 80120

RELOADING TOOLS AND ACCESSORIES

A & W Eng., Inc., 6520 Rampart St., Houston, Tex. 77036 (bullet puller)
Alcan, (See: Smith & Wesson-Fiocchi, Inc.)
Alpha-Molykote, Dow Corning Corp., 45 Commerce, Trumbull, Ct. 06601
Anchor Alloys, Inc., 966 Meeker Ave., Brooklyn, N.Y. 11222 (chilled shot)
Anderson Mfg. Co., Royal, Ia. 51357 (Shotshell Trimmers)
Aurands, 229 E. 3rd St., Lewistown, Pa. 17044
Automatic Reloading Equipment, Inc., 1602 Babcock St., Costa Mesa, CA 92627
B-Square Eng. Co., Box 11281, Ft. Worth, Tex. 76110
Bahler Die Shop, Box 386, Florence, Ore. 97439
Bair Machine Co., Box 4407, Lincoln, Neb. 68504
Bill Ballard, P.O. Box 656, Billings, Mont. 59103
Belding & Mull, P.O. Box 428, Philipsburg, Pa. 16866
H. S. Beverage, New Gloucester, Me. 04260 (brass bullet mould)
Blackhawk East, C2274 POB, Loves Park, Ill. 61111
Bonanza Sports, Inc., 412 Western Ave., Faribault, Minn. 55021
Gene Bowlin, 3602 Hill Ave., Snyder, Tex. 79549 (arbor press)
Brown Precision Co., 5869 Indian Ave., San Jose, Calif. 95123
A. V. Bryant, East Hartford, Ct. 06424
C-H Tool & Die Corp., Box L, Owen, Wis. 54460
Camdex, Inc., 15339 W. Michaels, Detroit, Mich. 48235
Carbide Die & Mfg. Co., Box 226, Covina, Calif. 91706
C'Arco, P.O. Box 2943, San Bernardino, CA 92406 (Ransom rest)
Carter Gun Works, 2211 Jefferson Pk. Ave., Charlottesville, Va. 22903

Ponsness-Warren Shotshell Reloaders

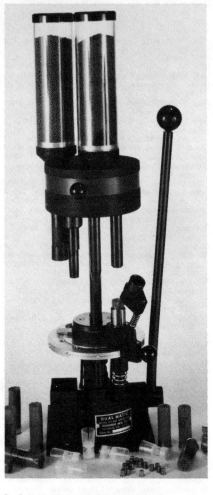

Primer feed system of the Size-O-Matic 800B.

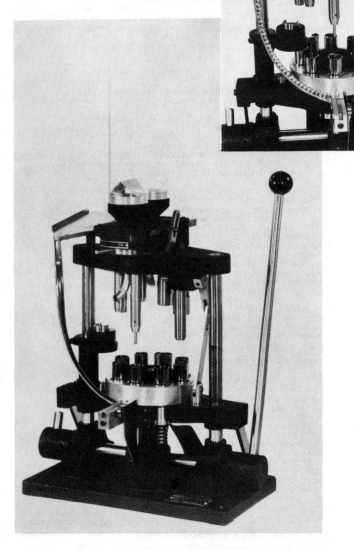

Size-O-Matic Model 800B Shotshell Reloader.

Du-O-Matic Model 375 Shotshell Reloader.

Du-O-Matic head with two sets of tooling attached.

Ponsness-Warren of Eugene, Oregon, manufactures two shotshell reloaders, the Du-O-Matic 375 and the Size-O-Matic Model 800B, that will reload shotshells to feed and chamber into any shotgun. Their tools utilize a full-length sizing die through the entire loading operation thus ensuring a completely resized case including brass and rim.

The Model 800B Size-O-Matic, an 8-station tool, has a unique gravity feed primer system, adjustable wad pressure and shut-off/drain valves for the powder and shot reservoirs. The basic unit in 12 or 20 gauge sells for $449.00.

The Model 375 Du-O-Matic offers the reloader the versatility of a partial set-up for two different gauges at the same time. The headplate holds tooling for two gauges and conversion from one to the other takes less than five minutes, including time for draining shot and powder. The basic unit with tooling for one gauge retails at $119.50.

Cascade Cartridge, Inc., (See Omark)
Chellife Corp., R.D. 1, Box 260 A1, Felton, Del. 19943
Lester Coats, 416 Simpson St., No. Bend, Ore. 97459 (core cutter)
Cole's Acku-Rite Prod., P.O. Box 25, Kennedy, N.Y. 14747 (die racks)
Containter Development Corp., 424 Montgomery St., Watertown, Wis. 53094
Cooper Engineering, 612 E. 20th Houston, Tex. 77008
Cooper-Woodward, Box 972, Riverside, Calif. 92502 (Perfect Lube)
Design & Development Co., 1002 N. 64th St., Omaha, Neb. 68132
Clarence Detsch, 135 Larch Rd., St. Mary's, Pa. 15857 (bullet dies)
J. Dewey Gun Co., Clinton Corners, N.Y. 12514 (bullet spinner)
Division Lead Co., 7742 W. 61st Pl., Summit, Ill. 60502
Dom Enterprises, 3985 Lucas, St. Louis, Mo. 63103
Eagle Products Co., 1520 Adelia Ave., So. El Monte, Cal. 91733
W. H. English, 4411 S. W. 100th, Seattle, Wash. 98146 (Paktool)
Ellwood Epps Sptg. Goods, 80 King St., Clinton, Ont., Canada
The Fergusons, 27 W. Chestnut St., Farmingdale, N.Y. 11735
Fitz, Box 49797, Los Angeles, Calif. 90049 (Fitz Flipper)
Flambeau Plastics, 801 Lynn, Baraboo, Wis. 53913
Fordwad Inc., 4322 W. 58th St., Cleveland, O. 44109
Forster-Appelt Mfg. Co., Inc., 82 E. Lanark Ave., Lanark, Ill. 61046
Full Ed'z Creel Co., 717 W. 9th St., Cheyenne, Wyo. 82001
Gene's Gun Shop, 3602 Hill Ave., Snyder, Tex. 79549 (arbor press)
Gopher Shooter's Supply, Box 246, Faribault, Minn. 55021
The Gun Clinic, 81 Kale St., Mahtomedi, Minn. 55115
H & H Sealants, Box 448, Saugerties, N.Y. 12477 (Loctite)
Hart Products, 401 Montgomery St., Nescopeck, Pa. 18635
Frank A. Hemsted, Box 281, Sunland, Cal. 91040 (swage dies)
Hensley & Gibbs, Box 10, Murphy, Ore. 97533
E. C. Herkner Co., Box 5007, Boise, Ida. 83702
Herter's Inc., RR1, Waseca, Minn. 56093
B. E. Hodgdon, Inc., 7710 W. 50 Hiway, Shawnee Mission, Kans. 66202
Hollywood Reloading, Inc., 19540 Victory, Reseda, CA 91335
Hulme Firearm Serv., Box 83, Millbrae, Calif. 94030 (Star case feeder)
I and I Co., 709 Twelfth St., Altoona, Pa. 16601 (multi-shellcatcher)
Independent Mach. & Gun Shop, 1416 N. Hayes, Pocatello, Ida. 83201
JASCO, Box 49751, Los Angeles, Calif. 90049
J & G Rifle Ranch, Turner, Mont. 59542 (case tumblers)
Javelina Products, Box 337, San Bernardino, Cal. 92402 (Alox beeswax)
Jay's Sports Inc., Menomonee Falls, Wis. 53051 (powd. meas. stand)
Kexplore, Box 22084, Houston, Tex. 77027
Kuharsky Bros., 2425 W. 12th, Erie, Pa. 16500 (primer pocket cleaner)
Lachmiller Div. of Peng. Ind., P.O. Box 97, Parkesburg, Pa. 19365
Lee Engineering, 46 E. Jackson, Hartford, Wis. 53027
Leon's Reloading Service, 3945 No. 11 St., Lincoln, Neb. 68521
L. L. F. Die Shop, 1281 Highway 99 N., Eugene, Ore. 97402
Liberty Arms, P.O. Box 308, Montrose, CA 91020
Ljutic Industries, 918 N. 5th Ave., Yakima, Wash. 98902
Lock's Phila. Gun Exch., 6700 Rowland, Philadelphia, Pa. 19149
J. T. Loos, Pomfret, CT. 06258 (primer pocket cleaner)
Lyman Gun Sight Products, Middlefield, Conn. 06455
McKillen & Heyer, Box 627, Willoughby, O. 44094 (case gauge)
Paul McLean, 2670 Lakeshore Blvd., W., Toronto 14, Ont., Canada (Universal Cartridge Holder)
Pat B. McMillan, 4908 E. Indianola, Phoenix, Ariz. 85018
MTM Molded Prod. Co., P.O. Box 14092, Dayton, OH 45414
Magma Eng. Co., P.O. Box 881, Chandler, AZ 85224
Mayville Eng. Co., Box 267, Mayville, Wis. 53050 (shotshell loader)
Merit Gun Sight Co., P.O. Box 995, Sequim, Wash. 98382
Minnesota Shooters Supply, 1915 E. 22nd St., Minneapolis, Minn. 55404
Murdock Lead Co., Box 5298, Dallas, Tex. 75222
National Lead Co., Box 831, Perth Amboy, N.J. 08861
Normington Co., Box 156, Rathdrum, Ida. 83858 (powder baffles)
John Nuler, 12869 Dixie, Detroit, Mich. 48239 (primer seating tool)
Ohaus Scale Corp., 29 Hanover Rd., Florham Park, N.J. 07932
Omark-CCI, Inc., Box 856, Lewiston, Ida. 83501
Pacific Tool Co., Box 4495, Lincoln, Neb. 68504
C. W. Paddock, 1589 Payne Ave., St. Paul, Minn. 55101 (cartridge boxes)
Vernon Parks, 104 Heussy, Buffalo, N.Y. 14220 (loaders bench)
Perfection Die Co., 1614 S. Choctaw, El Reno, Okla. 73036
Personal Firearms Record Book, Box 201, Park Ridge, Ill. 60068
Phelps Reloader Inc., Box 4004, E. Orange N.J. 07019
Ferris Pindell, Connersville, Inc. 47331
Plano Gun Shop, 1521B 14th St., Plano, Tex. 75074 (powder measure)
Plum City Ballistics Range, Box 128, Plum City, Wis. 54761
Ponsness-Warren, Inc., Box 186, Rathdrum, Ida. 83858
Potter Eng. Co., 1410 Santa Ana Dr., Dunedin, Fla. 33528
Marian Powley, 19 Sugarplum Rd., Levittown, Pa. 10956
Quinetics Corp., 3740 Colony Dr., San Antonio, Tx. 78230 (kinetic bullet puller)
RCBS, Inc., Box 1919, Oroville, Calif. 95965
Raymor Industries, 5856 So. Logan Ct., Littleton, Colo. 80120 (primer mag.)
Redco, Box 15523, Salt Lake City, Utah 84115
Redding-Hunter, Inc., 114 Starr Rd., Cortland, N.Y. 13045
Remco, 1404 Whitesboro St., Utica, N.Y. 13502 (shot caps)
Rifle Ranch, Rte. 1, Prescott, Ariz, 86301
Rochester Lead Works, Rochester, N.Y. 14608 (leadwire)
Roman Prod., Box 891, Golden, Colo. 80401
Rorschach Precision Prods., P.O. Box 1613, Irving, Tex. 75060
Rotex Mfg., Co. (see Texan)
Ruhr-American Corp., So. East Hwy. 55, Glenwood, Minn. 56334
SAECO Rel. Inc., P.O. Box 778, Carpinteria, Calif. 93013
Savage Arms Co., Westfield, Mass. 01085
Scientific Lubricants Co., 3753 Lawrence Ave., Chicago, Ill. 60625
Shoffstalls Mfg. Co., 740 Ellis Place, E. Aurora N.Y. 14052
Shooters Accessory Supply, Box 50, No. Bend, Ore. 97459 (SAS)
Shooters Serv. & Dewey, Inc., Clinton Corners, N.Y. 12514 (SS&D) (bullet spinner)
Sil's Gun Prod., 490 Sylvan Dr., Washington, Pa. 15301 (K-spinner)
Jerry Simmons, 713 Middlebury St., Goshen, Ind. 46526 (Pope de- & recapper)

Rob. B. Simonson, Rte. 7, 2129 Vanderbilt Rd., Kalamazoo, Mich. 49002
Smith & Wesson-Fiocchi, Inc., 3640 Seminary Rd., Alton, IL 62002
Sport Ammo Corp., 8407 Center Dr., Minneapolis, Minn. 55432 (mini-kit tool)
Star Machine Works, 418 10th Ave., San Diego, Calif. 92101
Strathmore Gun Spec., Box 308, Strathmore, Calif. 93267
Sullivan Arms Corp., 5204 E. 24th St., Indianapolis, Ind. 46218
Swanson Co., Inc., 2205 Long Lake Rd., St. Paul Minn. 55112 (Safari loader)
Texan Reloaders, Inc., P.O. Box 5355, Dallas, Tex. 75222
VAMCO, Box 67, Vestal, N.Y. 13850
W. S. Vickerman, 505 W. 3rd Ave., Ellensburg, Wash. 98926
Wanda Cartr. Co., P.O. Box 45901, Houston, Tex. 77045 (plastics)
Weatherby, Inc., 2781 Firestone Blvd., South Gate, Calif. 90280
Webster Scale Mfg. Co., Box 188, Sebring, Fla. 33870
Whit's Shooting Stuf, 2121 Stampede Ave., Cody, Wyo. 82414
Whitney Cartridge Co., Box 5872, Pasadena, CA 91107 (shotshells)
L. E. Wilson, Inc., Box 324, Cashmere, Wash. 98815
Xelex, Ltd., Hawksbury, Ont., Canada (powder)
Zenith Ent., Rt. 1, Box 52z, Del Mar, Calif. 92014
A. Zimmerman, 127 Highland Trail, Denville, N.J. 07834 (case trimmer)

RIFLE BARREL MAKERS

P.O. Ackley, P.O. Box 17347, Salt Lake City, Utah 84117
Apex Rifle Co., 7628 San Fernando, Sun Valley, Calif. 91352
Christy Gun Works, 875 57th St., Sacramento, Calif. 95819
Clerke Technicorp., 2054 Broadway Ave., Santa Monica, Calif. 90404
Cuthbert Gun Shop, 715 So. 5th, Coos Bay, Ore. 97420
J. Dewey Gun Co., Clinton Corners, N.Y. 12514
Douglas Barrels Co., Inc., 5504 Big Tyler Rd., Charleston, W. Va. 25312
Federal Firearms Co., Inc., Box 145, Oakdale, Pa. 15071 (Star bbls., actions)
A. R. Goode, 3306 Sellman Rd., Adelphi, Md. 20783
Hart Rifle Barrels, Inc., RD 2, Lafayette, N.Y. 13084
Wm. H. Hobaugh, Box 657, Philipsburg, Mont. 59858
Hoffman Rifle Barrel Co., Bucklin, Kans. 67834
Intern'l Casting Co., 19453 Forrer, Detroit, Mich. 48235
Johnson Automatics, Box 306, Hope Valley, R.I. 02832
Les' Gun Shop, Box 511, Kalispell, Mont. 59901
McGowen Rifle Barrels, Rte. 3, St. Anne, Ill. 60964
Nauman Gun Shop, 1048 S. 5th, Douglas, Wyo. 82633
Nu-Line Guns, Inc., 3727 Jennings Rd., St. Louis, Mo. 63121
Numrich Arms, W. Hurley, N.Y. 12491
Bob Parks, Gettysburg, Pa. 17325
Rheinmetall (see John Weir)
SS & D, Inc., Clinton Corners, N.Y. 12514 (cold-formed bbls.)
Sanders Cust. Gun Serv., 2358 Tyler Lane, Louisville, Ky. 40205
Sharon Rifle Barrel Co., P.O. Box 106 Kalispell, Mont. 59901
Ed Shilen Rifles, 4510 Harrington Rd., Irving, Tex. 75060
Titus Barrel & Gun Co., Box 151, Heber City, Ut. 84032
John E. Weir, 4301 Cottage, Independence, Mo. 64055
Wilson Arms, Box 364, Stony Creek, Branford, Conn. 06405

SCOPES, MOUNTS, ACCESSORIES, OPTICAL EQUIPMENT

Alley Supply Co., P.O. Box 458, Sonora, Calif. 95370 (Scope collimator)
American Import Co., 1167 Mission, San Francisco, Calif. 94103
Anderson & Co., 1203 Broadway, Yakima, Wash. 98902 (lens cap)
Bausch & Lomb Inc., 635 St. Paul St., Rochester, N.Y. 14602
Bennett, 561 Delaware, Delmar, N.Y. 12054 (mounting wrench)
Bridge Mount Co., Box 3344, Lubbock, Tex. 79410 (one-piece target mts.)
Browning Arms, Rt. 4, Box 624-B, Arnold, Mo. 63010
Maynard P. Buehler, Inc., 17 Orinda Highway, Orinda, Calif. 94563
Bullitco, Box 40, Shepherdsville, Ky. 40165 (Scope collimator)
D. P. Bushnell & Co., Inc., 2828 E. Foothill Blvd., Pasadena, Calif. 91107
Chilford Arms Mfg. Co., 9 First St., San Francisco, Calif. 94105
Kenneth Clark, 18738 Highway 99, Madera, Calif. 93637
Collins Co., Box 40, Shepherdsville, Ky. 40165 (Scope collimator)
Colt's, Hartford, Conn. 06102
Compass Instr. & Optical Co., Inc., 104 E 25th St., New York, N.Y. 10010
Conetrol, Hwy 123 South, Seguin, Tex. 78155
Continental Arms Corp., 697-5th Ave., New York, N.Y. 10022 (Nickel)
Davis Optical Co., P.O. Box 6, Winchester, Ind. 47934
Del-Sports, Main St., Margaretville, N.Y. 12455 (Kahles)
Diana Imports, Main St., Margaretville, N.Y. 12455 (Habicht)
Don's Gun Shop, 128 Ruxton, Manitou Springs, Colo. 80829 (claw mtg. rings)
Duo-Gun Prod., 3213 Partridge Ave., Oakland, Calif. 94605 (mount)
Flaig's, Babcock Blvd., Millvale, Pa. 15209
Freeland's Scope Stands, Inc. 3734 14th, Rock Island, Ill. 61201
Bert Friedberg & Co., 820 Mission St., San Francisco, Cal. 94103
Griffin & Howe, Inc., 589-8th Ave., New York, N.Y. 10017
E. C. Herkner Co., Box 5007, Boise, Idaho 83702
Herter's Inc., Waseca, Minn. 56093
J. B. Holden Co., Box H-1495, Plymouth, Mich. 48170 (Ironsighter)
The Hutson Corp., P.O. 1127, Arlington, Tex. 76010
Hy-Score Arms Corp., 200 Tillary St., Brooklyn, N.Y. 11201
Paul Jaeger, 211 Leedom St., Jenkintown, Pa. 19046 (Nickel)
Jana Intl. Co., Box 1107, Denver, Colo. 80201
Jason Empire, 1211 Walnut, Kansas City, Mo. 64106
Kesselring Gun Shop, Box 350, Rt. 1, Burlington, Wash. 98283
Kuharsky Bros., 2425 W. 12th St., Erie, Pa. 16500
Kwik-Site, 27367 Michigan, Inkster, Mich. 48141 (rings)
T. K. Lee, Box 2123, Birmingham, Ala. 35201 (reticles)
E. Leitz, Inc., Rockleigh, N.J. 07647
Leupold & Stevens Inc., P.O. Box 688, Beaverton, Ore. 97005
Jake Levin and Son, Inc., 1211 Walnut, Kansas City, Mo. 64106
Lyman Gun Sight Products, Middlefield, Conn. 06455
Marble Arms Co., 1120 Superior St., Gladstone, Mich. 49837

TASCO'S SCOPE-GUIDE

Tasco's Scope-Guide is an inexpensive collimator for Tasco riflescopes. Based on the use of the existing optics of the riflescope itself, the Scope-Guide gives the shooter a collimating device which can be used in the field in the event a scope is dropped or knocked out of alignment. The device, which will fit all rifle calibers from 22 to 45, has no moving parts and is not subject to climatic or weather changes.

The Scope-Guide kit, complete with plastic case, includes: an adjustable, tapered bore stud to fit all caliber rifles; a grid pattern stanchion; 7 aperture caps to fit all Tasco scopes; and a scale to find the center line of the rifle's bore. Tasco's collimator utilizes vertical and horizontal adjustment of the riflescope's optics in connection with the grid pattern to achieve "sighting-in." The complete kit sells for $9.95.

Full information on the Tasco's Scope-Guide and other Tasco optical products is available from Tasco Sales, Inc., 1075 N.W. 71st St., Miami, Florida 33138.

Stainless Steel Automatic Pistols

Calibers
25 & 380 Auto

Lightweight and Blued Models Also Available

For literature write: American Firearms Mfg. Co., Inc.
5732 Kenwick Drive, San Antonio, Texas 78238

Marlin Firearms Co., 100 Kenna Dr., New Haven, Conn. 06473
Mashburn Arms Co., 112 W. Sheridan, Oklahoma City, Okla. 73102
O. F. Mossberg & Sons, Inc., 7 Grasso Ave., North Haven, Conn. 06473
Normark Corp., 1710 E. 78th St., Minneapolis, Minn. 55423 (Singlepoint)
Numrich Arms, West Hurley, N.Y. 12491
Nydar Div., Swain Nelson Co., Box 45, Glenview, Ill. 60025 (shotgun sight)
PGS, Peters' Inc., 622 Gratiot Ave., Saginaw, Mich. 48602 (scope shields)
R. J. Enorec Inc., 175 N. 5th St., Saddle Brook, N.J. 07662 (bullet mould)
Pachmayr Gun Works, 1220 S. Grand Ave., Los Angeles, Calif. 90015
Pacific Tool Co., Box 4495, Lincoln, Neb. 68504
Ed Paul's Sptg. goods, Inc., 172 Flatbush Ave., Brooklyn, N.Y. 11217 (Tops)
Pickering Co., 2110 Walnut, Unionville, Mo. 63565
Precise Imports Corp., 3 Chestnut, Suffern, N.Y. 10901 (PIC)
Premier Reticles, Ocala, Fla. 32670
Ranging Inc., P.O. Box 9106, Rochester, N.Y. 14625
Realist, Inc., N. 93 W. 16288, Megal Dr., Menomonee Falls, Wis. 53051
Redfield Gun Sight Co., 5800 E. Jewell Ave., Denver, Colo. 80222
S & K Mfg. Co., Box 247, Pittsburgh, Pa. 16340 (Insta-mount)
Sanders Cust. Gun Serv., 2358 Tyler Lane, Louisville, Ky. 402305 (MSW)
Savage Arms, Westfield, Mass. 01085
Scope Inst. Co., 25-20 Brooklyn-Queens Expressway West, Woodside, N.Y. 11377
Sears, Roebuck & Co., 825 S. St. Louis, Chicago, Ill. 60607
Selsi Co., 40 Veterans Blvd., Carlstadt, N.J. 07072
W. H. Siebert, 22443 S.E. 56th Pl., Issaquah, Wn. 98027
Singlepoint (see Normark)
Southern Precision Inst. Co., 710 Augusta St., San Antonio, Tex. 78215
Stoeger Arms Co., 55 Ruta Ct., S. Hackensack, N.J. 07606
Swift Instruments, Inc., 952 Dorchester Ave., Boston, Mass. 02125
Tasco, 1075 N.W. 71st, Miami, Fla. 33138
Thompson-Center Arms, P.O. Box 2405, Rochester, N.H. 03867 (handgun scope)
Tradewinds, Inc., Box 1191, Tacoma, Wash. 98401
John Unertl Optical Co., 3551-5 East St., Pittsburgh, Pa. 15214
United Binocular Co., 9043 S. Western Ave., Chicago, Ill. 60620
Universal Firearms Corp., 3746 E. 10th Ct., Hialeah, Fla. 33013
Vissing Co., Box 437 Idaho Falls, Idaho 83401 (lens cap)
H. P. Wasson, Box 181, Netcong, N.J. 07857 (eyeglass apertures)
Weatherby's, 2781 Firestone, South Gate, Calif. 90280
W. R. Weaver Co., 7125 Industrial Ave., El Paso, Tex. 79915
Williams Gun Sight Co., 7389 Lapeer Rd., Davison, Mich. 48423
Carl Zeiss Inc., 444 Fifth Ave., New York, N.Y. 10018 (Hensoldt)

STOCKS (Commercial and Custom)

W. S. Abe, 5124 Huntington Dr., Los Angeles, Calif. 90032
R. E. Anderson, 706 So. 23rd St., Laramie, Wyo. 82070
Dale P. Andrews, 7114 So. Albion, Littleton, Colo. 80120
R. J. Anton, 1016 Riehl St., Waterloo, Ia. 50703
Jim Baiar, Rt. 1-B, Box 352, Columbia Falls, Mont. 59912
Joe J. Balickie, Custom Stocks, 6108 Deerwood Pl., Raleigh, N.C. 27607
Bartas, Rte. 1, Box 129, Cato, Wis. 54206
John Bianchi, 212 W. Foothill Blvd., Monrovia, Calif. 91016 (U. S. carbines)
Al Biesen, West 2039 Sinto Ave., Spokane, Wash. 99201
E. C. Bishop & Son Inc., Box 7, Warsaw, Mo. 65355
Kay H. Bowles, Pinedale, Wyo. 82941
Wm. Buchele, 2832 Sagamore Rd., Toledo, O. 43606 (ML only)
Cadmus Ind., 6311 Yucca St., Hollywood, Calif. (U. C. carbines)
Calico, 1648 Airport Blvd., Windsor, Calif. 95492 (blanks)
Dick Campbell, 1445 So. Meade, Denver, Colo. 80219
Chuck's Custom Gun Stocks, P.O. Box 1123, Frederick, Md. 21701
J. K. Cloward, 2045 Eastlake Ave. E., Seattle, Wa. 98102
Mike Conner, Box 324, Cedar Crest, N.M. 87008
Crane Creek Gun Stock Co., Box 268, Waseca, Minn. 56093
Crest Carving Co., 14849 Dillow St., Westminster, CA. 92683
Charles De Veto, 1087 Irene Rd., Lyndhurst, O. 44124
Custom Gunstocks, 1445 So. Meade, Denver, Colo. 80219
Reinhart Fajen, Box 338, Warsaw, Mo. 65355
N. B. Fashingbauer, Box 366, Lac Du Flambeau, Wis. 54538
Ted Fellowes, 9245 16th Ave. S. W., Seattle, Wash. 98106
Clyde E. Fischer, Rt. 1, Box 170-M, Victoria, Tex. 77901
Jerry Fisher, 1244-4th Ave., Kalispell, Mont. 59901
Flaig's Lodge, Millvale, Pa. 15209
Horace M. Frantz, Box 128, Farmingdale, N.J. 07727
Freeland's Scope Stands, Inc., 3734 14th Ave., Rock Island, Ill. 61201
Aaron T. Gates, 3229 Felton St., San Diego, Calif. 92104
Dale Goens, Box 224, Cedar Crest, N.M. 87008
Gould's Myrtlewood, 1692 N. Dogwood, Coquille, Ore. 97423
Rolf R. Gruning, 315 Busby Dr., San Antonio, Tex. 78209
Gunstocks-Rarewoods, Haleiwa, Hawaii 96712
Gunwoods (N.Z.) Ltd., Box 18505, New Brighton, Christchurch, New Zealand (blanks)
Hank's Stock Shop, 1078 Alice Ave., Ukiah, Calif. 95482
Harper's Custom Stocks, 928 Lombrano St., San Antonio, Tex. 78207
Harris Gun Stocks, Inc., 12 Lake St., Richfield Springs, N.Y. 13439
Elden Harsh, Rt. 4, London, O. 43140
Hal Hartley, Box 147, Blairsfork Rd., Lenoir, N.C. 28654
Hayes Gunstock Service Co., 914 E. Turner St., Clearwater, Fla. 33516
Edward O. Hefti, 300 Fairview, College Sta., Tex. 77840
Herter's Inc., Waseca, Minn. 56093
Hollis Gun Shop, 917 Rex St., Carlsbad, N.M. 88220
Richard Hodgson, 1550 Alpine, Boulder, Colo. 80302
Hurst Custom Gunstocks, RFD 1, Box 1000, Exmore, Va. 23350
Jackson's, Box 416, Selman City, Tex. 75689 (blanks)
Paul Jaeger, 211 Leedom St., Jenkintown, Pa. 19046
Bob Johnson, 1730 E. Sprague, Spokane, Wash. 99202
I. D. Johnson, Rt. 1, Strawberry Point, Ia. 52076 (blanks)
Monte Kennedy, R.D. 2B, Kalispell Mont. 59901
Leer's Gun Barn, Rt. 3, Sycamore Hills, Elwood, Ind. 46036
LeFever Arms Co., Inc., R.D. 1, Lee Center, N.Y. 13363

Maryland Gun Exchange, Rt. 40 W., RD 5, Frederick, Md. 21701
Maurer Arms, 2366 Frederick Dr., Cuyahoga Falls, O. 44221
Leonard Mews, 6116 Hollywood Blvd., Hollywood, Calif. 90028
Robt. U. Milhoan & Son, Rt. 3, Elizabeth, W. Va. 26143
Mills (D.H.) Custom Stocks, 401 N. Ellsworth Ave., San Mateo, Calif. 94401
Nelsen's Gun Shop, 501 S. Wilson, Olympia, Wash. 98501
Oakley and Merkely, Box 2446, Sacramento, Calif. 95801 (blanks)
Ernest O. Paulsen, Chinook, Mont. 59523 (blanks)
Peterson Mach. Carving, Box 1065, Sun Valley, Calif. 91352
Andrew Redmond, Inc., No. Anson, Me. 04958 (birchwood blanks)
Richards Micro-Fit Stocks, P.O. Box 1066, Sun Valley, CA. 91352 (thumbhole)
Roberts Wood Prod., 1400 Melody Rd., Marysville, Calif. 95901
Carl Roth, Jr., P.O. Box 2593, Cheyenne, Wy. 82001
Royal Arms, Inc., 10064 Bert Acosta St., Santee, Calif. 92071
Sanders Cust. Gun Serv., 2358 Tyler Lane, Louisville, Ky. 40205 (blanks)
Santa Barbara of Amer. Ltd., 930 N. Beltline Rd., #132, Irving, Tx. 75060
Saratoga Arms Co., R.D. 3, Box 387, Pottstown, Pa. 19464
Roy Schaefer, 965 W. Hilliard Lane, Eugene, Ore. 97402 (blanks)
Shaw's, 1655 S. Euclid Ave., Anaheim, Calif. 92802
Walter Shultz, R.D. 3, Pottstown, Pa. 19464
Sile Dist., 7 Centre Market Pl., New York, N.Y. 10013
Ed Sowers, 8331 DeCelis Pl., Sepulveda, Calif. 91343
Sportsmen's Equip. Co., 915 W. Washington, San Diego, Calif. 92103 (carbine conversions)
Keith Stegall, Box 696, Gunnison, Colo. 81230
Stinehour Rifles, Box 84, Cragsmoor, N.Y. 12420
J. R. Sundra, 683 Elizabeth St., Bridgeville, Pa. 15017
Swanson Cust. Firearms, 1051 Broadway, Denver, Colo. 80203
V. S. Swenson, Rt. 1, Ettrick, Wis. 54627
Talmage Enterpr., 1309 W. 12 St., Long Beach, CA 90813
D. W. Thomas, Box 184, Vineland, N.J. 08360
Roy Vail, Rt. 1, Box 8, Warwick, N.Y. 10990
Harold Waller, 1288 Camillo Way, El Cajon, CA 92021
Weatherby's, 2781 Firestone, South Gate, Calif. 90280
Western Stocks & Guns, Inc., 2206 E 11th, Bremerton, Wash. 98311
Joe White, Box 8505, New Brighton, Christchurch, N.Z. (blanks)
Lou Williamson, 103 S. Jennings, Ft. Worth, Tex. 76104
Robert M. Winter, Box 484, Menno, S.D. 57045
Fred Wranic, 6919 Santa Fe, Huntington Park, Calif. 90255 (mesquite)
Paul Wright, 4504 W. Washington Blvd., Los Angeles, Calif. 90016

SURPLUS GUNS, PARTS AND AMMUNITION

Allied Arms Ltd., 655 Broadway, New York, N.Y. 10012
Century Arms, Inc., 3-5 Federal St., St. Albans, Vt. 05478
W. H. Craig, Box 927, Selma, Ala. 36701
Cummings Intl. Inc., 41 Riverside Ave., Yonkers, N.Y. 10701
Eastern Firearms Co., 790 S. Arroyo Pkwy., Pasadena, Calif. 91105
Fenwick's, P.O. Box 38, Weisburg Rd., Whitehall, Md. 21161
Hunter's Lodge, 200 S. Union, Alexandria, Va. 22313
Lever Arms Serv. Ltd., 771 Dunsmuir St., Vancouver 1, B.C., Canada
Mars Equipment Corp., 3318 W. Devon, Chicago, Ill. 60645
National Gun Traders, 251-55 W. 22nd, Miami, Fla. 33135
Pacific Intl. Imp. Co., 2416-16th St., Sacramento, CA. 95818
Plainfield Ordnance Co., Box 447, Dunellen, N.J. 08812
Potomac Arms Corp., Box 35, Alexandria, Va. 22313
Ruvel & Co., 3037 N. Clark St., Chicago, Ill. 60614
Service Armament Co., 689 Bergen Blvd., Ridgefield, N.J. 07657
Sherwood Distrib. Inc., 9470 Santa Monica Blvd., Beverly Hills, CA 90210
Z. M. Military Research Co., 9 Grand Ave., Englewood, N.J. 07631

TARGETS, BULLET & CLAYBIRD TRAPS

Black Products Co., 13513 Calumet Ave., Chicago, Ill. 60627
Caswell Target Carriers, Box 344, Anoka, Minn. 55303
Cole's Acku-Rite Prod., Box 25, Kennedy, N.Y. 14747 (Site Rite targets)
Detroit Bullet Trap Co., 2233 N. Palmer Dr., Schaumburg, Ill. 60172
Dupont Target Co., Dupont, Ind. 47231 (motorized target carrier)
Gopher Shooter's Supply, Box 246, Faribault, Minn. 55021 (Lok-A-Leg target holders)
Millard F. Lerch, Box 163, 10842 Front St., Mokena, Ill. 60448 (bullet target)
National Target Co., 4960 Wyaconda Rd., Rockville, Md. 20853
Outers Laboratories, Inc., Onalaska, Wis. 54650 (claybird traps)
Peterson Label Co., P.O. Box 186Z, Redding Ridge, CT 06876 (paste-ons)
Police Ordnance, 3027 Enterprise St., Costa Mesa, Calif. 92626 (Multi-Rotating target system)
Professional Tape Co., 355 E. Burlington Rd., Riverside, Ill. 60546 (Time Labels)
Ranger Arms Co., Box 704, Gainesville, Tex. 76240 (paper targets)
Realistic Target Corp., (See HITS)
Recreation Prods. Res. Inc., 158 Franklin Ave., Ridgewood, N.J. 07450 (Butts bullet trap)
Remington Arms Co., Bridgeport, Conn. 06602 (claybird traps)
Scientific Prod. Corp., 5417A Vine St., Alexandria, Va. 22310 (Targeteer)
Sheridan Products, Inc., 3205 Sheridan, Racine, Wis. 53403 (traps)
Shooting Equip. Inc., 2001 N. Parkside Ave., Chicago, Ill. 60639 (electric range)
Sterling-Fleischman Inc., 176 Penna Ave., Malvern, Pa. 19355
Time Products Co. (See Prof. Tape Co.)
Trius Prod., Box 25, Cleves, O. 45002 (claybird, can thrower)
Valentine Equip. Co., 2630 W. Arthington, Chicago, Ill. 60612 ("Crazy Quail" clay target game)
Winchester-Western, New Haven, Conn. 06504 (claybird traps)
Wisler Western Target Co., 1685 Industrial Way, Sparks, Nev. 89431 (NRA targets)
X-Ring Prod. Co., Outers Lab., Onalaska, Wis. 54650 (traps)